FOOTBALL OUTSIDERS™
ALMANAC 2019

THE ESSENTIAL GUIDE TO THE 2019 NFL AND COLLEGE FOOTBALL SEASONS

Edited by Aaron Schatz

With Thomas Bassinger • Ian Boyd • Bill Connelly • Brian Fremeau

Tom Gower • Derrik Klassen • Bryan Knowles • Rivers McCown • Chad Peltier

Andrew Potter • Mike Tanier • Vincent Verhei • Robert Weintraub • Carl Yedor

Copyright 2019 EdjSports, LLC

ISBN: 978-1080768035
All rights reserved

Table of Contents

Introduction

lowly but surely, the analytics revolution in the NFL marches forward.

More teams are following more of the precepts of football analytics. Teams are passing more than they ever have. Teams are using play-action on more passes than they ever have. And teams are spreading out defenses more than they ever have.

Perhaps most prominently, teams last year suddenly became more aggressive on fourth down—certainly not to the extent that analytics has advised for years, but to a greater extent than ever before in NFL history. It's a copycat league, and once the Philadelphia Eagles won Super Bowl LII in part thanks to following analytics on fourth down, other teams followed suit. Based on our Aggressiveness Index numbers, NFL teams in 2018 went for it on fourth down about 40 percent more often than we would expect based on the averages of the last 25 years.

Off the field, analytics aficionados have been developing all kinds of new ways to measure players and teams. The state of NFL analytics has moved forward substantially in just the last two or three years. Analysts working for the NFL have developed new metrics (a.k.a. "Next Gen Stats") using the tracking systems that are now installed in every player's pads and in every football used on the field. The NFL even provided older tracking data to students to create new analytics in their 2019 Big Data Bowl. Those who don't have access to this tracking data have created their own new metrics using game charting data, such as the data collected by our partners at Sports Info Solutions.

A whole community of analysts has sprouted up on Twitter, developing new ways to look at the game and debating the great questions of current NFL fandom. And beginning this offseason, those analysts began to move into NFL front offices when the Baltimore Ravens hired three of them at one time to create a new internal analytics department.

At its heart, the football analytics revolution is about learning more about the intricacies of the game instead of just accepting the boilerplate storylines produced by insipid pregame shows and crotchety old players from the past. It's about not accepting the idea that some guy "just wins." It's about understanding that the "skill players" aren't the only guys on the team with skills. It's about gaining insight into the complexity behind the modern offense, and why just shoving the ball into the line hoping to gain yardage is usually a bad idea. It's about understanding the dramatic way that strength of schedule affects the way we see a team's performance, especially at the college level. It's about figuring out which player skills translate from college to the pros, and which skills just produce meaningless scoutspeak. And it's about accepting that the pass dominates the run in the National Football League, and that it has been that way for at least 30 years.

As the original football analytics website, Football Outsiders is still doing our part to challenge conventional wisdom and look deeper inside the numbers. The book you hold in your hand (or see on your computer screen) compiles our updated breakdown of what happened in the NFL during the 2018 season and what's going to happen during the 2019 season.

There's more to this analysis than just numbers. Numbers are just one way to look at what happens on the football field. Words are the meat of our analysis; numbers are just the spice. There's a rumor that stat analysts don't watch game tape. In reality, stat analysts watch more tape than most beat writers or national Internet columnists, and *a lot* more tape than the average fan. We take everything we learn off the tape, synthesize it with the statistics, and deliver it to you.

Everybody who writes about football uses both statistics (whether they be basic yardage totals or more advanced stats like ours) and scouting (whether scouting reports by professionals or just their own eyes). The same goes for us, except that the statistics portion of our analysis is far more accurate than what you normally see from football coverage. Those numbers are based on two ideas:

1) Conventional football statistics are heavily dependent on context. If you want to see which teams are good and which are bad, which strategies work and which do not, you first need to filter out that context. Down and distance, field position, the current score, time left on the clock, the quality of the opponent—all of these elements influence the objective of the play and/or its outcome. Yet, the official NFL stats add together all yardage gained by a specific team or player without considering the impact of that particular yardage on wins and losses.

A close football game can turn on a single bounce of the ball. In a season of only 16 games, those effects can have a huge impact on a team's win-loss record, thus obscuring the team's true talent level. If we can filter out these bits of luck and random chance, we can figure out which teams are really more likely to play better for the rest of the season, or even in the following season.

2) On any one play, the majority of the important action is not tracked by the conventional NFL play-by-play. That's why we started the Football Outsiders game charting project in 2005. We now partner with both ESPN Stats & Info and Sports Info Solutions to collect data on every single NFL regular-season and postseason play. We know how many pass-rushers teams send on each pass, how often teams go three-wide or use two tight ends, how often teams use a play-action fake, and which defensive backs are in coverage, even when they don't get a tackle in the standard play-by-play.

There's also a third important precept that governs the work we do at Football Outsiders, although it's more about how to interpret numbers and not the numbers themselves. **A player's production in one year does not necessarily equal his production the next year.** This also applies to teams, of course. Even when stats are accurate, they're often extremely variable from year to year and subject to heavy forces of regression to the mean. Field goal percentage, red zone performance, third-down performance on defense, interceptions and fumble recoveries—these are but a few examples. In addition, the age curves for football players are much steeper than in other sports. Old players break down faster, and young players often improve faster. Many football analysts concentrate on looking at what players did last year. We'll talk about that as well, but we're more interested in what players are going to do *this* year. Which performances from a year ago are flukes, and which ones represent long-term improvement or decline? What will one more year of experience do to this player's production? And how will a player's role change this year, and what does it mean for the team?

As with past books, *Football Outsiders Almanac 2019* starts off with "Pregame Show" (reviewing the most important research we've done in past books) and "Statistical Toolbox" (explaining all our stats). Once again, we preserve the ridiculousness of the football season for posterity with another version of "The Year in Quotes" and we introduce you to some of the more promising (and lesser-known) young bench players with our 13th annual list of Top 25 Prospects chosen in the third round or later.

Each NFL team gets a full chapter covering what happened in 2018 and our projections for the upcoming season. Are there reasons to believe that the team was inherently better or worse than its record last year? What did the team do in the offseason, and what does that mean for the team's chances to win in 2019? Each chapter also includes all kinds of advanced statistics covering 2018 performance and strategic tendencies, plus detailed commentary on each of the major units of the team: offensive line, defensive front, defensive secondary, and special teams.

"Skill players" (by which we mean "players who get counted in fantasy football") get their own section in the back of the book. We list the major players at each position alphabetically, along with commentary and a 2019 KUBIAK projection that will help you win your fantasy football league. We also have the most accurate projections anywhere for two fantasy football positions that people wrongly consider impossible to predict: kickers and team defense.

Next comes our preview of the college football season. We go in-depth with the top 50 projected teams in the nation. Just like with our NFL coverage, the goal of our college previews is to focus as much as possible on "why" and how," not just "which team is better." We're not just here to rank the Football Bowl Subdivision teams from 1 to 130. We break things down to look at offense and defense, pass and run, and clear passing situations compared to all plays.

We hope our book helps you raise your level of football expertise, win arguments with your friends, and win your fantasy football league. Occasionally, there are also jokes. Just don't expect it all to be right. The unexpected is part of the fun.

Aaron Schatz
Auburn, MA
July 15, 2019

P.S. Don't forget to visit FootballOutsiders.com every day for fresh coverage of the NFL and college football, plus the most intelligent football discussion threads on the Internet.

Pregame Show

It has now been 16 years since we launched Football Outsiders. In that time, we've done a lot of primary research on the National Football League, and we reference that research in many of the articles and comments in *Football Outsiders Almanac 2019*. New readers may come across an offhand comment in a team chapter about, for example, the idea that fumble recovery is not a skill, and wonder what in the heck we are talking about. We can't repeat all our research in every new edition of *Football Outsiders Almanac*, so we start each year with a basic look at some of the most important precepts that have emerged from Football Outsiders research. You will see these issues come up again and again throughout the book.

You can also find this introduction online at http://www.footballoutsiders.com/info/FO-basics, along with links to the original research in the cases in which that research appeared online instead of (or as well as) in print.

Our various methods for projecting NFL success for college prospects are not listed below, but are referenced at times during the book. Those methods are detailed in an essay on page 441.

You run when you win, not win when you run.

If we could only share one piece of anti-conventional wisdom with you before you read the rest of our book, this would be it. The first article ever written for Football Outsiders was devoted to debunking the myth of "establishing the run." There is no correlation whatsoever between giving your running backs a lot of carries early in the game and winning the game. Just running the ball is not going to help a team score; it has to run successfully.

There is also no evidence that running the ball more early in the game creates the opportunity for longer gains late in the game, i.e. the so-called "body blows" thesis. And there is no evidence that passing the ball too frequently puts the defense on the field too much and tires it out.

Why does nearly every beat writer and television analyst still repeat the tired old school mantra that "establishing the run" is the secret to winning football games? The biggest issue is confusing cause and effect. There are exceptions, but for the most part, winning teams have a lot of carries because their running backs are running out the clock at the end of wins, not because they are running wild early in games.

A sister statement to "you have to establish the run" is "team X is 8-1 when running back John Doe runs for at least 100 yards." Unless John Doe is possessed by otherworldly spirits the way Adrian Peterson was a half-decade ago, the team isn't winning because of his 100-yard games. He's putting up 100-yard games because his team is winning.

At this point, it's hard to figure out why so many commentators and fans still overrate the importance of the running game. One problem has always been history. Older NFL analysts and fans came of age during the 1970s, when the rules favored the running game much more than those in the modern NFL. We used to have to explain that optimal strategies from 1974 are not optimal strategies for today. But this would seem to be a smaller problem now than it was ten years ago; most current NFL analysts played the game in the '90s or beyond, when the game was heavily pass-centric.

Another issue may be a confusion of professional football with other levels. As you go down the football pyramid, from NFL teams to FBS to FCS to Division II and so on down to high school, at every level further down the running game becomes more important. To give an example, the Carolina Panthers led the NFL in 2018 with 5.1 yards per carry—but that average was lower than five different teams in the SEC. Strategies that win on Saturday do not necessarily win on Sunday.

A great defense against the run is nothing without a good pass defense.

This is a corollary to the absurdity of "establish the run." With rare exceptions, teams win or lose with the passing game more than the running game—and by stopping the passing game more than the running game. Ron Jaworski puts it best: "The pass gives you the lead, and the run solidifies it." The reason why teams need a strong run defense in the playoffs is not to shut the run down early; it's to keep the other team from icing the clock if they get a lead. You can't mount a comeback if you can't stop the run.

Running on third-and-short is more likely to convert than passing on third-and-short.

On average, passing will always gain more yardage than running, with one very important exception: when a team is just 1 or 2 yards away from a new set of downs or the goal line. On third-and-1, a run will convert for a new set of downs 36 percent more often than a pass. Expand that to all third or fourth downs with 1 or 2 yards to go, and the run is successful 40 percent more often. With these percentages, the possibility of a long gain with a pass is not worth the tradeoff of an incompletion that kills a drive.

This is one reason why teams have to be able to both run and pass. The offense also has to keep some semblance of balance so they can use their play-action fakes—you can't run a play-fake from an empty set—and so the defense doesn't just run their nickel and dime packages all game. Balance also means that teams do need to pass occasionally in short-yardage situations; they just need to do it less than they do now. Teams pass roughly 60 percent of the time on third-and-2 even though runs in that situation convert 20 percent more often than passes. They pass 68 percent of the time on fourth-and-2 even though runs in that situation convert twice as often as passes.

You don't need to run a lot to set up play-action.

Of course, the idea that you have to run a little bit so play-action will work doesn't mean you have to run as often as NFL teams currently do. There's no correlation between a team's rushing frequency or success rate rushing and its play-action effectiveness over the course of either a single game or an entire season. That doesn't mean there wouldn't be a correlation at an extreme run/pass ratio, but we have yet to see an NFL team that even comes close to what that extreme might be.

Standard team rankings based on total yardage are inherently flawed.

Check out the schedule page on NFL.com, and you will find that each game is listed with league rankings based on total yardage. That is still how the NFL "officially" ranks teams, but these rankings rarely match up with common sense. That is because total team yardage may be the most context-dependent number in football.

It starts with the basic concept that rate stats are generally more valuable than cumulative stats. Yards per carry says more about a running back's quality than total yardage, completion percentage says more than just a quarterback's total number of completions. The same thing is true for teams; in fact, it is even more important because of the way football strategy influences the number of runs and passes in the game plan. Poor teams will give up fewer passing yards and more rushing yards because opponents will stop passing once they have a late-game lead and will run out the clock instead. For winning teams, the opposite is true. For example, which team had a better pass defense last year: Chicago or Tennessee? The answer is obviously the Bears, yet according to the official NFL rankings, Tennessee (3,471 net yards allowed on 572 passes and sacks, 6.1 net yards per pass) was a better pass defense than Chicago (3,515 net yards allowed on 665 passes and sacks, 5.3 net yards per pass).

Total yardage rankings are also skewed because some teams play at a faster pace than other teams. For example, last year Indianapolis (6,179) had more yardage than New Orleans (6,067). However, the Saints were the superior offense and much more efficient; they gained those yards on only 155 drives while the Colts needed 176 drives.

A team will score more when playing a bad defense and will give up more points when playing a good offense.

This sounds absurdly basic, but when people consider team and player stats without looking at strength of schedule, they are ignoring this. In 2012, for example, rookie Russell Wilson had a higher DVOA rating than fellow rookie Robert Griffin III because he faced a more difficult schedule, even though Griffin had slightly better standard stats. A more recent example: in 2018, Carolina and New England both had 5.9 yards per play on offense. New England was clearly the better offense by DVOA in part because New England played the fourth-hardest schedule of opposing defenses in the league while Carolina played the easiest schedule of opposing defenses.

If their overall yards per carry are equal, a running back who consistently gains yardage on every play is more valuable than a boom-and-bust running back who is frequently stuffed at the line but occasionally breaks a long highlight-worthy run.

Our brethren at Baseball Prospectus believe that the most precious commodity in baseball is outs. Teams only get 27 of them per game, and you can't afford to give one up for very little return. So imagine if there was a new rule in baseball that gave a team a way to earn another three outs in the middle of the inning. That would be pretty useful, right?

That's the way football works. You may start a drive 80 yards away from scoring, but as long as you can earn 10 yards in four chances, you get another four chances. Long gains have plenty of value, but if those long gains are mixed with a lot of short gains, you are going to put the quarterback in a lot of difficult third-and-long situations. That means more punts and more giving the ball back to the other team rather than moving the chains and giving the offense four more plays to work with.

The running back who gains consistent yardage is also going to do a lot more for you late in the game, when the goal of running the ball is not just to gain yardage but to eat clock time. If you are a Chargers fan watching your team with a late lead, you don't want to see three straight Melvin Gordon stuffs at the line followed by a punt. You want to see a game-icing first down.

A common historical misconception is that our preference for consistent running backs means that "Football Outsiders believes that Barry Sanders was overrated." Sanders wasn't just any boom-and-bust running back, though; he was the greatest boom-and-bust runner of all time, with bigger booms and fewer busts. Sanders ranked in the top five in DYAR five times (third in 1989, first in 1990, and second in 1994, 1996, and 1997).

Rushing is more dependent on the offensive line than people realize, but pass protection is more dependent on the quarterback himself than people realize.

Some readers complain that this idea contradicts the previous one. Aren't those consistent running backs just the product of good offensive lines? The truth is somewhere in between. There are certainly good running backs who suffer because their offensive lines cannot create consistent holes, but most boom-and-bust running backs contribute to their own problems by hesitating behind the line whenever the hole is unclear, looking for the home run instead of charging forward for the 4-yard gain that keeps the offense moving.

As for pass protection, some quarterbacks have better instincts for the rush than others, and are thus better at getting out of trouble by moving around in the pocket or throwing the ball away. Others will hesitate, hold onto the ball too long, and lose yardage over and over.

Note that "moving around in the pocket" does not necessarily mean "scrambling." In fact, a scrambling quarterback will often take more sacks than a pocket quarterback, because while he's running around trying to make something happen, a defensive lineman will catch up with him.

Shotgun formations are generally more efficient than formations with the quarterback under center.

From 2013 to 2017, offenses averaged roughly 5.9 yards per

play from Shotgun (or Pistol), but just 5.1 yards per play with the quarterback under center. In 2018 that gap closed a bit, but offenses still averaged 5.9 yards per play from Shotgun or Pistol compared to 5.5 yards per play with the quarterback under center. This wide split exists even if you analyze the data to try to weed out biases like teams using Shotgun more often on third-and-long, or against prevent defenses in the fourth quarter. Shotgun offense is more efficient if you only look at the first half, on every down, and even if you only look at running back carries rather than passes and scrambles.

It's hard to think of a Football Outsiders axiom that has been better assimilated by the people running NFL teams since we started doing this a decade ago. In 2001, NFL teams only used Shotgun on 14 percent of plays. Five years later, in 2006, that had increased slightly, to 20 percent of plays. By 2012, Shotgun was used on a 47.5 percent of plays (including the Pistol, but not counting the Wildcat or other direct snaps to non-quarterbacks). In 2016, the league as a whole was up to an average of 64.4 percent of plays from Shotgun or Pistol. Last year, that average was at 63.8 percent.

There's an interesting corollary here which we are just starting to study, because there does seem to be one split where offenses are *less* efficient from shotgun: play-action. In 2018, offenses averaged 8.2 yards per play when using play-action from an under-center formation, compared to 7.0 yards per play when using play-action from a Shotgun formation. A number of teams that are near the top of the league in play-action usage, such as the Rams and Patriots, are also near the bottom of the league in using Shotgun.

A running back with 370 or more carries during the regular season will usually suffer either a major injury or a loss of effectiveness the following year, unless he is named Eric Dickerson.

Terrell Davis, Jamal Anderson, and Edgerrin James all blew out their knees. Larry Johnson broke his foot. Earl Campbell and Eddie George went from legendary powerhouses to plodding, replacement-level players. Shaun Alexander broke his foot *and* became a plodding, replacement-level player. This is what happens when a running back is overworked to the point of having at least 370 carries during the regular season. DeMarco Murray was the latest player to follow up a high workload with a disappointing season.

The "Curse of 370" was expanded in our book *Pro Football Prospectus 2005* and includes seasons with 390 or more carries in the regular season and postseason combined. Research also shows that receptions don't cause a problem, only workload on the ground.

Plenty of running backs get injured without hitting 370 carries in a season, but there is a clear difference. On average, running backs with 300 to 369 carries and no postseason appearance will see their total rushing yardage decline by 15 percent the following year and their yards per carry decline by two percent. The average running back with 370 or more regular-season carries, or 390 including the postseason, will see their rushing yardage decline by 35 percent, and their yards per carry decline by eight percent. However, the Curse

of 370 is not a hard and fast line where running backs suddenly become injury risks. It is more of a concept where 370 carries roughly represent the point at which additional carries start to become more and more of a problem.

By the late 2010s, the Curse of 370 seems to have become a moot point. Since 2010, only two running backs have had more than 350 carries in a season: Murray with 392 in 2014 and Arian Foster with 351 in 2012.

Wide receivers must be judged on both complete and incomplete passes.

Here's an example from last season: Tyler Lockett had 1,147 receiving yards while Josh Gordon had just 853 receiving yards, even though the two receivers were just one target apart. Both receivers played with top quarterbacks, and each ran his average route roughly 15 yards downfield. But there was a big reason why Lockett had the best season in the history of our numbers, while Gordon merely had a good season: Lockett caught 81 percent of intended passes and Gordon caught just 58 percent.

Some work has been done on splitting responsibility for incomplete passes between quarterbacks and receivers, but not enough that we can incorporate this into our advanced stats at this time. We know that wide receiver catch rates are almost as consistent from year to year as quarterback completion percentages, but it is also important to look at catch rate in the context of the types of routes each receiver runs. A few years ago, we expanded on this idea with a new plus-minus metric, which is explained in the introduction to the chapter on wide receivers and tight ends.

The total quality of an NFL team is four parts offense, three parts defense, and one part special teams.

There are three units on a football team, but they are not of equal importance. Work by Chase Stuart, Neil Paine, and Brian Burke suggests a split between offense and defense of roughly 58-42, without considering special teams. Our research suggests that special teams contributes about 13 percent to total performance; if you measure the remaining 87 percent with a 58-42 ratio, you get roughly 4:3:1. When we compare the range of offense, defense, and special teams DVOA ratings, we get the same results, with the best and worst offenses roughly 130 percent stronger than the best and worst defenses, and roughly four times stronger than the best and worst special teams.

Offense is more consistent from year to year than defense, and offensive performance is easier to project than defensive performance. Special teams is less consistent than either.

Nobody in the NFL understood this concept better than former Indianapolis Colts general manager Bill Polian. Both the Super Bowl champion Colts and the four-time AFC champion Buffalo Bills of the early 1990s were built around the idea that if you put together an offense that can dominate the league year after year, eventually you will luck into a year where good health and a few smart decisions will give you a defense good enough to win a championship. (As the Colts learned in 2006, you don't even need a year, just four weeks.) Even the New England Patriots, who are led by a defense-first head coach in Bill Belichick, have been more consistent on offense than on defense since they began their run of success in 2001.

Teams with more offensive penalties generally lose more games, but there is no correlation between defensive penalties and losses.

Specific defensive penalties of course lose games; we've all sworn at the television when the cornerback on our favorite team gets flagged for a 50-yard pass interference penalty. Yet overall, there is no correlation between losses and the total of defensive penalties or even the total yardage on defensive penalties. One reason is that defensive penalties often represent *good* play, not bad. Cornerbacks who play tight coverage may be just on the edge of a penalty on most plays, only occasionally earning a flag. Defensive ends who get a good jump on rushing the passer will gladly trade an encroachment penalty or two for ten snaps where they get off the blocks a split-second before the linemen trying to block them.

In addition, offensive penalties have a higher correlation from year to year than defensive penalties. The penalty that correlates highest with losses is the false start, and the penalty that teams will have called most consistently from year to year is also the false start.

Recovery of a fumble, despite being the product of hard work, is almost entirely random.

Stripping the ball is a skill. Holding onto the ball is a skill. Pouncing on the ball as it is bouncing all over the place is not a skill. There is no correlation whatsoever between the percentage of fumbles recovered by a team in one year and the percentage they recover in the next year. The odds of recovery are based solely on the type of play involved, not the teams or any of their players.

The Chicago Bears are a good example. In 2017, the Bears recovered 12 of 14 fumbles by opponents (86 percent). The next year, the same defense recovered only eight of 18 fumbles by opponents (44 percent).

Fumble recovery is equally erratic on offense. In 2017, the Tennessee Titans recovered only two of nine fumbles on offense (22 percent). In 2018, the Titans recovered nine of 14 fumbles on offense (64 percent).

Fumble recovery is a major reason why the general public overestimates or underestimates certain teams. Fumbles are huge, turning-point plays that dramatically impact wins and losses in the past, while fumble recovery percentage says absolutely nothing about a team's chances of winning games in the future. With this in mind, Football Outsiders stats treat all fumbles as equal, penalizing them based on the likelihood of each type of fumble (run, pass, sack, etc.) being recovered by the defense.

Other plays that qualify as "non-predictive events" include two-point conversions, blocked kicks, and touchdowns during turnover returns. These plays are not "lucky," per se, but they have no value whatsoever for predicting future performance.

Field position is fluid.

As discussed in the Statistical Toolbox, every yard line on the field has a value based on how likely a team is to score from that location on the field as opposed to from a yard further back. The change in value from one yard to the next is the same whether the team has the ball or not. The goal of a defense is not just to prevent scoring, but to hold the opposition so that the offense can get the ball back in the best possible field position. A bad offense will score as many points as a good offense if it starts each drive 5 yards closer to the goal line.

A corollary to this precept: the most underrated aspect of an NFL team's performance is the field position gained or lost on kickoffs and punts. This is part of why players such as Cordarrelle Patterson can have such an impact on the game, even when they aren't taking a kickoff or punt all the way back for a touchdown.

The red zone is the most important place on the field to play well, but performance in the red zone from year to year is much less consistent than overall performance.

Although play in the red zone has a disproportionately high importance to the outcome of games relative to plays on the rest of the field, NFL teams do not exhibit a level of performance in the red zone that is consistently better or worse than their performance elsewhere, year after year. The simplest explanation why is a small(er) sample size and the inherent variance of football, with contributing factors like injuries and changes in personnel.

Injuries regress to the mean on the seasonal level, and teams that avoid injuries in a given season tend to win more games.

There are no doubt teams with streaks of good or bad health over multiple years. However, teams who were especially healthy or especially unhealthy, as measured by our adjusted games lost (AGL) metric, almost always head towards league average in the subsequent season. Furthermore, injury—or the absence thereof—has a huge correlation with wins, and a significant impact on a team's success. There's no doubt that a few high-profile teams have resisted this trend in recent years. The Patriots often deal with a high number of injuries, and the 2017 Eagles obviously overcame a number of important injuries to win the championship. Nonetheless, the overall rule still applies. Last year, six of the 11 teams with the lowest AGL made the playoffs: Baltimore, Chicago, the Los Angeles Rams, New Orleans, Kansas City, and Seattle. Meanwhile, only two of the 11 teams with the highest AGL made the playoffs: Indianapolis and Philadelphia.

By and large, a team built on depth is better than a team built on stars and scrubs.

Connected to the previous statement, because teams need to go into the season expecting that they will suffer an average number of injuries no matter how healthy they were the previous year. You cannot concentrate your salaries on a handful of star players because there is no such thing as avoiding injuries in the NFL. The game is too fast and the players too strong to build a team based around the idea that "if we can avoid all injuries this year, we'll win."

Running backs usually decline after age 28, tight ends after age 29, wide receivers after age 30, and quarterbacks after age 32.

This research was originally done by Doug Drinen (editor of pro-football-reference.com) in 2000. In recent years, a few players have had huge seasons above these general age limits, but the peak ages Drinen found a few years ago still apply to the majority of players.

As for "non-skill players," research we did in 2007 for *ESPN The Magazine* suggested that defensive ends and defensive backs generally begin to decline after age 29, linebackers and offensive linemen after age 30, and defensive tackles after age 31. However, because we still have so few statistics to use to study linemen and defensive players, this research should not be considered definitive.

The strongest indicator of how a college football team will perform in the upcoming season is their performance in recent seasons.

It may seem strange because graduation enforces constant player turnover, but college football teams are actually much more consistent from year to year than NFL teams. Thanks in large part to consistency in recruiting, teams can be expected to play within a reasonable range of their baseline program expectations each season. Our Program F/+ ratings, which represent a rolling five-year period of play-by-play and drive efficiency data, have an extremely strong (.76) correlation with the next year's F/+ rating.

Championship teams are generally defined by their ability to dominate inferior opponents, not their ability to win close games.

Football games are often decided by just one or two plays: a missed field goal, a bouncing fumble, the subjective spot of an official on fourth-and-1. One missed assignment by a cornerback or one slightly askew pass that bounces off a receiver's hands and into those of a defensive back five yards away and the game could be over. In a blowout, however, one lucky bounce isn't going to change things. Championship teams—in both professional and college football—typically beat their good opponents convincingly and destroy the cupcakes on the schedule.

Aaron Schatz

Statistical Toolbox

After 16 years of Football Outsiders, some of our readers are as comfortable with DVOA and ALY as they are with touchdowns and tackles. Yet to most fans, including our newer readers, it still looks like a lot of alphabet soup. That's what this chapter is for. The next few pages define and explain all of all the unique NFL statistics you'll find in this book: how we calculate them, what the numbers mean, and what they tell us about why teams win or lose football games. We'll go through the information in each of the tables that appear in each team chapter, pointing out whether those stats come from advanced mathematical manipulation of the standard play-by-play or tracking wat we see on television with the Sports Info Solutions game charting project. This chapter covers NFL statistics only. College metrics such as Highlight Yards and F/+ are explained in the introduction to the college football section on page 390.

We've done our best to present these numbers in a way that makes them easy to understand. This explanation is long, so feel free to read some of it, flip around the rest of the book, and then come back. It will still be here.

Defense-Adjusted Value Over Average (DVOA)

One running back runs for three yards. Another running back runs for three yards. Which is the better run?

This sounds like a stupid question, but it isn't. In fact, this question is at the heart of nearly all of the analysis in this book.

Several factors can differentiate one three-yard run from another. What is the down and distance? Is it third-and-2, or second-and-15? Where on the field is the ball? Does the player get only three yards because he hits the goal line and scores? Is the player's team up by two touchdowns in the fourth quarter and thus running out the clock, or down by two touchdowns and thus facing a defense that is playing purely against the pass? Is the running back playing against the porous defense of the Chiefs, or the stalwart defense of the Vikings?

Conventional NFL statistics value plays based solely on their net yardage. The NFL determines the best players by adding up all their yards no matter what situations they came in or how many plays it took to get them. Now, why would they do that? Football has one objective—to get to the end zone—and two ways to achieve that, by gaining yards and achieving first downs. These two goals need to be balanced to determine a player's value or a team's performance. All the yards in the world won't help a team win if they all come in six-yard chunks on third-and-10.

The popularity of fantasy football only exacerbates the problem. Fans have gotten used to judging players based on how much they help fantasy teams win and lose, not how much they help *real* teams win and lose. Typical fantasy scor-

ing further skews things by counting the yard between the one and the goal line as 61 times more important than all the other yards on the field (each yard worth 0.1 points, a touchdown worth 6.0). Let's say DeAndre Hopkins catches a pass on third-and-15 and goes 50 yards but gets tackled two yards from the goal line, and then Lamar Miller takes the ball on first-and-goal from the two-yard line and plunges in for the score. Has Miller done something special? Not really. When an offense gets the ball on first-and-goal at the two-yard line, they are going to score a touchdown five out of six times. Miller is getting credit for the work done by the passing game.

Doing a better job of distributing credit for scoring points and winning games is the goal of **DVOA**, or Defense-adjusted Value Over Average. DVOA breaks down every single play of the NFL season, assigning each play a value based on both total yards and yards towards a first down, based on work done by Pete Palmer, Bob Carroll, and John Thorn in their seminal book, *The Hidden Game of Football*. On first down, a play is considered a success if it gains 45 percent of needed yards; on second down, a play needs to gain 60 percent of needed yards; on third or fourth down, only gaining a new first down is considered success.

We then expand upon that basic idea with a more complicated system of "success points," improved over the past four years with a lot of mathematics and a bit of trial and error. A successful play is worth one point, an unsuccessful play zero points with fractional points in between (for example, eight yards on third-and-10 is worth 0.54 "success points"). Extra points are awarded for big plays, gradually increasing to three points for 10 yards (assuming those yards result in a first down), four points for 20 yards, and five points for 40 yards or more. Losing three or more yards is minus-1 point. Interceptions average minus-6 points, with an adjustment for the length of the pass and the location of the interception (since an interception tipped at the line is more likely to produce a long return than an interception on a 40-yard pass). A fumble is worth anywhere from minus-1.7 to minus-4.0 points depending on how often a fumble in that situation is lost to the defense—no matter who actually recovers the fumble. Red zone plays get a bonus: 20 percent for team offense, five percent for team defense, and 10 percent for individual players. There is a bonus given for a touchdown that acknowledges that the goal line is significantly more difficult to cross than the previous 99 yards (although this bonus is nowhere near as large as the one used in fantasy football).

(Our system is a bit more complex than the one in *Hidden Game* thanks to our subsequent research, which added larger penalty for turnovers, the fractional points, and a slightly higher baseline for success on first down. The reason why all fumbles are counted, no matter whether they are recovered by the offense or defense, is explained in the essay "Pregame Show.")

Every single play run in the NFL gets a "success value"

based on this system, and then that number gets compared to the average success values of plays in similar situations for all players, adjusted for a number of variables. These include down and distance, field location, time remaining in game, and the team's lead or deficit in the game score. Teams are always compared to the overall offensive average, as the team made its own choice whether to pass or rush. When it comes to individual players, however, rushing plays are compared to other rushing plays, passing plays to other passing plays, tight ends to tight ends, wideouts to wideouts, and so on.

Going back to our example of the three-yard rush, if Player A gains three yards under a set of circumstances in which the average NFL running back gains only one yard, then Player A has a certain amount of value above others at his position. Likewise, if Player B gains three yards on a play on which, under similar circumstances, an average NFL back gains four yards, that Player B has negative value relative to others at his position. Once we make all our adjustments, we can evaluate the difference between this player's rate of success and the expected success rate of an average running back in the same situation (or between the opposing defense and the average defense in the same situation, etc.). Add up every play by a certain team or player, divide by the total of the various baselines for success in all those situations, and you get VOA, or Value Over Average.

Of course, the biggest variable in football is the fact that each team plays a different schedule against teams of disparate quality. By adjusting each play based on the opposing defense's average success in stopping that type of play over the course of a season, we get DVOA, or Defense-adjusted Value Over Average. Rushing and passing plays are adjusted based on down and location on the field; passing plays are also adjusted based on how the defense performs against passes to running backs, tight ends, or wide receivers. Defenses are adjusted based on the average success of the *offenses* they are facing. (Yes, technically the defensive stats are "offense-adjusted." If it seems weird, think of the "D" in "DVOA" as standing for "opponent-Dependent" or something.)

The biggest advantage of DVOA is the ability to break teams and players down to find strengths and weaknesses in a variety of situations. In the aggregate, DVOA may not be quite as accurate as some of the other, similar "power ratings" formulas based on comparing drives rather than individual plays, but, unlike those other ratings, DVOA can be separated not just by player, but also by down, or by week, or by distance needed for a first down. This can give us a better idea of not just which team is better, but why, and what a team has to do in order to improve itself in the future. You will find DVOA used in this book in a lot of different ways—because it takes every single play into account, it can be used to measure a player or a team's performance in any situation. All Pittsburgh third downs can be compared to how an average team does on third down. Joe Flacco and Drew Lock can each be compared to how an average quarterback performs in the red zone, or with a lead, or in the second half of the game.

Since it compares each play only to plays with similar circumstances, it gives a more accurate picture of how much bet-

ter a team really is compared to the league as a whole. The list of top DVOA offenses on third down, for example, is more accurate than the conventional NFL conversion statistic because it takes into account that converting third-and-long is more difficult than converting third-and-short, and that a turnover is worse than an incomplete pass because it eliminates the opportunity to move the other team back with a punt on fourth down.

One of the hardest parts of understanding a new statistic is interpreting its scale, or what numbers represent good performance or bad performance. We've made that easy with DVOA. For each season, ratings are normalized so that 0% represents league average. A positive DVOA represents a situation that favors the offense, while a negative DVOA represents a situation that favors the defense. This is why the best offenses have positive DVOA ratings (last year, Kansas City led the NFL at 34.2%) and the best defenses have negative DVOA ratings (with Chicago on top at -26.0%).

The scale of offensive ratings is wider than the scale of defensive ratings. In most years, the best and worst offenses tend to rate around +/- 30%, while the best and worst defenses tend to rate around +/- 20%. For starting players, the scale tends to reach roughly +/-40% for passing and receiving, and +/- 30% for rushing. As you might imagine, some players with fewer attempts will surpass both extremes.

Team DVOA totals combine offense and defense by subtracting the latter from the former because the better defenses will have negative DVOA ratings. (Special teams performance is also added, as described later in this essay.) Certain plays are counted in DVOA for offense and not for defense, leading to separate baselines on each side of the ball. In addition, although the league ratings for offense and defense are always 0%, the league averages for passing and rushing separately are *not* 0%. Because passing is more efficient than rushing, the average for team passing is always positive and the average for team rushing is always negative. However, ratings for individual players only compare passes to other passes and runs to other runs, so the league average for individual passing is 0%, as are the league averages for rushing and the three separate league averages for receiving by wide receivers, tight ends, and running backs.

Some other important notes about DVOA:

- Only four penalties are included in DVOA. Two penalties count as pass plays on both sides of the ball: intentional grounding and defensive pass interference. The other two penalties are included for offense only: false starts and delay of game. Because the inclusion of these penalties means a group of negative plays that don't count as either passes or runs, the league averages for pass offense and run offense are higher than the league averages for pass defense and run defense.
- Aborted snaps and incomplete backwards lateral passes are only penalized on offense, not rewarded on defense.
- Adjustments for playing from behind or with a lead in the fourth quarter are different for offense and defense, as are adjustments for the final two minutes of the first

half when the offense is not near field goal range.
- Offense gets a slight penalty and defense gets a slight bonus for games indoors.

How well does DVOA work? Using correlation coefficients, we can show that only actual points scored are better than DVOA at indicating how many games a team has won (Table 1) and DVOA is a does a better job of predicting wins in the coming season than either wins or points scored in the previous season (Table 2).

(Correlation coefficient is a statistical tool that measures how two variables are related by using a number between 1 and minus-1. The closer to minus-1 or 1, the stronger the relationship, but the closer to 0, the weaker the relationship.)

Table 1. Correlation of Various Stats to Wins, 2006-2017

Stat	Offense	Defense	Total
Points Scored/Allowed	.759	-.693	.917
DVOA	.715	-.481	.864
Yards Gained/Allowed	.546	-.374	.672
Yards Gained/Allowed per Play	.543	-.353	.705

Table 2. Correlation of Various Stats to Wins Following Year, 2006-2017

Stat	Correlation
DVOA	.388
Point Differential	.385
Pythagorean Wins	.383
Yardage Differential	329
Wins	.328
Yards per Play Differential	.319

Special Teams

The problem with a system based on measuring both yardage and yardage towards a first down is what to do with plays that don't have the possibility of a first down. Special teams are an important part of football and we needed a way to add that performance to the team DVOA rankings. Our special teams metric includes five separate measurements: field goals and extra points, net punting, punt returns, net kickoffs, and kick returns.

The foundation of most of these special teams ratings is the concept that each yard line has a different value based on the likelihood of scoring from that position on the field. In *Hidden Game*, the authors suggested that the each additional yard for the offense had equal value, with a team's own goal line being worth minus-2 points, the 50-yard line 2 points, and the opposing goal line 6 points. (-2 points is not only the value of a safety, but also reflects the fact that when a team is backed up in its own territory, it is likely that its drive will stall, forcing a punt that will give the ball to the other team in good field position. Thus, the negative point value reflects the

fact that the defense is more likely to score next.) Our studies have updated this concept to reflect the actual likelihood that the offense or defense will have the next score from a given position on the field based on actual results from the past few seasons. The line that represents the value of field position is not straight, but curved, with the value of each yard increasing as teams approach either goal line.

Our special teams ratings compare each kick or punt to league average based on the point value of the position of the kick, catch, and return. We've determined a league average for how far a kick goes based on the line of scrimmage for each kick (almost always the 35-yard line for kickoffs, variable for punts) and a league average for how far a return goes based on both the yard line where the ball is caught and the distance that it traveled in the air.

The kicking or punting team is rated based on net points compared to average, taking into account both the kick and the return if there is one. Because the average return is always positive, punts that are not returnable (touchbacks, out of bounds, fair catches, and punts downed by the coverage unit) will rate higher than punts of the same distance which are returnable. (This is also true of touchbacks on kickoffs.) There are also separate individual ratings for kickers and punters that are based on distance and whether the kick is returnable, assuming an average return in order to judge the kicker separate from the coverage.

For the return team, the rating is based on how many points the return is worth compared to average, based on the location of the catch and the distance the ball traveled in the air. Return teams are not judged on the distance of kicks, nor are they judged on kicks that cannot be returned. As explained below, blocked kicks are so rare as to be statistically insignificant as predictors for future performance and are thus ignored. For the kicking team they simply count as missed field goals, for the defense they are gathered with their opponents' other missed field goals in Hidden value (also explained below).

Field goal kicking is measured differently. Measuring kickers by field goal percentage is a bit absurd, as it assumes that all field goals are of equal difficulty. In our metric, each field goal is compared to the average number of points scored on all field goal attempts from that distance over the past 15 years. The value of a field goal increases as distance from the goal line increases. Kickoffs, punts, and field goals are then adjusted based on weather and altitude. It will surprise no one to learn that it is easier to kick the ball in Denver or a dome than it is to kick the ball in Buffalo in December. Because we do not yet have enough data to tailor our adjustments specifically to each stadium, each one is assigned to one of four categories: Cold, Warm, Dome, and Denver. There is also an additional adjustment dropping the value of field goals in Florida (because the warm temperatures allow the ball to carry better).

The baselines for special teams are adjusted in each year for rule changes such as the introduction of the special teams-only "k-ball" in 1999, movement of the kickoff line, and the 2016 change in kickoff touchbacks. Baselines have also been adjusted each year to make up for the gradual improvement of kickers over the last two decades, and a new baseline was set two years ago for the longer distance on extra points.

Once we've totaled how many points above or below average can be attributed to special teams, we translate those points into DVOA so the ratings can be added to offense and defense to get total team DVOA.

There are three aspects of special teams that have an impact on wins and losses, but don't show up in the standard special teams rating because a team has little or no influence on them. The first is the length of kickoffs by the opposing team, with an asterisk. Obviously, there are no defenders standing on the 35-yard line, ready to block a kickoff after the whistle blows. However, over the past few years, some teams have deliberately kicked short in order to avoid certain top return men, such as Devin Hester and Cordarrelle Patterson. The special teams formula now includes adjustments to give teams extra credit for field position on kick returns if kickers are deliberately trying to avoid a return.

The other two items that special teams have little control over are field goals against your team, and punt distance against your team. Research shows no indication that teams can influence the accuracy or strength of field goal kickers and punters, except for blocks. As mentioned above, although blocked field goals and punts are definitely skillful plays, they are so rare that they have no correlation to how well teams have played in the past or will play in the future, thus they are included here as if they were any other missed field goal or botched punt, giving the defense no additional credit for their efforts. The value of these three elements is listed separately as "Hidden" value.

Special teams ratings also do not include two-point conversions or onside kick attempts, both of which, like blocks, are so infrequent as to be statistically insignificant in judging future performance.

Defense-Adjusted Yards Above Replacement (DYAR)

DVOA is a good stat, but of course it is not a perfect one. One problem is that DVOA, by virtue of being a percentage or rate statistic, doesn't take into account the cumulative value of having a player producing at a league-average level over the course of an above-average number of plays. By definition, an average level of performance is better than that provided by half of the league and the ability to maintain that level of performance while carrying a heavy work load is very valuable indeed. In addition, a player who is involved in a high number of plays can draw the defense's attention away from other parts of the offense, and, if that player is a running back, he can take time off the clock with repeated runs.

Let's say you have a running back who carries the ball 250 times in a season. What would happen if you were to remove this player from his team's offense? What would happen to those 250 plays? Those plays don't disappear with the player, though some might be lost to the defense because of the associated loss of first downs. Rather those plays would have to be distributed among the remaining players in the offense, with the bulk of them being given to a replacement running back. This is where we arrive at the concept of replacement level, borrowed from our friends at Baseball Prospectus. When a player is removed from an offense, he is usually not replaced by a player of similar ability. Nearly every starting player in the NFL is a starter because he is better than the alternative. Those 250 plays will typically be given to a significantly worse player, someone who is the backup because he doesn't have as much experience and/or talent. A player's true value can then be measured by the level of performance he provides above that replacement level baseline, totaled over all of his run or pass attempts.

Of course, the *real* replacement player is different for each team in the NFL. Last year, the player who was originally the third-string running back in Denver (Phillip Lindsay) ended up as the starter with a higher DVOA than original starter Royce Freeman. Sometimes a player such as Dion Lewis will be cut by one team and turn into a star for another. On other teams, the drop from the starter to the backup can be even greater than the general drop to replacement level. (The 2011 Indianapolis Colts will be the hallmark example of this until the end of time.) The choice to start an inferior player or to employ a sub-replacement level backup, however, falls to the team, not the starter being evaluated. Thus we generalize replacement level for the league as a whole as the ultimate goal is to evaluate players independent of the quality of their teammates.

Our estimates of replacement level are computed differently for each position. For quarterbacks, we analyzed situations where two or more quarterbacks had played meaningful snaps for a team in the same season, then compared the overall DVOA of the original starters to the overall DVOA of the replacements. We did not include situations where the backup was actually a top prospect waiting his turn on the bench, since a first-round pick is by no means a "replacement-level" player.

At other positions, there is no easy way to separate players into "starters" and "replacements," since unlike at quarterback, being the starter doesn't make you the only guy who gets in the game. Instead, we used a simpler method, ranking players at each position in each season by attempts. The players who made up the final 10 percent of passes or runs were split out as "replacement players" and then compared to the players making up the other 90 percent of plays at that position. This took care of the fact that not every non-starter is a freely available talent. (Think of Giovani Bernard or Duke Johnson, for example.)

As noted earlier, the challenge of any new stat is to present it on a scale that's meaningful to those attempting to use it. Saying that Andy Dalton's passes were worth 61 success value points over replacement in 2018 has very little value without a context to tell us if 61 is good total or a bad one. Therefore, we translate these success values into a number called "Defense-adjusted Yards Above Replacement, or DYAR. Thus, Dalton was fourth among quarterbacks with 404 passing DYAR. It is our estimate that a generic replacement-level quarterback, throwing in the same situations as Dalton, would have been worth 404 fewer yards. Note that this doesn't mean the replacement level quarterback would have gained exactly 404 fewer yards. First downs, touchdowns, and turnovers all have an estimated yardage value in this system, so what we are saying is that a generic replacement-level quarterback would have fewer yards and touchdowns (and more turnovers) that would total up to be equivalent to the value of 404 yards.

Problems with DVOA and DYAR

Football is a game in which nearly every action requires the work of two or more teammates—in fact, usually 11 teammates all working in unison. Unfortunately, when it comes to individual player ratings, we are still far from the point at which we can determine the value of a player independent from the performance of his teammates. That means that when we say, "In 2018, Christian McCaffrey had rushing DVOA of 9.7%," what we really are saying is, "In 2018, Christian McCaffrey, playing in Norv Turner's offensive system with the Carolina offensive line blocking for him and Cam Newton selling the fake when necessary, had a DVOA of 9.7%."

DVOA is limited by what's included in the official NFL play-by-play or tracked by our game charting partners (explained below). Because we need to have the entire play-by-play of a season in order to compute DVOA and DYAR, these metrics are not yet ready to compare players of today to players throughout the league's history. As of this writing, we have processed 33 seasons, 1986 through 2018, and we add seasons at a rate of roughly two per year (the most recent season, plus one season back into history.)

In addition, because we need to turn around DVOA and DYAR quickly during the season before charting can be completed, we do not yet have charting data such as dropped passes incorporated into these advanced metrics. Eventually we will have two sets of metrics, one incorporating charting data and going back to 2005 or 2006, and another that does not incorporate charting and can be used to compare current players and teams to players and teams all the way back to 1986 or earlier.

Pythagorean Projection

The Pythagorean projection is an approximation of each team's wins based solely on their points scored and allowed. This basic concept was introduced by baseball analyst Bill James, who discovered that the record of a baseball team could be very closely approximated by taking the square of team runs scored and dividing it by the sum of the squares of team runs scored and allowed. Statistician Daryl Morey, now general manager of the Houston Rockets, later extended this theorem to professional football, refining the exponent to 2.37 rather than 2.

The problem with that exponent is the same problem we've had with DVOA in recent years: the changing offensive levels in the NFL. 2.37 worked great based on the league 20 years

ago, but in the current NFL it ends up slightly underprojecting teams that play high-scoring games. The most accurate method is actually to adjust the exponent based on the scoring environment of each individual team. Kansas City games have a lot of points. Buffalo games feature fewer points.

This became known as Pythagenport when Clay Davenport of Baseball Prospectus started doing it with baseball teams. In the middle of the 2011 season, we switched our measurement of Pythagorean wins to a Pythagenport-style equation, modified for the NFL.[1] The improvement is slight, but noticeable due to the high-scoring teams that have dominated the last few years.

For a long time, Pythagorean projections did a remarkable job of predicting Super Bowl champions. From 1984 through 2004, 10 of 21 Super Bowls were won by the team that led the NFL in Pythagorean wins. Seven other Super Bowls during that time were won by the team that finished second. Super Bowl champions that led the league in Pythagorean wins but not actual wins include the 2004 Patriots, 2000 Ravens, 1999 Rams, and 1997 Broncos.

Super Bowl champions were much less predictable over the next few seasons. As of 2005, the 1980 Oakland Raiders held the mark for the fewest Pythagorean wins by a Super Bowl champion, 9.7. Then, between 2006 and 2012, four different teams won the Super Bowl with a lower Pythagorean win total: the 2006 Colts (9.6), the 2012 Ravens (9.4), the 2007 Giants (8.6), and the 2011 Giants (7.9), the first team in the 90-year history of the National Football League to ever be outscored during the regular season and still go on to win the championship. In the past six seasons, we've returned to more standard playoff results: eight of the last 12 Super Bowl teams ranked first or second in Pythagorean wins during the regular season. However, this was not the case last season, as the Rams finished third in Pythagorean wins and the Patriots were sixth.

Pythagorean wins are also useful as a predictor of year-to-year improvement. Teams that win a minimum of one full game more than their Pythagorean projection tend to regress the following year; teams that win a minimum of one full game less than their Pythagorean projection tend to improve the following year, particularly if they were at or above .500 despite their underachieving. No team qualified for this combination in 2018; Baltimore was closest, going 10-6 despite 10.8 Pythagorean wins. On the other side, there are teams that seem set for a reversion of luck. The Los Angeles Rams went 13-3 despite just 10.9 Pythagorean wins, the only team in 2018 with at least two more wins than projected wins.

Adjusted Line Yards

One of the most difficult goals of statistical analysis in football is isolating the degree to which each of the 22 men on the field is responsible for the result of a given play. Nowhere is this as significant as the running game, in which one

---

1 The equation, for those curious, is 1.5 x log ((PF+PA)/G).

player runs while up to nine other players—including not just linemen but also wideouts and tight ends—block in different directions. None of the statistics we use for measuring rushing—yards, touchdowns, yards per carry—differentiate between the contribution of the running back and the contribution of the offensive line. Neither do our advanced metrics DVOA and DYAR.

We do, however, have enough play-by-play data amassed that we can try to separate the effect that the running back has on a particular play from the effects of the offensive line (and other offensive blockers) and the opposing defense. A team might have two running backs in its stable: RB A, who averages 3.0 yards per carry, and RB B, who averages 3.5 yards per carry. Who is the better back? Imagine that RB A doesn't just average 3.0 yards per carry, but gets exactly 3 yards on every single carry, while RB B has a highly variable yardage output: sometimes 5 yards, sometimes minus-2 yards, sometimes 20 yards. The difference in variability between the runners can be exploited not only to determine the difference between the runners, but the effect the offensive line has on every running play.

At some point in every long running play, the running back passes all of his offensive line blocks as well as additional blocking backs or receivers. From there on, the rest of the play is dependent on the runner's own speed and elusiveness and the speed and tackling ability of the opposing defense. If David Johnson breaks through the line for 50 yards, avoiding tacklers all the way to the goal line, his offensive line has done a great job—but they aren't responsible for the majority of the yards gained. The trick is figuring out exactly how much they *are* responsible for.

For each running back carry, we calculated the probability that the back involved would run for the specific yardage on that play based on that back's average yardage per carry and the variability of their yardage from play to play. We also calculated the probability that the offense would get the yardage based on the team's rushing average and variability using all backs *other* than the one involved in the given play, and the probability that the defense would give up the specific amount of yardage based on its average rushing yards allowed per carry and variability.

A regression analysis breaks the value for rushing yardage into the following categories: losses, 0-4 yards, 5-10 yards, and 11+ yards. In general, the offensive line is 20 percent more responsible for lost yardage than it is for positive gains up to four yards, but 50 percent less responsible for additional yardage gained between five and ten yards, and not at all responsible for additional yardage past ten yards.

By applying those percentages to every running back carry, we were able to create **adjusted line yards (ALY)**, a statistic that measured offensive line performance. (We don't include carries by receivers, which are usually based on deception rather than straight blocking, or carries by quarterbacks, although we may need to reconsider that given the recent use of the read option in the NFL.) Those numbers are then adjusted based on down, distance, situation, opponent and whether or not a team is in the shotgun. (Because defenses are generally

playing pass when the quarterback is in shotgun, the average running back carry from shotgun last year gained 4.61 yards, compared to just 4.22 yards on other carries.) The adjusted numbers are then normalized so that the league average for adjusted line yards per carry is the same as the league average for RB yards per carry. Adjusted line yards numbers are normalized differently in each season, so that normalization is based on that year's average for RB yards per carry rather than a historical average.

The NFL distinguishes between runs made to seven different locations on the line: left/right end, left/right tackle, left/right guard, and middle. Further research showed no statistically significant difference between how well a team performed on runs listed as having gone up the middle or past a guard, so we separated runs into just five different directions (left/right end, left/right tackle, and middle). Note that there may not be a statistically significant difference between right tackle and middle/guard either, but pending further research (and for the sake of symmetry) we still list runs behind the right tackle separately. These splits allow us to evaluate subsections of a team's offensive line, but not necessarily individual linesmen, as we can't account for blocking assignments or guards who pull towards the opposite side of the line after the snap.

Success Rate

Success rate is a statistic for running backs that measures how consistently they achieve the yardage necessary for a play to be deemed successful. Some running backs will mix a few long runs with a lot of failed runs of one or two yards, while others with similar yards-per-carry averages will consistently gain five yards on first down, or as many yards as necessary on third down. This statistic helps us differentiate between the two.

Since success rate compares rush attempts to other rush attempts, without consideration of passing, the standard for success on first down is slightly lower than those described above for DVOA. In addition, the standard for success changes slightly in the fourth quarter when running backs are used to run out the clock. A team with the lead is satisfied with a shorter run as long as it stays in bounds. Conversely, for a team down by a couple of touchdowns in the fourth quarter, four yards on first down isn't going to be a big help.

The formula for running back success rate is as follows:
- A successful play must gain 40 percent of needed yards on first down, 60 percent of needed yards on second down, and 100 percent of needed yards on third or fourth down.
- If the offense is behind by more than a touchdown in the fourth quarter, the benchmarks switch to 50 percent, 65 percent, and 100 percent.
- If the offense is ahead by any amount in the fourth quarter, the benchmarks switch to 30 percent, 50 percent, and 100 percent.

The league-average success rate in 2018 was 47.8 percent. Success Rate is not adjusted based on defenses faced and is not calculated for quarterbacks and wide receivers who occasionally carry the ball. Note gain that our calculation of success rate for running back is different from the success rate we use as a basis for DVOA, and other success rate calculations you may find across the Internet.

Approximate Value

Approximate Value is a system created by Doug Drinen of Pro Football Reference. The goal is to put a single number on every season of every NFL player since 1950, using a very broad set of guidelines. The goal is not to make judgments on individual seasons, but rather to have a format for studying groups of seasons that is more accurate than measuring players with a very broad brush such as "games started" or "number of Pro Bowls." Skill players are rated primarily using basic stats, while offensive linemen and defensive players are rated in large part based on team performance as well as individual accolades and games started. Advanced stats from Football Outsiders play-by-play breakdown are not part of this system. It is obviously imperfect—"approximate" is right there in the name—but it's valuable for studying groups of draft picks, groups of players by age, and so on. The system is introduced and explained at https://www.pro-football-reference.com/blog/index37a8.html

KUBIAK Projection System

Most "skill position" players whom we expect to play a role this season receive a projection of their standard 2019 NFL statistics using the KUBIAK projection system. KUBIAK takes into account a number of different factors including expected role, performance over the past two seasons, age, height, weight, historical comparables, and projected team performance on offense and defense. When we named our system KUBIAK, it was a play on the PECOTA system used by our partners at Baseball Prospectus—if they were going to name their system after a long-time eighties backup, we would name our system after a long-time eighties backup. Little did we know that Gary Kubiak would finally get a head coaching job the very next season. After some debate, we decided to keep the name, although discussing projections for Denver players was a bit awkward for a while.

To clear up a common misconception among our readers, KUBIAK projects individual player performances only, not teams.

2018 Win Projection System

In this book, each of the 32 NFL teams receives a **2019 Mean Projection** at the beginning of its chapter. These projections stem from three equations that forecast 2019 DVOA for offense, defense, and special teams based on a number of different factors. This offseason, we overhauled and improved the team projection system for the first time in a few years. The new system starts by considering the team's DVOA over the past three seasons and, on offense, a separate projection for the starting quarterback. The new system also does a much better job of measuring the value of offseason personnel changes by incorporating a measure that's based on the net personnel change in DYAR among non-quarterbacks (for offense) and the net change in Approximate Value above replacement level (for defense). Other factors include coaching experience, recent draft history, certain players returning from injury, and combined tenure on the offensive line.

These three equations produce precise numbers representing the most likely outcome, but also produce a range of possibilities, used to determine the probability of each possible offensive, defensive, and special teams DVOA for each team. This is particularly important when projecting football teams, because with only 16 games in a season, a team's performance may vary wildly from its actual talent level due to a couple of random bounces of the ball or badly timed injuries. In addition, the economic structure of the NFL allows teams to make sudden jumps or drops in overall ability more often than in other sports.

This projection system was built using the years 2003-2014. For the four years since, 2015-2018, the mean DVOA forecast by this new projection system had a correlation coefficient with actual wins of .489. By comparison, previous year's point differential had a correlation of .400, and previous year's wins had a correlation of just .313.

The next step in our forecast involves simulating the season one million times. We use the projected range of DVOA possibilities to produce 1,000 different simulated seasons with 32 sets of DVOA ratings. We then plug those season-long DVOA ratings into the same equation we use during the season to determine each team's likely remaining wins for our Playoff Odds Report. The simulation takes each season game-by-game, determining the home or road team's chance of winning each game based on the DVOA ratings of each team as well as home-field advantage. A random number between 0 and 100 determines whether the home or road team has won that game. We ran 1,000 simulations with each of the 1,000 sets of DVOA ratings, creating a million different simulations. The simulation was programmed by Mike Harris.

We use a system we call a "dynamic simulation" to better approximate the true distribution of wins in the NFL. When simulating the season, each team had 2.0% DVOA added or subtracted after a win or loss, reflecting the fact that a win or loss tends to tell us whether a team is truly better or worse than whatever their mean projection had been before the season. Using this method, a team projected with 20.0% DVOA which goes 13-3 will have a 40.0% DVOA entering the playoffs, which is much more realistic. This change gave us more projected seasons at the margins, with fewer seasons at 8-8 and more seasons at 14-2 or 2-14. The dynamic simulation also meant a slight increase in projected wins for the best teams, and a slight decrease for the worst teams. However, the conservative nature of our projection system still means the distribution of mean projected wins has a much smaller spread than the actual win-loss records we will see by the end of December. We will continue to experiment with changes to the simulation in order to produce the most accurate possible forecast of the NFL season in future years.

Football Outsiders
Game Charting Data

Each of the formulas listed above relies primarily on the play-by-play data published by the NFL. When we began to analyze the NFL, this was all that we had to work with. Just as a television broadcast has a color commentator who gives more detail to the facts related by the play-by-play announcer, so too do we need some color commentary to provide contextual information that breathes life into these plain lines of numbers and text. We added this color commentary with game charting.

Beginning in 2005, Football Outsiders began using a number of volunteers to chart every single play of every regular-season and postseason NFL game. To put it into perspective, there were over 54,000 lines of play-by-play information in each NFL season and our goal is to add several layers of detail to nearly all of them.

It gradually became clear that attempting to chart so much football with a crew of volunteers was simply not feasible, especially given our financial resources compared to those of our competitors. Over the past few years, we have partnered with larger companies to take on the responsibilities of game charting so that we can devote more time to analysis.

In 2015, Football Outsiders reached an agreement with Sports Info Solutions, formerly Baseball Info Solutions, to begin a large charting project that would replace our use of volunteers. We also have a partnership with ESPN Stats & Info and use their data to check against the data collected by Sports Info Solutions. All charting data for the 2018 season is provided by one of these two companies.

Our partnership with Sports Info Solutions has also resulted in the expansion of Football Outsiders Premium with a new NFL Charting Data subscription that updates some of our data such as cornerback charting and broken tackles every week during the season. We also produce the Off The Charts podcast, which explores data from game charting in a weekly discussion of the NFL season.[1]

Game charting is significantly easier now that the NFL makes coaches' film available through NFL Game Rewind. This tape, which was not publicly available when we began charting with volunteers in 2005, includes sideline and end zone perspectives for each play, and shows all 22 players at all times, making it easier to see the cause-and-effect of certain actions taken on the field. Nonetheless, all game charting is still imperfect. You often cannot tell which players did their jobs particularly well or made mistakes without knowing the play call and each player's assignment, particularly when it comes to zone coverage or pass-rushers who reach the quarterback without being blocked. Therefore, the goal of game charting from both ESPN Stats & Info and Sports Info Solutions is *not* to "grade" players, but rather to attempt to mark specific events: a pass pressure, a blown block, a dropped interception, and so on.

We emphasize that all data from game charting is unofficial.

Other sources for football statistics may keep their own measurements of yards after catch or how teams perform against the blitz. Our data will not necessarily match theirs. Even ESPN Stats & Info and Sports Info Solutions have a number of disagreements, marking different events on the same play because it can be difficult to determine the definition of a "pressure" or a "dropped pass." However, any other group that is publicly tracking this data is also working off the same footage, and thus will run into the same issues of difficulty and subjectivity.

There are lots of things we would like to do with all-22 film that we simply haven't been able to do yet, such as charting coverage by cornerbacks when they aren't the target of a given pass, or even when pass pressure prevents the pass from getting into the air. Unfortunately, we are limited by what our partners are able to chart given time constraints.

In the description of data below, we have tried to designate which data from 2018 comes from ESPN Stats & Info group (ESPN S&I), which data comes from Sports Info Solutions (SIS), and where we have combined data from both companies with our own analysis.

Formation/Personnel

For each play, we have the number of running backs, wide receivers, and tight ends on the field courtesy of ESPN S&I. Players were marked based on their designation on the roster, not based on where they lined up on the field. Obviously, this could be difficult with some hybrid players or players changing positions in 2018, but we did our best to keep things as consistent as possible.

SIS also tracked this data and added the names of players who were lined up in unexpected positions. This included marking tight ends or wide receivers in the backfield, and running backs or tight ends who were lined up either wide or in the slot (often referred to as "flexing" a tight end). SIS also marked when a fullback or tight end was actually a sixth (or sometimes even seventh) offensive lineman, and they marked the backfield formation as empty back, single back, I formation, offset I, split backs, full house, or "other." These notations of backfield formation were recorded directly before the snap and do not account for positions before pre-snap motion.

SIS then marked defensive formations by listing the number of linemen, linebackers, and defensive backs. There will be mistakes—a box safety may occasionally be confused for a linebacker, for example—but for the most part the data for defensive backs will be accurate. Figuring out how to mark whether a player is a defensive end or a linebacker is a different story. The rise of hybrid defenses has led to a lot of confusion. Edge rushers in a 4-3 defense may play standing up because they used to play for a 3-4 defense and that's what they are used to. A player who is usually considered an outside linebacker for a 3-4 defense may put his hand on the ground on third down (thus looking like a 4-3 defensive end), but the tackle next to him is still two-gapping (which is generally a

3-4 principle). SIS marked personnel in a simplified fashion by designating any front seven player in a standing position as a linebacker and designating any front seven player in a crouching position as a defensive lineman.

For the last three years, we also have data from SIS on where receivers lined up before each of their pass targets (wide, slot, tight, or backfield) and what routes they ran.

Rushers and Blockers

ESPN Stats & Info provided us with two data points regarding the pass rush: the number of pass-rushers on a given play, and the number defensive backs blitzing on a given play. SIS also tracked this data for comparison purposes and then added a count of blockers. Counting blockers is an art as much as a science. Offenses base their blocking schemes on how many rushers they expect. A running back or tight end's assignment may depend on how many pass-rushers cross the line at the snap. Therefore, an offensive player was deemed to be a blocker if he engaged in an actual block, or there was some hesitation before running a route. A running back that immediately heads out into the flat is not a blocker, but one that waits to verify that the blocking scheme is working and then goes out to the flat would, in fact, be considered a blocker.

Pass Play Details

Both companies recorded the following data for all pass plays:

- Did the play begin with a play-action fake, including read-option fakes that developed into pass plays instead of being handed to a running back?
- Was the quarterback in or out of the pocket?
- Was the quarterback under pressure in making his pass?
- Was this a screen pass?

SIS game charting also marks the name of the defender who caused the pass pressure. Charters were allowed to list two names if necessary, and could also attribute a hurry to "overall pressure." No defender was given a hurry and a sack on the same play, but defenders were given hurries if they helped force a quarterback into a sack that was finished by another player. SIS also identified which defender(s) caused the pass pressure which forced a quarterback to scramble for yardage. If the quarterback wasn't under pressure but ran anyway, the play could be marked either as "coverage scramble" (if the quarterback ran because there were no open receivers) or "hole opens up" (if the quarterback ran because he knew he could gain significant yardage). All pressure data in this book is based on SIS data.

Some places in this book, we divide pass yardage into two numbers: distance in the air and yards after catch. This information is tracked by the NFL, but it can be hard to find and the official scorers often make errors, so we corrected the original data based on input from both ESPN S&I and SIS. Distance in the air is based on the distance from the line of scrimmage to the place where the receiver either caught or was supposed to catch the pass. We do not count how far the quarterback was behind the line or horizontal yardage if the quarterback threw across the field. All touchdowns are counted to the goal line,

so that distance in the air added to yards after catch always equals the official yardage total kept by the league.

Incomplete Passes

Quarterbacks are evaluated based on their ability to complete passes. However, not all incompletes should have the same weight. Throwing a ball away to avoid a sack is actually a valuable incomplete, and a receiver dropping an otherwise quality pass is hardly a reflection on the quarterback.

This year, our evaluation of incomplete passes began with ESPN Stats & Info, which marked passes as Overthrown, Underthrown, Thrown Away, Batted Down at the Line, Defensed, or Dropped. We then compared this data to similar data from SIS and made some changes. We also changed some plays to reflect a couple of additional categories we have kept in past years for Football Outsiders: Hit in Motion (indicating the quarterback was hit as his arm was coming forward to make a pass), Caught Out of Bounds, and Hail Mary.

ESPN S&I and SIS also marked when a defender dropped an interception; Football Outsiders volunteers then analyzed plays where the two companies disagreed to come up with a final total. When a play is close, we tend to err on the side of not marking a dropped interception, as we don't want to blame a defender who, for example, jumps high for a ball and has it tip off his fingers. We also counted a few "defensed" interceptions, when a quarterback threw a pass that would have been picked off if not for the receiver playing defense on the ball. These passes counted as dropped interceptions for quarterbacks but not for the defensive players.

Defenders

The NFL play-by-play lists tackles and, occasionally, tipped balls, but it does not definitively list the defender on the play. SIS charters attempted to determine which defender was primarily responsible for covering either the receiver at the time of the throw or the location to which the pass was thrown, regardless of whether the pass was complete or not.

Every defense in the league plays zone coverage at times, some more than others, which leaves us with the question of how to handle plays without a clear man assigned to that receiver. Charters (SIS employees in 2015-2018, and FO volunteers in previous seasons) had three alternatives:

- We asked charters to mark passes that found the holes in zone coverage as Hole in Zone, rather than straining to assign that pass to an individual defender. We asked the charter to also note the player who appeared to be responsible for that zone, and these defenders are assigned half credit for those passes. Some holes were so large that no defender could be listed along with the Hole in Zone designation.
- Charters were free to list two defenders instead of one. This could be used for actual double coverage, or for zone coverage in which the receiver was right between two close defenders rather than sitting in a gaping hole. When two defenders are listed, ratings assign each with half credit.
- Screen passes and dumpoffs are marked as Uncovered

unless a defender (normally a linebacker) is obviously shadowing that specific receiver on the other side of the line of scrimmage.

Since we began the charting project in 2005, nothing has changed our analysis more than this information on pass coverage. However, even now with the ability to view all-22 film, it can be difficult to identify the responsible defender except when there is strict man-to-man coverage.

Additional Details

All draw plays were marked, whether by halfbacks or quarterbacks. Option runs and zone reads were also marked.

Both SIS and ESPN S&I when the formation was pistol as opposed to shotgun; the official play-by-play simply marks these plays all as shotgun.

Both SIS and ESPN S&I track yards after contact for each play.

SIS charters marked each quarterback sack with one of the following terms: Blown Block, Coverage Sack, QB Fault, Failed Scramble, or Blitz/Overall Pressure. Blown Blocks were listed with the name of a specific offensive player who allowed the defender to come through. (Some blown block sacks are listed with two blockers, who each get a half-sack..) Coverage Sack denotes when the quarterback has plenty of time to throw but cannot find an open receiver. QB Fault represents "self sacks" listed without a defender, such as when the quarterback drops back, only to find the ball slip out of his hands with no pass-rusher touching him. Failed Scramble represents plays where a quarterback began to run without major pass pressure because he thought he could get a positive gain, only to be tackled before he passed the line of scrimmage.

SIS tracked "broken tackles" on all runs or pass plays. We define a "broken tackle" as one of two events: Either the ballcarrier escapes from the grasp of the defender, or the defender is in good position for a tackle but the ballcarrier jukes him out of his shoes. If the ballcarrier sped by a slow defender who dived and missed, that did not count as a broken tackle. If the defender couldn't bring the ballcarrier down because he is being blocked out of the play by another offensive player, this did not count as a broken tackle. It was possible to mark multiple broken tackles on the same play. Broken tackles are not marked for special teams.

How to Read the Team Summary Box

Here is a rundown of all the tables and stats that appear in the 32 team chapters. Each team chapter begins with a box in the upper-right hand corner that gives a summary of our statistics for that team, as follows:

2018 Record gives each team's actual win-loss record. **Pythagorean Wins** gives the approximate number of wins expected last year based on this team's raw totals of points scored and allowed, along with their NFL rank. **Snap-Weighted Age** gives the average age of the team in 2018, weighted

based on how many snaps each player was on the field and ranked from oldest (New England, first at 27.9) to youngest (Dallas, 32nd at 25.3). **Average Opponent** gives a ranking of last year's schedule strength based on the average DVOA of all 16 opponents faced during the regular season. Teams are ranked from the hardest schedule of 2018 (Oakland) to the easiest (Indianapolis).

Total DVOA gives the team's total DVOA rating, with rank. **Offense**, **Defense**, and **Special Teams** list the team's DVOA rating in each category, along with NFL rank. Remember that good offenses and special teams have positive DVOA numbers, while a negative DVOA means better defense, so the lowest defensive DVOA is ranked No. 1 (last year, Chicago).

2019 Mean Projection gives the average number of wins for this team based on the 2019 Win Projection System described earlier in this chapter. Please note that we do not expect any teams to win the exact number of games in their mean projection. First of all, no team can win 0.8 of a game. Second, because these projections represent a whole range of possible values, the averages naturally tend to drift towards 8-8. Obviously, we're not expecting a season where no team goes 4-12 or 12-4. For a better way to look at the projections, we offer **Postseason Odds**, which give each team's chance of making the postseason based on our simulation, and **Super Bowl Appearance** odds, which give each team's chance of representing its conference in Super Bowl LIV. The average team will make the playoffs in 37.5 percent of simulations, and the Super Bowl in 6.3 percent of simulations.

Projected Average Opponent gives the team's strength of schedule for 2019; like the listing for last year's schedule strength in the first column of the box, this number is based not on last year's record but on the mean projected DVOA for each opponent. A positive schedule is harder, a negative schedule easier. Teams are ranked from the hardest projected schedule (Denver, first) to the easiest (New England, 32nd). This strength of schedule projection does not take into account which games are home or away, or the timing of the bye week.

The final column of the box gives the team's chances of finishing in four different basic categories of success:
- On the Clock (0-4 wins; NFL average 12%)
- Mediocrity (5-7 wins; NFL average 32%)
- Playoff Contender (8-10 wins; NFL average 36%)
- Super Bowl Contender (11+ wins; NFL average 20%)

The percentage given for each category is dependent not only on how good we project the team to be in 2019, but the level of variation possible in that projection, and the expected performance of the teams on the schedule.

You'll also find a table with the team's 2019 schedule placed within each chapter, along with a graph showing each team's 2018 week-to-week performance by single-game DVOA. The second, dotted line on the graph represents a five-week moving average of each team's performance, in order to show a longer-term view of when they were improving and declining. After the essays come statistical tables and comments related to that team and its specific units.

Weekly Performance

The first table gives a quick look at the team's week-to-week performance in 2018. (Table 3) This includes the playoffs for those teams that made the postseason, with the four weeks of playoffs numbered 18 (wild card) through 21 (Super Bowl). All other tables in the team chapters represent regular-season performance only unless otherwise noted.

Looking at the first week for the Chicago Bears in 2018, the first five columns are fairly obvious: Chicago opened the season with a 24-23 loss on the road in Green Bay. **YDF** and **YDA** are net yards on offense and net yards against the defense. These numbers do not include penalty yardage or special teams yardage. **TO** represents the turnover margin. Unlike other parts of the book in which we consider all fumbles as equal, this only represents actual turnovers: fumbles lost and interceptions. So, for example, the Bears forced one more turnover than Detroit in Week 12 but committed two more turnovers than the New York Giants in Week 13.

Finally, you'll see DVOA ratings for this game: Total **DVOA** first, then offense (**Off**), defense (**Def**), and special teams (**ST**). Note that these are DVOA ratings, adjusted for opponent, so a loss to a good team will often be listed with a higher rating than a close win over a bad team. For example, the Bears have a positive DVOA for their Week 1 loss to Green Bay, but a negative DVOA for their Week 3 win over Arizona.

Trends and Splits

Next to the week-to-week performance is a table giving DVOA for different portions of a team's performance, on both offense and defense. Each split is listed with the team's rank among the 32 NFL teams. These numbers represent regular season performance only.

Total DVOA gives total offensive, and defensive DVOA in all situations. **Unadjusted VOA** represents the breakdown of play-by-play considering situation but not opponent. A team whose offensive DVOA is higher than its offensive VOA played a harder-than-average schedule of opposing defenses; a team with a lower defensive DVOA than defensive VOA player a harder-than-average schedule of opposing offenses.

Weighted Trend lowers the importance of earlier games to give a better idea of how the team was playing at the end of the regular season. The final four weeks of the season are full strength; moving backwards through the season, each week is given less and less weight until the first three weeks of the season, which are not included at all. **Variance** is the same as noted above, with a higher percentage representing less consistency. This is true for both offense and defense: Philadelphia, for example, was very consistent on offense (3.5%, third) but inconsistent on defense (8.3%, 30th). **Average Opponent** is that the same thing that appears in the box to open each chapter, except split in half: the average DVOA of all opposing defenses (for offense) or the average DVOA of all opposing offenses (for defense).

Passing and **Rushing** are fairly self-explanatory. Note that

Table 3. 2018 Bears Stats by Week

Wk	vs.	W-L	PF	PA	YDF	YDA	TO	Total	Off	Def	ST
1	at GB	L	23	24	294	370	+1	5%	-26%	-26%	6%
2	SEA	W	24	17	271	276	0	35%	-8%	-38%	4%
3	at ARI	W	16	14	316	221	+2	-35%	-37%	-8%	-6%
4	TB	W	48	10	483	311	+3	95%	44%	-44%	7%
5	BYE										
6	at MIA	L	28	31	467	541	0	-14%	10%	16%	-8%
7	NE	L	31	38	453	381	+1	-15%	9%	-9%	-34%
8	NYJ	W	24	10	395	207	0	23%	24%	-8%	-9%
9	at BUF	W	41	9	190	264	+3	50%	0%	-45%	5%
10	DET	W	34	22	402	305	+3	54%	49%	-29%	-24%
11	MIN	W	25	20	308	268	0	31%	-2%	-28%	5%
12	at DET	W	23	16	264	333	+1	3%	-18%	-22%	-1%
13	at NYG	L	27	30	376	338	-2	-33%	-54%	-22%	-1%
14	LAR	W	15	6	294	214	+1	47%	-37%	-85%	-2%
15	GB	W	24	17	332	323	0	30%	-11%	-20%	21%
16	at SF	W	14	9	325	279	-1	18%	10%	-17%	-9%
17	at MIN	W	24	10	332	164	0	45%	14%	-37%	-5%
18	PHI	L	15	16	356	300	+2	34%	5%	-25%	4%

rushing DVOA includes all rushes, not just those by running backs, including quarterback scrambles that may have begun as pass plays.

The next three lines split out DVOA on **First Down**, **Second Down**, and **Third Down**. Third Down here includes fourth downs on which a team runs a regular offensive play instead of punting or attempting a field goal. **First Half** and **Second Half** represent the first two quarters and last two quarters (plus overtime), not the first eight and last eight games of the regular season. Next comes DVOA in the **Red Zone**, which is any offensive play starting from the defense's 20-yard line through the goal line. The final split is **Late and Close**, which includes any play in the second half or overtime when the teams are within eight points of each other in either direction. (Eight points, of course, is the biggest deficit that can be made up with a single score, a touchdown and two-point conversion.)

Five-Year Performance

This table gives each team's performance over the past five seasons. (Table 4) It includes win-loss record, Pythagorean Wins, **Estimated Wins**, points scored and allowed, and turnover margin. Estimated wins are based on a formula that estimates how many games a team would have been expected to win based on 2018 performance in specific situations, normalized to eliminate luck (fumble recoveries, opponents' missed field goals, etc.) and assuming average schedule strength. The formula emphasizes consistency and overall DVOA as well as DVOA in a few specifically important situations. The next columns of this table give total DVOA along with DVOA for offense, defense, and special teams, and the rank for each among that season's 32 NFL teams.

The next four columns give the adjusted games lost (AGL) for starters on both offense and defense, along with rank. (Our

Table 4. Cincinnati Bengals Five-Year Performance

Year	W-L	Pyth W	Est W	PF	PA	TO	Total	Rk	Off	Rk	Def	Rk	ST	Rk	Off AGL	Rk	Def AGL	Rk	Off Age	Rk	Def Age	Rk	ST Age	Rk
2014	10-5-1	8.6	9.0	365	344	0	5.0%	12	-1.4%	18	-2.3%	14	4.2%	6	48.5	28	23.2	5	25.9	29	28.1	2	26.1	14
2015	12-4	11.7	12.3	419	279	+11	27.9%	2	18.6%	2	-7.1%	10	2.2%	8	10.0	1	18.2	6	26.2	23	28.1	2	26.5	10
2016	6-9-1	8.3	8.0	325	315	+3	4.0%	13	7.5%	11	0.8%	17	-2.7%	28	24.7	7	10.4	2	26.7	17	28.2	1	26.4	7
2017	7-9	6.2	6.7	290	349	-9	-12.6%	24	-6.5%	22	3.7%	17	-2.4%	21	43.4	22	37.5	19	26.6	19	26.4	14	25.1	29
2018	6-10	5.9	7.2	368	455	+1	-9.7%	23	-3.3%	19	9.0%	27	2.6%	7	61.1	28	43.8	23	25.6	29	25.8	25	25.6	23

total for starters here includes players who take over as starters due to another injury and then get injured themselves, such as Colt McCoy or Adrian Peterson last year. It also includes important situational players who may not necessarily start, such as pass-rush specialists and slot receivers.) Adjusted games lost was introduced in *Pro Football Prospectus 2008*; it gives a weighted estimate of the probability that players would miss games based on how they are listed on the injury report. Unlike a count of "starter games missed," this accounts for the fact that a player listed as questionable who does in fact play is not playing at 100 percent capability. Teams are ranked from the fewest injuries (2018: Cleveland on offense, Washington on defense) to the most (2018: Washington on offense, Tampa Bay on defense).

Individual Offensive Statistics

Each team chapter contains a table giving passing and receiving numbers for any player who either threw five passes or was thrown five passes, along with rushing numbers for any players who carried the ball at least five times. These numbers also appear in the player comments at the end of the book (except for runs by wide receivers). By putting them together in the team chapters we hope we make it easier to compare the performances of different players on the same team.

Players who are no longer on the team are marked with an asterisk. New players who were on a different team in 2018 are in italics. Changes should be accurate as of July 1. Rookies are not included.

All players are listed with DYAR and DVOA. Passing statistics then list total pass plays (**Plays**), net yardage (**NtYds**), and net yards per pass (**Avg**). These numbers include not just passes (and the positive yardage from them) but aborted snaps and sacks (and the negative yardage from them). Then comes average yards after catch (**YAC**), as determined by the game charting project. This average is based on charted receptions, not total pass attempts. The final three numbers are completion percentage (**C%**), passing touchdowns (**TD**), and interceptions (**Int**).

It is important to note that the tables in the team chapters contain Football Outsiders stats, while the tables in the player comments later in the book contain official NFL totals, at least when it comes to standard numbers like receptions and yardage. This results in a number of differences between the two:

- Team chapter tables list aborted snaps as passes, not runs, although aborted handoffs are still listed as runs. Net yardage for quarterbacks in the team chapter tables includes the lost yardage from aborted snaps, sacks, and intentional grounding penalties. For official NFL stats, all aborted snaps are listed as runs.
- Football Outsiders stats omit kneeldowns from run totals and clock-stopping spikes from pass totals.

Table 5: Eagles Passing

Player	DYAR	DVOA	Plays	NtYds	Avg	YAC	C%	TD	Int
C.Wentz	545	8.1%	430	2851	6.6	5.0	70.1%	21	7
N.Foles*	74	-5.4%	202	1370	6.8	5.2	73.1%	7	4
C.Kessler	-458	-59.7%	153	555	3.6	4.1	64.9%	2	2

Table 6: Eagles Rushing

Player	DYAR	DVOA	Plays	Yds	Avg	TD	Fum	Suc
J.Adams	-12	-11.0%	120	511	4.3	3	1	50%
W.Smallwood	41	3.1%	87	364	4.2	3	1	51%
C.Clement	-31	-19.9%	68	259	3.8	2	2	46%
J.Ajayi*	-19	-17.9%	45	184	4.1	3	1	47%
D.Sproles*	19	8.5%	29	120	4.1	1	0	41%
C.Wentz	7	-6.8%	25	101	4.0	0	0	--
N.Foles*	5	-2.7%	8	18	2.3	0	0	--
J.Howard	-28	-11.1%	250	935	3.7	9	2	50%
D.Jackson	23	29.8%	6	29	4.8	1	0	--

Table 7: Eagles Receiving

Player	DYAR	DVOA	Plays	Ctch	Yds	Y/C	YAC	TD	C%
N.Agholor	-69	-21.8%	97	64	747	11.7	5.5	4	66%
A.Jeffery	251	21.1%	92	65	840	12.9	4.1	6	71%
G.Tate*	-81	-36.9%	45	31	278	9.0	4.8	1	69%
J.Matthews*	84	28.8%	28	20	300	15.0	4.2	2	71%
K.Aiken*	-9	-31.0%	7	6	53	8.8	1.8	0	86%
D.Jackson	153	12.2%	74	41	774	18.9	4.4	4	55%
Z.Ertz	93	1.6%	155	115	1166	10.1	3.1	8	74%
D.Goedert	38	5.1%	44	33	334	10.1	5.2	4	75%
J.Perkins	-27	-42.2%	11	5	67	13.4	3.2	0	45%
W.Smallwood	49	11.2%	35	28	230	8.2	8.3	2	80%
C.Clement	29	5.8%	25	22	192	8.7	12.0	0	88%
D.Sproles*	16	-3.7%	23	15	160	10.7	8.5	2	65%
J.Adams	-19	-37.9%	13	7	58	8.3	9.3	0	54%
J.Ajayi*	-4	-24.7%	6	5	20	4.0	6.0	0	83%
J.Howard	-13	-21.9%	27	20	145	7.3	6.4	0	74%

- "Skill players" who played for multiple teams in 2018 are only listed in team chapters with stats from that specific team; combined stats are listed in the player comments section.

Rushing statistics start with DYAR and DVOA, then list rushing plays and net yards along with average yards per carry and rushing touchdowns. The final two columns are fumbles (**Fum**)—both those lost to the defense and those recovered by the offense—and Success Rate (**Suc**), explained earlier in this chapter. Fumbles listed in the rushing table include all quarterback fumbles on sacks and aborted snaps, as well as running back fumbles on receptions, but not wide receiver fumbles.

Receiving statistics start with DYAR and DVOA and then list the number of passes thrown to this receiver (**Plays**), the number of passes caught (**Catch**) and the total receiving yards (**Yds**). Yards per catch (**Y/C**) includes total yardage per reception, based on standard play-by-play, while yards after catch (**YAC**) is based on information from our game charting project. Finally we list total receiving touchdowns, and catch percentage (**C%**), which is the percentage of passes intended for this receiver which were caught. Wide receivers, tight ends, and running backs are separated on the table by horizontal lines.

Performance Based on Personnel

These tables provide a look at performance in 2018 based on personnel packages, as defined above in the section on marking formation/personnel as part of Sports Info Solutions charting. There are four different tables, representing:

- Offense based on personnel
- Offense based on opponent's defensive personnel
- Defense based on personnel
- Defense based on opponent's offensive personnel

Most of these tables feature the top five personnel groupings for each team. Occasionally, we will list the personnel group which ranks sixth if the sixth group is either particularly interesting or nearly as common as the fifth group. Each personnel group is listed with its frequency among 2018 plays, yards per play, and DVOA. Offensive personnel are also listed with how often the team in question called a running play instead of a pass play from given personnel. (Quarterback scrambles are included as pass plays, not runs.)

Offensive personnel are given in the standard two-digit format where the first digit is running backs and the second digit is tight ends. You can figure out wide receivers by subtracting that total from five, with a couple of exceptions. Plays with six or seven offensive linemen will have a three-digit listing such as "611" or "622." Any play with a direct snap to a non-quarterback, or with a specific running quarterback taking the snap instead of the regular quarterback, was counted as "Wildcat." Tennessee is the only team with Wildcat listed among its top five offensive personnel groups.

When defensive players come in to play offense, defensive backs are counted as wide receivers and linebackers as tight ends. Defensive linemen who come in as offensive linemen are counted as offensive linemen; if they come in as blocking fullbacks, we count them as running backs.

We no longer give giving personnel data based on the number of defensive linemen and linebackers. This is because of the difficulty in separating between the two, especially with our simplified designation of players as defensive linemen or linebackers based simply on who has a hand on the ground. There are just too many hybrid defensive schemes in today's game: 4-3 schemes where one or both ends rush the passer from a standing position, or hybrid schemes that one-gap on one side of the nose tackle and two-gap on the other. Therefore, defensive personnel is listed in only five categories:

- Base (four defensive backs)
- Nickel (five defensive backs)
- Dime+ (six or more defensive backs)
- Big (either 4-4-3 or 3-5-3)
- Goal Line (all other personnel groups with fewer than four defensive backs)

11, or three-wide personnel, was by far the most common grouping in the NFL last year, used on 64 percent of plays, followed the standard two-tight end set 12 personnel (16 percent of plays) and the more traditional 21 personnel (7.3 percent). Defenses lined up in Base on 25 percent of plays, Nickel on 60 percent of plays, Dime+ on 13 percent of plays, and either Big or Goal Line on 1.1 percent of plays. Table 8 lists the average performance from the ten most common personnel groups in 2018. Note that because we don't track personnel grouping on penalties, those negative plays are all missing from this analysis, so the average offensive DVOA for this table is 4.4% rather than 0.0%. On Table 9, which shows the same numbers from the defensive perspective, the average DVOA is still 0.0%.

Strategic Tendencies

The Strategic Tendencies table presents a mix of information garnered from the standard play-by-play a well as charting from both Sports Info Solutions and ESPN Stats & Information. It gives you an idea of what kind of plays teams run in what situations and with what personnel. Each category is given a league-wide **Rank** from most often (1) to least often (32) except as noted below. The sample table shown here lists the NFL average in each category for 2018.

The first column of strategic tendencies lists how often teams ran in different situations. These ratios are based on the type of play, not the actual result, so quarterback scrambles count as "passes" while quarterback sneaks, draws and option plays count as "runs."

Runs, first half and **Runs, first down** should be self-evident. **Runs, second-and-long** is the percentage of runs on second down with seven or more yards to go, giving you an idea of how teams follow up a failed first down. **Runs, power**

Table 8. NFL Offensive Performance by Personnel Group, 2018

Pers.	Plays	Pct	Yds	DVOA
11	20509	63.7%	5.9	7.0%
12	5260	16.3%	5.9	4.8%
21	2341	7.3%	5.9	2.4%
13	1030	3.2%	5.0	-12.1%
22	734	2.3%	4.7	-5.5%
10	391	1.2%	5.6	-6.9%
612	327	1.0%	5.1	-5.3%
20	256	0.8%	6.9	29.9%
611	213	0.7%	3.4	-28.3%
01	212	0.7%	5.8	-17.1%

Table 9. NFL Defensive Performance by Personnel Group, 2018

Pers.	Plays	Pct	Yds	DVOA
Nickel	19343	60.0%	5.9	1.6%
Base	7980	24.8%	5.6	-3.4%
Dime+	4255	13.2%	6.0	0.9%
Goal Line	262	0.8%	1.1	-4.9%
Big	108	0.3%	3.4	-38.3%

situations is the percentage of runs on third or fourth down with 1-2 yards to go, or at the goal line with 1-2 yards to go. **Runs, behind 2H** tells you how often teams ran when they were behind in the second half, generally a passing situation. **Pass, ahead 2H** tells you how often teams passed when they had the lead in the second half, generally a running situation.

In each case, you can determine the percentage of plays that were passes by subtracting the run percentage from 100 (the reverse being true for "Pass, ahead 2H," of course).

The second column gives information about offensive formations and personnel, as tracked by Sports Info Solutions.

The first two entries detail formation, i.e. where players were lined up on the field. **Form: Single Back** lists how often the team lined up with only one player in the backfield, and **Form: Empty Back** lists how often the team lined up with no players in the backfield.

The next three entries are based on personnel, no matter where players were lined up in the formation. **Pers: 3+ WR** marks how often the team plays with three or more wide receivers. **Pers: 2+ TE/6+ OL** marks how often the team plays with either more than one tight end or more than five offensive linemen. **Pers: 6+ OL** marks just plays with more than five offensive linemen. Finally, we give the percentage of plays where a team used **Shotgun or Pistol** in 2018. This does not count "Wildcat" or direct snap plays involving a non-quarterback.

The third column shows how the defensive **Pass Rush** worked in 2018.

Rush 3/Rush 4/Rush 5/Rush 6+: The percentage of pass plays (including quarterback scrambles) on which Sports Info Solutions recorded this team rushing the passer with three or

fewer defenders, four defenders, five defenders, and six or more defenders. These percentages do not include goal-line plays on the one- or two-yard line.

Int DL Sacks/Second Level Sacks: The goal of these numbers is to split out how many sacks each team got from players who were not edge rushers. **Int DL Sacks** track the percentage of sacks from interior defensive linemen: any 3-4 lineman, or a 4-3 defensive tackle. **Second Level Sacks** track sacks that come from linebackers who are not edge rushers, plus sacks from defensive backs.

The fourth column has more data on the use of defensive backs.

4 DB/5DB/6+ DB: The percentage of plays where this defense lined up with four, five, and six or more defensive backs, according to Sports Info Solutions.

CB by Sides: One of the most important lessons from game charting is that each team's best cornerback does not necessarily match up against the opponent's best receiver. Most cornerbacks play a particular side of the field and in fact cover a wider range of receivers than we assumed before we saw the charting data. This metric looks at which teams prefer to leave their starting cornerbacks on specific sides of the field.

To figure CB by Sides, we took the top two cornerbacks from each team and looked at the percentage of passes where that cornerback was in coverage on the left or right side of the field, ignoring passes marked as "middle." For each of the two cornerbacks, we took the higher number, right or left, and then we averaged the two cornerbacks to get the final CB by Sides rating. Teams which preferred to leave their cornerbacks in the same place last season, such as Chicago and Seattle, will have high ratings. Teams that did more to move their best cornerback around to cover the opponent's top targets, such as New England and Jacksonville, will have low ratings.

S/CB Cover Ratio: This is our attempt to track which teams like to use their safeties as hybrid safety/corners and put them in man coverage on wide receivers. This ratio takes

Table 10: 2018 NFL Average Strategic Tendencies

Run/Pass		Rk	Formation		Rk	Pass Rush		Rk	Secondary		Rk	Strategy		Rk
Runs, first half	38%	--	Form: Single Back	79%	--	Rush 3	8.1%	--	4 DB	25%	--	Play action	24%	--
Runs, first down	47%	--	Form: Empty Back	8%	--	Rush 4	67.5%	--	5 DB	61%	--	Avg Box (Off)	6.21	--
Runs, second-long	30%	--	Pers: 3+ WR	67%	--	Rush 5	18.4%	--	6+ DB	13%	--	Avg Box (Def)	6.21	--
Runs, power sit.	57%	--	Pers: 2+ TE/6+ OL	24%	--	Rush 6+	5.8%	--	CB by Sides	74%	--	Offensive Pace	31.11	--
Runs, behind 2H	26%	--	Pers: 6+ OL	3%	--	Int DL Sacks	28.2%	--	S/CB Cover Ratio	28%	--	Defensive Pace	31.06	--
Pass, ahead 2H	49%	--	Shotgun/Pistol	64%	--	Second Level Sacks	23.8%	--	DB Blitz	9%	--	Go for it on 4th	1.40	--

all pass targets with a defensive back in coverage, and then gives what percentage of those targets belonged to a player who is rostered as a safety, ranging from Miami, which used safety Minkah Fitzpatrick as a nickelback (45 percent) to the New York Jets, who had very defined roles for their two rookie starting safeties (17 percent).

DB Blitz: We have data on how often the defense used at least one defensive back in the pass rush courtesy of ESPN Stats & Info.

Finally, in the final column, we have some elements of game strategy.

Play action: The percentage of pass plays (including quarterback scrambles) which began with a play-action fake to the running back. This percentage does not include fake end-arounds unless there was also a fake handoff. It does include flea flickers.

Average Box: Another item added to our charting courtesy of ESPN Stats & Info is the number of defenders in the box before the snap. We list the average box faced by each team's offense and the average box used by this team's defense.

Offensive Pace: Situation-neutral pace represents the seconds of game clock per offensive play, with the following restrictions: no drives are included if they start in the fourth quarter or final five minutes of the first half, and drives are only included if the score is within six points or less. Teams are ranked from quickest pace (New England, 28.2 seconds) to slowest pace (Washington, 33.2 seconds).

Defensive Pace: Situation-neutral pace based on seconds of game clock per defensive play. This is a representation of how a defense was approached by its opponents, not the strategy of the defense itself. Teams are ranked from quickest pace (New England, 29.2 seconds) to slowest pace (Indianapolis, 32.4 seconds).

Go for it on fourth: This is the Aggressiveness Index (AI) introduced by Jim Armstrong in *Pro Football Prospectus 2006*, which measures how often a team goes for a first down in various fourth down situations compared to the league average. A coach over 1.00 is more aggressive, and one below 1.00 is less aggressive. Coaches are ranked from most aggressive to least aggressive.

You may notice on the Strategic Tendencies sample table that the average Aggressiveness Index for 2018 was 1.40, far above the multi-year average of 1.00. There is no question that

NFL coaches, some following the example of the Super Bowl LII Champion Philadelphia Eagles, were more aggressive on fourth down in 2018 than in any year in memory. Twenty-six out of 34 head coaches (including those who coached partial seasons) had an Aggressiveness Index above 1.00.

Following each strategic tendencies table, you'll find a series of comments highlighting interesting data from that team's charting numbers. This includes DVOA ratings split for things like different formations, draw plays, or play-action passing. Please note that all DVOA ratings given in these comments are standard DVOA with no adjustments for the specific situation being analyzed. The average DVOA for a specific situation will not necessarily be 0%, and it won't necessarily be the same for offense and defense. For example, the average offensive DVOA on play-action passes in 2018 was 23.0%, while the average defensive DVOA was 15.8%. The average offensive DVOA when the quarterback was hurried was -59.8%; even if we remove sacks, scrambles, and intentional grounding and only look at actual passes, the average offensive DVOA was -5.2%. On average last year, there was pressure marked on 30.9 percent of pass plays.

How to Read the Offensive Line Tables

SIS charters mark blown blocks not just on sacks but also on hurries, hits, and runs stuffed at the line. However, while we have blown blocks to mark bad plays, we still don't have a metric that consistently marks good plays, so blown blocks should not be taken as the end all and be all of judging individual linemen. It's simply one measurement that goes into the conversation.

All offensive linemen who had at least 160 snaps in 2018 (not including special teams) are listed in the offensive line tables along with the position they played most often and their **Age** as of the 2019 season, listed simply as the difference between birth year and 2019. Players born in January and December of the same year will have the same listed age.

Then we list games, games started, snaps, and offensive penalties (**Pen**) for each lineman. The penalty total includes declined and offsetting penalties. Finally, there are three numbers for blown blocks in 2018.

Table 11: New England Patriots Offensive Line

Player	Pos	Age	GS	Snaps	Pen	Sk	Pass	Run	Player	Pos	Age	GS	Snaps	Pen	Sk	Pass	Run
Joe Thuney	LG	27	16/16	1119	4	0.5	2	2	Marcus Cannon	RT	31	13/13	835	7	2.0	9	1
David Andrews	C	27	16/16	1103	4	0.5	3	3	LaAdrian Waddle*	RT	28	16/3	342	2	2.0	5	1
Trenton Brown*	LT	26	16/16	1089	9	2.0	7	3	Ted Karras	RG	26	12/2	171	1	1.0	1	0
Shaquille Mason	RG	26	14/14	953	3	0.5	2	3									

Year	Yards	ALY	Rank	Power	Rank	Stuff	Rank	2nd Lev	Rank	Open Field	Rank	Sacks	ASR	Rank	Press	Rank	F-Start	Cont.
2016	3.99	4.46	9	59%	22	20%	16	1.10	22	0.60	21	24	4.6%	6	25.6%	14	14	38
2017	4.43	5.05	1	65%	14	16%	3	1.35	2	0.60	20	35	6.4%	13	27.0%	7	13	29
2018	4.24	5.03	3	58%	29	16%	4	1.19	21	0.63	25	21	3.8%	1	22.9%	1	16	31
2018 ALY by direction:			Left End: 5.36 (6)			Left Tackle: 4.21 (16)			Mid/Guard: 5.02 (2)			Right Tackle: 6.15 (1)			Right End: 4.29 (15)			

- Blown blocks leading directly to sacks
- All blown blocks on pass plays, not only including those that lead to sacks but also those that lead to hurries, hits, or offensive holding penalties
- All blown blocks on run plays; generally, this means plays where the running back is tackled for a loss or no gain, but it also includes a handful of plays where the running back would have been tackled for a loss if not for a broken tackle, as well as offensive holding penalties on running plays

Players are given half a blown block when two offensive players are listed with blown blocks on the same play.

As with all player tables in the team chapters, players who are no longer on the team have an asterisk and those new to the team in 2019 are in italics.

The second offensive line table lists the last three years of our various line stats.

The first column gives standard yards per carry by each team's running backs (**Yds**). The next two columns give adjusted line yards (**ALY**) followed by rank among the 32 teams.

Power gives the percentage of runs in short-yardage "power situations" that achieved a first down or touchdown. Those situations include any third or fourth down with one or two yards to go, and any runs in goal-to-go situations from the two-yard line or closer. Unlike the other rushing numbers on the Offensive Line table, Power includes quarterbacks.

Stuff gives the percentage of runs that are stuffed for zero or negative gain. Since being stuffed is bad, teams are ranked from stuffed least often (1) to most often (32).

Second-Level (**2nd Lev**) Yards and **Open-Field** Yards represent yardage where the running back has the most power over the amount of the gain. Second-level yards represent the number of yards per carry that come five to ten yards past the line of scrimmage. Open-field yards represent the number of yards per carry that come 11 or more yards past the line of scrimmage. A team with a low ranking in adjusted line yards but a high ranking in open-field yards is heavily dependent on its running back breaking long runs to make the running game work, and therefore tends to have a less consistent running attack. Second-level yards fall somewhere in between.

The next five columns give information about pass protection. That starts with total sacks, followed by adjusted sack rate (**ASR**) and its rank among the 32 teams. Some teams allow a lot of sacks because they throw a lot of passes; adjusted sack rate accounts for this by dividing sacks and intentional grounding by total pass plays. It is also adjusted for situation (sacks are much more common on third down, particularly third-and-long) and opponent, all of which makes it a better measurement than raw sacks totals. Remember that quarterbacks share responsibility for sacks, and two different quarterbacks behind the same line can have very different adjusted sack rates. We've also listed **Pressure Rate**: this is the percentage of pass plays where we have marked pass pressure, based on Sports Info Solutions charting. Sacks or scrambles due to coverage are not counted as passes with pressure.

F-Start gives the number of false starts, which is the offensive penalty which best correlates to both wins and wins

the following season. This total includes false starts by players other than offensive linemen, but it does not include false starts on special teams. Cincinnati led the league with 27, Pittsburgh was last with 8, and the NFL average was 16.6. Finally, Continuity score (**Cont.**) tells you how much continuity each offensive line had from game-to-game in that season. It was introduced in the Cleveland chapter of *Pro Football Prospectus 2007*. Continuity score starts with 48 and then subtracts:

- The number of players over five who started at least one game on the offensive line;
- The number of times the team started at least one different lineman compared to the game before; and
- The difference between 16 and that team's longest streak where the same line started consecutive games.

The Los Angeles Rams led the NFL with a perfect continuity score of 48. The lowest score last season was 17 for Arizona.

Finally, underneath the table in italics we give 2018 adjusted line yards in each of the five directions with rank among the 32 teams. The league average was 4.40 on left end runs (**LE**), 4.28 on left tackle runs (**LT**), 4.43 on runs up the middle (**MID**), 4.25 on right tackle runs (**RT**), and 4.30 on right end runs (**RE**).

How to Read the Defensive Front Tables

Defensive players make plays. Plays aren't just tackles—interceptions and pass deflections change the course of the game, and so does the act of forcing a fumble or beating the offensive players to a fumbled ball. While some plays stop a team on third down and force a punt, others merely stop a receiver after he's caught a 30-yard pass. We can measure opportunities in pass coverage thanks to our charting partners at Sports Info Solutions.

Defensive players are listed in these tables if they made at least 20 plays during the 2018 season, or if they played at least eight games and played 25 percent of defensive snaps in those games. Defensive players who were with two teams last year are only listed with the final team they played with.

Defensive Linemen/Edge Rushers

This year, we are no longer referring to these as "front seven" tables. As nickel and dime defenses become more and more popular each year, what used to be the front seven is now more of a front six and sometimes just a front five.

As we've noted earlier in this toolbox: as hybrid defenses become more popular, it becomes more and more difficult to tell the difference between a defensive end and an outside linebacker. What we do know is that there are certain players whose job is to rush the passer, even if they occasionally drop into coverage. We also know that the defensive ends in a two-gapping 3-4 system have a lot more in common with run-stuffing 4-3 tackles than with smaller 4-3 defensive ends.

Therefore, we have separated defensive front players into

three tables rather than two. All defensive tackles and defensive ends from 3-4 teams are listed as **Defensive Linemen**, and all ranked together. Defensive ends from 4-3 teams and outside linebackers from 3-4 teams are listed as **Edge Rushers**, and all ranked together. Most 4-3 linebackers are ranked along with 3-4 inside linebackers and listed simply as **Linebackers**. For the most part this categorization puts players with similar roles together. Some players who have hybrid roles are ranked at the position more appropriate to their role, such as J.J. Watt as an edge rusher despite playing defensive end in a nominally 3-4 scheme.

The tables for defensive linemen and edge rushers are the same, although the players are ranked in two separate categories. Players are listed with the following numbers:

Age in 2019, determined by 2019 minus birth year, plus position (**Pos**) and the number of defensive **Snaps** played in 2018.

Plays (**Plays**): The total defensive plays including tackles, assists, pass deflections, interceptions, fumbles forced, and fumble recoveries. This number comes from the official NFL gamebooks and therefore does not include plays on which the player is listed by the Football Outsiders game charting project as in coverage but does not appear in the standard play-by-play. Special teams tackles are also not included.

Percentage of team plays (**TmPct**): The percentage of total team plays involving this defender. The sum of the percentages of team plays for all defenders on a given team will exceed 100 percent, primarily due to shared tackles. This number is adjusted based on games played, so an injured player may be fifth on his team in plays but third in **TmPct**.

Stops (**Stop**): The total number of plays which prevent a "success" by the offense (45 percent of needed yards on first down, 60 percent on second down, 100 percent on third or fourth down).

Defeats (**Dfts**): The total number of plays which stop the offense from gaining first down yardage on third or fourth down, stop the offense behind the line of scrimmage, or result in a fumble (regardless of which team recovers) or interception.

Broken tackles (**BTkl**): The number of broken tackles recorded by SIS game charters.

The next five columns represent runs only, starting with the number of plays each player made on **Runs**. Stop rate (**St%**) gives the percentage of these run plays which were stops. Average yards (**AvYd**) gives the average number of yards gained by the runner when this player is credited with making the play.

Finally, we have pass rush numbers, starting with standard NFL **Sack** totals.

Hit: To qualify as a quarterback hit, the defender must knock the quarterback to the ground in the act of throwing or after the pass is thrown. We have listed hits on all plays, including those cancelled by penalties. (After all, many of the hardest hits come on plays cancelled because the hit itself draws a roughing the passer penalty.) Our count of hits does not add

Table 12: Carolina Panthers Defensive Front

Defensive Line	Age	Pos	G	Snaps	Plays	TmPct	Rk	Stop	Dfts	BTkl	Runs	St%	Rk	RuYd	Rk	Sack	Hit	Hur	Dsrpt
						Overall							vs. Run				Pass Rush		
Kawann Short	30	DT	14	584	42	6.2%	21	38	16	2	36	89%	5	0.8	3	3.0	4	20	0
Dontari Poe	29	DT	16	515	16	2.1%	82	10	3	1	15	60%	81	3.1	74	1.0	2	6	0
Kyle Love	33	DT	16	467	20	2.6%	79	17	5	3	16	81%	21	1.5	11	1.5	2	10	1
Vernon Butler	25	DT	14	329	19	2.8%	--	16	5	0	17	88%	--	2.1	--	0.5	3	7	0

Edge Rushers	Age	Pos	G	Snaps	Plays	TmPct	Rk	Stop	Dfts	BTkl	Runs	St%	Rk	RuYd	Rk	Sack	Hit	Hur	Dsrpt
						Overall							vs. Run				Pass Rush		
Mario Addison	32	DE	16	666	33	4.3%	59	30	20	2	20	85%	16	1.0	7	9.0	2	28	0
Julius Peppers	39	DE	16	506	28	3.6%	75	23	13	0	16	69%	62	1.5	14	5.0	7	16	5
Wes Horton	29	DE	16	471	24	3.1%	83	15	5	6	20	55%	85	3.1	65	1.5	0	15	1
Bryan Cox	25	DE	11	200	10	1.9%	--	7	2	4	8	88%	--	2.4	--	0.0	1	5	0
Efe Obada	27	DE	10	187	10	2.1%	--	8	3	2	5	80%	--	2.8	--	2.0	5	12	2
Bruce Irvin	32	DE	16	470	19	2.3%	93	14	11	3	9	56%	83	3.9	88	6.5	7	11	0

Linebackers	Age	Pos	G	Snaps	Plays	TmPct	Rk	Stop	Dfts	BTkl	Runs	St%	Rk	RuYd	Rk	Sack	Hit	Hur	Tgts	Suc%	Rk	AdjYd	Rk	PD	Int
						Overall						vs. Run				Pass Rush				vs. Pass					
Luke Kuechly	28	MLB	16	927	136	17.6%	9	80	38	7	77	68%	15	3.3	22	2.0	3	9	29	62%	6	3.3	2	6	1
Thomas Davis*	36	OLB	12	650	85	14.7%	27	48	18	9	43	65%	22	3.6	31	0.0	3	8	35	51%	35	6.9	46	6	0
Shaq Thompson	25	OLB	14	597	77	11.4%	49	34	12	5	33	48%	78	4.9	77	3.5	2	6	33	45%	51	6.5	31	1	0

Year	Yards	ALY	Rank	Power	Rank	Stuff	Rank	2nd Level	Rank	Open Field	Rank	Sacks	ASR	Rank	Press	Rank
2016	3.83	3.61	4	78%	32	24%	5	1.10	10	0.73	17	47	7.3%	5	30.2%	7
2017	3.89	3.51	5	47%	2	26%	4	1.12	18	0.94	27	50	9.1%	3	32.9%	6
2018	4.71	3.97	8	78%	31	24%	7	1.40	27	1.32	31	35	6.8%	20	31.6%	10

| 2018 ALY by direction: | Left End: 2.74 (3) | Left Tackle: 4.71 (22) | Mid/Guard: 3.61 (2) | Right Tackle: 4.81 (26) | Right End: 4.89 (23) |

in sacks; that count is referred to elsewhere as "knockdowns."

Hurries (**Hur**): The number of quarterback hurries recorded by Sports Info Solutions game charters. This includes both hurries on standard plays and hurries that force an offensive holding penalty that cancels the play and costs the offense yardage.

Disruptions (**Dsprt**): This stat combines two different but similar types of plays. First, plays where a pass-rusher forced an incomplete pass or interception by hitting the quarterback as he was throwing the ball. These plays are generally not counted as passes defensed, so we wanted a way to count them. Second, plays where the pass-rusher batted the ball down at the line of scrimmage or tipped it in the air. These plays are usually incomplete, but occasionally they lead to interceptions, and even more rarely they fall into the hands of offensive receivers. As with the "hit in motion" disruptions, some plays counted as tips by Football Outsiders were not counted as passes defensed by the NFL.

Defensive linemen and edge rushers are both ranked by percentage of team plays, run stop rate, and average yards per run tackle. The lowest number of average yards earns the top rank (negative numbers indicate the average play ending behind the line of scrimmage). Defensive linemen and edge rushers are ranked if they played at least 40 percent of defensive snaps in the games they were active. There are 83 defensive linemen and 93 edge rushers ranked.

Linebackers

Most of the stats for linebackers are the same as those for defensive linemen. Linebackers are ranked in percentage of team plays, and also in stop rate and average yards for running plays specifically. Linebackers are ranked in these stats if they played at least five games and at least 35 percent of defensive snaps in the games they were active, with 88 linebackers ranked.

The final six columns in the linebacker stats come from Sports Info Solutions game charting.

Targets (**Tgts**): The number of pass players on which game charters listed this player in coverage.

Success rate (**Suc%**): The percentage plays of targeting this player on which the offense did not have a successful play. This means not only incomplete passes and interceptions, but also short completions which do not meet our baselines for success (45 percent of needed yards on first down, 60 percent on second down, 100 percent on third or fourth down).

Yards per pass (**Yd/P**): The average number of yards gained on plays on which this defender was the listed target.

Passes defensed (**PD**): Beginning with this book, we are using the NFL's count of passes defensed rather than computing our own separate total.

These stats are explained in more detail in the section on secondary tables. There are 80 linebackers are ranked in the charting stats, based on hitting one of two minimums: 14 charted passes with fewer than eight games started, or 11 charted passes with eight or more games started. As a result of the different thresholds, some linebackers are ranked in standard stats but not charting stats.

Further Details

Just as in the offensive tables, players who are no longer on the team are marked with asterisks, and players who were on other teams last year are in italics. Defensive front player statistics are not adjusted for opponent.

Numbers for defensive linemen and linebackers unfortunately do not reflect all of the opportunities a player had to make a play, but they do show us which players were most active on the field. A large number of plays could mean a strong defensive performance, or it could mean that the linebacker in question plays behind a poor part of the line. In general, defensive numbers should be taken as information that tells us what happened on the field in 2018, but not as a strict, unassailable judgment of which players are better than others—particularly when the difference between two players is small (for example, players ranked 20th and 30th) instead of large (players ranked 20th and 70th).

After the individual statistics for linemen and linebackers, the Defensive Front section contains a table that looks exactly like the table in the Offensive Line section. The difference is that the numbers here are for all opposing running backs against this team's defensive front. As we're on the opposite side of the ball, teams are now ranked in the opposite order, so the No. 1 defensive front is the one that allows the fewest adjusted line yards, the lowest percentage in Power situations, and has the highest adjusted sack rate. Directions for adjusted line yards are given from the offense's perspective, so runs left end and left tackle are aimed at the right defensive end and (assuming the tight end is on the other side) weakside linebacker.

How to Read the Secondary Tables

The first few columns in the secondary tables are based on standard play-by-play, not game charting, with the exception of broken tackles. Age, total plays, percentage of team plays, stops, and defeats are computed the same way they are for other defensive players, so that the secondary can be compared to the defensive line and linebackers. That means that total plays here includes passes defensed, sacks, tackles after receptions, tipped passes, and interceptions, but not pass plays on which this player was in coverage but was not given a tackle or passed defense by the NFL's official scorer.

The middle five columns address each defensive back's role in stopping the run. Average yardage and stop rate for running plays is computed in the same manner as for defensive linemen and linebackers.

The third section of statistics represents data from Sports Info Solutions game charting. We do not count pass plays on which this player was in coverage, but the incomplete was listed as Thrown Away, Batted Down, or Hit in Motion. Hail Mary passes are also not included.

Targets (**Tgts**): The number of pass plays on which game charters listed this player in coverage.

Target percentage (**Tgt%**): The number of plays on which

Table 13: Indianapolis Colts Defensive Secondary

Secondary	Age	Pos	G	Snaps	Plays	Overall TmPct	Rk	Stop	Dfts	BTkl	vs. Run Runs	St%	Rk	RuYd	Rk	vs. Pass Tgts	Tgt%	Rk	Dist	Suc%	Rk	AdjYd	Rk	PD	Int
Malik Hooker	23	FS	14	913	48	6.5%	66	9	5	9	19	16%	70	11.4	71	9	2.6%	1	25.7	33%	71	17.3	75	4	2
Kenny Moore	24	CB	15	911	87	11.0%	9	47	21	13	24	75%	1	2.3	2	57	16.7%	22	8.6	56%	22	6.1	12	11	3
Pierre Desir	29	CB	16	904	86	10.2%	16	28	12	3	22	41%	42	5.0	16	67	19.8%	49	12.2	51%	50	8.5	59	8	1
Clayton Geathers	27	SS	12	715	88	13.9%	6	27	5	6	42	33%	54	7.2	43	27	10.1%	45	8.4	56%	19	6.7	26	3	0
Quincy Wilson	23	CB	13	436	28	4.1%	--	10	8	6	7	43%	--	8.1	--	23	14.1%	--	12.3	48%	--	6.5	--	2	1
Nate Hairston	25	CB	13	413	30	4.4%	--	13	5	5	12	67%	--	4.4	--	26	16.8%	--	9.8	35%	--	9.4	--	1	0
Mike Mitchell*	32	FS	8	224	29	6.9%	--	14	9	4	13	46%	--	7.1	--	8	9.5%	--	6.1	38%	--	6.1	--	1	1
George Odum	26	FS	16	205	30	3.6%	--	13	5	5	17	53%	--	6.1	--	9	11.7%	--	8.2	44%	--	8.2	--	2	1
Matthias Farley	27	SS	5	151	21	8.0%	--	10	8	3	7	43%	--	5.1	--	11	19.5%	--	6.0	45%	--	7.5	--	4	1
Derrick Kindred	26	SS	16	497	39	4.4%	--	11	5	10	14	29%	--	8.7	--	14	6.8%	--	5.9	36%	--	10.2	--	1	1

Year	Pass D Rank	vs. #1 WR	Rk	vs. #2 WR	Rk	vs. Other WR	Rk	WR Wide	Rk	WR Slot	Rk	vs. TE	Rk	vs. RB	Rk
2016	26	13.7%	29	-3.3%	12	-1.1%	14	8.3%	27	1.7%	15	33.1%	31	38.5%	31
2017	32	7.6%	18	22.7%	27	28.5%	31	22.3%	32	18.4%	24	9.9%	23	27.9%	31
2018	20	1.8%	17	-27.9%	1	-3.8%	14	-12.1%	8	-8.4%	6	21.2%	29	12.3%	25

this player was targeted divided by the total number of charted passes against his defense, not including plays listed as Uncovered. Like percentage of team plays, this metric is adjusted based on number of games played.

Average depth of target (**aDOT**): The average distance in the air beyond the line of scrimmage of all passes targeted at this defender. It does not include yards after catch and is useful for seeing which defenders were covering receivers deeper or shorter. This is also often referred to as "Air Yards."

Success rate (**Suc%**): The percentage plays of targeting this player on which the offense did not have a successful play. This means not only incomplete passes and interceptions, but also short completions which do not meet our baselines for success (45 percent of needed yards on first down, 60 percent on second down, 100 percent on third or fourth down). Defensive pass interference is counted as a failure for the defensive player similar to a completion of equal yardage (and a new first down).

Yards per pass (**Yd/P**): The average number of yards gained on plays on which this defender was the listed target.

Passes defensed (**PD**) and Interceptions (**Int**) represent the standard NFL count for both stats.

Cornerbacks need 50 charted passes or eight games started to be ranked in the defensive stats, with 79 cornerbacks ranked in total. Safeties require 20 charted passes or eight games started, with 76 safeties ranked in total. Strong and free safeties are ranked together.

Add Sample of Team Statistics for Defensive Secondary

Just like the defensive front, the defensive secondary has a table of team statistics following the individual numbers. This table gives DVOA figured against different types of receivers. Each offense's wide receivers have had one receiver designated as No. 1, and another as No. 2. (Occasionally this is difficult, due to injury or a situation with "co-No. 1 receivers," but it's usually pretty obvious.) The other receivers form a third category, with tight ends and running backs as fourth and fifth categories. The defense is then judged on the performance of

each receiver based on the standard DVOA method, with each rating adjusted based on strength of schedule. (Obviously, it's a lot harder to cover the No. 1 receiver of the Houston Texans than to cover the No.1 receiver of the Washington Redskins.) **Pass D Rank** is the total ranking of the pass defense, as seen before in the Trends and Splits table, and combines all five categories plus sacks and passes with no intended target.

The "defense vs. types of receivers" table should be used to analyze the defense as a whole rather than individual players. The ratings against types of receivers are generally based on defensive schemes, not specific cornerbacks, except for certain defenses that really do move one cornerback around to cover the opponent's top weapon (i.e., Arizona). The ratings against tight ends and running backs are in large part due to the performance of linebackers.

In addition, we list each team's numbers covering receivers based on where they lined up before the snap, either wide or in the slot. The "vs. Other WR" number has sometimes been misrepresented as measuring coverage of slot receivers, but in the modern NFL, the team's No. 1 or No. 2 receiver will often be working predominantly out of the slot, while other receivers will switch back and forth between the two positions. The listing of coverage of wide receivers in the slot also includes wide receivers lined up tight in a tight end position.

How to Read the Special Teams Tables

The special teams tables list the last three years of kick, punt, and return numbers for each team.

The first two columns list total special teams DVOA and rank among the 32 teams. The next two columns list the value in actual points of field goals and extra points (**FG/XP**) when compared to how a league average kicker would do from the same distances, adjusted for weather and altitude, and rank among the 32 teams. Next, we list the estimated value in ac-

Table 14: San Francisco 49ers Special Teams

Year	DVOA	Rank	FG/XP	Rank	Net Kick	Rank	Kick Ret	Rank	Net Punt	Rank	Punt Ret	Rank	Hidden	Rank
2016	-0.3%	17	3.9	8	-2.7	23	-6.7	29	5.1	9	-0.9	14	-1.2	19
2017	2.9%	11	14.2	2	3.0	10	-6.4	32	3.6	13	0.0	16	4.9	10
2018	0.3%	14	6.6	7	-0.4	17	1.7	8	0.0	17	-6.4	30	3.6	10

tual points of field position over or under the league average based on net kickoffs (**Net Kick**) and rank that value among the 32 teams. That is followed by the estimated point values of field position for kick returns (**Kick Ret**), net punting (**Net Punt**), and punt returns (**Punt Ret**) and their respective ranks.

The final two columns represent the value of "**Hidden**" special teams, plays which throughout the past decade have usually been based on the performance of opponents without this team being able to control the outcome. We combine the opposing team's value on field goals, kickoff distance, and punt distance, adjusted for weather and altitude, and then switch the sign to represent that good special teams by the opponent will cost the listed team points, and bad special teams will effectively hand them points. We have to give the qualifier of "usually" because, as explained above, certain returners such as Cordarrelle Patterson will affect opposing special teams strategy, and a handful of the missed field goals are blocked. Nonetheless, the "hidden" value is still "hidden" for most teams, and they are ranked from the most hidden value gained (New Orleans, 23.5 points) to the most value lost (Chicago, -17.1 points).

We also have methods for measuring the gross value of kickoffs and punts. These measures assume that all kickoffs or punts will have average returns unless they are touchbacks or kicked out of bounds, then judge the kicker or punter on the value with those assumed returns. We also count special teams tackles; these include both tackles and assists, but do not include tackles on two-point conversions, tackles after onside kicks, or tackles of the player who recovers a fumble after the punt or kick returner loses the ball. The best and worst individual values for kickers, punters, returners, and kick gunners (i.e. tackle totals) are listed in the statistical appendix at the end of the book.

Administrative Minutia

Receiving statistics include all passes intended for the receiver in question, including those that are incomplete or intercepted. The word passes refers to both complete and incomplete pass attempts. When rating receivers, interceptions are treated as incomplete passes with no penalty.

For the computation of DVOA and DYAR, passing statistics include sacks as well as fumbles on aborted snaps. We do not include kneeldown plays or spikes for the purpose of stopping the clock. Some interceptions which we have determined to be "Hail Mary" plays that end the first half or game are counted as regular incomplete passes, not turnovers.

All statistics generated by ESPN Stats & Info or Sports Info Solutions game charting, or our combination of the two sources, may be different from totals compiled by other sources.

Unless we say otherwise, when we refer to third-down performance in this book we are referring to a combination of third down and the handful of rushing and passing plays that take place on fourth down (primarily fourth-and-1).

Aaron Schatz

The Year In Quotes

NO JOKING HERE

"@ChicagoBears yo I'm available.... vision, route running, pass protection etc... shooters shoot"

—Former Chicago Bears running back Matt Forte applies for a job online after news broke that retired linebacker De-Marcus Ware would be brought in as a pass-rushing consultant for the Denver Broncos. (Matt Forte/Twitter)

"Matt Forte jokingly asks the Bears for a job on Twitter"

—The title of a 247Sports blog post reporting on the Forte tweet. (Big Papa The Don/Twitter)

"I wasn't joking."

—Forte makes it clear this is no laughing matter. (Matt Forte/Twitter)

'I AM A REAL AMERICAN, PUNT FOR THE RIGHTS OF EVERY MAN'

"I was an American, in America, [wearing an American tank top], kicking an American football, blindfolded ... We had practiced it like three times before the actual event and they were nowhere near. Nowhere near. Nowhere close. Didn't think it was possible. Then the adjudicator shows up. He's got a little suit on with a little Guinness patch on, all high and mighty, judging me. Wham! Right down the middle ... You know, they called me 'officially awesome.' That's their thing, like when you get a record they go, 'You are officially awesome!' I go, 'Thanks, adjudicator. I already knew that. Take a hike. Gimme the book.'"

—Former Indianapolis Colts punter and renowned story-teller Pat McAfee recounts the time he set a Guinness World Record for Longest Field Goal Made While Blindfolded in a previously unreleased interview for NFL Films' *NFL Top 100* series. (NFL Films/Twitter)

BUTT STUFF

"When they're going through stretch lines, is he patting them on the butt and getting them going?"

—Buffalo Bills general manager Brandon Beane on what he was looking for in a quarterback when he was scouting Josh Allen. (WGR 550 radio)

"High fiving and slapping butts. That's what we do around here."

—Allen said this at rookie minicamp in May. Now that we know what Beane was watching for, it makes more sense in hindsight. (Joe Buscaglia, WKBW)

NUMBERS NEVER LIE

"Damn I got cut and I'm a 93."

—Houston Texans safety Tyrann Mathieu uses Madden 19's player rankings to prove that no one in the NFL is safe. Mathieu was the fifth-highest rated safety in the video game. He was also cut earlier that offseason by the Arizona Cardinals. (Tyrann Mathieu/Twitter)

A NUTRITION TAKE THAT ONLY HARBAUGH COULD HAVE

"Early in his Michigan tenure, Harbaugh pulled Speight aside and told him not to eat chicken, a protein that is considered fairly safe by nutritionists. When Speight asked why, Harbaugh said, 'because it's a nervous bird.'"

—Bleacher Report's Matt Hayes snuck this gem into his lengthy Michigan season preview, alleging that Wolverines coach Jim Harbaugh believes that eating chicken could make you mentally weak or more easily scared. Harbaugh passed this advice along to then-Michigan starting quarterback Wilton Speight. (Bleacher Report)

"He thinks some type of sickness injected its way into the human population when people began eating white meats instead of beef and pork. And he believes it, 100 percent."

—Speight, who has since transferred to UCLA, confirms that when it comes to eating white meat, Harbaugh is, for lack of a better term, chicken. (Detroit Free Press)

NEVER LEAVE US, WADE PHILLIPS

"Now you are 71 years old—"
"At least, yeah."
"It is a big accomplishment, to still be in the league—"
"To still be alive, yeah."

—Los Angeles Rams defensive coordinator Wade Phillips dives into a touch of dark humor as he's asked by a reporter about his age in the NFL. (Rich Hammond, Orange County Register/Twitter)

"Well, I've been poppin' since my demo, baby."

—Wade Phillips quotes rapper Future while being asked about his long resume as a defensive expert. (Los Angeles Rams via Twitter)

TAKE THIS ROSE BACK TO THE HOUSE FOR SIX

"Our return game is kind of like The Bachelor *right now. We have about 12 contestants all with roses. We don't know who our returner is going to be. And if she doesn't like any of them we will bring in more."*

—New Orleans Saints head coach Sean Payton likens his team's battle for the main return spot to hit reality show *The Bachelor*. (Adam Schefter, ESPN/Twitter)

UNFORTUNATE ORDERING OF LAST NAMES

"You gotta love Long Cox, right?"

—Philadelphia Eagles defensive end Fletcher Cox, accompanied by fellow defensive end Chris Long, gives an interesting answer when asked if everyone on the team loves each other. (Matt Mullin, Philly Voice via Twitter)

MINNESOTA FASHIONOVA

"Random fashion question ... Are fanny packs back in style now?"

—Minnesota Vikings quarterback Kirk Cousins reached out to Twitter to see if he's still up to date on all the hottest trends. (Kirk Cousins via Twitter)

THE ULTIMATE INSULT

"Dean Spanos—The Mark Davis Haircut of NFL Owners"

—Los Angeles Chargers controlling owner Dean Spanos gets roasted hard by a banner flown over a Chargers home game. (SD Sign Guy via Twitter)

LIFELONG DISAPPOINTMENT

"Lee has requested six Buffalo Bills players as pallbearers so they can let him down one last time."

—Lee Merkel, lifelong Buffalo Bills fan and season ticket holder, passed away at his home in Raleigh, North Carolina. This is an excerpt from his obituary. (Fox News)

WHAT ARE YOU, A WICKED WITCH?

"I really don't like water. I'm trying. I really just don't like it. You know when you get that stomach feeling and it's all slushy? I'm trying to stay hydrated. Sometimes, I just got to get an IV. It's just necessary."

—New York Giants wide receiver Odell Beckham explaining that he doesn't like water. Beckham had to leave the game before halftime to get an IV twice in a three-game stretch. (Ryan Dunleavy, NJ.com)

HIPAA VIOLATIONS

"ESPN said I had surgery? Interesting, I didn't know I had surgery. You're going to have to talk to ESPN about that."

—Miami Dolphins defensive end Cameron Wake refuting ESPN reports saying Wake underwent arthroscopic surgery on his knee. (Miami Sun Sentinel)

TRADES ALWAYS REQUIRE A REFRESHER COURSE IN GEOGRAPHY

"Never spent any time in Maryland before ... we are in Maryland, right? This whole part of the country kind of throws me for a loop. I don't know if I'm in Virginia or what."

—Baltimore Ravens running back Ty Montgomery was born and raised in Texas, attended Stanford University, and played in Green Bay before getting traded to the Ravens. (Yahoo! Sports)

TALK THAT TALK!

"Not interested in me? I'm not quick enough? Don't have enough stars next to my name to be worth your time? Well here ... enjoy this three-star stiff-arm to your damn chest."

—In an excerpt from his Players' Tribune piece, Kentucky (now Pittsburgh Steelers) running back Benny Snell Jr. describes his state of mind after being slighted throughout his recruiting process. (Players' Tribune)

YOU WOULDN'T KNOW THEM, THEY GO TO A DIFFERENT SCHOOL

"Since I left Buffalo, I had 11 letters to interview for head coach jobs, four of them didn't even have to interview, just show up and sign the contract."

—The decision to promote him may have looked questionable, but Cleveland Browns interim head coach Gregg Williams ensures the media that he has been highly sought after by several NFL teams. (Mary Kay Cabot, Cleveland.com via Twitter)

"One other thing, I thought this thing was going to come up and I want to address it. I have not been offered any head coaching jobs."

—Cleveland Browns offensive coordinator Freddie Kitchens pokes fun at Williams' comment during his introductory press conference with the team. (Mary Kay Cabot, Cleveland.com via Twitter)

RUN, CORDARRELLE, RUN

"Cordarrelle, where do you think you've improved on from last week to this week as a running back?"

"Probably yards. Yards."

—New England Patriots wide receiver-turned-running back Cordarrelle Patterson after rushing for 61 yards and a touchdown against the Green Bay Packers. (Christopher Price, Boston Sports Journal via Twitter)

ROETHLISBERGER (DEAD): QUESTIONABLE TO RETURN

"I thought I was dead for a second."

—Pittsburgh Steelers quarterback Ben Roethlisberger may have been hyperbolizing a bit after an awkward tackle pulled him out of a game against Baltimore with some shoulder pain. Big Ben returned a few plays later with seemingly no issues. (Steelers Depot via Twitter)

COMING TO A CHEAPLY PRINTED T-SHIRT NEAR YOU

"When I woke up this morning I was feeling pretty dangerous."

—Cleveland Browns quarterback Baker Mayfield gives Cleveland a new catchphrase. (Barstool Sports via Instagram)

WELL THAT WAS A FUN TWO-HOUR NEWS CYCLE

"I love my Browns —and I know they will hire an experienced coach to take us to the next level.

"On a more serious note, I do hope that the NFL will start to bring women into the coaching profession as position coaches and eventually coordinators and head coaches. One doesn't have to play the game to understand it and motivate players. But experience counts —and it is time to develop a pool of experienced women coaches.

"BTW —I'm not ready to coach but I would like to call a play or two next season if the Browns need ideas! And at no time will I call for a 'prevent defense.'"

—For a few hours on a November Sunday morning, former Secretary of State Condoleezza Rice was reported to be a candidate for the Cleveland Browns head coaching position. This was her official statement after Cleveland refuted reports by ESPN. (Condoleezza Rice via Facebook)

OAKLAND: INFINITY WAR

"It's like Thanos snapped his fingers and they all vanished."

—Oakland Raiders quarterback Derek Carr after wide receivers Jordy Nelson, Brandon LaFell, and Martavis Bryant all went down with injuries in a two-week span. (Scott Bair, NBCSports Bay Area via Twitter)

RULES TO LIVE BY

"Back in college I learned the MF rule. If there are a lot of MFers over there, go the (other) way."

—Arizona Cardinals quarterback Josh Rosen brought some advice he learned at UCLA to the pro level. This was the explanation Rosen gave when recalling an audible that led to a 59-yard touchdown by wide receiver Christian Kirk. (Scott Bordow, The Athletic via Twitter)

COMPUTERS CAN'T REPLACE THE REAL THING

"Hell yes, hell yes! On Madden, I used to play with him, and I'd say, 'Who is this sidearm guy?' Then they drafted me, and I got out there on the practice field, and it was amazing what he was able to do. It's fun playing with him, bro."

—Los Angeles Chargers rookie safety Derwin James admitted that before he worked with quarterback Philip Rivers, his only exposure to him was through Madden. James admitted that Rivers was much better in person. (Michael Silver, Sports Illustrated via Twitter)

NOT THE KIND OF 'SUPER BOWL' MARTY WANTS TO TAKE PART IN

*"Great win #Patriots you guys are really f***ing awesome."*

—Former New England Patriots tight end Martellus Bennett congratulates his former teammates on a quality win against the Minnesota Vikings.

"Can we talk you out of retirement for the stretch run Marty?!"

—A hopeful Patriots fan responds to Bennett's Patriots tweet.

"Currently holding a blunt. If you can talk me into not lighting it right now you can do anything."

—Bennett's response. (Martellus Bennett)

LIKE BEING CAUGHT CURSING IN FRONT OF MOM

"I love that sh-t! Yeah!"

—New Orleans Saints running back Mark Ingram got caught coming out of the locker room yelling some colorful language.

"Excuse me."

—Ingram's immediate follow-up, as he realized New Orleans Saints owner Gayle Benson was standing in the locker room with her game ball.

"Oh hey, Miss B!"

—Fellow New Orleans Saints running back Alvin Kamara actively making the situation more awkward. (Tom Pelissero, NFL Network via Twitter)

LET KHALIL RUN HIS ERRANDS IN PEACE

"Man, I pull up to Home Goods and people are waiting on me in the parking lot."

—Chicago Bears linebacker Khalil Mack struggled a bit with being the new face of the Chicago Bears. (NFL on ESPN)

TECHNICAL DIFFICULTIES

"On Madden 2003, we had a bug where all the players vanished. Just a stadium, a field, and a ball at midfield. A Jr. coder named James said: 'Did you check inside the ball?' Smirking, we checked w/ the debug cam. AND THERE THEY WERE. Tiny players, in formation, in the ball."

—EASports employee Jim Heji engaged in a Twitter thread of most embarrassing game dev errors, telling the story of how 22 players ended up inside of a football. (Jim Heji, EA via Twitter)

'CONGRATS ON A GREAT GAME, NOW PEE IN THIS CUP'

"Everyone was right, I did get called in for a drug test today."

—Atlanta Falcons punter Matt Bosher leveled a Carolina Panthers returner in Week 16, leading to a random drug test by the NFL.

"The NFL Random Drug test is basically considered a compliment these last few years. You ball out. You piss in a cup. It's as easy as that."

—Former Indianapolis Colts punter Pat McAfee summarizes the recent phenomenon that is the NFL random drug test. (Pat McAfee via Twitter)

SORRY IN ADVANCE FOR THE PROFANITY

"...that's stinkin' awesome."

—Indianapolis Colts quarterback Andrew Luck reacts in Andrew Luck fashion to making the playoffs following a 33-17 win against the Tennessee Titans. (NFL on ESPN via Twitter)

FAILING TO PREPARE IS PREPARING TO FAIL

"I've done zero. I have not returned one phone call. I have not done one piece of work for it. I refuse to. And that's it."

—Chicago Bears defensive coordinator Vic Fangio had preparation for head coaching interviews down. (Chicago Sun-Times)

FAMILY MATTERS, EXCEPT DURING THE PLAYOFFS

"They tell us to tune out the outside, you know, media, stuff like that, but you can't tune out your family. Unfortunately, I'm playing against my family this week. You've got to look at it as just another dude out there. He kind of looks like me, possibly, but on Sunday, we're not related, so I've got to focus on my job."

—Chicago Bears guard Kyle Long faced off against his brother, Philadelphia Eagles defensive end Chris Long, in the first round of the playoffs. (NFL Network)

HE CRUSHES DREAMS, HE DOESN'T ANALYZE THEM

"I'm not an analyst of nightmares."

—New England Patriots head coach Bill Belichick was asked during a press conference about pass-rusher Trey Flowers having a nightmare about being unable to set the edge. Bill gave his most Belichick-ian answer. (Nora Princiotti, Boston Globe via Twitter)

HE WHO SHALL NOT BE NAMED

"I want to be the Brady. I want to be the Brady of Baltimore if I could."

—Rookie quarterback Lamar Jackson in a conversation for Showtime's *Inside the NFL* with Baltimore Ravens legend and known Patriots-hater Ray Lewis.

"Or you can be me. I brought multiple, too."

—Stonefaced and unmoving, Ray Lewis gives Lamar an out.

"You too! But you know he played quarterback, so that's why I'm saying Tom Brady."

—The rookie doubles down on his Brady comparison.

"Don't play."

—Ray Lewis retorts. At this point Lamar breaks and begins to laugh; Ray barely cracks a smile. (Michael Hurley, WBZ via Twitter)

CUP O' NOODLES MADE BY A MICHELIN CHEF

"I'm top 2 all time in Ramen Noodle making...don't @ me"

—Green Bay Packers quarterback DeShone Kizer takes to Twitter to brag about his instant noodle game.

"Stop asking about what to put into it.. that's the last thing to worry about. We are talking water to noodle to bowl ratio, noodle density, timing of seasoning.. there's levels to this #IfYouKnowYouKnow"

—After some input from the masses, Kizer follows up his comments to teach us that ramen is a borderline form of art. (DeShone Kizer via Twitter)

WORST. BIRTHDAY. EVER.

"Pro Bowl is on my birthday .. And Ima alternate. & none of the safeties dropped out .. that's messed up lol bad friends."

—Baltimore Ravens safety Tony Jefferson was so close to celebrating his birthday on the field in Orlando. (Tony Jefferson via Twitter)

McVAY-NIA

"Kingsbury is friends with Rams coach Sean McVay —the 32-year-old offensive genius who has become the blueprint of many of the new coaching hires around the NFL —and McVay reached out to Kingsbury after Texas Tech let him go to see if Kingsbury wanted to join the Rams' staff for the stretch run and postseason as an offensive consultant. Kingsbury considered it but ultimately joined USC."

—The Arizona Cardinals press release announcing the hiring of new head coach Kliff Kingsbury makes sure to mention that he's friends with Sean McVay. (Kyle Bonagura, ESPN)

"Wes is a young offensive coach who knows Sean McVay, if anyone is looking for a head coach."

—Los Angeles Rams defensive coordinator Wade Phillips is pitching his nephew hard for a future head coaching job, given his "connection" to Rams head coach Sean McVay. Wes Phillips is currently a tight ends coach for the Washington Redskins. (Rich Hammond, Orange County Register via Twitter)

COMING TO YOU ON A DUSTY ROAD/ GOOD LOVING, I GOT A TRUCKLOAD

"He's a quarterback. I don't like quarterbacks. My impression is the same. I go into every week wanting to take the quarterback's soul. When you get to look in a man's eye and see fear in his heart, that's when you know you've got him. That's how I play the game, and that's how we're going to dictate the game."

—Dallas Cowboys defensive end Demarcus Lawrence had this to say about Los Angeles Rams quarterback Jared Goff prior to their divisional-round matchup. (Barstool Sports via Twitter)

"Thought somebody f-ckin' take somebody soul? He ain't takin' no f-ckin' soul out here!"

—Los Angeles Rams cornerback Aqib Talib interrupted quarterback Jared Goff's postgame on-field interview with some colorful language almost certainly directed at Lawrence. Lawrence was held to three tackles and zero sacks on the game. (Dan "Big Cat" Katz, Barstool Sports via Twitter)

THE START OF A BEAUTIFUL BROMANCE

"Uhh... 'I love you,' then give him a hug? 'Can you show me how to catch the ball with one hand?'"

—Cleveland Browns head coach Freddie Kitchens wonders what's the first thing he'll say to the newly acquired Odell Beckham Jr. (Kimberly A. Martin, Yahoo! Sports via Twitter)

I DIDN'T COME HERE TO PLAY SCHOOL

"I remember at LSU we had a 8-page paper due and I told [Jamal Adams] 'Man I don't even think I know that many words.'"

—Jacksonville Jaguars running back Leonard Fournette reflects on the rigorous academia he was forced to tackle during his college days. (Leonard Fournette via Twitter)

EAT THE PAIN AWAY

"Aw man, we just both need a cheeseburger."

—Chicago Bears head coach Matt Nagy and Kansas City Chiefs head coach Andy Reid talked to each other after their heartbreaking playoff losses to the Philadelphia Eagles and New England Patriots, respectively. After 15 minutes of talking, Reid dropped this gem. (Kevin Fishbain, The Athletic Chicago via Twitter)

CLEVELAND CRYPTIDS

"I mean Myles [Garrett] is weird because he's into dinosaurs. Those are long gone. Bigfoot's still running around. Myles does his own thing, like, we get it, bud. They've been dead for a while. Bigfoot's real ... [hunting Bigfoot]'s known as 'Squatching.' They range from 7 to 8 1/2 feet. Big suckers. I know if I went out there, I'd catch him."

—Cleveland Browns quarterback Baker Mayfield rags on defensive end and teammate Myles Garrett for being "into" dinosaurs while announcing his belief in Bigfoot in the same breath. (Laces Out Show, Barstool Sports via Instagram)

THE CAKE IS A LIE

"The thing with me is I have seven kids. So in January, we have three birthdays. We've got a family birthday party, which includes cake. And then, we've got a friend's birthday party, which includes cake. So that's six times in January. We've got three birthdays in March—March 1, March 6, and March 11— which, again, that's a tough stretch. That's cake six out of 10 or 11 days. Then, we've got an April birthday so it doesn't slow down. But now that the birthdays are behind me, I think I'm going to try to go from peak offseason form maybe down to peak in-season form. I'll be OK."

—Miami Dolphins quarterback Ryan Fitzpatrick fielded questions about his offseason weight gain during OTAs. Was it a new diet? A lack of work ethic? Old age? Nope. Birthday cake. Lots and lots of birthday cake. (USA Today)

DIDN'T HE THROW FOUR PICKS IN HIS DEBUT WITH THE BEARS?

"Major clogged ducts. Jay had to get them out for me, sucking harder than he's ever sucked."

—Former star of *The Hills* Kristin Cavallari revealed in a promo for her reality television show that husband, former NFL quarterback Jay Cutler, had to really suck hard to unclog her milk ducts. (Jezebel)

THE YEAR IN BORTLES

"So the plan was to buy a Tesla so that I could quit dipping, because then I wouldn't have to go to the gas station. So now I go to the gas station just to buy dip."

—Los Angeles Rams quarterback Blake Bortles had an unexpected reason for buying an electric car.

"I didn't cry, I poured water on my eyes."

—Bortles' counterargument when accused of crying after losing the 2018 AFC Championship Game to the New England Patriots.

"Wear a helmet. I've seen Sean Mannion wearing a helmet on the sideline all last year. ... Nah, I'd wear a visor, or ask for a headset just to cover it up."

—Bortles, who seamlessly hid his bald spot with hats throughout his tenure in Jacksonville, was posed a hypothetical where Rams head coach Sean McVay wouldn't allow him to wear a hat on the sideline. These are his backup plans. (Pardon My Take)

THAT DISGUISE WON'T FOOL ME

"Sources involved with Bills free-agency negotiations tells me team uninterested in Chad Ochocinco."

—The Athletic's Tim Graham reports that, despite a need at receiver, the Buffalo Bills are uninterested in wide receiver Chad Ochocinco.

"What about Chad Johnson?"

—Former NFL wide receiver Chad Johnson, who legally changed his last name to Ochocinco in 2008 and had it changed back in 2012, clarifies whether the Bills are interested in the real receiver and not just his "alias."

"Also no."

—Graham assures the free agent that the Bills want neither Chad Johnson nor Chad Ochocinco. (Tim Graham, The Athletic via Twitter)

THE ENEMY OF THE ENEMY IS MY FRIEND

"I think we need to put him on salary. I think we need to put him on salary. I mean, they need to protect Dave Gettleman at all costs up in New York, for sure. All costs, because he's winning for us, geez Louise."

—Washington Redskins cornerback Josh Norman hopes that the Giants protect Dave Gettleman, because his presence alone is a win for Washington. (The Rich Eisen Show via Twitter)

'HOW 'BOUT THAT RIDE IN? I GUESS THAT'S WHY THEY CALL IT SIN CITY.'

"For the record, we asked 112 kids if they'd be OK on a Las Vegas Strip, or is it going to be a problem. All 112 of them said, 'No, Coach. It's going to be fine.' We didn't find one guy that admitted Las Vegas would be an issue. So they all lied to us."

—Oakland Raiders general manager Mike Mayock's team will make their move to Las Vegas in 2020, so he made sure to include that as part of his draft interview process. Either every prospect is a liar, or this is the most tame draft class in recent memory. (Michael Gehiken, Las Vegas Review-Journal via Twitter)

QUOTES OF THE YEAR

"They were going to travel Marcus to [Michael Thomas] and that was fine by us. We thought we really liked that matchup, a lot."

—New Orleans Saints head coach Sean Payton in a postgame press conference after his team beat the Los Angeles Rams 45-35. Saints receiver Michael Thomas finished with 12 catches for 211 yards and a touchdown, with much of that damage done with Rams cornerback Marcus Peters in coverage.

"Tell Sean Payton to keep talking that sh-t. We're going to see him soon. You feel me? Yeah, because I like what he was saying on the sidelines, too. Tell him, 'Keep talking that sh-t. And I hope to see you soon.' You hear me? And then we'll have a nice little bowl of gumbo together."

—Peters after practice later in the week, unhappy with what Payton had said about him. The Rams, of course, went on to beat the Saints in the NFC Championship Game later that January. (Lakisha Jackson, NFL.com)

"I don't even like gumbo. I was just bullsh-tting y'all."

—Los Angeles Rams cornerback Marcus Peters retracts his affinity for gumbo after the Rams' NFC Championship victory in New Orleans. (Dan Wolken, USA Today via Twitter)

compiled by Cale Clinton

Full 2019 Projections

The following table lists the mean DVOA projections for all 32 NFL teams. We also list the average number of wins for each team in our one million simulations, along with how often each team made the playoffs, reached the Super Bowl, and won the NFL Championship.

Full 2019 Projections

Team	Avg Wins	Postseason Odds			Mean DVOA Projections								Schedule	
		Make Playoffs	Reach Super Bowl	Win Super Bowl	Total DVOA	Rk	Off DVOA	Rk	Def DVOA	Rk	ST DVOA	Rk	Average Opponent	Rk
NO	10.3	70.5%	21.9%	12.3%	20.5%	1	17.1%	1	-3.7%	10	-0.4%	19	-0.4%	20
NE	10.2	72.2%	17.2%	9.2%	13.8%	5	10.5%	5	0.3%	17	3.6%	2	-5.6%	32
LAC	10.2	68.3%	18.6%	10.5%	19.1%	2	15.6%	2	-4.2%	8	-0.7%	21	-0.3%	19
LAR	9.6	60.5%	14.4%	7.6%	14.0%	4	9.7%	6	-2.5%	13	1.8%	4	0.1%	17
PIT	9.4	58.5%	12.6%	6.7%	12.8%	6	8.5%	7	-5.0%	5	-0.7%	20	-0.9%	23
KC	9.3	56.1%	12.2%	6.5%	14.2%	3	15.0%	3	3.1%	24	2.2%	3	2.2%	8
PHI	9.2	55.2%	9.8%	4.7%	7.1%	8	3.5%	14	-4.3%	6	-0.8%	22	-4.2%	30
IND	8.9	49.9%	8.6%	4.3%	9.3%	7	7.5%	9	-1.0%	14	0.8%	6	0.6%	15
DAL	8.7	47.7%	7.7%	3.7%	4.3%	11	0.0%	16	-4.0%	9	0.4%	11	-2.0%	27
SEA	8.6	44.7%	7.5%	3.6%	6.5%	9	8.4%	8	0.8%	18	-1.1%	25	1.2%	10
GB	8.6	44.4%	7.5%	3.7%	5.5%	10	11.0%	4	4.0%	26	-1.5%	32	0.2%	16
BAL	8.5	42.9%	6.0%	2.8%	3.5%	13	-5.3%	23	-4.2%	7	4.6%	1	-0.5%	21
TEN	8.3	40.9%	5.8%	2.8%	3.7%	12	4.0%	12	0.8%	19	0.5%	8	1.1%	11
DET	8.3	39.8%	5.2%	2.3%	1.7%	15	2.7%	15	1.4%	21	0.4%	9	-1.0%	24
CAR	8.1	36.5%	5.0%	2.3%	1.4%	17	3.9%	13	2.9%	22	0.5%	7	0.8%	14
MIN	8.0	35.7%	4.5%	2.0%	1.3%	18	-4.4%	21	-5.9%	3	-0.2%	14	1.0%	12
Team	Avg Wins	Make Playoffs	Reach Super Bowl	Win Super Bowl	Total DVOA	Rk	Off DVOA	Rk	Def DVOA	Rk	ST DVOA	Rk	Average Opponent	Rk
HOU	8.0	35.2%	4.7%	2.2%	2.8%	14	-4.3%	20	-7.3%	1	-0.3%	17	3.3%	2
CLE	8.0	33.7%	3.6%	1.6%	-2.1%	21	4.2%	11	5.0%	27	-1.4%	30	-1.3%	25
CHI	7.9	35.1%	4.9%	2.2%	1.7%	16	-2.2%	18	-5.2%	4	-1.2%	28	2.8%	5
NYJ	7.7	32.4%	2.8%	1.1%	-7.2%	23	-8.3%	25	-0.3%	16	0.8%	5	-4.8%	31
SF	7.7	31.1%	3.5%	1.5%	-2.1%	20	-5.2%	22	-3.4%	11	-0.3%	18	0.9%	13
ATL	7.6	29.7%	3.4%	1.5%	-1.8%	19	6.6%	10	7.2%	30	-1.2%	27	2.6%	6
JAX	7.3	26.8%	2.5%	1.1%	-4.1%	22	-10.5%	27	-6.4%	2	0.0%	12	2.0%	9
NYG	7.2	24.7%	1.7%	0.6%	-11.5%	27	-8.7%	26	3.2%	25	0.4%	10	-3.8%	29
CIN	6.9	21.2%	1.5%	0.6%	-10.5%	25	-3.2%	19	7.1%	29	-0.3%	15	-0.6%	22
BUF	6.9	21.9%	1.3%	0.5%	-13.1%	29	-11.1%	28	0.9%	20	-1.2%	26	-3.8%	28
OAK	6.6	18.1%	1.3%	0.5%	-9.0%	24	-0.8%	17	6.9%	28	-1.4%	31	2.9%	4
ARI	6.4	16.9%	1.3%	0.5%	-11.3%	26	-14.5%	31	-3.2%	12	0.0%	13	2.2%	7
DEN	6.2	14.5%	0.9%	0.4%	-11.9%	28	-11.4%	29	-0.8%	15	-1.3%	29	3.4%	1
WAS	6.1	14.8%	0.8%	0.3%	-18.1%	31	-14.3%	30	3.0%	23	-0.8%	23	-1.4%	26
TB	6.0	12.6%	0.8%	0.3%	-15.0%	30	-6.6%	24	7.4%	31	-1.0%	24	3.1%	3
MIA	5.1	7.6%	0.2%	0.1%	-25.5%	32	-17.6%	32	7.6%	32	-0.3%	16	0.1%	18

Arizona Cardinals

2018 record: 3-13	**Total DVOA:** -40.7% (32nd)	**2019 Mean Projection:** 6.4 wins	**On the Clock (0-4):** 25%
Pythagorean Wins: 2.8 (32nd)	**Offense:** -41.1% (32nd)	**Postseason Odds:** 16.9%	**Mediocrity (5-7):** 43%
Snap-Weighted Age: 26.6 (10th)	**Defense:** 0.5% (18th)	**Super Bowl Odds:** 1.3%	**Playoff Contender (8-10):** 26%
Average Opponent: 3.0% (5th)	**Special Teams:** 1.0% (11th)	**Proj. Avg. Opponent:** 2.2% (7th)	**Super Bowl Contender (11+):** 7%

2018: Terrible football with no lasting legacy that will soon be forgotten. Is this the AAF?

2019: Still terrible, but a lot more entertaining.

Let's dive right into this: the 2019 Arizona Cardinals may be the most thrilling awful team we've seen in some time. It's Kliff Kingsbury. It's Kyler Murray. It's Air Raid! Air Raid! Air Raid!

Though its roots can be traced back to LaVell Edwards' tenure as head coach at BYU, the Air Raid offense was first used full-time by head coach Hal Mumme and offensive coordinator Mike Leach in the late 1980s, first at Iowa Wesleyan College and then at Valdosta State. In 1997, Mumme and Leach brought the Air Raid to the University of Kentucky, developing quarterback Tim Couch into the NFL's top draft pick in 1999. While Mumme has continued to coach at New Mexico State and smaller schools, Leach spent one year as coordinator at Oklahoma, then 18 seasons as a head coach, first at Texas Tech, and now at Washington State. Through the years, a number of coaches from the Mumme/Leach tree have also leaned heavily on the Air Raid. That includes Kingsbury, who set records as a quarterback under Leach at Texas Tech in the early part of this century and was the head coach there from 2013 until he was fired last December.

The principles of the Air Raid are simple: use spread formations almost exclusively to open natural seams in a defense, then throw the ball to those seams for easy completions. Most running plays are the results of zone-read or run-pass options, or audibles at the line when defenses overcommit to pass coverage and vacate the box near the line of scrimmage. There's also a bit of a hurry-up element to it—receivers and backs tend to swap places wholesale, like lines in hockey, as the offense tries to wear the defense out by sheer number of snaps.

The resulting numbers are extreme. In Kingsbury's six years at Texas Tech, the Red Raiders threw more than 3,600 passes, second in the nation only to Leach's Cougars at Washington State. They ran more than 6,000 total plays; only Clemson and Baylor ran more. They threw at least 535 passes every season; no other team in the Big 12 (one of the nation's most pass-happy conferences) hit that number even once. And those passes were spread across the roster. Sixteen times a Red Raiders player caught at least 50 passes in a season; no other Big 12 school had more than 11.

Into this scheme steps Kyler Murray, the first overall pick in this year's draft, who played in a similar offense at Oklahoma. Sooners coach Lincoln Riley, Kingsbury's old backup at Tex-

as Tech, later joined Leach's staff before moving to Norman, where he developed first Baker Mayfield and then Murray into Heisman Trophy winners and top overall draft picks.

In his only season as a college starter, Murray was unearthly great. He averaged 11.6 yards per pass, most by any qualifying quarterback since at least the 1950s. He joined Clemson's Deshaun Watson as the only players to ever throw for 4,000 yards and rush for a thousand more in the same year. His 199.2 NCAA passer efficiency rating would have been an all-time record, surpassing the mark set by his teammate Mayfield the year before, but Alabama's Tua Tagavailoa sneaked by him at 199.4. He won the AP Player of the Year award, the Davey O'Brien Award, and the Heisman Trophy. He was a big-play machine—his 12 touchdown runs averaged 24.2 yards apiece; his 42 touchdown passes, 30.5.

In May, Steven Ruiz wrote an excellent article at For The Win breaking down in detail what Kingsbury's offense in Arizona might look like. He included several notes on the Red Raiders from Sports Info Solutions charting, including that Texas Tech ran the ball out of 10 personnel 199 times, and that only Oklahoma ran more plays with pulling guards among Power 5 teams. By spreading to run and moving linemen around the field, the Cardinals can make best use of Murray's athleticism while also working around his one physical weakness: his diminutive 5-foot, 10-inch frame.

All of this makes the Cardinals offense the most difficult to project this season. Will Kingsbury use similar run/pass splits as he did at Texas Tech, or modify his scheme for the NFL? Will the Cardinals let Murray run wild, or cut back on his running plays to avoid punishing hits? Will they be able to pile up the snap counts, or will opponents play keepaway and slow the game to a halt? And how will the weapons around Murray be implemented?

In college, Kingsbury's most successful receivers were undersized—four of his five top receivers at Texas Tech stood 6 feet or shorter. That's a good sign for Christian Kirk, last year's second-rounder who was one of the few bright spots in a horrible season, as well as Andy Isabella, this year's second-rounder, acquired in a trade with Miami. Mind you, there's room for taller receivers too—T.J. Vasher, all 6 feet, 6 inches of him, caught 83 passes for 1,232 yards and 13 touchdowns over the last two years in Lubbock. Larry Fitzgerald (6-foot-3) and fourth-round rookie Hakeem Butler (6-foot-5) should

2019 Cardinals Schedule

Week	Opp.	Week	Opp.	Week	Opp.
1	DET	7	at NYG	13	LAR
2	at BAL	8	at NO	14	PIT
3	CAR	9	SF (Thu.)	15	CLE
4	SEA	10	at TB	16	at SEA
5	at CIN	11	at SF	17	at LAR
6	ATL	12	BYE		

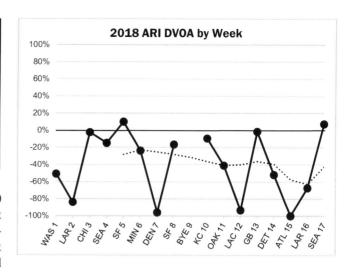

fit right in. And even though Kingsbury will use a lot of 10 personnel groupings with no tight ends on the field, he has put talented tight ends to good use in the past. Jace Amaro, a hold-over from the Tommy Tuberville era at Texas Tech, caught 106 passes under Kingsbury in 2013 before the Jets drafted him in the second round a year later. Incumbent Ricky Seals-Jones and free-agent signee Charles Clay should be more than just extra bodies at the goal line.

Finally, there is David Johnson, whose excellent receiving skills were mostly wasted in 2018. That should change this year. Kingsbury's running backs at Texas Tech fell into two groups: those who caught passes (DeAndre Washington, Justin Stockton, and Da'Leon Ward combined for 1,677 runs and 231 receptions under Kingsbury) and those who didn't (Tre King and Demarcus Felton had 325 runs but only caught 16 balls between them). The Cardinals won't force passes to running backs when there are more effective weapons available, but they will try to give a quality receiver like Johnson the targets he deserves. With so many new faces joining a team that is also making a drastic strategic conversion, it's difficult to project which players will get the most action or how they will fare. There's also the distinct possibility that the offensive line will collapse again, rendering all of Kingsbury's X's and O's moot. On paper, though, Kingsbury, Murray, and that diverse cast of weapons should give opposing defenses all sorts of headaches, which would be a huge change from last year.

Which brings us to a subject we have been trying to avoid for more than a thousand words now: the 2018 Arizona Cardinals offense. We've been putting this off for as long as possible because A) it's largely irrelevant at this point, since the head coach, quarterback and *both* coordinators responsible are all gone now; and B) it's a very unpleasant subject matter.

The Cardinals offense finished last in the league in DVOA, and last in weighted DVOA. They were last on first down, second down, and third down. They were last in the first half of games and last in the second half. They were last at home and last on the road. They were last when the game was close and last in the rare event they had a big lead. They were last out of shotgun formations. They were *next* to last on running plays, when losing big, in late and close games, or with the quarterback under center. Weirdly, they were 12th in the red zone … but then they only ran 95 red zone plays, which was also next to last.

It was a particularly tough year for quarterback Josh Rosen and tight end Ricky Seals-Jones, who put up historically bad seasons (Tables 1 and 2). Yes, in just 13 starts in the elevated passing environment of 2018, Josh Rosen put up the worst single-season passing DYAR we have ever measured. This is why he was traded away for a song just a year after he was drafted tenth overall. He's Miami's problem now, and you can read about him elsewhere in this book. But we should mention that it takes a team-wide collapse to produce a season this wretched. At the most basic level, there are four things a team can do to make life easier on its quarterback: the offensive line can give him time to throw, while his receivers can get open, catch the ball, and gain yards after the catch. The Cardinals were bad to horrible at all four of these things.

- The offensive line gave up a pressure rate of 35.4 percent, 29th in the NFL.

Table 1: Worst Single-Season Passing DYAR, 1986-2018

Year	Name	Team	Com	Att	C%	Yds	Avg.	TD	INT	Sacks	FUM	DYAR	DVOA
2018	Josh Rosen	ARI	217	393	55.2%	2278	5.80	11	14	45	10	-1145	-53.7%
2002	David Carr	HOU	233	444	52.5%	2592	5.84	9	15	76	21	-1130	-47.4%
2011	Blaine Gabbert	JAX	210	413	50.8%	2214	5.36	12	11	40	14	-1010	-46.5%
1998	Bobby Hoying	PHI	114	224	50.9%	961	4.29	0	9	35	6	-962	-68.2%
2014	Blake Bortles	JAX	280	475	58.9%	2908	6.12	11	17	55	7	-955	-40.7%
2016	Jared Goff	LAR	112	205	54.6%	1089	5.31	5	7	26	5	-881	-74.8%
2005	Alex Smith	SF	84	165	50.9%	875	5.30	1	11	29	10	-866	-88.6%
1992	Kelly Stouffer	SEA	92	190	48.4%	900	4.74	3	9	26	12	-837	-72.7%
2009	JaMarcus Russell	OAK	120	246	48.8%	1287	5.23	3	11	33	9	-834	-62.0%
2010	Jimmy Clausen	CAR	157	299	52.5%	1558	5.21	3	9	33	9	-760	-48.0%

- The team's top targets—Fitzgerald, Kirk, Seals-Jones, and rookie Chad Williams—each had an average separation of 2.7 yards or less per target according to NFL Next Gen Stats. None of them ranked higher than 80th among qualifying receivers. Their collective average was 2.4 yards of separation. Only Detroit had less separation among its top receivers.
- The Cardinals had 283 receptions and 25 drops. That's a drop rate of 8.1 percent, seventh-highest.
- Arizona averaged 4.4 yards after the catch per reception, second worst behind Tampa Bay. That includes just 2.7 yards after the catch on passes thrown past the line of scrimmage. No other offense was below 3.4.

Between those and other factors, NFL Next Gen Stats calculated Rosen's expected completion rate to be 59.4 percent, lowest among qualifying quarterbacks last season. Mind you, Rosen's actual completion rate of 55.2 percent was even worse than that—he had plenty of warts on his own. His fate was likely sealed as soon as Kingsbury was hired. Last October, when Kingsbury was still at Texas Tech and Murray had started all of eight games for the Sooners, Kingsbury called Murray "a freak" who had never had a bad outing and claimed he would draft Murray first overall if he could. As it turns out, he could, and he did. It was almost unprecedented to see one team take two quarterbacks so highly in back-to-back drafts. Since the 1970 merger with the AFL, only two teams have used more draft capital on quarterbacks in consecutive seasons: the 1982-83 Baltimore Colts and the 1989-90 Dallas Cowboys (Table 3). If anything, this is underselling Arizona's investment, because they actually traded up to draft Rosen.

Most of these teams were in similar situations to these Cardinals: they drafted a quarterback highly, it went terribly wrong, and so they grabbed another quarterback with the first overall pick the next year. Sometimes it worked, but sometimes it didn't—and when it didn't, that's often because spending all that draft capital on quarterbacks left teams unable to help their defense. In Arizona's case, it goes beyond quarterbacks—in the past two years, they have selected nine players in the first four rounds of the draft, and only two of those players play defense. That's bad news for a defense that wasn't capable of playing winning football either in 2018.

Despite going from James Bettcher's 3-4 in 2017 to Steve Wilks' 4-3 in 2018 and back to a 3-4 under Vance Joseph this fall,

the Cardinals defense is going to look quite familiar, schematically. All three coaches use a lot of blitzes, often with defensive backs, and move those corners and safeties around the field in man coverage. The biggest change this fall will be in personnel. The Broncos used a ton of base personnel (45 percent, leading the league); the Cardinals used almost none (10 percent, last in the league). When Joseph brought in more defensive backs, he was just as likely to go dime (fifth in the league in frequency) instead of nickel (31st), while the 2018 Cardinals were almost always in nickel. However, that nickel usually involved three safeties, not three cornerbacks. Arizona had three safeties on the field for a league-leading 76 percent of plays. The Dolphins and Chargers were the only other teams above 50 percent.

The problem for Arizona, however, isn't scheme, it's talent. The Cardinals have a Hall of Fame cornerback in Patrick Peterson, an All-Pro edge rusher in Chandler Jones, a playmaking young safety in Budda Baker, and few other defenders you would actually want starting on your team. Now subtract Peterson for a third of the season—he'll be suspended for the first six games due to a positive test for PEDs and a masking agent. Arizona general manager Steve Keim tried to fix the problem with an infusion of veteran talent; more than half the defensive starters on opening day could be veteran free-agent acquisitions. It sounds like a stop-gap measure, but acquiring veterans is the only thing at which Keim has been consistently successful. His drafting has been disastrous. Of the 42 players he drafted from 2013 to 2018, only 15 are still on the roster, and only five are expected to start this fall.

With turnover like that, it's no surprise the Cardinals have been in a constant state of flux. A year ago at this time, Keim was committed to Steve Wilks, Sam Bradford, and Josh Rosen; now, all are gone. Rosen's agent Ryan Williams told Robert Klemko of *Sports Illustrated* that Keim did not advise him to seek a trade until *after Murray was drafted*, showing a shocking lack of planning for a veteran GM. Kingsbury and Murray have their own questions about reliability. Kingsbury's greatest strength as a coaching candidate may have been his friendship with Rams coach Sean McVay, a relationship the Cardinals were sure to advertise in their press release announcing his hiring. (Kingsbury is also a former backup to Tom Brady, plus he looks like Ryan Gosling, so he should have no shortage of NFL opportunities going forward.) He was fired by a mid-level Big 12 team just last December, finishing with a los-

Table 2: Worst Single-Season Receiving DYAR, Tight Ends, 1986-2018

Year	Name	Team	Passes	Catches	Catch %	Yards	TD	Rec FUM	DYAR	DVOA
2011	Marcedes Lewis	JAX	85	39	46%	460	0	0	-161	-35.5%
2018	**Ricky Seals-Jones**	**ARI**	**69**	**34**	**49%**	**343**	**1**	**0**	**-158**	**-43.7%**
1998	Freddie Jones	SD	111	57	51%	602	3	1	-155	-29.1%
2010	Daniel Graham	DEN	37	18	49%	153	0	1	-140	-63.5%
2004	Boo Williams	NO	75	33	44%	362	2	2	-138	-35.0%
1997	Jamie Asher	WAS	99	49	49%	474	1	0	-129	-28.1%
2004	Stephen Alexander	DET	76	41	54%	377	1	0	-129	-32.5%
1989	Jay Novacek	PHX	53	23	43%	225	1	0	-129	-47.7%
1990	James Thornton	CHI	48	19	40%	254	1	1	-126	-47.4%
1996	Keith Cash	KC	33	14	42%	90	0	1	-124	-62.0%

ing record and only three bowl appearances. Within the next month he had accepted and then resigned from a job at USC. Murray, in the past five years, has committed to Texas A&M football, Texas A&M baseball, Oklahoma football, Oklahoma baseball, and Major League Baseball—and he failed to see any of those commitments through to the end. Kingsbury and Murray should be praised for doing whatever they can to maximize their earnings, and you could also credit Keim for being willing to admit his mistakes, but it's still concerning that everyone involved with this franchise seems to be making things up as they go along.

One thing is clear: The Cardinals have their most exciting offensive rookie since … Terry Metcalf? Ottis Anderson? The pickings here are pretty slim. They also have a coach who is not afraid to lean on that rookie and give him every opportunity to shine. In a division with the Rams, Seahawks, and 49ers—not to mention a schedule that also includes the strong AFC North and NFC South divisions—Arizona is not likely to win many games. But they're going to be the most intriguing losers the NFL has seen in recent memory.

Vincent Verhei

Table 3: Most Draft Capital Spent on QBs in Back-to-Back Years, 1970-2019

Team	Years	Year 1			Year 2			Total ExpAV*	5-Yr W-L
		Pick(s)	Player(s)	ExpAV*	Pick(s)	Player(s)	ExpAV*		
DAL	1989-1990	1	Troy Aikman	34.6	1	Steve Walsh*	34.6	69.2	44-36
BALC	1982-1983	4, 84	Art Schlichter, Mike Pagel	32.2	1, 280	John Elway, Jim Bob Taylor	34.7	66.9	28-51
ARI	2018-2019	10	Josh Rosen	19.9	1	Kyler Murray	34.6	54.5	—
CAR	2010-2011	48, 204	Jimmy Clausen, Tony Pike	10.6	1	Cam Newton	34.6	45.2	47-32-1
CLE	2017-2018	52	DeShone Kizer	9.4	1	Baker Mayfield	34.6	44.0	7-8-1
ATL	1974-1975	69	Kim McQuilken	7.6	1, 419	Steve Bartkowski, Mitch Anderson	34.7	42.3	30-44
HOU	2002-2003	1	David Carr	34.6	88, 192	Dave Ragone, Drew Henson	7.2	41.8	28-52
STL/LAR	2015-2016	89	Sean Mannion	6.0	1	Jared Goff	34.6	40.6	28-20
DAL	1988-1989	151	Scott Secules	2.7	1	Troy Aikman	34.6	37.3	35-45
ATL	2001-2002	1	Michael Vick	34.6	158	Kurt Kittner	2.4	37.0	40-39-1

* Expected AV based on Chase Stuart's Expected Approximate Value chart at FootballPerspective.com.
** After selecting Aikman first overall in 1989, the Cowboys took Walsh in the first round of the supplemental draft, forfeiting their first-round pick in 1990, which turned out to be the first overall pick.

2018 Cardinals Stats by Week

Wk	vs.	W-L	PF	PA	YDF	YDA	TO	Total	Off	Def	ST
1	WAS	L	6	24	213	429	-1	-51%	-43%	19%	11%
2	at LAR	L	0	34	137	432	0	-84%	-72%	-7%	-18%
3	CHI	L	14	16	221	316	-2	-2%	-30%	-31%	-3%
4	SEA	L	17	20	263	331	-1	-15%	-8%	-10%	-18%
5	at SF	W	28	18	220	447	+5	10%	0%	-4%	6%
6	at MIN	L	17	27	268	411	0	-24%	-29%	-4%	1%
7	DEN	L	10	45	223	309	-4	-96%	-80%	18%	2%
8	SF	W	18	15	321	267	-2	-17%	-29%	-10%	2%
9	BYE										
10	at KC	L	14	26	260	330	-2	-9%	-32%	-16%	7%
11	OAK	L	21	23	282	325	-2	-41%	-38%	11%	8%
12	at LAC	L	10	45	149	414	0	-93%	-49%	36%	-9%
13	at GB	W	20	17	315	325	0	-1%	-15%	-7%	7%
14	DET	L	3	17	279	218	0	-52%	-61%	-11%	-2%
15	at ATL	L	14	40	253	435	-3	-101%	-85%	23%	7%
16	LAR	L	9	31	263	461	+1	-67%	-33%	27%	-8%
17	at SEA	L	24	27	198	291	-1	8%	-45%	-30%	22%

Trends and Splits

	Offense	Rank	Defense	Rank
Total DVOA	-41.1%	32	0.5%	18
Unadjusted VOA	-40.2%	32	3.1%	21
Weighted Trend	-44.4%	32	4.0%	21
Variance	5.9%	11	3.9%	4
Average Opponent	0.9%	23	4.7%	4
Passing	-46.9%	32	-0.9%	8
Rushing	-21.4%	31	1.8%	29
First Down	-29.1%	32	2.0%	19
Second Down	-39.8%	32	6.2%	23
Third Down	-67.9%	32	-12.3%	8
First Half	-46.8%	32	-1.8%	12
Second Half	-35.8%	32	3.1%	20
Red Zone	9.6%	12	14.7%	25
Late and Close	-38.5%	31	-0.1%	18

Five-Year Performance

Year	W-L	Pyth W	Est W	PF	PA	TO	Total	Rk	Off	Rk	Def	Rk	ST	Rk	Off AGL	Rk	Def AGL	Rk	Off Age	Rk	Def Age	Rk	ST Age	Rk
2014	11-5	8.3	7.4	310	299	+8	-6.4%	22	-9.3%	23	-5.0%	7	-2.2%	21	24.0	8	48.8	24	27.3	10	27.1	9	26.4	5
2015	13-3	12.1	11.6	489	313	+9	27.4%	3	15.7%	4	-15.6%	3	-4.0%	29	21.2	4	41.3	25	28.2	3	26.0	26	25.8	21
2016	7-8-1	9.4	7.7	418	362	0	1.3%	16	-6.0%	21	-13.6%	3	-6.3%	30	35.4	17	42.4	21	28.3	1	25.9	29	25.5	27
2017	8-8	6.1	5.6	295	361	-4	-10.8%	22	-18.0%	30	-12.7%	4	-5.5%	28	74.8	32	30.8	13	28.6	1	28.1	2	26.5	6
2018	3-13	2.8	2.5	225	425	-12	-40.7%	32	-41.1%	32	0.5%	18	1.0%	11	61.5	29	34.2	15	26.1	25	27.2	4	26.2	9

2018 Performance Based on Most Common Personnel Groups

	ARI Offense					ARI Offense vs. Opponents					ARI Defense					ARI Defense vs. Opponents		
Pers	Freq	Yds	DVOA	Run%	Pers	Freq	Yds	DVOA	Run%	Pers	Freq	Yds	DVOA	Pers	Freq	Yds	DVOA
11	71%	4.1	-45.1%	28%	Base	25%	5.2	-16.4%	57%	Base	10%	4.2	-22.5%	11	64%	5.8	8.8%
12	17%	4.9	-17.5%	53%	Nickel	42%	4.2	-45.0%	31%	Nickel	84%	5.8	6.9%	12	15%	6.2	-3.3%
21	5%	4.6	-47.8%	65%	Dime+	17%	3.4	-48.4%	18%	Dime+	5%	4.4	-54.9%	21	11%	4.3	-13.2%
22	3%	3.3	1.7%	88%	Goal Line	0%	0.8	-26.8%	75%	Goal Line	1%	0.3	-30.0%	22	4%	3.2	-52.9%
13	2%	8.2	29.6%	60%	Big	1%	4.4	-48.6%	75%					13	2%	4.5	-8.8%

Strategic Tendencies

Run/Pass		Rk	Formation		Rk	Pass Rush		Rk	Secondary		Rk	Strategy		Rk
Runs, first half	39%	13	Form: Single Back	86%	6	Rush 3	3.8%	23	4 DB	10%	32	Play action	20%	26
Runs, first down	45%	21	Form: Empty Back	5%	28	Rush 4	61.2%	22	5 DB	84%	1	Avg Box (Off)	6.09	27
Runs, second-long	35%	7	Pers: 3+ WR	72%	12	Rush 5	28.2%	1	6+ DB	5%	19	Avg Box (Def)	6.43	1
Runs, power sit.	69%	5	Pers: 2+ TE/6+ OL	23%	17	Rush 6+	6.6%	12	CB by Sides	59%	24	Offensive Pace	31.46	20
Runs, behind 2H	30%	9	Pers: 6+ OL	0%	29	Int DL Sacks	23.5%	19	S/CB Cover Ratio	44%	2	Defensive Pace	32.13	30
Pass, ahead 2H	46%	21	Shotgun/Pistol	57%	23	Second Level Sacks	27.6%	10	DB Blitz	17%	1	Go for it on 4th	1.11	23

The Cardinals offense had the league's largest "reverse gap" on shotgun plays. Most teams are better from shotgun; the Cardinals were much worse. They gained 4.1 yards per play with -56.5% DVOA from shotgun, compared to 4.8 yards per play and -24.4% DVOA with the quarterback under center. ◉ Arizona was almost reasonable when they used play-action: 7.1 yards per pass, -3.3% DVOA. They had -54.3% DVOA on other passes. Only New England had a larger gap. ◉ In case they needed another way to struggle on offense, Arizona also ranked 30th in broken tackles—although they improved to 24th if you looked at the percentage of plays with at least one broken tackle. ◉ Arizona opponents threw deep (16-plus yards in the air) on a league-low 15 percent of passes. ◉ Arizona was surprisingly good on blitzes, particularly big blitzes of six or more pass-rushers. Their -38.6% DVOA allowed when blitzing was second behind Chicago, as was their -97.7% DVOA and measly 2.2 net yards per pass allowed on big blitzes. When specifically blitzing a defensive back, the Cardinals had a league-best -78.5% DVOA and just 2.9 net yards per pass allowed. ◉ The Cardinals only benefited from 118 opponent penalties, 22nd in the league. This was the first time since 2012 that the Cardinals did not rank in the top five.

Passing

Player	DYAR	DVOA	Plays	NtYds	Avg	YAC	C%	TD	Int
J.Rosen*	-1145	-53.7%	439	1943	4.4	4.5	55.5%	11	14
S.Bradford*	-213	-50.8%	86	366	4.3	3.8	62.5%	2	4
M.Glennon*	73	45.4%	22	166	7.5	5.6	71.4%	1	0

Receiving

Player	DYAR	DVOA	Plays	Ctch	Yds	Y/C	YAC	TD	C%
L.Fitzgerald	-23	-15.3%	112	69	734	10.6	3.0	6	62%
C.Kirk	57	-1.8%	68	43	590	13.7	5.3	3	63%
C.Williams	-142	-53.5%	46	17	171	10.1	0.9	1	37%
T.Sherfield	18	-4.3%	28	19	210	11.1	2.0	1	68%
J.J.Nelson*	-46	-41.6%	19	7	64	9.1	3.4	0	37%
J.Tolliver	-4	-20.8%	6	3	37	12.3	4.7	0	50%
K.White	15	10.1%	8	4	92	23.0	1.5	0	50%
R.Seals-Jones	-158	-43.7%	69	34	343	10.1	2.7	1	49%
J.Gresham*	-3	-11.4%	12	9	94	10.4	8.3	0	75%
C.Clay	-70	-38.3%	36	21	197	9.4	4.0	0	58%
M.Williams	18	8.2%	17	16	143	8.9	6.1	1	94%
D.Johnson	-13	-17.1%	76	50	443	8.9	7.7	3	66%
C.Edmonds	-19	-27.7%	23	20	103	5.2	6.1	0	87%
T.J.Logan	-10	-53.9%	7	7	37	5.3	5.6	0	100%

Rushing

Player	DYAR	DVOA	Plays	Yds	Avg	TD	Fum	Suc
D.Johnson	-42	-12.6%	258	940	3.6	7	2	38%
C.Edmonds	-27	-18.9%	60	208	3.5	2	1	45%
J.Rosen*	23	25.2%	14	145	10.4	0	1	--

Offensive Line

Player	Pos	Age	GS	Snaps	Pen	Sk	Pass	Run	Player	Pos	Age	GS	Snaps	Pen	Sk	Pass	Run
Mason Cole	C	23	16/16	942	3	3.5	5	2	Justin Pugh	RG	29	7/7	343	1	1.0	5	0
D.J. Humphries	LT	26	9/9	522	2	3.0	12	1	John Wetzel*	RT/G	28	8/5	339	4	1.5	4	1
Mike Iupati*	LG	32	10/10	477	3	2.0	8	2	Colby Gossett	LG	24	5/4	282	4	2.5	6	2
Andre Smith*	RT	32	11/8	452	5	6.0	11	1	J.R. Sweezy	LG	30	15/15	948	9	4.0	12	6
Oday Aboushi*	RG	28	8/6	407	3	4.5	7	2	Marcus Gilbert	RT	31	5/5	362	2	1.5	3	1
Joe Barksdale*	RT	30	10/5	388	4	0.0	4	0	Max Garcia	LG	28	9/4	242	3	1.0	4	5
Korey Cunningham	LT	24	6/6	349	4	2.0	8	4									

Year	Yards	ALY	Rank	Power	Rank	Stuff	Rank	2nd Lev	Rank	Open Field	Rank	Sacks	ASR	Rank	Press	Rank	F-Start	Cont.
2016	4.28	4.54	7	72%	5	21%	20	1.23	12	0.82	11	41	6.3%	21	30.9%	29	13	22
2017	3.38	4.02	17	68%	9	20%	13	0.90	32	0.30	32	52	8.1%	26	29.7%	11	17	26
2018	3.58	4.00	25	69%	10	16%	6	0.98	30	0.36	31	52	9.2%	26	35.4%	29	19	17
2018 ALY by direction:			Left End: 3.83 (22)			Left Tackle: 5.10 (4)			Mid/Guard: 4.03 (28)			Right Tackle: 3.24 (29)			Right End: 3.86 (23)			

A disaster the likes of which we have rarely seen. The Cardinals used 13 starters on the offensive line, tied for the most in our database going back to 1999. Throw in first-string center A.Q. Shipley, who missed the entire season with a torn ACL, and you get an unprecedented 14 offensive linemen expected to start at some point during the year. By the first week of December, all five of Arizona's preseason starters had been placed on IR or released outright; by Week 17 the Cardinals were starting three men who had been pulled from another team's practice squad or signed off the street. The Cardinals gave up 22 sacks in December alone—that's more sacks than the Patriots, Saints, or Colts allowed all season. ✎ Shipley signed a one-year, $2-million extension through 2019 just after his injury. He'll return to the starting lineup this fall, but he is now 33 with a bad leg. This is a player who bounced from the Colts to the Ravens back to the Colts and finally to the Cardinals before finally becoming a full-time starter at age 30, so his ceiling wasn't that high to begin with. And the player he replaces, rookie Mason Cole, was the only Cardinals lineman to start more than 10 games and had the highest rank at his position in snaps per blown block (17th). ✎ D.J. Humphries will return at left tackle, but at this point we can only assume his presence in the lineup will be temporary. The 2015 first-round pick spent his rookie year on the bench behind Bobby Massie and Jared Veldheer, and has missed three, 11, and seven games in the three years since. The Cardinals exercised his fifth-year option for $9.6 million to bring him back this year, but Kliff Kingsbury said he was "questionable" for OTAs as he recovers from a torn MCL and a dislocated kneecap. ✎ Justin Pugh left the Giants to join Arizona on a five-year, $45-million deal last season. He has his own sketchy injury history, missing 17 games in his last four seasons in New York, and missing nine more last year with knee and hand injuries. ✎ The Cardinals added two more veteran starters this offseason. Free agent left guard J.R. Sweezy missed all of 2016 with a back injury and failed to stick with Tampa Bay or Seattle since then. At right tackle, Arizona traded a sixth-round pick for Pittsburgh's Marcus Gilbert, who missed 11 games last year with a knee injury, and nine games in 2017 due to a hamstring problem and a suspension for PEDs. ✎ TL;DR: All five projected starters on Arizona's offensive line have had worrisome health issues in the past … which has us seriously worried about Kyler Murray's health in the present.

Defensive Front

Defensive Line	Age	Pos	G	Snaps	Plays	TmPct	Rk	Stop	Dfts	BTkl	Runs	St%	Rk	RuYd	Rk	Sack	Hit	Hur	Dsrpt
						Overall						**vs. Run**					**Pass Rush**		
Corey Peters	31	DT	15	733	50	6.1%	22	37	13	3	40	75%	41	2.1	35	2.5	1	10	1
Rodney Gunter	27	DT	16	641	45	5.1%	35	29	15	3	33	64%	77	3.0	71	4.5	6	11	1
Robert Nkemdiche	25	DT	10	426	32	5.8%	29	26	14	1	24	75%	41	2.0	30	4.5	5	6	1
Olsen Pierre*	28	DT	10	245	12	2.2%	--	11	2	0	9	100%	--	1.8	--	0.0	1	1	0
Darius Philon	*25*	*DT*	*16*	*607*	*33*	*4.2%*	*61*	*27*	*12*	*7*	*25*	*80%*	*24*	*1.3*	*5*	*4.0*	*5*	*15*	*0*

Edge Rushers	Age	Pos	G	Snaps	Plays	TmPct	Rk	Stop	Dfts	BTkl	Runs	St%	Rk	RuYd	Rk	Sack	Hit	Hur	Dsrpt
						Overall						**vs. Run**					**Pass Rush**		
Chandler Jones	29	DE	16	968	53	6.0%	22	41	26	4	29	69%	61	2.0	33	13.0	7	30	3
Benson Mayowa*	28	DE	15	550	40	4.8%	46	35	18	3	29	86%	12	1.6	18	4.0	7	13	4
Markus Golden*	28	DE	11	393	32	5.3%	38	25	9	3	25	80%	24	2.2	41	2.5	4	14	1
Cameron Malveaux	25	DE	9	173	11	2.3%	--	10	2	0	9	89%	--	1.9	--	1.0	0	4	1
Terrell Suggs	*37*	*OLB*	*16*	*744*	*38*	*5.0%*	*45*	*33*	*17*	*7*	*21*	*86%*	*13*	*1.4*	*12*	*7.0*	*7*	*36*	*5*
Brooks Reed	*32*	*DE*	*16*	*458*	*23*	*2.8%*	*87*	*14*	*3*	*2*	*18*	*72%*	*53*	*2.6*	*51*	*1.0*	*3*	*15*	*0*

Linebackers	Age	Pos	G	Snaps	Plays	TmPct	Rk	Stop	Dfts	BTkl	Runs	St%	Rk	RuYd	Rk	Sack	Hit	Hur	Tgts	Suc%	Rk	AdjYd	Rk	PD	Int
						Overall						**vs. Run**				**Pass Rush**				**vs. Pass**					
Haason Reddick	25	OLB	16	846	85	9.7%	60	47	18	19	45	56%	55	4.3	65	4.0	3	10	36	42%	59	6.8	37	5	0
Josh Bynes*	30	MLB	11	725	80	13.2%	36	49	16	4	41	80%	2	2.9	13	2.0	1	4	32	34%	74	8.1	64	5	0
Deone Bucannon*	27	OLB	13	389	36	5.0%	84	14	3	4	22	55%	60	4.5	69	1.0	1	6.5	11	45%	--	6.7	--	0	0
Gerald Hodges*	28	MLB	16	356	51	5.8%	--	19	6	7	35	46%	--	4.0	--	0.0	1	3	13	38%	--	6.2	--	0	0
Jordan Hicks	*27*	*MLB*	*12*	*705*	*95*	*16.2%*	*16*	*41*	*17*	*5*	*38*	*47%*	*82*	*4.7*	*73*	*3.0*	*2*	*3.5*	*27*	*37%*	*69*	*10.0*	*77*	*5*	*0*
Tanner Vallejo	*25*	*OLB*	*13*	*145*	*20*	*2.8%*	*--*	*15*	*4*	*4*	*12*	*92%*	*--*	*1.6*	*--*	*0.0*	*0*	*1*	*6*	*17%*	*--*	*9.8*	*--*	*0*	*0*

Year	Yards	ALY	Rank	Power	Rank	Stuff	Rank	2nd Level	Rank	Open Field	Rank	Sacks	ASR	Rank	Press	Rank
2016	3.30	3.58	3	61%	13	23%	6	0.95	3	0.31	2	48	7.5%	3	32.1%	2
2017	3.36	3.34	3	62%	12	23%	6	0.96	6	0.56	6	37	5.9%	24	30.2%	17
2018	4.92	4.32	14	80%	32	20%	12	1.46	30	1.28	30	49	8.8%	3	28.8%	22

2018 ALY by direction:　Left End: 4.16 (13)　Left Tackle: 2.51 (2)　Mid/Guard: 4.70 (24)　Right Tackle: 3.90 (12)　Right End: 4.47 (17)

Rushing the passer was about the only thing Arizona was good at last year—and as the pressure rate numbers in that table tell you, they weren't even consistent at that. Now they have lost two of their top three edge rushers, with Benson Mayowa and Markus Golden leaving for Oakland and the Giants, respectively. Replacing them will be the legendary Terrell Suggs, the former Defensive Player of the Year who was named to seven Pro Bowls in his time in Baltimore. Since Suggs was drafted tenth overall in 2003, only Julius Peppers, DeMarcus Ware, and Jared Allen have more sacks. Suggs turns 37 in October, but he's still productive—his 26.0 sacks over the last three years puts him in the top 20 in that category. 🏈 Suggs will line up across from Chandler Jones, who is moving back to outside linebacker in Vance Joseph's 3-4 scheme. The last time he played there, he led the NFL with 17.0 sacks in 2017. In preparation for the move, Jones has reportedly lost 25 pounds. Free-agent signee Brooks Reed offers depth at the position. 🏈 Also in the mix at edge rusher is third-round draftee Zach Allen out of Boston College. A 280-pounder noted as much for his run defense as his pass-rushing, Allen could move back and forth from inside to out on Arizona's line, much like Derek Wolfe did for Joseph in Denver last season. SackSEER ranked Allen sixth among this year's edge-rushing prospects, based largely on his knack for batting down passes at the line, which has often been a predictor of sack production in the NFL. 🏈 The Cardinals shouldn't have any problem finding bodies along the interior line. Incumbents Corey Peters, Robert Nkemdiche, and Rodney Gunter are all close to 300 pounds or more, as is free-agent signee Darius Philon, a 2015 sixth-round draft pick who developed into a starter for the Chargers. Peters will start at nose tackle with Gunter and Philon at the ends, but all four players (and Allen) will likely rotate in and out heavily. Gunter re-signed on a one-year deal in April. Nkemdiche, a first-rounder in 2016, has been a disappointment. The team declined his fifth-year option, and this fall will likely be an audition for him to win a starting job elsewhere. 🏈 Among their many other weaknesses, Arizona had some of the league's worst linebackers in 2018, especially once Josh Bynes went down with a thumb injury. (Bynes remains unsigned at press time.) No team allowed a higher total of second-level and open-field yards in the run game, and the Cardinals also ranked 30th on defense against passes to the short middle area of the field. 🏈 Haason Reddick, the 13th overall draft pick in 2017, has been something of a late bloomer, partly because he has switched back and forth from inside to outside linebacker. A permanent move to the inside can only help him. 🏈 Joining Reddick will be Jordan Hicks, who signed a four-year, $36-million contract in free agency. Hicks started each of his 35 games for Philadelphia over the past three years, but he missed 13 regular-season games over that span, plus the entire Super Bowl run in 2017. When healthy, he has been a very good player, but those missed games are a cause for concern.

Defensive Secondary

Secondary	Age	Pos	G	Snaps	Plays	TmPct	Rk	Stop	Dfts	BTkl	Runs	St%	Rk	RuYd	Rk	Tgts	Tgt%	Rk	Dist	Suc%	Rk	AdjYd	Rk	PD	Int
												vs. Run						**vs. Pass**							
Antoine Bethea*	35	FS	16	1111	125	14.2%	5	41	17	17	65	35%	50	8.2	50	46	12.1%	61	8.3	48%	44	5.8	10	4	0
Patrick Peterson	29	CB	16	1106	59	6.7%	68	22	6	8	25	28%	66	7.2	53	53	14.0%	4	12.4	60%	7	8.0	47	5	2
Tre Boston*	27	FS	14	950	87	11.3%	24	30	11	12	44	36%	47	9.6	61	33	10.1%	46	10.1	48%	41	6.4	17	9	3
Budda Baker	23	SS	14	938	101	13.1%	9	52	24	10	49	63%	4	4.3	6	44	13.7%	64	8.2	43%	56	8.4	53	1	0
Bene' Benwikere*	28	CB	15	592	54	6.5%	--	18	5	12	20	50%	--	5.5	--	49	24.6%	--	9.0	53%	--	6.0	--	4	1
Jamar Taylor*	29	CB	14	305	19	2.5%	--	3	3	4	4	25%	--	5.8	--	26	22.2%	--	13.0	27%	--	13.2	--	1	0
David Amerson*	28	CB	6	293	23	7.0%	--	10	2	5	9	67%	--	3.8	--	21	20.9%	--	10.2	57%	--	3.7	--	2	1
D.J. Swearinger	28	FS	15	961	63	8.3%	53	28	16	11	22	45%	30	4.6	9	40	9.9%	43	9.6	55%	23	7.9	46	10	4
Robert Alford	31	CB	15	957	61	7.8%	51	20	4	10	9	44%	30	5.8	29	75	18.0%	31	14.9	35%	79	11.8	79	11	0
Tramaine Brock	31	CB	12	437	29	4.7%	--	10	5	3	3	33%	--	10.7	--	38	21.9%	--	12.7	58%	--	6.6	--	6	0

Year	Pass D Rank	vs. #1 WR	Rk	vs. #2 WR	Rk	vs. Other WR	Rk	WR Wide	Rk	WR Slot	Rk	vs. TE	Rk	vs. RB	Rk
2016	3	-5.0%	10	17.2%	27	-1.2%	13	5.5%	23	1.4%	13	-19.7%	6	-43.5%	1
2017	10	11.4%	23	-19.8%	6	-9.9%	9	-4.7%	15	-8.4%	9	-14.6%	7	-0.5%	17
2018	8	-0.7%	14	13.6%	23	-6.7%	12	-9.8%	12	11.0%	24	3.0%	17	-3.1%	14

Patrick Peterson was perhaps the NFL's best cover corner in 2018. He started 16 games, usually following the opposition's top wideout across the field, and finished as one of three qualifying cornerbacks to make the top 10 in both target percentage and success rate. The others were San Francisco's Richard Sherman, who missed two games, and Philadelphia's Avonte Maddox, who only made nine starts. Peterson's yardage numbers are skewed because he was charged with a handful of long touchdowns, but on some of those plays (a 64-yarder by Denver's Emmanuel Sanders, a 39-yarder by L.A.'s Robert Woods), there was miscommunication between Peterson and the safety, and it's hard to pinpoint who was at fault. ♦ With Peterson suspended for six games, Arizona's cornerback depth chart looks awfully vulnerable. Robert Alford has started 72 games over the last five years in Atlanta, but at age 30 last year he declined from "reliable" to "replaceable." Tramaine Brock is on his fourth team in four years and is strictly a depth player at this point. David Amerson—who started five games for Arizona last year after being signed, cut, and re-signed in November—was released at the end of OTAs. That shows the faith Arizona has that Byron Murphy, the first pick in the second round in this year's draft, will be ready to start right away. Murphy lacks the typical size, speed, and grace you'd like to see in a top-flight cornerback, but he has elite ball skills—he was an All-American wide receiver in high school. ♦ Budda Baker was a monster in his second season, finishing second among safeties in defeats despite missing two games. His coverage numbers weren't nearly as good, which is one of the reasons Arizona struggled to cover slot receivers. ♦ Free safety D.J. Swearinger returned to Phoenix, where he started a dozen games in 2016, after Washington waived him near the end of last season. He was nothing special in 31 Washington starts over the past two years but should be an upgrade over what the Cardinals had at that position in 2018.

Special Teams

Year	DVOA	Rank	FG/XP	Rank	Net Kick	Rank	Kick Ret	Rank	Net Punt	Rank	Punt Ret	Rank	Hidden	Rank
2016	-6.3%	30	-8.9	30	-4.9	27	1.7	10	-14.7	31	-4.6	26	-2.8	20
2017	-5.5%	28	-8.9	28	-5.5	27	-2.1	20	-10.0	27	-0.9	20	-7.5	27
2018	1.0%	11	-5.1	25	2.6	11	-1.5	19	6.5	5	2.3	12	9.5	7

This is the one area where Steve Wilks' Cardinals improved over Bruce Arians' clubs. This may be a function of being so committed to special teams specialists—Arizona had five players (Dennis Gardeck, Joe Walker, Zeke Turner, Derrick Coleman, and Brandon Williams) who played at least 300 snaps in the kicking game but fewer than 100 snaps on offense or defense. There were only 34 such players in the NFL, and no other team had more than three. Turner was the star of the group, tied for the league lead with nine tackles on punt coverage (mind you, the Cardinals punted a lot) and second in total special teams tackles. ♦ Punt returns were also better under Wilks. Patrick Peterson has never recaptured the magic of his 2011 rookie season, when he returned four punts for touchdowns; last year he returned only nine punts for 64 yards, both career lows. Christian Kirk was the primary returner and fared much better—a 7.8-yard average on 21 returns, with a long of 44. The Cardinals also blocked a pair of punts in Week 17 against Seattle, though one didn't count as a block because the kick still gained 21 yards. ● Neither T.J. Logan nor Brandon Williams were anything special on kickoff returns. They certainly weren't good enough to ever turn down a touchback—Arizona's average kickoff return out of the end zone only reached the 18.9-yard line, worst in the league. ● Andy Lee led the league in gross punt value after finishing fifth in 2017 and 11th in 2016. He also led the league in gross average for the second time and total punts for the fourth time in his 15-year career. ● Placekicking remained a problem for Arizona. Phil Dawson tried and failed to play through a hip injury, going on injured reserve in November and likely bringing an end to his two-decade NFL career. Matthew McCrane was signed, kicked three extra points against Oakland, and then was waived, all in a span of 48 hours or so. Zane Gonzalez, last seen missing two extra points and two field goals in Cleveland's three-point loss to New Orleans in Week 2, was signed to finish the year. He hit 7-of-9 field goals (a perfect 5-for-5 inside 40 yards) and 5-of-6 extra points for Arizona, and will return in 2019 to handle placekicking and kickoffs … for now. ● Jeff Rodgers, who coordinated these special teams for Wilks, was retained by Kingsbury and given the additional title of assistant head coach. He is headed into his 16th season as an NFL special teams coach, having previously worked for the 49ers, Panthers, Broncos, and Bears.

Atlanta Falcons

2018 record: 7-9	Total DVOA: -3.0% (18th)	2019 Mean Projection: 7.6 wins	On the Clock (0-4): 13%
Pythagorean Wins: 7.8 (17th)	Offense: 8.8% (8th)	Postseason Odds: 29.7%	Mediocrity (5-7): 36%
Snap-Weighted Age: 27.1 (5th)	Defense: 13.3% (31st)	Super Bowl Odds: 3.4%	Playoff Contender (8-10): 36%
Average Opponent: -2.3% (22nd)	Special Teams: 1.4% (10th)	Proj. Avg. Opponent: 2.6% (6th)	Super Bowl Contender (11+): 14%

2018: Better offense. Injury-ravaged defense. Above-average special teams. Fire everyone!

2019: That stuff that didn't work from last season? Yeah, let's do more of that.

Everything we needed to know about the 2018 Atlanta Falcons, we learned in Week 1. On their first offensive drive of the season, they moved down the field with ease against the Eagles. Ten yards, 11 yards, 20 yards, 33 yards, 5 yards. It took them less than three minutes to get to the Philadelphia 1-yard line.

That's as far as they went. On fourth-and-goal, Devonta Freeman took a handoff to the left end, but Eagles linebacker Kamu Grugier-Hill stonewalled him, driving him back for a 1-yard loss. Atlanta started 2018 the same way it ended 2017: stuck at the Philadelphia 2. Curse you, Steve Sarkisian!

That wasn't the only ominous occurrence. Safety Keanu Neal left the game in the third quarter with what turned out to be a torn ACL; he missed the rest of the season. Freeman left in the fourth because of a knee bruise; he played in only one more game. Linebacker Deion Jones reported after the game that he felt soreness in his foot; it turned out to be broken, and he missed the next 10 games. Curse you, football gods!

In many ways, that was it. The Falcons' season was over as soon as it started. Sure, it wasn't all bad, Sarkisian included. The hope heading into the season was that the offense would improve in the coordinator's second season, and in general that happened—slightly. The offense gained more yards per drive (38.0 vs. 36.9), scored more points per drive (2.4 vs. 2.2) and increased its drive success rate (74.9 percent vs. 72.8 percent). Its overall DVOA increased from 8.1% to 8.8%.

The offense accomplished all this despite having the league's third-worst average starting field position (the 26.3-yard line). Imagine how much more it could have done if the defense forced more three-and-outs (17.6 percent of drives, 29th) or more than the occasional fumble (just eight, 30th). Another 5 yards of average field position might not seem like much, but over the course of a season, that's roughly a 50-point difference, based on Pro Football Reference's expected points data.

Table 1. Atlanta's Return to Shanahan Tendencies

Metric	2016	Rk	2017	Rk	2018	Rk
Situation-Neutral Pace	29.1	4	31.1	21	30.2	7
Play-Action Rate	26.6%	1	22.5%	13	26.2%	9
Red Zone Offense DVOA	3.0%	14	-11.8%	23	-0.9%	15

Of course, there was no way that Sarkisian was going to repeat the historic success that Atlanta enjoyed in 2016 under predecessor Kyle Shanahan. He did, however, restore elements of that offense (Table 1). The Falcons played with a faster pace. They used more play-action passes. Even their much-maligned red zone offense improved, to rank similarly to 2016.

Matt Ryan and the passing offense picked up most of the slack inside the 20, posting a 15.8% DVOA (11th), a 19.0% increase over 2017. Once Ryan handed the ball off, however, Atlanta's efficiency plummeted. The Falcons' -20.2% red zone rushing DVOA was the third worst. If there were ever a reason to put Sarkisian on blast, it's this: Atlanta was particularly bad at running to the outside, no matter the field position. Despite that, the Falcons kept trying in the red zone anyway. On runs to the outside left and right, they ranked 28th in yards per carry (2.7) and 27th in DVOA (-24.3%).

In most other seasons, an offense as productive and efficient as Atlanta's would be roundly praised. There are a couple of explanations why it wasn't. First, 2016 was still fresh in everyone's minds. Second, the offense couldn't score often enough to overcome an injury-ravaged defense that truly missed its Pro Bowl linebacker and Pro Bowl safety.

When Jones and Neal are on the field together—which happened for fewer than 40 snaps last season—the Falcons are a different defense. Since they entered the NFL in 2016, Atlanta has allowed a 63.5 percent completion rate, 6.7 yards per pass, and a touchdown rate of 3.6 percent when both are on the field, according to the NFL's Next Gen Stats. When one or both are off the field, the defense has allowed a 69.0 percent completion rate, 7.5 yards per attempt and a touchdown rate of 6.3 percent.

The loss of Jones was especially devastating, as the Falcons had an adequate replacement at safety (Damontae Kazee) but not at middle linebacker (Duke Riley). When Jones played (Week 1 and Weeks 13 to 17), Atlanta's pass defense produced an outstanding -10.8% DVOA. When he was absent (Weeks 2 to 12), the pass defense produced a ghastly 42.1% DVOA.

Jones' return likely also contributed to the Falcons defense extending a trend that dates back to 2016. For three straight seasons, it has improved significantly during the second half of the season, though the DVOA gap was largest last year (Table 2).

2019 Falcons Schedule

Week	Opp.	Week	Opp.	Week	Opp.
1	at MIN	7	LAR	13	NO
2	PHI	8	SEA	14	CAR
3	at IND	9	BYE	15	at SF
4	TEN	10	at NO	16	JAX
5	at HOU	11	at CAR	17	at TB
6	at ARI	12	TB		

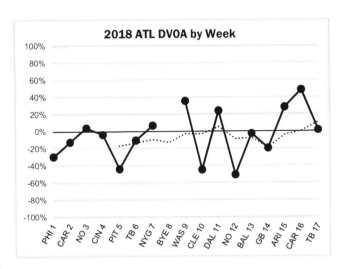

Jones' return and the subsequent improvement was too little too late. The Falcons won three straight meaningless games at the end of the season to finish 7-9 and cost themselves premium positioning in the draft. It marked the first time they finished below .500 under head coach Dan Quinn, so of course they didn't overreact in the offseason. They retreated to their Flowery Branch headquarters, took a deep breath, and pored over the data on the Football Outsiders website. Cooler heads prevailed.

Just kidding! They totally flipped out. They fired Sarkisian. They fired defensive coordinator Marquand Manuel. They fired longtime special teams coordinator Keith Armstrong. Rumor has it they even tried to fire Meatloaf and Gary Busey.

It's not uncommon for teams to replace their offensive and defensive coordinators. After all, Atlanta did so after the 2016 season, though only defensive coordinator Richard Smith was fired, ostensibly because the Falcons blew a 28-3 lead in Super Bowl LI. In reality, he was the fall guy for offensive coordinator Kyle Shanahan, who called for a pass instead of a run on third-and-1 late in the game, and for Devonta Freeman, who failed to block a blitzing Dont'a Hightower. Shanahan left to become head coach of the 49ers the next day.

What is rare is for a team to keep its head coach and enter the next season with three new coordinators. In fact, we found just nine such instances in the DVOA era, and for most of those teams at least one of the coordinators left of his own volition (Table 3). Only one team—the 1989 Colts—cleaned house like the Falcons. In the short term, their decision to keep Ron Meyer and overhaul his staff made little difference. In the long term, it set up Indianapolis for an extended run of irrelevance. Meyer ended up hanging onto his job long enough to persuade the team to trade offensive tackle Chris Hinton and receiver Andre Rison to, of all teams, the Falcons for the No. 1 overall pick in the 1990 draft. With that pick, the Colts chose ... Jeff George, future Falcons quarterback.

The other teams in our sample don't offer much hope, either. Most of them stayed the same. One—the 2007 Giants—won the Super Bowl, defeating the unbeaten Patriots in one of the unlikeliest upsets in NFL history. Technically, though, they don't meet the "three fired coordinators" criterion; their special teams coordinator, Mike Sweatman, retired after the 2006 season.

Given that Quinn is absorbing defensive coordinator responsibilities, the most interesting change on his staff is at offensive coordinator, where the Falcons said to hell with the space-time continuum, hopped in owner Arthur Blank's DeLorean, and re-

hired Dirk Koetter, their coordinator from 2012 to 2014.

It's a curious choice. It's not that Ryan was bad during Koetter's first stint; he just evolved into a different quarterback, after some initial struggles, once Koetter was fired. From 2012 to 2014, he was one of the league's more conservative quarterbacks. In that span, he never ranked higher than 28th among qualifying quarterbacks in average depth of target (8.2, 7.0, 8.0). After an uneven 2015 season (8.0), he has ranked in the top 12 every season since (9.0, 9.1, 9.0). He's pushing the ball deeper, a trend that must excite Koetter, whose Air Coryell offense in Tampa Bay was built around taking shots down the field. Ryan's ability to consistently connect on those shots must excite Koetter, too. "I think the thing I took for granted when I was away was his accuracy," he told the Atlanta media this offseason. Yeah, a couple seasons of watching Jameis Winston overthrow DeSean Jackson will do that.

The hiring of Koetter is more about familiarity than anything else. Quinn insists that the offense will continue to run outside zone concepts and that he wants Koetter to adjust the system to Ryan rather than Ryan adjusting (re-adjusting?) to the system. Quinn's seat is hotter these days. He can't risk the possibility of his quarterback floundering through the fall.

What should trouble Falcons fans is Quinn's call for "balance." "The thing I think for us to get back from an identity standpoint is the amount of run attempts," he said after hiring Koetter. That's right. Quinn's idea for getting Atlanta back to the playoffs is to do less of what it does well (pass) and more of what it doesn't do well (run).

Table 2. Atlanta's Second-Half Defensive Improvements, 2016-2018

Year	Wk 1-9 DVOA	Rk	Wk 1-9 Points Allowed	Rk	Wk 10-17 DVOA	Rk	Wk 10-17 Points Allowed	Rk
2016	10.3%	26	28.4	28	3.0%	23	21.0	13
2017	13.0%	28	21.5	14	-2.1%	11	16.6	5
2018	22.3%	31	28.3	29	4.0%	22	24.6	22

Table 3. Teams Who Retained Their Head Coach but Featured Three New Coordinators, 1986-2019

Season	Team	HC	New OC	DC	STC	DVOA Y-1 (rk)	Y-1 W-L	DVOA (rk)	W-L
2019	ATL*	D.Quinn	D.Koetter	D.Quinn	B.Kotwica	-3.0% (18)	7-9	—	—
2018	CAR	R.Rivera	N.Turner	E.Washington	C.Blackburn	13.0% (9)	11-5	0.5% (14)	7-9
2013	NYJ	R.Ryan	M.Morninweg	D.Thurman	B.Kotwica	-18.0% (27)	6-10	-7.7% (24)	8-8
2007	NYG	T.Coughlin	K.Gilbride	S.Spagnuolo	T.Quinn	13.7% (8)	8-8	1.9% (14)	10-6**
2007	SF	M.Nolan	J.Hostler	G.Manusky	A.Everest	-19.4% (27)	7-9	-33.4% (31)	5-11
2002	JAX	T.Coughlin	T.Coughlin	J.Pease	J.Bonamego	-6.1% (19)	6-10	-0.2% (18)	6-10
2000	CLE	C.Palmer	P.Carmichael Sr.	R.Crennel	M.Michaels	-39.7 (30)	2-14	-40.2% (31)	3-13
1994	DET	W.Fontes	D.Levy	H.Paterra	S.Kazor	-5.4% (19)	10-6	1.8% (12)	9-7
1989	IND*	R.Meyer	L.Kennan	B.Muir	B.Seely	1.1% (13)	9-7	-7.2% (17)	8-8

*Fired previous OC/DC/STC
**Won Super Bowl

Koetter's not a hard sell. For all his talk about explosive plays, he's also an establish-the-run guy. "We're going to be a run-first football team," he said in 2016, during his first training camp as head coach of the Buccaneers. "You've got to run the ball and stop the run to win in this league, and we're not going to change from that." Spoiler: they didn't do much winning in Tampa Bay.

Another red flag: Quinn's a believer in running the ball to set up the play-action pass. Football Outsiders research has shown that there is virtually no statistical relationship between run frequency or effectiveness and play-action pass success.[1] Atlanta was one of the most efficient play-action pass offenses in the league last season (38.5% DVOA, eighth in the NFL) and yet didn't have a credible run game. If the Falcons were to run the ball more early in games this season, they wouldn't be causing opponents harm; they would be doing them a favor.

As for the defense, Quinn is betting on two things: himself as a playcaller and himself as a shaman. Otherwise, Atlanta will look largely the same, aside from a handful of modest depth additions (free-agent defensive linemen Adrian Clayborn and Tyeler Davison, safety J.J. Wilcox, and a couple of late draft picks). We know Quinn can call plays—when he did so during the final quarter of the 2016 season, the defense produced a -0.9% DVOA—which makes counting on better injury luck the bigger gamble. Maybe Deion Jones, Keanu Neal, and Ricardo Allen will be healthy this season. Maybe they won't. Or maybe other players will suffer injuries. There's no reliable way to forecast that. Case in point: the Falcons already have lost defensive end Steven Means to a season-ending torn Achilles.

Even so, it's fair for Atlanta to blame last season's defensive struggles on injuries. The Falcons accumulated 44.6 adjusted games lost on defense, which ranked 25th. That's not an insurmountable amount, but it might feel that way for a defense that had been remarkably healthy under Quinn. It ranked third in defensive AGL in 2017 (5.1), 16th in 2016 (32.9), and fifth in 2015 (17.8). And AGL doesn't account for the quality of injured players, just the number of injuries. Atlanta fans have a good argument that the injuries to their young Pro Bowlers cost them more than similar injuries to average starters.

So as long as the Falcons avoid severe injuries going forward, they'll surge back into contention, right? Not so fast. Even when the defense has been healthy, it hasn't cracked the top 20 in DVOA (22nd in 2017, 26th in 2016, and 22nd in 2015). Our projections don't see it happening this season, either. Each year, fans expect the second-half defensive improvement to carry over to the next season. Each year, it doesn't happen.

To be sure, there's top-flight talent and upside throughout this win-now roster. Problem is, there are too many ifs. Atlanta will be bona fide contender ... if the defense can stay healthy. If the schedule isn't as tough as it looks. If Quinn can manufacture a pass rush. If Vic Beasley can be someone other than Vic Beasley. If the Ryan-Koetter reunion re-rejuvenates an already rejuvenated offense. If Quinn and Koetter don't really mean it when they talk about running the ball more often.

With this many question marks, the Falcons look more mediocre than super. But stranger things have happened to teams with three new coordinators. Just ask the 2007 Giants.

Thomas Bassinger

1 https://bit.ly/2Nwvfoy

2018 Falcons Stats by Week

Wk	vs.	W-L	PF	PA	YDF	YDA	TO	Total	Off	Def	ST
1	at PHI	L	12	18	299	232	+1	-30%	-54%	-21%	4%
2	CAR	W	31	24	442	439	0	-13%	21%	34%	1%
3	NO	L	37	43	407	534	0	4%	41%	23%	-15%
4	CIN	L	36	37	495	407	+1	-4%	28%	32%	-1%
5	at PIT	L	17	41	324	381	0	-44%	-6%	30%	-9%
6	TB	W	34	29	417	510	+2	-11%	22%	36%	4%
7	NYG	W	23	20	423	433	-1	7%	12%	11%	5%
8	BYE										
9	at WAS	W	38	14	491	366	0	35%	69%	38%	4%
10	at CLE	L	16	28	382	427	-1	-45%	9%	58%	4%
11	DAL	L	19	22	354	323	-1	24%	23%	5%	6%
12	at NO	L	17	31	366	312	-3	-51%	-38%	18%	5%
13	BAL	L	16	26	131	366	0	-3%	-21%	-11%	7%
14	at GB	L	20	34	344	300	-2	-20%	-21%	2%	3%
15	ARI	W	40	14	435	253	+3	28%	17%	-15%	-4%
16	at CAR	W	24	10	427	436	+2	48%	23%	-26%	-2%
17	at TB	W	34	32	489	433	0	2%	21%	30%	10%

Trends and Splits

	Offense	Rank	Defense	Rank
Total DVOA	8.8%	8	13.3%	31
Unadjusted VOA	11.7%	7	13.7%	30
Weighted Trend	7.8%	11	9.5%	26
Variance	9.4%	26	5.9%	19
Average Opponent	2.6%	30	0.7%	13
Passing	26.7%	7	21.7%	29
Rushing	-10.7%	22	2.4%	30
First Down	4.2%	12	14.5%	31
Second Down	8.4%	10	2.5%	21
Third Down	18.7%	6	28.3%	30
First Half	10.3%	8	4.5%	27
Second Half	7.3%	10	21.7%	31
Red Zone	-0.9%	15	14.9%	26
Late and Close	11.3%	9	12.3%	29

Five-Year Performance

Year	W-L	Pyth W	Est W	PF	PA	TO	Total	Rk	Off	Rk	Def	Rk	ST	Rk	Off AGL	Rk	Def AGL	Rk	Off Age	Rk	Def Age	Rk	ST Age	Rk
2014	6-10	7.1	7.2	381	417	+5	-5.4%	20	7.2%	10	15.7%	32	3.0%	9	60.6	30	33.2	12	26.8	16	26.6	21	26.4	7
2015	8-8	7.8	5.8	339	345	-7	-16.3%	26	-7.3%	23	6.9%	22	-2.1%	22	10.9	2	17.8	5	27.5	8	26.9	14	26.7	5
2016	11-5	10.9	11.8	540	406	+11	19.8%	3	24.6%	1	7.3%	26	2.5%	7	19.3	2	32.9	16	27.8	5	26.0	25	27.3	2
2017	10-6	9.1	8.5	353	315	-2	1.4%	15	8.1%	9	5.6%	22	-1.2%	19	11.2	3	5.1	3	27.4	8	25.7	25	26.5	5
2018	7-9	7.8	7.5	414	423	+1	-3.0%	18	8.8%	8	13.3%	31	1.4%	10	33.3	13	44.6	25	28.1	4	26.4	13	26.7	3

2018 Performance Based on Most Common Personnel Groups

ATL Offense					ATL Offense vs. Opponents					ATL Defense					ATL Defense vs. Opponents			
Pers	Freq	Yds	DVOA	Run%	Pers	Freq	Yds	DVOA	Run%	Pers	Freq	Yds	DVOA		Pers	Freq	Yds	DVOA
11	59%	6.7	21.7%	22%	Base	27%	5.9	5.7%	51%	Base	22%	5.9	-0.6%		11	72%	6.2	19.3%
12	17%	6.7	23.5%	46%	Nickel	56%	6.8	21.6%	28%	Nickel	74%	6.1	15.8%		12	15%	6.9	13.2%
21	10%	6.2	5.7%	38%	Dime+	15%	5.8	-0.5%	13%	Dime+	4%	8.9	80.3%		21	4%	6.2	-5.1%
13	4%	5.8	9.1%	61%	Goal Line	1%	0.7	-122.8%	67%	Goal Line	1%	0.8	6.8%		13	4%	4.1	-33.1%
22	3%	6.5	-45.7%	76%											22	2%	3.8	-18.3%
01	3%	4.7	-33.6%	8%														

Strategic Tendencies

Run/Pass		Rk	Formation		Rk	Pass Rush		Rk	Secondary		Rk	Strategy		Rk
Runs, first half	32%	29	Form: Single Back	73%	27	Rush 3	8.0%	14	4 DB	22%	18	Play action	26%	9
Runs, first down	37%	31	Form: Empty Back	11%	3	Rush 4	69.1%	16	5 DB	74%	8	Avg Box (Off)	6.14	24
Runs, second-long	32%	10	Pers: 3+ WR	65%	20	Rush 5	20.4%	9	6+ DB	4%	20	Avg Box (Def)	6.03	29
Runs, power sit.	45%	28	Pers: 2+ TE/6+ OL	25%	13	Rush 6+	2.3%	31	CB by Sides	87%	8	Offensive Pace	30.18	7
Runs, behind 2H	24%	21	Pers: 6+ OL	1%	22	Int DL Sacks	35.1%	8	S/CB Cover Ratio	25%	23	Defensive Pace	31.49	22
Pass, ahead 2H	56%	5	Shotgun/Pistol	50%	29	Second Level Sacks	17.6%	25	DB Blitz	6%	27	Go for it on 4th	1.10	24

Was the injury to Devonta Freeman part of the reason the Falcons dropped from fourth (70 percent) to 28th (45 percent) in frequency of running in short-yardage "power" situations? ● The Falcons were excellent with an empty backfield: 6.9 yards per play and 38.5% DVOA. ● The Atlanta offense and defense weirdly mirrored each other with extreme splits on second down. The offense ranked third passing but 29th running. Meanwhile, the defense ranked fifth against the pass but 31st against the run. We have no explanation for this. ● Atlanta recovered only three of 16 fumbles on defense. However, half of those fumbles were "unforced," and unforced fumbles are recovered by the offense at a higher rate. ● The Falcons ranked 30th with 10.0 average yards after the catch allowed on passes behind or at the line of scrimmage, but fifth with only 3.8 average YAC allowed on passes past the line of scrimmage.

Passing

Player	DYAR	DVOA	Plays	NtYds	Avg	YAC	C%	TD	Int
M.Ryan	1232	18.2%	649	4638	7.1	5.1	69.6%	35	7
M.Schaub	-52	-114.3%	8	12	1.5	1.6	71.4%	0	0

Rushing

Player	DYAR	DVOA	Plays	Yds	Avg	TD	Fum	Suc
T.Coleman*	14	-6.4%	167	800	4.8	4	1	43%
I.Smith	-19	-13.4%	90	318	3.5	4	1	48%
M.Ryan	68	33.9%	24	132	5.5	3	0	--
B.Hill	-2	-10.8%	20	157	7.9	0	1	50%
D.Freeman	1	-6.9%	14	68	4.9	0	0	50%
J.Langford	-8	-29.0%	9	35	3.9	0	0	56%
M.Sanu	47	77.3%	7	44	6.3	0	0	--
C.Ridley	15	10.7%	6	27	4.5	0	0	--
K.Barner	7	1.0%	19	71	3.7	0	0	63%

Receiving

Player	DYAR	DVOA	Plays	Ctch	Yds	Y/C	YAC	TD	C%
J.Jones	382	15.9%	170	113	1677	14.8	4.0	8	66%
M.Sanu	141	6.4%	94	66	838	12.7	6.1	4	70%
C.Ridley	167	10.2%	92	64	821	12.8	5.7	10	70%
J.Hardy	0	-12.8%	22	14	133	9.5	5.1	2	64%
M.Hall*	1	-12.0%	19	10	149	14.9	5.7	1	53%
R.Gage	-9	-24.2%	10	6	63	10.5	3.2	0	60%
A.Hooper	56	2.2%	88	71	660	9.3	3.3	4	81%
L.Paulsen	45	66.7%	9	9	91	10.1	6.4	1	100%
E.Saubert	-25	-46.1%	9	5	48	9.6	2.6	0	56%
L.Stocker	26	11.4%	21	15	165	11.0	4.3	2	71%
T.Coleman*	77	17.2%	44	32	276	8.6	8.6	5	73%
I.Smith	-8	-17.7%	32	27	152	5.6	5.9	0	84%
D.Freeman	-30	-109.8%	7	5	23	4.6	4.0	0	71%

Offensive Line

Player	Pos	Age	GS	Snaps	Pen	Sk	Pass	Run	Player	Pos	Age	GS	Snaps	Pen	Sk	Pass	Run
Alex Mack	C	34	16/16	1057	3	2.0	3	3	Zane Beadles*	RG	33	9/5	279	0	1.0	1	2
Jake Matthews	LT	27	16/16	1057	3	2.0	6	0	Ty Sambrailo	RT	27	16/4	266	3	0.0	2	0
Wes Schweitzer	LG	26	15/13	901	8	1.5	2	3	James Carpenter	LG	30	10/10	624	3	2.0	4	2
Ryan Schraeder*	RT	31	16/13	865	9	10.0	21	2	Jamon Brown	RG	26	13/8	537	8	3.5	10	3
Brandon Fusco*	RG	31	7/7	436	2	1.0	1	1	John Wetzel	RT/G	28	8/5	339	4	1.5	4	1
Ben Garland*	RG	31	14/4	371	2	2.5	5	2									

Year	Yards	ALY	Rank	Power	Rank	Stuff	Rank	2nd Lev	Rank	Open Field	Rank	Sacks	ASR	Rank	Press	Rank	F-Start	Cont.
2016	4.66	4.40	10	61%	17	22%	23	1.30	7	1.20	3	37	6.5%	23	29.5%	25	19	48
2017	4.25	4.35	8	64%	17	21%	20	1.25	6	0.85	10	24	4.8%	8	31.5%	19	17	34
2018	4.59	4.08	24	60%	27	25%	31	1.29	13	1.30	2	42	6.6%	14	28.2%	12	15	28
2018 ALY by direction:				Left End: 3.07 (26)			Left Tackle: 3.98 (20)			Mid/Guard: 4.58 (11)			Right Tackle: 5.11 (4)			Right End: 3.96 (19)		

Life comes at you fast. One moment you're feeling pretty good about your offensive line; the next you're scrambling to rebuild it. By the final quarter of the season, the Falcons were starting backups at left guard, right guard, and right tackle. ● Ryan Schraeder, who had been Atlanta's full-time starting right tackle since 2015, was the weakest link. He was one of only three linemen last season to allow 10 blown blocks that led directly to sacks. (Oakland rookies Kolton Miller and Brandon Parker were the others.) Schraeder ranked 63rd out of 70 qualifying tackles in snaps per blown block. In that context, the Falcons' trade up to select Kaleb McGary (Washington) 31st overall makes more sense. McGary is the rare first-round pick who spent his entire college career at right tackle. He's a run-game mauler, but some draftniks thought he would need to move inside in the NFL because of balance issues. ● Left tackle Jake Matthews and center Alex Mack return for their sixth and 11th NFL seasons, respectively. Since becoming teammates in 2016, neither has missed a game. ● Some NFL analysts called the selection of Chris Lindstrom at 14th overall a reach, but Atlanta had been cycling through veterans at right guard for years and needed a long-term solution. The Boston College product, who also has experience at tackle, will be the sixth Week 1 starter for the Falcons in seven seasons. ● Dan Quinn's hiring of Dirk Koetter as offensive coordinator has fueled speculation that the Falcons will move away from the zone-blocking scheme that Kyle Shanahan installed in 2015. Quinn, though, has maintained that there will be "adjustments" to the run game but not "wholesale changes." In Tampa Bay, Koetter indeed called gap runs. But he also called zone runs. Neither worked. The Buccaneers ranked 30th in rushing DVOA in 2016, 25th in 2017, and 24th in 2018. ● Atlanta lost yardage on 60 runs last season, tied for fifth-most. At 17.1 percent, it had the highest rate of negative runs. ● Assuming that the starters are Matthews at left tackle, newcomer James Carpenter at left guard, Mack at center, Lindstrom at right guard, and McGary at right tackle, the Falcons' first-string line will be composed entirely of former first-round picks.

Defensive Front

Defensive Line	Age	Pos	G	Snaps	Plays	TmPct	Rk	Stop	Dfts	BTkl	Runs	St%	Rk	RuYd	Rk	Sack	Hit	Hur	Dsrpt
						Overall						vs. Run				Pass Rush			
Grady Jarrett	26	DT	14	710	51	7.0%	14	37	17	2	43	70%	65	2.1	34	6.0	12	25	0
Jack Crawford	31	DT	16	623	36	4.3%	54	27	13	6	24	67%	72	3.3	79	6.0	3	19	0
Terrell McClain*	31	DT	13	374	17	2.5%	80	13	2	2	15	80%	24	2.2	44	1.0	0	2	0
Deadrin Senat	25	DT	15	371	30	3.8%	--	22	5	3	27	74%	--	2.5	--	0.0	3	6	0
Tyeler Davison	27	DT	14	421	24	3.4%	72	17	5	0	19	68%	69	2.2	41	2.0	1	5	0

Edge Rushers	Age	Pos	G	Snaps	Plays	TmPct	Rk	Stop	Dfts	BTkl	Runs	St%	Rk	RuYd	Rk	Sack	Hit	Hur	Dsrpt
						Overall						vs. Run				Pass Rush			
Vic Beasley	27	DE	16	700	23	2.8%	87	18	7	11	10	80%	24	1.9	31	5.0	3	27	2
Takkarist McKinley	24	DE	15	617	22	2.8%	86	15	10	5	13	54%	88	4.8	92	7.0	7	27	0
Bruce Irvin*	32	DE	16	470	19	2.3%	93	14	11	3	9	56%	83	3.9	88	6.5	7	11	0
Brooks Reed*	32	DE	16	458	23	2.8%	87	14	3	2	18	72%	53	2.6	51	1.0	3	15	0
Steven Means	29	DE	8	162	14	3.4%	--	13	5	0	13	92%	--	1.3	--	1.0	0	3	0
Adrian Clayborn	31	DE	14	318	11	1.6%	--	8	6	4	5	80%	--	1.6	--	2.5	10	29	0

Linebackers	Age	Pos	G	Snaps	Plays	TmPct	Rk	Stop	Dfts	BTkl	Runs	St%	Rk	RuYd	Rk	Sack	Hit	Hur	Tgts	Suc%	Rk	AdjYd	Rk	PD	Int
						Overall						vs. Run				Pass Rush				vs. Pass					
De'Vondre Campbell	26	OLB	16	899	94	11.3%	50	35	10	5	50	38%	88	6.3	88	1.5	1	4.5	42	43%	54	6.9	42	0	0
Foyesade Oluokun	24	OLB	16	527	89	10.7%	53	37	4	11	54	46%	85	4.1	54	0.0	2	4.5	35	57%	16	7.2	51	1	0
Duke Riley	25	MLB	16	407	59	7.1%	76	24	7	9	26	50%	76	3.9	44	0.0	1	0	25	48%	45	6.8	41	2	0
Deion Jones	25	MLB	6	383	59	18.8%	3	37	9	3	32	59%	45	4.2	57	1.0	0	1	26	54%	29	7.3	57	6	2

Year	Yards	ALY	Rank	Power	Rank	Stuff	Rank	2nd Level	Rank	Open Field	Rank	Sacks	ASR	Rank	Press	Rank
2016	4.28	4.47	25	63%	16	19%	18	1.29	26	0.64	13	34	5.4%	24	26.4%	20
2017	3.84	4.15	19	76%	29	20%	17	1.09	13	0.51	4	39	6.6%	16	29.5%	22
2018	4.66	5.07	31	74%	27	14%	32	1.25	18	0.80	15	37	6.6%	25	25.7%	30

2018 ALY by direction:	Left End: 5.55 (30)	Left Tackle: 3.88 (13)	Mid/Guard: 5.38 (32)	Right Tackle: 5.39 (31)	Right End: 4.13 (13)

"With the 13th pick in the 2019 NFL draft, the Miami Dolphins select … Christian Wilkins, defensive tackle, Clemson." Oof. One pick ahead of the Falcons. Good thing they beat the Buccaneers in Week 17. A disruptive interior force, Wilkins would have been an excellent fit for an Atlanta defense that ranked 30th in pressure rate and 30th in DVOA against the run. ● Grady Jarrett's 34 percent pass-rush win rate last season ranked fourth among defensive tackles, according to ESPN Stats & Info. After initially franchise tagging Jarrett, the Falcons eventually inked him to a longer-term contract that fully guarantees him $38 million and likely keeps him in Atlanta through the 2021 season. ● Atlanta signed run-stuffer Tyeler Davison, a starter for the Saints since 2016, to play next to Jarrett. Deadrin Senat, a 2018 third-round pick, and Jack Crawford will factor into the defensive tackle rotation. ● As was the case a year ago, the success of this unit hinges on the progression of pass-rushers Vic Beasley and Takk McKinley. Beasley's league-leading 15.5-sack performance in 2016 and relative lack of production since continues to define him. Four seasons into his career, perhaps it's time to reset expectations. That 2016 season was, of course, a mirage. His sack/hit/hurry total of 58.5 was nowhere near Oliver Vernon's NFL-high 94.0. The Beasley of 2017 and 2018 might be the real Beasley. After recording a hurry once every 17.7 snaps in 2016, he recorded one every 25.5 snaps in 2017 and every 25.9 snaps in 2018. At the NFL combine, Quinn said he was looking forward to taking a "hands-on approach" with Beasley, who will earn $12.8 million this season, the final year of his rookie deal. When the heavily scrutinized defensive end chose not to attend *voluntary* OTAs, the Atlanta media questioned his motivation and suggested he let his coach down. ● As for McKinley, the 2017 first-round draft pick came on strong down the stretch last season, registering 11 of his 27 hurries during Weeks 15 and 16. ● After a season in New England, Adrian Clayborn returns on a one-year deal. In 2017, the defensive end had a career-high 9.5 sacks, but six of those came in one game against the Cowboys' backup offensive tackles. ● When the Falcons lost Deion Jones for the season, strongside linebacker De'Vondre Campbell became responsible for relaying play calls. 🏈 Jones replacement, Duke Riley, struggled mightily, allowing three touchdowns (D.J. Moore in Week 2, Chris Godwin in Week 6, and Duke Johnson in Week 10).

Defensive Secondary

Secondary	Age	Pos	G	Snaps	Plays	TmPct	Rk	Stop	Dfts	BTkl	Runs	St%	Rk	RuYd	Rk	Tgts	Tgt%	Rk	Dist	Suc%	Rk	AdjYd	Rk	PD	Int
											Overall					vs. Run							vs. Pass		
Desmond Trufant	29	CB	16	1059	76	9.1%	34	28	9	5	11	27%	67	5.6	26	86	18.6%	39	11.0	48%	54	6.2	14	12	0
Damontae Kazee	26	FS	16	990	90	10.8%	32	22	12	16	42	19%	69	9.7	64	20	4.6%	5	9.9	50%	37	9.4	60	10	7
Robert Alford*	31	CB	15	957	61	7.8%	51	20	4	10	9	44%	30	5.8	29	75	18.0%	31	14.9	35%	79	11.8	79	11	0
Brian Poole*	27	CB	16	831	77	9.2%	31	34	16	16	23	52%	21	6.9	47	54	14.9%	12	8.7	41%	78	8.1	50	6	3
Sharrod Neasman	28	SS	12	434	45	7.2%	60	23	9	8	20	50%	21	5.2	15	26	13.7%	65	10.6	54%	28	7.0	33	4	0
Jordan Richards*	26	SS	15	428	40	5.1%	72	19	1	7	22	50%	21	5.1	14	20	10.7%	53	7.2	45%	52	7.9	47	3	0
Isaiah Oliver	22	CB	14	240	26	3.6%	--	12	4	1	4	25%	--	6.0	--	29	27.7%	--	11.7	52%	--	6.7	--	7	1
Ricardo Allen	28	SS	3	205	20	12.8%	--	6	2	2	5	20%	--	10.6	--	12	13.4%	--	8.7	58%	--	4.2	--	3	1

Year	Pass D Rank	vs. #1 WR	Rk	vs. #2 WR	Rk	vs. Other WR	Rk	WR Wide	Rk	WR Slot	Rk	vs. TE	Rk	vs. RB	Rk
2016	18	-3.4%	11	-5.6%	8	14.5%	27	-20.5%	3	14.5%	24	-5.6%	12	16.5%	25
2017	20	14.6%	25	19.3%	25	-7.9%	12	-2.3%	16	17.8%	23	-2.3%	14	8.4%	21
2018	29	15.8%	27	-6.3%	11	16.7%	27	14.7%	28	5.6%	21	0.9%	15	13.5%	28

The Falcons thought they were deep here, too. Until they weren't. In just one season, Robert Alford, their second-round draft pick in 2013, went from credible outside cornerback to arguably the worst cornerback in the NFL. He allowed the most receiving yards in the league last season, and his 34.7 percent coverage success rate was the lowest for a qualifying cornerback since 2016 (when Quinten Rollins' rate for the Packers was 31.9 percent). Atlanta released him on February 5, the two-year anniversary of his interception return for a touchdown in Super Bowl LI. 🏈 To replace Alford, the Falcons will look to another former second-round draft pick, Isaiah Oliver, whom they drafted 58th overall last year. He played well at times but also took his share of lumps, surrendering three touchdowns (to A.J Green, Antonio Brown, and Josh Doctson) in his first five games. His first career interception sealed Atlanta's Week 16 win over Carolina. "He got reps, he got experience, and I think he's one who is going to take a big step," Quinn said. He better. After Oliver and Desmond Trufant, the Falcons don't have many options. 🏈 Atlanta didn't offer a new contract to Brian Poole, the No. 3 cornerback last season. Damontae Kazee, who filled in at free safety for Ricardo Allen after he tore his Achilles in Week 3, got the snaps at nickel during offseason workouts. His seven interceptions last season were tied for the league lead. All other Falcons defensive backs had five total. 🏈 Five years ago, we watched Mike Smith cut Allen on HBO's *Hard Knocks*. "I'm going to show them that I can play in this league," he said then. The three-year contract extension he signed last August will pay him $3.5 million this season. That's solid starter money. What a journey. 🏈 In case Allen and strong safety Keanu Neal (knee) aren't ready for the opener, Atlanta could turn to Sharrod Neasman, Chris Cooper, or J.J. Wilcox.

Special Teams

Year	DVOA	Rank	FG/XP	Rank	Net Kick	Rank	Kick Ret	Rank	Net Punt	Rank	Punt Ret	Rank	Hidden	Rank
2016	2.5%	7	11.1	2	-3.0	25	-1.7	19	2.1	12	3.8	9	-4.3	22
2017	-1.2%	19	6.4	9	-4.5	25	-3.6	25	-1.0	19	-3.1	25	-3.0	16
2018	1.4%	10	12.0	1	-0.7	18	-2.4	22	1.0	16	-2.7	21	-11.3	28

Who says kickers aren't real football players? Money Matt Bryant put his body on the line when he kicked a 57-yard field goal at the end of the Falcons' Week 6 win over the Buccaneers. The kick was good, but Bryant's hammy was not. He clutched it immediately and missed the next three games. The kick turned out to be the beginning of the end for the 43-year-old, who was cut by the Arena Football League's Iowa Barnstormers nearly two decades ago. His injury allowed Atlanta to take a look at Giorgio Tavecchio. "Italian Ice" made a strong enough impression, converting all five of his field goals (including a 56-yarder in a Monday night win over the Giants) and all eight of his extra points, to win the job for this season. 🏈 Matt Bosher returns for his ninth straight season with the Falcons, though he's eligible to become a free agent in 2020. Bosher's gross punt value dropped into negative territory in 2018, but that was negated by strong Atlanta punt coverage. 🏈 While the defense was partly to blame for the offense's bad average starting field position, so was the Falcons' lousy return game. Free-agent acquisition Kenjon Barner and sixth-round rookie Marcus Green will compete with last year's punt returner Justin Hardy to be the primary returners. 🏈 The main reason for a poor "hidden" value on special teams: Opposing kickers went 22-of-22 on field goals against Atlanta, although they did miss three extra points.

Baltimore Ravens

2018 record: 10-6	**Total DVOA:** 17.0% (6th)	**2019 Mean Projection:** 8.5 wins	**On the Clock (0-4):** 7%
Pythagorean Wins: 10.8 (5th)	**Offense:** 0.9% (15th)	**Postseason Odds:** 42.9%	**Mediocrity (5-7):** 28%
Snap-Weighted Age: 26.7 (8th)	**Defense:** -13.1% (3rd)	**Super Bowl Odds:** 6.0%	**Playoff Contender (8-10):** 41%
Average Opponent: 1.3% (9th)	**Special Teams:** 2.9% (6th)	**Proj. Avg. Opponent:** -0.5% (21st)	**Super Bowl Contender (11+):** 24%

2018: *(Thom Yorke voice)* Ruuuuuuuuuuuuuuuuuuuuuuuuuuuunnnnnnn!!!

2019: The new forefront for applied football analysis. Are the experiments going to work?

The Baltimore Ravens turned on a dime last year, both in-season and in philosophy, when they benched Joe Flacco for rookie quarterback Lamar Jackson. For years, they had been something of a stagnant franchise, bloated by Flacco's large contract and lackluster play. In December, it even came to the point where there were whispers about the job status of John Harbaugh, one of the more successful coaches of the past 15 years.

The Ravens won the AFC North by reeling off wins in six of their final seven games. And although they lost their first playoff game, the 12-4 Chargers were one of the best wild-card teams in recent seasons. That loss shouldn't take anything away from what they did and the growth potential they have, because as the organization changed hands from Ozzie Newsome to Eric DeCosta, the analytics department only seemed to grow more powerful, with a public search this offseason bringing in even more of football's best and brightest minds that were freely available.

Assistant head coach Greg Roman spearheaded the team's Jackson-led offensive turnaround, and as a reward was officially elevated to offensive coordinator after the season. Roman, whose Buffalo Bills led the league in rushing offense DVOA in 2016 with Tyrod Taylor at quarterback, did what he knew his offense could. He ran the ball. He ran power, he ran traps, he ran counters, and he ran options with Jackson. He ran the ball so much that he turned the clock back 60 years. The 2018 Ravens compiled 1,607 rushing yards in Jackson's seven starts. Six NFL teams failed to hit that mark in 16 games. The Ravens attempted 547 rushes on the season, but they attempted 316 of those rushes over Jackson's seven starts. That pro-rates to a full-season effort of 723 rushes, on an average of 45 rushes a game. Since 2010, NFL teams have run the ball 45 times in a game just 73 times *total*. The 2018 Ravens had four of those games and are the only team to rush 45 or more times twice in the same season since 2014.

Jackson's first seven games as a quarterback are impacted a lot by how much the offense changed. You hear "scheme fit" offered a lot as a reason why a certain quarterback whose name you're all familiar with can't be signed as a backup, but this was a case where the offense legitimately had to change landmarks from the Flacco era. This was a case where offensive linemen had to change the way that they set and their timings. Wide receivers were completely out of sync with their new quarterback.

While the Ravens were prolific, they weren't exactly devastating as a rushing team. In Jackson's seven regular-season starts, Baltimore had the highest yards per carry of any team besides Tennessee, but they had just a 2.6% rushing DVOA because they fumbled 10 times during those seven games, including eight by Jackson alone. No other team fumbled even six times in that stretch, and though the Ravens kept seven of those 10 fumbles, DVOA punishes them because that was quite a fortuitous outcome for that level of sloppiness.

Combine that sudden offensive shift in the first season with Baltimore's second-year quarterback telling reporters that he "didn't know" that the scheme would shift again in OTAs and it's very easy to draw up a narrative where Jackson is implicated by circumstance as not a good quarterback. Don't get sucked into that idea quite so fast.

Roman simplified the Ravens offense to facilitate its midseason transition to Jackson, but Jackson still flashed his potential to become the franchise quarterback of a sophisticated offense. He saw the field well and understood progressions—he's not a runner playing quarterback, he's a play-extender that took way too many sacks trying to learn how far he can play into the down at the NFL level. When a player is as athletic and ridiculous with that athleticism as Jackson is, moves that made life easy in the pocket at the college level are a tough transition. He needed to learn how fast NFL linemen are. Jackson took 16 sacks with just 170 pass attempts, more than doubling Flacco's sack rate behind what was essentially the same offensive line. Seven of his sacks were charted as "failed scrambles," where Jackson still had time to throw but took off anyway and didn't make it past the line of scrimmage.

John Brown's skill set did not align with what Jackson did best in his rookie season. Jackson had problems with accurate placement to the boundary, and his longest completion that wasn't targeting a player that started in the slot or at tight end went 18 yards. The offseason portended a shift in that because the Ravens spent heavily in the draft on wide receivers, bringing in Marquise "Hollywood" Brown from Oklahoma with their first pick. Roman can now design the offense to counter defenses expecting the run with play-action passes that attack them downfield. Clearly they believe Jackson has the ability to do that even if it wasn't demonstrated last season.

Jackson has a history of improvement, which is a reason for optimism going forward. When he first started at Louisville,

2019 Ravens Schedule

Week	Opp.	Week	Opp.	Week	Opp.
1	at MIA	7	at SEA	13	SF
2	ARI	8	BYE	14	at BUF
3	at KC	9	NE	15	NYJ (Thu.)
4	CLE	10	at CIN	16	at CLE
5	at PIT	11	HOU	17	PIT
6	CIN	12	at LAR (Mon.)		

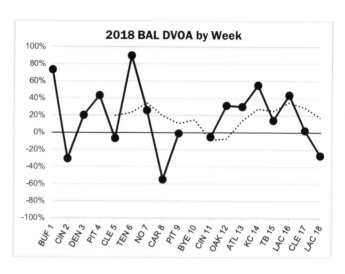

2018 BAL DVOA by Week

he was what people want to believe he is today: a running quarterback who was a chucker. But in 2016 and 2017 he developed further as a passer. His numbers didn't improve in 2017, but he also lost the three receivers from the 2016 team who had the most targets. The only one of his 2017 receivers that has made it to the NFL in any form is Jaylen Smith, a UDFA that signed with the Ravens.

The irony of all the attention paid to the Flacco-Jackson switch is that Baltimore's 6-1 drive to the playoffs was powered by defense and special teams, not by offense (Table 1). Baltimore's offensive DVOA was better with Flacco at quarterback, but Don Martindale's defense took a big step forward after the Week 10 bye. Only Chicago was better from Week 10 onwards.

Martindale's system is one of the most unusual in the NFL,

Table 1. Baltimore DVOA, Weeks 1-9 vs. Weeks 11-17

	Offense	Rk	Defense	Rk	Sp Tms	Rk
Weeks 1-9	4.3%	12	-8.0%	6	-0.5%	11
Weeks 11-17	-3.4%	21	-20.3%	2	7.4%	3

one where the players react to the offense rather than playing stagnant coverage. "We took all the different terms and simplified it," Martindale told *Sports Illustrated's* Robert Klemko before the playoff game. "Before it was like being in Spanish class, but for some reason there's a chapter on Chinese and another chapter on French. All we did was put it all in English. We really rely on those veterans. It's an elegant simplicity to us. We have pressure off of motion. Field and boundary."

Baltimore's defensive game is now as free-flowing and adjustable as the offenses they face, which is a big step that most NFL defenses simply haven't taken yet. It's a big reason the Ravens ranked sixth in the NFL in adjusted sack rate as a defense despite not having a truly dominant edge rusher. They finished third in defensive DVOA despite finding just 17 turnovers all season, a total that put them in the bottom third of the league. If Martindale can again pilot this defense into a top-five DVOA, he might be one of the most popular head coaching candidates in the NFL next offseason.

That's because the Ravens were decimated by free agency. They lost Eric Weddle, the on-field coach of their defense. They lost Terrell Suggs, the last link to the Ray Lewis defenses. They lost C.J. Mosley, one of the best linebackers in the

NFL, to a huge contract from the New York Jets. Za'Darius Smith, one of their rotational outside linebackers, found $20 million in guaranteed money from the Packers on his doorstep as free agency opened. All in all, the Ravens lost as much defensive AV over replacement as any team besides the 2009 Buccaneers (Table 2).

The Ravens already suffered some of Suggs' loss in a likely age-related second-half decline, and they replaced Weddle with their biggest free agent signing. But they don't have a clear replacement for Mosley who anchored their defense against the run and in coverage. The Ravens have players to replace him, but nobody who does it all quite like he did. 2018 rookie Kenny Young was good against the run, and Patrick Onwuasor was good in coverage. You may even see the Ravens go with dime coverage more often just to avoid putting Young in a bad position this season—they were already among the league leaders in using it in 2018.

This defense may not return several well-credentialed players, but let's talk a little bit about who they will have after the signing of future Hall of Fame safety Earl Thomas. Thomas has missed 19 regular-season games over the last three years. In the 19 games he missed, the Seattle defense allowed a completion rate of 64.1 percent, along with 31 touchdowns and seven interceptions. In the 29 games that Thomas played, they allowed a completion rate of 60.1 percent, along with 30 touchdowns and 30 interceptions. NFL Next Gen Stats noted that opponents were scared to target the deep middle of Seattle's defense when he was in the game. Passes to the deep middle were attempted 12 percent of the time while Thomas was in, and 18 percent of the time while Thomas was out.

We can't say for certain what Thomas has left after breaking his leg last season, but if he's anything like he's been for the last two years, the Ravens actually upgraded their defense by sending opposing offenses scattering away from the middle of the field, where a lot of the most valuable routes in football today are run. Passes to the deep middle were worth 38.5% DVOA against the Ravens last year. While still empirically not bad, it was their second-worst area of the field, and a healthy Thomas is one of those few players who breaks the normal football rules of demarcation. Especially given how effective Cover-3 zone blitzes were for Baltimore last year, the Thomas signing is a coup that could keep them from seeing much of a falloff in 2019.

Under Martindale, the Ravens blitz more than most teams would dare to. Not only were they second in the percentage of times they rushed five, but they were also second in the percentage of times they rushed six or more. Most coordinators tend to pick a happy spot—four rushers, five rushers—and stick there. In a big change from the unit that blitzed 29.4 percent of the time in 2017, the Ravens sent five or more pass-rushers on 38.4 percent of their snaps in 2018, which led the NFL. The only two other teams that even cracked 35 percent were Cleveland and Denver. The Ravens put the onus on the quarterback to make the quick decision, and they put players who are less often accustomed to dealing with that pressure—blocking backs and tight ends—in a position where they needed to succeed to win the play. The Ravens have a cadre of highly paid and highly skilled back-end players to clean up mistakes and win the pressured balls. Out of their six top defensive backs, the only one without a contract with $20 million in total value on it is Marlon Humphrey, a first-round pick who just might be the best player in the whole unit.

It remains to be seen just how effective the defense will be without its spiritual leaders, Mosley and Weddle. It remains to be seen what kind of leap, if any, Jackson will take in his second season. But there is heavy upside potential on the offense, and our projections believe the Ravens will retain a good defense despite the losses. If Jackson becomes an upper-crust quarterback in his second season, the Ravens will probably be one of the three best teams in the AFC. Even if he doesn't, Baltimore will likely be scrappy enough to compete for a wild-card spot.

More important than any of that to the casual fan flipping pages, we would make a plea to you that this is a team that deserves your attention in a sea of teams that don't really try to earn it. Most of our chapters in this book are about teams that are more or less stagnant. How many times do you want to see Andy Dalton check it down? How many Adam Gase offenses do you want to watch? How many fourth-and-1 punts do you want to see from teams who won't hire an analytics staff?

There are no promises that the Ravens will be great next year. What they will be, as they continue to try to push against the boundaries of current NFL norms, is interesting.

Rivers McCown

Table 2. Biggest Net Loss in AV Over Replacement on Defense, 2003-2019

Team	Year	Net AV Change	DVOA Y-1	Rk	DVOA	Rk	Change	Players Added	Players Lost
TB	2009	-32	-10.7%	6	8.0%	25	+18.6%	NONE	D.Brooks (8), G.Adams (6), P.Buchanon (5), K.Carter (5), J.Haye (4), C.June (4)
BAL	**2019**	**-27**	**-13.1%**	**3**	--	--	--	**E.Thomas (est. 7)***	**C.J.Mosley (12), T.Suggs (7), B.Urban (6), E.Weddle (6), Z Smith (3)**
NYJ	2013	-24	-4.2%	9	-5.6%	12	-1.3%	D.Landry (3)	B.Scott (7), L.Landry (5), Y.Bell (4), S.Pouha (4), B.Thomas (4), M.Devito (3)
CAR	2010	-23	-12.8%	6	-1.1%	16	+11.7%	NONE	J.Peppers (12), D.Lewis (5), C.Harris (4), N.Diggs (2)
PHI	2003	-20	-11.2%	4	3.0%	17	+14.2%	M.Coleman (4), N.Wayne (6)	H.Douglas (14), S.Barber (8), L.Kirkland (6), B.Bishop (2)
SF	2015	-20	-10.1%	5	9.9%	27	+20.0%	S.Wright (2)	J.Smith (5), P.Cox (4), C.Culliver (4), R.McDonald (4), C.Borland (3), D.Skuta (2)
ARI	2017	-19	-13.6%	3	-12.7%	4	+0.9%	A.Bethea (3), K.Dansby (2), J.Jones (2)	C.Campbell (13), K.Minter (5), M.Cooper (3), T.Jefferson (3), D.J.Swearinger (2)
CAR	2006	-18	-14.2%	2	-10.9%	4	+3.3%	K.Lucas (6), M.Kemoeatu (5), R.Howard (1)	W.Witherspoon (7), B.Buckner (6), K.Lucas (6), M.McCree (5), B.Short (5), R.Manning (1)
CAR	2016	-17	-18.4%	2	-5.3%	10	+13.1%	P.Soliai (2)	J.Norman (12), J.Allen (3), R.Harper (3), C.Tillman (1)
SD	2013	-17	2.0%	18	17.5%	32	+15.5%	D.Freeney (3), D.Cox (2)	Q.Jammer (5), S.Phillips (5), T.Spikes (4), A.Cason (3), V.Martin (2), A.Bigby (1), A.Franklin (1), D.Williams (1)
CLE	2011	-17	1.7%	18	4.2%	22	+2.6%	D.Patterson (1)	K.Coleman (5), A.Elam (4), M.Roth (4), E.Barton (3), D.Bowens (1), E.Wright (1)
CLE	2003	-17	-5.1%	10	-1.9%	14	+3.2%	NONE	E.Holmes (5), D.Hambrick (4), D.Rudd (4), D.Bush (2), C.Fuller (2)
	AVERAGE		-8.8%	7.5	0.5%	16.6	+9.3%		

*Thomas had only 2 AV in 2018 due to injury; for our projections, we estimated him at 10 AV to match what he earned in his last two full seasons.

2018 Ravens Stats by Week

Wk	vs.	W-L	PF	PA	YDF	YDA	TO	Total	Off	Def	ST
1	BUF	W	47	3	369	153	+1	73%	30%	-50%	-7%
2	at CIN	L	23	34	425	373	-3	-31%	-14%	19%	2%
3	DEN	W	27	14	342	293	+1	20%	16%	-15%	-10%
4	at PIT	W	26	14	451	284	+1	43%	15%	-27%	1%
5	at CLE	L	9	12	410	416	-1	-7%	-19%	-16%	-5%
6	at TEN	W	21	0	361	106	-1	90%	11%	-70%	9%
7	NO	L	23	24	351	339	+1	26%	30%	-1%	-5%
8	at CAR	L	21	36	325	386	-3	-55%	-29%	29%	3%
9	PIT	L	16	23	265	395	0	-1%	4%	12%	7%
10	BYE										
11	CIN	W	24	21	403	255	-1	-5%	0%	4%	-2%
12	OAK	W	34	17	416	249	-1	32%	-8%	-10%	29%
13	at ATL	W	26	16	366	131	0	30%	-19%	-45%	4%
14	at KC	L	24	27	321	442	0	55%	9%	-29%	18%
15	TB	W	20	12	370	241	-1	14%	-1%	-18%	-3%
16	at LAC	W	22	10	361	198	+2	44%	-6%	-50%	0%
17	CLE	W	26	24	463	426	+2	2%	5%	7%	5%
18	LAC	L	17	23	229	243	-2	-27%	-49%	-43%	-21%

Trends and Splits

	Offense	Rank	Defense	Rank
Total DVOA	0.9%	15	-13.1%	3
Unadjusted VOA	2.3%	14	-10.2%	5
Weighted Trend	-1.3%	19	-14.2%	4
Variance	2.9%	2	7.6%	28
Average Opponent	2.0%	27	4.5%	5
Passing	15.7%	14	-10.7%	3
Rushing	-1.9%	10	-16.9%	6
First Down	-4.5%	19	-14.1%	2
Second Down	-8.4%	24	-10.0%	7
Third Down	26.2%	4	-16.1%	6
First Half	-4.6%	21	-4.5%	7
Second Half	6.7%	13	-22.5%	1
Red Zone	-8.9%	19	3.9%	20
Late and Close	2.7%	15	-28.9%	1

Five-Year Performance

Year	W-L	Pyth W	Est W	PF	PA	TO	Total	Rk	Off	Rk	Def	Rk	ST	Rk	Off AGL	Rk	Def AGL	Rk	Off Age	Rk	Def Age	Rk	ST Age	Rk
2014	10-6	10.9	11.5	409	302	+2	21.9%	5	9.4%	9	-4.6%	8	8.0%	2	25.0	10	27.6	8	27.4	8	26.8	15	25.4	31
2015	5-11	6.0	7.5	328	401	-14	-3.0%	17	-5.2%	20	5.1%	20	7.3%	1	70.1	32	26.0	12	26.5	18	27.1	10	25.6	27
2016	8-8	8.6	9.1	343	321	+5	7.4%	12	-7.5%	24	-9.9%	6	4.9%	4	29.4	12	30.9	14	28.0	3	27.2	5	26.1	18
2017	9-7	10.5	10.4	395	303	+17	18.6%	7	-4.5%	21	-13.9%	3	9.2%	1	58.7	27	42.9	23	27.3	10	27.0	6	25.7	22
2018	10-6	10.8	11.0	389	287	-5	17.0%	6	0.9%	15	-13.1%	3	2.9%	6	17.2	4	12.4	2	26.3	20	27.6	2	25.7	21

2018 Performance Based on Most Common Personnel Groups

BAL Offense					BAL Offense vs. Opponents					BAL Defense					BAL Defense vs. Opponents			
Pers	Freq	Yds	DVOA	Run%	Pers	Freq	Yds	DVOA	Run%	Pers	Freq	Yds	DVOA		Pers	Freq	Yds	DVOA
11	54%	5.8	18.8%	39%	Base	39%	5.1	-13.1%	58%	Base	16%	5.2	1.7%		11	69%	5.0	-16.9%
12	23%	6.3	11.9%	47%	Nickel	61%	5.8	22.7%	40%	Nickel	57%	4.8	-15.2%		12	17%	5.0	3.6%
13	6%	3.9	-32.6%	54%	Dime+	14%	5.9	3.1%	26%	Dime+	26%	5.3	-19.9%		21	4%	5.4	-12.4%
22	6%	4.0	-11.9%	85%	Goal Line	1%	0.4	-25.0%	93%	Goal Line	0%	0.0	38.3%		13	3%	4.4	-12.9%
10	3%	6.2	19.3%	9%						Big	1%	2.0	-81.2%		22	3%	2.5	-83.2%
21	2%	4.5	-64.8%	46%											01	2%	5.9	-16.0%

Strategic Tendencies

Run/Pass		Rk	Formation		Rk	Pass Rush		Rk	Secondary		Rk	Strategy		Rk
Runs, first half	41%	9	Form: Single Back	67%	30	Rush 3	7.6%	15	4 DB	16%	29	Play action	28%	8
Runs, first down	55%	5	Form: Empty Back	10%	9	Rush 4	53.9%	31	5 DB	57%	23	Avg Box (Off)	6.49	2
Runs, second-long	37%	5	Pers: 3+ WR	59%	26	Rush 5	28.2%	2	6+ DB	26%	6	Avg Box (Def)	6.33	7
Runs, power sit.	74%	1	Pers: 2+ TE/6+ OL	37%	4	Rush 6+	10.2%	2	CB by Sides	77%	16	Offensive Pace	29.80	5
Runs, behind 2H	25%	18	Pers: 6+ OL	2%	17	Int DL Sacks	8.1%	32	S/CB Cover Ratio	28%	14	Defensive Pace	29.63	2
Pass, ahead 2H	34%	31	Shotgun/Pistol	80%	2	Second Level Sacks	31.4%	5	DB Blitz	13%	5	Go for it on 4th	2.25	2

As you can imagine, all of those run/pass splits changed dramatically after Lamar Jackson became the starting quarterback in Week 11. Here are the changes in the ratios; remember, planned quarterback runs count as runs here, but scrambles count as passes:

Split	Wk 1-9	Wk 11-17
Runs, first half	33%	52%
Runs, first down	43%	69%
Runs, second-long	29%	49%
Runs, power sit.	69%	83%
Runs, behind 2H	18%	53%
Pass, ahead 2H	43%	27%

As you might imagine, each of these run/pass ratios would have ranked No. 1 over the entire regular season (except the last one ranking No. 32). ✎ Baltimore had the league's biggest gap between DVOA on runs with one back (5.1 yards per carry, 14.0% DVOA) and runs with two backs (3.4, -25.4%). Related: Baltimore had the largest gap in yards per carry between runs from shotgun or pistol (5.1, 8.2%) and runs with the quarterback under center (3.1, -23.1%). ✎ Baltimore's defense was third with 33 dropped passes by opponents (second in rate of passes). ✎ The Ravens had the league's best defense against passes thrown at or behind the line of scrimmage. ✎ Baltimore had the league's best defense on plays where there was no pass pressure, by both net yards per pass (6.1) and DVOA (10.9%). ✎ John Harbaugh's high Aggressiveness Index includes the decision to go for it on eight of 10 qualifying fourth-and-1 opportunities, and that is even more impressive when you consider the quality of Baltimore's special teams.

Passing

Player	DYAR	DVOA	Plays	NtYds	Avg	YAC	C%	TD	Int
J.Flacco*	429	5.4%	392	2380	6.1	4.4	61.7%	12	6
L.Jackson	24	-9.2%	186	1119	6.0	5.2	58.6%	6	3
R.Griffin	0	-11.4%	6	21	3.5	13.0	33.3%	0	0

Rushing

Player	DYAR	DVOA	Plays	Yds	Avg	TD	Fum	Suc
G.Edwards	130	13.9%	137	718	5.2	2	0	63%
L.Jackson	-112	-27.2%	133	696	5.2	5	10	--
A.Collins*	-4	-9.4%	114	418	3.7	7	3	47%
K.Dixon	38	8.1%	60	337	5.6	2	2	55%
J.Allen*	-16	-16.3%	41	113	2.8	3	0	41%
T.Montgomery*	17	16.6%	16	83	5.2	0	0	69%
J.Flacco*	13	2.9%	13	46	3.5	0	1	--
C.Moore	7	-14.3%	5	17	3.4	0	0	--
M.Ingram	71	2.9%	138	645	4.7	6	2	57%

Receiving

Player	DYAR	DVOA	Plays	Ctch	Yds	Y/C	YAC	TD	C%
M.Crabtree*	-33	-16.6%	100	54	607	11.2	2.4	3	54%
J.Brown*	4	-12.2%	97	42	717	17.1	3.8	5	43%
W.Snead	21	-9.8%	95	62	651	10.5	4.5	1	65%
C.Moore	28	2.5%	25	19	196	10.3	3.1	1	76%
S.Roberts	86	4.7%	64	45	494	11.0	4.7	2	70%
M.Floyd	-58	-43.2%	24	10	100	10.0	2.9	1	42%
M.Andrews	159	36.2%	50	34	552	16.2	5.7	3	68%
N.Boyle	-50	-26.6%	37	23	213	9.3	6.1	0	62%
H.Hurst	-16	-17.5%	23	13	163	12.5	5.7	1	57%
M.Williams*	18	8.2%	17	16	143	8.9	6.1	1	94%
J.Allen*	-4	-15.4%	43	35	204	5.8	5.3	2	81%
A.Collins*	9	-6.6%	21	15	105	7.0	6.5	1	71%
T.Montgomery*	-29	-45.1%	17	10	65	6.5	6.4	0	59%
K.Dixon	5	-0.6%	7	6	51	8.5	9.0	0	86%
M.Ingram	-7	-18.8%	27	21	170	8.1	7.4	1	78%

Offensive Line

Player	Pos	Age	GS	Snaps	Pen	Sk	Pass	Run	Player	Pos	Age	GS	Snaps	Pen	Sk	Pass	Run
Matt Skura	C	26	16/16	1189	5	1.0	4	4	Alex Lewis	LG	27	10/10	707	6	3.0	8	1
Marshal Yanda	RG	35	16/16	1163	2	1.0	7	0	James Hurst	RT/LG	28	10/10	676	3	0.0	7	4
Ronnie Stanley	LT	25	15/15	1085	6	1.0	4	2	Bradley Bozeman	G	25	14/1	214	1	0.0	0	1
Orlando Brown	RT	23	16/10	760	3	1.0	3	0									

Year	Yards	ALY	Rank	Power	Rank	Stuff	Rank	2nd Lev	Rank	Open Field	Rank	Sacks	ASR	Rank	Press	Rank	F-Start	Cont.
2016	4.02	4.07	20	70%	9	20%	14	1.11	20	0.66	18	33	5.3%	8	26.9%	19	13	27
2017	4.22	4.36	6	69%	7	20%	14	1.27	5	0.70	17	27	4.3%	4	26.1%	6	11	30
2018	4.53	4.59	9	78%	1	15%	3	1.33	7	0.67	24	32	6.1%	8	28.5%	14	23	29

2018 ALY by direction: Left End: 4.12 (21) Left Tackle: 3.93 (21) Mid/Guard: 4.90 (4) Right Tackle: 4.27 (18) Right End: 3.14 (29)

A tale of two positions. The Ravens are quite well set at tackle now. First-round pick Ronnie Stanley continues to provide a fairly solid return on his draft position, improving from 11 blown blocks in pass protection in 2017 to just four in 2018. 2018 third-round pick Orlando Brown dropped in the pre-draft process because he was overweight and didn't run a good 40-yard dash, but it turns out that didn't mean much at the NFL level. Brown ranked No. 1 at his position in snaps per blown block as a rookie. James Hurst is an adequate swing tackle. ✱ Inside, though, things are getting thin. Marshal Yanda is a phenomenal player, but he's 35 and the end does tend to come quickly for NFL geriatrics. Yanda told the *Baltimore Sun* that good health was a big reason he returned for this season, noting that "If I was going to end the season on injured reserve, then I was probably going to hang it up." ✱ Alex Lewis and Matt Skura are both more limited players, with not much in the way of NFL success. Skura just has issues anchoring against true NFL power players. Lewis can't even point to much success staying on the field between concussions, ankles, and labrums. ✱ Fourth-round pick Ben Powers (Oklahoma) could see early playing time, particularly if Lewis is battling something in training camp. 2018 sixth-round pick Bradley Bozeman might also be in line for some more work after an uneven rookie season.

Defensive Front

Defensive Line	Age	Pos	G	Snaps	Plays	TmPct	Overall Rk	Stop	Dfts	BTkl	Runs	St%	vs. Run Rk	RuYd	Rk	Sack	Hit	Pass Rush Hur	Dsrpt
Brent Urban*	28	DE	16	522	29	3.8%	66	22	8	0	23	74%	48	2.2	42	0.5	1	12	2
Brandon Williams	30	DE	16	517	35	4.6%	45	26	3	3	32	75%	41	2.3	46	1.0	1	5	1
Chris Wormley	26	DT	16	401	21	2.8%	--	17	3	3	13	77%	--	2.8	--	1.0	1	15	4
Michael Pierce	27	DT	14	389	33	5.0%	41	24	7	2	28	71%	53	2.0	30	0.0	2	11	0

Edge Rushers	Age	Pos	G	Snaps	Plays	TmPct	Overall Rk	Stop	Dfts	BTkl	Runs	St%	vs. Run Rk	RuYd	Rk	Sack	Hit	Pass Rush Hur	Dsrpt
Terrell Suggs*	37	OLB	16	744	38	5.0%	45	33	17	7	21	86%	13	1.4	12	7.0	7	36	5
Za'Darius Smith*	27	OLB	16	690	46	6.1%	20	33	17	3	25	64%	70	3.2	72	8.5	17	30	0
Matt Judon	27	OLB	16	674	46	6.1%	20	28	14	6	25	60%	76	3.1	69	7.0	13	30	4
Shane Ray	*26*	*OLB*	*11*	*253*	*11*	*1.9%*	*--*	*8*	*4*	*1*	*5*	*80%*	*--*	*4.2*	*--*	*1.0*	*1*	*6*	*0*

Linebackers	Age	Pos	G	Snaps	Plays	TmPct	Overall Rk	Stop	Dfts	BTkl	Runs	St%	vs. Run Rk	RuYd	Rk	Sack	Hit	Hur	Tgts	Suc%	vs. Pass Rk	AdjYd	Rk	PD	Int
C.J. Mosley*	27	ILB	15	875	110	15.4%	20	62	17	9	63	67%	19	3.8	35	0.5	1	7.5	39	51%	37	6.0	21	5	1
Patrick Onwuasor	27	ILB	16	434	57	7.5%	74	30	13	6	31	55%	58	3.6	30	5.5	6	5	15	47%	48	6.1	22	3	1
Kenny Young	25	ILB	16	369	47	6.2%	80	28	7	9	28	61%	36	3.1	18	2.5	4	10	14	57%	--	5.6	--	1	0

Year	Yards	ALY	Rank	Power	Rank	Stuff	Rank	2nd Level	Rank	Open Field	Rank	Sacks	ASR	Rank	Press	Rank
2016	3.82	3.95	10	50%	3	21%	12	1.05	8	0.59	11	31	5.7%	22	26.7%	19
2017	4.12	3.85	7	62%	14	21%	15	1.10	14	0.87	26	41	6.8%	13	29.6%	20
2018	3.52	3.90	5	72%	25	19%	16	1.07	5	0.29	2	43	8.1%	6	32.8%	7
2018 ALY by direction:		*Left End: 5.48 (28)*			*Left Tackle: 3.19 (5)*			*Mid/Guard: 4.05 (7)*			*Right Tackle: 2.73 (2)*			*Right End: 3.59 (8)*	

The Ravens threw a big net out in trying to replace Terrell Suggs on the outside. They added Shane Ray and the returning Pernell McPhee as veteran free agents and then used a third-round pick on rookie Jaylon Ferguson, who merely broke D1's all-time sack record at Louisiana Tech. The guess here is that Ferguson and McPhee have the best shots at playing time. McPhee has a long history of solid NFL play and should be a steadying presence even if he's not a dominant pass-rusher. Ferguson slid in the draft due to a poor athletic profile, with an 8.08 3-cone drill time and a 4.82 40-yard dash. (He didn't get to work out at the combine after the NFL pulled his invite on account of a battery conviction in his freshman season—a $189 fine in a fight at McDonalds.) But Ferguson has NFL-ready skills and could force his way into the rotation sooner rather than later. ✱ Matt Judon and Michael Pierce are Ravens success stories. Judon has earned the lion's share of the playing time at edge rusher, and Pierce has been extremely good as an interior lineman after going undrafted. Both are also entering the final year of their rookie contracts, and the Ravens haven't balked at letting producers go. Pierce has the higher highs but has been less reliably on the field. This year could make the decision for Baltimore. ✱ Chris Wormley had an odd year, continuing to produce but losing playing time late in the season. He's in that special limbo where you have the talent to be an NFL starter, but you don't have the coaching staff buy-in. ✱ Brandon Williams is Baltimore's best nose tackle but has a wildly high cap figure compared to his on-field production at this point. This could be his last year with the Ravens as he hits the free-out years of the five-year, $52.5-million contract he signed in 2017. ✱ Patrick Onwausor and Kenny Young, as mentioned earlier in the chapter, are probably better platoon candidates than true starters at linebacker. Onwausor seems the more likely recipient of playing time. The only other middle linebacker to see real time last season was Chris Board, the UDFA special-teamer who had just 21 defensive snaps (but did lead the team with 10 special teams tackles). Baltimore seems like a good candidate to look at whatever inside linebackers get chopped in final cuts.

Defensive Secondary

Secondary	Age	Pos	G	Snaps	Plays	TmPct	Rk	Stop	Dfts	BTkl	Runs	St%	Rk	RuYd	Rk	Tgts	Tgt%	Rk	Dist	Suc%	Rk	AdjYd	Rk	PD	Int
Eric Weddle*	34	FS	16	1016	71	9.3%	45	24	7	8	34	38%	45	6.8	37	27	6.2%	14	11.4	48%	42	6.9	31	3	0
Brandon Carr	33	CB	16	876	56	7.4%	58	24	8	7	9	33%	56	8.9	68	74	19.6%	47	12.7	57%	19	7.4	33	11	2
Tony Jefferson	27	SS	14	863	80	12.0%	16	42	13	5	28	61%	7	4.9	10	36	9.7%	40	9.2	61%	13	6.6	20	6	1
Marlon Humphrey	23	CB	14	718	52	7.8%	49	24	13	6	10	40%	43	5.7	27	74	23.9%	66	12.0	66%	2	5.3	3	15	2
Jimmy Smith	31	CB	12	611	54	9.5%	28	16	5	6	9	44%	30	6.1	33	57	21.6%	57	12.8	51%	48	7.1	29	9	2
Tavon Young	25	CB	15	602	41	5.8%	--	19	9	5	8	38%	--	5.5	--	39	15.0%	--	9.0	51%	--	7.6	--	5	1
Anthony Levine	32	SS	16	280	29	3.8%	75	17	10	4	4	75%	1	3.5	2	20	16.6%	74	5.9	65%	7	5.7	9	8	1
Earl Thomas	30	FS	4	237	27	14.2%	--	11	5	0	11	18%	--	12.7	--	7	7.0%	--	11.6	71%	--	6.1	--	5	3

Year	Pass D Rank	vs. #1 WR	Rk	vs. #2 WR	Rk	vs. Other WR	Rk	WR Wide	Rk	WR Slot	Rk	vs. TE	Rk	vs. RB	Rk
2016	10	-5.9%	7	-6.3%	7	9.9%	22	-10.5%	8	7.9%	18	-28.8%	3	12.7%	24
2017	2	-24.7%	4	-39.7%	2	-1.0%	16	-26.7%	4	-17.4%	5	19.6%	29	-16.8%	6
2018	3	-9.7%	8	-26.2%	2	-11.6%	8	-32.5%	2	-4.4%	12	16.1%	22	-44.7%	1

Well, you don't get Earl Thomas and not play a ton of single-high and Cover-3, and that's exactly what Earl Thomas will be doing for the Ravens next year. It will be interesting to see just how disguised they let things be with the chess pieces around him. Thomas will spend 80 percent of his time directly in the middle of the field. ● Thomas will probably move Tony Jefferson into more of a dime linebacker/box role, which is how he blew up in Arizona en route to getting paid in the first place. ● Fun with weird splits for a really good cornerback: Marlon Humphrey allowed seven first downs and one touchdown in two games against the Browns. He allowed five first downs and three touchdowns in his other 14 games. ● Jimmy Smith's two-interception game against the Browns that clinched the AFC North in Week 17 is the perfect example of how good he is and why he's worth keeping even though he's always hurt and making a big chunk of cap space. At 31, on the last year of his contract, this might be his last hurrah with Baltimore. ● It's not very often you see a team surrender three years and $13 million guaranteed to their fourth corner, but the Ravens believe in Tavon Young. With respect to his numbers, Young did play with a sports hernia for all of last season. He's going to be the primary slot cornerback this season. ● Brandon Carr has outlived all of the insults he took for his work as the No. 1 guy in Dallas, and now he is what he is: A steady outside corner who will take away the deep stuff. It is worth noting that he definitely had the easiest wideout schedule of any Ravens corner last year. ● Four starting-quality cornerbacks give the Ravens a lot of flexibility when they play nickel or dime. If they prefer to play the three-safety dime look that has become so popular in the NFL in recent years, they also have a player for that, veteran Anthony Levine. ● The Ravens dropped a fourth-round pick on USC's Iman Lewis-Marshall, someone that NFL.com's Lance Zierlein projected as more of a safety than a corner because of his lack of functional long speed. He's certainly got space to develop on this depth chart. If anyone gets on the field beyond the top four corners, it will probably be 2018 fourth-rounder Anthony Averett, who showed some flashes in his playing time last season.

Special Teams

Year	DVOA	Rank	FG/XP	Rank	Net Kick	Rank	Kick Ret	Rank	Net Punt	Rank	Punt Ret	Rank	Hidden	Rank
2016	4.9%	4	25.5	1	7.0	3	-2.8	23	-1.0	16	-4.1	24	11.7	3
2017	9.2%	1	19.0	1	6.6	4	12.3	1	4.1	12	3.9	5	-7.0	24
2018	2.9%	6	11.0	3	0.9	15	-1.3	18	-3.4	25	7.5	2	8.3	9

Justin Tucker had his lowest field goal percentage since 2015 and missed an extra-point attempt for the first time in his career. But, nothing to see here—he's still probably the best kicker in the NFL, and he is continually asked to make the tough ones. The Ravens ranked second, behind only the Texans, by attempting field goals on 20.1 percent of their drives. Tucker is also one of the best kickoff artists in the league. ● Baltimore's weakest unit on special teams was punting. Sam Koch, who used to be one of the league's top punters, has been closer to average the last two seasons. ● Chris Moore handled the majority of the kick returns last year; he was around average but has a history of breaking some long ones. Cyrus Jones, a washout Patriots defensive back as a second-rounder, finished second in the NFL with 10.1 estimated points added on punt returns. ● Baltimore added three-time Pro Bowl special-teamer Justin Bethel in free agency; he was tied for third in the league with 14 special teams tackles for the 2018 Falcons.

Buffalo Bills

2018 record: 6-10	**Total DVOA:** -18.2% (28th)	**2019 Mean Projection:** 6.9 wins	**On the Clock (0-4):** 19%
Pythagorean Wins: 5.0 (30th)	**Offense:** -27.5% (31st)	**Postseason Odds:** 21.9%	**Mediocrity (5-7):** 41%
Snap-Weighted Age: 26.5 (14th)	**Defense:** -14.5% (2nd)	**Super Bowl Odds:** 1.3%	**Playoff Contender (8-10):** 30%
Average Opponent: 1.3% (8th)	**Special Teams:** -5.1% (32nd)	**Proj. Avg. Opponent:** -3.8% (28th)	**Super Bowl Contender (11+):** 9%

2018: The worst offense in modern franchise history is not going to lead to many wins.

2019: Josh Allen is going to prove a lot of people wrong, on one side or another.

To be fair, they warned us about this.

The 2017 season was a glorious fluke for the Buffalo Bills—the first playoff appearance of the 21st century in Sean McDermott's first year as head coach. Never mind their -9.8% DVOA, or the fact that they had the fifth-worst point differential for a playoff team in NFL history. The last time the Bills Mafia had gotten to experience January football was just after they had finished worrying about the Y2K bug. If that's not an event worth smashing a few tables over, I don't know what is.

It's also not remotely sustainable for long-term success, and to their credit, both head coach Sean McDermott and general manager Brandon Beane recognized this. Rather than rest on their rather fluky laurels, they admitted in March of 2018 that this was a team that was still rebuilding. They drafted centerpieces for both sides of the ball in Josh Allen and Tremaine Edmunds, knowing that both of them would need tons of development before they would be ready to excel. They (mostly) intentionally took on over $70 million in dead money, the most in NFL history, in order to clear the decks for future rebuilding. Cordy Glenn, Tyrod Taylor, Corey Coleman—anyone with a high price tag who wasn't in the long-term plans got jettisoned all at one time, in order to open a massive amount of cap space in 2019. They're in the middle of the "build" (never mind the rebuild), they said. "Respect the Process," they said.

"The Process" has become sports' favorite euphemism for rebuilding. It's short-term pain for long-term benefits. It's a promise to the fan base: we're going to suck now, but that will let us position ourselves for even greater success in the future.

The jury's still out on that second part, but man oh man, did Buffalo ever live up to the whole being terrible part of the plan, especially on offense.

Where even to begin? AJ McCarron couldn't beat out Nathan Peterman. Peterman's role as starting quarterback lasted precisely one half before he was yanked for Allen. Allen then got hurt, leading back to Peterman, who was still terrible, which led to street free agent Derek Anderson, who got hurt, which led to *another* street free agent in Matt Barkley, who gave way back to Allen in a game of "terrible quarterback musical chairs." Excluding Barkley's 26 pass attempts, the high-water DVOA mark for a Bills quarterback was Allen's -35.9%.

That would be enough for one nightmare season, but no, Buffalo spread it around. Kelvin Benjamin pouted his way to being released, refusing to even run routes with Allen. That,

plus the failed acquisitions of Corey Coleman and Terrelle Pryor, meant the Bills were running out a sub-JV collection of receivers by the end of the year. Meanwhile, LeSean McCoy had the worst season of his career by DVOA. The "skill" positions were anything but.

The end result of all this was a -27.5% offensive DVOA, the worst in franchise history. Worse than 2009, when Dick Jauron was fired midseason and Ryan Fitzpatrick replaced Trent Edwards. Worse than 2005, when Kelly Holcomb and J.P. Losman split starts replacing Drew Bledsoe. Worse than 1997, when Todd Collins replaced the retired Jim Kelly to predictable results. Our stats only go back to 1986, so it's possible there's a worse offense lurking out there in franchise history (check out 1968, where injuries to Jack Kemp and Tom Flores meant that running back Ed Rutkowski had to start at quarterback for the first time in six years!) but at least in the modern era, Buffalo fans have never had to sit through something this bad.

Now that the self-induced cap hell is over, however, Buffalo had the opportunity to revamp their roster, and boy howdy, did they ever go to town. The powers that be came in and used all that freed-up cap room to dramatically alter the shape of their offense, bringing in 15 free agents with a combined contract value of over $173 million, both the most in the league. All three of their Day 2 picks in the draft came on the offensive side of the ball, as well. It is entirely possible Buffalo's Week 1 offense will replace all 11 starters from a year ago (Table 1).

It's probable the Bills will retain a few holdover starters, with Dawkins, McCoy and Jones being the most likely candidates, but the size and scope of Buffalo's offensive changes are dramatic, and should have an immediate effect. There's competition at every position on the offensive side of the ball except quarterback. Buffalo had to make do with scraps and leftovers last season. While they didn't add any true superstars or gamechangers this year, the overall level of basic offensive competence should be much, much better.

The Bills haven't had a qualified receiver with a positive DVOA since Robert Woods in 2016. Enter Cole Beasley in the slot, John Brown out wide, and Tyler Kroft at tight end (assuming he recovers from his broken foot in time for the season). Beasley has never quite lived up to his epic 2016 season, but his 9.6% DVOA working out of the slot last season was sixth best among the pure slot receivers in the league; he'll be

\multicolumn{6}{c}{2019 Bills Schedule}

Week	Opp.	Week	Opp.	Week	Opp.
1	at NYJ	7	MIA	13	at DAL (Thu.)
2	at NYG	8	PHI	14	BAL
3	CIN	9	WAS	15	at PIT
4	NE	10	at CLE	16	at NE
5	at TEN	11	at MIA	17	NYJ
6	BYE	12	DEN		

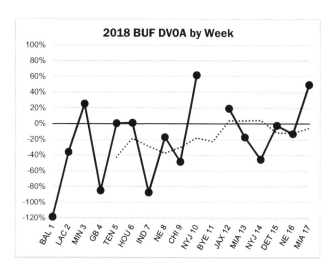

a security blanket in the short passing game. Brown's a logical choice for a quarterback with a huge arm; he was second among qualified receivers in average depth of target at 16.6 yards. When healthy, Kroft has been a solid red zone option, with a 21.5% red zone DVOA in 2017. None of that trio will knock your socks off, but considering the Bills were running out Isaiah McKenzie, Jason Croom, and Deonte Thompson in key roles by the end of the season, these are upgrades. Undrafted rookie Robert Foster came on strong in the second half of the season, with a 49.1% DVOA once he returned from the practice squad in Week 10. His skill set more or less duplicates Brown's, so there's some talk about keeping possession receiver Zay Jones as a starter instead. Foster's DVOA did drop to -4.6% on short passes from Allen, but Jones' was -27.6%. Whether Foster or Jones is starting on the outside, no one's going to mistake this group for an offensive powerhouse, but a below-average corps is leaps and bounds better than the terrible unit Buffalo trotted out last year.

The running back corps is a smorgasbord of *eh, maybe*. The aforementioned McCoy has declined each of the last two seasons and is a rumored cap cut, but perhaps limiting his carries and keeping him fresher will see the return of the McCoy who was second in the league in DVOA just three years ago. Frank Gore continues to defy age—the second-leading rusher in his draft class, Cedric Benson, has been retired for seven years! A trip to cold-weather Buffalo won't be great for his aging joints, but he's averaged 86.8 yards and 4.4 yards per carry in games under 40 degrees over the last four seasons, so the 36-year-old may still yet have gas in the tank. Rookie Devin Singletary is a broken-tackle machine with disappointing combine numbers, and T.J. Yeldon is a jack of all trades, albeit a master of none. The odds of any one of the four having a particularly good season in the backfield aren't great, but the odds of at least one or two of them turning out alright seem fairly high. At the very least, they should be better than last year's league-worst -15.8% DVOA and anemic 3.5 yards per carry when running backs carried the ball.

The offensive line, too, should be improved, with Mitch Morse arriving in free agency and Cody Ford added in the draft. Replacing Jordan Mills and Ryan Groy with leftover blocking sleds would probably have been an improvement; adding players with Morse's success and Ford's potential should make a massive difference. Like the rest of the offense, the rest of the line is still a work in progress. However, with veterans Spencer Long, Ty Nsekhe, and Jon Felciano coming in to battle for spots, there's every chance that Buffalo's

line could rise out of the bottom quartile in both adjusted line yards and adjusted sack rate.

This is still very much a rebuild, and there's plenty of work left to be done, but this offseason's spending spree should see tangible improvements at every level of the offense, whether you're looking at the Week 1 or Week 17 version. That means far fewer excuses for the hopes of the franchise under center, as Buffalo has done everything it can reasonably be expected to do to give Josh Allen a chance to succeed.

It would be fair to say that Allen's rookie season went better than we were expecting, though that's damning with fairly faint praise. Eighty quarterbacks have qualified for our tables as rookies since 1986; Allen's -35.9% DVOA ranks 68th out of that group. Limit that to top-10 picks, and Allen ranked 28th out of 36. That's still very bad, but considering the blind-leading-the-blind nature of the Bills' offense last season, not as bad as it was in our nightmares. Heck, it wasn't even the worst debut of 2018, considering Josh Rosen's struggles in Arizona.

The list of the ten worst first-round quarterback debuts includes some of the all-time worst selections, but it's not all terrible (Table 2). Matthew Stafford, Donovan McNabb, and Jared Goff became Pro Bowlers, after all. A terrible first step does not necessarily mean a terrible career to follow.

Table 1: Extreme Makeover, Buffalo Edition

Pos	2018 Week 1 Starter	Current Situation	Potential Replacement
QB	Nathan Peterman	Released, in OAK	Josh Allen
RB	LeSean McCoy	Potential cap casualty	Devin Singletary
WR	Zay Jones	-15.5% DVOA in 2018	Robert Foster
WR	Jeremy Kerley	Released; unsigned	Cole Beasley
WR	Kelvin Benjamin	Released; unsigned	John Brown
TE	Charles Clay	Released; in ARI	Tyler Kroft
LT	Dion Dawkins	24 blown blocks in 2018	Ty Nsekhe
LG	Vlad Ducasse	Lost job halfway through 2018	Quinton Spain
C	Ryan Groy	Left in free agency; in NO	Mitch Morse
RG	John Miller	Left in free agency; in CIN	Spencer Long
RT	Jordan Mills	Left in free agency; in MIA	Cody Ford

Table 2. Worst Rookie Seasons by First-Round QBs, 1986-2018

Player	Team	Year	DVOA	Y+1 DVOA	Career High DVOA
Tim Couch	CLE	1999	-28.4%	-15.1%	-8.0%
Josh Freeman	TB	2009	-31.1%	13.9%	13.9%
Christian Ponder	MIN	2011	-31.5%	-6.1%	-6.1%
Josh Allen	**BUF**	**2018**	**-35.9%**	**--**	**-35.9%**
Matthew Stafford	DET	2009	-36.6%	14.9%*	14.9%
Blake Bortles	JAX	2014	-40.7%	-9.9%	0.3%
Blaine Gabbert	JAX	2011	-46.5%	-25.3%	-15.6%
David Carr	HOU	2002	-47.4%	-7.0%	-3.2%
Donovan McNabb	PHI	1999	-51.6%	-1.4%	27.5%
Ryan Leaf	SD	1998	-51.8%	-35.5%*	-35.5%
Josh Rosen	**ARI**	**2018**	**-53.0%**	**--**	**-53.0%**
Jared Goff	LAR	2016	-74.8%	24.0%	24.0%

*This is the third season, not the second season, for Stafford (3 games in Year 2) and Leaf (did not play in Year 2).
Minimum 200 attempts.

The Bills' offensive outlook still hinges on Allen's development, and yes, the analytics community's consensus is still that he was a significant reach as a first-round player. We should be fair, however, and point out all the things that Allen did well. That mostly means forgetting about his arm and focusing on his legs.

Allen was Buffalo's leading rusher last season, and not just by default; his 192 rushing DYAR was the highest for a quarterback since Russell Wilson's 2014 season—and that's after missing a month. He trailed only Derrick Henry in rushing DYAR from Weeks 10 to 17. About 60 percent of Allen's runs last season were scrambles, putting him in a different class from players like Lamar Jackson or Cam Newton who had plenty of designed runs. Allen's DVOA on designed runs was -6.2%; it was 71.7% on his 48 scrambles. No one was better at running out of danger than Allen was last season, and he did it often—11.9 percent of Allen's dropbacks ended up with him scrambling, the most in the league by a significant margin. You don't want a quarterback scrambling that much, but it's nice to know that he can do it in a pinch, and the improved offensive line and receiving corps should mean Allen won't be running for his life quite so much in 2019.

There are three other signs Bills fans can hold on to from Allen's rookie performance. The first is that Allen saw legitimate improvement after he came back from his midseason injury. Allen was dead last in passing DVOA through the first six weeks of the season at -59.5%. Once he came back in Week 12, Allen had a -16.5% DVOA the rest of the way. This corresponds with Robert Foster breaking out, meaning Allen went from a disaster to merely replacement level when he had a receiver he could trust. That's not a terrible place for a rookie to be. He also saw 6.5 percent of his passes dropped, the fourth-highest rate in the league. Both of these point to the idea that, with some actually competent receivers, Allen would have done better as a rookie.

The other positive sign is that Allen could make big plays. Terrible quarterbacks like Peterman or Blake Bortles don't do anything particularly useful; there's no foundation to build off of there. Allen is the perfect Red Zone quarterback, by which we mean the channel, not the area of the field. He's good for several jaw-dropping plays a game—a scramble out of trouble, a bomb downfield to an open receiver, or a terrible interception right into the hands of an opponent. Allen made positive plays throughout 2018; he just made significantly more negative ones. Given the choice, I'd take a player like that over someone who doesn't make any positive plays at all.

But oh lord, was every criticism about Allen's arm, accuracy, and decision-making proven right in 2018. Allen's cannon meant that his passes were aimed the deepest last season, averaging 11.0 air yards per pass. And yet, his average completion was caught just 6.5 yards down the field. That 4.6-yard differential (rounding!) wasn't just the largest in the league; it was the largest in the league by a yard and a half. Allen had a ton of pretty arcing deep balls that didn't come within 3 yards of a receiver. A league-worst 22.0 percent of his passes were marked either as over or underthrown, and that doesn't include bullets thrown without touch. Those aren't receiver problems; those are accuracy problems.

Allen also did not handle pressure well, at all. The Bills had a -45.4% offensive DVOA when Allen was pressured, and that includes all of those positive-value scrambles he was so good at. When throwing the ball out of the pocket—so no scrambles and no sacks, just plays when Allen actually got the ball off—the team's DVOA dropped to -55.4%, third-worst in the league. When 27.4 percent of your passes come outside the pocket, the most in the league, that's terrible. Allen's accuracy tanks when he's asked to throw while moving; when he gets off-platform, his passes end up sprayed all over the field. He struggles to identify open receivers or recognize coverages and does not do well when asked to process information quickly. He averaged 3.22 seconds from snap to throw according to NFL Next Gen Stats—not just the slowest in the league, but the slowest since Tim Tebow in 2011. That figure doesn't include sacks, but a decent chunk of those throws were due to Allen holding the ball rather than checking down or going to a hot route. He holds on to the ball too long, passing up what the defense gives him in the hopes of hitting the home run. And those home-run balls don't come often enough to make it worthwhile; Allen's DVOA on deep passes was a league-worst -9.1%. To put that into context, the league DVOA for deep passes was 51.1%.

Allen isn't a hopeless cause at this point, but there are so many negative things he has to overcome for the Bills to be successful. Beane compares Allen's 2018 to Cam Newton's rookie year, noting that Newton ran more as a rookie as he got comfortable with the NFL game. That comparison doesn't really work when you go past the surface level, however—Newton was a much better passer as a rookie than Allen was. The comparison is based on the fact that both Newton and Allen ran, but a much higher chunk of Newton's runs have always been designed plays rather than scrambles. Newton wasn't reading the field, panicking, and taking off, even as a rookie; only 40 percent of his runs were listed as scrambles in his first season. Instead, Bills fans looking for hope in Allen's arm should look at Matthew Stafford, another big-armed rookie who struggled terribly with accuracy, injuries, and decision-making as a rookie before his team invested heavily in the offense around him. To misquote *Football Outsiders Almanac 2010*, "While [Allen's] rookie season does not end all hope that he can develop into a quality quarterback, another poor season will just about put the nail in the coffin."

The fate of the franchise is hinging on whether or not Allen can make those leaps and bounds in Year 2. Last year, the offense was bailed out somewhat by a fantastic defense, second only to Chicago in DVOA. The problem there is that defense is significantly less consistent from year-to-year than offense, so even adding a tremendous talent like Ed Oliver is unlikely to help Buffalo reproduce their success from last year.

Our projections hit Buffalo's defense hard—probably a little too hard, honestly. Even with some regression towards their previous performance (which ranked 15th in 2017), it's hard to believe the Bills will fall all the way to being a below-average unit in 2019. Oliver falling to the ninth pick is a great boon for Buffalo, Tremaine Edmunds will be a year older and a year more experienced, and the Bills added a couple of interesting corners in free agency in E.J. Gaines and Kevin Johnson. However, teams with a -10.0% defensive DVOA or better get worse by an average of 9.5% the year after, and there's no particular reason to believe Buffalo will be somehow immune to this.

If the defense does slip up—even just to the point where they're just good and not great—that just puts more pressure on the offense. The Tennessee and Minnesota wins, to pick two, were sparked by excellent defensive performances overcoming lackluster-at-best offensive days. Take that defense down a notch, and you're probably chalking up a couple more Ls. There's really nowhere for the Bills' defense to go *but* down, and the offense has to find a way to pull more of its own weight in 2019.

It feels reductive to say that everything depends on Allen's development, but that's the basket into which the Bills have decided to put all their eggs. A quarterback with the potential of developing into a solid NFL starter should be able to take these upgrades the Bills have given him and produce a significantly better season. He doesn't need to become an All-Pro overnight, but he needs to take that next step forward that will reassure fans—and management, for that matter—that their faith in Allen, in spite of his college film and the statistical evidence, was well-placed. If Allen can make that sort of second-year jump that we've seen people like Stafford or Donovan McNabb make, getting into sniffing range of a positive passing DVOA, the Bills could be a .500 team this season, possibly even making noise in the playoff race. We are highly dubious, however. Buffalo's massive offensive revamp is built on a shaky foundation, and while this offense shouldn't threaten to be one of the worst in Bills history yet again, it's not going to be good enough to get them out of double-digit losses.

Bryan Knowles

2018 Bills Stats by Week

Wk	vs.	W-L	PF	PA	YDF	YDA	TO	Total	Off	Def	ST
1	at BAL	L	3	47	153	369	-1	-119%	-84%	26%	-9%
2	LAC	L	20	31	293	349	-2	-36%	-19%	9%	-8%
3	at MIN	W	27	6	292	292	+3	25%	-22%	-33%	14%
4	at GB	L	0	22	145	423	-1	-85%	-109%	-24%	0%
5	TEN	W	13	12	223	221	+2	1%	-32%	-44%	-12%
6	at HOU	L	13	20	229	216	0	1%	-57%	-76%	-18%
7	at IND	L	5	37	303	376	-5	-87%	-55%	36%	3%
8	NE	L	6	25	333	387	-2	-17%	-34%	-10%	8%
9	CHI	L	9	41	264	190	-3	-49%	-50%	-2%	-1%
10	at NYJ	W	41	10	451	199	+2	62%	22%	-36%	3%
11	BYE										
12	JAX	W	24	21	327	333	+2	19%	30%	0%	-10%
13	at MIA	L	17	21	415	175	-2	-17%	-17%	-7%	-8%
14	NYJ	L	23	27	368	248	-1	-45%	-21%	-2%	-26%
15	DET	W	14	13	312	313	0	-2%	6%	6%	-3%
16	at NE	L	12	24	289	390	0	-13%	-33%	-27%	-7%
17	MIA	W	42	17	381	225	+3	50%	9%	-48%	-8%

Trends and Splits

	Offense	Rank	Defense	Rank
Total DVOA	-27.5%	31	-14.5%	2
Unadjusted VOA	-27.8%	31	-12.5%	2
Weighted Trend	-16.6%	29	-16.4%	2
Variance	13.6%	31	8.4%	32
Average Opponent	-2.1%	8	-1.7%	20
Passing	-36.0%	31	-18.4%	2
Rushing	-11.4%	23	-10.2%	14
First Down	-19.8%	28	-11.7%	4
Second Down	-28.9%	31	-11.8%	4
Third Down	-41.3%	31	-23.4%	4
First Half	-22.2%	31	-7.7%	4
Second Half	-32.5%	31	-21.9%	2
Red Zone	-22.2%	29	26.2%	31
Late and Close	-21.7%	28	-28.8%	2

Five-Year Performance

Year	W-L	Pyth W	Est W	PF	PA	TO	Total	Rk	Off	Rk	Def	Rk	ST	Rk	Off AGL	Rk	Def AGL	Rk	Off Age	Rk	Def Age	Rk	ST Age	Rk
2014	9-7	9.6	9.0	343	289	+7	10.5%	9	-11.2%	26	-15.5%	2	6.2%	4	27.2	14	31.9	11	26.6	21	26.1	26	26.1	15
2015	8-8	8.5	8.8	379	359	+6	2.7%	12	9.8%	9	8.6%	24	1.5%	12	37.2	19	43.3	28	26.2	21	26.4	21	26.5	9
2016	7-9	8.5	7.4	399	378	+6	1.0%	17	10.7%	10	7.8%	27	-1.9%	22	37.0	19	60.8	28	26.6	19	27.2	6	27.3	1
2017	9-7	6.3	6.8	302	359	+9	-9.8%	21	-11.1%	26	1.6%	15	2.9%	10	29.0	13	15.5	8	27.8	2	26.8	11	27.5	1
2018	6-10	5.0	6.5	269	374	-5	-18.2%	28	-27.5%	31	-14.5%	2	-5.1%	32	16.8	3	17.0	6	26.2	24	26.6	10	27.1	2

2018 Performance Based on Most Common Personnel Groups

BUF Offense					BUF Offense vs. Opponents					BUF Defense					BUF Defense vs. Opponents			
Pers	Freq	Yds	DVOA	Run%	Pers	Freq	Yds	DVOA	Run%	Pers	Freq	Yds	DVOA	Pers	Freq	Yds	DVOA
11	70%	5.1	-27.3%	31%	Base	25%	5.3	-3.3%	61%	Base	21%	4.5	-14.2%	11	59%	5.3	-12.4%
12	11%	5.2	-21.3%	55%	Nickel	65%	4.9	-22.2%	36%	Nickel	77%	5.4	-14.0%	12	17%	5.2	-22.9%
21	10%	4.8	-0.3%	54%	Dime+	13%	4.5	-88.5%	11%	Dime+	1%	2.0	-138.2%	21	10%	5.5	-18.9%
621	2%	2.6	-5.4%	100%	Goal Line	1%	2.6	14.5%	91%	Goal Line	1%	-0.2	-2.0%	22	4%	5.0	10.9%
20	1%	5.2	-13.7%	54%	Big	1%	1.8	-78.3%	82%					13	3%	4.7	-11.5%

Strategic Tendencies

Run/Pass		Rk	Formation		Rk	Pass Rush		Rk	Secondary		Rk	Strategy		Rk
Runs, first half	42%	6	Form: Single Back	75%	22	Rush 3	5.8%	18	4 DB	21%	20	Play action	24%	15
Runs, first down	47%	18	Form: Empty Back	8%	16	Rush 4	73.6%	12	5 DB	77%	4	Avg Box (Off)	6.25	14
Runs, second-long	39%	4	Pers: 3+ WR	72%	11	Rush 5	15.9%	21	6+ DB	1%	29	Avg Box (Def)	6.29	11
Runs, power sit.	73%	2	Pers: 2+ TE/6+ OL	16%	29	Rush 6+	4.5%	21	CB by Sides	69%	21	Offensive Pace	31.09	15
Runs, behind 2H	30%	7	Pers: 6+ OL	5%	5	Int DL Sacks	13.9%	30	S/CB Cover Ratio	32%	6	Defensive Pace	30.74	9
Pass, ahead 2H	41%	28	Shotgun/Pistol	57%	24	Second Level Sacks	44.4%	2	DB Blitz	10%	11	Go for it on 4th	1.62	9

Buffalo was the team least likely to throw passes in the "short middle" of the field (13 percent of targets), and the worst offense in the league on these passes (-29.1% DVOA). The Bills also had the worst DVOA in the league on passes to the deep middle (-73.3% DVOA). ● Josh Allen faced defensive back blitzes on 14.2 percent of passes, second only to Ryan Tannehill, but his -23.9% DVOA on these plays wasn't much worse than the league average of -12.8%. ● Buffalo's No. 2 ranking in "second-level sacks" is primarily based on categorizing Lorenzo Alexander as an off-ball linebacker; if we categorize him as an edge rusher, the Bills are at a much lower 26 percent (11th). ● The Bills led the league with -49.5% DVOA and allowed just 3.6 yards per pass on wide receiver screens. They also were excellent against running back screens, with -30.8% DVOA and 4.6 yards per pass. ● Buffalo's defense led the league in DVOA on passes to the short middle, the only defense to allow a negative DVOA in this area. ● The Bills had the league's second-best defense when there was no pass pressure, trailing only Baltimore by both net yards per pass (7.0, tied with Chicago) and DVOA (12.9%).

Passing

Player	DYAR	DVOA	Plays	NtYds	Avg	YAC	C%	TD	Int
J.Allen	-534	-35.9%	350	1840	5.3	5.6	53.0%	10	11
N.Peterman*	-380	-85.1%	88	252	2.9	4.2	55.0%	1	7
D.Anderson	-208	-56.9%	75	438	5.8	4.5	60.0%	0	4
M.Barkley	109	56.0%	26	224	8.6	5.1	60.0%	2	0

Rushing

Player	DYAR	DVOA	Plays	Yds	Avg	TD	Fum	Suc
L.McCoy	-109	-26.2%	161	514	3.2	3	0	37%
C.Ivory*	-27	-14.3%	115	385	3.3	1	1	44%
J.Allen	192	33.3%	81	638	7.9	8	3	--
M.Murphy	36	10.6%	52	250	4.8	0	0	42%
K.Ford	-6	-15.0%	21	79	3.8	0	0	43%
I.McKenzie	57	64.3%	10	66	6.6	2	0	--
N.Peterman*	18	19.3%	10	50	5.0	1	0	--
F.Gore	86	5.7%	156	722	4.6	0	1	50%
T.J.Yeldon	-17	-12.5%	104	414	4.0	1	1	48%

Receiving

Player	DYAR	DVOA	Plays	Ctch	Yds	Y/C	YAC	TD	C%
Z.Jones	-22	-15.5%	102	56	652	11.6	2.5	7	55%
K.Benjamin*	-68	-27.1%	62	23	354	15.4	2.7	1	37%
R.Foster	135	26.2%	44	27	541	20.0	6.2	3	61%
I.McKenzie	-25	-23.8%	30	18	179	9.9	4.2	0	60%
A.Holmes*	1	-11.8%	23	12	157	13.1	3.5	0	52%
D.Thompson*	-23	-39.9%	10	3	37	12.3	1.3	0	30%
T.Pryor*	-35	-71.0%	8	2	17	8.5	0.5	0	25%
R.McCloud	-6	-25.8%	6	5	36	7.2	5.6	0	83%
J.Brown	4	-12.2%	97	42	717	17.1	3.8	5	43%
C.Beasley	100	2.1%	87	65	672	10.3	3.3	3	75%
A.Roberts	-29	-34.3%	18	10	79	7.9	1.7	1	56%
C.Clay*	-70	-38.3%	36	21	197	9.4	4.0	0	58%
J.Croom	-27	-19.5%	35	22	259	11.8	6.2	1	63%
L.Thomas*	-37	-43.5%	17	12	77	6.4	2.8	0	71%
L.Smith	31	25.5%	11	10	73	7.3	5.5	3	91%
T.Kroft	-2	-11.7%	6	4	36	9.0	4.3	0	67%
L.McCoy	-26	-24.5%	46	34	238	7.0	8.5	0	74%
C.Ivory*	47	31.3%	21	13	205	15.8	15.7	0	62%
M.Murphy	-76	-82.6%	19	11	26	2.4	3.4	0	58%
T.J.Yeldon	76	3.0%	79	56	482	8.6	8.0	4	71%
F.Gore	49	35.4%	16	12	124	10.3	9.6	1	75%

Offensive Line

Player	Pos	Age	GS	Snaps	Pen	Sk	Pass	Run	Player	Pos	Age	GS	Snaps	Pen	Sk	Pass	Run
Dion Dawkins	LT	25	16/16	1057	15	7.5	19	5	Quinton Spain	LG	28	15/15	856	6	0.0	2	4
Jordan Mills*	RT	29	16/16	1011	9	4.0	16	2	Spencer Long	C/LG	29	13/13	805	5	2.5	5	7
John Miller*	RG	26	15/15	883	4	0.5	6	4	Mitch Morse	C	27	11/11	678	4	0.0	0	1
Russell Bodine	C	27	11/10	588	3	0.5	2	2	Ty Nsekhe	LT/LG	34	14/5	403	7	1.0	6	1
Vladimir Ducasse	LG	32	10/9	563	5	1.0	4	1	LaAdrian Waddle	RT	28	16/3	342	2	2.0	5	1
Ryan Groy*	C	29	15/6	528	1	1.0	4	0	Jon Feliciano	LG	27	13/4	227	4	1.5	3	2
Wyatt Teller	LG	25	8/7	475	5	0.0	4	3									

Year	Yards	ALY	Rank	Power	Rank	Stuff	Rank	2nd Lev	Rank	Open Field	Rank	Sacks	ASR	Rank	Press	Rank	F-Start	Cont.
2016	5.12	4.16	16	60%	20	22%	22	1.41	1	1.32	2	46	9.3%	31	31.8%	30	6	32
2017	3.96	3.67	27	61%	22	26%	27	1.17	15	0.90	8	47	9.3%	31	32.7%	23	10	34
2018	3.53	3.89	30	68%	14	21%	23	0.92	32	0.43	30	41	8.0%	23	35.3%	28	20	32
2018 ALY by direction:			Left End: 2.48 (31)			Left Tackle: 3.13 (31)			Mid/Guard: 4.24 (22)			Right Tackle: 3.51 (28)			Right End: 3.55 (27)		

Nearly 2,500 snaps walked out the door when Jordan Mills, John Miller, and Ryan Groy left town. These aren't precisely irreplaceable players, though it does mean this unit is going to look very different going forward. As you can tell from the number of italicized players on that table, the Bills threw a lot of darts at the offensive line in free agency. ✒ Dion Dawkins is the most likely returning starter. He'll be looking for a rebound season after leading Buffalo in sacks allowed, blown blocks, and penalties in 2018. The latter half of his rookie season was very strong, so the Bills are hoping he bounces back in 2019. ✒ Mitch Morse, fresh in from Kansas City, is the other starter with a defined position. Morse led all interior linemen with 339 snaps per blown block in 2018. The one issue Morse has is his health, as he has missed 14 games over the past two seasons. ✒ Second-round pick Cody Ford (Oklahoma) is penciled in as the starting right tackle, though he could also move inside to guard if necessary. His combination of size, athleticism, and overall fundamentals is among the top of the class, but he only had 21 starts in college and is a little raw. ✒ Assuming Ford plays at tackle, two of Quinton Spain, Joe Feliciano, Spencer Long, and Vlad Ducasse will start at the two guard positions. There are a lot of moving parts here, but Spain and Long would be the favorites with Feliciano providing valuable depth at all five positions. Ducasse was bad enough last season that his roster spot is in jeopardy. ✒ Ty Nsekhe, coming over from Washington, was penciled in at right tackle before the draft. The Ford pick makes it more likely Nsekhe serves as depth, but it gives Buffalo a solid option in case their other guards don't work out.

Defensive Front

Defensive Line	Age	Pos	G	Snaps	Plays	TmPct	Rk	Stop	Dfts	BTkl	Runs	St%	Rk	RuYd	Rk	Sack	Hit	Hur	Dsrpt
					Overall							vs. Run				Pass Rush			
Kyle Williams	36	DT	16	656	35	4.4%	50	25	16	3	23	70%	66	1.7	19	5.0	8	20	1
Star Lotulelei	30	DT	16	475	18	2.3%	81	11	5	2	16	63%	79	1.9	23	0.0	0	6	1
Jordan Phillips	27	DT	16	392	28	3.5%	--	24	8	4	19	89%	--	0.9	--	1.0	2	9	4
Harrison Phillips	23	DT	16	389	33	4.2%	--	24	4	1	32	75%	--	3.0	--	0.0	3	2	0

Edge Rushers	Age	Pos	G	Snaps	Plays	TmPct	Rk	Stop	Dfts	BTkl	Runs	St%	Rk	RuYd	Rk	Sack	Hit	Hur	Dsrpt
					Overall							vs. Run				Pass Rush			
Jerry Hughes	31	DE	16	668	37	4.7%	52	31	23	9	24	83%	18	1.3	11	7.0	13	39	2
Shaq Lawson	25	DE	14	440	35	5.0%	41	27	12	1	24	75%	44	1.7	25	4.0	8	18	5
Trent Murphy	29	DE	13	440	24	3.7%	71	17	11	6	14	57%	81	3.8	87	4.0	4	13	0
Eddie Yarbrough	26	DE	14	307	28	4.0%	--	22	7	2	24	83%	--	1.5	--	0.0	1	2	0

Linebackers	Age	Pos	G	Snaps	Plays	TmPct	Rk	Stop	Dfts	BTkl	Runs	St%	Rk	RuYd	Rk	Sack	Hit	Hur	Tgts	Suc%	Rk	AdjYd	Rk	PD	Int
					Overall							vs. Run				Pass Rush				vs. Pass					
Tremaine Edmunds	21	MLB	15	926	132	17.8%	7	65	23	18	60	55%	57	3.6	29	2.0	5	12.5	57	35%	73	7.5	59	12	2
Matt Milano	25	OLB	13	741	85	13.2%	37	51	24	18	47	68%	14	2.3	2	1.0	2	8	30	73%	3	3.5	3	7	3
Lorenzo Alexander	36	OLB	16	629	78	9.8%	57	47	20	4	39	62%	32	3.6	33	6.5	4	26.5	21	48%	46	4.8	10	9	2

Year	Yards	ALY	Rank	Power	Rank	Stuff	Rank	2nd Level	Rank	Open Field	Rank	Sacks	ASR	Rank	Press	Rank
2016	4.50	4.41	22	57%	6	19%	16	1.30	28	0.88	25	39	7.1%	7	29.0%	9
2017	4.48	4.18	21	76%	28	22%	10	1.36	32	1.00	29	27	5.4%	28	27.0%	31
2018	4.14	4.15	10	62%	9	26%	1	1.33	24	0.76	13	36	6.9%	19	33.3%	4

2018 ALY by direction:	Left End: 4.94 (20)	Left Tackle: 4.40 (16)	Mid/Guard: 4.07 (8)	Right Tackle: 5.05 (28)	Right End: 2.48 (3)

The big question about first-round pick Ed Oliver is what position he'll eventually settle into. No one questions his athletic ability, quickness, or explosiveness, but he measured up at just 6-foot-2, 287 pounds at the combine. That's very light for an interior defensive lineman, though not unheard of—Aaron Donald's only 280, and he has turned out alright. Buffalo won't use Oliver right on the nose like Houston did; he'll start as the 3-technique gap-shooting replacement for Kyle Williams. When Buffalo finds the right position for him, he's going to be a beast. 🖊 Star Lotulelei was pushed around a bit in his first season in Buffalo. While he ranked 23rd among interior linemen in run yards allowed per play at 1.9, his 63 percent stop rate was abysmal. If he struggles again in 2019, you might see Harrison Phillips taking more of his snaps. 🖊 The Bills are counting on a big rebound from Trent Murphy. He missed all of 2017 with a torn ACL and MCL and was fairly clearly not at full strength last season. He had nine sacks, 26 quarterback knockdowns, and 23 quarterback hurries the last time he was fully healthy. 🖊 Jerry Hughes' 38.5 quarterback hurries tied for ninth-most in the league last year, a career high. He may not have hit double-digit sacks since 2014, but he remains one of the most consistent pass-rushers in football. Only Hughes and Von Miller have recorded at least 30 hurries in each of the last five seasons. 🖊 2018 was very much a learning season for Tremaine Edmunds—something to be expected for someone who didn't turn 20 until his first OTAs. The game seemed to slow down for him some after he returned from his midseason concussion, so he'll look to take that momentum into Year 2. 🖊 Edmunds and Matt Milano each had 18 broken tackles, tied for seventh-most in the league. All in all, the Bills finished 26th on defense with 129 broken tackles and had the highest rate of plays with at least one broken tackle (13.1 percent of plays). 🖊 Lorenzo Alexander says that 2019 will be his last year in the NFL. The exceptionally versatile linebacker was one of only two players in the 20/20/20 club last season—20 quarterback hurries, 20 run stops, and 20 targets in pass coverage. (The other? Kyle Van Noy from the rival Patriots.) 🖊 Fifth-round linebacker Vosean Joseph (Florida) is inconsistently explosive, or explosively inconsistent, take your pick. He flies around with tremendous range, disrupting and blowing up plays all over the field. He's also often way out of position, lining up wrong and freestyling rather than sticking to his assignments. He's a great Day-3 flier; you can teach someone to overcome mental mistakes. You can't teach Joseph's speed and range.

Defensive Secondary

Secondary	Age	Pos	G	Snaps	Plays	Overall TmPct	Rk	Stop	Dfts	BTkl	vs. Run Runs	St%	Rk	RuYd	Rk	vs. Pass Tgts	Tgt%	Rk	Dist	Suc%	Rk	AdjYd	Rk	PD	Int
Jordan Poyer	28	FS	16	1009	101	12.7%	10	36	18	12	52	42%	37	6.6	30	24	6.4%	16	11.4	46%	50	10.1	65	6	4
Tre'Davious White	24	CB	16	960	62	7.8%	50	21	8	8	19	32%	63	5.7	28	65	18.2%	34	12.0	58%	15	5.9	9	8	2
Micah Hyde	29	SS	15	881	62	8.3%	52	24	9	9	34	35%	51	10.3	67	27	8.2%	25	8.9	52%	33	6.6	21	5	2
Rafael Bush	32	SS	15	452	44	5.9%	70	17	6	8	13	69%	2	5.0	11	28	16.7%	75	6.6	21%	75	8.7	55	0	0
Levi Wallace	24	CB	7	415	40	11.5%	--	17	5	8	25	36%	--	8.0	--	20	13.0%	--	10.5	65%	--	4.6	--	3	0
Taron Johnson	23	CB	11	405	44	8.1%	--	22	9	7	17	47%	--	5.0	--	24	15.9%	--	8.4	67%	--	3.0	--	3	1

Year	Pass D Rank	vs. #1 WR	Rk	vs. #2 WR	Rk	vs. Other WR	Rk	WR Wide	Rk	WR Slot	Rk	vs. TE	Rk	vs. RB	Rk
2016	21	3.1%	19	-0.4%	16	12.0%	25	-1.4%	17	11.8%	21	-5.9%	11	7.9%	21
2017	12	-0.1%	14	-29.7%	3	-28.0%	1	-10.0%	11	-22.7%	3	-3.9%	13	5.9%	20
2018	2	-11.2%	7	14.9%	24	-33.0%	2	-15.1%	6	-7.4%	8	-40.0%	2	-10.2%	9

Tre'Davious White improved upon his fantastic rookie season, raising his success rate from 54 percent to 58 percent and lowering his YAC allowed from 4.2 in 2017 to 2.9 last season. Interestingly, White's YAC and success rate were higher in the first half of the season, when he was shadowing opponents' top receivers. His stats all took a hit when he went back to playing mostly on the left starting in Week 10. ● The opposite corner position is anything but settled. Levi Wallace took over the job by the end of 2018 and played well in a limited sample size, but eight broken tackles in seven games is a bit concerning. He'll be competing with the returning E.J. Gaines, who struggled with injuries last year in Cleveland, and Kevin Johnson, who has only managed to appear in 19 games over the past three years. Wallace may win the job just by being the only one who can find the field. ● Micah Hyde's coverage success rate dropped from 60 percent to 52 percent from 2017 to 2018, but that's mostly because he didn't get any easy reps. Hyde faced barely 60 percent of the targets he saw two years ago, as opposing quarterbacks learned to mostly avoid him in coverage. ● Hyde and Jordan Poyer count a combined $10.9 million against the cap, which is a hell of a bargain for two players of their caliber. There are seven safeties in the league who make more than Hyde and Poyer combined. ● If there's a weak link in the secondary, it's nickel safety/corner Rafael Bush, who finished next-to-last in success rate among safeties last season with a 23 percent broken tackle rate. Ideally, 2018 fourth-round pick Taron Johnson will be healthier in 2019 and take snaps away from Bush.

Special Teams

Year	DVOA	Rank	FG/XP	Rank	Net Kick	Rank	Kick Ret	Rank	Net Punt	Rank	Punt Ret	Rank	Hidden	Rank
2016	-1.9%	22	-7.7	28	-2.6	21	-3.7	25	-2.9	21	7.6	5	-4.9	23
2017	2.9%	10	11.5	4	2.0	15	-4.9	29	4.3	11	1.8	11	-9.0	29
2018	-5.1%	32	-5.4	26	-1.6	25	-2.3	21	-9.1	27	-7.3	31	-5.2	22

Buffalo's special teams collapsed last season, finishing dead last in the league. They had negative value in all five major aspects of special teams, although they certainly couldn't match the 2000 Bills special teams, the worst ever measured in Football Outsiders history (-15.4% DVOA). ● Stephen Hauschka is coming off the worst season of his career, dropping below 80 percent in field goal percentage for the first time. He was playing through a hip injury for part of 2018, however, and the Bills' offensive struggles meant he only had 11 attempts from inside 40 yards. He's a bounce-back candidate. ● Of the three punters Buffalo employed last year, Corey Bojorquez provided the most negative value, being responsible for -4.3 of Buffalo's -9.1 points. He was still better on a per-punt basis than Colton Schmidt, but there's no reason to think he'll have much of a leg-up on Cory Carter in the punting competition. ● Isaiah McKenzie had negative value on both punt and kickoff returns. He was outperformed by Micah Hyde on punts and Marcus Murphy on kickoffs by significant margins. ● There's hope on the horizon with the arrival of ex-Jet Andre Roberts, who led the league in both kickoff and punt return value a year ago, finishing with +24.5 points of combined field-position value. Buyer beware, however—Roberts had a negative value in both kickoff and punt returns in 2017, and he was in the red on kickoffs in 2016 as well.

Carolina Panthers

2018 record: 7-9	**Total DVOA:** 0.5% (14th)	**2019 Mean Projection:** 8.1 wins	**On the Clock (0-4):** 10%
Pythagorean Wins: 7.8 (16th)	**Offense:** 6.0% (11th)	**Postseason Odds:** 36.5%	**Mediocrity (5-7):** 32%
Snap-Weighted Age: 27.6 (2nd)	**Defense:** 5.4% (22nd)	**Super Bowl Odds:** 5.0%	**Playoff Contender (8-10):** 39%
Average Opponent: -0.5% (17th)	**Special Teams:** -0.2% (18th)	**Proj. Avg. Opponent:** 0.8% (14th)	**Super Bowl Contender (11+):** 19%

2018: The quarterback's health defines the season.

2019: Can they keep the quarterback's health from defining the season again?

November 4, 2018. The 6-2 Carolina Panthers have just blown out the Buccaneers with another astonishing display of offensive football. Norv Turner is in the Coordinator of the Year conversation: his dynamic fusion of college concepts into his traditional offense has resulted in 99 points across the past nine quarters, including a 21-point fourth quarter on the road against the defending champion Eagles and 36 points against a Ravens defense that would finish No. 3 in DVOA. Third in total DVOA thanks largely to that top-five offense, the Panthers are widely considered a serious contender for the NFC South title, and potentially even for a playoff bye if they can overtake the division-leading Saints.

Four days later, the Panthers lose 52-21 in Pittsburgh. They do not win another game until Week 17, and even that comes only against a Saints team resting its starters with home-field advantage already sewn up. From 6-2 and NFC contention to 7-9 and nowhere close, the team's fortunes flip almost overnight.

The easy explanation for the reversal is Cam Newton's declining health. That Week 10 Thursday night road trip to Pittsburgh shortened Newton's recovery period between games, vital for the quarterback as he nursed a lingering shoulder issue that had first appeared on the injury report after the Eagles game. Newton never looked the same after the blowout loss, and the powder keg offense became more of a powder puff. After four straight weeks above 29.0% DVOA, the Panthers pass offense would not reach that level once between Week 9 and Kyle Allen's Week 17 start against the Saints backups. Newton's arm strength, already in question after Taylor Heinicke had been put in for a Hail Mary attempt against the Ravens, became a glaring problem: his DVOA on deep passes declined precipitously, from 42.3% in Weeks 1-9 to -79.5% from Week 10 to Week 15, and he did not complete a single pass over 25 air yards in the final six games of his season (0-for-7, one interception). His overall passing DVOA declined from 13.2% in Weeks 1-9 to -18.7% in Weeks 10-15; to put that in perspective, it was almost exactly the difference in passing efficiency between Andrew Luck and Blake Bortles. Newton was finally deactivated for the final two games of the season, had shoulder surgery in January, and the team hopes to have him back at full health for 2019.

Hoping for *full* health might prove optimistic. At the time of writing, Newton is still not throwing in team workout drills, and there is a faint but lingering whiff of concern that he might not be ready to play at the start of next season. Speaking to ESPN's David Newton[1] in January, owner David Tepper even raised the prospect of keeping Newton out for the full 2019 season, as the Colts did with Andrew Luck in 2017. The selection of Will Grier (West Virginia) in the third round of April's draft fits the contingency plan Tepper described for that eventuality. Though it is both an extreme and unlikely scenario—Newton has been throwing in individual drills—the mere fact that Tepper voiced the possibility is concerning. Newton's health is paramount: nobody is credibly suggesting that Grier or Kyle Allen is leading this team to the playoffs in Newton's absence.

That much, at least, the front office appears finally to understand. The major offseason moves on offense have demonstrated the importance they place on their quarterback's health. After long-time starting center Ryan Kalil retired, the team moved quickly to sign Broncos starter Matt Paradis to a three-year, $27-million contract. Paradis was a sixth-round pick in 2014 who started 60 straight games, (including the Super Bowl victory over his new team) from 2015 until a fractured ankle ended his 2018 season. Though he is likely to be a downgrade from peak Kalil, Kalil himself had not been at that level since injuries robbed him of most of the 2016 and 2017 seasons. Paradis should be better than 2018 Kalil, assuming he returns from his ankle fracture at something close to full strength. Trai Turner and former Packers (and Toronto Argonauts) guard Greg Van Roten—a 16-game starter last season following the departure of Andrew Norwell—both return alongside Paradis, which should give the Panthers a solid interior line quite capable of contributing a player or two to the Pro Bowl.

On the outside, the team invested significant resources in improving the tackle positions that have long been the weakest spots on the offense. At left tackle, they released Kalil's brother Matt—a big-money signing from 2017 who never came close to justifying his contract—and spent a second-round pick on his replacement, second-team All-American

---

1 https://es.pn/2RmLLFW

2019 Panthers Schedule

Week	Opp.	Week	Opp.	Week	Opp.
1	LAR	7	BYE	13	WAS
2	TB (Thu.)	8	at SF	14	at ATL
3	at ARI	9	TEN	15	SEA
4	at HOU	10	at GB	16	at IND
5	JAX	11	ATL	17	NO
6	at TB (U.K.)	12	at NO		

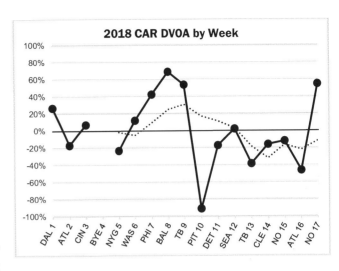

tackle Greg Little (Ole Miss). On the right, they re-signed one of the few successful tackles they have employed this decade, 2015 fifth-round pick Daryl Williams, to a one-year, $7-million contract. Williams missed the entire 2018 season after dislocating his kneecap and tearing his MCL during training camp, but he started 26 games at right tackle and performed well during 2016 and 2017. Taylor Moton, a 2017 second-round pick who started all 16 games in 2018 primarily as Williams' replacement, remains in contention at both ends of the line, with the winners of those position battles theoretically giving the Panthers their strongest pair of tackles since Jordan Gross and Byron Bell in 2013. Some offseason projections have all three prospective tackles starting, with Little and Moton as the tackles and Williams moving to left guard, but Van Roten will certainly have something to say about that. Whatever the combination, a line that ranked No. 11 in adjusted line yards and blocked for the No. 2 DVOA rushing offense has, in theory, improved significantly for both the short and long term this offseason.

Whether that will translate to a reduction in hits on Newton is another matter. Most research on the subject demonstrates quite conclusively that sacks and quarterback hits are primarily dependent on the quarterback, not the offensive line. Newton has proven willing—perhaps too willing—to absorb blows both as a runner and as a passer, and the coaching staff will need to rein in that tendency if they are truly focused on keeping him as healthy as possible. This is perhaps a more positive area in which they could look to the example of Luck: with a change of scheme, investment in the line, and a focus on Luck exposing himself to fewer hits, 2018 was both Luck's healthiest season since 2014 and the most efficient year of his career. In his first campaign under the tutelage of the adroit Norv Turner, an ailing Newton finished with his second-fewest rushing yards per game, his fewest touchdowns, and his third-fewest attempts. He also had the lowest sack rate of his career. Adding (or removing) further schematic elements to emphasize keeping the quarterback upright should not be too great a challenge for Turner and his staff.

If they can get their quarterback healthy and keep him that way, last season provides compelling evidence that the results could be spectacular. As mentioned above, before the shoulder injury sapped him of his arm strength, Newton's 13.2% passing DVOA would have been comfortably the best of his career. His previous best, 7.6%, was enough for him to win the league MVP as the Panthers reached the Super Bowl. The four games from Weeks 6-9, in which he averaged 51.2% DVOA,

was the third-best passing stretch of Newton's professional career, comparable to any four-game slice from that MVP campaign. (His best stretch was Weeks 11-14 of 2012, his second season, when he averaged an astounding 64.8% passing DVOA.) When Newton opined before the Week 13 disaster against Tampa Bay that he was playing the best football of his career, he was not without justification—though he was a few weeks removed from the peak of his 2018 performance, and would have the worst two games of his season in the ensuring three weeks. A multitalented group of receivers—and a running back who is comfortable both between the tackles and as a receiver—allowed Turner to craft an exciting offense that could attack all areas of the field in a variety of ways from a wide array of positions, and Newton excelled at the center of that array. The scoring pace from last October may be unsustainable, but between the line changes already covered and the addition of Chris Hogan in place of Devin Funchess, the talent around Newton is better now than it was then. It should not be out of the question for the Panthers to showcase their best offense since Newton's rookie season (2011: 18.2% DVOA, fourth). At the very least, they will hope to end the 2010s with as many finishes inside the DVOA top 10 (currently four) as outside (five).

If NFC South football has taught us anything over this decade, however, it is that a top offense alone carries no guarantees of a successful year. Newton's health was the easy explanation for what ailed the Panthers in November and December of last season, but it was not the *entire* explanation—the Panthers defense dropped off even more than the offense did, both from its 2017 level and from the first half of 2018 to the second half. At midseason, the defense's -2.0% DVOA ranked No. 14. They finished No. 24 in weighted DVOA, and their season-long performance was the second worst of the Ron Rivera era by both overall (5.4%, No. 22) and pass defense (14.8%, No. 24) DVOA. Not since Rivera's first year as Panthers head coach, when he was rebuilding a roster that had gone 2-14 the previous season, have the Panthers posted a positive defensive DVOA (remember, higher DVOA means bad defense). Their -7.0% run defense DVOA sounds good in comparison, but run defense is so much more efficient than pass defense that even this only ranked No. 18, and it was the third-worst mark of Rivera's time in charge. The Panthers defense only had two negative-DVOA games in the entire second half of the year, and one of those was the meaningless final game against Teddy Bridgewater's Saints—in which they still allowed Dwayne Washington to pile up over 100 yards on the ground.

Defensive success in Carolina typically begins with the pressure generated by the front seven, but last season's No. 20 rank by adjusted sack rate was the team's lowest since 2007 (the actual rate was lower in 2011, but because the overall league-wide rate was also lower that year, the 2011 defense ranked No. 16). To make matters worse, their second-best edge rusher, Julius Peppers, retired after the season, and their No. 3 defensive end, Wes Horton, signed with the division-rival Saints. That left only youngsters Bryan Cox Jr. and Efe Obada behind Mario Addison at defensive end. Somehow, a team that had spent five Day 1 or Day 2 picks on defensive linemen in five drafts from 2013 to 2017 was running short at that very position. Restocking that unit was *the* major offseason priority, especially as the team looked to add more variety to their defensive fronts.

Restock it, they certainly did. Given the draft's depth at the position, the team's first pick, No. 16 overall, was always pegged for use on an edge rusher. Still, the staff were particularly delighted to snag Florida State's Brian Burns, an explosive and adaptable pass-rusher who should be at ease on either end of those variable fronts regardless of his specific responsibilities. Burns had the No. 1 SackSEER projection of this year's deep edge rusher class, drawing comparisons to Texans standout Jadeveon Clowney for his athleticism and variety of pass-rush moves. He will probably have to bulk up to be more effective in run support, where his speed and play diagnosis were too often rendered ineffective by his size—but he added 14 pounds for the combine, and a professional diet and training regimen should see to the rest. In the meantime, expect to see him deployed in such a way that his primary skill set matches his primary responsibility: to make opposing quarterbacks uncomfortable.

Another important member of the restocked rotation is former Seahawks first-round pick Bruce Irvin, who joined from the Falcons in free agency as a situational veteran who, like Burns, can be deployed at both linebacker and defensive end. Other front seven changes included the departure of aging off-ball linebacker Thomas Davis, with 2015 first-round pick Shaq Thompson stepping up as a ready-made replacement, and another Day 3 selection at edge rusher in Christian Miller (Alabama). The biggest move was yet to come, as six-time Pro Bowl and three-time All-Pro defensive tackle Gerald McCoy signed in May following his release from Tampa Bay. The addition of McCoy to Dontari Poe, Kawann Short, and Vernon Butler should give the Panthers one of the league's strongest interior defensive line rotations. That should, in turn, benefit Addison, Burns, and Irvin on the edge, and help the Panthers front seven return to its usual dominance.

In a reversal of the team's usual fortunes, this offseason the secondary is the more stable of the defensive units. Since Rivera took charge in 2011, the Panthers have replaced at least half of the starting secondary in six out of seven offseasons. This time, the only expected change is the second safety spot vacated by outgoing veteran Mike Adams. Alas, there is no clear and obvious free safety on the current roster—even Adams himself, who remains unsigned, demonstrated last season that he is no longer suited to the demands of the role. Rashaan Gaulden is currently penciled in as the starter opposite Eric Reid: a 2018 third-round prospect, Gaulden projects more as a slot corner and box safety than the deep safety the Panthers seek. The coaching staff has drawn solid performance from less talented players in the past, but they can ill afford a repeat of last season's bottom-six DVOA against the deep pass. If a veteran upgrade can be found either from the remaining free-agent pool or, as with McCoy, from other teams' cuts later in the offseason, the Panthers should certainly be interested: a superior deep safety would embolden Reid to play closer to the line (and closer to his own strengths) and allow Gaulden to compete for the nickelback/third safety role that appears more suited to his talents. If no such player is available, Reid and Gaulden look set to be the starting safeties, and nickelback will likely be a straight contest between 2015 fifth-round pick Corn Elder and former Buccaneers nickel Javien Elliott. Assuming the front seven does return to form, those options should be adequate, but they could certainly stand to be upgraded for the Panthers to compete with the receiving talent that has become a hallmark of the modern NFC South.

The clearest issue we face in projecting the team's offseason changes is the sheer number of them, and how conditional they are. *If* Newton's shoulder is fully healed. *If* Paradis and Williams have recovered from last season's major injuries. *If* Greg Olsen can have his first healthy season in two years. *If* McCoy is still the player we remember from Tampa Bay; *if* the defensive line, restocked mostly with young draftees and budget veterans, can return to its previous level; *if* the scheme changes work out; and *if* the second safety outperforms the aging Adams. Our projections are lukewarm on Carolina, not because they do not have the talent, but because we do not usually see a team make so many changes to its starting lineup and be immediately successful. The Panthers do not have a strong track record of offensive success—only once in the past five seasons have they finished in the top 10 by DVOA, and their average rank is a bang-average No. 16. Despite the leaguewide passing explosion, Newton has now recorded negative passing DVOA in four of the past five seasons. Subjectively, we believe that the shoulder injury is what prevented him from bucking that trend in 2018; objectively, however impaired he was, it was still Newton who played the November and early-December games, and therefore Newton whose trend was sustained.

The Panthers do have a strong track record on defense, where we do project them to rebound somewhat—but to rebound to slightly above average, where they have spent most of the past four years, not to the top-three level of 2013 and 2015. Last year's midseason fade subsuming both the offense and the defense is an obvious concern, particularly because depth at most positions is no stronger now than it was then. Many of the best players on the defensive line—Addison, Irvin, McCoy, and Short—are on the wrong side of 30, and the backup front seven defenders are a very inexperienced group. The front seven's best player, Luke Kuechly, has a frightening concussion history. It is easy to see where improvement could come, but it is also easy to see why it might not.

To return once more to the realms of the hypothetical: If Turner can get the offense playing like it was last October, and second-year defensive coordinator Eric Washington can return the defense to its usual spot in the vicinity of the top 10, the Panthers could be very, very good in 2019. If the staff fails at either or both of those tasks, the Panthers could easily end the year with their third losing record in four seasons. Tepper was willing to overlook the second half of last season because of Newton's injury, but even that excuse is unlikely to suffice if we witness a repeat in 2019. This offseason has seen a lot of turnover among the playing staff in a bid to avert that possibility; this year's results will determine how much turnover we see among the coaching staff next time around.

Andrew Potter

2018 Panthers Stats by Week

Wk	vs.	W-L	PF	PA	YDF	YDA	TO	Total	Off	Def	ST
1	DAL	W	16	8	293	232	0	26%	10%	-12%	4%
2	at ATL	L	24	31	439	442	0	-17%	4%	26%	5%
3	CIN	W	31	21	377	396	+4	7%	18%	11%	0%
4	BYE										
5	NYG	W	33	31	350	432	+1	-24%	-28%	9%	13%
6	at WAS	L	17	23	350	288	-3	12%	22%	-1%	-11%
7	at PHI	W	21	17	371	342	+1	42%	38%	-7%	-2%
8	BAL	W	36	21	386	325	+3	69%	57%	-10%	2%
9	TB	W	42	28	407	301	+2	54%	36%	-15%	3%
10	at PIT	L	21	52	242	457	-2	-91%	-24%	65%	-2%
11	at DET	L	19	20	387	309	-1	-17%	4%	6%	-16%
12	SEA	L	27	30	476	397	-1	2%	11%	8%	-1%
13	at TB	L	17	24	444	315	-3	-39%	-23%	12%	-4%
14	at CLE	L	20	26	393	348	+1	-16%	9%	27%	2%
15	NO	L	9	12	247	346	0	-12%	-20%	-17%	-9%
16	ATL	L	10	24	436	427	-2	-46%	-39%	16%	9%
17	at NO	W	33	14	374	294	+1	55%	33%	-19%	3%

Trends and Splits

	Offense	Rank	Defense	Rank
Total DVOA	6.0%	11	5.4%	22
Unadjusted VOA	10.7%	9	6.4%	25
Weighted Trend	4.1%	12	5.4%	24
Variance	7.5%	21	4.6%	8
Average Opponent	3.5%	32	3.1%	9
Passing	9.2%	19	14.8%	24
Rushing	12.9%	2	-7.0%	18
First Down	-2.0%	16	-5.0%	9
Second Down	13.0%	6	8.3%	26
Third Down	11.7%	12	23.1%	28
First Half	11.8%	7	3.5%	25
Second Half	0.2%	17	7.4%	24
Red Zone	12.2%	11	17.9%	27
Late and Close	-9.9%	23	1.3%	21

Five-Year Performance

Year	W-L	Pyth W	Est W	PF	PA	TO	Total	Rk	Off	Rk	Def	Rk	ST	Rk	Off AGL	Rk	Def AGL	Rk	Off Age	Rk	Def Age	Rk	ST Age	Rk
2014	7-8-1	7.0	7.4	339	374	+3	-8.5%	24	-4.7%	20	-1.7%	15	-5.5%	30	39.7	25	11.7	1	26.4	26	27.2	8	26.4	6
2015	15-1	12.4	11.1	500	308	+20	26.0%	4	10.1%	8	-18.4%	2	-2.4%	23	28.2	14	22.7	8	27.0	14	28.1	3	26.8	3
2016	6-10	7.1	6.7	369	402	-2	-5.5%	24	-8.4%	25	-5.3%	10	-2.5%	25	36.9	18	19.6	7	27.0	12	26.2	23	26.6	6
2017	11-5	9.0	10.3	363	327	-1	13.0%	9	-0.5%	17	-8.8%	7	4.7%	6	31.9	14	11.0	5	26.3	25	28.4	1	26.6	4
2018	7-9	7.8	7.8	376	382	+1	0.5%	14	6.0%	11	5.4%	22	-0.2%	18	51.3	25	52.5	27	26.7	16	28.9	1	26.6	5

2018 Performance Based on Most Common Personnel Groups

CAR Offense				CAR Offense vs. Opponents					CAR Defense				CAR Defense vs. Opponents			
Pers	Freq	Yds	DVOA	Run%	Pers	Freq	Yds	DVOA	Run%	Pers	Freq	Yds	DVOA	Pers	Freq	Yds	DVOA
11	71%	6.6	13.7%	27%	Base	26%	5.4	-2.6%	56%	Base	39%	6.2	0.6%	12	21%	5.9	-1.8%
12	12%	4.6	-4.1%	56%	Nickel	72%	6.3	16.7%	32%	Nickel	60%	6.3	7.0%	21	7%	5.1	-0.1%
21	6%	6.8	14.0%	63%	Dime+	6%	7.3	-20.2%	8%	Goal Line	1%	1.0	99.5%	13	4%	8.9	51.1%
22	4%	4.8	14.0%	82%	Goal Line	2%	4.2	39.4%	68%					22	3%	7.6	-48.8%
10	2%	3.2	-13.8%	21%										10	3%	4.9	-33.1%
13	2%	5.1	7.1%	61%										01	2%	7.4	46.3%
620	2%	4.0	45.6%	71%										612	1%	4.1	-61.5%

Strategic Tendencies

Run/Pass		Rk	Formation		Rk	Pass Rush		Rk	Secondary		Rk	Strategy		Rk
Runs, first half	42%	4	Form: Single Back	73%	28	Rush 3	2.5%	29	4 DB	39%	4	Play action	29%	5
Runs, first down	44%	23	Form: Empty Back	9%	14	Rush 4	65.2%	20	5 DB	60%	19	Avg Box (Off)	6.15	21
Runs, second-long	28%	21	Pers: 3+ WR	73%	9	Rush 5	26.2%	5	6+ DB	0%	32	Avg Box (Def)	6.32	9
Runs, power sit.	61%	13	Pers: 2+ TE/6+ OL	19%	25	Rush 6+	5.5%	15	CB by Sides	57%	29	Offensive Pace	32.30	26
Runs, behind 2H	20%	27	Pers: 6+ OL	2%	15	Int DL Sacks	17.1%	27	S/CB Cover Ratio	22%	27	Defensive Pace	31.94	28
Pass, ahead 2H	51%	9	Shotgun/Pistol	77%	6	Second Level Sacks	30.0%	6	DB Blitz	12%	8	Go for it on 4th	1.91	6

Carolina's use of three-wide sets went up significantly, from 51 percent (27th) in 2017 to 73 percent (ninth) in 2018. 🏈 The Panthers were lousy on wide receiver screens, with just 3.6 yards per pass and -56.6% DVOA. 🏈 Overall, the Panthers ranked better rushing than passing and even had a higher raw DVOA rating rushing than they did passing. The big gap was on first down, where the Panthers were 27th passing and third rushing. But on third and fourth down, the Panthers ranked better passing the ball (10th) than rushing the ball (15th). 🏈 Let's talk about Cam Newton and blitzes. The rate at which opponents blitzed Cam Newton dropped last year for the third straight season, down to just 25 percent of plays. Just two years before, it was as high as 38 percent. Opponents keep blitzing Newton less even though Newton consistently has a less efficient performance against five or more pass rushers, year after year. In 2018, Carolina's DVOA with Newton at quarterback dropped from 55.8% with two or three pass-rushers to 18.0% with four pass-rushers and then -9.1% with five or more pass-rushers. The numbers were similar in 2017. 🏈 Carolina's offense recovered 13 of 17 fumbles. 🏈 The Panthers defense had one of the league's biggest differences between performance against shotgun (6.4 yards per play, 15.0% DVOA) and performance against under-center formations (5.8 yards per play, -8.4% DVOA).

Passing

Player	DYAR	DVOA	Plays	NtYds	Avg	YAC	C%	TD	Int
C.Newton	321	-1.4%	497	3159	6.4	5.4	68.7%	24	13
T.Heinicke	-140	-49.1%	58	303	5.2	4.3	62.5%	1	3
K.Allen	158	67.4%	31	266	8.6	4.6	64.5%	2	0

Rushing

Player	DYAR	DVOA	Plays	Yds	Avg	TD	Fum	Suc
C.McCaffrey	167	9.6%	219	1099	5.0	7	2	55%
C.Newton	71	2.7%	89	502	5.6	4	2	--
C.J.Anderson*	9	0.9%	24	104	4.3	0	0	50%
C.Artis-Payne	37	31.5%	19	69	3.6	1	0	58%
D.Moore	57	28.3%	13	172	13.2	0	2	--
T.Cadet*	-15	-41.7%	11	17	1.5	0	0	36%
A.Armah	0	-9.0%	9	15	1.7	2	0	44%
C.Samuel	60	111.1%	8	84	10.5	2	0	--
K.Allen	19	52.8%	5	19	3.8	1	0	--

Receiving

Player	DYAR	DVOA	Plays	Ctch	Yds	Y/C	YAC	TD	C%
D.J.Moore	109	4.1%	82	55	788	14.3	7.7	2	67%
D.Funchess*	13	-10.5%	79	44	549	12.5	1.7	4	56%
C.Samuel	39	-5.4%	65	39	494	12.7	2.8	5	60%
J.Wright	-12	-15.1%	59	43	447	10.4	4.6	1	73%
T.Smith	7	-10.0%	31	17	190	11.2	2.8	2	55%
C.Hogan	123	14.3%	55	35	532	15.2	5.5	3	64%
A.Robinson	47	4.0%	35	17	231	13.6	2.5	5	49%
I.Thomas	27	0.9%	49	36	333	9.3	4.4	2	73%
G.Olsen	57	14.6%	38	27	291	10.8	3.1	4	71%
C.McCaffrey	183	11.5%	124	107	867	8.1	8.0	6	86%

Offensive Line

Player	Pos	Age	GS	Snaps	Pen	Sk	Pass	Run	Player	Pos	Age	GS	Snaps	Pen	Sk	Pass	Run
Greg Van Roten	LG	29	16/16	1057	2	1.5	10	0	Trai Turner	RG	26	13/13	760	3	1.0	7	6
Taylor Moton	RT	25	16/16	1052	6	2.0	12	5	Tyler Larsen	RG	28	16/3	324	2	0.0	1	0
Ryan Kalil*	C	34	16/16	1027	2	1.5	8	4	Marshall Newhouse*	LT	31	13/2	210	5	1.5	4	1
Chris Clark*	LT	34	15/13	818	7	6.0	18	3	Matt Paradis	C	30	9/9	569	2	0.0	1	2

Year	Yards	ALY	Rank	Power	Rank	Stuff	Rank	2nd Lev	Rank	Open Field	Rank	Sacks	ASR	Rank	Press	Rank	F-Start	Cont.
2016	3.90	3.83	25	73%	3	22%	24	1.10	23	0.63	19	36	6.2%	19	26.8%	17	14	27
2017	3.61	3.78	25	72%	5	19%	12	0.94	30	0.53	22	35	7.1%	19	29.3%	9	9	30
2018	4.62	4.55	11	67%	18	17%	7	1.27	17	0.97	12	32	6.1%	10	28.9%	15	16	34
2018 ALY by direction:			Left End: 5.21 (12)			Left Tackle: 4.39 (10)			Mid/Guard: 4.48 (13)			Right Tackle: 4.50 (14)			Right End: 4.91 (9)			

2018's 6.1 percent adjusted sack rate was the Panthers' lowest since they drafted Cam Newton. The Panthers last ranked inside the top 10 in 2008, when Jake Delhomme was the starting quarterback. They had ranked 19th or lower in every other season with Newton as the starter. ❧ They also had their highest rank by adjusted line yards since 2011, and the second-best figure in franchise history. This translated to the highest average yards per carry in the league, the fourth-highest rate of first downs, and the No. 2 rushing DVOA. Despite this, the team's power success was its lowest since 2010. ❧ Despite generally being considered the weakest of the team's current projected starters, Greg Van Roten was the only Panthers lineman to rank in the top 10 at his position in snaps per blown block. Van Roten was one of six qualifying left guards not credited with a single blown block on run plays. Collectively, the Panthers were a shade below average in snaps per blown block. The two starters with the worst rates, Chris Clark and Ryan Kalil, have both left the team. ❧ The Panthers' 17 offensive holding penalties were the third-fewest, but they were merely average in total penalties. ❧ New center Matt Paradis was credited with fewer than 10 total blown blocks in three of his four seasons as a starter. In 2018, he had the best rate of his career prior to his season-ending fibula fracture. Only in 2017 was Paradis outside the top 10 at his position by this measure. Paradis is expected to start immediately for the Panthers, with Tyler Larsen again the primary backup on the interior line. ❧ The tackle positions are currently an open competition, with three players competing for two spots as detailed earlier in the chapter. Taylor Moton started games at both left and right tackle in 2018, and he appears to be the only one of the trio who is presently competing at both spots.

Defensive Front

Defensive Line	Age	Pos	G	Snaps	Plays	TmPct	Rk	Stop	Dfts	BTkl	Runs	St%	Rk	RuYd	Rk	Sack	Hit	Hur	Dsrpt
						Overall						vs. Run				Pass Rush			
Kawann Short	30	DT	14	584	42	6.2%	21	38	16	2	36	89%	5	0.8	3	3.0	4	20	0
Dontari Poe	29	DT	16	515	16	2.1%	82	10	3	1	15	60%	81	3.1	74	1.0	2	6	0
Kyle Love	33	DT	16	467	20	2.6%	79	17	5	3	16	81%	21	1.5	11	1.5	2	10	1
Vernon Butler	25	DT	14	329	19	2.8%	--	16	5	0	17	88%	--	2.1	--	0.5	3	7	0

Edge Rushers	Age	Pos	G	Snaps	Plays	TmPct	Rk	Stop	Dfts	BTkl	Runs	St%	Rk	RuYd	Rk	Sack	Hit	Hur	Dsrpt
						Overall						vs. Run				Pass Rush			
Mario Addison	32	DE	16	666	33	4.3%	59	30	20	2	20	85%	16	1.0	7	9.0	2	28	0
Julius Peppers	39	DE	16	506	28	3.6%	75	23	13	0	16	69%	62	1.5	14	5.0	7	16	5
Wes Horton	29	DE	16	471	24	3.1%	83	15	5	6	20	55%	85	3.1	65	1.5	0	15	1
Bryan Cox	25	DE	11	200	10	1.9%	--	7	2	4	8	88%	--	2.4	--	0.0	1	5	0
Efe Obada	27	DE	10	187	10	2.1%	--	8	3	2	5	80%	--	2.8	--	2.0	5	12	2
Bruce Irvin	32	DE	16	470	19	2.3%	93	14	11	3	9	56%	83	3.9	88	6.5	7	11	0

Linebackers	Age	Pos	G	Snaps	Plays	TmPct	Rk	Stop	Dfts	BTkl	Runs	St%	Rk	RuYd	Rk	Sack	Hit	Hur	Tgts	Suc%	Rk	AdjYd	Rk	PD	Int
						Overall						vs. Run				Pass Rush				vs. Pass					
Luke Kuechly	28	MLB	16	927	136	17.6%	9	80	38	7	77	68%	15	3.3	22	2.0	3	9	29	62%	6	3.3	2	6	1
Thomas Davis*	36	OLB	12	650	85	14.7%	27	48	18	9	43	65%	22	3.6	31	0.0	3	8	35	51%	35	6.9	46	6	0
Shaq Thompson	25	OLB	14	597	77	11.4%	49	34	12	5	33	48%	78	4.9	77	3.5	2	6	33	45%	51	6.5	31	1	0

Year	Yards	ALY	Rank	Power	Rank	Stuff	Rank	2nd Level	Rank	Open Field	Rank	Sacks	ASR	Rank	Press	Rank
2016	3.83	3.61	4	78%	32	24%	5	1.10	10	0.73	17	47	7.3%	5	30.2%	7
2017	3.89	3.51	5	47%	2	26%	4	1.12	18	0.94	27	50	9.1%	3	32.9%	6
2018	4.71	3.97	8	78%	31	24%	7	1.40	27	1.32	31	35	6.8%	20	31.6%	10
2018 ALY by direction:			Left End: 2.74 (3)			Left Tackle: 4.71 (22)			Mid/Guard: 3.61 (2)			Right Tackle: 4.81 (26)			Right End: 4.89 (23)

Offseason reports have the Panthers switching to a 3-4 base defense rather than their usual 4-3, though without much of the personnel upheaval such a move often entails. The most obvious configuration sees Dontari Poe, a 3-4 nose tackle in his Chiefs heyday, manning the nose with Kawann Short and Gerald McCoy to either side. Though listed as a defensive end, Mario Addison is about 25 to 30 pounds lighter than a prototypical 3-4 end, so he would likely function better as a stand-up edge rusher in a rotation with Brian Burns and Bruce Irvin. Heretofore disappointing 2016 first-round pick Vernon Butler should therefore have perhaps his final chance to impress in Carolina as the primary backup on the line, with few obvious rivals on the roster unless the front office adds a veteran or two later in the offseason. ◑ Luke Kuechly and Shaq Thompson are the obvious starters at off-ball linebacker, regardless of the alignment of the front. Kuechly led all defenders in total defeats, one ahead of Colts rookie sensation Darius Leonard. Despite technically starting at least 10 games in every season since he was selected in the first round in 2015, Thompson has never played more than 65 percent of defensive snaps in a season. He and Thomas Davis essentially split time alongside Kuechly in 2017 and 2018. ◑ Worryingly, the backup pool at every position of the front seven except edge rusher is an extremely shallow mix of young Day 3 draft picks and undrafted free agents. Even at edge rusher, the four players who are competing for probably three roster spots—Efe Obada, Bryan Cox Jr., Christian Miller, and Marquis Haynes—have only two NFL sacks between them, both by Obada. Miller and Haynes are fifth-round picks from the past two drafts, both of whom appear more suited to the role of 3-4 outside linebacker than 4-3 defensive end. Obada is a Nigerian-born former London Warriors (BAFA) defensive end who recorded two sacks and one interception in his first professional action last season. Cox is a 2017 undrafted free agent out of Florida who is currently more famous for being the son of three-time All-Pro former Dolphins linebacker Bryan Cox than for his own accomplishments.

Defensive Secondary

Secondary	Age	Pos	G	Snaps	Plays	TmPct	Rk	Stop	Dfts	BTkl	Runs	St%	Rk	RuYd	Rk	Tgts	Tgt%	Rk	Dist	Suc%	Rk	AdjYd	Rk	PD	Int
James Bradberry	26	CB	16	990	85	11.0%	8	39	15	7	16	63%	7	7.9	62	99	24.6%	68	13.2	54%	34	7.7	40	15	1
Mike Adams*	38	FS	16	938	81	10.5%	35	28	11	7	43	42%	39	6.7	32	30	7.9%	24	15.3	20%	76	17.9	76	6	3
Donte Jackson	24	CB	16	894	82	10.6%	10	36	12	14	24	42%	39	10.1	73	59	16.2%	21	13.4	46%	64	9.9	75	9	4
Eric Reid	28	SS	13	736	76	12.1%	15	27	10	12	42	40%	42	9.4	59	23	7.7%	23	9.0	65%	6	6.0	12	5	1
Captain Munnerlyn*	31	CB	16	630	56	7.3%	--	28	18	2	8	63%	--	3.9	--	50	19.5%	--	10.2	54%	--	7.6	--	9	1
Javien Elliott	26	CB	15	351	25	3.3%	--	10	6	7	7	57%	--	3.4	--	21	15.2%	--	9.6	38%	--	8.5	--	1	1

Year	Pass D Rank	vs. #1 WR	Rk	vs. #2 WR	Rk	vs. Other WR	Rk	WR Wide	Rk	WR Slot	Rk	vs. TE	Rk	vs. RB	Rk
2016	11	6.1%	24	-1.1%	15	10.1%	23	-3.6%	14	9.4%	19	-7.9%	9	-8.4%	12
2017	11	9.5%	19	5.4%	20	3.4%	19	1.6%	19	11.7%	20	-22.2%	4	-3.0%	14
2018	24	-15.0%	5	29.5%	32	-2.9%	15	-4.2%	20	5.4%	19	17.2%	24	-15.1%	5

Facing the fifth-highest average depth of target of any qualifying safety, Mike Adams had the worst success rate against the pass, allowed the fourth-highest average yards after catch, and therefore conceded the highest overall yards per pass target. Perhaps unsurprisingly, the veteran deep safety was not retained. ◑ Adams' prospective replacement, second-year professional Rashaan Gaulden, played only 143 snaps on defense as a rookie despite the veteran's struggles. The coaching staff appears to fancy Gaulden more as a nickelback than a true safety, but they also appear to have no other option: if eight-year veteran Colin Jones was the answer at free safety, one might reasonably assume that he would have seen more than 97 defensive snaps last season while teams were merrily torching Adams for big yardage twice a game. The only other safety with professional experience, 2017 undrafted free agent Kai Nacua, played 16 games for the 2017 Browns as the backup strong safety, but has not been on an active roster since. ◑ Nickelback Captain Munnerlyn joined Peppers and Davis on an auspicious list of departing veteran defenders. Munnerlyn remains a free agent at the time of writing, and the 31-year-old may be an option if neither potential nickelback takes hold of the job. He and James Bradberry were both among the top 20 cornerbacks in total defeats, with Donte Jackson also making the top 30. ◑ Other cornerback options include Ross Cockrell and Kevon Seymour. Cockrell is a 2014 fourth-round pick who started 54 games for the Bills, Steelers, and Giants between 2014 and 2017. He signed for the Panthers in 2018 on a two-year deal, in theory to start opposite Bradberry, but broke his fibula in training camp and missed the entire 2018 season. Seymour was also selected by the Bills, in the sixth round of the 2016 draft, but was traded to Carolina in exchange for Kaelin Clay on cutdown day the following year. He also missed the entire 2018 season after surgery to repair both labrums. Both players returned to practice this summer, but it is not yet clear what their respective roles will be in 2019.

Special Teams

Year	DVOA	Rank	FG/XP	Rank	Net Kick	Rank	Kick Ret	Rank	Net Punt	Rank	Punt Ret	Rank	Hidden	Rank
2016	-2.5%	25	-3.8	21	5.2	7	1.0	12	-10.4	29	-4.3	25	4.2	12
2017	4.7%	6	6.3	10	2.2	14	5.3	6	7.8	5	1.9	10	-0.2	13
2018	-0.2%	18	3.4	10	-1.2	20	-3.6	27	3.6	12	-3.1	24	-11.6	30

For the seventh time in eight seasons, Ron Rivera's Panthers finished outside the top 12 in our special teams ratings. ❧ Graham Gano missed four games with a knee injury last season, giving him his fewest field goal attempts since 2012, when he missed 10 games. Gano also had the fewest attempts per game since his rookie season (2009), though his 87.5 percent conversion rate was in line with his career average. He did record a career highlight against the Giants when he kicked a 63-yard game winner as time expired. That tied Tom Dempsey of the 1970 Saints for the longest game-winning field goal in NFL history. ❧ The 22.4 yards per kick return was exactly league average, ranking No. 16, but the lack of explosive returns—22 teams had at least one return longer than Carolina's longest—added to poor decision-making, and a fumble was enough to drop them to No. 27 in our kick return ratings. Receiver Curtis Samuel, who led the Panthers in kick returns, had -2.8 points of return value, fourth-worst of any kick returner. No other Panthers returner stood out, either for better or worse. ❧ Depth concerns up and down the roster, as detailed above, may have worrying implications for the special teams units. The team's leading special teams tacklers in 2018 were Ben Jacobs, who has since retired and joined the coaching staff, and Colin Jones, who is currently the only experienced backup safety. The next-most prolific special teams tacklers, Curtis Samuel and Rashaan Gaulden, are expected to assume larger roles on their respective units this year. Even the team's *next*-leading special teams tacklers are Shaq Thompson, recently elevated to a full-time starting role at linebacker, and David Mayo, who is now in San Francisco. It is not remotely clear who will even be on these units next season, besides specialists Gano and Michael Palardy, never mind how proficient those players are likely to be.

Chicago Bears

2018 record: 12-4	**Total DVOA:** 19.4% (5th)	**2019 Mean Projection:** 7.9 wins	**On the Clock (0-4):** 11%
Pythagorean Wins: 11.6 (1st)	**Offense:** -3.4% (20th)	**Postseason Odds:** 35.1%	**Mediocrity (5-7):** 33%
Snap-Weighted Age: 26.1 (26th)	**Defense:** -26.0% (1st)	**Super Bowl Odds:** 4.9%	**Playoff Contender (8-10):** 38%
Average Opponent: -6.2% (31st)	**Special Teams:** -3.2% (26th)	**Proj. Avg. Opponent:** 2.8% (5th)	**Super Bowl Contender (11+):** 18%

2018: Good fortune and a coaching change propel the Bears to their best finish in years.

2019: Now it's time for the fun part—fighting off regression.

Though Chicago's first playoff bid in eight seasons went as soon as it came, the brief venture into January football should be a proud moment for the franchise, not a disappointing cap to an otherwise fantastic season. The Bears had previously finished in fourth place in the NFC North four times in a row and had not won the division since 2010 under Lovie Smith, yet they broke both of those streaks in 2018. Their 12 wins under rookie head coach Matt Nagy were almost as many as the 14 total wins John Fox put together during his three-year reign over the team. The season also resulted in their best finish in DVOA since 2006, both times finishing fifth in the NFL. To say that last season was anything but a smashing success, especially given the circumstances of a first-year head coach, would be a farce.

Early in the year, the Bears landed their first true defensive star since Julius Peppers' departure after 2013. In trading for Raiders defensive end Khalil Mack, Chicago secured a proven superstar pass-rusher to build the defense around. Mack, with some help from a loaded secondary and top-tier coordinator in Vic Fangio, returned the Windy City to its status as the pinnacle of defense, something that has been critical to the fran-

chise's identity since its inception. The Bears were the best defense in the league by a country mile, finishing with one of the 10 best defensive DVOA ratings since 1986 (Table 1).

If that were not enough, quarterback Mitchell Trubisky, chosen second overall in 2017 after a trade up by the previous regime, showed signs of life after a lackluster rookie year. The spread-focused scheme Nagy installed put Trubisky in an offense more like the one he played in at North Carolina, a welcome change from the more traditional (but unfamiliar to Trubisky) under-center offense Fox threw him into. Trubisky did not play a perfect second season, but he statistically made a larger jump than the average second-year quarterback, and most importantly appeared to make some headway in regards to accuracy and decision-making. His progress is not akin to the electric early careers of 2017 draft peers Deshaun Watson and Patrick Mahomes, but it is fair to say Trubisky is coming along at his own pace.

On the surface, it is tough to see how the Bears are not prepared for future success. Their first-year coach put together the winningest season in roughly a decade, their young quarterback appears to be on track, and their identity as a pillar of defense in the NFL has been reestablished with a dominant force, Mack, at the forefront. How could this not be a team primed to contend for the NFC North title—not just next season, but for years to come?

The first part of the answer: regression to the mean. There is no use in stripping away the accomplishments of last year's team, but they benefited from a slew of factors on both sides of the ball that tend to regress year-over-year. Some of the key catalysts that propelled the Bears' return to prominence—league-high turnover rate on defense, unreasonably high defensive efficiency, and good fortune with regards to injuries—should not be expected to repeat again in 2019. That is not to say the Bears are doomed to crash and burn, but they will be brought back down to earth; to good, not great.

Table 2 shows the last 10 teams to lead the league in defensive DVOA. Each one of these teams saw its defensive rating rise (i.e., get worse) the following season, by an average of 14.3 percentage points. A similar change for the Bears would give them -11.7% defensive DVOA, which would have ranked fourth last year. Fourth would still make the Bears a menacing defense, but it is not the same caliber of dominance that can take over any game and carry a significant portion

Table 1. Best Defensive DVOA, 1986-2018

Team	Year	DVOA	DVOA Y+1	Rk Y+1
PHI	1991	-42.4%	-18.1%	2
CHI	1986	-33.6%	-6.3%	11
TB	2002	-31.8%	-17.6%	3
PIT	2008	-29.0%	-4.6%	9
BUF	2004	-28.5%	8.6%	25
BAL	2008	-27.8%	-14.2%	4
CHI	2012	-26.7%	8.7%	25
CHI	**2018**	**-26.0%**	--	--
MIN	1988	-25.9%	-17.8%	2
SEA	2013	-25.9%	-16.8%	1
DEN	2015	-25.8%	-18.3%	1
NYJ	2009	-25.5%	-10.9%	5
TEN	2000	-25.0%	10.3%	25
BAL	2003	-25.0%	-19.9%	2
NO	1991	-24.5%	-18.3%	1
AVERAGE		-28.4%	-9.7%	8.3

2019 Bears Schedule

Week	Opp.	Week	Opp.	Week	Opp.
1	GB (Thu.)	7	NO	13	at DET (Thu.)
2	at DEN	8	LAC	14	DAL (Thu.)
3	at WAS (Mon.)	9	at PHI	15	at GB
4	MIN	10	DET	16	KC
5	at OAK (U.K.)	11	at LAR	17	at MIN
6	BYE	12	NYG		

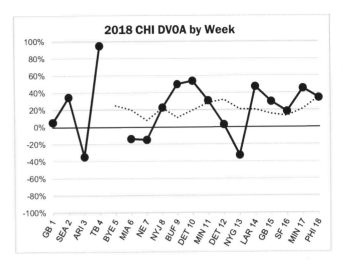

of the offense's load. And, in fact, our projections have them landing around that top-five range next year.

What propelled this Bears' defense, in addition to a fierce pass rush, was an absurd interception rate. Fangio's secondary ended 14.8 percent of drives with an interception, blowing the second-place Miami Dolphins at 11.8 percent out of the water. In an era with rules favored for passing offenses and offensive coordinators opting for safer approaches to the pass game, picking off as many passes as they did is stunning.

In fact, the rate at which the Bears' were intercepting passes had been unmatched over the previous four seasons (Table 3). Furthermore, their rate over the league average was wider than the gap for any league leader in interceptions since the 2011 Green Bay Packers. With cornerback Kyle Fuller making the most of an off-coverage role that allowed him to read quarterbacks' eyes and safety Eddie Jackson prowling all about the secondary to prey on faulty decision-making, it felt as though there was no safe area of the field to throw to. By season's end, the Bears' defense had only finished two games without recording at least one interception (Week 8 vs. Jets, Week 17 at Vikings).

Comparing the Bears to the DVOA and interception leaders of the past decade, we can see that Chicago's 2018 season is strikingly similar to the 2013 Seattle Seahawks—the peak of the Legion of Boom and a defense many would argue as the greatest of the modern era. They are nearly identical in DVOA, turnover rate, and interception rate over league av-

erage. Though the entire team did not match Seattle's Super Bowl run, Chicago's defense was as effective as that all-time unit and reached those heights in similar fashion.

There are two avenues to explore from here. Matching the success of an all-time squad may suggest the Bears can maintain similar success year-over-year, as the Seahawks did by repeating as DVOA champions. Conversely, to assume the Bears can replicate the sustained success of one of the most dominant defenses in league history seems optimistic. Never mind Chicago's circumstances heading into the new year; the unreasonable expectation to repeat is part of why the Seahawks' run was so impressive. The same goes for the Denver Broncos of 2015 and 2016. Considering what the Bears are losing on defense in 2019, the latter avenue of a steeper decline is more likely.

Fangio was one of the league's brightest defensive coordinators in the league and had been for some time, rivaling the likes of Wade Phillips (Rams), Jim Schwartz (Eagles), and Romeo Crennel (Texans). His San Francisco 49ers defenses in the early 2010s were among the best at the time and helped the team string together a number of playoff runs. Since Fangio joined the Bears in 2015, the team improved its DVOA

Table 2. Defensive DVOA Leaders, 2008-2018

Team	Year	DVOA	DVOA Y+1	Rk Y+1	INT/Dr	Rk
2008	PIT	-29.0%	-4.6%	9	10.9%	7
2009	NYJ	-25.5%	-10.9%	5	9.3%	13
2010	PIT	-20.7%	-9.4%	7	11.4%	5
2011	BAL	-17.1%	2.2%	19	8.2%	19
2012	CHI	-26.7%	8.7%	25	12.5%	1
2013	SEA	-25.9%	-16.8%	1	15.6%	1
2014	SEA	-16.8%	-15.2%	4	7.9%	20
2015	DEN	-25.8%	-18.3%	1	7.2%	17
2016	DEN	-18.3%	-5.5%	10	7.5%	16
2017	JAX	-16.1%	-9.4%	6	10.7%	3
2018	**CHI**	**-26.0%**	**--**	**--**	**14.8%**	**1**
AVERAGE		-22.2%	-7.9%	8.7	10.1%	10.2

Table 3. Interception Per Drive Leaders, 2008-2018

Team	Year	Int/Drive	Int/Dr over Avg	Int/Dr Y+1	Rk
CLE	2008	14.0%	5.8%	5.5%	29
GB	2009	16.3%	7.3%	13.2%	2
NE	2010	14.3%	5.6%	13.1%	2
GB	2011	17.4%	8.8%	9.8%	9
CHI	2012	12.5%	4.4%	11.0%	4
SEA	2013	15.6%	7.2%	7.9%	18
SF	2014	13.5%	5.6%	5.1%	27
CAR	2015	12.4%	4.8%	9.1%	7
KC	2016	10.3%	3.0%	9.2%	10
BAL	2017	11.6%	4.1%	6.9%	20
CHI	**2018**	**14.8%**	**7.3%**	**--**	**--**
AVERAGE		13.8%	5.7%	9.1%	12.8

rating each season, going from 31st when he inherited a desolate roster in his first season to first in 2018 once the defense was built in his image. Few other coordinators identified and exposed offenses' weaknesses the way Fangio did during his tenure in Chicago. He most recently and explicitly put that strength on display when his secondary picked off Jared Goff four times in Week 14 by hard-capping the seams to take away the middle of the field, by far the quarterback's most comfortable area to throw to.

Now Fangio has left to be the head coach of the Denver Broncos. Along with him went Ed Donatell, Fangio's defensive backs coach since joining forces in San Francisco in 2011. The coordinator-position coach duo was responsible for some of the most impressive defensive back development in recent years, including 2015 undrafted free agent Bryce Callahan and 2015 fifth-round pick Adrian Amos, and were near unrivaled in how well they put their players in positions to succeed. Callahan, a top nickel cornerback, even chose to follow the two to Denver when he could have signed anywhere. There is not a whole lot of science in measuring the value of a departing coordinator and position coach when there are a number of other variables to consider, but this pair of coaches is about as proven as one could ask for.

Stepping in for Fangio is Chuck Pagano. Pagano spent six years as the Colts' head coach before taking a "gap year" in 2018. It is hard to say Pagano is outright worse than Fangio considering we have not seen him work with this much defensive talent since he was with the Ravens, but if nothing else, his approach will be different and require adjustment from the players. In terms of broad stroke philosophy, Fangio believes in playing with a simple structure and not sending a ton of blitzes, while Pagano is more willing to move players around to create a wider variety of looks and be aggressive. Not only is he happier to send blitzes, Pagano evolved his defense over time in Indianapolis, favoring to less often lock his cornerbacks to one side of the field. Fangio, by comparison, almost never swapped his cornerbacks from their regular side of the field last season. Neither coach's approach is objectively better, but change is change and it is not always easy to rewire the muscle memory required to play defense at a high level.

A hemorrhage of talent from the secondary makes matters even worse. Callahan, as mentioned, left Chicago after four years with the team. He made his mark over the past few seasons as a feisty, fluid nickel cornerback, up there with the league's elite such as Chris Harris Jr. and Nickell Robey-Coleman. Amos also chose to sign elsewhere in free agency, sticking in the division to join Mike Pettine's revamped Green Bay Packers defense.

The Bears' answers to fill the vacancies are Buster Skrine and Ha Ha Clinton-Dix. Both players are coming off of a roller-coaster stretch in their respective careers and looking to get a fresh start. The drop from Amos to Clinton-Dix is not as severe, in part because safeties matter less than cornerbacks who get to directly match up with receivers. However, transitioning from an elite corner in Callahan to somewhat of a trainwreck in Skrine is going to put much more stress on Chicago's linebackers and safeties to pick up the slack in defending the middle of the field. Skrine was impressive early in his career with the Cleveland Browns, but his four-year stay with the New York Jets hardly produced the same results. He had more passes defensed in his final two seasons in Cleveland (35) than in four seasons in the Meadowlands (30) and only once posted a coverage success rate over 50 percent with the Jets (2017, 56 percent). The other three secondary stars in Jackson, Fuller, and Prince Amukamara may be able to keep the unit stable despite the changes, but there is no way to argue that this iteration of the secondary is as talented as last year's.

The loss of talent in the secondary is critical, because the Bears did not get better anywhere else on defense. Their defensive front, while good as a starting unit, did nothing to add much-needed depth, especially on the edge. If either Mack or Leonard Floyd goes out for an extended period of time, the Bears will be left with Aaron Lynch, a journeyman who found moderate success as a lightly used rotational player last year. 2017 undrafted free agent Isaiah Irving and 2018 sixth-round pick Kylie Fitts are the other two options, but they did not combine for even 200 snaps last season, and Irving recorded the lone sack between them. A healthy Bears front will be a force to reckon with, but it is disappointing to have little to look forward to in the future, and the lack of depth may lead to things turning sour in a hurry. The Bears defense ranked fourth in adjusted games lost last season, in part because their defensive line remained intact. They are walking a tightrope by hoping injury luck will not come back to bite them.

All of this is not to say Chicago's defense will collapse. By all means, this is still a top-10 unit, even top-five, and our projections say as much. Rather, there is evidence to suggest the Bears cannot match what they did a year ago, even with many of the same players still in place. It is more likely this defense looks something like Denver's or Minnesota's defense did last season—a little less productive, more hindered by injury, and not as capable of strapping the team on its back.

To make up for this likely regression, the Nagy-Trubisky marriage *must* take a step forward in 2019. Trubisky already looked considerably better in Nagy's offense, and there is still room to grow, as the young quarterback develops better mechanics, accuracy, and decision-making. With the help of Nagy's spread scheme and an influx of new pass-catchers last offseason, most notably tight end Trey Burton and wide receiver Allen Robinson, Trubisky was enabled to make better progress from his rookie year to his second year than many quarterbacks have since 2011, when the CBA changed practice regulations and offseason sessions.

Trubisky's rookie year was below average across the board, particularly in terms of scoring volume. Offensive coordinator Dowell Loggains, a remnant of the last coaching staff who previously served as a quarterbacks coach under Adam Gase, did a poor job putting together an offense under Fox's watch, but rookie Trubisky did not do the squad any favors after taking over for Mike Glennon. In his second season, he not only made up the gap to turn in at least an average Year 2, but Nagy's quick-hitting offense allowed him to dramatically increase his completion percentage and outpace average Year 2 adjusted net yards per attempt by a comfortable margin

(Table 4). There is more to crowning Trubisky than comparing him to a small sample in a few basic statistics, but it does provide some basis to say Trubisky is not trending the wrong way. That counts for something.

Table 4. Mitchell Trubisky vs. Average Year-2 QB Improvement

Player	C%	TD	INT	ANY/A**
Avg. Year 1*	59.4%	18.9	13.6	5.48
Avg. Year 2*	61.7%	25.2	11.9	6.24
Avg. Y2 - Y1 Difference*	2.3%	+6.3	-1.7	+0.76
Trubisky Year 1	59.4%	9.3	9.3	5.05
Trubisky Year 2	66.6%	27.4	13.7	6.59
Trubisky Y2 - Y1 Difference	7.2%	+18.1	+4.4	+1.54

* Includes all quarterbacks drafted 2011-2017 with at least six starts in each of their first two seasons, pro-rated to 16 games.
** Pro Football Reference's Adjusted Net Yards Per Attempt.

Yet, the door is open for a number of fair questions about the young quarterback. How much better can he become, how much of what he did last year can be expected to be replicable, and what happens when the Bears defense cannot carry as much of the burden and help cover up his flaws? Similar to the state of Chicago's defense, the answer is not as optimistic as many would hope.

No quarterback in the league had a smaller gap between play under pressure versus play without pressure. (Full table is listed in the Statistical Appendix, page 454.) This is in part because Trubisky was one of the best quarterbacks under pressure last year per DVOA, so it is easier for the gap to be smaller. Unfortunately, performance under pressure is simply not as consistent year-to-year as performance from a clean pocket. Even Trubisky himself, while a rookie, was abysmal under pressure in 2017 before posting a stellar year in 2018. Some quarterbacks, such as Jameis Winston, can maintain a relatively solid baseline for play under pressure, but even quarterbacks of that ilk cannot regularly be among the league's best. It is simply too volatile an environment.

To draw another example, Case Keenum and Tom Brady were the top two quarterbacks in DVOA under pressure in 2017 and the only two players with a positive figure. In 2018, both came in below average per DVOA in performance under pressure. Keenum and Brady are two wildly different quarterbacks with incomparable track records, yet neither could keep up their pace under pressure. There are endless such examples, but that is perhaps the most telling.

Trubisky Truthers must pay mind to this general principle because his performance when not being pressured was underwhelming. The average no-pressure DVOA rating in 2018 was 47.1%, with Cam Newton (46.6%) and Andrew Luck (47.7%) closely occupying either side of the average. Trubisky, on the other hand, came in at 37.9%, sandwiched between Dak Prescott (34.4%) and Kirk Cousins (39.2%), neither of whom operated in offenses as cohesive as Nagy's.

As of last season, Trubisky still struggles to find consistent accuracy and mental processing. He plays a clean, quick game when he can work the defense pre-snap based on either leverage or numbers, but the longer Trubisky has to hold the ball in the pocket, the worse he looks. His trigger on play-action and longer-developing plays needs considerable work, as do his mechanics. (Chicago was one of the rare offenses with better DVOA and yards per pass without play-action.) Trubisky is too volatile right now and needs to shake that in 2019. Being that Trubisky only started one season in college, two in the NFL, and only one in Nagy's system, there is some argument to be made that he has more room to develop than others because of his lack of experience. However, this is not an argument founded in anything other than assuming all players progress with the same arc. He is better than he was as a rookie, but high expectations from his "breakout" second season should be tempered. It is OK for him to be on his way without prematurely touting him as a strong franchise quarterback.

Skepticism about the young quarterback aside, the entire burden of the offense does not fall on Trubisky. He needs to continue to show improvement, but, like any developing passer, he needs help. Nagy, as well as offensive coordinator (and former Oregon head coach) Mark Helfrich, were brought in last year specifically for the purpose of giving Trubisky every opportunity to succeed to paint a clearer, quicker picture of what the Bears have in him. The offense underwent a complete schematic and aesthetic change that leaned into Trubisky's skill set and comfort—spread concepts, shotgun formations, and lighter personnel groupings all shot up under Nagy compared to Fox's final season—but some of Fox's outdated run-first and low play-action tendencies stuck around. For example, the Chiefs ran on just 32 percent of first-half plays in 2017, while the Bears ran on 46 percent. The 2018 Bears were much closer to the latter number, at 43 percent. Likewise, Nagy only increased Chicago's play-action frequency from 20 percent to 22 percent.

It is normal to not be able to overhaul every aspect of an offense in just one offseason. Resources are limited and reps are important for installing a new passing offense, especially with a young quarterback. However, with respect to a prevalent running game and minimal play-action, there is not enough evidence to suggest Nagy will change his tune significantly from Fox's.

Trading a strong, ground-and-pound back such as Jordan Howard would ordinarily suggest that the Bears were transitioning even further toward a spread passing offense that stresses the boundary—except the Bears had signed Mike Davis away from Seattle two weeks earlier and would use their first pick of the draft (a third-rounder) on Iowa State's David Montgomery a month later. Both additions provide a similar dynamic to Howard. Using their first pick on Montgomery signaled not only that they plan to maintain a relatively similar play style, but that they are willing to commit to maintaining a reliable rushing attack. Bringing in those two backs also raises the question about how Nagy views Tarik Cohen as a between-the-tackles runner, even moreso considering Cohen already played the fourth-most snaps at wide receiver among all running backs last season. Nagy's run game is a little more inside zone, a little less outside zone compared to Fox and Loggains, but it does not look like the downhill run-first principle is going away.

The mission for Nagy will be finding a way to be better on play-action and down the field in order to give the offense more effective options aside from quick passing and downhill running. Play-action, at least anecdotally, works better the more a pass concept looks like its run counterparts. If motions, shifts, alignments, personnel, and cadences are all indistinguishable between the two concepts, play-action should theoretically be more effective. Kyle Shanahan and Sean Mc-Vay are far and away the best at creating this mirage. It is no surprise they are two of the most frequent and productive play-action playcallers around.

As for deep passing, part of the blame for shortcomings there last season can be put on Trubisky's ball placement, but it would be encouraging to see Nagy unlock Taylor Gabriel's full potential as a deep threat. Gabriel's only two seasons of more than 12 yards per reception came under Shanahan, while

his 10.3 average with Nagy was his lowest since 2015. And if the Bears are lucky, undrafted free agent Emanuel Hall may surprise as a vertical menace like he did at Missouri with quarterback Drew Lock.

There is reason to believe in Nagy. He is a career Andy Reid disciple, and he made progress with the offense the moment he arrived. To what degree Nagy can up the ante and stave off Trubisky's volatility will make or break the coach-quarterback duo moving forward. With the defense sure to take a step back, even if just to a less-dominant first-place ranking, Nagy's offensive expertise will be put under a microscope that he managed to avoid in his rookie season.

The devil that is negative regression has its eyes on Chicago. No longer will the Bears be playing with a stacked deck. The true quality of the roster will be put to the test and their cornerstone pieces—Nagy, Trubisky, and Mack—will all need to be at their best if the Bears want to reach the heights that their city's fans have been led to believe they can.

Derrik Klassen

2018 Bears Stats by Week

Wk	vs.	W-L	PF	PA	YDF	YDA	TO	Total	Off	Def	ST
1	at GB	L	23	24	294	370	+1	5%	-26%	-26%	6%
2	SEA	W	24	17	271	276	0	35%	-8%	-38%	4%
3	at ARI	W	16	14	316	221	+2	-35%	-37%	-8%	-6%
4	TB	W	48	10	483	311	+3	95%	44%	-44%	7%
5	BYE										
6	at MIA	L	28	31	467	541	0	-14%	10%	16%	-8%
7	NE	L	31	38	453	381	+1	-15%	9%	-9%	-34%
8	NYJ	W	24	10	395	207	0	23%	24%	-8%	-9%
9	at BUF	W	41	9	190	264	+3	50%	0%	-45%	5%
10	DET	W	34	22	402	305	+3	54%	49%	-29%	-24%
11	MIN	W	25	20	308	268	0	31%	-2%	-28%	5%
12	at DET	W	23	16	264	333	+1	3%	-18%	-22%	-1%
13	at NYG	L	27	30	376	338	-2	-33%	-54%	-22%	-1%
14	LAR	W	15	6	294	214	+1	47%	-37%	-85%	-2%
15	GB	W	24	17	332	323	0	30%	-11%	-20%	21%
16	at SF	W	14	9	325	279	-1	18%	10%	-17%	-9%
17	at MIN	W	24	10	332	164	0	45%	14%	-37%	-5%
18	PHI	L	15	16	356	300	+2	34%	5%	-25%	4%

Trends and Splits

	Offense	Rank	Defense	Rank
Total DVOA	-3.4%	20	-26.0%	1
Unadjusted VOA	0.3%	17	-25.8%	1
Weighted Trend	-2.3%	21	-26.9%	1
Variance	8.1%	24	4.9%	10
Average Opponent	2.5%	29	-3.0%	23
Passing	8.5%	20	-25.2%	1
Rushing	-7.0%	19	-27.3%	2
First Down	-5.1%	20	-34.4%	1
Second Down	0.4%	17	-10.2%	6
Third Down	-6.3%	19	-33.9%	1
First Half	-2.5%	18	-44.6%	1
Second Half	-4.4%	20	-11.1%	6
Red Zone	29.4%	4	-29.4%	1
Late and Close	7.5%	12	-18.4%	4

Five-Year Performance

Year	W-L	Pyth W	Est W	PF	PA	TO	Total	Rk	Off	Rk	Def	Rk	ST	Rk	Off AGL	Rk	Def AGL	Rk	Off Age	Rk	Def Age	Rk	ST Age	Rk
2014	5-11	4.9	6.4	319	442	-5	-13.8%	26	-0.1%	14	10.6%	28	-3.1%	25	41.0	27	60.6	26	27.9	3	27.0	12	26.3	9
2015	6-10	6.3	6.8	335	397	-4	-5.7%	19	6.9%	10	11.3%	31	-1.2%	21	64.7	30	28.2	16	27.4	10	25.8	31	26.2	13
2016	3-13	4.7	6.2	279	399	-20	-8.3%	25	-2.6%	17	5.0%	23	-0.6%	18	84.0	31	71.1	32	26.7	16	26.0	24	26.2	11
2017	5-11	6.2	5.9	264	320	0	-16.0%	25	-15.1%	28	-1.5%	14	-2.4%	23	57.5	26	60.6	30	26.6	20	26.1	17	26.0	10
2018	12-4	11.6	10.7	421	283	+14	19.4%	5	-3.4%	20	-26.0%	1	-3.2%	26	20.7	6	15.9	4	26.1	26	26.0	22	26.1	11

2018 Performance Based on Most Common Personnel Groups

CHI Offense					CHI Offense vs. Opponents					CHI Defense				CHI Defense vs. Opponents			
Pers	Freq	Yds	DVOA	Run%	Pers	Freq	Yds	DVOA	Run%	Pers	Freq	Yds	DVOA	Pers	Freq	Yds	DVOA
11	62%	6.1	6.6%	36%	Base	15%	4.7	-18.3%	58%	Base	17%	4.7	-26.1%	11	78%	5.0	-23.2%
12	17%	4.6	-12.3%	47%	Nickel	64%	5.9	11.5%	44%	Nickel	76%	4.8	-23.6%	21	9%	4.5	-46.7%
21	12%	5.8	4.1%	46%	Dime+	21%	5.7	-20.3%	18%	Dime+	5%	6.2	-8.0%	12	8%	3.8	-29.5%
612	1%	2.0	-62.5%	67%	Goal Line	0%	0.8	28.0%	50%	Goal Line	0%	0.3	-67.6%	20	2%	5.7	39.0%
13	1%	9.0	1.4%	38%						Big	1%	0.6	-124.9%	10	1%	4.7	13.5%
22	1%	1.6	-13.8%	78%										13	1%	6.2	25.8%

Strategic Tendencies

Run/Pass		Rk	Formation		Rk	Pass Rush		Rk	Secondary		Rk	Strategy		Rk
Runs, first half	43%	3	Form: Single Back	83%	11	Rush 3	12.4%	7	4 DB	17%	26	Play action	22%	22
Runs, first down	49%	13	Form: Empty Back	8%	20	Rush 4	68.8%	17	5 DB	76%	6	Avg Box (Off)	6.15	23
Runs, second-long	32%	11	Pers: 3+ WR	64%	22	Rush 5	15.5%	23	6+ DB	5%	17	Avg Box (Def)	5.91	32
Runs, power sit.	63%	9	Pers: 2+ TE/6+ OL	22%	18	Rush 6+	3.3%	29	CB by Sides	95%	1	Offensive Pace	32.32	27
Runs, behind 2H	19%	28	Pers: 6+ OL	3%	8	Int DL Sacks	33.0%	10	S/CB Cover Ratio	24%	25	Defensive Pace	30.86	13
Pass, ahead 2H	52%	7	Shotgun/Pistol	80%	3	Second Level Sacks	26.0%	13	DB Blitz	6%	28	Go for it on 4th	1.58	10

Matt Nagy had trouble bringing Kansas City's success on short passes over to Chicago. The Bears ranked 31st in DVOA on passes at or behind the line of scrimmage, and dead last with 6.7 average yards after the catch on these plays. Kansas City, by comparison, was No. 1 in DVOA on these plays and fourth in YAC. ◣ A common short Chicago pass was the wide receiver screen. Only three teams ran more wide receiver screens than Chicago, but the Bears had just -2.4% DVOA on these passes, and 4.4 yards per pass ranked 29th in the league. ◣ For the second straight year, the Bears were better running in the red zone (third in 2018) than overall (19th in 2018). ◣ As noted earlier in the chapter, the Chicago offense had the league's biggest (opposite) yardage difference between play-action (5.8) and non-play-action (7.1) passes. However, the DVOA difference was much smaller (10.9% with play-action, 17.3% without play-action). ◣ Chicago had the league's biggest gap between performance in shotgun (6.1 yards per play, 4.5% DVOA) and performance with the quarterback under center (4.0 yards per play, -30.4% DVOA). ◣ Chicago was one of four teams that had less than 10 percent of its runs come against an eight-man box. ◣ The Bears defense led the league in DVOA against deep passes but was also third against shorter passes. They killed running back screens in particular, allowing just 3.1 yards per pass with -95.3% DVOA. ◣ How fumble-luck regression works: Chicago recovered 12 of 14 defensive fumbles in 2017 but only eight of 18 defensive fumbles in 2018.

Passing

Player	DYAR	DVOA	Plays	NtYds	Avg	YAC	C%	TD	Int
M.Trubisky	448	3.6%	457	3082	6.7	4.9	66.7%	24	12
C.Daniel	-152	-37.9%	87	462	5.3	3.2	69.7%	3	2

Rushing

Player	DYAR	DVOA	Plays	Yds	Avg	TD	Fum	Suc
J.Howard*	-28	-11.1%	250	935	3.7	9	2	50%
T.Cohen	-17	-12.9%	99	445	4.5	3	2	44%
M.Trubisky	114	22.9%	57	425	7.5	3	1	--
B.Cunningham*	-26	-64.8%	11	20	1.8	0	0	27%
T.Mizzell	-19	-63.9%	9	16	1.8	0	0	22%
T.Gabriel	37	41.4%	9	61	6.8	0	0	--
A.Miller	-9	-61.5%	6	26	4.3	0	1	--
C.Daniel	-26	-107.0%	5	0	0.0	0	1	--
M.Davis	80	9.0%	112	514	4.6	4	0	52%
C.Patterson	114	4.0%	42	228	5.4	1	0	--

Receiving

Player	DYAR	DVOA	Plays	Ctch	Yds	Y/C	YAC	TD	C%
A.Robinson	62	-4.8%	94	55	754	13.7	3.9	4	59%
T.Gabriel	19	-10.2%	93	67	688	10.3	3.2	2	72%
A.Miller	71	3.9%	54	33	423	12.8	5.2	7	61%
J.Bellamy*	-26	-25.5%	25	14	117	8.4	3.3	1	56%
K.White	15	10.1%	8	4	92	23.0	1.5	0	50%
M.Hall	1	-12.0%	19	10	149	14.9	5.7	1	53%
T.Burton	24	-2.7%	76	54	569	10.5	3.5	6	71%
A.Shaheen	9	14.0%	6	5	48	9.6	2.6	1	83%
T.Cohen	184	21.3%	91	71	725	10.2	7.3	5	78%
J.Howard*	-13	-21.9%	27	20	145	7.3	6.4	0	74%
T.Mizzell	15	8.1%	10	8	78	9.8	4.3	1	80%
M.Davis	31	-0.1%	42	34	214	6.3	6.9	1	81%

Offensive Line

Player	Pos	Age	GS	Snaps	Pen	Sk	Pass	Run	Player	Pos	Age	GS	Snaps	Pen	Sk	Pass	Run
Cody Whitehair	C	27	16/16	1075	3	0.5	3	3	Bryan Witzmann*	RG	29	10/7	533	1	3.0	8	8
Bobby Massie	RT	30	16/16	1070	6	2.5	17	5	Kyle Long	RG	31	8/8	511	3	1.5	3	2
Charles Leno	LT	28	16/16	1067	6	3.5	23	2	Eric Kush*	LG	30	15/7	344	2	0.5	4	2
James Daniels	LG	22	16/10	762	3	0.0	5	10	Ted Larsen	LG	32	15/13	751	4	3.0	11	7

Year	Yards	ALY	Rank	Power	Rank	Stuff	Rank	2nd Lev	Rank	Open Field	Rank	Sacks	ASR	Rank	Press	Rank	F-Start	Cont.
2016	4.69	4.48	8	75%	1	18%	11	1.27	10	1.06	5	28	4.9%	7	23.4%	9	18	29
2017	4.08	3.65	28	58%	26	26%	28	1.20	11	0.97	6	39	7.7%	23	30.3%	13	18	27
2018	3.83	3.92	28	67%	18	21%	22	0.96	31	0.63	26	33	6.0%	7	26.4%	8	16	33
2018 ALY by direction:			Left End: 4.26 (19)			Left Tackle: 4.04 (17)			Mid/Guard: 3.97 (30)			Right Tackle: 4.21 (19)			Right End: 2.92 (31)		

Chicago's significant improvement in adjusted sack rate can be linked to quarterback Mitchell Trubisky. As a rookie, he did not have a proper internal clock and often held onto the ball in the pocket for far too long, leading to a ton of sacks. It did not help that John Fox's offense often designed plays that asked him to hold the ball. Between Trubisky being more experienced in Year 2 and Matt Nagy installing a quarterback-friendly spread offense, the Bears were able to get the ball out quicker to help ease pressure off the line. ● The improved adjusted sack rate stands at odds with left tackle Charles Leno's charting results. His 23 blown blocks in pass protection were not only tied for fourth-most in the league, but were far more than the 13 and 14 he allowed in 2016 and 2017, respectively. However, Leno's 2018 season featured him alongside rookie James Daniels at left guard for 10 games. Daniels, while plenty capable for a rookie, may have put more of a burden on Leno due to his inexperience compared to veterans such as Kyle Long and Eric Kush, whom Leno previously played next to. Look for the Bears' left tackle to return to form as Cody Whitehair, a more experienced player, moves to left guard and Daniels kicks inside to play his college position of center. ● Though the Bears were comparatively no worse in adjusted line yards, they were dramatically worse at gaining second-level yards. Part of the disconnect is that Nagy's spread offense was not conducive to Jordan Howard's patient, smooth running style. Howard was better suited sifting through traffic in Fox's system, even if that offense was worse on the whole. Howard went from 43 and 32 10-plus-yard gains in 2016 and 2017, respectively, to just 18 in 2018. ● Former backup tackle Bradley Sowell is making a position switch to tight end. Last season he was featured in a gimmick goal-line play that had Sowell "sift" block down the line before breaking back outside on a rollout concept, resulting in his first and only career receiving touchdown. Sowell will now officially play the position after doing so unofficially last year.

Defensive Front

Defensive Line	Age	Pos	G	Snaps	Plays	Overall TmPct	Rk	Stop	Dfts	BTkl	Runs	vs. Run St%	Rk	RuYd	Rk	Pass Rush Sack	Hit	Hur	Dsrpt
Akiem Hicks	30	DE	16	780	60	7.4%	11	53	21	3	45	84%	13	1.7	17	7.5	9	28	6
Eddie Goldman	25	DT	16	552	40	4.9%	43	32	8	1	36	78%	32	2.1	38	3.0	0	13	0
Roy Robertson-Harris	26	DE	16	353	24	2.9%	--	19	11	2	15	73%	--	2.9	--	3.0	8	23	0
Bilal Nichols	23	DE	14	328	28	3.9%	--	20	9	0	23	65%	--	2.9	--	3.0	4	0	0
Jonathan Bullard	26	DE	16	298	19	2.3%	--	11	2	2	17	53%	--	3.2	--	0.0	2	4	2

Edge Rushers	Age	Pos	G	Snaps	Plays	Overall TmPct	Rk	Stop	Dfts	BTkl	Runs	vs. Run St%	Rk	RuYd	Rk	Pass Rush Sack	Hit	Hur	Dsrpt
Leonard Floyd	27	OLB	16	793	50	6.1%	19	36	14	9	31	84%	17	1.5	13	4.0	7	31	1
Khalil Mack	28	OLB	14	755	49	6.9%	10	35	22	7	27	63%	73	3.6	82	12.5	9	38	3
Aaron Lynch	26	OLB	13	353	17	2.6%	90	14	8	2	10	90%	4	1.5	14	3.0	5	13	0

Linebackers	Age	Pos	G	Snaps	Plays	Overall TmPct	Rk	Stop	Dfts	BTkl	Runs	vs. Run St%	Rk	RuYd	Rk	Pass Rush Sack	Hit	Hur	vs. Pass Tgts	Suc%	Rk	AdjYd	Rk	PD	Int
Danny Trevathan	29	ILB	16	986	108	13.2%	35	64	15	9	60	72%	8	3.8	38	2.0	3	15.5	43	47%	49	7.3	58	6	2
Roquan Smith	22	ILB	16	880	127	15.6%	19	61	18	11	57	60%	41	3.8	37	5.0	0	5	57	54%	25	5.0	11	5	1

Year	Yards	ALY	Rank	Power	Rank	Stuff	Rank	2nd Level	Rank	Open Field	Rank	Sacks	ASR	Rank	Press	Rank
2016	4.41	4.33	20	60%	10	17%	24	1.13	14	0.84	24	37	7.3%	4	28.1%	13
2017	4.16	4.50	30	79%	30	14%	32	1.06	9	0.62	11	42	7.6%	8	29.9%	19
2018	3.63	3.97	9	58%	4	20%	14	0.98	4	0.45	4	50	7.5%	12	33.4%	3

2018 ALY by direction:	Left End: 3.90 (11)	Left Tackle: 4.02 (14)	Mid/Guard: 3.93 (3)	Right Tackle: 3.87 (11)	Right End: 4.32 (15)

The addition of Khalil Mack didn't just juice the pass rush. The Bears jumped from 30th to ninth in adjusted line yards allowed; only the Jaguars defense jumped more spots last year. The addition of Mack forced many offenses to push attention toward him if they wanted to get anything done in the run game, allowing Chicago's talented interior and second-level players to thrive. It also helped that the Bears had much better health and depth on the defensive line compared to the year prior. As taxing as that position can be, health and depth are at a premium. ❧ Few defensive linemen play as consistently well as Akiem Hicks without finding themselves in the spotlight. Dating back to his days in New England, Hicks has been a force in both phases of the game, particularly adept at slashing through pass-pro schemes to open up his teammates on the edge. Three years running, Hicks has racked up at least seven sacks and 26 hurries, solidifying him as one of the best pocket-pushers around. ❧ No edge defender cracked 30 hurries in a season for the Bears between 2015 and 2017, though Leonard Floyd likely would have in 2017 had his season not been cut to just 10 games. Still, for the first time since Julius Peppers in 2011, the Bears had not only one player hit 30-plus hurries, but two in Mack and Floyd. ❧ Roquan Smith was overshadowed by two other fantastic rookie linebackers, Leighton Vander Esch (Cowboys) and Darius Leonard (Colts). That being said, Smith bested them in the area most pertinent to today's NFL: coverage. Smith scored a 54 percent success rate on a bountiful 57 targets, far outperforming Vander Esch's 41 percent and Leonard's 36 percent success rates. Among his young peers, Smith's range and instincts in coverage are unmatched.

Defensive Secondary

Secondary	Age	Pos	G	Snaps	Plays	TmPct	Rk	Stop	Dfts	BTkl	Runs	St%	Rk	RuYd	Rk	Tgts	Tgt%	Rk	Dist	Suc%	Rk	AdjYd	Rk	PD	Int
Adrian Amos*	26	SS	16	1028	81	9.9%	41	33	14	6	18	50%	21	7.1	42	39	8.7%	30	7.0	64%	9	4.3	3	9	2
Kyle Fuller	27	CB	16	1013	76	9.3%	29	37	18	9	11	55%	18	6.5	42	100	22.5%	61	12.1	54%	31	6.6	17	21	7
Prince Amukamara	30	CB	15	910	78	10.2%	17	26	13	6	12	33%	56	6.6	43	77	19.3%	44	12.4	47%	59	7.9	44	12	3
Eddie Jackson	27	FS	14	905	65	9.1%	49	30	11	12	20	20%	66	8.8	54	39	9.8%	41	11.9	79%	1	4.4	4	15	6
Bryce Callahan*	28	CB	13	675	51	7.7%	53	25	15	10	7	43%	36	7.6	56	37	12.5%	1	7.3	51%	43	6.9	23	6	2
Sherrick McManis	32	CB	15	236	25	3.3%	--	13	5	1	8	25%	--	6.9	--	20	19.3%	--	14.1	65%	--	3.2	--	4	1
Ha Ha Clinton-Dix	27	FS	16	1026	98	12.1%	14	20	11	10	44	11%	75	12.0	73	23	5.4%	11	9.0	48%	45	6.7	25	6	3
Buster Skrine	30	CB	14	694	65	9.0%	35	27	12	7	21	38%	50	5.6	24	61	21.8%	59	10.5	46%	63	8.3	55	8	0

Year	Pass D Rank	vs. #1 WR	Rk	vs. #2 WR	Rk	vs. Other WR	Rk	WR Wide	Rk	WR Slot	Rk	vs. TE	Rk	vs. RB	Rk
2016	17	12.3%	27	-1.7%	14	0.2%	15	10.2%	28	-2.2%	12	18.2%	28	-10.5%	11
2017	14	10.4%	20	-16.5%	7	19.4%	26	4.2%	23	5.6%	15	-6.2%	11	-3.4%	13
2018	1	-30.4%	1	-24.2%	3	-20.3%	4	-19.6%	3	-31.2%	1	-33.6%	3	-9.5%	10

As noted above, the Bears had the best DVOA in the league against deep passes (16 or more yards downfield). Just 15.9 percent of passes against the Bears were deep; only Arizona and Indianapolis were lower. Considering the Bears' fierce pass rush and ball-hawk secondary, it makes sense that teams would not risk going down the field too often. ❧ Not only did the Bears feature each of their cornerbacks to one side of the field more than any other team, but they were particular in the way they did it. Prince Amukamara, to the offense's left, often played press or bump coverage near the line of scrimmage. Kyle Fuller, right, tended to play a softer coverage alignment, setting up a cushion 8 to 10 yards off the line and playing what was in front of him. Seldom did they stray from this setup. ❧ Eddie Jackson asserted himself as an explosive, well-rounded cover safety. Whether flying over from a centerfield position to intercept Josh Rosen deep or closing from a half-field assignment for a pick-six to seal a game versus the Vikings, he is a threat to find the ball from anywhere on the field. ❧ Despite a strong start to his career, Ha Ha Clinton-Dix is a reclamation project at this point and a downgrade from Adrian Amos. He is too often lost in space with an inclination as to where he needs to be and does not offer the same caliber of versatility Amos did. He is still starting quality, but he needs to return to the heights he flashed early in his career with Green Bay. ❧ Throwing darts at cornerbacks Duke Shelley (Kansas State, sixth round) and Stephen Denmark (Valdosta State, seventh round) in the draft was the right call. Chicago's starting unit remains solid, but they do not have quality depth aside from Sherrick McManis, thankfully the only backup defensive back who had to play often last season.

Special Teams

Year	DVOA	Rank	FG/XP	Rank	Net Kick	Rank	Kick Ret	Rank	Net Punt	Rank	Punt Ret	Rank	Hidden	Rank
2016	-0.6%	18	-4.8	24	2.9	10	-1.5	17	-1.4	17	1.5	11	-12.9	32
2017	-2.4%	23	-6.0	25	-2.2	23	-1.2	17	-12.3	30	9.7	2	-12.3	31
2018	-3.2%	26	-10.2	29	-1.5	22	-6.2	31	-2.5	22	4.4	9	-17.1	32

The Bears cannot catch a break on special teams. Not only were they bottom-two in hidden value three years in a row, but they are the only team to even be in the bottom quarter of the league for three straight seasons. No other team matches the Bears' special teams misfortune, not even the Chargers. The biggest issue last season: opposing field goal kickers were 24-of-25 against Chicago (the only miss was Greg Zuerlein from 40 yards) and also hit all of their extra points. That made Chicago opponents a weather-adjusted, league-best 13.1 points above expectation. ● Three different players (Taquan Mizzell, Benny Cunningham, Anthony Miller) fielded at least five kicks for the Bears. None of them posted a positive return value by our ratings. ● If anyone can turn around the kick return game, it's Cordarrelle Patterson. He leads the league in attempts (176), yards (5,276), and touchdowns (six) since 2013, and ranks third in yards per return over that span at 30.0. He also finished fifth in kick return value last year. Patterson cannot run a proper route like many hoped he could out of college, but he is one of the best kick returners in history. ● Tarik Cohen's 33 punt return attempts were the most in the league and he was one of just two players to notch more than 30, along with Ryan Switzer (Steelers). ● Three different Bears had at least 10 special teams tackles in 2017. A year later, no Bears player had more than six special teams tackles, with DeAndre Houston-Carson and Joel Iyiegbuniwe as the leaders.

Cincinnati Bengals

2018 record: 6-10	Total DVOA: -9.7% (23rd)	2019 Mean Projection: 6.9 wins	On the Clock (0-4): 19%
Pythagorean Wins: 5.9 (24th)	Offense: -3.3% (19th)	Postseason Odds: 21.2%	Mediocrity (5-7): 41%
Snap-Weighted Age: 25.7 (29th)	Defense: 9.0% (27th)	Super Bowl Odds: 1.5%	Playoff Contender (8-10): 30%
Average Opponent: 5.8% (2nd)	Special Teams: 2.6% (7th)	Proj. Avg. Opponent: -0.6% (22nd)	Super Bowl Contender (11+): 9%

2018: Marvin Lewis finally runs out of prove-it years.

2019: Andy Dalton is in the waiting room.

In *The Road*, the Cormac McCarthy novel about the post-apocalyptic ruins of America, there's a scene where the main characters run into a wandering old man on … wait for it … the road. The unnamed protagonist man listens to his son, who wants to give the old man some of their food. They have a campfire and ask the old man some questions about his motivations. After some prompting, the old man says that he knew somebody or something would give him some food along the road. When asked if he made any preparations for it, the old man says "People were always getting ready for tomorrow. I didn't believe in that. Tomorrow wasn't getting ready for them. It didn't even know they were there."

Our long-starved Bengals fans finally got something new and different from the Marvin Lewis we have loved to poke fun at for so long. After 16 seasons and two successful rebuilds into playoff-caliber teams, Cincinnati ran out of juice. They chose not to pay all the members of their peak team, the 2015 Bengals, and watched as succession plans at tackle and injuries ravaged the perfect box they had built around Andy Dalton and Lewis' coaching faults. Instead, the Bengals continued to just bring back former Bengals, stay with Vontaze Burfict, and otherwise remain stuck in the past. They were never getting ready for tomorrow, they were constantly trying to relive 2015.

So deep in our hearts, we knew that one day the Bengals would have a different coach. Lewis could only do it for so long. It's one of 32 NFL jobs, yes, but there's a familial and cost-cutting ideal that the Bengals hold to so dearly. It will suck the life out of anybody, as you could see by watching Lewis' press photos get balder and grayer over the years.

The Bengals reached deep into the coaching candidate pool and came out with Zac Taylor, the quarterback coach for Sean McVay's Rams. Taylor does have a cup of coffee of offensive coordinator experience, as the guy who stepped into the role with the Dolphins during the Richie Incognito/Jonathan Martin scandal after all the other coaches were fired. He also has one year of offensive coordinator work at the University of Cincinnati. That's it.

Let's put aside Taylor's interim work with the Dolphins—because he didn't have much say in the preparation of the offense that year—and look at his work with the Bearcats. Cincinnati finished 99th in offensive S&P+ (FO associate/ESPN writer Bill Connelly's measure of empirical college football

production) in 2016. By FO colleague Bryan Fremeau's FEI ratings, Cincinnati was 109th. It was good enough to get Tommy Tuberville fired after seven straight losses. Granted, this wasn't exactly a bonanza of personnel: Gunner Kiel, Hayden Moore, and Tion Green were the big names the Bearcats had at this moment. The Bearcats also graduated their top six receivers by targets in 2015, including future Ravens wideout Chris Moore. So as an offense, the goal was to run the ball and ... they couldn't: They had five rushes of 20-plus yards *all season*. That turnover is pretty normal in college football and it's kind of startling how poorly Taylor's unit performed.

Hiring Taylor is an example of the Bengals leaning into their cheap roots. He's young enough to not have much of a background, and thus the market for his coaching services was lower than one would have been for a long-time NFL coordinator with success. That doesn't necessarily make Taylor a bad hire, and we would argue that the optics of the move make sense. After all, most of the best college football coordinators aren't coming from the NFL ranks. As the NFL starts to realize that being on the cutting edge of strategy is something that requires the ability to experiment, head coaching hires are skewing younger and NFL success shouldn't be a necessity for the job. However, the lack of empirical success for Taylor in any role but Rams quarterback coach—even if he was heavily involved—does make him a bit more of a risk, especially in an organization that likely will have no interest in paying two head coaches if Taylor fails.

Any inquiry into how the Bengals will do in 2019 depends on your reading of the head coach, and clues about how Taylor will run the team are more contextual than definitive. But for the sake of our educated guess, we're going to make a couple of Occam's Razor assumptions here: 1) The Bengals hired Taylor because they wanted an offense that is similar to the Rams, and 2) Taylor was a commodity because of his work with Jared Goff and Sean McVay.

It is in this context that we begin our overview of the Cincinnati Bengals by talking about how they drafted a blocking tight end in the second round. Drew Sample of Washington was not a draftnik favorite. He honestly wasn't anyone's favorite. NFL.com's Lance Zierlein gave him a fourth-round grade, comparing him to Jack Doyle. Sample was 11th among tight ends on Matt Miller's big board at Bleacher Report. He was 77th on Scouts Inc's big board, where their report on Sample noted "he

2019 Bengals Schedule

Week	Opp.	Week	Opp.	Week	Opp.
1	at SEA	7	JAX	13	NYJ
2	SF	8	at LAR (U.K.)	14	at CLE
3	at BUF	9	BYE	15	NE
4	at PIT (Mon.)	10	BAL	16	at MIA
5	ARI	11	at OAK	17	CLE
6	at BAL	12	PIT		

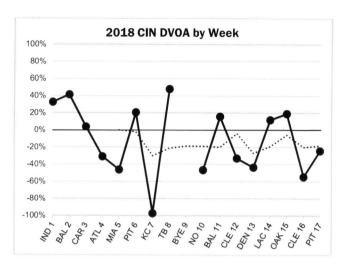

will never be a good starter in the NFL." Harsh! But Sample caught 25 passes in his senior season, and it takes some projection to see him as doing more than that as a receiver. It was a shocking reach for a team that we often think of as getting good value in the NFL draft from a media perspective.

However, if you view it in the context of playing like McVay's Rams, the move makes some sense because the Bengals don't have a tight end that can be a primary blocker/secondary receiver like Tyler Higbee. Tyler Eifert, on the rare occasions that he is healthy, fits more of a move tight end role. So does C.J. Uzomah. While McVay is often thought of as a passing-game guru because of Goff's production, he also is able to create better passing windows for Goff by having a dominant run game. It's the reason the Rams extended Todd Gurley and signed Andrew Whitworth, and it's the reason that they drafted Darrell Henderson in the third round even after making that cash outlay to Gurley.

The Rams also invested heavily in their offensive line, both before and after McVay was hired. Rodger Saffold and Rob Havenstein were already there, but McVay spent heavily to reel in Whitworth and John Sullivan in free agency. They also were able to replace incumbent Jamon Brown with Austin Blythe. The Bengals tried to do this, though we know the result is already not going to help them this year in the wake of Jonah Williams' injury. The first-round tackle got "dinged up" in OTAs and will miss the entire season after undergoing shoulder surgery, forcing a backpedal of creative Bengals offensive line plans such as "moving Cordy Glenn to guard."

The good news for Bengals fans is that to the extent that we can really separate things out, coaches really can make a bigger impact than most players by how they scheme the talent they do have. If nothing else, McVay proved that by turning around Goff from the sadness he endured under Jeff Fisher. The bad news for Bengals fans is that, should Taylor stay close to the McVay plan, the Bengals are arguably less talented than the Rams at every offensive position besides No. 1 wideout.

To the extent that the Bengals have any sort of breakout potential this year, it relies on an awful lot of returns to health or Taylor out-and-out "fixing" players. What's remarkable about the lack of talent in Cincinnati is that the Bengals have annually done quite well in our lists of top 25 "under the radar" prospects. It's failing at the early picks that has left them in this situation.

Since 2014, the Bengals have had their own first- and second-round picks in every season. The only player from their

2014 and 2015 draft classes still on the roster that was picked in those rounds is Darqueze Dennard, the 2014 first-rounder who re-signed a one-year deal this offseason once his free-agent market was discovered to be non-existent. In fact, every other player the Bengals drafted in the top 100 in each of those seasons is no longer on the roster. Even their early-round hits since then have taken time to establish themselves, with the exception of Jessie Bates. Tyler Boyd was almost completely left for dead after his puzzling sophomore season but came back to hit 1,000 receiving yards last year. William Jackson missed his first season due to injury. Joe Mixon has missed time to injuries in both of his first two seasons (he also entered the league as a domestic violence pariah, which complicates his future). Billy Price struggled when he did play last season and missed six starts to injury. We now know that Williams will also produce nothing in his first season, though that takes nothing away from his talent.

Table 1. Cincinnati Picks in Rounds 1-2, 2014-2018

Year	Pick	Pos	Player	AV	Rank Among Players Drafted in First Two Rounds
2014	24	CB	Darqueze Dennard	10	48
2014	55	RB	Jeremy Hill	21	37
2015	21	OT	Cedric Ogbuehi	13	39
2015	53	OT	Jake Fisher	6	57
2016	55	WR	Tyler Boyd	16	26
2016	24	CB	William Jackson	7	47
2017	48	RB	Joe Mixon	18	9
2017	9	WR	John Ross	2	57
2018	21	C	Billy Price	5	28
2018	54	SAF	Jessie Bates	5	28

Meanwhile, the Bengals continue churning out interesting young players late in the draft. Carl Lawson and Jordan Willis both made the top 10 of our top 25 prospects last year, with Andrew Billings (a staple of the lists who finally made the impact draftniks had been projecting for him last year) 16th on the list as well. Nick Vigil and AJ McCarron made the list in 2017, and Shawn Williams made it in 2015. Mohamed Sanu made it in 2013. It's to Cincinnati's credit that they continue to find useful players in the later rounds. Lawson, coming off an ACL tear, should be a big part of what the Bengals do, and everyone else from the 2015 to 2018 lists except McCarron will be in a position to start.

The most disappointing Bengals youngsters have been the ones meant to replace the stars of their 2015 team, A.J. Green and Whitworth. Neither Jake Fisher nor Cedric Ogbuehi are more than fringe NFL players, and John Ross has been injured and in Marvin Lewis' doghouse since the moment he was drafted.

The fulcrum point of this entire Bengals offense is probably what Ross can be with a fresh start. Coming out of Washington, Ross drew DeSean Jackson comparisons with his 4.22 40-yard dash and big-play profile. FO's Playmaker Score thought he was the best wide receiver in the first round of the draft, giving him a 96.9% rating and noting that his one-year wonder college career resembled similar statistical leaps for players such as Terry Glenn or Brandon Marshall. Ross caught seven touchdowns last season and 17 touchdowns in his last season with Washington. Five of Ross' seven touchdowns last year were on short passes, and 12 of his 17 touchdowns for the Huskies in his final season there were red zone touchdowns, pointing at his potential as more than just a deep-ball specialist

If you can draw up a future where Ross—who reportedly struggled with the offense in OTAs—is able to play up to his tools, everything gets a lot easier for the Bengals. They have three receivers who can win quickly, plus whatever Eifert

can give them before his body expires again. They're going to need that to deal with Dalton's shortcomings under pressure and Williams' injury forcing an offensive line full of retreads and castoffs to hold up. If Sample and a renewed focus on play-action passing can symbiotically exist with Mixon threatening the few holes that open up on the line, this offense could surprise.

With the Steelers finally winding down the Roethlisberger era and the Browns and Ravens loaded for bear, this feels like a year that Bengals fans will be used to: the one where they consolidate and take stock of what kind of shape their roster is in. But unlike under the Lewis era, you can at least tell yourself the story where Taylor is a transformative coach that changes the way things have been for far too long in Cincinnati. We believe the more likely scenario is one where Taylor learns that the Rams stuff works a lot better when you have the Rams personnel, including a quarterback with enough arm to target the deep middle consistently. The reality is that most coaches aren't Sean McVay and we don't know near enough about Taylor to project him to be the next McVay.

But like a wandering, starving man who has finally been given a can of peaches, the Bengals and their fan base now have some actual feedback to their right to believe. They don't necessarily have an original plan, but taking lieutenants from the best of the NFL's current offensive environment is a step in the right direction. The next step is probably for that coach to determine what does and doesn't work over 16 games, then let the roster bloodletting begin.

Rivers McCown

2018 Bengals Stats by Week

Wk	vs.	W-L	PF	PA	YDF	YDA	TO	Total	Off	Def	ST
1	at IND	W	34	23	330	380	0	32%	5%	-23%	5%
2	BAL	W	34	23	373	425	+3	41%	35%	-4%	2%
3	at CAR	L	21	31	396	377	-4	4%	13%	7%	-3%
4	at ATL	W	37	36	407	495	-1	-31%	17%	42%	-6%
5	MIA	W	27	17	332	297	+2	-46%	-36%	-11%	-22%
6	PIT	L	21	28	275	481	0	21%	26%	19%	14%
7	at KC	L	10	45	239	551	0	-97%	-56%	33%	-8%
8	TB	W	37	34	402	576	+4	48%	28%	-15%	5%
9	BYE										
10	NO	L	14	51	284	509	-2	-47%	-14%	36%	3%
11	at BAL	L	21	24	255	403	+1	16%	15%	4%	5%
12	CLE	L	20	35	372	342	-2	-33%	-2%	34%	3%
13	DEN	L	10	24	313	361	-2	-44%	-23%	19%	-1%
14	at LAC	L	21	26	295	288	0	12%	-6%	-8%	10%
15	OAK	W	30	16	294	297	+1	19%	-23%	-20%	23%
16	at CLE	L	18	26	209	493	0	-55%	-9%	51%	5%
17	at PIT	L	13	16	196	343	+1	-24%	-52%	-20%	8%

Trends and Splits

	Offense	Rank	Defense	Rank
Total DVOA	-3.3%	19	9.0%	27
Unadjusted VOA	-2.6%	19	12.2%	29
Weighted Trend	-10.0%	24	13.1%	31
Variance	7.7%	23	6.1%	21
Average Opponent	0.3%	18	7.0%	1
Passing	9.5%	18	15.7%	25
Rushing	-3.6%	14	1.0%	26
First Down	0.3%	14	10.4%	29
Second Down	-4.0%	21	0.7%	18
Third Down	-9.6%	22	18.9%	27
First Half	6.4%	11	17.7%	30
Second Half	-13.4%	25	-1.7%	13
Red Zone	27.3%	5	12.7%	24
Late and Close	-13.4%	25	-13.8%	6

Five-Year Performance

Year	W-L	Pyth W	Est W	PF	PA	TO	Total	Rk	Off	Rk	Def	Rk	ST	Rk	Off AGL	Rk	Def AGL	Rk	Off Age	Rk	Def Age	Rk	ST Age	Rk
2014	10-5-1	8.6	9.0	365	344	0	5.0%	12	-1.4%	18	-2.3%	14	4.2%	6	48.5	28	23.2	5	25.9	29	28.1	2	26.1	14
2015	12-4	11.7	12.3	419	279	+11	27.9%	2	18.6%	2	-7.1%	10	2.2%	8	10.0	1	18.2	6	26.2	23	28.1	2	26.5	10
2016	6-9-1	8.3	8.0	325	315	+3	4.0%	13	7.5%	11	0.8%	17	-2.7%	28	24.7	7	10.4	2	26.7	17	28.2	1	26.4	7
2017	7-9	6.2	6.7	290	349	-9	-12.6%	24	-6.5%	22	3.7%	17	-2.4%	21	43.4	22	37.5	19	26.6	19	26.4	14	25.1	29
2018	6-10	5.9	7.2	368	455	+1	-9.7%	23	-3.3%	19	9.0%	27	2.6%	7	61.1	28	43.8	23	25.6	29	25.8	25	25.6	23

2018 Performance Based on Most Common Personnel Groups

CIN Offense					CIN Offense vs. Opponents					CIN Defense				CIN Defense vs. Opponents			
Pers	Freq	Yds	DVOA	Run%	Pers	Freq	Yds	DVOA	Run%	Pers	Freq	Yds	DVOA	Pers	Freq	Yds	DVOA
11	75%	5.5	3.9%	31%	Base	17%	5.4	8.5%	50%	Base	30%	6.0	-4.9%	11	58%	6.4	10.6%
12	16%	6.1	14.1%	42%	Nickel	51%	5.6	-2.6%	33%	Nickel	63%	6.5	14.6%	12	18%	6.7	10.1%
13	2%	5.1	-27.7%	78%	Dime+	19%	5.4	24.0%	23%	Dime+	5%	6.2	12.5%	21	7%	6.4	-15.0%
21	2%	4.2	10.0%	22%	Goal Line	1%	0.4	-20.0%	64%	Goal Line	2%	1.5	23.7%	13	4%	4.0	-17.9%
611	1%	3.8	-4.3%	86%						Big	0%	9.4	79.8%	22	4%	6.6	25.9%
620	1%	0.0	-27.6%	57%										10	4%	6.8	28.6%

Strategic Tendencies

Run/Pass		Rk	Formation		Rk	Pass Rush		Rk	Secondary		Rk	Strategy		Rk
Runs, first half	36%	24	Form: Single Back	86%	7	Rush 3	3.6%	24	4 DB	30%	10	Play action	25%	12
Runs, first down	45%	19	Form: Empty Back	7%	21	Rush 4	76.3%	5	5 DB	63%	16	Avg Box (Off)	6.17	19
Runs, second-long	26%	24	Pers: 3+ WR	76%	5	Rush 5	15.9%	22	6+ DB	5%	16	Avg Box (Def)	6.09	27
Runs, power sit.	61%	12	Pers: 2+ TE/6+ OL	20%	23	Rush 6+	4.2%	25	CB by Sides	85%	10	Offensive Pace	30.83	12
Runs, behind 2H	30%	6	Pers: 6+ OL	3%	9	Int DL Sacks	44.1%	5	S/CB Cover Ratio	28%	16	Defensive Pace	30.83	12
Pass, ahead 2H	57%	3	Shotgun/Pistol	67%	12	Second Level Sacks	7.4%	32	DB Blitz	5%	30	Go for it on 4th	1.42	15

The Bengals were tied with Houston for the fewest broken tackles on offense. Joe Mixon was tied for 11th among running backs with 46, which means the entire rest of the team combined for just 35 broken tackles. ● Andy Dalton went from 5.4 net yards per pass against three or four pass-rushers to 7.7 net yards per pass against a blitz. He had a smaller but similar split in 2017, but in the years before that had not been particularly good against blitzes. Dalton was particularly good against defensive back blitzes, with 7.9 net yards per pass and a league-leading 69.3% DVOA. ● Cincinnati's use of safeties in coverage increased significantly after ranking dead last in 2017. ● Cincinnati had a gigantic "backwards" gap on defense between play-action passes and other passes. Their -16.3% DVOA against play-action ranked second in the league behind Pittsburgh; their 27.0% DVOA against non-play action ranked 31st in the league ahead of only Oakland. Play-action passes did gain more yardage, but only slightly, 7.6 to 7.4 yards. (The NFL average saw play-action passes gain 1.8 yards more than other passes last season.) ● The Bengals brought a league-low 36 percent pressure rate when blitzing. They went from 7.2 net yards per pass with three or four pass-rushers to 8.1 with five or more, although their DVOA barely changed. ● Opposing field goal kickers hit 33 of 36 attempts against the Bengals, with all three misses coming from 50 yards or more.

Passing

Player	DYAR	DVOA	Plays	NtYds	Avg	YAC	C%	TD	Int
A.Dalton	404	5.2%	383	2405	6.3	5.1	62.4%	21	10
J.Driskel	-61	-16.4%	193	872	4.5	4.8	59.7%	6	2

Rushing

Player	DYAR	DVOA	Plays	Yds	Avg	TD	Fum	Suc
J.Mixon	154	6.4%	237	1168	4.9	8	0	49%
G.Bernard	16	-1.6%	56	211	3.8	3	0	41%
J.Driskel	10	-2.8%	21	134	6.4	2	1	--
M.Walton*	-10	-21.8%	14	34	2.4	0	0	36%
A.Dalton	14	11.9%	13	101	7.8	0	0	--

Receiving

Player	DYAR	DVOA	Plays	Ctch	Yds	Y/C	YAC	TD	C%
T.Boyd	305	24.1%	108	76	1028	13.5	5.5	7	70%
A.J.Green	155	12.4%	77	46	694	15.1	3.5	6	60%
J.Ross	-96	-33.3%	58	21	210	10.0	2.8	7	36%
A.Erickson	-8	-16.4%	29	20	167	8.4	3.8	0	69%
C.Core	0	-12.8%	28	13	160	12.3	2.8	1	46%
A.Tate	-48	-65.0%	12	4	35	8.8	0.5	0	33%
C.Patterson	29	0.6%	28	21	247	11.8	7.7	3	75%
C.J.Uzomah	-18	-11.3%	65	43	439	10.2	4.5	3	66%
T.Eifert	36	21.1%	19	15	179	11.9	3.6	1	79%
M.Lengel*	-25	-50.6%	8	3	17	5.7	2.3	1	38%
T.Kroft*	-2	-11.7%	6	4	36	9.0	4.3	0	67%
J.Mixon	-5	-15.3%	55	43	296	6.9	7.7	1	78%
G.Bernard	5	-11.8%	48	35	218	6.2	6.5	0	73%
M.Walton*	-10	-40.1%	8	5	41	8.2	9.6	0	63%

Offensive Line

Player	Pos	Age	GS	Snaps	Pen	Sk	Pass	Run	Player	Pos	Age	GS	Snaps	Pen	Sk	Pass	Run
Bobby Hart	RT	25	16/16	994	13	7.5	15	4	Trey Hopkins	C/G	27	16/9	589	2	3.0	8	5
Clint Boling*	LG	30	16/16	969	5	4.0	7	5	Billy Price	C	24	10/10	558	5	1.5	4	7
Alex Redmond	RG	24	15/15	928	10	2.5	12	2	John Miller	RG	26	15/15	883	4	0.5	6	4
Cordy Glenn	LT	30	13/13	765	5	0.5	10	6									

Year	Yards	ALY	Rank	Power	Rank	Stuff	Rank	2nd Lev	Rank	Open Field	Rank	Sacks	ASR	Rank	Press	Rank	F-Start	Cont.
2016	3.91	4.20	14	60%	19	20%	15	1.04	26	0.55	23	41	7.3%	26	22.5%	8	15	38
2017	3.70	3.79	24	59%	24	18%	9	1.17	12	0.41	31	40	7.2%	20	28.9%	8	10	28
2018	4.61	4.10	22	71%	7	20%	20	1.30	11	1.19	3	37	7.0%	19	27.6%	10	27	30

2018 ALY by direction: Left End: 4.96 (14) Left Tackle: 3.43 (29) Mid/Guard: 4.2 (23) Right Tackle: 4.85 (6) Right End: 2.17 (32)

To the extent that the Bengals are going to emulate the Rams, the biggest place where they need to find improvement is on the offensive line. Last year's line was ghastly, and the unit returns with almost no changes after first-round pick Jonah Williams was lost to shoulder surgery in OTAs. ❧ Every year there's one offensive line contract that nobody understands, and this year that was the Bengals handing Bobby Hart a three-year extension worth $16.5 million, with another $5 million in incentives, after a year where he allowed 7.5 sacks. Hart has never performed at even an adequate NFL level, but the Bengals are paying him like he has. Bengals VP Troy Blackburn publicly defended the Hart re-signing, saying "There aren't perfect options out there. We asked (former Bengals tackle) Willie Anderson if he could go to a time machine and come back at age 25. We'd love to sign him, but you have to deal in your universe of options." You know it's a good signing when you have to run PR on it before you even get to camp. ❧ Cordy Glenn was a bit of a disappointment coming over from Buffalo, but he also allowed only 0.5 sacks. His problem, which has followed him for three seasons now, was staying on the field. He's an average-at-best left tackle. ❧ Inside, the best hope for the Bengals to be good is for last year's first-round pick, Billy Price, to be quick-fixed. Price was roundly worse than stop-gap Trey Hopkins, and his aborted snap was the one that ended Andy Dalton's season. The obvious story based on draft position and the first year of film: he has the power and speed, he didn't have the technique and patience. ❧ John Miller and John Jerry are also here taking up space. Christian Westerman has a good college pedigree and played well in a limited sample last year, but the Bengals can't seem to get over whatever is keeping them from giving him a full trial. ❧ Clint Boling retired just before we went to press due to a blood clot that developed into a pulmonary embolism. ❧ Fourth-round pick Michael Jordan will re-join Price on the line, as the two also shared time at Ohio State. Like His Original Airness in his later days, this Jordan can also be crossed over by a quick player. Still, the Bengals can't say there's a lot of proven depth that should stop them from giving Jordan a chance in 2019.

Defensive Front

Defensive Line	Age	Pos	G	Snaps	Plays	TmPct	Rk	Stop	Dfts	BTkl	Runs	St%	Rk	RuYd	Rk	Sack	Hit	Hur	Dsrpt
						Overall							vs. Run				Pass Rush		
Geno Atkins	31	DT	16	795	45	5.1%	35	35	13	5	33	76%	40	2.1	37	10.0	9	33	1
Andrew Billings	24	DT	16	632	32	3.6%	69	26	9	4	28	82%	20	1.4	8	2.5	4	15	1
Kerry Wynn	28	DE	14	394	33	4.5%	48	26	14	2	21	76%	38	3.3	79	1.5	2	12	2

Edge Rushers	Age	Pos	G	Snaps	Plays	TmPct	Rk	Stop	Dfts	BTkl	Runs	St%	Rk	RuYd	Rk	Sack	Hit	Hur	Dsrpt
						Overall							vs. Run				Pass Rush		
Carlos Dunlap	30	DE	16	839	55	6.3%	14	42	21	4	36	67%	64	2.4	46	8.0	17	32	10
Jordan Willis	24	DE	16	537	21	2.4%	91	18	4	6	16	94%	3	1.7	22	1.0	4	13	1
Sam Hubbard	24	DE	16	508	40	4.5%	55	24	16	4	27	48%	91	3.8	86	6.0	3	11	1
Michael Johnson*	32	DE	15	466	34	4.1%	63	22	2	6	30	60%	76	3.7	85	0.5	1	11	2
Carl Lawson	24	DE	8	225	6	1.4%	--	3	2	0	5	40%	--	8.6	--	1.0	8	12	0

Linebackers	Age	Pos	G	Snaps	Plays	TmPct	Rk	Stop	Dfts	BTkl	Runs	St%	Rk	RuYd	Rk	Sack	Hit	Hur	Tgts	Suc%	Rk	AdjYd	Rk	PD	Int
						Overall							vs. Run				Pass Rush				vs. Pass				
Nick Vigil	26	OLB	11	672	87	14.4%	29	44	9	13	48	63%	30	4.0	53	0.0	1	6.5	36	39%	66	8.3	67	3	0
Hardy Nickerson	25	MLB	16	538	54	6.1%	81	25	5	10	31	52%	73	5.5	84	0.0	0	0.5	27	44%	53	9.6	73	1	0
Jordan Evans	24	OLB	14	510	62	8.1%	69	31	7	6	40	53%	66	5.0	81	1.5	0	0	22	55%	24	6.3	26	3	1
Preston Brown	27	MLB	7	375	46	11.9%	46	22	3	5	23	52%	68	4.6	72	0.0	1	1.5	22	36%	71	7.2	49	4	2
Vontaze Burfict*	29	OLB	7	298	36	9.4%	61	18	4	9	23	52%	68	3.2	19	0.0	0	0	13	38%	--	9.2	--	3	0

Year	Yards	ALY	Rank	Power	Rank	Stuff	Rank	2nd Level	Rank	Open Field	Rank	Sacks	ASR	Rank	Press	Rank
2016	4.44	4.33	19	66%	23	17%	22	1.28	24	0.80	20	33	5.9%	16	30.8%	6
2017	4.06	4.38	29	70%	25	19%	25	1.26	26	0.49	3	41	6.3%	19	33.8%	5
2018	4.94	4.99	30	77%	29	14%	30	1.41	28	1.01	21	34	7.1%	16	26.5%	28

2018 ALY by direction:	Left End: 4.42 (16)	Left Tackle: 5.15 (28)	Mid/Guard: 5.14 (30)	Right Tackle: 4.45 (20)	Right End: 5.30 (27)

Defensive line is a major strength for the Bengals. Few teams can match their depth and star prowess here. One question will be just how much they can get from former FO No. 1 Top Prospect Carl Lawson, who tore his ACL just a few games into the season. He remains one of the brightest hopes this defense has for star-level production. ● Geno Atkins is already a star, remains a star, and will be slithering past a guard and into a quarterback's lap as you read this. ● Carlos Dunlap has never quite been a star but he's a solid No. 1 edge rusher who has finished in the top 30 in hurries in each of the last three seasons. He also has an unmatched talent for disturbing quarterbacks as they throw: for three straight years, Dunlap has finished first or second in our disruptions stat which combines batted passes with hitting the quarterback in motion. If Lawson can take some heat off of Dunlap, this unit could really get after the quarterback. ● It was a successful rookie season for Sam Hubbard, if not exactly one that disproved his pre-draft reputation as a pass rush-focused player. He should slide in as the fourth pass-rusher. ● The interior line looks well taken care of between a breakout year from Andrew Billings and the signing of solid Giants lineman Kerry Wynn. Jordan Willis playing on run downs at end also provides some bulk. All three of those players are solid run-stopping linemen. ● This unit springs a real leak at linebacker, where you can argue they don't have a single player who played well last season. Injuries sapped Nick Vigil of his speed, and he has never been a power linebacker that gets off blocks and tackles everybody in the open field. Preston Brown and Hardy Nickerson are stopgaps. ● A lot of Cincinnati's season will come down to two players we have barely seen play: 2018 third-round pick Malik Jefferson (Texas) and 2019 third-round pick Germaine Pratt (North Carolina State). New defensive coordinator Lou Anarumo has tried to make this more of a reaction defense, and that bodes well for Jefferson's speed, but preseason evidence shows him taking really awkward angles. Pratt is a converted safety and should have NFL athleticism, but his run defense has a few question marks and he may best be relied on as a third-down linebacker in his rookie season. On this defense, though, you could tell us any of these linebackers found 800 snaps and we wouldn't be surprised.

Defensive Secondary

Secondary	Age	Pos	G	Snaps	Plays	Overall TmPct	Rk	Stop	Dfts	BTkl	vs. Run Runs	St%	Rk	RuYd	Rk	vs. Pass Tgts	Tgt%	Rk	Dist	Suc%	Rk	AdjYd	Rk	PD	Int
Jessie Bates	22	FS	16	1114	118	13.4%	7	29	10	13	51	24%	63	9.6	62	38	8.5%	27	13.0	50%	38	9.7	62	7	3
William Jackson	27	CB	16	1063	54	6.1%	75	24	8	8	14	36%	53	8.7	66	65	15.2%	15	12.9	54%	32	6.7	19	13	0
Shawn Williams	28	SS	16	995	116	13.2%	8	36	11	15	54	33%	54	7.1	41	38	9.5%	35	11.7	45%	54	11.7	70	9	5
Dre Kirkpatrick	30	CB	13	774	50	7.0%	62	20	6	9	13	38%	48	5.4	20	64	20.5%	52	15.0	63%	4	6.7	21	9	0
Darqueze Dennard	28	CB	13	675	73	10.2%	15	37	14	4	20	65%	6	4.0	10	57	21.0%	53	8.1	51%	47	6.9	24	6	0
Darius Phillips	24	CB	15	232	21	2.5%	--	7	2	4	3	0%	--	11.3	--	19	20.3%	--	13.1	47%	--	6.8	--	2	0
Clayton Fejedelem	26	SS	16	169	22	2.5%	--	5	2	1	7	43%	--	5.9	--	6	8.8%	--	14.2	17%	--	14.3	--	0	0
B.W. Webb	29	CB	16	1005	65	7.8%	52	25	13	5	16	44%	33	7.2	52	60	14.8%	11	14.4	57%	20	7.8	42	6	1

Year	Pass D Rank	vs. #1 WR	Rk	vs. #2 WR	Rk	vs. Other WR	Rk	WR Wide	Rk	WR Slot	Rk	vs. TE	Rk	vs. RB	Rk
2016	14	-0.4%	13	8.1%	25	-2.2%	12	-14.9%	6	16.2%	29	-1.8%	17	-7.7%	14
2017	17	-14.4%	8	-4.4%	15	22.2%	28	-10.5%	9	11.9%	21	19.6%	30	-5.6%	11
2018	25	-2.6%	13	21.7%	28	-14.5%	7	7.9%	24	-3.8%	13	2.7%	16	22.0%	31

A free idea for entry-level fan Twitter account trolling: *DidDreKirkpatrickCommitPIToday?* Kirkpatrick has committed DPI three or more times in each of the last three seasons, including a league-high six times in 2017. Kirkpatrick is a steady NFL corner, but don't expect help in run support and don't expect highs. Also: why is his cap figure $10 million? 🏈 The spin-off of that account is obviously: *DidBWWebbCommitPIToday?* Webb led the NFL with six DPIs last year, and so you can see the Bengals had no choice but to sign him. Despite Webb's 5-foot-11, 187-pound frame, he played more outside last year than in the slot. The slot might be a more ideal fit for him. 🏈 Left for dead in free agency, Darqueze Dennard re-signed with the Bengals on March 25 after the league collectively shrugged at him. Family is there for each other, but given the three-year commitment to Webb, Dennard might just be depth, or waiting out a roster spot somewhere else due to injury. 🏈 William Jackson is the closest thing this unit has to a No. 1 corner, and even he got roughed up a bit as the pass defense was ravaged last year. If he bounces back to his 2017 form, though, the Bengals might have to pony up a big contract to keep him. Jackson's fifth-year option will hit in 2020, and after that free agency will be calling. It would behoove the Bengals to extend him sooner rather than later. 🏈 To put it mildly, one thing that is bad for your run defense is when your two starting safeties decide to team up and allow 28 broken tackles. Still, Jessie Bates showed great knowledge of angles and his struggles were only in open-field tackling. Williams' problems are longer-lasting and he may be entering the George Iloka zone, where he's a surprising cap casualty, if the Bengals can conjure up another player of Bates' ilk. 🏈 South Dakota State's Jordan Brown looms as a potential steal in the seventh round. He's got the right physical tools to be an outside cornerback but needs to be tougher at the catch point and learn more of the finer points of NFL technique.

Special Teams

Year	DVOA	Rank	FG/XP	Rank	Net Kick	Rank	Kick Ret	Rank	Net Punt	Rank	Punt Ret	Rank	Hidden	Rank
2016	-2.7%	28	-12.1	31	0.9	14	9.0	3	-2.7	20	-8.7	30	-11.4	29
2017	-2.4%	21	2.7	14	-2.9	24	-5.3	31	-6.0	22	-0.2	17	4.8	11
2018	2.6%	7	1.0	14	2.9	8	8.6	3	-1.2	18	1.6	13	-10.8	27

Randy Bullock has solidified a spot that was stuck in the vacuum that is Mike Nugent. He's been roundly average for the last couple of seasons in Cincinnati and is signed through 2020. Tristan Vizcaino (Washington) was signed as an UDFA but made only 12 of 19 field goal attempts for the Huskies last season. Vizcaino might be looked at as a kickoff specialist, and Bullock has only been average at that for the Bengals. 🏈 We don't know if it's possible for a punter to be more statistically average than Kevin Huber has been the last three years. Our gross punt values have him worth 1.5 points of field position in 2018, 1.5 points in 2017, and 0.1 points in 2016. If the coverage units are as solid as they were last year, he'll be fine. 🏈 Alex Erickson was one of two players to return more than 35 kicks in 2018 (Andre Roberts was the other) and Erickson provided the third-most kick return points in the league, at 8.6. He was also worth 2.7 points over average on punt returns, rebounding from a down 2017 where he was negative on both kick and punt returns. 🏈 Backup corner Brandon Wilson had the best season on the Bengals in kick coverage, with nine tackles and eight stops between kick and punt returns. 🏈 Kudos to new Bengals signing Kerry Wynn for adding seven tackles (all seven of which were stops) on special teams as a defensive lineman. No other defensive lineman in the league had more return stops last year—only 25 total players did, and most of them didn't have a steady role on offense or defense like Wynn did with the Giants.

Cleveland Browns

2018 record: 7-8-1	**Total DVOA:** -2.8% (17th)	**2019 Mean Projection:** 8.0 wins	**On the Clock (0-4):** 11%
Pythagorean Wins: 7.1 (20th)	**Offense:** -1.1% (17th)	**Postseason Odds:** 33.7%	**Mediocrity (5-7):** 33%
Snap-Weighted Age: 25.3 (31st)	**Defense:** -2.5% (12th)	**Super Bowl Odds:** 3.6%	**Playoff Contender (8-10):** 39%
Average Opponent: 4.7% (3rd)	**Special Teams:** -4.2% (30th)	**Proj. Avg. Opponent:** -1.3% (25th)	**Super Bowl Contender (11+):** 18%

2018: Baker Baker, Dream Maker.

2019: Don't dream about the Super Bowl quite yet, gang.

I've been writing for Football Outsiders since 2008, and in that period I've handled the Browns essay for the *Prospectus/Almanac* many times. Each of those essays, without exception, has centered on the same theme: "Can Quarterback X finally be the guy to turn this sorry franchise around?" From Derek Anderson to Colt McCoy to Brandon Weeden to Johnny Manziel, we have been forced to temper enthusiasm and dump cold analytical water on Cleveland's dreams while reminding them that the Factory of Sadness never closed.

Well, go ahead and padlock the factory doors, because it's going the way of all the other manufacturing plants in the Rust Belt. Don't blame automation or foreign competition for this one, however. The guy Making Cleveland Watchable Again is not a builder but a Baker.

Last year, rookie Baker Mayfield, the top overall pick in the draft, became the 30th starting quarterback in Cleveland since the team resumed operations in 1999. While predictions of this sort inevitably become fodder for the Freezing Cold Takes Twitter account, it would be a shock if that number was much higher by this point in 2029 and beyond. Mayfield led the Brownies to a 7-8-1 record, and he didn't play in the first two losses of the year. Not only was it a massive improvement on 2017's crushing 0-16 campaign, but it was three more victories than the Browns managed in the previous three seasons combined. For the first time since 2010 the Browns didn't finish last in the AFC North. Mayfield's performance in his initial season was so good, with so much promise for the future, that he electrified the team and the city more than all 29 other signal-callers put together (a quantifiable stat brought to you by the mathematical wizards at Football Outsiders).

Baker became an instant lakeside legend on a Thursday night in September. After two-plus weeks of Tyrod Taylor ineptitude, Mayfield entered the game against the Jets in a 14-0 hole. He led the Browns to a 21-17 win, the franchise's first in an unfathomable 635 days. Taylor's name didn't come up the rest of the season, and when head coach Hue Jackson, sporting a 3-36-1 record in Cleveland, was at long last relieved of his duties a bit more than a month later, everyone (except perhaps Michael Silver) rightly applauded the franchise for choosing Baker over Hue.

Mayfield broke the NFL's rookie record for passing touchdowns with 27, topping Peyton Manning and Russell Wilson. He tossed for a score in 13 straight games, something

no Browns quarterback had done since Frank Ryan—*in 1966*. Despite sitting for the first two-plus games of the year, he ended up 12th in the league in passing DYAR and 14th in DVOA, more than respectable numbers for a rookie. (ESPN's QBR equation was much less bullish, ranking Mayfield 25th.)

When assessing the Browns' improvement under Mayfield, his *cajones* get as much credit as his accuracy. Both were in evidence far beyond the usual rookie limits on such things. His 63.8 percent completion rate, to choose one basic stat, far outpaced the four other rookie quarterbacks who played in 2018 (Lamar Jackson was second, believe it or not, at 58.2 percent), and was the fourth-best of any rookie this decade. (The names ahead of Mayfield? Robert Griffin, Dak Prescott, and Teddy Bridgewater.)

Baker was no Charlie Checkdown, as the Browns threw it deep (16 or more yards downfield) on a league-leading 28 percent of passes. Mayfield's most glaring positive trait combined accuracy with stones, throwing pinpoint long passes, often despite close or double coverage. As just one example, in Week 14 against Carolina, Mayfield lasered passes far, wide, and handsome against myriad coverages and to eight different receivers in a clinical display of timing and bravado.

Sure, he had some clunkers. The Chargers made Mayfield look like an overmatched freshman, and he threw three ugly picks against the Texans. The finale against the Ravens was a good cross-section of Mayfield's campaign. Facing a top defense which needed a win to clinch a playoff berth, Mayfield forced some throws and hurried others, tossing a pair of first-half interceptions that put Cleveland in a hole. But then he rallied the Browns to within two points with a pair of touchdown passes. He was driving for a miracle win when he tossed his third interception under a heavy blitz on fourth-and-long. In other words, the sky is the limit for Baker, but there are still some issues to clean up.

In particular, Mayfield exploded in the second half of the year, when he got more reps in both practice and game situations, and he bonded with his new offensive coordinator. The combination of Hue and Todd Haley was less oil and water than lit match and gasoline, and Mayfield was caught in the resulting grease fire. When both coaches were fired, running backs coach Freddie Kitchens took over as playcaller and the Browns and Baker took off. Mayfield tossed 19 of his 27 touchdown passes in the season's last two months, and

2019 Browns Schedule

Week	Opp.	Week	Opp.	Week	Opp.
1	TEN	7	BYE	13	at PIT
2	at NYJ (Mon.)	8	at NE	14	CIN
3	LAR	9	at DEN	15	at ARI
4	at BAL	10	BUF	16	BAL
5	at SF (Mon.)	11	PIT (Thu.)	17	at CIN
6	SEA	12	MIA		

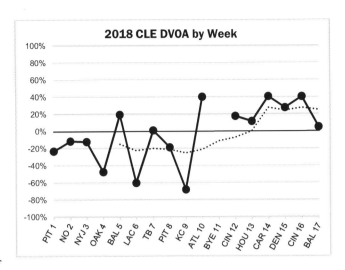

he threw for more yards in December than in September and October combined. Mayfield ended up with the third-highest second-half improvement in DVOA by any quarterback since 2004, and the best improvement by a first-year starter (Table 1). Mistakes were made, yes, but his play in the second half especially proved the future with Mayfield at the helm is incredibly promising and is certain to be exciting.

So can he sustain this level of play? Improve upon it, daresay? Or will he taste some regression in 2019?

Over and over throughout the history of Football Outsiders, we've looked at the idea that improvement or decline in the second half of the season predicts performance the following year. We've looked at it for offenses and for defenses. Here we're going to look at it for quarterbacks specifically. Always, we end up with a similar result. There simply doesn't seem to be a pattern where players or teams with outstanding second halves carry that momentum over to the following season. Full-season performance is more predictive than half-season performance, every time we look at it.

We looked at every quarterback since 2004 who had at least 80 pass attempts in each half of the year and at least 200 pass attempts the following year. For these quarterbacks, full-season DVOA in Year 1 predicted performance in Year 2 (corre-

lation: .50) better than looking at just DVOA from the second half of the season (correlation: .44).

What if we look only at quarterbacks who improved significantly in the second half of the year? If we limit ourselves to quarterbacks who improved by at least 10% DVOA after Week 10, we find … the same result. The correlation for full-season DVOA is .51 and the correlation for second-half DVOA is .45.

Of course, we want to believe that Mayfield's subpar performance in the first half was a rookie learning period, and the stellar Mayfield of the second half shows what he can do with more experience. So let's look only at other first-year starters. Surely, their improvement with more experience must carry over to Year 2? Nope, it doesn't. If we only look at first-year starters who improved in the second half, the correlation for full-season DVOA is .58 and the correlation for second-half DVOA is .48.

All evidence suggests that Mayfield's full-season perfor-

Biggest Second-Half Improvements in Passing DVOA, 2004-2018

Player	Year	Team	DVOA Wk 1-9	DVOA Wk 10-17	DVOA Change 2H	Age	Exp	Start Exp	DVOA	Plays +1	DVOA +1
Joey Harrington	2005	DET	-41.1%	24.7%	+65.9%	26.9	4	4	-15.2%	403	-14.9%
Russell Wilson	2015	SEA	-4.2%	54.3%	+58.5%	26.8	4	4	24.3%	600	4.0%
Baker Mayfield	**2018**	**CLE**	**-17.6%**	**39.9%**	**+57.5%**	**23.4**	**1**	**1**	**8.1%**		
Nick Foles	**2018**	**PHI**	**-37.5%**	**18.2%**	**+55.7%**	**29.6**	**7**	**6**	**-5.4%**		
Jon Kitna	2010	DAL	-34.7%	18.4%	+53.2%	37.9	14	12	-0.5%	10	-5.2%
Josh McCown	2007	OAK	-56.0%	-8.7%	+47.3%	28.2	6	4	-32.9%	0	0.0%
Josh Allen	**2018**	**BUF**	**-59.5%**	**-16.5%**	**+43.0%**	**22.3**	**1**	**1**	**-35.9%**		
Philip Rivers	2009	SD	22.5%	65.5%	+43.0%	27.7	6	4	41.7%	584	27.9%
Chris Simms	2005	TB	-34.3%	7.8%	+42.2%	25.0	3	1	-4.3%	110	-31.9%
JaMarcus Russell	2008	OAK	-38.9%	2.7%	+41.7%	23.1	2	1	-21.6%	280	-62.0%
Kurt Warner	2005	ARI	-16.0%	25.1%	+41.1%	34.2	12	7	8.2%	186	-4.5%
Carson Palmer	2004	CIN	-11.8%	28.9%	+40.8%	24.7	2	1	2.6%	537	33.4%
Matt Cassel	2008	NE	-20.6%	20.0%	+40.5%	26.3	4	1	1.1%	550	-29.3%
Jameis Winston	**2018**	**TB**	**-17.2%**	**23.4%**	**+40.5%**	**24.7**	**4**	**4**	**6.9%**		
Tom Brady	2010	NE	28.1%	67.8%	+39.7%	33.1	11	10	46.7%	648	35.3%
Sam Darnold	**2018**	**NYJ**	**-27.3%**	**12.3%**	**+39.6%**	**21.2**	**1**	**1**	**-15.2%**		
Drew Brees	2011	NO	22.0%	61.4%	+39.4%	32.6	11	10	38.3%	697	19.8%

Minimum 80 pass attempts in each half of the season.

mance is a better guide to how he'll do in 2019 than simply looking at the second half of the year. The fact that Mayfield led the league in passing DVOA from Week 10 onwards is not a good indicator that Mayfield will be the best quarterback in the league in 2018. And that's OK! Mayfield had the seventh-highest passing DVOA for a qualifying rookie since 1989, just ahead of Peyton Manning. Add some of the usual second-season improvement onto that and you have a top-ten quarterback.

Baker's sophomore season is inextricably linked with how the Browns perform in 2019, of course, but while we like Mayfield and presume he will be good in both short and long terms, the projection for the team is far less optimistic than the national consensus (Sports Blabber America will consider 2019 a failure if the Browns don't go undefeated).

Practically forgotten in all the offseason fireworks in Cleveland is that the team has a new head coach. Kitchens did such a good job running the offense and working with his star rookie that interim coach Gregg Williams was shown the door in order to give Kitchens his first head coaching job. Kitchens has been around the block, however, getting his start under Bill Parcells in Dallas in 2006 and doing every aspect of back office work on the Cardinals staff for over a decade, so it's heartening to see him succeed when he finally got his chance as a coordinator and parlay that into the top gig.

The only problem with that is, as we have seen on countless occasions (most recently his predecessor on the Browns sideline), being the head man is much different than succeeding as a coordinator. Kitchens is also in a trickier spot than the usual circumstances under which new coaches assume command—namely, a rebuilding team with little immediate pressure or a strong team whose coach retires or takes a better job. Cleveland is in an unusual position: talented, yet utterly unaccomplished; presumptive contenders, yet inexperienced; in need of some incognito development time, but poised to be the most closely scrutinized team of 2019. We know nothing of how Kitchens will handle the white-hot glare under which he is about to be thrust.

Baker is no stranger to controversy, going back to his college days and even as a pro, when he let his former coach, Jackson, know the Browns were better for his absence every chance he could. Mayfield is a loud presence for a quarterback, but he ain't beanbag next to his new toy. The Browns were already poised to be the league's darlings before they went and swiped Odell Beckham Jr. from the Giants, as general manager John Dorsey went all in to give his young quarterback advanced weaponry while Mayfield is still cheap.

Once Beckham was added to the fold, the Browns were guaranteed a surge in national TV games, segments on cable sports debate shows, and Twitter overreactions to every play. The Giants came to believe that OBJ's monumental talent and huge production (when healthy) wasn't worth the constant opera. Cleveland, the NFL's Chernobyl for nearly two decades, welcomed that particular tradeoff, at least for now. We will see what happens when Beckham initiates his De La Soul routine—"Me, Myself and I"—and if the wins that wallpaper over his antics don't come with the promised regularity. The team has already received a taste, with Beckham skipping vol-

untary minicamp in May, earning Kitchens' ire:
Q: "What is he missing by not being here?"
Kitchens: "The offense."

A player of Beckham's quality should manage to overcome missing some installation drills in the spring, but the incident highlighted another reason to not pencil the Browns in for a deep postseason run just yet.

Regardless of Beckham's volatility, Cleveland will score points in 2019. New offensive coordinator Todd Monken brings his schematic wizardry and "when in doubt, chuck it deep" mentality from Tampa Bay to help further unleash Mayfield. Running back Nick Chubb had nearly as high-quality a rookie season as his quarterback, likewise exploding once given a chance to do so post-Hue Jackson. Wideout Antonio Callaway was yet another rookie to do some special things, albeit not to the same degree. Rashard Higgins and David Njoku are young, talented pass-catchers, and for good measure the team added disgraced but highly productive back Kareem Hunt for the second half of the season, once he serves an eight-game suspension for off-field violence.

The offensive line might be the area that holds the team back, which is ironic given that for many years—the length of Joe Thomas' career, in fact—the front five was the team's strength, while the skill position guys were replacement-level. Not that Cleveland has a weak line, but it does have to replace star guard Kevin Zeitler (traded to the Giants for Olivier Vernon) and is reliant on another strong season from Greg Robinson at tackle, an iffy proposition given his history. But overall the unit was good in 2018, and anything close to a re-run will be just fine.

Mainly, our less-than-stellar projection is on the defense. There are a couple of factors here. First, the Browns were third in the NFL in ending drives with takeaways in 2018, forcing a turnover on 16.1 percent of enemy possessions. That's a number that is likely to regress, meaning Baker & Co. will be under even more pressure to score in bushels. In addition, the pass defense was ranked far better than the run defense in 2018. We've written about this elsewhere, but run defense is a better indicator for the following year's defensive DVOA than pass defense is. And while the mediocre pass rush got reinforcements in the form of Vernon and Sheldon Richardson, the run defense wasn't noticeably addressed in the offseason.

Tackling has been an issue in Cleveland seemingly since Clay Matthews Sr. was patrolling the field. The team led the league with 157 broken tackles and was 31st in percentage of plays with a broken tackle after ranking 30th in the same stat in 2017. Seven different defenders botched double-digit tackles. The poor run defense, as you would expect, was directly tied to the shoddy tackling. League-wide trends didn't help their cause. Cleveland was the worst defense in the NFL against shotgun and pistol runs, giving up a horrid 6.1 yards per carry and 26.4% DVOA. When the opposing quarterback was under center, however, the Browns got stout—sixth in the league in both yards per carry and DVOA. Alas, keeping the quarterback from touching his center's butt is the NFL's version of #MeToo, meaning the Browns need to spend plenty of time working on narrowing that gap.

Cleveland is also breaking in a new defensive scheme under a new coordinator. Steve Wilks presided as head coach over a single-season disaster in Arizona but while with the Panthers he coordinated sure-tackling, fast-moving defenses under his coaching rabbi, Ron Rivera. Clearly, the Browns won't be blitzing as much as they did under Williams, and the meeting rooms probably won't be quite so R-rated, either. Given all the noise on the offensive side of the ball, swapping out the voluble, oft-maniacal Williams for the far more stoic Wilks might be a stroke of genius, regardless of strategic tendencies.

Perhaps the biggest concern is depth. The Browns were quite healthy in 2018, with just 51.1 adjusted games lost, good for seventh in the league (for contrast, division rival Cincinnati lost more than twice as many, 104.9). While the boldface frontline talent is quite good, Dorsey hasn't had the opportunity to build up the back end of the roster in quite the same fashion. As is usually the case with teams on the rise, injury severity and timing will prove to be a key element in determining whether 2019 lives up to its promise or proves disappointing.

Cleveland is so thirsty for gridiron success, and the football public at large in general so eager to see them win at long last, that the Browns are in the hazardous waters of outsized expec-

tations. It bears remembering that the franchise hasn't had a winning (or even .500) season since 2007. They haven't made the postseason since 2002 or won a playoff game since 1994 (when the coach was Bill Belichick). Incredibly, the Browns haven't won as many as six games in consecutive seasons since 2001-02!

Last year, merely appearing on *Hard Knocks* caused the gambling crowd (read: suckers) to bet the Browns up to ridiculous odds to win the AFC North and even the AFC title, despite witnessing the toxic interplay between Jackson and his assistants. Now, with Beckham in town and the team looking "dangerous," to use Mayfield's favorite descriptor, hopes in the Dawg Pound are through the roof. Fans look around and see Le'Veon Bell and Antonio Brown gone from the hated Steelers, the Ravens playing a single-wing offense, and the Bengals in flux and foresee a cakewalk to the division title and beyond.

So once more, under very different circumstances to be sure, we're in the position of dampening the dreams of Browns Nation. Cleveland will be good in 2019, perhaps even playoff good. But you know about what happens when a starving person wolfs down a large meal, right?

Robert Weintraub

2018 Browns by Week

Wk	vs.	W-L	PF	PA	YDF	YDA	TO	Total	Off	Def	ST
1	PIT	T	21	21	327	472	+5	-23%	-34%	-28%	-16%
2	at NO	L	18	21	327	275	+1	-12%	-17%	-30%	-25%
3	NYJ	W	21	17	323	268	+3	-13%	-25%	-22%	-9%
4	at OAK	L	42	45	487	565	-2	-48%	-21%	9%	-17%
5	BAL	W	12	9	416	410	+1	19%	-2%	-26%	-5%
6	LAC	L	14	38	317	449	-1	-60%	-34%	36%	10%
7	at TB	L	23	26	305	456	+3	1%	-28%	-21%	8%
8	at PIT	L	18	33	237	421	+1	-19%	-3%	11%	-5%
9	KC	L	21	37	388	499	0	-68%	6%	69%	-5%
10	ATL	W	28	16	427	382	+1	40%	33%	-7%	0%
11	BYE										
12	at CIN	W	35	20	342	372	+2	18%	36%	12%	-6%
13	at HOU	L	13	29	428	384	-4	12%	13%	0%	-2%
14	CAR	W	26	20	348	393	-1	41%	27%	-2%	12%
15	at DEN	W	17	16	309	270	0	27%	6%	-17%	4%
16	CIN	W	26	18	493	209	0	40%	50%	-3%	-12%
17	at BAL	L	24	26	426	463	-2	5%	19%	17%	3%

Trends and Splits

	Offense	Rank	Defense	Rank
Total DVOA	-1.1%	17	-2.5%	12
Unadjusted VOA	1.3%	15	-2.1%	13
Weighted Trend	12.3%	8	3.7%	20
Variance	7.1%	19	6.8%	26
Average Opponent	1.3%	24	5.3%	3
Passing	7.8%	21	-3.5%	7
Rushing	-6.6%	17	-1.1%	25
First Down	2.3%	13	8.0%	26
Second Down	-10.5%	26	-7.4%	9
Third Down	6.8%	14	-17.3%	5
First Half	-7.7%	23	1.9%	21
Second Half	5.2%	15	-6.3%	10
Red Zone	21.2%	6	-12.5%	8
Late and Close	1.1%	16	-12.1%	8

Five-Year Performance

Year	W-L	Pyth W	Est W	PF	PA	TO	Total	Rank	Off	Rank	Def	Rank	ST	Rank	Off AGL	Rank	Def AGL	Rank	Off Age	Rank	Def Age	Rank	ST Age	Rank
2014	7-9	6.9	7.2	299	337	+6	-6.7%	23	-10.2%	24	-3.0%	11	0.4%	14	30.5	16	36.6	14	26.6	18	26.4	22	25.8	23
2015	3-13	4.0	4.5	278	432	-9	-23.0%	30	-13.2%	27	10.5%	29	0.7%	15	37.1	18	33.7	21	27.4	9	27.1	8	25.6	25
2016	1-15	3.3	1.5	264	452	-12	-30.4%	31	-13.4%	29	14.5%	30	-2.5%	26	46.2	23	50.2	23	26.7	15	25.1	32	24.5	32
2017	0-16	3.3	3.3	234	410	-28	-27.2%	32	-20.1%	32	2.0%	16	-5.1%	27	21.3	7	31.3	14	24.9	32	24.5	32	24.1	32
2018	7-8-1	7.1	7.5	359	392	+7	-2.8%	17	-1.1%	17	-2.5%	12	-4.2%	30	10.3	1	40.8	22	25.6	30	24.9	31	25.4	27

2018 Performance Based on Most Common Personnel Groups

	CLE Offense					CLE Offense vs. Opponents						CLE Defense					CLE Defense vs. Opponents			
Pers	Freq	Yds	DVOA	Run%		Pers	Freq	Yds	DVOA	Run%		Pers	Freq	Yds	DVOA		Pers	Freq	Yds	DVOA
11	62%	6.3	6.4%	26%		Base	26%	5.5	-10.5%	58%		Base	31%	5.2	-15.2%		11	65%	6.1	10.7%
12	16%	5.9	6.7%	48%		Nickel	44%	6.2	5.4%	32%		Nickel	66%	6.0	5.6%		12	17%	6.3	1.0%
13	12%	5.6	-17.7%	71%		Dime+	19%	6.7	17.1%	14%		Dime+	1%	6.9	24.6%		22	3%	4.7	-16.3%
10	3%	6.4	-3.3%	17%		Goal Line	1%	1.0	-3.4%	81%		Goal Line	1%	0.6	-55.8%		13	3%	1.4	-92.0%
21	2%	4.2	1.7%	30%													21	3%	4.3	-23.9%

Strategic Tendencies

Run/Pass		Rk	Formation		Rk	Pass Rush		Rk	Secondary		Rk	Strategy		Rk
Runs, first half	38%	16	Form: Single Back	73%	26	Rush 3	9.2%	12	4 DB	31%	7	Play action	23%	18
Runs, first down	44%	22	Form: Empty Back	10%	8	Rush 4	53.5%	32	5 DB	66%	15	Avg Box (Off)	6.25	13
Runs, second-long	31%	13	Pers: 3+ WR	66%	19	Rush 5	24.2%	7	6+ DB	1%	27	Avg Box (Def)	6.31	10
Runs, power sit.	50%	24	Pers: 2+ TE/6+ OL	29%	8	Rush 6+	12.9%	1	CB by Sides	82%	12	Offensive Pace	31.09	14
Runs, behind 2H	28%	15	Pers: 6+ OL	2%	16	Int DL Sacks	16.2%	28	S/CB Cover Ratio	24%	26	Defensive Pace	30.10	4
Pass, ahead 2H	51%	10	Shotgun/Pistol	63%	16	Second Level Sacks	36.5%	4	DB Blitz	11%	9	Go for it on 4th	2.24	3

Three years, three sets of quarterbacks, one very strange trend: Cleveland throws to the right side of the field much more than the left side. Last year, it was 46 percent of passes to the right and just 34 percent of passes to the left. Maybe it's a good idea considering that the Browns were ninth in DVOA on passes to the right and 28th in DVOA on passes to the left. ✎ Thankfully, Cleveland's ridiculous tendency to leave base defense on the field against 11 personnel was much less of a problem in 2018. The Browns more than doubled their use of nickel personnel. They still ranked second in frequency of using base defense against 11 personnel with 90 plays—Denver was No. 1 with 101 plays—but nearly a third of those came in one game, against Baltimore in Week 5. ✎ The Browns faced a league-high 51 wide receiver or tight end screens, with a -1.4% DVOA against these plays. ✎ The listed Aggressiveness Index of 2.24 belongs to Gregg Williams; Hue Jackson's AI in the first part of the season was 1.63, which would have ranked eighth if Williams were not included. ✎ Cleveland's defense tied with Oakland for the league high with 34 dropped passes by opponents. Of course, this was 7.5 percent of passes faced by Oakland but just 5.7 percent of passes faced by Cleveland (fifth).

Passing

Player	DYAR	DVOA	Plays	NtYds	Avg	YAC	C%	TD	Int
B.Mayfield	628	8.1%	509	3549	7.0	5.5	64.2%	27	14
T.Taylor*	-264	-53.5%	97	382	3.9	4.7	50.6%	2	2

Rushing

Player	DYAR	DVOA	Plays	Yds	Avg	TD	Fum	Suc
N.Chubb	80	1.1%	192	996	5.2	8	0	50%
C.Hyde*	10	-6.6%	114	399	3.5	5	1	38%
D.Johnson	24	7.2%	40	201	5.0	0	0	50%
B.Mayfield	-20	-28.6%	25	143	5.7	0	2	--
T.Taylor*	4	-6.8%	16	122	7.6	1	2	--
K.Hunt	134	9.1%	181	840	4.6	8	0	55%
O.Beckham	12	25.2%	5	19	3.8	0	0	--

Receiving

Player	DYAR	DVOA	Plays	Ctch	Yds	Y/C	YAC	TD	C%
J.Landry	-111	-22.2%	149	81	978	12.1	3.4	4	54%
A.Callaway	40	-6.3%	79	43	586	13.6	5.5	5	54%
R.Higgins	143	22.3%	53	39	572	14.7	3.7	4	74%
B.Perriman*	97	36.6%	25	16	340	21.3	4.7	2	64%
D.Ratley	-2	-14.3%	20	13	144	11.1	3.9	0	65%
O.Beckham	151	2.5%	124	77	1052	13.7	4.1	6	62%
D.Njoku	-63	-18.1%	88	56	639	11.4	5.5	4	64%
D.Fells*	52	53.9%	12	11	117	10.6	6.0	3	92%
S.DeValve	14	26.9%	7	5	74	14.8	3.0	1	71%
D.Harris	-14	-15.6%	25	12	164	13.7	6.3	3	48%
D.Johnson	103	12.9%	62	47	429	9.1	8.0	3	76%
N.Chubb	14	-4.6%	29	20	149	7.5	9.1	2	69%
D.Hilliard	43	70.4%	10	9	105	11.7	10.0	0	90%
C.Hyde*	-12	-41.7%	9	6	29	4.8	7.2	0	67%
K.Hunt	198	79.4%	35	26	378	14.5	13.0	7	74%

Offensive Line

Player	Pos	Age	GS	Snaps	Pen	Sk	Pass	Run	Player	Pos	Age	GS	Snaps	Pen	Sk	Pass	Run
Joel Bitonio	LG	28	16/16	1091	4	1.0	5	3	Greg Robinson	LT	27	16/8	498	10	0.0	4	6
Chris Hubbard	RT	28	16/16	1091	3	6.5	14	6	Kendall Lamm	RT	27	15/13	859	4	3.5	9	4
J.C. Tretter	C	28	16/16	1091	1	1.0	2	3	Bryan Witzmann	RG	29	10/7	533	1	3.0	8	8
Kevin Zeitler*	RG	29	16/16	1091	7	1.5	5	6	Eric Kush	LG	30	15/7	344	2	0.5	4	2
Desmond Harrison*	LT	26	8/8	595	10	2.5	8	4									

Year	Yards	ALY	Rank	Power	Rank	Stuff	Rank	2nd Lev	Rank	Open Field	Rank	Sacks	ASR	Rank	Press	Rank	F-Start	Cont.
2016	4.82	3.73	28	71%	7	22%	27	1.40	2	1.36	1	66	10.6%	32	30.5%	28	20	23
2017	4.15	4.09	14	74%	4	19%	11	1.23	8	0.75	15	50	7.6%	22	32.9%	24	11	39
2018	4.61	4.24	18	50%	32	23%	29	1.27	16	1.16	4	38	6.7%	16	27.7%	11	11	38

2018 ALY by direction: Left End: 4.88 (15) Left Tackle: 4.23 (13) Mid/Guard: 4.47 (14) Right Tackle: 3.19 (31) Right End: 4.40 (13)

Cleveland ranked eighth in the league in plays per blown block, including sixth on pass plays. ❧ Greg Robinson was the key to the line's solid effort in 2018, settling the left side down after project tackle Desmond Harrison was erratic during the season's first half. This was not a misprint. Robinson, the former No. 2 overall pick by the Rams, washed up in Cleveland and found new life on a veteran minimum deal, playing well enough to earn a $9-million contract for 2019. Meanwhile, Harrison was cut in early June. ❧ Chris Hubbard held down the right side after coming over from the Steelers, starting every game for his new club and providing good pass blocking, though we charted Cleveland runs at right tackle being second worst in adjusted line yards behind only the sieve in Houston. Hubbard also had 20 blown blocks, by far the most on the team. ❧ Center J.C. Tretter and superb guard Joel Bitonio are mainstays, but the line will be breaking in a replacement for the other guard, Kevin Zeitler, a stud traded to New York for Olivier Vernon. ❧ Austin Corbett, Cleveland's second-round pick in 2018, was a longtime left tackle while at Nevada, where he replaced Bitonio in the starting lineup. Now he is slated to line up alongside Bitonio as a fellow guard, provided he beats out Bryan Witzmann and Eric Kush, a pair of experienced free agents who provide excellent interior depth. Corbett may not be as good as Zeitler, especially in his first season of regular duty, but he has excellent agility and arm placement, and shouldn't be overmatched physically. That's important, for while the Browns line was effective enough in pass protection, it struggled with physicality on the ground. They were dead last in power situations, converting just half of their short-yardage runs, and fourth from the bottom in having their backs get tackled for loss or no gain. ❧ Cleveland runners, in the main Nick Chubb, were elusive once past the line of scrimmage, ranking fourth in open-field yards. A little better balance between line and backs would serve the Browns well in 2019.

Defensive Front

Defensive Line	Age	Pos	G	Snaps	Plays	TmPct	Rk	Stop	Dfts	BTkl	Runs	St%	Rk	RuYd	Rk	Sack	Hit	Hur	Dsrpt
Larry Ogunjobi	25	DT	16	930	52	5.9%	27	43	17	4	41	83%	19	1.5	10	5.5	8	17	0
Trevon Coley	25	DT	16	614	39	4.4%	51	29	10	4	32	84%	14	1.3	7	0.5	0	5	0
Sheldon Richardson	29	DT	16	718	48	5.9%	24	34	13	7	38	68%	69	2.8	67	4.5	13	21	0

Edge Rushers	Age	Pos	G	Snaps	Plays	TmPct	Rk	Stop	Dfts	BTkl	Runs	St%	Rk	RuYd	Rk	Sack	Hit	Hur	Dsrpt
Myles Garrett	24	DE	16	1011	47	5.3%	37	42	23	4	26	88%	8	1.8	27	13.5	17	33	2
Emmanuel Ogbah*	26	DE	14	806	48	6.2%	16	30	12	5	35	51%	90	3.4	77	3.0	5	28	6
Chris Smith	27	DE	16	336	23	2.6%	--	19	10	6	18	83%	--	0.6	--	1.0	1	7	1
Olivier Vernon	29	OLB	11	666	31	5.4%	36	26	10	2	19	79%	28	4.5	91	7.0	16	30	1

Linebackers	Age	Pos	G	Snaps	Plays	TmPct	Rk	Stop	Dfts	BTkl	Runs	St%	Rk	RuYd	Rk	Sack	Hit	Hur	Tgts	Suc%	Rk	AdjYd	Rk	PD	Int
Jamie Collins*	30	OLB	16	1067	108	12.2%	44	59	20	18	63	67%	19	3.6	32	4.0	3	9	45	42%	58	7.6	61	4	1
Joe Schobert	26	MLB	13	897	109	15.1%	24	51	17	20	70	53%	63	4.3	61	3.0	2	12	32	56%	18	5.3	16	6	1
Genard Avery	23	OLB	16	684	43	4.8%	85	28	14	1	20	70%	11	4.4	68	4.5	9	28.5	15	53%	--	6.4	--	4	0
Christian Kirksey	27	OLB	7	474	48	12.4%	43	22	7	11	26	62%	32	4.0	46	0.0	0	3	27	33%	75	10.9	79	5	2
Tanner Vallejo*	25	OLB	13	145	20	2.8%	--	15	4	4	12	92%	--	1.6	--	0.0	0	1	6	17%	--	9.8	--	0	0
Adarius Taylor	29	ILB	15	635	61	8.0%	70	31	7	5	36	50%	76	4.0	51	1.0	0	3	24	50%	40	6.7	35	5	1
Ray-Ray Armstrong	28	ILB	15	212	21	2.5%	--	11	1	2	15	67%	--	3.3	--	0.0	0	0.5	4	50%	--	11.8	--	0	0

Year	Yards	ALY	Rank	Power	Rank	Stuff	Rank	2nd Level	Rank	Open Field	Rank	Sacks	ASR	Rank	Press	Rank
2016	4.50	4.85	32	61%	12	15%	30	1.25	22	0.69	14	26	5.7%	21	23.7%	28
2017	3.35	3.27	2	56%	8	30%	1	1.08	12	0.60	8	34	6.5%	17	29.6%	21
2018	4.75	4.21	11	63%	10	23%	9	1.51	31	1.16	28	37	6.7%	23	27.1%	27

2018 ALY by direction:	Left End: 3.78 (9)	Left Tackle: 5.04 (27)	Mid/Guard: 4.03 (6)	Right Tackle: 4.35 (18)	Right End: 4.74 (20)

The Gregg Williams Effect: no team blitzed six or more players more often than Cleveland, and no team rushed only four less often. The all-out attack was necessary, as the Browns were just 23rd in adjusted sack rate, even with all the red doggin'. ● Myles Garrett emerged as the beast everyone expected when he was drafted first overall in 2017, with 50 hits/hurries to go with his 13.5 sacks. ● The rest of the front seven combined for just 21.5 sacks, however, so reinforcements were brought in. Olivier Vernon struggled with injury with the Giants, but he posted just four fewer hits/hurries than Garrett on nearly 400 fewer snaps. If he can stay on the field, Cleveland will be able to harass the passer from both sides. ● Pass rush will be coming up the gut as well, with Larry Ogunjobi now joined by Sheldon Richardson, who had a strong season rushing the passer in Minnesota before coming over to Cleveland on a three-year deal. A starting front four of Garrett, Ogunjobi, Richardson, and Vernon is terrifying and deserving of a nickname. Depth beyond "The Lake Effect" is a concern, however. ● In 2018, Richardson was average at best against the run, which was already Cleveland's main defensive weakness (25th in DVOA). ● Genard Avery emerged as a tremendous run-stuffer (we charted him with just one missed tackle in 684 snaps), but middle linebacker Joe Schobert continues to be the most slovenly on a team of sloppy tacklers (46 total missed tackles the last two years) and Christian Kirksey regressed from a solid 2017. ● With Jamie Collins not re-signed, the team drafted a pair of new linebackers. Mack Wilson began 2018 as the latest tackling stud from Alabama but didn't live up to the hype and fell to the fifth round. He is seen as a high-floor, low-ceiling prospect. BYU's Sione Takitaki profiles to be a depth player but he's got a Pro Bowl name. The third-rounder fits right into this unit because his biggest strength is range and his biggest weakness is tackling.

Defensive Secondary

Secondary	Age	Pos	G	Snaps	Plays	TmPct	Rk	Stop	Dfts	BTkl	Runs	St%	Rk	RuYd	Rk	Tgts	Tgt%	Rk	Dist	Suc%	Rk	AdjYd	Rk	PD	Int
Damarious Randall	27	FS	15	1082	93	11.2%	25	20	10	14	39	13%	74	12.8	74	41	9.1%	32	15.6	46%	49	8.9	57	9	4
T.J. Carrie	29	CB	16	907	81	9.1%	33	34	13	10	23	61%	10	3.5	5	73	19.4%	46	11.9	52%	39	6.7	18	8	1
Denzel Ward	22	CB	13	841	64	8.9%	38	25	15	11	16	31%	64	6.3	36	78	22.3%	60	10.5	63%	3	6.0	11	11	3
Jabrill Peppers*	24	SS	16	764	82	9.2%	47	32	10	9	39	51%	19	5.6	21	27	8.5%	28	9.9	41%	62	7.9	45	5	1
Briean Boddy-Calhoun*	26	CB	16	656	54	6.1%	76	16	7	8	12	17%	75	9.1	69	40	14.7%	9	6.6	45%	68	6.9	26	2	0
Derrick Kindred*	26	SS	16	497	39	4.4%	--	11	5	10	14	29%	--	8.7	--	14	6.8%	--	5.9	36%	--	10.2	--	1	1
Terrance Mitchell	27	CB	8	445	44	9.9%	--	18	6	3	10	30%	--	8.7	--	43	23.3%	--	9.8	58%	--	6.6	--	6	1
Phillip Gaines	28	CB	11	408	38	7.0%	--	11	2	2	18	33%	--	6.8	--	32	16.5%	--	13.7	41%	--	9.1	--	2	0
Eric Murray	25	FS	15	702	56	6.9%	63	12	5	4	21	29%	60	9.2	58	30	9.6%	36	13.2	40%	65	8.4	52	2	1
Morgan Burnett	30	SS	11	389	36	6.7%	65	21	11	0	12	58%	11	4.6	8	26	15.5%	72	14.2	62%	12	7.2	38	6	0
Jermaine Whitehead	26	FS	14	228	22	3.1%	--	9	3	2	11	45%	--	4.9	--	13	12.4%	--	7.1	38%	--	7.5	--	2	0

Year	Pass D Rank	vs. #1 WR	Rk	vs. #2 WR	Rk	vs. Other WR	Rk	WR Wide	Rk	WR Slot	Rk	vs. TE	Rk	vs. RB	Rk
2016	29	14.9%	30	6.0%	23	-4.5%	10	5.1%	22	10.6%	20	39.7%	32	3.5%	20
2017	26	22.0%	29	-7.5%	12	-6.4%	13	10.8%	27	1.4%	14	27.8%	32	24.9%	30
2018	7	-3.6%	12	-15.8%	8	-25.4%	3	-7.9%	15	-21.3%	2	-12.5%	9	4.4%	17

Baker Mayfield got all the hype, but another area of drastic improvement in Cleveland was pass defense. After finishing 26th, 29th, and 27th from 2015 to 17, the Browns leapt to seventh in DVOA. ● The addition of No. 4 overall pick Denzel Ward had an obvious effect on the secondary, fostering an improvement in covering enemy No. 1 wideouts (12th, up from 29th). The only concerns during Ward's tremendous first season were a pair of late-season concussions—his combination of small stature and willingness to stick his nose into combat is admirable but not necessarily conducive to a long, healthy career. ● T.J. Carrie came over from the Raiders and had a fantastic season in the slot—only Chicago defended inside receivers better than Cleveland, largely thanks to Carrie. ● Yet another key addition to the backfield was Damarious Randall, who went from playing out of position in Green Bay to a more natural free safety role in Browns Town. He brought swagger and stature to a position that has been a Browns weak spot for years. ● Randall's acquisition allowed Jabril Peppers to play nearer the line of scrimmage, where he was far more effective than he had been as a deep (*very* deep) safety in 2017. With him gone, the box safety role figures to be a battle between well-traveled veteran Morgan Burnett and fourth-round rookie Sheldrick Redwine, a physical force at Miami who lapsed in coverage but could emerge with some coaching. ● Another rookie, Greedy Williams, is likely to man the corner opposite Ward sooner rather than later. Thought to be a top-10 talent at LSU, Greedy fell in the draft when he coasted through his redshirt sophomore season, making several "business decisions" when it came to tackling enemy wideouts. He also reportedly did poorly on the Wonderlic and in team interviews. But as John Dorsey said, the NFL is a passing league, and Greedy can cover, and at 6-foot-2 with long arms he presents a much different challenge than Ward. Let's face it—his nickname (Greedy's given name is Andraez) virtually guarantees a player good enough to earn a second contract but also hold out in order to maximize his payday. That said, Williams was mainly a press-man corner at LSU, so if Wilks indeed sticks with the heavy zone looks as he has in the past, Greedy will have to become more altruistic to fit in.

Special Teams

Year	DVOA	Rank	FG/XP	Rank	Net Kick	Rank	Kick Ret	Rank	Net Punt	Rank	Punt Ret	Rank	Hidden	Rank
2016	-2.5%	26	-4.5	23	3.3	9	-6.6	28	-1.4	18	-3.6	23	4.5	9
2017	-5.1%	27	-3.5	21	-6.0	28	2.1	9	-11.5	29	-6.8	30	-4.8	21
2018	-4.2%	30	-9.8	28	0.8	16	-5.3	30	-10.8	30	4.2	10	0.4	15

The Browns remained consistently terrible pretty much across the special teams spectrum in 2018. 🏈 Zane Gonzalez was cut after missing a quartet of field goals and extra points to cost the team a game against the Saints. His replacement, Greg Joseph, missed seven kicks himself. 🏈 Even worse was punter Britton Colquitt, who regressed mightily, ranking 30th out of 34 punters in gross punt value. Punting is usually the most consistent of the special teams disciplines from year to year, but in three years Colquitt has gone from 21st to sixth to 30th in gross punt value. 🏈 The gunner units were poor, and Jabril Peppers and Antonio Callaway were mediocre return men, evidenced in part by the fact that only the Bears had worse average starting field position on offense. Dontrell Hilliard was better in a small sample, and thus has the inside track to return kicks in 2019. 🏈 In the fifth round, the Browns drafted Oklahoma's Austin Seibert, a kicking multitasker who placekicked, kicked off, and punted for the Sooners. Alas, he wasn't particularly great at any of the disciplines, so his capacity to beat out the incumbents looks limited. 🏈 Otherwise, all these specialists save the traded Peppers are set to have another go in 2019. Improvement in these areas is crucial if Cleveland is to achieve its lofty goals.

Dallas Cowboys

2018 record: 10-6	**Total DVOA:** -5.2% (21st)	**2019 Mean Projection:** 8.7 wins	**On the Clock (0-4):** 6%
Pythagorean Wins: 8.4 (14th)	**Offense:** -6.6% (24th)	**Postseason Odds:** 47.7%	**Mediocrity (5-7):** 25%
Snap-Weighted Age: 25.3 (32nd)	**Defense:** -3.5% (9th)	**Super Bowl Odds:** 7.7%	**Playoff Contender (8-10):** 42%
Average Opponent: -2.1% (21st)	**Special Teams:** -2.1% (23rd)	**Proj. Avg. Opponent:** -2.0% (27th)	**Super Bowl Contender (11+):** 27%

2018: Meet the Rutles.

2019: All you need is cash.

As ruts go, the Cowboys are stuck in a rather comfortable one.

The team is relatively successful, with three straight winning seasons and two playoff appearances in the last three years. The roster is young and talented. The cap situation, for once, is manageable. The franchise structure and coaching staff are stable. Perhaps a little too stable.

But a comfortable rut is still a rut. The last two Cowboys seasons have had a Groundhog Day vibe. Each year, the team endures a slump, then enjoys a surge. During each slump, Jason Garrett's future and Dak Prescott's franchise-quarterback worthiness are questioned. During each surge, Prescott is temporarily vindicated, and Garrett is granted another stay of execution.

Each year, the Cowboys lose a sliver of their mighty offensive line and overreact to the setback. Each year, the youthful defense looks a little bit better, but never arrives near excellence. Each offseason, Ezekiel Elliott gets in some sort of near-trouble that earns him a spin on the league's Wheel of Random Justice.

The Cowboys squandered two years of Prescott's magic-window rookie contract years spinning their wheels and taking care of old housecleaning items like Tony Romo's cap debts and Dez Bryant's departure. They have spent two years trying to recapture the 13-3 magic of their 2016 season instead of building on it. Now they are trying to climb back into contention before their young nucleus becomes prohibitively expensive to maintain. But it may already be too late.

The Cowboys won 10 games last year, outperforming their Estimated Wins (7.0) and Pythagorean Projection (8.4) thanks largely to some close late-season victories in games where they did not play all that well: Week 16 against the Buccaneers, Weeks 10 and 11 against the Falcons and Eagles. They beat a Seahawks team in the playoffs that decided to use a game plan from a 1970s high school coaching clinic before losing to the Rams in a game which wasn't as close as the 30-22 final score suggests. It was a fine season, but it hammered home the fact that the Cowboys were second-tier contenders with no clear plan for climbing into the top tier.

The Amari Cooper trade illustrates the Cowboys dilemma. The team tried to move on from the expensive, aging, user-unfriendly receiver Dez Bryant last summer without finding a suitable replacement. They kidded themselves with a Cole Beasley/Tavon Austin/Allen Hurns/Michael Gallup receiver committee for a few weeks, started the season with a 3-4 record and lots of sub-200-yard passing days, then traded their 2019 first-round pick to the Raiders for Cooper during the bye week.

With Cooper integrated into the offense, the Cowboys passing DVOA climbed from 28th in the league (-13.5%) in the first half of the season to 17th (9.1%) in the second half. Prescott and the passing game no longer flatlined every other week like they did at the start of the season, and the Cowboys rode a 7-1 second-half stretch into the playoffs.

So the Cooper trade worked out well … except that it left the Cowboys without a first-round pick in 2019. And Cooper is entering the option year of his rookie contract, so the team added to its queue of young veterans seeking their first big-time deals. The Cooper trade kept the Cowboys from back-sliding, but it is also one of the factors which could keep them from contending for the Super Bowl.

From a cap standpoint, the Cowboys now have a lot of mouths to feed. Tank Lawrence was the first of their current wave of young veterans to cash in, signing a five-year deal in April with $48 million in guarantees. Prescott is in the final year of that team-cuddly fourth-round rookie contract. Cooper, Elliott, and Byron Jones are also in the deli line. Jerry Jones must soon shell out some massive wads of dough just to keep his core intact, which wouldn't be so bad if it were an 11-Estimated Win core, not an 8.4-Estimated Win core.

The Cowboys planned for this bank run better than they have in years past, but even the planning has become part of the problem. In the past, the Cowboys scraped the roof of the salary cap each year, performing voodoo economics on Romo's contract and sometimes letting useful young veterans go in order to pay both their Romo-Bryant-Jason Witten-Demarcus Ware nucleus and anyone for whom Jerrah made it rain in free agency.

This year, the Cowboys entered the summer with $19 million in 2019 cap space and over $85 million for 2020 squirreled away after the Tank extension. That money represents a quarterback-sized line in the budget for the Prescott deal to squeeze into, plus some extra cash for Cooper and perhaps some others. Again: wise budgeting. But this new fiscal responsibility kept them out of the premium free-agent market at a point when they could have used another impact player or

2018 Cowboys Schedule

Week	Opp.	Week	Opp.	Week	Opp.
1	NYG	7	PHI	13	BUF (Thu.)
2	at WAS	8	BYE	14	at CHI (Thu.)
3	MIA	9	at NYG (Mon.)	15	LAR
4	at NO	10	MIN	16	at PHI
5	GB	11	at DET	17	WAS
6	at NYJ	12	at NE		

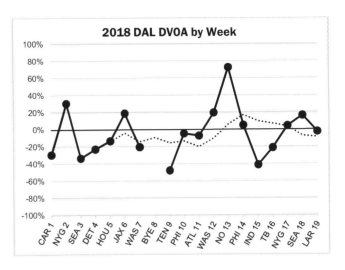

2018 DAL DVOA by Week

two to vault them into the Super Bowl.

With austerity measures preventing them from doing much in free agency—Randall Cobb, their biggest-name acquisition, is merely a short-term replacement for Beasley, signed away by the Bills—and the Cooper trade leaving them with limited draft capital, the Cowboys hope to close the gap separating them from the true NFC contenders with the help of some returning veterans and improvement across their young defense.

Whether because they lack imagination, felt the need for more locker room leadership, or simply couldn't bear to see a beloved legend roasted every week for his Monday Night Football broadcast caterwauling, the Cowboys chose to lure Jason Witten out of retirement with a one-year, $5-million contract. As ludicrous as the signing looks on paper, it's not disastrous. Expectations for Witten are low: a 30- to 40-snap per game package role. At age 37, after a year of making Lou Reed's *Metal Machine Music* sound soothing compared to his color commentary, Witten is still a likely upgrade over Geoff Swaim, now with the Jaguars, and can mentor/platoon with Blake Jarwin, who came on strong late in the year.

Soon after re-signing Witten, the Cowboys restructured Sean Lee's contract to keep him in Dallas through this year. Lee had a typical Lee season in 2019: he started out relatively strong, injured a hamstring, missed a few games, tried to come back, reaggravated the same hamstring, missed even more games, then hobbled back to attempt some Kirk Gibson playoff heroics.

Lee has never been healthy for 16 games, has battled hamstring ailments for two years, and rarely looked like much more than a shell of himself after the first injury last year. Lee already has an heir apparent on the roster: Leighton Vander Esch played very well at middle linebacker in his absence. The Cowboys may see Lee as a situational player at this point, perhaps as a designated pass-rusher; like Witten, he could help a little, but shouldn't be counted upon for much.

Center Travis Frederick, who missed all of last season with Guillain-Barré Syndrome, could have a much bigger impact on the Cowboys' 2019 fortunes than Witten or Lee. In Frederick's absence, the interior line of All-Pro Zach Martin and journeymen/rookies Joe Looney, Connor Williams, and Xavier Su'a-Filo was adequate on its best days and got its soul devoured by Fletcher Cox-types on its worst.

The Cowboys finished a respectable eighth in the league in adjusted line yards without Frederick last year, and Prescott's tendency to hold the ball too long had as much an impact on their 56 sacks allowed and 28th-ranked finish in adjusted sack rate as the protection issues. But the Cowboys system (and payroll) is built around dominance on the offensive line, not above-averageness.

Frederick was a full participant at the start of OTAs, which is great news from both a Cowboys standpoint and a human standpoint. If the Cowboys' line can have another 2016-caliber season, the team could enjoy another 13-3 finish. The problem is that any setback to the Frederick-Martin-Tyron Smith Big Three has immediately caused an offense-wide derailment in the past. That's a coaching-scheme issue, and the Cowboys refuse to make any meaningful changes in that department.

The Cowboys are also counting on broad-based improvements on defense. The Cowboys fielded the youngest snap-weighted defense in the NFL last season, at 24.7 years old. Nearly every significant defensive contributor from last season—Lawrence, Vander Esch, Byron Jones, Jaylon Smith, Chidobe Awuzie, Xavier Woods, Maliek Collins, Antwaun Woods, Anthony Brown—is 27 years old or younger. The young defense improved as last season went on, climbing from 16th to ninth in overall defense and 26th to 11th in pass defense in the second half of last season. With discount free agent Robert Quinn joining the fold as a pass-rusher and Taco Charlton still capable of a breakout year, the Cowboys defense could take another step forward in 2019.

Defensive backs coach, passing game coordinator, and de facto defensive coordinator Kris Richard may be more important to the Cowboys' defensive success in 2019 than any player. One of the principal architects of the Legion of Boom in Seattle, Richard arrived in Dallas last year and rapidly climbed the coaching org chart; Rod Marinelli is still the official defensive coordinator, but Richard has assumed many of the responsibilities that matter.

The Cowboys got lucky when Richard was passed over on the head coaching carousel in favor of all the Sean McVay clones. They won't be so lucky this year. If Richard elevates this defense into a top-ten unit, the Cowboys will lose their best coach. That's one more reason, along with the rapidly expanding payroll, why the Cowboys can't afford to remain mired in 9-7 purgatory for another year.

As good as many elements of the current roster and coaching staff are, the Cowboys may be stuck in this rut because they lack excellence at the top. Jerrah and Stephen Jones can't quite find any of the middle gears between free-spending impatience and thrifty over-patience. Jason Garrett's talents lie in massaging the egos above and below him and keeping everyone on the same page of his one-page game plans: he's not going to win any chess matches or bring new ideas to the table. Prescott has settled into the middle of the starting quarterback pack, and there is no reason to expect him to climb out with this receiving corps and coaching staff just because he's about to be overpaid.

Our projections find the Cowboys rebounding from their two-year offensive slide thanks to Cooper, Frederick, and old-fashioned regression to the mean. They may also enjoy a slight uptick on defense, and a schedule full of Giants, Skins, and AFC East opponents will have plenty of soft spots. But those improvements will only offset the gap between their Pythagorean and Expected Wins and their actual record last season, and they're unlikely to catch the Eagles in injury crisis mode twice again this year. So the Cowboys are even spinning their wheels from a mathematical modeling standpoint.

If 2019 turns out to be another comfortable rut season, it will be the last for the Cowboys. Something's gotta give, capwise. The core of the offensive line is climbing toward age 30. Jerrah will either give up on Garrett, lose Richard, or both. Despite its youth, the Cowboys roster isn't built to last. Despite its stability, the Cowboys coaching staff is one slump away from upheaval.

This has to be the year in which everything breaks right. But that's precisely the problem: everything has to break right, and the Cowboys just spent two years proving that they don't have a plan for when it doesn't.

Mike Tanier

2018 Cowboys Stats by Week

Wk	vs.	W-L	PF	PA	YDF	YDA	TO	Total	Off	Def	ST
1	at CAR	L	8	16	232	293	0	-30%	-20%	-4%	-14%
2	NYG	W	20	13	298	255	+1	30%	15%	-18%	-3%
3	at SEA	L	13	24	303	295	-3	-34%	-44%	-4%	6%
4	DET	W	26	24	414	382	0	-23%	8%	33%	2%
5	at HOU	L	16	19	292	462	0	-14%	-26%	-13%	0%
6	JAX	W	40	7	378	204	+2	19%	-1%	-13%	7%
7	at WAS	L	17	20	323	305	-2	-21%	-7%	7%	-6%
8	BYE										
9	TEN	L	14	28	297	340	0	-48%	-23%	18%	-8%
10	at PHI	W	27	20	410	421	+1	-5%	18%	13%	-10%
11	at ATL	W	22	19	323	354	+1	-7%	-9%	1%	3%
12	WAS	W	31	23	404	331	+3	20%	3%	-20%	-4%
13	NO	W	13	10	308	176	-1	72%	-7%	-73%	6%
14	PHI	W	29	23	576	256	-2	5%	-3%	-8%	1%
15	at IND	L	0	23	292	370	0	-41%	-30%	8%	-4%
16	TB	W	27	20	232	383	+2	-22%	-24%	1%	4%
17	at NYG	W	36	35	419	441	+1	4%	26%	7%	-14%
18	SEA	W	24	22	380	299	-1	16%	8%	-8%	0%
19	at LAR	L	22	30	308	459	0	-2%	6%	7%	-1%

Trends and Splits

	Offense	Rank	Defense	Rank
Total DVOA	-6.6%	24	-3.5%	9
Unadjusted VOA	-3.4%	21	-4.2%	10
Weighted Trend	-4.2%	23	-3.9%	11
Variance	3.7%	4	5.3%	13
Average Opponent	2.2%	28	-1.2%	17
Passing	-0.8%	26	7.4%	16
Rushing	-6.9%	18	-17.6%	5
First Down	-12.4%	25	-10.0%	5
Second Down	1.7%	14	3.1%	22
Third Down	-8.3%	20	-1.3%	17
First Half	-5.3%	22	-13.3%	2
Second Half	-7.9%	22	5.7%	23
Red Zone	-34.3%	31	-4.3%	13
Late and Close	-4.5%	19	2.3%	22

Five-Year Performance

Year	W-L	Pyth W	Est W	PF	PA	TO	Total	Rk	Off	Rk	Def	Rk	ST	Rk	Off AGL	Rk	Def AGL	Rk	Off Age	Rk	Def Age	Rk	ST Age	Rk
2014	12-4	10.8	10.3	467	352	+6	13.7%	6	16.8%	4	4.0%	22	0.9%	13	9.3	2	66.8	28	26.4	25	26.1	25	25.6	29
2015	4-12	5.2	4.4	275	374	-22	-18.0%	27	-15.6%	31	4.1%	19	1.8%	11	24.1	11	27.6	15	26.9	15	25.9	29	25.7	23
2016	13-3	11	11.8	421	306	+5	20.3%	2	19.9%	3	1.1%	18	1.6%	9	37.5	20	33.1	17	26.6	20	26.3	20	26.1	16
2017	9-7	8.6	8.9	354	332	-1	5.3%	13	6.5%	10	5.8%	25	4.6%	7	7.8	2	29.4	12	26.8	18	25.1	30	25.9	15
2018	10-6	8.4	7.0	339	324	+2	-5.2%	21	-6.6%	24	-3.5%	9	-2.1%	23	44.1	20	34.5	16	25.5	31	24.7	32	25.8	14

2018 Performance Based on Most Common Personnel Groups

DAL Offense					DAL Offense vs. Opponents					DAL Defense					DAL Defense vs. Opponents			
Pers	Freq	Yds	DVOA	Run%	Pers	Freq	Yds	DVOA	Run%	Pers	Freq	Yds	DVOA	Pers	Freq	Yds	DVOA
11	67%	5.6	-2.3%	30%	Base	26%	5.9	-6.6%	60%	Base	28%	4.6	-13.0%	11	65%	5.7	0.6%
12	14%	5.9	-0.1%	62%	Nickel	68%	5.4	-2.9%	35%	Nickel	69%	5.9	1.4%	12	19%	5.7	-1.7%
21	7%	5.6	-17.8%	62%	Dime+	9%	5.5	-10.8%	4%	Dime+	3%	5.1	-39.8%	10	4%	5.3	-12.4%
13	4%	5.6	-24.6%	68%	Goal Line	1%	1.3	20.8%	75%	Goal Line	0%	1.0	109.6%	21	3%	4.9	-9.3%
10	3%	4.0	-11.8%	40%										13	2%	2.8	-28.4%
														612	2%	3.7	-31.4%

Strategic Tendencies

Run/Pass		Rk	Formation		Rk	Pass Rush		Rk	Secondary		Rk	Strategy		Rk
Runs, first half	39%	14	Form: Single Back	80%	16	Rush 3	2.0%	30	4 DB	28%	11	Play action	25%	13
Runs, first down	50%	11	Form: Empty Back	8%	18	Rush 4	79.1%	3	5 DB	69%	12	Avg Box (Off)	6.29	7
Runs, second-long	30%	17	Pers: 3+ WR	73%	8	Rush 5	13.7%	27	6+ DB	3%	21	Avg Box (Def)	6.13	24
Runs, power sit.	69%	6	Pers: 2+ TE/6+ OL	20%	22	Rush 6+	5.1%	16	CB by Sides	92%	2	Offensive Pace	31.67	21
Runs, behind 2H	24%	22	Pers: 6+ OL	1%	26	Int DL Sacks	17.9%	24	S/CB Cover Ratio	26%	22	Defensive Pace	31.71	25
Pass, ahead 2H	49%	14	Shotgun/Pistol	62%	18	Second Level Sacks	21.8%	18	DB Blitz	6%	25	Go for it on 4th	1.24	18

Dallas was one of three offenses tied for last place in usage of max protect (defined as seven or more blockers with at least two more blockers than pass-rushers), just 3.7 percent of pass plays. ● The Cowboys ranked 29th in DVOA on passes to the short middle portion of the field. ● The Dallas defense was fifth against the pass on first down, then declined to 28th against the pass on second down and 21st on third down. ● Of teams that generally played only two safeties, the Cowboys had the smallest gap between where the safeties made their average plays, with Jeff Heath making his average play at 10.0 yards and Xavier Woods at 9.8 yards. ● Dallas was the beneficiary of a league-low 104 penalties and just 681 penalty yards.

Passing

Player	DYAR	DVOA	Plays	NtYds	Avg	YAC	C%	TD	Int
D.Prescott	112	-8.1%	582	3532	6.1	5.3	67.7%	22	8

Rushing

Player	DYAR	DVOA	Plays	Yds	Avg	TD	Fum	Suc
E.Elliott	149	2.9%	304	1436	4.7	6	6	50%
D.Prescott	45	2.0%	58	320	5.5	6	4	--
R.Smith*	-8	-12.8%	44	127	2.9	1	0	39%
D.Jackson	-8	-48.6%	6	16	2.7	0	0	17%
T.Austin	34	66.4%	6	55	9.2	0	0	--

Receiving

Player	DYAR	DVOA	Plays	Ctch	Yds	Y/C	YAC	TD	C%
C.Beasley*	100	2.1%	87	65	672	10.3	3.3	3	75%
A.Cooper	120	6.8%	76	53	725	13.7	6.0	6	70%
M.Gallup	-9	-14.3%	68	33	507	15.4	5.2	2	49%
A.Hurns	9	-9.3%	35	20	295	14.8	3.9	2	57%
D.Thompson*	-4	-15.1%	20	14	124	8.9	2.4	0	70%
T.Austin	19	5.1%	13	8	140	17.5	4.6	2	62%
N.Brown	-11	-29.6%	8	5	54	10.8	4.0	0	63%
R.Cobb	-45	-22.1%	61	38	384	10.1	6.2	2	62%
B.Jarwin	68	24.0%	36	27	307	11.4	4.1	3	75%
G.Swaim*	-9	-11.6%	32	26	242	9.3	6.3	1	81%
D.Schultz	4	-4.0%	17	12	116	9.7	5.5	0	71%
R.Gathers	-24	-53.9%	7	3	45	15.0	9.0	0	43%
E.Elliott	52	-3.2%	95	77	567	7.4	7.5	3	81%
R.Smith*	3	-9.0%	12	9	60	6.7	6.3	0	75%

Offensive Line

Player	Pos	Age	GS	Snaps	Pen	Sk	Pass	Run	Player	Pos	Age	GS	Snaps	Pen	Sk	Pass	Run
Joe Looney	C	29	16/16	1077	4	0.0	11	7	Connor Williams	LG	22	13/10	689	5	4.5	7	2
La'el Collins	RT	26	16/16	1076	11	6.0	15	3	Xavier Su'a-Filo	LG	28	8/8	494	1	2.5	8	6
Zack Martin	RG	29	14/14	877	1	3.0	4	3	Cameron Fleming	LT	27	14/3	233	2	1.0	2	1
Tyron Smith	LT	29	13/13	849	10	3.5	7	1									

Year	Yards	ALY	Rank	Power	Rank	Stuff	Rank	2nd Lev	Rank	Open Field	Rank	Sacks	ASR	Rank	Press	Rank	F-Start	Cont.
2016	4.68	4.63	4	73%	3	15%	5	1.36	5	0.98	8	28	5.6%	13	28.8%	24	14	37
2017	4.26	4.66	4	77%	3	17%	4	1.16	16	0.67	19	32	6.4%	15	31.9%	21	10	30
2018	4.46	4.61	8	75%	3	18%	11	1.31	9	0.87	14	56	9.7%	28	34.1%	26	11	32

2018 ALY by direction: Left End: 5.06 (13)   Left Tackle: 4.83 (6)   Mid/Guard: 4.62 (10)   Right Tackle: 4.74 (8)   Right End: 3.67 (25)

Travis Frederick, who missed all of last season with Guillain-Barré Syndrome, was participating in individual drills in June minicamp. Frederick told the team website that his return to the field was like climbing back on a bike. "A very rusty bike," he admitted. ❧ Tyron Smith missed three games with a neck injury and committed seven holding penalties, but he otherwise enjoyed another All-Pro season. Smith vowed in May to come back "faster and stronger" this year, which should be a sight to see. ❧ Zach Martin remains freakin' awesome, and the Cowboys still have the league's best offensive line on the increasingly rare occasions when Frederick, Martin, and Smith are all available. ❧ La'el Collins is slow-footed and slow to react against quicker pass-rushers at right tackle, but the Cowboys insist on keeping him there. ❧ That leaves left guard as the only spot on the line with any questions or competition. Connor Williams had an up-and-down rookie season—in fact, we think we saw Fletcher Cox shake him up and down once or twice. Third-round pick Connor McGovern of Penn State has the size to be a Cowboys-style mauler and could also slide to center if Frederick suffers a setback.

Defensive Front

Defensive Line	Age	Pos	G	Snaps	Plays	TmPct	Rk	Stop	Dfts	BTkl	Runs	St%	Rk	RuYd	Rk	Sack	Hit	Hur	Dsrpt
						Overall							vs. Run				Pass Rush		
Antwaun Woods	26	DT	15	585	35	4.6%	46	24	6	4	27	67%	72	1.6	12	1.5	4	8	1
Maliek Collins	24	DT	13	496	19	2.9%	76	14	7	2	14	79%	31	0.1	1	3.0	5	16	0
Daniel Ross	26	DT	13	249	14	2.1%	--	12	7	0	11	82%	--	1.0	--	1.0	6	10	0
Caraun Reid*	28	DT	10	185	10	2.0%	--	8	4	1	8	75%	--	1.0	--	0.5	2	8	0
Christian Covington	26	DE	12	257	15	2.4%	--	14	8	1	8	88%	--	2.0	--	3.5	4	7	0

Edge Rushers	Age	Pos	G	Snaps	Plays	TmPct	Rk	Stop	Dfts	BTkl	Runs	St%	Rk	RuYd	Rk	Sack	Hit	Hur	Dsrpt
						Overall							vs. Run				Pass Rush		
Demarcus Lawrence	27	DE	16	734	65	8.0%	5	54	30	7	49	78%	38	1.7	24	10.5	13	44	0
Tyrone Crawford	30	DE	15	633	35	4.6%	53	30	13	5	23	83%	19	0.6	3	5.5	7	24	2
Randy Gregory	27	DE	14	457	24	3.4%	80	18	10	2	17	65%	69	3.1	68	6.0	11	21	0
Taco Charlton	25	DE	11	401	28	5.0%	44	20	6	1	23	70%	58	1.9	30	1.0	3	16	1
Dorance Armstrong	22	DE	15	273	13	1.7%	--	7	2	3	12	50%	--	3.3	--	0.5	2	6	0
Robert Quinn	29	DE	16	635	38	4.6%	54	26	14	10	27	63%	73	2.6	53	6.5	10	26	1

Linebackers	Age	Pos	G	Snaps	Plays	TmPct	Rk	Stop	Dfts	BTkl	Runs	St%	Rk	RuYd	Rk	Sack	Hit	Hur	Tgts	Suc%	Rk	AdjYd	Rk	PD	Int
						Overall							vs. Run				Pass Rush				vs. Pass			
Jaylon Smith	24	MLB	16	976	124	15.3%	22	64	20	18	67	66%	21	3.1	15	4.0	2	8	34	35%	72	7.3	55	4	0
Leighton Vander Esch	22	OLB	16	784	145	17.9%	5	65	14	7	72	56%	55	3.7	34	0.0	1	2	49	41%	63	6.4	29	7	2
Damien Wilson	26	OLB	16	286	32	3.9%	--	15	5	9	19	63%	--	2.3	--	1.0	1	2	16	25%	80	9.6	74	0	0
Sean Lee	33	OLB	7	220	31	8.7%	64	21	4	5	20	70%	11	2.9	12	0.5	1	1	10	30%	--	14.4	--	1	0

Year	Yards	ALY	Rank	Power	Rank	Stuff	Rank	2nd Level	Rank	Open Field	Rank	Sacks	ASR	Rank	Press	Rank
2016	4.02	4.01	13	69%	25	22%	8	1.28	25	0.58	10	36	6.5%	12	23.1%	29
2017	4.12	3.95	11	83%	32	22%	11	1.25	25	0.76	20	38	6.7%	14	35.5%	2
2018	3.88	3.87	3	67%	20	25%	5	1.16	10	0.76	14	39	6.5%	27	32.2%	8

2018 ALY by direction: Left End: 3.31 (6)   Left Tackle: 3.25 (6)   Mid/Guard: 4.15 (10)   Right Tackle: 4.57 (24)   Right End: 3.61 (9)

Rookie Leighton Vander Esch finished fourth in the NFL in total defensive plays (tackles + assists + sacks + interceptions + anything else a defender can do that shows up on the stat sheet) and third in the NFL in total pass plays. The Cowboys trusted him in coverage against Zach Ertz-caliber tight ends, Saquon Barkley-caliber running backs, and even the occasional slot receiver, and he handled most of those assignments very well. Vander Esch has Luke Keuchly-level potential. ❧ Tank Lawrence finished fifth in the NFL in pressures and could challenge for the league lead in sacks if the Cowboys can find a reliable complementary pass-rusher. Taco Charlton was effective against weaker offensive lines (Texans, Giants) but invisible against better blockers and offenses. Randy Gregory failed a fourth drug test and is once again on the NFL's suspension list. Robert Quinn was miscast as a starter for the Dolphins but is still an effective pure pass-rusher. He could cause trouble in a 20- to 25-snap role 🏈 Keep an eye on second-round pick Trysten Hill, who is an Ed Oliver-type Tasmanian Devil at defensive tackle. Hill was sometimes the best player on the field for Central Florida, at least when he got onto the field; Josh Heupel and his staff frequently benched Hill for reasons those of us who aren't dictatorial college football princelings cannot fathom. Hill and 2018 rookie free-agent discovery Antwaun Woods could form the core of a reliable and (importantly) affordable interior defensive line.

Defensive Secondary

Secondary	Age	Pos	G	Snaps	Plays	TmPct	Rk	Stop	Dfts	BTkl	Runs	St%	Rk	RuYd	Rk	Tgts	Tgt%	Rk	Dist	Suc%	Rk	AdjYd	Rk	PD	Int
								Overall					**vs. Run**						**vs. Pass**						
Byron Jones	27	CB	16	1019	79	9.7%	23	34	12	6	19	42%	38	7.7	57	70	17.0%	24	13.8	61%	5	6.8	22	14	0
Jeff Heath	28	SS	16	998	83	10.2%	38	33	9	21	36	47%	29	7.4	45	39	9.6%	39	9.4	54%	29	7.7	42	5	1
Chidobe Awuzie	24	CB	16	884	83	10.2%	14	22	5	8	17	29%	65	6.4	41	82	22.9%	62	12.4	43%	76	8.0	45	12	1
Xavier Woods	24	FS	14	882	64	9.0%	50	15	5	10	21	14%	72	9.6	63	27	7.6%	22	8.6	41%	63	8.9	59	9	2
Anthony Brown	26	CB	15	689	50	6.6%	71	24	10	8	14	50%	22	6.8	46	43	15.4%	17	11.5	51%	44	8.5	60	8	1

Year	Pass D Rank	vs. #1 WR	Rk	vs. #2 WR	Rk	vs. Other WR	Rk	WR Wide	Rk	WR Slot	Rk	vs. TE	Rk	vs. RB	Rk
2016	19	-5.0%	9	3.1%	18	-11.9%	8	-19.0%	5	13.2%	22	31.2%	30	-2.2%	18
2017	18	10.7%	21	13.5%	23	-14.9%	8	-15.2%	6	18.8%	25	12.5%	25	14.5%	28
2018	16	-11.7%	6	-24.1%	4	6.9%	22	-4.6%	19	-8.1%	7	4.7%	19	12.5%	26

Depth is the key to this unit, and Kris Richard's coaching is the key to that depth. Richard transformed Byron Jones from a solid-but-unspectacular safety into Richard Sherman Lite at right cornerback. Chidobe Awuzie overcame an ankle injury and some miserable early-season performances for some great games down the stretch. Anthony Brown is a versatile nickel defender who handles No. 1 receivers hiding in the slot very well and is a sure tackler on screens and running plays. Jourdain Lewis escaped Richard's early-season doghouse to take on a late-season role as an Alvin Kamara Buster against speedy receiver-backs. 🏈 The depth at cornerback, the coverage ability at linebacker, and a scheme full of Cover-3 concepts mean that the Cowboys safeties spend a lot of time in deep zones. Xavier Woods, who settled in at free safety last year after playing a slot/hybrid role as a rookie (the pre-Richard Cowboys may have gotten a little carried away with the hybrid roles in the secondary) has the range to be effective in an Earl Thomas-like role. Former Bengal and Raider George Iloka will challenge Jeff Heath, who finished second in the NFL in missed tackles, for the strong safety job, but Iloka worked with the second string throughout OTAs.

Special Teams

Year	DVOA	Rank	FG/XP	Rank	Net Kick	Rank	Kick Ret	Rank	Net Punt	Rank	Punt Ret	Rank	Hidden	Rank
2016	1.6%	9	4.5	7	1.0	13	-2.0	20	6.1	7	-1.8	19	10.2	5
2017	4.6%	7	-7.0	26	4.5	8	2.3	8	16.9	2	6.2	3	14.8	2
2018	-2.1%	23	-2.6	23	-3.4	26	-0.8	15	-2.5	21	-1.1	18	-4.1	21

The disaster potential was high when the Cowboys released reliable Dan Bailey in a cost-cutting move at the end of training camp last year. But former CFL kicker Brett Maher had a solid year, converting six-of-seven 50-plus-yarders (though the lone miss was a 52-yarder that would have forced overtime against Washington in Week 7). Maher was average on kickoffs, with poor coverage dragging the Cowboys down below average in net kickoff value. 🏈 Punter Chris Jones had his first year with negative gross punt value since 2013. 🏈 Cole Beasley's departure opens a competition for the return jobs. Tavon Austin is the best candidate when healthy and focused, but the Cowboys need a plan for the other 14 weeks of the season. Fourth-round rookie running back Tony Pollard got a long look as a kickoff returner in OTAs. He has the combination of quickness and power to excel at the task.

Denver Broncos

For decades, the Denver Broncos were synonymous with organizational competence. Perhaps they weren't always at the top of the league, but you could count on them bouncing back very quickly. Denver hadn't experienced consecutive losing seasons since 1972. The next-longest streak in the NFL belonged to the Packers, and they had back-to-back stinkers as recently as 1990-91. That's two entire decades of success over anyone else in the league, an extended period of organizational competence most other fanbases would die for. If you're a Broncos fan under the age of 55, you had never experienced an extended down period.

The past tense can be so harsh.

Whatever luster was still left on John Elway's tenure as an executive was wiped right off with last year's 6-10 record. It wasn't just back-to-back losing seasons, it was back-to-back *double-digit*-losing seasons, a first for the Broncos in the NFL. Banners fly forever, and that Super Bowl 50 title means that Elway's reign won't be a failure no matter what, but he has also overseen his team falling into a pit the likes of which they haven't seen since bell bottoms and *Soul Train* ruled the world. With that in mind, Elway has done the electric slide over to the reset button in an effort to get the Broncos back in the general direction of the right track.

Out goes Vance Joseph, who leaves with the worst winning percentage for a full-time Broncos head coach since Lou Saban. Out goes Case Keenum, whose 2017 season looks more and more like a one-hit wonder. Out go starters Matt Paradis, Jared Veldheer, Domata Peko, Brandon Marshall, Darian Stewart, and Bradley Roby. It's time for a brand-new head coach, a half-dozen new starters on offense, and the fifth starting quarterback in the past four years.

Joseph was unprepared to be an NFL head coach. We could talk about Denver's slow starts, or their clock management issues. We could wonder about the lack of an organizational vision or guiding philosophy around which the team could grow. We could poke holes in the depth chart and personnel decisions, or list all the fourth-down and red zone errors. But the Vance Joseph experience can perhaps best be summed up by one play: in Week 15, against the Cleveland Browns, down by four with 5:29 left in the game, the Broncos faced a fourth-and-1 from the Browns' 6-yard line. Joseph elected to run the clock down all the way, take a delay of game penalty, and then kick a 29-yard field goal. Per EdjSports' Game-Winning

Chance (GWC) metric, the decision cost Denver 33.1 percent GWC. It was the worst play call made since tracking began in 2011. That just about sums up the Vance Joseph experience.

Elway has since admitted, in an interview with Peter King, that he was wrong to hire Joseph; that he had an idea that Joseph was "kind of [his] guy" before the hiring process began. That meant Denver passed on candidates Sean McVay and Kyle Shanahan as Elway zeroed in on his target. This time around, a more extensive interview process led Elway and the Broncos to settle on longtime defensive coordinator Vic Fangio as their new head coach.

At age 60, Fangio is old for a first-time head coach, but he brings with him an impressive resume. Fangio has spent more years as an NFL defensive coordinator alone than Vance Joseph had spent as a coach or assistant on any level prior to his hire in 2017. It's not just bygone success, either; half of Fangio's defenses have ranked in the top 10 in DVOA, and he ended up taking Chicago from 31st in defense to first in four years, showing improvement in every season. His players love him; his rivals rave about his schematic ingenuity. We have no idea what he'll be like as a head coach, but as a strictly *defensive* hire, Fangio's the real deal. While the offense got most of the talent acquisition this offseason, Fangio's job is to take the remaining defensive parts and squeeze the most out of them.

Fangio's defense, like what Joseph trotted out the past couple seasons, is a 3-4 front on paper, but they have very different philosophies when it comes to how the defense actually plays.

First, there are the play-calling differences. Expect far fewer blitzes than we have seen in recent years; while Denver ranked in the top 10 last season in both five- and six-man rushes, Fangio's defenses always rank towards the bottom of the pack. Instead, he relies on his down linemen to occupy blockers inside and allow his outside linebackers to win in one-on-one opportunities. Whereas Joseph's defense was designed around being aggressive towards the passer and using tight press-man coverage to force quarterbacks to make quick decisions, Fangio's is more about confusion and misdirection. He likes to mix zone and man coverages on the same play, creating combo coverages trying to get quarterbacks to misdiagnose the defenses pre-snap. When it works, this results in creative yet safe pressure packages.

To make that work, however, Fangio's defense needs versa-

2019 Broncos Schedule

Week	Opp.	Week	Opp.	Week	Opp.
1	at OAK (Mon.)	7	KC (Thu.)	13	LAC
2	CHI	8	at IND	14	at HOU
3	at GB	9	CLE	15	at KC
4	JAX	10	BYE	16	DET
5	at LAC	11	at MIN	17	OAK
6	TEN	12	at BUF		

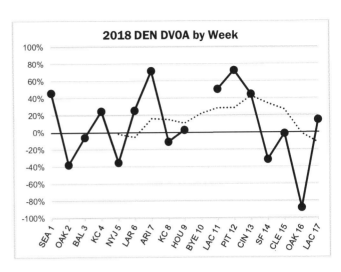

2018 DEN DVOA by Week

tile players who can play a wide variety of different roles. For the past few years, Denver's defense has been based around specialists: players asked to do one or two things particularly well. That is going to change under Fangio, and the transition could cause some growing pains.

In the secondary, Fangio keeps his cornerbacks on one side of the field or the other, rather than having his top guy shadow the offense's top guy. The Broncos have been top-corner-on-top-guy for a decade at this point, so that's a massive shift in philosophy. Fangio's safeties are interchangeable, needing to play in the box and cover deep. They'll be asked to cover less than safeties were under Joseph, however, because Fangio's team is in nickel nearly all the time. Joseph's Broncos were in their base defense a league-leading 45 percent of the time, and then jumped right to dime in passing situations, almost never running five defensive backs. Fangio is much more likely to ask a safety to move up in the box on early downs and then drop an inside linebacker back when extra coverage is required; there's no need for substitutions to tip his hand as to what his team will be doing. That means Chris Harris will be joined by Bryce Callahan and either Kareem Jackson or Isaac Yiadom as essentially full-time starters.

Up front, Joseph's 3-4 was fairly standard, with both ends generally playing 5- or 4i-technique roles, lining up opposite the offensive tackles. Fangio's system uses more of a 4-3 under front, however. That means one of those ends will often kick in and play a 3-technique, like a 4-3 defensive tackle across from a guard. It's a position both ends need to be able to play, as Fangio likes to switch around his 3- and 5-techniques based on matchups and situation. Because Fangio doesn't blitz very often, it's important for those interior linemen to be able to generate pressure on their own—it's what made Akiem Hicks and Justin Smith Pro Bowlers in Fangio defenses. Neither Derek Wolfe nor Adam Gotsis has shown the ability to generate the sort of interior pressure the role dictates to this point.

And then we get to the linebackers, which are the most important roles in Fangio's defenses. It is no surprise that his Bears shot to No. 1 when adding Khalil Mack and rookie Roquan Smith, or that Fangio prioritized adding Danny Trevathan in his second year in Chicago. Fangio's history is loaded with linebacker units stellar both inside and out. From the Dome Patrol in New Orleans to Kevin Greene and Sam Mills in Carolina to Patrick Willis and NaVorro Bowman in San Francisco, Fangio's successful defenses have included a who's who of linebacker talent. It's critical to Fangio's defense being successful.

The Broncos certainly have the outside linebackers to make Fangio's system go. Von Miller fits in any discussion of the best rushing linebackers of all time, and Bradley Chubb's 34.5 pass pressures as a rookie were just one behind the veteran. That being said, their jobs, too, will change some in Fangio's system. The weakside linebacker typically plays up on the line of scrimmage as the fourth man in the 4-3 under front. He pins his ears back and charges after the quarterback, so no problems there. The strongside linebacker, however, is more likely to jam the tight end and drop into a short zone, or set the edge against the run. I'm not sure Miller even remembers what it's like to drop into coverage, but Fangio's edge rushers are asked to handle more targets than most. Fangio's not exactly going to ask Miller or Chubb to cover Travis Kelce one-on-one or anything, though, and each player should be just fine in Fangio's system. They could even become the first pair of linebackers to rack up double-digit sacks for Fangio since Greene and Lamar Lathon back in 1996.

Inside linebacker is another story. Fangio requires elite athleticism from both inside linebackers, who are asked to cover far more than you would expect from a standard 3-4 defense. Chicago's Roquan Smith led all inside linebackers last season with 57 targets, and Danny Trevathan wasn't far behind. Josey Jewell and Todd Davis *combined* for 57 targets a year ago. Fangio's inside linebackers are asked to handle inside gap responsibility against the run, match up with tight ends and running backs in man coverage, and rush the passer from both the inside and outside. To handle all of that, Fangio's inside linebackers are generally top-level athletes, which Jewell and Davis most decidedly are not. It's difficult to picture either managing to slow down the likes of Kelce or Hunter Henry one-on-one on a regular basis. Neither were three-down players under Joseph, but that's the role Fangio's linebackers play. This is by far the toughest defensive transition the team faces, and it may require someone like Su'a Cravens to play out of position at linebacker to make things work.

All of that might start to explain Denver's curiously low defensive projection. The Broncos defense hasn't been worse than *good* in at least five years, and they have arguably been very good or great in five of the last seven, with a low point of a -0.2% DVOA back in 2013. Yet our projections have them downright average in 2019, and that defensive coordinator flip is a large part of it. It generally takes time to adapt to a new defensive coordinator and a new system, as the previous system's square pegs find their places in the new scheme's round holes. Fangio is no exception; it generally takes a couple seasons for his defenses to really start clicking (Table 1). Fangio's first year in Chicago saw the Bears rank 31st in DVOA, though the Bears were *just a skosh* less talented than last year's Broncos were. There's a floor to how bad a defense with this much talent can be, but some transitional pains are to be expected in 2019.

Table 1: Vic Fangio's Defenses

Year	Team	DVOA	Rank	Year	Team	DVOA	Rank
2018	CHI	-26.0%	1	2003	HOU	11.7%	29
2017	CHI	-1.5%	14	2002	HOU	2.3%	21
2016	CHI	5.0%	23	2001	IND	15.3%	29
2015	CHI	11.3%	31	2000	IND	5.7%	23
2014	SF	-10.1%	5	1999	IND	9.1%	26
2013	SF	-4.6%	13	1998	CAR	6.2%	21
2012	SF	-14.4%	3	1997	CAR	4.7%	23
2011	SF	-14.6%	3	1996	CAR	-12.2%	6
2005	HOU	20.1%	32	1995	CAR	-12.5%	5
2004	HOU	1.9%	18				

If the defense does drop off, it will be up to the offense to pick up the slack—an offense that continues to be charitably described as a work in progress.

Compared to 2017, 2018's offense was a roaring success, which is a little bit like saying "compared to being on fire, these third-degree burns are a fantastic thing to have." The Broncos saw improvements in both the running game and passing game, and they had the second-largest offensive DVOA increase last season. The problem is that 2017's offense had the lowest DVOA we've ever recorded for Denver, so even a significant improvement left plenty to be desired. Case Keenum was better than the three-headed monster of Trevor Siemian, Brock Osweiler, and Paxton Lynch, but only really lifted the passing offense from "terrible" to "bad." Philip Lindsay was a tremendous find in the running game, but there's only so much even a top-five rushing attack can do to bolster a floundering pass offense in the modern NFL.

Furthermore, the Broncos' offense came up smallest in the most crucial situations. They ranked 28th in DVOA on third downs. They ranked 29th when passing in the red zone, and they compounded that by passing on 56 percent of their red zone plays, 11th most in the league—and they ranked fifth in red zone rushing DVOA, so it's not like Lindsay and Royce Freeman weren't producing. When they did take a lead, they were worst of all. When leading by seven points or less, the Broncos' offense dropped from 14th to 29th in DVOA. Denver had just two touchdowns all year long holding on to those one-score leads, tied for last in the NFL with Arizona. If Denver could have held on to fourth-quarter leads against Kansas City, Houston, and Cleveland, we'd be talking about a 9-7 team just missing the playoffs against a very tough schedule.

There's plenty of blame to go around: a quarterback who wasn't able to live up to what appears to be a flukish season in Minnesota, a very young set of skill position players experiencing growing pains, an offensive line that had the second-most blown blocks in football. But when you have so many problems in situational football, you have to turn to the guy calling the plays.

Bill Musgrave's game plan rarely seemed to be adapted to the players under his control. Denver boasted an offensive line ranked sixth in adjusted line yards, an undrafted sensation at running back, and a quarterback who found significantly more success when using play-action. Yet Denver favored not runs nor play-action but rather standard dropbacks. Only 10 teams threw the ball more frequently than the Broncos did last season, but they were just middle of the pack in frequency of play-action fakes. It felt like Musgrave made no efforts to adjust his offense to the strengths of the actual team he was coaching.

So out goes Musgrave, and in comes Rich Scangarello, the latest fruit from the McVay/Shanahan tree. He'll be working with a significantly changed offensive unit which should feature a half-dozen different starters compared to December of last season thanks to players returning from injury, veterans added in the offseason, and a draft strategy that saw Denver make three offensive selections in the first 42 picks. The change everyone is talking about, however, is at quarterback.

Bringing in Case Keenum was a gambit that always had a high likelihood of failure. His 2017 season in Minnesota was legitimately outstanding, but that was the only season in his career where he had been anywhere close to solid as a starter. It says something when his own franchise would rather spend $84 million guaranteed on a free-agent quarterback rather than re-sign the guy who led them to the NFC Championship Game.

This has been the path of the post-Peyton Manning Broncos: stuck on the quarterback carousel, trying to get by with below-average quarterbacks at mid-range costs. Osweiler begat Siemian. Siemian begat Lynch. Lynch begat Keenum, and round and round we go. With each passing year, it feels more like Elway lucked into getting a Hall of Fame quarterback at the tail end of his powers, as every attempt to find a long-term answer at the position since then has failed. But it's alright now. Elway has learned his lesson and has traded in his moderately expensive non-franchise veteran quarterback for... a different, even more expensive non-franchise veteran quarterback, albeit one with a shiny Super Bowl ring.

Saying Joe Flacco is the pinnacle of mediocre is an insult to mediocrity, and has been for years. From 2015 through 2017, Flacco had negative double-digit passing DVOA, never ranking in the top 25 at the position. His 2018 season was his best in four years, and that saw him getting benched for a rookie quarterback whom the Ravens barely trusted to throw the ball. Baltimore fans are tired of the list of Flacco "accomplishments," but as he's new to the Denver fan base, it might be nice to list some of his biggest hits.

- Flacco has now been below league average in adjusted net yards per attempt in each of the past four seasons, yet remained Baltimore's starter. He is only the 11th quarterback since the merger to manage that extended feat of below-average play without getting benched, joining luminaries such as Mark Sanchez, Joey Harrington, and Rick Mirer.

- Despite his reputation for being a solid deep-ball passer, Flacco regularly ranks near the bottom of our failed completion statistics. A failed completion is a dump-off or checkdown that doesn't meaningfully advance the ball; think 2-yard screens on first-and-10, or any third-down completion that ends short of the sticks. Flacco's 2016 season had 144 failed completions, the all-time record. Second-place was Flacco's 2017 season.

- Flacco's pretty deep ball is often listed as one of his strengths, but it's overstated. His average pass traveled 8.4 yards through the air in 2018, which ranked 13th in the league, but his average completion was went just 5.9 yards through the air, so there were a lot of beautiful deep balls bouncing off the turf—13.5 percent of his passes were listed as overthrown in 2018. Flacco ranked 28th out of 34 qualified quarterbacks in DVOA on passes that traveled at least 15 yards downfield, below such noted deep-ball slingers such as Nick Foles, Derek Carr, and—yes—Case Keenum.

Elway's response to all this is to claim that the 34-year-old Flacco is "just getting into his prime," noting that he "plays the position exactly how [Denver] envisions it being played." He points to Flacco's decent 2014 season under Gary Kubiak as reason for optimism, as Scangarello's offense will presumably be similar to Kyle Shanahan's offense, which bears some resemblance to Kubiak's system as Shanahan was Kubiak's offensive coordinator for two years in Houston. That's a game of telephone tag, not a reason for optimism, even when filtered through the lens of preseason platitudes. Flacco has been an anchor for Baltimore for years; there's little reason to suspect that he's going to have a breakout season and reverse years of decline just because his zip code changed.

Flacco will do some things better than Keenum did. His strong arm may mesh better with deep options such as Courtland Sutton and first-round pick Noah Fant. Flacco will do some things worse than Keenum did. He is an immobile statue in the pocket, turning his linemen's blown blocks into sacks. The point is, both players would likely have been in the same ballpark in 2019 and switching between them is just re-arranging deck chairs on the Titanic. Bringing in Flacco as a free agent would have been questionable; giving up a fourth-round pick for the right to his services is certifiable.

At least Denver did bring in an alternative. The Broncos were often mocked Missouri quarterback Drew Lock in the pre-draft process, usually at their No. 10 draft slot. Instead, Denver picked Lock up with the 42nd pick, a much more reasonable value for him. Before the draft, QBASE, our rookie quarterback projection system, had Lock as the fourth-best quarterback in the class, just above sixth-overall pick Daniel Jones. Lock is an average prospect—almost prototypically so. As a senior, all of his stats QBASE uses to measure players—adjusted yards per pass attempt, completion rate, team passing S&P+—were within 0.1 standard deviations of the mean for all quarterback prospects over the last 20 years. As a first-round pick, that's underwhelming. As a second-round pick, he's more than worth a kick of the tires.

You don't have to go back far into Broncos history to find a passer Lock resembles—he's Jay Cutler, only more congenial off the field. Like Cutler, Lock has a cannon for an arm and is willing to trust it to make the big throws, sometimes to his detriment. He's mobile enough and has the pocket awareness to step up and avoid sacks. His field vision is excellent as well, and he can quickly scan through and process coverages. He needs to work on his touch and accuracy, and his footwork could use an overhaul as well, but there are enough positives there to be worth considering.

Most importantly, he at least has the potential to be a long-term starter. Even if Flacco repeats his best season of the past four years in Denver, he's still both old and mediocre. Flacco is not the quarterback who will take the Broncos back to the playoffs. Lock probably isn't either, but at least he's an unknown quantity. The best thing Denver can do this season is evaluate and develop the young talent that will make up the core of the team for the next five years. If sanity prevails, Flacco will at some point be benched for a rookie quarterback yet again in 2019.

There's plenty of that young talent to go around. The Broncos are likely to trot out half a dozen different offensive starters than they had by the end of 2018, as new arrivals and healthy returnees come in droves. Fant is a receiver trapped in a tight end's body; not many tight ends run a 4.5 40 while still showing adequate blocking chops. He'll be an immediate contributor, alongside last year's crop of rookies. Courtland Sutton and DaeSean Hamilton had promising campaigns, while Philip Lindsay was an undrafted star. The Broncos have a set of skill players who could form the basis for a solid offense when a quarterback finally does arrive, assuming they haven't all aged out of the league and retired by that point.

The biggest question mark is the most important veteran, 32-year-old Emmanuel Sanders, who isn't expected back from a torn Achilles until mid-July at the earliest. If he has a setback, that bumps everyone else on the depth chart up to a level they're likely not ready to handle just yet. When Sanders went down in December, Sutton became the top target, where he averaged just 37 yards and a -12.1% DVOA over the last four games. Sutton and Hamilton are still developing; they're not ready to be the top targets quite yet. If Sanders is hurt, the young players will have to take major strides forward for the passing game to be above remedial.

The changes continue on the offensive line. The Broncos also added Ja'Wuan James, who should be a massive improvement over Jared Veldheer at right tackle, and look to get guard Ron Leary back from injury. Second-round pick Dalton Risner (Kansas State) is another rookie who should be starting from Day 1. He'll be penciled in at guard, but he's versatile enough to play anywhere along the line of scrimmage. Losing Matt Paradis hurts, but the offensive line could be much improved if all the "ifs" work out. If Leary and James are fully healthy. If Risner is able to contribute right away. If Garrett Bolles can finally take that step forward Denver has been waiting for. Really, that's the best way to describe Denver's offensive prospects going forward: iffy.

No, there's no reason to suspect that the Broncos have licked their quarterback conundrum just yet, and the rest of their offense is more potential and possibility than it is a functioning NFL unit at this point in time. Combine that with some transitional pains on defense, and you get a very bleak picture for the 2019 Broncos. The Broncos may be in a better place looking ahead now than they were before the offseason began, but for now, they continue to wander in the post-Manning wilderness. The collection of young offensive talent makes sense for a team that's looking to 2020 or 2021 as a realistic shot to get back into competitive football. It won't make for a fun season, but it's medicine that Denver has to take in order to get

back to sustainable success.

However, if that's the philosophy, then the Flacco trade sticks out like a sore thumb. You don't trade for a 34-year-old veteran to facilitate a rebuilding project. That move seems to be designed to try to win now, with the always-competitive Elway feeling the pressure to try to avoid a third straight losing season. If that's the standard we're judging this team by, then 2019 is likely to be another highly disappointing year. The failures of the last two seasons have cost a head coach, two offensive coordinators, and four quarterbacks their jobs. There aren't many scapegoats left, and one more poor season might well put even a franchise legend like Elway on the hot seat.

Bryan Knowles

2018 Broncos Stats by Week

Wk	vs.	W-L	PF	PA	YDF	YDA	TO	Total	Off	Def	ST
1	SEA	W	27	24	470	306	0	46%	5%	-41%	0%
2	OAK	W	20	19	385	373	-1	-38%	-11%	25%	-2%
3	at BAL	L	14	27	293	342	-1	-6%	-1%	4%	-1%
4	KC	L	23	27	385	446	-1	25%	21%	-11%	-8%
5	at NYJ	L	16	34	436	512	+1	-36%	1%	27%	-10%
6	LAR	L	20	23	357	444	0	25%	17%	-16%	-7%
7	at ARI	W	45	10	309	223	+4	72%	15%	-50%	6%
8	at KC	L	23	30	411	340	-1	-11%	-8%	-5%	-9%
9	HOU	L	17	19	348	290	-1	3%	4%	-9%	-9%
10	BYE										
11	at LAC	W	23	22	325	479	+2	50%	34%	-17%	0%
12	PIT	W	24	17	308	527	+4	72%	44%	-17%	11%
13	at CIN	W	24	10	361	313	+2	45%	14%	-26%	5%
14	at SF	L	14	20	274	389	+1	-32%	-32%	-7%	-7%
15	CLE	L	16	17	270	309	0	-1%	-10%	-7%	2%
16	at OAK	L	14	27	300	273	-2	-88%	-31%	24%	-34%
17	LAC	L	9	23	370	276	0	15%	-13%	-34%	-6%

Trends and Splits

	Offense	Rank	Defense	Rank
Total DVOA	1.1%	14	-9.7%	5
Unadjusted VOA	3.3%	13	-7.6%	7
Weighted Trend	-0.4%	17	-13.6%	5
Variance	4.4%	6	5.0%	11
Average Opponent	1.5%	25	3.7%	7
Passing	0.4%	24	-10.6%	4
Rushing	7.7%	5	-8.5%	16
First Down	14.8%	6	-0.9%	15
Second Down	1.1%	15	-10.8%	5
Third Down	-25.5%	28	-25.4%	3
First Half	-3.9%	20	-1.3%	13
Second Half	5.9%	14	-18.6%	4
Red Zone	-2.2%	16	0.5%	18
Late and Close	12.5%	7	-5.8%	14

Five-Year Performance

Year	W-L	Pyth W	Est W	PF	PA	TO	Total	Rk	Off	Rk	Def	Rk	ST	Rk	Off AGL	Rk	Def AGL	Rk	Off Age	Rk	Def Age	Rk	ST Age	Rk
2014	12-4	11.0	13.3	482	354	+5	29.5%	2	20.0%	3	-13.2%	4	-3.7%	27	11.7	4	25.2	6	28.6	2	25.7	31	25.6	27
2015	12-4	9.7	10.7	355	296	-4	17.7%	8	-8.7%	25	-25.8%	1	0.7%	14	42.9	22	13.8	2	28.3	2	26.5	19	25.6	26
2016	9-7	9.1	8.5	333	297	+2	3.7%	14	-12.3%	28	-18.3%	1	-2.3%	24	26.0	8	34.2	18	26.6	18	26.7	12	25.1	30
2017	5-11	5.4	5.6	289	382	-17	-21.1%	29	-19.0%	31	-5.3%	10	-7.4%	30	28.1	11	37.8	20	27.1	14	26.7	12	25.0	30
2018	6-10	7.4	8.7	329	349	+7	6.6%	13	1.1%	14	-9.7%	5	-4.2%	31	48.9	23	27.3	11	26.6	18	26.9	7	25.4	28

2018 Performance Based on Most Common Personnel Groups

DEN Offense					DEN Offense vs. Opponents					DEN Defense					DEN Defense vs. Opponents			
Pers	Freq	Yds	DVOA	Run%	Pers	Freq	Yds	DVOA	Run%	Pers	Freq	Yds	DVOA		Pers	Freq	Yds	DVOA
11	63%	5.5	-1.9%	26%	Base	29%	5.8	8.2%	56%	Base	45%	5.5	-6.2%		11	61%	5.8	-17.3%
21	12%	5.3	-0.6%	65%	Nickel	50%	5.7	-0.6%	33%	Nickel	27%	6.4	0.3%		12	19%	6.0	6.0%
12	11%	5.9	7.3%	44%	Dime+	20%	5.3	3.3%	18%	Dime+	28%	5.7	-29.6%		21	7%	7.3	-11.4%
20	4%	7.6	38.2%	40%	Goal Line	1%	0.7	36.7%	67%	Goal Line	0%	0.7	32.6%		22	5%	4.4	-4.2%
22	4%	7.0	29.1%	69%											13	5%	3.9	-20.6%

Strategic Tendencies

Run/Pass		Rk	Formation		Rk	Pass Rush		Rk	Secondary		Rk	Strategy		Rk
Runs, first half	36%	21	Form: Single Back	70%	29	Rush 3	4.6%	21	4 DB	45%	1	Play action	25%	14
Runs, first down	42%	25	Form: Empty Back	11%	6	Rush 4	60.1%	25	5 DB	27%	31	Avg Box (Off)	6.28	8
Runs, second-long	37%	6	Pers: 3+ WR	69%	15	Rush 5	27.6%	4	6+ DB	28%	5	Avg Box (Def)	6.36	4
Runs, power sit.	54%	20	Pers: 2+ TE/6+ OL	18%	27	Rush 6+	7.7%	6	CB by Sides	58%	27	Offensive Pace	30.23	8
Runs, behind 2H	29%	13	Pers: 6+ OL	2%	11	Int DL Sacks	20.5%	22	S/CB Cover Ratio	32%	8	Defensive Pace	30.40	7
Pass, ahead 2H	34%	32	Shotgun/Pistol	56%	26	Second Level Sacks	8.0%	31	DB Blitz	6%	25	Go for it on 4th	1.13	21

Denver got a league-leading 72 percent of sacks from edge rushers. This is another thing that might change with a Fangio defense, as the Bears were near the bottom of the league at 41 percent. ● The Broncos went from 6.2 net yards per pass (-10.2% DVOA) with three or four pass-rushers to 7.5 net yards per pass (0.1% DVOA) with a blitz. But those blitz numbers were split further into bad defense with five pass-rushers (16.2% DVOA, 8.2 yards) and then really good defense with six or more (-59.3% DVOA, 5.0 yards). ● Denver was one of only two teams (along with the Chargers) where three different running backs had at least 20 broken tackles. But since all three were also under 40, the Broncos were only tied for tenth in broken tackles. ● Once again, Denver was much better running from one-back sets (5.2 yards, 11.3% DVOA) than two-back sets (4.3 yards, -10.0% DVOA). ● Denver receivers dropped a league-high 38 passes. ● New quarterback Joe Flacco was blitzed on a league-high 31.5 percent of passes last season. His yards per pass actually went up from 6.4 to 7.9 against a five-man pass-rush, but Flacco had a dismal 3.6 net yards per pass with -53.5% DVOA against a big blitz or six or more.

Passing

Player	DYAR	DVOA	Plays	NtYds	Avg	YAC	C%	TD	Int
C.Keenum*	-63	-12.7%	620	3634	5.9	4.9	62.6%	18	14
J.Flacco	429	5.4%	392	2380	6.1	4.4	61.7%	12	6

Rushing

Player	DYAR	DVOA	Plays	Yds	Avg	TD	Fum	Suc
P.Lindsay	203	17.3%	192	1037	5.4	9	0	49%
R.Freeman	10	-6.8%	130	521	4.0	5	1	46%
D.Booker	27	9.6%	34	183	5.4	1	0	50%
C.Keenum*	40	31.2%	15	101	6.7	2	1	--
J.Flacco	13	2.9%	13	46	3.5	0	1	--

Receiving

Player	DYAR	DVOA	Plays	Ctch	Yds	Y/C	YAC	TD	C%
E.Sanders	113	2.0%	99	72	877	12.2	4.3	4	73%
C.Sutton	95	1.3%	84	42	704	16.8	3.9	4	50%
D.Thomas*	64	1.6%	56	36	402	11.2	3.7	3	64%
D.Hamilton	-20	-18.1%	46	30	243	8.1	2.3	2	65%
T.Patrick	-16	-17.6%	41	23	315	13.7	4.9	1	56%
J.Heuerman	-70	-29.7%	48	31	281	9.1	4.8	2	65%
M.LaCosse*	-1	-7.6%	37	24	250	10.4	6.0	1	65%
J.Butt	-26	-38.7%	13	8	85	10.6	5.5	0	62%
B.Parker*	-40	-65.0%	10	5	33	6.6	5.8	0	50%
D.Booker	1	-13.5%	51	38	275	7.2	6.3	0	75%
P.Lindsay	9	-10.4%	47	35	241	6.9	8.5	1	74%
R.Freeman	-20	-32.2%	20	14	72	5.1	4.2	0	70%
A.Janovich	47	75.0%	10	8	112	14.0	7.9	1	80%

Offensive Line

Player	Pos	Age	GS	Snaps	Pen	Sk	Pass	Run	Player	Pos	Age	GS	Snaps	Pen	Sk	Pass	Run
Garett Bolles	LT	27	16/16	1062	13	5.5	24	4	Elijah Wilkinson	RG	24	12/7	520	0	2.0	6	4
Connor McGovern	RG/C	26	16/15	1056	6	1.5	16	4	Ronald Leary	LG	30	6/6	383	2	0.0	3	0
Billy Turner*	LG/RT	28	16/11	824	2	1.0	14	10	Max Garcia	LG	28	9/4	242	3	1.0	4	5
Jared Veldheer*	RT	32	12/12	704	8	2.0	11	2	Ja'Wuan James	RT	27	15/15	815	7	3.5	9	5
Matt Paradis*	C	30	9/9	569	2	0.0	1	2	Jake Brendel	LG	27	4/3	176	2	2.0	3	1

Year	Yards	ALY	Rank	Power	Rank	Stuff	Rank	2nd Lev	Rank	Open Field	Rank	Sacks	ASR	Rank	Press	Rank	F-Start	Cont.
2016	3.78	4.09	18	51%	29	21%	21	1.19	13	0.50	26	40	7.4%	27	24.6%	12	20	32
2017	4.03	4.31	9	65%	15	18%	7	1.11	18	0.51	26	52	9.1%	29	31.1%	16	17	28
2018	4.88	4.75	6	71%	7	18%	14	1.42	5	1.01	10	34	6.3%	11	32.1%	20	9	31

2018 ALY by direction:	Left End: 5.29 (10)	Left Tackle: 3.57 (27)	Mid/Guard: 4.74 (8)	Right Tackle: 4.53 (13)	Right End: 5.44 (4)

The Broncos ranked in the top 10 in adjusted line yards for the first time since 2013, but they also had the third-highest blown block rate in the league, sixth highest on running plays. In short: when the blocking held, they were very effective. They just failed to hold far too often. ❧ Maybe "hold" was a poor choice of words—Garrett Bolles led the league with ten holding flags. He led the league in accepted holding penalties the year before, too. He also ranked 61st among tackles in snaps per blown block and had the third-most blown pass blocks in the league. Other than that, it was a good year. ❧ Ja'Wuan James comes over from Miami to handle right tackle duties. He ranked 32nd among tackles last season with 58.2 snaps per blown block. That's not exactly stellar, but it's better than Jared Veldheer, Menelik Watson, or Donald Stephenson managed over the past three seasons. ❧ If Dalton Risner was just a little bit faster and light on his feet, he could have been an early Day 1 pick as a tackle. His stiffness matters less inside, even in Denver's zone-blocking scheme. His experience playing all across the line at Kansas State certainly won't hurt, either. If Bolles continues to struggle, don't be surprised to see James moved to left tackle and Risner given a chance on the right side. ❧ Risner started at left guard at OTAs, which would move Ronald Leary back to the right side. That presumes that Leary is fully recovered from his Week 6 Achilles tear and manages to play a full season for the first time since 2013. For what it's worth, he's reportedly going to be fully ready for training camp. ❧ Connor McGovern is moving from guard to center full time to replace Matt Paradis, and that's a downgrade. McGovern is playing out of position, and his play notably decreased when asked to move inside last season. A full offseason at center may help.

Defensive Front

Defensive Line	Age	Pos	G	Snaps	Plays	TmPct	Rk	Stop	Dfts	BTkl	Runs	St%	Rk	RuYd	Rk	Sack	Hit	Hur	Dsrpt
Derek Wolfe	29	DE	16	710	49	5.9%	25	40	12	2	37	81%	22	2.4	51	1.5	4	18	4
Domata Peko*	35	DT	16	522	33	4.0%	65	28	3	4	27	85%	11	2.5	56	0.5	2	3	2
Adam Gotsis	27	DE	16	512	44	5.3%	34	34	9	2	32	75%	41	1.9	26	3.0	6	9	6
Zach Kerr	29	DE	16	394	34	4.1%	--	23	5	3	29	69%	--	2.7	--	1.5	1	5	1
Shelby Harris	28	DT	16	390	42	5.1%	--	29	9	1	34	65%	--	2.9	--	1.5	5	12	5

Edge Rushers	Age	Pos	G	Snaps	Plays	TmPct	Rk	Stop	Dfts	BTkl	Runs	St%	Rk	RuYd	Rk	Sack	Hit	Hur	Dsrpt
Bradley Chubb	23	OLB	16	844	60	7.2%	8	46	22	9	41	73%	49	2.1	38	12.0	11	35	0
Von Miller	30	OLB	16	844	51	6.2%	17	46	29	6	27	89%	7	2.1	36	14.5	11	36	2
Shaquil Barrett*	27	OLB	13	275	25	3.7%	--	19	8	3	15	80%	--	2.9	--	3.0	4	5	0
Shane Ray*	26	OLB	11	253	11	1.9%	--	8	4	1	5	80%	--	4.2	--	1.0	1	6	0

Linebackers	Age	Pos	G	Snaps	Plays	TmPct	Rk	Stop	Dfts	BTkl	Runs	St%	Rk	RuYd	Rk	Sack	Hit	Hur	Tgts	Suc%	Rk	AdjYd	Rk	PD	Int
Todd Davis	27	ILB	16	842	121	14.6%	28	61	11	14	76	53%	65	4.8	75	0.5	4	10	36	42%	60	8.3	65	7	1
Brandon Marshall*	30	ILB	11	468	43	7.6%	73	17	5	3	27	52%	71	4.7	74	0.0	0	3	16	63%	5	4.4	6	1	0
Josey Jewell	25	ILB	16	459	53	6.4%	79	29	7	5	38	58%	51	3.9	43	0.0	0	2	21	52%	32	8.3	66	3	0

Year	Yards	ALY	Rank	Power	Rank	Stuff	Rank	2nd Level	Rank	Open Field	Rank	Sacks	ASR	Rank	Press	Rank
2016	4.03	4.60	28	65%	20	11%	32	0.91	1	0.52	7	42	7.6%	2	32.2%	1
2017	3.44	3.37	4	45%	1	26%	3	0.91	3	0.60	9	33	6.9%	11	32.7%	7
2018	4.78	4.58	23	73%	26	14%	30	1.14	8	1.16	29	44	8.0%	9	30.2%	17

2018 ALY by direction:	Left End: 4.29 (14)	Left Tackle: 5.17 (29)	Mid/Guard: 4.40 (14)	Right Tackle: 4.51 (22)	Right End: 5.47 (29)

In an interview, Von Miller stated that coverage was a huge part of his game, and that he's excited to be doing it more in 2019 under Fangio. For the record, Miller has been targeted 11 times in the past three seasons and hasn't had a successful play in coverage since 2016. That's not a deal-breaker—Khalil Mack went 0-for-4 in pass coverage for Fangio's Bears in 2018—but let's not exaggerate things too much here. ✎ Bradley Chubb's 34.5 pass pressures are the most we've ever recorded for a rookie. ✎ Stick a pin in fifth-round pick Justin Hollins out of Oregon. He's not going to see the field too often with Miller and Chubb in the way, but he's more of the type of linebacker Fangio looks for, blending both pass-rushing talent and zone coverage potential. ✎ Josey Jewell got a big vote of confidence when Denver passed on Devin Bush in the draft. Going from Brandon Marshall to Jewell is a drop-off in pass coverage, but Jewell's instincts made him a much more involved and successful player in run support. ✎ Todd Davis is still an above-average tackler, but he has seen his broken tackle rate increase in each of the last two seasons. ✎ In Chicago, Fangio's top interior rusher (Akiem Hicks) averaged 27.3 quarterback pressures over the past three seasons. Derek Wolfe averaged 15.2 over that time period and hasn't topped two sacks in a season since 2016. He's a solid run defender, but he's just not an interior presence against the pass. ✎ Something to keep an eye on: Wolfe, Adam Gotsis, and Shelby Harris are all free agents after this season. It is highly unlikely Denver will have the cap space to re-sign all three, so seeing how well each player adapts to Fangio's system will be key to figuring out who will be wearing orange next season. ✎ Gotsis was second in the league in pass disruptions (balls tipped at the line plus incompletes caused by hitting the quarterback) with six. Harris was just behind him, tied in fifth. ✎ Dre'Mont Jones is going to fight his way into the lineup sooner rather than later. The Ohio State product might have been the best interior pass-rusher in the draft. He fell to the third round because he's skinny for a lineman at 281 pounds and tested out fairly poorly at the combine, but he might just be the 3-technique Fangio is looking for.

Defensive Secondary

Secondary	Age	Pos	G	Snaps	Plays	Overall TmPct	Rk	Stop	Dfts	BTkl	Runs	vs. Run St%	Rk	RuYd	Rk	Tgts	vs. Pass Tgt%	Rk	Dist	Suc%	Rk	AdjYd	Rk	PD	Int
Justin Simmons	26	FS	16	1077	101	12.2%	12	30	10	9	38	45%	33	9.2	57	49	11.4%	56	9.2	47%	48	7.0	35	4	3
Bradley Roby*	27	CB	15	926	62	8.0%	47	27	11	12	9	56%	15	6.3	38	78	21.2%	55	12.0	46%	62	10.3	76	12	1
Darian Stewart*	31	SS	14	874	63	8.7%	51	18	8	12	25	24%	62	8.8	54	18	5.2%	9	9.8	56%	20	9.4	61	3	2
Chris Harris	30	CB	12	747	59	9.5%	27	28	11	3	13	54%	19	6.2	35	64	21.6%	56	8.7	50%	51	6.9	25	10	3
Will Parks	25	SS	16	572	43	5.2%	71	21	8	7	20	65%	3	4.5	7	25	11.0%	55	10.2	48%	43	6.2	14	4	1
Tramaine Brock*	31	CB	12	437	29	4.7%	--	10	5	3	3	33%	--	10.7	--	38	21.9%	--	12.7	58%	--	6.6	--	6	0
Isaac Yiadom	23	CB	13	263	20	3.0%	--	8	6	3	3	33%	--	5.3	--	30	28.7%	--	12.1	50%	--	7.0	--	3	1
Kareem Jackson	31	CB	16	985	104	12.3%	3	55	21	13	40	55%	17	3.7	8	59	15.0%	14	11.3	51%	49	6.4	16	17	2
Bryce Callahan	28	CB	13	675	51	7.7%	53	25	15	10	7	43%	36	7.6	56	37	12.5%	1	7.3	51%	43	6.9	23	6	2

Year	Pass D Rank	vs. #1 WR	Rk	vs. #2 WR	Rk	vs. Other WR	Rk	WR Wide	Rk	WR Slot	Rk	vs. TE	Rk	vs. RB	Rk
2016	1	-29.6%	2	-58.5%	1	-24.0%	4	-9.1%	11	-54.4%	1	-20.7%	5	-7.1%	15
2017	15	-33.6%	2	-13.3%	9	28.5%	30	-28.6%	3	-2.1%	12	19.8%	31	5.6%	19
2018	4	-5.8%	11	0.1%	17	-36.4%	1	-7.7%	16	-14.2%	3	-9.3%	12	5.4%	18

Kareem Jackson is the most interesting player to watch in this secondary. For his first nine years in Houston, Jackson was primarily a cornerback, but he started making the transition to safety in 2018, and has lined up there in Denver's early workouts. Fangio loves his defenders to be versatile, so Jackson's ability to play both corner and safety was impossible to resist. Fangio has been mum as to where Jackson will line up come Week 1, and he might well end up playing plenty of both corner and safety as the year goes on. ✎ If Jackson plays corner for most of the year, that puts either Will Parks or Su'a Cravens into the starting lineup. If he sticks to safety, last year's third-round pick Isaac Yiadom would be in line for a starting boundary corner role. ✎ Fangio brought one player with him from Chicago: slot corner Bryce Callahan. Callahan was targeted on just 12.5 percent of his snaps last season, fewest in the league—opponents didn't want to challenge him. He's a perfect fit for Fangio's scheme when healthy, but he has never managed to play all 16 games in a season. ✎ Callahan's arrival likely ends Chris Harris' career as a regular slot corner. As Denver's top corner last season, he ended up splitting time between the slot and boundary roughly 60/40, moving inside whenever they went into nickel or dime. It's the end of an era for arguably the best slot corner of the 2010s. Fortunately, he's just as good playing outside. ● Justin Simmons saw his charting stats drop across the board in 2018. His down season was in part due to having to play not only both safety positions, but plenty of fill-in snaps at corner for a depleted secondary. It was too much on his plate all at once, and he struggled handling it all. Being able to focus just on playing safety will hopefully bounce him back to where he was in 2017.

Special Teams

Year	DVOA	Rank	FG/XP	Rank	Net Kick	Rank	Kick Ret	Rank	Net Punt	Rank	Punt Ret	Rank	Hidden	Rank
2016	-2.3%	24	1.6	12	-8.6	29	-0.9	14	3.3	11	-6.8	28	4.3	11
2017	-7.4%	30	-10.3	29	-9.8	31	-3.6	24	-8.8	26	-4.5	27	-2.6	15
2018	-4.2%	31	0.3	15	-1.4	21	-6.4	32	-9.3	28	-4.3	27	11.4	4

If anything, Vance Joseph had too much faith in Brandon McManus. McManus was a perfect 18-for-18 from within 50 yards, but only 2-for-7 past that. McManus has never been particular good at long field goals (11-for-21 lifetime coming in to the season, despite kicking at altitude half the time) and hasn't made one from more than 55 yards out since 2016. With that in mind, asking him to kick a 58-yarder against Oakland and a *62-yarder* against Houston was a bit daft. At least the 58-yarder came as the first half expired; the miss against Houston directly led to a Texans field goal in a game Denver lost by two points. ● Colby Wadman replaced Marquette King early last season, to somewhat disappointing results. Denver's net punt value of -9.3 points was their worst since Britton Colquitt's rookie season in 2010. ● The Broncos also had their worst kick return season since 2014, as Devontae Booker and Phillip Lindsay were unable to make much of a splash. Booker averages 21.3 yards per kick return; that's the third-worst total in the league over the past two seasons. An open competition would be advised. ● Pacman Jones and River Cracraft split punt return duties last season. Jones is now retired, and Cracraft isn't a lock to make the 53-man roster. Brendan Langley, a third-round pick in 2017 who converted from corner to wideout last season, might be an option going forward.

Detroit Lions

2018 record: 6-10	**Total DVOA:** -15.2% (26th)	**2019 Mean Projection:** 8.3 wins	**On the Clock (0-4):** 8%
Pythagorean Wins: 7.0 (21st)	**Offense:** -5.2% (23rd)	**Postseason Odds:** 39.8%	**Mediocrity (5-7):** 30%
Snap-Weighted Age: 26.5 (15th)	**Defense:** 9.0% (28th)	**Super Bowl Odds:** 5.2%	**Playoff Contender (8-10):** 41%
Average Opponent: -1.4% (19th)	**Special Teams:** -0.9% (20th)	**Proj. Avg. Opponent:** -1.0% (24th)	**Super Bowl Contender (11+):** 22%

2018: Matt Patricia stripped the team to its core and suffered consequential growing pains.

2019: It's time for Patricia to show promise with the roster reconstructed in his vision.

No two coaching changes are the same. Some new coaches get the luxury of stepping into a ready-made team that underwhelmed under the previous staff, while others are stuck with the burden of building the team up from scraps. The NFC North's two rookie head coaches in 2018, Matt Nagy (Bears) and Matt Patricia (Lions), encapsulated how different those circumstances and the lenses through which each coach should be judged can be.

Nagy is the former example. The Bears already had a top-10 defense and the shell of a quality offense when he took over. With a few key additions during the offseason and early in the year—primarily wide receiver Allen Robinson and outside linebacker Khalil Mack—the Bears were able to make the leap from competitors to contenders. Nagy still did his fair share of work and helped develop the offense better than John Fox had previously, but it is hard to make a case that Chicago's 2018 season was all his doing. The Bears were already teetering toward being a top team.

Patricia, conversely, took over an incomplete Lions club. Detroit had won nine games the previous season under Jim Caldwell, but the offense overachieved through favorable turnover luck (particularly with respect to Matt Stafford's interceptions) and unreal seasons from Marvin Jones and Kenny Golladay doing their best pterodactyl impressions. That offense also had tight end Eric Ebron, who went on to catch 13 touchdowns with the Colts the next year, and a full season of Golden Tate. Likewise, the 2017 defense had a mostly healthy Ezekiel Ansah and the league's second-highest turnover rate. Patricia got the benefit of neither in 2018: Ansah started just two games, and the Lions plummeted to 31st in defensive turnover rate. The team was stripped down and all its overachievements caved in on Patricia.

Last season was effectively a Year 0. Patricia was hindered by a defense not yet sculpted in his image, which is especially troubling for a hybrid scheme such as his. As for the offense, not only did it lose much of its firepower either before the season (Ebron) or during the year through injury or trade, but offensive coordinator Jim Bob Cooter remained on hand as a remnant of the last coaching staff. After "fixing" Stafford in 2015 when he first took over play-calling duties, Cooter had organized one of the most vanilla offenses in the league. It was an offense even a remedial viewer could pick up tendencies on. That remained true in 2018. Without as many high-

end skill players to carry the water for him, Cooter's offense crashed.

2019 is about brushing off the last of the previous staff and barreling full steam ahead with the new one. Patricia took control of re-envisioning the defense by signing three players who spent time with him in New England: defensive end Trey Flowers and cornerbacks Justin Coleman and Rashaan Melvin. Draft weekend was further aimed at restructuring the defense as the Lions selected four defenders within their first five picks—first-round tight end T.J. Hockenson (Iowa) being the exception.

Patricia also got the opportunity to put in place his own offensive coordinator and see the offense retooled. He decided to hire Darrell Bevell, the former Seahawks offensive coordinator during the franchise's reign atop the NFC. Bevell was underappreciated toward the end of his tenure in Seattle. Sometimes team-coach pairings just need a change, and Bevell now gets that in Detroit. He has often been one to mold well to whatever the situation calls for, best displayed when he shifted the Seahawks' offense away from a run-heavy, under-center approach to more of a shotgun pass approach as running back Marshawn Lynch departed and the offensive line eroded (thanks, Tom Cable).

At Bevell's disposal are a handful of new toys to supplement the star receiving duo of Jones and Golladay. Detroit signed wide receivers Danny Amendola, another former Patriot, and Jermaine Kearse, who played under Bevell in Seattle. In addition to drafting Hockenson with the ninth overall pick, the Lions signed tight end Jesse James away from the Steelers early in the free-agency period and took a flier on Georgia tight end Isaac Nauta in the seventh round. They also signed the human bowling ball himself, running back C.J. Anderson, after a peculiar season in which he was cut by the Panthers only to become the Rams' lead back through their playoff run.

Admittedly, there is no star power in that bunch aside from Hockenson. The two receivers' best football is behind them, James can do everything well but nothing spectacularly, and Anderson will likely see the third-most running back touches behind Kerryon Johnson and Theo Riddick. Nevertheless, even just fielding five functional skill players and having proper depth was not on the table for the Lions last year. Their tight ends were pitiful and the receiving corps after Golladay and Jones was poor, especially once Tate was traded to

2019 Lions Schedule

Week	Opp.	Week	Opp.	Week	Opp.
1	at ARI	7	MIN	13	CHI (Thu.)
2	LAC	8	NYG	14	at MIN
3	at PHI	9	at OAK	15	TB
4	KC	10	at CHI	16	at DEN
5	BYE	11	DAL	17	GB
6	at GB (Mon.)	12	at WAS		

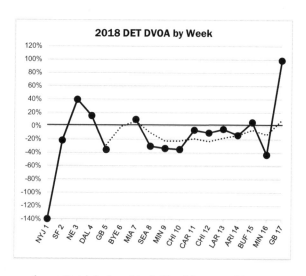

Philadelphia at the deadline. Defenses only had to respect two of the five potential pass-catchers the Lions were putting on the field—which became one when Jones lost the final seven games to a knee injury. Having a full cupboard should do wonders for Bevell and Stafford in their efforts to get the offense moving again.

To appreciate where the Lions are heading, it is worth dissecting what went wrong in Patricia's inaugural season and how exactly they plan to fix it. It is not enough to add talent for the sake of doing so. The defense needs to blend its new pieces together to create the hybrid defense Patricia could not fully develop last season, and the offense needs to find a new personality to pair well with a defense that wants to attack.

The defense's capitulation last year was discouraging but not surprising given the circumstances. By any standard, no matter the style they wanted to play, the Lions simply did not have the talent to field a proper defense. For Patricia's unique, multiple defense, the talent void was only amplified. He tried to make it work but to little avail.

The outside pass rush was non-existent. Ansah battled shoulder issues that sidelined him for much of the year, while Kerry Hyder failed to regain his impressive 2016 form after missing the entire 2017 season with an Achilles injury. Edge-rushing responsibilities were left up to Romeo Okwara, a career backup with one sack in the previous two seasons, and Devon Kennard, a hybrid SAM linebacker in Steve Spagnuolo's Giants defense before converting almost exclusively to the edge in Detroit. No team was starting worse—or at least less conventional—outside pass-rushers than Detroit.

The Lions' secondary was not well put together either. While cornerback Darius Slay was among the league's elite and cornerback Nevin Lawson and strong safety Quandre Diggs weren't too shabby, the unit was incomplete. Its weak links were clear, abusable, and ultimately unfixable during the season. In fact, the Lions defense was increasingly worse the more defensive backs they put on the field. They allowed a decent -2.9% defensive DVOA when in base personnel but fell to 7.6% in nickel and 22.2% in dime. More than anything, only having two quality corners hurt the Lions. Slay could lock down one side. Lawson could play outside in base and slot in nickel. Beyond those two, the Lions' secondary was a circus act, with Jamal Agnew, Mike Ford, DeShawn Shead, and Teez Tabor all seeing at least 200 snaps. Save for Agnew, they all finished the year with a sub-40 percent coverage success rate.

Not having a well-rounded secondary or a proper outside pass rush put Patricia in a bind. The Lions could not pressure effectively without extra rushers but also could not cover well with or without extra defenders in coverage. There was no right answer.

Patricia's defense rushed three more often than all but one other team. Rushing three at a high rate is not inherently bad, nor is it out of Patricia's norm if his tendencies in New England are any indicator; the Patriots were top-two in rush-three percentage in all but one of Patricia's six seasons as the coordinator. The problem is that if a defense rushes three at a high rate and hardly blitzes with five or more pass-rushers, while not having a legit No.1 pass-rush threat, quality coverage linebackers, or a full secondary, a situation arises where the defense is neither pressuring in time nor covering well despite the numbers advantage. The opposing quarterback gets extra time to pick on weak coverages. It's no wonder Detroit's pass defense DVOA was better than only Oakland's.

The Lions were excellent when they did blitz, too. Patricia is a mastermind at moving gaps, creating leverage, and opening up pathways for his blitz packages to get to the quarterback. He liked to send linebacker Jarrad Davis when he could. Davis is a devastating blitzer and Patricia maximized that strength at every opportunity, but because the secondary needed so much help when the base pass-rushers weren't pulling their weight, it was tough for Patricia to justify leaving the coverage short-handed very often. Maybe he should have blitzed more anyway given how poor a coverage piece Davis is, but it's understandable that Patricia in his first season with full control wanted to take a conservative approach by just putting bodies in coverage.

Patricia made it a point to change course in 2019. He brought in "his" guys en masse, setting up for a handful of new faces in the starting lineup. Flowers and Coleman are surefire starters. Assuming Tabor does not take a meaningful step forward this season, Melvin will likely take the starting spot opposite Slay. Second-round linebacker Jahlani Tavai (Hawaii) may not start out of the gate, but if all goes well, he can compete for snaps over Davis and Jones. Considering Patricia's desire for man coverage ability from all of his defensive backs, third-round safety Will Harris (Boston College) can earn a significant portion of the snaps over Miles Killebrew. Two Day 3 picks, Clemson defensive end Austin Bryant and Penn State cornerback Amani Oruwariye, fit Patricia's mold to a T and may also be able to play themselves into a contributing role. The Lions will see at least two new quality starters and as many as five, depending on how a few position battles turn out. There is still a way to go before this defense is a finished product, but these additions give Patricia personnel that he can mold into his scheme seamlessly.

Flowers alone overhauls what the defense can do with its base defensive line. Detroit's front can now be self-sufficient in their base pass-rush with Flowers; some combination of Damon Harrison, A'Shawn Robinson, and Da'Shawn Hand inside; and Devon Kennard or Romeo Okwara at the other end. Tack on Hand's and Flowers' versatility across the line, as well as Kennard's flexibility to slide out into coverage, and it's easy to see why Patricia was adamant about securing Flowers to unlock the rest of the front.

The cornerbacks are looking to match that independence with Coleman and Melvin solidifying a three-man core alongside Slay. Patricia's goal is to have a stable of cornerbacks who can play well in man coverage. His defense is predicated on playing man on the back end with the front seven being the source of confusion for the quarterback. The Lions did not have enough of those guys last year, but the hope is that 2019 will be different.

If both units can play better in their own right, Patricia will have the freedom to better mix up his approach, because neither unit will desperately need help on every play. He will have more autonomy to play with different packages, move his fronts around, and get creative with his safety assignments and rotations. The leeway to do more of what he wants, rather than what he has to do to protect a bad roster, will make for a more aggressive Patricia—the version that Detroit was seeking when they moved on from Caldwell's dull and conservative ways.

Though less directly, Patricia's influence will also leak into the offense. He is on track to mimic many of his defensive-minded peers by asking for an offense that controls the clock, puts an emphasis on running the ball, and does not surrender turnovers. Cooter was forced to go down that road in 2018, but it ran contrary to everything he had done in Detroit to that point, which only added to his struggles. This offseason, on the other hand, Bevell already appears to be ahead of the curve on leading an offense that prioritizes running the ball. It's true that Bevell ran more of a spread-gun offense toward the end of his stint in Seattle, but he has also coordinated run-first offenses in Minnesota with Adrian Peterson and early on in Seattle with Marshawn Lynch. The Lions don't have a Peterson or a Lynch, but they won't necessarily need one.

Establishing a run-first offense to help out the defense is a fallacy many defensive-minded head coaches fall for. Mike Zimmer had some of the most run-happy offenses in the league early in his career with the Vikings, and last year's pass-first approach under offensive coordinator John DeFilippo blew up before the season ended. Ron Rivera's Panthers have ranked in the top eight in first-half runs since 2014, steadily climbing each season before peaking at fourth in 2017 and 2018.

Jack Del Rio, who lasted just three seasons as Oakland's head coach, often rolled out run-first offenses, yet it was during a 2016 season in which the Raiders ran less than Del Rio's norm that they had their most success under him. In Todd Bowles' final season with the Jets in 2018, he moved on from pseudo-Air Raid coordinator John Morton in favor of then-quarterbacks coach Jeremy Bates before the season, in part because the players and staff were not happy with Morton's propensity to forget about running the ball. The Jets did not actually end up running more often under Bates, but the intent was there when he was promoted. Though there is some success sprinkled across these coaches, many of their best seasons (Rivera 2015, Del Rio 2016, Bowles 2017) came on the back of career years from their respective quarterbacks, including an MVP campaign from Cam Newton for Rivera. Passing is king no matter how much these coaches convince themselves running the ball is a priority.

As such, it is not an offensive philosophy change that needs to reignite the Lions offense. Aimlessly running the ball is not going to fix anything. Regardless of philosophy or scheme, the offense must become less predictable and more dynamic. Cooter's offenses, even when they were performing fairly well, weren't the toughest to decipher. For example, when Cooter began calling a decent amount of pistol formation during the 2017 season, almost anybody could tell you the play call would be inside zone or a quick screen to a wide receiver out of a stack formation. The creativity to mix in pistol formations in a league that is slow to embrace them was impressive, but Cooter painfully telegraphed what he wanted to do out of those formations. It was the most obvious tell in the sport at the time. New York Jets linebacker Darron Lee said he and his teammates were calling out the Lions' plays before the ball was snapped following their Week 1 matchup on Monday Night Football.

Bevell has to bring more variety and give his players a chance to catch defenders off guard; hopefully a deeper skill group can give him the tools he needs to do so. If the type of players that Detroit brought in is telling of anything, it is not hard to see where the offense is going. In addition to Bevell's proclamation about running the ball, Detroit's new stable of pass-catchers suggests they want to mix in more personnel groups and reestablish an efficient passing game.

Drafting Hockenson after signing James is an obvious point of change. The Lions' best tight end last year was Levine Toilolo, and they were not going to suffer like that for another season. Hockenson is the perfect dual-threat tight end who can blow someone up in the run game, then beat a linebacker down the seam on the next play. James provides a similar dynamic, though without the same tantalizing potential as his rookie counterpart. The two receivers Detroit signed, Amendola and Kearse, are at their best working the short to intermediate area of the field, particularly over the middle. They operate best on timing routes and when sifting through zones. All four pickups, to one degree or another, signal that the Lions want a pass game that can reliably take the easy yards, instead of needing to rely on riskier downfield throws to the two skyscrapers they play on the outside. The two passing styles can live in harmony to make for a more complete Lions offense that forces defenses to respect every blade of grass. Ideally, the Lions find their footing as a passing offense with these new pieces and do not feel pressured to run the ball too often.

The offense's shift and development all comes to a head with Stafford. Ten years into his career, Stafford has played himself out of the bottom tier of quarterbacks. Maintaining his status as a top-flight quarterback has been a struggle, though. Stafford showed immense potential early on—expected from a first-overall pick—but has since become a watered-down version of Ben Roethlisberger. His highs show up too infrequently for a passer whose baseline level of play is not elite. Stafford was excellent down the stretch in 2017 when fighting for a playoff spot, for instance, but was lackluster during the first half of that season and reverted back to mediocrity in 2018. Granted, the offense was not geared for success in 2018, but it's not as though Stafford made a Herculean effort to make up lost ground. Given that the Lions have an option to cut Stafford for a portion of his salary after the 2020 season, now is the time for him to step up.

Luckily for Stafford, Bevell's offense should give him the opportunity to rebound as well as give Patricia the opportunity to properly evaluate him as the long-term option. In three of the past four seasons, Detroit's pass game has been better on play-action passes than non-play-action passes per DVOA, with 2015 being the odd year out. Cooter's offense has regularly ranked in the bottom third of the league in play-action usage over that period, though. Bevell's Seattle offenses, conversely, ranked top-10 in play-action percentage. Those concepts, both out of shotgun and from under center, helped drive Russell Wilson's success over the years. Considering the Lions have two towering deep threats on the outside and an ath-

letic tight end who can sell run-action before torching across the field, Bevell and Stafford have all the tools they need to produce an explosive play-action game.

Added skill talent, a heavier focus on the run game, and a more thorough and extensive play-action pass game should all serve to relieve stress from Stafford. He has long carried a significant burden for this franchise. It's keen of Patricia to notice the weight Stafford has had to carry, even through injury, and do what he can to redistribute responsibility. Nobody should expect the Lions' offense to ascend to the top of the league, but if Stafford can sustain above-average play and the offense can be an effective complement to an improved defense, Detroit will be in good position to compete in the division.

2019 may not be the year the Lions become an elite team, but it doesn't have to be. Now that Patricia is getting a legitimate go at coaching "his" team, Detroit's goals should be to put Stafford on the right track and for the defense to show signs of life. This is their chance to climb out of the abyss to become a competitive team again and set up for a prosperous future with their fresh coaching staff.

With the Bears expected to regress and the Vikings potentially stuck in mediocrity, it may only take a few things going the Lions' way for them to be duking it out for the division title. To be fair, the NFC North is going to look like a Big Ten bloodbath in which each team within the division beats up on the others enough so that no club rises to the top of the league, but a solid, efficient offense and a semi-competent defense could make Detroit a more complete team than their peers. Coming off a down season in a chaotic division, a dose of stability is just what the Lions need now and moving forward.

Derrik Klassen

2018 Lions Stats by Week

Wk	vs.	W-L	PF	PA	YDF	YDA	TO	Total	Off	Def	ST
1	NYJ	L	17	48	339	349	-3	-143%	-68%	32%	-44%
2	at SF	L	27	30	427	346	-1	-22%	7%	32%	3%
3	NE	W	26	10	414	209	0	40%	7%	-32%	0%
4	at DAL	L	24	26	382	414	0	15%	31%	16%	1%
5	GB	W	31	23	264	521	+3	-36%	-17%	25%	5%
6	BYE										
7	at MIA	W	32	21	457	322	0	10%	34%	27%	4%
8	SEA	L	14	28	331	413	-3	-31%	-2%	23%	-6%
9	at MIN	L	9	24	209	283	+1	-34%	-31%	1%	-2%
10	at CHI	L	22	34	305	402	-3	-35%	1%	44%	8%
11	CAR	W	20	19	309	387	+1	-6%	-2%	18%	14%
12	CHI	L	16	23	333	264	-1	-10%	-10%	-3%	-3%
13	LAR	L	16	30	310	344	0	-5%	-19%	-12%	3%
14	at ARI	W	17	3	218	279	0	-14%	-13%	0%	-2%
15	at BUF	L	13	14	313	312	0	6%	30%	18%	-6%
16	MIN	L	9	27	223	340	0	-43%	-28%	12%	-3%
17	at GB	W	31	0	402	175	+1	99%	15%	-70%	13%

Trends and Splits

	Offense	Rank	Defense	Rank
Total DVOA	-5.2%	23	9.0%	28
Unadjusted VOA	-7.2%	24	7.2%	26
Weighted Trend	-2.7%	22	5.1%	23
Variance	6.8%	15	8.0%	29
Average Opponent	-3.0%	3	-3.3%	24
Passing	3.7%	22	24.7%	31
Rushing	-12.0%	25	-10.6%	13
First Down	-15.6%	27	10.8%	30
Second Down	4.0%	13	14.6%	30
Third Down	0.6%	18	-3.6%	16
First Half	-1.7%	17	3.8%	26
Second Half	-9.2%	24	14.2%	29
Red Zone	-11.3%	24	2.6%	19
Late and Close	1.0%	17	20.7%	31

Five-Year Performance

Year	W-L	Pyth W	Est W	PF	PA	TO	Total	Rk	Off	Rk	Def	Rk	ST	Rk	Off AGL	Rk	Def AGL	Rk	Off Age	Rk	Def Age	Rk	ST Age	Rk
2014	11-5	9.2	8.7	321	282	+7	4.4%	14	-3.8%	19	-13.9%	3	-5.7%	31	26.4	13	41.1	21	27.0	15	27.5	6	25.9	20
2015	7-9	6.9	7.4	358	400	-6	1.2%	13	1.8%	13	1.6%	16	1.0%	13	21.7	5	55.0	30	26.2	24	27.3	6	26.2	15
2016	9-7	7.7	5.3	346	358	-1	-15.6%	27	-0.6%	15	18.5%	32	3.5%	6	40.0	22	29.4	13	26.2	25	26.4	18	25.9	21
2017	9-7	8.9	8.4	410	376	+10	5.5%	12	4.4%	12	4.0%	19	5.1%	5	27.9	10	44.8	24	26.6	21	26.0	21	26.0	9
2018	6-10	7.0	6.1	324	360	-5	-15.2%	26	-5.2%	23	9.0%	28	-0.9%	20	41.8	18	35.0	17	26.8	15	26.2	17	26.5	8

2018 Performance Based on Most Common Personnel Groups

DET Offense					DET Offense vs. Opponents					DET Defense					DET Defense vs. Opponents			
Pers	Freq	Yds	DVOA	Run%	Pers	Freq	Yds	DVOA	Run%	Pers	Freq	Yds	DVOA		Pers	Freq	Yds	DVOA
11	58%	5.8	4.6%	29%	Base	30%	4.1	-22.1%	63%	Base	15%	5.6	-2.9%		11	66%	6.1	11.2%
12	12%	4.7	-24.8%	55%	Nickel	70%	5.7	0.9%	28%	Nickel	58%	5.7	7.6%		12	14%	5.2	2.4%
21	10%	4.5	0.9%	50%	Dime+	8%	6.9	55.2%	15%	Dime+	26%	6.5	22.2%		21	9%	5.2	-1.2%
10	5%	6.9	1.2%	0%	Goal Line	1%	0.5	-65.8%	100%	Goal Line	1%	0.5	2.3%		13	4%	6.6	23.4%
20	4%	6.1	39.8%	7%	Big	1%	7.5	22.8%	83%						613	1%	5.8	-5.6%

Strategic Tendencies

Run/Pass		Rk	Formation		Rk	Pass Rush		Rk	Secondary		Rk	Strategy		Rk
Runs, first half	41%	8	Form: Single Back	81%	15	Rush 3	19.0%	2	4 DB	15%	30	Play action	18%	29
Runs, first down	49%	14	Form: Empty Back	4%	29	Rush 4	66.3%	19	5 DB	58%	20	Avg Box (Off)	6.28	9
Runs, second-long	27%	22	Pers: 3+ WR	67%	17	Rush 5	11.9%	31	6+ DB	26%	7	Avg Box (Def)	5.95	31
Runs, power sit.	48%	26	Pers: 2+ TE/6+ OL	19%	24	Rush 6+	2.7%	30	CB by Sides	59%	23	Offensive Pace	32.64	29
Runs, behind 2H	22%	24	Pers: 6+ OL	7%	3	Int DL Sacks	15.1%	29	S/CB Cover Ratio	29%	12	Defensive Pace	31.93	27
Pass, ahead 2H	46%	24	Shotgun/Pistol	66%	14	Second Level Sacks	39.5%	3	DB Blitz	3%	32	Go for it on 4th	0.79	30

Even with Jim Bob Cooter still serving as offensive coordinator, there were some significant changes in the Detroit offense: more runs, more six-lineman sets, and less shotgun compared to Cooter's past offenses. ● With T.J. Hockenson in town, the Lions will no longer be dead last in the percent of targets thrown to tight ends (12 percent). ● Detroit was very good on running back screens—7.0 yards per pass, 43.2% DVOA—and only Philadelphia used the play more often. ● The Lions need to figure out how to maintain their fast starts because they were great last year for the first 15 minutes of the game. In the first quarter, they ranked eighth in offensive DVOA and fourth in defensive DVOA. For the rest of the game, they ranked 26th in offensive DVOA and 30th in defensive DVOA. ● Lions opponents threw deep (16 or more air yards) on 23.8 percent of passes. Only the Patriots faced more deep passes, and Detroit was 23rd in DVOA on these passes. ● Detroit's defense ranked third against the run in the red zone but 25th against the pass. ● The Lions also ranked No. 1 in defense against the run on third and fourth downs. On every other combination of down and play type, they ranked 24th or worse.

Passing

Player	DYAR	DVOA	Plays	NtYds	Avg	YAC	C%	TD	Int
M.Stafford	396	-0.8%	594	3521	5.9	5.5	66.2%	21	11
M.Cassel*	-96	-90.7%	18	46	2.6	4.1	41.2%	0	1

Receiving

Player	DYAR	DVOA	Plays	Ctch	Yds	Y/C	YAC	TD	C%
K.Golladay	250	13.3%	119	70	1063	15.2	5.0	5	59%
G.Tate*	-53	-22.3%	69	44	517	11.8	6.4	3	64%
M.Jones	142	15.7%	62	35	508	14.5	3.1	5	56%
B.Ellington*	-75	-44.9%	30	23	132	5.7	3.7	0	77%
T.J.Jones*	30	1.6%	27	19	190	10.0	1.9	2	70%
A.Jones	-31	-29.0%	24	11	80	7.3	2.4	1	46%
B.Powell	4	-9.2%	17	11	129	11.7	10.5	0	65%
D.Amendola	38	-6.2%	79	59	575	9.7	3.9	1	75%
J.Kearse	-95	-28.8%	76	37	371	10.0	3.4	1	49%
L.Toilolo*	75	37.3%	24	21	263	12.5	5.2	1	88%
M.Roberts*	1	-6.7%	20	9	100	11.1	2.6	3	45%
L.Willson*	-28	-28.6%	19	13	87	6.7	4.5	0	68%
J.James	96	27.3%	39	30	423	14.1	6.2	2	77%
L.Thomas	-37	-43.5%	17	12	77	6.4	2.8	0	71%
T.Riddick	4	-12.7%	74	61	384	6.3	6.7	0	82%
K.Johnson	20	-4.8%	39	32	213	6.7	8.3	1	82%
L.Blount*	-38	-52.5%	15	10	67	6.7	8.7	0	67%
Z.Zenner	-11	-32.2%	10	7	56	8.0	9.3	0	70%
C.J.Anderson	-12	-34.4%	9	5	41	8.2	9.0	1	56%

Rushing

Player	DYAR	DVOA	Plays	Yds	Avg	TD	Fum	Suc
L.Blount*	-125	-27.9%	154	418	2.7	5	1	37%
K.Johnson	124	17.5%	118	641	5.4	3	1	53%
Z.Zenner	68	19.3%	55	265	4.8	3	0	56%
T.Riddick	5	-4.7%	40	171	4.3	0	0	43%
M.Stafford	12	1.9%	16	85	5.3	0	1	--
C.J.Anderson	141	41.2%	67	403	6.0	2	0	67%

Offensive Line

Player	Pos	Age	GS	Snaps	Pen	Sk	Pass	Run	Player	Pos	Age	GS	Snaps	Pen	Sk	Pass	Run
Graham Glasgow	C	27	16/16	1074	9	0.5	2	3	Kenny Wiggins	RG	31	16/10	796	3	4.0	9	5
Frank Ragnow	LG	23	16/16	1074	6	5.0	15	9	T.J. Lang*	RG	32	6/6	282	0	0.0	2	1
Taylor Decker	LT	26	16/16	1062	7	3.5	9	8	Oday Aboushi	RG	28	8/6	407	3	4.5	7	2
Rick Wagner	RT	30	15/15	984	6	4.0	7	2	Luke Bowanko	LG	28	7/3	244	3	2.5	4	0

Year	Yards	ALY	Rank	Power	Rank	Stuff	Rank	2nd Lev	Rank	Open Field	Rank	Sacks	ASR	Rank	Press	Rank	F-Start	Cont.
2016	3.64	3.49	31	56%	26	23%	29	1.10	21	0.47	27	37	6.1%	18	27.1%	20	16	30
2017	3.31	3.16	32	45%	32	27%	31	0.94	29	0.52	23	47	7.5%	21	30.6%	15	10	16
2018	4.10	4.14	20	68%	14	22%	27	1.18	22	0.74	23	41	6.3%	12	27.0%	9	10	28
2018 ALY by direction:			Left End: 4.30 (18)			Left Tackle: 4.23 (14)			Mid/Guard: 4.37 (18)				Right Tackle: 3.22 (30)			Right End: 4.00 (18)		

The Detroit Lions were Dr. Jekyll and Mr. Hyde when it came to bodies on the line of scrimmage. They ran 7.0 percent of plays with six offensive linemen, third in the league. Conversely, they also ran 9.3 percent of plays *without* either a tight end or a sixth lineman; that was most in the league, well ahead of the second-place Broncos at 5.9 percent. 🏈 Adding guard Frank Ragnow in the first round last year knocked out two birds with one stone. He assumed the left guard position and played fairly well for a rookie, allowing Graham Glasgow to move back to center after playing left guard in 2017. Ragnow was an upgrade over Glasgow, while Glasgow held his own in place of a discarded Travis Swanson. Ragnow lacked consistency, as he ranked 29th in snaps per blown block among left guards, but the promise and overall impact he showed in his first season ever playing the position is a good sign of things to come. 🏈 More specifically, Ragnow was a boon for the line's power success. They sat at the bottom of the league in that area for the past two seasons, but Ragnow—with all that Arkansas Razorbacks nastiness—helped turn the Lions into a team that could get push when they needed it. The team's adjusted line yards to the left tackle and middle tell a similar story. Now moving back to center, his best position in college, Ragnow may be able to more evenly spread his strength to both sides of the line. 🏈 Right guard was Detroit's weak point last season whenever T.J. Lang was out of the lineup. They did little to address that this offseason. Kenny Wiggins, Lang's stand in, is a backup quality player who struggled for much of last season, but he is currently slated to start. Free agent Oday Aboushi, a cast-off from an atrocious Cardinals offensive line, and rookie undrafted free agent Beau Benzschawel (Wisconsin) are Wiggins' only real competition. They should at least spark a battle for the starting job, but neither player would be a significant upgrade. 🏈 Ricky Wagner has ranked among the top eight right tackles in snaps per blown block each of the past three years, peaking at second in 2018.

Defensive Front

Defensive Line	Age	Pos	G	Snaps	Plays	TmPct	Rk	Stop	Dfts	BTkl	Runs	St%	Rk	RuYd	Rk	Sack	Hit	Hur	Dsrpt
						Overall						vs. Run					Pass Rush		
Damon Harrison	31	DT	17	606	81	10.2%	1	69	21	4	74	84%	16	1.6	13	3.5	4	10	1
A'Shawn Robinson	24	DT	13	415	48	7.9%	6	34	5	3	47	70%	60	2.1	39	1.0	4	12	0
Ricky Jean Francois*	33	DT	16	405	30	4.0%	64	21	7	2	27	70%	59	2.4	50	2.0	0	6	0

Edge Rushers	Age	Pos	G	Snaps	Plays	TmPct	Rk	Stop	Dfts	BTkl	Runs	St%	Rk	RuYd	Rk	Sack	Hit	Hur	Dsrpt
						Overall						vs. Run					Pass Rush		
Romeo Okwara	24	DE	15	716	40	5.7%	29	28	12	5	27	59%	78	3.4	76	7.5	6	22	1
Da'Shawn Hand	24	DE	13	455	26	4.3%	58	21	6	0	23	78%	33	2.3	43	3.0	0	14	0
Trey Flowers	26	DE	15	732	58	8.0%	4	46	16	3	42	74%	48	2.3	44	7.5	12	43	3

Linebackers	Age	Pos	G	Snaps	Plays	TmPct	Rk	Stop	Dfts	BTkl	Runs	St%	Rk	RuYd	Rk	Sack	Hit	Hur	Tgts	Suc%	Rk	AdjYd	Rk	PD	Int
						Overall						vs. Run				Pass Rush				vs. Pass					
Jarrad Davis	24	MLB	16	976	105	14.1%	31	58	19	16	58	60%	38	3.5	28	6.0	4	17	33	48%	44	5.8	20	5	0
Devon Kennard	28	OLB	15	864	46	6.6%	78	30	12	5	35	57%	53	3.5	26	7.0	7	29	3	33%	--	9.7	--	0	0
Christian Jones	28	OLB	16	643	72	9.7%	59	31	5	5	48	44%	86	4.9	76	1.0	3	3	17	29%	77	6.8	39	3	0

Year	Yards	ALY	Rank	Power	Rank	Stuff	Rank	2nd Level	Rank	Open Field	Rank	Sacks	ASR	Rank	Press	Rank
2016	4.35	4.40	21	73%	31	15%	29	1.20	20	0.73	15	26	5.4%	25	23.1%	30
2017	4.18	4.32	25	61%	11	17%	29	1.23	24	0.66	13	35	6.1%	22	28.1%	27
2018	4.68	4.47	20	52%	1	15%	28	1.20	14	1.10	26	43	8.1%	5	26.3%	29

2018 ALY by direction:	Left End: 3.43 (7)	Left Tackle: 4.98 (26)	Mid/Guard: 4.46 (20)	Right Tackle: 5.10 (29)	Right End: 3.89 (12)

The Lions dealt a fourth-round pick to the Giants to acquire Damon "Snacks" Harrison before the trade deadline, and Harrison was every bit as good as he was supposed to be. The Lions ranked 29th in run defense DVOA through the first nine weeks, but skyrocketed to first in Weeks 10 to 17 once Harrison settled in. His sense of flow for running plays and command over multiple gaps at a time is unrivaled. ● Matt Patricia was one of the least blitz-happy play callers last season, yet his defense ranked third in second-level sacks. Part of the explanation is that Detroit's base edge rushers were middling and Devon Kennard, effectively an edge defender in this defense, is listed as a linebacker. Additionally, Patricia made fantastic use of middle linebacker Jarrad Davis, an effective blitzer who shouldn't always be dropping into coverage. ● However, luck also played a major role in Detroit's sack success. The Lions were 29th in pressure rate, in part because they only had one "traditional" defensive end in career backup Romeo Okwara, but came in fifth in adjusted sack rate. Specifically, the Lions ranked 29th in adjusted sack rate on first down, then improved to seventh on second down and third on third down. Patricia deserves some credit for being able to scheme open guys on the downs that matter most, but that disparity won't hold. Also, Detroit's defense had 15 sacks last year that were coded by charters as "coverage sacks." No other team had more than seven. ● Last year's fourth-round pick Da'Shawn Hand looks like a hit. He was a menacing run defender and provided decent help as a pass-rusher. Though listed at edge, he is more of a hybrid player who can move all over the line, including 0-tech on pass downs. With added help off the edge and a more flexible front, Hand should blossom into a solid cornerstone in Patricia's defense. ● Aside from signing Trey Flowers, Patricia's most Patriots-esque move as head coach was drafting Hawaii linebacker Jahlani Tavai in the second round. The Patriots, with some exceptions, have long preferred smart, hard-nosed linebackers over pure athletes. Tavai is not a sideline-to-sideline specialist, but he sees the field well, can eat up the run game, and has experience at defensive end. Patricia is hoping he has found his own Dont'a Hightower.

Defensive Secondary

Secondary	Age	Pos	G	Snaps	Plays	Overall TmPct	Rk	Stop	Dfts	BTkl	vs. Run Runs	St%	Rk	RuYd	Rk	vs. Pass Tgts	Tgt%	Rk	Dist	Suc%	Rk	AdjYd	Rk	PD	Int
Quandre Diggs	26	SS	16	948	86	11.5%	21	40	15	10	32	56%	13	6.7	31	46	11.9%	57	9.2	43%	55	7.8	43	8	3
Darius Slay	28	CB	15	875	60	8.6%	42	26	15	4	6	50%	22	4.8	15	82	23.0%	64	15.7	59%	13	5.7	7	17	3
Glover Quin*	33	FS	16	829	76	10.2%	39	24	6	11	35	43%	35	7.3	44	25	7.4%	19	9.6	52%	32	6.9	32	3	0
Mike Ford	24	CB	7	316	25	7.7%	--	4	1	3	2	50%	--	8.0	--	31	24.0%	--	13.2	23%	--	13.1	--	1	0
Tavon Wilson	29	SS	15	304	32	4.6%	--	15	5	3	11	64%	--	3.5	--	17	13.7%	--	8.1	59%	--	6.5	--	0	0
Teez Tabor	24	CB	12	275	23	4.1%	--	6	2	1	4	50%	--	10.8	--	29	25.8%	--	13.0	38%	--	12.5	--	0	0
Tracy Walker	24	SS	16	267	16	2.1%	--	4	3	1	5	20%	--	9.8	--	9	8.3%	--	16.0	78%	--	6.4	--	2	1
DeShawn Shead*	30	CB	12	247	10	1.8%	--	2	2	3	1	100%	--	-3.0	--	17	16.9%	--	14.1	24%	--	13.7	--	0	0
Justin Coleman	26	CB	16	672	52	6.9%	--	26	7	11	9	44%	--	6.9	--	58	20.4%	--	7.3	62%	--	5.4	--	10	1
Rashaan Melvin	30	CB	14	604	65	9.7%	24	24	8	4	17	59%	12	3.7	9	67	30.6%	79	11.0	45%	69	8.9	67	9	1
Andrew Adams	27	FS	13	370	45	6.8%	64	22	16	12	12	58%	11	5.8	22	24	16.5%	73	10.1	58%	17	6.7	24	9	4

Year	Pass D Rank	vs. #1 WR	Rk	vs. #2 WR	Rk	vs. Other WR	Rk	WR Wide	Rk	WR Slot	Rk	vs. TE	Rk	vs. RB	Rk
2016	32	11.5%	26	5.0%	21	27.4%	32	13.9%	29	14.7%	26	21.7%	29	34.4%	29
2017	16	-25.6%	3	11.3%	22	5.8%	20	-5.0%	12	-2.5%	11	12.9%	26	-12.7%	8
2018	31	21.5%	32	19.4%	27	39.5%	32	19.3%	31	34.0%	31	19.4%	26	-6.6%	11

Patricia uses man coverage at very high rates, not surprising for a Bill Belichick coaching descendent. (Sports Info Solutions charted the Lions in man coverage on 52 percent of passes, fifth in the league; the Patriots were first at 57 percent.) ● Rookie safety Will Harris, a third-round pick out of Boston College, is an investment in that style of defense. Harris is an excellent athlete who can roam around the back end as well as roll down to cover slot receivers, tight ends, and backs. ● Cornerback Darius Slay is elite, full stop. Slay's 56 passes defensed over the past three seasons are the most of any player, and his 13 interceptions over that span only trails Marcus Peters (14). He is one of the few cornerbacks in the league who can successfully follow any receiver, fulfill any assignment, play any coverage, and dominate. For as often as Slay was targeted in 2018, especially down the field, his success rate and adjusted yards allowed speak for themselves. ● Prepare for 2017 second-round cornerback Teez Tabor to be phased out under Patricia's reign. He is slow and has a propensity to be beaten early in dramatic fashion. Patricia already used him sparingly last season; bringing in Justin Coleman and Rashaan Melvin may seal the young corner's fate. ● Melvin should be the expected starter in place of Tabor, but do not be surprised if rookie Amani Oruwariye (Penn State) earns playing time. His man-zone versatility and ball skills are premium for the position, especially in Patricia's defense. Oruwariye was widely viewed as a Day 2 cornerback, coming in as the seventh corner per *The Athletic's* Arif Hasan's consensus big board, but Detroit snagged him in the fifth round as the 16th corner off the board. ● Safety Andrew Adams is a sneaky good depth signing with potential to take over a starting role. He played well in relief/emergency roles the past two seasons with the Giants and Bucs, respectively.

Special Teams

Year	DVOA	Rank	FG/XP	Rank	Net Kick	Rank	Kick Ret	Rank	Net Punt	Rank	Punt Ret	Rank	Hidden	Rank
2016	3.5%	6	2.5	11	-2.9	24	-1.5	16	10.7	5	8.5	3	2.4	14
2017	5.1%	5	7.3	8	5.8	5	-4.0	27	-1.5	20	17.9	1	6.4	6
2018	-0.9%	20	0.2	16	2.6	10	-0.7	14	-3.1	24	-3.5	25	20.0	2

On top of missing more than half the season with a knee injury, punt returner Jamal Agnew's effectiveness took a nosedive in 2018. His 17.3 added points of value were unrivaled as a rookie in 2017. Last season, though, Agnew did not return any punt further than 16 yards in his 12 attempts. ● No alternative proved himself well enough to retain the job over Agnew moving forward. Three of the five players who fielded at least one punt in his place are no longer on the roster, including T.J. Jones, who fared well (2.1 points of value) in his eight attempts. ● Detroit's drop in FG/XP value can be explained in part by volume. Kicker Matt Prater was a quality 8-of-12 (67 percent) on field goals of 40-plus yards in 2018, but that pales in comparison to his 14-of-19 (74 percent) rate in 2017. On a per-kick basis, he was only slightly more effective in 2017, but the increased success on top of the huge boost in volume creates a noticeable discrepancy. It's not so much that Prater got worse, he just didn't get as much action. ● Punter Sam Martin had another strong year of gross punt value, but Detroit's coverage team was weak. The Lions allowed 8.3 estimated points worth of field position over average on returns, more than any other punt coverage team in the NFL. ● Detroit's high "hidden" special teams value comes from a lot of good luck on field goals that is unlikely to continue in 2019. Opposing field goal kickers were just 19-for-28 against Detroit, with six of those misses coming from 42 yards or less. They also missed four extra points.

Green Bay Packers

2018 record: 6-9-1	Total DVOA: -3.1% (19th)	2019 Mean Projection: 8.6 wins	On the Clock (0-4): 7%
Pythagorean Wins: 7.4 (19th)	Offense: 11.1% (7th)	Postseason Odds: 44.4%	Mediocrity (5-7): 27%
Snap-Weighted Age: 26.4 (18th)	Defense: 10.1% (29th)	Super Bowl Odds: 7.5%	Playoff Contender (8-10): 40%
Average Opponent: -3.9% (30th)	Special Teams: -4.1% (29th)	Proj. Avg. Opponent: 0.2% (16th)	Super Bowl Contender (11+): 25%

2018: The power structure in Green Bay finally collapsed once and for all.

2019: Can an overhauled Packers organization rediscover a level of success that eluded them the past two seasons?

The curtains have closed on the Mike McCarthy era. After more than a decade with the team, McCarthy was not given the grace to finish out his final season in Lambeau. A Week 13 loss at home to a putrid Arizona Cardinals club sealed the coach's fate, leaving the frustrated franchise little choice but to fire him before the night's end. McCarthy was canned, offensive coordinator Joe Philbin took over the interim position in his place, and the Packers stumbled through the final four games to a 6-9-1 record. The mediocre results barred Green Bay from the playoffs, the first time the Packers missed the playoffs in back-to-back seasons since 2005-2006, and making 2018 the first season with six or fewer wins since 2008.

The irony is that McCarthy, after years of a dull and recycled West Coast system that relied exclusively on one-on-one receiver victories, spiced up the offense to offset the lack of talent and experience on the roster. His offense was on the forefront of manufacturing light defensive boxes to run into, a common-sense "revelation" trickling up from the high school and college ranks. To account for Rodgers' questionable health, McCarthy leaned into more pistol formations, giving Rodgers the safety and vision of shotgun while also providing him with the comfort and success he has shown from under center. The passing offense was also more aggressive than it has been in years despite two of the team's four top receivers being rookie Day 3 draft picks. It did not prove to be enough, in large part because the defense was a disaster, but the longtime head coach went down swinging.

By most standards, McCarthy's tenure was a success. It would not take much to convince anyone that he underachieved considering he had arguably the most talented quarterback of all-time at his disposal, but the Packers won six division championships, 10 playoff games, and a Super Bowl in his 13 seasons. McCarthy could have accomplished more, but his run was not a failure.

That did not stop the Packers from ushering in a new era. It was time for a change. Thirteen seasons in and with new general manager Brian Gutekunst stepping up in 2018, the Packers did not feel McCarthy was the best option to milk the most out of Rodgers' final stretch. At age 35, Rodgers has just a handful of potential peak-performance years left before age wears on him. Gutenkunst, with the help of his star quarterback, landed a bright-eyed Matt LaFleur to be the new head coach.

LaFleur, just four years older than Rodgers, is one of many proteges from the Kyle Shanahan-Sean McVay tree, coaching under both in different capacities before branching out on his own to call plays for the Tennessee Titans last season. In most every way imaginable, LaFleur was the antithesis of McCarthy (Table 1). Most coaching changes come in the form of going from one extreme to another; authoritarian to player's coach, offensive-minded to defensive-minded, old to young, etc. Centering a coaching change around a major philosophical difference on offense is not as dramatic a change as the Bears going from John Fox to Matt Nagy, for example, but there is no doubt that Green Bay wanted to rid themselves of anything that resembled McCarthy's approach.

Table 1. Strategic Tendencies, McCarthy vs. LaFleur in 2018

	McCarthy (Rank)	LaFleur (Rank)
Avg. Box (Offense)	5.89 (32)	6.60 (1)
Shotgun/Pistol	73% (8)	58% (27)
Single Back	87% (5)	74% (23)
3+ WR	78% (4)	58% (28)
Play-Action	20% (27)	29% (6)
Runs, First Half	33% (28)	43% (2)
Runs, 2nd and Long	23% (31)	44% (1)
Runs, Behind 2H	17% (30)	37% (3)

Some of the disparity between the strategies of these two coaches can be explained by the personnel each had on hand, especially at quarterback, but the tangible difference between them is not up for debate. In the same vein, LaFleur's offense will adapt to the Packers' roster, even if his general principles remain. LaFleur wants to use heavier personnel sets, condense the formation, operate from under center, and lean on the run game and play-action as the engine of the offense. The influence from McVay and Shanahan is written all over him. McVay's offense operates almost exclusively out of 11 personnel and Shanahan runs more two-back sets than anyone in the league by far, while LaFleur leaned on 12 personnel in his one season as a stand-alone playcaller, but a handful of the same underlying themes remain.

A shift away from 11 personnel suits the Packers. Wide receiver Davante Adams has enjoyed a meteoric rise over the

2019 Packers Schedule

Week	Opp.	Week	Opp.	Week	Opp.
1	at CHI. (Thu.)	7	OAK	13	at NYG
2	MIN	8	at KC	14	WAS
3	DEN	9	at LAC	15	CHI
4	PHI (Thu.)	10	CAR	16	at MIN (Mon.)
5	at DAL	11	BYE	17	at DET
6	DET (Mon.)	12	at SF		

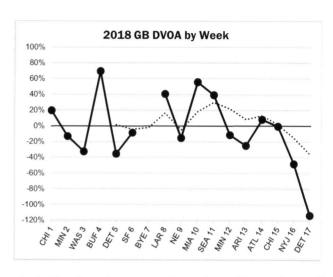

past couple seasons, but he cannot shoulder the load of receiving production by himself. Randall Cobb and Geronimo Allison, ideally the team's No. 2 and No. 3 options last year, were injured for large stretches. Cobb left this offseason to join the Cowboys. Though good before injury last season, Allison could be stepping into the No. 2 or No. 3 role having never caught more than 23 passes in his three-year career. Equanimous St. Brown and Marquez Valdes-Scantling impressed in infrequent bursts as rookies, but to ask them to play instrumental roles in the offense's success is asking for a lot. Of the two, Valdes-Scantling has the best chance to emerge as a legitimate contributor, though he needs to show he can be more than a post/go-route player.

Conversely, Green Bay drafted Texas A&M tight end Jace Sternberger in the third round. A grad transfer from Kansas, Sternberger is a decent athlete who functions more as a pass-catcher than a blocker, but he is more than willing to get his hands dirty. He can also be flexed all around the formation in such a way that LaFleur should be able to take creative advantage of. Pairing Sternberger with Jimmy Graham does not give LaFleur the same dynamic he had with Delanie Walker and Jonnu Smith in Tennessee, but the pass-catching prowess of his new tight end duo is going to be a headache for opposing defenses.

Going back to more under-center formations will be of aid to Rodgers, too. In each of the past three seasons, the Packers finished top-10 in non-shotgun DVOA. Their worst finish over that stretch was ninth in 2017, the year Rodgers broke his collarbone seven games in. It has been a quiet strength for him hidden in McCarthy's shotgun-centric offense.

One reason Rodgers was so effective under center and slightly less so out of shotgun is that he often struggles coming back to his checkdown or "rush" routes. He will bypass safe, short throws in favor of potentially finding the home run. McCarthy's shotgun spread concepts were regularly designed around the quarterback taking layups and coming back to his checkdowns properly rather than going for riskier throws over the middle or down the field, but Rodgers of late is not the best maximizing those outlets. That is not to say Rodgers is reckless—his career interception ratio proves his risk calculation—but he sometimes makes drives harder on himself than he needs to. Rodgers, for all his greatness, is prone to holding the ball longer than advised to find those explosive passes. In each of his past two full seasons (2016, 2018), Rodgers finished in the top six for time to throw at 2.87 seconds and 2.95 seconds, respectively, per NFL's Next Gen Stats.

In LaFleur's under-center, play-action offense, plays will more frequently be designed to hit deep or intermediate routes at the top of the quarterback's drop. Rodgers will not have to do as much to manufacture vertical aggression out of the offense. LaFleur, like McVay, is also privy to designing two-man stop or comeback combos out of max-protection play-action concepts. These serve as great complements to many of the other hard play-action concepts in their offenses. Those plays often require little from the quarterback aside from timing and top-shelf accuracy. Rodgers checks both of those boxes.

The glue that will hold together the overwhelming change is the offensive line. All-Pro left tackle David Bakhtiari, left guard Lane Taylor, center Corey Linsley, and right tackle Bryan Bulaga are going on their fourth consecutive season together. A few minor injuries have tweaked this lineup here and there, but they have become one of the most reliable lines in football.

Right guard has been the lone point of uncertainty plaguing the unit since the Packers allowed longtime starter T.J. Lang to walk following the 2016 season. They put forth a carousel of different types of players at the position over the past two years: Jahri Evans in 2017 and—even worse—Byron Bell and Justin McCray in 2018. Early this offseason, Gutekunst set out to solve the problem once and for all by signing Billy Turner and drafting Mississippi State offensive lineman Elgton Jenkins. Turner, drafted by Miami in 2014, was a fringe starter for most of his career before stepping up in Denver last season. Playing mostly left guard for the Broncos, Turner helped re-establish a mean run game and held his own in pass protection despite playing next to Garrett Bolles, one of the worst left tackles in the NFL. Jenkins, conversely, started two years at center in college, but also spent time at both tackle spots as well as left guard. The two can duke it out for the starting job at right guard and the loser of that camp battle can provide good play off the bench at a number of spots.

A healthy and rejuvenated Rodgers should return in 2019 as well. He was not at full capacity last season. The severity of Rodgers' knee injury in Week 1 versus the Bears was up in the air throughout the year, by some fault of his own because he returned in that same game to launch a fourth-quarter comeback. After the season, he confirmed that he had a tibial plateau fracture in addition to a sprained MCL. Rodgers managed to start the rest of the season on one good knee, but it was clear he wasn't fully himself. His short accuracy in particular took a hit, perhaps best epitomized in Week 11 when he threw at Valdes-Scantling's feet on a third-and-2 late in the fourth quarter against the Seahawks on Thursday Night Football. To say Rodgers gave up after that moment would be reckless, but something seemed to switch within him and for the rest of the team.

Through the first 10 games of the season, Rodgers averaged 53.9 DYAR per game while playing with a busted knee. In the four games after the loss to the Seattle—a stretch Green Bay desperately needed to crush in order to make the playoffs—Rodgers dropped to 30.8 DYAR per game. It does not help that he faced Minnesota and Chicago on the road, but the decline in production was instrumental to Green Bay dropping three of four games during that stretch, including the embarrassing home loss to the Cardinals.

Physically, emotionally, and mentally, Rodgers was taxed to the maximum last season. There was a sense that he had shouldered the entire burden of the franchise on his shoulders and it finally came crashing down in the last few games of the year. A fresh start in an inventive offense with a stable line and a clean bill of health is the right recipe for a Rodgers revival, if he and LaFleur can get on the same page.

The star quarterback is not the only one in Green Bay looking to bounce back. Coming in at 29th in defensive DVOA, the Packers produced their worst finish since 2013. Defensive coordinator Mike Pettine was a strong addition to the staff before last season, but with an inexperienced secondary, one good linebacker, and mediocre firepower off the edge, he was trying to make lemonade without lemons and sugar. It was never going to be a good unit regardless of health, but injuries piled on throughout the year and Green Bay's defense devolved from below average (23rd through Week 9) to a full-blown liability (31st in Weeks 10 to 17). The small handful of stars couldn't pull the weight of an otherwise replacement-level defense.

Pettine had to make the best of an incomplete roster. Desperation spurned innovation as he crafted the most unique defense in the league. Pettine called a fluid secondary that often put six defensive backs on the field and asked them to play man coverage. Six defensive backs usually meant a linebacker came off the field—or, for long stretches, was never on the field in the first place. Blake Martinez played almost every snap on defense but was the only linebacker to play more than 30 percent of the team's snaps and was regularly the only traditional linebacker on the field. The Los Angeles Chargers received all the attention for deploying six defensive backs late in the season because they were one of the most exciting teams in the league, and because they took a game from the Baltimore Ravens in the playoffs in large part by swarming the run game with their faster defensive backs. Not to take away from the Chargers' success, but the Packers were doing the same thing for a good portion of the season. Pettine just didn't have Derwin James and reliable edge rushers to tie it all together.

In an effort to bypass inconsistent cover skills, Green Bay's defensive backs were sent on blitzes more than almost every other secondary in the league. Pettine also frequently peppered offenses with five-man pressure packages. Rushing four was futile if the Packers wanted any chance to disrupt the quarterback, but rushing six with an all-out blitz was asking for his beat-up secondary to get torched. With some help from a strong stable of pass-rushing interior defensive linemen, Green Bay quietly managed to rank 14th in pressure rate. Unfortunately, the sack numbers weren't as impressive.

When coordinators go off the beaten path the way Pettine had to, they don't always stick with it. They tend to revert back to "standard" approaches and secure the right personnel to prevent them from having to go down that road again. That doesn't appear to be the case with Pettine. If anything, Green Bay's offseason proved they are willing to invest in this unique brand of defense.

Previous Packer regimes were not big spenders in free agency. Ted Thompson, specifically, believed in strict draft tendencies, undrafted gems, and paying homegrown talent. Gutekunst tossed that out the window. On March 12, the Packers went all-in on two of the top pass-rushers on the market: Preston Smith from the Redskins and Za'Darius Smith from the Ravens.

Preston Smith has long been a player who racks up pressures with the best of 'em, but never quite finds the sack totals to match. He has generated 88 pressures the past three seasons with just 17 sacks to show for it. Rocking a thick, long build, he is quicker than he looks and can be devastating around the arc. The other Smith, Za'Darius, is more of a tweener. He is an outside linebacker in base and an interior defensive lineman on pass-rush downs. There is not as much bend or quickness to his game as his new counterpart on the edge, but he is overwhelming when he gets going. He is the outside linebacker equivalent of a battering ram.

With the 13th overall pick, the Packers also selected Rashan Gary, an edge defender out of Michigan. Gary is a former blue-chip recruit who struggled to convert athleticism into production but possesses all the tools NFL coaches salivate over. After signing the Smiths, it seemed as though the Packers would be set at outside linebacker. Drafting Gary a month later smells of Pettine wanting Za'Darius to be more of an inside player.

Theoretically, a front Pettine could frequently rollout is: Preston Smith and Gary on the outside, Za'Darius Smith at 3-technique/4i, and Kenny Clark at nose. Za'Darius Smith could rotate with either of the two outside linebackers and Mike Daniels could step in as the 3-technique. Daniels may even come in for Clark on obvious pass downs to get the best four pass-rushers on the field. There will always be players subbing in and out, on top of the inevitable injury or two, but that group of four could be their most popular grouping outside of a "base" set of Smith-Daniels-Clark-Smith. It seems counterintuitive to move an outside linebacker to a frequent inside role with regards to defending the run, but it may be the case that Pettine wants lighter players on the field to cook up dangerous blitz packages.

Contrasted by the heavy investment in pass-rushers, Green Bay did close to nothing at linebacker. 2018 third-round pick Oren Burks converted from safety to linebacker in college and served primarily as a special-teamer as a rookie. Betting on him for meaningful contributions, especially behind a potentially light defensive front, may be a tad optimistic. Every other off-ball linebacker on the roster is a seventh-round pick or undrafted free agent from the past two years. Martinez remains the lone reliable force up front. He is a mean run defender and a better cover player than his athletic profile suggests, but it will be a tall order for him to be the only significant linebacker again.

The secondary, like the front, is somewhat of a mystery. Kevin King is a lock to play on the outside. The same can be said of Adrian Amos, another notable free-agent signing, at safety. Everything else could see tweaks throughout the preseason and regular season, depending on where Pettine's vision leads him.

First-round safety Darnell Savage Jr. (Maryland) and cornerback Jaire Alexander are the two key chess pieces in Green Bay's back end. Under head coach D.J. Durkin, formerly Florida's defensive coordinator, Savage played a lot of quarters and was regularly rolled down to play as a true nickel cornerback. He is a hybrid player who can play both safety positions and man coverage from the slot. Paired with Amos, also capable of playing both safety spots, Savage unlocks what Pettine can do with his safeties. Similarly, Alexander is on his way to being a top-tier cornerback, both outside and in the slot. He played both spots last year and thrived in both, akin to players such as Casey Hayward and Chris Harris Jr. Sprinkle on top the possibility of Josh Jackson seeing snaps at safety instead of cornerback, as well as Josh Jones being a hybrid linebacker/safety, and it paints a secondary that could be mixed and matched every which way, with the exception of King sticking on the outside.

In isolation, there's nothing unique about this kind of flexibility on each of the three levels of defense. Plenty of other teams around the league can match at least one level of the defense, be it the Chargers' defensive back-laden scheme or the Lions' ability to morph their front into a number of interesting looks. Together, though, all three levels of the defense being able to stray from the norm in some way or another is significant. If the Packers lean into the style they played in the back half of last season the way they have positioned themselves to, there will not be any defense in the league that functions quite the same way. With added star power up front and a secondary with fewer weak links, the fresh look on defense should bear far better results than in 2018.

Unique or not, Green Bay's defense almost has to improve. There is not much room to get worse compared to last season. There is likely to be regression in injury luck, as the Packers were 30th in adjusted games lost on defense. Combine that with a handful of talent upgrades, and Pettine's defense is poised to climb out of the abyss. For them to spring from 29th into the top third of the league is an optimistic proposition, but if the Packers' defense can be average or slightly below average, an improved offense under LaFleur will have a considerably easier time carrying the team back into the postseason.

The Packers of the past half-decade will feel like a distant memory compared to this new-look squad. LaFleur's rendition of the offense will look quite different from McCarthy's, while Pettine leans into a lighter, faster, more versatile style of defense than many are used to seeing. Morale and energy is difficult to quantify, but this team no longer feels like the downtrodden team of the past two seasons.

With that, the green and gold are set to earn a first-place finish in the division. The NFC North being the tightest division in the NFL leaves less room for error, but with a dash of regression and a breath of fresh air throughout the franchise, the title is theirs for the taking. It's high time Rodgers reclaimed his throne atop the conference.

Derrik Klassen

2018 Packers Stats by Week

Wk	vs.	W-L	PF	PA	YDF	YDA	TO	Total	Off	Def	ST
1	CHI	W	24	23	370	294	-1	20%	6%	-16%	-2%
2	MIN	T	29	29	351	480	+1	-13%	15%	20%	-8%
3	at WAS	L	17	31	340	386	0	-33%	12%	48%	3%
4	BUF	W	22	0	423	145	+1	69%	7%	-57%	5%
5	at DET	L	23	31	521	264	-3	-36%	19%	10%	-44%
6	SF	W	33	30	521	401	+3	-9%	20%	32%	3%
7	BYE										
8	at LAR	L	27	29	359	416	-1	41%	23%	-16%	2%
9	at NE	L	17	31	367	433	-1	-15%	-5%	12%	2%
10	MIA	W	31	12	377	294	+1	56%	34%	-23%	-2%
11	at SEA	L	24	27	359	378	+1	39%	36%	-2%	1%
12	at MIN	L	17	24	254	416	-1	-12%	14%	29%	3%
13	ARI	L	17	20	325	315	0	-25%	11%	36%	0%
14	ATL	W	34	20	300	344	+2	8%	2%	-2%	4%
15	at CHI	L	17	24	323	332	0	0%	16%	15%	-1%
16	at NYJ	W	44	38	540	370	-1	-48%	32%	50%	-31%
17	DET	L	0	31	175	402	-1	-114%	-79%	34%	-1%

Trends and Splits

	Offense	Rank	Defense	Rank
Total DVOA	11.1%	7	10.1%	29
Unadjusted VOA	8.9%	10	10.1%	28
Weighted Trend	10.4%	10	13.1%	30
Variance	6.9%	17	8.3%	31
Average Opponent	-2.3%	5	-5.9%	29
Passing	18.0%	12	20.1%	28
Rushing	12.4%	3	-2.0%	23
First Down	13.8%	7	9.0%	28
Second Down	7.3%	12	22.3%	32
Third Down	11.9%	11	-6.5%	12
First Half	8.5%	9	22.0%	32
Second Half	13.5%	6	-3.3%	12
Red Zone	14.9%	10	23.4%	29
Late and Close	11.4%	8	2.7%	24

Five-Year Performance

Year	W-L	Pyth W	Est W	PF	PA	TO	Total	Rk	Off	Rk	Def	Rk	ST	Rk	Off AGL	Rk	Def AGL	Rk	Off Age	Rk	Def Age	Rk	ST Age	Rk
2014	12-4	11.2	10.8	486	348	+14	23.3%	3	24.7%	1	-1.0%	16	-2.3%	22	11.0	3	31.0	9	25.7	30	26.7	18	25.9	19
2015	10-6	9.3	9.9	368	323	+5	9.9%	10	2.2%	11	-7.3%	9	0.4%	17	29.7	15	26.5	14	26.7	16	26.3	23	25.5	28
2016	10-6	9.1	9.8	432	388	+8	12.3%	7	16.6%	4	2.5%	20	-1.9%	21	35.2	16	35.3	19	26.8	14	25.8	30	25.4	28
2017	7-9	6.2	7.7	320	384	-3	-3.3%	17	0.3%	15	4.9%	20	1.3%	14	46.0	24	38.8	21	27.0	16	25.5	28	25.2	28
2018	6-9-1	7.4	8.0	376	400	0	-3.1%	19	11.1%	7	10.1%	29	-4.1%	29	28.4	8	64.3	30	27.6	8	25.8	24	25.2	31

2018 Performance Based on Most Common Personnel Groups

GB Offense					GB Offense vs. Opponents					GB Defense					GB Defense vs. Opponents			
Pers	Freq	Yds	DVOA	Run%	Pers	Freq	Yds	DVOA	Run%	Pers	Freq	Yds	DVOA		Pers	Freq	Yds	DVOA
11	77%	6.0	22.0%	23%	Base	13%	5.9	9.9%	45%	Base	18%	5.5	6.9%		11	66%	5.5	2.2%
12	16%	6.3	13.9%	39%	Nickel	79%	5.8	19.6%	28%	Nickel	40%	6.0	10.8%		12	12%	6.6	22.9%
13	4%	4.5	-9.0%	75%	Dime+	10%	6.6	-3.1%	11%	Dime+	41%	5.7	7.5%		21	9%	7.6	38.2%
21	1%	0.3	-103.3%	75%	Goal Line	1%	0.4	-27.8%	38%	Goal Line	0%	1.5	113.3%		612	3%	8.3	37.5%
14	1%	0.4	-12.7%	43%											22	2%	2.7	-19.0%
															13	2%	6.1	23.3%

Strategic Tendencies

Run/Pass		Rk	Formation		Rk	Pass Rush		Rk	Secondary		Rk	Strategy		Rk
Runs, first half	33%	28	Form: Single Back	87%	5	Rush 3	14.0%	5	4 DB	18%	24	Play action	20%	27
Runs, first down	36%	32	Form: Empty Back	5%	27	Rush 4	56.1%	28	5 DB	40%	28	Avg Box (Off)	5.89	32
Runs, second-long	23%	31	Pers: 3+ WR	78%	4	Rush 5	25.5%	6	6+ DB	41%	2	Avg Box (Def)	6.06	28
Runs, power sit.	30%	32	Pers: 2+ TE/6+ OL	20%	21	Rush 6+	4.5%	22	CB by Sides	80%	14	Offensive Pace	31.46	19
Runs, behind 2H	17%	30	Pers: 6+ OL	0%	31	Int DL Sacks	28.4%	15	S/CB Cover Ratio	37%	3	Defensive Pace	30.13	5
Pass, ahead 2H	65%	1	Shotgun/Pistol	73%	8	Second Level Sacks	26.1%	12	DB Blitz	14%	4	Go for it on 4th	2.63	1

At 64.8 percent, the Packers were more likely to pass when leading in the second half than any team since the 2013 Atlanta Falcons. ● The Packers in 2017 ranked third in empty backfields and 28th in single-back formations. Last year, that switched to 27th and fifth, respectively. ● The Packers ran 50 wide receiver or tight end screens, second in the league behind Pittsburgh, although they gained just 5.1 yards per play with 0.7% DVOA on these plays. ● Green Bay had the No. 1 DVOA running in the red zone but ranked 22nd passing in the red zone. ● Not only did the Packers defense rank near the top of the league in defensive back blitzes, they also brought pass pressure 62 percent of the time when they blitzed a defensive back, third in the league. However, their -20.7% DVOA allowed on these plays was just 14th in the league. ● Green Bay and Pittsburgh tied for the league lead with 34 penalties on special teams. ● The listed Aggressiveness Index is for Mike McCarthy; interim coach Joe Philbin had an AI of zero, never going for it on a qualifying fourth down during his four-game stint. McCarthy only went for it on 1-of-4 fourth-and-1 opportunities but earned a high AI for tougher decisions such as going for fourth-and-4 in the second quarter against both San Francisco in Week 6 and Arizona in Week 13.

Passing

Player	DYAR	DVOA	Plays	NtYds	Avg	YAC	C%	TD	Int
A.Rodgers	817	8.1%	644	4032	6.3	5.7	62.9%	25	2
D.Kizer	-262	-102.7%	45	152	3.4	3.2	48.8%	0	2

Rushing

Player	DYAR	DVOA	Plays	Yds	Avg	TD	Fum	Suc
A.Jones	146	17.1%	133	728	5.5	9	1	55%
J.Williams	52	1.7%	121	464	3.8	3	0	45%
A.Rodgers	66	18.4%	38	274	7.2	2	2	--
T.Montgomery*	0	-9.0%	26	105	4.0	1	1	50%

Receiving

Player	DYAR	DVOA	Plays	Ctch	Yds	Y/C	YAC	TD	C%
D.Adams	246	6.1%	169	111	1386	12.5	4.3	13	66%
M.Valdes-Scantling	8	-11.3%	73	38	581	15.3	5.6	2	52%
R.Cobb*	-45	-22.1%	61	38	384	10.1	6.2	2	62%
E.St.Brown	16	-7.2%	36	21	328	15.6	5.7	0	58%
G.Allison	66	16.8%	30	20	303	15.2	5.3	2	67%
J.Kumerow	19	8.8%	11	8	103	12.9	2.9	1	73%
J.Davis	-11	-29.1%	8	4	40	10.0	1.0	0	50%
J.Graham	4	-6.6%	89	55	636	11.6	4.7	2	62%
L.Kendricks*	12	-0.1%	25	19	170	8.9	5.9	1	76%
R.Tonyan	19	38.7%	6	4	77	19.3	2.5	1	67%
J.Williams	11	-9.3%	41	27	210	7.8	8.5	0	66%
A.Jones	33	2.2%	35	26	206	7.9	8.5	1	74%
T.Montgomery*	28	8.6%	23	15	170	11.3	9.9	0	65%

Offensive Line

Player	Pos	Age	GS	Snaps	Pen	Sk	Pass	Run	Player	Pos	Age	GS	Snaps	Pen	Sk	Pass	Run
Corey Linsley	C	28	16/16	1075	1	2.0	8	5	Justin McCray	RG	27	13/5	481	3	4.0	10	1
David Bakhtiari	LT	28	16/16	1032	5	3.0	11	3	Jason Spriggs	RT	25	13/2	291	7	4.0	8	0
Lane Taylor	LG	30	15/14	881	2	4.0	10	4	Lucas Patrick	LG/RG	26	14/4	279	2	1.0	5	1
Bryan Bulaga	RT	30	14/14	782	8	4.0	11	0	Billy Turner	LG/RT	28	16/11	824	2	1.0	14	10
Byron Bell*	RG	30	12/9	527	1	1.0	4	2									

Year	Yards	ALY	Rank	Power	Rank	Stuff	Rank	2nd Lev	Rank	Open Field	Rank	Sacks	ASR	Rank	Press	Rank	F-Start	Cont.
2016	4.36	4.08	19	49%	30	20%	17	1.15	15	0.94	9	35	5.5%	11	26.3%	16	13	33
2017	4.13	4.60	5	66%	11	16%	2	1.10	19	0.51	24	51	8.6%	28	35.1%	28	11	21
2018	4.70	4.71	7	65%	21	18%	12	1.49	2	0.80	20	53	7.9%	21	29.0%	16	16	33

2018 ALY by direction:	Left End: 5.33 (8)	Left Tackle: 4.01 (18)	Mid/Guard: 4.76 (6)	Right Tackle: 4.77 (7)	Right End: 4.21 (16)

The Packers used six offensive linemen on just one play the entire season. Only the Los Angeles Rams had zero plays with six or more offensive linemen. ● The Packers faced, on average, the lightest boxes in the NFL. A league-leading 68 percent of Green Bay's running back carries came against small boxes (less than seven). They regularly created light boxes by operating out of 11 personnel spread formations that featured tight end Jimmy Graham as a slot or wideout. In turn, the Packers' offensive line had an easier job resetting the line of scrimmage further up the field and the backs were able to capitalize at the second level against the lighter boxes. ● Signing Billy Turner for four years, $28 million dollars after starting just one of the past four seasons is a gamble, especially considering he had one of the worst blown-block rates in the league. The idea behind signing Turner is that he is a stronger pass-blocker than Byron Bell and considerably better than Justin McCray, and the Packers want to put a premium on pass protection to better enable their star quarterback. ● Patience is running thin for 2016 second-round tackle Jason Spriggs. An impressive athlete out of Indiana, Spriggs has yet to clean up his technique and develop a stout, physical play style. He too often sets himself up to fail and does not have the raw strength to mask it. Drafting him three years ago came with the intention for him to eventually supplant Bryan Bulaga, but Spriggs has not proven he is up for the task. ● Second-round pick Elgton Jenkins (Mississippi State), like many Packers linemen, started his career as a left tackle before transitioning to a different position; center, in his case. Jenkins is no threat to take Corey Linsley's starting job, but Linsley's contract is up after 2020 and Jenkins can take over as a cheaper option then while providing quality depth at multiple spots right now.

Defensive Front

Defensive Line	Age	Pos	G	Snaps	Plays	TmPct	Rk	Stop	Dfts	BTkl	Runs	St%	Rk	RuYd	Rk	Sack	Hit	Hur	Dsrpt
						Overall					vs. Run					Pass Rush			
Kenny Clark	24	DT	13	721	58	8.8%	3	48	13	3	47	83%	18	2.4	52	6.0	3	20	2
Dean Lowry	25	DE	16	698	47	5.8%	30	34	7	7	40	70%	62	2.6	57	3.0	2	16	3
Mike Daniels	30	DE	10	419	19	3.7%	68	17	2	2	16	88%	8	2.4	54	2.0	3	24	1
Tyler Lancaster	25	DT	11	271	26	4.6%	--	24	3	1	25	92%	--	2.2	--	0.0	1	5	1
Fadol Brown	26	DE	12	214	21	3.7%	--	18	4	2	19	84%	--	2.1	--	0.0	4	4	1
Montravius Adams	24	DT	16	212	20	2.5%	--	10	5	2	16	50%	--	3.4	--	1.5	0	2	0

Edge Rushers	Age	Pos	G	Snaps	Plays	TmPct	Rk	Stop	Dfts	BTkl	Runs	St%	Rk	RuYd	Rk	Sack	Hit	Hur	Dsrpt
						Overall					vs. Run					Pass Rush			
Clay Matthews*	33	OLB	16	756	42	5.2%	40	33	15	8	32	78%	36	3.3	75	3.5	11	21	1
Kyler Fackrell	28	OLB	16	623	41	5.0%	43	31	15	7	25	76%	42	3.5	80	10.5	2	6	1
Reggie Gilbert	26	OLB	16	486	39	4.8%	48	29	9	3	27	81%	21	3.0	60	2.5	5	15	2
Nick Perry*	29	OLB	9	301	26	5.7%	30	18	6	2	19	63%	72	3.4	79	1.5	1	8	3
Preston Smith	27	OLB	16	832	56	6.9%	9	40	14	8	42	69%	60	2.5	48	4.0	13	33	1
Za'Darius Smith	27	OLB	16	690	46	6.1%	20	33	17	3	25	64%	70	3.2	72	8.5	17	30	0

Linebackers	Age	Pos	G	Snaps	Plays	TmPct	Rk	Stop	Dfts	BTkl	Runs	St%	Rk	RuYd	Rk	Sack	Hit	Hur	Tgts	Suc%	Rk	AdjYd	Rk	PD	Int
						Overall					vs. Run					Pass Rush			vs. Pass						
Blake Martinez	25	ILB	16	1049	147	18.0%	4	70	18	12	89	48%	80	4.2	59	5.0	1	11.5	37	57%	17	5.0	14	3	0
Antonio Morrison*	25	ILB	16	299	45	5.5%	--	24	8	6	33	61%	--	3.6	--	1.0	1	2.5	7	14%	--	11.4	--	0	0

Year	Yards	ALY	Rank	Power	Rank	Stuff	Rank	2nd Level	Rank	Open Field	Rank	Sacks	ASR	Rank	Press	Rank
2016	4.12	3.84	9	72%	30	20%	13	1.16	17	0.82	22	40	7.0%	8	27.0%	16
2017	3.81	3.93	9	56%	7	20%	21	1.08	10	0.57	7	37	7.3%	9	29.0%	26
2018	4.32	4.78	27	63%	10	15%	29	1.15	9	0.62	7	44	7.7%	10	30.8%	14

2018 ALY by direction: Left End: 5.64 (31)   Left Tackle: 3.85 (11)   Mid/Guard: 4.84 (26)   Right Tackle: 3.74 (9)   Right End: 5.82 (32)

Defensive tackle Kenny Clark is steadily on his way to stardom. He is a prototype modern interior defender. Clark sports the size and power to work between the guards as a run-stopping nose tackle, yet also possesses enough wiggle and explosiveness to threaten as a pass-rusher from a number of alignments. Both in nickel and base, Clark can be a foundation that the rest of the defense is built around. ● Kyler Fackrell is this year's most obvious candidate for sack regression. He stunned with 10.5 sacks, twice as many as he had in the past two years combined, despite just six hurries. Fackrell wound up in the right place at the right time with uncanny regularity. That should not be expected to happen again. After all, the Packers sought out three new pass-rushers for a reason. ● One of those new pass-rushers is Za'Darius Smith, a Baltimore-bred hybrid player. His best role is as an edge defender in base packages who will then slide inside to 3-technique on clear passing downs and third downs, as he did in Baltimore. Do not expect him to play outside the tackles all the time. ● Selecting Michigan's Rashan Gary in the first round came as a bit of a surprise. He is a hyper-athletic, former five-star defensive end out of Don Brown's four-down lineman defense. However, he is a raw pass-rusher who desperately needs to develop a better toolset in getting to the passer. Gary also battled a shoulder issue during his final college season and plans to play through it again as a rookie. He may not undergo surgery until after 2019. A lot needs to go right for Gary to progress properly, both in terms of health and skill.

Defensive Secondary

Secondary	Age	Pos	G	Snaps	Plays	TmPct	Rk	Stop	Dfts	BTkl	Runs	St%	Rk	RuYd	Rk	Tgts	Tgt%	Rk	Dist	Suc%	Rk	AdjYd	Rk	PD	Int
Tramon Williams	36	FS	16	1059	56	6.9%	62	14	4	9	19	16%	70	10.4	68	49	12.0%	60	10.1	55%	21	6.3	15	2	0
Jaire Alexander	22	CB	13	760	74	11.2%	7	27	12	10	15	27%	68	11.6	76	73	24.9%	70	11.5	52%	40	8.2	53	11	1
Josh Jackson	23	CB	16	718	55	6.7%	67	21	5	13	13	38%	48	6.3	37	52	18.8%	41	11.4	44%	71	9.5	73	10	0
Kentrell Brice*	25	FS	14	646	52	7.3%	59	14	2	14	27	37%	46	6.8	36	26	10.4%	49	8.8	23%	74	13.3	72	2	0
Josh Jones	25	SS	13	501	53	8.0%	--	21	3	8	27	59%	--	4.3	--	19	9.8%	--	7.8	37%	--	8.1	--	2	0
Bashaud Breeland*	27	CB	7	329	24	6.7%	--	11	4	6	8	63%	--	3.3	--	25	19.7%	--	12.6	60%	--	7.8	--	4	2
Tony Brown	24	CB	11	287	34	6.1%	--	11	8	3	7	43%	--	4.0	--	37	33.5%	--	10.7	49%	--	6.3	--	5	0
Jermaine Whitehead*	26	FS	14	228	22	3.1%	--	9	3	2	11	45%	--	4.9	--	13	12.4%	--	7.1	38%	--	7.5	--	2	0
Adrian Amos	26	SS	16	1028	81	9.9%	41	33	14	6	18	50%	21	7.1	42	39	8.7%	30	7.0	64%	9	4.3	3	9	2

Year	Pass D Rank	vs. #1 WR	Rk	vs. #2 WR	Rk	vs. Other WR	Rk	WR Wide	Rk	WR Slot	Rk	vs. TE	Rk	vs. RB	Rk
2016	23	12.3%	28	18.0%	28	13.7%	26	7.7%	26	19.1%	31	-17.4%	7	-7.9%	13
2017	27	31.9%	32	22.1%	26	-9.4%	10	8.3%	26	28.1%	31	4.1%	21	17.3%	29
2018	28	9.0%	22	14.9%	25	-4.1%	13	4.1%	22	13.6%	25	20.8%	27	25.1%	32

Jaire Alexander posted as impressive a rookie season as anyone could ask for. Many of his efficiency numbers are average or slightly above, but considering he saw the most targets on the team by far, he performed exceptionally well. Both outside and in the slot, Alexander has the smooth hips, downfield speed, and ball tracking skills to be a dominant corner. ● Mike Pettine's Packers finished second in using six or more defensive backs, third in CB/S cover ratio, and fourth in defensive back blitz percentage. They were the only defense to rank in the top 10 in all three categories, never mind top five. Drafting safety/nickel hybrid Darnell Savage Jr. (Maryland) and signing versatile safety Adrian Amos further leans into Green Bay's unique, fluid secondary situation. ● Do not be surprised if Josh Jackson finds himself playing more safety instead of cornerback. He has the size, discipline, and ball skills of a quality outside corner, but he can be stiff as a board and often struggles to match receivers through their breaks. Being able to play more off of his eyes and instincts in deep zones may better suit him. ● In turn, Savage may play the nickel, allowing Alexander and Kevin King to man the outside. Savage played a nickel/safety hybrid role in college, similar to Tyrann Mathieu or Budda Baker. In terms of getting the best five defensive backs on the field, this would be the way to go. ● Box safety/dime linebacker Josh Jones expressed a desire to be traded this summer, but that story quickly went away and he will stay in Green Bay. Jones is not a better safety option than Amos, Savage, or even Jackson. Instead, his role will most likely be as a dime and pseudo linebacker next to Blake Martinez; it has been his most succesful role in his first two NFL seasons. ● A rare age-defying cornerback, Tramon Williams is moving back to his natural position after taking over at safety in place of Ha Ha Clinton-Dix midway through last season. Williams played well on the back end for Green Bay, but with a fresh pair of starting safeties, he no longer has to start there. The Packers now have the safety talent to allow Williams to start as an outside cornerback and be shifted around during the season in the event of injury, if need be. Williams posted 49 percent (2016, Cleveland) and 55 percent (2017, Arizona) coverage success rates in his previous two seasons as a full-time cornerback.

Special Teams

Year	DVOA	Rank	FG/XP	Rank	Net Kick	Rank	Kick Ret	Rank	Net Punt	Rank	Punt Ret	Rank	Hidden	Rank
2016	-1.9%	21	0.7	13	-8.7	30	-2.5	22	0.1	14	1.1	13	-8.4	26
2017	1.3%	14	-2.8	19	0.1	17	0.2	13	5.1	9	4.0	4	-12.0	30
2018	-4.1%	29	-0.1	18	-4.5	28	-4.5	29	-2.1	19	-9.2	32	1.1	13

Getting Trevor Davis back from injury will revive the Packers' punt return game. Davis was effective in a part-time return role as a rookie in 2016 before turning in a third-place finish in punt return value as the full-time man in 2017. Hamstring issues kept him out for most of 2018, however, forcing the Packers to try out five different returners in his absence. As a receiver, Davis has always been at his best after the catch, and those skills translate well to returning punts. ● A 35-year-old Tramon Williams fielded the most punts (12) in Davis' stead. That is all you need to know about why the Packers' return game was not as electric as before. ● Mason Crosby is a fairly successful kickoff artist, often finding himself in the top third of the league in kick value. The 10 special teamers around him, though, seldom return the favor. Only three teams gave up more return value in 2018. ● Bashaud Breeland and Ty Montgomery accounted for 18 of the team's 30 kick returns last year, but neither is on the roster now. Granted, Davis will likely assume the role like he did before his injury, but Green Bay has still lost a lot of recent kick return experience. ● J.K. Scott was fairly average as a rookie and will be the first punter to return to the Packers since Tim Masthay in 2014 and 2015.

Houston Texans

2018 record: 11-5	Total DVOA: 7.1% (11th)	2019 Mean Projection: 8.0 wins	On the Clock (0-4): 10%
Pythagorean Wins: 10.3 (8th)	Offense: -3.5% (21st)	Postseason Odds: 35.2%	Mediocrity (5-7): 33%
Snap-Weighted Age: 26.0 (27th)	Defense: -7.1% (7th)	Super Bowl Odds: 4.7%	Playoff Contender (8-10): 39%
Average Opponent: -3.5% (29th)	Special Teams: 3.5% (5th)	Proj. Avg. Opponent: 3.3% (2nd)	Super Bowl Contender (11+): 18%

2018: Nine straight wins couldn't mask glaring fundamental flaws in coverage and on the offensive line.

2019: Houston, Rivers won't let us use this cliché.

What role do you think NASA has in your day-to-day life? We're long past the era of space flight being interesting or relevant news. There's nobody to fight in space at the moment. Certainly, NASA is a funded government agency that is doing something up there. According to their website, they're studying what travel to Mars would be like, they're studying what long-term life in space does to humans, and they're developing advanced planes to try to cut flight times. But on a day-to-day basis, normal people don't get much news about it. We would wager you've heard more about Elon Musk or Jeff Bezos attempting to fly themselves to space than NASA in the last year or so.

We're not here to dunk on NASA—it's just that they (likely by design) have no great leadership ethos or direction. There is no primary public directive at this point, and the people who do talk about what NASA should be doing outside of documentaries use phrases like "space armies" instead of wrestling with what humankind's role in space should be as we go further towards the future. Is it sustainable life off the planet? Is it a way to help climate control? Is it searching for alien life? NASA just sort of sits there, directionless, waiting for a focal point.

We assume you're smart enough to understand the transition point here: what is Houston Texans football about? Houston Texans football had forever been designed on the ethos of "not having enough." Sometimes, like in 2005, that literally meant that the whole roster had been deprived of talent. Sometimes, like in 2008, it meant that the defense would never allow them to keep up with Peyton Manning's Colts. Sometimes, like in 2012, it meant that they did not have the proper quarterback to win a tough game against a top-tier AFC opponent.

Then, in 2017, the Texans traded up to draft Deshaun Watson. It was somewhat of a bold move, because Watson wasn't a flawless NFL projection and the Texans were banking on him to turn out great or a lot of people were going to be out of a job. Watson, a cunning quarterback with a knack for making plays out of structure and keeping things alive, went 3-3 with three close losses to playoff teams in 2017 before tearing his ACL. The makeshift offense head coach Bill O'Brien built around Watson's talents averaged 34.6 points per game. The Texans won exactly one game without him, to a Cardinals team starting Blaine Gabbert on purpose.

So while we come at this from a highly advanced statistical reasoning side of things—understanding that Watson would regress from that sample is not news to anybody—the coronation was expected in 2018. To some extent, the coronation happened. The Texans went 11-5 and won the AFC South.

Upon closer examination, though, the Texans went 11-5 against the fourth-easiest schedule in the NFL. It was a roller coaster where the Texans started 0-3, then won nine straight games before finishing the season 2-2 and then getting convincingly dropped by Indianapolis in the first round of the playoffs. Watson's sophomore season was marred by a league-worst 62 sacks taken, the highest number of sacks any NFL quarterback has taken since Mike Martz and Jon Kitna made seven-step-dropback magic together in 2006. The offense finished 26th in rushing DVOA despite the fact that Watson finished second in the NFL in quarterback rushing attempts and did so with a DVOA of 7.7%; remove Watson's carries, and the Texans would have finished dead last in rushing DVOA. The pass defense struggled any time Jadeveon Clowney and J.J. Watt couldn't get to the quarterback before he could get the ball out of his hands. The New York Giants had their highest single-game passing DVOA of the season against the Texans solely by competently executing easy underneath routes. This was a coronation in the way that a one-dimensional *Game of Thrones* character gets to sit on the throne for a while, with the seeds of their own destruction already blooming below their feet.

So with open question marks all around them, the Texans went into the offseason and did exactly nothing of interest to stabilize the team for 2019. They lost Tyrann Mathieu to free agency, then replaced him with ex-Jaguars safety Tashaun Gipson in what Houston is hoping will be a lateral move. They lost Kareem Jackson to the Broncos without even making an offer, and replaced him with Bradley Roby, who finished 76th of 79 qualifying cornerbacks in yards per pass allowed last year. Roby's market was so down he took a one-year prove-it deal. Their biggest holes were at offensive line and cornerback, and the Texans exited the offseason with Roby, Matt Kalil's staggered kickstep, and dice rolls from the draft.

Tackle and cornerback are not often positions where you can just plug in a rookie and be fine. Maybe the Texans will get lucky there, but Texans fans should remember that former star tackle Duane Brown was smacked around in his rookie season to the point where he was platooning with Ephraim Salaam. Al-

2019 Texans Schedule

Week	Opp.	Week	Opp.	Week	Opp.
1	at NO (Mon.)	7	at IND	13	NE
2	JAX	8	OAK	14	DEN
3	at LAC	9	at JAX (U.K.)	15	at TEN
4	CAR	10	BYE	16	at TB
5	ATL	11	at BAL	17	TEN
6	at KC	12	IND (Thu.)		

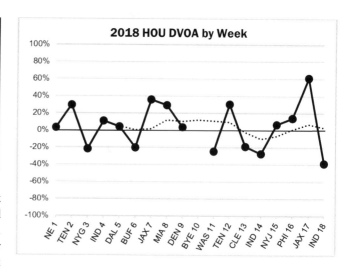

2018 HOU DVOA by Week

abama State's Tytus Howard has the tools to play left tackle, but also a developmental curve that doesn't make him a clean and easy starter. Kalil has been an offseason punchline for years. The Texans did absolutely nothing else to address an interior line that was in shambles last year, and if the rookies aren't ready to play right away, they might wind up throwing Julie'n Davenport back at left tackle and shrugging their shoulders.

The history of teams drafting two offensive linemen in the first two rounds of the draft has not revealed much instant help either (Table 1). The average team received only a small boost from awful to slightly bad, and a lot of the boosts get explained away easily by coaching or quarterback changes. Last year's Colts, for example, also had changes both at quarterback and head coach. The 2015 Bengals didn't start Cedric Ogbuehi or Jake Fisher. The 2003 Panthers rolled with Jake Delhomme. And so on. The Texans have a more stagnant profile than most of these teams.

The Texans as of this writing have roughly $41 million in cap space still available and currently are set up to have the most cap space in the NFL in 2019, but they lost out on free agent Rodger Saffold in direct competition with the Titans. They lost despite having the single-most valuable commod-

ity an NFL team can have—a star quarterback on a cost-controlled rookie contract—as well as the thing that a rookie-contract star quarterback gives you: endless reserves of cap space. A lot of the tone and tenor around losing Saffold was that the Texans don't want to go over their "value" for a player. That's an adorable concept to cling to as the salary cap has nearly doubled in the last 10 years, creating an environment where every signing that's a hit becomes underpaid in a couple of seasons.

At the core of all these issues is head coach Bill O'Brien. It would be unfair to say that O'Brien is a bad coach. (We did *just* praise his adjustment coaching with Watson's rookie season.) But it is fair to say at this point that O'Brien is an extremely conservative head coach, and one who falls heavily into his preferred method of doing things. When O'Brien needs to pull something out of his pre-game bag of tricks, it tends to go pretty well. In Week 17, after 23 running back

Table 1. Teams that Drafted Two Offensive Linemen in the First or Second Rounds, 1996-2019

Year	Team	Players (Draft Spot)	Combined Player AV (to date)*	Y-1 ALY	Y-1 ASR	ALY	ASR
1997	IND	Tarik Glenn (19), Adam Meadows (48)	136	3.53 (29)	8.3% (25)	3.93 (20)	11.7% (30)
2001	DET	Jeff Backus (18), Dominic Raiola (50)	130	4.11 (13)	9.7% (27)	3.50 (29)	10.6% (29)
2003	CAR	Jordan Gross (8), Bruce Nelson (50)	73	3.67 (30)	8.6% (28)	4.23 (13)	5.5% (8)
2004	OAK	Robert Gallery (2), Jake Grove (45)	58	4.37 (7)	8.1% (28)	4.11 (18)	5.5% (6)
2006	NYJ	D'Brickashaw Ferguson (4), Nick Mangold (29)	112	3.80 (24)	10.3% (31)	3.89 (25)	6.7% (17)
2006	TB	Davin Joseph (23), Jeremy Trueblood (59)	81	3.85 (21)	8.4% (26)	3.77 (30)	5.9% (10)
2009	JAX	Eugene Monroe (8), Eben Britton (39)	68	4.16 (12)	7.9% (24)	4.23 (11)	8.5% (29)
2009	BUF	Eric Wood (28), Andy Levitre (51)	102	4.12 (14)	8.1% (25)	4.22 (12)	9.9% (32)
2010	SF	Anthony Davis (11), Mike Iupati (17)	91	3.53 (32)	8.1% (26)	4.14 (13)	8.9% (30)
2011	IND	Anthony Castonzo (22), Ben Ijalana (49)	57	3.82 (22)	2.8% (1)	3.91 (25)	6.9% (18)
2015	CIN	Cedric Ogbuehi (21), Jake Fisher (53)	19	4.03 (11)	4.6% (5)	4.21 (1)	5.9% (15)
2015	TB	Donovan Smith (34), Ali Marpet (61)	57	3.21 (32)	9.4% (29)	4.00 (9)	5.8% (14)
2018	IND	Quenton Nelson (6), Braden Smith (37)	20	3.98 (18)	10.0% (32)	4.83 (4)	4.1% (2)
2019	ATL	Chris Lindstrom (14), Kaleb McGary (31)	N/A	4.08 (24)	6.6% (14)	--	--
2019	HOU	Tytus Howard (23), Max Scharping (55)	N/A	3.93 (27)	11.6% (32)	--	--
Averages (post-2011 not included for AV)			90.8	3.87	8.16%	4.07	7.37%

* Pro Football Reference's Approximate Value

carries for 27 yards in Week 15 and 16 combined, O'Brien shifted the run game to involve more Watson and it worked. The Texans ran for 134 yards on the Jaguars in a 20-3 win that clinched the AFC South.

But until he is down far enough on his prospects to actually have to try something new, O'Brien's base philosophy is not interesting. He wants to control the clock and win games 20-13. He wants to take one of this generation's most mobile and innovative quarterbacks and turn him into a comebacks-and-flats completion-percentage monster who never gets picked.

It wasn't surprising that Watson regressed from his 2017 season; what was surprising is that O'Brien was at the head of the charge. Watson ran play-action on 82 of his 248 drop-backs per Sports Info Solutions in 2017; in 2018, that number dropped to 144 of 651 dropbacks. In other words, the frequency of play-action dropped nearly 11 percent over the course of last season despite averaging about 9.3 yards per pass with it in 2017. Meanwhile, the Texans ran 72 of 188 run plays in 2017 with Watson on the field that were categorized as zone-read or option plays per SIS. In 2018, that number plummeted to eight. Instead of letting Watson's legs be the threat that they could be to open up the offense, the Texans wound up running mostly inside zone with a line that couldn't combo block to save their lives. It isn't hard to make the argument that the biggest problem Watson ran into last year was his own coaching staff. It certainly looked that way when the Texans managed just seven points against Indy in the playoffs. The offense looked completely ill-prepared for the cornerback slot blitz despite it being a big focal point of the Colts game plan against them in Week 14.

When O'Brien's preferred game scripts don't manifest themselves, the Texans lose. Since 2014, the Texans are 4-32 when they allow 22 or more points. They're 3-15 in one-score games in which they allow 22 or more points. Two of those wins are overtime wins. O'Brien certainly doesn't help matters by being a poor in-game clock manager, but it's jarring to see just how one-sided this is. The team has been built to win in only one way.

Which is exactly the sort of thing you don't want to talk about when you look at Houston's schedule next season. The Texans have our hardest projected schedule in the NFL with games against the AFC West and NFC South as well as improving AFC South teams. The list of quarterbacks the Texans will get this year includes Patrick Mahomes, Tom Brady, Andrew Luck twice, Drew Brees, Philip Rivers, Cam Newton, and Matt Ryan. The worst quarterback is probably either Joe Flacco or maybe Lamar Jackson if Jackson doesn't improve. How many of those quarterbacks will the Texans be holding under 22 points? Even the lower tier of starters they'll play involves quarterbacks who have had success in small sizes: Jameis Winston, Marcus Mariota, Nick Foles, Derek Carr, and so on. There are no Blake Bortles or Zach Mettenbergers to gobble up.

There are not many Houston fans left who need to be converted to the idea that O'Brien isn't the kind of head coach with whom you win a championship. They've endured five long years of this, and O'Brien's contract extension that kicks in this year runs four more seasons. It's hard to know exactly what to say at this point because the Texans never seemed to operate with any urgency as an organization under Bob McNair, and McNair passed away during last season's run, leaving his son Cal as the primary ownership figurehead. And then, out of nowhere, they canned general manager Brian Gaine in June, forcing the team into a hilarious game of "figure out which person that O'Brien knows will be named GM." The winner, after Patriots second-in-command Nick Caserio was effectively blocked from the job, was ... Bill O'Brien! It's not the first time he has won a power struggle, and you can ask the knife in Rick Smith's back if you believe otherwise.

What happens if the Texans finish this year 6-10? Is that enough to dismiss O'Brien with three years left on his deal? It took a complete and utter 2-14 flameout to get Gary Kubiak canned in Houston, so this is actually a hard question to answer, especially when you consider that O'Brien is the only person in the building with any experience in managing a football team. By all accounts, it sure seems that O'Brien is safe to continue showing just enough to make you wonder why he's not a better coach regardless of what happens this year.

The more likely scenario is that Houston's top-tier talent continues to pull its weight. Watson, DeAndre Hopkins, Watt, and Clowney can erase a lot of sins. Well, Clowney can if the Texans actually choose to pay him rather than letting him flounder in franchise-tag purgatory. The impending standoff could be a flashpoint moment for the franchise. But let's assume they pay him. The way the Texans build on last year's success is a dead-cat bounce on the offensive line, continued good health for their stars and near-stars (like Will Fuller), and winning the close high-scoring games they haven't demonstrated much ability to win. If they run somewhere near last year's ratings, as we're projecting, they'll lose about three wins. Keep in mind we currently have the Texans with the best defensive projection in the NFL, with some of the guiding philosophy there being that DVOA run defense often correlates to good defense the following season. The 2018 Texans were one of the ten best run defenses in DVOA history, and all the active pieces of that are still in place outside of Kareem Jackson. However, given the split the Texans run against bad quarterbacks and good quarterbacks, that shouldn't necessarily be objective solace to Texans fans. The offense needs to take a step forward for this to be a playoff team.

But as far as the actual question of what the Texans are about? They're a team that has now, finally, "enough." But they're still operating like they're not. What they did this offseason is no different than going up to the microphone, muttering "space armies" a few times, then moving on to the next talking point in a speech. The Texans are in a malaise that's easy to understand, easy to fix, and somehow way too difficult for them to confront right now.

Rivers McCown

2018 Texans Stats by Week

Wk	vs.	W-L	PF	PA	YDF	YDA	TO	Total	Off	Def	ST
1	at NE	L	20	27	325	389	+1	3%	-29%	-19%	13%
2	at TEN	L	17	20	437	283	-1	30%	19%	-18%	-7%
3	NYG	L	22	27	427	379	-2	-22%	-11%	24%	13%
4	at IND	W	37	34	466	478	+1	11%	4%	-7%	-1%
5	DAL	W	19	16	462	292	0	4%	-17%	-29%	-8%
6	BUF	W	20	13	216	229	0	-20%	-65%	-35%	9%
7	at JAX	W	20	7	272	259	+3	36%	5%	-31%	-1%
8	MIA	W	42	23	427	370	+1	29%	40%	7%	-4%
9	at DEN	W	19	17	290	348	+1	4%	7%	6%	2%
10	BYE										
11	at WAS	W	23	21	320	278	-1	-25%	-38%	-20%	-7%
12	TEN	W	34	17	462	365	+1	31%	38%	11%	4%
13	CLE	W	29	13	384	428	+4	-19%	3%	33%	11%
14	IND	L	21	24	315	436	+1	-27%	-16%	17%	6%
15	at NYJ	W	29	22	286	318	+1	7%	-9%	2%	18%
16	at PHI	L	30	32	371	519	+2	14%	12%	-2%	1%
17	JAX	W	20	3	342	119	+1	61%	4%	-51%	7%
18	IND	L	7	21	322	422	0	-39%	-16%	22%	0%

Trends and Splits

	Offense	Rank	Defense	Rank
Total DVOA	-3.5%	21	-7.1%	7
Unadjusted VOA	-3.2%	20	-11.4%	3
Weighted Trend	-1.4%	20	-5.2%	10
Variance	7.1%	20	5.4%	16
Average Opponent	-2.3%	6	-6.5%	31
Passing	17.8%	13	8.8%	19
Rushing	-13.0%	26	-30.1%	1
First Down	-11.3%	24	-4.2%	10
Second Down	9.7%	9	-12.2%	3
Third Down	-9.9%	23	-5.1%	14
First Half	1.0%	13	-12.9%	3
Second Half	-7.9%	23	-1.2%	17
Red Zone	-23.0%	30	25.3%	30
Late and Close	-8.4%	22	-7.0%	13

Five-Year Performance

Year	W-L	Pyth W	Est W	PF	PA	TO	Total	Rk	Off	Rk	Def	Rk	ST	Rk	Off AGL	Rk	Def AGL	Rk	Off Age	Rk	Def Age	Rk	ST Age	Rk
2014	9-7	9.8	6.7	372	307	+12	-4.5%	19	-6.8%	21	-6.2%	6	-3.9%	28	18.8	6	41.1	20	27.2	12	26.0	28	26.1	17
2015	9-7	8.8	7.8	339	313	+5	-4.8%	18	-8.5%	24	-9.3%	8	-5.7%	32	49.8	26	15.0	3	26.5	17	26.2	24	25.8	20
2016	9-7	6.5	4.6	279	328	-7	-21.9%	29	-21.2%	30	-5.8%	9	-6.5%	31	51.8	27	40.0	20	25.7	30	26.5	17	26.2	12
2017	4-12	5.5	5.1	338	436	-12	-20.0%	28	-9.9%	24	5.6%	23	-4.5%	26	62.2	30	45.1	26	26.1	30	26.0	18	26.1	8
2018	11-5	10.3	9.1	402	316	+13	7.1%	11	-3.5%	21	-7.1%	7	3.5%	5	44.6	21	44.9	26	25.5	32	26.7	9	25.7	20

2018 Performance Based on Most Common Personnel Groups

HOU Offense

Pers	Freq	Yds	DVOA	Run%
11	54%	5.9	1.4%	31%
12	37%	5.9	7.6%	46%
13	3%	2.9	-20.1%	82%
20	2%	10.4	35.4%	41%
21	2%	3.5	-28.0%	53%

HOU Offense vs. Opponents

Pers	Freq	Yds	DVOA	Run%
Base	27%	6.1	10.3%	54%
Nickel	67%	5.6	-2.2%	37%
Dime+	8%	5.9	26.2%	4%

HOU Defense

Pers	Freq	Yds	DVOA
Base	30%	5.8	-9.1%
Nickel	50%	5.1	-7.4%
Dime+	19%	5.9	-4.7%
Goal Line	1%	3.1	6.7%
Big	1%	2.2	-56.1%

HOU Defense vs. Opponents

Pers	Freq	Yds	DVOA
11	59%	5.5	-0.7%
12	18%	5.7	-11.8%
21	7%	3.4	-63.5%
13	5%	7.2	9.6%
10	3%	4.7	-52.7%
22	3%	5.2	14.8%
612	3%	8.1	25.1%

Strategic Tendencies

Run/Pass		Rk	Formation		Rk	Pass Rush		Rk	Secondary		Rk	Strategy		Rk
Runs, first half	40%	10	Form: Single Back	78%	20	Rush 3	16.7%	3	4 DB	30%	9	Play action	24%	16
Runs, first down	55%	3	Form: Empty Back	13%	2	Rush 4	60.9%	23	5 DB	50%	26	Avg Box (Off)	6.20	15
Runs, second-long	24%	28	Pers: 3+ WR	56%	30	Rush 5	18.0%	13	6+ DB	19%	11	Avg Box (Def)	6.13	25
Runs, power sit.	43%	30	Pers: 2+ TE/6+ OL	41%	2	Rush 6+	4.5%	23	CB by Sides	55%	31	Offensive Pace	30.27	9
Runs, behind 2H	28%	17	Pers: 6+ OL	1%	25	Int DL Sacks	17.4%	26	S/CB Cover Ratio	28%	15	Defensive Pace	30.99	15
Pass, ahead 2H	51%	12	Shotgun/Pistol	70%	9	Second Level Sacks	22.1%	17	DB Blitz	9%	12	Go for it on 4th	0.80	29

Once again, the Texans offense was built around one receiver more than any other offense in the league. They threw to De-Andre Hopkins on 33 percent of passes; no other offense threw to a single receiver on more than 30 percent of passes. On the flip side, Houston only threw 13 percent of passes to running backs, dead last. No team had fewer running back screens than the Texans, who ran the play just five times all year for 16 yards. ● Related: Houston threw exactly one-sixth of passes behind or at the line of scrimmage. They ranked 27th in DVOA on these passes, but fifth in DVOA on passes thrown anywhere beyond the line of scrimmage. ● The Texans had a league-low 12 dropped passes. They were tied for third-lowest with 21 the year before. ● A year after they led the league by using six linemen on 18 percent of plays, the Texans used six linemen on only 10 plays all season. ● The Texans ranked 31st in broken tackles on offense for the third straight season, dropping from 95 in 2016 to 85 in 2017 and now 81 in 2018. ● Despite the lack of broken tackles, Houston running backs were more successful with more men in the box. They gained 5.5 yards per carry against eight in the box (-14.6% DVOA), compared to 3.7 yards per carry (-27.0% DVOA) on other runs. Only two other offenses had a similar (albeit much smaller) "reverse split" by yards per carry, although 11 other offenses had a similar reverse split by DVOA. ● Houston's defense ranked sixth on passes to the short right but 25th on passes to the short left. ● Houston allowed only 3.3 yards per pass and -51.1% DVOA when blitzing a defensive back.

Passing

Player	DYAR	DVOA	Plays	NtYds	Avg	YAC	C%	TD	Int
D.Watson	737	9.5%	562	3779	6.7	5.1	69.1%	26	9

Rushing

Player	DYAR	DVOA	Plays	Yds	Avg	TD	Fum	Suc
L.Miller	28	-5.3%	210	973	4.6	5	0	44%
A.Blue*	-93	-23.0%	150	499	3.3	2	0	41%
D.Watson	95	7.8%	89	550	6.2	6	2	--
D.Foreman	-37	-177.7%	7	-1	-0.1	0	1	0%

Receiving

Player	DYAR	DVOA	Plays	Ctch	Yds	Y/C	YAC	TD	C%
D.Hopkins	455	22.6%	163	115	1572	13.7	3.4	11	71%
W.Fuller	180	34.6%	45	32	503	15.7	5.2	4	71%
K.Coutee	7	-10.5%	41	28	287	10.3	7.5	1	68%
D.Thomas*	31	-0.3%	33	23	275	12.0	6.3	2	70%
D.Carter	18	-2.3%	23	20	195	9.8	6.8	0	87%
B.Ellington*	19	10.6%	12	8	92	11.5	3.0	1	67%
V.Smith	8	-3.3%	10	5	91	18.2	1.2	1	50%
R.Griffin*	-18	-13.5%	43	24	305	12.7	6.3	0	56%
J.Thomas	38	12.5%	27	20	215	10.8	4.8	4	74%
J.Akins	24	8.3%	25	17	225	13.2	7.2	0	68%
D.Fells	52	53.9%	12	11	117	10.6	6.0	3	92%
L.Miller	-10	-19.9%	35	25	163	6.5	6.8	1	71%
A.Blue*	-10	-20.5%	27	20	154	7.7	5.4	0	74%

Offensive Line

Player	Pos	Age	GS	Snaps	Pen	Sk	Pass	Run	Player	Pos	Age	GS	Snaps	Pen	Sk	Pass	Run
Nick Martin	C	26	16/16	1094	2	0.0	1	7	Zach Fulton	RG	28	13/13	817	4	2.0	6	4
Julie'n Davenport	LT	24	16/15	1014	14	8.0	28	2	Martinas Rankin	LT	25	16/4	430	5	6.0	16	1
Senio Kelemete	LG	29	15/14	895	2	3.5	14	3	Greg Mancz	RG	27	16/4	368	1	0.5	4	2
Kendall Lamm*	RT	27	15/13	859	4	3.5	9	4									

Year	Yards	ALY	Rank	Power	Rank	Stuff	Rank	2nd Lev	Rank	Open Field	Rank	Sacks	ASR	Rank	Press	Rank	F-Start	Cont.
2016	4.14	4.16	15	61%	18	16%	6	1.14	16	0.61	20	32	5.6%	12	30.2%	27	7	29
2017	3.78	3.89	20	63%	18	21%	18	0.99	26	0.51	25	54	9.2%	30	36.9%	31	20	23
2018	4.01	3.93	27	63%	23	20%	21	1.09	26	0.83	17	62	11.6%	32	38.5%	32	24	23
2018 ALY by direction:			Left End: 2.86 (29)			Left Tackle: 4.37 (11)			Mid/Guard: 4.27 (21)			Right Tackle: 2.29 (32)			Right End: 5.37 (6)			

Of Houston's early picks, Max Scharping is the one who appears most pro-ready. Northern Illinois' four-year starter has the ability to redirect quickly, and he looks alive and anchors well enough in the run game that he could get an early look at right tackle. He struggled the most against stunts and good handplay—but we could say that for 90 percent of NCAA tackles. ● Meanwhile, Tytus Howard's bizarre NFL combine involved him running an 8.49 3-cone drill time, one that would put him in the sixth percentile among all NFL tackles. The Texans had to pounce on someone with left tackle attributes, and Howard has those if he can be taught the technique it will take to hang with NFL edge rushers. But between the leap from Southern Alabama and the fact that Howard had just 115 college reps before his senior season, it would not be surprising if he struggles early. ● Julie'n Davenport was what Howard is: a good small-school tackle with an athletic profile and little idea how to deal with the more nuanced pass-rushers of the NFL. Maybe he has a future in the league, but it's probably at right tackle. ● Center Nick

Martin is often regarded as the best player on this line, but he did not have a smooth season. He struggled to combo-block with his guards, and a lot of blown-up run plays ended with Martin on the ground. He's a better athlete than he plays. "Does this team have an offensive line coach?" you might be asking. Mike Devlin is the offensive line coach, and his list of notable successes include "whatever happened to Brian Winters in his early career with the Jets." He's yet to develop any young player on this line. ● Last year's free-agent targets, Senio Kelemete and Zach Fulton, were average in their best games. Kelemete struggled to stay healthy, and neither of them helped much. ● One thing that Matt Kalil and Seantrel Henderson have in common is that the two of them never play. Henderson has started two games in three seasons, while Kalil didn't play last year and started twice in 2016. When Kalil did see action in 2017, he played like his shoe was stuck in the turf and he had to push off the ground as hard as he could to get out of it. It wasn't pretty. Nothing about this line is.

Defensive Front

Defensive Line	Age	Pos	G	Snaps	Plays	Overall TmPct	Rk	Stop	Dfts	BTkl	Runs	St%	vs. Run Rk	RuYd	Rk	Sack	Hit	Pass Rush Hur	Dsrpt
D.J. Reader	25	DT	16	638	32	3.8%	67	27	6	1	25	88%	7	2.0	28	2.0	3	10	0
Angelo Blackson	27	DE	16	430	27	3.2%	75	17	3	1	20	60%	81	2.4	49	1.0	1	5	0
Brandon Dunn	27	DT	14	347	24	3.3%	--	18	6	3	18	83%	--	1.3	--	0.0	0	5	0
Christian Covington*	26	DE	12	257	15	2.4%	--	14	8	1	8	88%	--	2.0	--	3.5	4	7	0

Edge Rushers	Age	Pos	G	Snaps	Plays	Overall TmPct	Rk	Stop	Dfts	BTkl	Runs	St%	vs. Run Rk	RuYd	Rk	Sack	Hit	Pass Rush Hur	Dsrpt
J.J. Watt	30	DE	16	963	64	7.6%	6	61	28	12	42	95%	1	0.9	6	16.0	15	42	4
Jadeveon Clowney	26	OLB	15	901	47	5.9%	25	42	24	7	33	88%	9	0.8	4	9.0	11	35	3

Linebackers	Age	Pos	G	Snaps	Plays	Overall TmPct	Rk	Stop	Dfts	BTkl	Runs	St%	vs. Run Rk	RuYd	Rk	Sack	Hit	Pass Rush Hur	Tgts	Suc%	vs. Pass Rk	AdjYd	Rk	PD	Int
Benardrick McKinney	27	ILB	16	920	111	13.2%	38	62	17	11	74	59%	44	4.3	64	1.5	4	9.5	24	50%	39	4.6	7	7	1
Whitney Mercilus	29	OLB	16	785	38	4.5%	87	26	11	4	22	86%	1	2.1	1	4.0	9	28	7	14%	--	9.6	--	0	0
Zach Cunningham	25	ILB	14	753	110	14.9%	25	61	18	14	63	60%	39	3.4	25	0.0	2	5	41	49%	43	6.9	44	5	1

Year	Yards	ALY	Rank	Power	Rank	Stuff	Rank	2nd Level	Rank	Open Field	Rank	Sacks	ASR	Rank	Press	Rank
2016	3.86	4.16	17	60%	10	17%	23	1.10	12	0.48	6	31	5.8%	18	26.2%	22
2017	3.93	3.86	8	70%	25	22%	7	1.11	17	0.75	17	32	6.2%	21	29.0%	24
2018	3.11	3.56	1	67%	18	25%	3	0.88	2	0.21	1	43	7.4%	13	29.0%	20

2018 ALY by direction: Left End: 3.86 (10) — Left Tackle: 5.29 (31) — Mid/Guard: 3.49 (1) — Right Tackle: 2.42 (1) — Right End: 3.53 (7)

While J.J. Watt is still the predominant player on this side of the ball, Houston's desire to put him on the edge last year really shook up the way that they played. It was never communicated to media what the desire was to play Watt on the edge. The Occam's Razor explanation is simply getting his bad back away from the interior trenches. ● Whitney Mercilus suffered the most for this, being played as a true stand-up linebacker in many of Houston's packages. It was a position he was not prepared to play, and one that presented to observers why he was not a standout zone coverage defender at Illinois. ● Jadeveon Clowney had almost as much impact as Watt as a pass-rusher last year. The surprising thing was just how much of it he did as a stand-up linebacker. Romeo Crennel, suffering from a lack of interior rush, would just put Clowney up in an A-gap and see what offensive lines could do about it. Not much. ● D.J. Reader is entering a contract year as a big, dominant run-stuffing defensive tackle who can move all around the line and has great instincts reading plays at the line of scrimmage. Houston's cap space makes keeping him attainable—but how much do they value him? ● Benardrick McKinney made the Pro Bowl last year but is more of a zone-coverage linebacker than someone you want man-on-man outside. Same goes for Zach Cunningham, honestly—he was roasted early on by backs like Saquon Barkley. They're excellent in downhill pursuit though, and fit Crennel's preferences. ● Most of Houston's other interior linemen are passable run-stuffers stretched when asked to get after the passer. Fifth-round pick Charles Omenihu (Texas) might find himself with an early role after 9.5 sacks in his senior season on the Forty Acres.

Defensive Secondary

Secondary	Age	Pos	G	Snaps	Plays	TmPct	Rk	Stop	Dfts	BTkl	Runs	St%	Rk	RuYd	Rk	Tgts	Tgt%	Rk	Dist	Suc%	Rk	AdjYd	Rk	PD	Int
						Overall						vs. Run							vs. Pass						
Tyrann Mathieu*	27	FS	16	1045	97	11.5%	22	42	17	12	27	59%	9	5.0	13	43	10.3%	48	9.7	53%	30	8.1	50	8	2
Kareem Jackson*	31	CB	16	985	104	12.3%	3	55	21	13	40	55%	17	3.7	8	59	15.0%	14	11.3	51%	49	6.4	16	17	2
Justin Reid	22	SS	16	906	90	10.7%	33	26	14	10	36	33%	54	7.4	46	33	9.1%	33	15.7	42%	58	13.1	71	10	3
Johnathan Joseph	35	CB	14	811	71	9.6%	25	36	12	15	12	67%	4	4.3	11	84	26.0%	74	10.9	58%	16	6.7	20	13	2
Shareece Wright*	32	CB	12	505	37	5.9%	--	17	6	5	6	100%	--	1.2	--	43	21.4%	--	13.8	47%	--	7.4	--	5	0
Aaron Colvin	28	CB	10	318	30	5.7%	--	10	7	3	6	33%	--	7.7	--	22	17.4%	--	9.9	50%	--	6.3	--	1	0
Andre Hal*	27	FS	8	237	16	3.8%	--	7	7	2	3	0%	--	10.3	--	8	8.5%	--	18.5	63%	--	14.1	--	5	3
Jahleel Addae	29	SS	16	1025	78	9.8%	43	22	7	7	38	34%	53	7.0	39	17	4.2%	3	15.9	41%	61	14.1	73	3	1
Tashaun Gipson	29	FS	16	1007	61	8.0%	56	28	9	7	30	50%	21	5.9	24	32	8.4%	26	13.4	69%	4	5.3	6	7	1
Bradley Roby	27	CB	15	926	62	8.0%	47	27	11	12	9	56%	15	6.3	38	78	21.2%	55	12.0	46%	62	10.3	76	12	1
Briean Boddy-Calhoun	26	CB	16	656	54	6.1%	76	16	7	8	12	17%	75	9.1	69	40	14.7%	9	6.6	45%	68	6.9	26	2	0

Year	Pass D Rank	vs. #1 WR	Rk	vs. #2 WR	Rk	vs. Other WR	Rk	WR Wide	Rk	WR Slot	Rk	vs. TE	Rk	vs. RB	Rk
2016	5	1.8%	17	-38.1%	2	1.8%	17	-8.6%	12	-10.9%	6	-40.6%	2	23.3%	28
2017	25	12.4%	24	37.8%	30	16.6%	24	6.3%	24	33.6%	32	15.2%	27	-16.7%	7
2018	18	19.6%	31	0.9%	18	3.8%	20	-6.3%	18	25.9%	28	16.3%	23	-21.3%	3

Johnathan Joseph has seen it all, and that makes him a valuable zone cornerback. But at 35 years old, he doesn't have the deep speed to stay with your T.Y. Hilton-esque receivers, and he winds up leaving at least two or three games a season with some kind of small injury. He's a warrior, and Texans fans should be grateful they had his prime. They should also be hopeful that they don't need him after this season. ● Second-round pick Lonnie Johnson (Kentucky) has a body that can play NFL cornerback and little experience doing it in college. Johnson struggled in run support, only picked off one pass in his entire college career, and the only things he really seemed to do well involved downhill zone reads. But at 6-foot-1, 210 pounds, with a 4.4 40-yard dash at his pro day, the Texans are betting he can learn how to play corner. ● Bringing over Bradley Roby in free agency to replace Kareem Jackson was going to be a net negative from the beginning. Jackson's 2018 season is statistically improbable for any corner to replicate, no matter how good they are. The remarkable part was not Jackson's performance in coverage, though 6.4 yards per pass and 17 passes defensed are very good numbers. The remarkable part was Jackson making 40 run tackles when Logan Ryan (30) was the only other cornerback in the NFL with more than 25. Some of that came from playing safety early in the season, but injuries changed that plan after September, and Jackson kept making plays on running backs regardless. ● In theory, Roby is a younger player who is a better man-cover corner than Jackson is at this point. In actuality, Roby spent a lot of 2018 tackling curl routes from a huge cushion and getting roasted by slants and in-breaking Cover-3 beaters. ● Big plays were the name of Justin Reid's season—he gave up some big ones later in the season but also made some big picks and pass breakups downfield. He definitely outplayed his draft slot and should be effective in either safety role because of his sure tackling. Improvement will come with more experience. ● The other safety spot will be a straight swap of Tyrann Mathieu for Tashaun Gipson. Gipson is the steadier player, and they're both fairly versatile. Mathieu had more of the flare for the big play, though the way the Texans used him last season was asking a lot. Often he'd draw tight end coverage against players that towered over him.

Special Teams

Year	DVOA	Rank	FG/XP	Rank	Net Kick	Rank	Kick Ret	Rank	Net Punt	Rank	Punt Ret	Rank	Hidden	Rank
2016	-6.5%	31	-5.9	26	-12.9	32	-7.5	30	-13.0	30	6.7	6	1.4	15
2017	-4.5%	26	-5.8	24	0.1	18	-5.3	30	-10.7	28	-1.1	21	-16.9	32
2018	3.5%	5	4.4	8	7.8	1	0.5	11	4.5	11	0.5	14	-2.5	19

Can you believe the Texans have a great special teams unit? Neither can we. We complained for so many years in these pages, but last year things finally came together under former Pats assistant Brad Seely. The Texans had by far the best kickoff coverage in the league, and the punt coverage was strong as well. Opponent returns combined to be worth an estimated 12.2 points worth of field position below average. ● The Texans invested heavily in special-teamers on last year's roster. A.J. Moore and Greg Howell, two UDFAs, saw three offensive and defensive snaps between them but hung on the roster all year while adding 17 return stops on 20 tackles. ● Neither kicker Kai'imi Fairbairn nor punter Trevor Daniel inspired a ton of confidence last year. Fairbairn's five misses come with the territory since he attempted more field goals than any player in the NFL, but it was clear that the Texans didn't have Justin Tucker-level confidence in him. Houston punted 11 times last year from inside the opposing 42-yard line; no other team had more than eight such punts. Daniel shanked a few punts of his own and probably qualifies as close to an average punter. The Texans didn't seem completely satisfied with him but didn't bring in any real competition this offseason. ◗   DeAndre Carter and Keke Coutee profile as the main returners this year. The Texans claimed Carter off waivers from the Eagles in the middle of last season, letting Tyler Ervin go for the chance. Carter fumbled four times in just seven games for the Texans, but he did show off burst and speed when he actually held on to the ball.

Indianapolis Colts

2018 record: 10-6	**Total DVOA:** 12.6% (8th)	**2019 Mean Projection:** 8.9 wins	**On the Clock (0-4):** 5%
Pythagorean Wins: 10.3 (9th)	**Offense:** 8.2% (10th)	**Postseason Odds:** 49.9%	**Mediocrity (5-7):** 23%
Snap-Weighted Age: 25.6 (30th)	**Defense:** -3.4% (10th)	**Super Bowl Odds:** 8.6%	**Playoff Contender (8-10):** 43%
Average Opponent: -6.3% (32nd)	**Special Teams:** 0.9% (12th)	**Proj. Avg. Opponent:** 0.6% (15th)	**Super Bowl Contender (11+):** 29%

2018: After a slow start, the Colts come roaring down the stretch and end up in the playoffs.

2019: This is a strong contender, but life is about to get much harder for the defense.

Through six weeks, Frank Reich's project to remake the Indianapolis Colts appeared to be in pretty rough shape. Andrew Luck looked good after missing the 2017 season, but the Colts were just 1-5 after falling to a New York Jets team that would only win one more game all year. Then Indianapolis started winning and kept winning, with a loss in Jacksonville as the only blemish on their record until the Chiefs ended their season in Arrowhead in January.

The basic view of this turnaround might center around the Colts allowing at least 34 points four times in the first six games, but not once after that point. The defense will be an important factor in just how good the Colts will be in 2019, no doubt, but our numbers point to a different explanation. The biggest culprit in the early struggles was a sputtering offense. Notwithstanding Luck, Indianapolis had DVOA's 25th-best offense through six weeks, near the bottom of our table alongside their AFC South brethren. The defense was not nearly as bad as the point totals suggested—not actually good, mind you, but in the great muddled middle at 1.6%.

The defense was better the second half of the season, but the real change came on offense. After those early struggles, only playoff foe Kansas City had a better offensive DVOA than Indianapolis from Weeks 7 to 17. The change was wholesale and comprehensive, affecting many aspects of the Colts offense (Table 1).

There was no single reason for the turnaround. The offensive line, highlighted by rookie sixth overall pick Quenton Nelson, took plenty of credit for the Colts' offensive jump after a lousy 2017. The unit was significantly improved as a whole, despite no more continuity than they had had in past mediocre seasons. Even in the first six weeks of the season, though, the Colts already had the fourth-best adjusted sack rate in the league and ranked in the top ten by adjusted line yards. Reich, whom Andrew Luck described as being in almost every meeting he had, and offensive coordinator Nick Sirianni deserve much of the credit for those numbers. They completely overhauled a Colts offense centered around too

many long-lasting drops where quarterbacks get sacked more frequently. According to the NFL's Next Gen Stats, Luck had the fourth-highest average time to throw among qualifying quarterbacks in 2016, while Jacoby Brissett had the sixth-highest time to throw in 2017. In 2018, Luck had the ninth-lowest time to throw, a significant change in how the Colts tried to play offense. Those offensive line numbers would get even better the second half of the season with the rest of the offensive numbers, but the real improvement was elsewhere.

Some of the early-season trouble was surely the normal friction that came from a quarterback who missed a season getting together with a mostly new group of receivers while first-time head coach Reich and first-time coordinator Sirianni got used to running their own show. But one thing that changed significantly was T.Y. Hilton's role. His efficiency jump nearly doubled even that made by Luck's other targets, while at the same time his target share went from 14 percent before Week 7 to 24 percent from Week 7 on. Most of that target-share jump is explained by Hilton's injury-related absence in a couple of high-volume pass games in Weeks 5 and 6, but availability remains one of the most important NFL abilities.

One of general manager Chris Ballard's offseason priorities was to find answers at the receiver position instead of once again trotting out Hilton and a bunch of question marks. (It got so bad that by the end of the year, midseason street free-agent addition Dontrelle Inman was the Colts' second-best wide receiver.) Devin Funchess is the less exciting of the two additions, coming from a history of mostly underwhelming play in Carolina, albeit in a role that with Cam Newton has never produced great efficiency numbers. The $10-million part of his contract suggests he will be the starter opposite Hilton; the one-year part of his contract suggests that's just until the Colts get a better option.

The more intriguing addition is Parris Campbell, a second-round pick out of Ohio State. Our Playmaker Score projection system is not a fan of Campbell because he was a senior prospect who did not put up overwhelming numbers even as a senior. Schematically, however, he should fit smoothly in as

Table 1. Indianapolis Offensive Turnaround

Weeks	Off DVOA	Rk	Pass DVOA	Rk	Run DVOA	Rk	Suc Rate	Rk	Yd/Play	Rk
Weeks 1-6	-11.1%	25	-1.1%	24	-18.6%	27	45%	16	5.36	27
Weeks 7-17	20.8%	2	39.0%	4	3.9%	8	52%	1	6.47	3

2019 Colts Schedule

Week	Opp.	Week	Opp.	Week	Opp.
1	at LAC	7	HOU	13	TEN
2	at TEN	8	DEN	14	at TB
3	ATL	9	at PIT	15	at NO (Mon.)
4	OAK	10	MIA	16	CAR
5	at KC	11	JAX	17	at JAX
6	BYE	12	at HOU (Thu.)		

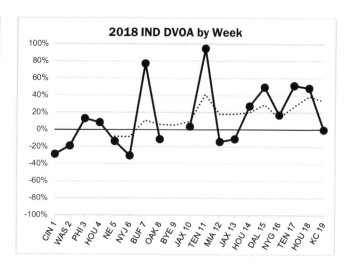

a slot receiver. His best NFL trait is his speed, but his experience for the Buckeyes was not using that speed on deep routes. Rather, he ran primarily crosses and other short routes to create yards-after-catch opportunities. Reich and Sirianni came from offenses more oriented around getting yards after the catch, but outside of Hilton, Colts receivers had trouble getting it in 2018. Indianapolis averaged the third-lowest yards after catch in the NFL, and not because they were throwing passes not intended to produce yards after catch. Outside of Hilton, who ranked ninth in YAC+ among receivers with a minimum of 50 targets, no Colts player was better than average. Funchess, with the lowest YAC and fourth-lowest YAC+ among such receivers, does nothing to change that.

Defensively, the Colts are in an interesting place. Coordinator Matt Eberflus may be the best thing Josh McDaniels did for Indianapolis, signing off on Eberflus as defensive coordinator before backing out of the head coaching job. In *Football Outsiders Almanac 2018*, we chronicled the Colts' positional instability, with only a handful of starters remaining the same from 2016 to 2017 to 2018. However, right from the start of the season, the results of last year's defensive changes were better than anyone, even our moderately bullish projection system, saw coming. The defense's reasonable start was made even more impressive by the fact that the most acclaimed player in 2018, Darius Leonard, was a rookie coming from low-level South Carolina State and had missed the entire offseason.

With Eberflus' roots working for Rod Marinelli and the Tampa-2, the easy comparison for his transition away from Chuck Pagano's defense is to what Tony Dungy did when he brought the Tampa-2 from the Buccaneers. Eberflus gave the Colts a relatively simple defense focused on letting fast players play fast and forcing opposing offenses to execute against it. The results were terrific, but a note of caution may be in order.

Indianapolis benefited from an exceptionally easy slate of opposing offenses in 2018, the easiest in the league according to average DVOA of opponent. They played one regular-season game against one of DVOA's top dozen offenses, compared to a dozen against the bottom dozen. Even if their AFC South foes remain in that lower grouping, this year's schedule includes a number of foes who were very good last year and should be good again, including three of DVOA's top four 2018 offenses between Kansas City, New Orleans, and the Los Angeles Chargers.

While Ballard's offseason was more muted than it could have been given the Colts' oodles of cap space, he and Eberflus recognized the need for better schematic diversity and more pass

rush. Like wide receiver, they addressed it in both free agency and the draft. The Colts were one of the heaviest four-man rush teams (76 percent of pass plays, seventh in the NFL), but did not have the overwhelming defensive line talent to make that work. Enter, as a first step, Justin Houston from Kansas City. Though Houston has plenty of 3-4 experience, the Colts are treating him as almost exclusively a right defensive end, charged with setting the edge and getting after the quarterback rather than regularly dropping back in coverage. He will be 30 when the season begins and was the Chiefs' third-best pass-rusher last year, but he will be a better complement for Jabaal Sheard than Indianapolis had last year and move second-year man Kemoko Turay into more of a rotational rusher role where he should be better suited. Second-round pick Ben Banogu (TCU) will also fit into the defensive end mix. The Colts initially announced him as an outside linebacker, and he showed some ability to drop into space, but ended up working with his hand in the dirt in the offseason. Either he or Turay needs to develop into a long-term option beyond Houston and an aging Sheard, as the Colts have yet to get even 8.0 career sacks from a player they drafted since Robert Mathis in 2003.

An improved pass rush to disrupt opposing offenses will be an important challenge for the 2019 Colts defense. The Colts made their share of big plays on defense in 2018, but for the most part, they didn't get those plays through pass pressure.

To show this, we're going to look at a metric our own Bill Connelly developed for looking at college football defenses called Havoc Rate. It adds up tackles for loss, passes defensed, and forced fumbles into order to see how much defenses are disrupting opposing offenses.

The first and most basic question is whether an offense or a defense is more responsible for a given stat. The way we answered this question was straightforward: calculate the rates of tackles for loss, fumbles, and passes defensed for each offense and defense, and see how those correlate with offensive DVOA and defensive DVOA. In some ways, this might seem almost facile. Of course, the teams with more tackles for loss are better on defense, because tackles for loss are good plays for defenses. Unsurprisingly, we do in fact find that offensive DVOA and defensive DVOA are both correlated in the direction you would expect with having fewer or more of those sorts of disruptive plays. More significantly for our research, though, is that tackles for loss, fumbles, and passes defensed, plus the three of them combined, are all better predicted by the offense than by the defense (Table 2).

Using this knowledge, we can then further adjust a defense's Havoc Rate to account for the offense it faces. Table 3 shows that the Colts defense's 13th-place ranking in Havoc Rate was definitely a product of the offenses they faced. The Colts had the highest Expected Havoc Rate based on their opponents, and thus finished 18th in Havoc Rate vs. Expectation. In particular, they had the league's third-lowest rate of (unadjusted) passes defensed, suggesting secondary upgrades as a particular area of concern.

When creating Havoc Rate, Connelly also tried to include hurries, but lacking a reliable wide data source on that for college football, did not include that in his final formula. Through our partnership with Sports Info Solutions, we do have that data for the NFL, so let's examine what information that adds.

Like the three statistics included in Havoc Rate, pressure rate is associated in the direction you would expect with both offensive DVOA and defensive DVOA. Unlike the other three statistics, pressure rate is more closely correlated with defensive DVOA than with offensive DVOA. The correlation coefficient between pressure rate (hurries per pass play) and defensive DVOA is -.48, compared to just -.31 between pressure rate and offensive DVOA. This is especially bad news for the Colts because they ranked just 25th in pressure rate on defense. A Colts defense just as good as last year's, against a tougher slate of opposing offenses, will not be as disruptive and consequently put more pressure on the Colts offense to be as good as they were the second half of last season.

We have found historically that predicting a team to match its full-season performance from one season to the next gives the best results, even if there are sometimes distinct reasons to downplay part of the season. Consequently, our projection is for the Colts offense to most likely be good but not elite, just as it was when measured over the entire 2018 season. Perhaps if Funchess can be a reliable chains-moving option and Campbell can team up with Hilton to produce more short gains that become longer ones, they can defy our projections. The defense, likewise, should be about as good as it was last year, around average and still part of the great muddled middle. This combination, plus solid special teams play, makes the Colts the favorites in the AFC South and puts them in the Super Bowl conversation, though not as one of the prime contenders. A transformed pass rush could put them there, while defensive backsliding could put them out of the playoffs entirely.

Tom Gower

Table 2. Correlation between Havoc Rate and DVOA

Metric	Offense	Defense
Tackles for Loss	-.63	-.49
Fumbles	-.49	-.37
Passes Defensed	-.33	-.24
Havoc Rate Total	-.73	-.59
Total Pressures	-.10	-.52
Pressure Rate	-.31	-.48

Table 3. Havoc Rate, 2018

Team	Def DVOA	Rk	Havoc Rate	Rk	Expected Havoc Rate	Havoc vs. Expectation	Rk
CAR	5.4%	22	17.6%	1	14.9%	2.67%	1
BAL	-13.1%	3	16.8%	4	14.6%	2.23%	2
BUF	-14.5%	2	16.8%	5	14.7%	2.16%	3
PIT	-0.9%	13	15.9%	8	14.0%	1.90%	4
CHI	-26.0%	1	17.1%	2	15.4%	1.72%	5
HOU	-7.1%	7	17.0%	3	15.5%	1.44%	6
NO	-2.9%	11	16.8%	6	15.3%	1.43%	7
MIN	-10.3%	4	15.9%	10	15.0%	0.92%	8
DAL	-3.5%	9	16.4%	7	15.5%	0.88%	9
CLE	-2.5%	12	15.0%	14	14.2%	0.73%	10
SEA	-0.1%	14	15.6%	11	15.2%	0.44%	11
PHI	0.0%	15	15.9%	9	15.5%	0.44%	12
TB	14.8%	32	15.4%	12	15.0%	0.39%	13
LAC	-4.7%	8	14.9%	17	14.7%	0.22%	14
LAR	0.5%	17	14.9%	15	15.1%	-0.20%	15
KC	6.9%	26	14.4%	18	14.7%	-0.25%	16
ARI	0.5%	18	14.9%	16	15.3%	-0.36%	17
IND	**-3.4%**	**10**	**15.3%**	**13**	**15.8%**	**-0.57%**	**18**
NYJ	3.3%	21	14.2%	19	14.8%	-0.65%	19
DEN	-9.7%	5	14.1%	20	14.8%	-0.75%	20
CIN	9.0%	27	12.7%	30	14.3%	-1.51%	21
DET	9.0%	28	13.6%	22	15.2%	-1.55%	22
WAS	1.7%	20	13.6%	23	15.4%	-1.83%	23
JAX	-9.4%	6	13.3%	25	15.1%	-1.85%	24
SF	5.7%	23	13.0%	27	14.9%	-1.89%	25
ATL	13.3%	31	12.8%	29	14.7%	-1.93%	26
MIA	6.5%	25	12.9%	28	14.8%	-2.00%	27
NYG	5.8%	24	13.7%	21	15.7%	-2.04%	28
TEN	0.6%	19	13.5%	24	15.6%	-2.15%	29
GB	10.1%	29	13.1%	26	15.7%	-2.52%	30
OAK	12.3%	30	11.6%	32	14.5%	-2.84%	31
NE	0.4%	16	12.7%	31	15.6%	-2.85%	32

2018 Colts by Week

Wk	vs.	W-L	PF	PA	YDF	YDA	TO	Total	Off	Def	ST
1	CIN	L	23	34	380	330	0	-29%	-21%	5%	-4%
2	at WAS	W	21	9	281	334	-1	-19%	-12%	7%	0%
3	at PHI	L	16	20	209	379	+2	13%	-13%	-13%	13%
4	HOU	L	34	37	478	466	-1	8%	2%	-6%	1%
5	at NE	L	24	38	439	438	-1	-14%	-6%	8%	0%
6	at NYJ	L	34	42	428	374	-2	-31%	-21%	14%	4%
7	BUF	W	37	5	376	303	+5	77%	43%	-34%	-1%
8	at OAK	W	42	28	461	347	+1	-11%	38%	51%	2%
9	BYE										
10	JAX	W	29	26	366	415	0	3%	33%	18%	-11%
11	TEN	W	38	10	397	267	+2	95%	37%	-46%	12%
12	MIA	W	27	24	455	314	-2	-14%	-2%	3%	-9%
13	at JAX	L	0	6	265	211	-1	-11%	-32%	-23%	-2%
14	at HOU	W	24	21	436	315	-1	28%	20%	-11%	-4%
15	DAL	W	23	0	370	292	0	50%	27%	-21%	2%
16	NYG	W	28	27	402	392	0	17%	18%	9%	9%
17	at TEN	W	33	17	436	258	+1	51%	31%	-17%	4%
18	at HOU	W	21	7	422	322	0	49%	31%	-16%	1%
19	at KC	L	13	31	266	433	0	0%	-10%	-14%	-5%

Trends and Splits

	Offense	Rank	Defense	Rank
Total DVOA	8.2%	10	-3.4%	10
Unadjusted VOA	7.9%	11	-8.9%	6
Weighted Trend	15.9%	5	-5.7%	8
Variance	6.1%	12	5.3%	14
Average Opponent	-0.7%	14	-8.6%	32
Passing	21.3%	10	8.8%	20
Rushing	-3.2%	13	-18.8%	4
First Down	11.8%	9	-5.5%	8
Second Down	0.8%	16	-4.7%	12
Third Down	12.8%	10	2.5%	21
First Half	-0.9%	16	1.5%	19
Second Half	18.6%	4	-8.3%	7
Red Zone	34.6%	2	-4.2%	14
Late and Close	16.1%	5	-11.5%	10

Five-Year Performance

Year	W-L	Pyth W	Est W	PF	PA	TO	Total	Rk	Off	Rk	Def	Rk	ST	Rk	Off AGL	Rk	Def AGL	Rk	Off Age	Rk	Def Age	Rk	ST Age	Rk
2014	11-5	10.2	8.8	458	369	-5	4.5%	13	-1.1%	17	-2.3%	13	3.3%	8	56.6	29	48.2	23	26.2	28	28.3	1	26.1	12
2015	8-8	6.0	5.5	333	408	-5	-12.9%	23	-15.6%	30	-2.2%	13	0.5%	16	22.0	6	43.1	26	27.1	13	28.6	1	26.3	11
2016	8-8	8.5	7.0	411	392	-5	-4.6%	23	3.7%	12	12.5%	29	4.1%	5	27.3	9	51.1	24	25.8	27	28.0	2	25.9	20
2017	4-12	4.2	4.3	263	404	+5	-22.8%	31	-17.8%	29	8.7%	27	3.7%	8	56.4	25	44.8	25	26.4	24	25.7	24	25.3	27
2018	10-6	10.3	10.0	433	344	+2	12.6%	8	8.2%	10	-3.4%	10	0.9%	12	59.7	27	56.8	29	25.8	28	25.3	28	25.7	19

2018 Performance Based on Most Common Personnel Groups

IND Offense					IND Offense vs. Opponents					IND Defense					IND Defense vs. Opponents			
Pers	Freq	Yds	DVOA	Run%	Pers	Freq	Yds	DVOA	Run%	Pers	Freq	Yds	DVOA	Pers	Freq	Yds	DVOA
11	64%	5.9	11.8%	28%	Base	25%	6.1	-5.8%	51%	Base	27%	5.2	-3.2%	11	62%	5.7	-4.7%
12	16%	6.5	18.7%	37%	Nickel	70%	6.1	19.0%	32%	Nickel	52%	5.5	-3.3%	12	21%	5.7	-1.7%
612	7%	6.8	9.2%	63%	Dime+	11%	6.0	8.2%	8%	Dime+	20%	6.3	-3.1%	21	6%	5.9	2.4%
13	4%	5.3	-32.4%	55%	Goal Line	1%	-0.2	-7.7%	60%	Goal Line	0%	0.3	-36.5%	13	5%	5.9	9.9%
21	3%	8.4	57.6%	52%										22	2%	1.6	-51.1%
611	3%	3.1	-72.7%	76%										02	1%	7.4	21.6%
10	2%	8.8	78.3%	0%										611	1%	5.4	31.3%
														10	1%	4.3	-8.9%

Strategic Tendencies

Run/Pass		Rk	Formation		Rk	Pass Rush		Rk	Secondary		Rk	Strategy		Rk
Runs, first half	35%	25	Form: Single Back	88%	3	Rush 3	6.5%	16	4 DB	27%	13	Play action	22%	19
Runs, first down	38%	29	Form: Empty Back	9%	15	Rush 4	75.7%	7	5 DB	52%	25	Avg Box (Off)	6.07	30
Runs, second-long	32%	12	Pers: 3+ WR	67%	18	Rush 5	13.6%	28	6+ DB	20%	9	Avg Box (Def)	5.98	30
Runs, power sit.	52%	23	Pers: 2+ TE/6+ OL	28%	9	Rush 6+	4.0%	27	CB by Sides	56%	30	Offensive Pace	28.53	2
Runs, behind 2H	22%	25	Pers: 6+ OL	11%	2	Int DL Sacks	23.7%	17	S/CB Cover Ratio	27%	18	Defensive Pace	32.42	32
Pass, ahead 2H	51%	11	Shotgun/Pistol	74%	7	Second Level Sacks	25.0%	15	DB Blitz	8%	18	Go for it on 4th	1.17	19

One thing Frank Reich brought with him was an increase in tempo, as the Colts went from 23rd (31.2 seconds) to second (28.5 seconds) in situation-neutral pace. ✎ The Colts offense ranked in the bottom six in broken tackles for the fourth straight season. ✎ It's a small sample size, just 18 plays, but the Colts averaged just 0.2 yards on running back screens. They were much better on wide receiver or tight end screens, running 44 of them (fifth in the league) for 7.6 average yards and 41.3% DVOA. ✎ Andrew Luck had 9.2 net yards per pass against the blitz, second only to Nick Foles (in a much smaller sample size). The Colts' 54.1% offensive DVOA when blitzed ranked third in the league. ✎ The Indianapolis defense ranked third against passes to the offensive left but 30th against passes to the offensive right. You might think that's related to specific personnel, but the Colts didn't tend to play their cornerbacks on specific sides.

Passing

Player	DYAR	DVOA	Plays	NtYds	Avg	YAC	C%	TD	Int
A.Luck	1070	13.3%	656	4430	6.8	4.6	67.7%	39	15

Rushing

Player	DYAR	DVOA	Plays	Yds	Avg	TD	Fum	Suc
M.Mack	216	16.8%	195	912	4.7	9	1	54%
N.Hines	-12	-11.8%	85	313	3.7	2	1	46%
J.Wilkins	61	15.0%	60	336	5.6	1	0	58%
A.Luck	51	25.3%	26	171	6.6	0	0	--
R.Turbin*	-21	-120.8%	4	10	2.5	0	1	50%
S.Ware	38	9.0%	51	246	4.8	2	0	45%

Receiving

Player	DYAR	DVOA	Plays	Ctch	Yds	Y/C	YAC	TD	C%
T.Y.Hilton	359	23.4%	120	76	1270	16.7	6.0	6	63%
C.Rogers	17	-9.7%	72	53	485	9.2	4.9	2	74%
R.Grant*	12	-9.8%	52	35	334	9.5	2.7	1	67%
Z.Pascal	-28	-20.5%	46	27	268	9.9	3.0	2	59%
D.Inman*	69	9.1%	39	28	304	10.9	2.1	3	72%
M.Johnson	43	59.8%	8	6	102	17.0	4.7	1	75%
D.Funchess	13	-10.5%	79	44	549	12.5	1.7	4	56%
E.Ebron	68	2.0%	110	66	750	11.4	3.8	13	60%
J.Doyle	0	-7.4%	33	26	245	9.4	4.2	2	79%
M.Alie-Cox	16	9.5%	13	7	133	19.0	7.1	2	54%
E.Swoope*	41	47.4%	10	8	87	10.9	2.1	3	80%
N.Hines	79	3.5%	81	63	425	6.7	5.5	2	78%
M.Mack	-10	-21.3%	26	17	110	6.5	7.2	1	65%
J.Wilkins	-34	-47.8%	17	16	85	5.3	6.6	0	94%
S.Ware	85	56.1%	23	20	224	11.2	12.3	0	87%

Offensive Line

Player	Pos	Age	GS	Snaps	Pen	Sk	Pass	Run	Player	Pos	Age	GS	Snaps	Pen	Sk	Pass	Run
Quenton Nelson	LG	23	16/16	1137	9	1.0	3	2	Matt Slauson*	RG	33	5/5	376	1	0.0	1	1
Braden Smith	RT	23	15/13	854	3	2.5	9	3	Joe Haeg	RG/RT	26	8/6	367	3	0.0	4	1
Ryan Kelly	C	26	12/12	778	4	0.0	1	2	Le'Raven Clark	LT	26	12/4	365	3	1.0	4	3
Anthony Castonzo	LT	31	11/11	745	4	2.0	12	1	Evan Boehm	C	26	11/4	357	2	0.5	4	2
Mark Glowinski	RG	27	11/9	602	6	0.0	3	3									

Year	Yards	ALY	Rank	Power	Rank	Stuff	Rank	2nd Lev	Rank	Open Field	Rank	Sacks	ASR	Rank	Press	Rank	F-Start	Cont.
2016	3.83	4.69	2	63%	15	13%	1	1.01	28	0.26	32	44	7.6%	28	33.3%	31	18	24
2017	3.63	3.98	18	81%	2	20%	16	1.00	25	0.44	29	56	10.0%	32	37.0%	32	20	20
2018	4.55	4.83	4	59%	28	18%	9	1.34	6	0.74	22	18	4.1%	2	25.9%	6	15	24

2018 ALY by direction: Left End: 5.37 (5)   Left Tackle: 5.39 (3)   Mid/Guard: 4.76 (7)   Right Tackle: 3.96 (23)   Right End: 4.66 (10)

Penalties were the main blemish on Quenton Nelson's outstanding rookie season. Adjusting to the NFL more smoothly than other highly touted guards, he showcased outstanding pulling ability both in the run and in pass protection. ✎ Ryan Kelly looked better healthy and with better guards surrounding him. He had the third-lowest blown block rate among centers, and Evan Boehm's starts in his absence reminded you of how good Kelly was. ● Braden Smith was projected as a guard after he went in the second round last year, but kicked outside. He will never be the smoothest pass protector, but did fine. ● Anthony Castonzo is heading into the final year of his deal and will probably get a reasonable extension rather than see Chris Ballard gamble on a replacement. ● Mark Glowinski was surprisingly effective filling in at right guard after Matt Slauson was injured in Week 5. He was re-signed to a three-year deal after the season, while the oft-injured Slauson retired. ● Depth remains a bit of a question mark, especially should Castonzo go down. ● Indianapolis ranked second in usage of six-offensive lineman sets, using them on 10.5 percent of plays. They particularly preferred the extra tackle to a second tight end when Jack Doyle was out. The Colts led the league with 5.5 yards per play with six linemen, thanks to a few deep completions to T.Y. Hilton, but only had -8.8% DVOA because of a low success rate. ● One surprise departure: line coach Dave DeGuglielmo was fired after leading the turnaround. Familiar face Howard Mudd returns as senior offensive assistant, while Chris Strausser takes over as position coach.

Defensive Front

Defensive Line	Age	Pos				Overall							vs. Run					Pass Rush		
			G	Snaps	Plays	TmPct	Rk	Stop	Dfts	BTkl	Runs	St%	Rk	RuYd	Rk	Sack	Hit	Hur	Dsrpt
Denico Autry	29	DT	12	554	37	5.9%	28	32	19	4	24	88%	8	1.0	4	9.0	3	19	0
Al Woods*	32	DT	14	375	24	3.3%	74	16	4	2	21	71%	53	2.2	43	0.0	2	10	1
Grover Stewart	26	DT	15	292	17	2.2%	--	13	2	4	16	75%	--	3.3	--	0.0	0	3	0
Caraun Reid	28	DT	10	185	10	2.0%	--	8	4	1	8	75%	--	1.0	--	0.5	2	8	0

Edge Rushers	Age	Pos				Overall							vs. Run					Pass Rush		
			G	Snaps	Plays	TmPct	Rk	Stop	Dfts	BTkl	Runs	St%	Rk	RuYd	Rk	Sack	Hit	Hur	Dsrpt
Jabaal Sheard	30	DE	16	813	54	6.4%	12	42	24	6	36	78%	37	1.6	17	5.5	7	28	3
Margus Hunt	32	DE	15	724	31	3.9%	68	30	16	3	21	95%	1	0.0	1	5.0	3	12	1
Al-Quadin Muhammad	24	DE	15	415	29	3.7%	73	25	11	1	27	85%	15	0.6	2	0.0	2	10	2
Kemoko Turay	24	DE	14	384	15	2.0%	--	10	5	2	6	50%	--	4.0	--	4.0	8	24	0
Tyquan Lewis	24	DE	8	339	14	3.3%	81	10	4	0	7	71%	55	2.6	52	2.0	7	14	0
Justin Houston	30	OLB	12	665	38	5.8%	26	29	19	6	20	75%	44	2.4	45	9.0	5	26	1

Linebackers	Age	Pos				Overall							vs. Run			Pass Rush			vs. Pass				
			G	Snaps	Plays	TmPct	Rk	Stop	Dfts	BTkl	Runs	St%	Rk	RuYd	Rk	Sack	Hit	Hur	Tgts	Suc%	Rk	AdjYd	Rk	PD	Int
Darius Leonard	24	OLB	15	956	171	21.6%	1	89	37	10	90	61%	34	4.0	48	7.0	1	3.5	55	36%	70	6.6	33	8	2
Anthony Walker	24	MLB	15	694	108	13.7%	34	68	16	14	62	76%	4	2.3	3	1.0	1	5	37	51%	36	6.9	45	4	1
Matthew Adams	24	OLB	16	215	26	3.1%	--	14	6	3	17	76%	--	2.6	--	0.0	2	4	8	13%	--	12.0	--	0	0
Zaire Franklin	23	OLB	16	177	26	3.1%	--	14	2	1	12	83%	--	2.8	--	0.0	0	0	10	40%	--	9.0	--	1	0

Year	Yards	ALY	Rank	Power	Rank	Stuff	Rank	2nd Level	Rank	Open Field	Rank	Sacks	ASR	Rank	Press	Rank
2016	4.81	4.83	31	48%	2	16%	28	1.42	31	0.82	21	33	6.3%	13	19.0%	32
2017	3.96	4.09	16	64%	18	20%	20	1.11	16	0.69	15	25	4.5%	31	31.7%	10
2018	3.84	3.96	7	65%	14	25%	4	1.10	7	0.69	10	38	5.3%	29	28.0%	25
2018 ALY by direction:		Left End: 4.82 (19)			Left Tackle: 3.86 (12)			Mid/Guard: 4.12 (9)			Right Tackle: 3.18 (4)			Right End: 3.03 (4)	

Margus Hunt started off the season with his best J.J. Watt impression. The Estonian has always been a great athlete, but his play finally showed that with four sacks in the first four games before returning to his previous useful but not elite level of performance. His excellent stop rate is a product of not making plays outside his area, thus the below-average number of plays. ● The hope is that Justin Houston's arrival will not only put Jabaal Sheard in more favorable situations, working at left end with a genuine threat opposite him, but also let him convert more of his total pressures into sacks. Only seven defensive linemen had more defeats than Sheard, and he ranked in the top 15 against both the run and the pass. ● Darius Leonard led the league with 111 primary tackles, and they were not all just empty tackles either. Only Luke Kuechly (38) had more defeats. The wild-card win against the Texans showed what he could do, with 13 tackles and an interception. The loss to the Chiefs showed what he was not yet, as they attacked him early, often, and with success by stressing his ability to pattern-match in zone coverage. ● Anthony Walker broke through from special teams player to starter. At least as much as Leonard, he emphasized the scheme transition and what Matt Eberflus allowed players to be. His ability to hold on to the starting middle linebacker job is no lock, though, after the Colts selected Bobby Okereke (Stanford) in the third round. Okereke is instinctual and rangy but a bit undersized and has issues with broken tackles. ● If Ben Banogu ends up at defensive end, where he practiced in June, Matthew Adams returns as the third starting linebacker, a minor position for the Colts likely to only see action against run-heavy teams that feature base personnel.

Defensive Secondary

Secondary	Age	Pos	G	Snaps	Plays	TmPct	Rk	Stop	Dfts	BTkl	Runs	St%	Rk	RuYd	Rk	Tgts	Tgt%	Rk	Dist	Suc%	Rk	AdjYd	Rk	PD	Int
						Overall						vs. Run							vs. Pass						
Malik Hooker	23	FS	14	913	48	6.5%	66	9	5	9	19	16%	70	11.4	71	9	2.6%	1	25.7	33%	71	17.3	75	4	2
Kenny Moore	24	CB	15	911	87	11.0%	9	47	21	13	24	75%	1	2.3	2	57	16.7%	22	8.6	56%	22	6.1	12	11	3
Pierre Desir	29	CB	16	904	86	10.2%	16	28	12	3	22	41%	42	5.0	16	67	19.8%	49	12.2	51%	50	8.5	59	8	1
Clayton Geathers	27	SS	12	715	88	13.9%	6	27	5	6	42	33%	54	7.2	43	27	10.1%	45	8.4	56%	19	6.7	26	3	0
Quincy Wilson	23	CB	13	436	28	4.1%	--	10	8	6	7	43%	--	8.1	--	23	14.1%	--	12.3	48%	--	6.5	--	2	1
Nate Hairston	25	CB	13	413	30	4.4%	--	13	5	5	12	67%	--	4.4	--	26	16.8%	--	9.8	35%	--	9.4	--	1	0
Mike Mitchell*	32	FS	8	224	29	6.9%	--	14	9	4	13	46%	--	7.1	--	8	9.5%	--	6.1	38%	--	6.1	--	1	1
George Odum	26	FS	16	205	30	3.6%	--	13	5	5	17	53%	--	6.1	--	9	11.7%	--	8.2	44%	--	8.2	--	2	1
Matthias Farley	27	SS	5	151	21	8.0%	--	10	8	3	7	43%	--	5.1	--	11	19.5%	--	6.0	45%	--	7.5	--	4	1
Derrick Kindred	26	SS	16	497	39	4.4%	--	11	5	10	14	29%	--	8.7	--	14	6.8%	--	5.9	36%	--	10.2	--	1	1

Year	Pass D Rank	vs. #1 WR	Rk	vs. #2 WR	Rk	vs. Other WR	Rk	WR Wide	Rk	WR Slot	Rk	vs. TE	Rk	vs. RB	Rk
2016	26	13.7%	29	-3.3%	12	-1.1%	14	8.3%	27	1.7%	15	33.1%	31	38.5%	31
2017	32	7.6%	18	22.7%	27	28.5%	31	22.3%	32	18.4%	24	9.9%	23	27.9%	31
2018	20	1.8%	17	-27.9%	1	-3.8%	14	-12.1%	8	-8.4%	6	21.2%	29	12.3%	25

We were cautiously optimistic about the Colts' secondary in *Football Outsiders Almanac 2018*, noting that with good work by Eberflus and the pass rush, we could see significant defensive improvement. And so it was. ● Kenny Moore completed the elevation from waiver-wire find to terrific slot corner. The extension he earned in June was a bit of a surprise, as our statistics on slot corners tend to vary wildly from one season to the next, but good slot corner money is not too bad and rewarding your own was a good move by Chris Ballard. ● On the spectrum of strong to free safeties, Malik Hooker is even more the last line of defense than the Omega Sector was in *True Lies*, and his numbers should be considered accordingly. ● Clayton Geathers staying healthy enough to play in 12 games was not a bad total by his standards. If Hooker is playing back, Geathers is the one playing up. His on-field presence was not quite as dramatic being paired with run-and-chase linebackers in Leonard and Moore instead of Chuck Pagano's thumpers, but he was still effective enough in his role. Geathers' persistent injury issues helped lead the Colts to select Khari Willis, who filled a similar role at Michigan State, in the fourth round. Matthias Farley has experience filling in for Hooker and Geathers. Also, the Colts are high on George Odum's potential, and ex-Brown Derrick Kindred gives them another veteran option. ● Finding a good outside corner counterpart for Pierre Desir is a priority. Former second-round pick Quincy Wilson finally emerged into a consistent role the second half of 2018 and is the favorite to play outside in nickel, when Moore shifts to the slot. If he cannot keep up that consistency, it may be second-round pick Rock Ya-Sin (Temple) earning that job. Ya-Sin spent his first three years of college at FCS Presbyterian and lacks elite deep speed, so he projects as a better early fit if the Colts continue to play more zone coverage.

Special Teams

Year	DVOA	Rank	FG/XP	Rank	Net Kick	Rank	Kick Ret	Rank	Net Punt	Rank	Punt Ret	Rank	Hidden	Rank
2016	4.1%	5	8.9	4	1.6	12	9.0	4	3.5	10	-2.3	21	4.4	10
2017	3.7%	8	0.4	16	1.6	16	-1.2	18	20.2	1	-2.6	23	5.0	9
2018	0.9%	12	-1.9	22	-1.5	24	-1.1	17	9.1	3	0.1	15	-8.6	26

Missing only one field goal from under 40 yards and hitting four of six from 50 and beyond might have gotten you to the Pro Bowl when Adam Vinatieri started his career. Now, along with three missed extra points from the newer distance, that sort of season is below average by advanced metrics. ● Rigoberto Sanchez had a below-average season on kickoffs and was only slightly above average on punt value, but the Colts had the third-best punt coverage unit in the league. ● Zach Pascal had a below-average season as a kickoff returner, but he was barely needed. The Colts only tried to return 19 percent of kickoffs, the second-lowest (to Dallas) rate in the league. Parris Campbell is a candidate to return kicks if Pascal can't make the bottom of the receiver depth chart. ● Like Pascal, Chester Rogers was barely needed as a punt returner. The Colts had the fifth-lowest rate of returned punts. Rogers was average when he did try to make a return. ● One big reason for the negative hidden special teams value: in gross punt value, opposing punters were a league-best 10.1 points of estimated field position better than expectation against the Colts.

Jacksonville Jaguars

2018 record: 5-11	Total DVOA: -8.1% (22nd)	2019 Mean Projection: 7.3 wins	On the Clock (0-4): 15%
Pythagorean Wins: 5.7 (26th)	Offense: -22.0% (30th)	Postseason Odds: 26.8%	Mediocrity (5-7): 39%
Snap-Weighted Age: 26.2 (23rd)	Defense: -9.4% (6th)	Super Bowl Odds: 2.5%	Playoff Contender (8-10): 34%
Average Opponent: 0.9% (11th)	Special Teams: 4.4% (4th)	Proj. Avg. Opponent: 2.0% (9th)	Super Bowl Contender (11+): 13%

2018: Bortles V: The Final Bortling. No, really, we mean it this time.

2019: The defense is good, but will Nick Foles deliver the Super Bowl magic every week?

For nine seasons now, the Jacksonville Jaguars have struggled with the two quarterbacks they've drafted in the top 10: Blaine Gabbert and Blake Bortles. It was impossible to talk about the franchise as a whole without discussing these two players: their potential, what was needed to coax it to the "next step," or how the Jaguars got by while managing games with them. That's not to totally dismiss Bortles' 2015 as smoke and mirrors, or to say that the two of them had zero upside between them. But it was clear that they were quarterbacks that you won in spite of, not because of. When the Jaguars used the 2017 fourth overall pick on Leonard Fournette, it was clear they were trying to make a commitment to Bortles by ensuring that his margin for error was higher than ever. Given that it led to an AFC Championship Game appearance in the 2017 season, it seemed like they had found a proper balance.

But last year, that proper balance collapsed. Yards per attempt were down and sack rate was up. Bortles' touchdown rate dropped to a level unseen since his rookie year. He proved incapable of consistently threatening deeper holes in zone coverage. Bortles attempted just 13 throws of more than 20 yards against zone, and he completed only four of them. The final straw was a 24-21 loss against the Bills where even with the Jaguars running game going, Bortles completed just 12 passes for 127 yards, getting picked twice. Jacksonville benched Bortles, bringing him back only after Cody Kessler proved even more inept. Watching Bortles try to play quarterback last year was like watching the burglars from *Home Alone* try to catch Kevin: periods of quiet, cautious play, followed by a dumbfounding mistake that hit the Jaguars like a 100-pound bag of cement.

Now, for the first time since David Garrard and Byron Leftwich were donning the teal, the Jaguars finally have a quarterback that can be thought of as capable. "Can be thought of" is carrying a lot of weight in that sentence, yes. It's former Super Bowl MVP Nick Foles! Foles played extremely well down the stretch, carrying the Eagles to yet another playoff berth after a Carson Wentz injury. Philadelphia was not an offensive juggernaut under Foles, but with the running game completely off the rails, they had to put the entire game plan on his back.

Of course, the thing with Foles is that he's kind of a divining rod for how good your offensive coaching staff is. He didn't do much with Jeff Fisher's Rams and he fell apart in his first stint with the Eagles right around the same time Chip

Kelly's game plan fell into the sea. In normal circumstances, that's probably not a guy to whom you want to give a four-year, $88-million contract. The Jaguars tried to rekindle what worked with Foles in the past by bringing in former Eagles quarterback coach John DeFilippo as offensive coordinator. DeFilippo flopped in his lone season as Vikings offensive coordinator, earning a pink slip after the Seahawks held Minnesota to seven points on Monday Night Football in Week 14. That said, Kirk Cousins finished the season with a 70 percent completion rate and many of Minnesota's struggles could be traced back to an offensive line that seemed impervious to improvement. One of the common criticisms of DeFilippo last year with the Vikings is that he ignored the run game to an extreme. This was mentioned not only by fans and media, but also by Vikings head coach Mike Zimmer. While Jaguars head coach Doug Marrone was publicly forward-thinking about the play calling ("I don't have a problem with that," he said per NFL.com), it's going to be an interesting year in Jacksonville if they don't get an instant offensive turnaround. DeFilippo's preference for the pass does not seem to mesh with Tom Coughlin's philosophies.

So what do we know about DeFilippo's play calling last year in Minnesota? Outside of his reluctance to run without a lead, the offense was good at changing things up. They were in the middle of the pack of most formation groupings and, with 61 percent of their plays coming in shotgun or pistol, did not overdo things. One area that might play to Foles' strengths is how often DeFilippo targeted slot receivers. Adam Thielen led the league with a staggering 89 targets through the first seven weeks and was targeted at least seven times in every game DeFilippo coached. Meanwhile, Foles targeted 88 of his 193 regular-season throws at the slot receiver. That number was 46 out of 102 in 2017, so it's a sustained trend. This is a potential fantasy football blowup spot for whomever Jacksonville manages to put in that spot—probably the agile Dede Westbrook. It also puts a lot of strain on the Jaguars to make sure they have the best receiver they can there.

One thing that might be interesting to key on is how little the Vikings used play-action. Only 21 percent of their passing plays were play-action in 2018, whereas Foles' Eagles teams used play-action on 32 percent of passes in 2018 and 27 percent in 2017. Those were both top-five rates in the league. The Jaguars used play-action less than only three other NFL teams

2019 Jaguars Schedule

Week	Opp.	Week	Opp.	Week	Opp.
1	KC	7	at CIN	13	TB
2	at HOU	8	NYJ	14	LAC
3	TEN (Thu.)	9	HOU (U.K.)	15	at OAK
4	at DEN	10	BYE	16	at ATL
5	at CAR	11	at IND	17	IND
6	NO	12	at TEN		

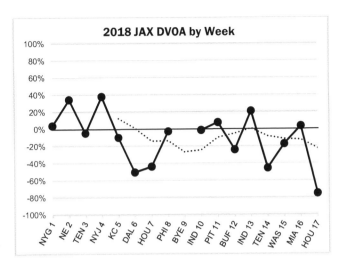

in 2018, but also had the worst DVOA in the NFL on play-action throws. Foles does not have a hose, but if he can just bring the Jaguars up to a reasonable play-action success rate, maybe they'll consider using it at the Philadelphia rate rather than the Minnesota rate.

The Jaguars should also get some positive regression from Foles' supporting cast. The Jaguars were third in adjusted games lost at wideout, second in AGL at tight end, and second in AGL on the offensive line; they lost a combined 81.6 AGL just to those three positions. To put that into perspective, the division-winning Texans lost 89.6 games on the entire roster. The only team that had more offensive AGL than the Jaguars was Washington (Table 1), which started *Futurama* presidential hopefuls at quarterback in December. It was the third-most offensive AGL since 2011.

Table 1. Most Injured Offenses, 2011-2018

Year	Team	Off AGL	Off DVOA	Off DVOA Y+1	Off AGL Y+1
2016	MIN	92.1	-9.8%	12.0%	42.8
2018	**WAS**	**88.9**	**-19.5%**	--	--
2018	**JAX**	**88.4**	**-22.0%**	--	--
2016	CHI	84.0	-2.6%	-15.1%	57.5
2014	SD	82.1	7.0%	0.9%	55.7
2013	NYG	82.1	-22.0%	-0.3%	65.9
2013	TB	75.6	-10.4%	-26.3%	31.1
2013	IND	75.5	4.3%	-1.1%	56.6
2017	ARI	74.8	-18.4%	-41.1%	61.5
2017	WAS	70.6	-3.0%	-19.5%	88.9

We're not surprised to see that most teams with that many AGL had a bad offense. The only two teams with a positive DVOA were those confounding mid-2010s Chargers that fielded offensive lines of witness protection agents like "Johnnie Troutman" and the Pagano-era Colts that were literally a one-Luck show. While not every team in this group improved on offense the next season, they all did at least get a little healthier. The surprising thing about this table is that the majority of the teams in it didn't get better next season at all. That said, it's a very small sampling of teams, one of which purposely used John Fox's offense in 2017.

Injury concerns also helped the Jaguars in the draft as one of the consensus three best offensive tackles in the draft, Flor-

ida's Jawaan Taylor, fell into their laps in the second round. Several draft media members described teams giving him a medical red flag on his knees and possibly even his back. Taylor has a chance to be an instant starter replacing the released Jermey Parnell, and with Cam Robinson coming back off a torn ACL, Foles should have a solid offensive line—perhaps not what he had with the Eagles, but there's a lot of upside if everyone actually manages to stay on the field.

A lot of the burden of this offense is going to on skill position players who haven't proven themselves on a grand statistical level yet. That's what will make or break this year for Jacksonville. Marqise Lee is coming off an ACL tear. Westbrook has a Top 25 Prospects List pedigree but hasn't cracked 700 yards receiving yet. Keelan Cole has low catch rates but has at times charmed observers into thinking he can be a real difference-maker. Leonard Fournette has as legitimate an argument to the easy sports radio trope of "he always has to face stacked boxes" as any running back does. Fournette finished third with a 35.3 percent rate of eight in the box in 2018 and fifth with a 48.5 percent rate of eight in the box in 2017, per NFL Next Gen Stats. All of these players have been able to proudly wear the "Yeah, but that's because he plays with Blake Bortles" excuse over the past two seasons. That's over. They now have a capable NFL quarterback and an offensive coordinator who has shown the ability to rack up some yards. If the skill position youth thrives in 2019, it ratchets up expectations for this team. If it's Nick Foles leading an offense on his lonesome, well, that didn't work too well for the Rams.

What else went wrong to lead to a 5-11 season? The common sentiment was that the defense crumbled, but it didn't crumble as much as you might think; the Jaguars ranked sixth in defensive DVOA and fourth in points allowed. And our projection is that the Jaguars will have one of the best chances of any NFL team of having a good defense in 2019. Yes, that's even after we told you in last year's *Almanac* that all the data was projecting a Jacksonville defensive regression. Why did it fall apart in 2018? Let us introduce you to our friend turnover luck (Table 2).

We don't expect a 16.2 percent turnover rate to hold up very well. We were not exactly calling for it to drop all the way to 27th in the NFL. To be fair, some of that drop came because

Table 2. Jacksonville Turnover Luck, 2017 vs. 2018

Year	Int	PD	FF	FR	Fum TD	TO/Drive
2017	21	77	17	12	5	0.162
2018	11	49	8	6	0	0.086

teams were less apt to challenge Jalen Ramsey and A.J. Bouye (when healthy) last year, leading to a lower interception total as well as many fewer passes defensed. But forcing only eight fumbles all season is not something you would expect, no matter how light Jacksonville's linebackers are.

Another reason our projection system likes Jacksonville's defense this year is because they now have a three-year trend of marked consistency. The Jaguars have posted a negative defensive DVOA in each of the last three years. Finally, as readers of last year's chapter know, our projection system is much more sanguine about projecting good things from a defense if it has a good run defense. Jacksonville boosted their run defense DVOA from 27th in the NFL in 2017 to seventh last year. The Jaguars will have some turnover after releasing players to make cap room for Foles, but Malik Jackson's departure should be countered by growth from last year's first-

round pick, Taven Bryan. Meanwhile, seventh overall pick Josh Allen should have some instant impact as a pass-rusher and let Calais Campbell play inside on passing downs.

The middle of the field is going to be a bit more questionable this year after the release of Tashaun Gipson. The Jaguars don't have an easy replacement for him and will be expecting Jarrod Wilson and Ronnie Harrison to make strides. Telvin Smith's apparent gap year is also a bit of a blow, even if Smith didn't have a great 2018 season. Former Packers linebacker Jake Ryan is probably the replacement there.

Our mean projection for the Jaguars has them rebounding to respectability rather than contending for the AFC South crown, but none of the AFC South teams have a marked edge in what looks to be a tight race. Plus, of our projections, Jacksonville's offense is the unit that has the most potential to bounce forward—it's the lowest-rated unit in the division— and the Jaguars also draw the last-place schedule benefit. Games against the Bengals and Jets could be quite a boon in a tight divisional race.

So, with the Bortles excuse erased, how good is this offense? A positive answer could mean a return to football in January.

Rivers McCown

2018 Jaguars Stats by Week

Wk	vs.	W-L	PF	PA	YDF	YDA	TO	Total	Off	Def	ST
1	at NYG	W	20	15	305	324	+1	4%	-23%	-24%	2%
2	NE	W	31	20	480	302	-1	34%	20%	-13%	2%
3	TEN	L	6	9	232	233	-1	-5%	-27%	-21%	2%
4	NYJ	W	31	12	503	178	-3	38%	7%	-30%	1%
5	at KC	L	14	30	502	424	-3	-10%	-34%	-25%	-2%
6	at DAL	L	7	40	204	378	-2	-51%	-40%	5%	-6%
7	HOU	L	7	20	259	272	-3	-44%	-41%	1%	-2%
8	PHI	L	18	24	335	395	+1	-3%	-6%	15%	18%
9	BYE										
10	at IND	L	26	29	415	366	0	-1%	9%	10%	0%
11	PIT	L	16	20	243	323	+2	8%	-22%	-28%	2%
12	at BUF	L	21	24	333	327	-2	-24%	-4%	25%	5%
13	IND	W	6	0	211	265	+1	21%	-38%	-52%	7%
14	at TEN	L	9	30	255	426	0	-46%	-25%	28%	8%
15	WAS	L	13	16	192	245	-2	-18%	-57%	-10%	29%
16	at MIA	W	17	7	244	183	+1	4%	-36%	-36%	3%
17	at HOU	L	3	20	119	342	-1	-75%	-76%	2%	2%

Trends and Splits

	Offense	Rank	Defense	Rank
Total DVOA	-22.0%	30	-9.4%	6
Unadjusted VOA	-21.8%	29	-7.4%	8
Weighted Trend	-26.6%	30	-5.4%	9
Variance	6.2%	13	5.3%	15
Average Opponent	-0.9%	10	-1.2%	18
Passing	-24.3%	30	-5.2%	6
Rushing	-10.6%	21	-14.3%	7
First Down	-22.3%	29	-13.1%	3
Second Down	-24.3%	30	-5.3%	11
Third Down	-18.1%	26	-8.9%	11
First Half	-15.6%	28	-7.5%	5
Second Half	-28.4%	30	-11.6%	5
Red Zone	-21.0%	28	-3.6%	16
Late and Close	-48.6%	32	-14.7%	5

Five-Year Performance

Year	W-L	Pyth W	Est W	PF	PA	TO	Total	Rk	Off	Rk	Def	Rk	ST	Rk	Off AGL	Rk	Def AGL	Rk	Off Age	Rk	Def Age	Rk	ST Age	Rk
2014	3-13	3.6	3.3	249	412	-6	-29.5%	32	-24.3%	31	1.5%	20	-3.6%	26	33.5	19	44.3	22	24.7	32	26.1	27	25.5	30
2015	5-11	6.2	5.8	376	448	-10	-16.0%	25	-5.4%	21	9.7%	26	-0.9%	20	25.7	12	43.2	27	25.6	30	26.4	22	25.4	29
2016	3-13	5.8	5.4	318	400	-16	-10.4%	26	-11.3%	27	-3.1%	12	-2.3%	23	47.6	26	25.0	10	25.6	31	25.9	28	25.5	26
2017	10-6	11.9	9.0	417	268	+10	13.2%	8	-0.3%	16	-16.2%	1	-2.7%	24	33.3	15	5.0	2	26.1	28	25.9	22	26.0	11
2018	5-11	5.7	6.1	245	316	-12	-8.1%	22	-22.0%	30	-9.4%	6	4.4%	4	88.4	31	16.2	5	26.3	21	26.2	16	25.6	24

2018 Performance Based on Most Common Personnel Groups

JAX Offense					JAX Offense vs. Opponents					JAX Defense					JAX Defense vs. Opponents			
Pers	Freq	Yds	DVOA	Run%	Pers	Freq	Yds	DVOA	Run%	Pers	Freq	Yds	DVOA		Pers	Freq	Yds	DVOA
11	65%	5.2	-16.8%	22%	Base	32%	4.1	-24.7%	64%	Base	21%	5.0	-19.7%		11	59%	5.4	-4.8%
12	12%	3.8	-28.3%	56%	Nickel	65%	5.0	-21.1%	23%	Nickel	78%	5.5	-6.0%		12	22%	4.7	-14.0%
21	9%	5.4	0.3%	66%	Dime+	6%	8.2	51.6%	7%	Dime+	0%	2.0	-63.1%		21	6%	5.3	-17.3%
22	5%	4.0	-9.2%	89%	Goal Line	1%	1.0	15.1%	57%	Goal Line	0%	0.0	-36.6%		13	4%	6.9	-6.7%
13	4%	3.1	-41.9%	63%	Big	1%	3.1	-23.5%	100%						22	2%	3.9	-4.8%
10	3%	3.6	-74.2%	13%														

Strategic Tendencies

Run/Pass		Rk	Formation		Rk	Pass Rush		Rk	Secondary		Rk	Strategy		Rk
Runs, first half	42%	5	Form: Single Back	79%	18	Rush 3	2.6%	28	4 DB	21%	22	Play action	19%	28
Runs, first down	45%	20	Form: Empty Back	3%	32	Rush 4	75.6%	8	5 DB	78%	3	Avg Box (Off)	6.26	12
Runs, second-long	30%	18	Pers: 3+ WR	70%	13	Rush 5	13.9%	26	6+ DB	0%	30	Avg Box (Def)	6.26	14
Runs, power sit.	57%	17	Pers: 2+ TE/6+ OL	21%	19	Rush 6+	7.7%	5	CB by Sides	57%	28	Offensive Pace	32.27	25
Runs, behind 2H	17%	29	Pers: 6+ OL	1%	23	Int DL Sacks	17.6%	25	S/CB Cover Ratio	27%	17	Defensive Pace	31.60	24
Pass, ahead 2H	55%	6	Shotgun/Pistol	69%	11	Second Level Sacks	20.3%	20	DB Blitz	10%	10	Go for it on 4th	0.99	25

The Jaguars offense ranked eighth when running the ball on third or fourth down but ranked 20th or worse on every other combination of down and play type. ● Jacksonville receivers dropped a league-high 7.4 percent of passes (37 total drops). ● The Jaguars ranked third in the league in how often they went without a tight end (4.6 percent of plays) but they were awful on these plays with -34.2% DVOA and just 4.8 yards per play. ● Although the Jaguars were a top-ten run defense overall, they ranked dead last against the run in the red zone. ● The Jacksonville defense was second in DVOA on passes to the deep middle portion of the field, and fourth in DVOA on passes to the short middle. But they were susceptible on passes to the deep left (28th).

Passing

Player	DYAR	DVOA	Plays	NtYds	Avg	YAC	C%	TD	Int
B.Bortles*	-221	-18.9%	435	2549	5.9	6.1	60.3%	13	10
C.Kessler*	-458	-59.7%	153	555	3.6	4.1	64.9%	2	2
N.Foles	74	-5.4%	202	1370	6.8	5.2	73.1%	7	4

Rushing

Player	DYAR	DVOA	Plays	Yds	Avg	TD	Fum	Suc
L.Fournette	-4	-9.3%	133	439	3.3	6	0	47%
T.J.Yeldon*	-17	-12.5%	104	414	4.0	1	1	48%
C.Hyde*	-28	-19.7%	58	189	3.3	0	1	41%
B.Bortles*	107	26.8%	51	370	7.3	1	2	--
C.Kessler*	20	7.5%	18	124	6.9	0	0	--
C.Grant*	-16	-38.5%	13	40	3.1	0	0	31%
D.Westbrook	47	32.8%	9	98	10.9	0	0	--
D.Williams*	9	18.8%	8	36	4.5	0	0	38%
J.Charles*	-9	-48.5%	6	7	1.2	0	0	0%
B.Wilds*	-13	-67.9%	6	15	2.5	0	0	33%
A.Blue	-93	-23.0%	150	499	3.3	2	0	41%
B.Cunningham	-26	-64.8%	11	20	1.8	0	0	27%
N.Foles	5	-2.7%	8	18	2.3	0	0	--

Receiving

Player	DYAR	DVOA	Plays	Ctch	Yds	Y/C	YAC	TD	C%
D.Westbrook	-25	-15.7%	102	67	717	10.7	5.4	5	66%
D.Moncrief*	-14	-14.8%	89	48	672	14.0	5.0	3	54%
K.Cole	-48	-21.3%	70	38	493	13.0	3.6	1	54%
DJ Chark	-90	-47.4%	32	14	174	12.4	3.2	0	44%
R.Greene*	-36	-68.6%	8	6	60	10.0	2.5	0	75%
C.Conley	48	-1.0%	52	32	334	10.4	4.4	5	62%
T.Pryor	42	6.1%	30	16	252	15.8	3.9	2	53%
J.O'Shaughnessy	-49	-28.9%	38	24	214	8.9	5.1	0	63%
A.Seferian-Jenkins*	-24	-25.9%	19	11	90	8.2	2.7	1	58%
N.Paul*	-9	-18.8%	13	10	98	9.8	3.2	0	77%
B.Bell*	1	-5.0%	11	8	67	8.4	4.8	0	73%
D.Grinnage*	6	4.7%	8	6	61	10.2	3.0	0	75%
G.Swaim	-9	-11.6%	32	26	242	9.3	6.3	1	81%
T.J.Yeldon*	76	3.0%	79	56	482	8.6	8.0	4	71%
L.Fournette	37	9.6%	26	22	185	8.4	9.7	1	85%
C.Grant*	15	6.2%	12	9	67	7.4	9.2	0	75%
T.Bohanon*	1	-12.3%	9	6	41	6.8	5.8	0	67%
C.Hyde*	-39	-105.7%	7	4	4	1.0	4.0	0	57%
A.Blue	-10	-20.5%	27	20	154	7.7	5.4	0	74%

Offensive Line

Player	Pos	Age	GS	Snaps	Pen	Sk	Pass	Run	Player	Pos	Age	GS	Snaps	Pen	Sk	Pass	Run
A.J. Cann	RG	28	15/15	934	2	5.5	13	6	Tyler Shatley	C	28	16/7	543	5	0.5	3	11
Jermey Parnell*	RT	33	13/13	869	9	1.0	8	2	Brandon Linder	C	27	9/9	508	0	1.0	4	0
Andrew Norwell	LG	28	11/11	726	3	2.5	6	4	Josh Wells	LT/RT	28	7/5	306	0	1.5	6	0
Patrick Omameh*	LG/RG	30	14/11	679	2	4.0	13	4	Josh Walker*	LT	28	5/4	293	2	2.0	11	1
Ereck Flowers*	LT	25	14/9	588	6	2.5	12	2	Chris Reed*	G	27	9/1	178	3	2.0	7	0

Year	Yards	ALY	Rank	Power	Rank	Stuff	Rank	2nd Lev	Rank	Open Field	Rank	Sacks	ASR	Rank	Press	Rank	F-Start	Cont.
2016	3.80	3.73	27	58%	24	20%	18	1.06	24	0.55	24	34	5.3%	9	22.2%	7	18	28
2017	4.16	4.12	13	62%	19	19%	10	0.98	27	0.96	7	24	4.4%	5	33.2%	25	17	26
2018	3.47	4.12	21	69%	12	19%	19	0.98	29	0.29	32	53	9.3%	27	33.6%	25	14	22

2018 ALY by direction:	Left End: 3.25 (25)	Left Tackle: 3.53 (28)	Mid/Guard: 4.30 (19)	Right Tackle: 5.22 (3)	Right End: 3.81 (24)

In 2017, Sports Info Solutions charted the Jaguars with more blown blocks than any other offensive line. Last year, they improved to third, behind Minnesota and Denver. 🏈 The problem with losing Cam Robinson to a torn ACL in Week 2 wasn't that Robinson was some sort of superstar—it's that there is almost no tackle depth in the NFL. Robinson's injury forced the team into a revolving door of names with little positive experience. Josh Walker, Josh Wells, and Ereck Flowers all saw time at the position in 2019. Robinson's health will improve the situation simply because he's not those guys. 🏈 Right guard A.J. Cann was somewhat of a disappointment in 2018. He struggled to deal with interior linemen who could move in the middle, and he didn't show much in the way of recovery speed once a rusher got a step on him. Part of the poor statistical output may have just been how often he was matched with the best in the game: his sacks allowed reel includes Leonard Williams, Chris Jones, and Jadeveon Clowney. Cann's three-year contract jumps in value in 2020 and the Jags have outs—this could be his last year here. 🏈 With the release of Jermey Parnell, right tackle figures to be a battle between second-rounder Jawaan Taylor (Florida) and last year's fourth-rounder, Will Richardson (North Carolina State). Taylor is more of a road-grader type, a true right tackle who demonstrated good pop on his punch in college. Richardson was never healthy last season and profiles as an athletically competent swing tackle without a true plus-plus trait. 🏈 Neither Andrew Norwell nor Brandon Linder had great 2018 seasons when compared to their past track records, but it's not like they lost talent, and both missed time to injury. Norwell had some issues pulling in Jacksonville's scheme, particularly against the Steelers in Week 11.

Defensive Front

Defensive Line	Age	Pos	G	Snaps	Plays	TmPct	Rk	Stop	Dfts	BTkl	Runs	St%	Rk	RuYd	Rk	Sack	Hit	Hur	Dsrpt
						Overall						vs. Run				Pass Rush			
Malik Jackson*	29	DT	16	628	33	4.3%	57	25	13	3	24	79%	29	2.0	27	3.5	8	23	1
Marcell Dareus	29	DT	15	563	33	4.6%	47	24	7	2	29	72%	51	2.3	48	1.0	1	7	1
Abry Jones	28	DT	15	498	31	4.3%	55	28	7	1	24	92%	2	1.8	20	1.0	1	10	0
Taven Bryan	23	DT	16	301	20	2.6%	--	14	4	1	19	68%	--	2.3	--	1.0	1	7	0

Edge Rushers	Age	Pos	G	Snaps	Plays	TmPct	Rk	Stop	Dfts	BTkl	Runs	St%	Rk	RuYd	Rk	Sack	Hit	Hur	Dsrpt
						Overall						vs. Run				Pass Rush			
Calais Campbell	33	DE	16	817	74	9.6%	1	68	32	2	58	90%	6	1.0	8	10.5	11	36	2
Yannick Ngakoue	24	DE	16	767	28	3.7%	74	25	19	9	14	79%	31	2.8	56	9.5	24	38	1
Dawuane Smoot	24	DE	8	172	4	1.0%	--	4	3	2	3	100%	--	1.7	--	0.0	3	6	0

Linebackers	Age	Pos	G	Snaps	Plays	TmPct	Rk	Stop	Dfts	BTkl	Runs	St%	Rk	RuYd	Rk	Sack	Hit	Hur	Tgts	Suc%	Rk	AdjYd	Rk	PD	Int
						Overall						vs. Run				Pass Rush				vs. Pass					
Myles Jack	24	MLB	16	1025	108	14.1%	32	65	15	14	73	67%	18	3.8	36	2.5	2	8.5	27	59%	12	6.5	32	1	1
Telvin Smith*	28	OLB	16	1020	136	17.7%	8	72	21	20	83	63%	29	5.0	78	1.0	2	8	55	47%	47	6.2	23	2	2
Ramik Wilson	27	ILB	16	161	33	4.3%	--	22	7	0	17	59%	--	3.2	--	0.0	0	0	16	75%	1	5.0	13	2	0

Year	Yards	ALY	Rank	Power	Rank	Stuff	Rank	2nd Level	Rank	Open Field	Rank	Sacks	ASR	Rank	Press	Rank
2016	3.76	3.73	7	64%	18	21%	11	0.96	4	0.74	18	33	5.9%	17	27.2%	15
2017	4.27	4.37	28	59%	9	20%	19	1.16	20	0.76	19	55	9.1%	2	34.3%	3
2018	4.07	3.87	4	61%	7	21%	11	0.90	3	1.03	22	37	7.1%	15	33.2%	5

2018 ALY by direction:	Left End: 3.30 (5)	Left Tackle: 2.15 (1)	Mid/Guard: 3.93 (4)	Right Tackle: 4.24 (17)	Right End: 4.77 (21)

There are free agents that bust, and free agents that hit so hard they change the entire team. Calais Campbell is one of the latter, with 24 sacks, 73 hurries, and 27 quarterback hits over his first two seasons with the Jaguars. Campbell is entering his age-33 season, with two years left on his contract that would be easy to renegotiate. The NFL's best pass-rushers have tended to show more longevity than expected lately. Campbell could very well cash in again before he's done. He'll play more inside this year with the departure of Malik Jackson. 🦅 SackSEER doesn't have anything that says Josh Allen is super-unique as a first-round edge prospect, but it also doesn't have any reason to doubt him. Allen was uniformly good across the board—sacks, passes defensed, combine numbers—and SackSEER sees him a lot like it saw Ryan Kerrigan. 🦅 Yannick Ngakoue is on a crash course for Franchise Tag Purgatory with 29.5 sacks in his first three seasons. He's heading into the final year of his rookie deal and, while he doesn't have much to offer on run defense, he's one of the best young pass-rushers in the NFL. That's why it wasn't much of a surprise to see him holding out in OTAs. 🦅 The likely favorite to play inside on passing downs next to Campbell is last year's first-round pick, Taven Bryan. Bryan's lone start in his rookie season was the game Derrick Henry ran for 238 yards, though Bryan wasn't on the field for the 99-yard touchdown run. He did show a lack of power at times in that game and will need to show heavier hands to start. 🦅 With Telvin Smith MIA, Myles Jack will likely have to take on his workload as the main coverage linebacker. Jack has the speed for the role, but last year was in more read-and-react situations. This will be a bit more of a test for Jack mentally. 🦅 After tearing his ACL and being usurped by Antonio Morrison and Oren Burks in Green Bay, Jake Ryan is the only depth on this roster with much in the way of starting experience at linebacker. Ryan wasn't counted on in the passing game by the Packers at all. It's possible a youngster (2018 seventh-rounder Leon Jacobs?) or someone unexpected comes in to win the starting job on passing downs next to Jack.

Defensive Secondary

Secondary	Age	Pos	G	Snaps	Plays	TmPct	Rk	Stop	Dfts	BTkl	Runs	St%	Rk	RuYd	Rk	Tgts	Tgt%	Rk	Dist	Suc%	Rk	AdjYd	Rk	PD	Int
Jalen Ramsey	25	CB	16	1020	79	10.3%	12	30	11	8	17	41%	41	5.9	31	89	23.1%	65	14.1	55%	27	7.4	34	14	3
Tashaun Gipson*	29	FS	16	1007	61	8.0%	56	28	9	7	30	50%	21	5.9	24	32	8.4%	26	13.4	69%	4	5.3	6	7	1
A.J. Bouye	28	CB	13	828	62	9.9%	22	24	9	5	14	36%	53	7.8	59	57	18.2%	35	10.0	49%	53	6.3	15	8	1
Barry Church*	31	SS	11	671	40	7.6%	57	18	6	6	22	59%	10	6.0	25	25	9.9%	42	11.8	56%	18	10.1	64	2	1
D.J. Hayden	29	CB	10	457	49	10.2%	--	21	10	4	14	36%	--	4.9	--	34	19.7%	--	5.6	56%	--	5.0	--	4	1
Ronnie Harrison	22	SS	14	328	34	5.1%	73	18	7	4	16	63%	5	3.6	3	11	8.9%	31	7.5	55%	24	4.1	2	3	1
Tyler Patmon*	28	CB	12	232	15	2.6%	--	5	1	1	2	50%	--	4.0	--	14	16.0%	--	12.4	36%	--	9.6	--	1	0

Year	Pass D Rank	vs. #1 WR	Rk	vs. #2 WR	Rk	vs. Other WR	Rk	WR Wide	Rk	WR Slot	Rk	vs. TE	Rk	vs. RB	Rk
2016	15	0.9%	15	4.4%	19	16.1%	29	23.6%	32	-10.1%	7	-1.9%	16	-28.5%	2
2017	1	-58.4%	1	-14.1%	8	-8.5%	11	-36.4%	1	-23.9%	2	2.3%	20	-1.6%	16
2018	6	-15.9%	4	-1.6%	16	-8.3%	11	-8.0%	14	-9.1%	5	-5.9%	13	-12.9%	8

While most outlets were quick to label Jalen Ramsey as having a bad year, most of our statistics don't agree with that. Keep in mind that 39 of his 92 targets came defending Odell Beckham, DeAndre Hopkins, Antonio Brown, and T.Y. Hilton. He had a 59 percent success rate against those players, with three interceptions. 🦅 If you're looking for the player who had a down year, A.J. Bouye is here. He was dinged up and had a 41 percent success rate against 17 combined slant and out routes. 🦅 It was quite unlikely that anybody was going to replicate Aaron Colvin's strong 2017 season, but D.J. Hayden powerfully did not replace it. And, as usual, Hayden got hurt, leaving Tyler Patmon and Tre Herndon to get pasted. 🦅 With Tashaun Gipson off to Houston, and Barry Church mercifully released in December and unsigned as we go to press, the Jaguars are going to be relying on youth at safety. Ronnie Harrison took over for Church and was decent in coverage but poor in run support. Former Michigan UDFA Jarrod Wilson, a converted corner, will probably fit in as the deep safety. The Jags went ahead and re-signed Wilson to a three-year deal after the standard UDFA contract ran out, so they think highly of him. He has still never received a full complement of snaps, so he might be someone who gets exposed as more film comes to the coaches. 🦅 The Jaguars signed a few interesting UDFAs who could get some run this year, including Alabama's Saivion Smith. Smith was the top cornerback recruit in the country in 2016, and has the tall, built profile to play press-man. He also gave up five touchdowns last year with the Crimson Tide, so clearly there's some work to be done.

Special Teams

Year	DVOA	Rank	FG/XP	Rank	Net Kick	Rank	Kick Ret	Rank	Net Punt	Rank	Punt Ret	Rank	Hidden	Rank
2016	-2.3%	23	0.5	14	0.0	16	8.9	5	-8.9	28	-11.8	32	-3.7	21
2017	-2.7%	24	-3.6	22	-8.8	30	-0.5	15	-4.4	21	3.8	6	-7.0	23
2018	4.4%	4	3.7	9	4.0	5	-0.9	16	10.7	1	4.5	8	0.2	16

While the Jaguars crushed it as a punting unit, most of it wasn't from Logan Cooke's punting. He was just about league-average in gross punt value, worth -0.7 points. The coverage though, was outstanding. Corey Davis—the journeyman special-teamer formerly of the Rams, not the Titans No. 1 wideout—led the team with five punt stops and eight total tackles. Second-round pick DJ Chark added four punt stops of his own.   Dede Westbrook added 8.9 return points in 2018, sixth among all punt returners. Kickoffs were more average under the jurisdiction of Rashad Greene, Chark, and Jaydon Mickens. Chark figures to be the main returner of kickoffs this year.   Josh Lambo is established as below average on kickoffs, but when you convert 92.7 percent of your field goals over a two-year period, you get a $15.5-million contract for your troubles anyway.

Kansas City Chiefs

2018 record: 12-4	**Total DVOA:** 32.9% (1st)	**2019 Mean Projection:** 9.3 wins	**On the Clock (0-4):** 4%
Pythagorean Wins: 11.0 (4th)	**Offense:** 34.2% (1st)	**Postseason Odds:** 56.1%	**Mediocrity (5-7):** 20%
Snap-Weighted Age: 26.1 (25th)	**Defense:** 6.9% (26th)	**Super Bowl Odds:** 12.2%	**Playoff Contender (8-10):** 41%
Average Opponent: 0.5% (12th)	**Special Teams:** 5.6% (2nd)	**Proj. Avg. Opponent:** 2.2% (8th)	**Super Bowl Contender (11+):** 35%

2018: All offense and no defense makes Patrick something something.

2019: Always harder the second time around.

"Bringing [Patrick] Mahomes along and seeing him deliver on his potential would be as important as anything else the Chiefs could realistically accomplish this season. Though the record may not reflect it right away, the Chiefs are bringing on a better, more exciting identity."

—*Football Outsiders Almanac 2018*

"Better and more exciting" makes an excellent subtitle for the 2018 Chiefs season. It may not quite have ended like fans would have hoped, but holy cow, was it a fantastic ride to get there. The 2018 Chiefs were the best team in football. Their 32.9% DVOA was the highest we've ever recorded for the franchise, going back to 1986. They reached their first conference championship game since 1993, winning their first home playoff game in a quarter century.

Their offense thrilled; the most explosive and exciting attack in a year defined by explosive and exciting attacks. The Chiefs had the fifth-best offensive DVOA we have ever recorded; they lapped the field in in almost any metric you choose to look at, especially if you focus on the passing game. And they were led by Patrick Mahomes, the most valuable asset in football. Taking a first-round quarterback when they were already a playoff contender with a perfectly serviceable player like Alex Smith under center was a huge gamble, but it paid off better than anyone could possibly have dreamed. Mahomes became just the fourth quarterback since the merger to win an MVP award in his first two seasons, and the first to do it under the current CBA put into place in 2011. Analysis from salary cap experts Spotrac put Mahomes' value on the open market at around $35.2 million a year; the Chiefs get him for three more seasons at an average of just over $4 million. That gives Kansas City a championship window rarely rivalled in the modern NFL.

Yes, the defense was bad, but that just means the Chiefs had a clear area to work on in the offseason. They fired defensive coordinator Bob Sutton and brought in Steve Spagnuolo to implement his 4-3 defense. Keep the offense up to speed, crank the defense back in the general direction of league average, and you surely have the Super Bowl favorites, right?

Well, maybe not quite the *favorites*. We still have the Chiefs as major contenders in 2019, but just half a rung behind the top trio in the league. In fact, we don't even have Kansas City as favorites in the AFC West, as the Chargers join the Patriots and Saints atop our DVOA projections.

Please, put down the pitchforks and torches.

It is very, very difficult to repeat an offensive performance like the Chiefs had in 2018. The unspoken corollary of being the fifth-best offense in the DVOA era is that teams aren't able to consistently perform at that high level on a year-after-year basis. To put up a DVOA above 25.0%, you need to be lucky as well as really good—players having career seasons, a lack of key injuries, missing out on December snowstorms, and so forth. Those aren't things that a team can control, and it is very difficult to keep that momentum going year after year.

Not including the 2018 Chiefs, 28 teams have had an offensive DVOA of 25.0% or higher. These teams dropped by an average of 14.2% DVOA the next season, and 27 out of those 28 teams saw at least some regression. The average DVOA for those 28 teams in the following season was 16.8%—generally a top-five unit, because we're talking about some of the best offenses we've ever seen. But that's a far cry from 34.2%.

Three teams have managed to put together consecutive excellent offensive years, shrugging off the effects of regression to the mean. The Patriots did it four straight years from 2009 to 2012, with the 2009 team being the one team to actually see their great offensive DVOA improve. The 1992-93 49ers pulled off the feat as well, as did the 2002-04 Chiefs, the last time Kansas City tried an all-offense, no-defense spectacular. It's not inconceivable that Kansas City could join that list with a smaller-than-average drop-off; it's easier to stay above that 25.0% DVOA water line when you're nearly ten points above it. But it's hard, and it's rare, and it's not the only thing that indicates a potential decline in 2019.

The Plexiglass Principle, first coined by baseball stats legend Bill James, states that teams which significantly improve (or decline) in one season have a tendency to relapse or bounce back in the next. Progress is generally slow and gradual; personnel changes and standard player development tend not to produce large season-to-season fluctuations. A large jump indicates that that a significant chunk of luck was involved, on top of any sustainable on-field gains. That doesn't mean that the team's underlying talent level *didn't* improve, or that all the gains were phantom, just that at least some of the leap can be chalked up to the randomness present in a 16-game sample size.

The Chiefs saw their overall DVOA increase by 22.3 percentage points last year. Historically, teams in that 20- to

2019 Chiefs Schedule

Week	Opp.	Week	Opp.	Week	Opp.
1	at JAX	7	at DEN (Thu.)	13	OAK
2	at OAK	8	GB	14	at NE
3	BAL	9	MIN	15	DEN
4	at DET	10	at TEN	16	at CHI
5	IND	11	at LAC (Mon./Mex.)	17	LAC
6	HOU	12	BYE		

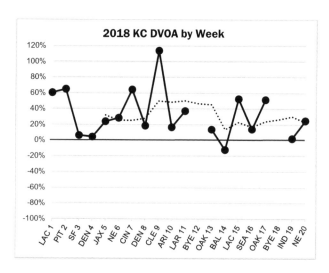

30-point increase range have lost between a third and half of those gains the season after (Table 1). About 40 percent of them fall right back to where they started, erasing essentially all their gains from the year prior. Last season, three teams had entered the 20/20 club—teams with at least a 20.0% DVOA and a 20-point improvement from the year before. All three of them (Saints, Rams, and Vikings) had a lower DVOA last season. It wouldn't be unprecedented if the Chiefs topped the DVOA charts again in 2019, but they almost certainly will come back towards the pack at least somewhat.

Table 1. Plexiglass Bounces, 1987-2017

DVOA Change	Teams	DVOA Change Y+1	Win Change Y+1	Pct of Teams Improving	Pct of Teams Declining
+30% or better	44	-9.0%	-1.1	25.0%	75.0%
+20% to 30%	84	-10.3%	-1.9	26.2%	73.8%
+10% to +20%	170	-5.9%	-1.0	35.9%	64.1%
0% to +10%	169	-0.3%	+0.3	46.7%	53.3%
-10% to 0%	205	+1.1%	+0.4	51.2%	48.8%
-20% to -10%	142	+3.5%	+0.1	59.2%	40.8%
-30% to -20%	83	+11.0%	+2.3	77.1%	22.9%
-30% or worse	48	+14.5%	+2.2	83.3%	16.7%

It's not all doom and gloom, mind you. Two of those three 20/20 club members were the Saints and Rams, who had 13-win seasons and played each other in the NFC Championship Game. When you start high enough, even a season of regression leaves you among the contenders. The Chiefs were a good team in 2017, so even losing all of last year's gains would keep them in playoff contention. And, of course, most teams in the sample set didn't add the league MVP to their starting lineup.

While Plexiglass hits everyone, the regression isn't as severe when the improvement comes alongside changes at either head coach, quarterback, or both. Kansas City fans should be familiar with that already. The biggest year-to-year improvement we've ever recorded came from the 2013 Chiefs, who saw their DVOA shoot up 57.6 points. The fact that that improvement came at the same time Romeo Crennel and Matt Cassel were replaced by Andy Reid and Alex Smith is not coincidental. The 2014 Chiefs did slip back a little bit, but the franchise has ranked in the top 10 in DVOA every year since.

Because the Chiefs' improvement came alongside Mahomes taking the reins from Smith, there's reason to believe Kansas City can fight off some of that regression. Teams that saw a 20.0% DVOA increase without swapping quarterbacks saw their DVOA fall by 13.0% the year after. Teams that saw that increase while replacing the man under center only fell 6.8%. Mahomes replacing Smith, Smith replacing Cassel, Trent Green replacing Elvis Grbac—Chiefs fans have seen, time and time again, just how much an upgrade at quarterback can do for the franchise as a whole.

A season like Mahomes' 2018 doesn't come along every year. Mahomes didn't just lead the league in DYAR; he had the highest DYAR for someone 25 or under we've ever recorded (Table 2). That does come with an asterisk as we do not yet have full play-by-play to analyze Dan Marino's 1984 MVP year yet, but outside of that, we have never seen a quarterback dominate at such a young age like Mahomes—and it's not like the top of that table is filled with a bunch of one-and-done flukes, either. To make matters even juicier for Chiefs fans, Mahomes' 2,039 DYAR shattered the record for most DYAR in a first year as a starter. It was a hell of a debut for 2017's first-round pick.

Table 2. Best Passing DYAR, 25 and Under

Player	Year	Team	Age	DYAR	DVOA	Year Starting
Patrick Mahomes	2018	KC	23	2039	40.1%	First
Peyton Manning	2000	IND	24	1888	38.3%	Third
Dan Marino	1986	MIA	25	1693	29.2%	Fourth
Peyton Manning	1999	IND	23	1581	34.0%	Second
Daunte Culpepper	2000	MIN	23	1352	30.1%	First
Dak Prescott	2016	DAL	23	1302	31.6%	First
Bernie Kosar	1987	CLE	24	1284	36.3%	Third
Jim Everett	1988	LAR	25	1281	23.6%	Second
Boomer Esiason	1986	CIN	25	1268	28.6%	Second
Jay Cutler	2008	DEN	25	1172	17.0%	Second

The previous record for DYAR by a first-year starter belonged to 28-year-old Kurt Warner with 1,586 DYAR in 1999.

A season like that is a tough act to follow. The only quarterback to have more than one season at or above Mahomes' 2018 DYAR is Peyton Manning. The only other quarterback to have multiple seasons above 2,000 DYAR is Tom Brady. It's not something mere mortals have been able to manage. There's no reason to expect that Mahomes won't be among the very best quarterbacks in the league this year—our KUBIAK projections have him with the most yards and touchdowns, and ranked in the top five in DVOA—but a season as good as his 2018 isn't something that can be counted on year after year.

Luck might even itself out some in 2019. Mahomes only had 12 interceptions on the year, but threw 10 more passes that were dropped by defenders per Sports Info Solutions' charting. That tied for the most in the league. Even when you take away Mahomes' one Hail Mary interception, he finished the season with 21 adjusted picks, tied for the most in the league and entering the bottom ten in adjusted interception rate. If you were going to critique anything about last season, it would be his decision-making; he trusts his arm enough to throw it into traffic rather than throw the ball away. The ending to the Rams-Chiefs game is a perfect example; Mahomes threw an interception to Lamarcus Joyner in double coverage to end the game, rather than tossing it out of bounds and facing second-and-10. He spent most of last season not getting burned for poor decisions. We're not saying he's due for a boatload of picks in 2019, just that his exceptional luck when making those bad decisions isn't a sustainable skill.

Mahomes' supporting cast also got a little bit weaker over the offseason. Mitch Morse is gone to Buffalo. Chris Conley's departure leaves a question mark at the third receiver position. The Chiefs' offense did get worse when Kareem Hunt was cut after multiple off-field assault accusations, although they lost more from his receiving value than his rushing value. Carlos Hyde has been brought in to compete with Damien Williams there, but neither is the game-changer Hunt can be. And then…

Just before draft day, disturbing reports broke about Tyreek Hill and an investigation into child abuse of his three-year-old son, complete with a disturbing audio release. Hill categorically denies the child abuse claims but does not deny spanking his child with a belt. At time of writing, the police investigation into the matter is not active, but the Child Protection Services investigation and an existing family court case both still are. Hill was suspended by the team from offseason activities but appears set to re-join the team for training camp. The NFL has not yet indicated if, and for how long, Hill will be suspended. It's a mess of a situation with disturbing elements all around, and it's not approaching anything like a clear conclusion as of press time.[1]

The entire situation and the NFL's delay on ruling on Hill's punishment, is frustrating and disturbing on a wide number of levels, the *least* important of which is the implications on Kansas City's offensive projection. Still, as distasteful as it is, we must talk about it some, because losing a player of Hill's skills will have a significant effect on the Chiefs' passing game. Adrian Peterson received an indefinite stay on the Commissioner's Exempt List after using corporal punishment on his child, but he was indicted by a grand jury; Hill does not currently face any criminal charges. More recently, Jimmy Smith was suspended four games for threatening and emotionally abusive behaviors, but he didn't have a college assault conviction on his record; Hill does. Those would seem to be the ceiling and floor for potential Hill suspensions, and we won't be able to say much more about it until the commissioner makes a final say on the matter. One way or another, until Hill is cleared to play, the Chiefs will be missing three of their top five receivers from 2018.

The timing of the Hill news meant that the Chiefs had little time and even less certainty when it came to responding at a personnel level. They ended up addressing the situation in the draft, trading up to take receiver Mecole Hardman out of Georgia with their first selection. Hardman was a bit of a reach at 52, though we were in the middle of a wideout run and Hardman was a combine superstar, perhaps just needing an MVP-caliber quarterback to turn his speed and quickness into actual production. However, it's easy to imagine, in a world where Hill is still in everyone's good graces, that the Chiefs would have used their first pick on defensive help, as they did with their subsequent three picks.

The Chiefs did bring in a bunch of defensive talent this offseason. Virginia safety Juan Thornhill and Western Illinois defensive tackle Khalen Saunders were excellent Day 2 picks. Free agent Tyrann Mathieu was once arguably the top safety in the league and now is another year removed from his torn ACL. Frank Clark and Emmanuel Ogbah came over in trades to provide a pass rush, as did free agent Alex Okafor. That's a pretty good group of additions, an excellent start to a rebuilding process.

The trouble is, the Chiefs also saw a significant amount of talent go *out*. Eric Berry, Justin Houston, Dee Ford, Steven Nelson, and Allen Bailey are all gone, so it's not a case of the Chiefs simply adding talent to their defense for 2019; they're *replacing* a lot of players who have been significant contributors. The Chiefs added more talent than they lost, especially when you factor in the switch from a 3-4 to a 4-3 front. That doesn't mean it was a case of addition by subtraction by getting rid of so many of last year's starters; it's a step back that's hopefully obscured by multiple steps forward.

Adding talent to the defense, coupled with some simple regression back towards the mean, gives Chiefs fans two reasons for expecting their defense to be notably better in 2019. Our projections have them as a below-average unit, which would still be an improvement over the past couple seasons. Expecting them to be much better than that, however, doesn't really stand up to scrutiny.

One argument some have made in favor of the defense is how it improved down the stretch. They may have ranked

26th with a 6.9% DVOA overall, but by the end of the year, they were firmly in the middle of the pack in weighted DVOA at 2.5%. That's something to build on going forward, right? Well, maybe not. There is no indication that having a better weighted DVOA than total season DVOA carries over to the next year, especially when it's not accompanied by an obvious sparking factor like a rookie entering the starting lineup. The season-long stats are better to look at when projecting future success, and the season-long stats for the Chiefs were bad.

The other argument is that Spagnuolo is going to come in and fix all of Sutton's issues, getting more out of the players that remain and employing a better, more aggressive strategy. Spagnuolo's defense is definitely very different from Sutton's, for reasons that go far beyond the change to an even front. Sutton's defenses were often criticized for being too complex; Spagnuolo's defenses are more straightforward, with easier-to-understand roles and assignments on any given play. He tends to favor more exotic blitzes, and a greater number of them than Sutton utilized. You'll see more zone coverage under Spags, with more corners and safeties joining in on the pass rush. It'll be different, at the very least, and that's something.

But it takes time for a new defensive coordinator to put his stamp on a team. It takes a year or two for the right personnel to get into place, and for existing players to truly understand the nuances of the new system. New defensive coordinators rarely provide instant success unless they are named "Wade Phillips." The Chiefs are unlikely to be better defensively in 2019 because of their scheme; improvement will come from the new talent added and positive regression.

To be clear, we still expect the Chiefs to be among the top teams in the league. We expect that their offense will still be explosive and exciting, just not quite at the level it was last season. We expect that their defense will be improved, just not to the level where it makes up for the offensive regression. We would not be remotely surprised if the 2019 season ends with Andy Reid standing in Hard Rock Stadium, finally lifting the Lombardi that has been so elusive throughout his career. We've been negative and nitpicky throughout this essay, because finding flaws in the Chiefs' offense requires picking nits.

But we have the Chiefs as *a* top team, and not *the* top team, and that's a significant difference. Vegas has the Chiefs as odds-on favorites to win the Super Bowl this year, and we just can't get on board with that. There's every reason to believe that the Chiefs will be in the championship conversation for years to come, but we can't quite put them at the very top of the league for 2019.

Bryan Knowles

2018 Chiefs by Week

Wk	vs.	W-L	PF	PA	YDF	YDA	TO	Total	Off	Def	ST
1	at LAC	W	38	28	362	541	+2	60%	44%	19%	36%
2	at PIT	W	42	37	449	475	-1	65%	78%	19%	6%
3	SF	W	38	27	384	406	0	6%	32%	30%	4%
4	at DEN	W	27	23	446	385	+1	4%	30%	23%	-3%
5	JAX	W	30	14	424	502	+3	24%	15%	1%	10%
6	at NE	L	40	43	446	500	-1	29%	10%	10%	28%
7	CIN	W	45	10	551	239	0	64%	45%	-29%	-9%
8	DEN	W	30	23	340	411	+1	19%	22%	1%	-3%
9	at CLE	W	37	21	499	388	0	114%	119%	9%	4%
10	ARI	W	26	14	330	260	+2	17%	23%	6%	1%
11	at LAR	L	51	54	546	455	-3	37%	31%	1%	7%
12	BYE										
13	at OAK	W	40	33	469	442	+2	14%	41%	24%	-4%
14	BAL	W	27	24	442	321	0	-12%	18%	10%	-20%
15	LAC	L	28	29	294	407	+2	53%	29%	-11%	12%
16	at SEA	L	31	38	419	464	-2	14%	21%	26%	19%
17	OAK	W	35	3	409	292	+3	52%	14%	-38%	1%
18	BYE										
19	IND	W	31	13	433	266	0	2%	12%	-15%	-26%
20	NE	L	31	37	290	524	+2	25%	24%	-2%	-1%

Trends and Splits

	Offense	Rank	Defense	Rank
Total DVOA	34.2%	1	6.9%	26
Unadjusted VOA	33.1%	1	6.1%	24
Weighted Trend	30.6%	1	2.5%	17
Variance	7.7%	22	3.6%	2
Average Opponent	-0.9%	11	0.6%	14
Passing	62.9%	1	4.7%	12
Rushing	11.0%	4	9.8%	32
First Down	20.0%	4	4.3%	22
Second Down	43.9%	1	-0.3%	16
Third Down	51.0%	1	25.1%	29
First Half	42.4%	1	1.7%	20
Second Half	25.6%	1	12.2%	28
Red Zone	40.0%	1	5.6%	21
Late and Close	29.6%	2	6.1%	25

Five-Year Performance

Year	W-L	Pyth W	Est W	PF	PA	TO	Total	Rk	Off	Rk	Def	Rk	ST	Rk	Off AGL	Rk	Def AGL	Rk	Off Age	Rk	Def Age	Rk	ST Age	Rk
2014	9-7	10.1	9.4	353	281	-3	10.4%	10	5.0%	12	1.3%	19	6.7%	3	36.0	20	62.8	27	26.6	19	26.6	20	25.7	26
2015	11-5	11.2	11.4	405	287	+14	25.2%	5	11.7%	6	-11.6%	6	2.0%	9	26.3	13	28.6	18	25.8	28	27.4	5	25.8	19
2016	12-4	10.1	9.7	389	311	+16	13.5%	6	2.9%	13	-2.8%	14	7.8%	1	33.2	14	66.1	30	25.9	26	26.5	16	25.1	31
2017	10-6	10.0	10.0	415	339	+15	10.6%	10	15.9%	4	10.7%	30	5.3%	4	43.1	21	36.9	18	26.3	26	27.1	5	25.9	16
2018	12-4	11.0	13.1	565	421	+11	32.9%	1	34.2%	1	6.9%	26	5.6%	2	36.5	16	24.3	9	26.0	27	26.2	15	25.7	18

2018 Performance Based on Most Common Personnel Groups

KC Offense					KC Offense vs. Opponents					KC Defense				KC Defense vs. Opponents			
Pers	Freq	Yds	DVOA	Run%	Pers	Freq	Yds	DVOA	Run%	Pers	Freq	Yds	DVOA	Pers	Freq	Yds	DVOA
11	61%	7.1	46.7%	32%	Base	16%	6.1	33.5%	51%	Base	23%	6.5	16.7%	11	71%	6.0	3.6%
12	27%	7.3	40.0%	34%	Nickel	55%	6.8	33.8%	37%	Nickel	61%	5.9	-2.3%	12	10%	6.6	23.2%
21	6%	6.2	19.4%	50%	Dime+	19%	8.3	72.9%	15%	Dime+	15%	6.5	36.0%	21	10%	6.8	24.2%
22	3%	4.3	33.8%	59%						Goal Line	1%	0.5	-15.0%	22	5%	6.6	27.3%
01	2%	8.7	20.3%	10%										13	2%	3.3	-54.3%

Strategic Tendencies

Run/Pass		Rk	Formation		Rk	Pass Rush		Rk	Secondary		Rk	Strategy		Rk
Runs, first half	30%	31	Form: Single Back	83%	12	Rush 3	11.2%	10	4 DB	23%	17	Play action	29%	7
Runs, first down	41%	27	Form: Empty Back	9%	12	Rush 4	66.7%	18	5 DB	61%	18	Avg Box (Off)	6.09	28
Runs, second-long	26%	23	Pers: 3+ WR	63%	23	Rush 5	17.2%	15	6+ DB	15%	13	Avg Box (Def)	6.22	19
Runs, power sit.	52%	22	Pers: 2+ TE/6+ OL	30%	6	Rush 6+	4.9%	18	CB by Sides	86%	9	Offensive Pace	29.92	6
Runs, behind 2H	21%	26	Pers: 6+ OL	1%	24	Int DL Sacks	46.2%	3	S/CB Cover Ratio	22%	28	Defensive Pace	29.66	3
Pass, ahead 2H	51%	13	Shotgun/Pistol	81%	1	Second Level Sacks	8.7%	30	DB Blitz	5%	29	Go for it on 4th	1.55	13

Kansas City led the league with 163 penalties; no other team was above 150. The Chiefs were first in defensive penalties and second in offensive penalties. ✎ The Chiefs were much less likely to run in short-yardage power situations compared to the year before, with 52 percent (22nd) runs last year but 74 percent (first) in 2017. ✎ Running on second-and-long is usually a terrible strategy, but it was a great one for the Chiefs in 2018. They led the league with 39.4% DVOA and 6.8 yards per carry on these runs. ✎ Kansas City had the league's largest (opposite) DVOA difference between play-action and not using play-action. But this gap came mostly because the Chiefs were just so good on all pass plays. Kansas City's 74.8% DVOA without play-action was double any other offense; their 43.4% DVOA with play-action still ranked sixth. ✎ Kansas City threw the ball at or behind the line of scrimmage on 22.8 percent of passes, third-most in the league. They had the league's best DVOA on these passes and ranked fourth with 10.9 average yards after the catch. But again, Kansas City was good at everything. On passes beyond the line of scrimmage, only Seattle had a better DVOA and only San Francisco and Pittsburgh had more average yards after the catch. ✎ Another place where the Chiefs offense excelled: with an empty backfield they ranked second with both 9.1 yards per play and 82.7% DVOA. ✎ Oh, and the Chiefs had an obscene 11.2 yards per play and 168.3% DVOA on running back screens; they were tied for third in how frequently they used the play. ✎ The one thing the Chiefs had trouble with on offense? They ranked just 25th in DVOA running the ball on third or fourth down. ✎ Patrick Mahomes had a league-leading 13.1 net yards per play against a three-man pass rush—over 4 yards higher than any other offense—even though the Chiefs also led the league in pass pressure allowed against three-man rushes (43 percent). ✎ Kansas City was the only team which ran zero plays all year without a tight end on the field. ✎ Kansas City used dime personnel on defense roughly one-third as often as they did the year before. ✎ The Chiefs defense was excellent against screens, seventh with -14.9% DVOA against wide receiver screens and third with -76.5% DVOA against running back screens. ✎ An example of how time of possession doesn't necessarily correlate with winning: Kansas City ranked 27th in the NFL with an average of 28:51 time of possession per game.

Passing

Player	DYAR	DVOA	Plays	NtYds	Avg	YAC	C%	TD	Int
P.Mahomes	2031	39.9%	607	4910	8.1	6.8	66.4%	50	11

Rushing

Player	DYAR	DVOA	Plays	Yds	Avg	TD	Fum	Suc
K.Hunt*	134	9.1%	181	840	4.6	8	0	55%
S.Ware*	38	9.0%	51	246	4.8	2	0	45%
Dam.Williams	79	26.4%	50	257	5.1	4	1	62%
P.Mahomes	39	3.0%	47	276	5.9	2	1	--
T.Hill	89	29.7%	21	154	7.3	1	0	--
Dar.Williams	-1	-10.2%	13	44	3.4	0	0	62%
S.Watkins	3	-31.0%	5	52	10.4	0	1	--
C.Hyde	-18	-11.0%	172	588	3.4	5	2	39%

Receiving

Player	DYAR	DVOA	Plays	Ctch	Yds	Y/C	YAC	TD	C%
T.Hill	387	23.8%	137	87	1479	17.0	6.1	12	64%
S.Watkins	161	24.1%	55	40	519	13.0	6.0	3	73%
C.Conley*	48	-1.0%	52	32	334	10.4	4.4	5	62%
D.Robinson	68	13.5%	33	22	288	13.1	5.3	4	67%
T.Kelce	196	11.5%	150	103	1336	13.0	5.5	10	69%
D.Harris*	-14	-15.6%	25	12	164	13.7	6.3	3	48%
B.Bell	1	-5.0%	11	8	67	8.4	4.8	0	73%
N.Sterling	-8	-22.8%	8	6	47	7.8	4.8	0	75%
K.Hunt*	198	79.4%	35	26	378	14.5	13.0	7	74%
Dam.Williams	74	33.9%	24	23	160	7.0	9.3	2	96%
S.Ware*	85	56.1%	23	20	224	11.2	12.3	0	87%
A.Sherman	48	77.7%	9	8	96	12.0	7.0	1	89%
C.Hyde	-51	-73.3%	16	10	33	3.3	5.9	0	63%

Offensive Line

Player	Pos	Age	GS	Snaps	Pen	Sk	Pass	Run	Player	Pos	Age	GS	Snaps	Pen	Sk	Pass	Run
Mitchell Schwartz	RT	30	16/16	1045	5	5.0	18	5	Mitch Morse*	C	27	11/11	678	4	0.0	0	1
Eric Fisher	LT	28	16/16	1042	8	4.5	16	5	Laurent Duvernay-Tardif	RG	28	5/5	331	5	0.0	2	0
Cameron Erving	LG	27	14/13	830	12	2.0	14	5	Austin Reiter	C	28	11/4	265	0	1.0	2	1
Andrew Wylie	RG	25	16/10	687	2	2.0	6	2	Jeff Allen*	LG	29	10/4	224	2	0.5	4	1

Year	Yards	ALY	Rank	Power	Rank	Stuff	Rank	2nd Lev	Rank	Open Field	Rank	Sacks	ASR	Rank	Press	Rank	F-Start	Cont.
2016	3.91	4.10	17	59%	21	18%	10	1.04	27	0.57	22	32	5.7%	14	21.0%	5	23	32
2017	4.66	4.14	12	82%	1	18%	8	1.23	9	1.17	2	37	6.7%	17	31.4%	18	18	24
2018	4.66	4.37	16	72%	4	18%	13	1.27	18	1.01	11	26	5.4%	5	33.2%	24	24	28

2018 ALY by direction: Left End: 2.67 (30)   Left Tackle: 5.97 (2)   Mid/Guard: 4.29 (20)   Right Tackle: 5.64 (2)   Right End: 3.95 (20)

Kansas City's high ranking in adjusted sack rate is slightly inflated by how good Patrick Mahomes was. The Chiefs allowed just 16 sacks on blown blocks, but had 65 blown pass blocks in total. That's one sack per four blown blocks, the fifth-highest rate in the league. ❧ Mitchell Schwartz surprisingly ranked very high with 23 blown blocks, the third-highest total among right tackles. That goes well against his public perception, but it's mostly the result of one bad day. Ten of those blown blocks came against Baltimore in Week 14, as Matt Judon and Terrell Suggs routinely beat him around the edge. Apart from that, he mostly lived up to his All-Pro billing, with an 86 percent pass-block win rate per ESPN. ❧ While Schwartz was a first-team All-Pro, he ended up staying at home during Pro Bowl weekend. Instead, it was Eric Fisher who earned a nod as the Chiefs' tackle going to Orlando. Schwartz was certainly a better player than Fisher was, but Fisher has improved significantly over the past few seasons, going from top-pick bust to a solid, if unspectacular, player. ❧ Cameron Erving had 15 flags thrown against him last season, second-most in the league. He ranked 94th out of 107 interior linemen with a blown block every 43.7 snaps. He is, by far, the weakest link on the line; rookie Andrew Wylie was better last season and may end up taking the job from him. ❧ Wylie got his snaps while replacing Laurent Duvernay-Tardif, who broke his leg in October. The return of LDT, M.D., at RG should be OK for the KC OL. ❧ With Mitch Morse gone to Buffalo, journeyman Austin Reiter will slide into the starting center spot. He started four games, allowing three blown blocks and a sack. That's more of each than Morse gave up all year.

Defensive Front

Defensive Line	Age	Pos	G	Snaps	Plays	Overall TmPct	Rk	Stop	Dfts	BTkl	vs. Run Runs	St%	Rk	RuYd	Rk	Pass Rush Sack	Hit	Hur	Dsrpt
Allen Bailey*	30	DE	16	847	37	4.2%	59	34	12	8	28	89%	4	1.8	22	6.0	4	25	0
Chris Jones	25	DE	16	773	44	5.0%	38	36	27	6	20	65%	74	2.6	58	15.5	15	35	4
Derrick Nnadi	23	DT	16	448	35	4.0%	--	29	2	5	35	83%	--	2.5	--	0.0	0	10	0
Xavier Williams	27	DT	16	424	47	5.4%	--	30	4	7	41	63%	--	3.0	--	2.5	1	6	0

Edge Rushers	Age	Pos	G	Snaps	Plays	TmPct	Rk	Stop	Dfts	BTkl	Runs	St%	Rk	RuYd	Rk	Sack	Hit	Hur	Dsrpt
Dee Ford*	28	OLB	16	1021	52	6.0%	24	38	21	3	31	68%	63	2.1	35	13.0	18	49	1
Justin Houston*	30	OLB	12	665	38	5.8%	26	29	19	6	20	75%	44	2.4	45	9.0	5	26	1
Breeland Speaks	24	OLB	16	476	24	2.8%	89	11	4	6	16	44%	92	5.1	93	1.5	7	12	0
Emmanuel Ogbah	26	DE	14	806	48	6.2%	16	30	12	5	35	51%	90	3.4	77	3.0	5	28	6
Frank Clark	26	DE	16	728	41	5.4%	35	34	21	11	19	79%	28	2.4	47	13.0	13	34	1
Alex Okafor	28	DE	16	656	36	4.5%	56	29	8	3	28	82%	20	2.9	58	4.0	7	25	1

Linebackers	Age	Pos	G	Snaps	Plays	TmPct	Rk	Stop	Dfts	BTkl	Runs	St%	Rk	RuYd	Rk	Sack	Hit	Hur	Tgts	Suc%	Rk	AdjYd	Rk	PD	Int
Anthony Hitchens	27	ILB	15	944	131	16.0%	18	54	17	13	82	48%	81	5.0	80	0.0	3	3	37	32%	76	8.4	68	0	0
Reggie Ragland	26	ILB	16	582	87	10.0%	56	33	6	15	72	42%	87	4.4	67	0.5	0	2	12	50%	41	7.3	53	1	1
Dorian O'Daniel	25	ILB	16	302	30	3.4%	--	19	5	5	12	75%	--	3.3	--	0.0	1	2	13	62%	67	4.2	61	1	0
Terrance Smith*	26	ILB	7	172	21	5.5%	--	7	4	4	3	33%	--	5.7	--	1.0	0	1.5	15	47%	--	7.1	--	0	0
Darron Lee	25	ILB	12	808	78	12.6%	41	46	12	5	43	65%	22	2.8	11	0.0	2	3	34	62%	7	4.1	5	5	3

Year	Yards	ALY	Rank	Power	Rank	Stuff	Rank	2nd Level	Rank	Open Field	Rank	Sacks	ASR	Rank	Press	Rank
2016	4.43	4.72	30	65%	22	18%	19	1.39	30	0.47	5	28	5.1%	26	24.4%	27
2017	4.23	4.35	26	60%	10	20%	23	1.35	31	0.55	5	31	5.8%	26	30.3%	16
2018	4.97	5.28	32	78%	30	15%	27	1.57	32	0.72	12	52	8.0%	7	31.5%	11

2018 ALY by direction: Left End: 6.10 (32) Left Tackle: 4.03 (15) Mid/Guard: 5.19 (31) Right Tackle: 6.55 (32) Right End: 5.25 (26)

With Kansas City shifting from a 3-4 to a 4-3 front, there was plenty of turnover in the front seven this offseason. The Chiefs had to focus on finding players to fit Steve Spagnuolo's roles, rather than replacing like-for-like, so some of the moves were really lateral ones for 2019. ● Dee Ford and Justin Houston are out; Frank Clark is in. While Clark had as many sacks as Ford did in 2018, Ford out-pressured him 48.5 to 33.5, which was a career high for Clark. He's young and undeniably talented, but 2018 was the first season where it felt like Clark truly hit his potential, hitting his high-water mark in essentially any pass-rushing stat you care to use. Kansas City will need to hope Clark's Superman turn wasn't an imaginary tale. ● Clark will be joined by Alex Okafor and Emmanuel Ogbah in the All-New, All-Different edge rushing corps. Okafor's a better run-stuffer than pass-rusher, while Ogbah has only managed 12.5 sacks over the past three years. The unit as a group is not improved over Ford/Houston in 2018, though they will likely be better than Ford and Houston would be in a 4-3 front. ● By the time you're reading this, Chris Jones may have joined Clark as the second $20 million man on Kansas City's front line. Jones was second only to Aaron Donald among interior linemen in yards per play allowed, and he ranked near the top of the league in pass pressures, finishing second in the league in pass-rush win rate among defensive tackles. A contract extension is an absolute must for the Chiefs' front office. ● Derrick Nnadi showed promise as a run-stuffer as a rookie; had he enough snaps to qualify, he would have been in the top 20 in run stop rate. ● Third-round pick Khalen Saunders from Western Illinois should start in a rotational role as he bulks up to NFL size. He dominated double-teams at the FCS level and flashed some of that disruption in the Senior Bowl. An interesting one-gap prospect to watch. ● Off-ball linebacker was arguably Kansas City's worst position a year ago, and now they'll need three of them. Reggie Ragland will presumably take over the Mike role; he had a 26 percent broken tackle rate and the second-worst run stop rate among linebackers a year ago. ● Anthony Hitchens was a free-agent bust replacing Derrick Johnson a year ago; he'll have to fight for his job against Jets bust Darron Lee, looking for a fresh start in a new system. ● Ex-Cowboys reserve Damien Wilson was brought in to compete at strongside linebacker. Dorian O'Daniel will fight for the spot; he was the best sideline-to-sideline player the Chiefs had a year ago but should not be asked to read interior gaps.

Defensive Secondary

Secondary	Age	Pos	G	Snaps	Plays	TmPct	Rk	Stop	Dfts	BTkl	Runs	St%	Rk	RuYd	Rk	Tgts	Tgt%	Rk	Dist	Suc%	Rk	AdjYd	Rk	PD	Int
Steven Nelson*	26	CB	16	1164	83	9.5%	26	29	11	13	18	22%	72	8.3	63	109	21.0%	54	14.3	59%	12	7.0	28	15	4
Kendall Fuller	24	CB	15	1078	94	11.5%	6	41	19	14	23	39%	45	7.3	54	88	18.3%	36	9.7	47%	60	8.2	52	12	2
Ron Parker*	32	FS	15	1026	82	10.0%	40	19	6	12	29	21%	65	10.8	69	44	9.6%	37	14.4	39%	67	11.4	69	5	2
Orlando Scandrick*	32	CB	15	788	57	7.0%	63	29	10	6	6	17%	75	9.8	72	87	24.8%	69	12.2	60%	10	5.4	4	13	1
Eric Murray*	25	FS	15	702	56	6.9%	63	12	5	4	21	29%	60	9.2	58	30	9.6%	36	13.2	40%	65	8.4	52	2	1
Daniel Sorensen	29	SS	7	354	28	7.3%	--	11	2	5	13	38%	--	7.5	--	16	10.1%	--	9.8	63%	--	6.2	--	2	1
Jordan Lucas	26	FS	16	262	30	3.4%	--	6	4	5	14	14%	--	7.4	--	13	11.1%	--	10.5	31%	--	11.2	--	2	1
Charvarius Ward	23	CB	13	139	21	3.0%	--	5	1	0	4	0%	--	7.5	--	17	27.4%	--	12.1	35%	--	10.1	--	3	0
Tyrann Mathieu	27	FS	16	1045	97	11.5%	22	42	17	12	27	59%	9	5.0	13	43	10.3%	48	9.7	53%	30	8.1	50	8	2
Bashaud Breeland	27	CB	7	329	24	6.7%	--	11	4	6	8	63%	--	3.3	--	25	19.7%	--	12.6	60%	--	7.8	--	4	2

Year	Pass D Rank	vs. #1 WR	Rk	vs. #2 WR	Rk	vs. Other WR	Rk	WR Wide	Rk	WR Slot	Rk	vs. TE	Rk	vs. RB	Rk
2016	7	0.2%	14	-10.0%	6	-24.9%	3	-9.4%	10	-13.4%	4	3.4%	20	-20.5%	4
2017	23	29.5%	31	-6.0%	14	0.8%	18	2.3%	20	19.6%	26	-5.9%	12	-23.1%	3
2018	12	-9.2%	9	-23.8%	5	21.6%	29	-9.8%	13	-0.1%	16	19.1%	25	7.3%	21

As bad as Kansas City's defense was last year, the secondary managed to hold its own—they were one of five teams to rank in the top 10 covering both No. 1 and No. 2 receivers. It was just every *other* aspect of pass coverage that let the Chiefs down last season. Kendall Fuller is the one returning cornerback who qualified for our cornerback charting stats a year ago; he finished just 60th out of 79 in success rate. He'll once again start outside and then move to the slot in nickel. Bashaud Breeland will be moving back to the outside for Kansas City after a year in the slot in Green Bay. This is better for his skill set and he has had more success when getting to play the boundary. He's an up-and-down player who peaks at slightly above average. Charvarius Ward, who had 139 snaps last season, is penciled in as the other starter at the moment. That lack of experience could give someone like AAF standout Keith Reaser a chance to crack the starting lineup. Tyrann Mathieu will replace Eric Berry as the Chiefs' standout safety. Like Berry, health issues have limited Mathieu's snaps, but there are few better at the position when he's in the lineup. Mathieu can be lined up anywhere on the field, and his fantastic run-thumping presence in the box is likely to be a huge sigh of relief to Kansas City's overmatched linebackers. The other safety position will be a toss-up between second-round pick Juan Thornhill (Virginia), 2017 starter Daniel Sorensen, and Jordan Lucas. The only real question is how quickly Thornhill is ready to start; he's the future. As a converted corner, Thornhill's ball skills are excellent for a safety, and he can fill in as a cover guy in some big nickel packages without looking totally lost out there.

Special Teams

Year	DVOA	Rank	FG/XP	Rank	Net Kick	Rank	Kick Ret	Rank	Net Punt	Rank	Punt Ret	Rank	Hidden	Rank
2016	7.8%	1	0.5	15	0.5	15	5.7	7	11.3	4	20.8	1	3.2	13
2017	5.3%	4	11.8	3	7.1	2	0.0	14	6.2	8	1.7	12	5.0	8
2018	5.6%	2	3.1	11	5.3	3	6.8	4	7.0	4	6.0	3	10.9	5

The Chiefs were one of only three teams to have a positive value in all five aspects of special teams. Harrison Butker's field goal attempts provided the least value to Kansas City's special teams, though part of that is due to the fact that Kansas City was scoring so many touchdowns. Butker only attempted 27 field goals, down from 42 with the Alex Smith-led 2017 Chiefs. Butker also led the league in gross kickoff value, including a league-leading 72 touchbacks and a pleasingly round 7,000 yards exactly. Dustin Colquitt is the longest-tenured Chief in franchise history for a reason. Kansas City has had a positive net punting value in our stats in 12 of Colquitt's 14 seasons, as opposed to just eight out of 18 years before he arrived. Tyreek Hill's ongoing domestic assault and child abuse allegations also mean Kansas City will have to find someone else to fill in returning punts for however long the inevitable suspension ends up being. A 4.32-second 40 at his pro day was enough to give Tremon Smith a look as a returner, and he delivered; he had the fourth-most kick return value in the league last season. Charvarius Ward dominated the Chiefs' coverage teams, with twice as many special teams tackles (12) as anyone else on the club.

Los Angeles Chargers

2018 record: 12-4	**Total DVOA:** 22.6% (3rd)	**2019 Mean Projection:** 10.2 wins	**On the Clock (0-4):** 2%
Pythagorean Wins: 10.6 (7th)	**Offense:** 20.7% (3rd)	**Postseason Odds:** 68.3%	**Mediocrity (5-7):** 13%
Snap-Weighted Age: 26.5 (16th)	**Defense:** -4.7% (8th)	**Super Bowl Odds:** 18.6%	**Playoff Contender (8-10):** 36%
Average Opponent: -0.1% (14th)	**Special Teams:** -2.8% (25th)	**Proj. Avg. Opponent:** -0.3% (19th)	**Super Bowl Contender (11+):** 49%

2018: Despite their best season in over a decade, they still play second fiddle in their division *and* city.

2019: We're ready for our close-up, Mr. Goodell.

Only the Chargers. Only a team that has seen such a bizarre series of ups and downs over the past decade could have a season as good as their 2018 and still end up in the "others receiving votes" column when it came to memorable years.

The Chargers finished 2018 with a 22.6% DVOA. That was their best mark since 2006, Philip Rivers' first season as a starter and Marty Schottenheimer's last year on the sidelines. They suffered the usual bout of Chargers bad luck, this time in the form of injuries to Hunter Henry, Joey Bosa, and essentially the entire linebacker corps, and yet they still managed at least a dozen wins for the first time since 2009, plus their first playoff win since 2013. They finished third in our DVOA rankings and were the only team in football to rank in the top quarter of the league on both offense and defense. They tied for the best record in the AFC, for heaven's sake! By any reasonable measure, they should have been the talk of the NFL.

But, of course, third place means two teams outdid them, and it's just the Chargers' luck that they would finish behind *those* two. Of course, in their best season in a dozen years, their new crosstown rival, the Rams, would end up going to the Super Bowl. The Chargers were already playing second fiddle, crammed into their makeshift soccer stadium with their much smaller local fanbase. Their first playoff run in Los Angeles should have drawn attention and finally gotten them the respect they deserved, but the runaway McVay display meant that nearly all the headlines in town went to the Rams.

And of course, the biggest story of the regular season was the rise of Patrick Mahomes and the Chiefs, so the Chargers couldn't even boast their first AFC West title of the 2010s. The two teams finished with identical records, with the Chargers only losing out on the division thanks to tiebreakers (curse that Week 11 loss to Denver!). That means they had to go out and win a wild-card playoff game while the Chiefs got to sit at home, presumably eating barbeque. Both teams went 12-4, won their first playoff game, and then lost to the Patriots to see their season end, but because the Chiefs did all that *one week later* than the Chargers did, they're the ones with the best Super Bowl LIV odds in Vegas.

Chargers fans have had to put up with a lot of bad luck like that, so naturally they would be the ones playing double-second fiddle. They have finished second in the AFC West in six of the nine seasons in the 2010s, two more runner-up finishes than any other team in the league. Four times, they've been one win away from winning the division, with another season of being one win out of the wild card to boot. Add in the years of special teams disasters, bizarre and unusual losses, and injury epidemics (not to mention the team, you know, leaving its home of 56 years…), and rooting for the Chargers has been one of the NFL's most frustrating experiences. It's not that they've always been terrible—though, yes, the Mike McCoy era got pretty bad. It's that they've been *so close* to being one of the premier teams of the league time in and time out, and have fallen just short. Always the bridesmaids, never the brides.

Well, just in time for the long overdue return of the powder blues, it's time for the Chargers to take the spotlight. Our projections have the Chargers right atop the AFC, neck-and-neck with the Patriots as the top team in the conference. Our numbers think the common wisdom around the division is wrong. It's not that the Chargers have to go through Arrowhead and Mahomes' record-setting offense to win the division crown. The bigger challenge may be the Chiefs heading down to Carson and hoping they can keep up with the well-balanced Chargers attack.

That's not to say that you should pencil in the AFC Championship Game to be held at Dignity Health Sports Park just yet, and not only because the NFL would really like their championship games not to be held in a converted soccer stadium. The Chargers were a balanced team, alright—so balanced that even their flaws showed up equally on offense and defense. If the Chargers want to be playing football into February, they need to focus on third downs and quarterback pressures on *both* sides of the ball, and that means shoring up questionable play up near the line of scrimmage.

The Chargers' offense, their best in five years, was fun to watch last season. After a three-year stretch where it seemed Philip Rivers had begun a slow decline into the twilight stages of his career, he's roared back over the past two seasons. He's one of only three quarterbacks to top 1,200 DYAR in both 2017 and 2018, alongside Drew Brees and Ben Roethlisberger. At the moment, Los Angeles' playoff window and Rivers' remaining years of effectiveness are intertwined. Rivers turns 38 in August, and the Chargers have opted not to draft a developmental quarterback to sit behind him, so they're all-in on Rivers until he collapses into dust. Rivers has shown signs of late-season fatigue in the past few seasons; his DVOA dropped from 36.9% from September through November last

2019 Chargers Schedule

Week	Opp.	Week	Opp.	Week	Opp.
1	IND	7	at TEN	13	at DEN
2	at DET	8	at CHI	14	at JAX
3	HOU	9	GB	15	MIN
4	at MIA	10	at OAK (Thu.)	16	OAK
5	DEN	11	KC (Mon./Mex.)	17	at KC
6	PIT	12	BYE		

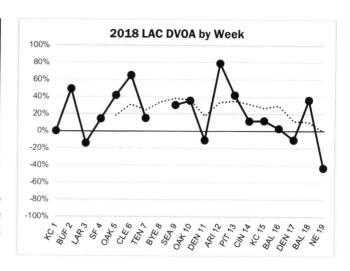

2018 LAC DVOA by Week

season to 6.8% in December to 2.8% in the postseason, and he had a similar (albeit less pronounced) drop in December the year before. Still, he remains near the top of his game, helped by a cornucopia of skill players.

The one-two receiving punch of Keenan Allen and Mike Williams was dynamite last season. Williams' rookie season was derailed by injuries, but he came roaring back to finish second in DVOA and 13th in DYAR—a bit boom-or-bust, being held to 30 or fewer receiving yards in seven games, but his booms were gigantic. He'll move up to the second receiver slot with Tyrell Williams out of town; he had already passed Williams in production and was a better deep threat last year, anyway. Allen remains one of the top slot receivers in the game, an outstanding route-runner who routinely appears near the top of our route leaderboards on outs, curls, digs, and any other short route where you need excellent hands and quick separation. Adding the returning Hunter Henry, who ranked in the top ten in both DYAR and DVOA in 2016 and 2017, is almost unfair.

Melvin Gordon and Austin Ekeler are a fantastic one-two combo in the backfield, as well. Gordon ranked third in rushing DVOA, Ekeler was fourth in receiving DVOA among running backs, and neither was too shabby at handling the other's specialty, either. No other team boasted a back in the top five in both rushing and receiving. They were explosive, too; the Chargers tied for the league lead with 36 runs of 15 yards or more. The Chargers' 144 plays of 15 yards or more were fourth in the league; few teams could boom as often or as effectively as Los Angeles.

The problem is that the Chargers were highly reliant on boom plays to keep their offensive ticking. The Chargers' offense had the best DVOA in the league on first down, but ranked fourth on second down and 16th on third down. Among the playoff teams, only the Ravens had a lower success rate on third down. The Chargers' -39.5% DVOA on third-and-longs was, by a wide margin, the worst of any playoff team, and 26th in the league as a whole. The Chargers were basically either picking up huge gains on first and second down, or they were bogging down quickly and giving the ball back up after failing on third down. On a per-play basis, which DVOA measures, the Chargers were the third-best offense in the league. On a per-*drive* basis, however, they were closer to the bottom of the top 10—still good, obviously, but not as good as one might expect.

You get a clearer picture when you look at Los Angeles' drive and third-down stats when compared to the rest of the league, to the playoff field in general, and to the four conference championship game teams (table 1). On a per-drive basis,

the Chargers aren't any more successful than an average playoff team in terms of points per drive or percentage of drives which succeed at *something*, be it a first down or a touchdown. They're a clear rung down below the Chiefs, Patriots, Rams, and Saints—the sorts of teams you'd expect a 12-4 team with title aspirations to want to compare themselves to. The disconnect between their per-play success and their per-drive success is due in large part to their struggles on third down, where they perform at or below the league average, well underneath what even a middling playoff team could manage. Failure to perform on third downs means that a disproportionally high percentage of Chargers drives ended poorly, at least compared to the cream of the cream. They punted or turned the ball over on 47.8 percent of their drives—that's pretty good, and the ninth-lowest rate in the league, but the top teams were doing that less than 40 percent of the time.

Table 1. The Chargers and Their Third-Down Problems

Team	Off DVOA	Yds/Dr	Pts/Dr	Plays/Dr	Third Down DVOA	Third-and-Long DVOA
Chargers	20.7%	34.84	2.43	5.81	-0.3%	-39.5%
Conf Champ Teams	22.3%	37.80	2.70	6.13	23.9%	54.8%
Playoff Teams	9.5%	35.45	2.44	6.20	12.6%	20.1%
NFL	0.0%	32.31	2.04	5.93	-0.2%	0.4%

The Chargers were too good to be just pretty good on offense. Sustaining drives at the same rate as teams like the Chiefs, Rams, or Saints is the missing piece of their offensive puzzle. It's the kind of success that can turn 24-point games into 31-point games, close losses into close wins, and divisional playoff teams into conference champs.

Some of the Chargers' issues were caused by a conservative mindset from head coach Anthony Lynn and offensive coordinator Ken Whisenhunt—and that problem stretches beyond just third downs. The Chargers' average third down saw them facing 7.4 yards to go, barely squeaking into the top 20, and second-worst only to Dallas among playoff teams. This comes, in part, from how they set up their third-down plays. Rush-rush-pass is one of the least effective play sequences an offense can have, making them predictable and easier to defend. The Chargers used run-run-pass sequences 20 percent of the time in 2018, fourth-most in the league per FiveThirtyEight, and had a below-average success rate and EPA. When the Chargers *did* pass on first and second downs, they had an ALEX of -2.4, the fourth-lowest total in the league. They relied on receivers making moves in the open field to try to pick up first downs, rather than simply throwing the ball past the sticks to begin with. In other words, the Chargers regularly put themselves in poor third-down situations and had to fight their way out of it.

On third down itself, the Chargers did try—they had the fewest failed rushes in the league on third down and an above-average +1.3 ALEX—but the conservative play calling on first and second down put them in terrible third-down situations time and time again, at least compared to the league's best offenses. Third-and-long was their real issue all season long, and yet they did very little on first and second down to try to stay out of those situations.

Whisenhunt calls the plays, but Lynn is the one who makes the big decisions, and he too showed a frustrating conservative streak at times. Aggressiveness Index is our measure of how more (or less) likely each coach is to go for it on fourth down compared to his peers, and Lynn ended up in dead last in 2018. His score of 0.58 means the average NFL coach—a superstitious, cowardly lot on the whole—was nearly twice as likely to go for it on fourth down as Lynn was. Lynn had 90 opportunities for an aggressive call on fourth down—excluding obvious catch-up situations — and pulled the trigger only four times, all on fourth-and-1 situations. The Chargers turned down 11 opportunities to go for it on fourth-and-1, the most in the league. They never went for it on fourth-and-2. They never went for it in that awkward 31- to 37-yard-line range, instead settling for five long field goals. It should be noted that, in total, the Chargers ran eight fourth-down plays in 2018. Seven of them picked up first downs, and the eighth might have as well had Austin Ekeler not fumbled. A little bit more aggression with one of the best offenses in football would likely be justified.

Conservatism may have kept the Chargers in third-and-long situations, but it was their inability to stop opposing pass-rushers that turned those plays into failures. Los Angeles allowed a pressure 32.4 percent of the time, 22nd in the league. The offensive line blew a block every 7.2 pass snaps, 31st in the league. It's hard to convert third-and-long when you have two seconds to throw the ball.

This was supposed to be fixed by now. The 2017 draft saw guards Forrest Lamp and Dan Feeney taken on the second day, with tackle Sam Tevi coming in the sixth round. They were supposed to be the anchors of the line going forward. Instead, Tevi and Feeney tied for the fifth-most blown blocks in football last season. Lamp remains mostly unknown, having missed his entire rookie season with a torn ACL and only getting into two games in 2018.

The Chargers didn't really address the interior of the line at all this offseason, but they did grab tackle Trey Pipkins out of

Sioux Falls in the third round. For most teams, a player such as Pipkins would sit for a year as he builds up strength and gets up to speed after coming out of a small school. Pipkins may instead be the Chargers' opening day right tackle, if for no other reason than a collection of sandbags might do a better job setting the edge than Tevi. As for the two guard spots, the Chargers are simply counting on Feeney to go back to the promise he had as a rookie, and for Lamp to physically exist on a football field. The Chargers are taking a leap of faith with their front line.

The defense struggled with the same things the offense did, albeit to a lesser degree. They had a pressure rate of 30.8 percent, 16th in the league. They dropped from eighth to 18th in defensive DVOA on third downs. These issues, more than anything else, are what reared their head in the playoff loss to New England. The Chargers couldn't get anywhere near Tom Brady, nor could they get the Patriots off the field on third down.

One major contributor to the defensive slowdown, especially later in the year, was injuries. The Chargers were 28th with 52.5 adjusted games lost on defense. They were 30th at linebacker with 20.6, mostly fueled by Kyzir White missing 13 games with a knee injury and Denzel Perryman tearing his ACL in Week 11. Joey Bosa missed half the year with a foot injury, while Corey Liuget missed the *other* half with a knee injury. Jatavis Brown's ankle injury came late enough to not add much to the AGL, but he missed the playoffs. The Chargers that closed the year in New England had five different defensive starters than they had in Week 1. A stunning 41.3 percent of their defensive snaps against the Patriots came from players who had less than a dozen snaps in the first game of the season. That's a lot of in-season turnover, and the Chargers had struggles dealing with it.

Desperate times call for desperate measures, and the Chargers responded to the injuries by running the most dime snaps we have seen since we started tracking in 2011: 627 snaps, more than 200 more than anyone else in the league last year and 50 more than the previous record holder, the 2014 Arizona Cardinals. It culminated in the divisional game against the Ravens, where the Chargers were in dime personnel for 46 out of 47 plays and absolutely shut down the Baltimore offense, before New England was able to defeat them the week after.

It's a growing trend in the NFL for dime packages, especially in non-traditional dime situations, to go big by playing three safeties. That was very much true for the Chargers. SIS charters listed three safeties on the field for the Chargers on 58 percent of regular-season snaps, second behind only Arizona. One of those "safeties" was rookie Derwin James, and he was the lynchpin that made sure this huge number of dime packages worked at all. Yes, he's listed on the roster as a safety, but his versatility is what made the Chargers' defense hum last season. He lined up deep and in the box. He lined up as an outside corner and as a slot corner. He lined up as both an outside and inside linebacker. Honestly, you can put him anywhere on the defense except for nose tackle and get value out of him. His stat profile is unique: 13 pass deflections with three interceptions, a 60 percent coverage success rate, 3.5 sacks with six quarterback knockdowns and 25 stops in run support. With James able to handle any assignment given, the Chargers all-dime, all-the-time strategy was feasible. Move James into the box, and you're essentially down into a smaller-than-average nickel, which is basically base defense in this 11-personnel world, anyway.

Still, it turns out linebackers are important, as the Patriots were more than happy to prove in the divisional round. The good news is that injury levels tend to regress towards the mean from year to year. While certainly not impossible, it seems highly unlikely that the Chargers will have to make do without so many defensive starters again in 2019. The Chargers have been heavy dime users ever since Gus Bradley took over the defensive coordinator job from John Pagano, and the versatility of James means that the Chargers can afford to have an extra defensive back on the field most of the time. They'll still probably be near the top in dime usage, just perhaps slightly less often than a record-setting 64 percent of the time.

The defense should also be improved thanks to an influx of talent. Adding Thomas Davis to Perryman and Brown suddenly makes the linebacker corps a real strength. Even at age 36, Davis is still a very good pass defender and ranked in the top 30 in both run and total stop rate among linebackers. Add in Kyzir White and the linebacker corps is deep, if they can stay healthy.

First-round pick Jerry Tillery should be an instant starter on the defensive line, which will help with some of the Chargers' pressure issues. Tillery was arguably the best interior pass-rusher available in the draft; a highly athletic tackle who racked up 13 sacks and 25.5 tackles for loss in 40 starts at Notre Dame. He was good for at least a pressure per game in college. When coupled with a healthy Bosa and a rebound season from Melvin Ingram, it's more than reasonable to ex-

pect the Chargers pass rush to be much improved going forward. At the very least, Tillery's addition should offset any pain from losing Darius Philon.

Safety should be the strength of the team. Jahleel Addae is gone after finishing 61st out of 76 qualified safeties in pass coverage success and with a history of poor tackling. Instead, the Chargers dime package will feature James, All-Pro special-teamer Adrian Phillips, and second-round rookie Nasir Adderley (Delaware). Adderley's a perfect fit for the Chargers; a dynamic, fluid free safety with great range, excellent ball skills, and experience playing corner. He's still developing a little bit on the mental side of the game in terms of play recognition and the like, but he should be part of the Chargers' dime sets from Day 1. All three should see significant playing time, and no other team in the league can match that top three at safety. Add in Desmond King and Casey Hayward at corner, and you can see why the Chargers are in dime all the time.

If the offensive line can take a step forward, the Chargers should be the most complete team in all of football. They don't have some of the glaring weaknesses other top teams in the conference have—they don't have the defensive issues of the Chiefs, or the question marks at receiver that the Patriots have, or the tumultuous offseason we saw in Pittsburgh. They may not be the best in the league at any one thing, but it's hard to find a team as solid from top to bottom as Los Angeles. The Bolts have spent a decade playing second fiddle. With a little bit of luck—and we know how terrifying *that* concept is for Chargers fans—it could finally be time for the Chargers to steal the spotlight.

Either way, they'll at least look better in the powder blues, right?

Bryan Knowles

2018 Chargers Stats by Week

Wk	vs.	W-L	PF	PA	YDF	YDA	TO	Total	Off	Def	ST
1	KC	L	28	38	541	362	-2	0%	44%	2%	-42%
2	at BUF	W	31	20	349	293	+2	49%	34%	-4%	12%
3	at LAR	L	23	35	356	521	0	-14%	16%	14%	-16%
4	SF	W	29	27	368	364	+1	14%	-4%	-12%	7%
5	OAK	W	26	10	412	289	+2	42%	37%	-10%	-6%
6	at CLE	W	38	14	449	317	+1	65%	37%	-30%	-2%
7	TEN	W	20	19	344	390	+1	15%	26%	6%	-5%
8	BYE										
9	at SEA	W	25	17	375	356	+1	30%	40%	-10%	-19%
10	at OAK	W	20	6	335	317	0	36%	16%	-17%	2%
11	DEN	L	22	23	479	325	-2	-11%	9%	22%	3%
12	ARI	W	45	10	414	149	0	79%	59%	-19%	1%
13	at PIT	W	33	30	371	336	+1	42%	38%	8%	12%
14	CIN	W	26	21	288	295	0	12%	3%	1%	9%
15	at KC	W	29	28	407	294	-2	12%	7%	-13%	-8%
16	BAL	L	10	22	198	361	-2	3%	-14%	-12%	5%
17	at DEN	W	23	9	276	370	0	-11%	-17%	-4%	3%
18	at BAL	W	23	17	243	229	+2	36%	-24%	-47%	13%
19	at NE	L	28	41	335	498	-2	-43%	-9%	28%	-6%

Trends and Splits

	Offense	Rank	Defense	Rank
Total DVOA	20.7%	3	-4.7%	8
Unadjusted VOA	21.2%	3	-5.1%	9
Weighted Trend	17.1%	3	-5.9%	7
Variance	4.9%	8	1.8%	1
Average Opponent	0.3%	17	0.7%	12
Passing	41.6%	2	1.2%	10
Rushing	4.2%	7	-12.0%	10
First Down	32.6%	1	-8.3%	6
Second Down	13.4%	4	-2.7%	14
Third Down	4.6%	16	-0.8%	18
First Half	22.9%	3	-4.5%	8
Second Half	18.7%	3	-5.0%	11
Red Zone	31.9%	3	-23.5%	5
Late and Close	19.8%	4	1.2%	20

Five-Year Performance

Year	W-L	Pyth W	Est W	PF	PA	TO	Total	Rk	Off	Rk	Def	Rk	ST	Rk	Off AGL	Rk	Def AGL	Rk	Off Age	Rk	Def Age	Rk	ST Age	Rk
2014	9-7	8.0	8.0	348	348	-5	-0.6%	16	7.0%	11	4.9%	25	-2.7%	23	82.1	32	37.0	15	27.9	4	26.7	17	26.6	4
2015	4-12	5.9	6.0	320	398	-4	-14.8%	24	0.9%	15	10.4%	28	-5.3%	31	55.7	27	25.7	10	27.6	7	25.9	30	26.5	7
2016	5-11	7.7	6.9	410	423	-7	-1.1%	19	-3.2%	18	-6.8%	7	-4.8%	29	61.7	29	66.0	29	27.9	4	25.7	31	25.7	24
2017	9-7	10.5	8.4	355	272	+12	7.9%	11	10.6%	7	-4.7%	12	-7.5%	31	35.9	17	31.7	15	27.6	5	25.7	26	25.4	25
2018	12-4	10.6	11.0	428	329	+1	22.6%	3	20.7%	3	-4.7%	8	-2.8%	25	31.5	11	52.5	28	27.8	7	25.7	26	25.4	29

2018 Performance Based on Most Common Personnel Groups

LAC Offense					LAC Offense vs. Opponents					LAC Defense				LAC Defense vs. Opponents			
Pers	Freq	Yds	DVOA	Run%	Pers	Freq	Yds	DVOA	Run%	Pers	Freq	Yds	DVOA	Pers	Freq	Yds	DVOA
11	63%	6.6	34.6%	29%	Base	29%	6.3	7.1%	61%	Base	20%	5.7	-0.1%	11	68%	5.5	-7.6%
12	13%	6.6	11.3%	47%	Nickel	52%	6.5	35.5%	34%	Nickel	15%	5.4	-17.0%	12	14%	5.5	-7.1%
21	11%	5.5	6.6%	64%	Dime+	14%	6.6	28.8%	19%	Dime+	64%	5.6	-2.8%	21	8%	8.0	24.0%
22	8%	6.3	6.7%	84%	Goal Line	0%	0.5	-2.1%	100%	Goal Line	1%	0.5	-68.1%	13	3%	6.1	18.6%
10	1%	5.8	64.9%	0%										611	2%	2.3	-84.8%
13	1%	10.5	68.1%	42%										613	1%	4.7	25.4%

Strategic Tendencies

Run/Pass		Rk	Formation		Rk	Pass Rush		Rk	Secondary		Rk	Strategy		Rk
Runs, first half	36%	22	Form: Single Back	76%	21	Rush 3	5.2%	19	4 DB	20%	23	Play action	22%	20
Runs, first down	53%	7	Form: Empty Back	9%	11	Rush 4	80.1%	1	5 DB	15%	32	Avg Box (Off)	6.27	10
Runs, second-long	30%	16	Pers: 3+ WR	65%	21	Rush 5	12.5%	29	6+ DB	64%	1	Avg Box (Def)	6.33	6
Runs, power sit.	59%	15	Pers: 2+ TE/6+ OL	24%	15	Rush 6+	1.8%	32	CB by Sides	59%	25	Offensive Pace	31.25	16
Runs, behind 2H	30%	10	Pers: 6+ OL	2%	19	Int DL Sacks	26.3%	16	S/CB Cover Ratio	34%	4	Defensive Pace	31.11	17
Pass, ahead 2H	48%	15	Shotgun/Pistol	57%	25	Second Level Sacks	27.6%	9	DB Blitz	6%	24	Go for it on 4th	0.58	32

Los Angeles had the best DVOA in the league when running from shotgun, 18.6% with 5.5 yards per carry. With that in mind, maybe the Chargers should have used more shotgun on third down. Los Angeles dropped to 13th in DVOA when passing on third down, and even worse, to 30th when running the ball. Los Angeles ranked third in the league in broken tackles; Denver was the only other team where three different running backs were recorded with 20 or more broken tackles. The Chargers ranked third in DVOA when blitzing a defensive back. Los Angeles had the only defense in the league that was not credited by charters with a "rusher untouched" sack all season.

Passing

Player	DYAR	DVOA	Plays	NtYds	Avg	YAC	C%	TD	Int
P.Rivers	1316	27.2%	540	4104	7.6	6.1	68.3%	32	12
T.Taylor	-264	-53.5%	97	382	3.9	4.7	50.6%	2	2

Rushing

Player	DYAR	DVOA	Plays	Yds	Avg	TD	Fum	Suc
M.Gordon	210	20.8%	175	885	5.1	10	0	53%
A.Ekeler	59	4.9%	106	554	5.2	3	0	52%
J.Jackson	6	-6.0%	50	206	4.1	2	0	56%
D.Newsome	-6	-22.7%	11	49	4.5	0	0	36%
P.Rivers	-55	-96.5%	10	10	1.0	0	1	--
K.Allen	37	60.9%	8	75	9.4	0	0	--
M.Williams	16	7.6%	7	28	4.0	1	0	--
T.Benjamin	14	11.0%	7	41	5.9	0	0	--
D.Watt	-6	-37.8%	4	11	2.8	0	0	50%
T.Taylor	4	-6.8%	16	122	7.6	1	2	--

Receiving

Player	DYAR	DVOA	Plays	Ctch	Yds	Y/C	YAC	TD	C%
K.Allen	320	18.1%	136	97	1196	12.3	4.2	6	71%
M.Williams	262	39.2%	66	43	664	15.4	2.7	10	65%
T.Williams*	128	12.3%	65	41	653	15.9	4.8	5	63%
T.Benjamin	2	-11.7%	24	12	186	15.5	5.4	1	50%
A.Gates*	0	-7.4%	45	28	333	11.9	4.5	2	62%
V.Green	-2	-8.2%	27	19	210	11.1	5.4	1	70%
M.Gordon	72	5.5%	66	50	490	9.8	10.7	4	76%
A.Ekeler	131	30.3%	53	39	404	10.4	10.5	3	74%
J.Jackson	37	29.9%	19	15	135	9.0	10.1	0	79%

Offensive Line

Player	Pos	Age	GS	Snaps	Pen	Sk	Pass	Run	Player	Pos	Age	GS	Snaps	Pen	Sk	Pass	Run
Dan Feeney	LG	25	16/16	995	5	7.0	23	3	Sam Tevi	RT	25	16/15	871	5	6.8	22	4
Michael Schofield	RG	29	16/16	978	1	4.8	16	9	Russell Okung	LT	31	15/15	866	7	3.5	9	1
Mike Pouncey	C	30	16/16	954	6	0.5	3	4									

Year	Yards	ALY	Rank	Power	Rank	Stuff	Rank	2nd Lev	Rank	Open Field	Rank	Sacks	ASR	Rank	Press	Rank	F-Start	Cont.
2016	3.92	3.97	23	66%	13	21%	19	1.01	30	0.76	12	36	6.6%	24	28.7%	23	19	37
2017	3.93	3.71	26	58%	25	24%	26	1.17	13	0.78	12	18	4.2%	3	31.8%	20	17	26
2018	4.91	4.80	5	67%	18	18%	16	1.46	4	1.05	7	34	6.4%	13	32.4%	22	10	38

2018 ALY by direction:	Left End: 5.58 (4)	Left Tackle: 4.22 (15)	Mid/Guard: 4.49 (12)	Right Tackle: 4.62 (12)	Right End: 6.09 (2)

The Chargers' above-average adjusted sack rate can be credited to Philip Rivers and his quick release. Los Angeles blew a block in pass protection every 7.2 pass plays, second-worst in the league. ❧ The Chargers must especially improve at guard, where Michael Schofield and Dan Feeney ranked 99th and 103rd among 107 qualifying interior linemen in snaps per blown block. In fact, the Chargers haven't had a guard rank inside the top 60 in blown blocks in any of the past three seasons. ❧ Forrest Lamp's 2018 season was somewhat of a mystery. The second-round pick missed all of 2017 with a knee injury and wasn't able to practice until August. But he was on the active roster throughout 2018, the guards ahead of him were playing very poorly and still, nothing. Lamp has just 17 career snaps through his first two seasons; his lack of playing time last season does not bode well for the coaching staff's confidence in his abilities. ❧ Sam Tevi wasn't much better than the guards, ranking 67th out of 70 tackles in snaps per blown block. Lamp will get some tackle snaps in preseason to see if he can't beat Tevi out. ❧ The Chargers used their third-round pick on Trey Pipkins out of Sioux Falls—he's another option at right tackle. He allowed just two sacks in 43 starts, but that's at the Division II level. He needs significant developmental time to become a starter, but could be forced into action thanks to the lack of depth. ❧ Mike Pouncey was a huge relief after years of Spencer Pulley and Matt Slauson at center. He allowed just half a sack and was the fifth-best player to switch teams last season according to Pro Football Reference's Approximate Value. ❧ Okung had a much better season in 2018, jumping from 25th to eighth among left tackles in snaps per blown block. His pass protection numbers are still a bit behind the top of the league, but SIS only recorded Okung with one blown run block all season long.

Defensive Front

Defensive Line	Age	Pos	G	Snaps	Plays	TmPct	Rk	Stop	Dfts	BTkl	Runs	St%	Rk	RuYd	Rk	Sack	Hit	Hur	Dsrpt
						Overall							**vs. Run**				**Pass Rush**		
Darius Philon*	25	DT	16	607	33	4.2%	61	27	12	7	25	80%	24	1.3	5	4.0	5	15	0
Damion Square	30	DT	16	530	34	4.3%	58	27	7	2	24	75%	41	2.7	63	3.0	3	8	3
Brandon Mebane	34	DT	12	405	41	6.9%	17	27	5	1	38	63%	78	3.2	77	1.0	2	7	0
Justin Jones	23	DT	15	300	17	2.3%	--	7	1	1	15	40%	--	3.6	--	0.5	1	7	0

Edge Rushers	Age	Pos	G	Snaps	Plays	TmPct	Rk	Stop	Dfts	BTkl	Runs	St%	Rk	RuYd	Rk	Sack	Hit	Hur	Dsrpt
						Overall							**vs. Run**				**Pass Rush**		
Melvin Ingram	30	DE	16	913	46	5.8%	27	38	19	7	31	77%	39	1.6	16	7.0	10	43	1
Isaac Rochell	24	DE	16	536	28	3.5%	77	25	10	3	21	86%	13	2.5	49	5.0	1	17	0
Joey Bosa	24	DE	7	314	22	6.3%	13	16	7	3	14	71%	55	3.0	60	5.5	3	13	1

Linebackers	Age	Pos	G	Snaps	Plays	TmPct	Rk	Stop	Dfts	BTkl	Runs	St%	Rk	RuYd	Rk	Sack	Hit	Hur	Tgts	Suc%	Rk	AdjYd	Rk	PD	Int
						Overall							**vs. Run**				**Pass Rush**				**vs. Pass**				
Jatavis Brown	25	OLB	15	636	97	13.0%	39	39	13	13	33	48%	78	5.2	82	1.0	0	2	41	46%	50	6.3	25	5	0
Denzel Perryman	27	MLB	9	387	53	11.9%	47	29	3	8	35	63%	28	3.5	27	0.0	1	3	20	65%	4	3.3	1	2	1
Uchenna Nwosu	23	OLB	16	265	19	2.4%	--	13	6	2	10	70%	--	2.4	--	3.5	6	15.5	2	50%	142	4.0	45	1	0
Kyle Emanuel*	28	OLB	16	216	26	3.3%	--	16	8	4	18	72%	--	2.1	--	1.0	1	1.5	10	40%	--	7.7	--	0	0
Thomas Davis	36	OLB	12	650	85	14.7%	27	48	18	9	43	65%	22	3.6	31	0.0	3	8	35	51%	35	6.9	46	6	0

Year	Yards	ALY	Rank	Power	Rank	Stuff	Rank	2nd Level	Rank	Open Field	Rank	Sacks	ASR	Rank	Press	Rank
2016	3.85	3.65	6	71%	28	24%	4	1.18	18	0.73	16	35	5.9%	15	26.8%	18
2017	4.82	4.31	24	64%	18	20%	16	1.27	28	1.26	32	43	7.8%	7	30.6%	15
2018	4.38	4.37	17	71%	23	19%	18	1.21	15	0.83	16	38	6.7%	24	30.8%	15
2018 ALY by direction:		Left End: 4.37 (15)			Left Tackle: 5.28 (30)			Mid/Guard: 4.53 (21)			Right Tackle: 4.06 (16)			Right End: 2.29 (2)	

Were the Chargers a bad run defense? No and yes. Los Angeles put up a -12.0% run defense DVOA for the season, but that dropped to 1.9% when looking at runs up the middle, 27th in the league. ❧ First-round pick Jerry Tillery will eventually be the replacement for Brandon Mebane, though he may open the season as a 25-snap-a-game rotational guy as he adapts to the NFL game. While still a useful player, age is catching up to the 34-year-old Mebane. His run stop rate was down to 63 percent, and he hasn't been in the top 75 there since 2015 in Seattle. ❧ Joey Bosa ranked in the top 25 among edge rushers in pass pressures per snap—impressive for a guy who was in a cast in September. He's still facing some soreness in his foot, and you have to be a little worried about a guy who's missed 13 of his 32 career games, but when he's out there, there are few who are better. ❧ The narrative is that Melvin Ingram had a "down year," handling the load with Bosa out. Ingram was sixth in the league in pressures and saw his run stop rate increase from 64 percent to 77 percent. Some down year. ❧ While he's no longer at the very top of the charts, Thomas Davis is one of only two linebackers who has ranked in the top 35 in pass coverage success rate every year since 2012. ❧ Denzel Perryman is yet to play all 16 games in a season. In 2018, it was an LCL and hamstring that cost him seven games. When healthy, he's a force. When healthy… ❧ Fourth-round pick Drue Tranquill converted from safety to linebacker at Notre Dame, giving him a good chance to fit in with Los Angeles' all-dime, all-the-time packages. He's probably a special teams guy who backs up all three linebacker positions rather than a future starter, but goodness knows the Chargers needed, like, eight of him last season.

Defensive Secondary

Secondary	Age	Pos	G	Snaps	Plays	TmPct	Rk	Stop	Dfts	BTkl	Runs	St%	Rk	RuYd	Rk	Tgts	Tgt%	Rk	Dist	Suc%	Rk	AdjYd	Rk	PD	Int
						Overall							**vs. Run**					**vs. Pass**						
Derwin James	23	SS	16	1027	118	14.9%	4	58	18	16	58	43%	34	7.0	39	42	10.3%	47	9.4	60%	15	6.5	19	13	3
Jahleel Addae*	29	FS	16	1025	78	9.8%	43	22	7	7	38	34%	53	7.0	39	17	4.2%	3	15.9	41%	61	14.1	73	3	1
Casey Hayward	30	CB	16	1016	54	6.8%	66	21	7	3	23	39%	45	7.4	55	58	14.4%	8	12.3	52%	41	7.8	43	8	0
Desmond King	25	CB	16	801	70	8.8%	39	37	13	16	16	44%	33	7.1	49	57	17.9%	30	6.9	58%	17	5.6	5	10	3
Adrian Phillips	27	SS	16	684	86	10.8%	31	43	18	7	41	51%	20	4.1	5	39	14.3%	67	11.7	69%	3	6.4	16	9	1
Michael Davis	24	CB	16	626	52	6.5%	72	27	11	4	8	63%	7	7.1	49	57	22.9%	63	10.1	56%	23	6.9	27	8	0
Trevor Williams	26	CB	9	410	26	5.8%	--	7	5	5	2	0%	--	5.5	--	28	17.2%	--	12.0	32%	--	10.3	--	4	1

Year	Pass D Rank	vs. #1 WR	Rk	vs. #2 WR	Rk	vs. Other WR	Rk	WR Wide	Rk	WR Slot	Rk	vs. TE	Rk	vs. RB	Rk
2016	9	-10.4%	6	5.7%	22	-25.0%	2	-20.3%	4	4.0%	16	-2.1%	15	-3.5%	17
2017	9	-11.8%	10	0.5%	17	-25.2%	3	-17.3%	5	-6.1%	10	0.9%	18	-21.3%	5
2018	10	10.3%	23	-2.6%	15	3.1%	19	7.2%	23	4.6%	18	-52.4%	1	9.7%	23

The Chargers ranked 10th in pass defense DVOA overall but had a massive deep-short split. Once we remove passes thrown away on purpose or tipped at the line, the Chargers had the best DVOA in the league on short passes, up to 15 yards through the air. But they were 29th in DVOA against deep passes. This may partially be caused by their own success. They faced the fifth-fewest deep passes in football because their coverage was good enough to force other teams to go with shorter options. When other teams did go long, however, it resulted in a first down 49.4 percent of the time and a turnover only 2.4 percent of the time, both second-worst in the league. ● The Chargers also had the second-best DVOA against tight ends of any defense since 1999, trailing only the 2016 Philadelphia Eagles. Los Angeles wasn't particularly low in yards allowed to tight ends, but that's because opponents threw to tight ends over 120 times. However, the Chargers allowed just 6.2 yards per pass on throws to tight ends (third in NFL) and were tied for the league lead with eight picks on throws to tight ends. ● If you had to give Derwin James a positional alignment, it'd be box safety; he played about 40 percent of his snaps there. The other 60 percent were just about evenly distributed as a deep safety, slot corner, and edge rusher. James led all defensive backs in QB hurries, had the fourth-most run tackles, and ranked in the top 15 in pass success rate among safeties. That's insane versatility. ● Second-round pick Nasir Adderley played both corner and safety at Delaware, making him yet another Swiss Army knife for Gus Bradley to use in the secondary. On many teams, he'd start out behind Rayshawn Jenkins or Adrian Phillips at the beginning of the year as he gained experience as a full-time deep safety, but almost no one uses three-safety packages as much as the Chargers do. He'll be in the lineup from Day 1, replacing the departed Jahleel Addae. ● Trevor Williams and Michael Davis will compete for the second starting corner position across from Casey Hayward. Williams' success rate dropped from 56 percent in 2017 to 32 percent last year, at least in part due to ankle and knee injuries which ended up shutting his season down. 2017 Williams is the best option, but the 2018 version of Davis filled in quite well despite not having an interception. ● Desmond King ranked sixth among qualified corners in yards per pass allowed, and 17th in success rate. Part of that comes from facing the shortest average pass depth in the league, but don't let that take away from King's excellence in the slot. ● Hayward missed the Pro Bowl for the first time since 2015, in part because he didn't have an interception. It's hard to get interceptions, however, when no one targets you. Hayward went from around 80 targets a year in previous seasons to just 58 last year.

Special Teams

Year	DVOA	Rank	FG/XP	Rank	Net Kick	Rank	Kick Ret	Rank	Net Punt	Rank	Punt Ret	Rank	Hidden	Rank
2016	-4.8%	29	-8.7	29	-2.6	20	-4.7	26	-5.8	25	-2.2	20	-12.3	31
2017	-7.5%	31	-22.2	32	-7.4	29	-3.9	26	-6.1	24	2.3	9	-4.7	20
2018	-2.8%	25	-5.9	27	1.5	13	-3.2	26	-11.3	31	4.8	7	-3.4	20

The Chargers still were very bad at field goal/extra point value, but at least they were only very bad and not soul-crushingly terrible. Baby steps! It should be noted that Caleb Sturgis put up -11.9 points of value in his six games, which is what happens when you go 3-for-7 from beyond 40 yards and miss 40 percent of your extra points. Undrafted free agent Mike Badgley was responsible for +6.0 points, which would have ranked eighth in the league. Once again, don't draft kickers. ● Tyler Newsome and Ty Long will battle for the open punting job. Long's a multi-time CFL All-Star who handled kicking and punting for the BC Lions, so he has versatility. Newsome's a UDFA who leaves Notre Dame with multiple school punting records, rocks a mullet, and benched 30 reps at the combine. Newsome's the more fun player; Long may be better. Punter battles! Woo! ● It's not always the best plan for your return guy to play more than three quarters of your defensive snaps as well, but Desmond King was too good at both his jobs to bench. King's All-Pro performance was more based on his punt returning than kick returning, so if the Chargers do want to give him a bit of a rest, Austin Ekeler is another possibility. ● Adrian Phillips led the NFL with 17 special teams tackles on punts and kickoffs, 13 of which stopped the opposition short of an average return.

Los Angeles Rams

2018 record: 13-3	Total DVOA: 24.0% (2nd)	2019 Mean Projection: 9.6 wins	On the Clock (0-4): 3%
Pythagorean Wins: 11.2 (3rd)	Offense: 24.6% (2nd)	Postseason Odds: 60.5%	Mediocrity (5-7): 17%
Snap-Weighted Age: 26.6 (11th)	Defense: 0.5% (17th)	Super Bowl Odds: 14.4%	Playoff Contender (8-10): 41%
Average Opponent: -2.4% (25th)	Special Teams: -0.2% (17th)	Proj. Avg. Opponent: 0.1% (17th)	Super Bowl Contender (11+): 39%

2018: McVay's brilliance takes the Rams to the brink of ultimate glory.

2019: Better make this one count or risk becoming a what-if story.

After a massive turnaround in head coach Sean McVay's first season in Los Angeles, the Rams made aggressive moves heading into 2018 to try to vault themselves into championship contention. The Rams had finished second in DVOA, but they further bolstered their squad by adding Marcus Peters, Aqib Talib, Ndamukong Suh, and Brandin Cooks, raising expectations for a team that many already had pegged as one of the teams to beat in the NFC.

Although we were somewhat skeptical that the improvement would stick due to the plexiglass principle, the Los Angeles offense ascended to even greater heights, finishing second in offensive DVOA. The Rams led the league in rushing offense DVOA by a mile, and the team's three starting wide receivers all finished in the top 25 in receiving DYAR, a feat made even more impressive by the fact that slot receiver Cooper Kupp missed half the year due to injury.

Kupp may not have been on the field as much as the Rams would have liked, but he certainly made an impact when he was available. Even though he only played the equivalent of seven full games (he left in the first half of the Rams' Week 6 contest with the Broncos after spraining the MCL in his left knee, missed the following two games, and then tore the ACL in the same knee against the Seahawks in Week 10), Kupp served as a crucial security blanket for Jared Goff and still finished 23rd in receiving DYAR on the year despite how often he was stuck in the training room.

In 2017, the Rams had used Sammy Watkins in the deep-threat role for their wide receiver trio. While he had performed efficiently, finishing sixth in receiving DVOA that year, Los Angeles elected to not re-sign him in free agency; Kansas City then handed him a hefty three-year contract worth up to $48 million. Watkins followed up in 2018 by exactly matching his prior season's receiving DVOA of 24.1%. Sounds like a recipe for a drop-off in the Rams' receiving corps, no?

Well, not if you immediately find an upgrade. Enter Cooks, who was acquired in a trade with the Patriots during the offseason. Watkins posted impressive efficiency numbers in Kansas City, but due to a foot injury, he only played in ten games; that top-five DVOA mark took place on only 55 targets. Cooks nearly matched Watkins' receiving DVOA (21.5% vs. 24.1%), but he also did so on more than *double* the number of targets, obtaining 117 in the Rams' high-flying offense. Cooks had been a high-volume receiving threat in both New England and

New Orleans, and his addition helped add a new dimension to the Los Angeles offense, as he was not limited to running deep routes to take the top off the defense.

Fellow wide receiver Robert Woods also took a major step forward in his second season with his hometown Rams. Woods was a major piece of the offense in 2017, but a combination of an increase in target volume (8.1 per game in 2018 vs. 7.1 in 2017), improved health, and increased volume in the running game allowed him to have a much larger total impact in the Los Angeles offense. Woods started all 16 games for the first time in his career and made the most of his increased opportunities, setting career highs in rushing and receiving yards, receiving DYAR, and receiving DVOA. While he never exceeded three carries in any game, the mere threat of Woods taking the ball on a jet sweep, particularly from the tight bunch formations the Rams used so effectively, was a consistent problem for defenses that already had enough things to worry about when trying to counter the Rams' play-action-heavy offensive assault.

In case you were worried that the Rams did not have enough offensive weapons, their rushing attack was a force to be reckoned with in its own right. The Rams led the league in rushing offense DVOA at 21.3%, which gets even more impressive with additional context. As we know, pass plays are generally more efficient than runs, but the Rams rushing attack was more efficient than all but the best passing attacks in the NFL. Indianapolis finished with the No. 10 passing offense by DVOA, and their pass offense DVOA of 21.3% was identical to Los Angeles' mark in the rushing category. Only nine teams in the entire league finished with a rushing DVOA better than 0.0%, and the Rams' rushing DVOA was the highest since the 2014 Seahawks unit led by Marshawn Lynch and Russell Wilson.

While running back Todd Gurley received MVP votes in 2017 and continued to play at a high level when healthy in 2018, the Rams' offensive line deserves a massive amount of credit for the run game's strength. Los Angeles' 5.49 adjusted line yards was the highest in our database going back to 1996, surpassing the 5.25 mark of the 2011 Saints. They also led the league in second-level yards (yards earned between 5 and 10 yards beyond the line of scrimmage) per carry and finished second in stuffed rate. The Rams' heavy use of play-action passes that forced defenders to hesitate before flying to the

2019 Rams Schedule

Week	Opp.	Week	Opp.	Week	Opp.
1	at CAR	7	at ATL	13	at ARI
2	NO	8	CIN (U.K.)	14	SEA
3	at CLE	9	BYE	15	at DAL
4	TB	10	at PIT	16	at SF
5	at SEA (Thu.)	11	CHI	17	ARI
6	SF	12	BAL (Mon.)		

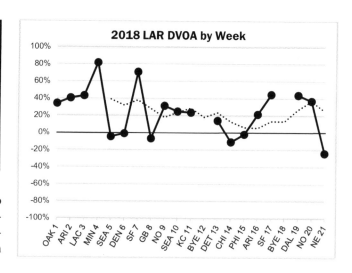

ball and tendency to avoid running into stacked boxes also helped their rushing metrics overall, but even with those caveats, the numbers are just staggering. The Rams' pass blocking was also quite impressive, finishing sixth in the league in adjusted sack rate.

Add all those weapons up and you end up with an incredibly potent offense, which should come as a surprise to exactly no one. The Rams may not have been the Chiefs' equal on offense in 2018, but it was still plenty good enough to make up for the team's decline in performance on defense and special teams and carry them to the Super Bowl for the first time since 2001. The end result may not have been what the team was hoping for, as the Patriots shut down the Rams in a 13-3 win, but even still, the Rams' 2018 season was a huge success.

Given that Goff is still on his rookie contract, you would expect that the Rams would be set up well for the long haul. The Rams should still be excellent in 2019, but there are some key questions about the future beyond this season, once Goff starts getting paid a market rate after the Rams (presumably) extend him on a long-term contract. Goff's rookie deal has provided the Rams with extra wiggle room to add veterans on market-rate deals to bolster the team's roster, but if he and the Rams do not agree to a contract extension prior to 2020 that lowers his cap hit in the first year, he will play that season on a fifth-year option that would be equal to the transition tag for quarterbacks. Los Angeles' ability to plug holes with veterans thanks to the savings from Goff's deal has papered over some issues that might have otherwise been a bigger deal.

The Rams' young quarterback is a good place to start. While Goff underwent an absolutely massive transformation under the tutelage of head coach McVay after spending his rookie year trapped in Jeff Fisher-world, he regressed some as a passer in Year 3 by both passing DYAR and DVOA. That decline seemed particularly stark late in the season, as Goff and the rest of the Rams offense turned in complete stinkers against the Bears and Patriots in particular. There are legitimate injury-based reasons for the team's poor showings against those two teams, but therein lies the problem.

Cooper Kupp's presence on the field was a key bellwether for how the Rams offense would perform as a whole, even with Cooks and Woods in the fold. While understandable for a talented player like Kupp, it raises the question of how much Goff's supporting cast elevates him versus the other way around.

Kupp missed half of Week 6, all of Weeks 7 and 8, and then every game from Week 11 onward. Counting the game against the Broncos as a game where Kupp appeared, the Rams' of-

fensive DVOA dropped nearly 30 percentage points when Kupp was out of the lineup (Table 1). With Kupp on the field, the Rams had four games with offensive DVOA above 50%, but they never managed to hit that mark without him in the fold. That split has to be somewhat concerning as the Rams prepare to offer Goff a massive contract that will force spending cuts elsewhere on the roster.

Table 1: The Kupp Factor

	Off DVOA	Pts/G	Goff DVOA	Goff DYAR/G
With Kupp (Weeks 1-6, 9-10)	39.1%	33.4	37.3%	117
Without Kupp (Weeks 7-8, 11-17)	10.9%	29.0	-2.2%	23

Todd Gurley also spent some time on the shelf with knee issues late in the year, being primarily replaced in the lineup by veteran back C.J. Anderson, and while the Rams offense continued to churn out yards on the ground both in his absence and with him playing a smaller role in the offense upon his return, Gurley's knee injuries appear to be a long-term problem. Given his medical track record from his time in college at Georgia, it is not completely surprising that he would go on to have knee problems as a professional. Make no mistake, this is incredibly unfortunate for Gurley, as the electric young runner may never be a true workhorse back again.

In addition to Gurley's own injury history, the nature of his position also leads to players getting hurt often. The Rams traded up to draft Memphis running back Darrell Henderson in the third round this year and made sure to bring back incumbent backup Malcolm Brown to add to the depth behind Gurley. It seems like Los Angeles has a good succession plan in place; the only issue is Gurley's contract. Prior to the 2018 season, the team signed Gurley to a four-year extension that reset the market at the running back position and made him the highest-paid back in the league. It is not that difficult to find starting-caliber running backs on rookie contracts or street free-agent deals, and completely resetting the market exposed the Rams to some serious downside risk.

They're now seeing what is one of the worst possible outcomes for the early extension. Gurley will likely not be able to handle workhorse duties, forcing the Rams to commit additional resources to the running back position, and Gurley's base salary and roster bonus for 2020 have already become guaranteed. Normally, a running back losing his effectiveness due to injury would not be a huge deal, especially in McVay's system with a high-quality offensive line. However, the Rams cannot save any money against the salary cap from Gurley's current contract until 2021 at the earliest, and even then they would have to take a decent-sized dead money hit if they were to release him.

The amount of money tied up in Gurley's contract will hinder Los Angeles' ability to add supplemental pieces to the team in the next few seasons that might otherwise put them over the edge and bring them back to the Super Bowl. By the time they get out from under Gurley's deal, the currently formidable Rams offensive line may not be the same either, as star left tackle Andrew Whitworth is 37 years old and already considered retiring this offseason. After this season, the Rams could find themselves needing to replace at least two starters on the offensive line as well as their starting tight end, and if second-year players Joseph Noteboom and Brian Allen do not replace the departed Rodger Saffold and John Sullivan effectively at left guard and center, the offensive line may be in need of an even greater overhaul. The Rams do at least have all their studs at wide receiver locked up through 2020, with Cooks in particular signed through 2023, but after a Goff extension, fitting all the other offensive pieces in around his and Gurley's contracts will be a challenge.

These potential offensive issues would be mitigated slightly if the defense were able to pick up the slack, but Los Angeles' 2018 unit left a lot to be desired. After trying to upgrade their secondary by bringing in cornerbacks Talib and Peters, the Rams likely were not happy with the results. Talib was effective when on the field, but he missed half of 2018 with injuries and will be 33 this year. Peters also struggled, failing to play at the Pro Bowl level we have seen from him in the past, with teams taking advantage of his tendency to gamble for interceptions and being rewarded with big plays. Both Talib and Peters will be free agents at the end of 2019, so the team will have some key decisions to make in the secondary.

Suh was underwhelming for much of the regular season before turning it up in the playoffs, and the Rams felt comfortable letting him depart for Tampa Bay. Los Angeles did not replace Suh with anyone of note, which could be worrisome for a run defense that was already one of the league's worst in 2018. Los Angeles added a run-stuffing nose tackle in the fourth round in Washington's Greg Gaines, but relying on a Day 3 draft pick to step in and play a real role is a risk for a team that has its sights set on not only returning to the Super Bowl but winning it this time.

Aaron Donald was his normal dominant self at defensive tackle, winning Defensive Player of the Year again in runaway fashion, but he alone does not a strong defense make.

His pass-rushing prowess helped make the Rams an above-average pass defense unit, but the Rams' problems against the run dragged the unit down from sixth in defensive DVOA in 2017 to just 18th in 2018. We expect the defense to bounce back to become a slightly above-average unit in 2019, but outside of Donald there is a good amount of uncertainty on the defensive side of the ball both this year and beyond. (There is no uncertainty with Aaron Donald, only scared quarterbacks.)

The Rams are hoping they can get more pass-rush juice out of their edge rushers in 2019—they brought back Dante Fowler after trading for him at midseason, then added Clay Matthews in free agency. The Rams got a league-low 15 percent of their sacks from their edge rushers in 2018, and the hope is that the combination of Fowler and Matthews will provide a stronger complementary threat to Donald. Fowler flashed at times after being brought into the fold at midseason, and even though he is entering his fifth year in the league, he is still only 25. Matthews was a perennial Pro Bowler early in his career due in large part to his pass-rushing prowess. However, Matthews is very much on the decline, and Fowler never lived up to the expectations that came with being drafted third overall by the Jaguars in 2015. Outside of those two, the Rams are essentially running it back with an edge rusher group that did not offer a ton in support for Donald in 2018.

There are also questions on the back end of the defense, as Lamarcus Joyner departed for Oakland after playing 2018 on the franchise tag at free safety. Former Chargers and Ravens star Eric Weddle will get the first crack at replacing Joyner as the starter, though at 34, it's fair to wonder how much Weddle has left in the tank. John Johnson is entrenched as the starter at strong safety and seems like a key building block moving forward, but the Rams' long-term solution at free safety is very much up in the air. Second-round rookie Taylor Rapp of Washington played some free safety in college but does not profile particularly well there at the next level. Add all that to the question of whether the team will bring back Peters and/or Talib after 2019, and the Rams will soon have some major personnel decisions to make about their defensive backfield.

Most of these questions are about the long-term future of the team, so at least for 2019, the Rams do not have a ton to worry about. Goff is still on his rookie contract and has a deep, talented group surrounding him on offense. The reigning two-time Defensive Player of the Year is not going anywhere and will continue to destroy worlds on the defensive line. With all the talent that the Rams bring back from last year, it's no surprise that we again project the Rams to contend for a first-round bye in the NFC and potentially even a repeat trip to the Super Bowl. But McVay's nigh-invincible offense showed some cracks late in 2018, and with major financial decisions looming, they better make the most of their chances while they can. If they don't, there's no guarantee they'll make it back.

Carl Yedor

2018 Rams Stats by Week

Wk	vs.	W-L	PF	PA	YDF	YDA	TO	Total	Off	Def	ST
1	at OAK	W	33	13	365	395	+3	34%	30%	-6%	-1%
2	ARI	W	34	0	432	137	0	40%	8%	-15%	18%
3	LAC	W	35	23	521	356	0	43%	52%	-6%	-15%
4	MIN	W	38	31	556	446	+1	82%	99%	6%	-12%
5	at SEA	W	33	31	468	373	-2	-5%	23%	24%	-3%
6	at DEN	W	23	20	444	357	0	-1%	15%	12%	-4%
7	at SF	W	39	10	339	228	+4	71%	18%	-47%	6%
8	GB	W	29	27	416	359	+1	-7%	-1%	8%	1%
9	at NO	L	35	45	483	487	0	31%	50%	20%	2%
10	SEA	W	36	31	456	414	+1	25%	53%	28%	0%
11	KC	W	54	51	455	546	+3	24%	27%	-6%	-9%
12	BYE										
13	at DET	W	30	16	344	310	0	14%	-2%	-10%	7%
14	at CHI	L	6	15	214	294	-1	-11%	-46%	-35%	0%
15	PHI	L	23	30	407	381	-2	-2%	9%	10%	-1%
16	at ARI	W	31	9	461	263	-1	22%	47%	27%	1%
17	SF	W	48	32	377	391	+4	45%	27%	-11%	8%
18	BYE										
19	DAL	W	30	22	459	308	0	44%	37%	-1%	5%
20	at NO	W	26	23	378	290	0	37%	-4%	-33%	7%
21	NE	L	3	13	260	407	0	-24%	-49%	-23%	2%

Trends and Splits

	Offense	Rank	Defense	Rank
Total DVOA	24.6%	2	0.5%	17
Unadjusted VOA	24.1%	2	-3.1%	11
Weighted Trend	19.3%	2	0.3%	14
Variance	10.1%	28	4.5%	7
Average Opponent	-0.2%	15	-1.9%	21
Passing	32.9%	5	-0.1%	9
Rushing	21.3%	1	1.1%	27
First Down	31.7%	2	3.0%	20
Second Down	23.2%	2	0.9%	19
Third Down	10.3%	13	-5.8%	13
First Half	27.5%	2	2.3%	24
Second Half	21.5%	2	-1.5%	15
Red Zone	19.8%	9	-3.6%	15
Late and Close	31.5%	1	-11.6%	9

Five-Year Performance

Year	W-L	Pyth W	Est W	PF	PA	TO	Total	Rk	Off	Rk	Def	Rk	ST	Rk	Off AGL	Rk	Def AGL	Rk	Off Age	Rk	Def Age	Rk	ST Age	Rk
2014	6-10	7.1	6.1	324	354	-2	-3.8%	18	-11.1%	25	-3.8%	9	3.5%	7	37.6	21	26.5	7	26.5	23	25.0	32	25.2	32
2015	7-9	6.5	7.9	280	330	+5	-2.2%	16	-15.0%	29	-10.5%	7	2.4%	7	32.3	16	48.0	29	25.2	32	26.1	25	24.9	32
2016	4-12	3.3	4.6	224	394	-11	-28.6%	30	-37.8%	32	-2.0%	15	7.1%	3	7.7	1	21.3	8	25.5	32	26.0	26	25.4	29
2017	11-5	11.6	11.3	478	329	+7	27.7%	2	11.1%	6	-9.8%	6	6.8%	2	3.6	1	12.0	6	26.0	31	26.0	19	25.0	31
2018	13-3	11.2	12.5	527	384	+11	24.0%	2	24.6%	2	0.5%	17	-0.2%	17	10.9	2	28.7	13	27.1	12	26.5	11	25.8	15

2018 Performance Based on Most Common Personnel Groups

LAR Offense					LAR Offense vs. Opponents					LAR Defense					LAR Defense vs. Opponents			
Pers	Freq	Yds	DVOA	Run%	Pers	Freq	Yds	DVOA	Run%	Pers	Freq	Yds	DVOA	Pers	Freq	Yds	DVOA	
11	92%	6.7	29.2%	37%	Base	7%	5.1	1.0%	53%	Base	43%	6.2	-0.3%	11	52%	6.3	11.2%	
12	7%	5.6	19.4%	77%	Nickel	83%	6.9	33.1%	42%	Nickel	34%	6.2	4.4%	12	26%	6.0	-10.3%	
					Dime+	17%	6.0	14.0%	21%	Dime+	22%	6.0	-7.8%	21	11%	6.3	-7.8%	
					Goal Line	0%	2.0	69.6%	100%	Goal Line	1%	0.8	49.3%	22	3%	3.2	-41.7%	
					Big	1%	6.5	-32.9%	83%					612	2%	8.4	59.9%	

Strategic Tendencies

Run/Pass		Rk	Formation		Rk	Pass Rush		Rk	Secondary		Rk	Strategy		Rk
Runs, first half	37%	20	Form: Single Back	89%	2	Rush 3	4.6%	20	4 DB	43%	2	Play action	36%	1
Runs, first down	49%	12	Form: Empty Back	11%	4	Rush 4	74.9%	10	5 DB	34%	29	Avg Box (Off)	6.11	25
Runs, second-long	25%	25	Pers: 3+ WR	93%	1	Rush 5	16.4%	19	6+ DB	22%	8	Avg Box (Def)	6.27	13
Runs, power sit.	62%	10	Pers: 2+ TE/6+ OL	7%	32	Rush 6+	4.1%	26	CB by Sides	81%	13	Offensive Pace	29.05	3
Runs, behind 2H	28%	14	Pers: 6+ OL	0%	32	Int DL Sacks	70.7%	1	S/CB Cover Ratio	33%	5	Defensive Pace	32.20	31
Pass, ahead 2H	48%	16	Shotgun/Pistol	39%	32	Second Level Sacks	14.6%	28	DB Blitz	4%	31	Go for it on 4th	1.76	8

The Rams had a league-best 70 percent fumble recovery rate, not counting special teams muffs or aborted snaps where a quarterback still got off a pass. They recovered nine of 15 offensive fumbles, 11 of 13 defensive fumbles, and one of two special teams fumbles. ❧ The Rams used empty backfields roughly three times as often as they did the year before. ❧ For the second straight year, the Rams were the only team not to use a single play with six offensive linemen. ❧ The Rams used play-action fakes more than any team we've tracked since the 2012 Washington Redskins, who were at a remarkable 42 percent because of read-option fakes. The Rams used play-action on over 50 percent of first-down passes. ❧ The Rams were second in the league with 11.1 average YAC on passes behind or at the line of scrimmage. They led the league with 11.4 YAC the year before. On wide receiver screens, the Rams ranked second with 54.0% DVOA and fourth with 7.6 yards per play. On running back screens, they were tenth with 38.5% DVOA but third with 9.5 yards per play. ❧ The Rams ran 77 percent of the time when they were in 12 personnel; no other offense was above 62 percent. ❧ Not only were the Rams the team that used the least amount of shotgun in the league, they were basically telegraphing pass when they went shotgun. They ran only 14 times all year out of shotgun, 33 less than any other offense, and had just 3.8 yards per carry on these runs. ❧ On the other hand, the Rams gave up a ton of yardage to opponents who were running from shotgun or pistol: 6.1 yards per carry and 17.2% DVOA. Against handoffs from under-center formations, they only allowed 3.7 yards per carry with -24.9% DVOA. ❧ The Rams were the only defense where opponents threw to wide receivers on less than half of all pass targets. The Rams were No. 1 facing passes to running backs (26 percent) and No. 2 facing passes to tight ends (24 percent). ❧ Los Angeles was an excellent tackling team, second behind Minnesota with just 86 broken tackles. ❧ The Rams were last in the league with just 38 penalties on offense, but fourth in the league with 25 penalties on special teams.

Passing

Player	DYAR	DVOA	Plays	NtYds	Avg	YAC	C%	TD	Int
J.Goff	1114	17.0%	593	4450	7.5	5.8	65.2%	32	10
B.Bortles	-221	-18.9%	435	2549	5.9	6.1	60.3%	13	10

Rushing

Player	DYAR	DVOA	Plays	Yds	Avg	TD	Fum	Suc
T.Gurley	366	23.6%	256	1251	4.9	17	0	57%
C.J.Anderson*	132	61.4%	43	299	7.0	2	0	77%
M.Brown	36	9.7%	43	212	4.9	0	0	67%
J.Kelly	-15	-22.3%	27	74	2.7	0	0	44%
J.Goff	0	-11.8%	26	118	4.5	2	1	--
R.Woods	96	40.7%	19	157	8.3	1	0	--
B.Cooks	63	65.8%	10	68	6.8	1	0	--
B.Bortles	107	26.8%	51	370	7.3	1	2	--

Receiving

Player	DYAR	DVOA	Plays	Ctch	Yds	Y/C	YAC	TD	C%
R.Woods	316	17.5%	130	86	1219	14.2	4.9	6	66%
B.Cooks	318	21.5%	117	80	1205	15.1	4.3	5	68%
C.Kupp	158	23.8%	55	40	566	14.2	7.6	6	73%
J.Reynolds	62	1.9%	53	29	402	13.9	4.4	5	55%
G.Everett	2	-6.6%	50	33	319	9.7	4.4	3	66%
T.Higbee	54	15.0%	34	24	292	12.2	5.7	2	71%
T.Gurley	98	6.9%	81	59	580	9.8	9.9	4	73%
M.Brown	23	43.5%	7	5	52	10.4	7.8	1	71%
C.J.Anderson*	-17	-59.6%	6	4	17	4.3	4.3	0	67%

Offensive Line

Player	Pos	Age	GS	Snaps	Pen	Sk	Pass	Run	Player	Pos	Age	GS	Snaps	Pen	Sk	Pass	Run
Austin Blythe	RG	27	16/16	1100	2	1.0	4	4	John Sullivan*	C	34	16/16	1054	7	3.5	5	4
Rob Havenstein	RT	27	16/16	1100	2	2.5	6	6	Andrew Whitworth	LT	38	16/16	1037	8	7.5	11	0
Rodger Saffold*	LG	31	16/16	1068	6	1.0	9	6									

Year	Yards	ALY	Rank	Power	Rank	Stuff	Rank	2nd Lev	Rank	Open Field	Rank	Sacks	ASR	Rank	Press	Rank	F-Start	Cont.
2016	3.23	3.66	29	61%	16	22%	28	0.89	31	0.30	30	49	8.1%	29	28.0%	21	20	29
2017	4.53	4.70	3	50%	29	22%	23	1.42	1	0.82	11	28	5.6%	9	29.8%	12	20	42
2018	5.00	5.49	1	68%	13	15%	2	1.58	1	0.84	16	33	5.4%	6	25.2%	4	11	48
2018 ALY by direction:			Left End: 4.49 (16)			Left Tackle: 6.24 (1)			Mid/Guard: 5.81 (1)			Right Tackle: 4.73 (9)			Right End: 4.38 (14)		

The Los Angeles offensive line was one of the NFL's very best once again, and a large part of that was due to excellent play from its two bookends. Andrew Whitworth and Rob Havenstein ranked 12th and 13th, respectively, in snaps per blown block among tackles. Whitworth had some issues in pass protection, allowing 7.5 sacks on the season, but he did not have a single blown run block charted in his age-37 season. The Rams ranked first in the league in adjusted line yards on runs to the left tackle at 6.24. On the other hand, Havenstein's infrequent missteps were more evenly distributed between runs and passes, and the

Rams were not quite as dominant running to the right. 🏈 Former seventh-round pick Austin Blythe took advantage of Jamon Brown's early-season suspension and stepped in as the starter at right guard for the duration of his third season. Blythe's excellent play led to Brown being waived in October. After spending 2017 as a backup, Blythe made the most of his opportunity; he is entering a contract year, and he should be due for a nice raise. 🏈 Rodger Saffold got a big free-agent contract from Tennessee after nine seasons as a mainstay on the Rams' line, primarily at left guard and tackle. Center John Sullivan was not as lucky, as the Rams declined to exercise the option in his contract for 2019, and Sullivan is still looking for a new team at press time. 🏈 2018 third-round pick Joseph Noteboom has the inside track to taking over for Saffold at left guard, and may may be a long-term replacement for Whitworth once he decides to hang it up. Fellow 2018 draftee Brian Allen looks like the eventual starter at center. The two of them combined for only 114 snaps last year due to the excellent health of the rest of the line, so there is still some uncertainty surrounding how they'll perform with more responsibility. Noteboom was a three-year starter at TCU, spending time at both left and right tackle. He entered the league with consistency questions about his blocking technique, particularly when dealing with power, but after what was essentially a redshirt season, the Rams are optimistic that his flashes of strong hand usage and his athleticism in space will translate effectively to the professional level. Allen's athletic testing left a lot to be desired, raising some questions about his fit in a zone-blocking scheme, but he drove defenders off the ball effectively in the run game at Michigan State.

Defensive Front

Defensive Line	Age	Pos	G	Snaps	Plays	Overall TmPct	Rk	Stop	Dfts	BTkl	Runs	St%	vs. Run Rk	RuYd	Rk	Sack	Pass Rush Hit	Hur	Dsrpt
Aaron Donald	28	DE	16	917	60	7.7%	7	57	36	4	38	92%	1	0.3	2	20.5	22	59	2
Ndamukong Suh*	32	DT	16	891	63	8.1%	5	44	10	4	48	69%	68	3.1	73	4.5	15	30	4
Michael Brockers	29	DE	16	683	53	6.8%	18	39	10	3	50	76%	39	2.3	47	1.0	3	10	1
John Franklin-Myers	23	DE	16	301	10	1.3%	--	8	2	0	7	71%	--	3.7	--	2.0	6	17	0

Edge Rushers	Age	Pos	G	Snaps	Plays	Overall TmPct	Rk	Stop	Dfts	BTkl	Runs	St%	vs. Run Rk	RuYd	Rk	Sack	Pass Rush Hit	Hur	Dsrpt
Samson Ebukam	24	OLB	16	695	39	5.0%	42	26	10	8	30	67%	64	3.0	63	3.0	5	28	0
Dante Fowler	25	OLB	15	578	31	4.3%	60	21	10	4	20	65%	68	2.9	59	4.0	4	27	1
Matt Longacre*	28	OLB	13	281	17	2.7%	--	10	3	1	15	60%	--	4.3	--	1.0	5	11	0
Clay Matthews	33	OLB	16	756	42	5.2%	40	33	15	8	32	78%	36	3.3	75	3.5	11	21	1

Linebackers	Age	Pos	G	Snaps	Plays	Overall TmPct	Rk	Stop	Dfts	BTkl	Runs	St%	vs. Run Rk	RuYd	Rk	Sack	Pass Rush Hit	Hur	Tgts	vs. Pass Suc%	Rk	AdjYd	Rk	PD	Int
Cory Littleton	26	ILB	16	967	138	17.8%	6	82	26	10	72	58%	49	4.1	55	4.0	1	11.5	54	52%	34	7.0	47	13	3
Mark Barron*	30	ILB	12	569	60	10.3%	54	36	6	7	40	68%	16	3.9	39	1.0	1	1	24	54%	27	6.9	43	1	0
Ramik Wilson*	27	ILB	16	161	33	4.3%	--	22	7	0	17	59%	--	3.2	--	0.0	0	0	16	75%	1	5.0	13	2	0

Year	Yards	ALY	Rank	Power	Rank	Stuff	Rank	2nd Level	Rank	Open Field	Rank	Sacks	ASR	Rank	Press	Rank
2016	3.99	3.43	1	64%	19	29%	1	1.10	11	1.04	30	31	5.0%	29	28.4%	11
2017	4.65	4.36	27	63%	16	18%	28	1.14	19	1.19	31	48	7.9%	5	31.5%	11
2018	4.91	4.49	21	68%	21	16%	22	1.36	25	1.12	27	41	7.0%	17	36.0%	1

2018 ALY by direction:	Left End: 5.18 (25)	Left Tackle: 4.66 (21)	Mid/Guard: 4.39 (13)	Right Tackle: 4.00 (14)	Right End: 4.52 (18)

Not much more needs to be said about Aaron Donald, but the two-time Defensive Player of the Year was his normal dominant self, leading the league in run stop rate at 92 percent in addition to his impressive sack total. 🏈 The rest of the front seven left a bit to be desired against the run, which may be why the team felt comfortable letting Ndamukong Suh leave for Tampa Bay after his one season in Los Angeles. The Rams are hoping John Franklin-Myers can help fill Suh's shoes as the 2018 fourth-rounder heads into his second season. Los Angeles also added University of Washington nose tackle Greg Gaines in the fourth round of this year's draft, and he profiles as a run-stuffer. 🏈 Michael Brockers is entering the last year of the extension he signed in 2016; though he did not offer nearly as much as Suh rushing the passer in 2018, Brockers has been a mainstay on the Rams' defensive line since the Jeff Fisher days. 🏈 Filling the role of veteran ring-seeking pass-rusher on this year's edition of the Rams will be Clay Matthews, who joins the team after a decorated tenure in Green Bay. While Matthews is no longer the game-wrecking star he once was, he should help provide an extra boost rushing off the edge in addition to incumbents Dante Fowler and Samson Ebukam. 🏈 Fowler signed a one-year prove-it deal after joining the team at midseason from Jacksonville and flashing as a pass-rusher, while Ebukam stepped into the starting lineup at outside linebacker in his second season, serving as an inexpensive counterbalance to all the other highly compensated talent in the Los Angeles front seven. After making four starts as a fill-in in 2017, Cory Littleton held down the starting job at inside linebacker all season. His play likely helped the Rams with their decision to waive Mark Barron, who is now plying his trade with the Steelers. After playing sparingly as a rookie, Micah Kiser will get a shot to replace Barron at inside linebacker. Ramik Wilson served as a useful depth piece against the run, posting 22 stops on just 161 snaps, but the team let him walk over the offseason.

Defensive Secondary

Secondary	Age	Pos	G	Snaps	Plays	TmPct	Rk	Stop	Dfts	BTkl	Runs	St%	Rk	RuYd	Rk	Tgts	Tgt%	Rk	Dist	Suc%	Rk	AdjYd	Rk	PD	Int
													vs. Run						vs. Pass						
John Johnson	24	SS	16	965	129	16.6%	1	50	21	10	67	42%	40	7.5	47	44	10.7%	52	8.5	48%	46	6.5	18	11	4
Marcus Peters	26	CB	16	918	51	6.6%	70	20	6	7	10	40%	43	10.3	74	67	17.1%	26	11.1	49%	52	9.7	74	8	3
Lamarcus Joyner*	29	FS	15	911	81	11.1%	27	19	8	7	36	22%	64	11.5	72	22	5.7%	12	12.6	55%	26	9.9	63	3	1
Nickell Robey-Coleman	27	CB	16	558	39	5.0%	--	18	11	5	7	29%	--	11.4	--	39	16.4%	--	7.6	67%	--	4.4	--	4	1
Troy Hill	28	CB	16	426	39	5.0%	--	19	4	4	10	60%	--	5.2	--	39	21.5%	--	14.8	56%	--	10.6	--	5	2
Aqib Talib	33	CB	8	392	28	7.2%	61	9	3	0	2	50%	22	7.0	48	23	13.8%	3	12.2	52%	38	8.4	57	5	1
Marqui Christian	25	FS	16	348	34	4.4%	74	13	9	5	7	43%	35	6.4	29	35	23.6%	76	8.6	54%	27	6.9	30	1	0
Sam Shields*	32	CB	16	339	23	3.0%	--	8	4	5	7	29%	--	5.0	--	37	25.6%	--	11.3	43%	--	12.6	--	4	1
Eric Weddle	34	FS	16	1016	71	9.3%	45	24	7	8	34	38%	45	6.8	37	27	6.2%	14	11.4	48%	42	6.9	31	3	0

Year	Pass D Rank	vs. #1 WR	Rk	vs. #2 WR	Rk	vs. Other WR	Rk	WR Wide	Rk	WR Slot	Rk	vs. TE	Rk	vs. RB	Rk
2016	20	3.7%	21	-3.8%	11	17.8%	30	20.5%	31	-3.3%	11	-6.0%	10	-20.1%	6
2017	3	-5.4%	12	-24.8%	4	-16.8%	7	-10.4%	10	-16.0%	6	1.2%	19	-9.8%	9
2018	9	15.9%	28	-12.2%	9	9.9%	24	3.0%	21	10.2%	23	-22.1%	5	-18.1%	4

Los Angeles brought in a pair of first-team All-Pros at cornerback in Aqib Talib and Marcus Peters, to mixed results. Talib's play was generally positive when he was on the field, but he missed half the season due to injuries. Peters was fairly inconsistent, with his ballhawk tendencies occasionally working against him and getting him burned on big plays deep down the field. The Rams' secondary strategy changed dramatically when Talib was injured. With Talib healthy, they mostly kept Peters on the right side with Talib on the left (CB by Sides: 92 percent). When Talib was out, Peters moved around to cover specific receivers (CB by Sides: 66 percent). The aptly named Nickell Robey-Coleman held down the nickel role throughout the year; Robey-Coleman was not targeted particularly frequently, but had he qualified for our rankings, his success rate of 67 percent would have been among the very best. Sam Shields and Troy Hill added depth in a defensive backfield that had to handle Talib's absence for half the year. While neither did enough to earn a starting role heading into 2019 (either in Los Angeles or elsewhere), the pair did combine for nine passes defensed and three interceptions. Hill remains with the Rams as a backup, but Shields is not under contract with a team. The fact that Shields was on the field at all last year was impressive considering that he had played in one game between 2016 and 2017 combined due to a debilitating concussion. Third-round rookie David Long of Michigan could play a larger role in the future, as Talib and Peters are both entering the final year of their contracts. Long stood out with the top 3-cone and 20-yard shuttle times at this year's combine. Second-round rookie Taylor Rapp lined up all over the defensive backfield at Washington, even at free safety, as his safety partner was much better suited to playing in the box. At the professional level, Rapp profiles as more of a versatile box safety; he lacks the range needed to play single-high safety in the NFL but tackles well and should be able to match up with tight ends in man coverage. John Johnson started all 16 games at strong safety in his second season and not only led the team with 11 passes defensed but also had the third-most run stops on the team. Marqui Christian saw his first notable playing time in his third season and will be back to provide additional depth at safety in 2019.

Special Teams

Year	DVOA	Rank	FG/XP	Rank	Net Kick	Rank	Kick Ret	Rank	Net Punt	Rank	Punt Ret	Rank	Hidden	Rank
2016	7.1%	3	3.8	9	4.0	8	1.3	11	29.2	1	-2.6	22	0.7	16
2017	6.8%	2	11.3	5	-0.3	19	9.2	2	10.3	3	3.7	7	40.6	1
2018	-0.2%	17	-4.9	24	1.1	14	-3.0	25	3.4	13	2.6	11	10.4	6

After back-to-back top-three finishes in special teams DVOA, the Rams fell all the way to 17th. It was the first time they had ranked outside the top ten since all the way back in 2012, which was Jeff Fisher's first season with the team. ◥ A major component of that mediocrity was the struggles of the team's placekickers. Greg Zuerlein dealt with injuries over the course of the year, forcing Sam Ficken, Cairo Santos, and even punter Johnny Hekker to step in at times during the season. Unsurprisingly, Ficken and Santos were nowhere near Zuerlein's level, which explains a lot of why they were available to begin with. Hekker outperformed the two of them in net points of field position from kickoffs. ◥ Hekker turned in another solid season punting the ball, but it still represented a step down from his outstanding 2016 and 2017 seasons. He also tied his career high for pass attempts in a season with four, completing two of them on fake punts. ◥ JoJo Natson finished just outside the top ten in punt return value in 2018 while replacing former All-Pro returner Pharoh Cooper, who went on injured reserve before being released in December. ◥ Blake Countess did not make much of an impact returning kicks in Cooper's absence and has since signed with the Eagles. ◥ Rookie safety Nick Scott, a seventh-round pick from Penn State, will likely get a chance in the return game after serving as the Nittany Lions' special teams captain for the past two years.

Miami Dolphins

2018 record: 7-9	**Total DVOA:** -16.5% (27th)	**2019 Mean Projection:** 5.1 wins	**On the Clock (0-4):** 44%
Pythagorean Wins: 5.1 (29th)	**Offense:** -8.9% (26th)	**Postseason Odds:** 7.6%	**Mediocrity (5-7):** 40%
Snap-Weighted Age: 26.5 (17th)	**Defense:** 6.5% (25th)	**Super Bowl Odds:** 0.2%	**Playoff Contender (8-10):** 14%
Average Opponent: -3.3% (28th)	**Special Teams:** -1.1% (21st)	**Proj. Avg. Opponent:** 0.1% (18th)	**Super Bowl Contender (11+):** 2%

2018: The Ryan Tannehill era fizzles on the vine.

2019: It's a Fish Rebuild, not a Fish Tank.

The Dolphins are not tanking. They're rebuilding.

It's easy to equate the two when trying to sound edgy on social media, but it's important to be precise here at *Football Outsiders Almanac*, especially when it comes to Moneyball-flavored topics. "Tanking" means constructing the weakest conceivable roster in order to obtain future high draft choices and extra draft capital while saving gobs of money for future signings. "Rebuilding" means constructing the youngest and least expensive conceivable roster in order to cut losses on past mistakes and develop young talent, while also stockpiling some cap space and draft capital. Rebuilding carries a built-in sense of urgency, not to compete for the playoffs, but to at least accomplish something. Tanking suggests that the losing itself is the accomplishment, which is one reason why NFL decision-makers scoff at the concept.

Rebuilding is a well-established tool of roster construction. Tanking in the NFL is mostly a sports-radio talking point and thought experiment. Even Sashi Brown's Browns weren't planning to be so weak that they went 1-31 over two seasons, although that ultimately turned out to be the best thing that they did.

The Dolphins are now led by general manager Chris Grier and head coach Brian Flores, a Bill Parcells and a Bill Belichick disciple who would never abide by constructing a purposely terrible team. That's why the Dolphins did not gut their roster to the degree which would suggest "tanking."

But perhaps they should have.

Our projections for the Dolphins average just 5.1 wins this year, likely earning the league's worst record and the first pick in the 2020 draft. But why should the Dolphins leave anything to chance? With some roster tweaks, they could have ended up with something like a 4.1-win projection, a near guarantee of that top pick, millions more in future cap space, and a slightly bigger draft haul this year.

The handful of concessions they made to being semi-competitive in 2019 could actually cost the Dolphins a few opportunities down the line. But it's more likely that the Dolphins made the prudent move by taking a step back and trimming the fat from their roster without going full *Major League*.

The Dolphins' boldest move of the offseason, of course, was the Josh Rosen trade. Acquiring Rosen from the Cardinals in exchange for a second-round pick was shrewd from an analytical, cap management, and risk-reward standpoint.

The Dolphins exploited a unique and extreme market inefficiency—the Cardinals underwent the most severe "culture change" since the Chip Kelly Eagles this offseason—to acquire a potential young franchise quarterback from a team suddenly lurching in a new direction. The Cardinals were in such a mad dash to begin the Kliff Kingsbury/Kyler Murray era that they ate Rosen's rookie signing bonus (the most expensive chunk of his contract), and the Dolphins even picked up a 2020 second-round pick from the Saints as the brokerage fee in what became a three-way trade because the Cardinals procrastinated until draft weekend before pursuing trade talks for some reason.

Rosen landed in awful circumstances last season, and quarterbacks of his pedigree are never traded after one year, so any projection of his potential based on last season's performance would be mostly speculative. If Rosen spent last year on the Cardinals bench watching Sam Bradford get richer instead of playing, we'd still base his future on his QBASE projection in the 2018 draft: 22.3 percent chance of becoming an elite or upper-tier quarterback, a 50.8 percent bust risk. Even if the percentages are now skewed another point or two toward "bust," Rosen still grades out as a similar prospect to Dwayne Haskins (51 percent bust, 21 percent upper tier/elite) and a better one than Drew Lock (59 percent/14 percent) or Daniel Jones (56 percent/19 percent).

So the Dolphins now have a viable franchise quarterback prospect at an affordable price for three years with no obligations. That certainly qualifies as an important future asset. But they also signed Ryan Fitzpatrick to a two-year, $11-million contract as a mentor, caretaker, insurance policy, and beat-reporter flypaper.

Fitzpatrick's contract is budget friendly, but it still represents money that the Dolphins did not need to spend if their 2019 goal is an extended tryout and development period for Rosen. Since 2008, Fitzpatrick has started at least three games and led his teams to at least two wins each year, making him an expert at emerging from cloudy quarterback situations with playing time and just enough success to take his team out of the running for the top pick in the draft. From a long-range standpoint, Rosen losses would be much more useful to the Dolphins than feel-good Fitzmagic moments, even if those losses only prove that the Rosen won't be the answer. And the value of a mentor quarterback as anything more than an

2019 Dolphins Schedule

Week	Opp.	Week	Opp.	Week	Opp.
1	BAL	7	at BUF	13	PHI
2	NE	8	at PIT (Mon.)	14	at NYJ
3	at DAL	9	NYJ	15	at NYG
4	LAC	10	at IND	16	CIN
5	BYE	11	BUF	17	at NE
6	WAS	12	at CLE		

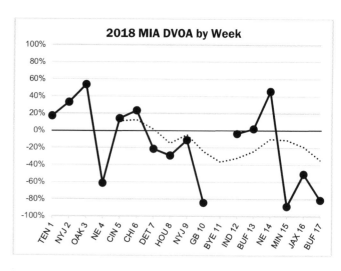

2018 MIA DVOA by Week

anxiety pet for the offensive coordinator is grossly overstated (see: Bradford).

The Dolphins signed Fitzpatrick before trading for Rosen, anticipating that they would want a caretaker quarterback for some young quarterback (possibly a draft pick). It was a hedged bet, and the Dolphins offseason was full of similar decisions.

The Dolphins traded Ryan Tannehill and Robert Quinn and released Danny Amendola, Andre Branch, Josh Sitton and some minor veterans before the start of free agency. They also let Frank Gore and stalwart Cameron Wake walk in free agency. They will eat $38 million in dead cap space this year, most of it from Tannehill (they had to swallow his old signing bonus as part of the sign-and-trade terms with the Titans) and Ndamukong Suh (though it feels like it's been 10 years since Suh played for the Dolphins).

The departures both officially signaled the organization's commitment to rebuild and erased their most recent series of baffling decisions. The Dolphins were fooled by their 10-6 playoff season in 2016—built upon a Jets-Bills sweep and narrow wins over the Browns, Kelly 49ers, and Jeff Fisher Rams—into thinking that loading up on veterans would somehow make them Super Bowl contenders. The veteran purge and a 2019 commitment to credit repair left the Dolphins with $62 million in 2020 cap space after cornerback Xavien Howard's mid-May contract extension.

The Dolphins could have cut even closer to the quick this offseason by getting rid of expensive, expendable veterans such as wide receivers Kenny Stills and DeVante Parker and linebacker Kiko Alonso. (Safety Reshad Jones, with three years and $47 million left on his contract, was trade bait at press time.) But by doing so, they risked pushing well past the point of diminishing returns between "rebuilding" and "tanking."

Quinn netted only a sixth-round pick from the Cowboys in trade compensation. The Dolphins stopped just short of paying the Titans to haul Tannehill away after six seasons as their starter. Stills and Parker weren't going to fetch much on a buyer's market for damaged goods and fading prospects, but getting rid of them could leave Rosen with no one to throw the ball to. That would place him in the same predicament he faced with the Cardinals.

As for shedding even more salary in the name of hoarding cap space, right now the Dolphins have no one to spend it on. Last year's roster was larded with old-timers like Wake, Quinn, Gore, and Amendola, all of them still playing just well enough for Adam Gase to play escape-the-doghouse with

prospects such as Parker, running back Kenyan Drake, and edge rusher Charles Harris.

Howard, the only true blue-chip player on the current roster, signed a five-year, $75-million extension in early May. Left tackle Laremy Tunsil is due for an extension before he plays for a $10.3-million fifth-year option in 2020. There is no one else on the payroll who is both due for a big contract and has proven to be worth one. So while the Dolphins may make a few more cost-cutting trims over the next year, the Dolphins' top priority should not be saving money. It should be identifying and developing players worth paying.

That's where the new decision-makers come in.

Faith in the Dolphins rebuilding plan hinges on faith in Grier and Flores. Nurturing that faith is tricky, because Grier is a Dolphins lifer (in-house politics are the reason the Dolphins have spent over a decade fielding mostly sub-.500 teams full of failed prospects and 30-somethings) and Flores is a Belichick Buddy (the track record of Patriots assistants who go on to head coaching jobs is less than spectacular) .

Neither Grier nor Flores presents a dynamic public persona, which may be a good thing: it brings into focus who they are not, if not who they are. The soft-spoken Flores is not a self-promoter famous for shouting at Tom Brady, strutting the sideline with a pencil behind his ear, or engaging in other acts of both on-camera and behind-the-scenes self-promotion. Flores rose slowly from the Patriots scouting ranks through special teams, offense, and defense before replacing Matt Patricia as Belichick's chief defensive lieutenant and making the Patriots significantly better in 2018 than they were under Patricia. The slow organizational cooking may have allowed Flores to internalize more of "The Patriots Way" than most of the Patriots assistants who preceded him.

Flores hired several well-regarded assistants to fill out his staff, including offensive coordinator Chad O'Shea, the Patriots' long-time wide receivers coach; quarterbacks coach Jim Caldwell of Playoff Flacco fame; and running backs coach Eric Studesville, a beloved Broncos assistant fired during a John Elway mood swing. It's a solid mix of new faces and lifers, Patriots Way types, and outsiders with fresh voices.

Grier's Dolphins career began in 2000, and he rose to the rank of director of college scouting in 2008 when Bill Parcells (who groomed the young Grier in Foxborough) briefly took over the organization. So Grier survived the post-Parcells Jeff Ireland era, the Dennis Hickey era, and the Tannenbaum era, which means he's going straight to heaven when he dies. Grier was never directly implicated in the endless politicking that has defined the Dolphins organizational culture for a decade. He doesn't have the ink from any regrettable contracts on his hands, and the Dolphins weak draft history has more to do with the bad decisions of the GMs than a scouting issue. Grier is a methodical executive who survived in a front office that operated on pure impulse for over a decade, making him an ideal choice for a rebuild that won't happen overnight.

Flores, Grier, and Rosen all have the potential to be great, making them the Dolphins most important assets right now. But all they have is potential, and the Dolphins' only other assets are Howard and Tunsil, second-tier prospects like Drake and White, this year's draft class, and the extra picks and cap space they added for next year. That's why the tanking-versus-rebuilding distinction is largely academic for 2019: after three years of Gase and 15 years of organizational faction wars, the Dolphins barely had anything worth giving away, let alone keeping.

The new Dolphins regime emblazoned giant letters "T.N.T." onto a wall next to the team's practice fields. That stands for "Takes No Talent," a slogan that can easily be turned into a punchline, but words painted within the block letters clarify what T.N.T. is all about: hustling, enthusiasm, conditioning, knowing the rules and game situations, trusting, believing, competing, communicating, and all that stuff that most teams take for granted but can be easily damaged by "tanking" tactics and rhetoric.

Flores and Grier will be teaching the basics this year. Instilling those basics may or may not be worth more than winning an extra game and losing a little draft capital. But Flores and Grier are rebuilding the Dolphins the way they were taught to rebuild a team. And they were taught by the best in the business.

Mike Tanier

2018 Dolphins Stats by Week

Wk	vs.	W-L	PF	PA	YDF	YDA	TO	Total	Off	Def	ST
1	TEN	W	27	20	342	336	+1	17%	-7%	-37%	-13%
2	at NYJ	W	20	12	257	362	+1	33%	-7%	-27%	13%
3	OAK	W	28	20	373	434	+2	54%	60%	11%	5%
4	at NE	L	7	38	172	449	0	-61%	-57%	1%	-3%
5	at CIN	L	17	27	297	332	-2	14%	-23%	-15%	22%
6	CHI	W	31	28	541	467	0	23%	34%	16%	6%
7	DET	L	21	32	322	457	0	-22%	20%	36%	-5%
8	at HOU	L	23	42	370	427	-1	-29%	10%	48%	9%
9	NYJ	W	13	6	168	282	+4	-11%	-45%	-32%	2%
10	at GB	L	12	31	294	377	-1	-84%	-51%	31%	-3%
11	BYE										
12	at IND	L	24	27	314	455	+2	-4%	-9%	-3%	3%
13	BUF	W	21	17	175	415	+2	2%	8%	13%	7%
14	NE	W	34	33	412	421	0	46%	74%	1%	-27%
15	at MIN	L	17	41	193	418	+1	-89%	-35%	33%	-21%
16	JAX	L	7	17	183	244	-1	-51%	-45%	-7%	-13%
17	at BUF	L	17	42	225	381	-3	-81%	-46%	35%	0%

Trends and Splits

	Offense	Rank	Defense	Rank
Total DVOA	-8.9%	26	6.5%	25
Unadjusted VOA	-14.3%	26	4.9%	23
Weighted Trend	-11.9%	26	13.4%	32
Variance	15.8%	32	6.8%	23
Average Opponent	-2.3%	7	-6.1%	30
Passing	-3.7%	27	14.4%	23
Rushing	-4.4%	15	-1.6%	24
First Down	-2.7%	17	1.8%	18
Second Down	-9.9%	25	17.0%	31
Third Down	-19.9%	27	-0.7%	19
First Half	0.2%	14	-1.9%	11
Second Half	-19.5%	26	15.2%	30
Red Zone	-9.3%	21	-4.9%	11
Late and Close	-29.4%	29	7.3%	26

Five-Year Performance

Year	W-L	Pyth W	Est W	PF	PA	TO	Total	Rk	Off	Rk	Def	Rk	ST	Rk	Off AGL	Rk	Def AGL	Rk	Off Age	Rk	Def Age	Rk	ST Age	Rk
2014	8-8	8.4	8.8	388	373	+2	3.5%	15	10.1%	8	0.5%	17	-6.1%	32	40.3	26	39.1	18	26.2	27	27.3	7	25.7	25
2015	6-10	5.8	5.8	310	389	-3	-19.0%	29	-7.3%	22	9.0%	25	-2.7%	24	23.0	7	40.5	24	25.5	31	26.6	16	25.3	30
2016	10-6	7.5	8.9	363	380	+2	1.0%	18	1.8%	14	1.6%	19	0.8%	12	46.3	24	52.8	25	26.3	23	26.9	10	25.6	25
2017	6-10	4.9	5.6	281	393	-14	-19.8%	27	-13.1%	27	9.4%	28	2.6%	12	61.8	29	53.6	29	27.3	11	27.1	4	25.8	19
2018	7-9	5.1	5.0	319	433	+5	-16.5%	27	-8.9%	26	6.5%	25	-1.1%	21	67.0	30	28.3	12	27.3	10	26.1	20	25.8	17

2018 Performance Based on Most Common Personnel Groups

MIA Offense					MIA Offense vs. Opponents					MIA Defense				MIA Defense vs. Opponents			
Pers	Freq	Yds	DVOA	Run%	Pers	Freq	Yds	DVOA	Run%	Pers	Freq	Yds	DVOA	Pers	Freq	Yds	DVOA
11	75%	5.3	-3.1%	36%	Base	12%	5.7	-21.4%	49%	Base	40%	6.1	6.9%	11	59%	6.5	3.4%
12	12%	6.3	-0.6%	48%	Nickel	62%	5.3	0.3%	41%	Nickel	58%	6.6	3.6%	12	18%	6.5	4.6%
21	3%	9.1	55.8%	46%	Dime+	11%	5.6	-9.2%	21%	Dime+	0%	15.5	223.4%	21	13%	6.5	27.7%
13	3%	2.2	-58.5%	65%						Goal Line	1%	1.5	19.7%	13	4%	5.6	-13.7%
20	2%	7.0	23.9%	53%						Big	0%	6.2	49.0%	22	1%	5.2	16.6%

Strategic Tendencies

Run/Pass		Rk	Formation		Rk	Pass Rush		Rk	Secondary		Rk	Strategy		Rk
Runs, first half	40%	11	Form: Single Back	81%	14	Rush 3	1.4%	32	4 DB	40%	3	Play action	22%	21
Runs, first down	50%	10	Form: Empty Back	8%	19	Rush 4	75.5%	9	5 DB	58%	21	Avg Box (Off)	6.08	29
Runs, second-long	40%	3	Pers: 3+ WR	80%	3	Rush 5	17.0%	17	6+ DB	0%	31	Avg Box (Def)	6.42	2
Runs, power sit.	48%	27	Pers: 2+ TE/6+ OL	15%	30	Rush 6+	5.7%	14	CB by Sides	59%	26	Offensive Pace	32.74	31
Runs, behind 2H	32%	5	Pers: 6+ OL	0%	28	Int DL Sacks	19.4%	23	S/CB Cover Ratio	45%	1	Defensive Pace	31.96	29
Pass, ahead 2H	47%	20	Shotgun/Pistol	66%	13	Second Level Sacks	19.4%	21	DB Blitz	9%	17	Go for it on 4th	0.89	28

Most teams are more efficient running from shotgun and pistol formations than they are on more traditional handoffs with the quarterback under center. However, Miami had a strong lean the other way. The Dolphins gained 5.4 yards per carry with 6.6% DVOA on runs with the quarterback under center, compared to 4.2 yards per carry and -21.0% DVOA from shotgun. ● Miami actually used play-action more frequently on second-down passes (30.4 percent) than on first-down passes (28.7 percent). Philadelphia was the only other offense to do so. ● The Dolphins ran against small boxes (less than seven) on 66 percent of their running back carries, second behind Green Bay. ● Miami's quarterbacks combined for -60.7% DVOA against blitzes; only Arizona was worse. ● Fumble luck regression watch: Miami recovered only three of 13 fumbles on offense and only five of 14 fumbles on defense. ● Overall, the Dolphins defense ranked about the same against the run and the pass, but how they got there was sort of weird.

Miami Defense Run/Pass DVOA Splits by Down, 2018

	Pass	Rk	Run	Rk
1st Down	3.0%	8	1.0%	29
2nd Down	40.5%	32	-7.4%	17
3rd/4th Down	-2.3%	17	2.7%	15
All Plays	14.4%	23	-1.6%	24

If Brian Flores brings along the Patriots' defensive scheme, get ready for some big changes in Miami's strategic tendencies next season. There will be more dime personnel and a lot less base personnel, and there will be more three-man rushes but also more big blitzes. ● Miami's nickel was usually three safeties, not three cornerbacks, but that's something Flores is comfortable with. Miami used three safeties on 55 percent of plays, third in the NFL, while the Patriots used three safeties on 45 percent of plays, fourth in the NFL. ● Hopefully, another thing Flores will be able to bring is tackling discipline. The Dolphins were 31st in the NFL last year with 145 broken tackles. By comparison, Flores' Patriots and ex-boss Matt Patricia's Lions were tied for third in fewest broken tackles with just 87 each. ● The Dolphins were horrible last year when they blitzed, allowing 71.9% DVOA and 10.2 net yards per pass when they rushed five or more defenders. No other defense allowed more than 8.3 yards on average. This was the worst performance when blitzing of any defense in our game charting database, back to 2011.

Passing

Player	DYAR	DVOA	Plays	NtYds	Avg	YAC	C%	TD	Int
R.Tannehill*	-186	-20.8%	309	1694	5.5	6.1	64.5%	17	9
B.Osweiler*	-85	-17.7%	195	1112	5.7	5.9	63.8%	7	4
J.Rosen	-1145	-53.7%	439	1943	4.4	4.5	55.5%	11	14
R.Fitzpatrick	473	16.8%	260	2283	8.8	5.3	66.7%	17	12

Rushing

Player	DYAR	DVOA	Plays	Yds	Avg	TD	Fum	Suc
F.Gore*	86	5.7%	156	722	4.6	0	1	50%
K.Drake	58	4.7%	120	535	4.5	4	2	45%
K.Ballage	16	1.0%	36	186	5.2	1	1	42%
R.Tannehill*	39	34.9%	21	154	7.3	0	0	--
B.Bolden*	32	99.6%	8	91	11.4	2	1	63%
A.Wilson	10	-15.4%	8	16	2.0	0	0	--
B.Osweiler*	-3	-24.0%	5	23	4.6	0	0	--
J.Rosen	23	25.2%	14	145	10.4	0	1	--
M.Walton	-10	-21.8%	14	34	2.4	0	0	36%

Receiving

Player	DYAR	DVOA	Plays	Ctch	Yds	Y/C	YAC	TD	C%
D.Amendola*	38	-6.2%	79	59	575	9.7	3.9	1	75%
K.Stills	127	12.6%	64	37	553	14.9	3.5	6	58%
D.Parker	-52	-26.6%	48	25	309	12.4	3.9	1	52%
A.Wilson	63	10.8%	35	26	391	15.0	12.9	4	74%
J.Grant	21	-4.6%	34	21	268	12.8	6.7	2	62%
B.Butler	21	16.5%	9	6	60	10.0	0.2	1	67%
M.Gesicki	-70	-37.3%	32	22	202	9.2	4.4	0	69%
D.Smythe	-17	-31.2%	11	6	50	8.3	1.2	0	55%
N.O'Leary	27	29.3%	10	8	86	10.8	8.1	1	80%
K.Drake	123	14.0%	74	54	477	8.8	7.8	5	73%
F.Gore*	49	35.4%	16	12	124	10.3	9.6	1	75%
K.Ballage	-17	-39.6%	11	9	56	6.2	8.4	0	82%
M.Walton	-10	-40.1%	8	5	41	8.2	9.6	0	63%

Offensive Line

Player	Pos	Age	GS	Snaps	Pen	Sk	Pass	Run	Player	Pos	Age	GS	Snaps	Pen	Sk	Pass	Run
Jesse Davis	RG	28	16/16	920	5	6.5	15	9	Daniel Kilgore	C	32	4/4	182	2	0.0	0	5
Laremy Tunsil	LT	25	15/15	819	9	2.0	9	3	Jake Brendel*	LG	27	4/3	176	2	2.0	3	1
Ja'Wuan James*	RT	27	15/15	815	7	3.5	9	5	Jordan Mills	RT	29	16/16	1011	9	4.0	16	2
Ted Larsen*	LG	32	15/13	751	4	3.0	11	7	Chris Reed	G	27	9/1	178	3	2.0	7	0
Travis Swanson*	C	28	12/11	643	1	2.0	9	8									

Year	Yards	ALY	Rank	Power	Rank	Stuff	Rank	2nd Lev	Rank	Open Field	Rank	Sacks	ASR	Rank	Press	Rank	F-Start	Cont.
2016	4.59	3.97	22	52%	28	24%	31	1.40	3	1.13	4	30	6.3%	21	26.8%	18	14	25
2017	4.09	3.26	30	71%	6	27%	30	1.09	20	1.07	4	33	5.8%	11	29.6%	10	21	30
2018	4.79	4.47	14	62%	24	18%	15	1.29	12	1.02	8	52	10.5%	31	36.3%	31	16	26

2018 ALY by direction:	Left End: 5.68 (3)	Left Tackle: 4.71 (7)	Mid/Guard: 4.44 (17)	Right Tackle: 3.79 (25)	Right End: 4.60 (12)

Laremy Tunsil has developed into a dependable left tackle despite a penchant for penalties: 21 of them in the last two seasons, with 11 false starts and six holds. Tunsil should receive an extension on his rookie contract soon. He's the anchor of the Dolphins line. Everything else is in flux. ✎ Former 49ers center Daniel Kilgore, acquired to replace Mike Pouncey last year, started just four games before suffering a triceps injury. Kilgore is now 31 and has started 16 games only once, losing much of past seasons to knee injuries and a broken ankle. ✎ Right tackle Ja'Wuan James (signed away by the Broncos) and guard Ted Larsen (back with the Bears after a bad year) are gone. Jesse Davis, who started 16 games at right guard last season, slid over to right tackle in minicamp. Davis will compete with journeyman Jordan Mills, one of those veterans the Dolphins grabbed in the offseason to make sure the wheels don't fall off the wagon. ✎ Third-round pick Michael Deiter, your basic Wisconsin rookie lineman, took starter's reps in minicamp. Sixth-round pick Isaiah Prince (Ohio State) was not as far along in minicamp as Deiter but figures to be in the mix for one of the interior line positions, as is former Jaguars backup Chris Reed and some even more obscure players. ✎ In summary, this is not going to be a very good offensive line, though it should still be better than the one Josh Rosen played behind in Arizona last year.

Defensive Front

Defensive Line	Age	Pos	G	Snaps	Plays	TmPct	Rk	Stop	Dfts	BTkl	Runs	St%	Rk	RuYd	Rk	Sack	Hit	Hur	Dsrpt
						Overall							**vs. Run**				**Pass Rush**		
Davon Godchaux	25	DT	16	674	48	5.7%	31	37	11	3	43	77%	34	1.7	14	1.0	3	6	0
Akeem Spence	28	DT	16	665	41	4.9%	42	25	10	6	37	62%	80	3.9	83	2.0	8	12	0
Sylvester Williams*	31	DT	14	376	13	1.8%	83	9	0	4	13	69%	67	3.2	75	0.0	0	5	0
Ziggy Hood*	32	DT	13	217	10	1.5%	--	7	0	1	8	75%	--	1.9	--	0.0	0	6	1
Vincent Taylor	25	DT	8	204	27	6.5%	--	18	7	3	20	70%	--	2.5	--	2.0	0	3	0

Edge Rushers	Age	Pos	G	Snaps	Plays	TmPct	Rk	Stop	Dfts	BTkl	Runs	St%	Rk	RuYd	Rk	Sack	Hit	Hur	Dsrpt
						Overall							**vs. Run**				**Pass Rush**		
Robert Quinn*	29	DE	16	635	38	4.6%	54	26	14	10	27	63%	73	2.6	53	6.5	10	26	1
Cameron Wake*	37	DE	14	517	35	4.8%	47	28	11	4	23	78%	33	2.8	55	6.0	10	37	1
Andre Branch*	30	DE	14	483	26	3.6%	76	18	10	6	17	59%	80	2.2	39	1.5	4	15	1
Charles Harris	24	DE	11	347	19	3.3%	82	9	3	2	15	33%	93	4.4	89	1.0	4	13	0

Linebackers	Age	Pos	G	Snaps	Plays	TmPct	Rk	Stop	Dfts	BTkl	Runs	St%	Rk	RuYd	Rk	Sack	Hit	Hur	Tgts	Suc%	Rk	AdjYd	Rk	PD	Int
						Overall							**vs. Run**				**Pass Rush**				**vs. Pass**				
Kiko Alonso	29	OLB	15	1004	130	16.6%	13	64	17	13	77	51%	75	5.6	85	0.0	3	4.5	42	52%	33	9.5	72	6	3
Raekwon McMillan	24	MLB	16	830	106	12.7%	40	70	12	13	78	74%	5	3.3	21	0.0	0	1	22	41%	62	8.8	70	1	0
Jerome Baker	23	OLB	16	679	78	9.3%	62	43	10	8	40	68%	16	3.3	20	3.0	2	2	35	43%	57	10.1	78	3	1

Year	Yards	ALY	Rank	Power	Rank	Stuff	Rank	2nd Level	Rank	Open Field	Rank	Sacks	ASR	Rank	Press	Rank
2016	4.54	4.32	18	57%	6	22%	10	1.45	32	0.82	23	33	4.7%	31	31.4%	4
2017	4.13	3.94	10	50%	3	24%	5	1.26	27	0.85	25	30	5.7%	27	27.7%	29
2018	4.53	4.36	16	65%	15	20%	15	1.29	21	1.04	23	31	6.3%	28	28.5%	23

| 2018 ALY by direction: | Left End: 4.60 (17) | Left Tackle: 3.64 (8) | Mid/Guard: 4.44 (19) | Right Tackle: 3.86 (10) | Right End: 4.97 (24) |

The Dolphins lost 12.5 of their 31 sacks and 63 pressures with the departures of Cameron Wake and Robert Quinn. They won't get many of those sacks and pressures back this year. ✦ You could almost hear Bill Parcells nodding with satisfaction when the Dolphins selected Clemson defensive tackle Christian Wilkins with the 13th overall pick. The 314-pounder from Framingham, Massachusetts, is not just a classic "Planet Theory" defensive lineman: he earned a master's degree in three-and-a-half years and worked as a substitute teacher during offseasons. Wilkins' presence will upgrade the pass rush. Now the Dolphins just need to find some edge rushers. ✦ Brian Flores said he "can't say enough good things" in OTAs about Charles Harris, the 2017 first-round pick with just three career sacks. Harris, who was working through a wrist injury in the offseason, is moving from defensive end into a Patriots-style hybrid edge rusher role. Jerome Baker bulked up to 227 pounds in the offseason and is expected to generate pressure as a 3-4 outside linebacker. Former prospects like Nate Orchard and Tank Carradine fill the bottom of the depth chart at the pass-rush positions; Flores and Grier are either mining for talent Patriots-style, buttressing the roster with pros to turn the heat up in camp battles, or both. ✦ As for the rest of the Dolphins front seven: Raekwon McMillan can thump between the tackles but is one of the league's worst coverage linebackers, Kiko Alonso is bad at everything but keeps getting opportunities, and Wilkins will be joined at defensive tackle by Davon Godchaux, who may be the son of that husband-and-wife duo who joined the Grateful Dead in the mid-'70s (though this Godchaux can actually play a little). ✦ In summary, this is not going to be a very good defensive front seven.

Defensive Secondary

Secondary	Age	Pos	G	Snaps	Plays	TmPct	Rk	Stop	Dfts	BTkl	Runs	St%	Rk	RuYd	Rk	Tgts	Tgt%	Rk	Dist	Suc%	Rk	AdjYd	Rk	PD	Int
						Overall							**vs. Run**						**vs. Pass**					
T.J. McDonald	28	SS	14	952	89	12.2%	13	33	9	14	48	50%	21	6.7	33	32	9.6%	38	9.5	38%	69	8.0	49	5	3
Minkah Fitzpatrick	23	FS	16	944	88	10.5%	34	35	15	11	35	40%	44	6.8	35	50	15.2%	70	13.7	60%	14	7.3	39	9	2
Reshad Jones	31	FS	14	825	81	11.1%	29	35	17	8	39	41%	41	8.8	56	27	9.4%	34	10.1	59%	16	5.3	7	9	3
Bobby McCain	26	CB	14	823	64	8.8%	40	25	6	11	25	44%	32	6.4	40	52	18.1%	33	9.3	42%	77	8.4	58	5	1
Xavien Howard	26	CB	12	803	47	7.5%	57	24	12	8	11	36%	51	14.7	78	50	17.8%	29	15.3	60%	8	7.1	30	12	7
Torry McTyer	24	CB	15	346	32	4.1%	--	13	4	7	8	50%	--	4.5	--	24	19.9%	--	14.3	33%	--	14.4	--	3	0

Year	Pass D Rank	vs. #1 WR	Rk	vs. #2 WR	Rk	vs. Other WR	Rk	WR Wide	Rk	WR Slot	Rk	vs. TE	Rk	vs. RB	Rk
2016	16	-15.1%	5	-15.6%	4	22.9%	31	-20.5%	2	13.2%	23	4.7%	21	-11.1%	10
2017	29	11.2%	22	-8.2%	11	15.4%	23	0.0%	17	9.7%	19	17.1%	28	1.8%	18
2018	23	7.0%	21	5.5%	21	-2.2%	17	26.0%	32	-5.7%	10	-0.3%	14	20.2%	30

Xavien Howard is very good, very reliable, and now very rich. He's the anchor of the Dolphins secondary. Everything else is in flux. ❧ Safety Reshad Jones is now 31 and has three years and over $46 million on his contract. The Dolphins made some overtures about trading Jones, but the market on veteran safeties was gutted by Eric Weddle- and Earl Thomas-types in the offseason. Cutting Jones would force the Dolphins to gulp down a monstrous $25-million cap hit this year, due to past restructurings and the typical bananapants guarantees and bonuses included in any Mike Tanenbaum contract. Unless some suitor appears with a late-round pick and a credit-repair opportunity, the Dolphins will keep Jones as a very expensive sage in the secondary for at least a year. ❧ Miami dropped from seeing the most opponent passes to tight ends (26 percent) to ranking 29th (16 percent). The Minkah Fitzpatrick effect? Not really; we only registered five tight end targets with Fitzpatrick in coverage. Instead, it was usually T.J. McDonald and Jerome Baker covering tight ends. ❧ Fitzpatrick struggled as an outside cornerback but fared much better as a slot safety/cornerback hybrid last year. Brian Flores said in May that he plans to move Fitzpatrick all over the defense this season. "I'll know what he's doing," Flores said, per Charles Trainor Jr.'s *Miami Herald* report in May (a major source for this section). "You guys probably won't." ❧ Veteran Bobby McCain is also better suited to slot/dime duty, leaving Eric Rowe as the favorite to start opposite Howard. Rowe matches up well with tall receivers on paper but had a knack for getting torched in spot duty for the Patriots. Rowe told reporters in May that he was playing hurt last year, and of course he's the kind of "knows the system" guy defensive-minded head coaches love to add to their rosters while they figure other stuff out. Cordrea Tankersley is also attempting a comeback from both an ACL tear and the Adam Gase doghouse. ❧ Other than Fitzpatrick (and Howard, who is just 26), there's not a lot of young talent in the secondary. The most interesting rookie on the depth chart is UDFA Nik Needham of UTEP, a hard-hitting hybrid defender who at times looked like Minkah Fitzpatrick Lite on tape.

Special Teams

Year	DVOA	Rank	FG/XP	Rank	Net Kick	Rank	Kick Ret	Rank	Net Punt	Rank	Punt Ret	Rank	Hidden	Rank
2016	0.8%	12	-6.2	27	6.0	5	6.6	6	-3.5	22	1.2	12	21.0	1
2017	2.6%	12	3.4	12	5.3	6	-1.5	19	6.6	6	-0.6	19	6.4	5
2018	-1.1%	21	1.9	13	-5.8	29	2.9	6	-10.5	29	6.0	4	11.8	3

Tiny Jakeem Grant returned both a punt and a kickoff for a touchdown last season before suffering a lower leg injury. Grant was limited in OTAs but is expected to be at full speed for training camp. ❧ Kicker Jason Sanders performed well as a rookie, with a 78.6 percent touchback rate (55-of-70, second in the league to Washington's Dustin Hopkins among regulars) and just two missed field goals and one missed extra point. Sanders won't get many field goal opportunities this year. ❧ Matt Haack, on the other hand, may lead the league in total punts after finishing second to Arizona's Andy Lee last year. ❧ Kick coverage units were a sore spot last year but should improve now that the organization is being run competently.

Minnesota Vikings

2018 record: 8-7-1	Total DVOA: 8.1% (10th)	2019 Mean Projection: 8.0 wins	On the Clock (0-4): 10%
Pythagorean Wins: 8.5 (12th)	Offense: -1.3% (18th)	Postseason Odds: 35.7%	Mediocrity (5-7): 32%
Snap-Weighted Age: 26.6 (12th)	Defense: -10.3% (4th)	Super Bowl Odds: 4.5%	Playoff Contender (8-10): 39%
Average Opponent: -2.7% (27th)	Special Teams: -0.9% (19th)	Proj. Avg. Opponent: 1.0% (12th)	Super Bowl Contender (11+): 18%

2018: The offense doesn't hold up its end of the bargain.

2019: Our projections think the offense won't hold up its end of the bargain, but coaching stability may favor a more positive outcome.

Week 2 visiting the Green Bay Packers, tie ballgame, four seconds remain in overtime. With the ball between the hashes on Green Bay's 17-yard line, Minnesota Vikings kicker Daniel Carlson has a 2-0 start for the team lined up in his sights. The snap is crisp, the holder gets the ball down in time, but Carlson hooks the ball wide right. The Vikings leave Lambeau that evening with half a win in their pockets. Unbeknownst to them, the other half of that win would be the difference between making the playoffs and not.

Come late December, the Vikings would lose the sixth seed in the NFC to the Philadelphia Eagles. The Eagles finished 9-7, while the Vikings finished just shy of them at 8-7-1. Minnesota had beaten Philadelphia in Week 5, giving them the head-to-head tiebreaker in the event both teams finished with the same record. Without that elusive half of a win in Week 2, the Vikings could not match the Eagles' record and conceded the final playoff spot in the conference.

Every team can go through "what ifs"—made up scenarios that save or sink the perception and tangible success of a season. Even heading into Week 17, had Minnesota won or Philadelphia lost their final game, the Vikings would have been playing in January. Nevertheless, that the Vikings ultimately missed out on the postseason by a half of a win that eluded them via a missed chip-shot field goal is too on the nose.

Narrowly missing the playoffs was a fitting ending for a Vikings season that was the center of offseason discussion and overzealous hype. After a 13-3 regular season in 2017, capped off by the Minnesota Miracle, adding quarterback Kirk Cousins in place of Case Keenum and hiring Eagles quarterback coach John DeFilippo to be the offensive coordinator seemed like clear upgrades to an offense already in a decent spot.

Maybe 13-3 was unrepeatable, but Cousins was a more capable and proven quarterback than journeyman Keenum, and DeFilippo was coming off a season in which his quarterback, Carson Wentz, put up MVP-caliber numbers. With two elite receivers in Stefon Diggs and Adam Thielen, a rock-solid tight end in Kyle Rudolph, and a blossoming running back in Dalvin Cook, the two had the tools they needed to succeed. On paper, they were the perfect quarterback-coordinator duo to sustain success following Keenum's anomalous season, while the defense could stick to their same old ways and stomp the rest of the league.

The latter rang true. Mike Zimmer's defense dropped a negligible distance in DVOA, going from a second-place -13.9% rating in 2017 to a fourth-place -10.3% rating in 2018. They were effectively just as dominant as they were the year before. However, the offense did not make good on their potential. With one issue after another, the new-look offense unraveled over the course of the season.

Most of the offense's demise can be linked to the line and the coordinator change. The offensive line dropped from 19th to 23rd in adjusted line yards and sixth to ninth in adjusted sack rate. Those may not seem like steep drops in isolation, but on top of the rest of the line's shortcomings, it was bad. They also plummeted from 10th to 30th in power success and from 19th to 25th in stuff percentage. Most damning of all, Minnesota's line ended with 28 percent more blown blocks than any other offensive line in the league (Table 1). Not only was Minnesota less efficient across the board, they completely lost their effectiveness in short-yardage situations and were more prone to negative plays. In turn, the offensive line's collapse put DeFilippo in an impossible position in balancing the run-pass ratio.

Table 1. Fewest Plays per Blown Block by Offensive Line, 2018

Team	Blown Blocks	All Plays	Plays per Blown Block
MIN	141	998	7.1
MIA	105	868	8.3
DEN	110	1009	9.2
JAX	108	998	9.2
LAC	99	933	9.4
ARI	93	897	9.6
SF	101	996	9.9
HOU	101	1030	10.2
CHI	95	1006	10.6
CIN	88	937	10.6
OAK	92	980	10.7
WAS	89	960	10.8

Offensive line only; based on Sports Info Solutions charting

DeFilippo is already inclined to throw the ball. Since 2014, every offense with DeFilippo as either offensive coordinator or quarterback coach has ranked in the top half of the league in passing attempts, often in the top 10. Among those sea-

2019 Vikings Schedule

Week	Opp.	Week	Opp.	Week	Opp.
1	ATL	7	at DET	13	at SEA (Mon.)
2	at GB	8	WAS (Thu.)	14	DET
3	OAK	9	at KC	15	at LAC
4	at CHI	10	at DAL	16	GB (Mon.)
5	at NYG	11	DEN	17	CHI
6	PHI	12	BYE		

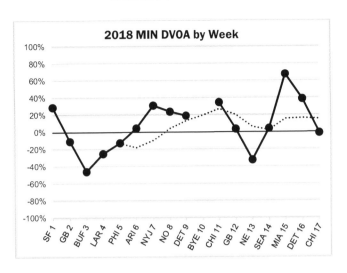

sons were Derek Carr's rookie year in Oakland (2015, fourth in attempts) and Carson Wentz's rookie year in Philadelphia (2016, sixth in attempts). The 2015 Browns offense that he coordinated finished 11th in attempts with 609. Conversely, Zimmer's Vikings had only finished in the top half of the league in attempts once in four seasons prior to DeFilippo, when Sam Bradford quarterbacked the 2016 team. The Vikings even finished dead last in attempts in 2015 with a second-year Teddy Bridgewater. There is more to passing attempt totals than general philosophy, but the difference between the two is not hard to see.

Between DeFilippo's inclination to throw and the offensive line's poor adjusted line yards in the run game, running the ball was both an afterthought and a challenge. Even still, Zimmer wanted to be committed to the run, going so far as to state in a Week 11 post-game interview that the Vikings needed to "stick with the run," just three weeks before he ultimately fired DeFilippo.

Tangentially, Minnesota did not make use of play-action often enough, either. The Vikings used play-action on a league-high 30 percent of their passing attempts in 2017 but fell to a 25th-ranked 21 percent in 2018. Furthermore, they ranked in the bottom five in play-action percentage on first down at just 28 percent. For comparison, league average on first down was 36 percent, and the Los Angeles Rams led the league at 59 percent.

While their rushing attack was considerably worse and less a part of the offense in 2018, Ben Baldwin wrote in last year's *Almanac* that play-action has little to do with how well or often a team runs the ball. His findings were such that poor rushing success should not have steered the Vikings away from play-action. Of course, Zimmer being the old-school coach he is may firmly believe good play-action stems from rushing success, not that it is independent of it. What is more troubling is that the Vikings still ranked a solid 11th in yards per play on play-action, so it was not as though ineffectiveness pushed them off course. There was both an issue with being unable to trust the offensive line even with extra blockers and a fault in DeFilippo's game-planning and Zimmer's dated beliefs.

The drop in play-action was par for the course for DeFilippo. Though the Eagles consistently used play-action when he was the quarterback coach, DeFilippo's one season as the offensive coordinator for Cleveland in 2015 landed the Browns in 28th place with just 15 percent of passes being off play-action. Anecdotally, it makes sense that teams who get and stay ahead may be afforded more believability in their play-action fakes considering teams run more often with a lead, but the

Vikings not playing from ahead as often in 2018 as in 2017 does not necessarily excuse DeFilippo in this instance.

DeFilippo was fired after the team's Week 14 loss to the Seattle Seahawks. Zimmer promoted Kevin Stefanski to be the interim offensive coordinator for the final three games. Stefanski has been on the Vikings' coaching staff in some capacity since 2006, most recently serving as the quarterbacks coach. He was promoted over DeFilippo in part because he was assumed to follow through with Zimmer's run-first vision, and he did. The first two games Stefanski called ranked among the team's top five games in rushing attempts for the season. Granted, the first game was a blowout versus a broken Miami Dolphins defense, but Stefanski stuck with the run the following week versus the Detroit Lions despite averaging 3.6 yards per attempt.

Ultimately, the switch to Stefanski was not enough as the Vikings were held to just 10 points when a Week 17 win over the Chicago Bears could have sent them to the playoffs. Stefanski's offense better fit Zimmer's vision, but his three-game stint suggested little else other than philosophical redirection. It only served as a precursor of what the offense will look like this season, not a salve for what ailed the offense in 2018. The offense was too far gone, and it was too late in the season to right the ship, if that was even possible given the offensive line issues.

Those who were not blaming the line or offensive coordinator turned to Cousins, the $84 million quarterback who was supposed to be an upgrade over Keenum. While Cousins was statistically a steep decline from what Keenum had done the year before, the confluence of poor offensive line performance and questionable, or at least ill-fitting, play calling put the new quarterback in an unreasonable position.

The crime is not necessarily that Cousins shouldered a portion of the blame he did not deserve, but that he did so in what felt like his most developed season as a pro. His ball placement, ball security, and pocket command and poise were as impressive on film as they have ever been. Per NFL's Next Gen Stats, Cousins posted the third-best completion percentage above expectation in the league, sporting a +5.3 percent difference from his 70.1 percent completion rate versus the expected 64.8 percent (Table 2). Football Outsiders' passing plus-minus ratings agreed, ranking Cousins second behind Drew Brees with 30 receptions more than we would otherwise expect given the location of his pass targets. Cousins also posted a career-best 1.7 percent interception rate. Still, the mitigating factors around him did not allow these developments to bear out in the all-encompassing statistics.

Table 2. 2018 Leaders, Next Gen Stats Completion Rate Above Expectation and FO Passing +/- Rate

Player	Comp % Over Exp	Player	Passing +/- %
Drew Brees	+7.4%	Drew Brees	+8.5%
Nick Foles	+5.7%	Kirk Cousins	+5.4%
Kirk Cousins	+5.3%	Russell Wilson	+5.1%
Russell Wilson	+5.2%	Deshaun Watson	+3.7%
Matt Ryan	+4.6%	Matt Ryan	+3.5%
Ryan Fitzpatrick	+3.9%	Ryan Fitzpatrick	+3.4%
Deshaun Watson	+3.9%	Derek Carr	+3.4%
Carson Wentz	+3.2%	Jared Goff	+2.9%
Cam Newton	+3.1%	Carson Wentz	+2.7%
Cody Kessler	+2.3%	Nick Foles	+2.6%

Completion Rate Above Expectation courtesy NFL Next Gen Stats

Despite being the best version of himself, Cousins posted his second-lowest adjusted net yards per attempt (6.48) and DYAR (596) since becoming a full-time starter in 2015. Only his 2017 season in Washington featured slightly lower marks, when Cousins was surrounded by a cratered offensive line and a subpar, oft-injured group of pass-catchers. Though not particularly his fault, Cousins now has back-to-back middling seasons on paper, making it difficult to fault Vikings fans for being down on Cousins just one year into his deal.

Minnesota's saving grace was Zimmer's defense. The collapse of the offense should have been enough to sink any team out of the playoff hunt, but the Vikings defense played at an elite level despite issues of its own. It makes sense that Zimmer would better be equipped to stabilize the defense than the offense given his defensive expertise, but it is not as though this season was a walk in the park for him compared to De-Filippo and Stefanski.

Between losing safety Andrew Sendejo in Week 5, defensive end Everson Griffen missing five games early in the year citing mental health concerns, and the pitfalls of linebackers Anthony Barr and Eric Kendricks in coverage, the defense was tougher to manage than the year prior. Even before the season began, soon-to-be free agent Barr was asking to be used more as a pass-rusher, likely in an effort to boost his market value. Both on the field and in handling the locker room, Zimmer had a full plate.

The Sendejo injury should have crippled Minnesota's defensive structure. The Vikings were one of the most frequent two-deep safety teams in the league thanks to the flexibility to swap Harrison Smith and Sendejo between the free and strong safety roles. Sendejo was not an elite player by any means, but he did well to play what was in front of him both versus the run and in coverage, as any good two-deep safety should. Though his coverage success rate of 43 percent was shaky in 2018, the sample size was limited, and he had posted a team-high 55 percent success rate the year before.

In Sendejo's absence, Zimmer turned career backup Anthony Harris into a wildly productive safety partner for Smith. Harris could not match Sendejo's energy and prowess as a run defender, but he cleaned up as one of the best cover safeties in the league. Zimmer also put Harris in a different position to win than Sendejo. Harris made his average play 7.4 yards off the line of scrimmage, whereas Sendejo made his about 12.8 yards off the ball. Part of that is a small sample for Sendejo that featured a gauntlet of teams that like to push the ball down the field, but the change was still apparent. That Zimmer could insert a career backup into a stable starter's position, tweak the role to suit him better, and get Pro Bowl-caliber production out of him is one of many testaments to Zimmer's brilliance.

Minnesota's linebackers' disappearance in coverage could have sunk the defense, too. Barr and Kendricks had always been lauded for their range in coverage, but for whatever reason, both of them crashed in 2018. Barr regularly looked lost in picking up his assignments, most famously put on display against the Rams in Week 4. Kendricks, conversely, was still fine in spot dropping and reading the quarterback's eyes, but if he was asked to match or carry skill players, he was often beaten with ease.

And yet, the middle of the Vikings' defense being in turmoil almost did not matter to Zimmer. He still managed to steer the Vikings to a top-five defensive DVOA ranking. It helped to have two star cornerbacks in Xavier Rhodes and Trae Waynes and one of the best young pass-rushers in Danielle Hunter, but Zimmer still had to fill in the holes. Defense is about consistency and making sure there are no weak links to be exposed. Zimmer did as best he could to shore up weaknesses to enable his stars to shine.

Where the Vikings go from here is dependent on a revival from the offense and sustained dominance from the defense. For as ugly as last year's offense was, there is reason to believe they can make the turnaround, even if our own projections do not suggest they will.

In our average projection, the Vikings rock a below-average offense similar to the level of play they had last season. Where they may be able to work around the system is in the intangibles, primarily through their coaching staff via offensive coordinator and offensive line coach. The Vikings' offense will be more stable behind the scenes than last season.

Losing offensive line coach Tony Sparano to an untimely passing a month before the season in 2018 was surely a factor in the unit's dip in play, but the impact of a position coach is not necessarily quantifiable. Heading into 2019, Rick Dennison will be the offensive line coach and run game coordinator. Dennison is attached to the hip of Gary Kubiak, who will also be on the staff, and has helped craft some of the most successful zone-running offenses of the past decade, including the surprising (and devastating) 2014 Ravens ground game spearheaded by running back Justin Forsett.

Similarly, there was a clear rift between Zimmer and De-Filippo that resulted in a disjointed, uncomfortable offensive approach. Zimmer wants a run-first, ball-control offense that can best set up his defense to succeed and command the flow of the game. That is the philosophy the Vikings rode to a 13-3 finish in 2017 and, to a different extent, an 11-5 finish in 2015. Those two seasons are Zimmer's only playoff appearances in his five-year tenure with the Vikings. It is only natural he prefers that style given the success he perceives to be associated with it, even if analysts have proven over and over again that running the ball is less valuable than passing. Running the ball often was never going to be DeFilippo's M.O., though, and Zimmer will now better be able to mold the team to his liking with Stefanski coordinating the offense.

The beneficiary of both coaching positions being more stable is Cousins. The addition of a successful offensive line coach and the continuity in Stefanski as the offensive coordinator should take pressure off of Cousins' shoulders. It is not as projectable in the way adding a star receiver may be, but consistency is key for quarterbacks. Being able to more comfortably rely on his offensive line, even if only slightly, and having a clearer picture of the offense's goals will help Cousins better settle into the Vikings offense than he was able to last year. Tack on the fact that Cousins is typically at his best when throwing off of pre-snap leverage and in the rhythm of the play, and consistency is even more of a benefit to him. The blend of stability around him and lowered expectations compared to last season gives Cousins the perfect opportunity to bounce back and reclaim his status as one of the better passers in the league.

However, one element that may not rebound as much as fans expect is play-action usage. Kubiak's Denver and Houston teams were routinely around the league average in play-

action frequency, although even that would be a step in the right direction after last season.

On defense, staying the course is the goal. The Vikings are the only team to post a top-10 DVOA rating in each of the last three seasons and would only further separate themselves from the pack with a fourth-straight top-10 finish. For a handful of reasons, the Vikings should be able to complete the feat.

For one, Minnesota is the most consistent tackling team in the league. They have ranked in the top five in fewest percentage of missed tackles in each of the last three seasons, including a league-best 7.6 percent in 2018. No Vikings defender had double-digit missed tackles last season. Simply not giving the opponent chances for extra yards is critical to Zimmer's formula. Additionally, they lost a minimal number of starters this offseason. Only Sendejo and defensive tackle Sheldon Richardson will not be back. Sendejo was absent for most of last season anyway. Richardson will be missed given his disruption as a pass-rusher from the interior, but it would be a stretch to assume his absence alone is enough to ripple through the rest of the defense and cause it to crumble. There are too many other stars, and Zimmer has a reliable track record of defensive success.

The Vikings are a good candidate to surprise relative to our projections. Our forecast has them vying for third place in the division with the Chicago Bears, while the Green Bay Packers and Detroit Lions duke it out for the top spot. However, despite being projected near the bottom of the division, the Vikings are league-average overall, and an offensive rebound would be enough to boost them to battling for the top of the division. With plenty of reason to believe in their defense staying strong, buying into an offensive revival to boost the Vikings upward is an enticing prospect. Consistency and stability are key for the Vikings in 2019, and both would go a long way in making them a force to reckon with again.

Derrik Klassen

2018 Vikings Stats by Week

Wk	vs.	W-L	PF	PA	YDF	YDA	TO	Total	Off	Def	ST
1	SF	W	24	16	343	327	+3	29%	-20%	-46%	2%
2	at GB	T	29	29	480	351	-1	-11%	22%	2%	-31%
3	BUF	L	6	27	292	292	-3	-46%	-31%	13%	-3%
4	at LAR	L	31	38	446	556	-1	-26%	25%	52%	2%
5	at PHI	W	23	21	375	364	+1	-13%	11%	13%	-11%
6	ARI	W	27	17	411	268	0	4%	-11%	-12%	3%
7	at NYJ	W	37	17	316	263	+4	31%	-10%	-34%	7%
8	NO	L	20	30	423	270	-1	24%	13%	-19%	-9%
9	DET	W	24	9	283	209	-1	19%	-23%	-37%	5%
10	BYE										
11	at CHI	L	20	25	268	308	0	35%	11%	-19%	5%
12	GB	W	24	17	416	254	+1	4%	12%	-2%	-10%
13	at NE	L	10	24	278	471	-1	-33%	-13%	15%	-4%
14	at SEA	L	7	21	276	274	0	4%	-13%	-24%	-7%
15	MIA	W	41	17	418	193	-1	67%	10%	-38%	20%
16	at DET	W	27	9	340	223	0	39%	-3%	-37%	5%
17	CHI	L	10	24	164	332	0	-1%	-8%	5%	12%

Trends and Splits

	Offense	Rank	Defense	Rank
Total DVOA	-1.3%	18	-10.3%	4
Unadjusted VOA	-5.6%	22	-10.8%	4
Weighted Trend	-1.1%	18	-14.4%	3
Variance	2.8%	1	6.9%	27
Average Opponent	-0.9%	9	-2.8%	22
Passing	13.4%	16	-9.7%	5
Rushing	-16.3%	28	-11.0%	11
First Down	5.5%	11	-3.7%	11
Second Down	-4.2%	22	-6.7%	10
Third Down	-9.5%	21	-30.2%	2
First Half	-0.5%	15	-0.7%	14
Second Half	-2.2%	19	-20.2%	3
Red Zone	-6.2%	18	-27.0%	3
Late and Close	-17.3%	27	-19.3%	3

Five-Year Performance

Year	W-L	Pyth W	Est W	PF	PA	TO	Total	Rk	Off	Rk	Def	Rk	ST	Rk	Off AGL	Rk	Def AGL	Rk	Off Age	Rk	Def Age	Rk	ST Age	Rk
2014	7-9	7.5	7.2	325	343	-1	-8.7%	25	-7.4%	22	4.3%	23	3.0%	10	39.0	23	17.1	3	26.7	17	25.9	29	25.6	28
2015	11-5	9.8	9.5	365	302	+5	5.7%	11	0.0%	16	-1.8%	14	3.9%	4	36.5	17	22.5	7	26.4	19	27.5	4	25.7	22
2016	8-8	8.6	8.6	327	307	+11	-1.7%	20	-9.8%	26	-6.6%	8	1.5%	10	92.1	32	28.6	12	27.1	10	27.8	3	26.3	10
2017	13-3	11.7	12.0	382	252	+5	25.0%	4	12.0%	5	-13.9%	2	-0.9%	18	42.8	20	4.9	1	26.9	17	27.9	3	25.7	23
2018	8-7-1	8.5	8.9	360	341	0	8.1%	10	-1.3%	18	-10.3%	4	-0.9%	19	36.3	15	37.6	20	26.9	13	26.7	8	25.5	25

2018 Performance Based on Most Common Personnel Groups

MIN Offense					MIN Offense vs. Opponents					MIN Defense					MIN Defense vs. Opponents			
Pers	Freq	Yds	DVOA	Run%	Pers	Freq	Yds	DVOA	Run%	Pers	Freq	Yds	DVOA	Pers	Freq	Yds	DVOA	
11	67%	5.7	3.0%	23%	Base	24%	5.1	3.5%	54%	Base	21%	4.5	-17.2%	11	57%	5.6	-6.2%	
12	19%	5.7	7.8%	50%	Nickel	62%	5.7	-0.5%	30%	Nickel	77%	5.3	-7.9%	12	17%	4.5	-19.9%	
21	7%	5.0	-4.4%	52%	Dime+	15%	6.3	17.0%	6%	Dime+	1%	6.8	-14.2%	21	10%	4.9	-1.3%	
22	2%	5.5	-13.2%	71%	Goal Line	1%	0.5	-27.3%	91%	Goal Line	1%	0.8	-21.4%	13	3%	4.5	-29.5%	
13	2%	3.9	-37.4%	67%										612	3%	4.5	-2.4%	
														611	2%	4.4	-21.0%	

Strategic Tendencies

Run/Pass		Rk	Formation		Rk	Pass Rush		Rk	Secondary		Rk	Strategy		Rk
Runs, first half	33%	27	Form: Single Back	85%	9	Rush 3	1.5%	31	4 DB	21%	19	Play action	21%	25
Runs, first down	42%	24	Form: Empty Back	5%	26	Rush 4	71.6%	15	5 DB	77%	5	Avg Box (Off)	6.17	18
Runs, second-long	31%	14	Pers: 3+ WR	69%	16	Rush 5	20.1%	10	6+ DB	1%	28	Avg Box (Def)	6.34	5
Runs, power sit.	41%	31	Pers: 2+ TE/6+ OL	25%	14	Rush 6+	6.8%	10	CB by Sides	71%	19	Offensive Pace	31.77	22
Runs, behind 2H	16%	31	Pers: 6+ OL	2%	18	Int DL Sacks	23.0%	20	S/CB Cover Ratio	26%	21	Defensive Pace	31.47	21
Pass, ahead 2H	47%	19	Shotgun/Pistol	61%	19	Second Level Sacks	29.0%	7	DB Blitz	9%	13	Go for it on 4th	1.57	11

Minnesota's offense recovered only four of 14 fumbles. ● Mike Zimmer was much more aggressive in 2018 after ranking dead last in Aggressiveness Index in 2017. ● For the second straight year, Minnesota's defense ranked in the top three of both yards allowed per pass (4.8) and DVOA (-34.0%) when blitzing. ● The Vikings had the league's biggest gap in defense against play-action passes compared to other passes. They allowed 28.7% DVOA and 8.6 yards per play against play-action, but just -20.2% DVOA and 5.5 yards per play otherwise. The good news for the Vikings is that this is a fixable problem, as there generally isn't any year-to-year consistency in these defensive gaps against play-action. In fact, the Vikings defense actually had a slightly better DVOA against play-action than against other passes the year before. ● The 2018 Vikings defense also had the league's largest "reverse gap" defending shotgun plays. They allowed a league-low 4.8 yards per play with -17.7% DVOA (second) against shotgun. But when the quarterback was under center, Vikings opponents gained 5.6 yards per play with -0.6% DVOA. ● The Vikings defense ranked 24th in DVOA in the first quarter. From the second quarter onwards, only Chicago had a better defense.

Passing

Player	DYAR	DVOA	Plays	NtYds	Avg	YAC	C%	TD	Int
K.Cousins	595	2.7%	646	3988	6.2	4.6	70.5%	30	10

Rushing

Player	DYAR	DVOA	Plays	Yds	Avg	TD	Fum	Suc
L.Murray*	25	-4.2%	140	578	4.1	6	0	46%
D.Cook	-27	-13.7%	133	616	4.6	2	2	41%
K.Cousins	-2	-13.2%	31	124	4.0	1	1	--
M.Boone	2	-4.2%	11	47	4.3	0	0	36%
S.Diggs	37	53.0%	10	62	6.2	0	0	--
R.Thomas	-7	-32.7%	8	30	3.8	0	0	38%
C.J.Ham	-16	-60.5%	6	8	1.3	0	0	17%
A.Thielen	12	6.8%	5	30	6.0	0	0	--

Receiving

Player	DYAR	DVOA	Plays	Ctch	Yds	Y/C	YAC	TD	C%
A.Thielen	341	15.2%	153	113	1373	12.2	3.7	9	74%
S.Diggs	8	-12.0%	149	102	1021	10.0	4.3	9	68%
L.Treadwell	-27	-19.1%	53	35	302	8.6	3.4	1	66%
A.Robinson*	47	4.0%	35	17	231	13.6	2.5	5	49%
K.Rudolph	91	8.6%	82	64	634	9.9	3.9	4	78%
T.Conklin	20	37.6%	7	5	77	15.4	6.2	0	71%
D.Morgan	1	-4.0%	6	5	36	7.2	5.4	0	83%
D.Cook	45	2.1%	49	40	305	7.6	9.3	2	82%
L.Murray*	9	-7.5%	26	22	141	6.4	5.2	0	85%
C.J.Ham	14	1.3%	15	11	85	7.7	7.6	0	73%

Offensive Line

Player	Pos	Age	GS	Snaps	Pen	Sk	Pass	Run	Player	Pos	Age	GS	Snaps	Pen	Sk	Pass	Run
Mike Remmers*	RG	30	16/16	1048	8	4.5	19	8	Rashod Hill	RT/LT	27	16/8	529	3	4.5	18	4
Pat Elflein	C	25	14/13	863	5	1.5	7	9	Danny Isidora	LG	25	14/2	214	1	2.5	8	4
Tom Compton*	LG	30	14/14	837	7	7.0	11	7	Brett Jones	C	28	14/3	191	0	0.0	0	3
Brian O'Neill	RT	24	15/11	800	4	1.0	12	7	Josh Kline	RG	30	16/16	975	4	3.5	8	6
Riley Reiff	LT	31	13/13	793	4	5.5	19	4									

Year	Yards	ALY	Rank	Power	Rank	Stuff	Rank	2nd Lev	Rank	Open Field	Rank	Sacks	ASR	Rank	Press	Rank	F-Start	Cont.
2016	3.15	3.64	30	47%	31	22%	26	0.81	32	0.28	31	38	6.0%	17	23.6%	10	18	23
2017	3.98	3.96	19	67%	10	21%	19	1.11	17	0.77	13	27	4.4%	6	36.1%	29	11	27
2018	4.29	4.09	23	58%	30	21%	25	1.16	23	1.02	9	40	6.1%	9	34.1%	27	14	31

2018 ALY by direction: Left End: 3.79 (23)   Left Tackle: 4.40 (9)   Mid/Guard: 4.11 (26)   Right Tackle: 4.03 (22)   Right End: 3.95 (21)

Minnesota's offensive line was not materially worse in terms of pressures allowed last season despite the feeling that they were. They went from 36.1 percent in 2017 to 34.1 percent in 2018. The real difference was the difference between Case Keenum, who has a daring, scrambling style of play, and Kirk Cousins, a more stationary and scheduled passer. ◥ Statistically, Rashod Hill was the worst qualifying tackle in the league, sporting a last-place rate of 24.0 snaps per blown block. On film, Hill's feet are often clunky or slow to react, and he does not have the raw athletic ability to make up the lost ground he concedes. Second-round rookie Brian O'Neill was not markedly better when he took over, but he showed a more stable base in pass pro and has the benefit of the doubt through potential development that Hill, 27 years old, no longer has. ◥ Amidst the team's offensive line scrambles, Mike Remmers was moved permanently from right tackle to right guard after playing some guard in 2017. When moved to guard full time, Remmers suffered. Despite blown blocks being recorded at a much lower rate across the league last season, Remmers' snaps per blown block rate actually got worse, going from 42.0 in 2017 to 38.9 in 2018. ◥ Former Patriot and Titan Josh Kline is a clear upgrade at right guard, as he is more capable and more reliable. He has experience both with gap and pulling schemes, via Mike Mularkey in 2016 and 2017, and in more zone-oriented schemes with Matt LaFleur in 2018. With Gary Kubiak and Rick Dennison on staff, surely the offense will be more zone-oriented, and Kline fared well in such a system last season. ◥ Similarly, first-round pick Garrett Bradbury (North Carolina State) is the right center for a team looking to establish a strong zone running game. He erupted at the NFL combine, posting some of the best numbers in the class in the 40-yard dash, three-cone drill, and short-shuttle, all of which highlight what he showed on film with his ability to thrive in space and climb to the second level.

Defensive Front

Defensive Line	Age	Pos	G	Snaps	Plays	TmPct	Rk	Stop	Dfts	BTkl	Runs	St%	Rk	RuYd	Rk	Sack	Hit	Hur	Dsrpt
Sheldon Richardson*	29	DT	16	718	48	5.9%	24	34	13	7	38	68%	69	2.8	67	4.5	13	21	0
Linval Joseph	31	DT	15	669	58	7.7%	8	41	10	1	51	71%	58	3.2	76	1.0	3	10	0
Tom Johnson*	35	DT	14	381	24	3.4%	73	14	9	0	15	53%	83	2.7	64	4.5	2	8	0
Jaleel Johnson	25	DT	16	261	13	1.6%	--	7	3	1	12	50%	--	2.7	--	0.5	1	3	0
Shamar Stephen	*28*	*DT*	*15*	*494*	*25*	*3.5%*	*70*	*17*	*2*	*1*	*21*	*71%*	*53*	*2.6*	*60*	*2.0*	*1*	*3*	*0*

Edge Rushers	Age	Pos	G	Snaps	Plays	TmPct	Rk	Stop	Dfts	BTkl	Runs	St%	Rk	RuYd	Rk	Sack	Hit	Hur	Dsrpt
Danielle Hunter	25	DE	16	877	71	8.8%	3	47	27	5	50	56%	82	3.5	81	14.5	3	39	1
Everson Griffen	32	DE	11	584	34	6.1%	18	26	8	4	26	69%	59	3.3	73	5.5	7	17	1
Stephen Weatherly	25	DE	16	523	35	4.3%	57	25	9	5	24	79%	26	2.5	50	3.0	7	26	1

Linebackers	Age	Pos	G	Snaps	Plays	TmPct	Rk	Stop	Dfts	BTkl	Runs	St%	Rk	RuYd	Rk	Sack	Hit	Hur	Tgts	Suc%	Rk	AdjYd	Rk	PD	Int
Eric Kendricks	27	MLB	14	875	115	16.3%	15	52	17	9	72	47%	84	4.0	51	1.0	1	6.5	47	49%	42	8.4	69	7	2
Anthony Barr	27	OLB	13	808	57	8.7%	65	27	12	1	37	51%	74	4.5	71	3.0	2	14.5	13	38%	67	11.5	80	2	0
Eric Wilson	25	OLB	16	336	31	3.8%	--	17	8	5	16	56%	--	4.1	--	2.0	3	4	12	50%	--	5.9	--	0	0
Ben Gedeon	25	OLB	15	310	46	6.1%	--	24	4	3	35	54%	--	5.0	--	0.0	0	0.5	10	50%	--	10.0	--	2	0

Year	Yards	ALY	Rank	Power	Rank	Stuff	Rank	2nd Level	Rank	Open Field	Rank	Sacks	ASR	Rank	Press	Rank
2016	4.17	4.46	24	59%	9	15%	31	1.08	9	0.56	8	41	7.8%	1	31.2%	5
2017	3.56	3.99	13	55%	5	19%	26	0.91	2	0.33	2	37	6.3%	18	31.1%	13
2018	4.05	4.60	24	66%	17	16%	25	1.09	6	0.48	5	50	9.3%	2	32.0%	9
2018 ALY by direction:		Left End: 4.79 (18)		Left Tackle: 4.75 (24)		Mid/Guard: 4.73 (25)		Right Tackle: 4.93 (27)		Right End: 3.35 (6)						

Minnesota's interior defensive line swapped out run defense for pass rush last year. Following the 2017 season, the team let Shamar Stephen walk to sign with Seattle, then picked up Sheldon Richardson for themselves. Richardson's explosive pass-rush skills helped boost the team's pressure rate and interior sack total, but he fell short compared to Stephen as a run defender. The Vikings are now reversing the move in 2019, letting Richardson sign with Cleveland while they reacquired Stephen from Seattle, where he had a quietly nice season. 🏈 In part because of the decreased run-defending presence up front, star linebackers Anthony Barr and Eric Kendricks posted their lowest success rates over the past three seasons at 51 percent and 47 percent, respectively. Considering both are space-oriented linebackers who do not necessarily want to get into scrums, it makes sense that the loss of beef up front directly affected them. 🏈 Only two front-seven defenders age 25 or younger recorded at least 35 hurries in each of the past two seasons: Danielle Hunter and Trey Flowers. 🏈 Career backup Stephen Weatherly was sneaky effective in the absence of Everson Griffen. Weatherly is purely a speed rusher, but he can fly off the line similarly to Hunter and punish tackles for not respecting him on the edge. 🏈 Of Minnesota's two front-seven rookies, defensive tackle Armon Watts (sixth round, Arkansas) and linebacker Cameron Smith (fifth round, USC), the former has a better chance to crack into a semi-regular role. For one, defensive tackle is a more heavily rotated position because of the physical toll it takes, but the third spot at the position is also up for grabs. Jaleel Johnson struggled in limited snaps during both phases of the game last year, while Jalyn Holmes, an unproductive college player at Ohio State, hardly saw action as a rookie. Watts did not break out until his senior season, but his seven sacks trailed only Quinnen Williams (Jets) and Isaiah Buggs (Steelers) among SEC defensive tackles in 2018.

Defensive Secondary

Secondary	Age	Pos	G	Snaps	Plays	Overall TmPct	Rk	Stop	Dfts	BTkl	Runs	vs. Run St%	Rk	RuYd	Rk	Tgts	vs. Pass Tgt%	Rk	Dist	Suc%	Rk	AdjYd	Rk	PD	Int
Harrison Smith	30	FS	16	1024	89	11.0%	30	36	17	6	47	40%	43	6.8	34	39	10.8%	54	11.4	62%	10	6.2	13	6	3
Xavier Rhodes	29	CB	14	769	54	7.6%	55	22	10	5	10	60%	11	5.1	18	68	25.0%	71	11.0	51%	42	6.2	13	7	1
Trae Waynes	27	CB	14	692	52	7.4%	59	27	4	4	15	73%	2	2.3	1	53	21.7%	58	12.9	55%	28	7.4	36	8	1
Anthony Harris	28	FS	15	623	48	6.3%	68	16	6	3	20	30%	59	6.3	28	14	6.4%	15	10.6	64%	8	4.6	5	6	3
Mackensie Alexander	26	CB	15	564	53	7.0%	--	35	21	5	13	54%	--	2.8	--	35	17.6%	--	8.8	69%	--	5.4	--	10	0
Holton Hill	22	CB	16	374	40	5.0%	--	15	6	5	8	0%	--	8.9	--	27	20.4%	--	16.1	63%	--	5.1	--	7	1
Andrew Sendejo*	32	SS	5	324	28	11.1%	--	8	0	4	11	55%	--	5.5	--	7	6.1%	--	9.3	43%	--	9.0	--	1	0
Mike Hughes	22	CB	6	243	24	7.9%	--	12	5	6	7	71%	--	5.3	--	24	28.0%	--	11.2	50%	--	8.7	--	3	1
Jayron Kearse	25	SS	16	202	20	2.5%	--	14	4	1	9	78%	--	2.2	--	11	15.4%	--	6.5	64%	--	4.4	--	2	0

Year	Pass D Rank	vs. #1 WR	Rk	vs. #2 WR	Rk	vs. Other WR	Rk	WR Wide	Rk	WR Slot	Rk	vs. TE	Rk	vs. RB	Rk
2016	8	-1.9%	12	-4.2%	10	-23.9%	5	-3.2%	15	-19.1%	3	12.3%	24	-12.1%	8
2017	4	-13.1%	9	-22.2%	5	-3.5%	15	-4.9%	13	-15.3%	7	-24.2%	2	-37.6%	1
2018	5	-23.8%	3	-20.0%	6	-11.4%	9	-33.9%	1	-4.6%	11	22.6%	30	12.5%	27

Xavier Rhodes has posted a success rate between 51 and 53 percent in each of the last three seasons. Likewise, his yards per pass allowed over that span has been between 6.2 and 6.7 yards, which always puts him in the top 20. Rhodes may not have elite shutdown seasons like other top cornerbacks, but he is a model of consistency at a position that often lacks it. The feat is made more impressive by Mike Zimmer's willingness to allow Rhodes to follow top receivers in certain games or situations. ❧ The Mackensie Alexander pick from 2016 finally paid off last year. He hardly played as a rookie and struggled in a semi-regular role in 2017, but he erupted down the stretch in 2018 as he grew into the nickel position. He showed a sense of urgency, explosiveness, and scrappiness that he was not able to put together in previous seasons, making him one of the most effective nickel corners in the league alongside Nickell Robey-Coleman and Justin Coleman. ❧ In part because of Alexander's emergence over the second half of the year, the Vikings went from the ninth-rated (-0.8%) DVOA pass defense in Weeks 1 to 9 to the fourth-rated (-22.3%) in Weeks 10 to 17. Injuries to Andrew Sendejo and first-round pick Mike Hughes in Weeks 5 and 6, Alexander's early hot/cold play, and the linebackers' particularly poor start to the season (we all remember the Rams game) all culminated in a slightly disappointing first half of the year in pass coverage. ❧ Anthony Harris did a fantastic job filling in for Sendejo, but backup Jayron Kearse also showed promise. Though in a small sample and more of a box-oriented role, he put up nearly identical coverage numbers to Harris in terms of efficiency. 2018 was the first time Kearse played more than 100 snaps in his three-year career. ❧ Seventh-round pick Kris Boyd (Texas) was a steal and is a good candidate to surprise if forced into action. His press skills and aggressive nature when the ball is in the air fit well in a Zimmer defense.

Special Teams

Year	DVOA	Rank	FG/XP	Rank	Net Kick	Rank	Kick Ret	Rank	Net Punt	Rank	Punt Ret	Rank	Hidden	Rank
2016	1.5%	10	-5.5	25	-10.7	31	9.4	2	5.9	8	8.3	4	-6.4	25
2017	-0.9%	18	-3.1	20	-5.0	26	-2.6	21	2.9	17	3.1	8	-4.2	19
2018	-0.9%	19	-15.2	32	-1.5	23	1.2	10	5.8	8	5.3	5	-11.4	29

One has to admire how the Vikings leaned into the joke in regards to their kicking woes. Though they had only been below-average, not disastrous, since the Blair Walsh blunder, 2018 was a full nosedive back into the abyss. Between Daniel Carlson and Dan Bailey, the Vikings' -15.2 points was worst value in the league by a good margin, in large part because the two kickers were a combined 6-of-14 on kicks of 40 yards or more. ❧ Punt returner Marcus Sherels has long been a staple of the Minnesota special teams unit. Of the 15 players with at least 100 returns since Sherels started fielding them in 2011, Sherels ranks fourth in yards per return (10.59) and is tied with Darren Sproles for most touchdowns (five). Losing him this offseason will hurt more than losing most any other punt returner would. ❧ Backup receiver Brandon Zylstra, cornerback Mike Hughes, and star receivers Adam Thielen and Stefon Diggs are the only players on the roster to have fielded punts for the Vikings recently. The two stars are likely out of the running for that role this year, and Hughes should not be expected to take on the burden given the first-round investment in him. Expect the job to go to Zylstra or an outsider, like undrafted rookie Davion Davis, who returned two touchdowns in just 13 tries as a junior at Sam Houston State in 2017. ❧ A different player has led the Vikings in special teams tackles in each of the last three seasons (Kentrell Brothers, Ben Gedeon, Jayron Kearse). With Kearse potentially assuming a larger role on defense, it is possible a fourth unique tackler emerges. Linebacker Eric Wilson, who was second last year, is the most probable candidate.

New England Patriots

2018 record: 11-5	Total DVOA: 14.2% (7th)	2019 Mean Projection: 10.2 wins	On the Clock (0-4): 2%
Pythagorean Wins: 10.8 (6th)	Offense: 14.5% (5th)	Postseason Odds: 72.2%	Mediocrity (5-7): 13%
Snap-Weighted Age: 27.9 (1st)	Defense: 0.4% (16th)	Super Bowl Odds: 17.2%	Playoff Contender (8-10): 35%
Average Opponent: -2.4% (24th)	Special Teams: 0.1% (16th)	Proj. Avg. Opponent: -5.6% (32nd)	Super Bowl Contender (11+): 50%

2018: The latest last Super Bowl run of the Brady-Belichick era.

2019: The next last Super Bowl run of the Brady-Belichick era.

Tom Brady is getting old, and the Patriots benefit from playing in an easy division.

We thought we'd start with the "controversial" stuff, though there shouldn't be anything controversial about pointing out that the 42-year-old Brady is starting to decline, or that the AFC East has put up slightly more resistance than a JV scout team for many years. These talking points only spark controversy because there's a noisy quadrant of the Patriots fanbase that bristles at anything that sounds remotely like criticism of Brady or the team. But getting past hang-ups about the obvious is important if we hope to understand how the Patriots keep winning Super Bowls, and why they remain in fine position to win yet another one.

Signs of age were visible all across Brady's statistics last season. He finished with his lowest DYAR (1,034) and DVOA (15.4 percent) since 2013. He ranked seventh in the NFL in DVOA, his lowest finish since 2013, and ninth in DYAR, his lowest finish since way back in 2003.

In a season when passing statistics around the league dramatically increased, Brady posted his lowest QBR (68.8) since 2015, his lowest passer rating (97.7) since 2014, his lowest touchdown total (29) and rate (5.1 percent) since 2013, his highest interception rate (1.9 percent) since 2011, his lowest yards per attempt (7.6) since 2015 and yards per completion (11.6) since 2014. Pick just about any other meaningful metric, and Brady posted his lowest figure of the last three to seven years.

I dove into the NFL's Next Gen Stats for a Bleacher Report column in January and found further evidence of Brady's decline:

- Brady's average pass attempt traveled just 7.6 yards downfield, which ranked 24th in the NFL. His average completion traveled just 5.6 yards, 23rd in the NFL.
- Brady's average throw traveled to a distance of 1.1 yards in front of the sticks, 21st in the NFL.
- Brady's "Aggressiveness," or willingness to throw into what the GPS gizmos determine to be tight windows, was just 13.8 percent, 27th in the NFL.

Brady's air yards per attempt, air yards per completion, and aggressiveness metrics were three-year lows in stats which have only been kept for three years. So while he hasn't exactly been a mad bomber since Randy Moss left town, both statistical analysis and a sober look at the game film showed that he became increasingly reliant on extremely short passes last season, with diminished (though still very good) results.[1]

The counterarguments to the suggestion that Brady's statistical dip and preference for shorter throws were signs of age can be lumped into three categories:

- Brady's decline was due to a weak supporting cast;
- It was a change in the offensive system, you dummy; and
- UR a Hater.

The supporting cast argument amounts to special pleading. Yes, Rob Gronkowski and Julian Edelman were unavailable for chunks of the year. They were also unavailable for chunks of many signature Brady years. Brady's 2018 stats were weaker than his 2016 stats, when Gronk started just six games and Malcolm Mitchell was one his primary receivers (and Brady himself missed four games). Brady posted higher DVOA and DYAR than last season in 2014, when Brandon LaFell was the third option in the passing game (and Gronk and Edelman both missed some time). Arguing the merits of Gronk's backups or various iterations of Chris Hogan in various years is missing the forest for the trees and advancing an over-engineered hypothesis in place of a simple but unpopular one.

As for the changes to the offensive system, that's a chicken-or-egg argument. The Patriots did indeed become more run-and short-pass oriented last season than in years past. Passes made up just 54.9 percent of their plays, the lowest figure since the 2008 Matt Cassel run. As noted above, Brady's throws were shorter than ever. But it's much more likely that the team downshifted into ground-'n'-pound mode in response to Brady's declining skills than because they just felt like doing things differently and emphasizing a rookie running back over a Hall of Fame quarterback.

And if you subscribe to the Hater argument, you aren't going to like the next segment any more than the last one.

The Patriots enjoyed the 24th easiest schedule in the NFL last season, according to DVOA. Their schedule ranked 28th in 2017, 32nd in 2016, and 23rd in 2015. Their projected schedule strength for 2019 is once again dead last. Thanks to

---

1 https://bit.ly/2NvvlfQ

2019 Patriots Schedule

Week	Opp.	Week	Opp.	Week	Opp.
1	PIT	7	at NYJ (Mon.)	13	at HOU
2	at MIA	8	CLE	14	KC
3	NYJ	9	at BAL	15	at CIN
4	at BUF	10	BYE	16	BUF
5	at WAS	11	at PHI	17	MIA
6	NYG (Thu.)	12	DAL		

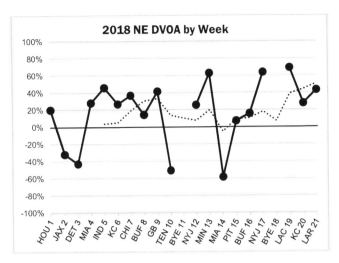

2018 NE DVOA by Week

playing three upside-down turtles in the AFC East twice each, the Patriots enjoy perennial easy schedules despite a system that forces them to face the winners of two other AFC divisions every season.

This is another unpopular sentiment with a familiar counterargument: the Patriots are 77-21 in divisional games since 2003 (78.6 percent) but 150-45 (76.9 percent) in non-divisional games. If they get such a boost from facing the Jets, Bills, and Dolphins, how do you explain near-identical winning percentages against the rest of the league? Huh? HUH?

Well, taking things all the way back to 2003 or 2001 is a little precious. The Patriots' schedule was pretty tough when the Rex Ryan Jets were in their prime (seventh-hardest in the league in 2009 and 2010) and the AFC East was pretty competitive in the mid-2000s as well. The utter ineptitude of all three divisional challengers is a relatively recent development. It was caused, in part, by Patriots dominance (the Jets-Dolphins-Bills keep cycling through regimes due to lack of success, which prevents continuity, which forestalls success, causing regime changes), but it also coincides with this late run of Super Bowl appearances by a Patriots team that would have gotten beaten pretty badly by the 2007 or 2004 Patriots teams.

Furthermore, only the Cheatriots truther weirdos would suggest that the Patriots were some ordinary team transformed into a dynasty by their weak division. They're a great team that beats most of their opponents, strong and weak, at a rate that would seem unsustainable if they didn't keep sustaining it. Comparisons of win-loss records ignore the simple fact that the AFC East hasn't thrown up a true challenger since the Ryan Jets flamed out, making the division easier to win and all but ensuring playoff byes and home games that contenders in other divisions are forced to fight harder for.

This was particularly obvious in 2018, when the Jets and Bills arrived in Foxboro with their rookie quarterbacks for their traditional late-season bludgeonings just as the Patriots fell to 9-5. The two end-of-year cakewalks ensured the Patriots a first-round bye and a home game against a Chargers team with a superior record playing its third straight road game. To claim that playing in the AFC East wasn't an advantage for the Patriots last season is simply being dense.

There are two reasons we spent the first 1,000 words of this essay riling up the Patriots fanbase. First, Brady's age and the soft AFC East are both relevant to our 10.2-win Patriots projection. More importantly, accepting Brady's mortality and the annual tribute the Patriots get from their divisional serfs

is the first step toward recognizing how brilliant the organization has become at both leveraging advantages (like the annual cushy schedule) and mitigating disadvantages (including Brady's slow decline).

The Patriots have conducted a post-doctorate course in how to extend a Super Bowl window over the last two seasons, rebuilding and reshaping the roster around Brady in a variety of clever and sometimes counterintuitive ways, including:

Acquiring and deploying draft capital: Over the past two years, the Patriots acquired an extra first-round pick in the Brandin Cooks trade, an extra second-rounder in the Jimmy Garoppolo trade, and a pair of third-round compensatory picks. They then traded up and down the board (as they do), turning those picks and their own into a multitude of players, several of whom are expected to play major roles in 2019: Isaiah Wynn, who is the favorite to start at left tackle this season; running back Sony Michel; and a deep , diverse 2019 draft class led by receiver N'Keal Harry.

The fact that the Patriots possessed five Day 2 draft picks the year after winning the Super Bowl (though they ended up only using four of them after trades) speaks volumes about their ability to manage draft capital and blend their short- and long-term roster plans. Some of their selections may not adhere to strict analytical guidelines (Michel), but the big-picture effort to squeeze the most value from picks in the 30th-to-110th overall range has kept the Patriots from aging into an overpriced geezer squad.

Reclamation projects: Dumpster-diving for players who failed in other systems is a long-time staple of The Patriots Way. The defense got a lot of mileage last season out of players like Jason McCourty, Kyle Van Noy, and Danny Shelton, all of whom were deemed expendable by inferior teams. Michael Bennett joins them this year as part of his tour of NFL teams that aren't scared away by a player's politics.

The Patriots are also sifting once again through the wide receiver bargain bin in search of useful role players, with Demaryius Thomas, Dontrelle Inman, and returning tight end Benjamin Watson vying for jobs which are by no means guaranteed to them.

The succession game: Offensive linemen David Andrews, Marcus Cannon, Shaq Mason. and Joe Thuney are all draft-and-develop (or in Andrews' case, sign as an undrafted free agent-and-develop) in-house projects who grew into one of the league's best units last season.

Addition by subtraction: Danny Amendola, Malcolm Butler, Cooks, Trey Flowers, Dion Lewis, Logan Ryan, and Nate Solder, all starters or key contributors in 2017, were allowed to depart in trades or as free agents over the last two seasons, as were one-year rentals who played significant roles like Trent Brown and Martellus Bennett. Cooks is the only one the Patriots truly missed so far.

The Patriots remain masters of buying low and selling high in both the draft and free agency. Trent Brown, for example, arrived in a draft-weekend swap of midround picks with the 49ers in 2018. He replaced Solder at left tackle, earned a Super Bowl ring, then signed a four-year, $66-million deal with the Raiders. Flowers, drafted with the fourth-round pick acquired in the 2015 Logan Mankins trade, blossomed into a versatile, high-effort starter for three seasons, then earned his first big contract ($90 million) from the Lions. The Raiders and 49ers appear to be overpaying for cogs in the Patriots' well-oiled machine. In return, the Patriots can keep oiling the machine with cap flexibility and compensatory picks.

Resource re-allocation: The Patriots have spent more money and cap space on backups, role players, special teamers, and low-cost veterans than most teams for several years. As of 2019, they will allocate a higher percentage of their salary cap to low-cost players (those making less than $4.6 million per season) than any other team in the NFL, per OverTheCap. com. Nearly one-third (33.1 percent) of their cap space goes towards affordable players such as Andrews, Jason McCourty, James White, and Stephen Gostkowski. The Patriots rank fourth in the NFL in allocations for middle-income ($4.6- to $9.1 million per year), allocating 24 percent of their cap space to a tier which includes Cannon, Mason, Edelman, Stephone Gilmore, and others.

The low cap numbers of big-name players like Edelman and rising stars like Mason are the remarkable result of the Patriots staying ahead of the market and signing core players before they come close to free agency. The Patriots accomplish this by being the Patriots (guys will sign early in search of more rings) and by letting expensive/expendable Trent Brown-types walk.

All of these team-building concepts work in harmony with one another. Trent Brown became expendable because Wynn is in the pipeline, and the Patriots invested one of their extra Day 2 picks on West Virginia tackle Yodny Cajuste to restock the pipeline. Compensatory picks develop into solid starters who are either extended at below-market salaries or set free in search of more compensatory picks. A well-established coaching pipeline makes everything else possible: Bill Belichick's defensive lieutenants know how to wring the most out of Van Noy types, and offensive line wizard Dante Scarnecchia can slow-cook a Cannon or Mason or flash-fry a Brown into a worthy protector for Brady.

The Patriots had the oldest snap-weighted roster in the NFL last season (average age: 27.9). They will still field a very old roster this year, but much of that age is concentrated in Brady, Edelman, the McCourty Twins, and Gostkowski, all of them still championship-caliber performers, plus some rentals like Watson and Thomas. The offensive line is relatively young, and the veteran role players scattered all over the roster fall mostly into those low- to middle-tier tax brackets. The Patriots have the sort of deep, balanced roster that shouldn't be possible to maintain after three-straight Super Bowl appearances, not to mention 18 years of general dominance in the salary cap era.

The Patriots only lost one truly irreplaceable part this off-season, but he's a biggie: Gronk retired in the spring after nine punishing seasons. Gronk's absence robs the Patriots not just of one of Brady's best receivers but of an exceptional blocker who made the Patriots unpredictable in their base personnel package. Gronk's presence facilitated both the Patriots running game and their short passing package, pulling coverage away from Edelman and the running backs while pummeling opponents such as the Chargers who tried to contain him by playing whole games in their nickel packages.

The Patriots didn't try to replace Gronk by trading up for one of the Iowa tight ends or overpaying for a Jared Cook-type. That's not how they use their resources. Instead, they're more likely to continue their metamorphosis into a run-oriented team. The ability to change offensive styles every few seasons (run-heavy and traditional from 2001 to 2006; Moss Bombs Away from 2007 to 2010; Gronks-and-slots from 2011 to 17; back to the run from 2018-???) is yet another innovation which allows the Patriots to adjust to the talent market, league defensive tendencies, their own strengths and weaknesses, and yes, the rise and decline of their most important player.

The secret behind the Patriots' late-era series of Super Bowl runs isn't some TB12 fountain of eternal youth or a division full of fluffy buttermilk pancakes. It's the fact that Brady reached such a lofty peak at the height of his career that he remains a very effective quarterback even in decline, and the team's ability to keep adapting and reinventing itself, mixing short-term fixes with long-range draft and cap strategies, has lasted for so long that its rivals have become trapped in endless rebuilding loops.

The Patriots are going to win their division again, even as age and the loss of Gronk force Brady to creep another step backward. At least a portion of the playoffs will once again roll through Foxborough, probably with predictable results. Perhaps 2020 will be the year when the Patriots finally collapse and/or the young quarterbacks of the AFC East rise up in rebellion. We'll revisit that possibility after this season. For now, it's all business as usual, and while the inevitable is indeed inevitable, it remains in its familiar position of being at least a year away.

Mike Tanier

2018 Patriots Stats by Week

Wk	vs.	W-L	PF	PA	YDF	YDA	TO	Total	Off	Def	ST
1	HOU	W	27	20	389	325	-1	20%	10%	-18%	-8%
2	at JAX	L	20	31	302	480	+1	-32%	15%	42%	-5%
3	at DET	L	10	26	209	414	0	-43%	-24%	16%	-2%
4	MIA	W	38	7	449	172	0	28%	6%	-24%	-2%
5	IND	W	38	24	438	439	+1	46%	28%	-15%	3%
6	KC	W	43	40	500	446	+1	27%	22%	-16%	-11%
7	at CHI	W	38	31	381	453	-1	37%	31%	11%	16%
8	at BUF	W	25	6	387	333	+2	14%	23%	-5%	-13%
9	GB	W	31	17	433	367	+1	41%	19%	-12%	11%
10	at TEN	L	10	34	284	385	0	-51%	-28%	25%	2%
11	BYE										
12	at NYJ	W	27	13	498	338	+1	26%	35%	12%	3%
13	MIN	W	24	10	471	278	+1	63%	41%	-23%	-2%
14	at MIA	L	33	34	421	412	0	-59%	7%	62%	-3%
15	at PIT	L	10	17	368	376	+1	7%	7%	5%	4%
16	BUF	W	24	12	390	289	0	16%	1%	-9%	6%
17	NYJ	W	38	3	375	239	+3	64%	23%	-36%	4%
18	BYE										
19	LAC	W	41	28	498	335	+2	69%	50%	-15%	4%
20	at KC	W	37	31	524	290	-2	28%	6%	-10%	12%
21	LAR	W	13	3	407	260	0	43%	-11%	-56%	-2%

Trends and Splits

	Offense	Rank	Defense	Rank
Total DVOA	14.5%	5	0.4%	16
Unadjusted VOA	13.9%	5	-2.4%	12
Weighted Trend	16.1%	4	-0.1%	13
Variance	3.7%	5	6.8%	25
Average Opponent	-2.5%	4	-5.3%	28
Passing	33.0%	4	5.0%	13
Rushing	2.5%	9	-7.0%	19
First Down	18.0%	5	-3.5%	12
Second Down	10.6%	7	8.3%	25
Third Down	14.0%	9	-4.1%	15
First Half	20.4%	4	2.2%	23
Second Half	7.7%	9	-1.5%	16
Red Zone	-2.8%	17	-7.6%	10
Late and Close	27.0%	3	8.8%	27

Five-Year Performance

Year	W-L	Pyth W	Est W	PF	PA	TO	Total	Rk	Off	Rk	Def	Rk	ST	Rk	Off AGL	Rk	Def AGL	Rk	Off Age	Rk	Def Age	Rk	ST Age	Rk
2014	12-4	11.8	10.8	468	313	+12	22.1%	4	13.5%	6	-3.0%	12	5.7%	5	24.4	9	37.6	16	27.7	5	26.6	19	26.1	16
2015	12-4	11.7	10.9	465	315	+7	22.6%	6	15.4%	5	-3.3%	12	3.9%	5	60.6	29	32.7	19	27.2	12	25.9	27	25.9	18
2016	14-2	12.8	11.9	441	250	+12	24.9%	1	20.8%	2	-1.8%	16	2.3%	8	47.2	25	7.3	1	27.3	7	26.6	14	26.3	9
2017	13-3	12.0	11.0	458	296	+6	22.6%	6	27.3%	1	10.9%	31	6.3%	3	36.7	18	24.6	10	27.7	3	26.3	15	26.7	3
2018	11-5	10.8	10.0	436	325	+10	14.2%	7	14.5%	5	0.4%	16	0.1%	16	42.8	19	35.8	18	28.5	1	27.2	5	27.9	1

2018 Performance Based on Most Common Personnel Groups

NE Offense					NE Offense vs. Opponents					NE Defense					NE Defense vs. Opponents			
Pers	Freq	Yds	DVOA	Run%	Pers	Freq	Yds	DVOA	Run%	Pers	Freq	Yds	DVOA	Pers	Freq	Yds	DVOA	
11	56%	6.8	30.3%	31%	Base	33%	5.8	15.8%	62%	Base	12%	5.1	-4.6%	11	65%	5.7	-0.8%	
21	28%	5.8	6.5%	56%	Nickel	59%	6.3	17.8%	33%	Nickel	54%	5.9	1.9%	12	18%	6.5	3.1%	
12	5%	6.0	16.1%	42%	Dime+	12%	7.5	45.8%	25%	Dime+	33%	6.1	0.6%	21	5%	6.4	9.0%	
22	4%	3.6	-0.6%	79%	Goal Line	2%	0.8	4.5%	95%	Goal Line	1%	1.4	-67.9%	612	2%	3.6	-51.2%	
10	2%	5.2	20.4%	6%	Big	1%	1.1	-168.9%	88%					13	2%	4.5	24.5%	

Strategic Tendencies

Run/Pass		Rk	Formation		Rk	Pass Rush		Rk	Secondary		Rk	Strategy		Rk
Runs, first half	39%	15	Form: Single Back	59%	31	Rush 3	12.8%	6	4 DB	12%	31	Play action	31%	4
Runs, first down	53%	6	Form: Empty Back	9%	13	Rush 4	59.2%	26	5 DB	54%	24	Avg Box (Off)	6.42	3
Runs, second-long	24%	27	Pers: 3+ WR	59%	27	Rush 5	18.8%	12	6+ DB	33%	4	Avg Box (Def)	6.16	22
Runs, power sit.	71%	3	Pers: 2+ TE/6+ OL	12%	31	Rush 6+	9.3%	3	CB by Sides	53%	32	Offensive Pace	28.18	1
Runs, behind 2H	33%	4	Pers: 6+ OL	2%	12	Int DL Sacks	13.3%	31	S/CB Cover Ratio	29%	11	Defensive Pace	29.21	1
Pass, ahead 2H	46%	22	Shotgun/Pistol	47%	30	Second Level Sacks	28.3%	8	DB Blitz	9%	15	Go for it on 4th	1.29	17

New England was the NFL's best team on play-action last season, by leaps and bounds. They had both the largest gap in yards per play (9.8 vs. 6.2) and DVOA (76.4% vs. 16.4%). Appropriately, the Patriots also used play-action more often than any other team in the AFC. ● New England used two players in the backfield on a 57 percent of running plays; San Francisco was the only other team in the league above 40 percent. The Patriots were slightly better with two backs (4.3 yards per carry, 1.5% DVOA) than with one (4.2, -13.9%). ● The Patriots ranked second in the league in how well they ran on second-and-long, with 22.7% DVOA and 5.8 yards per carry. Kansas City was the only other offense with DVOA above 5.5% when running in second-and-long. ● New England surprisingly led the league in the percentage of their runs that came with eight in the box: 32 percent, compared to an NFL average of 17 percent. The Patriots gained only 3.2 yards per carry with eight in the box compared to 4.8 yards per carry with lighter boxes, but because a lot of those eight-man boxes were in short-yardage situations, New England's offensive DVOA was the same either way. ● Tom Brady was blitzed on a league-low 16.9 percent of pass plays. Brady's performance against five pass-rushers was virtually identical to his performance against three or four pass-rushers. He had a lousy -83.0% DVOA against six pass-rushers, but with a tiny sample of 14 plays. ● New England's own frequency of big blitzes (sending six or more pass-rushers) more than tripled from the year before, and the Patriots only rushed three about half as much as they had the previous couple of seasons. ● New England opponents threw deep (16 or more yards in the air) a league-leading 24.5 percent of the time, even though this was a strength of the Patriots defense. Chicago was the only defense that had a better DVOA against these passes than the Patriots. ● Patriots opponents used shotgun on a league-leading 74 percent of plays.

Passing

Player	DYAR	DVOA	Plays	NtYds	Avg	YAC	C%	TD	Int
T.Brady	1034	15.4%	589	4197	7.1	5.7	66.1%	29	11

Rushing

Player	DYAR	DVOA	Plays	Yds	Avg	TD	Fum	Suc
S.Michel	58	-2.7%	209	933	4.5	6	1	53%
J.White	42	1.6%	94	425	4.5	5	0	47%
R.Burkhead	1	-8.2%	57	186	3.3	0	1	40%
C.Patterson*	114	4.0%	42	228	5.4	1	0	--
K.Barner*	7	1.0%	19	71	3.7	0	0	63%
T.Brady	30	18.1%	12	44	3.7	2	0	--
J.Edelman	82	119.4%	9	107	11.9	0	0	--
J.Develin	42	88.0%	6	8	1.3	4	0	83%
J.Hill*	15	73.3%	4	25	6.3	0	0	75%
B.Bolden	32	99.6%	8	91	11.4	2	1	63%

Receiving

Player	DYAR	DVOA	Plays	Ctch	Yds	Y/C	YAC	TD	C%
J.Edelman	122	1.7%	108	74	850	11.5	4.7	6	69%
J.Gordon	183	20.3%	68	40	720	18.0	6.6	3	59%
C.Hogan*	123	14.3%	55	35	532	15.2	5.5	3	64%
P.Dorsett	56	5.4%	42	32	290	9.1	3.1	3	76%
C.Patterson*	29	0.6%	28	21	247	11.8	7.7	3	75%
D.Thomas	96	0.9%	89	59	677	11.5	4.7	5	66%
M.Harris	-73	-33.2%	47	28	304	10.9	3.6	0	60%
D.Inman	69	9.1%	39	28	304	10.9	2.1	3	72%
R.Gronkowski	98	13.3%	72	47	682	14.5	3.9	3	65%
B.Watson	73	15.2%	46	35	400	11.4	2.5	2	76%
M.LaCosse	-1	-7.6%	37	24	250	10.4	6.0	1	65%
J.White	194	13.5%	123	87	751	8.6	7.6	7	71%
R.Burkhead	5	-9.1%	20	14	131	9.4	8.6	1	70%
J.Develin	-32	-44.5%	17	12	61	5.1	3.0	0	71%
S.Michel	-3	-18.4%	11	7	50	7.1	7.1	0	64%

Offensive Line

Player	Pos	Age	GS	Snaps	Pen	Sk	Pass	Run	Player	Pos	Age	GS	Snaps	Pen	Sk	Pass	Run
Joe Thuney	LG	27	16/16	1119	4	0.5	2	2	Marcus Cannon	RT	31	13/13	835	7	2.0	9	1
David Andrews	C	27	16/16	1103	4	0.5	3	3	LaAdrian Waddle*	RT	28	16/3	342	2	2.0	5	1
Trenton Brown*	LT	26	16/16	1089	9	2.0	7	3	Ted Karras	RG	26	12/2	171	1	1.0	1	0
Shaquille Mason	RG	26	14/14	953	3	0.5	2	3									

Year	Yards	ALY	Rank	Power	Rank	Stuff	Rank	2nd Lev	Rank	Open Field	Rank	Sacks	ASR	Rank	Press	Rank	F-Start	Cont.
2016	3.99	4.46	9	59%	22	20%	16	1.10	22	0.60	21	24	4.6%	6	25.6%	14	14	38
2017	4.43	5.05	1	65%	14	16%	3	1.35	2	0.60	20	35	6.4%	13	27.0%	7	13	29
2018	4.24	5.03	3	58%	29	16%	4	1.19	21	0.63	25	21	3.8%	1	22.9%	1	16	31
2018 ALY by direction:			Left End: 5.36 (6)			Left Tackle: 4.21 (16)			Mid/Guard: 5.02 (2)			Right Tackle: 6.15 (1)			Right End: 4.29 (15)			

Last year continued New England's remarkable run of success in adjusted line yards: the Patriots have now ranked in the top ten in every season since 2007, and only missed the top five once (2016). They have also ranked in the top ten of rushing DVOA in 11 of the past 15 seasons, and their 132.7 rushing yards per game was the third-highest figure of the Tom Brady era. (They also had 142.4 yards per game in 2008, with Matt Cassel at quarterback.) 🐾 For the first time in the history of the metric, the Patriots ranked No. 1 in adjusted sack rate, though they did have a better rate when they finished No. 2 behind Peyton Manning's Colts in 2009. 🐾 Every primary starter on the line finished in the top ten at his position in snaps per blown block. Thuney's 280 snaps per blown block ranked third among all qualifying linemen. 🐾 Left tackle Trent Brown, who was brought in via trade from the 49ers last season, left to sign a big-money deal with the Raiders in free agency. The favorite to replace him is 2018 first-round pick Isaiah Wynn, who missed his entire rookie season with a torn Achilles. Wynn's relative lack of height (6-foot-3) meant he projected more as a guard out of Alabama, but his unquestioned pass-blocking ability and long reach should stand him in good stead at tackle. 🐾 Backup tackle LaAdrian Waddle also left in free agency, and incoming veteran free agent Jared Veldheer retired within a month of signing, so third-round pick Yodny Cajuste (West Virginia) is expected to be the primary backup at tackle. 🐾 Fourth-round pick Hjalte Froholdt (Arkansas) will have to push ahead of Ted Karras and Brian Schwenke to be assured of a roster spot. Former Titans fourth-round pick Schwenke is listed as a guard, but most of his starts in Tennessee came at center. He was inactive for all but three games last year but signed a one-year extension in February to remain with the team. Karras appeared in 13 games, starting two, and again looks set to be the primary backup on the interior line.

Defensive Front

Defensive Line	Age	Pos	G	Snaps	Plays	TmPct	Rk	Stop	Dfts	BTkl	Runs	St%	Rk	RuYd	Rk	Sack	Hit	Hur	Dsrpt
					Overall						vs. Run					Pass Rush			
Lawrence Guy	29	DT	16	518	59	7.7%	9	41	7	1	57	70%	61	2.8	66	1.0	10	14	2
Malcom Brown*	25	DT	15	458	39	5.4%	33	27	2	3	34	76%	35	2.9	70	0.0	1	5	0
Adam Butler	25	DT	16	379	19	2.5%	--	13	5	1	12	58%	--	3.5	--	3.0	2	10	3
Danny Shelton	26	DT	13	324	21	3.4%	--	15	1	3	20	75%	--	2.4	--	0.0	2	10	0
Mike Pennel	28	DT	16	359	28	3.4%	--	26	2	2	26	92%	--	1.9	--	0.0	2	6	0

Edge Rushers	Age	Pos	G	Snaps	Plays	TmPct	Rk	Stop	Dfts	BTkl	Runs	St%	Rk	RuYd	Rk	Sack	Hit	Hur	Dsrpt
					Overall						vs. Run					Pass Rush			
Trey Flowers*	26	DE	15	732	58	8.0%	4	46	16	3	42	74%	48	2.3	44	7.5	12	43	3
Deatrich Wise	25	DE	16	432	30	3.9%	70	20	9	2	22	59%	79	3.0	64	4.5	11	14	0
Adrian Clayborn*	31	DE	14	318	11	1.6%	--	8	6	4	5	80%	--	1.6	--	2.5	10	29	0
John Simon	29	DE	11	185	17	3.2%	--	13	4	0	12	75%	--	2.7	--	2.0	1	9	0
Michael Bennett	34	DE	16	716	31	4.0%	67	25	18	7	17	76%	41	1.1	9	9.0	20	34	1

Linebackers	Age	Pos	G	Snaps	Plays	TmPct	Rk	Stop	Dfts	BTkl	Runs	St%	Rk	RuYd	Rk	Sack	Hit	Hur	Tgts	Suc%	Rk	AdjYd	Rk	PD	Int
					Overall						vs. Run					Pass Rush				vs. Pass					
Kyle Van Noy	28	OLB	16	946	91	11.8%	48	47	14	19	52	52%	70	3.9	44	3.5	7	27.5	29	59%	14	6.7	36	2	1
Dont'a Hightower	29	OLB	15	774	49	6.8%	77	25	5	4	31	55%	58	5.3	83	1.0	5	16.5	21	43%	56	7.6	60	1	1
Elandon Roberts	25	MLB	16	430	67	8.7%	66	44	14	10	44	70%	10	2.8	10	1.0	1	4	24	54%	26	6.8	38	4	0
Jamie Collins	30	OLB	16	1067	108	12.2%	44	59	20	18	63	67%	19	3.6	32	4.0	3	9	45	42%	58	7.6	61	4	1

Year	Yards	ALY	Rank	Power	Rank	Stuff	Rank	2nd Level	Rank	Open Field	Rank	Sacks	ASR	Rank	Press	Rank
2016	3.61	3.96	11	63%	14	17%	21	1.03	7	0.27	1	34	5.0%	27	24.7%	26
2017	4.69	4.51	31	62%	15	16%	30	1.28	29	0.95	28	42	7.1%	10	27.5%	30
2018	4.79	4.67	26	67%	18	16%	24	1.31	23	0.91	19	30	5.0%	30	33.0%	6

2018 ALY by direction:	Left End: 5.18 (26)	Left Tackle: 4.63 (19)	Mid/Guard: 4.91 (27)	Right Tackle: 2.77 (3)	Right End: 4.64 (19)

The run defense is less encouraging than the run offense. The team was below average in every sub-category of adjusted line yards and in every direction except right tackle. 🐾 The 2018 pass rush had both the team's lowest adjusted sack rate (5.0 percent) and its lowest rank (30) in the history of the statistic. However, they did rank No. 6 in pressure rate on pass plays, and No. 2 in third-down pressure rate. This is very unusual: though sack rate is less consistent than pressure rate, we would usually expect to see a team's sack rate increase the higher its pressure rate. The exact opposite happened to the Patriots: their sack rate was much higher in 2017, when their pressure rate was much lower. The Patriots converted only 12 percent of their pressures into sacks; only the Giants and Raiders did so at a worse rate. 🐾 Despite their poor ALY numbers, the Patriots also allowed the second-fewest rushing touchdowns (seven) behind only the Chicago Bears (five). 🐾 The edge position will look significantly different in 2018. Leading edge defender Trey Flowers left for Detroit as a free agent, to be replaced via a trade with Philadelphia for three-time Pro Bowl veteran Michael Bennett. The team's third-leading edge rusher, Adrian Clayborn, was released after a disappointing 2.5-sack campaign and rejoined the Falcons. He will be replaced by third-round pick Chase Winovich (Michigan), who received a second-round grade as the No. 12 edge rusher in our SackSEER projections. Winovich joins the crowd of recent draftees (Derek Rivers, Deatrich Wise) alongside veterans Bennett and John Simon. Wise's 9.5 sacks rank second on the team behind Flowers over the past two seasons. 🏈 The only change at the second level sees weakside linebacker Jamie Collins return on a one-year deal following his three-year exile in Cleveland. During his previous spell in New England, Collins developed a reputation for making splash plays—mostly on A-gap blitzes—then frittering away the goodwill from those big plays by freelancing, but he was named second-team All-Pro by the Associated Press in 2015. 🏈 The Patriots are an excellent tackling defense. They had the third-best rate of broken tackles, the fifth year of the last six where they were in the top five. But there was one weak spot: Kyle Van Noy's 19 broken tackles last season ranked third-most among linebackers and fifth-most overall. The incoming Collins also had 18 broken tackles, his third straight year averaging more than one broken tackle per game played.

Defensive Secondary

Secondary	Age	Pos	G	Snaps	Plays	Overall TmPct	Rk	Stop	Dfts	BTkl	vs. Run Runs	St%	Rk	RuYd	Rk	vs. Pass Tgts	Tgt%	Rk	Dist	Suc%	Rk	AdjYd	Rk	PD	Int
Stephon Gilmore	29	CB	16	1013	66	8.6%	43	34	16	3	9	67%	4	6.0	32	90	18.7%	40	15.0	67%	1	4.9	2	20	2
Devin McCourty	32	FS	16	1004	80	10.4%	36	22	9	3	35	29%	60	9.9	65	48	10.1%	44	8.1	42%	60	6.8	27	4	1
Patrick Chung	32	SS	15	887	84	11.6%	19	36	9	4	32	50%	21	6.3	27	60	14.3%	66	8.5	55%	22	6.7	22	3	1
Jason McCourty	32	CB	16	833	78	10.1%	18	34	18	3	15	53%	20	4.8	13	73	18.5%	38	13.5	56%	21	8.0	48	10	1
Duron Harmon	28	SS	16	636	42	5.4%	--	7	6	4	16	13%	--	16.1	--	13	4.3%	--	10.9	38%	--	14.1	--	4	4
Jonathan Jones	26	CB	16	516	57	7.4%	--	25	14	9	9	33%	--	7.4	--	62	25.3%	--	10.5	50%	--	8.4	--	7	3
J.C. Jackson	24	CB	13	395	30	4.8%	--	11	8	2	6	33%	--	11.7	--	43	22.9%	--	14.5	53%	--	5.8	--	6	3

Year	Pass D Rank	vs. #1 WR	Rk	vs. #2 WR	Rk	vs. Other WR	Rk	WR Wide	Rk	WR Slot	Rk	vs. TE	Rk	vs. RB	Rk
2016	22	3.6%	20	-5.6%	9	4.0%	19	2.2%	20	1.4%	14	-3.4%	14	9.2%	22
2017	21	18.9%	26	4.9%	19	6.8%	22	-4.9%	14	24.2%	29	-11.6%	8	10.1%	22
2018	13	0.0%	16	-6.1%	12	-17.4%	5	-14.0%	7	-2.5%	15	-12.8%	8	9.5%	22

Only Arizona played less "base" defense in 2018, and more than 40 percent of New England's defensive plays featured three safeties. Devin McCourty, Patrick Chung, and Duron Harmon combined to play 2,527 snaps. 🏈 Cornerback Eric Rowe is the only defensive back who played more than 10 snaps on defense for the 2018 Patriots and is not still on the roster. A starter during the team's 2017 Super Bowl run, Rowe played 74 snaps as a Week 1 starter last year but injured his groin in Week 2 and only played 62 snaps total the rest of the year. He signed with the Dolphins as a free agent. 🏈 A major factor in Rowe's departure was the emergence of undrafted rookie J.C. Jackson. Jackson did not have enough targets or starts to qualify for our leaderboards, but his 5.8 yards allowed per pass target would have ranked in the top ten if he had. Jackson also outperformed 2016 UDFA Jonathan Jones in both success rate and yards per target. 🏈 First-team All-Pro Stephon Gilmore had an out-standing season in coverage, topping the charts in success rate while ranking second in both yards per pass target and average yards allowed after the catch. Only Kyle Fuller had more pass deflections than Gilmore's 20. 🏈 Jason McCourty's coverage numbers were less noteworthy than Gilmore's, but he did lead all Patriots defenders with 18 defeats despite only snagging a single interception. 🏈 The Patriots tied with the Rams for the third-most interceptions in 2018, and with the Broncos and Dolphins for the fifth-most total takeaways. 🏈 Second-round pick Joejuan Williams (Vanderbilt) is a big, physical cornerback with good ball skills who excels in run support, but his inconsistency, lack of short-area quickness, and slow 40-yard dash at the combine saw some analysts project him as a third-round pick and possible safety conversion. Williams will compete for playing time with 2018 second-round pick Duke Dawson, a versatile nickel cornerback with safety traits and experience who missed his entire rookie year after injuring his hamstring in September. The pair appear to be in direct competition to be the seventh of seven active defensive backs, and their initial playing time is likely to depend heavily on specific matchups.

Special Teams

Year	DVOA	Rank	FG/XP	Rank	Net Kick	Rank	Kick Ret	Rank	Net Punt	Rank	Punt Ret	Rank	Hidden	Rank
2016	2.3%	8	0.2	17	10.4	2	-3.6	24	12.1	3	-7.7	29	11.6	4
2017	6.3%	3	8.9	6	8.4	1	6.4	4	8.2	4	-0.6	18	13.1	3
2018	0.1%	16	0.1	17	-8.7	32	5.3	5	4.5	10	-0.6	17	8.5	8

The Patriots just barely continued one of the most remarkable runs in football, with an above-average special teams DVOA for the 23rd straight season. Nonetheless, 2018 was New England's lowest finish in our special teams rankings since 2004, and the franchise's lowest rating since 1995. The Patriots were in the top eight in every year from 2010 to 2017. ❧ Most of 2018's decline came on kick returns, where the Patriots allowed a league-worst 11.5 points of return value. No other team allowed more than 8.2 points of value on kick returns. This is likely to be a one-year blip, as the Patriots had ranked in the top four of that statistic in each of the previous five seasons. Also, most teams with a rating that low rebound: only the 2016-17 Packers have ranked in the bottom four in consecutive seasons since at least 2013. ❧ Fifth-round pick Jake Bailey (Stanford) was a kickoff specialist in college, as well as a three-time All-Pac-12 punter. If Bailey makes the roster ahead of incumbent Ryan Allen, his ability on kickoffs is likely to be a factor. Allen was a free agent this offseason but signed a one-year deal to remain in New England. He and Bailey will face an open competition over the summer. ❧ Cordarrelle Patterson ranked in the top five of our kick returner numbers for the fourth time in six seasons, but he signed with the Bears in free agency. Sony Michel's four kick returns were not enough to qualify for the table, but his average return was almost ten yards shorter than Patterson's. Several players on the Patriots have experience returning kicks, including Michel and stalwarts such as James White and Devin McCourty, but this is very much an open spot as of mid-June. ❧ Julian Edelman had at least ten punt returns for the eighth time in the past nine seasons, but he has not been above average in our punt return numbers since 2014. ❧ Returning from a torn ACL suffered against Miami in November 2017, Nate Ebner again led the Patriots with 13 special teams tackles, but he made most of those tackles after hefty returns; his 31 percent stop rate was the lowest of any player with at least 10 tackles. Teammate Brandon King, who had 12 special teams tackles, tied for the third-worst stop rate by the same criteria. (A special teams stop is any tackle that stops the returner short of an average return based on kick distance and catch location.)

New Orleans Saints

2018 record: 13-3	**Total DVOA:** 20.5% (4th)	**2019 Mean Projection:** 10.3 wins	**On the Clock (0-4):** 2%
Pythagorean Wins: 11.5 (2nd)	**Offense:** 15.9% (4th)	**Postseason Odds:** 70.5%	**Mediocrity (5-7):** 12%
Snap-Weighted Age: 26.7 (9th)	**Defense:** -2.9% (11th)	**Super Bowl Odds:** 21.9%	**Playoff Contender (8-10):** 35%
Average Opponent: -0.5% (16th)	**Special Teams:** 1.7% (9th)	**Proj. Avg. Opponent:** -0.4% (20th)	**Super Bowl Contender (11+):** 50%

2018: The Saints are at the top of the mountain...

2019: ... but can they be the ones who plant the flag?

By almost any measure, 2018 was one of the most successful seasons in the 52-year history of the New Orleans Saints. For only the sixth time, the team completed consecutive seasons with a winning record. For the first time, they successfully defended a division title—even the Super Bowl winners of 2009 had to settle for a wild card berth (and the infamous Beastquake defeat) in 2010. The Saints had never won a playoff game in consecutive seasons, but now they have. In a deep and volatile NFC playoff field, the Saints are one of the few consistent contenders, and last year's team continued their record of earning a playoff appearance every time they pair Drew Brees with a defense outside the bottom quartile of the DVOA table.

The advanced figures make even more encouraging reading. Not since the Dome Patrol defense roamed the *Mardi Grass* turf had the Saints finished in the top five by overall DVOA in consecutive seasons. The current team followed 2017's No. 1 rank with a fourth-place finish in 2018 to eclipse even that great squad's two-year peak. The offense and defense declined slightly from 2017 to 2018, but after recovering from yet another rocky start (more on that later), the Saints finished with both the best record in the league and the No. 2 weighted DVOA. Even though they failed to emulate the playoff achievements of the 2009 squad, it is quite possible to make the argument that the Saints of the past two seasons have been the best overall team in the history of the franchise.

Yet for all their regular-season proficiency, an undercurrent of disappointment threatens to submerge this squad's perception precisely *because* they have failed to emulate those playoff achievements. The nature of the playoff defeats has both helped and hindered that perspective: the extreme, highly improbable misfortune of the two critical plays (Stefon Diggs' walk-off touchdown, and *that* pass interference no-call) is offered in mitigation, but their impact was magnified by allowing two winnable games against arguably inferior opponents to each come down to a single play. A reversal of either game's outcome would have considerable impact on the perception of the current team. The Saints cannot keep rolling critical failures at critical junctures indefinitely, but similarly should never have allowed a single critical failure to define their season. As the tenth anniversary of the club's lone title looms, anything less than a serious tilt at repeating that achievement will be viewed as insufficient for a team of this standard.

Fortunately, both our projections and the Vegas odds agree that the Saints look extremely well-placed to make such a tilt. Though the team lost several significant starters in Benjamin Watson, Max Unger, Alex Okafor, and Tyeler Davison during the offseason, the replacements for those players are all either established starters themselves (Jared Cook, Nick Easton, Malcom Brown) or highly-regarded prospects looking to mature into a starting role (Marcus Davenport). Injured defensive tackle Sheldon Rankins is unlikely to be ready for the start of the year, but the star lineman should return partway through to enhance the defensive rotation. The team may have lost a good deal of its experience—the four departing starters were all valuable veterans—but not even a former All-Pro such as Unger should be considered irreplaceable. As is well-established by now, Drew Brees is the conductor of the Saints orchestra, and around him the other key players—Michael Thomas, Alvin Kamara, Cameron Jordan, and Marshon Lattimore—have not changed a bit.

As a result, we expect to see a very similar Saints team to the one which ranked No. 1 in DVOA in 2017 and No. 2 in weighted DVOA at the end of 2018. 2017's sudden, dramatic leap forward on defense, so often the source of predictable regression (see the 2018 Jaguars or, more extreme, the 2017 Buccaneers), appears to have stuck. The team benefited from above-average health (50.7 adjusted games lost, sixth), defensive turnover rate (0.149 turnovers per drive, eighth), and pass rush (adjusted sack rate of 8.7 percent, fourth), all of which are volatile statistics that are likely to regress somewhat. They also had by far the worst defensive DVOA on deep passes (62.2%), which is likely to regress to the team's benefit, and a superior run defense DVOA to pass defense DVOA—important because run defense DVOA is usually a better predictor of the team's DVOA the following year than pass defense DVOA. And of course, they have an offense that has not finished outside the top ten in DVOA since 2010. The Saints have demonstrated over the past ten years that, although competence on defense is historically far from guaranteed, competence on defense is also all they require to be one of the top two or three contenders in the NFC.

Whether it be the result of extreme good fortune, excellent scouting, strong coaching, or a combination of the three, competence at least ought to be guaranteed from the current defense. The 2017 draft class, which landed four impact start-

2019 Saints Schedule

Week	Opp.	Week	Opp.	Week	Opp.
1	HOU (Mon.)	7	at CHI	13	at ATL (Thu.)
2	at LAR	8	ARI	14	SF
3	at SEA	9	BYE	15	IND (Mon.)
4	DAL	10	ATL	16	at TEN
5	TB	11	at TB	17	at CAR
6	at JAX	12	CAR		

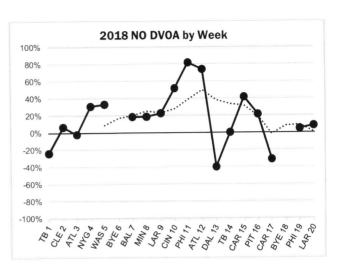

ers and two valuable contributors from the first three rounds, is rightly lauded for the immediate and lasting impact it made on the fortunes of the team, but the 2016 haul of Sheldon Rankins, Michael Thomas, Vonn Bell, and David Onyemata is also impressive. Those successful picks were vital: expensive mistakes in free agency have kept the team tight against the salary cap over the past few seasons, so the draft was the sole available means by which to significantly improve the team. Even there, past decisions impaired the front office's ability to improve the roster this offseason: the decision to trade away a valuable 2019 first-round pick ahead of a deep class of defensive linemen to move up for a rotational edge rusher in 2018 (Marcus Davenport) was somewhat confusing at the time, and left the Saints with only a single pick from the first three rounds of this year's draft.

Still, given the average age of their defensive starters (defensive snap-weighted age of 25.3, fourth-youngest) and standard of their recent performances, the front office could reasonably argue that the gain from another draft selection, compared to a year of professional experience for Davenport, would be marginal at best. The recent infusion of talent means considerably fewer opportunities for a young player to break into the Saints defensive lineup now than there were in 2016 and 2017. This year's defense will see *some* change, of course, particularly on the defensive line. Okafor's departure should see Davenport ascend into the starting role opposite Jordan. 2017 SackSEER sleeper Trey Hendrickson will again be involved in the pass-rush rotation, with recent free-agent addition Wes Horton providing additional bulk against the run. Brown should slot in for Davison on the interior, with Onyemata temporarily starting until Rankins returns from his Achilles tear (Onyemata himself will be out for the opener against Houston, serving a one-game suspension following an offseason arrest for marijuana possession). That would not necessarily translate to opportunities for another draftee, however: the preferred starting four shows three players who were heavily involved last year, and just the one incoming replacement.

The back seven will probably see even less change. The midseason acquisition of Eli Apple worked out well for both player and team, though not quite well enough for the Saints to pick up his $13 million fifth-year option. Patrick Robinson should return at full strength from his early-season ankle fracture. Of the ten back-seven defenders who averaged at least 10 defensive snaps per game last year, only depth safety Kurt Coleman does not return. The roster is two-deep at every spot except Coleman's—the Saints have not yet reprised their recent habit of

signing a veteran safety for a rotational role behind two younger starters, but such a signing would alleviate the depth concerns there—so even a predictable number of injuries should not be cause for concern. Just two short years ago, the Saints were coming off their worst multi-year stretch of defensive performance in DVOA history. Now, with back-to-back finishes in the top third of the DVOA table for the first time since the turn of the century, they are coming off one of their best.

The offense has responded to that defensive improvement with its own best stretch of performance in ten years. The Super Bowl squad of 2009 was the last Saints offense to finish consecutive seasons in the top five of the DVOA table. That squad ranked No. 1 in cumulative DVOA over 2008 and 2009; the current incarnation ranks No. 2 over the past two seasons behind only Kansas City. (The 2017 Chiefs offense led by Alex Smith had the exact same DVOA as the 2018 Saints, whereas the 2018 Chiefs with Patrick Mahomes at quarterback were more efficient than the 2017 Saints.) While the offense has seen slightly more turnover than the defense—Mark Ingram's departure effectively brings the total to three starters rather than two—the result may well be a net gain, with the likely drop-off at center more than compensated for by the addition of a superior receiving threat at tight end. The configuration of the receiving group beyond No. 1 target Michael Thomas remains very much to be determined, but shuffling between Ted Ginn, Tre'Quan Smith, Cameron Meredith, Austin Carr, and even Keith Kirkwood was barely enough to impair the Saints passing game in 2018. The pass offense has improved its efficiency by DVOA in each of the past five seasons, and though it will be tough to improve on 2018's third-ranked 34.5% DVOA, neither should we expect a drastic drop-off even if the depth chart remains more of a flip chart.

The biggest question mark is probably still the age of the quarterback, but Brees and his contemporaries have been hard at work in recent years demonstrating that age is not quite the barrier it once was. Even if the worst was to happen to Brees, through either injury or age-related decline, Teddy Bridgewater in theory provides one of the better insurance plans in the league—even at quarterback, the Saints have both depth and top-level talent, further emphasizing just how strong this roster is from top to bottom.

That is not to say that there are no lingering areas for concern. For one, as we mentioned earlier, the Saints have an alarming habit of making extremely slow starts to their season. The 21-18 win over Cleveland last September was the first win the Saints have recorded in either Week 1 or 2 since, astoundingly, 2013, and even that win over Hue Jackson's squad depended on a last-minute field goal miss (and to a lesser extent two extra-point failures) by Zane Gonzalez. Starting well is less important than finishing well—witness all the concern about the Patriots after they started 1-2 last season—but in a fiercely competitive NFC field, three September games against the Rams, Seahawks, and Cowboys could easily prove the difference between hosting the conference championship game and a tough road trip in the divisional round.

Everybody would prefer to host their playoff games rather than travel, but the difference between those two prospects is especially stark for this team. The Saints' home playoff record in the Sean Payton era is 6-1, whereas their road record is a perfectly converse 1-6. At home in 2018, Brees' passing DVOA was 64.1%. On the road, it fell to 9.8%, and the three-game road trip in December was easily his least efficient stretch of the season. No playoff quarterback saw a larger difference between his home and road performance last season. If the Saints are to make a serious tilt at repeating their achievement from a decade ago, their ability to secure home-field advantage could be key to their success. The surest way to scupper that prospect would be another 0-2 start.

Also, for all the improvement on defense, some of the same issues that plagued the team in their terrible 2014-16 run showed up again in last year's numbers. When Marshon Lattimore had his outstanding rookie season in 2017, the Saints ranked sixth in DVOA against No. 1 receivers, league average

against No. 2 receivers, and slightly above average (No. 12) against receiving backs. Last year, those numbers all dropped back to where they had been before: No. 30 against top receivers, No. 31 against No. 2 receivers, and No. 29 against receiving backs. Those teams were also terrible against the deep pass, particularly in 2014 and 2015, so there may be a schematic element at play, but this is a division packed with deep passers, talented receivers, and offenses that are not afraid to attack the deep areas of the field. The weaknesses in these specific areas did not translate to a poor overall DVOA, but they bear watching as the season unfolds.

Still, absent some unpredictable disaster, the Saints should be looking to extend their first-ever streak of division wins to three, and to once again compete for home-field advantage as arguably the most complete team in the NFL. Last offseason, most criticism of the team focused on their lack of splash compared to other teams around them—while the Rams were aggressive throughout the offseason, the Vikings added Sheldon Richardson and Kirk Cousins, and the Eagles added Michael Bennett, the Saints' headline signings were the twin returns of Benjamin Watson and Patrick Robinson. This offseason has a similar feel in New Orleans, but with a bit more confidence in the maturing defense and with fewer splashy moves from the other top teams in the conference. The Saints are unlikely to have changed much from last year, but as last year's No. 1 seed they had very little room to improve anyway—it's hard to complain about the team scrambling to retain its position when that position is the top of the mountain. The biggest question now is whether they can scale that same mountain again, and perhaps this time be the ones to plant the flag at the pinnacle.

Andrew Potter

2018 Saints Stats by Week

Wk	vs.	W-L	PF	PA	YDF	YDA	TO	Total	Off	Def	ST
1	TB	L	40	48	475	529	-2	-24%	25%	48%	-2%
2	CLE	W	21	18	275	327	-1	7%	-8%	-21%	-6%
3	at ATL	W	43	37	534	407	0	-2%	22%	27%	3%
4	at NYG	W	33	18	389	299	+2	31%	31%	4%	3%
5	WAS	W	43	19	447	283	+1	33%	30%	-6%	-3%
6	BYE										
7	at BAL	W	24	23	339	351	-1	19%	24%	10%	5%
8	at MIN	W	30	20	270	423	+1	19%	10%	0%	9%
9	LAR	W	45	35	487	483	0	23%	39%	16%	-1%
10	at CIN	W	51	14	509	284	+2	52%	43%	-2%	6%
11	PHI	W	48	7	546	196	+3	82%	42%	-37%	3%
12	ATL	W	31	17	312	366	+3	74%	26%	-50%	-1%
13	at DAL	L	10	13	176	308	+1	-40%	-51%	-14%	-3%
14	at TB	W	28	14	298	279	-1	0%	-22%	-19%	4%
15	at CAR	W	12	9	346	247	0	42%	-6%	-39%	8%
16	PIT	W	31	28	370	429	+1	21%	27%	5%	-1%
17	CAR	L	14	33	294	374	-1	-31%	-13%	23%	5%
18	BYE										
19	PHI	W	20	14	420	250	+1	5%	-6%	-16%	-5%
20	LAR	L	23	26	290	378	0	8%	-19%	-21%	6%

Trends and Splits

	Offense	Rank	Defense	Rank
Total DVOA	15.9%	4	-2.9%	11
Unadjusted VOA	17.5%	4	-1.9%	14
Weighted Trend	13.4%	7	-9.8%	6
Variance	7.0%	18	6.8%	24
Average Opponent	3.4%	31	3.1%	8
Passing	34.5%	3	10.6%	22
Rushing	3.3%	8	-24.9%	3
First Down	23.5%	3	-2.3%	13
Second Down	7.5%	11	-12.7%	2
Third Down	14.1%	8	10.4%	24
First Half	16.1%	6	2.1%	22
Second Half	15.6%	5	-8.0%	8
Red Zone	21.0%	7	-16.5%	7
Late and Close	13.0%	6	-9.2%	11

Five-Year Performance

Year	W-L	Pyth W	Est W	PF	PA	TO	Total	Rk	Off	Rk	Def	Rk	ST	Rk	Off AGL	Rk	Def AGL	Rk	Off Age	Rk	Def Age	Rk	ST Age	Rk
2014	7-9	7.4	7.6	401	424	-13	-0.9%	17	10.6%	7	13.1%	31	1.6%	11	26.4	12	31.6	10	29.0	1	26.2	24	25.9	22
2015	7-9	6.4	5.2	408	476	+2	-18.7%	28	10.5%	7	26.1%	32	-3.2%	26	19.7	3	36.3	23	28.2	4	26.5	20	26.7	4
2016	7-9	8.3	8.6	469	454	-3	-1.9%	21	15.4%	6	14.6%	31	-2.6%	27	22.4	5	58.9	27	28.3	2	26.8	11	27.0	4
2017	11-5	11.1	13.4	448	326	+7	30.7%	1	21.6%	2	-7.9%	8	1.2%	15	33.6	16	62.3	31	27.5	6	24.9	31	25.7	21
2018	13-3	11.5	11.1	504	353	+9	20.5%	4	15.9%	4	-2.9%	11	1.7%	9	29.1	9	21.6	8	28.2	3	25.3	29	26.6	7

2018 Performance Based on Most Common Personnel Groups

NO Offense					NO Offense vs. Opponents					NO Defense				NO Defense vs. Opponents			
Pers	Freq	Yds	DVOA	Run%	Pers	Freq	Yds	DVOA	Run%	Pers	Freq	Yds	DVOA	Pers	Freq	Yds	DVOA
11	55%	6.6	28.5%	34%	Base	32%	5.9	4.3%	61%	Base	16%	5.2	-12.1%	11	71%	6.2	-1.5%
12	16%	6.8	15.0%	44%	Nickel	60%	6.4	23.0%	38%	Nickel	79%	6.1	-1.5%	12	13%	5.2	-0.1%
21	13%	6.1	-1.2%	55%	Dime+	8%	8.0	49.3%	16%	Dime+	2%	9.1	63.2%	21	4%	7.5	23.8%
22	6%	5.3	-4.3%	74%	Goal Line	1%	0.6	35.3%	64%	Goal Line	2%	4.0	-26.1%	10	2%	8.2	21.6%
13	2%	3.6	11.3%	64%										01	2%	5.4	-22.1%
20	2%	12.2	131.1%	14%										13	2%	3.8	-52.8%

Strategic Tendencies

Run/Pass		Rk	Formation		Rk	Pass Rush		Rk	Secondary		Rk	Strategy		Rk
Runs, first half	38%	17	Form: Single Back	73%	25	Rush 3	9.5%	11	4 DB	16%	28	Play action	21%	24
Runs, first down	51%	8	Form: Empty Back	10%	10	Rush 4	63.5%	21	5 DB	79%	2	Avg Box (Off)	6.32	6
Runs, second-long	34%	9	Pers: 3+ WR	57%	29	Rush 5	17.9%	14	6+ DB	2%	23	Avg Box (Def)	6.22	18
Runs, power sit.	65%	8	Pers: 2+ TE/6+ OL	27%	10	Rush 6+	9.0%	4	CB by Sides	66%	22	Offensive Pace	31.07	13
Runs, behind 2H	40%	1	Pers: 6+ OL	3%	7	Int DL Sacks	31.6%	12	S/CB Cover Ratio	19%	30	Defensive Pace	30.49	8
Pass, ahead 2H	39%	29	Shotgun/Pistol	51%	28	Second Level Sacks	26.5%	11	DB Blitz	9%	16	Go for it on 4th	1.51	14

Drew Brees didn't take a single sack all year that could be considered a "non-pressure sack," marked as coverage sack, failed scramble, or QB fault. The Saints did have one coverage sack, but it came with Teddy Bridgewater at quarterback in Week 17. 🦅 The Saints had the No. 31 defense in the first quarter of games, then ranked sixth on defense from the second quarter onwards. 🦅 New Orleans was one of the top defenses for sending big blitzes of six or more, but they were not good on these plays: they allowed 9.7 net yards per pass (30th) and 22.6% DVOA (25th). 🦅 Sean Payton went for it a league-high 12 times on fourth-and-1s that qualified for Aggressiveness Index … but the Saints also led the league with 18 such opportunities. 🦅 The Saints played with a lot of referees who swallowed their whistles last year, ranking 31st with just 109 penalties and 30th with just 106 penalties by opponents.

Passing

Player	DYAR	DVOA	Plays	NtYds	Avg	YAC	C%	TD	Int
D.Brees	1631	36.7%	506	3854	7.6	5.0	74.6%	32	5
T.Bridgewater	-46	-39.7%	25	110	4.4	3.8	60.9%	1	1
T.Hill	-19	-40.8%	8	61	7.6	6.0	42.9%	0	1

Rushing

Player	DYAR	DVOA	Plays	Yds	Avg	TD	Fum	Suc
A.Kamara	238	18.5%	194	896	4.6	14	0	58%
M.Ingram*	71	2.9%	138	645	4.7	6	2	57%
T.Hill	12	-7.1%	37	194	5.2	2	1	--
D.Washington	12	3.1%	27	154	5.7	0	0	41%
M.Gillislee*	-40	-60.9%	16	43	2.7	0	1	56%
D.Brees	43	29.0%	13	40	3.1	4	0	--
Z.Line	20	25.2%	9	41	4.6	0	0	78%
L.Murray	25	-4.2%	140	578	4.1	6	0	46%
J.Allen	-16	-16.3%	41	113	2.8	3	0	41%

Receiving

Player	DYAR	DVOA	Plays	Ctch	Yds	Y/C	YAC	TD	C%
M.Thomas	442	23.1%	147	125	1405	11.2	4.1	9	85%
T.Smith	126	22.7%	44	28	427	15.3	4.1	5	64%
T.Ginn	-21	-21.6%	30	17	209	12.3	2.8	2	57%
K.Kirkwood	58	23.5%	21	13	209	16.1	3.8	2	62%
A.Carr	35	17.3%	14	9	97	10.8	2.4	2	64%
C.Meredith	21	16.9%	10	9	114	12.7	4.2	1	90%
T.Hill	-56	-111.8%	7	3	4	1.3	1.7	0	43%
B.Watson*	73	15.2%	46	35	400	11.4	2.5	2	76%
J.Hill	12	0.1%	24	16	185	11.6	10.6	1	67%
D.Arnold	-18	-21.0%	19	12	150	12.5	2.5	1	63%
J.Cook	146	13.8%	101	68	896	13.2	5.0	6	67%
A.Kamara	197	19.4%	105	81	709	8.8	7.9	4	77%
M.Ingram*	-7	-18.8%	27	21	170	8.1	7.4	1	78%
Z.Line	-2	-16.8%	10	5	14	2.8	1.4	2	50%
J.Allen	-4	-15.4%	43	35	204	5.8	5.3	2	81%
L.Murray	9	-7.5%	26	22	141	6.4	5.2	0	85%

Offensive Line

Player	Pos	Age	GS	Snaps	Pen	Sk	Pass	Run	Player	Pos	Age	GS	Snaps	Pen	Sk	Pass	Run
Max Unger*	C	33	16/16	1012	0	3.5	6	7	Jermon Bushrod*	LT	35	11/6	372	2	0.5	5	5
Ryan Ramczyk	RT	25	15/15	996	3	1.5	8	4	Josh LeRibeus*	LG	30	6/3	179	2	0.0	1	0
Larry Warford	RG	28	15/15	980	2	1.5	5	6	Cameron Tom	G	24	12/1	178	1	0.0	0	1
Andrus Peat	LG	26	13/13	739	4	1.0	4	5	Ryan Groy	C	29	15/6	528	1	1.0	4	0
Terron Armstead	LT	28	10/10	602	1	0.0	0	1	Marshall Newhouse	LT	31	13/2	210	5	1.5	4	1

Year	Yards	ALY	Rank	Power	Rank	Stuff	Rank	2nd Lev	Rank	Open Field	Rank	Sacks	ASR	Rank	Press	Rank	F-Start	Cont.
2016	4.53	4.93	1	70%	9	14%	2	1.11	19	0.85	10	27	4.5%	5	18.9%	3	19	21
2017	5.11	4.93	2	69%	7	15%	1	1.30	3	1.37	1	20	4.0%	2	20.9%	1	6	23
2018	4.60	5.19	2	70%	9	14%	1	1.28	14	0.77	21	20	4.4%	3	23.9%	3	11	24

2018 ALY by direction:	Left End: 7.31 (1)	Left Tackle: 3.83 (23)	Mid/Guard: 5.01 (3)	Right Tackle: 5.09 (5)	Right End: 5.70 (3)

Since Drew Brees and Sean Payton arrived in 2006, the Saints have ranked in the top seven of adjusted sack rate every year except 2014, when they ranked No. 12. No team allowed fewer quarterback knockdowns and only the Colts allowed fewer sacks. ◗ Former All-Pro center Max Unger retired this offseason after earning his third Pro Bowl berth, his first in New Orleans. Unger started 63 of 64 possible games during his time with the Saints. Former 49ers and Vikings guard Nick Easton, who played center at Harvard, was signed to a four-year, $24-million contract as a potential veteran replacement for Unger, but the 2015 undrafted free agent will now compete with 2019 second-round pick Erik McCoy (Texas A&M) for the vacant spot. ◗ Left tackle Terron Armstead still has not started more than 14 games in any season of his six-year career. He did at least reach double figures for the fourth time, and he has started every playoff game since being drafted in 2013, but Armstead has now missed 21 regular-season games in the past three years. ◗ When he is on the field, however, Armstead remains excellent. SIS charting credits him with only a single blown block all season, by far the lowest number among starting left tackles. The rest of his linemates also grade well by this measure: of the five preferred starters only the now-retired Unger did not rank in the top 12 at his position in snaps per blown block, and no team had fewer sacks attributed to blown blocks by the offensive line.

Defensive Front

Defensive Line	Age	Pos	G	Snaps	Plays	TmPct	Rk	Stop	Dfts	BTkl	Runs	St%	Rk	RuYd	Rk	Sack	Hit	Hur	Dsrpt
						Overall							vs. Run				Pass Rush		
Sheldon Rankins	25	DT	16	641	40	5.0%	40	33	14	1	24	79%	29	2.4	53	8.0	7	21	0
David Onyemata	27	DT	16	616	36	4.5%	49	32	10	3	23	87%	10	1.7	15	4.5	3	17	0
Tyeler Davison*	27	DT	14	421	24	3.4%	72	17	5	0	19	68%	69	2.2	41	2.0	1	5	0
Taylor Stallworth	24	DT	14	318	8	1.1%	--	5	1	0	7	57%	--	2.7	--	1.0	0	1	0
Malcom Brown	25	DT	15	458	39	5.4%	33	27	2	3	34	76%	35	2.9	70	0.0	1	5	0
Sylvester Williams	31	DT	14	376	13	1.8%	83	9	0	4	13	69%	67	3.2	75	0.0	0	5	0

Edge Rushers	Age	Pos	G	Snaps	Plays	TmPct	Rk	Stop	Dfts	BTkl	Runs	St%	Rk	RuYd	Rk	Sack	Hit	Hur	Dsrpt
						Overall							vs. Run				Pass Rush		
Cameron Jordan	30	DE	16	883	54	6.8%	11	46	24	2	33	79%	30	1.2	10	12.0	9	49	3
Alex Okafor*	28	DE	16	656	36	4.5%	56	29	8	3	28	82%	20	2.9	58	4.0	7	25	1
Marcus Davenport	23	DE	13	417	24	3.7%	72	21	10	1	16	88%	10	0.8	5	4.5	9	20	3

Linebackers	Age	Pos	G	Snaps	Plays	TmPct	Rk	Stop	Dfts	BTkl	Runs	St%	Rk	RuYd	Rk	Sack	Hit	Hur	Tgts	Suc%	Rk	AdjYd	Rk	PD	Int
						Overall							vs. Run				Pass Rush				vs. Pass				
Demario Davis	30	OLB	16	877	114	14.3%	30	62	20	14	54	59%	46	3.3	23	5.0	7	10.5	39	51%	38	7.3	54	4	0
A.J. Klein	28	OLB	16	669	73	9.1%	63	44	14	7	51	65%	25	2.6	6	2.0	2	7	20	60%	10	5.4	17	3	1
Alex Anzalone	25	MLB	16	486	61	7.6%	72	22	14	5	19	58%	51	4.2	56	2.0	4	9	23	39%	65	5.0	12	2	1

Year	Yards	ALY	Rank	Power	Rank	Stuff	Rank	2nd Level	Rank	Open Field	Rank	Sacks	ASR	Rank	Press	Rank
2016	4.21	4.09	15	65%	20	20%	14	1.13	13	0.94	27	30	5.0%	28	27.3%	14
2017	4.11	4.10	17	66%	21	21%	13	1.08	11	0.80	22	42	7.8%	6	32.3%	8
2018	3.22	3.61	2	57%	3	24%	6	0.87	1	0.40	3	49	8.7%	4	31.2%	13

2018 ALY by direction:	Left End: 2.10 (2)	Left Tackle: 2.65 (3)	Mid/Guard: 4.41 (17)	Right Tackle: 3.72 (8)	Right End: 1.43 (1)

The Achilles injury suffered during the playoffs is likely to keep star defensive tackle Sheldon Rankins on PUP beyond the start of the regular season. If that prognosis is accurate, he would not be eligible to return until Week 6. Rankins had the best year of his young career in 2018, setting career highs in tackles, sacks, and tackles for a loss. ◾ Stand-in starter David Onyemata will miss the first game of the season, a Monday nighter against Houston, due to suspension for violating the league's substance abuse policy. ◾ Cameron Jordan has now played 128 consecutive games since being drafted in 2011. The 29-year-old played his fewest snaps since our records began (2012), but he has still played more snaps than any other Saints defensive lineman in every season for which we have data. Per SIS charting, Jordan's 49 pass pressures were the second-most in 2018 behind only Aaron Donald. ◾ 2018 first-round draft pick Marcus Davenport is expected to assume the starting role opposite Jordan following the departure of Alex Okafor. Davenport had more sacks, defeats, and quarterback hits than Okafor in 2018 despite not even playing two-thirds as many snaps as the veteran. ◾ The defense's 8.7 percent adjusted sack rate was its highest mark since 2001, and only the fifth top-half finish by that mark in Sean Payton's 13 seasons as head coach. Last year's defense also ranked second with 3.61 adjusted line yards per carry, the team's best-ever mark in that metric. The previous highest was ninth, with 3.70 ALY. ◾ Demario Davis was the first Saints off-ball linebacker to have 5.0 sacks or more in a single season since Charlie Clemons in 2001. He was also the first to record 10 or more tackles for a loss since Jonathan Vilma in 2009.

Defensive Secondary

Secondary	Age	Pos	G	Snaps	Plays	TmPct	Rk	Stop	Dfts	BTkl	Runs	St%	Rk	RuYd	Rk	Tgts	Tgt%	Rk	Dist	Suc%	Rk	AdjYd	Rk	PD	Int
						Overall							vs. Run					vs. Pass						
Marcus Williams	23	FS	16	955	57	7.1%	61	7	5	5	21	14%	72	11.0	70	15	3.5%	2	11.4	40%	64	7.1	36	3	2
Eli Apple	24	CB	15	905	88	11.7%	5	32	12	14	12	42%	39	5.1	17	106	26.7%	76	13.8	54%	33	7.6	39	14	2
Marshon Lattimore	23	CB	16	905	71	8.9%	37	25	10	9	12	33%	56	8.7	65	71	17.5%	27	14.0	44%	72	10.7	77	12	2
Vonn Bell	25	SS	16	752	89	11.1%	28	35	13	10	40	53%	18	5.3	17	41	12.2%	62	8.8	49%	40	6.8	28	3	0
P.J. Williams	26	CB	15	693	62	8.3%	44	26	11	5	16	56%	14	2.8	3	60	19.3%	45	10.6	43%	74	8.9	68	9	1
Ken Crawley	26	CB	10	409	37	7.4%	--	13	3	1	5	60%	--	4.0	--	42	22.9%	--	13.1	36%	--	11.3	--	6	0
Kurt Coleman*	31	SS	16	359	30	3.8%	76	12	4	8	20	55%	14	4.1	4	7	4.4%	4	6.7	29%	72	8.0	48	0	0

Year	Pass D Rank	vs. #1 WR	Rk	vs. #2 WR	Rk	vs. Other WR	Rk	WR Wide	Rk	WR Slot	Rk	vs. TE	Rk	vs. RB	Rk
2016	30	5.5%	23	11.3%	26	15.3%	28	16.0%	30	4.4%	17	4.8%	22	43.4%	32
2017	5	-19.1%	6	0.6%	18	-21.8%	5	-31.6%	2	7.9%	16	-17.0%	6	-5.5%	12
2018	22	17.7%	30	28.4%	31	-16.4%	6	13.5%	27	5.6%	20	-22.2%	4	19.8%	29

The midseason acquisition of Eli Apple was key to the improvement of the Saints defense last year. In the six games prior to the trade, the Saints allowed a DVOA of 23.9% to opposing passers. That would have ranked No. 29 over the full season. In the ten games Apple started, from Weeks 8-17, that figure improved to -6.2%, which would have ranked sixth. ✎ Apple's arrival almost completely displaced 2017 starter Ken Crawley from the lineup. Crawley played at least 59 snaps on defense in five of the first six games. From Week 8 until the end of the season, Crawley played a total of only 61 defensive snaps. ✎ Apple's 7.6 yards allowed per target was the best figure among the team's top four cornerbacks; Crawley's 11.3 was not only the worst among Saints defensive backs, it would have been the third-worst figure in the league if he had faced enough targets to qualify. ✎ Apple and Crawley both struggled with penalties. Apple had a league-leading seven DPI penalties and three defensive holding calls against him in his ten games for the Saints, plus another defensive holding while still in New York. (One of each was declined.) Crawley conceded a further four DPIs, one defensive holding, and a facemask. No team conceded more than New Orleans' 19 DPI penalties (two of which were declined). However, no team had more than New Orleans' 14 DPIs called against their opponents either, making DPI the one exception to the refereeing tendency noted in the Strategic Tendencies section. ✎ Reigning Defensive Rookie of the Year Marshon Lattimore had a much tougher second season. His yards allowed per pass, success rate, defeats, and interception total all declined significantly from 2017. Among qualifying cornerbacks, only Jalen Mills and Robert Alford allowed more than Lattimore's 10.7 yards per target. ✎ Marcus Williams also had a rougher sophomore year. Only Buccaneers rookie Isaiah Johnson and Minnesota's Andrew Sendejo made their average pass play farther than Williams' 17.4 yards downfield, and Williams didn't have a single tackle to prevent a pass reception from gaining successful yardage. Some of that was due to his role: The Saints had the league's second-largest gap between where their top two safeties made their average play (pass and run combined), with Williams at 15.0 yards downfield and Vonn Bell at just 8.0 yards downfield. However, the deep safety's struggles were also reflected in the defense as a whole: New Orleans ranked dead last in DVOA against deep passes (16-plus yards in the air), but tenth against shorter passes.

Special Teams

Year	DVOA	Rank	FG/XP	Rank	Net Kick	Rank	Kick Ret	Rank	Net Punt	Rank	Punt Ret	Rank	Hidden	Rank
2016	-2.6%	27	0.0	18	-5.1	28	-8.0	31	0.8	13	-1.0	15	-6.3	24
2017	1.2%	15	-0.9	17	-0.3	20	5.6	5	6.5	7	-5.0	28	10.3	4
2018	1.7%	9	6.8	6	-0.9	19	-0.2	13	5.3	9	-2.4	19	23.5	1

Last year's Saints finished in the top ten of our special teams table for the first time in the Sean Payton era. Their previous high finish was No. 11. ✎ Wil Lutz improved his field goal accuracy for the third straight season and had the best performance for a Saints kicker in our numbers since 2002. The three seasons since Lutz was drafted are now the best, second-best, and third-best seasons for the Saints field goal unit since 2006. ✎ The Saints punt coverage allowed the third-shortest average return; their mark of exactly 5.0 yards per return trailed Jacksonville (4.98) by a rounding error. They tied with the Rams for both the fewest returns allowed (12) and the fewest total punts (43). Remarkably, there was also less than half a foot of difference between Thomas Morstead and Johnny Hekker's average punt distance. ✎ Punt gunner Justin Hardee had seven punt stops, tied for the league lead alongside Vikings safety Jayron Kearse. Every one of Hardee's 10 total special teams tackles counted as a stop, defined as preventing a longer than average return. ✎ Taysom Hill did most of the kick returns and was close to league average; Alvin Kamara had only four returns but they averaged 31.5 yards. ✎ Tommylee Lewis was the team's most effective punt returner, averaging 7.5 yards per return, but Lewis is now in Detroit. To replace him, the Saints signed return specialist Marcus Sherels on a one-year deal from the Vikings, where he holds the franchise record for punt return touchdowns. They also signed college return specialist Deonte Harris (Assumption College), who holds the NCAA record for most combined kick and punt return touchdowns, as an undrafted free agent. ✎ One positive that's unlikely to carry over into 2019: New Orleans led the league in "hidden" special teams value, for a couple of reasons. Saints opponents finished last in gross punt value once blocked punts are removed from the equation. Saints opponents also finished next-to-last in field goal value, missing six field goals and five extra points.

New York Giants

2018 record: 5-11	Total DVOA: 0.0% (15th)	2019 Mean Projection: 7.2 wins	On the Clock (0-4): 16%
Pythagorean Wins: 6.9 (22nd)	Offense: 1.3% (13th)	Postseason Odds: 24.7%	Mediocrity (5-7): 40%
Snap-Weighted Age: 26.4 (19th)	Defense: 5.8% (24th)	Super Bowl Odds: 1.7%	Playoff Contender (8-10): 33%
Average Opponent: -2.3% (23rd)	Special Teams: 4.5% (3rd)	Proj. Avg. Opponent: -3.8% (29th)	Super Bowl Contender (11+): 11%

2018: Saquon Barkley will surely be worth the No. 2 overall pick!

2019: Daniel Jones will surely be worth the No. 6 overall pick?

erhaps you've seen this message from Weird Twitter user @wint:

Food $200
Data $150
Rent $800
Candles $3,600
Utility $150
someone who is good at the economy please help me budget this. my family is dying.

This tweet essentially summarizes the entire Dave Gettleman era with the New York Giants. Gettleman's moves in the past two offseasons have been the surreal sports equivalent of Weird Twitter, even more than the idea of a baseball team sharing two new stadiums in Tampa and Montreal. Like a circus juggler, general manager Dave Gettleman's work has been so effervescent, so fluid in its dumbness, that you have a hard time focusing on each individual bad move.

Gettleman's most important decision last year was drafting Saquon Barkley with the second overall pick. Not only did it turn the phrase "generational talent" into a meme that was impossible to avoid, but it actually worked if you could ignore the big picture. There was never a question whether or not Barkley was a good player. He made the Pro Bowl as a rookie and he led the NFL in broken tackles by more than 30 per Sports Info Solutions' charting data. While Barkley did not produce much in the way of DVOA last season as a receiver, he was targeted with more passes than any back besides Christian McCaffrey and James White. Most of those catches came in a bad offense that never threw past the line of scrimmage, but Barkley was surprisingly effective when told to go deep as well. The scouts were right: Barkley truly is a generational talent at running back. The Giants drafted him and improved from a 3-13 team to a 5-11 team, because getting a generational talent at running back in today's NFL is like spending $3,600 on candles. All you get to do is enjoy a well-lit vantage point of your family dying.

Eli Manning's career has been dying for years. He last made the Pro Bowl in 2015 and arguably didn't deserve it at that point. The only time in the last six seasons that the Giants made the playoffs was in 2016; the Packers spanked them 38-13 while Manning barely completed half his passes. Last year's move from Ben McAdoo's system to Pat Shurmur's even-quicker-throws invigorated Manning's completion rate to the highest point it's ever been, but Manning's diminished arm strength continued to miss open receivers farther down the field.

Manning may or may not make the Hall of Fame. He's certainly deserving if all you focus on is the word "fame." But between the Giants' reaction to him being benched in 2017 and Gettleman's continuing obsession with talking about how Manning is still good even to this day, the team has completely distanced itself from reality on the issue. The mythos of Eli was always ahead of his play and conveniently ignored the clutchness of those around him, but without any checks from within it has consumed the entire organization. As McAdoo said to *Sports Illustrated* in a column about what he learned from the situation that developed from benching Manning: "if there's one thing I want fans of the Giants to know, it's that I made this call to try to make the Giants stronger for the future. It probably got me fired, but I believe I did the right thing for the right reasons." The future of good Giants football is with a quarterback not named Eli Manning. That is readily apparent to anybody not currently in the building.

But when a team gets as bad as the Giants are, and the quarterback is as old as Manning is, they have an obligation to sniff at any quarterback who so much as passes their franchise starter baselines. They ignored that in 2018 to select Barkley, leaving Sam Darnold on the board for the Jets and letting three other first-round quarterbacks get selected. They then entered 2019 with the hole at the position festering under the weight of wasted third-round picks. It led them to select Duke's Daniel Jones, by most accounts a second-round pick at best, with the sixth overall pick.

QBASE, Football Outsiders' projection model, looks at three different statistical indicators for quarterbacks: adjusted yards per attempt, completion rate, and team passing S&P+. Of all the quarterbacks QBASE projected last year, Jones finished last in each category. He got a tiny bump in the projection system because Duke was not flooded with other top-flight prospects, as well as because they played a tough defensive schedule last season. He still finished with a mean projection of just 279 DYAR in his third through fifth years. To put that into context, 279 DYAR is 63 DYAR worse than Manning had *last year*. If you're looking for a projection system based more on intricate charting data, Josh Hermsmeyer

2019 Giants Schedule

Week	Opp.	Week	Opp.	Week	Opp.
1	at DAL	7	ARI	13	GB
2	BUF	8	at DET	14	at PHI (Mon.)
3	at TB	9	DAL (Mon.)	15	MIA
4	WAS	10	at NYJ	16	at WAS
5	MIN	11	BYE	17	PHI
6	at NE (Thu.)	12	at CHI		

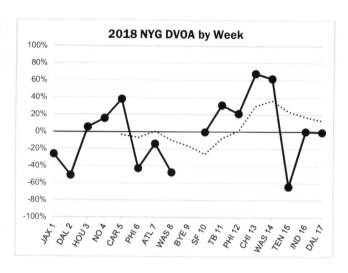

of FiveThirtyEight created a statistical study around Completion Percentage Over Expectation, which weighed each quarterback's completion percentage against his average depth of target. Jones had the second-lowest average depth of target among the quarterbacks Hermsmeyer listed, ahead of only Gardner Minshew. The CPOE model puts Jones behind undrafted free agents such as Brett Rypien and Jake Browning, and gives him just a 17 percent chance of averaging 7.1 yards per attempt in the NFL.

Even if the stats don't like Jones, surely he must stand out on film, right? Not so much. Both his foot speed and mental processing were slow at Duke. His receivers miscommunicated with him multiple times in some games, something that is an obvious red flag. His deep ball was as lacking as the average depth of target would tell you, and his accuracy was negatively impacted by his ball placement in the short and intermediate area. However, Jones does have several positives. He was coached by Peyton Manning's quarterback coach, David Cutcliffe, at Duke. He is tall and fits old school NFL prototypes of weight and body composition. Just as Buffalo's selection of Josh Allen last year resembles the mistake that the Titans made with Jake Locker, the bust Jones most resembles is Christian Ponder—and even Ponder had some stats that would at least let you dream a little. So why did Gettleman pick him?

"To me it's very important that you see quarterbacks play [live]. Seeing them in the environment is very important … I had decided to stay for the [Senior Bowl] … [Jones] walked out there and I saw a professional quarterback, after the three series that I watched. I saw a professional quarterback, so that's when I was in full bloom love." Gettleman picked a quarterback—an investment that could define his entire tenure—like he was trying to decide which ice cream to pick up for solo Netflix runs on a Saturday night.

And we haven't even gotten yet to the absurd trade that sent Odell Beckham to the Browns for a low first-round pick, a low third-round pick, and Jabril Peppers. Beckham had become a bit of a tabloid rag staple, constantly blamed as one of the main reasons for the Giants' losing record. This is pretty much par for the course for any objectively great player stuck on a crummy team. Yes, Beckham had made some emotional outbursts because he wanted to win. He'd also broken a fibula in 2017 and missed time with a quad injury towards the end of 2018. Beckham's not a perfect player—he's merely one of the best receivers in the NFL, one that the Giants signed to a huge extension before the 2018 season, and one who did nothing on the field to disprove his greatness last season. Gettleman

himself said that the team "didn't sign [Beckham] to trade him." Then … he traded him. And not for a great return either. Gettleman got the No. 17 overall selection, the last non-supplemental pick of the third round, and a safety with one solid NFL season.

That huge extension marks a big difference between the Beckham deal and other recent deals for players of the same caliber. This offseason Frank Clark was dealt for first- and second-round picks, plus a swap of third-rounders. Brandin Cooks, a less productive receiver than Beckham, was worth a late first for the Rams. The difference is that both of these players immediately signed new deals at market rates. Essentially, the Browns got Beckham at a discount because the Giants were already on the hook for his entire signing bonus. What's left on the contract is an annual salary that was a pretty solid deal in 2018 and will only become better as the cap grows larger. This cap savings should have made Beckham worth more than similar players who required new contracts after a trade. ESPN's Adam Schefter all but said that he knew that the Giants had better offers on the table than the one they accepted for Beckham. A deep dive on the trade by Jordan Raanan and Pat McManamon on ESPN.com implied that the Giants never returned a call to the 49ers—Beckham's most aggressive suitors—after they got Cleveland's offer.

A defiant Gettleman talked up how great Peppers was, referring to him as a second first-round pick that he received in the trade. What he didn't say is that the Giants refused to franchise-tag one of the 10 best free agents in the NFL, safety Landon Collins, and let him walk in free agency without so much as a legitimate offer. Collins walked to divisional rival Washington.

And then, rather than using the No. 6 overall pick on a true difference-maker and using the 17th pick to draft an iffy quarterback, the Giants instead used their initial first-round pick on Jones and their second on Dexter Lawrence. Lawrence is a very good prospect for what he does—he's a huge, 340-pound Planet Theory candidate who can stuff the run and has shown some instinct for pass-rushing in his early Clemson days. But the recent history of players that big has been … well, not good (Table 1). Recent first-round picks that were over 320 pounds include Vernon Butler, Danny Shelton, Dontari Poe, Dan Williams, Phil Taylor, Sylvester Williams, Malcom Brown, Vita Vea, and Marcell Dareus. Dareus is the only player on that list that made a second contract with his original team—and he was traded to the Jaguars a few years after signing it. Dareus is also the only player of the group to get more than 10 sacks in a season. And none of the players created a dominating run defense on their own.

Table 1. Run Defenses and the Impact of 320-Pound First-Round Nose Tackles, 2010-2019

Team	Year	Player	Career Sacks	Run Def DVOA Y-1	Run Def DVOA	Run Def DVOA Y+1
ARI	2010	Dan Williams	3.5	-7.7% (14)	2.3% (29)	1.5% (24)
BUF	2011	Marcell Dareus	37	3.8% (31)	5.5% (28)	7.9% (31)
CLE	2011	Phil Taylor	7	-1.1% (22)	3.8% (26)	-4.7% (18)
KC	2012	Dontari Poe	16.5	-5.9% (17)	3.0% (28)	-6.4% (15)
DEN	2013	Sylvester Williams	5.5	-18.1% (4)	-14.3% (9)	-23.6% (3)
CLE	2015	Danny Shelton	1.5	5.2% (31)	-2.9% (26)	1.6% (27)
NE	2015	Malcom Brown	8.5	-10.3% (13)	-16.2% (10)	-23.3% (5)
CAR	2016	Vernon Butler	2	-18.6% (6)	-15.1% (9)	-16.9% (6)
TB	2018	Vita Vea	3	-5.1% (19)	3.0% (31)	--
NYG	**2019**	**Dexter Lawrence**	**N/A**	**-5.9% (20)**	--	--

You'll notice the Giants already had a decent run defense last year. That's because they had one of the best nose tackles in the NFL—Snacks Harrison. He got traded to Detroit mid-season because the team was trying to save cap space. By the way, New York has $33 million in dead cap space because of their trades, and Manning's cap number is $23 million. Just thought it might be an appropriate time in the chapter to mention those facts.

The Giants also shipped out Olivier Vernon—a good edge rusher who hasn't been able to stay on the field the last two years—to the Browns for guard Kevin Zeitler. We don't have a problem with this trade in a vacuum, but it's another one that points to Gettleman's inability to square value with the current game. The most valuable positions in today's NFL are generally perceived to be quarterback, wideout, edge rusher, and corner-

back. The Giants have acquired a lot of talent, but it's at guard instead of tackle, and at safety instead of corner. They might have the worst group of wide receivers in the NFL, even after dropping $30 million on Golden Tate. Their edge rushing corps is made up of youngsters without much NFL success and Arizona Cardinals castoffs. The cornerback crew is Janoris Jenkins and four players selected in the last two drafts.

Hidden at the core of all of this crisis is a fact that is hard to square with what happened at the Meadowlands this offseason: our numbers kind of like the Giants.

The Giants were incredibly unlucky last season. They ranked 15th in DVOA, which is not normally where you would find a team that's 5-11. Their Pythagorean projection was nearly two wins higher than their actual record. They were 4-8 in games decided by one score. On top of that, the Giants have one of the easiest schedules in the NFL. They get two games with the rebuilding Redskins, three games with the non-Patriots AFC East, four games with an NFC North division our projections are lukewarm about, plus games with Tampa Bay and Arizona because of finishing fourth last year. In a normal world with a normal offseason, this is a team we would expect to take a few steps forward if it returned the same quality of play the next year. Yes, there would have been collapse potential because of the aging quarterback, but this should have been a team we projected for a rebound.

But after all that's gone on this offseason, there aren't many ways to sugarcoat the mess that the New York Giants have become. Because of the high-profile New York media market focus, Giants pessimism is unavoidable. This team's offseason exploded all over the kitchen like an Italian sausage left on the stovetop too long. There's almost no reason to believe in their quarterback of the future and there's definitely no reason to believe in their quarterback of the past. The passing offense is going to be incredibly reliant on yards after the catch, and Barkley is going to be run into the ground because nobody else is any good.

Daniel Jones is 6-foot-4. To paraphrase one last bit of Weird Twitter: the worst part about being that tall is having a lot of time to think about your mistakes while your franchise sinks into the quicksand.

Rivers McCown

2018 Giants by Week

Wk	vs.	W-L	PF	PA	YDF	YDA	TO	Total	Off	Def	ST
1	JAX	L	15	20	324	305	-1	-26%	-13%	9%	-5%
2	at DAL	L	13	20	255	298	-1	-51%	-17%	35%	1%
3	at HOU	W	27	22	379	427	+2	6%	27%	9%	-13%
4	NO	L	18	33	299	389	-2	16%	22%	10%	3%
5	at CAR	L	31	33	432	350	-1	38%	8%	-25%	5%
6	PHI	L	13	34	401	379	-1	-43%	-18%	15%	-10%
7	at ATL	L	20	23	433	423	+1	-14%	5%	22%	3%
8	WAS	L	13	20	303	360	-1	-48%	-32%	22%	6%
9	BYE										
10	at SF	W	27	23	277	374	+2	-1%	1%	6%	4%
11	TB	W	38	35	359	510	+4	31%	31%	9%	9%
12	at PHI	L	22	25	402	341	-1	21%	13%	12%	20%
13	CHI	W	30	27	338	376	+2	68%	16%	-28%	24%
14	at WAS	W	40	16	402	288	+2	62%	8%	-44%	9%
15	TEN	L	0	17	260	301	-2	-64%	-58%	3%	-3%
16	at IND	L	27	28	392	402	0	0%	11%	12%	1%
17	DAL	L	35	36	441	419	-1	-1%	11%	31%	19%

Trends and Splits

	Offense	Rank	Defense	Rank
Total DVOA	1.3%	13	5.8%	24
Unadjusted VOA	-1.2%	18	3.9%	22
Weighted Trend	1.1%	15	4.2%	22
Variance	5.5%	9	4.5%	6
Average Opponent	-0.8%	13	-3.6%	25
Passing	14.9%	15	16.0%	26
Rushing	-6.5%	16	-5.9%	20
First Down	-4.3%	18	4.6%	23
Second Down	-1.5%	18	-14.3%	1
Third Down	17.2%	7	39.4%	32
First Half	-2.7%	19	1.4%	17
Second Half	5.1%	16	10.0%	26
Red Zone	-17.1%	27	8.1%	22
Late and Close	-5.7%	20	2.3%	22

Five-Year Performance

Year	W-L	Pyth W	Est W	PF	PA	TO	Total	Rk	Off	Rk	Def	Rk	ST	Rk	Off AGL	Rk	Def AGL	Rk	Off Age	Rk	Def Age	Rk	ST Age	Rk
2014	6-10	7.5	7.0	380	400	-2	-5.8%	21	-0.3%	15	4.9%	24	-0.6%	15	65.9	31	71.3	30	26.6	20	27.6	5	26.7	3
2015	6-10	7.5	7.4	420	442	+7	-7.1%	20	-1.8%	19	10.7%	30	5.4%	2	66.9	31	71.8	31	26.2	22	27.0	13	26.5	8
2016	11-5	8.8	9.8	310	284	-2	9.6%	8	-6.0%	22	-14.5%	2	1.2%	11	27.7	11	24.7	9	26.3	22	25.9	27	26.2	13
2017	3-13	4.0	4.4	246	388	-3	-22.3%	30	-9.1%	23	5.7%	24	-7.5%	32	59.9	28	36.4	17	26.5	23	26.0	20	25.6	24
2018	5-11	6.9	7.9	369	412	+2	0.0%	15	1.3%	13	5.8%	24	4.5%	3	34.0	14	19.2	7	26.9	14	26.1	21	26.0	12

2018 Performance Based on Most Common Personnel Groups

NYG Offense					NYG Offense vs. Opponents						NYG Defense					NYG Defense vs. Opponents			
Pers	Freq	Yds	DVOA	Run%	Pers	Freq	Yds	DVOA	Run%		Pers	Freq	Yds	DVOA		Pers	Freq	Yds	DVOA
11	60%	5.9	10.4%	25%	Base	30%	6.4	13.7%	54%		Base	17%	5.7	7.8%		11	65%	5.8	2.0%
12	23%	6.4	-1.3%	48%	Nickel	59%	5.7	6.6%	27%		Nickel	68%	6.0	5.2%		12	17%	6.7	17.8%
21	8%	6.4	18.5%	54%	Dime+	6%	6.8	-19.0%	12%		Dime+	15%	6.4	7.4%		21	8%	6.3	-5.6%
22	2%	5.3	24.8%	57%	Goal Line	0%	0.3	-39.9%	100%		Goal Line	1%	0.3	-9.5%		13	4%	4.5	-1.2%
13	2%	6.6	40.1%	50%	Big	1%	1.0	-86.3%	67%							10	2%	8.6	56.0%

Strategic Tendencies

Run/Pass		Rk	Formation		Rk	Pass Rush		Rk	Secondary		Rk	Strategy		Rk
Runs, first half	36%	23	Form: Single Back	84%	10	Rush 3	6.3%	17	4 DB	17%	27	Play action	24%	17
Runs, first down	47%	17	Form: Empty Back	4%	30	Rush 4	72.2%	14	5 DB	68%	14	Avg Box (Off)	6.18	16
Runs, second-long	31%	15	Pers: 3+ WR	62%	24	Rush 5	16.5%	18	6+ DB	15%	12	Avg Box (Def)	6.23	17
Runs, power sit.	57%	18	Pers: 2+ TE/6+ OL	30%	7	Rush 6+	4.8%	19	CB by Sides	84%	11	Offensive Pace	31.25	17
Runs, behind 2H	25%	19	Pers: 6+ OL	3%	10	Int DL Sacks	33.3%	9	S/CB Cover Ratio	32%	7	Defensive Pace	31.32	20
Pass, ahead 2H	47%	18	Shotgun/Pistol	59%	22	Second Level Sacks	21.7%	19	DB Blitz	12%	7	Go for it on 4th	1.95	5

The Giants ranked 31st in frequency of using wide receiver or tight end screens, ahead of only Seattle. However, they were among the top 10 teams in running back screens and had 80.3% DVOA on these plays. ● The Giants only ran on 14 percent of shotgun snaps, but those were some of their biggest plays. They gained a league-leading 5.8 yards per carry with 8.6%

DVOA on these runs, compared to 4.3 yards per carry and -14.5% DVOA on runs with the quarterback under center. ◥ The Giants led the league by going max protect on 13.9 percent of pass plays (defined as seven or more blockers with at least two more blockers than pass-rushers). ◥ Only two teams went empty backfield less often than the Giants, but in that small sample size the Giants actually had the best empty-backfield offense in the league, with 89.9% DVOA and 9.3 yards per play. ◥ After leading the league in dropped passes in 2017, the Giants were just about average with 28 drops in 2018. ◥ The Giants had the largest gap in the league between where their top two safeties made their average play, with Curtis Riley making his average play 15.3 yards downfield and Landon Collins making his average play just 8.0 yards downfield.

Passing

Player	DYAR	DVOA	Plays	NtYds	Avg	YAC	C%	TD	Int
E.Manning	337	-2.5%	622	3946	6.3	5.7	66.1%	21	11

Rushing

Player	DYAR	DVOA	Plays	Yds	Avg	TD	Fum	Suc
S.Barkley	127	3.3%	261	1307	5.0	11	0	41%
W.Gallman	30	7.3%	51	176	3.5	1	0	39%
E.Manning	4	-7.4%	11	24	2.2	1	0	--
E.Penny	-6	-30.1%	7	25	3.6	0	0	57%
J.Stewart*	3	4.7%	6	17	2.8	0	0	50%
O.Beckham*	12	25.2%	5	19	3.8	0	0	--
R.Smith	-8	-12.8%	44	127	2.9	1	0	39%

Receiving

Player	DYAR	DVOA	Plays	Ctch	Yds	Y/C	YAC	TD	C%
O.Beckham*	151	2.5%	124	77	1052	13.7	4.1	6	62%
S.Shepard	97	-0.9%	107	66	872	13.2	4.7	4	62%
B.Fowler	-12	-18.4%	27	16	199	12.4	4.8	1	59%
R.Shepard	47	20.5%	19	10	188	18.8	1.6	2	53%
C.Latimer	40	19.7%	16	11	190	17.3	2.1	1	69%
C.Coleman	23	19.6%	8	5	71	14.2	1.6	0	63%
J.Davis*	-11	-29.1%	8	4	40	10.0	1.0	0	50%
E.Engram	50	4.8%	64	45	577	12.8	8.6	3	70%
R.Ellison	48	14.4%	34	25	272	10.9	5.2	1	74%
S.Simonson	-5	-11.6%	14	9	86	9.6	3.4	1	64%
S.Barkley	86	-0.7%	121	91	721	7.9	8.4	4	75%
W.Gallman	-47	-63.8%	22	14	89	6.4	5.8	0	64%
E.Penny	4	-5.2%	9	8	50	6.3	6.4	0	89%
R.Smith	3	-9.0%	12	9	60	6.7	6.3	0	75%

Offensive Line

Player	Pos	Age	GS	Snaps	Pen	Sk	Pass	Run	Player	Pos	Age	GS	Snaps	Pen	Sk	Pass	Run
Will Hernandez	LG	24	16/16	1028	3	4.3	7	2	Jamon Brown*	RG	26	13/8	537	8	3.5	10	3
Nate Solder	LT	31	16/16	1028	6	5.8	15	4	John Greco*	C/RG	34	14/7	489	4	3.0	8	1
Chad Wheeler	RT	25	15/14	858	3	6.3	12	8	Kevin Zeitler	RG	29	16/16	1091	7	1.5	5	6
Spencer Pulley	C	26	13/9	567	1	2.0	3	2	Mike Remmers	RG	30	16/16	1048	8	4.5	19	8

Year	Yards	ALY	Rank	Power	Rank	Stuff	Rank	2nd Lev	Rank	Open Field	Rank	Sacks	ASR	Rank	Press	Rank	F-Start	Cont.
2016	3.70	3.89	24	63%	14	17%	9	1.01	29	0.40	29	22	3.9%	2	21.6%	6	11	30
2017	4.02	4.06	15	50%	29	17%	6	1.02	24	0.68	18	34	5.8%	10	25.5%	5	13	20
2018	4.69	3.90	29	69%	10	21%	24	1.10	25	1.60	1	47	7.4%	20	30.7%	17	17	29
2018 ALY by direction:			Left End: 3.00 (28)			Left Tackle: 3.59 (26)			Mid/Guard: 3.99 (29)			Right Tackle: 4.66 (11)			Right End: 3.65 (26)		

Pairing youngster Will Hernandez, who was solid in his rookie season, with ex-Cleveland guard Kevin Zeitler should give this unit some strength up front. While not quite the same player he was in his prime with the Bengals, Zeitler is a premier pass-blocker and will hopefully help buy some time for the incoming checkdowns. Hernandez didn't blow many run blocks, but also didn't get a ton of push in his rookie year. If he can improve his technique, look out. Hernandez told NFL.com's Grant Gordon this offseason that he "feel(s) like I'm a lot more comfortable here and I feel like I can breathe. I'm not struggling to learn the whole playbook, cram everything down, learn everything, make sure I don't mess up." ◥ Left tackle Nate Solder took advantage of a down free-agent market to get a ridiculous contract from the Giants, then promptly struggled early on. However, he pulled it together later in the season and wound up with fairly average blown block numbers. He's not worth the contract he got, but only about three NFL tackles are, and none of them were available for the Giants to pay. ◥ Right tackle, however, proved a harder spot to hide after the GIants pushed the eject button on Ereck Flowers. Chad Wheeler was pressed into work and was a major liability. The Giants signed former Dave Gettleman employee Mike Remmers, who was a guard last year in Minnesota, as competition outside. He shouldn't provide much. ◥ Spencer Pulley got most of the center reps last season after Jon Halapio went down with broken leg in Week 2. Halapio should be the favorite to win the job, but nothing is assured after an injury that nasty. ◥ Adding to the right-tackle mix will be the Giants' seventh-rounder, Kentucky's George Asafo-Adjei, who has an NFL body and not much NFL technique.

Defensive Front

Defensive Line	Age	Pos	G	Snaps	Plays	Overall TmPct	Rk	Stop	Dfts	BTkl	Runs	vs. Run St%	Rk	RuYd	Rk	Pass Rush Sack	Hit	Hur	Dsrpt
B.J. Hill	24	DT	16	643	50	6.0%	23	39	11	1	38	76%	37	1.9	25	5.5	3	18	2
Dalvin Tomlinson	25	DT	16	628	58	6.9%	15	43	15	0	55	76%	36	1.8	21	0.0	0	15	0
Kerry Wynn*	28	DE	14	394	33	4.5%	48	26	14	2	21	76%	38	3.3	79	1.5	2	12	2
Josh Mauro*	28	DE	12	270	28	4.5%	--	22	12	0	27	78%	--	1.4	--	1.0	1	4	0

Edge Rushers	Age	Pos	G	Snaps	Plays	Overall TmPct	Rk	Stop	Dfts	BTkl	Runs	vs. Run St%	Rk	RuYd	Rk	Pass Rush Sack	Hit	Hur	Dsrpt
Olivier Vernon*	29	OLB	11	666	31	5.4%	36	26	10	2	19	79%	28	4.5	91	7.0	16	30	1
Kareem Martin	27	OLB	16	610	50	6.0%	23	40	12	5	39	87%	11	1.7	26	1.5	8	16	2
Lorenzo Carter	24	OLB	15	442	43	5.5%	32	28	13	0	26	54%	88	3.7	84	4.0	7	16	3
Connor Barwin*	33	OLB	15	289	16	2.0%	--	10	5	1	9	33%	--	3.7	--	1.0	3	11	4

Linebackers	Age	Pos	G	Snaps	Plays	Overall TmPct	Rk	Stop	Dfts	BTkl	Runs	vs. Run St%	Rk	RuYd	Rk	Pass Rush Sack	Hit	Hur	Tgts	vs. Pass Suc%	Rk	AdjYd	Rk	PD	Int
Alec Ogletree	28	ILB	13	885	101	14.9%	26	59	24	18	54	59%	46	3.3	23	1.0	3	8.5	38	55%	21	6.4	28	8	5
B.J. Goodson	26	ILB	15	514	64	8.2%	68	34	12	4	40	53%	66	4.0	50	0.5	2	6	26	58%	15	5.6	18	4	2
Tae Davis	23	ILB	14	344	33	4.5%	88	20	6	7	18	72%	7	3.1	14	2.0	2	1.5	22	45%	52	7.9	62	1	0
Ray-Ray Armstrong*	28	ILB	15	212	21	2.5%	--	11	1	2	15	67%	--	3.3	--	0.0	0	0.5	4	50%	--	11.8	--	0	0

Year	Yards	ALY	Rank	Power	Rank	Stuff	Rank	2nd Level	Rank	Open Field	Rank	Sacks	ASR	Rank	Press	Rank
2016	3.64	4.12	16	63%	14	17%	20	0.91	2	0.45	4	35	5.5%	23	29.2%	8
2017	4.22	4.30	23	53%	4	22%	12	1.23	22	0.79	21	27	4.9%	30	29.0%	25
2018	4.25	4.38	18	64%	12	20%	13	1.21	16	0.85	17	30	4.9%	31	30.8%	16

2018 ALY by direction: Left End: 4.00 (12) Left Tackle: 4.77 (25) Mid/Guard: 4.42 (18) Right Tackle: 4.35 (19) Right End: 4.28 (14)

Joining first-round pick Dexter Lawrence up front will be B.J. Hill and Dalvin Tomlinson. Tomlinson is more of a traditional power player at 6-foot-3, 318 pounds, so he might wind up at the nose rather than Lawrence. Either way, the two of them will provide plenty of beef up the middle and stop those pesky Giants from running on themselves in practice. ● Hill is a more versatile player, providing disruption that nobody else on the interior can at this point. He definitely overperformed expectations coming out of North Carolina State, where a lot of teams thought he wouldn't be anything more than a run-stuffer. Hey, Gettleman's got a type. ● The most interesting edge player in the league as far as "what is this player actually?" is Lorenzo Carter. Carter's speed and size suggest he should be a good edge rusher, but he wasn't that guy last year. However, he did show really well as a coverage player last year, and should his edge rushing improve, he might be one of the most unique weapons in the NFL. Defensive coordinator James Bettcher is betting on improvement from Carter, telling *Forbes*' Patricia Traina that "Now, you see a guy that is aware of how he wants to rush, aware of techniques that he wants to rush with." ● Another player who might get big playing time is third-rounder Oshane Ximines, out of Old Dominion. Ximines tickled SackSEER from a production standpoint after 30 sacks and 13 passes defended, but his athletic testing wasn't great at the combine, with only average results in all the explosive drills. Obviously, at Old Dominion, he didn't face the best of the best, and he might need a sub-package role as he gets used to NFL run defense. The Giants praised his first step in post-draft pressers and thought he was advanced as far as how many rush moves he knew. ● Markus Golden had 12.5 sacks for Arizona in 2016, then tore his ACL in the 2017 offseason and didn't show much in his 2018 campaign. Reunited with his old defensive coordinator, he's a good bet to be the starter opposite Carter. ● Alec Ogletree's entire career has felt like a bit of a disappointment. He was supposed to be one of the stars for the Rams after being acquired in the RGIII trade bounty, but he has never lived up to his tools. With an $11.75-million cap figure in each of the next two years, we'd be surprised if he was a Giant in 2020. ● B.J. Goodson is the closest thing this team has to a good middle linebacker, which is something we feel like we write over and over again even though he's no great shakes. ● Fifth-rounder Ryan Connelly (Wisconsin) projects as a slower Mike linebacker, but the Giants praised his instincts and believed he could play sideline-to-sideline. He certainly doesn't have much in front of him on the depth chart.

Defensive Secondary

Secondary	Age	Pos	G	Snaps	Plays	TmPct	Rk	Stop	Dfts	BTkl	Runs	St%	Rk	RuYd	Rk	Tgts	Tgt%	Rk	Dist	Suc%	Rk	AdjYd	Rk	PD	Int
Janoris Jenkins	31	CB	16	1089	84	10.0%	20	33	16	9	23	26%	69	5.6	23	84	19.2%	43	12.5	45%	66	8.8	66	15	2
Janoris Jenkins	31	CB	16	1089	84	10.0%	20	33	16	9	23	26%	69	5.6	23	84	19.2%	43	12.5	45%	66	8.8	66	15	2
Curtis Riley*	27	FS	16	1048	78	9.3%	46	13	8	22	24	8%	76	13.2	76	20	4.7%	7	15.0	50%	36	8.9	58	5	4
B.W. Webb*	29	CB	16	1005	65	7.8%	52	25	13	5	16	44%	33	7.2	52	60	14.8%	11	14.4	57%	20	7.8	42	6	1
Landon Collins*	25	SS	12	804	99	15.8%	2	43	16	15	52	54%	15	5.0	11	49	15.1%	69	7.9	45%	53	8.1	51	4	0
Michael Thomas	29	SS	16	522	53	6.3%	69	27	8	5	25	60%	8	5.5	19	25	11.9%	58	6.9	68%	5	3.8	1	6	2
Grant Haley	23	CB	10	427	34	6.5%	73	12	6	3	9	56%	15	5.2	19	31	18.0%	32	7.8	45%	67	8.4	56	2	0
Antoine Bethea	35	FS	16	1111	125	14.2%	5	41	17	17	65	35%	50	8.2	50	46	12.1%	61	8.3	48%	44	5.8	10	4	0
Jabrill Peppers	24	SS	16	764	82	9.2%	47	32	10	9	39	51%	19	5.6	21	27	8.5%	28	9.9	41%	62	7.9	45	5	1

Year	Pass D Rank	vs. #1 WR	Rk	vs. #2 WR	Rk	vs. Other WR	Rk	WR Wide	Rk	WR Slot	Rk	vs. TE	Rk	vs. RB	Rk
2016	4	-29.7%	1	-12.8%	5	-14.2%	7	-37.4%	1	-4.8%	8	15.7%	26	-25.8%	3
2017	19	-2.8%	13	42.4%	32	-17.3%	6	2.8%	22	8.9%	17	-0.4%	15	-2.8%	15
2018	26	15.0%	26	-18.8%	7	20.0%	28	-18.7%	4	30.3%	30	3.1%	18	-14.6%	6

Outside corner Janoris Jenkins is getting up there in age and doesn't have the same sort of read-and-react speed he had at 27. But he's still a solid corner who had some real successful games last year, including holding DeAndre Hopkins to 61 yards on nine targets in Week 3. ● Meanwhile, free safety Antoine Bethea, the ageless wonder, reunites with his old defensive coordinator after two years in Arizona. The good news is that Bethea knows everything that can ever happen on a football field. The bad news is that he allowed 17 broken tackles last year and is only a minor improvement in that area over the deposed Curtis Riley. ● We wrote a whole chapter and barely even mentioned that the Giants A) had one of the best safeties in the NFL last year, and B) let that safety walk in free agency for no reason. Did we mention their offseason was kind of a disaster? Anyway, Jabrill Peppers will step into the spot that Landon Collins vacated. Peppers has amazing athleticism and he should make up for some of Bethea's tackling deficiencies. ● Grant Haley, the other returning cornerback from last year, mostly played in the second half of the season as a slot corner. His early returns weren't promising in a small sample, particularly because the players he was matched up against just weren't all that good. Haley allowed touchdowns to Chester Rogers, Jamison Crowder, Anthony Miller, and Adam Humphries last year. Not exactly a murderer's row. ● The Giants have three different (essentially) rookies who could play this year at corner. First is Georgia's DeAndre Baker, the one first-round pick they didn't reach for. In their post-draft pressers, they called Baker the best cover corner in the draft, talked up how he stood up to the challenge when tested—including holding down D.K. Metcalf—and noted that he'd probably play outside. ● That leaves the inside to Sam Beal (Western Michigan), last year's supplemental third-rounder, and fourth-round pick Julian Love (Notre Dame). Love is more of a shifty slot corner and the Giants brass specifically mentioned his speed when talking about him. Beal (who lost his rookie year to a shoulder injury) has outside pedigree and has a leg up on the OTA snaps, but has technique questions. It's likely both players will see extended playing time in 2019. ● Just in case the secondary wasn't young enough, the Giants selected Corey Ballantine out of football powerhouse Washburn in the sixth round as a height-weight-speed dart throw. There's so much unsettled on this depth chart that it's not out of the question he plays. ● The primary backup safety should be Michael Thomas, who is steady and functional depth if not anything super exciting at 30 years old.

Special Teams

Year	DVOA	Rank	FG/XP	Rank	Net Kick	Rank	Kick Ret	Rank	Net Punt	Rank	Punt Ret	Rank	Hidden	Rank
2016	1.2%	11	4.6	6	-3.0	26	2.5	9	10.6	6	-8.7	31	-11.3	27
2017	-7.5%	32	-12.2	30	-0.8	22	-3.5	23	-16.5	32	-4.5	26	-3.5	17
2018	4.5%	3	11.5	2	5.3	2	2.2	7	9.6	2	-5.8	29	-16.5	31

Aldrick Rosas went from hitting 72 percent of his field goals in 2017 to 97 percent in 2018, with a similar boost on extra points. Rosas will be a restricted free agent next summer, and a team with kicking issues might consider making an offer he can't refuse if the Giants don't slap a high tender on him. ● Brad Wing's exile in favor of former Broncos punter Riley Dixon could not have turned out better. Dixon posted -7.5 points worth of gross value on his punts in 2017, not much better than Wing, but was worth 3.2 points above average in 2018. That was combined with excellent coverage as only Jacksonville and Minnesota allowed less value on punt returns compared to expectations. ● Corey Coleman was solid on kickoff returns in 2018 and figures to be the main returner in 2019. Meanwhile, Jabrill Peppers isn't just a first-round quality player, he's also a pretty good punt returner! Peppers added 3.3 points of estimated field position in 2018 and should take over for Jawill Davis and Quadree Henderson.

New York Jets

2018 record: 4-12	Total DVOA: -14.7% (25th)	2019 Mean Projection: 7.7 wins	On the Clock (0-4): 12%
Pythagorean Wins: 5.3 (28th)	Offense: -19.5% (29th)	Postseason Odds: 32.4%	Mediocrity (5-7): 35%
Snap-Weighted Age: 26.1 (24th)	Defense: 3.3% (21st)	Super Bowl Odds: 2.8%	Playoff Contender (8-10): 37%
Average Opponent: -1.3% (18th)	Special Teams: 8.1% (1st)	Proj. Avg. Opponent: -4.8% (31st)	Super Bowl Contender (11+): 16%

2018: Hope at quarterback amidst a third straight last-place finish.

2019: Gase upon my works, ye mighty, and despair.

It was the best of offseasons. It was the worst of offseasons. It was the Jets-iest of offseasons.

It was a winter and spring of hope and despair, weeks of wisdom and foolishness, a time when the Jets lurched in one direction one week and the other the next. It was an offseason very much like so many other Jets offseasons, only much, much more so.

The story of the Jets offseason would make a tight 12-part Netflix series. The supporting cast alone groans with compelling side characters: Christopher Johnson (the brother of a team owner in ambassadorial absentia, ruling like Robin Hood's Prince John), Mike Maccagnan (the deposed general manager, a bumbling Polonius behind the curtains of his own downfall), Kliff Kingsbury and Jim Harbaugh (the Rosencrantz-and-Guildenstern college coaches Johnson and Maccagnan surreptitiously conspired with before Todd Bowles was even fired), Matt Ruhle (Baylor's brash young Mark Antony; Maccagnan's doomed choice as puppet regent), Gregg Williams (the Rasputin-like defensive coordinator whose results never quite match his reputation), near-miss free-agent acquisition Anthony Barr (Sir Not Appearing in This Film) and Peyton Manning (Adam Gase's Deus Ex Machina).

But this is an analytical almanac, not the last exposé Seth Wickersham writes before researching it sends him spiraling into gibbering madness. So we'll assume you know most of the details of the Shakespearean/Dickensian past (Johnson and Maccagnan fired Bowles and chose Gase over Ruhle based on Peyton's recommendation; Johnson then fired Maccagnan, presumably due to Gase's orchestrations) and focus instead on the four characters who will decide the Jets' future:

- Sam Darnold: Bonny Prince of Florham Park and Jets quarterback of the present and future. Darnold rebounded from a midseason swoon and November ankle injury with a string of encouraging December performances.
- Le'Veon Bell: the reluctant mercenary lured back to the battlefield in search of both fortune and validation.
- Joe Douglas: the new general manager/prime minister/ voice of reason, a canny talent evaluator with a near-spotless record, for now. And finally:
- Adam Gase: The Man Who Would Be King, the fulcrum upon which the Jets future hinges.

The four Jets puzzle pieces don't quite fit snuggly together,

in part because Gase—who earned a reputation as a high-maintenance boardroom politician while coaching the Dolphins and has exceeded expectations on that front in his six months with the Jets—is all jagged edges.

Douglas was Gase's hand-picked choice to run the personnel department. He's a vast upgrade over Maccagnan, whose primary managerial skills consisted of milking four years of employment out of one fluky 10-win season and inspiring ride-or-die loyalty from some high-profile members of the New York media. Douglas worked his way through Ozzie Newsome's tightly organized Ravens front office for over a decade before crossing paths with Gase on the 2015 Bears (Douglas was director of college scouting, Gase offensive coordinator), en route to joining Howie Roseman's Eagles staff and using his scouting acumen to help build a world champion.

Douglas' job will be to rebuild a roster that nearly crumbled to dust after four years of abysmal drafting by Maccagnan, and he's the right man for the long-term job. But Douglas arrived too late to make his mark on this year's roster. Furthermore, despite apparent mutual respect and admiration between Gase and Douglas, there's reason to worry about how the pair will coexist.

To be blunt, it sure looked like Gase wanted absolute roster control for himself: he flexed his muscles by trading Darron Lee, cutting Jordan Leggett, and re-signing Bilal Powell before Douglas was hired. The Jets may have only offered 53-man roster control to Douglas as an enticement and to ensure that the Jets would receive permission to interview him. (The Eagles could have declined permission for a lateral move, no matter the official title.) Johnson then appeared to drag out the interview process and add alternate candidates simply to reign in Gase. None of this sounds like a formula for healthy collaboration or respect for the chain of command.

The Gase-Bell relationship also started out on the wrong foot. Gase was reportedly displeased with the Bell signing, more because of the size of the contract than because of any doubts about the former Steelers running back's ability. But that post-coup narrative sounds fishy, as if someone within the organization was trying to thread the needle of blaming Maccagnan for a bad decision without alienating one of the most important players on the roster. (Narrator: that "someone" was Gase).

Bell's reported four-year, $52-million deal is really a two-

2019 Jets Schedule					
Week	Opp.	Week	Opp.	Week	Opp.
1	BUF	7	NE (Mon.)	13	at CIN
2	CLE (Mon.)	8	at JAX	14	MIA
3	at NE	9	at MIA	15	at BAL (Thu.)
4	BYE	10	NYG	16	PIT
5	at PHI	11	at WAS	17	at BUF
6	DAL	12	OAK		

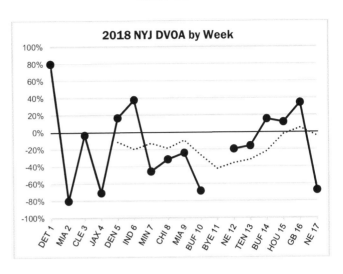

2018 NYJ DVOA by Week

year, $19-million deal with lots of padding, and the Jets had both a critical need for a playmaker and cap space to burn in 2019 and 2020. Far from another Maccagnan bungle, it may have been his shrewdest move as a general manager. And with 160 receptions and second- and 11th-place finishes in receiving DYAR alone in 2016 and 2017, Bell's receiving ability alone will be a major asset for the Jets and provide a boost to Darnold's development.

For his part, Bell skipped all of OTAs except mandatory minicamp. Skipping voluntary workouts was well within Bell's rights, of course, but you would figure he had spent enough time working out independently during his year-long holdout and might be eager to report to his new job a wee bit early. Gase, who managed to have a personality conflict with the saintly Frank Gore in Miami, didn't voice any public displeasure over Bell's absence, but now more than ever, it's important to read reports from Jets headquarters through an Orwellian lens.

Douglas and Bell aside, it's the Gase-Darnold dynamic which matters most to the Jets organization. Gase's calling card reads "Quarterback Guru," although he is still waiting to guru his first quarterback. If Gase turns Darnold into an All-Pro, no one will care if Bell disappears out the back door or who is found sprawled on the conference room floor with a dagger in his back.

The problem is that Gase is an ineffective offensive coach, and his system threatens to ruin Darnold, burying his potential under an avalanche of failed completions.

At Football Outsiders, we define a failed completion as any completed pass that fails to gain 45 percent of needed yards on first down, 60 percent on second down, or 100 percent on third or fourth down. Failed completions make completion percentages and quarterback ratings look great but end up starving out an offense with screen passes on third-and-20.

As I reported for Bleacher Report in May, Gase's Dolphins quarterbacks were always among the league's leaders in failed completion rates:

* 29.5 percent of Ryan Tannehill's completions last year were failed completions, ranking him 32nd among qualifying quarterbacks. Failed completions accounted for 16.7 percent of his total pass attempts, which ranked 29th.
* 28.1 percent of Jay Cutler's completions and 17.4 percent of his attempts in 2017 were failed completions. Both figures ranked 25th among eligible quarterbacks.
* 29.9 percent of Ryan Tannehill's completions (31st) and

20.2 percent of his attempts (31st) were failed completions during the Dolphins' triumphant wild-card season in 2016.

One reason the Dolphins were often among the league leaders in failed completions was Gase's preference for throwing well short of the sticks on both second-and-long and third-and-long. Last season, for example, Tannehill completed 36 of 55 passes on second-and-long (65.5 percent) for 375 yards, three touchdowns and two interceptions. He was 24-of-45 (53.3 percent) with 287 yards, three touchdowns and three interceptions on third-and-long. Superficially, these are decent numbers. Further, Brock Osweiler completed 21 of 33 second-and-long passes and a stunning 17 of 22 third-and-long passes. Yet the Dolphins ranked 31st in DVOA on second-and-long and 28th in DVOA on third-and-long.

The numbers were similar in 2017. Cutler's raw numbers in long-yardage situations that year were slightly better than Tannehill's last year: a 69.7 percent completion rate (62-of-89) on second-and-long and a 56.3 percent rate (36-of-64) on third-and-long. Yet the Dolphins finished dead last in second-and-long DVOA and 26th in third-and-long DVOA that year.

Some of the blame for all of the failed completions falls on Tannehill, Cutler, and Osweiler. Both Tannehill and Cutler were among the league leaders in failed completions before they were coached by Gase. But Gase has repeatedly gone to great rhetorical lengths to defend his short-passing philosophy, perhaps because Miami reporters constantly questioned him about the wisdom of it.

For example, Gase justified his preference for the short pass to reporters after a preseason game full of dump-offs last August. "If they come up and play Cover-1, we'll have some shots to push the ball down the field," he said. "If they play off, and we have to take things underneath, then we have to do a good job of going 12 plays and scoring through the goal line."

That sure sounds like an invitation for the defense to play "off" and test Gase's quarterbacks to determine how many Peyton Manning-esque 12-play touchdown drives they have in them.

What's most discouraging about the Gase-Darnold pairing is that Darnold was successful last year because he was *not* a Gase-like dink-and-dunker. Darnold threw failed completions on only 21.8 percent of his completions (ninth in the NFL) and 11.7 percent of his attempts (a remarkable fourth). Uniquely among rookie quarterbacks, Darnold took his share of downfield shots last season, and they were starting to pay off late in the year. The Jets finished just 30th in DVOA on second-and-long (still better than Gase's Dolphins, despite fewer weapons and reps split between the rookie Darnold and the soon-to-retire Josh McCown) but a respectable 15th on third-and-long.

So there's a risk that Gase will take away one thing that made Darnold unique and effective last season. And Gase will have plenty of justifications for doing so. The Jets offensive line was not addressed in the offseason and remains weak after years of Maccagnan negligence. Bell, Quincy Enunwa, and new arrival Jamison Crowder provide a trio of enticing short-range pass targets, with Robbie Anderson as the lone deep threat. Gase could turn Darnold into a quarterback with decent stats but poor habits, which is precisely what he did to Tannehill.

Gase's Jets, like most of his Dolphins teams, have the look of a sub-.500 team with a few expensive pieces but too many critical weaknesses: the talent-poor line, a thin cornerback corps, question marks at the edge rush positions, and so forth. Our forecast for the Jets is remarkably sanguine, thanks to probable improvement by both Darnold and the defense combined with one of the league's easiest schedules. If they finish around our 7.7-win projection, Gase can simultaneously take credit for the team's progress and blame Maccagnan for the failure to reach the playoffs, and he won't hesitate to do both.

As for future years, there's a lot to like about Darnold, Douglas, and youngsters like Anderson, Jamal Adams, rookie Quinnen Williams and others. But this essay would have been far more optimistic and charitable if Ruhle, Kingsbury, or some Andy Reid knockoff won the head coaching job instead of Gase.

Gase was a terrible choice as head coach, made as the result of an incomprehensibly muddled search. And he has already buttressed his job security, not just by hiring Douglas but by filling his staff with unsuitable in-house replacements in the event of an insurrection. Gregg Williams' Bountygate history and "Lost Ryan Twin" personality make him a tough sell as an interim head coach (that's precisely why Hue Jackson kept Williams around in Cleveland) and offensive coordinator Dowell Loggains is a long-time Gase hanger-on. Gase's staff, like his game plans, is designed to look good on paper.

The Jets have stumbled into some good results from a bad process in recent years. They were only in position to draft Darnold because Maccagnan whiffed on past quarterback experiments and mired the Jets near the bottom of the standings until the quarterback class was deep and the Giants had a hankerin' for Saquon Barkley. Douglas is only in Florham Park because of Gase, who is only the head coach because the Maccagnan-Ruhle alliance fell apart. Adams and other youngsters are merely testament to the fact that even someone drafting out of a Phil Steele college annual is going to hit on a few picks. For all of the drama of this offseason, the Jets are still blind squirrels; they just stumbled over a few more acorns than usual.

The Jets needed to fix their power structure this offseason more than they needed to surround Darnold with talent. They somehow made things worse. Based on Gase's history, he'll quarrel with those above and below him, squander a lot of resources on "culture changes" and other hobgoblins of the mediocre coach's mind, deflect criticism and blame at every turn, and linger a little too long before the Johnson brothers realize they are better off starting over from scratch the way the Dolphins are now doing.

But that will all happen in 2020 and beyond. Until then, Viva La Revolution!

Mike Tanier

2018 Jets Stats by Week

Wk	vs.	W-L	PF	PA	YDF	YDA	TO	Total	Off	Def	ST
1	at DET	W	48	17	349	339	+3	80%	1%	-47%	32%
2	MIA	L	12	20	362	257	-1	-80%	-79%	-2%	-4%
3	at CLE	L	17	21	268	323	-3	-3%	-32%	-22%	7%
4	at JAX	L	12	31	178	503	+3	-71%	-41%	31%	1%
5	DEN	W	34	16	512	436	-1	17%	30%	15%	2%
6	IND	W	42	34	374	428	+2	38%	5%	-22%	12%
7	MIN	L	17	37	263	316	-4	-46%	-41%	2%	-3%
8	at CHI	L	10	24	207	395	0	-32%	-13%	21%	3%
9	at MIA	L	6	13	282	168	-4	-24%	-64%	-41%	-1%
10	BUF	L	10	41	199	451	-2	-68%	-30%	38%	-1%
11	BYE										
12	NE	L	13	27	338	498	-1	-20%	-7%	24%	11%
13	at TEN	L	22	26	280	403	0	-16%	-25%	4%	13%
14	at BUF	W	27	23	248	368	+1	16%	3%	5%	18%
15	HOU	L	22	29	318	286	-1	12%	-2%	-14%	0%
16	GB	L	38	44	370	540	+1	35%	26%	26%	35%
17	at NE	L	3	38	239	375	-3	-68%	-57%	17%	7%

Trends and Splits

	Offense	Rank	Defense	Rank
Total DVOA	-19.5%	29	3.3%	21
Unadjusted VOA	-22.7%	30	2.5%	20
Weighted Trend	-16.3%	27	9.9%	28
Variance	9.7%	27	6.4%	22
Average Opponent	-4.0%	1	-4.1%	26
Passing	-8.2%	28	8.8%	18
Rushing	-20.7%	30	-3.9%	21
First Down	-28.7%	31	8.0%	27
Second Down	-23.2%	29	7.1%	24
Third Down	2.8%	17	-12.1%	9
First Half	-15.9%	29	-2.8%	9
Second Half	-23.0%	29	9.3%	25
Red Zone	-9.3%	20	-3.0%	17
Late and Close	-15.3%	26	10.5%	28

Five-Year Performance

Year	W-L	Pyth W	Est W	PF	PA	TO	Total	Rk	Off	Rk	Def	Rk	ST	Rk	Off AGL	Rk	Def AGL	Rk	Off Age	Rk	Def Age	Rk	ST Age	Rk
2014	4-12	4.8	5.9	283	401	-11	-15.5%	27	-11.2%	27	3.5%	21	-0.8%	16	18.7	5	22.8	4	27.3	9	27.0	11	26.1	13
2015	10-6	10.0	9.7	387	314	+6	12.4%	9	1.6%	14	-13.8%	5	-2.9%	25	48.7	25	13.2	1	28.5	1	27.1	9	26.6	6
2016	5-11	4.4	4.6	275	409	-20	-32.4%	32	-21.9%	31	3.7%	21	-6.8%	32	67.6	30	42.9	22	27.5	6	26.4	19	26.0	19
2017	5-11	5.6	5.2	298	382	-4	-17.2%	26	-10.3%	25	3.9%	18	-3.0%	25	39.0	19	8.4	4	27.1	13	25.6	27	25.9	13
2018	4-12	5.3	5.9	333	441	-10	-14.7%	25	-19.5%	29	3.3%	21	8.1%	1	49.7	24	24.9	10	26.4	19	26.0	23	26.0	13

2018 Performance Based on Most Common Personnel Groups

NYJ Offense					NYJ Offense vs. Opponents					NYJ Defense				NYJ Defense vs. Opponents			
Pers	Freq	Yds	DVOA	Run%	Pers	Freq	Yds	DVOA	Run%	Pers	Freq	Yds	DVOA	Pers	Freq	Yds	DVOA
11	55%	5.0	-11.7%	30%	Base	25%	4.7	-22.9%	59%	Base	21%	5.8	2.5%	11	72%	6.0	5.4%
12	21%	4.7	-35.2%	50%	Nickel	55%	4.7	-25.3%	35%	Nickel	75%	6.1	6.9%	12	11%	5.8	-2.0%
13	9%	5.5	-3.2%	63%	Dime+	11%	7.4	81.4%	10%	Dime+	3%	2.8	-91.7%	21	8%	6.3	22.8%
21	6%	5.4	9.3%	60%	Goal Line	0%	0.0	-17.7%	100%	Goal Line	2%	1.9	-27.5%	13	3%	3.2	-44.4%
612	3%	4.1	-44.2%	50%										20	2%	7.9	39.1%

Strategic Tendencies

Run/Pass		Rk	Formation		Rk	Pass Rush		Rk	Secondary		Rk	Strategy		Rk
Runs, first half	42%	7	Form: Single Back	79%	19	Rush 3	15.3%	4	4 DB	21%	21	Play action	26%	10
Runs, first down	47%	16	Form: Empty Back	10%	7	Rush 4	55.5%	29	5 DB	75%	7	Avg Box (Off)	6.17	17
Runs, second-long	35%	8	Pers: 3+ WR	59%	25	Rush 5	22.1%	8	6+ DB	3%	22	Avg Box (Def)	6.26	15
Runs, power sit.	62%	11	Pers: 2+ TE/6+ OL	34%	5	Rush 6+	6.7%	11	CB by Sides	88%	6	Offensive Pace	32.51	28
Runs, behind 2H	30%	12	Pers: 6+ OL	4%	6	Int DL Sacks	30.8%	13	S/CB Cover Ratio	17%	32	Defensive Pace	30.24	6
Pass, ahead 2H	48%	17	Shotgun/Pistol	61%	21	Second Level Sacks	25.6%	14	DB Blitz	17%	2	Go for it on 4th	1.41	16

Revenge of the unsustainable splits: In 2017, the Jets were 26th in run offense DVOA overall but somehow the No. 1 run offense on third downs. Last year, the Jets were 30th in run offense DVOA overall, in part because third-down running had fallen back to 24th in the league. ● New York was dead last in the league when running on second-and-long, with -60.8% DVOA and 3.5 yards per carry. ● The Jets were second in the league going max protect, using seven or more blockers with at least two more blockers than pass-rushers on 12.6 percent of pass plays. ● The Jets ranked fifth with 10.0 average yards after catch on passes thrown at or behind the line of scrimmage, but they ranked 28th with just 3.8 average YAC on passes thrown past the line of scrimmage. ● Gregg Williams loves to get sacks from those second-level defenders, so watch for defensive back blitz numbers to stay high under the new Jets regime. Both of the last two years, Cleveland ranked in the top five in percentage of their sacks coming from second-level defenders. ● It's hard to tell how aggressive Adam Gase is going to be on fourth downs; Miami ranked No. 1 in Aggressiveness Index in 2017 but 28th in 2018.

Passing

Player	DYAR	DVOA	Plays	NtYds	Avg	YAC	C%	TD	Int
S.Darnold	-110	-15.2%	445	2653	6.0	5.4	57.9%	17	15
J.McCown*	-184	-36.5%	116	504	4.3	5.1	55.0%	1	4

Rushing

Player	DYAR	DVOA	Plays	Yds	Avg	TD	Fum	Suc
I.Crowell*	37	-1.9%	143	685	4.8	7	0	36%
E.McGuire	-90	-32.1%	92	276	3.0	3	2	36%
B.Powell	-34	-19.9%	80	343	4.3	0	2	44%
T.Cannon	-10	-14.7%	38	113	3.0	1	0	37%
S.Darnold	23	0.2%	30	146	4.9	1	2	--
J.McCown*	6	14.2%	5	32	6.4	0	0	--
T.Montgomery	17	0.9%	42	188	4.5	1	1	57%

Receiving

Player	DYAR	DVOA	Plays	Ctch	Yds	Y/C	YAC	TD	C%
R.Anderson	6	-11.8%	94	50	752	15.0	3.6	6	53%
J.Kearse*	-95	-28.8%	76	37	371	10.0	3.4	1	49%
Q.Enunwa	-105	-32.2%	68	38	449	11.8	7.5	1	56%
T.Pryor*	77	34.0%	22	14	235	16.8	4.4	2	64%
A.Roberts*	-29	-34.3%	18	10	79	7.9	1.7	1	56%
D.Burnett	37	19.7%	15	10	143	14.3	2.5	0	67%
J.Crowder	23	-6.2%	49	29	388	13.4	7.0	2	59%
J.Bellamy	-26	-25.5%	25	14	117	8.4	3.3	1	56%
D.Thompson	-27	-24.1%	30	17	161	9.5	2.2	0	57%
C.Herndon	50	6.3%	56	39	502	12.9	4.7	4	70%
J.Leggett*	-16	-17.4%	25	14	114	8.1	3.5	1	56%
E.Tomlinson	-23	-37.4%	14	8	72	9.0	11.1	0	57%
N.Sterling*	-8	-22.8%	8	6	47	7.8	4.8	0	75%
E.McGuire	38	8.1%	31	19	193	10.2	8.9	1	61%
I.Crowell*	10	-6.8%	28	21	152	7.2	8.2	0	75%
T.Cannon	-23	-30.2%	25	17	144	8.5	6.9	0	68%
B.Powell	-1	-14.4%	18	11	110	10.0	7.6	1	61%
T.Montgomery	-1	-14.1%	40	25	235	9.4	8.5	0	63%

Offensive Line

Player	Pos	Age	GS	Snaps	Pen	Sk	Pass	Run	Player	Pos	Age	GS	Snaps	Pen	Sk	Pass	Run
Kelvin Beachum	LT	30	16/16	1001	9	3.0	12	5	James Carpenter*	LG	30	10/10	624	3	2.0	4	2
Brian Winters	RG	28	16/16	1001	6	6.0	11	12	Jonotthan Harrison	C	28	16/8	506	4	0.0	3	0
Brandon Shell	RT	27	14/14	850	5	2.0	5	4	Tom Compton	LG	30	14/14	837	7	7.0	11	7
Spencer Long*	C/LG	29	13/13	805	5	2.5	5	7	Kelechi Osemele	LG	30	11/11	739	5	2.2	8	7

Year	Yards	ALY	Rank	Power	Rank	Stuff	Rank	2nd Lev	Rank	Open Field	Rank	Sacks	ASR	Rank	Press	Rank	F-Start	Cont.
2016	4.25	4.30	12	74%	2	16%	7	1.24	11	0.66	17	35	6.3%	20	24.9%	13	16	20
2017	3.96	3.40	29	48%	31	26%	29	1.03	23	1.04	5	47	8.6%	27	32.2%	22	14	27
2018	4.05	3.59	32	61%	26	26%	32	1.05	28	1.06	6	37	6.7%	18	32.4%	21	21	28

2018 ALY by direction: Left End: 3.00 (27)   Left Tackle: 4.36 (12)   Mid/Guard: 3.49 (32)   Right Tackle: 4.39 (17)   Right End: 3.34 (28)

This unit needed an offseason overhaul but did not get one. Left guard James Carpenter and center Spencer Long left for the Falcons and Bills, respectively, and the Jets hope to replace them with trade acquisition Kelechi Osemele, coming off an injury-plagued and disappointing year for the Raiders, and incumbent backup center Jonotthan Harrison, who has never been very good. ✎ Kelvin Beachum and Brandon Shell form an adequate-at-best tackle tandem. Both are in the final years of their contracts. Beachum turned 30 in June but could be targeted for an extension: Joe Douglas' Eagles were always willing to pay a little extra for dependability and experience on the offensive line. Shell suffered a knee injury last year and was brought along slowly in OTAs. ✎ Third-round pick Chuma Edoga is a massive dude with some of the quickest feet in this draft class, but his USC tape ran hot and cold. Edoga's development will determine Beachum's long-term fate. ✎ There is no other young talent on the depth chart, because Edoga was the only offensive lineman Mike Maccagnan drafted in the first three rounds in four seasons as a general manager. Judging by Maccagnan's overall record, any lineman he drafted early probably would have stunk, anyway.

Defensive Front

Defensive Line	Age	Pos	G	Snaps	Plays	TmPct	Rk	Stop	Dfts	BTkl	Runs	St%	Rk	RuYd	Rk	Sack	Hit	Hur	Dsrpt
													vs. Run			Pass Rush			
Leonard Williams	25	DE	16	867	42	5.1%	37	36	14	7	32	84%	14	1.7	16	5.0	15	22	3
Henry Anderson	28	DE	16	668	39	4.7%	44	33	13	4	24	83%	17	1.7	18	7.0	8	19	3
Steve McLendon	33	DT	16	471	34	4.1%	62	24	4	2	30	70%	62	2.9	69	0.0	1	5	1
Mike Pennel*	28	DT	16	359	28	3.4%	--	26	2	2	26	92%	--	1.9	--	0.0	2	6	0
Nathan Shepherd	26	DT	16	343	15	1.8%	--	11	2	1	15	73%	--	2.9	--	0.0	5	9	0

Edge Rushers	Age	Pos	G	Snaps	Plays	TmPct	Rk	Stop	Dfts	BTkl	Runs	St%	Rk	RuYd	Rk	Sack	Hit	Hur	Dsrpt
													vs. Run			Pass Rush			
Jordan Jenkins	25	OLB	16	660	34	4.1%	64	25	11	4	23	74%	47	2.6	54	7.0	7	15	1
Brandon Copeland	28	OLB	16	612	35	4.2%	62	27	9	5	24	79%	26	3.2	71	5.0	9	22	1
Frankie Luvu	23	OLB	14	443	22	3.0%	84	17	7	5	12	67%	64	3.2	70	3.0	8	16	1

Linebackers	Age	Pos	G	Snaps	Plays	TmPct	Rk	Stop	Dfts	BTkl	Runs	St%	Rk	RuYd	Rk	Sack	Hit	Hur	Tgts	Suc%	Rk	AdjYd	Rk	PD	Int
											vs. Run					Pass Rush				vs. Pass					
Avery Williamson	27	ILB	16	1115	126	15.3%	23	64	20	6	71	61%	37	3.9	40	3.0	1	8	39	41%	61	7.3	56	6	1
Darron Lee*	25	ILB	12	808	78	12.6%	41	46	12	5	43	65%	22	2.8	11	0.0	2	3	34	62%	7	4.1	5	5	3
Neville Hewitt	26	ILB	16	268	28	3.4%	--	15	3	3	15	80%	--	2.6	--	1.5	3	3	14	50%	--	5.5	--	0	0
C.J. Mosley	27	ILB	15	875	110	15.4%	20	62	17	9	63	67%	19	3.8	35	0.5	1	7.5	39	51%	37	6.0	21	5	1

Year	Yards	ALY	Rank	Power	Rank	Stuff	Rank	2nd Level	Rank	Open Field	Rank	Sacks	ASR	Rank	Press	Rank
2016	3.99	3.62	5	51%	4	27%	2	1.16	16	0.91	26	27	4.3%	32	26.3%	21
2017	3.67	3.77	6	70%	24	22%	8	0.93	4	0.66	12	28	5.8%	25	30.0%	18
2018	4.31	4.28	13	55%	2	22%	10	1.25	19	0.87	18	39	6.7%	21	28.1%	24

2018 ALY by direction:	Left End: 5.00 (22)	Left Tackle: 2.97 (4)	Mid/Guard: 4.37 (12)	Right Tackle: 4.47 (21)	Right End: 3.73 (10)

Rookie nose tackle Quinnen Williams is as close to a sure thing as exists in this world of doubt and uncertainty (or at least the annual NFL draft of doubt and uncertainty). Williams is stout and tenacious, has some of the strongest hand technique of any interior line prospect in recent years, and gets high character grades. The Alabama product joins Leonard Williams and Henry Anderson on a defensive line that will remain solid against the run. ⬛ Third-round pick Jachai Polite, unlike Williams, has boom-or-bust potential. Polite had the tape of a top-15 pick but had a rep for immaturity at Florida, looked flabby (and a little unfocused) at both the combine and his pro day, and pulled up with minor hamstring injuries after both workouts. SackSEER split the uprights of Polite's production and workout results with a so-so 15.7-sack projection for his early career and a mediocre 30.3% rating. ⬛ The Jets need Polite to step up and help fill an utter void at the edge rush positions. Jordan Jenkins recorded seven sacks against the likes of Brock Osweiler, Tyrod Taylor, Matt Barkley, and Deshaun Watson (with his coffee-filter offensive line) and worked out with pass-rush guru Chuck Smith this offseason in search of a breakout 2019 season. If all the defenders who worked out with Smith had breakout seasons, there would be no quarterbacks left. Brandon Copeland, penciled in at the other edge position, owns a real estate business and taught an "economics life skills" class in the offseason. No word on whether Mike Maccagnan attended. The good news is that Williams, Williams, and Johnson should produce more pass rush than the typical 3-4 front, and that safety Jamal Adams is an excellent blitzer. ⬛ Adam Gase was said to be as upset about linebacker C.J. Mosley's reported $85-million contract as he was about the Le'Veon Bell deal. On the one hand, Gase has a point: inside linebacker, like running back, is a position at which good organizations develop inexpensive talent and bad ones overpay. On the other hand, Mosley can play, and it's unusual for a first-year coach to micromanage the payroll the way Gase did (or does). Anyway, Mosley is an upgrade over Darron Lee, who played well last year but was traded soon after Gase's coup in what may have been a one-man purge of Maccagnan's midround draft success stories.

Defensive Secondary

Secondary	Age	Pos	G	Snaps	Plays	TmPct	Rk	Stop	Dfts	BTkl	Runs	St%	Rk	RuYd	Rk	Tgts	Tgt%	Rk	Dist	Suc%	Rk	AdjYd	Rk	PD	Int
												vs. Run						vs. Pass							
Jamal Adams	24	SS	16	1120	126	15.3%	3	62	27	7	64	50%	21	6.0	25	39	8.7%	29	11.5	62%	11	7.0	34	12	1
Morris Claiborne*	29	CB	15	1003	71	9.2%	32	28	11	10	18	50%	22	3.6	6	74	18.3%	37	13.8	55%	25	8.0	46	14	2
Darryl Roberts	29	CB	16	726	52	6.3%	74	19	10	8	19	16%	77	12.2	77	41	14.0%	7	14.6	59%	14	9.2	70	7	1
Buster Skrine*	30	CB	14	694	65	9.0%	35	27	12	7	21	38%	50	5.6	24	61	21.8%	59	10.5	46%	63	8.3	55	8	0
Trumaine Johnson	29	CB	10	671	45	8.7%	41	18	8	6	6	33%	56	7.8	61	55	20.4%	51	12.1	55%	29	8.7	64	5	4
Marcus Maye	26	FS	6	393	35	11.3%	--	7	2	4	18	17%	--	10.2	--	9	5.7%	--	14.1	56%	--	8.7	--	2	1
Doug Middleton	26	FS	7	231	24	6.6%	--	4	2	1	8	0%	--	11.8	--	3	3.2%	--	29.0	33%	--	16.0	--	3	0
Brian Poole	27	CB	16	831	77	9.2%	31	34	16	16	23	52%	21	6.9	47	54	14.9%	12	8.7	41%	78	8.1	50	6	3

Year	Pass D Rank	vs. #1 WR	Rk	vs. #2 WR	Rk	vs. Other WR	Rk	WR Wide	Rk	WR Slot	Rk	vs. TE	Rk	vs. RB	Rk
2016	31	11.5%	25	25.1%	32	7.7%	21	7.5%	25	24.1%	32	0.9%	19	-5.9%	16
2017	22	21.1%	28	-7.0%	13	-26.7%	2	13.7%	28	-15.0%	8	-7.4%	9	13.3%	26
2018	19	11.5%	24	-3.5%	14	9.7%	23	-10.5%	10	21.1%	27	7.8%	20	-13.4%	7

Jamal Adams led all NFL safeties in total defeats and has emerged as the tone-setter and spokesman for the Jets defense. So it's encouraging to hear that he loves new coordinator Gregg Williams. "It's kind of like an uncle, really," Adams said of Williams, per Scott Thompson of SNY. "He's coaching us hard, he wants the best out of us, and you can run through a wall for a coach like that, you know what I mean?" Based on minicamp beat reports, Uncle Gregg won't be asking Adams to play 30 yards from the line of scrimmage the way Jabrill Peppers did in Cleveland, which is an encouraging sign. ● Marcus Maye joins Adams to make the Jets safety corps the strength of the roster, as long as he's healthy: he lost time to foot, thumb, and shoulder injuries last season. ● Cornerback is another matter. As with the offensive line, the Jets allowed a pair of so-so veterans to depart (Morris Claiborne and Buster Skrine) despite a lack of obvious available upgrades, leaving Trumaine Johnson as the one sure thing on the depth chart. Brian Poole, penciled in as the starter opposite Johnson, was let go by the Falcons, and the charting and tape show exactly the kind of player who is not quite good enough to stick in the secondary for a team that allowed 26.4 points per game. Poole has ranked 61st, 70th, and 78th in coverage success rate over the last three seasons. ● Depth will have to wait, because Mike Maccagnan never drafted a cornerback in the first three rounds in four seasons as general manager. We may need a federal investigation to figure out just who Maccagnan did draft in the first three rounds.

Special Teams

Year	DVOA	Rank	FG/XP	Rank	Net Kick	Rank	Kick Ret	Rank	Net Punt	Rank	Punt Ret	Rank	Hidden	Rank
2016	-6.8%	32	0.3	16	-0.4	17	-6.2	27	-21.1	32	-6.6	27	-11.8	30
2017	-3.0%	25	2.8	13	3.9	9	-3.4	22	-6.0	23	-12.2	32	5.8	7
2018	8.1%	1	10.3	4	5.1	4	13.6	2	2.7	14	8.8	1	0.8	14

With all respect to Jets MVP Jamal Adams, Andre Roberts was arguably the Jets most important player for long chunks of last season. Roberts scored two touchdowns on returns and provided 10 kickoff returns of 40-plus yards, setting set up scoring drives during stretches when the Jets offense could barely move the ball on its own. Roberts is in Buffalo now, and the battle for the return chores was wide open in the spring. Trenton Cannon (who excelled as a gunner, with 10 tackles) and Ty Montgomery (who got kicked out of Green Bay for ignoring Mike McCarthy even more than everyone else did) are the favorites on kickoffs, Jamison Crowder on punts. ● Chandler Catanzaro is back to replace Jason Myers, signed by the Seahawks as a free agent. Catanzaro had a disastrous season for the Buccaneers, missing four extra points and going 0-for-3 from 40 to 49 yards, before mopping up some late-season games for Carolina. The Jets did not bring in a young challenger for Catanzaro because it's hard to focus on signing camp kickers while staging a boardroom adaptation of *Macbeth*. ● Punter Lachlan Edwards will once again be very busy.

Oakland Raiders

2018 record: 4-12	**Total DVOA:** -21.0% (31st)	**2019 Mean Projection:** 6.6 wins	**On the Clock (0-4):** 22%
Pythagorean Wins: 3.7 (31st)	**Offense:** -7.1% (25th)	**Postseason Odds:** 18.1%	**Mediocrity (5-7):** 43%
Snap-Weighted Age: 27.2 (4th)	**Defense:** 12.3% (30th)	**Super Bowl Odds:** 1.3%	**Playoff Contender (8-10):** 28%
Average Opponent: 6.6% (1st)	**Special Teams:** -1.6% (22nd)	**Proj. Avg. Opponent:** 2.9% (4th)	**Super Bowl Contender (11+):** 8%

2018: And with a mighty snap, half of Oakland's roster crumbled into dust.

2019: Just what *is* Jon Gruden's Endgame?

Did you miss this year's Sloan Sports Analytics Conference? You really should try to go sometime; it's like ComicCon, except people know more about Nate Silver and VORP than the Silver Surfer or MODOK.

… Actually, there's more crossover in those groups than you'd think, but I digress. Anyway…

Alongside the speakers from across the sports analytics world and the panel discussions covering everything from machine learning to tracking data, the conference also presented the Alpha Awards, recognizing the best uses of analytics in sports. And, wouldn't you know it, the award for best transaction of 2018 in all of sports went to the Oakland Raiders for the trade of Khalil Mack.

Yes, the trade (The Trade?) that was widely panned by sports media as a whole, sent a million Twitter accounts bursting into flame, and had even players on the Raiders scratching their heads won an analytics award for Jon Gruden, who infamously said that he was trying to "throw the game back to 1998" and dismissed the value of analytic data at the 2018 combine. Oakland team president Marc Badain assumed the call to inform them of the award was a practical joke at first, and had to be convinced that, no, some people actually did support the decision. I'm sure the giant plexiglass "α" sits right next to the pair of Lombardis in Oakland's trophy cabinet.

The logic behind such an award is simple. One of the worst places to be in any sport is stuck right around .500—not good enough to compete for championships, not bad enough to get high draft picks to get players that will help you complete for championships. If you do not feel you can be competitive

right away, you should do everything you can to exchange current assets for future ones. A dozen sacks and an All-Pro nod on a losing season doesn't mean anything in the long run; if it can be exchanged for the nucleus of a championship-caliber team two or three years from now, that's the right thing to do. Mack is just the tenth player in the DVOA era to be traded for multiple first-round draft picks, a set of deals which have generally gone better for the teams gaining the picks than the teams gaining the players (Table 1).

It's safe to say that Oakland embraced that "future assets" motto with gusto. No team lost more talent from 2017 to 2018 than the Raiders did. Mack made his third All-Pro team in Chicago. Amari Cooper averaged more than 80 yards a game after a midseason trade to Dallas. Michael Crabtree and Cordarrelle Patterson combined for over 1,000 yards from scrimmage with their new clubs. Denico Autry had nine sacks in a breakout year in Indianapolis. The list goes on.

But instead of having those players, the Raiders acquired three first-round picks and three later-round selections. They also avoided paying $51.3 million in average salary and handing out nearly $120 million in guarantees. Would they have been a better team last season with some of that escaped talent on their team? Almost assuredly. Would that have made them a contender? Probably not. With that in mind, from an analytical perspective, it makes plenty of sense to jettison that talent for more potential and flexibility down the road. Award-winning sense, apparently.

Still…

Take another look at that list of players traded for multiple

Table 1. Trading Stars for Draft Picks Pays Dividends

Player	Year	From	To	AV*	Best players drafted	AV*
Jay Cutler	2009	DEN	CHI	74	Demaryius Thomas, Eric Decker	133
Ricky Williams	2002	NO	MIA	56	Charles Grant, Jon Stinchcomb	130
Keyshawn Johnson	2000	NYJ	TB	37	John Abraham	58
Joey Galloway	2000	SEA	DAL	32	Shaun Alexander, Koren Robinson	113
Jeff George	1994	IND	ATL	21	Marvin Harrison	165
Herschel Walker	1989	DAL	MIN	23	Emmitt Smith, Darren Woodson	336
Fredd Young	1987	SEA	IND	19	Cortez Kennedy, Terry Wooden	197
Eric Dickerson	1987	LAR	IND	48	Cleveland Gary	85
Jim Everett	1986	HOU	LAR	77	Cris Dishman, Haywood Jeffries	137

AV with given team only.

2019 Raiders Schedule

Week	Opp.	Week	Opp.	Week	Opp.
1	DEN (Mon.)	7	at GB	13	at KC
2	KC	8	at HOU	14	TEN
3	at MIN	9	DET	15	JAX
4	at IND	10	LAC (Thu.)	16	at LAC
5	CHI (U.K.)	11	CIN	17	at DEN
6	BYE	12	at NYJ		

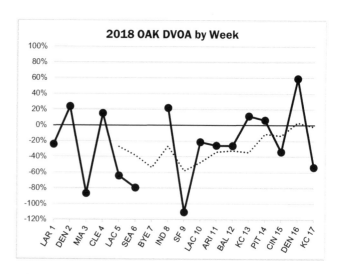

2018 OAK DVOA by Week

draft picks. It's not a bad list of players, but there's really not a Khalil Mack on it. Those nine players combined for four All-Pro nods and nine Pro Bowl appearances before being traded; Mack had two and three, respectively. The traded nine averaged an Approximate Value of 28 in the three years before they were traded, with none topping Eric Dickerson's 39. Mack's AV in his last three seasons in Oakland was 41. You can build a strong case that Mack is the best player of the bunch. When you look at the successful Trust the Process teams in other sports, such as the World Series-winning Astros and Cubs, you'll struggle to find many assets traded away that were as valuable as Mack was.

Mack is the sort of player you build a defense around. Admittedly, it's easier to swallow a $23.5 million-per-year contract when your quarterback is on a rookie deal, but the point of finding cost-effective deals is to be able to afford players like Mack. Trading away Cooper for a first-round draft pick makes loads of sense, and most of the other players Oakland opted not to re-sign in 2018 have already moved on to new teams or are still struggling to find employment in 2019. Mack's a different caliber of player, however, and it's unlikely that any player the Raiders get with all their assets will be a better player than Mack was. Edge rushers like Mack do not grow on trees, and that should be taken into account when considering the value of a trade.

The other major issue with the Raiders' analytics award was the timing. The Sloan Conference gave out their awards in early March, after the season but before the beginning of free agency or the draft. Acquiring a boatload of draft picks is great, but a future first-rounder doesn't catch touchdown passes, and cap space doesn't sack the quarterback. Acquiring these assets is only half the battle; teams need to have a good process in place to *use* them in order for these huge deals to pay off. And here's where Oakland's offseason begins to get puzzling.

On one hand, the payload of the Mack deal doesn't fully arrive until the 2020 season. Add in developmental time for the rookies drafted this year, and it would make sense to think of 2019 as Year 0 for the Las Vegas Raiders as opposed to Year 25 of the Oakland Raiders, Mark II. Continue to add young players through the draft, trading down when need be to stockpile assets. Spend one more year evaluating Derek Carr—is he the quarterback that will lead the Raiders back to the playoffs, or do they take advantage of the potential $16.5 million in cap savings from cutting Carr after 2019 and enter Vegas with someone like Tua Tagovailoa or Justin Herbert

under center? Gruden was signed to a ten-year deal; he has the job security to spend as much time as he needs tinkering and assembling until he has a team that can compete for the long term. The Raiders could have taken things slowly, and gradually built up a foundation of young, cheap players that could grow up together, gain chemistry, and peak in time for a contending season in two or three years.

On the other hand, the $75 million in cap space created by getting rid of Mack, Cooper, and the lot arrives now. That's a lot of extra room and money to quickly inject the team with veteran talent, launching the team from the doldrums up to a competitive level right away. Gruden has never been one to put too much stock in rookie starters; use those extra draft picks and that cap space to bring in experienced veterans to get the most out of your quarterback, inject some life into your defense, and propel yourself into the leaguewide conversation right away. Historically, more than 45 percent of Gruden's starters have been 30-somethings. That's how he builds his teams.

The Raiders did not choose between these two options. Instead, after bringing Mike Mayock in to run the front office, the Raiders hit the gas pedal, and chose option C: all of the above. They spent the most draft capital of any team in the league, using all three of their first-rounders and adding seven players in the first four rounds, all of whom should be contending for playing time in 2019. They also signed the most players in free agency, adding 22 new players to the mix; they could theoretically trot out a lineup consisting only of free-agent acquisitions. They handed out three of the largest 20 free-agent contracts, finishing second only to the Bills in cap space used in free agency. And they started the whole shebang by trading for Antonio Brown, arguably the best player to switch teams this offseason.

You can't accuse Gruden and company of doing anything by half-measures. With so many new bodies on the roster, we assume the first episode of *Hard Knocks* will be filled with getting-to-know-you games as players try to figure out just who the heck is in the locker room.

Oakland's offseason was dramatic. It was headline-grabbing. It was transformative. It was confusing and self-contradictory. The Raiders had so many assets this offseason they tried to both build for the future *and* create a competitive team right off the bat. That's crazy—and it might just be crazy enough to work. Most of the Raiders' moves make sense when considered individually; it's certainly a more talented bunch than last season's aging veterans and high-risk rookies. There are just a lot of question marks that start popping up when you try to look at the offseason as a whole and make all the moves make sense with one another. The Raiders are trying to serve two masters here, and that's a tough tightrope to walk.

The shadow of the Mack trade brings up questions for every move intended to win in 2019, as the Raiders would be better right now had they kept Mack on the franchise tag. The $85 million in guaranteed money shelled out brings up questions for every move intended to build the team over the long term, as these veterans are pretty much financially locked in to the team for the next two years, while the players drafted with all those extra picks won't really enter their prime until after that. The end result of the offseason should be a Raiders team that is more competitive and better all-around than Gruden's first year in charge. Yet questions remain as to how much better the team will be, how wisely they've used their resources, and whether or not it all meshes together with what seemed to be the long-term strategy when Mack, Cooper, and the rest left town last season.

Carr's performance will play a major role in figuring out the team's direction for 2020 and beyond. Carr's MVP candidacy in 2016 was overblown even at the time, but he was a legit top-10 quarterback that season, and the Raiders paid him as such. He has not looked the same since his back injury in early 2017, handling pressure extraordinarily poorly, looking timid when asked to throw downfield, and generally requiring everything around him to be working perfectly in order to look like an above-average quarterback. Carr's stats last year were the worst since his rookie season, though a lot of the blame can be placed on his dismal supporting cast. Oakland went out and invested a lot to give Carr more protection up front and an actual NFL-caliber fleet of receivers to work with in 2019, so this is a put-up or shut-up year for the young quarterback. A top-10 Carr means the Raiders can say that they always trusted him, which is why they signed so much talent this offseason. Anything else gives the Raiders leave to cut him next offseason, point to their multiple first-round picks, and say that they're building a new solid foundation. It's a convenient out either way.

Carr will have a much better chance to succeed now that Antonio Brown is in town. Any time you can trade two midround picks for one of the top five receivers in football, it's a no-brainer. Yes, last season was Brown's worst in years, the first time he dropped out of the top 10 in DYAR since 2012. No, he's not likely to put up the same numbers with Carr throwing him the ball that he did with Ben Roethlisberger. But the Raiders arguably didn't even have a No. 2 receiver after Cooper left town, and now they have one of the best No. 1 receivers in the game.

Heck, Brown's signing gives the Raiders *two* new top targets, as Tyrell Williams cited the Brown signing as one of the reasons he came to Oakland. That's worth far more than a couple of midround picks, even if Brown's very best years are probably behind him. Going from Jordy Nelson and Seth Roberts to Brown and Williams is a quantum leap in terms of talent at the wideout position.

It's not all sunshine and roses, however. Williams has been primarily a deep threat; his average target last season came 12.5 yards downfield, and that's actually lower than his career average. Brown's more of an all-around receiver, but his average target came 11.2 yards downfield last season. These are players designed for deep shots. Brown was targeted on 49 deep passes last season (16 or more yards through the air), and Williams added 19 more.

That has not been Derek Carr's game, to put it mildly. The Raiders only attempted 76 deep shots last season, the fewest in the league, while Nelson led the team last season with a 9.1-yard average depth of target. Carr had the second-lowest aDOT in the league last year and the fourth-lowest ALEX; he is not comfortable with throwing deep on a regular basis. The additions of Brown and Williams will hopefully entice Carr to throw deeper, or else some of the value gained by adding these players will be lost. The questions don't end there, though. If the Raiders wanted to put together the best receiving corps they could for 2019, why not re-sign Jared Cook? Oakland still has nearly $28 million in free salary-cap space as of writing; they could have beaten New Orleans' $8-million guaranteed offer if they had really wanted to. Yes, Cook is 32, but Brown turns 31 this year, so it's not like they're too concerned about an aging roster entering the Vegas years, and Cook had the higher DVOA despite playing in the worse offense…

No time for questions! No time for introspection—that's not the Raider way! To shore up the offensive line, the Raiders went out and brought in Trent Brown, arguably the best tackle on the market. That's a hugely needed upgrade as the Raiders had the worst tackles in the league last season, partially contributing to Carr's need to throw the ball away as quickly as possible. But, again, questions: why are the Raiders moving Brown back to the right side, after his breakout season on the left? And why are they paying a player who's never even made the Pro Bowl, much less an All-Pro team, more money than any other tackle in history?

So the Oakland Browns are each the highest-paid player at their position now, with Antonio pulling in $16.7 million per year and Trent bringing in $16.5 million. Even if you consider both players worth that much, the Raiders have to field a 53-man roster and there are some implications to having two players making that much money. And if you don't like that thought, remember, that's not us saying it: that's a direct quote from coach Gruden in 2018, explaining why Khalil Mack had to go. There were obviously other factors going into the Mack decision—for one, the two Browns wanted to play in Oakland, while Mack was actively holding out while pushing for a new contract—but Oakland could have had Mack on the franchise tag for $17.5 million this season, and Mack's actual cap hit in Chicago this year is under $12 million, less than either Brown. Again, the Raiders still have $28 million in cap space this year and bringing in the highest-priced players at multiple positions does not scream "building for the long term."[1] It's a case of last year's philosophy and this year's philosophy not fully lining up.

But, hey, adding the most talented players at their positions is the kind of big flashy signing that blots out those sorts of questions. Other offseason acquisitions don't shine quite so bright, even if they're all upgrades to what Oakland trotted out a year ago. Lamarcus Joyner and Brandon Marshall are big-time names to spruce up a moribund defense; never mind that both are coming off of off years. Vontaze Burfict and Richie Incognito are massive character risks—Burfict for his constant suspensions for violent play on the field, Incognito for an appalling record off of it. Those last two are the most confounding of all, considering how frequently Mayock stressed the importance of finding high-character guys in press interviews after the draft. The inconstant public stances make it feel like the Raiders are making moves first and justifying them later, rather than working out of a common playbook.

Don't think about that—more headlines! The Raiders became the third team this millennium to make three first-round picks; the perfect base for a long-term rebuilding project! They grabbed a much-needed force on the edge in Clelin Ferrell! (… an admitted reach, even by Oakland; later media reports said that the Raiders hoped to trade back and pick up Ferrell in the low teens but could not find a taker on draft day). The best running back in the class in Josh Jacobs! (… still a first-round running back, which is grounds for automatic revoking of any analytics kudos ever given). The top safety available, Johnathan Abram! (… OK, even we can't snark on that one; Abram's probably the best player the Raiders picked up in the first round and should be their best defensive back by the end of the year). This year's draft class is the foundation for years of future success, just after the high-priced free agents from this offseason see their contracts expire.

Every player mentioned here is an upgrade over what the Raiders had a year ago, make no mistake. Raiders fans should be far more optimistic about this year's signings, rather than trying to make the fading Jordy Nelson and Doug Martin a

thing to get excited about. Oakland has made so many moves, and were in such desperate need of everyone and anyone of any talent whatsoever that they could hardly help from being improved in 2019. Antonio (and, to a lesser extent, Trent) Brown should help significantly, and Oakland had a positive offensive DVOA in 2016 and 2017, so there should be some plexiglass rebound effect. Our projections have the Raiders with an average offense even without Carr returning to his 2016 form. It just feels so haphazardly done.

A successful NFL program is like a NASA launch—years of planning, carefully and painstakingly balancing components, leading to an organized ascent into the stratosphere. The Raiders feel more like a Kerbal Space Program launch, strapping 19 different rockets to a pod and flinging themselves upwards in a gigantic fireball. Yes, they're gaining altitude, but they're spinning wildly and half of those rockets are going to fall off at any moment unless someone can fix the guidance system mid-flight.

The Raiders are going to be one of the most fun teams to watch this season. They are a mess, but the best kind of mess—an improving, chaotic mash of big players and even bigger question marks. They're the perfect team for *Hard Knocks*; watching Gruden try to will shape and form onto this mass of new arrivals is going to be must-see TV.

Oakland should take a step forward this season. The pain they suffered through last season will not go unrewarded. It just isn't likely to get them out of the bottom quarter of the league; not right away, at any rate. There also doesn't seem to be a clear plan on how to take the next step forward, or the next and the next to avoid getting caught in a trap of long-term mediocrity. There's a long distance between winning offseason headlines and awards and actually winning games on the field. Gruden and company have yet to show us that they understand how to handle a long-term rebuilding project, and the future of the franchise remains in questionable hands.

Bryan Knowles

---

1 Technically, Odell Beckham's deal remains the largest for any wide receiver. However, because the Giants are paying for his signing bonus, Oakland's annual payment to Brown is higher than Cleveland's annual payment to Beckham.

2018 Raiders by Week

Wk	vs.	W-L	PF	PA	YDF	YDA	TO	Total	Off	Def	ST
1	LAR	L	13	33	395	365	-3	-25%	-15%	11%	2%
2	at DEN	L	19	20	373	385	+1	24%	31%	1%	-6%
3	at MIA	L	20	28	434	373	-2	-87%	-7%	71%	-9%
4	CLE	W	45	42	565	487	+2	15%	13%	-3%	-1%
5	at LAC	L	10	26	289	412	-2	-64%	-28%	27%	-9%
6	SEA	L	3	27	185	369	-1	-79%	-63%	10%	-7%
7	BYE										
8	IND	L	28	42	347	461	-1	22%	57%	31%	-4%
9	at SF	L	3	34	242	405	0	-111%	-51%	45%	-14%
10	LAC	L	6	20	317	335	0	-22%	-14%	7%	0%
11	at ARI	W	23	21	325	282	+2	-26%	0%	22%	-5%
12	at BAL	L	17	34	249	416	+1	-26%	1%	11%	-17%
13	KC	L	33	40	442	469	-2	12%	23%	16%	5%
14	PIT	W	24	21	354	340	0	7%	8%	1%	-1%
15	at CIN	L	16	30	297	294	-1	-34%	-40%	-9%	-3%
16	DEN	W	27	14	273	300	+2	59%	21%	-8%	31%
17	at KC	L	3	35	292	409	-3	-54%	-62%	4%	12%

Trends and Splits

	Offense	Rank	Defense	Rank
Total DVOA	-7.1%	25	12.3%	30
Unadjusted VOA	-9.5%	25	16.2%	31
Weighted Trend	-10.5%	25	9.6%	27
Variance	11.8%	29	4.4%	5
Average Opponent	-0.8%	12	6.2%	2
Passing	12.0%	17	28.3%	32
Rushing	-16.5%	29	-3.3%	22
First Down	-8.2%	22	0.2%	16
Second Down	-3.6%	20	9.4%	27
Third Down	-11.2%	24	39.1%	31
First Half	-8.1%	24	-5.3%	6
Second Half	-6.0%	21	30.0%	32
Red Zone	-11.5%	25	-4.9%	12
Late and Close	8.9%	10	39.3%	32

Five-Year Performance

Year	W-L	Pyth W	Est W	PF	PA	TO	Total	Rk	Off	Rk	Def	Rk	ST	Rk	Off AGL	Rk	Def AGL	Rk	Off Age	Rk	Def Age	Rk	ST Age	Rk
2014	3-13	3.1	4.8	253	452	-15	-27.4%	29	-19.4%	30	6.3%	26	-1.7%	18	26.1	11	77.5	32	26.5	22	27.7	4	26.2	11
2015	7-9	6.9	7.4	359	399	+1	0.1%	14	-1.3%	18	-1.5%	15	-0.1%	19	23.7	8	33.9	22	26.2	20	26.6	17	27.2	1
2016	12-4	8.8	8.9	416	385	+16	8.2%	10	12.2%	8	4.3%	22	0.3%	14	32.5	13	32.4	15	26.5	21	26.6	13	26.9	5
2017	6-10	6.0	7.7	301	373	-14	-6.6%	19	4.0%	13	10.3%	29	-0.2%	17	12.1	5	32.0	16	27.6	4	26.6	13	25.8	17
2018	4-12	3.7	4.7	290	467	-7	-21.0%	31	-7.1%	25	12.3%	30	-1.6%	22	41.5	17	40.2	21	27.6	9	27.1	6	26.7	4

2018 Performance Based on Most Common Personnel Groups

OAK Offense					OAK Offense vs. Opponents					OAK Defense					OAK Defense vs. Opponents			
Pers	Freq	Yds	DVOA	Run%	Pers	Freq	Yds	DVOA	Run%	Pers	Freq	Yds	DVOA	Pers	Freq	Yds	DVOA
11	68%	5.7	-0.3%	30%	Base	26%	5.3	-10.8%	58%	Base	25%	6.2	-1.8%	11	65%	6.9	18.6%
12	11%	5.5	23.5%	35%	Nickel	52%	5.8	5.8%	34%	Nickel	68%	6.7	17.6%	12	13%	7.2	12.6%
21	7%	7.9	17.0%	53%	Dime+	22%	5.5	3.0%	17%	Dime+	5%	9.7	50.5%	21	8%	6.4	2.7%
22	5%	2.4	-40.7%	84%	Goal Line	2%	0.5	-20.9%	80%	Goal Line	2%	0.8	-8.7%	13	4%	5.0	-17.9%
13	4%	4.7	-27.5%	56%										22	3%	4.7	14.0%

Strategic Tendencies

Run/Pass		Rk	Formation		Rk	Pass Rush		Rk	Secondary		Rk	Strategy		Rk
Runs, first half	38%	18	Form: Single Back	80%	17	Rush 3	9.1%	13	4 DB	25%	15	Play action	18%	30
Runs, first down	49%	15	Form: Empty Back	6%	25	Rush 4	73.8%	11	5 DB	68%	13	Avg Box (Off)	6.26	11
Runs, second-long	24%	26	Pers: 3+ WR	69%	14	Rush 5	11.9%	30	6+ DB	5%	18	Avg Box (Def)	6.17	20
Runs, power sit.	59%	16	Pers: 2+ TE/6+ OL	23%	16	Rush 6+	5.0%	17	CB by Sides	88%	7	Offensive Pace	32.07	24
Runs, behind 2H	28%	16	Pers: 6+ OL	2%	13	Int DL Sacks	46.2%	3	S/CB Cover Ratio	32%	9	Defensive Pace	31.22	18
Pass, ahead 2H	41%	27	Shotgun/Pistol	61%	20	Second Level Sacks	23.1%	16	DB Blitz	7%	19	Go for it on 4th	0.90	27

Oakland recovered only seven of 21 fumbles on offense and only three of 10 fumbles on defense. ❧ The Raiders offense had a huge gap between runs from shotgun (5.5 yards per carry, 1.4% DVOA) and runs with the quarterback under center (3.6, -27.6%). ❧ The Oakland defense had the league's smallest DVOA gap between performance with and without pressure. On the rare plays where the Raiders actually got pressure, they were the only team in the NFL to allow a positive DVOA (8.5%). But on plays without pressure, they allowed 35.5% DVOA, 12th in the league. ● Oakland ranked 30th in the NFL with just 31 percent of sacks coming from edge rushers. Tennessee and the Los Angeles Rams were lower. ● Oakland faced play-action on a league-leading 33 percent of pass plays; no other defense was above 30 percent. The Raiders were one of only two defenses to allow fewer yards per play to play-action passes (7.6 yards, 21.4% DVOA) compared to non-play-action passes (8.1 yards, 34.1% DVOA). ● Oakland tied for the league high with 34 dropped passes by opponents. This was 7.5 percent of passes; no other defense was higher than 6.2 percent. ● The Raiders allowed a league-high 6.7 average yards after the catch, including 11.7 average YAC on passes at or behind the line of scrimmage. Only one other defense, Seattle, was above 10.0. ● Oakland's defense ranked sixth in DVOA before halftime, then dead last after halftime.

Passing

Player	DYAR	DVOA	Plays	NtYds	Avg	YAC	C%	TD	Int
D.Carr	392	-1.0%	598	3734	6.2	5.2	69.8%	19	10
N.Peterman	-380	-85.1%	88	252	2.9	4.2	55.0%	1	7

Rushing

Player	DYAR	DVOA	Plays	Yds	Avg	TD	Fum	Suc
D.Martin	-27	-12.2%	172	725	4.2	4	3	53%
M.Lynch*	25	-2.3%	90	376	4.2	3	0	53%
J.Richard	-28	-20.3%	55	259	4.7	1	2	45%
D.Washington	-16	-19.6%	29	111	3.8	0	1	55%
D.Carr	8	-0.3%	13	57	4.4	1	0	--
I.Crowell	37	-1.9%	143	685	4.8	7	0	36%
N.Peterman	18	19.3%	10	50	5.0	1	0	--

Receiving

Player	DYAR	DVOA	Plays	Ctch	Yds	Y/C	YAC	TD	C%
J.Nelson*	130	5.7%	88	63	739	11.7	3.8	3	72%
S.Roberts*	86	4.7%	64	45	494	11.0	4.7	2	70%
A.Cooper*	67	13.2%	31	22	280	12.7	4.4	1	71%
M.Ateman	-38	-28.5%	31	15	154	10.3	2.1	1	48%
M.Bryant*	13	-6.7%	27	19	266	14.0	6.9	0	70%
B.LaFell*	48	26.9%	16	12	135	11.3	4.4	2	75%
D.Harris	-24	-63.5%	6	6	40	6.7	7.8	0	100%
A.Brown	191	1.7%	168	104	1297	12.5	4.7	15	62%
T.Williams	128	12.3%	65	41	653	15.9	4.8	5	63%
R.Grant	12	-9.8%	52	35	334	9.5	2.7	1	67%
J.Cook*	146	13.8%	101	68	896	13.2	5.0	6	67%
D.Carrier	-4	-12.4%	12	7	67	9.6	2.3	1	58%
L.Smith*	31	25.5%	11	10	73	7.3	5.5	3	91%
D.Waller	15	26.7%	6	6	75	12.5	9.3	0	100%
L.Willson	-28	-28.6%	19	13	87	6.7	4.5	0	68%
J.Richard	138	17.4%	81	68	607	8.9	7.3	0	84%
D.Martin	3	-11.7%	24	18	116	6.4	5.2	0	75%
M.Lynch*	-17	-28.5%	20	15	84	5.6	6.0	0	75%
K.Smith	-9	-31.9%	7	5	23	4.6	3.6	0	71%
I.Crowell	10	-6.8%	28	21	152	7.2	8.2	0	75%

Offensive Line

Player	Pos	Age	GS	Snaps	Pen	Sk	Pass	Run	Player	Pos	Age	GS	Snaps	Pen	Sk	Pass	Run
Rodney Hudson	C	30	16/16	1046	1	0.5	3	3	Denzelle Good	RG/RT	28	6/4	306	2	2.5	6	2
Kolton Miller	LT	24	16/16	1012	8	10.7	20	6	Jon Feliciano*	LG	27	13/4	227	4	1.5	3	2
Gabe Jackson	RG	28	13/13	859	5	4.0	7	1	Donald Penn*	RT	36	4/4	192	1	2.0	2	1
Brandon Parker	RT	24	15/12	780	11	10.7	20	1	Trenton Brown	LT	26	16/16	1089	9	2.0	7	3
Kelechi Osemele*	LG	30	11/11	739	5	2.2	8	7									

Year	Yards	ALY	Rank	Power	Rank	Stuff	Rank	2nd Lev	Rank	Open Field	Rank	Sacks	ASR	Rank	Press	Rank	F-Start	Cont.
2016	4.66	4.39	11	59%	23	17%	8	1.28	8	1.00	7	18	3.4%	1	17.7%	1	24	31
2017	4.14	4.17	11	62%	21	22%	22	1.17	14	0.73	16	24	4.6%	7	23.1%	3	18	26
2018	4.24	4.49	13	53%	31	18%	10	1.31	8	0.60	28	52	8.7%	25	28.3%	13	22	28

2018 ALY by direction:	Left End: 4.37 (17)	Left Tackle: 3.99 (19)	Mid/Guard: 4.79 (5)	Right Tackle: 3.82 (24)	Right End: 4.06 (17)

Tom Cable has been an NFL offensive line coach or head coach for 13 seasons now. He has never had an offensive line rank higher than 20th in adjusted sack rate. ● Even though Oakland tied for fifth in sacks allowed, Derek Carr wasn't charted with a coverage sack all season. Thirty-five of Oakland's sacks were blamed on blown blocks by charters; no other offense was above 30. Kolton Miller and Brandon Parker tied for the league lead in sacks allowed, with 10.7 each. Yes, both were rookies, and Parker won't be starting in 2019, but that's not an ideal start to either player's career. Miller will need to bounce back big-time if he's going to continue on the blind side. ● Trent Brown has ranked in the top 10 at his position in snaps per blown block in each of the past two years. His 108.9 snaps per blown block is a significant upgrade over Parker's 37.1. ❧ The newly-signed Richie Incognito will likely start at left guard. If he faces league discipline for his myriad off-field incidents, Denzelle Good would presumably start the season at the position. ❧ Gabe Jackson played most of 2018 with a torn pectoral, and then fractured his elbow before finally going on IR in December. The fact that he continued to play at a decently high level, the second-best lineman Oakland had last season, is a testament to his toughness, a reflection of his great run-blocking ability, and a condemnation of most of the rest of Oakland's line. ❧ Rodney Hudson has been among the top ten centers in snaps per blown blocks in each of the last three seasons. He has given up just one sack combined since 2016. There may not be a better pass-blocking center in all of football.

Defensive Front

Defensive Line	Age	Pos	G	Snaps	Plays	Overall TmPct	Rk	Stop	Dfts	BTkl	Runs	vs. Run St%	Rk	RuYd	Rk	Pass Rush Sack	Hit	Hur	Dsrpt
Johnathan Hankins	27	DT	15	573	36	5.0%	39	27	5	3	32	75%	41	2.2	40	0.0	2	5	0
P.J. Hall	24	DT	14	511	23	3.4%	71	21	6	2	19	89%	3	1.5	9	0.0	4	11	3
Maurice Hurst	24	DT	13	472	34	5.5%	32	26	8	1	24	71%	57	3.4	81	4.0	1	6	3
Clinton McDonald*	32	DT	15	419	31	4.3%	53	24	5	2	26	77%	33	3.0	72	2.0	0	5	0
Josh Mauro	28	DE	12	270	28	4.5%	--	22	12	0	27	78%	--	1.4	--	1.0	1	4	0

Edge Rushers	Age	Pos	G	Snaps	Plays	Overall TmPct	Rk	Stop	Dfts	BTkl	Runs	vs. Run St%	Rk	RuYd	Rk	Pass Rush Sack	Hit	Hur	Dsrpt
Arden Key	23	DE	16	644	30	3.9%	69	19	6	9	25	64%	70	3.4	77	1.0	12	28	1
Frostee Rucker*	36	DE	15	550	39	5.4%	34	29	7	6	35	77%	40	1.9	29	0.0	4	13	2

Linebackers	Age	Pos	G	Snaps	Plays	Overall TmPct	Rk	Stop	Dfts	BTkl	Runs	vs. Run St%	Rk	RuYd	Rk	Pass Rush Sack	Hit	Hur	Tgts	vs. Pass Suc%	Rk	AdjYd	Rk	PD	Int
Tahir Whitehead	29	OLB	16	1025	130	17.0%	11	62	22	11	84	56%	54	4.3	61	0.0	1	4	32	38%	68	9.8	76	5	1
Marquel Lee	24	MLB	16	448	61	8.0%	71	37	7	5	47	64%	27	2.7	8	0.0	3	6	15	53%	30	5.1	15	3	0
Nicholas Morrow	24	OLB	16	416	39	5.1%	83	21	10	8	27	52%	71	6.2	87	1.0	2	4	17	53%	31	8.8	71	3	0
Jason Cabinda	23	MLB	10	164	21	4.4%	--	12	0	1	18	61%	--	5.8	--	0.0	1	2	4	75%	--	5.5	--	0	0
Brandon Marshall	30	ILB	11	468	43	7.6%	73	17	5	3	27	52%	71	4.7	74	0.0	0	3	16	63%	5	4.4	6	1	0
Vontaze Burfict	29	OLB	7	298	36	9.4%	61	18	4	9	23	52%	68	3.2	19	0.0	0	0	13	38%	--	9.2	--	3	0

Year	Yards	ALY	Rank	Power	Rank	Stuff	Rank	2nd Level	Rank	Open Field	Rank	Sacks	ASR	Rank	Press	Rank
2016	4.52	4.43	23	63%	17	16%	26	1.13	15	0.98	28	25	4.9%	30	26.9%	17
2017	4.10	4.26	22	67%	22	19%	24	1.11	15	0.68	14	31	6.1%	23	27.8%	28
2018	4.76	4.63	25	65%	16	17%	20	1.29	22	1.05	25	13	3.5%	32	22.0%	32

2018 ALY by direction:	Left End: 3.46 (8)	Left Tackle: 4.73 (23)	Mid/Guard: 4.69 (23)	Right Tackle: 4.73 (25)	Right End: 5.53 (30)

Clemson's Clelin Ferrell would be an instant starter even if Oakland had gotten more than 13 sacks in 2018. He still has some mechanical issues and awkward moves, but the optimist's view is that those can be straightened out. SackSEER is more pessimistic, rating Ferrell as an average prospect instead of a high first-rounder because of mediocre college production and a poor 3-cone time. ❧ While the Raiders did finish dead last in sacks and pressure rate last season, Arden Key's 27.5 pressures kept him in the top 50 overall, ahead of five other teams' leaders in pressures. He had more than half of Oakland's pressures by himself. ❧ Fourth-round pick Maxx Crosby (Eastern Michigan) is an intriguing prospect, with great athleticism and an aggressive pass-rushing style. He needs to spend a year or two in the weight room to get up to NFL size, but there's potential there to become the starting end across from Ferrell, perhaps in 2020. ❧ Maurice Hurst tumbled down draft boards last season after being diagnosed with a heart condition. So far, so good: Hurst played 472 quality snaps for Oakland with nary an issue. Moving from nose tackle to the 3-technique has helped him, too. ❧ The Raiders re-signed Johnathan Hankins to plug holes as the nose tackle. He may rotate some with Justin Ellis, who missed ten games with sprained ligaments in his foot last season. ❧ From 2014 to 2016, Brandon Marshall was a very good off-ball linebacker. He has struggled with injuries over the past couple seasons but managed a top-five success rate in pass coverage last year (albeit with a small sample size). Even 70 percent of Marshall's prime is better than anyone Oakland trotted out there last year. ❧ It's not a surprise that Paul Guenther brought Vontaze Burfict in thanks to their Cincinnati connections. Burfict hasn't played a full season since 2013, missing 10 games with suspensions and 27 more with injuries. The NFL offices in charge of player safety presumably have a picture of Burfict on their dartboard; his violent style is precisely what the league is trying to legislate out of the game. ❧ Tahir Whitehead played 99.7 percent of Oakland's defensive snaps last season. He may not even hit half that in 2019.

Defensive Secondary

Secondary	Age	Pos	G	Snaps	Plays	TmPct	Rk	Stop	Dfts	BTkl	vs. Run					vs. Pass									
											Runs	St%	Rk	RuYd	Rk	Tgts	Tgt%	Rk	Dist	Suc%	Rk	AdjYd	Rk	PD	Int
Marcus Gilchrist*	31	FS	16	871	62	8.1%	55	20	10	8	23	35%	52	10.2	66	46	14.6%	68	12.6	52%	31	6.8	29	6	3
Gareon Conley	24	CB	15	679	52	7.3%	60	24	11	5	10	20%	73	9.8	71	42	17.0%	25	12.2	60%	11	9.5	71	15	3
Rashaan Melvin*	30	CB	14	604	65	9.7%	24	24	8	4	17	59%	12	3.7	9	67	30.6%	79	11.0	45%	69	8.9	67	9	1
Karl Joseph	26	SS	13	509	46	7.4%	58	16	4	8	33	36%	47	8.0	49	11	6.0%	13	13.9	36%	70	14.5	74	2	1
Daryl Worley	24	CB	11	505	40	7.6%	56	15	9	3	11	36%	51	6.2	34	36	19.6%	48	12.1	47%	57	8.1	51	7	1
Erik Harris	29	SS	16	433	49	6.4%	67	20	11	4	20	45%	31	5.2	15	24	15.3%	71	14.8	71%	2	5.3	8	7	2
Reggie Nelson*	36	FS	11	370	27	5.1%	--	7	3	8	12	33%	--	8.5	--	14	10.4%	--	17.6	29%	--	13.4	--	2	2
Leon Hall*	35	CB	10	366	28	5.9%	--	14	5	4	11	36%	--	5.2	--	17	12.8%	--	6.1	59%	--	9.7	--	3	0
Nick Nelson	23	CB	10	311	18	3.8%	--	6	2	3	9	44%	--	7.1	--	24	21.3%	--	14.8	54%	--	9.0	--	1	0
Curtis Riley	27	FS	16	1048	78	9.3%	46	13	8	22	24	8%	76	13.2	76	20	4.7%	7	15.0	50%	36	8.9	58	5	4
Lamarcus Joyner	29	FS	15	911	81	11.1%	27	19	8	7	36	22%	64	11.5	72	22	5.7%	12	12.6	55%	26	9.9	63	3	1
Jordan Richards	26	SS	15	428	40	5.1%	72	19	1	7	22	50%	21	5.1	14	20	10.7%	53	7.2	45%	52	7.9	47	3	0

Year	Pass D Rank	vs. #1 WR	Rk	vs. #2 WR	Rk	vs. Other WR	Rk	WR Wide	Rk	WR Slot	Rk	vs. TE	Rk	vs. RB	Rk
2016	25	-17.0%	4	5.0%	20	6.0%	20	-0.8%	18	-4.1%	10	7.7%	23	9.8%	23
2017	30	22.3%	30	14.9%	24	25.8%	29	15.2%	29	28.0%	30	0.1%	16	13.9%	27
2018	32	-27.0%	2	-5.3%	13	27.8%	30	-16.0%	5	0.1%	17	39.7%	32	7.2%	20

Oakland had the worst pass defense in football last season, but don't blame it on the starting corners. Oakland ranked second in the league against No. 1 receivers with a -27.0% DVOA. Credit most of that to Gareon Conley. He missed most of his rookie year with injuries, but came back strong in his sophomore season. He just missed the top 10 in success rate at 60 percent. Conley was the only Oakland corner to finish in the top 50 in success rate. Rashaan Melvin was the worst, but he's gone. Daryl Worley wasn't far behind him, and he has to worry about losing his job to 2018 fourth-round pick Nick Nelson. Neither player was great, but at least Nelson put up a success rate above 50 percent. Second-round pick Trayvon Mullen (Clemson) lacks top-level agility, but he's a big, physical, disruptive corner. He could jump Nelson and Worley to start right away on the outside, leaving free-agent pickup Nevin Lawson as the nickel corner. Don't count out fourth-round pick Isaiah Johnson (Houston) from the competition, either. He probably needs another year or two to develop, as he's a recent convert from wide receiver, but early returns from the position switch have been very promising. Oakland's secondary was really lacking any sort of playmaker, so free agent Lamarcus Joyner should be a major help. He had somewhat of a down year in 2018, but was great in coverage as a free safety and nickel corner the two years prior. The other safety spot will likely go to first-round pick Jonathan Abram (Mississippi State). All you really need to know about Abram's style is that he was once ejected for targeting a teammate in a spring practice game; he has an aggressive attitude that borders on reckless. He's not just a whirling dervish of headshots though; he's fantastic at diagnosing plays and shutting them down with his speed. With a little more technique and restraint, he'll become a great all-purpose safety.

Special Teams

Year	DVOA	Rank	FG/XP	Rank	Net Kick	Rank	Kick Ret	Rank	Net Punt	Rank	Punt Ret	Rank	Hidden	Rank
2016	0.3%	14	-1.6	19	5.3	6	-1.4	15	-5.5	24	4.9	7	13.2	2
2017	-0.2%	17	-4.3	23	2.2	13	4.7	7	4.8	10	-8.6	31	-3.8	18
2018	-1.6%	22	2.8	12	-4.4	27	0.1	12	-12.0	32	5.3	6	2.2	11

Fourth time was the charm for the Raiders at kicker last season. UDFA Eddy Pineiro went on injured reserve before the season, and veteran Mike Nugent joined him there after just three weeks. Matt McCrane was a disaster, with a field goal value of -6.2 points after missing four field goals in three weeks. Fortunately, Daniel Carlson was there to right the ship, after he himself was cut for a disastrous performance in Minnesota. Kickers, man. Oakland surprisingly cut punter Marquette King and drafted Johnny Townsend in the fifth round. This did not work out at all; while King got hurt and missed most of 2018, Townsend was the worst punter in football in both gross (-8.6 points) and net (-12.0 points) punting value. After leading the NCAA in gross punting average, Townsend was second-to-last in the NFL last season. Punters, man. Dwayne Harris was much more effective as a punt returner (9.2 points of estimated field position) than a kickoff returner (0.1 points). Oakland may want to consider someone like Nick Nelson on kickoffs; he was a very good returner at Wisconsin.

Philadelphia Eagles

2018 record: 9-7	**Total DVOA:** -0.1% (16th)	**2019 Mean Projection:** 9.2 wins	**On the Clock (0-4):** 5%
Pythagorean Wins: 8.5 (13th)	**Offense:** -0.3% (16th)	**Postseason Odds:** 55.2%	**Mediocrity (5-7):** 21%
Snap-Weighted Age: 27.4 (3rd)	**Defense:** 0.0% (15th)	**Super Bowl Odds:** 9.8%	**Playoff Contender (8-10):** 41%
Average Opponent: -0.2% (15th)	**Special Teams:** 0.2% (15th)	**Proj. Avg. Opponent:** -4.2% (30th)	**Super Bowl Contender (11+):** 33%

2018: Philadelphia fights off offensive regression and defensive injuries to return to the postseason.

2019: Strong potential to rebound on both sides of the ball makes Philly a Super Bowl contender once again.

Among the 18 Super Bowl champions that preceded the 2017 Philadelphia Eagles, eight missed the playoffs the following season. If the New England Patriots, who hold a 4-1 record in returning to the playoffs, are excluded from the equation, then seven of 13 Super Bowl champions missed the postseason the following year. To drive the point home even further, only two non-Patriots teams in that span won a playoff game following their Super Bowl run.

While we generally expect good teams to stay good, the randomness of the sport lends itself to extreme swings in fortune from year to year, be that through injuries, situational play, turnovers, close-game wins and losses, or otherwise. It is tougher to stay at the height of competition in the NFL than intuition may suggest, and bringing home the Lombardi trophy is not a golden ticket to future success.

That is why the 2018 Eagles season was less of a disappointment than it may appear on the surface. Their 9-7 record was lackluster compared to how spectacular the previous 13-3 season had been, but the Eagles made the playoffs and won a playoff game. That they made it to January already made them more impressive than half of the recent Super Bowl champions who came before them, and their win over the Chicago Bears in the wild-card round put them in rare company. Sure, they failed to secure back-to-back titles, but the Eagles battled through post-Super Bowl hangover about as well as they could have reasonably been expected to.

In the Eagles' case, injury luck was a primary cause for the swing in success. They finished with the 13th-fewest adjusted games lost (53.5) due to injury during their 2017 Super Bowl season. That is not a supremely fortunate year, especially considering that quarterback Carson Wentz tore his ACL down the stretch, but they fared better than more than half the league. In 2018, however, they finished with 118.5 adjusted games lost, most in the league. The 65.0-game difference year over year was the second-largest increase in AGL behind the Jacksonville Jaguars at 66.3. Among other teams to rank in the bottom five in AGL or year-over-year difference in AGL, only the Eagles and the Indianapolis Colts made the playoffs.

The defense in particular was ravaged by a lengthy injury report every week. The Eagles ranked third in adjusted games lost across the defensive line at 25.7. Defensive tackle Timmy Jernigan (back) missed the first three-fourths of the season and defensive end Derek Barnett (rotator cuff) did not see action following Week 7. Both players were supposed to be staples up front.

Likewise, the secondary was constantly in disarray. Rodney McLeod, who allowed the Eagles to play single-high coverages far better than any other safety on the roster, tore his ACL in Week 3. Ronald Darby (foot), one of the best all-around cornerbacks in the league, and fellow starting corner Jalen Mills (ACL) also went down with season-ending injuries in Weeks 9 and 10, respectively. In turn, defensive coordinator Jim Schwartz had to field a secondary that gave significant snaps to washed-up safety Corey Graham, cornerback and emergency safety Avonte Maddox, and depth cornerbacks Rasul Douglas and Cre'Von LeBlanc. Each of these players saw the field for at least 50 percent of defensive snaps in games they were active. LeBlanc, cut by Detroit midseason, was starting in Philadelphia by Week 13. It was as patchwork as a secondary could get.

And yet, Schwartz managed to maintain a respectable defense despite the slew of injuries that ravaged his starting lineup. The absence of Jernigan and Barnett along the defensive line forced Schwartz to adapt the way he aligns his fronts. With two starters out, Schwartz had to bend the front to what he had on hand. Star defensive tackle Fletcher Cox mostly remained in his normal role, and defensive tackle Haloti Ngata slotted next to him as a 1-technique for about 35 percent of the team's snaps, but what the Eagles did with the rest of the front was unique.

Schwartz was willing to move Michael Bennett, and to a lesser extent Brandon Graham, inside and outside of the tackles. He often looked to slot one of them inside with Cox, while the other played outside with veteran defensive end Chris Long on the opposite end. Of course, some clear run-heavy situations did not call for it, but when the freedom was there, Schwartz took the liberty of putting his best four players on the field and letting them figure it out. The malleable front was Schwartz's answer to maintaining a functional pass rush without the typical tools to do so. Despite the injuries to two starters, the Eagles still managed a 29.7 percent pressure rate, good for a middle-of-the-pack ranking of 19th. Not great, but better than most defensive lines would fare with two starters missing for most of the year.

On the back end, Maddox and Douglas played better than expected, even if not exceptional. Maddox granted Schwartz a player with cornerback/safety flexibility. He could be a nickel corner on one play, then play a two-deep shell on the next. Having McLeod's true centerfielder prowess in the lineup

2019 Eagles Schedule

Week	Opp.	Week	Opp.	Week	Opp.
1	WAS	7	at DAL	13	at MIA
2	at ATL	8	at BUF	14	NYG (Mon.)
3	DET	9	CHI	15	at WAS
4	at GB (Thu.)	10	BYE	16	DAL
5	NYJ	11	NE	17	at NYG
6	at MIN	12	SEA		

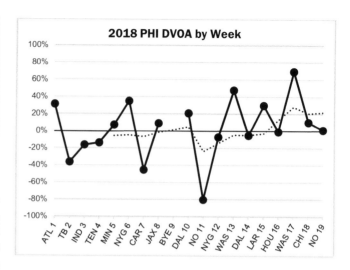

2018 PHI DVOA by Week

would have been better, but in his absence, Schwartz made do with a different, more versatile player in Maddox. Douglas, on the other hand, was not overtly impressive, but he held his own for a second-year player who was not supposed to be starting. His ability to work the sideline and match up with bigger, stronger receivers was a plus, and he proved himself to be a fiery and effective run defender on the perimeter.

Not only do the defense's injuries help explain why they fell from elite status last season, but they also suggest the Eagles can return to dominance come 2019. Assuming the Eagles do not suffer catastrophic injury luck again, they are poised to be a top-10 defense. Getting back a good single-high safety in McLeod, a top-tier cover corner in Darby, and a couple of starters on the defensive line is the perfect recipe for Philadelphia to find its footing on defense again.

There are a couple roadblocks they need to clear to earn their status among the league's best again, however. For one, the Eagles are now without Bennett (traded to Patriots) and Long (retired), two primary contributors up front. Youngsters Josh Sweat and Shareef Miller are waiting in the wings, and the team brought back Vinny Curry after he spent one season with the Buccaneers, but it would be a stretch to say right now that any of those players will match Long's production, much less Bennett's. The burden falls on Barnett to continue the development he showed before injuring his rotator cuff last season.

In similar fashion, someone in the cornerback room will have to step up across from Darby. Douglas was fine as a bench player thrust into the starting lineup but did not appear to be a Week 1 starter. Mills is in similar standing and was arguably worse than Douglas despite starting over him. The hope is that 2017 second-round pick Sidney Jones can finally develop and finish a season with his health intact, but that is wishful thinking. Maybe the return of McLeod at safety shores this issue up by proximity, but one has to imagine Schwartz is looking for better individual play across from Darby.

The real story of Philadelphia's upcoming season is not the defense, though. Many fans and analysts trust Schwartz as a top defensive mind, the team made a number of solid additions (including linebacker Zach Brown and safety Andrew Sendejo), and injury fortune will likely swing in their favor. Positive regression is more a matter of "how much" than "if." It is the Eagles offense, particularly Carson Wentz, that shoulders most of the pressure heading into 2019.

Philadelphia's 2018 offense was not up to the standard many expected of them. In 2017, they ranked eighth in offensive DVOA and Wentz, in just his second season, was com-

peting with Tom Brady for the MVP award. The offense was explosive, efficient, and painfully difficult for defenses to deal with on third down and in the red zone. With such a young quarterback at the helm and a creative offensive staff on hand, the Eagles seemed to be equipped for sustained success.

The offense tumbled down to mediocrity in 2018, and that decline could not be as easily explained away by injury the way the defense's could. Losing running backs Jay Ajayi and Darren Sproles for most of the year certainly did not help, nor did losing deep threat wide receiver Mike Wallace in Week 2. However, considering they were almost completely healthy at offensive line and tight end—especially important as the most tight end-oriented team in the league—it was not as though the offense was completely ravaged. They were mostly healthy in all the right areas until Wentz suffered a stress fracture in his back late in the season.

In terms of calling an offense the "right" way, the Eagles also did well. Though they lost offensive coordinator Frank Reich to the Colts and quarterback coach John DeFilippo to the Vikings last offseason, head coach Doug Pederson and Co. maintained a sound, smart offensive strategy that consistently played to the way analytics suggest an offense should be called. Namely, the Eagles were a shotgun offense with liberal use of play-action and a keen understanding of when to run the ball (read: not much and not too often on second-and-long). They were also hyper aggressive on fourth down and were more than willing to take necessary risks.

Moreover, Pederson consistently did his best to craft the offense to fit the personnel he had on hand. The initial plan was to sport a balanced 11- and 12-personnel offense, with Wallace taking the top off the defense out of 11 and rookie tight end Dallas Goedert serving as a pseudo receiver out of 12. With Wallace's early injury, though, the Eagles learned their 11-personnel approach was not going to work. Nelson Agholor was more of a YAC-oriented underneath threat in place of Wallace's deep threat. Agholor's average yards after the catch went from 4.9 in 2017 to 5.5 in 2018, but his YAC+, representing his YAC compared to expectation on those passes, stayed the same at -0.2. And Agholor struggled when he had more responsibility, particularly early in the year with -33.1% receiving DVOA through Week 9.

In response, the Eagles shifted over the year to be more of a 12-personnel team as Goedert grew more comfortable. Only Houston, by a handful of plays, used more 12 personnel than the Eagles did in 2018. The offense as a whole became more controlled and reliant on getting the ball out quicker, resulting in Wentz's average depth of target dropping from 10.4 yards in 2017 to just 8.2 yards last season.

In an attempt to open the offense back up, the Eagles traded for Lions receiver Golden Tate at the deadline. The thinking was that if Tate could assume Agholor's role as the YAC player, then Agholor might have been able to move to a role where space could be opened up for him to win down the field. In theory, the offense would have more options and personnel groupings to toy with. Unfortunately, Tate did not find much success in Philadelphia. He was less effective in the short-yardage YAC department than they had hoped and he provided little else beyond that, which was not the case when he was in Detroit. With Ertz, Agholor, and Jordan Matthews already taking up snaps from the slot, the Eagles were left with an abundance of slot threats with little vertical presence to open them up. The lackluster move for Tate was just one of many things that did not swing Philly's way in 2018.

Against their best efforts to call the offense properly and craft it to their personnel, the breaks just did not favor them. They saw major dips in red zone effectiveness, turnover differential, and third-down conversion rates, the former two of which tend to be volatile year to year. The regression back to the mean was not necessarily surprising considering the volatility of those statistics, but the predictability of regression did not soften the blow. That regression, combined with an offense that was forced to play with more short passes and fewer explosive plays, resulted in a disappointing, even if functional, unit.

The down year served to further complicate the value of Wentz. The second overall pick in 2016, Wentz put together a solid rookie season before erupting for a near-MVP campaign in his second year in 2017. That season was buoyed in part by an unsustainable touchdown rate and drives regularly starting in favorable field position, but he clearly made strides in his mechanics, accuracy, and overall game sense. He was far from complete but proved what the peak of his skill set looks like. With an ACL tear late in the year, however, Wentz did not get to finish the season, and backup quarterback Nick Foles went on to lead the team to a Super Bowl victory. Of course, Foles' surprising success sparked a conversation: how impressive was Wentz, really, if Foles could pull off such a feat in his place?

Wentz, on film, silenced that conversation in 2018. He blossomed into a more complete and controlled quarterback, proving to be as efficient as he could be explosive. Whereas Wentz had previously been someone who relied on broken plays and designed deep shots, his third season in the pros showed a quarterback who could pick apart defenses in the quick game, play a more patient style of offense, and stand strong in the pocket more consistently instead of bailing to scramble. As the cherry on top, Wentz further cleaned up his mechanics, displaying better ease of motion and platform adaptability than he had before. In turn, he was more accurate from all platforms and to all areas of the field than he had been even

during his MVP-caliber season. By every measure of the eye test, Wentz was a better quarterback than the one who led the Eagles to an 11-2 record before his injury in 2017.

And yet, for all of Wentz's progress, the offense was not better due to the aforementioned regression of the unit at large. It was an odd case of a near-MVP quarterback coming off a torn ACL, returning from injury a better player than before, and the offense still getting worse. As if the offense's dip in production was not enough to complicate Wentz's story to this point, the stress fracture he suffered at the end of the season only added to the concern that he is injury-prone, a label Wentz has battled dating back to his college days at North Dakota State. Foles departing in free agency to sign with the Jacksonville Jaguars heightens the fear of another Wentz injury even further.

Now Wentz is heading into Year 4 with back-to-back season-ending injuries and is coming off a season in which his subjective progress didn't translate into objective progress for the team. With the way quarterback salaries are trending, Wentz's mixed circumstances and success to this point make this upcoming season sort of a tipping point for how comfortable the Eagles should be about paying him the going rate. They paid him handsomely this offseason with a four-year, $128-million extension, giving him a $32-million average annual salary, just lower than Russell Wilson's new deal. In terms of talent and development, Wentz clears the bar, but he will need to prove he can return the offense to glory and remain healthy while doing it.

The good news is the Eagles are giving Wentz everything he needs to prove himself. General manager Howie Roseman spent the team's first three draft picks on offensive players: offensive tackle Andre Dillard (Washington State), running back Miles Sanders (Penn State), and wide receiver J.J. Arcega-Whiteside (Stanford). Dillard, if nothing else, will be a strong swing tackle this year before replacing Jason Peters in 2020. Sanders should slot in immediately to a prominent role as a receiving and change-of-pace back. Arcega-Whiteside is suited more to be a role player than a starter right away, but his Mike Evans-lite play style should serve well to boost the Eagles' red zone production back up.

Philadelphia also traded for running back Jordan Howard from the Bears and signed fan-favorite wide receiver DeSean Jackson. Howard can be the downhill back to complement Sanders' more slippery running style, while Jackson will give Pederson the deep threat he wanted last season in Wallace.

Assuming Pederson has not lost his touch as a forward thinker, the Eagles' offense is equipped to be one of the most versatile, creative units in the league. They will be able to flow between 10, 11, and 12 personnel with high-end players across the board out of all three sets, while they also can mix up their rushing attack with Howard and Sanders. So many of the skill players, particularly Ertz and Goedert, also have the flexibility to play from a number of alignments, lending to even more creativity within each personnel set. Unless right guard Brandon Brooks hits a roadblock in his return from a torn Achilles, it's tough to find a spot where the Eagles' offensive line falls short. Even the line's weak link, Isaac Seumalo, has been good enough for the Eagles to sign him to a three-year extension this offseason.

The potential for Philadelphia to rebound on both sides of the ball coincides well with how weak the rest of the NFC East is. The Eagles only slightly edge out the Dallas Cowboys as top dog in our division projections, but the New York Giants and Washington Redskins trail well behind. It is a two-horse race for the NFC East title, and the Eagles have a hair more firepower and coaching prowess to give them the upper hand.

The Eagles handled the offseason as well as they could have.

They understood the defense's issue was not talent, but health, and instead chose to dump most of their resources into an offense searching for the final component to get them back on track. As they return key contributors on defense and add new ones to the offense, they are positioned to look more like the team that brought home the organization's first Lombardi Trophy than the one that narrowly skidded into last year's playoffs.

Derrik Klassen

2018 Eagles Stats by Week

Wk	vs.	W-L	PF	PA	YDF	YDA	TO	Total	Off	Def	ST
1	ATL	W	18	12	232	299	-1	31%	-28%	-60%	-1%
2	at TB	L	21	27	412	436	0	-36%	-3%	21%	-12%
3	IND	W	20	16	379	209	-2	-16%	-21%	-22%	-18%
4	at TEN	L	23	26	432	397	0	-14%	-7%	13%	6%
5	MIN	L	21	23	364	375	-1	7%	19%	15%	3%
6	at NYG	W	34	13	379	401	+1	35%	12%	-18%	5%
7	CAR	L	17	21	342	371	-1	-46%	-15%	24%	-7%
8	at JAX	W	24	18	395	335	-1	9%	26%	13%	-3%
9	BYE										
10	DAL	L	20	27	421	410	-1	21%	28%	18%	10%
11	at NO	L	7	48	196	546	-3	-80%	-40%	38%	-2%
12	NYG	W	25	22	341	402	+1	-7%	11%	12%	-6%
13	WAS	W	28	13	436	235	0	48%	1%	-36%	11%
14	at DAL	L	23	29	256	576	+2	-5%	-1%	8%	4%
15	at LAR	W	30	23	381	407	+2	30%	4%	-17%	10%
16	HOU	W	32	30	519	371	-2	-1%	4%	5%	0%
17	at WAS	W	24	0	360	89	0	69%	9%	-55%	5%
18	at CHI	W	16	15	300	356	-2	10%	4%	-3%	4%
19	at NO	L	14	20	250	420	-1	1%	-10%	-11%	0%

Trends and Splits

	Offense	Rank	Defense	Rank
Total DVOA	-0.3%	16	0.0%	15
Unadjusted VOA	0.8%	16	1.7%	18
Weighted Trend	3.7%	14	2.9%	18
Variance	3.5%	3	8.3%	30
Average Opponent	0.6%	20	-0.8%	15
Passing	18.0%	11	6.7%	15
Rushing	-13.6%	27	-12.3%	9
First Down	-12.5%	26	1.1%	17
Second Down	10.4%	8	-1.6%	15
Third Down	6.3%	15	0.4%	20
First Half	-8.3%	25	0.6%	16
Second Half	7.2%	11	-0.6%	18
Red Zone	-10.2%	22	-20.0%	6
Late and Close	8.3%	11	-7.6%	12

Five-Year Performance

Year	W-L	Pyth W	Est W	PF	PA	TO	Total	Rk	Off	Rk	Def	Rk	ST	Rk	Off AGL	Rk	Def AGL	Rk	Off Age	Rk	Def Age	Rk	ST Age	Rk
2014	10-6	9.7	9.7	474	400	-8	12.8%	7	1.1%	13	-3.3%	10	8.3%	1	32.2	18	16.4	2	27.2	11	26.9	13	26.9	1
2015	7-9	6.7	6.8	377	430	-5	-11.2%	22	-10.1%	26	3.0%	17	1.9%	10	23.7	10	28.3	17	27.2	11	26.7	15	26.9	2
2016	7-9	9	9.9	367	331	+6	14.4%	5	-5.5%	20	-12.4%	4	7.5%	2	20.6	3	17.8	5	27.0	11	26.9	9	27.0	3
2017	13-3	12.0	11.1	457	295	+11	23.4%	5	10.1%	8	-12.3%	5	0.9%	16	28.5	12	25.0	11	27.1	12	26.9	9	26.4	7
2018	9-7	8.5	8.0	367	348	-9	-0.1%	16	-0.3%	16	0.0%	15	0.2%	15	47.2	22	71.3	31	27.9	5	27.6	3	25.5	26

2018 Performance Based on Most Common Personnel Groups

PHI Offense					PHI Offense vs. Opponents					PHI Defense				PHI Defense vs. Opponents			
Pers	Freq	Yds	DVOA	Run%	Pers	Freq	Yds	DVOA	Run%	Pers	Freq	Yds	DVOA	Pers	Freq	Yds	DVOA
11	55%	5.9	0.6%	34%	Base	17%	5.4	15.6%	46%	Base	18%	6.4	0.0%	11	70%	6.1	4.0%
12	36%	5.8	14.5%	35%	Nickel	81%	5.8	1.0%	35%	Nickel	61%	6.1	2.3%	12	16%	5.4	-9.9%
13	5%	6.0	34.6%	52%	Dime+	6%	6.8	34.7%	9%	Dime+	19%	5.3	-5.3%	21	6%	6.7	6.0%
612	1%	2.9	-39.5%	64%	Goal Line	0%	0.5	-2.2%	0%	Goal Line	1%	0.3	-16.6%	13	2%	3.6	-68.5%
611	1%	1.9	-63.3%	75%						Big	1%	4.3	-25.5%	10	1%	2.0	-145.5%
														20	1%	8.0	73.8%
														22	1%	10.0	108.5%

Strategic Tendencies

Run/Pass		Rk	Formation		Rk	Pass Rush		Rk	Secondary		Rk	Strategy		Rk
Runs, first half	35%	26	Form: Single Back	92%	1	Rush 3	3.1%	26	4 DB	18%	25	Play action	32%	3
Runs, first down	41%	26	Form: Empty Back	7%	22	Rush 4	79.6%	2	5 DB	61%	17	Avg Box (Off)	6.15	22
Runs, second-long	29%	20	Pers: 3+ WR	56%	31	Rush 5	10.0%	32	6+ DB	19%	10	Avg Box (Def)	6.16	21
Runs, power sit.	57%	18	Pers: 2+ TE/6+ OL	43%	1	Rush 6+	7.1%	8	CB by Sides	88%	5	Offensive Pace	32.69	30
Runs, behind 2H	30%	8	Pers: 6+ OL	2%	14	Int DL Sacks	31.8%	11	S/CB Cover Ratio	19%	31	Defensive Pace	30.88	14
Pass, ahead 2H	57%	4	Shotgun/Pistol	79%	5	Second Level Sacks	17.0%	27	DB Blitz	7%	21	Go for it on 4th	1.96	4

With the arrival of Dallas Goedert, the Eagles went from around league average to the No. 1 team in frequency of two-tight end sets. Philadelphia threw 36 percent of passes to tight ends when no other team was above 31 percent. ✎ Both of the last two seasons, Philadelphia has used more play-action on third down than any other offense. Last year, they used it 11.2 percent of the time; no other offense was above 7.3 percent. The Eagles also led the league by using play-action on 39.3 percent of passes on second down. But on first down (39.0 percent) they were close to the league average. Miami and Philadelphia were the only two teams to use play-action at a higher rate on second down than on first down. ✎ The Eagles threw to the right side on a league-leading 47 percent of passes, to the left side on just 34 percent of passes, and to the middle on a league-low 19 percent of passes. That low rate of middle passes looks like it may be a quirk of the official scorers in Philadelphia, but Eagles opponents did not show a similar left/right split. This trend was stronger with Nick Foles at quarterback (28/22/50) than it was with Carson Wentz (37/17/46). ✎ The Eagles led the league in running back screens and had a good 30.6% DVOA on these plays. ✎ Philadelphia was one of four teams that had less than 10 percent of its runs come against an eight-man box. ✎ The Eagles are somewhat unique in their blitz rates, where they send a big blitz (six or more) almost as often as they rush five. Jacksonville was the only other defense in the top dozen of "Rush 6+" that wasn't also in the top half of the league for "Rush 5." ✎ Philadelphia was the only defense all year that was not credited with a coverage sack by charters. ✎ In 2017, the Eagles were excellent when blitzing a defensive back, -45.7% DVOA and 5.3 net yards per pass. Last year, they allowed a league-worst 8.9 net yards per pass on these plays with 35.0% DVOA.

Passing

Player	DYAR	DVOA	Plays	NtYds	Avg	YAC	C%	TD	Int
C.Wentz	545	8.1%	430	2851	6.6	5.0	70.1%	21	7
N.Foles*	74	-5.4%	202	1370	6.8	5.2	73.1%	7	4
C.Kessler	-458	-59.7%	153	555	3.6	4.1	64.9%	2	2

Rushing

Player	DYAR	DVOA	Plays	Yds	Avg	TD	Fum	Suc
J.Adams	-12	-11.0%	120	511	4.3	3	1	50%
W.Smallwood	41	3.1%	87	364	4.2	3	1	51%
C.Clement	-31	-19.9%	68	259	3.8	2	2	46%
J.Ajayi*	-19	-17.9%	45	184	4.1	3	1	47%
D.Sproles*	19	8.5%	29	120	4.1	1	0	41%
C.Wentz	7	-6.8%	25	101	4.0	0	0	--
N.Foles*	5	-2.7%	8	18	2.3	0	0	--
J.Howard	-28	-11.1%	250	935	3.7	9	2	50%
D.Jackson	23	29.8%	6	29	4.8	1	0	--

Receiving

Player	DYAR	DVOA	Plays	Ctch	Yds	Y/C	YAC	TD	C%
N.Agholor	-69	-21.8%	97	64	747	11.7	5.5	4	66%
A.Jeffery	251	21.1%	92	65	840	12.9	4.1	6	71%
G.Tate*	-81	-36.9%	45	31	278	9.0	4.8	1	69%
J.Matthews*	84	28.8%	28	20	300	15.0	4.2	2	71%
K.Aiken*	-9	-31.0%	7	6	53	8.8	1.8	0	86%
D.Jackson	153	12.2%	74	41	774	18.9	4.4	4	55%
Z.Ertz	93	1.6%	155	115	1166	10.1	3.1	8	74%
D.Goedert	38	5.1%	44	33	334	10.1	5.2	4	75%
J.Perkins	-27	-42.2%	11	5	67	13.4	3.2	0	45%
W.Smallwood	49	11.2%	35	28	230	8.2	8.3	2	80%
C.Clement	29	5.8%	25	22	192	8.7	12.0	0	88%
D.Sproles*	16	-3.7%	23	15	160	10.7	8.5	2	65%
J.Adams	-19	-37.9%	13	7	58	8.3	9.3	0	54%
J.Ajayi*	-4	-24.7%	6	5	20	4.0	6.0	0	83%
J.Howard	-13	-21.9%	27	20	145	7.3	6.4	0	74%

Offensive Line

Player	Pos	Age	GS	Snaps	Pen	Sk	Pass	Run	Player	Pos	Age	GS	Snaps	Pen	Sk	Pass	Run
Brandon Brooks	RG	30	16/16	1087	3	0.0	2	7	Stefen Wisniewski	LG	30	16/7	643	3	1.0	2	5
Jason Kelce	C	32	16/16	1037	4	1.0	6	1	Isaac Seumalo	LG	26	13/9	548	1	1.0	8	2
Lane Johnson	RT	29	15/15	962	6	2.5	14	3	Halapoulivaati Vaitai	OT	26	16/1	334	2	3.0	6	2
Jason Peters	LT	37	16/16	868	8	4.5	15	2									

Year	Yards	ALY	Rank	Power	Rank	Stuff	Rank	2nd Lev	Rank	Open Field	Rank	Sacks	ASR	Rank	Press	Rank	F-Start	Cont.
2016	4.28	4.28	13	57%	25	18%	12	1.36	6	0.67	16	33	5.4%	10	25.7%	15	26	26
2017	4.52	3.85	22	64%	16	21%	21	1.30	4	1.14	3	36	6.2%	12	34.4%	26	16	28
2018	4.12	4.14	19	62%	25	21%	26	1.28	15	0.61	27	40	6.7%	17	26.0%	7	18	30

2018 ALY by direction:	Left End: 3.63 (24)	Left Tackle: 1.98 (32)	Mid/Guard: 4.45 (15)	Right Tackle: 4.15 (21)	Right End: 4.97 (8)

After a revolving door situation at left guard between Stefen Wisniewski, Chance Warmack, and Isaac Seumalo in 2017, the Eagles trotted out Wisniewski again for the first four games of 2018 before he surrendered the job to Seumalo, a significantly worse pass-blocker. Seumalo is slated to start in 2019, hopefully with more to offer. ● Franchise left tackle Jason Peters is not done, but he is over the hill. Once a dominant force with outstanding athletic ability to work the perimeter, the two-time All-Pro has lost his juice. He surrendered a blown block once per 51.1 snaps, just below average among qualifying left tackles, as a result of diminished quickness. ● The Eagles' average rushing yards per attempt took a major hit in 2018, but not because of the line. The offensive line improved their adjusted line yards and found similar success in stuff rate and power rate. A slew of injuries at running back, however, left them with lackluster runners such as Josh Adams, Wendell Smallwood, and Corey Clement, none of whom could match the injured Jay Ajayi's explosiveness in the open field from the year prior. Look for rookie running back Miles Sanders to uncork the running game again. ● First-round offensive tackle Andre Dillard was a bit of a surprise pick as Peters is still plenty capable, but Philadelphia seems confident enough in the current roster to invest in the future. Dillard started for three seasons at Washington State under Air Raid savant Mike Leach. As such, he has an immense number of reps in pass protection, which is important for a technique-based position that requires reps to refine. There may be concern that Dillard will struggle because pass pro in the Air Raid is different from traditional pass pro, but he faced plenty of pro-level talent in the Pac-12 and the NFL is increasingly embracing Air Raid players they may have overlooked in the past. He is also the first tackle drafted from a Leach offense since Daniel Loper in 2005, who barely found playing time in his career when he transitioned to guard. Dillard, hopefully, is at the forefront of change in the NFL. If anything, Dillard's run-blocking may be more of a concern, as he will be playing more in a phone booth than he did in college. Like Philadelphia's current starting tackles, Dillard is also a fantastic athlete with light feet, putting up performances in the 89th percentile or better in the 40-yard dash, broad jump, 3-cone drill, and short shuttle at the combine. He likely will not be needed in 2019, but he sets the Eagles up to sustain success post-Peters.

Defensive Front

Defensive Line	Age	Pos	G	Snaps	Plays	TmPct	Rk	Stop	Dfts	BTkl	Runs	St%	Rk	RuYd	Rk	Sack	Hit	Hur	Dsrpt
Fletcher Cox	29	DT	16	830	46	5.9%	26	39	20	4	25	80%	24	1.9	24	10.5	24	49	2
Haloti Ngata*	35	DT	13	368	18	2.8%	77	15	6	2	15	80%	24	1.3	6	1.0	2	5	1
Treyvon Hester	27	DT	12	226	13	2.2%	--	10	2	1	12	75%	--	1.6	--	1.0	2	5	0
Malik Jackson	29	DT	16	628	33	4.3%	57	25	13	3	24	79%	29	2.0	27	3.5	8	23	1

Edge Rushers	Age	Pos	G	Snaps	Plays	TmPct	Rk	Stop	Dfts	BTkl	Runs	St%	Rk	RuYd	Rk	Sack	Hit	Hur	Dsrpt
Brandon Graham	31	DE	16	753	41	5.3%	39	33	16	4	28	79%	31	1.6	19	4.0	7	35	2
Michael Bennett*	34	DE	16	716	31	4.0%	67	25	18	7	17	76%	41	1.1	9	9.0	20	34	1
Chris Long*	34	DE	16	613	23	2.9%	85	17	8	4	11	73%	51	3.0	60	6.5	12	24	0
Vinny Curry	31	DE	12	445	21	3.4%	78	14	10	2	16	63%	75	1.7	22	2.5	4	11	0

Linebackers	Age	Pos	G	Snaps	Plays	TmPct	Rk	Stop	Dfts	BTkl	Runs	St%	Rk	RuYd	Rk	Sack	Hit	Hur	Tgts	Suc%	Rk	AdjYd	Rk	PD	Int
Nigel Bradham	30	OLB	15	919	100	13.7%	33	55	16	7	48	63%	30	4.0	47	2.0	2	10	36	61%	9	4.8	9	4	0
Jordan Hicks*	27	MLB	12	705	95	16.2%	16	41	17	5	38	47%	82	4.7	73	3.0	2	3.5	27	37%	69	10.0	77	5	0
Kamu Grugier-Hill	25	OLB	16	329	36	4.6%	--	19	9	5	20	60%	--	2.9	--	1.0	0	1	6	17%	--	6.7	--	2	1
Nathan Gerry	24	OLB	13	134	20	3.2%	--	12	2	2	11	64%	--	4.3	--	0.0	0	0	5	60%	--	6.0	--	2	1
Zach Brown	30	ILB	16	703	97	12.0%	45	60	16	5	50	80%	3	2.4	5	1.0	1	6	37	54%	28	6.3	24	1	0
L.J. Fort	29	ILB	15	305	43	5.9%	--	29	12	3	22	86%	--	2.0	--	1.0	2	7	22	59%	13	6.8	40	0	0

Year	Yards	ALY	Rank	Power	Rank	Stuff	Rank	2nd Level	Rank	Open Field	Rank	Sacks	ASR	Rank	Press	Rank
2016	4.20	3.44	2	70%	27	24%	3	1.20	19	1.13	31	34	6.6%	11	31.6%	3
2017	3.35	2.99	1	55%	6	29%	2	0.88	1	0.83	23	38	6.3%	19	32.2%	9
2018	4.56	3.93	6	62%	8	26%	2	1.22	17	1.44	32	44	6.5%	26	29.7%	19

2018 ALY by direction:	Left End: 1.79 (1)	Left Tackle: 3.77 (10)	Mid/Guard: 4.25 (11)	Right Tackle: 3.25 (5)	Right End: 5.43 (28)

Losing Michael Bennett means losing the team's most effective and versatile pass-rusher. Not only did Bennett post the team's best pass-rushing numbers, almost across the board, but he did so from a number of alignments. He could play 3-technique (between tackle and guard), 5-technique (tackle's outside shoulder), and from a traditional defensive end alignment. The versatility was especially useful with injuries to defensive tackle Timmy Jernigan and defensive end Derek Barnett. ✎ Assuming he returns close to full strength, getting Jernigan back from injury will strengthen an already good run defense. Jernigan's average 1.1 yards allowed on run tackles in 2017 was fourth among defensive tackles and helped propel the team to the best adjusted line yards in the league. ✎ Signing Malik Jackson also serves to bolster the interior defensive line. Whereas Jernigan is primarily a 1-technique, Jackson is an explosive 3-technique who thrives as a gap-shooter in the run game and when let loose as a pass-rusher. Fletcher Cox was the team's only effective full-time defensive tackle versus the pass last season. Adding Jackson to the mix for some big-play threat could transform the unit. ✎ To a lesser extent, the same can be said about the return of Barnett. Barnett is not a special player and does not possess the athletic ability to ascend to true stardom, but he has the technique, strength, and motor of a staple defensive end. 2019 will be a big year for him considering his lackluster rookie year in 2017 and an incomplete 2018 season. ✎ The Eagles will be looking to put more speed off the edge with second-year end Josh Sweat and fourth-round rookie Shareef Miller (Penn State). The two ran 4.53 and 4.69 in the 40-yard dash, respectively, which are both above the 80th percentile among defensive ends. Sweat also tore up the rest of the combine but ended up on the bench for most of last year despite his tools. In the absence of a retiring Chris Long, Sweat taking the next step would be huge. ✎ The linebacker spot is getting a massive overhaul, save for Nigel Bradham. Jordan Hicks, a former Pro Bowler who struggled with injuries and showed a decline in play last season, is being replaced by Zach Brown (ex-Washington), an underrated stalwart in the run game with solid coverage skills to boot. The addition of L.J. Fort (ex-Pittsburgh) also gives the Eagles a better, more well-rounded third linebacker than Kamu Grugier-Hill.

Defensive Secondary

Secondary	Age	Pos	G	Snaps	Plays	TmPct	Rk	Stop	Dfts	BTkl	Runs	St%	Rk	RuYd	Rk	Tgts	Tgt%	Rk	Dist	Suc%	Rk	AdjYd	Rk	PD	Int
Malcolm Jenkins	32	SS	16	1038	99	12.7%	11	48	16	13	39	54%	15	5.5	20	48	10.6%	50	11.0	50%	34	6.7	23	8	1
Corey Graham*	34	FS	13	655	58	9.2%	48	21	10	5	25	36%	49	8.5	52	15	5.2%	10	15.1	27%	73	10.7	67	5	1
Rasul Douglas	24	CB	16	544	61	7.8%	48	29	16	5	10	70%	3	5.5	21	64	26.9%	77	11.7	47%	58	8.6	62	4	3
Ronald Darby	25	CB	9	542	55	12.5%	2	24	9	10	6	50%	22	3.3	4	65	27.4%	78	11.9	57%	18	6.0	10	12	1
Avonte Maddox	23	CB	13	540	36	5.7%	79	8	6	3	8	13%	78	16.6	79	33	14.0%	5	12.7	61%	6	4.6	1	4	2
Jalen Mills	25	CB	8	457	50	12.8%	1	21	7	9	8	63%	7	4.8	12	51	25.5%	72	13.5	43%	75	11.7	78	9	0
Cre'Von LeBlanc	25	CB	11	378	26	4.8%	--	7	2	3	7	43%	--	6.0	--	34	20.5%	--	8.3	50%	--	7.8	--	1	0
Sidney Jones	23	CB	9	321	27	6.2%	--	10	5	7	7	29%	--	4.0	--	31	22.1%	--	10.0	45%	--	7.0	--	2	0
Tre Sullivan	25	SS	12	219	12	2.1%	--	4	3	6	3	67%	--	3.3	--	4	4.2%	--	12.5	50%	--	4.0	--	0	0
Andrew Sendejo	32	SS	5	324	28	11.1%	--	8	0	4	11	55%	--	5.5	--	7	6.1%	--	9.3	43%	--	9.0	--	1	0

Year	Pass D Rank	vs. #1 WR	Rk	vs. #2 WR	Rk	vs. Other WR	Rk	WR Wide	Rk	WR Slot	Rk	vs. TE	Rk	vs. RB	Rk
2016	2	-18.5%	3	1.6%	17	2.3%	18	-2.3%	16	-12.0%	5	-52.8%	1	-11.9%	9
2017	8	-15.8%	7	-48.5%	1	5.9%	21	-12.1%	7	-25.4%	1	0.7%	17	-6.1%	10
2018	15	0.0%	15	6.5%	22	-2.7%	16	8.1%	25	-6.6%	9	-16.1%	7	11.2%	24

One of Philadelphia's young cornerbacks has to fully emerge this year to challenge Jalen Mills for a starting spot. Mills has posted a sub-50 percent success rate two years in a row, and his 43 percent success rate in 2018 is especially alarming considering how often the Eagles gave him a cushion to work with while they asked Ronald Darby to often play press or bump. ✎ Though not a high bar, cornerback Rasul Douglas has posted a higher success rate than Mills two seasons in a row despite seeing less playing time. Douglas sports clear strengths that Mills just does not, namely being able to match up with bigger receivers and better play the ball in the air. ✎ Time is running out for cornerback Sidney Jones to show signs of life. He missed nearly his entire rookie season with a torn Achilles in 2017 and did not start a game in 2018 until Week 10 against the Giants, one week before he was part of a 48-7 beatdown the Eagles suffered against the Saints in their first game without Darby. He looked rusty in his second career start, particularly in defending downfield routes in New Orleans' wide-open offense. ✎ Jim

Schwartz's defenses have been top-seven in playing their cornerbacks predominantly to one side of the field since he joined the team in 2016. They finished fifth in cornerback by sides in 2018 (88 percent), in part because Darby is one of the best all-around cornerbacks in the league and is capable of playing man, press, and zone coverage, effectively allowing the rest of the secondary to play off his strength while he shuts off one side of the field. ✦ Signing Andrew Sendejo, a former Viking, gives the Eagles the flexibility to play with three safeties. Rodney McLeod is a true free safety, but Sendejo and Malcolm Jenkins can each be flex safeties to play the run, play "rat in the hole" over the middle, or match up with tight ends. If nothing else, they will have a fantastic rotational safety who can help keep the secondary fresh.

Special Teams

Year	DVOA	Rank	FG/XP	Rank	Net Kick	Rank	Kick Ret	Rank	Net Punt	Rank	Punt Ret	Rank	Hidden	Rank
2016	7.5%	2	3.5	10	14.3	1	15.1	1	0.1	15	4.8	8	-11.3	28
2017	0.9%	16	3.9	11	-0.8	21	0.6	12	3.4	14	-2.5	22	0.8	12
2018	0.2%	15	-0.5	19	3.1	7	-2.6	23	6.4	6	-5.3	28	-6.7	24

The Eagles' return game has diminished with each passing season. In 2016, they were the most effective kick return team with a stable of Kenjon Barner, Wendell Smallwood, and Josh Huff, and eighth in punt return value with Darren Sproles leading the charge. They dropped 11 and 14 spots, respectively, the following season, and fell even further to 23rd and 28th place in 2018. The 2017 drop in punt return value can be explained by switching from Sproles to a less spry Barner, while the plummet in 2018 can be explained in part by an entirely new set of players in both return spots. ✦ With Sproles and DeAndre Carter—the team's two leading punt returners last year—off the roster, there is a new vacancy at the position. Corey Clement could take over, but he struggled in the role when thrust into it early in 2018. Smallwood, Braxton Miller, and DeSean Jackson, though all rather inexperienced punt returners as of late, should be top candidates vying for the position. Clement will likely return kicks, but that could be up in the air as well. ✦ Linebacker Kamu Grugier-Hill has led the team in special teams tackles for two seasons in a row. The feat was especially impressive last season considering he became a more regular part of the defense, which was not the case in 2017 when he was almost exclusively a special teams ace. ✦ First-year starting punter Cameron Johnston posted the best gross punting value the Eagles have seen in three seasons, but got the least amount of help from the coverage team in corralling the returner. Still, Johnston's efforts propelled the unit to a higher net value than the previous two seasons.

Pittsburgh Steelers

2018 record: 9-6-1	**Total DVOA:** 11.2% (9th)	**2019 Mean Projection:** 9.4 wins	**On the Clock (0-4):** 4%
Pythagorean Wins: 9.7 (11th)	**Offense:** 13.8% (6th)	**Postseason Odds:** 58.5%	**Mediocrity (5-7):** 18%
Snap-Weighted Age: 26.9 (7th)	**Defense:** -0.9% (13th)	**Super Bowl Odds:** 12.6%	**Playoff Contender (8-10):** 42%
Average Opponent: 3.8% (4th)	**Special Teams:** -3.5% (27th)	**Proj. Avg. Opponent:** -0.9% (23rd)	**Super Bowl Contender (11+):** 36%

2018: As The Steelers Turn.

2019: Fewer B's, Still Killer.

No one around the National Football League feels any sympathy for the Pittsburgh Steelers, who have had mostly unbridled success since the early 1970s, not to mention six Super Bowls to savor. But 2018 saw an insanely talented team self-destruct in ways unprecedented in the annals of such a proud franchise. The unending Steel City soap opera caused the team to not just fall short of the Super Bowl, for which they were projected to compete by many (including us), but to miss the postseason entirely. It was a season to forget, but one that will be long remembered in Yinzer Town.

Le'Veon Bell, the Steelers' top runner and arguably the best back in the NFL, decided the league's enlightened refusal to pay top dollar for his position was a worthy hill to die upon, and sat out the entire season in a contract dispute. From the franchise's perspective, it was a worse situation than if he had blown out a knee in training camp, or even simply declared himself over and out, smell ya later. Bell leveraged the drama for all he could, dropping social media teasers and hinting to fans and media that he would return after six games, or ten, or maybe just zip in for a playoff contest the team wouldn't qualify for. In the end, Bell sat on his couch for the duration, then signed with the Jets in the offseason for less than he was offered by Pittsburgh.

Then there was Antonio Brown, a.k.a. the self-styled "Mr. Big Chest," who has been a behind-the-scenes provocateur for several seasons while maintaining his status as one of the best wideouts in football. After quarterback Ben Roethlisberger threw blame Brown's way for an end zone interception in a stunning loss to Denver in late November, the moody, mercurial receiver began acting out for reals, as the kids say. It culminated in Brown playing hooky from the team's finale against the Bengals, a must-win game with the Steelers' postseason hopes on life support. It was a stunning middle finger to the rest of the team, not to mention all those fans decked out in their black No. 84 jerseys, and it made Bell's contractual squabbling look Lincolnesque in its rectitude. The Steelers dumped Brown on Oakland in the spring, getting back a third- and a fifth-round draft choice, puny renumeration for one of the top players in the league.

Even with all the *sturm und drang*, Pittsburgh had no business watching the playoffs on TV. They were ninth in DVOA, ninth in Estimated Wins, and put up a 10-win pace via Pythagorean Theory. They were 7-2-1 after ten games,

widely considered a viable championship contender. They still had Roethlisberger, who continues to be excellent well into his (football) dotage. Their offensive line was among the league's best. T.J. Watt emerged as the leader of a pass rush that led the league in sacks. While the team continued to miss Ryan Shazier, the linebacker whose awful 2017 neck injury forced him from the game, the defense still performed well enough. In a year in which all three division rivals changed or lost starting quarterbacks to injury, there was no reason the Steelers shouldn't have made the playoffs regardless of all the noise around them.

Give the team credit for this much—at least they didn't turn in the "typical" Pittsburgh underachieving season. To wit: Instead of the annual one inexplicable loss on the road to a doormat, there were two. The AFC West swept the Steelers, and while getting outslugged by the Chiefs was excusable, and even blowing a big halftime lead to the Chargers wasn't the end of the world, conjuring ways to lose to both Denver and Oakland on the road brought twice as much opprobrium as usual upon the team and head coach Mike Tomlin.

Meanwhile, Pittsburgh is usually aces at home against good teams, to the tune of 12-5 over the last four years. But in 2018 they lost to the Chiefs, Ravens, and Chargers at their supposed Heinz Field fortress. The lone good team Pittsburgh did defeat at home was, of all squads, their longtime *bête noires* from New England. Indeed, the 17-10 victory nine days before Christmas was the last time the Pats lost en route to the Lombardi Trophy. That the Steelers would at long last best Bill Belichick and Co. and still not make the playoffs was a bitter pill for wavers of the Terrible Towel.

So the 2019 Steelers are coming off one of the most disappointing campaigns in franchise history, down two of their best players. Tomlin is still on the sidelines, meaning the serial damp squibs against weak competition will continue, if nothing else. One would imagine that would cause us to dampen our hopes, but actually, the projection remains quite strong. For the fourth straight season, Pittsburgh has one of our top five win projections. They project to have a top-10 offense and defense, along with a much weaker schedule (23rd) than last year, when they played the fourth-hardest. In other words, the Steelers remain strong Super Bowl contenders.

How can that be? Start with Roethlisberger, obviously. Last year he turned in his highest average net yards per attempt

2019 Steelers Schedule

Week	Opp.	Week	Opp.	Week	Opp.
1	at NE	7	BYE	13	CLE
2	SEA	8	MIA (Mon.)	14	at ARI
3	at SF	9	IND	15	BUF
4	CIN (Mon.)	10	LAR	16	at NYJ
5	BAL	11	at CLE (Thu.)	17	at BAL
6	at LAC	12	at CIN		

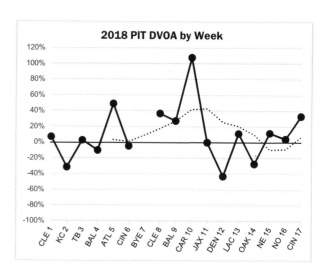

since 2015, and his best rating in ESPN's Total QBR since 2007. He has a new contract extension and perhaps a new mission to prove to the world that he made AB, not the other way around. For all the production and excitement Bell and Brown provided, losing a franchise quarterback of Big Ben's caliber would be far more devastating to any team.

Elsewhere, our projection system digs their consistency on the offensive line and at head coach as well. (Losing O-line coach Mike Munchak is a blow not accounted for by the system, however.) The offense has been top-seven in DVOA for five straight years, and remember Bell only played 49 of a possible 80 games in that span. And we foresee a key element that hurt the team last year, a very low turnover rate (just 7.9 percent of opponent's drives ended with a takeaway, about 4 percent below the league average), regressing towards the mean this season. That would push the overall defensive numbers up, even if the pass rush isn't quite so potent.

Meanwhile, the Bengals have a new coach, as do the Browns (though they have fortified the roster considerably), and the Ravens are fully committed to a quarterback who was inconsistent, to put it mildly, as a rookie passer in 2018. Add in a little "addition by subtraction" motivation and it's quite easy to foresee another AFC North flag flying at Heinz Field, at minimum.

Cleaning up a few small-scale areas of performance would go a long way towards achieving loftier ambitions. While not as obvious as, say, an interception on the goal line late in the Denver game, when added together these shortcomings may have tipped the team into just missing the postseason rather than just making it.

Kicker Chris Boswell got lost a bit in the Brown and Bell dramas, but he was a Killer B in the most literal sense, as in he killed the team with his inaccurate leg. Boswell missed seven field goals and five extra points in a disaster of a season that came hard on the heels of a new contract and a Pro Bowl appearance. His misses directly affected the endings of the Raiders loss and the Browns tie, and more consistency would almost certainly have propelled Pittsburgh into the playoffs.

It wasn't just Boswell's inaccuracy that dragged down the special teams, which underwhelmed across the disciplines. Indeed, the Steelers were 27th in this area in DVOA, and while overall, Pittsburgh wasn't a heavily penalized team (111 accepted hankies, in the bottom half of the league), Pitt and Green Bay were tied for the league lead with 34 special teams flags apiece. The Steelers struggled with field position all year, and all those penalties setting them back 10 yards at a

time were a big reason they were 31st in average starting line of scrimmage per drive. They were fifth in yards per drive, so a few shorter fields might have resulted in the scoring of a handful of critical points. Indeed, the team committed five special teams penalties in both of the narrow home losses to Kansas City and San Diego (they had six in Tampa Bay but managed to hold off FitzMagic that night).

In the loss to the Chiefs, Travis Kelce ripped Pittsburgh's defense apart, to the tune of 109 yards and two scores. In the Tampa Bay game, Cameron Brate and O.J. Howard combined for 106 yards and a touchdown. The inability to defend tight ends was a massive weakness in the Steelers defense, which was odd; in 2017 Pittsburgh was first in defending passes to tight ends by a country mile. But they lost the plot in the middle of the field in 2018, going from -34.6% DVOA to 25.5% and 31st in the NFL, a staggering drop-off that is the second steepest since we've tracked this stat (Table 1).

Table 1: Biggest Drop in DVOA vs. Tight Ends from Previous Year, 2004-2018

Year	Team	DVOA Y-1	Rk	DVOA	Rk	Dif
2015	NO	-26.7%	1	46.0%	32	72.7%
2018	**PIT**	**-34.6%**	**1**	**25.5%**	**31**	**60.1%**
2016	DAL	-25.0%	3	31.2%	30	56.3%
2017	HOU	-40.6%	2	15.2%	27	55.8%
2006	NYG	-31.9%	3	23.2%	30	55.1%
2009	CLE	-11.9%	10	41.7%	32	53.6%
2017	PHI	-52.8%	1	0.7%	17	53.5%
2006	DEN	-47.4%	1	1.0%	17	48.4%
2017	BAL	-28.8%	3	19.6%	29	48.3%
2018	MIN	-24.2%	2	22.6%	30	46.7%

Unfortunately for Pittsburgh, the general rule is that teams don't rebound mightily the year after a big collapse in covering tight ends. Of the teams in Table 1, only the 2017 Eagles reappeared in the top ten the following season.

The hope in the Steel City is that the addition of rookie

linebacker Devin Bush figures to alleviate that weak spot somewhat. Steelers fans have placed an awful lot of hope on the shoulders of the former Michigan standout. Shazier's speed and instinct for the big play have been missed so much that the Steelers were forced into drastic (by their standards) action. They traded up ten spots in the first round of the draft in order to procure Bush, a linebacker with similar traits to Shazier. The big move cost the Steelers their second-round pick and a third in next year's draft, but the benefits of adding a player perfectly designed to fix their most glaring issue was worth the price. The secondary remains short on blue-chip talent, but Bush's ability to assist in pass coverage would figure to mitigate that, though that may not take effect immediately as the rookie learns the ropes.

Last year's defense was helped considerably by a stellar pass rush—but surprisingly was also hurt by that pass rush. For the second straight year, the Steelers led the league in both adjusted sack rate and total sacks (where they actually had four fewer than in 2017). They also finished second in pressure rate. But there was a key exception—on third down, the Steelers fell all the way to 19th in pressure rate and 28th in adjusted sack rate. Needless to say, that's a bad time for the pass-rushers to break for some Gatorade. It's also likely an anomaly that bounces back to normal this season.

On offense, we talk a lot in these parts about how the wide receiver screen on third down needs to be consigned to the dustbin of history like the leather helmet and the forearm shiver. Pittsburgh was Exhibit A. They led the NFL in wideout/tight end screens in 2018 with 61, and overall it was a worthwhile tactic (26.9% DVOA). But on the 18 times they used a wideout screen on third down (also a league high), the efficiency plummeted to -34.5%. Eight of those plays were on third-and-3 or less, and half either went for no gain or lost yards. Obviously, the tendency had been sussed out by opponents, but the Steelers under new offensive coordinator Randy Fichtner stubbornly refused to abandon the play. Perhaps with Brown elsewhere the offensive brain trust will realize 'tis better to throw downfield on third down.

Or maybe they'll realize they need to hand the ball to James Conner when it's third-and-short. Overall, Bell's Greta Garbo

turn forced the Steelers to go absurdly pass-heavy, with 689 attempts, 99 more than in 2017. The franchise of Franco, the Bus, and Fast Willie had just 345 rushing attempts (only Green Bay had fewer) and 1,445 yards (ahead of only Arizona). They went with an empty backfield over 18 percent of the time, leading the league with a rate over twice the NFL average of 8.2 percent. In general, analytics suggest this is a good thing— NFL teams generally run too much and don't pass enough, and the Steelers were certainly more efficient when passing (including 18.6% DVOA from those empty backfields). But analytics also suggest there are times when running is a good thing. The Steelers were 29th in frequency of running in power (short-yardage) situations even though they converted 71 percent of the time, fifth in the NFL. It's as though the offense had Bell's absence on the brain, overthinking the few, but important, situations where running still is the preferred method.

While no one but the old-school diehards wearing Rocky Bleier jerseys is calling for a return to smashmouth football, the team seems likely to address the imbalance at least somewhat. Theoretically, Fichtner will adjust a bit in his second season at the helm, and thanks in part to Brown's departure, we project the pass-run ratio to narrow a bit in 2019. But Pittsburgh will remain an offense carried by Roethlisberger.

The NFL commentariat seems eager to move on from Pittsburgh and to embrace the "Baker vs. Lamar will decide the division for the next decade" theme. Perhaps in time that will play out, but dismissing the AFC North team with the best quarterback, the head coach without a losing season, and the front office that has far more hits than misses seems extremely foolish and premature. What has hurt the Steelers in recent seasons most isn't drama but complacency, manifested by a sense of looking ahead to the next game while losing the one in which they were actually competing. With the pigskin world writing them off as done without Bell and Brown, that self-regard is gone, replaced by a determination to shove it back at their doubters. And a team this talented with something to prove is a dangerous team indeed.

Robert Weintraub

2018 Steelers Stats by Week

Wk	vs.	W-L	PF	PA	YDF	YDA	TO	Total	Off	Def	ST
1	at CLE	T	21	21	472	327	-5	7%	-16%	-27%	-4%
2	KC	L	37	42	475	449	+1	-32%	32%	50%	-14%
3	at TB	W	30	27	413	455	+3	3%	-7%	-16%	-6%
4	BAL	L	14	26	284	451	-1	-10%	-2%	10%	2%
5	ATL	W	41	17	381	324	0	49%	29%	-18%	2%
6	at CIN	W	28	21	481	275	0	-5%	20%	17%	-8%
7	BYE										
8	CLE	W	33	18	421	237	-1	37%	25%	-8%	3%
9	at BAL	W	23	16	395	265	0	27%	41%	8%	-6%
10	CAR	W	52	21	457	242	+2	108%	77%	-18%	12%
11	at JAX	W	20	16	323	243	-2	0%	-13%	-15%	-3%
12	at DEN	L	17	24	527	308	-4	-43%	1%	32%	-13%
13	LAC	L	30	33	336	371	-1	11%	29%	6%	-13%
14	at OAK	L	21	24	340	354	0	-28%	0%	12%	-16%
15	NE	W	17	10	376	368	-1	12%	13%	0%	-2%
16	at NO	L	28	31	429	370	-1	4%	11%	8%	2%
17	CIN	W	16	13	343	196	-1	33%	-21%	-46%	8%

Trends and Splits

	Offense	Rank	Defense	Rank
Total DVOA	13.8%	6	-0.9%	13
Unadjusted VOA	12.9%	6	2.4%	19
Weighted Trend	15.0%	6	-0.4%	12
Variance	6.4%	14	5.5%	17
Average Opponent	0.8%	22	4.4%	6
Passing	25.5%	8	7.5%	17
Rushing	-2.4%	12	-13.1%	8
First Down	10.8%	10	-6.6%	7
Second Down	13.2%	5	0.3%	17
Third Down	21.6%	5	10.3%	22
First Half	18.8%	5	-2.6%	10
Second Half	8.1%	8	0.7%	19
Red Zone	5.9%	13	8.7%	23
Late and Close	7.3%	13	0.4%	19

Five-Year Performance

Year	W-L	Pyth W	Est W	PF	PA	TO	Total	Rk	Off	Rk	Def	Rk	ST	Rk	Off AGL	Rk	Def AGL	Rk	Off Age	Rk	Def Age	Rk	ST Age	Rk
2014	11-5	9.7	9.4	436	368	0	12.1%	8	22.5%	2	11.3%	30	0.9%	12	4.1	1	38.7	17	26.5	24	27.8	3	26.2	10
2015	10-6	10.7	10.8	423	319	+2	21.3%	7	17.3%	3	-3.8%	11	0.1%	18	43.2	23	23.9	9	28.2	5	27.0	11	26.2	14
2016	11-5	9.9	10.2	399	327	+5	17.1%	4	12.5%	7	-4.7%	11	-0.1%	16	35.2	15	26.7	11	27.1	9	26.5	15	25.7	23
2017	13-3	10.6	11.3	406	308	+2	27.1%	3	17.6%	3	-6.4%	9	3.1%	9	15.2	6	15.3	7	27.4	7	25.7	23	25.9	14
2018	9-6-1	9.7	9.2	428	360	-11	11.2%	9	13.8%	6	-0.9%	13	-3.5%	27	25.7	7	14.8	3	27.9	6	26.2	18	26.1	10

2018 Performance Based on Most Common Personnel Groups

PIT Offense					PIT Offense vs. Opponents					PIT Defense					PIT Defense vs. Opponents			
Pers	Freq	Yds	DVOA	Run%	Pers	Freq	Yds	DVOA	Run%	Pers	Freq	Yds	DVOA		Pers	Freq	Yds	DVOA
11	71%	6.4	23.0%	25%	Base	20%	6.1	-3.0%	55%	Base	30%	4.9	-13.6%		11	61%	5.8	2.8%
12	8%	7.5	19.6%	43%	Nickel	59%	6.7	28.9%	27%	Nickel	33%	5.3	-3.7%		12	14%	5.5	2.4%
01	6%	6.3	-15.5%	7%	Dime+	25%	5.8	0.8%	14%	Dime+	36%	6.3	15.8%		21	9%	6.1	4.4%
621	3%	3.9	-19.8%	92%	Goal Line	2%	1.4	-2.5%	80%	Goal Line	0%	0.3	-2.0%		13	5%	4.8	-1.0%
22	3%	7.5	23.9%	64%	Big	1%	9.4	96.3%	60%						22	4%	3.8	-11.1%
00	3%	7.8	46.1%	3%											10	2%	5.2	-6.9%

Strategic Tendencies

Run/Pass		Rk	Formation		Rk	Pass Rush		Rk	Secondary		Rk	Strategy		Rk
Runs, first half	27%	32	Form: Single Back	74%	24	Rush 3	11.3%	9	4 DB	30%	8	Play action	12%	32
Runs, first down	40%	28	Form: Empty Back	18%	1	Rush 4	54.2%	30	5 DB	33%	30	Avg Box (Off)	6.16	20
Runs, second-long	21%	32	Pers: 3+ WR	80%	2	Rush 5	28.0%	3	6+ DB	36%	3	Avg Box (Def)	6.11	26
Runs, power sit.	45%	29	Pers: 2+ TE/6+ OL	18%	26	Rush 6+	6.5%	13	CB by Sides	70%	20	Offensive Pace	30.42	11
Runs, behind 2H	10%	32	Pers: 6+ OL	6%	4	Int DL Sacks	40.4%	6	S/CB Cover Ratio	26%	19	Defensive Pace	30.81	11
Pass, ahead 2H	51%	8	Shotgun/Pistol	79%	4	Second Level Sacks	19.2%	22	DB Blitz	14%	3	Go for it on 4th	1.12	22

Once again, the Steelers used less play-action than any other team in the NFL. It was by a good margin, too; every other team was at 17 percent or more, while the Steelers were just at 12 percent. But maybe there's method to this madness. In general, if you separate it from overall passing performance, we haven't found much year-to-year consistency in which teams are most and least efficient using play-action. Is Pittsburgh an exception? For four straight years, the Steelers have a better DVOA *without* play-action, even though the league as a whole always has a better DVOA *with* play-action.

Pittsburgh on Play-Action, 2015-2018

Year	PA Pct	Rank	Yds w/PA	DVOA w/PA	Yds (no PA)	DVOA (no PA)	Yds Dif	DVOA Dif
2015	14%	31	8.3	3.6%	7.7	39.0%	+0.6	-35.4%
2016	14%	32	8.3	12.7%	6.9	33.7%	+1.4	-21.0%
2017	11%	32	6.6	31.5%	7.6	37.8%	-0.9	-6.2%
2018	12%	32	7.0	9.0%	7.2	30.0%	-0.2	-21.0%

Note: includes scrambles and Defensive Pass Interference

There's a bit of chicken-and-egg problem going on here. Do the Steelers consistently not use play-action because they aren't good at it, or are they consistently not good at it because they don't do it enough or practice it enough? Does Ben Roethlisberger, specifically, not have a convincing play fake? Or is this four-year streak just random chance, and like the rest of the league, the Steelers would prove to be more efficient over the long run when using play-action passing? ● Interestingly, on defense Pittsburgh *faced* the least amount of play-action, just 15 percent of pass plays, and also had a huge "backwards" gap between performance with and without play-action. The Steelers had league-best -26.8% DVOA and allowed just 5.9 yards per play when opponents used play-action. Those numbers were 18.9% DVOA and 6.6 yards per play without play-action. Oakland was the only other defense to allow fewer yards per play with play-action than without. ● Pittsburgh used four or more wide receivers in personnel 9.3 percent of the time, the only team to use this personnel over 5 percent of the time. ● With Le'Veon Bell out of the picture, the Steelers dropped from third (41 percent) to dead last (21 percent) in run/pass ratio on second-and-long. In 2017, the Steelers were the best offense in the league when running in second-and-long (20.3% DVOA); in 2018, they ranked 31st with -59.2% DVOA and had just 3.9 yards per carry. ● Ben Roethlisberger had a league-high 10.4 net yards per pass with 54.4% DVOA against defensive back blitzes. ● Somehow, the Steelers allowed more pass pressure the fewer pass-rushers they faced. The Steelers allowed pressure on 35 percent of three-man rushes, but 28 percent of four-man rushes and then 25 percent of blitzes. Every other offense allowed pressure on at least 32 percent of blitzes. ● Pittsburgh had the league's biggest gap between DVOA when running from shotgun (7.5% DVOA, 5.1 yards per carry) and running with the quarterback under center (-24.0% DVOA, 3.6 yards). ● The Pittsburgh defense, in turn, had the biggest defensive DVOA gap between performance against offenses in shotgun (7.3% DVOA, 5.8 yards per play) and performance against offenses with the quarterback under center (-16.4% DVOA, 4.8 yards). ● Pittsburgh was the beneficiary of a league-high 154 opponent penalties for 1,170 penalty yards.

Passing

Player	DYAR	DVOA	Plays	NtYds	Avg	YAC	C%	TD	Int
B.Roethlisberger	1204	14.5%	696	4944	7.1	6.2	67.4%	34	16
J.Dobbs	-85	-124.0%	12	43	3.6	3.2	50.0%	0	1

Rushing

Player	DYAR	DVOA	Plays	Yds	Avg	TD	Fum	Suc
J.Conner	99	2.3%	215	972	4.5	12	3	49%
J.Samuels	17	-1.3%	56	256	4.6	0	0	52%
S.Ridley*	-45	-48.0%	29	80	2.8	1	1	34%
B.Roethlisberger	62	37.8%	19	111	5.8	3	0	--
R.Switzer	-3	-50.9%	6	21	3.5	0	0	--

Receiving

Player	DYAR	DVOA	Plays	Ctch	Yds	Y/C	YAC	TD	C%
A.Brown*	191	1.7%	168	104	1297	12.5	4.7	15	62%
J.Smith-Schuster	235	4.4%	167	112	1426	12.7	5.8	7	67%
R.Switzer	5	-11.1%	44	36	253	7.0	3.8	1	82%
J.Washington	-37	-25.1%	38	16	217	13.6	3.3	1	42%
E.Rogers	-10	-20.8%	14	12	79	6.6	3.3	0	86%
J.Hunter*	-54	-64.2%	13	3	21	7.0	0.7	0	23%
D.Moncrief	-14	-14.8%	89	48	672	14.0	5.0	3	54%
V.McDonald	51	3.6%	72	50	609	12.2	7.7	4	69%
J.James*	96	27.3%	39	30	423	14.1	6.2	2	77%
X.Grimble	-4	-14.8%	8	6	86	14.3	9.3	0	75%
J.Conner	112	15.2%	71	55	497	9.0	10.0	1	77%
J.Samuels	79	36.4%	29	26	199	7.7	8.3	3	90%
R.Nix	-8	-32.0%	6	4	38	9.5	10.8	0	67%

Offensive Line

Player	Pos	Age	GS	Snaps	Pen	Sk	Pass	Run	Player	Pos	Age	GS	Snaps	Pen	Sk	Pass	Run
Ramon Foster	LG	33	16/16	1116	3	1.5	5	4	Matt Feiler	RT	27	11/10	676	0	1.0	6	1
Alejandro Villanueva	LT	31	16/16	1116	6	4.0	11	2	Marcus Gilbert*	RT	31	5/5	362	2	1.5	3	1
Maurkice Pouncey	C	30	16/16	1102	5	0.0	3	1	B.J. Finney	RG	28	16/2	164	0	0.0	2	1
David DeCastro	RG	29	14/14	958	3	0.5	6	3									

Year	Yards	ALY	Rank	Power	Rank	Stuff	Rank	2nd Lev	Rank	Open Field	Rank	Sacks	ASR	Rank	Press	Rank	F-Start	Cont.
2016	4.47	4.68	3	71%	7	15%	4	1.40	4	0.52	25	21	4.1%	4	18.6%	2	21	31
2017	4.07	4.36	7	65%	12	17%	5	1.22	10	0.48	27	24	3.9%	1	22.7%	2	14	26
2018	4.36	4.44	15	71%	5	16%	5	1.20	20	0.80	19	24	4.4%	4	23.2%	2	8	28

2018 ALY by direction: Left End: 5.24 (11)   Left Tackle: 4.91 (5)   Mid/Guard: 4.16 (24)   Right Tackle: 4.44 (16)   Right End: 6.33 (1)

Pittsburgh sported one of the league's top front fives once again in 2018, combining agile movement with punishing drive blocking. This is a continuing, underrated key to Pittsburgh's success, and last season the unit started 72 of a possible 80 games together. ◐ The high quality of the starters led to hardly any use of max-protection schemes—just 3.7 percent of pass plays, tied for last in the NFL. (This is defined as seven or more blockers and at least two more blockers than pass-rushers.) ◐ However, this unit is getting up there in age. The interior combo of 33-year-old Ramon Foster, 30-year-old Maurkice Pouncey, and 29-year-old David DeCastro is set to begin its eighth season together, an extraordinary run of cohesiveness that is otherwise unseen in today's NFL. Their left tackle teammate, Alejandro Villanueva, turns 31 early in the season. Foster seemed likely to depart in the offseason but was suddenly re-signed when the team just couldn't face breaking up the band. ◐ The lone spot where youth is served is right tackle, where Marcus Gilbert sustained his usual injury in October, and has since been shipped to Arizona. Matt Feiler took over for Gilbert, started ten games, and was decent enough, though not so dominant that last year's third-round pick, Chukwuma Okorafor, can't win the spot in training camp. ◐ The biggest issue facing the line is probably the loss of its coach, Mike Munchak, who moved to Denver to be closer to his family. He is replaced by fellow alliterative Shaun Sarrett, who was Munchak's assistant. Sarrett won't be inclined to change what isn't broken, but it's also unlikely he will command the respect that Munchak had.

Defensive Front

Defensive Line	Age	Pos	G	Snaps	Plays	TmPct	Rk	Stop	Dfts	BTkl	Runs	St%	Rk	RuYd	Rk	Sack	Hit	Hur	Dsrpt
						Overall							vs. Run				Pass Rush		
Cameron Heyward	30	DE	16	841	54	6.9%	16	41	15	2	36	72%	52	2.8	65	8.0	10	36	2
Stephon Tuitt	26	DE	14	693	48	7.0%	13	41	16	2	36	81%	23	2.1	36	5.5	16	23	4
Javon Hargrave	26	DT	16	456	49	6.3%	20	38	11	5	38	74%	49	3.2	77	6.5	1	9	1
Tyson Alualu	32	DE	15	312	22	3.0%	--	18	3	2	18	83%	--	2.6	--	0.0	1	5	0

Edge Rushers	Age	Pos	G	Snaps	Plays	TmPct	Rk	Stop	Dfts	BTkl	Runs	St%	Rk	RuYd	Rk	Sack	Hit	Hur	Dsrpt
						Overall							vs. Run				Pass Rush		
T.J. Watt	25	OLB	16	903	69	8.8%	2	54	24	14	39	90%	5	1.8	28	13.0	11	33	1
Bud Dupree	26	OLB	16	869	45	5.8%	28	31	18	4	23	78%	33	2.8	57	5.5	7	27	3
Anthony Chickillo	27	OLB	16	295	20	2.6%	--	17	8	1	11	82%	--	1.5	--	1.5	1	8	1

Linebackers	Age	Pos	G	Snaps	Plays	TmPct	Rk	Stop	Dfts	BTkl	Runs	St%	Rk	RuYd	Rk	Sack	Hit	Hur	Tgts	Suc%	Rk	AdjYd	Rk	PD	Int
						Overall							vs. Run				Pass Rush				vs. Pass				
Vince Williams	30	ILB	14	745	76	11.1%	51	43	17	11	52	60%	43	5.0	79	4.5	6	8.5	28	43%	55	7.3	52	2	1
Jon Bostic*	28	ILB	16	562	76	9.7%	58	38	12	4	40	65%	24	3.1	16	2.5	1	8	24	29%	78	9.8	75	3	0
L.J. Fort*	29	ILB	15	305	43	5.9%	--	29	12	3	22	86%	--	2.0	--	1.0	2	7	22	59%	13	6.8	40	0	0
Mark Barron	30	ILB	12	569	60	10.3%	54	36	6	7	40	68%	16	3.9	39	1.0	1	1	24	54%	27	6.9	43	1	0

Year	Yards	ALY	Rank	Power	Rank	Stuff	Rank	2nd Level	Rank	Open Field	Rank	Sacks	ASR	Rank	Press	Rank
2016	4.39	4.07	14	67%	24	22%	9	1.24	21	0.99	29	38	5.8%	19	24.7%	24
2017	4.47	3.96	12	82%	31	20%	18	1.31	30	1.04	30	56	9.8%	1	34.3%	4
2018	4.04	4.24	12	69%	22	19%	17	1.17	11	0.63	8	52	9.3%	1	34.5%	2

2018 ALY by direction: Left End: 3.01 (4)   Left Tackle: 3.65 (9)   Mid/Guard: 4.41 (16)   Right Tackle: 4.04 (15)   Right End: 3.87 (11)

The Steelers were all over the quarterback in 2018, and it was a balanced effort—six different players had at least 4.5 sacks. ◗ Classically, Pittsburgh has built defenses around pairs of blitzing linebackers, but recent vintages are focused on two of the three down linemen. Cameron Heyward and Stephon Tuitt had strong seasons once again. They combined for 10.5 more sacks/hits/hurries than in 2017 and continued to play well against the run. ◗ Javon Hargrave is a strong third man up front, possessor of a quick step that belies his bulk. ◗ T.J. Watt posted the first double-digit sack season (13) by a Steelers edge rusher since LaMarr Woodley and James Harrison did the trick in 2010, and he was excellent with a 90 percent run stop rate. ◗ The other linebackers didn't match Watt's high standards, especially against the run and in coverage. Bud Dupree had his moments rushing the passer, but inside, Vince Williams, Jon Bostic, and L.J. Fort struggled, particularly against the pass (though Bostic did play well against the run). ◗ The franchise clearly was after a game-changer at inside linebacker this offseason and traded up in the draft to get one. Rookie Devin Bush has the talent to be that player. Speedy with great instincts and the taste for violence that the position requires, Bush should become a popular figure in the 'Burgh. At Michigan he was susceptible to being shown up in coverage by good passing attacks (Dwayne Haskins and Ohio State ate Bush alive in the 2018 rout), but he has the skills to improve and give Pittsburgh the totemic inside player it has lacked since Ryan Shazier's injury.

Defensive Secondary

Secondary	Age	Pos	G	Snaps	Plays	TmPct	Rk	Stop	Dfts	BTkl	Runs	St%	Rk	RuYd	Rk	Tgts	Tgt%	Rk	Dist	Suc%	Rk	AdjYd	Rk	PD	Int
Sean Davis	26	FS	15	979	86	11.8%	18	21	8	13	31	19%	68	8.8	53	21	5.0%	8	9.9	48%	47	11.1	68	7	1
Terrell Edmunds	22	SS	16	967	77	9.9%	42	25	6	6	31	42%	38	6.9	38	30	7.2%	18	9.2	50%	35	8.5	54	4	1
Joe Haden	30	CB	15	937	76	10.4%	11	26	13	12	16	19%	74	5.9	30	81	20.0%	50	13.6	56%	24	5.6	6	12	2
Coty Sensabaugh*	31	CB	15	745	50	6.8%	65	16	5	2	17	24%	71	8.4	64	49	15.2%	16	13.0	55%	26	5.7	8	6	0
Mike Hilton	25	CB	15	593	64	8.8%	--	34	19	5	15	80%	--	2.1	--	56	21.9%	--	8.2	52%	--	7.2	--	8	1
Morgan Burnett*	30	SS	11	389	36	6.7%	65	21	11	0	12	58%	11	4.6	8	26	15.5%	72	14.2	62%	12	7.2	38	6	0
Artie Burns	24	CB	16	308	20	2.6%	--	7	2	1	6	33%	--	4.5	--	24	18.1%	--	14.3	42%	--	10.3	--	1	0
Cameron Sutton	24	CB	15	241	22	3.0%	--	8	3	1	2	50%	--	9.0	--	26	25.0%	--	13.4	31%	--	10.5	--	3	1
Steven Nelson	26	CB	16	1164	83	9.5%	26	29	11	13	18	22%	72	8.3	63	109	21.0%	54	14.3	59%	12	7.0	28	15	4

Year	Pass D Rank	vs. #1 WR	Rk	vs. #2 WR	Rk	vs. Other WR	Rk	WR Wide	Rk	WR Slot	Rk	vs. TE	Rk	vs. RB	Rk
2016	12	19.8%	32	-18.9%	3	-30.4%	1	7.0%	24	-21.0%	2	-4.4%	13	3.3%	19
2017	7	4.3%	17	-10.9%	10	17.5%	25	-10.7%	8	21.7%	28	-34.6%	1	12.5%	23
2018	17	-6.0%	10	2.4%	19	10.8%	25	-6.8%	17	10.0%	22	25.5%	31	1.6%	15

Pittsburgh had the league's best adjusted sack rate and their opponents dropped the third-highest percentage of passes; otherwise, their 17th-rated pass defense could have been much worse. ◗ Joe Haden held up his end at one corner well enough. Coty Sensabaugh's charting stats were very similar to Haden's, a surprising result that certainly belies the eye test. Artie Burns was toasty badness in his six starts. ◗ Given the reputation of the Steelers cornerbacks, it is very odd that opponents threw it 40 percent of the time to Haden's preferred left side (offensive right) instead of focusing on the weaker links on the other side. Indeed, the 28 percent thrown at the offensive left side was the lowest rate in the league. It would seem a missed opportunity. Perhaps quarterbacks under duress defaulted to the easier throw to their right. ◗ Two new corners replace the unsigned (as of press time) Sensabaugh in the Steel City. Free agent Steven Nelson had a solid season with the Chiefs despite being targeted a league-leading 109 times. Part of that, of course, is situational—with K.C. ahead so much, opponents were throwing often on them, and Nelson's coverage success rate was actually better than Haden's. ◗ Pittsburgh also drafted Justin Layne of Michigan State in the third round. Layne is a big and long but slow player who needs to improve in run support. ◗ Safeties Sean Davis and rookie Terrell Edmunds are similar players, punishing hitters with range who struggle in coverage and with sophisticated route concepts. Both are certainly young enough to improve in that area, especially Edmunds, who came on as the season progressed. ◗ As mentioned earlier in the chapter, Pittsburgh's ability to defend tight ends fell off a cliff in 2018. Teams ate up Morgan Burnett, who struggled with injury, and Cameron Sutton when they matched up on tight ends as the Steelers "dimebacker" or third safety. 2018 fifth-rounder Marcus Allen (sorry, no relation) will get the opportunity to step in and do better. He didn't sniff the field as a rookie, but Pittsburgh's options in this area are limited. ◗ The Steelers may not have had a ton of good players in the secondary, but they were used often and in a variety of ways—only two teams played six defensive backs more often, and Pittsburgh was also third in blitzing defensive backs, though the secondary only provided two of the team's 52 sacks. It's reminiscent of the old Borscht Belt joke about a couple reviewing a restaurant; "The food here is terrible!" "And such small portions!"

Special Teams

Year	DVOA	Rank	FG/XP	Rank	Net Kick	Rank	Kick Ret	Rank	Net Punt	Rank	Punt Ret	Rank	Hidden	Rank
2016	-0.1%	16	9.1	3	-2.2	19	-1.6	18	-4.4	23	-1.3	17	-0.2	17
2017	3.1%	9	8.4	7	5.2	7	1.3	10	3.3	15	-2.9	24	-8.0	28
2018	-3.5%	27	-11.0	30	3.7	6	-4.2	28	-5.5	26	-0.5	16	1.2	12

As noted earlier in the chapter, poor special teams play was a little-remarked-upon factor in Pittsburgh's disappointing 2018.
⬤ One particular domain of incompetence was in punt coverage; only Detroit gave up more estimated points of field position in this area. The kickoff coverage was excellent by contrast, and punter Jordan Berry was average but not terrible, so it should be a correctable issue (though punt coverage performance has trended downward in Pittsburgh over the last three seasons). ⬤ Kicker Chris Boswell's fall from grace was well documented, going from Pro Bowl and contract extension to the precipice of unemployment before an injury ended his season. Matt McCrane earned a game ball for making all three of his kicks against Cincinnati in the finale but was cut after the season. Boswell will instead face a camp battle with rookie Matthew Wright from Central Florida, whose 77.5 percent field goal rate in college seems a bit underwhelming. ⬤ Ryan Switzer remains the primary returner as well, though he was weak on kickoffs and merely average on punts in 2018.

San Francisco 49ers

2018 record: 4-12	**Total DVOA:** -20.7% (30th)	**2019 Mean Projection:** 7.7 wins	**On the Clock (0-4):** 12%
Pythagorean Wins: 5.6 (27th)	**Offense:** -15.4% (27th)	**Postseason Odds:** 31.1%	**Mediocrity (5-7):** 35%
Snap-Weighted Age: 25.7 (28th)	**Defense:** 5.7% (23rd)	**Super Bowl Odds:** 3.5%	**Playoff Contender (8-10):** 37%
Average Opponent: 1.1% (10th)	**Special Teams:** 0.3% (14th)	**Proj. Avg. Opponent:** 0.9% (13th)	**Super Bowl Contender (11+):** 15%

2018: The Handsome Jimmy G era stumbles out of the blocks.

2019: Don't trust an offense built on overpaying running backs.

By now, we were supposed to know more about this 49ers regime. It was January of 2017 when John Lynch was yanked off the Fox Sports studios set and placed behind the general manager's desk, with Kyle Shanahan joining him as head coach shortly thereafter. That fall, a midseason trade for Jimmy Garoppolo looked to set the franchise in the right direction, as the 49ers won each of his five starts to close the year. When Garoppolo signed a massive extension after that season, most observers in San Francisco felt that the foundation had been built. Even if immediate postseason contention was unrealistic, 2018 should have seen enough improvement that the team would need only minor tweaks to make a playoff push in 2019.

Unfortunately, things didn't work out that way. Jerick McKinnon, Lynch's shiny new free-agent signee, tore his ACL in practice before the season even started. Garoppolo tore his own ACL just three weeks into the year. Each of the top three wide receivers was also lost for a significant chunk of time. A six-game losing streak all but eliminated San Francisco from the playoff race before Halloween, and save for a handful of individual highlights—a practice-squad quarterback leading the team to victory here, a tight end setting records there—the 2018 season for the San Francisco 49ers was largely a waste of time. One year later, we are left with unanswered questions concerning Lynch's ability to build a roster, Shanahan's proficiency at managing a team, and Garoppolo's chances of living up to his contract extension.

We'll begin with Lynch, who if nothing else has managed to rebuild his roster through the draft. Lynch has now selected 27 players in his three NFL drafts, and at least 25 of them will still likely be on the team heading into training camp this year. Pending training camp battles, that includes somewhere between six and nine starters between offense and defense. There's a difference, though, between starters and *good* starters. Only two of Lynch's draftees—tight end George Kittle and linebacker Fred Warner—have proven themselves to be impact players in the NFL. The others have either struggled to stay healthy or show they belong in NFL lineups. It's worth noting that Kittle was a fifth-round pick in 2017, while Warner was a third-round pick the next year. Lynch's success rate on earlier picks is highly dubious. The first-round selections in his first two drafts include Solomon Thomas, the third overall pick in 2017 who is already in danger of losing his starting job;

Reuben Foster, the linebacker who was released after he was arrested three separate times in 2018; and Mike McGlinchey, the right tackle who led the NFL in blown blocks last year.

Will the 2019 draft class have more success in Santa Clara? Nick Bosa will likely be a good NFL player, but our Sack-SEER projections say he may have been a reach with the second overall pick. His production at Ohio State was modest, and his performance at the combine was below average for most successful edge rushers. Our projections aren't thrilled about the wide receivers Lynch found in the second and third rounds either. Neither South Carolina's Deebo Samuel nor Baylor's Jalen Hurd did much to stand out in a mediocre pool of wideout talent.

The obvious caveat here is that all of these players are young and still have time to develop into solid pros. The point is not to condemn Lynch for his failures, only to show that the jury remains very much out on his drafting acuity.

It is more fair, though, to evaluate Lynch's free-agent spending, where his prevailing strategy seems to be "solve all problems by severely overpaying a running back." Our cost-benefit analysis found that Kyle Juszczyk was the most overpaid free-agent running back of 2017, and Lynch doubled down on that by making McKinnon the most overpaid free-agent running back of 2018. This year he added another veteran runner: Tevin Coleman, formerly of Atlanta. That contract seems much more reasonable on the surface but given San Francisco's existing surplus at the position, there were better ways to spend that money. The roster still includes Juszczyk, McKinnon, Matt Breida, Jeff Wilson, and Raheem Mostert, who was re-signed to a three-year deal just days after Coleman was acquired. Per Over The Cap, 49ers running backs have a combined cap hit of $20.4 million in 2019, over $3 million more than any other team.

To be fair to Lynch, he's not tunnel-focused on overpaying running backs; he has also overpaid offensive linemen, guaranteeing $16.5 million to center Weston Richburg and $4 million to guard Jonathan Cooper in 2018. Richburg went on to provide 15 disappointing starts, but that is more than we can say for Cooper, who was released before the season started. This year's passenger on the John Lynch gravy train is Kwon Alexander, a 25-year-old linebacker coming off a torn ACL. He's a good player, but Lynch gave him a contract worth $54 million over four years. That's an average of $13.5 million per

2019 49ers Schedule

Week	Opp.	Week	Opp.	Week	Opp.
1	at TB	7	at WAS	13	at BAL
2	at CIN	8	CAR	14	at NO
3	PIT	9	at ARI (Thu.)	15	ATL
4	BYE	10	SEA (Mon.)	16	LAR
5	CLE (Mon.)	11	ARI	17	at SEA
6	at LAR	12	GB		

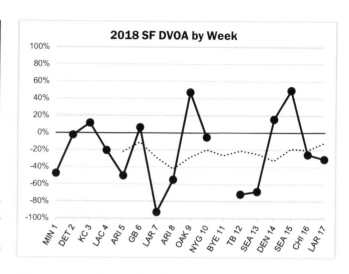

year, second-highest in the league among off-ball linebackers. If Alexander is anything less than a first-team All-Pro this season, he'll be grossly overpaid.

We're cherry-picking some of Lynch's worst deals here. He has had other acquisitions—Marquise Goodwin, Pierre Garcon, Earl Mitchell, Malcolm Smith, Richard Sherman—that were perfectly reasonable and more or less successful. His best move this year was to acquire edge rusher Dee Ford from Kansas City. Lynch gave up just a 2020 second-rounder for Ford, then signed him to a five-year deal worth up to $87.5 million, but he maintained some cap flexibility -- Ford is guaranteed nearly $20 million upfront, but the deal is structured so that no further money is guaranteed until April of 2020.

The biggest problem with Lynch's offseason is that he ignored some clear areas of need. We've already discussed his fetish for acquiring running backs every year, but let's not forget that he spent two Day 2 draft picks on wide receivers, and also signed free-agent wideout Jordan Matthews. This on a team that already had plenty of weapons—Goodwin and Dante Pettis out wide, Kittle at tight end, and a dozen or so running backs, several of whom can split out wide or in the slot themselves. Perhaps Deebo Samuel and Jalen Hurd will develop into good players—Samuel could even be a Day 1 starter in the slot—but the 49ers had bigger needs. The interior offensive line was denied a needed infusion of new talent. The secondary is left with an aging Sherman as one cornerback and question marks everywhere else. Lynch even used a fourth-round pick on a punter, Utah's Mitch Wishnowsky, rather than adding a useful blocker or corner.

Sherman's first season in San Francisco was largely successful, but you can't win with one star cornerback if the players on the other side can't hold up their end of the deal. "Throw away from No. 25" was an all-too-easy strategy for quarterbacks facing the 49ers in 2018. Opposing quarterbacks threw 44 percent of their passes to the left side of the field (away from Sherman), the highest rate in the league. And those passes usually worked—the 49ers ranked 26th in DVOA against passes in that direction. San Francisco gave up a league-high 17 touchdown passes to quarterbacks throwing to their left last year, three more than anyone else and nearly double the average of 8.9. At the same time, they were the only defense that failed to intercept a single pass thrown to that side of the field.

Of course, interceptions were a problem everywhere for San Francisco—they only had two all season, and one of those was thrown by Josh Rosen so it should only get half credit.

(The other was thrown by Philip Rivers.) Every other defense had at least seven interceptions. Fifty-two individual players had more interceptions than the 49ers last year. That includes Seattle's Earl Thomas, who had three interceptions before a broken leg ended his season in September. On top of that, San Francisco recovered only five of 18 fumbles on defense. That's seven turnovers in 174 drives, a rate of 0.040 turnovers per drive that is the lowest of any defense in our drive stats database going back to 1993.

This is partly because turnovers are down for everyone these days; last year's Lions also show up on the list of defenses with the fewest takeaways per drive, and the Steelers (0.079 takeaways per drive) and Packers (0.080) just missed (Table 1). Nonetheless, this is a stat that usually sees very strong regression towards the mean from year to year. Interceptions and fumble recoveries both roughly doubled the following season for the defenses in Table 1, and 14 of the 18 teams listed prior to 2018 improved in DVOA the following year. However, that improvement was less than you might expect, just 7.9% on average, and the overall results were often still quite mediocre. More turnovers will help, but the 49ers will need more than that to become a championship-caliber defense.

There's plenty of blame to go around for San Francisco's defensive failures—this is on Lynch for selecting the players and the performance of players themselves, but also on Shanahan and his coaching staff. Defensive coordinator Robert Saleh, a product of the Pete Carroll coaching tree, gained experience in Seattle and Jacksonville before joining Shanahan in San Francisco. He must carry much of the burden of San Francisco's defensive performance, but as head coach Shanahan must bear responsibility for the whole operation. Besides, Shanahan's own offensive scheme has its own share of warts to deal with.

In the tables in this chapter, you'll see that San Francisco finished dead last in rush offense DVOA—but you'll also see that the offensive line was in the top 10 in adjusted line yards, and they got plenty of big plays in the running game, finishing in the top five in both second-level yards and open-field yards. How can a team that moved the ball so well finish last in rushing offense? The first issue is fumbles—San Francisco running backs fumbled a league-high eight times on running plays. Another issue is that all three of San Francisco's starting quarterbacks—Garoppolo, C.J. Beathard, and Nick Mullens—had terrible rushing results. Even after removing kneel-downs, the trio combined for 31 carries that gained a total of 95 yards (and also three more fumbles). That average of 3.1 yards apiece was third-worst in the league for quarterback runs, just ahead of Philip Rivers and the Chargers (1.7) and Eli Manning and the Giants (2.2), and barely half the league average (5.9). All told, the 49ers had -69 rushing DYAR by quarterbacks, next to last behind Baltimore. (You can read about the Ravens elsewhere in this book but suffice to say our system is not designed to measure quarterbacks who run as frequently as Lamar Jackson.) Shanahan also deprives his running backs of easy third-down conversions—the average 49ers handoff on third down came with 6.97 yards to go, third-most in the league. That's a good way to get yardage without the kind of efficiency that leads to a strong DVOA rating.

Shanahan's passing schemes leave room for criticism as well. His offense is very good at getting receivers open for easy completions but not nearly so effective at keeping quarterbacks upright. Between sacks and hits, 49ers were put on the ground 127 times last season, 21.6 percent of all pass plays, second-most in both categories behind the Houston Texans. Each of the three quarterbacks who started for San Francisco last year—Garoppolo, C.J. Beathard, and Nick Mullens—had knockdown rates of 20 percent or higher. This was not a one-year anomaly, either. Beathard had the highest knockdown rate of any qualifying quarterback in 2017. Even in 2016, when Shanahan and the Falcons made it to the Super Bowl, Matt Ryan's knockdown rate of 18.9 percent was the highest of his career. Each of those teams allowed a higher pressure rate than average, but overall they were closer to the middle of the pack than not. What's going on here?

It appears that Shanahan coaches his quarterbacks to deal with pressure by hanging in the pocket and reading through progressions rather than panicking and going to Plan B. According to Sports Info Solutions charting, the most common route thrown by quarterbacks under pressure was "broken play." This is not the case in San Francisco, however, where digs, drags, and curls were all thrown under pressure more frequently than broken plays. 49ers quarterbacks also threw fewer checkdowns to the flat under pressure than most quarterbacks. Shanahan may have gotten away with this in the past—even including last season, his teams have suffered fewer adjusted games lost at the quarterback position than average—but given those trends, it was almost inevitable that one of his quarterbacks eventually suffered a serious injury.

Those are the weaknesses in the Shanahan offense, but then, there are strengths too. Specifically, he's very good at using play-action and pass patterns to scheme receivers open. According to NFL's Next Gen Stats, San Francisco's most frequently targeted receivers—Kittle, Bourne, Garcon, Pettis, and Goodwin—averaged 3.11 yards of separation, better than the top targets on all teams but the Giants. Based on a number of factors—including receiver separation, pass length, pressure, and more—Beathard had the highest expected completion percentage in the league. Furthermore, San Francisco led all teams by averaging 7.0 yards after the catch per reception. Kittle led all players with 870 YAC. In short, the job requirements for San Francisco quarterbacks were often "throw the ball to the wide-open receiver, then watch as he takes off downfield for an easy gain."

So if playing quarterback for Shanahan is so easy, why did

Table 1: Fewest Turnovers Forced per Drive, 1993-2018

Year	Team	Year N						Year N+1					
		Drives	TOs/Drive	INT	FR	DVOA	W-L	Drives	TOs/Drive	INT	FR	DVOA	W-L
2018	SF	174	0.040	2	5	5.7%	4-12	--	--	--	--	--	--
2014	NYJ	178	0.056	6	7	3.5%	4-12	187	0.150	18	12	-13.8%	10-6
2006	WAS	172	0.058	6	6	15.0%	5-11	187	0.128	14	10	-7.9%	9-7
2013	HOU	187	0.059	7	4	2.5%	2-14	193	0.166	20	14	-6.2%	9-7
2015	DAL	168	0.060	8	3	4.1%	4-12	166	0.114	9	11	1.1%	13-3
2016	JAX	182	0.060	7	6	-3.1%	3-13	197	0.162	21	12	-16.2%	10-6
2016	CLE	176	0.063	10	3	14.5%	1-15	179	0.073	7	6	2.0%	0-16
2012	KC	173	0.064	7	6	13.0%	2-14	201	0.159	21	15	-6.7%	11-5
2015	BAL	181	0.066	6	8	5.1%	5-11	184	0.141	18	10	-9.9%	8-8
2016	CHI	163	0.067	8	3	5.0%	3-13	169	0.118	8	14	-1.5%	5-11
2015	SF	176	0.068	9	3	9.9%	5-11	183	0.202	10	10	12.1%	2-14
2014	OAK	186	0.070	9	5	6.3%	3-13	188	0.117	14	11	-1.5%	7-9
2014	KC	170	0.071	6	8	1.3%	9-7	179	0.156	22	7	-11.6%	11-5
2017	OAK	166	0.072	5	9	10.3%	6-10	168	0.101	14	3	12.3%	4-12
2017	CLE	179	0.073	7	6	2.0%	0-16	193	0.161	17	14	-2.5%	7-8-1
2018	DET	165	0.073	7	7	9.0%	6-10	--	--	--	--	--	--
2016	NYJ	174	0.075	8	6	3.7%	5-11	186	0.108	11	9	3.9%	5-11
2017	CIN	183	0.077	11	3	3.7%	7-9	172	0.105	12	6	9.0%	6-10
2005	HOU	166	0.078	7	9	20.1%	2-14	165	0.133	11	11	13.7%	6-10
2004	STL	178	0.079	6	9	14.2%	8-8	188	0.133	13	14	12.7%	6-10
Average		*174.9*	*0.066*	*7.1*	*5.8*	*7.3%*	*4.2-11.8*	*182.5*	*0.135*	*14.4*	*10.5*	*-0.6%*	*7.2-8.8*

Garoppolo often make it look so hard? NFL Next Gen Stats lists a stat called "aggressiveness" that measures the percentage of throws a quarterback attempts into tight windows with a defender within 1 yard of the intended receiver. Mullens' aggressiveness of 12.0 percent was the second-lowest among qualifying quarterbacks. Beathard's rate of 14.8 percent was also lower than average, but high for him—he was lowest in 2017 at 12.5 percent. In his three starts, however, Garoppolo's aggressiveness rate was 27.0 percent. Consider that Josh Rosen's aggressiveness of 21.6 percent was the highest of all qualified passers. Garoppolo also threw much deeper (9.2-yard average depth of target) than either Mullens (6.8) or Beathard (6.6). This may have been a three-game fluke—Garoppolo's aggressiveness in 2017 was 15.2 percent, though his pass distance was again 9.2.

Still, this brings us to the heart of the matter with Garoppolo—how can anyone know what to expect from a quarterback who has seen so little action? Garoppolo turns 28 this season, but in terms of on-field experience he remains a rookie—he has fewer career pass attempts than Baker Mayfield, Sam Darnold, or Josh Rosen. Nobody can be certain how good

those rookies will eventually be, so how can we be certain of what Garoppolo is? Garoppolo played well for 361 passes before tearing his ACL. Robert Griffin played well for 393 passes before tearing his ACL, but he has not been good since. Garoppolo plays the position very differently than Griffin, obviously, but that doesn't guarantee that he will improve in the future—and he will need to improve if San Francisco is going to win in the postseason.

In the long term, there is still hope for the 49ers, and for Lynch, Shanahan, and Garoppolo. In the short term, though, things won't be easy. The 49ers will face a murderer's row of quarterbacks—two games each against Jared Goff, Russell Wilson, and Kyler Murray, plus Ben Roethlisberger, Baker Mayfield, Lamar Jackson, Drew Brees, Matt Ryan, Cam Newton, and Aaron Rodgers in 2019. It looks like a tough schedule for a San Francisco team where so many important people are still learning on the job. The 49ers should be better this year than they were in 2018, but a return to the playoffs will likely be at least one more year away.

Vincent Verhei

2018 49ers Stats by Week

Wk	vs.	W-L	PF	PA	YDF	YDA	TO	Total	Off	Def	ST
1	at MIN	L	16	24	327	343	-3	-48%	-53%	-5%	0%
2	DET	W	30	27	346	427	+1	-3%	11%	9%	-5%
3	at KC	L	27	38	406	384	0	11%	19%	4%	-4%
4	at LAC	L	27	29	364	368	-1	-21%	-19%	-17%	-18%
5	ARI	L	18	28	447	220	-5	-50%	-14%	25%	-12%
6	at GB	L	30	33	401	521	-3	6%	18%	17%	5%
7	LAR	L	10	39	228	339	-4	-93%	-74%	8%	-11%
8	at ARI	L	15	18	267	321	+2	-55%	-30%	24%	0%
9	OAK	W	34	3	405	242	0	47%	12%	-27%	9%
10	NYG	L	23	27	374	277	-2	-5%	-7%	3%	5%
11	BYE										
12	at TB	L	9	27	342	412	-2	-72%	-35%	37%	0%
13	at SEA	L	16	43	452	331	-3	-69%	-32%	31%	-5%
14	DEN	W	20	14	389	274	-1	16%	-10%	-24%	2%
15	SEA	W	26	23	351	385	-1	49%	10%	-8%	31%
16	CHI	L	9	14	279	325	+1	-26%	-8%	20%	3%
17	at LAR	L	32	48	391	377	-4	-31%	-30%	8%	7%

Trends and Splits

	Offense	Rank	Defense	Rank
Total DVOA	-15.4%	27	5.7%	23
Unadjusted VOA	-14.4%	27	9.4%	27
Weighted Trend	-16.5%	28	7.0%	25
Variance	6.9%	16	3.7%	3
Average Opponent	0.6%	21	2.6%	10
Passing	2.9%	23	19.6%	27
Rushing	-22.4%	32	-11.0%	12
First Down	-7.2%	21	7.9%	25
Second Down	-20.0%	28	-4.6%	13
Third Down	-27.0%	29	16.8%	26
First Half	-10.2%	27	6.0%	28
Second Half	-20.5%	27	5.3%	22
Red Zone	-53.0%	32	22.4%	28
Late and Close	-31.1%	30	-0.9%	16

Five-Year Performance

Year	W-L	Pyth W	Est W	PF	PA	TO	Total	Rk	Off	Rk	Def	Rk	ST	Rk	Off AGL	Rk	Def AGL	Rk	Off Age	Rk	Def Age	Rk	ST Age	Rk
2014	8-8	7.0	9.0	306	340	+7	6.6%	11	-0.4%	16	-10.1%	5	-3.0%	24	30.0	15	71.8	31	27.6	6	26.8	16	26.4	8
2015	5-11	3.8	4.1	238	387	-5	-27.5%	32	-14.0%	28	9.9%	27	-3.6%	27	58.2	28	25.8	11	27.7	6	25.4	32	25.1	31
2016	2-14	3.9	4.6	309	247	-5	-19.6%	28	-7.2%	23	12.1%	28	-0.3%	17	39.0	21	58.5	26	27.0	13	26.2	22	26.1	17
2017	6-10	6.6	6.7	331	383	-3	-8.4%	20	-3.0%	19	8.3%	26	2.9%	11	24.7	8	66.8	32	27.3	9	25.4	29	25.8	18
2018	4-12	5.6	4.8	342	435	-25	-20.7%	30	-15.4%	27	5.7%	23	0.3%	14	54.0	26	44.2	24	26.7	17	25.1	30	25.2	30

2018 Performance Based on Most Common Personnel Groups

SF Offense					SF Offense vs. Opponents					SF Defense				SF Defense vs. Opponents			
Pers	Freq	Yds	DVOA	Run%	Pers	Freq	Yds	DVOA	Run%	Pers	Freq	Yds	DVOA	Pers	Freq	Yds	DVOA
21	42%	6.4	-1.5%	51%	Base	45%	6.7	-0.5%	54%	Base	26%	5.3	-10.1%	11	62%	5.8	13.5%
11	39%	5.2	-11.4%	17%	Nickel	40%	5.7	-9.9%	30%	Nickel	72%	5.8	12.7%	12	18%	5.2	-3.0%
12	10%	7.5	-6.2%	56%	Dime+	12%	4.2	-23.8%	11%	Dime+	2%	4.2	-40.0%	21	6%	4.9	-28.4%
22	6%	4.4	-29.4%	69%	Goal Line	1%	0.0	-110.8%	75%	Goal Line	0%	0.8	-1.8%	22	2%	4.0	15.6%
13	1%	4.1	-46.1%	78%										613	2%	5.3	8.2%
01	1%	5.3	-62.0%	0%										10	2%	4.6	-11.0%

Strategic Tendencies

Run/Pass		Rk	Formation		Rk	Pass Rush		Rk	Secondary		Rk	Strategy		Rk
Runs, first half	40%	12	Form: Single Back	52%	32	Rush 3	3.6%	25	4 DB	26%	14	Play action	26%	11
Runs, first down	50%	9	Form: Empty Back	11%	5	Rush 4	77.3%	4	5 DB	72%	10	Avg Box (Off)	6.38	4
Runs, second-long	29%	19	Pers: 3+ WR	40%	32	Rush 5	14.4%	24	6+ DB	2%	24	Avg Box (Def)	6.32	8
Runs, power sit.	60%	14	Pers: 2+ TE/6+ OL	17%	28	Rush 6+	4.6%	20	CB by Sides	89%	4	Offensive Pace	30.39	10
Runs, behind 2H	30%	11	Pers: 6+ OL	0%	30	Int DL Sacks	37.8%	7	S/CB Cover Ratio	26%	20	Defensive Pace	30.77	10
Pass, ahead 2H	46%	23	Shotgun/Pistol	46%	31	Second Level Sacks	18.9%	23	DB Blitz	9%	14	Go for it on 4th	0.78	31

The modern NFL in a nutshell: the 49ers were dead last in usage of single-back sets and still used them on more than half their offensive plays. The 49ers were the only team in 2018 with 21 instead of 11 as its most common personnel set. ◗ San Francisco used two players in the backfield on a league-leading 59 percent of running plays; New England was the only other team in the league above 40 percent. The 49ers performance running the ball was basically the same with one back (4.9 yards, -21.6% DVOA) as it was with two backs (4.8, -19.6%). ◗ What happens when you don't spread the field: the 49ers ran just 29 percent of their running back carries against small boxes (less than seven); only Tennessee ran a higher percentage of the time against seven or more in the box. ◗ San Francisco averaged 5.9 yards after the catch on passes thrown past the line of scrimmage. No other offense was above 5.2. Yet despite all that YAC, San Francisco was actually below-average in DVOA on these passes (49.6% DVOA versus a league average of 55.4%). ◗ The 49ers ranked seventh in defensive DVOA on third-and-short, but 28th on all other third downs. ◗ San Francisco opponents threw a league-high 26 percent of targets to tight ends. ◗ For a forward-thinking young head coach, Kyle Shanahan is distinctively conservative on fourth downs, ranking 27th and 31st in Aggressiveness Index in his two seasons.

Passing

Player	DYAR	DVOA	Plays	NtYds	Avg	YAC	C%	TD	Int
N.Mullens	286	4.2%	287	2151	7.5	7.0	65.2%	13	10
C.J.Beathard	-156	-24.3%	188	1101	5.9	7.1	60.4%	8	7
J.Garoppolo	-9	-12.5%	102	620	6.1	6.9	59.6%	5	3

Rushing

Player	DYAR	DVOA	Plays	Yds	Avg	TD	Fum	Suc
M.Breida	58	1.3%	153	814	5.3	3	1	46%
A.Morris*	-103	-30.5%	111	429	3.9	2	2	41%
J.Wilson	-2	-9.4%	66	266	4.0	0	3	52%
R.Mostert	40	19.4%	34	261	7.7	1	1	65%
C.J.Beathard	-13	-25.2%	18	68	3.8	1	1	--
K.Juszczyk	-29	-86.7%	8	30	3.8	0	1	38%
J.Garoppolo	-14	-48.2%	7	31	4.4	0	1	--
N.Mullens	-43	-118.6%	6	-4	-0.7	0	1	--
T.Coleman	14	-6.4%	167	800	4.8	4	1	43%

Receiving

Player	DYAR	DVOA	Plays	Ctch	Yds	Y/C	YAC	TD	C%
K.Bourne	42	-4.5%	67	42	488	11.6	3.5	4	63%
P.Garcon*	-31	-21.3%	46	24	286	11.9	4.1	1	52%
D.Pettis	109	16.8%	45	27	467	17.3	7.6	5	60%
M.Goodwin	51	1.7%	44	23	395	17.2	5.5	4	52%
T.Taylor	-21	-19.4%	40	26	215	8.3	4.0	1	65%
R.James	11	-2.8%	14	9	130	14.4	11.2	1	64%
J.Matthews	84	28.8%	28	20	300	15.0	4.2	2	71%
G.Kittle	207	15.1%	136	88	1377	15.6	9.9	5	65%
G.Celek	38	60.6%	8	5	90	18.0	8.6	2	63%
L.Toilolo	75	37.3%	24	21	263	12.5	5.2	1	88%
K.Juszczyk	76	18.7%	41	30	324	10.8	5.8	1	73%
M.Breida	105	44.8%	31	27	261	9.7	8.7	2	87%
J.Wilson	17	4.9%	15	12	98	8.2	8.1	0	80%
A.Morris*	6	-6.7%	13	8	73	9.1	8.4	0	62%
R.Mostert	-6	-32.1%	7	6	25	4.2	7.3	0	86%
T.Coleman	77	17.2%	44	32	276	8.6	8.6	5	73%

Offensive Line

Player	Pos	Age	GS	Snaps	Pen	Sk	Pass	Run	Player	Pos	Age	GS	Snaps	Pen	Sk	Pass	Run
Mike McGlinchey	RT	25	16/16	1053	3	4.5	25	7	Mike Person	RG	31	16/16	998	7	3.5	13	6
Laken Tomlinson	LG	27	16/16	1026	8	3.0	9	8	Weston Richburg	C	28	15/15	967	4	3.5	10	7
Joe Staley	LT	35	16/16	1005	5	4.0	9	1	*Ben Garland*	*RG*	*31*	*14/4*	*371*	*2*	*2.5*	*5*	*2*

Year	Yards	ALY	Rank	Power	Rank	Stuff	Rank	2nd Lev	Rank	Open Field	Rank	Sacks	ASR	Rank	Press	Rank	F-Start	Cont.
2016	3.99	3.46	32	69%	11	22%	25	1.12	17	0.72	14	47	8.4%	30	28.6%	22	15	32
2017	4.13	4.20	10	62%	20	23%	25	1.24	7	0.76	14	43	6.8%	18	31.3%	17	22	28
2018	4.84	4.56	10	68%	16	19%	18	1.47	3	1.13	5	48	8.0%	22	31.9%	19	25	37

2018 ALY by direction:	Left End: 5.31 (9)	Left Tackle: 4.56 (8)	Mid/Guard: 4.63 (9)	Right Tackle: 3.59 (26)	Right End: 4.63 (11)

As noted earlier in the chapter, right tackle Mike McGlinchey led the NFL in blown blocks in 2018. In addition, Weston Richburg ranked second among centers, and Laken Tomlinson and Mike Person both made the top ten at left and right guard, respectively. Joe Staley, meanwhile, ranked 28th among left tackles. All five starters return, so we are left with two questions for 2019: can Staley maintain that high level of play? And is there hope for improvement among the others? ✎ Staley, of course, has been a high-quality player for a long time, but he can't last forever. He turns 35 at the end of August; only two starting offensive linemen were that old in the NFL in 2019. Those two players were Jason Peters and Andrew Whitworth, and they will be starting again for the Eagles and Rams this fall, so success at this age certainly isn't unprecedented. Still, at his age, Staley is more likely than not to decline. The 49ers clearly disagree—they signed Staley to a two-year extension that will last through 2021. ✎ As for the others, the outlook is brightest for McGlinchey. He was a first-round pick for a reason, and NFL history is littered with players who struggled as rookies but improved with more experience. ✎ There is less cause for optimism in the interior. Tomlinson ranked among the worst guards in blown blocks in 2017 as well, and there is a reason the 49ers were able to acquire him for a fifth-round pick just two years after Detroit drafted him in the first round. Richburg has spent too much time in the trainer's room—he has missed time with concussions and battled through hand injuries, and he may miss part of training camp after offseason leg surgery. Before arriving in San Francisco, Person spent time with the Seahawks, Rams, Falcons, and Colts; the 49ers are the first team that thought it was a good idea to bring him back as a starter for a second season. ✎ Stability at the running back position would help the line, which had radically different results depending on who was in the backfield. San Francisco's adjusted line yards were below 4.00 when Alfred Morris or Kyle Juszczyk carried the ball, but 4.64 or higher when Matt Breida, Jeff Wilson, or Raheem Mostert toted the rock.

Defensive Front

Defensive Line	Age	Pos	G	Snaps	Plays	TmPct	Rk	Stop	Dfts	BTkl	Runs	St%	Rk	RuYd	Rk	Sack	Hit	Hur	Dsrpt
DeForest Buckner	25	DT	16	852	70	9.1%	2	52	22	4	50	70%	62	2.5	55	12.0	7	30	3
Earl Mitchell*	32	DT	14	363	28	4.2%	--	18	3	2	23	74%	--	3.1	--	0.0	3	6	0
Sheldon Day	25	DT	12	275	13	2.2%	--	9	3	0	9	56%	--	3.1	--	2.0	1	14	2
D.J. Jones	24	DT	10	239	17	3.5%	--	13	1	3	17	76%	--	1.8	--	0.0	1	4	0

Edge Rushers	Age	Pos	G	Snaps	Plays	TmPct	Rk	Stop	Dfts	BTkl	Runs	St%	Rk	RuYd	Rk	Sack	Hit	Hur	Dsrpt
Solomon Thomas	24	DE	16	644	31	4.0%	66	17	5	3	24	54%	87	3.1	67	1.0	7	20	0
Arik Armstead	26	DE	16	608	48	6.2%	15	28	8	8	42	55%	86	3.1	66	3.0	9	20	0
Cassius Marsh*	27	DE	16	550	36	4.7%	50	27	20	5	22	73%	51	3.6	83	5.5	10	20	0
Ronald Blair	26	DE	16	534	36	4.7%	50	28	16	3	25	76%	42	1.6	20	5.5	8	12	0
Dee Ford	*28*	*OLB*	*16*	*1021*	*52*	*6.0%*	*24*	*38*	*21*	*3*	*31*	*68%*	*63*	*2.1*	*35*	*13.0*	*18*	*49*	*1*

Linebackers	Age	Pos	G	Snaps	Plays	TmPct	Rk	Stop	Dfts	BTkl	Runs	St%	Rk	RuYd	Rk	Sack	Hit	Hur	Tgts	Suc%	Rk	AdjYd	Rk	PD	Int
Fred Warner	23	MLB	16	1060	129	16.7%	12	66	18	11	73	60%	40	3.9	41	0.0	3	6	52	56%	20	5.6	19	6	0
Elijah Lee	23	OLB	16	476	63	8.2%	67	33	13	5	31	65%	26	4.3	63	1.0	1	5.5	25	40%	64	6.6	34	2	0
Reuben Foster*	25	OLB	6	337	29	10.0%	55	15	5	6	17	59%	48	4.2	58	0.0	2	4	15	67%	--	5.5	--	1	0
Malcolm Smith	30	OLB	13	336	36	5.7%	82	24	5	4	23	70%	13	3.1	17	0.0	3	2.5	11	64%	--	8.7	--	1	0
Kwon Alexander	*25*	*MLB*	*6*	*366*	*47*	*15.4%*	*21*	*24*	*13*	*7*	*17*	*53%*	*62*	*2.6*	*7*	*1.0*	*3*	*4.5*	*10*	*40%*	*--*	*8.9*	*--*	*2*	*0*

Year	Yards	ALY	Rank	Power	Rank	Stuff	Rank	2nd Level	Rank	Open Field	Rank	Sacks	ASR	Rank	Press	Rank
2016	4.97	4.68	29	71%	28	16%	27	1.27	23	1.29	32	33	5.8%	20	22.6%	31
2017	3.82	4.09	15	64%	17	22%	9	1.05	8	0.62	10	30	5.0%	29	29.4%	23
2018	4.08	4.39	19	61%	6	17%	21	1.19	12	0.59	6	37	6.9%	18	29.9%	18

2018 ALY by direction:	Left End: 5.50 (29)	Left Tackle: 4.64 (20)	Mid/Guard: 4.40 (15)	Right Tackle: 3.35 (6)	Right End: 3.21 (5)

Most of San Francisco's success against the pass last season came on blitzes. When they used exactly five pass-rushers, they were second behind New England with a 63 percent success rate, allowing 4.8 yards per play (third) with a -16.5% DVOA (ninth). They were even better on defensive back blitzes, leading the league with a 70 percent success rate and finishing second at 2.9 yards allowed per play. They didn't use either of those tactics very often, however—77 percent of the time, they used a vanilla four-man rush, fourth-most. ◉ Since San Francisco likes to rush four, it's critical they get the best four pass-rushers they can find. Enter Nick Bosa, the second overall pick in this year's draft, and Dee Ford, John Lynch's big-money free-agent acquisition this year (well, one of them). Bosa collected 5.0 sacks as a freshman at Ohio State and added 8.5 as a sophomore. He had 4.0 in the first three games of his junior season, then underwent surgery to treat a "core muscle injury" and missed the rest of the year. Ford, a 2014 first-round pick in Kansas City, was a late bloomer. He didn't hit ten sacks in a season until 2016, then was limited to 2.0 sacks and only six games played in 2017 due to back injuries. He rebounded last season with 13.0 sacks and a league-high seven forced fumbles. In a best-case scenario, Bosa and Ford become the league's premier rushing bookends and the 49ers lead the league in sacks; worst-case, both men are struck with injuries and have trouble just getting on the field. ◉ We would be remiss if we didn't note Bosa's history on Twitter, a history that includes liking multiple Tweets that include homophobic and racial slurs that could make life difficult for a white man going to work in a mostly black locker room. Richard Sherman, who has never been shy about sharing his opinion, told Chris Biderman of the *Sacramento Bee* that it would not be an issue: "If he can play, he can play. If he can't play, he won't be here. But at the end of the day, that's all that matters in football. Is he getting sacks on Sunday? Is he helping our team? Is he being a good teammate? Those are things that matter." ◉ In addition to Bosa and Ford, the 49ers have three other former first-round picks on the defensive line: Arik Armstead (2015), DeForest Buckner (2016), and Solomon Thomas (2017). Results there have been mixed at best. Buckner is a rock, starting 47 of a possible 48 games in his career and posting a dozen sacks last year, third-most among interior linemen. Thomas, however, has just 4.0 sacks after starting 25 games at defensive end in his first two years. He'll move to 3-technique this season; curiously, he has prepared for the move inside by dropping to 270 pounds, 10 pounds lighter than he played last year. Armstead, meanwhile, has frequently been injured, and though he started all 16 games last year, he had little production to show for it. Trade rumors circled both Armstead and Thomas over the offseason, but each will get one last chance to live up to their draft stock in San Francisco. ◉ At linebacker, Fred Warner was a pleasant surprise in the third round. The BYU alum started all 16 games, finished third among rookies in total tackles, and might have made the All-Rookie team in a non-Darius Leonard season. ◉ Joining Warner will be Kwon Alexander, who has superstar potential (he was third in the league in total plays made in 2016) but has missed at least four games in three of his four seasons and is coming off a torn ACL. ◉ Warner and Alexander will be the key players responsible for solving San Francisco's problems against screen passes. The 49ers were 28th on defense in DVOA on passes thrown to receivers behind the line of scrimmage last year. Mind you, they were 29th on passes thrown to receivers beyond the line of scrimmage, so the secondary needs work too. Speaking of which…

Defensive Secondary

Secondary	Age	Pos	G	Snaps	Plays	TmPct	Rk	Stop	Dfts	BTkl	Runs	St%	Rk	RuYd	Rk	Tgts	Tgt%	Rk	Dist	Suc%	Rk	AdjYd	Rk	PD	Int
											Overall					**vs. Run**				**vs. Pass**					
Richard Sherman	31	CB	14	836	41	6.1%	77	15	6	3	9	33%	56	6.3	38	45	14.0%	6	12.0	60%	9	7.4	35	4	0
Ahkello Witherspoon	24	CB	14	700	41	6.1%	77	13	1	7	14	43%	36	7.7	58	69	25.6%	73	14.0	52%	37	7.1	31	4	0
K'Waun Williams	28	CB	14	595	47	7.0%	64	18	11	4	15	33%	56	5.5	22	36	15.7%	18	7.7	47%	56	7.5	37	2	0
Antone Exum	28	SS	15	594	44	6.1%	--	16	4	8	22	36%	--	9.1	--	14	6.1%	--	14.9	36%	--	11.5	--	7	1
Jaquiski Tartt	27	SS	8	437	43	11.2%	26	20	9	5	21	62%	6	3.5	1	18	10.7%	51	7.3	39%	66	7.3	40	2	1
Jimmie Ward	28	CB	9	388	23	5.3%	--	2	0	1	8	13%	--	9.1	--	21	14.1%	--	12.9	52%	--	8.1	--	0	0
D.J. Reed	23	FS	15	360	36	5.0%	--	14	4	4	19	37%	--	7.5	--	15	10.8%	--	10.5	53%	--	6.9	--	0	0
Marcell Harris	25	SS	8	358	30	7.8%	--	18	6	9	16	81%	--	2.8	--	12	8.7%	--	6.6	50%	--	6.8	--	0	0
Adrian Colbert	26	FS	7	320	21	6.2%	--	3	2	4	6	0%	--	11.7	--	7	5.7%	--	13.3	14%	--	13.9	--	1	0
Tarvarius Moore	23	CB	16	232	21	2.7%	--	8	2	2	6	50%	--	6.2	--	17	19.0%	--	12.1	47%	--	5.8	--	2	0

Year	Pass D Rank	vs. #1 WR	Rk	vs. #2 WR	Rk	vs. Other WR	Rk	WR Wide	Rk	WR Slot	Rk	vs. TE	Rk	vs. RB	Rk
2016	28	19.1%	31	7.6%	24	-7.0%	9	-4.9%	13	16.1%	28	17.5%	27	17.1%	27
2017	28	21.1%	27	-1.6%	16	30.7%	32	17.3%	30	20.2%	27	-19.5%	5	13.2%	24
2018	27	4.8%	19	18.5%	26	36.9%	31	-9.9%	11	36.7%	32	9.6%	21	5.7%	19

That defensive backs table for San Francisco is an absolute mess—which means it's an accurate summation of the 2018 49ers secondary. Six different players started at safety, but none of them started more than eight games. Six *other* players started at corner, and most of them were negatives. The only one here who was uncategorically good was Richard Sherman, and even he looked more vulnerable than usual. He gave up four catches for 81 yards to the Cardinals (the *Cardinals!*) in Week 8 and four catches for 100 yards to the Bucs in Week 12. Sherman turned 31 in March; at that age, it's quite likely that his best days are behind him. 🏈 Mind you, Sherman at 80 percent would still have been San Francisco's best corner last year. There is hope that Ahkello Witherspoon could rebound to his rookie form, when he was among the top four cornerbacks in both success rate and yards allowed per target, albeit in just nine starts. As for K'Waun Williams, 2018 was the first time in his five NFL seasons he played enough to qualify for our tables. A 47 percent success rate is less than ideal, but teams did not pick on him as much as you think, and he didn't surrender many big plays. 🏈 The wild card here is Jason Verrett, who made the Pro Bowl with the Chargers in 2015 but has played in only five games since. Verrett's injuries include both a torn ACL and a torn Achilles, but if he could somehow play a meaningful chunk of the season at anything close to his former level, San Francisco's whole defense would start to look a lot better. 🏈 Speaking of players with severe injury concerns, let's discuss hypothetical starting safeties Jaquiski Tartt and Adrian Colbert. Tartt, the box safety, has tantalizing playmaking potential, as seen in his superlative run-tackling stats. He has 19 defeats the last two years despite playing in only 17 games (to put that in perspective, only three safeties had more than that in 2018), and at 215 pounds showed surprising speed running down Tyler Lockett from behind on a long kickoff return against Seattle in Week 13. Colbert, the deep man, has started a dozen games by default since he was drafted in the seventh round in 2017 and has failed to make any kind of impact. 🏈 For the sake of completeness, we will point out that Jimmie Ward—who has spent five years bouncing back and forth from safety to nickelback but failing to play well or stay healthy at either—has already suffered his first significant injury of 2019, breaking his collarbone in OTAs. He is expected to recover by Week 1; he was playing free safety before the injury and would likely replace Colbert as the starter.

Special Teams

Year	DVOA	Rank	FG/XP	Rank	Net Kick	Rank	Kick Ret	Rank	Net Punt	Rank	Punt Ret	Rank	Hidden	Rank
2016	-0.3%	17	3.9	8	-2.7	23	-6.7	29	5.1	9	-0.9	14	-1.2	19
2017	2.9%	11	14.2	2	3.0	10	-6.4	32	3.6	13	0.0	16	4.9	10
2018	0.3%	14	6.6	7	-0.4	17	1.7	8	0.0	17	-6.4	30	3.6	10

Since joining San Francisco two years ago, Robbie Gould leads the NFL in both total field goals (72) and conversion rate (96 percent) … so of course he is now the center of a nasty contract dispute. John Lynch slapped the franchise tag on him. Gould responded by pulling out of contract negotiations and demanding a trade, a trade which the 49ers have refused to consider. Ordinarily we'd caution a team against overpaying for a kicker, let alone one who turns 37 this season, but this might not be an issue if the team hadn't spent more than $20 million on running backs. (Just before we went to press, Gould signed a four-year, $19-million deal with the 49ers.) 🏈 Bradley Pinion had negative punting value in each of the last three seasons, so he's gone, replaced by fourth-round draftee Mitch Wishnowsky. Wishnowsky won the Ray Guy award as the nation's best punter at Utah in 2016. His next two seasons weren't quite as spectacular, but he should be reliable at avoiding returns and pinning opponents inside the 20, though there are questions about his ability to boom long punts out of his own end. 🏈 The 49ers were strong on kick returns, thanks in large part to rookie Richie James, who had a 97-yard touchdown against Seattle in Week 15. D.J. Reed, another rookie, added his own kickoff return for a touchdown against Detroit, though it was called back due to his own face mask penalty. 🏈 Things weren't nearly as good on punt returns. Dante Pettis averaged 14.2 yards with an NCAA record nine touchdowns at the University of Washington but gained only 27 total yards on nine returns in his rookie year in San Francisco. James and Trent Taylor were hardly any better.

Seattle Seahawks

2018 record: 10-6	**Total DVOA:** 6.7% (12th)	**2019 Mean Projection:** 8.6 wins	**On the Clock (0-4):** 7%
Pythagorean Wins: 10.1 (10th)	**Offense:** 8.8% (9th)	**Postseason Odds:** 44.7%	**Mediocrity (5-7):** 27%
Snap-Weighted Age: 26.3 (22nd)	**Defense:** -0.1% (14th)	**Super Bowl Odds:** 7.5%	**Playoff Contender (8-10):** 41%
Average Opponent: -1.8% (20th)	**Special Teams:** -2.2% (24th)	**Proj. Avg. Opponent:** 1.2% (10th)	**Super Bowl Contender (11+):** 25%

2018: A somewhat unlikely playoff run fueled by the quarterback and memes.

2019: For Russell Wilson, more money than in his wildest dreams.

When Earl Thomas broke his leg against the Arizona Cardinals in Week 4 and subsequently flipped off the Seattle sideline, we knew that the reboot of the Seattle Seahawks was complete. While his days in Seattle were already numbered at that point, as Thomas had been the subject of trade rumors throughout the offseason, it was a stark reminder that this would not be the same fearsome Legion of Boom of old. Sure, some of the cast of characters remained in the form of mainstay linebackers Bobby Wagner and K.J. Wright as well as young defensive end Frank Clark, but make no mistake: the Seattle defense was nowhere near its past heights.

At the time of Thomas' injury, Seattle ranked an impressive sixth in defensive DVOA, but that had been inflated slightly by the team creating nine turnovers (including three Thomas interceptions) in its first four games. As the season progressed, the turnovers stopped coming as frequently, and the Seahawks' defensive performance suffered accordingly. They finished the year as a barely better-than-average unit. A unit built around Wagner, Wright, Clark, defensive tackle Jarran Reed, and safety Bradley McDougald did everything it could to hold down the fort, but it did not measure up to some of the stronger defenses around the league.

Wagner turned in another strong year, earning first-team All-Pro honors, but he alone was not enough to hold it down for the linebacker corps. Wright spent most of 2018 unavailable while dealing with a knee injury. For a while, it looked like the Seahawks lucked into a high-quality replacement in Mychal Kendricks, whom they signed after Cleveland cut him for his involvement in an insider trading scheme, but Kendricks would only appear in four games due to suspension (for said insider trading scheme) and injuries of his own.

There was more room for optimism along the defensive line in the form of Clark's and Reed's big pass-rushing seasons, as the pair both eclipsed the ten-sack mark, something former stalwart defensive ends Michael Bennett and Cliff Avril were never able to accomplish in the same season in Seattle. At ages 25 and 26, respectively, Clark and Reed looked poised to form the anchor of the Seattle defensive line for the foreseeable future. However, 2018 represented the final year of Clark's rookie contract, and without an extension in place prior to the end of the season, Seattle placed the franchise tag on him.

The Seahawks intended to sign him to a long-term deal,

but after the Cowboys helped reset the market for defensive ends by agreeing to an extension with their star pass-rusher Demarcus Lawrence, it became clear that Seattle and Clark would not be able to come to terms on an extension. Seattle subsequently traded Clark to Kansas City, where he summarily signed his extension as part of the deal. The trade brought back some serious draft capital in the form of a 2019 first-round pick and a 2020 second-round pick, but it simultaneously left a big hole at edge rusher for the Seahawks to fill.

Seattle attempted to address that gap by signing former Lions defensive end Ezekiel Ansah to a one-year prove-it deal in addition to drafting TCU's L.J. Collier in the first round to fill a 5-technique role on the opposite side. While Ansah has been a productive player when healthy, he was injured for much of 2018 and is recovering from an offseason shoulder surgery. Collier had a solid senior season in college, but he is only a rookie (and at 24, will be an older one). Expecting the two of them to fill the pass-rush gap left by Clark's departure may be too much to ask.

In the halcyon days of the Legion of Boom, a relatively lackluster pass rush did not derail the defense's overall performance, but with stars like Thomas, Richard Sherman, and Kam Chancellor all gone, it will be harder to overcome. In 2012, Seattle finished second in overall defensive DVOA and third against the pass while ranking only 21st in adjusted sack rate. However, with a lesser cast of characters in the defensive backfield in 2018, Seattle's defense finished 14th against the pass despite an adjusted sack rate of 7.3 percent, better than the 6.1 percent of 2012.

Given the youth movement currently underway in the defensive backfield—other than McDougald, none of the expected starters at defensive back have started for more than two seasons in the NFL—we can expect a bumpy road ahead for Seattle's defense. As was the case in 2018, a drop-off in defensive performance will put the onus on the Seattle offense to carry the load in 2019 if the Seahawks are going to make a trip to the playoffs.

Fortunately for Seattle, that offense was enough in 2018, improving from barely above average in 2017 to the ninth-ranked unit in the league in 2018. Much of the narrative surrounding Seattle's offensive resurgence focused on an improved rushing attack. Seattle's running game took a massive step forward, finishing sixth in rushing DVOA in 2018 after

2019 Seahawks Schedule

Week	Opp.	Week	Opp.	Week	Opp.
1	CIN	7	BAL	13	MIN (Mon.)
2	at PIT	8	at ATL	14	at LAR
3	NO	9	TB	15	at CAR
4	at ARI	10	at SF (Mon.)	16	ARI
5	LAR (Thu.)	11	BYE	17	SF
6	at CLE	12	at PHI		

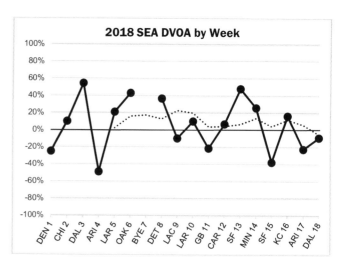

ranking 23rd the year before. The improvement of the offensive line had a lot to do with that, as Seattle jumped from 31st in adjusted line yards in 2017 all the way to a very respectable 12th.

Over the course of the 2018 offseason, Seattle had organizationally recommitted to running the ball effectively, and many of their coaching and personnel changes reflected that aim. The Seahawks fired offensive line coach Tom Cable and replaced him with Mike Solari, who introduced more power-blocking schemes in the run game to complement what had previously been an almost exclusively zone-blocking system. Seattle then went out in free agency and added right guard D.J. Fluker, a former first-round pick who was primarily known for his run-blocking in his time with the Chargers and Giants. They also drafted tight end Will Dissly, a stout run-blocker, in the fourth round.

In addition to their efforts to improve their run-blocking, the Seahawks also selected running back Rashaad Penny in the first round to bolster a backfield that already had Chris Carson and Mike Davis, but that move did not go as smoothly as their other rushing-related decisions. Carson and Davis had question marks entering the offseason, so it made sense that Seattle was not entirely comfortable rolling with just those two at running back. With all the other needs on Seattle's roster, though, using a first-round pick on Penny was still a high price to pay at the time. Hindsight did not make that decision look much better, as Penny spent the majority of his rookie season third on the depth chart. Penny did flash periodically over the course of the season, most notably on the road against the Rams in Week 10, but with other concerns on both sides of the ball, it would have made more sense to go in a different direction in Round 1.

Given how much Seattle wanted to run the football, improving in that area was an absolute necessity if they were to sustain any sort of offensive success in 2018. It's hard to overstate just how transformative Brian Schottenheimer's offense was to Seattle's run/pass ratios. The year before, the Seahawks had ranked 30th in run/pass ratio on first downs and in the first half. Last year, they led the league in both. They went from 28th to second in runs when behind in the second half and dropped from third to 23rd in passes when ahead in the second half.

However, while their rushing attack clearly represented a step up from 2017, their dogged insistence on running the ball held them back in terms of their season-long offensive output, and not just in their loss to the Cowboys in the wild-card round.

It is a little strange to say the Seattle offense had issues that held it back when it finished in the top ten of offensive DVOA, passing DVOA, and rushing DVOA, but Seattle's distribution of runs and passes resulted in worse overall offensive output in the long run. To illustrate this problem, we can use a Simpson's paradox example comparing Seattle's offense with that of Pittsburgh, which finished sixth overall in offensive DVOA (Table 1). For those unfamiliar with Simpson's paradox, the simple explanation here is that one team can outperform another in two individual areas (in this case, rushing offense and passing offense DVOA) but show worse overall results in the aggregate depending on the distribution of each group.

Table 1: A Simpson's Paradox Explanation of Seattle's Rushing Problem

Team	Rush Off	Rk	Runs	Pass Off	Rk	Passes	Overall Off	Rk	Plays
SEA	4.3%	6	534	27.2%	6	427	8.8%	9	961
PIT	-2.4%	12	345	25.5%	8	689	13.8%	6	1,034

Let's walk through this step by step. Seattle had a very run-heavy play distribution, while Pittsburgh had an incredibly pass-heavy distribution. As we can see from the table, both offenses were much better when passing than they were while running, though that gap was larger for Pittsburgh. This is a trend that we typically see across the league, as passing is more efficient than rushing.

Seattle performed better in both rushing offense and passing offense than Pittsburgh, but each team's distribution of runs versus passes played a major role in flipping the expected offensive rankings in Pittsburgh's favor. Even though Pittsburgh was not as good as Seattle at either rushing or passing, the fact that Pittsburgh passed on roughly two-thirds of their plays while Seattle passed the ball less than half the time allowed the Steelers to perform more efficiently on offense in the aggregate.

This is a bit of an extreme example, given that Seattle and Pittsburgh were on the complete opposite ends of the run-heavy versus pass-heavy offensive spectrum, and Seattle still finished in the top ten in offensive DVOA. That's nothing to sneeze at! But if Seattle is going to take the next step as an offensive team in 2019, a more efficient offensive play distribution would likely help, especially when you consider the huge gap in performance between the Seahawks and teams like the Chiefs, Rams, and Chargers at the top. The offensive DVOA gap between the No. 9 Seahawks and the No. 3 Chargers (11.9%) was similar to the gap between the Seahawks and the No. 19 Bengals (12.1%). With all the question marks on defense, adding more juice to the offense would go a long way toward improving Seattle's playoff chances.

Beyond Seattle's stated objectives of getting back to its identity as a pound-the-rock team, there were other reasons that the Seahawks might have wanted to avoid throwing the ball all the time. Wide receiver Doug Baldwin spent the season dealing with a series of nagging injuries that limited his effectiveness when he was on the field. While the Seattle offensive line improved its run-blocking, it still finished 30th in adjusted sack rate, which left Russell Wilson dodging defenders again and again. Of course, a large part of that is due to Wilson's own tendency to hold onto the ball in search of an opportunity to throw deep, but that is a tradeoff the Seahawks have decided to live with at this point in his career.

Frankly, that's a fair tradeoff given what Wilson can do with his deep ball. Seattle had the best passing DVOA in the league on deep passes (Table 2). Wide receiver Tyler Lockett posted the highest receiving DVOA that we have measured since 1986 (minimum 50 targets) due in large part to his rapport with Wilson on throws deep down the field. Seattle used play-action at one of the highest rates in the league in 2018, and Lockett was often a deep target on those plays, making for a very fruitful offensive pairing.

Table 2. Best Pass DVOA on Deep Passes, 2018

Team	Passes	Yd/Pass	TD	INT	DVOA
SEA	94	16.6	16	1	225.2%
LAC	91	14.9	9	5	165.4%
KC	126	15.3	12	9	143.9%
NYG	115	14.0	6	4	133.8%
GB	137	13.2	10	0	118.9%
NO	95	15.2	9	4	114.6%
DET	80	14.4	6	5	112.6%
HOU	88	14.9	8	6	112.3%
NE	101	13.1	9	4	109.7%
LAR	111	14.0	9	6	107.0%

Includes passes of 16 or more yards in the air. Pass interference gains included. Passes batted down, thrown away, or with QB hit in motion not included.

Lockett will have to shoulder more of the offensive load through the air in 2019, as the cumulative effect of Baldwin's injuries forced him to effectively retire from the NFL. (Baldwin was officially released with an injury designation so he could keep signing bonus money that he had already received.) While Baldwin was clearly not operating at his best in 2018, losing him altogether will have a knock-on effect for Seattle's other receivers, forcing them to step into roles for which they may not be ready.

In addition to holdovers David Moore and Jaron Brown, Seattle added two receivers in the draft's first four rounds: Gary Jennings Jr. (West Virginia) and viral shirtless sensation D.K. Metcalf (Ole Miss). Both rookie receivers project well as deep threats, which will allow Lockett to move into the slot on a more frequent basis. Lockett had spent a good deal of time in the slot in 2018 due to Baldwin's absence, so it would not be a surprise if he continues to take on that role as Wilson's favorite target.

The future is a bit murky for Seattle's aerial attack without Baldwin, but armed with a fresh new $140-million contract extension, Wilson will have to make it work. When you make top-of-the-market money at quarterback, that expectation comes with the territory. Wilson's deep passing proficiency allowed the offense to get away with running the ball at an incredibly high rate and lining up backup offensive tackle George Fant at "tight end," and he will likely have to do it again to take Seattle back to the playoffs, especially with all the question marks on the defensive side of the ball.

Our projections give Wilson good odds to lead the Seahawks back to the postseason once again, but his margin of error is much smaller than it was in the early stages of his career. Gone are all but the last remnants of the preeminent defense of its era. Gone is Wilson's favorite safety blanket in the originally overlooked Baldwin. If there was any doubt before, this is Wilson's show now. In every year that he has been healthy, Wilson has piloted an above-average offense (the only exception being 2016 when he spent a sizable portion of the season dealing with knee and ankle injuries). If he does it again, it should mean another wild-card berth, even with all the turnover and uncertainty on defense.

If Pete Carroll and company are able to rebuild the Seattle defense to a level that even comes close to approximating the Legion of Boom's heights, the ceiling for the 2019 Seattle squad will be higher, and the Seahawks could even challenge the Rams for NFC West supremacy. But if the defense continues on a downward trend or Wilson ends up having to miss any amount of time due to injury, Seattle will be sitting at home come playoff time, longing for the days of its DVOA dynasty.

Carl Yedor

2018 Seahawks Stats by Week

Wk	vs.	W-L	PF	PA	YDF	YDA	TO	Total	Off	Def	ST
1	at DEN	L	24	27	306	470	0	-25%	-25%	1%	1%
2	at CHI	L	17	24	276	271	0	10%	-2%	-12%	-1%
3	DAL	W	24	13	295	303	+3	54%	14%	-39%	1%
4	at ARI	W	20	17	331	263	+1	-49%	-15%	23%	-10%
5	LAR	L	31	33	373	468	+2	21%	38%	2%	-15%
6	at OAK	W	27	3	369	185	+1	43%	-4%	-44%	2%
7	BYE										
8	at DET	W	28	14	413	331	+3	36%	33%	3%	6%
9	LAC	L	17	25	356	375	-1	-10%	5%	22%	7%
10	at LAR	L	31	36	414	456	-1	10%	35%	30%	4%
11	GB	W	27	24	378	359	-1	-22%	-12%	16%	6%
12	at CAR	W	30	27	397	476	+1	7%	17%	12%	1%
13	SF	W	43	16	331	452	+3	48%	44%	9%	13%
14	MIN	W	21	7	274	276	0	26%	-3%	-20%	9%
15	at SF	L	23	26	385	351	+1	-38%	3%	20%	-21%
16	KC	W	38	31	464	419	+2	16%	27%	-4%	-15%
17	ARI	W	27	24	291	198	+1	-23%	-14%	-15%	-24%
18	at DAL	L	22	24	299	380	+1	-9%	9%	13%	-6%

Trends and Splits

	Offense	Rank	Defense	Rank
Total DVOA	8.8%	9	-0.1%	14
Unadjusted VOA	11.0%	8	-1.8%	15
Weighted Trend	11.3%	9	3.1%	19
Variance	4.6%	7	4.7%	9
Average Opponent	0.2%	16	-0.9%	16
Passing	27.2%	6	5.1%	14
Rushing	4.3%	6	-7.6%	17
First Down	-9.7%	23	-1.1%	14
Second Down	19.6%	3	10.9%	28
Third Down	29.4%	2	-15.1%	7
First Half	7.0%	10	1.4%	18
Second Half	10.7%	7	-1.6%	14
Red Zone	20.2%	8	-26.0%	4
Late and Close	5.6%	14	-1.0%	15

Five-Year Performance

Year	W-L	Pyth W	Est W	PF	PA	TO	Total	Rk	Off	Rk	Def	Rk	ST	Rk	Off AGL	Rk	Def AGL	Rk	Off Age	Rk	Def Age	Rk	ST Age	Rk
2014	12-4	11.9	12.7	394	254	+10	31.9%	1	16.8%	5	-16.8%	1	-1.7%	19	39.5	24	35.3	13	25.3	31	26.3	23	25.8	24
2015	10-6	11.8	12.5	423	277	+7	38.1%	1	18.7%	1	-15.2%	4	4.2%	3	23.7	9	16.4	4	25.9	25	27.0	12	26.3	12
2016	10-5-1	9.8	9.1	354	292	+1	8.0%	11	-2.6%	16	-10.6%	5	-0.1%	15	23.8	6	17.3	4	25.7	29	27.2	7	26.4	8
2017	9-7	9.0	8.5	366	332	+8	3.8%	14	2.0%	14	-3.8%	13	-2.0%	20	45.5	23	42.7	22	26.1	29	27.0	8	25.8	20
2018	10-6	10.1	8.9	428	347	+16	6.7%	12	8.8%	9	-0.1%	14	-2.2%	24	32.8	12	32.9	14	27.2	11	25.5	27	25.8	16

2018 Performance Based on Most Common Personnel Groups

SEA Offense					SEA Offense vs. Opponents					SEA Defense					SEA Defense vs. Opponents			
Pers	Freq	Yds	DVOA	Run%	Pers	Freq	Yds	DVOA	Run%	Pers	Freq	Yds	DVOA		Pers	Freq	Yds	DVOA
11	65%	5.8	13.7%	41%	Base	32%	6.5	16.9%	60%	Base	34%	6.1	5.3%		11	68%	6.2	-0.1%
12	8%	7.9	40.4%	42%	Nickel	57%	5.8	12.4%	49%	Nickel	49%	6.4	4.0%		12	14%	6.1	0.0%
612	8%	6.7	24.9%	71%	Dime+	15%	5.0	12.3%	21%	Dime+	14%	5.0	-25.9%		21	10%	5.5	1.9%
613	7%	4.6	15.3%	79%	Goal Line	1%	1.1	26.6%	75%	Goal Line	1%	0.6	-32.9%		22	3%	7.2	18.1%
21	3%	8.1	23.9%	47%						Big	2%	4.8	-23.2%		13	2%	6.7	-6.9%
611	3%	4.9	3.6%	73%														

Strategic Tendencies

Run/Pass		Rk	Formation		Rk	Pass Rush		Rk	Secondary		Rk	Strategy		Rk
Runs, first half	50%	1	Form: Single Back	88%	4	Rush 3	4.2%	22	4 DB	34%	5	Play action	33%	2
Runs, first down	61%	1	Form: Empty Back	4%	31	Rush 4	75.7%	6	5 DB	49%	27	Avg Box (Off)	6.32	5
Runs, second-long	41%	2	Pers: 3+ WR	74%	7	Rush 5	16.3%	20	6+ DB	14%	14	Avg Box (Def)	6.15	23
Runs, power sit.	71%	4	Pers: 2+ TE/6+ OL	25%	12	Rush 6+	3.8%	28	CB by Sides	89%	3	Offensive Pace	31.36	18
Runs, behind 2H	37%	2	Pers: 6+ OL	20%	1	Int DL Sacks	29.1%	14	S/CB Cover Ratio	29%	13	Defensive Pace	31.07	16
Pass, ahead 2H	42%	26	Shotgun/Pistol	69%	10	Second Level Sacks	18.6%	24	DB Blitz	7%	22	Go for it on 4th	1.15	20

The Seahawks not only used six offensive linemen way more than any other team (20 percent of plays ... the Colts were next at 10.5 percent), they were the only offense that used six linemen on more than 3 percent of plays *and* had a positive offensive DVOA with six linemen (9.4% DVOA, 5.3 yards per play). ✎ Seattle ran on 40 percent of their shotgun plays, while no other team ran more than 30 percent of the time when in shotgun. The Seahawks had 4.8% DVOA and 4.8 yards per carry from shotgun, compared to -10.3% DVOA and 4.4 yards per carry with the quarterback under center. ✎ The NFC West loves its play fakes, as the Rams and Seahawks ranked one-two in percentage of passes with play-action. Both teams used play-action on over 50 percent of their first-down passes. ✎ Seattle's offense recovered 13 of 17 fumbles. ✎ The Seahawks had the best DVOA in the league when they threw the ball past the line of scrimmage. But they ranked 30th when they threw the ball at or behind the line of scrimmage, ahead of just Arizona and Chicago. The issue isn't screen passes, per se, because Seattle threw fewer wide receiver screens than any other offense (11) and was also near the bottom with 15 running back screens. ✎ Not related, but ironic: Seattle also ranked 31st in the league on defense against passes at or behind the line of scrimmage. Only Oakland was worse. In particular, the Seahawks were bad against running back screens. They faced more of them than any other defense (37) and allowed 8.6 yards per play with 42.5% DVOA. ✎ Seattle's defense faced the lowest percentage of passes to opposing No. 1 wide receivers, just 16 percent. ✎ The Seahawks had a below-average pressure rate on first and second downs but ranked second behind only the Rams with a 44.3 percent pressure rate on third and fourth downs.

Passing

Player	DYAR	DVOA	Plays	NtYds	Avg	YAC	C%	TD	Int
R.Wilson	673	11.3%	471	3090	6.6	4.9	66.8%	35	6

Rushing

Player	DYAR	DVOA	Plays	Yds	Avg	TD	Fum	Suc
C.Carson	133	3.9%	247	1151	4.7	9	3	51%
M.Davis*	80	9.0%	112	514	4.6	4	0	52%
R.Penny	56	8.9%	85	419	4.9	2	0	40%
R.Wilson	83	23.3%	50	382	7.6	0	2	--
T.Lockett	25	-2.7%	14	69	4.9	0	0	--

Receiving

Player	DYAR	DVOA	Plays	Ctch	Yds	Y/C	YAC	TD	C%
D.Baldwin*	113	6.0%	73	50	618	12.4	3.1	5	68%
T.Lockett	464	66.3%	70	57	965	16.9	3.7	10	81%
D.Moore	20	-7.4%	53	26	445	17.1	3.6	5	49%
B.Marshall*	-16	-22.3%	23	11	136	12.4	2.1	1	48%
J.Brown	100	58.0%	19	14	166	11.9	3.3	5	74%
N.Vannett	2	-6.5%	43	29	269	9.3	4.8	3	67%
W.Dissly	36	30.6%	14	8	156	19.5	11.6	2	57%
E.Dickson	56	61.4%	13	12	143	11.9	6.5	3	92%
M.Davis*	31	-0.1%	42	34	214	6.3	6.9	1	81%
C.Carson	43	21.2%	24	20	163	8.2	8.2	0	83%
R.Penny	12	8.3%	12	9	75	8.3	8.1	0	75%

Offensive Line

Player	Pos	Age	GS	Snaps	Pen	Sk	Pass	Run	Player	Pos	Age	GS	Snaps	Pen	Sk	Pass	Run
Duane Brown	LT	34	16/16	1067	1	2.5	11	4	George Fant	OT	27	16/7	371	7	3.0	3	2
Germain Ifedi	RT	25	15/15	989	11	7.0	10	5	Ethan Pocic	LG	24	10/4	296	4	2.5	5	2
Justin Britt	C	28	16/15	989	4	0.0	2	6	Jordan Simmons	RG	25	6/3	195	1	1.5	5	1
J.R. Sweezy*	LG	30	15/15	948	9	4.0	12	6	Mike Iupati	LG	32	10/10	477	3	2.0	8	2
D.J. Fluker	RG	28	10/9	607	9	0.0	2	4									

Year	Yards	ALY	Rank	Power	Rank	Stuff	Rank	2nd Lev	Rank	Open Field	Rank	Sacks	ASR	Rank	Press	Rank	F-Start	Cont.
2016	3.82	3.77	26	53%	27	23%	30	1.12	18	0.70	15	42	6.9%	25	33.7%	32	26	28
2017	3.30	3.18	31	55%	27	30%	32	0.97	28	0.54	21	43	8.1%	25	36.9%	30	20	29
2018	4.64	4.50	12	71%	5	17%	8	1.30	10	0.85	15	51	10.4%	30	35.7%	30	20	26

2018 ALY by direction:	Left End: 5.35 (7)	Left Tackle: 3.42 (30)	Mid/Guard: 4.44 (16)	Right Tackle: 4.47 (15)	Right End: 5.39 (5)

After joining the Seahawks via trade during the 2017 season, left tackle Duane Brown signed a three-year contract extension in the offseason and subsequently provided some much-needed stability on Russell Wilson's blind side, only committing one penalty all season long. ✎ On the opposite side, third-year tackle Germain Ifedi and backup tackle/sixth offensive lineman George Fant mauled people in the run game, helping Seattle finish fifth in adjusted line yards to the right end. The pass protection was not as impressive, as Ifedi allowed seven sacks over the course of the year. This may have contributed to Seattle not picking up the fifth-year option on Ifedi's rookie contract. Fant had been slated to start at left tackle in 2017 before tearing his ACL in the preseason and missing the entire year. ✎ The road-grading D.J. Fluker stepped in at right guard after being brought in as a free agent, and while he dealt with injuries over the course of the season, he provided a major upgrade running to the offensive right. Fluker's play earned him a new two-year contract this offseason. ✎ After being released by Tampa Bay, J.R. Sweezy returned to where his career began and wound up holding down the left guard spot. Sweezy allowed four sacks in 2018 (Aaron Donald welcomed him back rather rudely), then signed a two-year deal in free agency with the Cardinals. ❧ Sweezy was essentially exchanged for ex-Cardinal Mike Iupati; he in turn gets the first crack at replacing Sweezy at left guard, though the four-time Pro Bowler does not represent a long-term solution at this stage of his career. The future might belong to Phil Haynes, a fourth-round rookie from Wake Forest who filled in for an injured Iupati during OTAs. Haynes started for four years with the Demon Deacons and will have a chance to push for playing time. ❧ Former second-round pick Ethan Pocic started four games at guard as an injury fill-in, but it appears he has fallen out of favor with the Seattle coaching staff. He may be fighting for a roster spot in training camp.

Defensive Front

Defensive Line	Age	Pos	G	Snaps	Plays	TmPct	Rk	Stop	Dfts	BTkl	Runs	St%	Rk	RuYd	Rk	Sack	Hit	Hur	Dsrpt
						Overall						vs. Run					Pass Rush		
Jarran Reed	27	DT	16	773	50	6.6%	19	44	14	6	35	89%	6	2.1	32	10.5	14	25	1
Shamar Stephen*	28	DT	15	494	25	3.5%	70	17	2	1	21	71%	53	2.6	60	2.0	1	3	0
Poona Ford	24	DT	11	231	21	4.0%	--	16	3	0	21	76%	--	2.8	--	0.0	2	4	0
Al Woods	32	DT	14	375	24	3.3%	74	16	4	2	21	71%	53	2.2	43	0.0	2	10	1

Edge Rushers	Age	Pos	G	Snaps	Plays	TmPct	Rk	Stop	Dfts	BTkl	Runs	St%	Rk	RuYd	Rk	Sack	Hit	Hur	Dsrpt
						Overall						vs. Run					Pass Rush		
Frank Clark*	26	DE	16	728	41	5.4%	35	34	21	11	19	79%	28	2.4	47	13.0	13	34	1
Quinton Jefferson	26	DE	16	558	26	3.4%	79	22	9	4	16	81%	22	2.2	40	3.0	11	18	2
Dion Jordan*	29	DE	12	295	23	4.0%	--	13	7	2	14	57%	--	1.8	--	1.5	4	14	1
Branden Jackson	27	DE	9	258	10	2.3%	92	8	4	2	8	75%	44	2.3	42	1.0	1	6	0
Rasheem Green	22	DE	10	201	9	1.9%	--	6	2	2	7	57%	--	4.7	--	1.0	0	7	0
Cassius Marsh	27	DE	16	550	36	4.7%	50	27	20	5	22	73%	51	3.6	83	5.5	10	20	0

Linebackers	Age	Pos	G	Snaps	Plays	TmPct	Rk	Stop	Dfts	BTkl	Runs	St%	Rk	RuYd	Rk	Sack	Hit	Hur	Tgts	Suc%	Rk	AdjYd	Rk	PD	Int
					Overall							vs. Run				Pass Rush				vs. Pass					
Bobby Wagner	29	MLB	15	925	148	20.8%	2	72	21	4	84	58%	49	4.3	60	1.0	7	8	41	56%	19	6.4	27	11	1
Barkevious Mingo	29	OLB	16	517	36	4.7%	86	13	7	7	19	47%	82	5.7	86	1.0	2	5.5	15	27%	79	8.0	63	1	0
Austin Calitro	25	MLB	16	282	42	5.5%	--	21	6	5	26	54%	--	3.5	--	0.5	0	1	13	54%	--	7.3	--	1	0
K.J. Wright	30	OLB	5	223	26	11.0%	52	12	4	2	13	54%	61	4.0	49	0.0	0	1	14	36%	--	8.1	--	3	0
Mychal Kendricks	29	OLB	4	183	20	10.5%	--	13	4	5	14	57%	--	4.1	--	2.0	1	2	7	71%	36	4.3	62	1	0

Year	Yards	ALY	Rank	Power	Rank	Stuff	Rank	2nd Level	Rank	Open Field	Rank	Sacks	ASR	Rank	Press	Rank
2016	3.42	3.81	8	58%	8	23%	7	0.97	6	0.40	3	42	6.7%	10	28.6%	10
2017	4.01	4.10	18	67%	22	18%	27	1.00	7	0.75	18	39	6.6%	15	30.9%	14
2018	4.55	4.55	22	58%	5	19%	19	1.28	20	0.91	20	43	7.3%	14	28.9%	21

| 2018 ALY by direction: | Left End: 5.09 (24) | Left Tackle: 4.40 (17) | Mid/Guard: 4.62 (22) | Right Tackle: 3.42 (7) | Right End: 5.70 (31) |

Seattle attempted to fill the hole left by K.J. Wright's injury in a few ways. Rookie fifth-round pick Shaquem Griffin had the first crack at it but struggled in Week 1 against Denver, and he spent the rest of the season primarily on special teams. Seattle will try to get him more involved in Year 2 as a pass-rusher, something at which he excelled in college at Central Florida. ❧ Mychal Kendricks joined the team after being cut by Cleveland as a result of his insider trading case and filled in effectively as a pass-rusher before missing most of the year due to injury and suspension. At press time, his legal situation is still unresolved, though he is under contract for 2019. ❧ Barkevious Mingo signed a two-year deal in 2018 to play strongside linebacker and occasionally rush the passer, but he may be a cap casualty by the end of training camp. ❧ Defensive tackle Jarran Reed and defensive end Frank Clark provided the vast majority of the pass-rush juice in 2018, but with Clark off to Kansas City, Seattle will need Rasheem Green, Jacob Martin, and Quinton Jefferson to play a larger role getting after the quarterback. None of those three made a huge impact in 2018, but with more pass-rush snaps available this year, they will have their chance. ❧ Rookie undrafted free agent Poona Ford came out of nowhere to take over the starting nose tackle role by season's end, which helped with Seattle's decision to not resign Shamar Stephen. Stephen returned to Minnesota after spending one season with the Seahawks. ❧ First-round pick L.J. Collier from Texas Christian will slot in at 5-technique in the old Michael Bennett role. The team had hoped Dion Jordan could take over Bennett's spot effectively, but he failed to make an impact in 2018 and is currently unsigned. 2017 third-round pick Nazair Jones will also get a shot at 5-technique, but it remains to be seen how he will take to the role after spending his first two seasons as more of a defensive tackle.

Defensive Secondary

Secondary	Age	Pos	G	Snaps	Plays	Overall TmPct	Rk	Stop	Dfts	BTkl	vs. Run Runs	St%	Rk	RuYd	Rk	vs. Pass Tgts	Tgt%	Rk	Dist	Suc%	Rk	AdjYd	Rk	PD	Int
Shaquill Griffin	24	CB	16	941	70	9.2%	30	27	13	7	22	45%	29	9.5	70	70	17.6%	28	12.9	44%	70	8.7	65	8	2
Tre Flowers	24	CB	15	903	73	10.3%	13	19	9	12	21	24%	70	8.8	67	73	19.1%	42	13.0	47%	61	9.5	72	6	0
Bradley McDougald	29	SS	16	874	87	11.5%	23	37	16	8	30	53%	17	5.8	23	47	12.7%	63	7.7	49%	39	7.3	41	9	3
Justin Coleman*	26	CB	16	672	52	6.9%	--	26	7	11	9	44%	--	6.9	--	58	20.4%	--	7.3	62%	--	5.4	--	10	1
Tedric Thompson	24	FS	14	656	55	8.3%	54	8	6	13	20	20%	66	13.1	75	21	7.6%	21	13.1	38%	68	8.8	56	3	1
Lano Hill	24	SS	13	320	24	3.9%	--	9	3	2	14	50%	--	7.1	--	11	8.1%	--	10.3	64%	--	4.5	--	1	0
Earl Thomas*	30	FS	4	237	27	14.2%	--	11	5	0	11	18%	--	12.7	--	7	7.0%	--	11.6	71%	--	6.1	--	5	3
Jamar Taylor	29	CB	14	305	19	2.5%	--	3	3	4	4	25%	--	5.8	--	26	22.2%	--	13.0	27%	--	13.2	--	1	0

Year	Pass D Rank	vs. #1 WR	Rk	vs. #2 WR	Rk	vs. Other WR	Rk	WR Wide	Rk	WR Slot	Rk	vs. TE	Rk	vs. RB	Rk
2016	13	1.3%	16	22.3%	31	-3.2%	11	-9.4%	9	15.8%	27	-1.3%	18	-20.3%	5
2017	3	0.9%	16	38.9%	31	-5.3%	14	20.2%	31	0.8%	13	-23.9%	3	-33.0%	2
2018	14	13.1%	25	4.6%	20	-10.3%	10	18.8%	30	-3.7%	14	-12.3%	10	-3.7%	13

Richard Sherman's offseason departure left some big shoes to fill at left cornerback, and that unenviable task fell to Shaquill Griffin, who slid over from the right side where he spent most of his rookie season as the starter. Rookie fifth-round pick Tre Flowers took over Griffin's old spot on the right and showed some promise in his first year as a cornerback after playing safety at Oklahoma State. Flowers actually had a better success rate than Griffin while simultaneously being targeted more frequently. ◗ Nickel cornerback Justin Coleman earned a four-year deal from Detroit in free agency, so Akeem King, Kalan Reed, journeyman Jamar Taylor, and 2019 fifth-round pick Ugo Amadi will compete to fill that spot. King saw more run late in the season when Seattle went to its dime package, and Reed spent most of 2018 on the practice squad. Taylor played a small role in Arizona and was unsigned until the later stages of free agency. Amadi played both free safety and nickel in college at Oregon, so he has a decent chance to get on the field in some form as a rookie despite his small stature at 5-foot-9. ◗ Earl Thomas' leg injury left a gaping hole in the secondary alongside veteran Bradley McDougald, and the young safeties Seattle trotted out there in his absence did not impress. McDougald switched back and forth from strong to free safety depending on which of Tedric Thompson and Lano (formerly Delano) Hill was out there with him, and the team also experimented with some three-safety looks. Thompson got the first crack at replacing Thomas, though his 38 percent coverage success rate left a lot to be desired. When Hill played, he was more of a strong safety, with McDougald switching over to free safety. Seattle also nabbed hard-hitting Marquise Blair, who profiles as more of a box safety, from Utah in the second round and will add him to the competition.

Special Teams

Year	DVOA	Rank	FG/XP	Rank	Net Kick	Rank	Kick Ret	Rank	Net Punt	Rank	Punt Ret	Rank	Hidden	Rank
2016	-0.3%	17	3.9	8	-2.7	23	-6.7	29	5.1	9	-0.9	14	-1.2	19
2017	2.9%	11	14.2	2	3.0	10	-6.4	32	3.6	13	0.0	16	4.9	10
2018	0.3%	14	6.6	7	-0.4	17	1.7	8	0.0	17	-6.4	30	3.6	10

Seattle has not finished with an above average special teams unit by DVOA since 2015, and this year's team represented the low point of the Pete Carroll era. ◗ Despite rookie punter Michael Dickson finishing fourth in gross punt value, the unit as a whole was below average. Seattle's kickoff coverage units struggled as well, finishing near the bottom in kickoff value despite the ancient Sebastian Janikowski ranking in the top ten in estimated field position value from kickoffs alone. Special teams coordinator Brian Schneider needs to turn around those downfield coverage units quickly. ◗ While Janikowski's swan song represented an improvement over the 2017 Blair Walsh experience, Seattle was hoping for something more at kicker and paid top dollar for free agent Jason Myers on a four-year deal. Myers was with the team during the 2018 offseason, but the Seahawks decided to roll with Janikowski instead. While Myers undoubtedly had the better year in 2018, it seems unlikely that he will hit nearly 90 percent of his field goals from further than 40 yards again when his career high prior to last year was only 75 percent. ◗ As Tyler Lockett will be forced to take on a larger role as a No. 1 receiver in the Seattle offense, he will likely cede return duties to a younger player like J.D. McKissic, now listed as a return specialist on the team roster. McKissic had shown promise as a pass-catching back in 2017 but missed most of 2018 due to injury.

Tampa Bay Buccaneers

2018 record: 5-11	**Total DVOA:** -13.0% (24th)	**2019 Mean Projection:** 6.0 wins	**On the Clock (0-4):** 30%
Pythagorean Wins: 6.4 (23rd)	**Offense:** 5.9% (12th)	**Postseason Odds:** 12.6%	**Mediocrity (5-7):** 44%
Snap-Weighted Age: 26.3 (21st)	**Defense:** 14.8% (32nd)	**Super Bowl Odds:** 0.8%	**Playoff Contender (8-10):** 21%
Average Opponent: 1.6% (7th)	**Special Teams:** -4.1% (28th)	**Proj. Avg. Opponent:** 3.1% (3rd)	**Super Bowl Contender (11+):** 5%

2018: Jameis Winston is Ryan Fitzpatrick, Ryan Fitzpatrick is Jameis Winston, and the Buccaneers are still the Buccaneers.

2019: A make-or-break season for Winston. For real this time. Can Bruce Arians turn him and the Buccaneers into a winner?

It was the day the Tampa Bay Buccaneers were afraid of, the day they hoped would never come. On July 26, 2018, Jameis Winston, the face of the franchise, stood before a throng of reporters and television cameras. He looked as at ease as a man in front of a firing squad. For the next 10 minutes, he was bombarded with questions. *Have you apologized to the team? Can you explain how you put yourself in this position? What do you say to the fans that are disappointed in you? Is alcohol a banned substance for you? Should you still be considered the face of this team? What did you learn from this?*

A month earlier, the NFL had announced it was suspending Winston for the first three games of the regular season. The league determined that he touched an Uber driver "in an inappropriate and sexual manner without her consent" in March 2016. It wasn't the first time he had been accused of sexual misconduct. A Florida State student said that he had raped her late in 2012. Winston was never charged, but in April 2015, his accuser filed a civil lawsuit against him. Two weeks later, the Buccaneers drafted him anyway.

We're not here to evaluate Winston's character or second-guess Tampa Bay's decision to draft him. That late July afternoon, however, is where the story of the 2018 Buccaneers—and the 2019 Buccaneers—begins. It's the day Winston's once-unbreakable hold on the starting quarterback job began to slip. During practice, he split first-team reps with his early-season replacement, 175-year-old Civil War veteran Ryan Fitzpatrick. The Buccaneers' opening stretch was a daunting one—at the NFC South champion Saints, home against the Super Bowl champion Eagles, and home against the AFC North champion Steelers—and coach Dirk Koetter needed to see whether Fitzpatrick's arm was still alive.

It was alive all right. Over the first three weeks of the season, Fitzpatrick took Tampa Bay over, sideways, and under on a magic carpet ride. The Buccaneers did what they couldn't do with Winston. They had normal pregame hype speeches. They threw complete passes to DeSean Jackson. They even ate a couple of Ws. Fitzpatrick performed better than Winston ever had, throwing for at least 400 yards and three touchdowns in each game. His 54.9% passing DVOA in that span was second to only Patrick Mahomes' 71.1% DVOA. You have to go back to 2015 to find a comparable three-game stretch from Winston (he posted a 45.4% DVOA against Jacksonville, Washington, and Atlanta that season).

And then it was over. The 48-10 loss to the Bears in Week 4, during which Fitzpatrick was benched at halftime, made that clear, so resoundingly clear that Koetter suggested afterward that everyone should be fired, including himself. Ownership would have been doing him a favor. Instead, it held him captive for three more months.

It's not as if the bloodbath in Chicago came out of nowhere. There were warning signs. Like Steelers tight end Vance McDonald's hellacious stiff arm to Chris Conte en route to a 75-yard touchdown. Like Isaiah Johnson's full-speed sprint into a wall while defending a deep pass from Ben Roethlisberger. Like Fitzpatrick's entire career. Like Winston's entire career.

Koetter spent the rest of the season navigating the most frustrating quarterback controversy in the NFL, a real-life re-enactment of the Spider-Man pointing at Spider-Man meme. After regaining the starting job, Winston proceeded to remind us of who he is at this stage of his career: Fitzpatrick, without the beard. In any given game, he's capable of throwing four touchdown passes, as he did against the Falcons in Week 6. He's just as capable of throwing four interceptions, as he did against the Bengals in Week 8. He's the quintessential no-risk-it, no-biscuit quarterback.

Which brings us to new coach Bruce Arians. What a find. Good thing the Buccaneers enlisted executive recruiting firm Korn Ferry to help them in their search. Otherwise, they would have hired Bruce Arians. According to his LinkedIn profile, the 66-year-old last coached in Arizona from 2013 to 2017 and is a certified self-proclaimed quarterback whisperer who doesn't actually whisper. In Tampa Bay, he'll be responsible for developing Winston, who is in the final season of his rookie deal, into the franchise quarterback ownership desperately wants him to be.

Perhaps Arians can deliver the validation the Buccaneers are seeking. His work with Peyton Manning, Ben Roethlisberger, and Carson Palmer (he also coached Andrew Luck for a season) suggests as much, but it might not happen right away. By DVOA, all three were adequate quarterbacks in their first seasons under Arians. Manning made the leap in his second season while Roethlisberger and Palmer did so in their third seasons (Table 1). One often overlooked counterpoint: Tim Couch.

Though Winston has yet to meet the expectations that come with being a No. 1 overall draft pick, he has proven that his

2019 Buccaneers Schedule

Week	Opp.	Week	Opp.	Week	Opp.
1	SF	7	BYE	13	at JAX
2	at CAR (Thu.)	8	at TEN	14	IND
3	NYG	9	at SEA	15	at DET
4	at LAR	10	ARI	16	HOU
5	at NO	11	NO	17	ATL
6	CAR (U.K.)	12	at ATL		

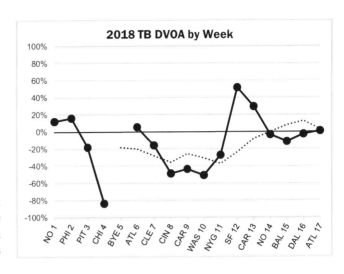

2018 TB DVOA by Week

floor is league average. Overall, he took a step backward last season (his passing DVOA fell from 14.3% to 6.2%), but he also teased a potential breakout. Despite his early-season struggles, he was one of the best at moving the chains. His rate of first downs per pass (41.2 percent) ranked sixth. No. 1 was, of course, Fitzpatrick (46.3 percent). Winston's success in this department is no fluke. He ranked second in 2017, sixth in 2016, and sixth in 2015. Since 2015, only Matt Ryan has a higher rate of first downs per pass (39.9 percent) than Winston (39.6 percent). Winston also bounced back nicely after hitting bottom against the Bengals. His 23.4% passing DVOA from Week 10 on ranked fifth, behind Baker Mayfield, Andrew Luck, Patrick Mahomes, and Drew Brees.

The challenge for Arians (and offensive playcaller Byron Leftwich) will be to minimize Winston's head-scratching mistakes, an issue that dates back to his final season at Florida State. Since 2015, he has thrown an interception on 3.0 percent of his passes, the second-highest rate among quarterbacks who have thrown 1,000 passes. The owner of the highest rate? Ding! Fitzpatrick! And when Winston is off, he's really off. More than 70 percent of his interceptions have come in less than 30 percent of his games. He has thrown multiple interceptions in a game 16 times, a total matched by only one other quarterback, whose name, surprisingly enough, isn't Ryan Fitzpatrick. It's Blake Bortles, though Fitzpatrick (13) isn't far behind.

One way Arians and Leftwich could help Winston is by incorporating more play-action fakes, because actual handoffs to Peyton Barber and Ronald Jones, behind this offensive line, aren't a good idea. Though Tampa Bay didn't call much play-action last season—the Buccaneers' rate of 17.2 percent ranked 31st—it's unlikely we'll see a spike in frequency. Arians' Arizona offenses ranked higher than 26th just once—in 2015, when the Cardinals' 17.4 percent rate ranked 21st.

There has been no shortage of excuses for Winston's interception problem. You name it, someone in Tampa Bay has blamed it—DeSean Jackson's moodiness, Mike Smith's defense, Dirk Koetter's love for Bit-O-Honey candy bars, Mike

Smith's defense, the run game's ineffectiveness, Mike Smith's defense, Hillary's e-mails, Mike Smith's defense. Even Arians has gotten in on the act, arguing that the ping-ponging between Winston and Fitzpatrick last season hurt both of them. "I think sometimes, they were both looking over their shoulder," he said. Never mind that it was Winston's suspension that set the back-and-forth in motion.

Arians also has suggested that the defense was part of the problem, though he was kind enough to not mention Mike Smith by name. "When you're 21 down and you're throwing it 50 times, you're going to throw some damn interceptions," he said. It's hyperbole, of course, and while there's some truth to his claim, it's grossly misleading. Winston isn't a victim. His interceptions contribute to those deficits. Since 2015, his 12 interceptions in the first quarter rank second, his 15 in the second quarter rank fourth, his 12 in the third quarter rank third, and his 18 in the fourth quarter rank fourth. Far too often, he is a liability.

That's not to excuse the defense, which has been cover-your-eyes awful. It was bad in 2017 and got worse in 2018, a rare feat in the DVOA era. Of all the teams that finished last in defensive DVOA in a season, only four failed to improve the next season—the 1997-98 Bengals, the 2002-03 Cardinals, the 2007-08 Lions, and the 2017-18 Buccaneers. These dreadful performances have indeed put Winston and the offense at a disadvantage—not as extreme as Arians suggested, but significant nonetheless. In 2017, when the offense began a drive, it trailed, on average, by 4.1 points, a margin that ranked 28th. In 2018, when the offense began a drive, it trailed by 3.6 points, a margin that ranked 25th.

It makes sense then that Tampa Bay's primary focus this offseason has been overhauling the defense. In just about

Table 1. Arians' Quarterback-Whispering Record

Role	Team	Quarterback	DVOA Y-1 (rank)	DVOA Y1 (rank)	DVOA Y2 (rank)	DVOA Y3 (rank)
Quarterbacks coach	IND	Peyton Manning	-	7.7% (18)	34.0% (2)	38.3% (1)
Offensive coordinator	CLE	Tim Couch	-15.1% (34)	-24.7% (35)	-7.9% (29)	-14.1% (34)
Offensive coordinator	PIT	Ben Roethlisberger	8.2% (15)	12.7% (13)	-8.1% (27)	23.2% (8)
Head coach	ARI	Carson Palmer	-2.2% (18)	2.7% (17)	8.5% (12)	34.4% (1)
Head coach	TB	Jameis Winston	6.2% (15)	-	-	-

every way—coaching, scheme, personnel—the Buccaneers will look dramatically different. Arians will be entrusting the don't-call-it-a-rebuild rebuild to Todd Bowles, who before coaching the Jets from 2015 to 2018 was the Cardinals' coordinator in 2013 and 2014. By now, you know what to expect from Bowles: an amorphous, attacking defense that three-quarters of the time won't be in its "base" 3-4 grouping. Oh, and he'll blitz. His Jets defenses tended to be among the most aggressive in the NFL, though his blitz rate dropped about five percentage points last season, from 35 to 30, which was still above the league average. He gets his defensive backs involved, too; they will crash the box and rush off the edge, and they will do so often. The bend-and-OH MY GOD IT'S BROKEN AGAIN era in Tampa Bay is over.

An attack-style defense sounds cool, but it puts a lot of pressure on the back end, especially if pass-rushers fail to disrupt the quarterback. When the Buccaneers didn't generate pressure last season, which was often (their 25.8 percent rate was the second-lowest), opponents picked them apart. Their 58.7% DVOA in such situations was the worst in the NFL. It's no coincidence then that the team chose three defensive backs on Day 2 of the draft—cornerback Sean Murphy-Bunting (Central Michigan), cornerback Jamel Dean (Auburn), and safety Mike Edwards (Kentucky). Murphy-Bunting and Jamel Dean are your prototypical Bowles corners; they're tall, fast, and physical in press man coverage. Edwards' most attractive attribute is his versatility. He can play safety; he can play nickel corner. He can cover; he can blitz. Because of a mix of injuries and inexperience in Tampa Bay's secondary, all three have a path to substantial playing time, which will be either a credit to their competitiveness or an indictment of the Buccaneers' previous personnel decisions.

The trio's knack for attacking the ball no doubt stood out to Tampa Bay, which allowed a 72.5 completion percentage and a 110.9 passer rating last season, both of which were the second-highest marks of all time. Murphy-Bunting, Dean, and Edwards intercepted a combined six passes in 2018; the Buccaneers intercepted nine passes, and four of them came in one game. Overall, Tampa Bay ranked 28th in takeaways per drive (8.6 percent), forcing only one when trailing, and that was with six minutes left in the season. Regardless of how often the rookies see the field, the Buccaneers should improve in the turnover department anyway thanks to good old-fashioned regression. Every team that ranked in the bottom five in takeaways per drive in 2017 improved in 2018.

Things will be different in the front seven, too. Tampa Bay said goodbye to linebacker Kwon Alexander, who was a fan favorite but also a missed-tackles machine. Equestrian Devin White, the fifth overall pick in April's draft, is eager to quiet his naysayers (or are they neigh-sayers?) and fill the void.

The Buccaneers also said goodbye to defensive tackle Gerald McCoy but much more awkwardly. Initially, Arians said McCoy, the team leader in quarterback knockdowns, was still a premier pass-rusher. Then he looked at Tampa Bay's salary-cap situation and suddenly McCoy wasn't "as disruptive as he was four years ago." The Buccaneers replaced McCoy with Ndamukong Suh, who presumably also got older over the past four years. Even with Suh in the fold, the defensive front is perilously thin. Jason Pierre-Paul could miss the season after suffering a neck fracture in a car crash in May, a worst-case scenario for a team that already needs a series of best-case scenarios to fall its way.

If the defense improves—and our projections say it will—the turnaround will be attributed to Bowles and his scheme. To be sure, coaching will be an influence, but one factor will have almost nothing at all to do with coaching: injuries. Tampa Bay was among the least healthy teams in the NFL last season, and the defense was especially hard hit. The Buccaneers accumulated 109.3 adjusted games lost, 92.0 of which were on defense, obliterating the previous record of 77.5 set by the 2014 Raiders. They had the most games lost at linebacker and the second-most at defensive back. Better injury luck alone could elevate the defense to respectability.

Upon his arrival in Tampa Bay, Arians said the Buccaneers have the core to win quickly. What else would you expect him to say? That they have the core to win … eventually? That wouldn't inspire a fanbase that hasn't seen a playoff appearance in 11 years and a playoff win in 16 years. That wouldn't inspire the locker room, either. There are some things we can't measure, and one of them is a coach's confidence and how it influences a team. After all, it's easier for a team to win when it expects to win. This is, to some degree, what Tampa Bay is counting on.

The more realistic outlook is that the Buccaneers have missed their optimal window for contention and that it might be too late for a course correction. Their core players are no longer bargains, which is problematic given that those core players have produced 10 wins over the past two seasons. Almost 55 percent of Tampa Bay's salary cap is tied up in just eight players—Winston, Mike Evans, Pierre-Paul, Donovan Smith, Ali Marpet, Ryan Jensen, Lavonte David, and Suh. Only the Chargers and Vikings have a greater percentage of their salary cap tied up in eight players. During an NFL season, things are going to go wrong, and usually the survivors are the ones who made contingency plans. That's not the Buccaneers. They're built on hope, not depth. Chances are the offense will decline some, the defense will improve, and we'll be just as skeptical a year from now as we are today.

Thomas Bassinger

2018 Buccaneers Stats by Week

Wk	vs.	W-L	PF	PA	YDF	YDA	TO	Total	Off	Def	ST
1	at NO	W	48	40	529	475	+2	12%	54%	31%	-10%
2	PHI	W	27	21	436	412	0	16%	29%	9%	-4%
3	PIT	L	27	30	455	413	-3	-18%	-11%	-1%	-8%
4	at CHI	L	10	48	311	483	-3	-84%	-21%	63%	0%
5	BYE										
6	at ATL	L	29	34	510	417	-2	6%	33%	26%	-1%
7	CLE	W	26	23	456	305	-3	-16%	-15%	-7%	-7%
8	at CIN	L	34	37	576	402	-4	-49%	-17%	30%	-1%
9	at CAR	L	28	42	301	407	-2	-44%	-17%	31%	4%
10	WAS	L	3	16	501	286	-4	-51%	-16%	17%	-17%
11	at NYG	L	35	38	510	359	-4	-27%	13%	35%	-5%
12	SF	W	27	9	412	342	+2	52%	39%	-4%	9%
13	CAR	W	24	17	315	444	+3	30%	17%	-10%	2%
14	NO	L	14	28	279	298	+1	-3%	-5%	-29%	-27%
15	at BAL	L	12	20	241	370	+1	-11%	1%	12%	-1%
16	at DAL	L	20	27	383	232	-2	-3%	-5%	-2%	0%
17	ATL	L	32	34	433	489	0	1%	30%	31%	3%

Trends and Splits

	Offense	Rank	Defense	Rank
Total DVOA	5.9%	12	14.8%	32
Unadjusted VOA	4.9%	12	17.7%	32
Weighted Trend	4.0%	13	10.9%	29
Variance	5.8%	10	5.2%	12
Average Opponent	0.5%	19	1.7%	11
Passing	24.0%	9	24.3%	30
Rushing	-11.9%	24	3.0%	31
First Down	13.4%	8	19.2%	32
Second Down	-16.5%	27	11.6%	29
Third Down	26.8%	3	10.3%	23
First Half	4.8%	12	19.0%	31
Second Half	7.1%	12	10.7%	27
Red Zone	-10.2%	23	41.0%	32
Late and Close	-10.9%	24	15.9%	30

Five-Year Performance

Year	W-L	Pyth W	Est W	PF	PA	TO	Total	Rk	Off	Rk	Def	Rk	ST	Rk	Off AGL	Rk	Def AGL	Rk	Off Age	Rk	Def Age	Rk	ST Age	Rk
2014	2-14	4.4	4.1	277	410	-8	-28.3%	30	-26.3%	32	1.1%	18	-0.8%	17	31.1	17	56.1	25	27.5	7	25.7	30	26.0	18
2015	6-10	6.0	6.7	342	417	-5	-9.1%	21	-1.1%	17	3.3%	18	-4.7%	30	42.2	21	32.8	20	25.9	27	25.9	28	26.2	16
2016	9-7	7.6	7.2	354	369	+2	-3.0%	22	-4.1%	19	-2.9%	13	-1.8%	20	59.6	28	17.9	6	25.7	28	26.2	21	25.8	22
2017	5-11	6.7	6.2	335	382	-1	-12.0%	23	5.2%	11	11.7%	32	-5.5%	29	26.3	9	52.3	28	26.2	27	27.0	7	25.9	12
2018	5-11	6.4	5.5	396	464	-18	-13.0%	24	5.9%	12	14.8%	32	-4.1%	28	17.3	5	92.0	32	26.3	22	26.5	12	25.6	22

2018 Performance Based on Most Common Personnel Groups

TB Offense					TB Offense vs. Opponents					TB Defense					TB Defense vs. Opponents			
Pers	Freq	Yds	DVOA	Run%	Pers	Freq	Yds	DVOA	Run%	Pers	Freq	Yds	DVOA	Pers	Freq	Yds	DVOA	
11	70%	6.7	16.0%	24%	Base	22%	5.7	-3.2%	48%	Base	31%	5.6	3.7%	11	61%	6.8	25.7%	
12	18%	5.3	-13.0%	48%	Nickel	76%	6.6	13.1%	27%	Nickel	57%	6.8	16.7%	12	17%	5.9	4.2%	
21	4%	8.7	39.8%	55%	Dime+	7%	8.0	32.0%	4%	Dime+	10%	7.1	50.7%	21	10%	7.3	14.3%	
10	3%	8.4	36.2%	13%	Goal Line	1%	0.6	20.4%	88%	Goal Line	1%	0.8	18.6%	13	5%	5.1	-0.6%	
13	2%	1.1	-111.9%	57%	Big	1%	0.0	-136.4%	80%					22	2%	3.4	-67.5%	

Strategic Tendencies

Run/Pass		Rk	Formation		Rk	Pass Rush		Rk	Secondary		Rk	Strategy		Rk
Runs, first half	32%	30	Form: Single Back	83%	13	Rush 3	2.7%	27	4 DB	31%	6	Play action	17%	31
Runs, first down	38%	30	Form: Empty Back	6%	23	Rush 4	73.3%	13	5 DB	57%	22	Avg Box (Off)	6.04	31
Runs, second-long	24%	29	Pers: 3+ WR	75%	6	Rush 5	17.1%	16	6+ DB	10%	15	Avg Box (Def)	6.26	16
Runs, power sit.	53%	21	Pers: 2+ TE/6+ OL	21%	20	Rush 6+	6.9%	9	CB by Sides	78%	15	Offensive Pace	29.59	4
Runs, behind 2H	24%	23	Pers: 6+ OL	1%	27	Int DL Sacks	23.7%	17	S/CB Cover Ratio	31%	10	Defensive Pace	31.51	23
Pass, ahead 2H	61%	2	Shotgun/Pistol	63%	17	Second Level Sacks	17.1%	26	DB Blitz	7%	20	Go for it on 4th	1.90	7

One thing to watch for with the new offense: the Arizona Cardinals ranked first or second in use of empty backfields for all five years of the Bruce Arians regime. In addition, Arians' last four offenses ranked between 10th and 16th in two-tight end sets, so we should expect to see more of O.J. Howard and Cameron Brate on the field together. ● Can Arians possibly do something about Tampa Bay's recent troubles gaining yards after the catch? The Buccaneers were last with 4.3 average YAC last season. This was the fourth time in six years that they have ranked last in YAC, and they were 29th and 27th the other two years. The problem goes back to before Jameis Winston was drafted four years ago. However, Arians' recent offenses don't suggest a lot of change here; those Cardinals offenses also tended to be near the bottom of the league in YAC. ● Another similarity between the old Tampa Bay offense and the Arians offense: they don't run much from shotgun. Tampa Bay ran on 12.6 percent of shotgun snaps, 29th in the league. When Tampa Bay ranked 31st in this stat in 2016 and 2017, Arians' Arizona offense was ranked 32nd. ● The Buccaneers threw a league-low 10.1 percent of passes at or behind the line of scrimmage. ● Surprising for a team that goes deep so much: Tampa Bay was one of three offenses tied for last place in usage of max protect (defined as seven or more blockers with at least two more blockers than pass-rushers), just 3.7 percent of pass plays. ● Winston faced a defensive back blitzing on a league low 5.0 percent of pass plays. ● Somehow, the Buccaneers defense finished sixth with three-and-outs on 24.6 percent of drives despite being dead last in defensive DVOA. ● Tampa Bay ranked sixth in DVOA against passes in the "deep middle," but it ranked in the bottom ten against deep passes to each side. ● The Buccaneers benefited from a league low 14 dropped passes by opponents, or just 2.7 percent of passes against them.

Passing

Player	DYAR	DVOA	Plays	NtYds	Avg	YAC	C%	TD	Int
J.Winston	470	6.9%	405	2824	7.0	3.7	64.7%	19	13
R.Fitzpatrick*	473	16.8%	260	2283	8.8	5.3	66.7%	17	12
B.Gabbert	-154	-35.5%	106	576	5.4	4.9	61.0%	4	4

Rushing

Player	DYAR	DVOA	Plays	Yds	Avg	TD	Fum	Suc
P.Barber	-37	-12.4%	234	871	3.7	6	1	44%
J.Winston	37	4.7%	43	283	6.6	1	3	--
J.Rodgers*	1	-7.6%	33	106	3.2	1	0	33%
R.Fitzpatrick*	40	15.9%	29	157	5.4	2	0	--
R.Jones	-15	-24.3%	23	44	1.9	1	0	30%
S.Wilson*	3	7.8%	6	29	4.8	0	0	50%
D.Jackson*	23	29.8%	6	29	4.8	1	0	--

Receiving

Player	DYAR	DVOA	Plays	Ctch	Yds	Y/C	YAC	TD	C%
M.Evans	420	26.3%	138	86	1524	17.7	3.3	8	62%
A.Humphries*	152	6.7%	105	76	816	10.7	5.5	5	72%
C.Godwin	105	1.3%	95	59	842	14.3	4.2	7	62%
D.Jackson*	153	12.2%	74	41	774	18.9	4.4	4	55%
B.Perriman	97	36.6%	25	16	340	21.3	4.7	2	64%
C.Brate	2	-6.8%	49	30	289	9.6	1.7	6	61%
O.J.Howard	169	44.0%	48	34	565	16.6	6.1	5	71%
A.Auclair	2	-2.5%	8	7	48	6.9	1.1	0	88%
J.Leggett	-16	-17.4%	25	14	114	8.1	3.5	1	56%
J.Rodgers*	49	7.1%	45	38	304	8.0	6.3	0	84%
P.Barber	-34	-35.1%	29	20	92	4.6	3.2	1	69%
R.Jones	-15	-42.4%	9	7	33	4.7	6.0	0	78%

Offensive Line

Player	Pos	Age	GS	Snaps	Pen	Sk	Pass	Run	Player	Pos	Age	GS	Snaps	Pen	Sk	Pass	Run
Ryan Jensen	C	28	16/16	1116	11	1.5	6	7	Caleb Benenoch	RG	25	16/16	844	7	5.5	9	6
Ali Marpet	LG	26	16/16	1116	2	2.0	12	3	Evan Smith	G	33	7/0	168	2	0.0	3	0
Donovan Smith	LT	26	16/16	1116	7	7.0	16	8	Josh LeRibeus	LG	30	6/3	179	2	0.0	1	0
Demar Dotson	RT	34	15/15	1005	11	2.5	8	3									

Year	Yards	ALY	Rank	Power	Rank	Stuff	Rank	2nd Lev	Rank	Open Field	Rank	Sacks	ASR	Rank	Press	Rank	F-Start	Cont.
2016	3.61	4.01	21	47%	32	24%	32	1.06	25	0.45	28	35	5.9%	16	29.9%	26	16	32
2017	3.53	4.06	16	65%	12	20%	17	0.93	31	0.41	30	40	6.5%	16	30.5%	14	18	34
2018	3.55	3.78	31	64%	22	25%	30	1.06	27	0.49	29	41	6.6%	15	31.4%	18	14	40

2018 ALY by direction: Left End: 1.33 (32)   Left Tackle: 3.78 (25)   Mid/Guard: 4.14 (25)   Right Tackle: 4.20 (20)   Right End: 3.00 (30)

Laboring in obscurity. Starving and struggling. This is an offensive line that Keanu Reeves would approve of. No team embraces its mediocre nothingness like the Buccaneers. After handing out contract extensions to left tackle Donovan Smith and left guard Ali Marpet, Tampa Bay will spend close to $50 million on its line this season, or about a quarter of the salary cap. According to Over The Cap, that's third in the league behind Dallas and Green Bay. Teams like the Steelers, Colts, and Eagles all spend substantially less to field substantially better lines. ● Smith, who will earn $12.5 million this season (a nearly 900 percent raise), had the fewest snaps per blown block on the team and ranked 25th among 35 qualifying left tackles. That was actually an improvement over 2017, when he ranked 30th. ● Whether it was Caleb Benenoch, Evan Smith, or Alex Cappa, it didn't matter who played right guard. They were all liabilities, especially in pass protection. The Buccaneers signed Earl Watford, who played for Arians in Arizona, to compete with Cappa for the starting right guard job, but he isn't an upgrade. Tampa

Bay is counting on Cappa, a 2017 third-round pick out of Humboldt State (a Division II school in northern California, near the border with Oregon), to make a leap. ✇ Benenoch is transitioning to tackle, where the Buccaneers are sorely lacking in depth. Right tackle Demar Dotson, who turns 34 in October, played through various leg injuries last season and is on borrowed time.

Defensive Front

Defensive Line	Age	Pos	G	Snaps	Plays	TmPct	Rk	Stop	Dfts	BTkl	Runs	St%	Rk	RuYd	Rk	Sack	Hit	Hur	Dsrpt
						Overall						vs. Run				Pass Rush			
Gerald McCoy*	31	DT	14	732	29	4.1%	63	22	13	5	17	65%	75	2.1	33	6.0	15	22	1
Vita Vea	24	DT	13	493	28	4.2%	60	21	4	0	22	68%	71	2.7	61	3.0	1	9	0
Beau Allen	28	DT	14	386	20	2.8%	78	17	2	2	20	85%	12	2.6	58	0.0	4	6	0
Ndamukong Suh	32	DT	16	891	63	8.1%	5	44	10	4	48	69%	68	3.1	73	4.5	15	30	4

Edge Rushers	Age	Pos	G	Snaps	Plays	TmPct	Rk	Stop	Dfts	BTkl	Runs	St%	Rk	RuYd	Rk	Sack	Hit	Hur	Dsrpt
						Overall						vs. Run				Pass Rush			
Jason Pierre-Paul	30	DE	16	933	60	7.4%	7	45	22	10	37	73%	50	2.0	34	12.5	9	27	1
Carl Nassib	26	DE	15	598	31	4.1%	65	27	18	8	21	81%	23	1.7	21	6.5	10	19	1
Vinny Curry*	31	DE	12	445	21	3.4%	78	14	10	2	16	63%	75	1.7	22	2.5	4	11	0
William Gholston	28	DE	16	402	10	1.2%	--	7	5	0	8	63%	--	2.4	--	1.0	6	12	0
Shaquil Barrett	27	OLB	13	275	25	3.7%	--	19	8	3	15	80%	--	2.9	--	3.0	4	5	0

Linebackers	Age	Pos	G	Snaps	Plays	TmPct	Rk	Stop	Dfts	BTkl	Runs	St%	Rk	RuYd	Rk	Sack	Hit	Hur	Tgts	Suc%	Rk	AdjYd	Rk	PD	Int
						Overall						vs. Run				Pass Rush				vs. Pass					
Lavonte David	29	OLB	14	922	123	17.3%	10	77	30	7	62	73%	6	2.3	3	3.5	3	6	42	55%	22	6.5	30	3	0
Adarius Taylor*	29	MLB	15	635	61	8.0%	70	31	7	5	36	50%	76	4.0	51	1.0	0	3	24	50%	40	6.7	35	5	1
Kwon Alexander*	25	MLB	6	366	47	15.4%	21	24	13	7	17	53%	62	2.6	7	1.0	3	4.5	10	40%	--	8.9	--	2	0
Devante Bond	26	OLB	11	248	19	3.4%	--	9	2	3	15	53%	--	4.9	--	0.0	1	2	7	29%	--	19.6	--	0	0
Deone Bucannon	27	OLB	13	389	36	5.0%	84	14	3	4	22	55%	60	4.5	69	1.0	1	6.5	11	45%	--	6.7	--	0	0

Year	Yards	ALY	Rank	Power	Rank	Stuff	Rank	2nd Level	Rank	Open Field	Rank	Sacks	ASR	Rank	Press	Rank
2016	4.20	4.53	26	57%	5	19%	17	1.29	27	0.57	9	38	7.1%	6	24.7%	25
2017	4.18	4.16	20	62%	13	21%	14	1.19	21	0.84	24	22	4.3%	32	24.8%	32
2018	4.59	4.36	15	71%	24	23%	8	1.45	29	1.04	24	38	8.0%	8	25.0%	31
2018 ALY by direction:		Left End: 5.28 (27)			Left Tackle: 3.35 (7)			Mid/Guard: 4.03 (5)			Right Tackle: 5.31 (30)			Right End: 4.45 (16)	

The Tampa-2 is ancient history. The 4-3 front is out, and the 3-4 front is in, which is probably a good thing because there isn't much defensive line depth here. "I know Tampa traditionally had a front four for years," Arians said this spring. "We don't have a front four, per se. We've got a bunch of guys coming after the quarterback. Now, it could be four, could be three, could be eight, and it's that unknown, that's how you create a pass rush." ✇ The Buccaneers' attempt to emulate the Super Bowl champion Eagles' pass-rush rotation failed miserably, even after importing a pair of players from Philadelphia, defensive end Vinny Curry and defensive tackle Beau Allen. Curry, who dealt with an ankle injury throughout the season and eventually lost his job to Carl Nassib, was Arians' first major cut. Tampa Bay retained Allen, but only after restructuring his contract to lower his 2019 salary-cap hit. His $4 million salary signals the Buccaneers are counting on him to be more than a role player, a curious decision given that he's a run-stopping interior lineman who isn't particularly good at stopping the run. When he was on the field last season, opponents averaged 4.9 yards per carry; when he was off it, they averaged 4.5 yards per carry. On the relatively rare occasions when the defense is in its 3-4 base alignment, the primary linemen likely will be Allen, Vita Vea, and Ndamukong Suh. ✇ In addition to Curry and Allen, Tampa Bay traded for edge rusher Jason Pierre-Paul. The net result: The defense's pressure rate improved from worst to second-worst. On the surface, the trade of a third-round pick for Pierre-Paul seemed worthwhile. He recorded 12.5 sacks, the most by a Buccaneers player since Simeon Rice recorded 14 in 2005. Pierre-Paul, though, was likely to regress this season, as he converted pressures into sacks at a significantly higher rate last season than he had during his previous eight seasons. Even if his neck heals and he returns around midseason, the 30-year-old has racked up a lot of mileage. He played 1,011 snaps in 2017 (second in the league among edge rushers) and 939 snaps in 2018 (fifth). ✇ Aside from Lavonte David, the Tampa Bay defense will feature a revamped linebacker corps, led by first-round draft pick Devin White on the inside. One reason White could be a sneaky good upgrade in the middle of the field: Tampa Bay had the league's worst defensive DVOA last year against passes in the "short middle" portion of the field. Former Cardinals moneybacker Deone Bucannon will back up David and White. ✇ New faces on the outside include Shaquil Barrett, who had 32 hurries as a starter for the 2017 Broncos, and Anthony Nelson, a fourth-round bargain out of Iowa with an 82.7% SackSEER rating.

Defensive Secondary

Secondary	Age	Pos	G	Snaps	Plays	TmPct	Rk	Stop	Dfts	BTkl	Runs	St%	Rk	RuYd	Rk	Tgts	Tgt%	Rk	Dist	Suc%	Rk	AdjYd	Rk	PD	Int
												Overall						vs. Run				vs. Pass			
Brent Grimes*	36	CB	13	791	54	8.2%	45	14	4	7	19	11%	79	10.8	75	46	14.8%	10	12.4	43%	73	9.0	69	6	0
Carlton Davis	23	CB	13	718	44	6.7%	69	22	8	9	17	59%	12	3.6	7	45	16.0%	19	13.6	51%	45	8.2	54	4	0
Jordan Whitehead	22	SS	15	660	79	10.4%	37	31	9	17	40	48%	28	7.8	48	31	12.0%	59	11.6	42%	59	7.8	44	4	0
Justin Evans	24	SS	10	605	61	12.0%	17	20	11	4	32	31%	57	9.6	60	11	4.6%	6	11.6	45%	51	10.1	66	2	1
Ryan Smith	26	CB	16	419	39	4.8%	--	18	5	4	13	54%	--	4.2	--	34	20.7%	--	12.8	50%	--	7.6	--	6	1
Isaiah Johnson	27	FS	15	404	47	6.2%	--	9	1	0	22	23%	--	12.4	--	18	11.4%	--	10.7	33%	--	11.0	--	2	1
Andrew Adams*	27	FS	13	370	45	6.8%	64	22	16	12	12	58%	11	5.8	22	24	16.5%	73	10.1	58%	17	6.7	24	9	4
Javien Elliott*	26	CB	15	351	25	3.3%	--	10	6	7	7	57%	--	3.4	--	21	15.2%	--	9.6	38%	--	8.5	--	1	1
M.J. Stewart	24	CB	11	300	32	5.7%	--	14	8	4	3	100%	--	-0.7	--	31	26.3%	--	8.5	35%	--	9.9	--	3	0
Kentrell Brice	25	FS	14	646	52	7.3%	59	14	2	14	27	37%	46	6.8	36	26	10.4%	49	8.8	23%	74	13.3	72	2	0

Year	Pass D Rank	vs. #1 WR	Rk	vs. #2 WR	Rk	vs. Other WR	Rk	WR Wide	Rk	WR Slot	Rk	vs. TE	Rk	vs. RB	Rk
2016	6	-5.5%	8	-2.1%	13	-18.5%	6	-12.5%	7	-4.7%	9	-22.4%	4	16.6%	26
2017	31	0.9%	15	8.4%	21	21.0%	27	2.5%	21	14.6%	22	6.1%	22	13.3%	25
2018	30	16.0%	29	25.1%	29	-1.4%	18	-11.2%	9	28.7%	29	21.1%	28	2.2%	16

Brent Grimes' coverage success rate dropped from 53.7 percent in 2017, which ranked 28th, to 43.5 percent in 2018, which ranked 73rd. Only six cornerbacks were worse. The reason for his poor performance? Grimes said on his wife's podcast that coaches destroyed his "vibe" for the whole season because they asked him to shadow Antonio Brown in Week 3. That's a job for cornerbacks who earn $13 million to $15 million, he said, not for cornerbacks who earn $7 million. In related news, the 36-year-old Grimes isn't shadowing anyone right now and is set to make $0 million this season. ◥ The new old man in the secondary is 24-year-old Vernon Hargreaves. The 2016 first-round draft pick has yet to fulfill his promise and is entering a prove-it season. In 26 career games (he missed almost all of last season because of a shoulder injury), he has intercepted one pass. His coverage success rate has never been greater than 45 percent. Tampa Bay picked up his fifth-year option, which is worth $9 million. ◥ The Buccaneers' rookie defensive backs—M.J. Stewart, Carlton Davis, and Jordan Whitehead—did little to slow quarterbacks. Between them, they had 11 passes defensed. Two Falcons players, one Panthers player, and two Saints players had at least that many. Inexperience? Perhaps, but they weren't known as ballhawks when Tampa Bay drafted them. Their lack of comfort in the Buccaneers' off-coverage scheme likely was a factor in their struggles, particularly for Stewart and Davis. They're physical defenders who prefer to play press man coverage, and thus better fits for Todd Bowles' scheme. Davis will compete for one of the starting outside cornerback jobs, while Stewart, who lacks the speed to play on the outside, will get looks at nickel cornerback and safety.

Special Teams

Year	DVOA	Rank	FG/XP	Rank	Net Kick	Rank	Kick Ret	Rank	Net Punt	Rank	Punt Ret	Rank	Hidden	Rank
2016	-1.8%	20	-15.0	32	2.6	11	-8.9	32	13.6	2	-1.2	16	9.6	6
2017	-5.5%	29	-13.2	31	-14.4	32	-0.6	16	0.2	18	0.3	14	-1.2	14
2018	-4.1%	28	-12.9	31	1.7	12	-2.2	20	-2.9	23	-4.0	26	-8.3	25

The Buccaneers extended their streak of below-average special teams play to seven seasons. The special teams DVOA rankings of Bruce Arians' Cardinals teams: 27th, 21st, 29th, 30th, and 28th. ◥ When general manager Jason Licht drafted kicker Roberto Aguayo in the second round in 2016, he said he wanted to stop the team's kicker carousel. Well, the carousel continued in 2018. Tampa Bay signed Chandler Catanzaro to replace Patrick Murray but ended up releasing him after he missed two field goals in a Week 11 loss to Washington. He landed in Carolina, where he made all five of his field goals and all but one of his extra points. ◥ The carousel continues this summer, as fifth-round draft pick Matt Gay (Utah) challenges incumbent Cairo Santos. You read that right. Even after the Aguayo debacle, the Buccaneers drafted another kicker. They're calling this a competition, but Gay would have to lose his mind and/or feet for Tampa Bay to consider cutting him. ◥ Bradley Pinion comes over from San Francisco because Tampa Bay was willing to make him the league's 10th-highest paid punter. The thinking was that Pinion would handle kickoffs, but then … Matt Gay. It's a wonder that the Buccaneers are in salary-cap trouble and have had just one compensatory draft pick since 2011. ◥ Tampa Bay rotated three kick returners last season, but receiver Bobo Wilson was the one with positive value. ◥ With Adam Humphries gone, the punt return job is up for grabs. The Buccaneers will look to a couple of rookies to fill the role—sixth-rounder Scotty Miller and second-rounder Sean Murphy-Bunting. Miller at least has some experience; he returned seven punts in his four seasons at Bowling Green. Murphy-Bunting didn't return any during his four seasons at Central Michigan.

Tennessee Titans

2018 record: 9-7	Total DVOA: -4.9% (20th)	2019 Mean Projection: 8.3 wins	On the Clock (0-4): 8%
Pythagorean Wins: 8.2 (15th)	Offense: -5.1% (22nd)	Postseason Odds: 40.9%	Mediocrity (5-7): 29%
Snap-Weighted Age: 26.3 (20th)	Defense: 0.6% (19th)	Super Bowl Odds: 5.8%	Playoff Contender (8-10): 40%
Average Opponent: 0.2% (13th)	Special Teams: 0.8% (13th)	Proj. Avg. Opponent: 1.1% (11th)	Super Bowl Contender (11+): 22%

2018: The more things change, the more they stay the same.

2019: The more things stay the same, the more they stay the same.

From where the Tennessee Titans were when general manager Jon Robinson arrived in 2016, 9-7 looked pretty good. After all, the team he inherited had gone just 5-27 the previous two seasons and had not had a winning record since 2011. After three consecutive seasons with that mark, though, 9-7 starts looking stale. Not stale enough for Robinson to be in danger of getting sacked like Mike Mularkey was despite winning a playoff game two years ago, but now the Titans are looking for more and better. It comes as no surprise a mantra heard repeatedly from St. Thomas Sports Park this offseason has been about going from "good to great."

Fortunately for the Titans, they are far from the first organization looking to make that transition. The challenge is common enough even beyond the field of sports to have inspired a classic business book. *Good to Great* by Jim Collins addresses precisely that challenge and outlines the characteristics of companies that successfully made the transition. What can those characteristics, however they might be applied to football, tell us about the Titans' chances of making that transition to true Super Bowl contender?

Collins' first trait is **"Level 5 Leadership."** The typical view of successful leaders is that those who effectively lead an organization do so through personal vision and driving performance. The Level 5 leaders that led the companies Collins identified as making the transition are of a different cloth, combining professional will and personal humility in a way that creates enduring success for their organizations.

An NFL team of 53 players, plus practice-squadders, a dozen or more assistant coaches, and support staff—which may (scouting) or may not (ticket sales) have much to do with the on-field product—is not of the same scale that Collins considered.Even the reigning dean of NFL coaches, Bill Belichick, looks more like a Level 4 leader, the singular genius who produces a great organization so long as he is present but who may not create enduring success.

Indeed, Collins' second trait is **"First Who ... Then What."** Briefly, the organizations that made the transition emphasized well-qualified people, not just the right one, in contrast to the "genius with a thousand helpers" model. As Collins described the Level 4 leadership problem, "When the genius leaves, the helpers are often lost. Or, worse, they try to mimic their predecessor with bold, visionary moves (trying to act like a genius, without being a genius) that prove unsuccessful." That sounds like the fate of former Belichick assistants.

A couple of approaches to these two traits seem particularly apposite for the Titans. The first is the current head coach and former Belichick player, Mike Vrabel, hired after Mike Mularkey was fired last offseason. By the standard of most NFL coaching hires, Vrabel had a thin background: just eight years as an assistant, half that in college, and a single season as a coordinator with mediocre results. He had spent most of his coaching time engrossed in the details of tight end, the same position where he once moonlighted on the field. The risk in such a hire is that while he might be able to succeed as a leader of men, he might not have the requisite background knowledge and experience to succeed as a leader of football strategy. Tennessee, though not Robinson, saw a similar scenario play out earlier this decade with Mike Munchak. Vrabel rallied the team from midseason disappointment to the verge of the playoffs, suggesting he has those leadership qualities, but more remains to be seen.

The second relates to first-round pick Jeffery Simmons. Robinson in his first three seasons has held to a bright line rule on character, eschewing any real clear character risks, let alone embracing the deeply troubled like his predecessor Ruston Webster did. But there he was with the 19th pick, a selection which ESPN followed by showing not the film of Simmons disrupting offenses at Mississippi State, but rather him attacking a woman as a high school senior.

This is not the forum for going into all the details and potential ramifications and wherefores about what Simmons did, rather than emphasizing that it seemed a departure from Robinson's oft-repeated mantra of "faith, family, and football." Or perhaps not—Simmons was assisting his sister in a fight, not attacking his girlfriend.[1]

A clean record and fine references from Starkville made Simmons an acceptable risk for a team that had heretofore shied away from even that and showed a new wrinkle in the team philosophy on how to find the best players.

The third trait from *Good to Great* is **"Confront the Brutal**

---

1 See https://es.pn/2mZD1sW on why this is an important distinction.

2019 Titans Schedule

Week	Opp.	Week	Opp.	Week	Opp.
1	at CLE	7	LAC	13	at IND
2	IND	8	TB	14	at OAK
3	at JAX (Thu.)	9	at CAR	15	HOU
4	at ATL	10	KC	16	NO
5	BUF	11	BYE	17	at HOU
6	at DEN	12	JAX		

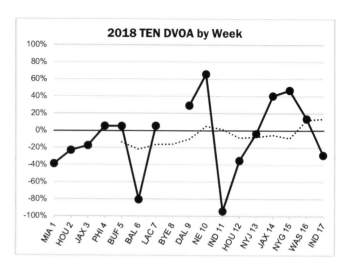

Facts." Self-delusion, about how good you are and how you will likely be, is a most human trait, and an NFL populated by humans is no different. Denying brutal facts—that inaccurate college quarterbacks are extremely unlikely to become competent NFL quarterbacks or winning a lot of close games means less than winning games by large margins—is commonplace.

The Titans' most likely refusal to confront the brutal facts revolves around their defense. By our numbers, this was in fact the best Titans' defense since 2011, but that means very little. Their defensive DVOA was just average at 0.6% and ranked just 19th. Naturally, the talk out of St. Thomas Sports Park has revolved around their much more impressive conventional statistics, where they ranked eighth-best in yards allowed and third in points against.

Without rehashing all the reasons that our numbers differ from the NFL's official rankings, such as yards allowed ignoring both schedule strength and turnovers, it is worth thinking about some of the reasons a big jump by the Titans defense might be possible and also why you might share the skepticism of our projection system that the defense will be above average for the first time in a decade.

The first is red zone performance. The Titans were an outstanding red zone team in 2018. They led the league by allowing only 4.15 points per red zone possession and allowed touchdowns at the third-lowest rate. Only the Bears had a better red zone defensive DVOA. Our research has shown, however, that outside of perhaps New England, red zone defense tends to regress toward the mean from one season to the next.

A second factor to consider is performance in key games. The Titans' three most important games last year were probably a two-game division road trip to Indianapolis and Houston at midseason and a for-the-postseason home game against the Colts in Week 17. The defense was shredded in all three contests, giving up a combined 105 points. Those were also their three worst games of the year by defensive DVOA, and a continued mastery over Blake Bortles belies any argument that divisional games were a particular problem.

Whatever else he has done, Jon Robinson has invested in the defense. Even without Simmons, likely to miss at least the first half of the season after tearing his ACL in February, Robinson has significant resources invested at defensive line, the side's thinnest position. Jurrell Casey ranks behind only Aaron Donald and J.J. Watt in average salary per year among 3-4 defensive ends. DaQuan Jones is in the top 15 at the position. Austin Johnson is a second-round pick on a rookie deal.

The same story is true at virtually every position. With a cou-

ple of exceptions, the Titans defense will be made up of younger players picked in the first three rounds or established veterans being paid good money. That is the sort of unit that, chosen and led well, could reasonably be expected to have a performance that matches those impressive conventional statistics.

The fourth trait is **"The Hedgehog Concept (Simplicity within the Three Circles)."** Building off Isaiah Berlin's distinction between the hedgehog and the fox, Collins found the companies that made the good-to-great transition were hedgehogs that knew one thing. They knew what they could be the best at and were not the best at, what drove their success, and what they were passionate about.

In what was mostly a dismal offensive season for the Titans, the particular bright spot was Derrick Henry's remarkable play the second half of the season. Henry has always had the highlight reel runs, many of them featuring his powerful stiff-arm, but his down-to-down performance also included tentative play between the tackles and a tendency to go down on leg contact. A bye week meeting with franchise legend Eddie George led to a transformation in his play. The first half of the season he was on the wrong end of a split with Dion Lewis, whose greater versatility between run and pass made the Titans less predictable. The second half of the season, Henry asserted control over the job not because of an ability to pass block but because of a more assertive running style. Gone was the Le'Veon Bell-like hesitation and the ensuing leg tackles that came without Bell's lateral agility. Instead, he ran powerfully behind his large frame and showed he could be a sustaining runner (Table 1).

Table 1. Derrick Henry, Before and After Eddie George

	DVOA	Success Rate	Yds/Run
Weeks 1-8	-4.5%	43%	3.3
Weeks 10-17	40.6%	56%	6.0

New offensive coordinator Arthur Smith seems likely to try to get Henry to recapture that form for the entirety of the season, but that may be up to Henry more than anyone else.

Further, passing is more important than running to the point where even having 100 DYAR more than any other back from Week 10 onwards could not make the Titans more than an average offense in the second half of the season.

The fifth trait is **"A Culture of Discipline."** Collins specifically distinguishes this from the tyrant who disciplines, a generally unsustainable model. Rather, "[it] is about disciplined *people* who engage in disciplined *thought* and who *then* take disciplined action." From a broader management perspective, it is fanatical adherence to the things the company is trying to be the best at and not doing activities that fall outside their area of excellence.

Translating this trait to the culture of the NFL requires some lateral thinking. One particular aspect of discipline that seems obvious is penalties. It seemed like a curious strategy a few years ago when Mularkey emphasized in offseason work that the team that was penalized for the third-fewest yards in the NFL the year before needed to commit fewer penalties. The few who paid attention and noticed Mularkey's Titans then had the seventh-most penalty yards had a chuckle and moved on. Vrabel's comments this offseason have a same feel. After all, Tennessee was dead last in the NFL with just 31 defensive penalties and 99 penalties total. Why, then, would Vrabel be emphasizing penalty avoidance?

Our research has emphasized that many penalties are not actually that bad. The line between offensive holding and a good block or illegal contact and good sticky pass defense is not always obvious, even to insiders. What Mularkey might have been emphasizing, and what Vrabel's similar comments this offseason might actually be about, is creating precisely this sort of culture of discipline. Our research has found that some penalties are actually bad. Coaches across the years at all levels have emphasized reducing and eliminating mental errors, and those do lead to penalties like too many men and illegal shift that are indeed just bad.

The sixth trait is **"Technology Accelerators."** Collins found in his research that the companies that made the transition from good to great were not necessarily at the forefront of the technological frontier. However, neither did they ignore technology. They aggressively incorporated it to advance their core businesses and assist them in making better strategic decisions.

A gross generalization of the past 40 years of NFL history, since the 1978 passing rules liberalization, is a growing realization that passing can be done safely and efficiently, enabling offenses to be more proficient even on regular downs. It is not clear how much this lesson sunk in for the 2018 Titans.

Offensive coordinator Matt LaFleur came from the Rams, a team which unsophisticated measures might suggest was run-oriented. What looked like the Rams' run orientation, though, came from a team that threw at above-average rates on early downs early in the game to get a lead, and then ran to preserve that lead. What he did in Tennessee was not that.

While not reaching the same depths as the insanely run-oriented Seattle Seahawks, the Titans were the second-most extreme team in their run orientation. They were the only other team to rank in the top five in run/pass ratio on first downs

in the first quarter, the second quarter before the two-minute warning, and the third quarter. They were especially enamored of the second-and-long run, ranking first in the league by running 44 percent of the time. They fared well in those situations, ranking fourth in the league with 5.4 yards per carry and a DVOA of 4.5%, but even that was not as good as their 16.3% passing DVOA in the same situation.

LaFleur now gets to deal with Aaron Rodgers and the weather in Green Bay, so Arthur Smith gets to deal with Marcus Mariota and company. Smith is a long-time Titans assistant across multiple regimes, originally joining the team as a defensive quality control coach before eventually becoming tight ends coach. Just what he will want to do with the offense is an open question. LaFleur's background was outside zone and more outside zone with Gary Kubiak, the Shanahans, and Sean McVay. By contrast, Smith has worked under Chris Palmer's modified run-and-shoot, Dowell Loggains' tight end-heavy zone run-oriented offense, Ken Whisenhunt's protection-optional three-wideout bunch and trips sets, Mike Mularkey's tight end-heavy gap run-oriented condensed-field offense, and LaFleur's wide receiver-heavy (in Los Angeles) or tight end-heavier (in Tennessee), pass-oriented (in Los Angeles) or run-oriented (in Tennessee), zone run game with the field condensed to spread. Smith was sold as a continuity hire and preliminary indications suggest he will keep at least LaFleur's verbiage and try to build on Henry's success the second half of the season.

One complicating factor for this whole analysis is that the 2018 Titans did not really have enough receivers to run a pass-oriented offense, especially after the relationship with their only real veteran receiver, Rishard Matthews, broke down and led to his virtual benching and release early in the season. LaFleur might have wanted to throw the ball more, but the lack of depth at receiver and Mariota's Week 1 arm injury (which limited his ability to throw the ball down the field even after he returned) may have convinced him he simply could not.

Robinson addressed wide receiver in a big way this offseason, adding Adam Humphries from Tampa Bay in free agency and selecting A.J. Brown from Ole Miss in the second round. Robinson was with the Bucs when they signed Humphries as an undrafted free agent, and the Titans did not have a traditional slot receiver who could take advantage of the two-way go opportunity. Brown was primarily a big slot receiver with the Rebels and might project to a role similar to the one Robert Woods has played with the McVay Rams.

Is that combination of philosophy and personnel additions going to be enough to help take the Titans from good to great? Much of the potential offensive improvement depends on Mariota establishing less of a variably average level of play and being more consistently reliable, not just interspersing or fluctuating from one game to the next from quite good to not so good at all. Even Blake Bortles was able to succeed relatively consistently in structured situations when the Jaguars made their run to the 2017 AFC Championship Game, and Mariota's level of play has been clearly above that of Bortles.

Most likely, though, the Titans will be improved on offense

from 2018 but still no better than average. An average offense and an average defense, against a schedule we project to be around average, suggests another pretty average season in Nashville. That is still much better than the 5-27 of the 2014-15 Titans, but making that transition from good to great depends on a several factors going in ways we do not expect them to go.

Even if the Titans do make this transition, well, the future was not as bright as the past for the companies that made Collins' precise cut for companies that had made the transition from good to great. Over the next decade, they did not outperform the market as a whole. Even making the *Good to Great*

transition does not by itself make for enduring success. Fortunate, then, that Collins wrote a whole other significant book about that process. If the theme of next year's Titans chapter is about how a newly great team can indeed be *Built to Last*, that will be a success. More likely, though, the Titans will be about as good as they have been and next year's chapter will cover Robinson's offseason quarterback decision and whether it will be Mariota, newly-acquired backup Ryan Tannehill, or some shiny new passer who gets to battle Andrew Luck and Deshaun Watson for long-term AFC South supremacy.

Tom Gower

2018 Titans Stats by Week

Wk	vs.	W-L	PF	PA	YDF	YDA	TO	Total	Off	Def	ST
1	at MIA	L	20	27	336	342	-1	-39%	-51%	1%	13%
2	HOU	W	20	17	283	437	+1	-23%	-2%	27%	5%
3	at JAX	W	9	6	233	232	+1	-18%	-17%	-5%	-6%
4	PHI	W	26	23	397	432	0	5%	5%	-5%	-4%
5	at BUF	L	12	13	221	223	-2	5%	-30%	-18%	18%
6	BAL	L	0	21	106	361	+1	-80%	-61%	12%	-8%
7	at LAC	L	19	20	390	344	-1	6%	10%	9%	4%
8	BYE										
9	at DAL	W	28	14	340	297	0	29%	28%	-11%	-9%
10	NE	W	34	10	385	284	0	66%	24%	-37%	4%
11	at IND	L	10	38	267	397	-2	-94%	-55%	35%	-5%
12	at HOU	L	17	34	365	462	-1	-35%	-3%	36%	4%
13	NYJ	W	26	22	403	280	0	-4%	-2%	-12%	-14%
14	JAX	W	30	9	426	255	0	40%	41%	-6%	-6%
15	at NYG	W	17	0	301	260	+2	47%	-1%	-48%	0%
16	WAS	W	25	16	291	292	+2	14%	13%	6%	7%
17	IND	L	17	33	258	436	-1	-29%	-19%	21%	11%

Trends and Splits

	Offense	Rank	Defense	Rank
Total DVOA	-5.1%	22	0.6%	19
Unadjusted VOA	-6.3%	23	-1.6%	16
Weighted Trend	0.8%	16	0.4%	15
Variance	8.9%	25	5.5%	18
Average Opponent	-3.6%	2	-5.0%	27
Passing	-0.2%	25	9.4%	21
Rushing	-2.3%	11	-9.4%	15
First Down	-0.8%	15	6.1%	24
Second Down	-5.1%	23	1.7%	20
Third Down	-13.3%	25	-11.0%	10
First Half	-9.6%	26	8.7%	29
Second Half	-0.3%	18	-7.7%	9
Red Zone	1.1%	14	-28.3%	2
Late and Close	-6.4%	21	-13.4%	7

Five-Year Performance

Year	W-L	Pyth W	Est W	PF	PA	TO	Total	Rk	Off	Rk	Def	Rk	ST	Rk	Off AGL	Rk	Def AGL	Rk	Off Age	Rk	Def Age	Rk	ST Age	Rk
2014	2-14	3.3	4.0	254	438	-10	-29.3%	31	-16.4%	29	11.2%	29	-1.8%	20	38.8	22	40.9	19	27.0	14	27.0	10	26.7	2
2015	3-13	4.8	4.4	299	423	-14	-26.6%	31	-15.7%	32	7.1%	23	-3.8%	28	38.7	20	26.5	13	25.6	29	26.5	18	25.7	24
2016	9-7	8.1	8.7	381	378	0	3.5%	15	10.8%	9	6.4%	24	-1.0%	19	21.0	4	11.0	3	26.2	24	27.0	8	26.2	14
2017	9-7	7.4	7.6	334	356	-4	-5.7%	18	-2.2%	18	5.0%	21	1.6%	13	11.2	4	16.4	9	26.5	22	26.9	10	26.8	2
2018	9-7	8.2	7.7	310	303	-1	-4.9%	20	-5.1%	22	0.6%	19	0.8%	13	31.2	10	37.5	19	26.2	23	26.4	14	26.6	6

2018 Performance Based on Most Common Personnel Groups

TEN Offense					TEN Offense vs. Opponents					TEN Defense				TEN Defense vs. Opponents			
Pers	Freq	Yds	DVOA	Run%	Pers	Freq	Yds	DVOA	Run%	Pers	Freq	Yds	DVOA	Pers	Freq	Yds	DVOA
11	57%	5.1	-14.0%	31%	Base	34%	5.8	5.8%	62%	Base	25%	6.2	7.6%	11	62%	5.4	0.5%
12	28%	5.9	8.3%	56%	Nickel	47%	5.4	0.3%	38%	Nickel	73%	5.3	0.0%	12	21%	6.8	20.1%
13	10%	5.5	-3.7%	72%	Dime+	12%	4.8	-51.3%	16%	Dime+	2%	3.9	-2.9%	21	5%	5.5	0.3%
WC	2%	8.1	78.4%	89%	Goal Line	1%	1.3	31.1%	75%	Goal Line	1%	0.1	-43.4%	13	4%	5.0	-13.0%
21	1%	4.9	-3.6%	31%	Big	1%	5.4	62.5%	40%					612	3%	4.5	-12.0%
610	1%	0.3	7.0%	100%										611	2%	3.6	-18.7%

Strategic Tendencies

Run/Pass		Rk	Formation		Rk	Pass Rush		Rk	Secondary		Rk	Strategy		Rk
Runs, first half	43%	2	Form: Single Back	74%	23	Rush 3	11.8%	8	4 DB	25%	16	Play action	29%	6
Runs, first down	55%	4	Form: Empty Back	6%	24	Rush 4	60.7%	24	5 DB	73%	9	Avg Box (Off)	6.60	1
Runs, second-long	44%	1	Pers: 3+ WR	58%	28	Rush 5	20.0%	11	6+ DB	2%	25	Avg Box (Def)	6.38	3
Runs, power sit.	67%	7	Pers: 2+ TE/6+ OL	40%	3	Rush 6+	7.2%	7	CB by Sides	72%	17	Offensive Pace	31.93	23
Runs, behind 2H	37%	3	Pers: 6+ OL	1%	21	Int DL Sacks	20.5%	21	S/CB Cover Ratio	21%	29	Defensive Pace	31.29	19
Pass, ahead 2H	39%	30	Shotgun/Pistol	53%	27	Second Level Sacks	50.0%	1	DB Blitz	12%	6	Go for it on 4th	1.57	12

Tennessee hired an all-new coaching staff and yet their rankings in these strategic tendencies categories are almost all roughly the same as they were the year before. The big changes: way more sacks from second-level defenders (led by nine sacks from defensive backs and six from Jayon Brown) and more aggressive play calling on fourth down from Mike Vrabel. ● Marcus Mariota may have learned his craft in the Chip Kelly shotgun spread, but the Titans once again were a much better offense last year with Mariota under center: ninth in DVOA compared to 27th with the quarterback in shotgun. The year before, those ranks were sixth and 25th. In 2016, however, the performance was reversed: third in shotgun, 18th under center. ● Mariota was big-blitzed (six or more pass-rushers) more than any quarterback in the league, 11 percent of pass plays, and was terrible with just 4.2 net yards per pass and -63.6% DVOA against big blitzes. ● Tennessee threw a league-high 24.5 percent of passes at or behind the line of scrimmage despite a -17.8% DVOA on these passes, which ranked 25th in the league. ● The Titans led the league with 158 broken tackles on offense. Both Derrick Henry and Dion Lewis had over 50 broken tackles, and Mariota finished second among quarterbacks with 28. ● It's a good thing Titans running backs could break tackles, because the Titans ran a league-low 27 percent of their running back carries against small boxes (less than seven). ● Department of fumble recovery luck reversal: the Titans recovered nine of 14 offensive fumbles after recovering just two of nine the year before. ● The Titans' defensive DVOA improved with each additional pass-rusher: 42.3% DVOA allowed with three pass-rushers, 17.6% with the standard four, -5.9% with five, and -18.0% with six or more.

Passing

Player	DYAR	DVOA	Plays	NtYds	Avg	YAC	C%	TD	Int
M.Mariota	65	-8.5%	373	2289	6.1	5.6	68.9%	11	8
B.Gabbert*	-154	-35.5%	106	576	5.4	4.9	61.0%	4	4
R.Tannehill	-186	-20.8%	309	1694	5.5	6.1	64.5%	17	9

Receiving

Player	DYAR	DVOA	Plays	Ctch	Yds	Y/C	YAC	TD	C%
C.Davis	104	-1.2%	112	65	891	13.7	4.1	4	58%
T.Taylor	43	-2.7%	56	37	466	12.6	4.4	1	66%
T.Sharpe	30	-4.9%	47	26	316	12.2	3.2	2	55%
D.Jennings	-1	-13.2%	15	11	101	9.2	3.4	0	73%
C.Batson	15	4.7%	11	8	88	11.0	6.8	0	73%
R.Matthews*	-35	-91.5%	6	3	11	3.7	1.7	0	50%
A.Humphries	152	6.7%	105	76	816	10.7	5.5	5	72%
J.Smith	11	-1.8%	30	20	258	12.9	9.0	3	67%
L.Stocker*	26	11.4%	21	15	165	11.0	4.3	2	71%
A.Firkser	85	59.3%	20	19	225	11.8	5.1	1	95%
M.Pruitt	28	32.1%	11	9	102	11.3	3.1	1	82%
D.Walker	-9	-25.9%	7	4	52	13.0	5.0	0	57%
D.Lewis	15	-9.8%	67	59	400	6.8	8.1	1	88%
D.Henry	-4	-18.0%	18	15	99	6.6	7.7	0	83%

Rushing

Player	DYAR	DVOA	Plays	Yds	Avg	TD	Fum	Suc
D.Henry	281	23.1%	215	1059	4.9	12	0	51%
D.Lewis	-69	-20.1%	155	517	3.3	1	1	34%
M.Mariota	86	15.1%	59	361	6.1	2	3	--
C.Davis	25	38.5%	6	55	9.2	0	0	--
D.Fluellen	-2	-20.2%	4	16	4.0	0	0	25%
R.Tannehill	39	34.9%	21	154	7.3	0	0	--

Offensive Line

Player	Pos	Age	GS	Snaps	Pen	Sk	Pass	Run	Player	Pos	Age	GS	Snaps	Pen	Sk	Pass	Run
Ben Jones	C	30	16/16	986	2	2.0	3	8	Jack Conklin	RT	25	9/9	498	7	6.0	10	0
Josh Kline*	RG	30	16/16	975	4	3.5	8	6	Dennis Kelly	RT	29	11/5	376	1	1.0	3	2
Quinton Spain*	LG	28	15/15	856	6	0.0	2	4	Rodger Saffold	LG	31	16/16	1068	6	1.0	9	6
Taylor Lewan	LT	28	15/15	852	9	2.0	7	6									

Year	Yards	ALY	Rank	Power	Rank	Stuff	Rank	2nd Lev	Rank	Open Field	Rank	Sacks	ASR	Rank	Press	Rank	F-Start	Cont.
2016	4.39	4.63	5	68%	12	19%	13	1.27	9	0.72	13	28	5.7%	15	20.8%	4	15	33
2017	4.00	3.85	23	60%	23	23%	24	1.09	21	0.90	9	35	6.4%	14	24.5%	4	12	36
2018	4.25	4.33	17	67%	17	19%	17	1.15	24	0.83	18	47	10.2%	29	25.7%	5	13	24

2018 ALY by direction: Left End: 6.45 (2) Left Tackle: 3.93 (22) Mid/Guard: 4.04 (27) Right Tackle: 3.59 (27) Right End: 5.15 (7)

Bringing back all five offensive linemen for their third season together was supposed to create the rock upon which the Titans offense was built. A continuity score of just 24 shows it did not work out that way. ● Jack Conklin missed the first month of the season recovering from the ACL he tore in the previous year's playoff loss, then another game with a concussion, and eventually went to IR with a knee injury. How much of his struggles were a player coming off an ACL injury, and how much getting exposed by more one-on-one reps in pass protection? The Titans are hopeful for a better season but still unsurprisingly declined his fifth-year option. ● Only two left tackles had more blown blocks in the run game than Taylor Lewan, but he had the sixth-lowest blown block rate in the pass game among left tackles. ● The big difference between Quinton Spain and big free-agent acquisition Rodger Saffold at left guard will come on the second level. Spain did a fine job of blocking the players in front of him, with the fourth-lowest blown block rate among left guards. ● Neither another season of fan discontent nor the third-most blown blocks in the run game among centers was enough to threaten Ben Jones' job security. Backup Corey Levin showed no more oomph to his game in a small sample size, so outside hopes for improvement fall on Hroniss Grasu, Mariota's center at Oregon and a former third-round pick yet to establish himself as a starter. ● At right guard, the early favorite to re-place Josh Kline, released one season after he signed a big extension, is veteran swing man Kevin Pamphile, but the job will go to third-round pick Nate Davis (Charlotte) eventually. ● The Titans' best five includes either Conklin or Dennis Kelly, who played very well in Conklin's stead last year, at right guard. However, the Titans have firmly rebuffed all public suggestions of a move inside for either player to this point.

Defensive Front

Defensive Line	Age	Pos	G	Snaps	Plays	TmPct	Rk	Stop	Dfts	BTkl	Runs	St%	Rk	RuYd	Rk	Sack	Hit	Hur	Dsrpt
Jurrell Casey	30	DT	15	745	62	8.1%	4	47	23	8	50	74%	47	2.2	45	7.0	5	23	0
DaQuan Jones	28	DE	16	587	35	4.3%	56	28	6	3	34	79%	28	2.0	29	0.0	5	6	2
Austin Johnson	25	DT	16	400	24	3.0%	--	19	3	1	21	76%	--	2.4	--	1.0	0	3	2
Brent Urban	28	DE	16	522	29	3.8%	66	22	8	0	23	74%	48	2.2	42	0.5	1	12	2

Edge Rushers	Age	Pos	G	Snaps	Plays	TmPct	Rk	Stop	Dfts	BTkl	Runs	St%	Rk	RuYd	Rk	Sack	Hit	Hur	Dsrpt
Harold Landry	23	OLB	15	592	42	5.5%	31	28	15	6	26	65%	67	3.3	74	4.5	9	24	2
Brian Orakpo*	33	OLB	13	573	31	4.7%	49	22	10	6	17	71%	57	2.1	37	1.5	8	17	3
Derrick Morgan*	30	OLB	13	532	28	4.2%	61	16	3	5	18	56%	83	4.4	90	0.5	5	15	3
Kamalei Correa	25	OLB	13	321	18	2.7%	--	12	7	4	11	55%	--	2.5	--	3.5	3	6	0
Sharif Finch	24	OLB	15	207	20	2.6%	--	11	6	1	13	62%	--	2.7	--	1.5	1	3	0
Cameron Wake	37	DE	14	517	35	4.8%	47	28	11	4	23	78%	33	2.8	55	6.0	10	37	1

Linebackers	Age	Pos	G	Snaps	Plays	TmPct	Rk	Stop	Dfts	BTkl	Runs	St%	Rk	RuYd	Rk	Sack	Hit	Hur	Tgts	Suc%	Rk	AdjYd	Rk	PD	Int
Jayon Brown	24	ILB	16	850	102	12.5%	42	55	20	10	57	60%	41	4.5	70	6.0	4	7.5	34	62%	8	4.6	8	6	1
Wesley Woodyard	33	ILB	14	713	114	16.0%	17	58	20	4	70	53%	63	3.9	42	4.5	2	6	32	59%	11	7.2	50	2	0
Rashaan Evans	23	ILB	15	495	54	7.1%	75	33	8	4	42	71%	9	2.7	9	0.0	2	6	10	60%	74	3.4	38	1	0

Year	Yards	ALY	Rank	Power	Rank	Stuff	Rank	2nd Level	Rank	Open Field	Rank	Sacks	ASR	Rank	Press	Rank
2016	3.80	3.97	12	45%	1	20%	15	0.96	5	0.60	12	40	6.2%	14	24.9%	23
2017	3.44	4.07	14	65%	20	20%	22	0.94	5	0.23	1	43	6.9%	12	31.4%	12
2018	4.29	4.82	28	64%	13	16%	23	1.19	13	0.64	9	39	6.7%	22	27.6%	26

2018 ALY by direction: Left End: 5.01 (23) Left Tackle: 4.58 (18) Mid/Guard: 5.00 (29) Right Tackle: 3.99 (13) Right End: 4.97 (25)

Austin Johnson and DaQuan Jones combining for nine hurries in nearly 1,000 snaps tells you all you need to know about why the Titans spent a first-round pick on Jeffery Simmons. Even for two players valued more for their ability to stop the run and control the line of scrimmage, that was not good enough. Jurrell Casey needed help, and Tennessee was toothless when he missed the season finale. ◦ Brent Urban spent time with Dean Pees in Baltimore and will help cover the time until Simmons is ready, whether that is November or 2020. ◦ The Titans used a nose tackle so rarely that Bennie Logan didn't even qualify to be listed in our tables, but the team still needs someone at the position with Logan gone in free agency. Veteran depth is practically nil, so expect to see Tennessee connected with every available free-agent defensive lineman until they sign one. ◦ Both Derrick Morgan and Brian Orakpo went from very good players in 2017 to looking old and not very good in 2018. Orakpo did not show the same power in the run game or as a pass-rusher and retired at the end of the season. Morgan, never Orakpo's equal as a pass-rusher, also looked punchless much of the time. He was still a free agent in early June. ◦ Second-round pick Harold Landry had a great start to his rookie season, until opposing teams learned to concentrate on his outside move. Whether he can develop a quality inside counter move is the key to his NFL future. If he can, he could be a double-digit-sack player. ◦ Cameron Wake was a surprising free-agent addition. Like Landry, he is primarily a speed-oriented outside rusher who is not the ideal run-down defender. ◦ As Wake is 37 and will likely be held to some snap count to keep him fresh, finding a third quality outside linebacker is critical. The Titans are high on Sharif Finch, who did a good job setting the edge as an undrafted rookie. Rookie fifth-round pick D'Andre Walker (Georgia) also offers edge-setting potential thanks to a good wingspan, though uncertainty about how well his pass-rush skills translate meant he fell to the third day. ◦ Figuring out how to dole out inside linebacker snaps will be Pees' most pleasant challenge in 2019 ◦ Jayon Brown had a terrific second season, excelling particularly in sub packages as both a cover player and as a rusher. ◦ Wesley Woodyard did not look like he would likely be part of the solution to covering running backs the past couple of seasons, so his 2018 play was a pleasant surprise. He made more plays against the run than any other Titans defender, and tied Casey for most successful plays in the run game. ◦ First-round pick Rashaan Evans improved over the course of the year after missing training camp and the start of the season with a hamstring injury. He improved his ability to read plays, going from getting caught standing still on long runs at midseason to attacking runs downhill by the end of the year. The key for his second season is how much he improves in pass coverage. He flashed some feel as a blitzer, a key for Pees, but needs to stay stickier in coverage or else the Titans will primarily go with Woodyard and Brown in their two-linebacker sub packages.

Defensive Secondary

Secondary	Age	Pos	G	Snaps	Plays	TmPct	Rk	Stop	Dfts	BTkl	Runs	St%	Rk	RuYd	Rk	Tgts	Tgt%	Rk	Dist	Suc%	Rk	AdjYd	Rk	PD	Int
						Overall						vs. Run							vs. Pass						
Kevin Byard	26	FS	16	1043	94	11.6%	20	31	13	4	52	31%	58	8.3	51	28	6.9%	17	7.0	43%	57	5.9	11	8	4
Adoree' Jackson	24	CB	16	957	82	10.1%	19	32	10	7	17	47%	28	4.8	14	98	26.2%	75	12.9	51%	46	7.6	38	10	2
Logan Ryan	28	CB	14	856	84	11.8%	4	36	17	2	30	43%	35	6.7	45	46	13.7%	2	11.3	46%	65	8.1	49	8	0
Malcolm Butler	29	CB	16	833	81	10.0%	21	27	9	8	17	35%	55	7.2	51	78	23.9%	67	13.6	47%	55	8.7	63	12	3
Kenny Vaccaro	28	SS	13	747	62	9.4%	44	27	7	4	29	45%	32	5.3	18	22	7.5%	20	8.0	55%	25	7.1	37	4	1
Kendrick Lewis*	31	FS	13	275	26	3.9%	--	6	2	3	14	36%	--	7.2	--	11	10.2%	--	14.9	36%	--	13.8	--	1	0

Year	Pass D Rank	vs. #1 WR	Rk	vs. #2 WR	Rk	vs. Other WR	Rk	WR Wide	Rk	WR Slot	Rk	vs. TE	Rk	vs. RB	Rk
2016	27	2.5%	18	21.7%	30	0.2%	16	2.7%	21	14.6%	25	-14.8%	8	36.3%	30
2017	24	-8.1%	11	29.2%	28	-0.3%	17	0.1%	18	9.5%	18	10.1%	24	28.0%	32
2018	21	5.8%	20	26.1%	30	5.3%	21	8.5%	26	19.2%	26	-10.6%	11	-31.6%	2

The optimistic case for Adoree' Jackson was that teams would go from targeting him often as a rookie to avoiding him in his second season. That was not the case, as he went from the most-targeted corner in the NFL to just one of the most targeted while maintaining average coverage numbers. ◦ Malcolm Butler's transition to Tennessee was rough, with blown coverage leading to long touchdowns a too-common early sight. He began the season as a starter, but shifted to an outside role in nickel coverages and was much better the second half of the season. ◦ Logan Ryan had his second consecutive season with no interceptions, though the passes defensed total again suggests they will be coming. ◦ Expect Kevin Byard to get a mega-extension around the time this book is released. His mediocre stats are a product of his role as often the last line of defense as a free safety. He is one of the best all-around safeties in the league, capable in man coverage, coming up in run support, as a blitzer, or as a deep safety. ◦ Kenny Vaccaro was a training camp addition after Johnathan Cyprien tore his ACL and played well enough at strong safety to lead to Cyprien's release and a four-year, $26-million extension for himself. He is not as versatile as Byard but was a key part of the Titans' improvement against tight ends. ◦ Fourth-round pick Amani Hooker (Iowa) likely backs up both Byard and Vaccaro and gives Pees the option to play dime defense, a past Pees feature not seen in Tennessee in 2018.

Special Teams

Year	DVOA	Rank	FG/XP	Rank	Net Kick	Rank	Kick Ret	Rank	Net Punt	Rank	Punt Ret	Rank	Hidden	Rank
2016	-1.0%	19	8.1	5	-2.7	22	-2.5	21	-6.4	26	-1.4	18	5.1	8
2017	1.6%	13	0.6	15	2.9	12	0.8	11	3.0	16	0.7	13	-5.8	22
2018	0.8%	13	-1.8	21	-7.2	31	13.6	1	2.3	15	-2.8	23	-5.6	23

Ryan Succop missed his first field goal under 40 yards since 2013, almost enough by itself to make him a below-average kicker in today's hyper-accurate NFL. He was average on kickoffs, but Tennessee allowed the second-most kick return value, thus the No. 31 ranking. ● Brett Kern had his second consecutive Pro Bowl season, and for the second consecutive season our numbers were less impressed by the Titans punting game. As in 2017, the difference was punt coverage. Kern led the AFC in gross punt value, but the Titans were below average in coverage here as well. ● Darius Jennings wrested the kick return job away from Adoree' Jackson and it paid dividends in Week 1 as he took one back for a score in the longest game in NFL history, a 7:08 affair thanks to multiple lightning delays. Jennings was only tackled behind the 20 on one kickoff return all season. ● Jackson's electric return ability at USC has yet to translate to the NFL, as he was below average on punt returns again. With his importance on defense and mediocre results, expect competition there. That may be Jennings, but more likely Adam Humphries, backup slot receiver Cameron Batson, Amani Hooker, or someone else.

Washington Redskins

2018 record: 7-9	**Total DVOA:** -18.6% (29th)	**2019 Mean Projection:** 6.1 wins	**On the Clock (0-4):** 28%
Pythagorean Wins: 5.7 (25th)	**Offense:** -19.5% (28th)	**Postseason Odds:** 14.8%	**Mediocrity (5-7):** 43%
Snap-Weighted Age: 26.9 (6th)	**Defense:** 1.7% (20th)	**Super Bowl Odds:** 0.8%	**Playoff Contender (8-10):** 23%
Average Opponent: -2.7% (26th)	**Special Teams:** 2.5% (8th)	**Proj. Avg. Opponent:** -1.4% (26th)	**Super Bowl Contender (11+):** 6%

2018: Another year in 7-9 purgatory.

2019: A talented rookie quarterback falls into their laps, but his initial supporting cast looks weak.

The Washington Redskins organization lacks object permanence.

Like an infant or a kitten, the Skins only perceive reality in the present, with just the vaguest conception of a past to learn from or a future to prepare for. Objects which are not in the Skins' direct line of sight do not exist to them. If you play peek-a-boo with Bruce Allen, he thinks the whole world disappears when you cover his eyes, and he's probably not particularly upset about it.

Each season, Allen and his loyal lieutenants get caught off guard by the need to assemble an NFL roster, so they hastily build a team based on random impulses and instincts buried in the cerebellum. The team then bobs along around .500 on the currents of NFL parity for a year, and Allen rewards himself by firing some challengers to his power, because Allen's primary goal as the team's chief executive is to ensure that Allen remains the team's chief executive.

Allen ascended to the Iron Cerrato Throne when general manager Scot McCloughan was fired amid rumors of an alcoholism relapse in 2017 (rumors which, per the *Washington Post*, came from within the organization, and which McCloughan grieved and denied in court). Allen then consolidated power by building an insulation layer of yes-men between him and accountability: cap manager Eric Schaffer, 34-year-old college scouting director Kyle Smith, pro scouting director and organizational survivor Alex Santos, and senior personnel executive Doug Williams. All report directly to Allen, who reports only to Dan Snyder, who spends his days wondering why ticket sales have tanked (it's because the team is bad, the stadium is worse, and no one even wants to type your organization's name, chief) and watching IMAX movies on his $100-million yacht.

Schaffer, acting under Snyder and Allen's auspices, is so generous with contracts that he's basically Mike Tannenbaum on Super Spender's Serum. Smith runs the draft with an Alabama media guide in one hand and some shredded McCloughan notes that he taped back together in the other. Williams' and Santos' primary functions appear to be taking the fall for bad decisions and making the organization look a little less racist. Whatever talents they may possess are blunted by the need to run all decisions through Allen, who has no concept of prioritizing short-term, long-term, cap, draft, or free-agent needs or resources. All the subordinates adhere strictly to Allen's party line, lest they get fired like the public relations executives who were canned after mere months on the job in December for failing to put a positive spin on Allen's decision to sign Reuben Foster (and more importantly, for operating independently of Allen).

The parlor drama and resulting yes-man culture have left the Skins operating like it's their first year in a fantasy football keeper league, constantly caught by surprise by such NFL subtleties as the need to have a quarterback on the roster under contract beyond the current season.

Kirk Cousins friend-zoned Allen and the Skins in 2016 and 2017 after early low-ball offers (and Allen's habits of taking his side of the story to the press and calling his starting quarterback "Kurt") soured the contract negotiations. Cousins played two seasons under the franchise tag while the organization sabotaged its own bargaining leverage by refusing to draft or acquire any potential challengers or successors. When Allen finally realized that Cousins would cost him $34 million for one season if tagged for a third year, the Skins hastily traded a second-round pick and defensive back Kendall Fuller (a very solid young role player) to the Chiefs for Alex Smith. Schaffer then used his cap acumen to reward Smith with a four-year extension with $55 million in guaranteed money spread across three years. As further insurance against a scrambling just-better-than-journeyman 34-year-old suffering an injury or decline in ability the Skins … still didn't bother drafting or acquiring any young quarterbacks.

Smith suffered one of the most gruesome injuries in NFL history, which could not have been foreseen, though the need to have a successor in the wings in case of less dramatic circumstances could be foreseen by anyone outside of Ashburn, Virginia. The Skins, 6-3 at the time of Smith's injury thanks to a soft schedule and some narrow wins, fell apart as Colt McCoy, Mark Sanchez, and finally Josh Johnson took their turns under center. Everyone, including head coach Jay Gruden, got to blame the injuries for the team's disappointing finish and keep their jobs. Except the public relations department.

Dwayne Haskins' arrival heralds the end of three years of expensive procrastination at quarterback, but he's the almost-accidental good result of a bad process. The organization is on record stating that they didn't set out to acquire Haskins or any other young quarterback in the offseason; he was just one of several good players they hoped would fall to them with the

2019 Redskins Schedule

Week	Opp.	Week	Opp.	Week	Opp.
1	at PHI	7	SF	13	at CAR
2	DAL	8	at MIN (Thu.)	14	at GB
3	CHI (Mon.)	9	at BUF	15	PHI
4	at NYG	10	BYE	16	NYG
5	NE	11	NYJ	17	at DAL
6	at MIA	12	DET		

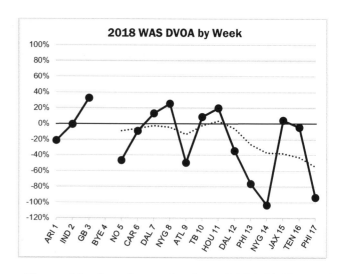

2018 WAS DVOA by Week

15th pick in the draft. The Skins even traded for Case Keenum as yet another veteran placeholder in March and spent early spring touting a Keenum-McCoy quarterback competition. (The fired PR execs, like those immediately vaporized by an atomic blast, must have felt like the lucky ones for a while).

Meanwhile, the impact of the Cousins-Smith overspending remained noticeable on the Skins roster. Smith will eat up $20 million in cap space this season, and while we hope he enjoys every penny after what happened to him last year, that's money that won't help the team. A core group of veterans whose contracts were shaped to accommodate a franchise-tagged quarterback—Ryan Kerrigan, Josh Norman, Jordan Reed, and Trent Williams—eat up another $53 million.

The Skins entered the summer with just over $8 million in cap space, but most of their money was spent on a quarterback on crutches and veterans who peaked around 2016. Also, Williams held out of OTAs and minicamp, reportedly because he felt the team's medical department botched an offseason procedure. There's a chance that the Skins will be forced to trade away their least replaceable player due to a lack of organizational professionalism.

Allen and his minions did find space in the budget for one free-agent splurge this offseason, signing Landon Collins away from the Giants for six years and $84 million, with $44.5 million in guarantees. Collins is a very good player, but in-the-box safeties have limited marginal value, and cap constraints forced the team to backload his base salary and bonus into future years. The Skins already have $162 million in cap liabilities on the books for 2020, including $52 million for four of the previously mentioned veterans; $14.2 million for a safety they didn't really need; and $21 million for Smith who, sadly, may still be on crutches by then. There's no flexibility in the budget for something useful like, say, a financial apology to Williams.

The Skins also cleared room for Collins by allowing Preston Smith, Ha Ha Clinton-Dix, Jamison Crowder, Zach Brown, and Ty Nsekhe to depart as free agents. Crowder and Nsekhe could have aided Haskins' development as a slot receiver and provided a dependable backup offensive lineman/Williams holdout insurance, respectively. The three starting defenders were, well, three starting defenders: Smith a capable young pass-rusher; Brown a versatile, productive middle linebacker; and Clinton-Dix a capable-enough safety who didn't require an $84 million upgrade. The Skins got thinner and more expensive in the offseason. At least they didn't also somehow get older.

The combination of poor planning, wishful thinking, and budget tomfoolery has left Haskins with one of the weakest supporting casts in the NFL. In 2015 and 2016, when McCloughan was still the general manager, Cousins produced gaudy stats throwing to Reed, Crowder, Pierre Garcon, DeSean Jackson, and Vernon Davis, with Williams anchoring an offensive line that also included Spencer Long and Shawn Lauvao (with Nsekhe as an oft-used super sub). Long, Garcon, Jackson, and now Crowder and Nsekhe all left on Allen's watch, with Lauvao aging out and Reed and Davis growing old expensively at tight end. Replacements like Josh Doctson (a McCloughan draft whiff) and Terrelle Pryor (an Allen genius-move fantasy) flunked at wide receiver, an injury rash forced the Skins to turn to Adrian Peterson at running back, and the offensive line is now tissue-thin, with Ereck Flowers—THE Ereck Flowers—penciled in at one of the guard spots.

So Haskins' receiving corps now consists of Paul Richardson (grossly overpaid, undersized speedster coming off an injury), Doctson (on the final year of his scholarship), Terry McLaurin (a receiver Haskins didn't often throw to much when they were Ohio State teammates), Kelvin Harmon (size-speed-effort project), Brian Quick (a size-speed-effort project from the Jeff Fisher Rams days, somehow still employed), and a variety of Jehu Chesson types. Reed and Davis still top the tight end depth chart and will be lucky to spend a combined ten weeks off the injury report. Derrius Guice, Chris Thompson, and Bryce Love will either try to get healthy to challenge for running back roles or be scavenged for spare parts to keep Peterson running. Oh, and if Flowers really does win a starting job, Haskins might not survive to see October.

The prognosis is better on defense, if only because assembling a mid-2010s Alabama alumni team guarantees a certain baseline competitiveness, no matter how much money, draft capital and fan goodwill is spent putting it together. But the Skins defense exemplifies the same indifference to long-range planning that plagues the offense.

Thanks to their long-term contracts, Norman and Kerrigan are entering the diminishing-returns stages of their careers at critical positions. The team has not prioritized finding a partner for or successor to Norman, and while Montez Sweat arrived late in the first round to provide Kerrigan with edge-rushing help, he won't do much more as a rookie than offset the loss of Preston Smith. The Skins prefer to spend the bulk of their resources at lower-impact positions like strong safety (Collins) and the interior line (Jonathan Allen, Da'Ron Payne). Reuben Foster's minicamp ACL tear absolves us from having to say anything about him.

The Skins defense hovered around league average in DVOA for most of last season, but good luck played a factor in that modest near-success. The Skins had the NFL's healthiest defense last year, with just 10.3 adjusted games lost, all while suffering a league-worst 88.9 adjusted games lost on offense. So while the Skins offense will improve the moment they place a quarterback under center whom they didn't grab off an AAF roster in November, the defense is likely to get worse due to departures, age at critical positions, and some regression to the mean when it comes to injuries and takeaways.

At best, the Skins will hover around .500 again this year. At worst, the Williams drama will cause a domino effect that results in Haskins laboring through a Josh Rosen-like rookie season. Either way, Gruden's job depends more on Allen's whims than the results. Gruden is basically Jason Garrett

with a famous brother and a slightly smarter offense, a useful scapegoat to be sacrificed if Allen wants to save face after a bad season, but also a handy functionary if he wants to reframe 2019 as a rebuilding year. Allen will decide where to hang the bullseye after he's shot all his arrows.

As for 2020 and beyond, there is no plan besides "hope Haskins is awesome."

The New York Giants took a lot of justified roasting during this offseason. But at least the Giants had a plan, or two or maybe three, illogical and contradictory as they were. The Giants drafted the quarterback they wanted (for better or worse), not merely the one on the board when it was their turn. They traded away a superstar they soured on (again, for better or worse) and got value back for him. The Giants have a better core of young offensive players than the Skins, and they are in far better cap shape.

The Skins are just the Giants without the comic timing. They can't even be bad in a funny way, and with dysfunction well entrenched in their front office, their routine is going to go on far, far too long.

Mike Tanier

2018 Redskins Stats by Week

Wk	vs.	W-L	PF	PA	YDF	YDA	TO	Total	Off	Def	ST
1	at ARI	W	24	6	429	213	+1	-21%	-1%	9%	-12%
2	IND	L	9	21	334	281	+1	-1%	-15%	-18%	-4%
3	GB	W	31	17	386	340	0	33%	31%	-3%	-1%
4	BYE										
5	at NO	L	19	43	283	447	-1	-47%	-22%	27%	2%
6	CAR	W	23	17	288	350	+3	-9%	-15%	12%	18%
7	DAL	W	20	17	305	323	+2	13%	1%	-11%	1%
8	at NYG	W	20	13	360	303	+1	26%	0%	-25%	0%
9	ATL	L	14	38	366	491	0	-50%	4%	58%	4%
10	at TB	W	16	3	286	501	+4	9%	-10%	-9%	10%
11	HOU	L	21	23	278	320	+1	20%	-21%	-41%	1%
12	at DAL	L	23	31	331	404	-3	-35%	-36%	14%	16%
13	at PHI	L	13	28	235	436	0	-76%	-79%	8%	10%
14	NYG	L	16	40	288	402	-2	-103%	-96%	9%	2%
15	at JAX	W	16	13	245	192	+2	4%	-13%	-37%	-20%
16	at TEN	L	16	25	292	291	-2	-5%	-6%	6%	8%
17	PHI	L	0	24	89	360	0	-94%	-86%	13%	5%

Trends and Splits

	Offense	Rank	Defense	Rank
Total DVOA	-19.5%	28	1.7%	20
Unadjusted VOA	-15.4%	28	0.7%	17
Weighted Trend	-28.6%	31	1.1%	16
Variance	12.3%	30	6.0%	20
Average Opponent	1.6%	26	-1.7%	19
Passing	-19.5%	29	2.1%	11
Rushing	-7.1%	20	1.3%	28
First Down	-28.3%	30	4.0%	21
Second Down	-2.9%	19	-8.7%	8
Third Down	-28.4%	30	15.1%	25
First Half	-16.4%	30	0.0%	15
Second Half	-22.4%	28	3.6%	21
Red Zone	-11.6%	26	-10.5%	9
Late and Close	-2.8%	18	-0.8%	17

Five-Year Performance

Year	W-L	Pyth W	Est W	PF	PA	TO	Total	Rk	Off	Rk	Def	Rk	ST	Rk	Off AGL	Rk	Def AGL	Rk	Off Age	Rk	Def Age	Rk	ST Age	Rk
2014	4-12	4.5	4.4	301	438	-12	-27.0%	28	-11.8%	28	9.9%	27	-5.4%	29	21.9	7	67.6	29	27.1	13	26.9	14	25.9	21
2015	9-7	8.2	7.8	388	379	+5	-0.3%	15	1.9%	12	5.4%	21	3.2%	6	44.0	24	75.1	32	25.9	26	27.1	7	26.0	17
2016	8-7-1	8.3	9.7	396	383	0	9.5%	9	15.8%	5	6.8%	25	0.4%	13	27.6	10	68.9	31	27.1	8	27.4	4	26.1	15
2017	7-9	6.8	7.2	342	388	-4	-0.6%	16	-3.1%	20	-4.9%	11	-2.4%	22	70.6	31	50.4	27	27.1	15	26.3	16	25.3	26
2018	7-9	5.7	6.0	281	359	+7	-18.6%	29	-19.5%	28	1.7%	20	2.5%	8	88.9	32	10.3	1	28.4	2	26.2	19	25.1	32

2018 Performance Based on Most Common Personnel Groups

WAS Offense					WAS Offense vs. Opponents					WAS Defense				WAS Defense vs. Opponents			
Pers	Freq	Yds	DVOA	Run%	Pers	Freq	Yds	DVOA	Run%	Pers	Freq	Yds	DVOA	Pers	Freq	Yds	DVOA
11	72%	5.1	-18.1%	32%	Base	19%	5.0	-6.7%	51%	Base	28%	6.0	5.6%	11	68%	6.0	0.4%
12	18%	4.8	-19.0%	44%	Nickel	63%	5.3	-15.1%	40%	Nickel	70%	5.9	-4.1%	12	20%	6.4	9.5%
13	7%	6.0	13.1%	60%	Dime+	15%	4.4	-28.4%	8%	Dime+	1%	12.2	189.6%	13	5%	5.4	4.8%
620	1%	1.8	28.8%	100%	Goal Line	1%	1.6	40.4%	91%	Goal Line	0%	1.3	99.4%	21	4%	4.6	-29.8%
21	1%	4.0	-55.0%	57%										22	2%	4.4	-3.0%

Strategic Tendencies

Run/Pass		Rk	Formation		Rk	Pass Rush		Rk	Secondary		Rk	Strategy		Rk
Runs, first half	38%	19	Form: Single Back	86%	8	Rush 3	23.9%	1	4 DB	28%	12	Play action	21%	23
Runs, first down	56%	2	Form: Empty Back	8%	17	Rush 4	57.6%	27	5 DB	70%	11	Avg Box (Off)	6.11	26
Runs, second-long	23%	30	Pers: 3+ WR	73%	10	Rush 5	14.1%	25	6+ DB	1%	26	Avg Box (Def)	6.27	12
Runs, power sit.	49%	25	Pers: 2+ TE/6+ OL	26%	11	Rush 6+	4.4%	24	CB by Sides	71%	18	Offensive Pace	33.19	32
Runs, behind 2H	25%	20	Pers: 6+ OL	1%	20	Int DL Sacks	46.7%	2	S/CB Cover Ratio	25%	24	Defensive Pace	31.84	26
Pass, ahead 2H	46%	25	Shotgun/Pistol	65%	15	Second Level Sacks	12.0%	29	DB Blitz	6%	23	Go for it on 4th	0.91	26

Washington was worst in the league with 80 offensive penalties (including declined and offsetting). ✎ Washington ranked a dismal 30th when running the ball on first down but improved to fifth running on second down and then second running on third down. ✎ Washington's offense recovered 12 of 16 fumbles. ✎ Greg Manusky more than tripled the frequency of Washington sending just three pass-rushers compared to the year before. ✎ Washington faced the league's highest rate of passes thrown to WR2 (26 percent) and "Other WR" (24 percent) but the lowest rate of passes thrown to tight ends (13 percent) and the second-lowest thrown to WR1 (19 percent). ✎ Washington was killed by wide receiver screens (8.6 yards per pass, 53.1% DVOA, both the worst in the league) but was exceptional against running back screens (4.8 yards per pass, -86.2% DVOA). ✎ Washington was dead last on third-and-short defense, but 21st on third-and-medium (3 to 6 yards to go) and eighth on third-and-long (7-plus yards to go).

Passing

Player	DYAR	DVOA	Plays	NtYds	Avg	YAC	C%	TD	Int
A.Smith	-53	-13.5%	350	2033	5.8	4.8	63.3%	10	5
J.Johnson*	-87	-25.8%	100	520	5.2	5.8	57.1%	3	3
C.McCoy	-119	-40.8%	58	338	5.8	4.4	65.4%	3	3
M.Sanchez*	-300	-154.6%	42	96	2.3	4.6	54.3%	0	3
C.Keenum	-63	-12.7%	620	3634	5.9	4.9	62.6%	18	14

Rushing

Player	DYAR	DVOA	Plays	Yds	Avg	TD	Fum	Suc
A.Peterson	26	-6.0%	251	1042	4.2	7	2	47%
C.Thompson	-35	-30.7%	43	178	4.1	0	1	30%
A.Smith	42	13.8%	34	173	5.1	1	1	--
J.Johnson*	27	12.1%	22	122	5.5	1	0	--
K.Bibbs*	59	55.2%	20	101	5.1	3	0	65%
C.McCoy	30	48.3%	9	64	7.1	0	0	--
S.Perine	9	19.3%	8	32	4.0	0	0	63%
R.Kelley*	-5	-36.4%	4	8	2.0	0	0	50%
C.Keenum	40	31.2%	15	101	6.7	2	1	--

Receiving

Player	DYAR	DVOA	Plays	Ctch	Yds	Y/C	YAC	TD	C%
J.Doctson	7	-11.5%	78	44	532	12.1	3.0	2	56%
J.Crowder*	23	-6.2%	49	29	388	13.4	7.0	2	59%
M.Harris*	-73	-33.2%	47	28	304	10.9	3.6	0	60%
P.Richardson	48	4.1%	35	20	262	13.1	2.3	2	57%
M.Floyd*	-58	-43.2%	24	10	100	10.0	2.9	1	42%
T.Quinn	22	14.9%	10	9	75	8.3	1.9	1	90%
J.Reed	-80	-22.2%	84	54	554	10.3	4.2	2	64%
V.Davis	60	19.0%	36	25	367	14.7	6.7	2	69%
J.Sprinkle	-4	-13.6%	9	5	41	8.2	4.2	1	56%
C.Thompson	-10	-17.3%	56	42	272	6.5	5.3	1	75%
A.Peterson	50	22.3%	26	20	208	10.4	10.1	1	77%
K.Bibbs*	-12	-26.7%	18	13	102	7.8	7.7	1	72%
B.Marshall	3	-6.3%	6	4	30	7.5	7.0	0	67%

Offensive Line

Player	Pos	Age	GS	Snaps	Pen	Sk	Pass	Run	Player	Pos	Age	GS	Snaps	Pen	Sk	Pass	Run
Chase Roullier	C	26	16/16	1020	4	1.5	7	5	Ty Nsekhe*	LT/LG	34	14/5	403	7	1.0	6	1
Morgan Moses	RT	28	16/16	965	16	5.0	20	3	Shawn Lauvao*	LG	32	5/5	284	2	2.0	3	1
Trent Williams	LT	31	13/13	792	12	3.5	9	5	Luke Bowanko*	LG	28	7/3	244	3	2.5	4	0
Tony Bergstrom	RG/C	33	13/8	509	1	0.5	8	1	Jonathan Cooper*	LG	29	4/4	201	3	1.0	3	0
Brandon Scherff	RG	28	8/8	506	2	1.0	1	5	Ereck Flowers	LT	25	14/9	588	6	2.5	12	2

Year	Yards	ALY	Rank	Power	Rank	Stuff	Rank	2nd Lev	Rank	Open Field	Rank	Sacks	ASR	Rank	Press	Rank	F-Start	Cont.
2016	4.67	4.57	6	72%	5	15%	3	1.15	14	1.06	6	23	3.9%	3	24.2%	11	25	28
2017	3.65	3.86	21	55%	27	20%	15	1.04	22	0.45	28	41	7.7%	24	34.9%	27	16	25
2018	4.16	3.96	26	76%	2	23%	28	1.24	19	0.93	13	44	8.5%	24	32.7%	23	24	19

2018 ALY by direction: Left End: 4.12 (20)   Left Tackle: 3.79 (24)   Mid/Guard: 3.67 (31)   Right Tackle: 4.66 (10)   Right End: 3.92 (22)

Trent Williams had what was variously described as a "growth" or "tumor" removed from his scalp sometime before the combine. By April, NFL.com reported that Williams was fine. But something about the way the organization handled the procedure ticked Williams off, because he held out of minicamp and multiple reports indicated that he no longer wanted to play for Washington. If the organization can smooth things over, Williams will continue to provide Pro Bowl-caliber play at left tackle between his annual football-related aches and pains. If not—and this is an organization that got into a two-year pee-pee contest with Kirk Cousins, who's like the friendliest counselor at the Christian summer camp—the Skins are in big trouble, because long-time backup tackle Ty Nsekhe is now in Buffalo. Geron Christian is the most likely replacement for Williams, but the 2018 third-round pick was limited during OTAs with a knee injury. As of late May, the Skins were shuffling the bottom of the tackle depth chart, adding randos like Blake Hance and Jerald Foster. ✎ Guard Brandon Scherff played very well last season before suffering a season-ending pectoral injury against the Falcons. At press time, Scherff was still playing under the $12.5-million fifth-year option of his 2015 rookie contract, with no timetable for an extension. The Skins may be waiting to see whether Scherff is fully healthy, which will make him prohibitively expensive as a pending free agent, or still limited by the injury, in which case they paid $12.5 million for an injured guard they need to replace. In Washington, they call this "planning." ✎ Former Giants first-round regret and professional blocking sled Ereck Flowers got manhandled by rookie Montez Sweat early in OTAs. Coaches responded by (you guessed it) giving him some left tackle reps in Williams' absence; Michael Phillips of the *Richmond Post-Dispatch* reported in June that Flowers "was picked up and moved around like a piece of unwanted furniture" by Ryan Anderson and others. If Flowers makes the 53-man roster, everyone in the Skins college and pro scouting department should be fired. If he ends up the starting left tackle on opening day, the franchise itself should be disbanded for the good of society.

Defensive Front

Defensive Line	Age	Pos	G	Snaps	Plays	TmPct	Rk	Stop	Dfts	BTkl	Runs	St%	Rk	RuYd	Rk	Sack	Hit	Hur	Dsrpt
Da'Ron Payne	22	DT	16	796	59	7.3%	12	43	10	4	44	73%	50	2.9	68	5.0	3	13	3
Jonathan Allen	24	DE	16	778	61	7.6%	10	41	15	7	47	64%	76	2.7	62	8.0	7	19	0
Matt Ioannidis	25	DE	14	439	31	4.4%	52	24	9	1	21	71%	53	3.6	82	7.5	3	14	1
Stacy McGee*	29	DE	8	137	9	2.2%	--	8	1	0	7	86%	--	2.0	--	1.0	0	0	0

Edge Rushers	Age	Pos	G	Snaps	Plays	TmPct	Rk	Stop	Dfts	BTkl	Runs	St%	Rk	RuYd	Rk	Sack	Hit	Hur	Dsrpt
Preston Smith*	27	OLB	16	832	56	6.9%	9	40	14	8	42	69%	60	2.5	48	4.0	13	33	1
Ryan Kerrigan	31	OLB	16	818	44	5.5%	33	37	20	0	25	72%	54	1.9	32	13.0	6	38	0

Linebackers	Age	Pos	G	Snaps	Plays	TmPct	Rk	Stop	Dfts	BTkl	Runs	St%	Rk	RuYd	Rk	Sack	Hit	Hur	Tgts	Suc%	Rk	AdjYd	Rk	PD	Int
Mason Foster	30	ILB	16	1014	133	16.5%	14	72	22	10	74	61%	35	4.4	66	1.0	1	7	53	55%	23	7.0	48	4	2
Zach Brown*	30	ILB	16	703	97	12.0%	45	60	16	5	50	80%	3	2.4	5	1.0	1	6	37	54%	28	6.3	24	1	0
Josh Harvey-Clemons	25	ILB	16	196	22	2.7%	--	12	9	4	4	50%	--	6.5	--	1.0	1	5.5	19	74%	2	3.7	4	4	0
Shaun Dion Hamilton	24	ILB	16	129	22	2.7%	--	11	4	2	13	54%	--	4.2	--	1.5	3	3	3	0%	--	14.7	--	0	0
Jon Bostic	28	ILB	16	562	76	9.7%	58	38	12	4	40	65%	24	3.1	16	2.5	1	8	24	29%	78	9.8	75	3	0
Reuben Foster	25	OLB	6	337	29	10.0%	55	15	5	6	17	59%	48	4.2	58	0.0	2	4	15	67%	--	5.5	--	1	0

Year	Yards	ALY	Rank	Power	Rank	Stuff	Rank	2nd Level	Rank	Open Field	Rank	Sacks	ASR	Rank	Press	Rank
2016	4.52	4.54	27	69%	26	17%	25	1.37	29	0.76	19	38	6.9%	9	28.4%	12
2017	4.49	4.91	32	74%	27	15%	31	1.23	23	0.71	16	42	8.1%	4	36.7%	1
2018	4.57	4.97	29	76%	28	16%	26	1.37	26	0.71	11	46	7.6%	11	31.3%	12

2018 ALY by direction:	Left End: 4.97 (21)	Left Tackle: 5.62 (32)	Mid/Guard: 4.93 (28)	Right Tackle: 4.54 (23)	Right End: 4.86 (22)

Alabama alum Jonathan Allen has developed into a quality, all-purpose, two-gap defensive lineman, while rookie Alabama alum Da'Ron Payne handled himself well as a run-stuffer before fading down the stretch. ◥ Alabama alum Ryan Anderson saw spot duty as a situational pass-rusher last year but had a strong offseason and should see more snaps this season. ◥ Troubled Alabama alum Reuben Foster was expected to be the replacement at linebacker for cap casualty Zach Brown, who led the team in rush defeats, was second in rush stops and was highly regarded in coverage. Foster suffered an ACL tear in OTAs, so journeyman Jon Bostic, notoriously vulnerable in coverage, is expected to start at inside linebacker next to reliable Mason Foster. Alabama alum Shaun Dion Hamilton may also get a look. ◥ OK, enough with the Alabama jokes: there's talent here, but depth up the middle was an issue last year, and the defense suffered when the young starters were on the field too long (a huge problem late in the year) or when their subs were in the lineup. ◥ Montez Sweat posted an impressive 89.7% SackSEER rating, with a projection of 25.7 sacks through his first five seasons, which ranked third in this year's loaded edge rusher class. Sweat ate his share of souls during Senior Bowl pit drills, blew up the combine, and drew some high OTA praise. A rotation of Sweat, Anderson, and Ryan Kerrigan on the edge, with both Allen and Matt Ioannidis capable of rushing from the inside, should keep the Skins pass rush credible, despite the loss of Preston Smith.

Defensive Secondary

Secondary	Age	Pos	G	Snaps	Plays	TmPct	Rk	Stop	Dfts	BTkl	Runs	St%	Rk	RuYd	Rk	Tgts	Tgt%	Rk	Dist	Suc%	Rk	AdjYd	Rk	PD	Int
Josh Norman	32	CB	16	1028	72	8.9%	36	30	12	11	15	33%	56	7.8	60	70	16.2%	20	10.5	54%	30	7.2	32	9	3
Ha Ha Clinton-Dix*	27	FS	16	1026	98	12.1%	14	20	11	10	44	11%	75	12.0	73	23	5.4%	11	9.0	48%	45	6.7	25	6	3
D.J. Swearinger*	28	SS	15	961	63	8.3%	53	28	16	11	22	45%	30	4.6	9	40	9.9%	43	9.6	55%	23	7.9	46	10	4
Fabian Moreau	25	CB	16	840	62	7.7%	54	20	10	4	18	39%	47	5.6	25	53	15.0%	13	11.0	53%	36	8.6	61	5	1
Montae Nicholson	24	FS	14	466	39	5.5%	--	13	3	9	20	40%	--	7.1	--	13	6.6%	--	5.2	54%	--	7.5	--	1	0
Greg Stroman	23	CB	15	386	42	5.6%	--	15	6	4	11	36%	--	5.6	--	35	21.6%	--	12.4	43%	--	10.7	--	4	1
Quinton Dunbar	27	CB	7	373	48	13.6%	--	19	6	3	8	38%	--	5.4	--	44	28.1%	--	9.3	45%	--	7.5	--	9	2
Landon Collins	25	SS	12	804	99	15.8%	2	43	16	15	52	54%	15	5.0	11	49	15.1%	69	7.9	45%	53	8.1	51	4	0

Year	Pass D Rank	vs. #1 WR	Rk	vs. #2 WR	Rk	vs. Other WR	Rk	WR Wide	Rk	WR Slot	Rk	vs. TE	Rk	vs. RB	Rk
2016	24	4.4%	22	18.1%	29	10.5%	24	-0.5%	19	18.9%	30	13.0%	25	-16.4%	7
2017	6	-20.1%	5	31.2%	29	-23.0%	4	6.5%	25	-18.0%	4	-6.5%	10	-23.0%	4
2018	11	3.9%	18	-7.2%	10	13.8%	26	17.8%	29	-9.3%	4	-17.4%	6	-6.1%	12

There was spring scuttlebutt about the Skins releasing Josh Norman as a June 1 cap cut. Doing so would have saved the Skins $8.5 million in cap space in 2019 and over $20 million overall and, coupled with the arrival of Dwayne Haskins, would have signaled a rebuilding era in Washington. With Norman's skills in noticeable decline—his charting numbers are down, he committed five holding penalties last year, and he got burned deep by some very ordinary receivers—releasing him would have made a lot of sense, even if it temporarily weakened the Skins. Naturally, it did not happen. ◥ Quinton Dunbar was back on the field in minicamp after missing much of last season with a pinched nerve in his leg. When Dunbar is healthy, he typically locks down right cornerback, with Norman on the left side. After Dunbar's injury, Norman began floating with the opponent's top receiver, an assignment he doesn't handle as well as he did in the past. If Dunbar's injury recurs, Fabian Moreau will again take over as the starter, with Dominique Rodgers-Cromartie (playing for his 96th NFL team) also on the depth chart. ◥ It's unclear who will play free safety opposite Landon Collins, who is exceptional in the box but ordinary at best when playing deep. Deshazor Everett, who got most of the starter's reps in OTAs, has always been more of a box safety; he made last year's average tackle 5.9 yards from the line of scrimmage, though he saw more action at free safety in 2017. Montae Nicholson played some free safety last year but desperately needs to improve his open-field tackling. Last year, Washington had the fourth-highest tackle distance gap between its two safeties, with Ha Ha Clinton-Dix making his average tackle 13.2 yards from the line of scrimmage and D.J. Swearinger 7.1 yards.

Special Teams

Year	DVOA	Rank	FG/XP	Rank	Net Kick	Rank	Kick Ret	Rank	Net Punt	Rank	Punt Ret	Rank	Hidden	Rank
2016	0.4%	13	-3.7	20	-1.5	18	0.6	13	-2.4	19	9.3	2	-0.2	18
2017	-2.4%	22	-1.6	18	6.9	3	-4.1	28	-7.8	25	-5.5	29	-7.3	25
2018	2.5%	8	9.2	5	2.8	9	-3.0	24	6.1	7	-2.5	20	-1.1	17

At 80 percent, Dustin Hopkins had the league's highest touchback rate (minimum 20 kickoffs). Hopkins hasn't missed a field goal inside of 40 yards in two seasons. He was also 4-of-5 on 50-plus-yarders last year but 5-of-13 in his career before that, so don't read too much into what may be random noise. Still, Hopkins is a good kicker, giving Washington one less thing to worry about. ◟ Tress Way ranked second in our measurement of gross punt value, but Washington's net punt value was less impressive because the Skins gave up an estimated 5.1 points worth of return value, fourth-worst. ◟ Greg Stroman, who returned four punts for touchdowns at Virginia Tech, averaged just 3.4 yards per return after winning the job as a seventh-round pick last year. Stroman took most of the return reps in OTAs, so look for him to reprise his role this year. He has the skills to be a difference-maker, but keep in mind that his college production may have been inflated by playing for a program which has fielded the nation's best special teams for decades.

Quarterbacks

On the following pages, we provide the last three years of statistics for the top two quarterbacks on each team's depth chart, as well as a number of other quarterbacks who played significant time in 2018.

Each quarterback gets a projection from our KUBIAK fantasy football projection system, based on a complicated regression analysis that takes into account numerous variables including projected role, performance over the past two years, performance on third down vs. all downs, experience of the projected offensive line, historical comparables, collegiate stats, height, age, and strength of schedule.

It is difficult to accurately project statistics for a 162-game baseball season, but it is exponentially more difficult to accurately project statistics for a 16-game football season because of the small size of the data samples involved. With that in mind, we ask that you consider the listed projections not as a prediction of exact numbers, but the mean of a range of possible performances. What's important is not so much the exact number of yards and touchdowns we project, but whether or not we're projecting a given player to improve or decline. Along those same lines, rookie projections will not be as accurate as veteran projections due to lack of data.

Our quarterback projections look a bit different than our projections for the other skill positions. At running back and wide receiver, second-stringers see plenty of action, but, at quarterback, either a player starts or he does not start. We recognize that, when a starting quarterback gets injured in Week 8, you don't want to grab your *Football Outsiders Almanac* to find out if his backup is any good only to find that we've projected that the guy will throw 12 passes this year. Therefore, each year we project all quarterbacks to start all 16 games. If Patrick Mahomes goes down in November, you can look up Chad Henne, divide the stats by 16, and get an idea of what we think he will do in an average week (and then, if you are a Kansas City fan, pass out). There are full-season projections for the top two quarterbacks on all 32 depth charts.

The first line of each quarterback table contains biographical data—the player's name, height, weight, college, draft position, birth date, and age. Height and weight are the best data we could find; weight, of course, can fluctuate during the offseason. **Age** is very simple: the number of years between the player's birth year and 2019, but birthdate is provided if you want to figure out exact age.

Draft position gives draft year and round, with the overall pick number with which the player was taken in parentheses. In the sample table, it says that Ben Roethlisberger was chosen in the first round of the 2004 NFL draft, with the 11th overall pick. Undrafted free agents are listed as "FA" with the year they came into the league, even if they were only in training camp or on a practice squad.

To the far right of the first line is the player's Risk variable for fantasy football in 2019, which measures the likelihood of the player hitting his projection. The default rating for each player is Green. As the risk of a player failing to hit his projection rises, he's given a rating of Yellow or, in the worst cases, Red. The Risk variable is not only based on age and injury probability, but how a player's projection compares to his recent performance as well as our confidence (or lack thereof) in his offensive teammates. A few players with the strongest chances of surpassing their projections are given a Blue rating. Most players marked Blue will be backups with low projections, but a handful are starters or situational players who can be considered slightly better breakout candidates.

Next, we give the last three years of player stats. The majority of these statistics are passing numbers, although the final five columns on the right are the quarterback's rushing statistics.

The first few columns after the year and team the player played for are standard numbers: games and games started (**G/GS**), offensive **Snaps**, pass attempts (**Att**), pass completions (**Cmp**), completion percentage (**C%**), passing yards (**Yds**), passing touchdowns (**TD**). These numbers are official NFL totals and therefore include plays we leave out of our own metrics, such as clock-stopping spikes, and omit plays we include in our metrics, such as sacks and aborted snaps. (Other differences between official stats and Football Outsiders stats are described in the "Statistical Toolbox" introduction at the front of the book.)

The column for interceptions contains two numbers, representing the official NFL total for interceptions (**Int**) as well as our own metric for adjusted interceptions (**Adj**). For example, if you look at our sample table, Ben Roethlisberger had 16 interceptions and 20 adjusted interceptions in 2018. Adjusted interceptions use game charting data to add dropped interceptions, plays where a defender most likely would have had an interception but couldn't hold onto the ball. Then we remove Hail Mary passes and interceptions thrown on fourth down when losing in the final two minutes of the game. We also remove "tipped interceptions," when a perfectly catchable ball

Ben Roethlisberger			Height: 6-5		Weight: 240		College: Miami (Ohio)			Draft: 2004/1 (11)		Born: 2-Mar-1982		Age: 37		Risk: Yellow	
Year	Team	G/GS	Snaps	Att	Comp	C%	Yds	TD	INT/Adj	FUM	ASR	NY/P	Rk	DVOA	Rk	DYAR	Rk	YAR	Runs	Yds	TD	DVOA	DYAR	QBR
2016	PIT	14/14	921	509	328	64.4%	3819	29	13/25	8	4.0%	7.0	8	12.1%	9	807	8	790	16	14	1	14.8%	7	66.3
2017	PIT	15/15	1038	561	360	64.2%	4251	28	14/18	3	3.6%	7.4	5	21.8%	8	1270	5	1247	28	47	0	-2.1%	6	63.2
2018	PIT	16/16	1086	675	452	67.0%	5129	34	16/20	7	4.4%	7.1	9	14.5%	8	1204	5	1070	31	98	3	37.8%	62	71.8
2019	PIT			612	406	66.3%	4668	31	14	5		6.9		17.1%					28	65	1	-1.3%		

| 2017: | 50% Short | 28% Mid | 14% Deep | 9% Bomb | aDOT: 9.6 (7) | YAC: 5.7 (9) | ALEX: 2.4 | 2018: | 54% Short | 28% Mid | 10% Deep | 8% Bomb | aDOT: 8.0 (22) | YAC: 6.2 (3) | ALEX: 1.4 |

deflected off the receiver's hands or chest and into the arms of a defender.

Overall, adjusted interception rate is higher than standard interception rate, so most quarterbacks will have more adjusted interceptions than standard interceptions. On average, a quarterback will have one additional adjusted interception for every 120 pass attempts. Once this difference is accounted for, adjusted interceptions are a better predictor of next year's interception total than standard interceptions.

The next column is fumbles (**FUM**), which adds together all fumbles by this player, whether turned over to the defense or recovered by the offense (explained in the essay "Pregame Show"). Even though this fumble total is listed among the passing numbers, it includes all fumbles, including those on sacks, aborted snaps, and rushing attempts. By listing fumbles and interceptions next to one another, we're giving readers a general idea of how many total turnovers the player was responsible for.

Next comes Adjusted Sack Rate (**ASR**). This is the same statistic you'll find in the team chapters, only here it is specific to the individual quarterback. It represents sacks per pass play (total pass plays = pass attempts + sacks) adjusted based on down, distance, and strength of schedule. For reference, the NFL average was 6.1 percent in 2016, 6.7 percent in 2017, and 7.1 percent in 2018.

The next two columns are Net Yards per Pass (**NY/P**), a standard stat but a particularly good one, and the player's rank (**Rk**) in Net Yards per Pass for that season. Net Yards per Pass consists of passing yards minus yards lost on sacks, divided by total pass plays.

The five columns remaining in passing stats give our advanced metrics: **DVOA** (Defense-Adjusted Value Over Average), **DYAR** (Defense-Adjusted Yards Above Replacement), and **YAR** (Yards Above Replacement), along with the player's rank in both DVOA and DYAR. These metrics compare each quarterback's passing performance to league-average or replacement-level baselines based on the game situations that quarterback faced. DVOA and DYAR are also adjusted based on the opposing defense. The methods used to compute these numbers are described in detail in the "Statistical Toolbox" introduction at the front of the book. The important distinctions between them are:

- DVOA is a rate statistic, while DYAR is a cumulative statistic. Thus, a higher DVOA means more value per pass play, while a higher DYAR means more aggregate value over the entire season.
- Because DYAR is defense-adjusted and YAR is not, a player whose DYAR is higher than his YAR faced a harder-than-average schedule. A player whose DYAR is lower than his YAR faced an easier-than-average schedule.

To qualify for a ranking in Net Yards per Pass, passing DVOA, and passing DYAR in a given season, a quarterback must have had 200 pass plays in that season. 34 quarterbacks ranked for 2016, 35 for 2017, and 34 for 2018.

The final five columns contain rushing statistics, starting with **Runs**, rushing yards (**Yds**), and rushing touchdowns (**TD**). Once again, these are official NFL totals and include kneeldowns, which means you get to enjoy statistics such as Nick Mullens rushing 18 times for -16 yards. The final two columns give **DVOA** and **DYAR** for quarterback rushing, which are calculated separately from passing. Rankings for these statistics, as well as numbers that are not adjusted for defense (YAR and VOA) can be found on our website, FootballOutsiders.com.

The last number listed is the Total QBR metric from ESPN Stats & Information. Total QBR is based on the expected points added by the quarterback on each play, then adjusts the numbers to a scale of 0-100. There are five main differences between Total QBR and DVOA:

- Total QBR incorporates information from game charting, such as passes dropped or thrown away on purpose.
- Total QBR splits responsibility on plays between the quarterback, his receivers, and his blockers. Drops, for example, are more on the receiver, as are yards after the catch, and some sacks are more on the offensive line than others.
- Total QBR has a clutch factor which adds (or subtracts) value for quarterbacks who perform best (or worst) in high-leverage situations.
- Total QBR combines passing and rushing value into one number and differentiates between scrambles and planned runs.

The italicized row of statistics for the 2019 season is our 2019 KUBIAK projection, as detailed above. Again, in the interest of producing meaningful statistics, all quarterbacks are projected to start a full 16-game season, regardless of the likelihood of them actually doing so.

The final line below the KUBIAK projection represents data on how far the quarterback throws his passes. First, we break down charted passes based on distance: **Short** (5 yards or less), **Mid** (6 to 15 yards), **Deep** (16 to 25 yards), and **Bomb** (26 or more yards). These numbers are based on distance in the air only and include both complete and incomplete passes. Passes thrown away or tipped at the line are not included, nor are passes on which the quarterback's arm was hit by a defender while in motion. We also give average depth of target (**aDOT**) and average yards after catch (**YAC**) with the rank in parentheses for the 34 quarterbacks who qualify. The final number listed here is **ALEX**, which stands for Air Less EXpected, and measures the distance of each quarterback's average third-down throw compared to how many yards were needed for a first down. Patrick Mahomes' ALEX of 4.5 means his average third-down pass was thrown 4.5 yards deeper than the sticks, the highest in the league; Dak Prescott had the lowest ALEX at -1.0.

A number of third- and fourth-string quarterbacks are briefly discussed at the end of the chapter in a section we call "Going Deep."

Top 20 QB by Passing DYAR (Total Value), 2018

Rank	Player	Team	DYAR
1	Patrick Mahomes	KC	2,039
2	Drew Brees	NO	1,632
3	Philip Rivers	LAC	1,321
4	Matt Ryan	ATL	1,233
5	Ben Roethlisberger	PIT	1,208
6	Jared Goff	LAR	1,092
7	Andrew Luck	IND	1,072
8	Tom Brady	NE	1,034
9	Aaron Rodgers	GB	821
10	Deshaun Watson	HOU	742
11	Russell Wilson	SEA	679
12	Baker Mayfield	CLE	630
13	Kirk Cousins	MIN	596
14	Carson Wentz	PHI	549
15	Ryan Fitzpatrick	TB	473
16	Jameis Winston	TB	453
17	Joe Flacco	BAL	432
18	Mitchell Trubisky	CHI	418
19	Andy Dalton	CIN	405
20	Matthew Stafford	DET	402

Minimum 200 passes

Top 20 QB by Passing DVOA (Value per Pass), 2018

Rank	Player	Team	DVOA
1	Patrick Mahomes	KC	40.1%
2	Drew Brees	NO	36.8%
3	Philip Rivers	LAC	27.3%
4	Matt Ryan	ATL	18.2%
5	Ryan Fitzpatrick	TB	16.8%
6	Jared Goff	LAR	16.4%
7	Tom Brady	NE	15.4%
8	Ben Roethlisberger	PIT	14.6%
9	Andrew Luck	IND	13.4%
10	Russell Wilson	SEA	11.6%
11	Deshaun Watson	HOU	9.6%
12	Carson Wentz	PHI	8.2%
13	Aaron Rodgers	GB	8.2%
14	Baker Mayfield	CLE	8.1%
15	Jameis Winston	TB	6.2%
16	Joe Flacco	BAL	5.5%
17	Andy Dalton	CIN	5.2%
18	Nick Mullens	SF	4.2%
19	Kirk Cousins	MIN	2.7%
20	Mitchell Trubisky	CHI	2.5%

Minimum 200 passes

Josh Allen

Height: 6-5   Weight: 237   College: Wyoming   Draft: 2018/1 (7)   Born: 21-May-1996   Age: 23   ^t Red

Year	Team	G/GS	Snaps	Att	Comp	C%	Yds	TD	INT/Adj	FUM	ASR	NY/P	Rk	DVOA	Rk	DYAR	Rk	YAR	Runs	Yds	TD	DVOA	DYAR	QBR
2018	BUF	12/11	719	320	169	52.8%	2074	10	12/16	8	8.4%	5.3	33	-35.9%	33	-534	33	-476	89	631	8	33.3%	192	52.0
2019	BUF			480	284	59.2%	3317	16	14	12		6.0		-15.8%					111	654	7	25.2%		

2018:	44% Short	26% Mid	19% Deep	11% Bomb	aDOT: 11.1 (2)	YAC: 5.6 (11)	ALEX: 3.6

You know the basics about Allen from the Buffalo chapter: rocket arm, horrible accuracy, fantastic scrambling, and the weight of the entire franchise on his shoulders. Despite that much-touted arm, Allen struggled on deep passes (16+ air yards) last season. The league as a whole sees DVOA go way up on deep passes -- after all, the gains are much larger, which more than counters the lower completion rate. But Allen saw his DVOA decline slightly, with a -7.8% DVOA on the short stuff falling to -9.1% when going deep. He also had an interesting side-to-side bias: Allen managed 16.4% DVOA on passes to the left but -39.9% DVOA on passes to his right, worst in the league. No other quarterback came anywhere close to having that large of a gap from one direction to the other.

Kyle Allen

Height: 6-3   Weight: 211   College: Houston   Draft: 2018/FA   Born: 8-Mar-1996   Age: 23   Risk: Yellow

Year	Team	G/GS	Snaps	Att	Comp	C%	Yds	TD	INT/Adj	FUM	ASR	NY/P	Rk	DVOA	Rk	DYAR	Rk	YAR	Runs	Yds	TD	DVOA	DYAR	QBR
2018	CAR	2/1	68	31	20	64.5%	266	2	0/0	0	0.0%	8.6	--	67.4%	--	158	--	170	5	19	1	52.8%	19	95.7
2019	CAR			512	331	64.6%	3700	22	18	9		6.4		-3.4%					55	163	1	-3.9%		

2018:	50% Short	30% Mid	7% Deep	13% Bomb	aDOT: 10.4 (--)	YAC: 4.6 (--)	ALEX: 4.2

To lose one backup quarterback to injury in the final couple of games may be regarded as a misfortune; to lose both looks like carelessness. Like Taylor Heinicke, Kyle Allen made his starting debut after Cam Newton was shut down for the season last December. Like Heinicke, Allen was injured in that debut and had to leave the game early. Unlike Heinicke, Allen looked impressive prior to his injury: he threw for two touchdowns and ran for a third, with no turnovers in a 33-14 victory at New Orleans, albeit against a vanilla Saints defense mostly focused on staying healthy for the postseason.

That victorious performance as a rookie may be enough to give the youngest of the four Panthers quarterbacks the inside track in the race to back Newton up in 2019. At the very least, it probably makes it impossible for the Panthers to stash Allen on the practice squad again—he spent most of 2018 there, only being promoted to the active roster when Newton was deactivated for Week 16. Allen was a highly regarded prospect out of high school, but struggled with inconsistency and turnovers in college and was benched at both Texas A&M and Houston. If he can improve the mental side of his game, he has the potential to at least be a long-time backup in the mold of Chase Daniel. However, the 2018 undrafted free agent faces stiff competition to hold onto that spot in Carolina this year.

Derek Anderson

Height: 6-6 Weight: 229 College: Oregon State Draft: 2005/6 (213) Born: 15-Jun-1983 Age: 36 Risk: N/A

Year	Team	G/GS	Snaps	Att	Comp	C%	Yds	TD	INT/Adj	FUM	ASR	NY/P	Rk	DVOA	Rk	DYAR	Rk	YAR	Runs	Yds	TD	DVOA	DYAR	QBR
2016	CAR	5/2	86	53	36	67.9%	453	2	5/4	1	0.8%	8.5	--	-17.9%	--	-27	--	-41	1	4	0	-200.4%	-13	18.2
2017	CAR	3/0	16	8	2	25.0%	17	0	0/0	0	0.0%	2.1	--	-41.5%	--	-18	--	-24	2	-2	0	--	--	0.2
2018	BUF	2/2	118	70	42	60.0%	465	0	4/6	3	8.0%	5.8	--	-56.9%	--	-208	--	-180	1	-1	0	--	--	26.9

2017: 25% Short 50% Mid 25% Deep 0% Bomb aDOT: 11.5 (--) YAC: 3.0 (--) ALEX: -0.3 2018: 44% Short 30% Mid 21% Deep 5% Bomb aDOT: 9.3 (--) YAC: 4.5 (--) ALEX: 1.3

The Bills re-signed Anderson to be Josh Allen's backup, but he retired in May after 13 seasons in the NFL. Anderson's 2007 Pro Bowl season remains one of the weirdest outliers in modern NFL history—an 8.7% DVOA for a player who never again topped -17.5% as a starter. A league-leading 12.7 yards per completion and 29 touchdowns for a guy who only threw 31 in his other 12 seasons combined. The Browns' only 10-win season since returning to the NFL. Not since Don Majkowski have we seen a quarterback have a season so good without ever being a relevant starting quarterback again. Anderson transitioned into a long career as Cam Newton's caddy in Carolina before the desperate Bills dragged him off the golf course last season. Two games, four interceptions, and a concussion later, Anderson was done.

Matt Barkley

Height: 6-2 Weight: 230 College: USC Draft: 2013/4 (98) Born: 8-Sep-1990 Age: 29 Risk: Yellow

Year	Team	G/GS	Snaps	Att	Comp	C%	Yds	TD	INT/Adj	FUM	ASR	NY/P	Rk	DVOA	Rk	DYAR	Rk	YAR	Runs	Yds	TD	DVOA	DYAR	QBR
2016	CHI	7/6	412	216	129	59.7%	1611	8	14/14	4	2.7%	7.1	7	-10.9%	26	4	26	127	7	2	0	-321.8%	-34	39.2
2018	BUF	1/1	73	25	15	60.0%	232	2	0/1	0	3.7%	8.6	--	56.0%	--	109	--	111	3	-2	0	-97.9%	-11	87.0
2019	BUF			483	284	58.8%	3248	15	19	10		5.9		-30.8%					45	18	1	-25.0%		

2018: 36% Short 32% Mid 24% Deep 8% Bomb aDOT: 12.4 (--) YAC: 5.1 (--) ALEX: 4.4

Technically, Barkley was the Bills' best quarterback in 2018. Signed off the street on Halloween, Barkley was deemed a better option than Nathan Peterman after just 12 days of practice time; the fact that this was correct says more about Peterman than it does about Barkley. Barkley threw for 232 yards and two touchdowns on his way to a 41-10 victory over the Jets; that gave him a DVOA of 56.0% in what we like to call "small sample size theatre." That wasn't enough to keep the starting job because, hey, he's still Matt Barkley, but it was enough to earn him a contract extension and a locked in spot as Josh Allen's backup for the next two years for a cool $4 million. There are worse jobs than being a backup quarterback.

C.J. Beathard

Height: 6-2 Weight: 219 College: Iowa Draft: 2017/3 (104) Born: 16-Nov-1993 Age: 26 Risk: Red

Year	Team	G/GS	Snaps	Att	Comp	C%	Yds	TD	INT/Adj	FUM	ASR	NY/P	Rk	DVOA	Rk	DYAR	Rk	YAR	Runs	Yds	TD	DVOA	DYAR	QBR
2017	SF	7/5	390	224	123	54.9%	1430	4	6/4	3	8.5%	5.3	32	-23.1%	31	-176	30	-271	26	136	3	44.6%	73	32.0
2018	SF	6/5	340	169	102	60.4%	1252	8	7/8	5	8.7%	5.9	--	-24.3%	--	-156	--	-188	19	69	1	-25.2%	-13	43.3
2019	SF			520	312	59.9%	3566	19	16	10		5.7		-21.7%					62	241	2	-5.1%		

2017: 59% Short 28% Mid 8% Deep 5% Bomb aDOT: 7.6 (31) YAC: 5.2 (18) ALEX: 1.3 2018: 54% Short 31% Mid 12% Deep 3% Bomb aDOT: 7.0 (--) YAC: 7.1 (--) ALEX: -1.1

Only three quarterbacks lost to the Arizona Cardinals last year, and two of them were C.J. Beathard. Through two seasons, Beathard has probably played better than his raw numbers would suggest—he's one of the few quarterbacks with more actual interceptions than adjusted interceptions—but then his raw numbers are dreadful, so that's not saying much. He goes into training camp the clear underdog in a battle with Nick Mullens for the backup spot behind Jimmy Garoppolo, though the 49ers might keep all three, especially if they're still worried about Garoppolo's knee come Week 1. (By the way, the other quarterback to lose to the Cardinals last year was Aaron Rodgers, because football is weird.)

Blake Bortles

Height: 6-4 | Weight: 232 | College: Central Florida | Draft: 2014/1 (3) | Born: 16-Dec-1991 | Age: 28 | Risk: Red

Year	Team	G/GS	Snaps	Att	Comp	C%	Yds	TD	INT/Adj	FUM	ASR	NY/P	Rk	DVOA	Rk	DYAR	Rk	YAR	Runs	Yds	TD	DVOA	DYAR	QBR
2016	JAX	16/16	1111	625	368	58.9%	3905	23	16/17	8	5.3%	5.6	30	-10.0%	24	52	23	3	58	359	3	23.3%	90	49.2
2017	JAX	16/16	1110	523	315	60.2%	3687	21	13/16	9	4.4%	6.7	13	0.3%	16	408	15	597	57	322	2	25.1%	84	55.6
2018	JAX	13/12	777	403	243	60.3%	2718	13	11/9	8	7.5%	5.9	30	-18.9%	31	-221	32	-177	58	365	1	26.8%	107	45.7
2019	LAR			516	322	62.3%	3744	23	13	10		6.3		-7.5%					60	309	2	14.1%		

2017:   56% Short   25% Mid   12% Deep   7% Bomb   aDOT: 8.3 (22)   YAC: 6.1 (4)   ALEX: 0.7   2018:   58% Short   26% Mid   10% Deep   6% Bomb   aDOT: 7.4 (29)   YAC: 6.1 (4)   ALEX: 0.2

After being cut by the Jaguars, Bortles became the second former Jacksonville No. 3 overall pick to join the Rams in a matter of months, after pass-rusher Dante Fowler was traded there in mid-2018. Bortles performed serviceably in 2017 for a team that made the AFC Championship Game, but that season clearly was the exception, not the rule. At the very least, Bortles has a nice, lucrative career as a clipboard-holder to look forward to, but if Jared Goff goes down and Sean McVay can get above-average play out of the former Jaguars starter, that might be his most impressive achievement yet.

Sam Bradford

Height: 6-4 | Weight: 236 | College: Oklahoma | Draft: 2010/1 (1) | Born: 8-Nov-1987 | Age: 32 | Risk: N/A

Year	Team	G/GS	Snaps	Att	Comp	C%	Yds	TD	INT/Adj	FUM	ASR	NY/P	Rk	DVOA	Rk	DYAR	Rk	YAR	Runs	Yds	TD	DVOA	DYAR	QBR
2016	MIN	15/15	978	552	395	71.6%	3877	20	5/9	10	6.3%	6.1	24	2.2%	17	510	16	571	20	53	0	54.3%	23	49.2
2017	MIN	2/2	91	43	32	74.4%	382	3	0/0	0	9.2%	7.1	--	44.2%	--	169	--	131	2	-3	0	--	--	72.4
2018	ARI	3/3	135	80	50	62.5%	400	2	4/4	3	6.2%	4.3	--	-50.8%	--	-213	--	-268	2	7	0	32.5%	4	30.3

2017:   55% Short   21% Mid   17% Deep   6% Bomb   aDOT: 8.2 (--)   YAC: 4.8 (--)   ALEX: -1.7   2018:   58% Short   27% Mid   12% Deep   4% Bomb   aDOT: 6.6 (--)   YAC: 3.8 (--)   ALEX: 2.2

Say goodbye to the Duke of Dumpoffs, the Champion of Checkdowns, the Thelonious Monk of the Dink-and-Dunk. Bradford's average completed pass in his career has gained only 10.5 yards, the fewest in NFL history among the 117 quarterbacks with at least 1,500 completions. And it's not just because he played in an era that encourages short throws—the league average over the course of his career (weighted by his number of completions each season) is 11.6 yards completion, over a full yard higher. That's the largest gap for any quarterback since the 1950s. Obviously, yards per completion isn't the most important stat for quarterbacks—Jameis Winston and Cam Newton are the active leaders in this category, while Tom Brady is in the middle of the pack and Drew Brees is way below normal. Bradford's pop-gun style has also been effective at times; for most of his career he was an average starter by DVOA, and he set a single-season completion percentage record (since broken) with Minnesota in 2016. And if the leading wide receivers in your career were Danny Amendola and Brandon Gibson, you'd check down a lot too. Still, for a first overall draft pick who has collected nearly $130 million in NFL paychecks, you'd like more than a guy who took what the defense gave him and almost never more than that.

If Bradford were healthy, he might have found another GM to pay him $10 million to throw 3-yard passes on third-and-8. But he's not—after two ACL tears, the cartilage in his left knee is reportedly gone, leaving him bone on bone in that leg and barely able to practice, let alone play.

Tom Brady

Height: 6-4 | Weight: 225 | College: Michigan | Draft: 2000/6 (199) | Born: 3-Aug-1977 | Age: 42 | Risk: Yellow

Year	Team	G/GS	Snaps	Att	Comp	C%	Yds	TD	INT/Adj	FUM	ASR	NY/P	Rk	DVOA	Rk	DYAR	Rk	YAR	Runs	Yds	TD	DVOA	DYAR	QBR
2016	NE	12/12	819	432	291	67.4%	3554	28	2/3	5	4.2%	7.8	2	33.4%	2	1286	5	1361	28	64	0	-18.9%	-9	83.0
2017	NE	16/16	1118	581	385	66.3%	4577	32	8/13	7	6.4%	7.4	6	27.8%	2	1595	1	1621	25	28	0	-12.2%	0	67.4
2018	NE	16/16	1092	570	375	65.8%	4355	29	11/12	4	3.8%	7.1	8	15.4%	7	1034	8	1051	23	35	2	18.1%	30	70.6
2019	NE			560	382	68.3%	4218	29	13	7		6.7		11.0%					26	38	2	-4.1%		

2017:   51% Short   29% Mid   12% Deep   8% Bomb   aDOT: 9.6 (8)   YAC: 5.0 (21)   ALEX: 2.9   2018:   50% Short   32% Mid   12% Deep   6% Bomb   aDOT: 8.2 (18)   YAC: 5.7 (10)   ALEX: 2.8

Brady's age-41 season led him into almost-uncharted waters not only for quarterbacks, but for any player. Brady became only the seventh player ever to start 10 or more games at age 41 or older. Not even in the pre-merger days had a quarterback ever led a team that finished with a winning record at 41 or older, never mind won a championship. Naturally, Brady set records in every meaningful statistical category for quarterbacks his age and posted his 14th straight season ranked among the top 11 passers by DVOA (obviously excluding 2008, when he tore his ACL in Week 1).

The lack of precedent severely limits our ability to predict what lies in store for 2019. Only Warren Moon and Vinny Testaverde have even started more than a single game at quarterback at age 42 or older. Both Moon's 1998 and Testaverde's 2005 (and 2007) were in their bottom five career seasons by Pro Football Reference's Adjusted Net Yards Per Attempt, but neither player was nearly as effective as Brady at age 41 either. Brady's 2018 DVOA was his second-lowest since 2003, but it still made him the second-most efficient passer in the AFC—and when the playoffs came around, Brady's 31.0% DVOA was the highest of any postseason quarterback.

What we can perhaps more confidently expect, given both the shift in focus of the Patriots offense and Brady's own postseason success, is that Brady's regular-season volume will continue to be limited whenever possible. 2018 saw Brady's fewest pass attempts per game since 2010, resulting in his second-lowest DYAR since 2006. His lowest three seasons since 2011 by total attempts have all come in the past three years, and his yards per game has also declined in each of those campaigns. As long as he remains healthy, Brady will probably remain a highly efficient quarterback—if not quite as efficient last year as in years previous—but we are so far outside the boundaries of a normal aging curve that we simply don't have precedent for anything we could project for Brady in 2019.

Drew Brees

Height: 6-0 • Weight: 209 • College: Purdue • Draft: 2001/2 (32) • Born: 15-Jan-1979 • Age: 40 • Risk: Yellow

Year	Team	G/GS	Snaps	Att	Comp	C%	Yds	TD	INT/Adj	FUM	ASR	NY/P	Rk	DVOA	Rk	DYAR	Rk	YAR	Runs	Yds	TD	DVOA	DYAR	QBR
2016	NO	16/16	1151	673	471	70.0%	5208	37	15/14	5	4.5%	7.3	5	23.3%	4	1599	2	1473	23	20	2	17.2%	21	72.0
2017	NO	16/16	1034	536	386	72.0%	4334	23	8/12	5	4.0%	7.5	3	27.4%	3	1390	3	1402	33	12	2	-5.6%	6	59.0
2018	NO	15/15	978	489	364	74.4%	3992	32	5/7	5	4.0%	7.6	3	36.7%	2	1631	2	1679	31	22	4	29.0%	43	80.8
2019	NO			513	369	71.9%	4185	31	9	6		7.6		31.1%					31	29	2	-9.4%		

2017:	62% Short	22% Mid	11% Deep	6% Bomb	aDOT: 6.7 (35)	YAC: 6.1 (2)	ALEX: -0.2	2018:	55% Short	26% Mid	14% Deep	5% Bomb	aDOT: 7.6 (27)	YAC: 5.0 (25)	ALEX: 0.1

Brees' apparent late-season swoon, in which he had three of his five interceptions versus only three touchdowns in his final four regular-season games, has evoked comparisons to 2014 Peyton Manning among sections of the NFL commentariat this offseason, leading to significant concern about his prospects for 2019. While we might expect to see some decline from a quarterback entering his age-40 season, we also need to be careful not to extrapolate too heavily from such a limited sample.

Brees' swoon in our numbers was really confined to the three-game road trip from Weeks 13 to 15: Thursday Night Football at Dallas, then back-to-back outdoor division games in Carolina and Tampa Bay. Brees was unquestionably poor in those games: his -40.8% DVOA ranked 30th of 36 passers with at least 30 attempts over that period, and they were his three worst individual games of the season. However, Brees then had 24.5% DVOA in Weeks 16, 19, and 20, and ranked fourth in passing DVOA during the playoffs—ahead of Patrick Mahomes, Andrew Luck, and Philip Rivers. The Saints offense is prone to mid-season productivity lulls—see Weeks 12 and 13 of 2016, or Weeks 5 to 9 of 2017—and that is not *necessarily* more significant for coming in December rather than October in 2018.

That is not to say that Brees will not decline at all next season. Even with that three-game skid, he posted the second-highest DVOA of his career and his third-highest DYAR. Brees is therefore highly likely to regress at least toward his own career mean—but that mean is still a top-six quarterback in both figures. The only thing that really *has* changed significantly for Brees over the past couple of seasons is volume: now that the Saints are winning again, and the defense is performing like honest-to-goodness professionals, Brees has posted his fewest and third-fewest attempts of his time in New Orleans over the past two seasons. That matters not a jot for the Saints' prospects when he is leveraging those attempts so efficiently, but it does dampen the enthusiasm for him in certain circles. As with a certain other elder quarterback, Brees may not be quite the enticing fantasy option that he was in the early 2010s, but rumors of his impending demise appear somewhat premature.

Teddy Bridgewater

Height: 6-2 • Weight: 214 • College: Louisville • Draft: 2014/1 (32) • Born: 10-Nov-1992 • Age: 27 • Risk: Yellow

Year	Team	G/GS	Snaps	Att	Comp	C%	Yds	TD	INT/Adj	FUM	ASR	NY/P	Rk	DVOA	Rk	DYAR	Rk	YAR	Runs	Yds	TD	DVOA	DYAR	QBR
2017	MIN	1/0	9	2	0	0.0%	0	0	1/0	0	0.0%	0.0	--	-493.2%	--	-68	--	-66	3	-3	0	--	--	0.0
2018	NO	5/1	71	23	14	60.9%	118	1	1/1	0	8.6%	4.4	--	-39.7%	--	-46	--	-40	11	5	0	-58.4%	-13	33.6
2019	NO			513	333	65.0%	3637	24	15	7		6.0		-1.3%					41	136	2	8.3%		

2017:	100% Short	0% Mid	0% Deep	0% Bomb	aDOT: 3.5 (--)	YAC: 0.0 (--)	ALEX: -1.0	2018:	57% Short	29% Mid	14% Deep	0% Bomb	aDOT: 6.7 (--)	YAC: 3.8 (--)	ALEX: 1.0

Bridgewater's Week 17 start against the Panthers was his first meaningful action since dislocating his knee in the summer of 2016. It had been three full years since the former Vikings first-round pick started a regular-season game. Though his performance in a 33-14 defeat was nothing to write home about, the mere fact he was healthy enough to start and play the entire game is a major development for a player whose career was feared to be over after that devastating injury.

Still only 26—the five-year veteran is barely two years older than rookie Ryan Finley—Bridgewater has enough time to get his career as a starting quarterback back on track. Though he was below average in DVOA during both of his seasons as a starter for the Vikings, he showed enough potential to believe that he could develop into a franchise passer. To that end, re-signing with the Saints this offseason was a slight surprise given the greater chance of playing time elsewhere. If he can continue to progress and impress the coaching staff, it remains possible that we could see Bridgewater as the heir apparent to Drew Brees at the center of the talent-rich Saints offense. Even if he never returns as an established starter though, Bridgewater returning to the field at all has to be considered a success after the longest of long roads back.

Jacoby Brissett

Height: 6-4   Weight: 231   College: North Carolina State   Draft: 2016/3 (91)   Born: 11-Dec-1992   Age: 27   Risk: Yellow

Year	Team	G/GS	Snaps	Att	Comp	C%	Yds	TD	INT/Adj	FUM	ASR	NY/P	Rk	DVOA	Rk	DYAR	Rk	YAR	Runs	Yds	TD	DVOA	DYAR	QBR
2016	NE	3/2	156	55	34	61.8%	400	0	0/0	3	9.4%	5.9	--	-10.0%	--	4	--	-4	16	83	1	-24.4%	-8	44.8
2017	IND	16/15	989	469	276	58.8%	3098	13	7/11	8	9.8%	5.5	29	-14.4%	27	-105	28	-178	63	260	4	-13.7%	-4	39.6
2018	IND	4/0	18	4	2	50.0%	2	0	0/0	0	1.2%	0.5	--	-70.3%	--	-16	--	-16	7	-7	0	--	--	100.0
2019	IND			563	342	60.7%	3966	24	15	12		6.2		-10.6%					68	264	4	6.5%		

2017: 59% Short 29% Mid 8% Deep 5% Bomb aDOT: 7.7 (30) YAC: 5.7 (8) ALEX: 0.3 2018: 67% Short 0% Mid 0% Deep 33% Bomb aDOT: 9.3 (--) YAC: 0.5 (--) ALEX: 18.0

Brissett wasn't terrible in a bad situation in 2017, so with Andrew Luck coming off a healthy season and ensconced as the Colts' starting quarterback for the long haul, the question is whether the Colts let him play out the final year of his rookie deal or trade him for a longer-lasting asset. General manager Chris Ballard has indicated the asking price is pretty high, so barring a training camp injury elsewhere, expect Brissett to stick around. With Luck missing offseason workouts and no other quarterbacks of note on the roster, that's probably the smart move for now.

Derek Carr

Height: 6-3   Weight: 220   College: Fresno St.   Draft: 2014/2 (36)   Born: 3/28/1991   Age: 28   Risk: Red

Year	Team	G/GS	Snaps	Att	Comp	C%	Yds	TD	INT/Adj	FUM	ASR	NY/P	Rk	DVOA	Rk	DYAR	Rk	YAR	Runs	Yds	TD	DVOA	DYAR	QBR
2016	OAK	15/15	1048	560	357	63.8%	3937	28	6/12	5	3.3%	6.7	12	19.8%	6	1164	7	1038	39	70	0	-50.3%	-39	62.1
2017	OAK	15/15	937	515	323	62.7%	3496	22	13/19	8	4.3%	6.6	14	9.7%	13	709	12	721	23	66	0	-66.5%	-35	46.7
2018	OAK	16/16	1034	553	381	68.9%	4049	19	10/20	12	8.6%	6.3	21	-1.0%	22	392	21	281	24	47	1	-0.3%	8	48.9
2019	OAK			554	371	67.0%	4093	25	14	6		6.3		5.0%					23	43	0	-12.6%		

2017: 53% Short 29% Mid 10% Deep 9% Bomb aDOT: 8.7 (17) YAC: 5.0 (20) ALEX: 1.4 2018: 56% Short 30% Mid 10% Deep 4% Bomb aDOT: 7.1 (33) YAC: 5.2 (19) ALEX: 0.3

We've come a long way from Al Davis' vertical passing attack. Carr has yet to see a deep pass enticing enough to pass up a checkdown for. He had the second-worst aDOT in the league and the fourth-lowest ALEX (all downs). Just 14.1 percent of his passes traveled more than 15 yards downfield, the lowest rate in the league. Carr seems uncomfortable when asked to hold the ball for longer than a couple seconds, though that's entirely understandable considering the state of his tackles last season. Carr's -110.5% DVOA when pressured last season was second-worst in the league, and he had the largest drop-off between clean and pressured pockets last season. The thing is, Carr has shown that he has the accuracy and arm strength to be a better quarterback than he has been the past two seasons. He doesn't need to be as hesitant as he is about throwing into even moderately tight windows. At some point, he lost trust in something—his offensive line protecting him, his receivers getting open deep, or his own arm to make NFL-quality throws. Whether it's out of necessity or by design, Carr has prioritized getting the ball out quickly rather than standing in and letting a play develop. Now, equipped with the best receiving corps he's ever had and an upgraded offensive line, Carr must regain the form that made him a top-ten quarterback in 2016. If not, his contract makes it very easy for the Las Vegas Raiders to start fresh behind center.

Kirk Cousins

Height: 6-3   Weight: 214   College: Michigan State   Draft: 2012/4 (102)   Born: 19-Aug-1988   Age: 31   Risk: Yellow

Year	Team	G/GS	Snaps	Att	Comp	C%	Yds	TD	INT/Adj	FUM	ASR	NY/P	Rk	DVOA	Rk	DYAR	Rk	YAR	Runs	Yds	TD	DVOA	DYAR	QBR
2016	WAS	16/16	1063	606	406	67.0%	4917	25	12/16	9	3.9%	7.6	3	20.9%	5	1317	3	1197	34	96	4	1.9%	18	71.7
2017	WAS	16/16	1012	540	347	64.3%	4093	27	13/20	13	7.7%	6.5	16	-0.6%	18	395	16	318	49	179	4	-2.3%	21	52.3
2018	MIN	16/16	1051	606	425	70.1%	4298	30	10/13	9	6.1%	6.2	23	2.7%	20	595	13	573	44	123	1	-13.2%	-2	62.0
2019	MIN			550	371	67.4%	3947	28	12	7		6.2		7.9%					42	124	2	-2.3%		

2017: 57% Short 28% Mid 9% Deep 6% Bomb aDOT: 8.1 (24) YAC: 6.1 (3) ALEX: 0.7 2018: 57% Short 27% Mid 9% Deep 7% Bomb aDOT: 7.6 (28) YAC: 4.6 (31) ALEX: 1.0

Minnesota's team-wide struggles drowned out any narrative that did not simply say "Kirk Cousins was a waste of money," but in reality Cousins played one of the most interesting seasons across all quarterbacks. In three years as the starter in Washington, he always scored above average in passing DVOA without pressure, but at or below average when pressured. The script flipped in 2019 as Cousins ranked top-10 in DVOA under pressure and plummeted into the bottom 10 in DVOA without pressure, sandwiched between Marcus Mariota and Mitchell Trubisky. In addition to good fortune, Cousins' under-pressure success can be explained by his genuine growth in that area over the years compounded with two fantastic safety blankets at wide receiver. Without pressure, though, Cousins struggled in part because the passing game was stripped down to a barebones approach that threw short more than any team other than Oakland while also being one of the worst yards-after-catch offenses in the league. Cousins can play that way, but he is often at his best moving 1-2-3 through his reads on play-action and intermediate concepts that allow him to play in a rhythm. The hope is that an offensive coaching stable of Kevin Stefanski, Gary Kubiak, and Rick Dennison can craft a more fitting and balanced offense.

Andy Dalton

Height: 6-2   Weight: 215   College: TCU   Draft: 2011/2 (35)   Born: 29-Oct-1987   Age: 32   Risk: Green

Year	Team	G/GS	Snaps	Att	Comp	C%	Yds	TD	INT/Adj	FUM	ASR	NY/P	Rk	DVOA	Rk	DYAR	Rk	YAR	Runs	Yds	TD	DVOA	DYAR	QBR
2016	CIN	16/16	1085	563	364	64.7%	4206	18	8/16	9	7.3%	6.6	15	7.6%	12	738	10	667	46	184	4	20.6%	60	58.3
2017	CIN	16/16	941	496	297	59.9%	3320	25	12/16	4	7.3%	5.8	23	-8.6%	24	87	24	75	38	99	0	11.3%	24	41.1
2018	CIN	11/11	627	365	226	61.9%	2566	21	11/13	1	5.8%	6.3	20	5.2%	17	404	19	406	16	99	0	11.9%	14	61.9
2019	CIN			542	341	62.8%	3890	27	13	5		6.2		1.3%					36	145	1	9.2%		

2017: 53% Short   31% Mid   10% Deep   7% Bomb   aDOT: 8.6 (20)   YAC: 5.8 (6)   ALEX: 2.2   2018: 48% Short   34% Mid   12% Deep   6% Bomb   aDOT: 8.5 (17)   YAC: 5.1 (23)   ALEX: 1.1

Listen to Andy Dalton's story. This may be his last chance. Dalton has been a competent game manager quarterback hooked up with A.J. Green boosts throughout his career, except for 2015, when he got to play with one of the most talented offenses assembled in this decade. Dalton is the kind of quarterback who is just good enough to tell you how good the team around him is. Praising Zac Taylor's offense in minicamp, Dalton pointed out to MMQB's Albert Breer that now that the whole offense gets the play call, everyone has a better idea of why they're doing what they're doing. We're going to learn very fast whether Taylor's system is good enough to carry Dalton to some extent. Entering the second-to-last year of his contract, if Dalton doesn't rebound this year, he's likely to enter the Ryan Fitzpatrick portal and never become a full-time starter again.

Chase Daniel

Height: 6-0   Weight: 225   College: Missouri   Draft: 2009/FA   Born: 7-Oct-1986   Age: 33   Risk: Red

Year	Team	G/GS	Snaps	Att	Comp	C%	Yds	TD	INT/Adj	FUM	ASR	NY/P	Rk	DVOA	Rk	DYAR	Rk	YAR	Runs	Yds	TD	DVOA	DYAR	QBR
2016	PHI	1/0	6	1	1	100.0%	16	0	0/0	0	0.0%	11.0	--	360.8%	--	16	--	13	0	0	0	--	--	99.5
2017	NO	1/0	5	0	0	0.0%	0	0	0/0	0	--	--	--	--	--	--	--	--	3	-2	0	--	--	--
2018	CHI	5/2	148	76	53	69.7%	515	3	2/3	4	10.7%	5.6	--	-37.9%	--	-152	--	-87	13	3	0	-107.0%	-26	29.6
2019	CHI			503	321	63.9%	3403	19	11	10		5.8		-14.3%					41	83	1	-23.9%		

2018: 45% Short   36% Mid   13% Deep   6% Bomb   aDOT: 8.6 (--)   YAC: 3.2 (--)   ALEX: -3.9

Despite starting just two games in 2018, Daniel managed to crack into the 20 worst quarterback DYAR performances of the year. On 44 dropbacks against the Giants, Daniel threw for only 285 yards with one touchdown, two interceptions, and five sacks. At first glance, that stat line is not egregious, but remember that New York was one of the worst pass defenses in the league. Daniel ended the day with -170 total DYAR. Other quarterbacks to start fewer than three games and still land on the bottom-20 single-performance list include Taylor Heinicke (Panthers), Derek Anderson (Bills), Nathan Peterman (Bills), DeShone Kizer (Packers), and Mark Sanchez (Washington). Daniel has long made his name as a stable veteran presence and a quick, mobile passer, but his lackluster arm and shoddy decision-making make it tough for him to maintain any level of success. Some backup quarterbacks surprise in limited action and earn opportunities elsewhere, but it's not a mystery as to why Daniel's two starts in 2018 were as many as he had made in the previous eight seasons combined.

Sam Darnold

Height: 6-3   Weight: 221   College: USC   Draft: 2018/1 (3)   Born: 5-Jun-1997   Age: 22   Risk: Green

Year	Team	G/GS	Snaps	Att	Comp	C%	Yds	TD	INT/Adj	FUM	ASR	NY/P	Rk	DVOA	Rk	DYAR	Rk	YAR	Runs	Yds	TD	DVOA	DYAR	QBR
2018	NYJ	13/13	810	414	239	57.7%	2865	17	15/21	5	6.7%	6.0	27	-15.2%	30	-110	30	-139	44	138	1	0.2%	23	48.4
2019	NYJ			538	328	61.1%	3702	24	16	10		6.0		-8.9%					57	232	2	-0.3%		

2018: 40% Short   39% Mid   14% Deep   6% Bomb   aDOT: 9.4 (7)   YAC: 5.4 (16)   ALEX: 1.1

Remove Darnold's four-interception fiasco in a 13-6 loss to the Dolphins in Week 9 last year and his DYAR climbs from -109 to 94 and his DVOA rises to -7.3%; he basically moves up from Case Keenum-Ryan Tannehill territory to Nick Foles-Dak Prescott territory. Darnold had other bad games last year (against the Vikings in Week 7, most notably), but he played at least some of the Dolphins game on the foot injury which sidelined him for a month, so there's good reason to quarantine that game from the rest of his season, at least for academic purposes. The Dolphins game was not removed from the KUBIAK projection, because line-item vetoing games doesn't make for accurate or objective projections, which is one reason why Darnold's projection is modest and his interception total is high. The relative weakness of his supporting cast is another reason. We're excited about Darnold's potential but as cautious about projecting a breakout season based on a few good games as we would be about projecting a bust based on one or two bad ones.

Jeff Driskel

Height: 6-4   Weight: 234   College: Louisiana Tech   Draft: 2016/6 (207)   Born: 23-Apr-1993   Age: 26   Risk: Red

Year	Team	G/GS	Snaps	Att	Comp	C%	Yds	TD	INT/Adj	FUM	ASR	NY/P	Rk	DVOA	Rk	DYAR	Rk	YAR	Runs	Yds	TD	DVOA	DYAR	QBR
2018	CIN	9/5	372	176	105	59.7%	1003	6	2/8	4	9.4%	4.5	--	-16.4%	--	-61	--	-109	25	130	2	-2.8%	10	31.6
2019	CIN		535	326	60.9%	3325	20	15	12		5.3		-20.1%					62	291	3	9.1%		

2018: 48% Short   30% Mid   15% Deep   7% Bomb   aDOT: 8.5 (--)   YAC: 4.8 (--)   ALEX: -2.0

On eight deep balls targeting Tyler Boyd, Driskel was 5-of-8 for 114 yards, four first downs, and a touchdown. On deep balls to anyone else, he was 5-for-28 with five first downs and two interceptions. Driskel, to his credit, didn't get to play with A.J. Green, which would have helped a bit. But if you're going to be advertised as an arm-strength guy, you better be able to take advantage of that arm strength. Driskel was competent enough underneath, but the Bengals saw enough of him in 2018 to draft Ryan FInley, which isn't exactly a glowing endorsement of his future in the tiger stripes.

Ryan Finley

Height: 6-4   Weight: 210   College: North Carolina State   Draft: 2019/4 (104)   Born: 26-Dec-1994   Age: 25   Risk: Green

Year	Team	G/GS	Snaps	Att	Comp	C%	Yds	TD	INT/Adj	FUM	ASR	NY/P	Rk	DVOA	Rk	DYAR	Rk	YAR	Runs	Yds	TD	DVOA	DYAR	QBR
2019	CIN			516	311	60.3%	3251	18	17	10		5.2		-22.6%					33	50	0	-18.7%		

The Bengals traded up to the top of the fourth round for Finley, a tall signal-caller who helped North Carolina State remain undefeated well in to November. His early practices in Cincinnati had beat writers wondering why he looked so bad, so perhaps set expectations for him to not pass Jeff Driskel on the depth chart this year. However, Finley did show some advanced pocket movement at N.C. State as well the ability to throw off-platform and make some big plays. He fell to the fourth round because his intermediate arm strength is questionable and he didn't show well against the best of the best in the NCAA. If he doesn't grow from here, he could be the next Cody Kessler. If he takes some steps forward, he's a potential starter who has some similarities to another former N.C. State quarterback, Philip Rivers.

Ryan Fitzpatrick

Height: 6-2   Weight: 221   College: Harvard   Draft: 2005/7 (250)   Born: 24-Nov-1982   Age: 37   Risk: Yellow

Year	Team	G/GS	Snaps	Att	Comp	C%	Yds	TD	INT/Adj	FUM	ASR	NY/P	Rk	DVOA	Rk	DYAR	Rk	YAR	Runs	Yds	TD	DVOA	DYAR	QBR
2016	NYJ	14/11	765	403	228	56.6%	2710	12	17/20	10	4.8%	6.2	23	-22.6%	32	-319	32	-329	33	130	0	-19.5%	-11	45.4
2017	TB	6/3	299	163	96	58.9%	1103	7	3/3	0	5.2%	6.3	--	17.3%	--	307	--	315	15	78	0	17.5%	17	54.4
2018	TB	8/7	428	246	164	66.7%	2366	17	12/14	4	5.5%	8.8	1	16.8%	6	473	15	459	36	152	2	15.9%	40	63.7
2019	MIA		479	295	61.6%	3593	18	22	6		6.5		-20.2%					66	261	2	-7.2%		

2017: 50% Short   31% Mid   11% Deep   8% Bomb   aDOT: 9.5 (--)   YAC: 4.1 (--)   ALEX: 1.0   2018: 40% Short   33% Mid   17% Deep   10% Bomb   aDOT: 10.6 (3)   YAC: 5.3 (17)   ALEX: 1.9

Fitzpatrick's never-ending career provides a useful illustration of the difference between "average value" and "replacement level," particularly at quarterback.

Fitzpatrick has posted a negative DVOA in five seasons since his breakthrough year with the Bills in 2010. But he has been at least 120 yards over replacement level in every year since 2010 except for 2016, when the Jets cratered and he played hurt for part of the year. Fitzpatrick was even above replacement level in 2011, when he led the NFL in interceptions, and last year, when he led the league in interception rate by 1.1 percentage points; his high-risk, high-reward style is more effective than the typical veteran backup's game plan of checking down and playing not to lose.

So Fitzpatrick often hovers in the range between average and below average for a starting quarterback, but he is almost always better than the random backup pulled off the bench. Therefore, he has earned his late-career role as a custodian, "push" guy for a faltering prospect, and so forth.

Fitzpatrick may not be the glowing paragon of leadership he's made out to be by fawning reporters who love a quotable beardo (none of Fitzpatrick's young protégés have really developed), but if a young quarterback can't outperform Fitzpatrick, he's probably never going to establish himself as a starter. And that goes for Josh Rosen, too.

Joe Flacco

Height: 6-6 Weight: 236 College: Delaware Draft: 2008/1 (18) Born: 16-Jan-1985 Age: 34 Risk: Red

Year	Team	G/GS	Snaps	Att	Comp	C%	Yds	TD	INT/Adj	FUM	ASR	NY/P	Rk	DVOA	Rk	DYAR	Rk	YAR	Runs	Yds	TD	DVOA	DYAR	QBR
2016	BAL	16/16	1111	672	436	64.9%	4317	20	15/19	5	5.4%	5.8	28	-14.6%	29	-155	30	-44	21	58	2	15.8%	21	58.4
2017	BAL	16/16	1027	549	352	64.1%	3141	18	13/17	6	4.5%	5.2	33	-19.3%	30	-301	32	-102	25	54	1	37.0%	24	43.0
2018	BAL	9/9	641	379	232	61.2%	2465	12	6/11	3	4.3%	6.1	25	5.4%	16	429	18	329	19	45	0	2.9%	13	57.4
2019	DEN			559	355	63.6%	3712	19	13	7		5.7		-8.8%					26	63	0	-1.8%		

2017: 60% Short 27% Mid 9% Deep 5% Bomb aDOT: 7.0 (34) YAC: 4.1 (34) ALEX: 0.5   2018: 46% Short 32% Mid 14% Deep 8% Bomb aDOT: 9.5 (6) YAC: 4.4 (33) ALEX: 1.7

Thirty quarterbacks have thrown at least 1,000 passes over the past four seasons. Flacco has the lowest yards per attempt at 6.32, and ranks 29th in both passer rating and Pro Football Reference's adjusted net yards per attempt, in both cases finishing just ahead of Brock Osweiler. "Better than Osweiler" may not be the battlecry Broncos fans have been waiting for.

Flacco has more completions, attempts, passing yards, and touchdowns than any other player who has never been named to the Pro Bowl, in an era when it's easier than ever to be named to the Pro Bowl. Guys like Matt Cassel, Vince Young, and David Garrard have taken trips to Hawaii; Flacco hasn't managed to scrape up so much as an injury replacement bid. It has been a long time since we were arguing about whether or not Flacco was elite; now, the argument is about whether or not he should still be starting.

Nick Foles

Height: 6-5 Weight: 243 College: Arizona Draft: 2012/3 (88) Born: 20-Jan-1989 Age: 30 Risk: Red

Year	Team	G/GS	Snaps	Att	Comp	C%	Yds	TD	INT/Adj	FUM	ASR	NY/P	Rk	DVOA	Rk	DYAR	Rk	YAR	Runs	Yds	TD	DVOA	DYAR	QBR
2016	KC	3/1	106	55	36	65.5%	410	3	0/1	0	7.1%	6.4	--	-9.9%	--	5	--	26	4	-4	0	--	--	35.3
2017	PHI	7/3	212	101	57	56.4%	537	5	2/2	6	5.4%	4.8	--	-28.5%	--	-114	--	-63	11	3	0	-123.1%	-19	28.0
2018	PHI	5/5	357	195	141	72.3%	1413	7	4/5	4	4.4%	6.8	13	-5.4%	25	74	26	142	9	17	0	-2.7%	5	67.4
2019	JAX			554	358	64.6%	3952	21	12	10		6.2		-3.0%					32	65	0	-18.8%		

2017: 51% Short 30% Mid 14% Deep 5% Bomb aDOT: 8.7 (--) YAC: 4.2 (--) ALEX: 0.9   2018: 60% Short 24% Mid 10% Deep 6% Bomb aDOT: 7.0 (34) YAC: 5.2 (20) ALEX: -0.3

In his small sample size last year, Foles was cool under pressure. When defenses rushed five or more at Foles, he was 26-of-33 for 323 yards, two touchdowns, and 16 first downs. He took just two sacks on those plays. The (then-healthy) Falcons in Week 1 had the right idea: play Foles straight up and force him to stick the tight-window throws. Foles doesn't get enough credit for how much he has improved in the pocket, cutting his sack rate from his 2013 Pro Bowl season (8.1 percent) almost in half. The biggest question about his success is going to be how that holds up on a team that doesn't have blue-chippers entrenched all over the offensive line—although Brandon Linder and Andrew Norwell are a good start.

Blaine Gabbert

Height: 6-4 Weight: 234 College: Missouri Draft: 2011/1 (10) Born: 15-Oct-1989 Age: 30 Risk: Red

Year	Team	G/GS	Snaps	Att	Comp	C%	Yds	TD	INT/Adj	FUM	ASR	NY/P	Rk	DVOA	Rk	DYAR	Rk	YAR	Runs	Yds	TD	DVOA	DYAR	QBR
2016	SF	6/5	344	160	91	56.9%	925	5	6/8	0	5.5%	5.1	--	-25.4%	--	-158	--	-205	40	173	2	13.3%	52	60.3
2017	ARI	5/5	345	171	95	55.6%	1086	6	6/9	7	10.6%	5.1	--	-26.4%	--	-189	--	-304	22	82	0	-36.0%	-21	30.7
2018	TEN	8/3	211	101	61	60.4%	626	4	4/7	0	5.7%	5.4	--	-35.5%	--	-154	--	-102	6	0	0	39.6%	8	28.4
2019	TB			583	342	58.6%	4109	22	19	7		6.0		-18.0%					42	108	1	-11.5%		

2017: 50% Short 33% Mid 12% Deep 6% Bomb aDOT: 9.8 (--) YAC: 4.3 (--) ALEX: 0.2   2018: 55% Short 30% Mid 13% Deep 2% Bomb aDOT: 7.2 (--) YAC: 4.9 (--) ALEX: 0.5

"I love Blaine," head coach Bruce Arians said this spring just before the Buccaneers officially announced signing the former first-round pick, who played for Arians in Arizona in 2017. That brings the total number of people who love Gabbert to … two. If you count his mother. But why, Tampa Bay? Gabbert has never even produced a replacement-level season, he has one of the NFL's highest interception rates since joining the league in 2011, and he buys just enough time to … take a sack. The answer: the Buccaneers wanted a backup who didn't stand a chance of competing with Jameis Winston for the starting job. Mission accomplished.

Jimmy Garoppolo

Height: 6-2 Weight: 226 College: Eastern Illinois Draft: 2014/2 (62) Born: 11-Feb-1991 Age: 28 Risk: Red

Year	Team	G/GS	Snaps	Att	Comp	C%	Yds	TD	INT/Adj	FUM	ASR	NY/P	Rk	DVOA	Rk	DYAR	Rk	YAR	Runs	Yds	TD	DVOA	DYAR	QBR
2016	NE	6/2	144	63	43	68.3%	502	4	0/0	2	3.6%	7.3	--	44.4%	--	225	--	182	10	6	0	-4.3%	1	89.9
2017	2TM	6/5	353	178	120	67.4%	1560	7	5/8	1	3.2%	8.2	--	39.1%	--	598	--	556	15	11	1	-8.8%	2	80.5
2018	SF	3/3	197	89	53	59.6%	718	5	3/3	4	11.3%	6.1	--	-12.5%	--	-9	--	-20	8	33	0	-48.2%	-14	29.9
2019	SF			545	346	63.4%	4314	24	14	5		6.8		6.2%					46	132	1	-11.4%		

2017: 41% Short 42% Mid 14% Deep 4% Bomb aDOT: 9.2 (--) YAC: 6.0 (--) ALEX: 1.7 2018: 43% Short 39% Mid 11% Deep 7% Bomb aDOT: 9.5 (--) YAC: 6.9 (--) ALEX: -1.9

Garoppolo has averaged an outstanding 8.22 yards per pass in his career, but his completion, touchdown, and interception rates are more mundane, leaving him with an NFL passer rating of "only" 97.3. Those numbers would have ranked seventh and 14th among qualifying quarterbacks last season. As it turns out, this style of passing—routinely producing explosive plays at the relative expense of efficiency or ball security—has been a hallmark of quarterbacks who began their career as backups before developing into successful starters in recent NFL history. Tony Romo and Matt Schaub each had three seasons with at least 200 passes and 8.0 yards per attempt, but a passer rating below 100.0. Marc Bulger and Kirk Cousins have done it twice (so far). Kurt Warner, Trent Green, and Colin Kaepernick did it once each. There may be something about spending time on the sidelines that drives a quarterback to take more risks when he finally gets a chance to play, but that is a question for a psychologist, not stat analysts.

The 49ers took a cautious approach with Garoppolo this summer, limiting his participation during OTAs. He was expected to be fully cleared by training camp, but there is a small chance he could miss the first week or two of the regular season, just as Carson Wentz did last year.

When he does return, one area where Garoppolo must improve is pocket presence in the red zone. In just three starts last season, he took six sacks inside the opponents' 20. Only six other quarterbacks took that many red zone sacks all year. This may have been a fluke, however—he didn't take a single red zone sack in 2017.

Mike Glennon

Height: 6-6 Weight: 218 College: North Carolina State Draft: 2013/3 (73) Born: 12-Dec-1989 Age: 30 Risk: Red

Year	Team	G/GS	Snaps	Att	Comp	C%	Yds	TD	INT/Adj	FUM	ASR	NY/P	Rk	DVOA	Rk	DYAR	Rk	YAR	Runs	Yds	TD	DVOA	DYAR	QBR
2016	TB	2/0	15	11	10	90.9%	75	1	0/0	0	1.7%	6.8	--	65.8%	--	65	--	64	0	0	0	--	--	96.9
2017	CHI	4/4	264	140	93	66.4%	833	4	5/7	6	5.4%	5.0	--	-37.1%	--	-231	--	-151	4	4	0	-114.7%	-13	21.9
2018	ARI	2/0	26	21	15	71.4%	174	1	0/0	0	5.0%	7.5	--	45.4%	--	73	--	79	0	0	0	--	--	76.4
2019	OAK			547	349	63.9%	3584	20	15	11		5.6		-16.3%					28	26	1	-25.0%		

2017: 62% Short 29% Mid 7% Deep 2% Bomb aDOT: 6.5 (--) YAC: 3.6 (--) ALEX: -1.5 2018: 40% Short 45% Mid 10% Deep 5% Bomb aDOT: 8.9 (--) YAC: 5.6 (--) ALEX: -8.3

Glennon served last year as Arizona's third quarterback, a role that was necessary because Sam Bradford's bones are made of glass and an injury was more or less inevitable. Glennon has made the most out of a couple of below-average seasons in Tampa Bay in 2013 and 2014, earning a massive contract to be Chicago's starter for four games before his eight turnovers and -231 DYAR earned him a permanent seat on the bench. He'll be competing with Nathan Peterman for the backup role behind Derek Carr, as Jon Gruden continues to sign every player who once appeared on his Gruden's QB Camp specials on ESPN. Hey, scouting is scouting, right?

Jared Goff

Height: 6-4 Weight: 215 College: California Draft: 2016/1 (1) Born: 14-Oct-1994 Age: 25 Risk: Green

Year	Team	G/GS	Snaps	Att	Comp	C%	Yds	TD	INT/Adj	FUM	ASR	NY/P	Rk	DVOA	Rk	DYAR	Rk	YAR	Runs	Yds	TD	DVOA	DYAR	QBR
2016	LAR	7/7	393	205	112	54.6%	1089	5	7/8	5	11.1%	3.8	34	-74.8%	34	-881	34	-819	8	16	1	-22.8%	-3	22.2
2017	LAR	15/15	937	477	296	62.1%	3804	28	7/10	8	5.4%	7.4	4	24.0%	5	1125	6	1041	28	51	0	-20.6%	-6	52.0
2018	LAR	16/16	1064	561	364	64.9%	4688	32	12/18	12	5.5%	7.5	5	17.0%	5	1114	6	1110	43	108	2	-11.8%	0	66.4
2019	LAR			549	357	65.0%	4440	31	13	11		7.3		15.5%					49	154	1	0.0%		

2017: 52% Short 29% Mid 12% Deep 7% Bomb aDOT: 8.5 (21) YAC: 6.8 (1) ALEX: 0.2 2018: 45% Short 34% Mid 14% Deep 7% Bomb aDOT: 9.0 (11) YAC: 5.8 (7) ALEX: -0.3

At the helm of the impressive Rams offense, Goff was again one of the most efficient quarterbacks in the league in 2018, but if you could force him into an obvious passing situations, his effectiveness plummeted. While he finished with 24.9% passing DVOA on first downs and 17.9% passing DVOA on second downs, his DVOA on third or fourth down dropped all the way to -0.2%. This represented a stark shift from 2017, when he started off as slightly above average at 6.5% on first down before jumping all the way up to 46.7% on third and fourth downs. Whether that change is a function of teams adjusting to Sean Mc-

Vay's offensive schemes on third downs or just simple year-to-year variance remains to be seen, but it's still impressive that the Rams offense was so effective in spite of Goff's relative struggles on third and fourth down.

Will Grier			Height: 6-2		Weight: 217		College: West Virginia				Draft: 2019/3 (100)		Born: 3-Apr-1995			Age: 24		Risk: Green
Year	Team	G/GS	Snaps	Att	Comp	C%	Yds	TD	INT/Adj	FUM	ASR	NY/P	Rk	DVOA	Rk	DYAR	Rk	YAR	Runs	Yds	TD	DVOA	DYAR	QBR
2019	CAR		538	334	62.0%	3720	17	16	10		5.8		-14.3%					32	48	1	-10.1%		

The oldest quarterback to be drafted in the first two days in April, Grier only started for two-and-a-bit seasons of his five-year college career—in part due to byzantine NCAA transfer rules, in part due to a PED suspension ending his 2015 season in mid-October while at Florida. He missed the second half of that 2015 season due to the suspension, then his transfer to West Virginia rendered him ineligible to play in 2016. After returning to start 11 games in each of 2017 and 2018, he was named second-team All-Big-12 in his senior year behind only No. 1 overall pick Kyler Murray.

Partly as a result of that lack of full-season starting experience, Grier had the lowest QBASE projection of any projected Day 1 or Day 2 quarterback in our pre-draft analysis, below even eventual fourth-rounders Jarrett Stidham and Ryan Finley. We should note, however, that our projection came out very differently from a projection by FiveThirtyEight.com, based on charting data of completion percentage over expectation. Grier had a strong senior performance with a high average depth of target, so he finished second in those projections behind only Murray.

Robert Griffin			Height: 6-2		Weight: 223		College: Baylor				Draft: 2012/1 (2)		Born: 12-Feb-1990			Age: 29		Risk: Red
Year	Team	G/GS	Snaps	Att	Comp	C%	Yds	TD	INT/Adj	FUM	ASR	NY/P	Rk	DVOA	Rk	DYAR	Rk	YAR	Runs	Yds	TD	DVOA	DYAR	QBR
2016	CLE	5/5	302	147	87	59.2%	886	2	3/5	4	12.9%	4.4	--	-36.0%	--	-270	--	-331	31	190	2	17.0%	39	45.0
2018	BAL	3/0	21	6	2	33.3%	21	0	0/1	0	0.0%	3.5	--	-11.4%	--	0	--	3	0	0	0	--	--	2.2
2019	BAL		482	291	60.4%	3310	19	14	12		6.0		-19.6%					96	458	3	-4.3%		

2018: 40% Short   20% Mid   20% Deep   20% Bomb   aDOT: 10.8 (--)   YAC: 13 (--)   ALEX: 4.5

For the second time in four seasons, Griffin actually got some run. For the first time, it wasn't as a potential answer at quarterback. Griffin probably left his best attributes on a busted FedEx Field turf in January 2013, but he is a good fit for a backup quarterback in a Greg Roman offense given his speed and how he can work off of play-action. RG3 will probably continue to get more run on *Fixer Upper* than he will in the NFL. Say, have they ever tried to make an ACL out of shiplap?

Dwayne Haskins			Height: 6-3		Weight: 218		College: Ohio State				Draft: 2019/1 (15)		Born: 3-May-1997			Age: 22		Risk: Red
Year	Team	G/GS	Snaps	Att	Comp	C%	Yds	TD	INT/Adj	FUM	ASR	NY/P	Rk	DVOA	Rk	DYAR	Rk	YAR	Runs	Yds	TD	DVOA	DYAR	QBR
2019	WAS		510	314	61.7%	3491	20	17	9		5.9		-13.7%					42	84	2	-10.5%		

Haskins is an African-American quarterback, but he is not a scrambler. Repeat: Haskins is black, but not a scrambler. Let's turn that into a fun little bumper-sticker slogan: "BLACK QB" DOES NOT MEAN "SCRAMBLING QB." Feel free to save that phrase in Auto Type. That way, when your father-in-law complains on Facebook that the Redskins need to make better use of Haskins' mobility, you can just paste it on in. When the wisdom of the comment thread switches to Jay Gruden adding more options to make use of Haskins' "athleticism"—BOOM—paste that bad boy right in there and save yourself some keystrokes. Haskins threw for 4,831 yards and 50 touchdowns last season in a typically loaded Ohio State offense. He's at his best when sitting in a clean pocket and tossing underneath throws to playmakers. But then, who isn't? Haskins has a little Kirk Cousins in him (high-effort pocket guy) and a little Robert Griffin (pigment, college rep, high-maintenance dad you will surely hear more about in the months to come). The apotheosis of Washington quarterbacking will come when he somehow loses a quarterback competition to himself.

Taylor Heinicke

Height: 6-1 | Weight: 210 | College: Old Dominion | Draft: 2015/FA | Born: 15-Mar-1993 | Age: 26 | Risk: Red

Year	Team	G/GS	Snaps	Att	Comp	C%	Yds	TD	INT/Adj	FUM	ASR	NY/P	Rk	DVOA	Rk	DYAR	Rk	YAR	Runs	Yds	TD	DVOA	DYAR	QBR
2017	HOU	1/0	9	1	1	100.0%	10	0	0/0	0	50.0%	-3.0	--	-32.9%	--	-3	--	-7	1	2	0	-96.9%	-4	1.3
2018	CAR	6/1	91	57	35	61.4%	320	1	3/3	1	4.4%	5.2	--	-49.1%	--	-140	--	-112	5	31	0	-49.7%	-5	19.9
2019	CAR			559	353	63.2%	3631	18	21	11		5.7		-21.8%					53	145	1	-17.5%		

2018: 60% Short | 23% Mid | 8% Deep | 9% Bomb | aDOT: 7.5 (--) | YAC: 4.3 (--) | ALEX: 4.1

Heinicke is a 2015 undrafted free agent who, despite only one regular-season pass attempt in his first three seasons, has missed time with injuries every year since he turned pro. His first career sack resulted in a concussion while with the Texans in 2017. He spent most of last year as Cam Newton's backup and occasional Hail Mary chucker before injuring his triceps in his first career start to once again land on injured reserve.

Heinicke has worked with Norv Turner in both Carolina and Minnesota, but a three-interception day against the woeful 2018 Falcons suggests that Heinicke's main asset in Carolina is simply his knowledge of Turner's offense. He is the most experienced backup on the current roster, which might put him in good stead, but the 26-year-old also appears to be the least enticing prospect of the three Panthers backup candidates.

Chad Henne

Height: 6-2 | Weight: 230 | College: Michigan | Draft: 2008/2 (57) | Born: 2-Jul-1985 | Age: 34 | Risk: Green

Year	Team	G/GS	Snaps	Att	Comp	C%	Yds	TD	INT/Adj	FUM	ASR	NY/P	Rk	DVOA	Rk	DYAR	Rk	YAR	Runs	Yds	TD	DVOA	DYAR	QBR
2016	JAX	1/0	1	0	0	0.0%	0	0	0/0	0	--	--	--	--	--	--	--	--	1	-2	0	--	--	--
2017	JAX	2/0	23	2	0	0.0%	0	0	0/1	0	0.0%	0.0	--	-87.5%	--	-10	--	-12	5	-5	0	--	--	3.0
2018	KC	1/0	13	3	2	66.7%	29	0	0/0	0	3.9%	9.7	--	38.8%	--	11	--	17	1	3	0	-51.8%	-2	71.8
2019	KC			559	348	62.3%	3841	24	13	6		5.7		-8.6%					38	143	0	-0.7%		

2017: 100% Short | 0% Mid | 0% Deep | 0% Bomb | aDOT: 2.0 (--) | YAC: 0.0 (--) | ALEX: -7.0 | 2018: 67% Short | 33% Mid | 0% Deep | 0% Bomb | aDOT: 6.0 (--) | YAC: 7.5 (--) | ALEX: 3.0

Henne was brought in as insurance in case Patrick Mahomes ended up struggling; Mahomes did, after all, have just one professional start under his belt coming into 2018. Suffice it to say, Henne's services were not particularly necessary, though he did throw more passes last season than he did in the previous two years combined. At the best of times, Henne was a below-average starter, though that was enough for him to battle head-to-head with Blake Bortles in Jacksonville. He's professional and prepared, and you can trust him under center for a game or two without everything falling apart, but no more than that. On the other hand, he doesn't put ketchup on his mac and cheese, so maybe he secretly is Kansas City's best option at quarterback.

Taysom Hill

Height: 6-2 | Weight: 221 | College: Brigham Young | Draft: 2017/FA | Born: 23-Aug-1990 | Age: 29 | Risk: Yellow

Year	Team	G/GS	Snaps	Att	Comp	C%	Yds	TD	INT/Adj	FUM	ASR	NY/P	Rk	DVOA	Rk	DYAR	Rk	YAR	Runs	Yds	TD	DVOA	DYAR	QBR
2018	NO	16/4	181	7	3	42.9%	64	0	1/1	1	14.4%	7.6	--	-40.8%	--	-19	--	-15	37	196	2	-7.1%	12	43.5
2019	NO			6	3	50.0%	50	0	0	0		6.4		0.0%					32	159	2	0.0%		

2018: 33% Short | 17% Mid | 17% Deep | 33% Bomb | aDOT: 19.7 (--) | YAC: 6.0 (--) | ALEX: 0.0

Hill has carved out an odd niche of fame, particularly among color commentators, as the One Gadget Player to Rule Them All: though listed as a quarterback, you are more likely to see him running routes or Quarterback Power than throwing a pass. So valuable is he as a potential quarterback of the future that the Saints frequently deploy him as a punt gunner. Nobody does this with a quarterback of any promise. No, not even Sean Payton. Hill's projection is the only one in this section that isn't for 16 games started, and it includes three receptions for 15 yards to go with his carries and a handful of trick passes.

Brian Hoyer

Height: 6-2 | Weight: 215 | College: Michigan State | Draft: 2009/FA | Born: 13-Oct-1985 | Age: 34 | Risk: Yellow

Year	Team	G/GS	Snaps	Att	Comp	C%	Yds	TD	INT/Adj	FUM	ASR	NY/P	Rk	DVOA	Rk	DYAR	Rk	YAR	Runs	Yds	TD	DVOA	DYAR	QBR
2016	CHI	6/5	314	200	134	67.0%	1445	6	0/0	3	2.5%	7.1	6	19.4%	7	404	18	506	7	-2	0	-47.9%	-3	61.1
2017	2TM	11/6	381	211	123	58.3%	1287	4	4/8	3	7.7%	5.2	34	-16.7%	28	-80	27	-111	9	4	1	-96.7%	-29	31.9
2018	NE	5/0	27	2	1	50.0%	7	0	0/0	0	0.0%	3.5	--	-41.8%	--	-3	--	-5	11	-8	0	32.7%	3	0.5
2019	NE			551	357	64.8%	3699	20	11	9		5.8		-5.4%					32	42	0	-20.6%		

2017: 57% Short | 27% Mid | 11% Deep | 4% Bomb | aDOT: 8.1 (25) | YAC: 4.6 (30) | ALEX: 0.1 | 2018: 50% Short | 50% Mid | 0% Deep | 0% Bomb | aDOT: 2.0 (--) | YAC: 10.0 (--) | ALEX: -15.0

As expected, Hoyer has not taken a snap of meaningful action since returning to the Patriots after the Jimmy Garoppolo trade. By all accounts a valuable contributor on the scout team and in defensive meetings, Hoyer should also be an adequate veteran stand-in in the unfortunate event that Tom Brady misses time in 2019. That role—a quarterback whom you don't want as the primary starter but who would be OK for a game or two—appears to fit Hoyer's level perfectly. Even the selection of Jarrett Stidham (Auburn) is unlikely to affect him; the Patriots are more likely to move forward with three quarterbacks in 2019 than to cut Hoyer in favor of the fourth-round rookie.

Brett Hundley

Height: 6-3   Weight: 226   College: UCLA   Draft: 2015/5 (147)   Born: 15-Jun-1993   Age: 26   Risk: Red

Year	Team	G/GS	Snaps	Att	Comp	C%	Yds	TD	INT/Adj	FUM	ASR	NY/P	Rk	DVOA	Rk	DYAR	Rk	YAR	Runs	Yds	TD	DVOA	DYAR	QBR
2016	GB	4/0	22	10	2	20.0%	17	0	1/0	1	0.0%	1.7	--	-109.2%	--	-80	--	-75	3	-2	0	--	--	6.3
2017	GB	11/9	622	316	192	60.8%	1836	9	12/12	4	9.1%	4.8	35	-28.3%	34	-396	34	-517	36	270	2	40.3%	100	41.2
2019	ARI			520	307	58.9%	3431	19	21	10		5.6		-30.7%					69	283	3	-4.0%		

2017:   61% Short   23% Mid   9% Deep   7% Bomb   aDOT: 8.1 (23)   YAC: 5.3 (17)   ALEX: 2.0

Hundley was the backup in Green Bay before the Packers decided they preferred DeShone Kizer, then he was the backup in Seattle before the Seahawks decided they preferred Paxton Lynch and Geno Smith. Now he's the backup in Arizona, but history says he won't last there. Hundley has shined in the preseason (career numbers: 185 passes, 11 touchdowns, three interceptions, 102.1 passer rating), so there's definitely some talent here. But he has never been able to replicate those results in the regular season, and he's running out of chances.

Lamar Jackson

Height: 6-2   Weight: 216   College: Louisville   Draft: 2018/1 (32)   Born: 17-Jan-1997   Age: 22   Risk: Red

Year	Team	G/GS	Snaps	Att	Comp	C%	Yds	TD	INT/Adj	FUM	ASR	NY/P	Rk	DVOA	Rk	DYAR	Rk	YAR	Runs	Yds	TD	DVOA	DYAR	QBR
2018	BAL	16/7	585	170	99	58.2%	1201	6	3/6	12	10.2%	6.0	--	-9.2%	--	24	--	69	147	695	5	-27.2%	-112	45.2
2019	BAL			439	271	61.7%	3084	17	10	13		6.2		-8.3%					155	847	6	-1.2%		

2018:   35% Short   49% Mid   10% Deep   5% Bomb   aDOT: 9.1 (--)   YAC: 5.2 (--)   ALEX: 0.2

From 2010 to 2019, 117 quarterbacks ran 10 or more times in a game. That number includes every one of Lamar Jackson's starts. The list of players who have ran that many times in five games in one season since 2010: Michael Vick, Cam Newton, Tim Tebow, Robert Griffin, and Jackson. Nobody can maintain that much quarterback rushing and keep the quarterback healthy, but the guess here is that Jackson continues to be allowed to showcase his wheels at a historical rate. His next step as a quarterback is to work on his accuacy to the boundary. On 46 targets to players lined up on the outside, Jackson averaged 4.1 yards per attempt and picked up only 10 first downs and one touchdown. None of those completions came on the nine outside attempts that were deep balls. Teams are going to line up and force Jackson to prove that he can hit those throws early in the season. It's not dramatic to suggest that how Jackson performs on those throws could determine the direction of Baltimore's offense.

Josh Johnson

Height: 6-3   Weight: 213   College: San Diego   Draft: 2008/5 (160)   Born: 15-May-1986   Age: 33   Risk: N/A

Year	Team	G/GS	Snaps	Att	Comp	C%	Yds	TD	INT/Adj	FUM	ASR	NY/P	Rk	DVOA	Rk	DYAR	Rk	YAR	Runs	Yds	TD	DVOA	DYAR	QBR
2018	WAS	4/3	204	91	52	57.1%	590	3	4/6	2	9.4%	5.2	--	-25.8%	--	-87	--	-110	23	120	1	12.1%	27	50.1

2018:   52% Short   24% Mid   17% Deep   7% Bomb   aDOT: 9.5 (--)   YAC: 5.8 (--)   ALEX: 1.6

Johnson had stints on ten different NFL rosters, plus the Sacramento Mountain Lions of the long-forgotten UFL and the San Diego Fleet of the soon-to-be-forgotten AAF, between the end of his three-year run as the Buccaneers backup quarterback in 2011 and the moment Washington called upon him to be their desperation quarterback last December. Johnson scrambled his way to a 16-13 win over the Jaguars before it became obvious that he only knew a fraction of the playbook, the team around him was crumbling, and he's not that good. Johnson then needed postseason ankle surgery, preventing him from playing in the AAF. He may well surface on an XFL roster unless some other team decides it needs a scrambler to get through an emergency and decides to select an obviously inferior one for political reasons.

Daniel Jones

| | | Height: 6-5 | | Weight: 220 | | College: Duke | | | Draft: 2019/1 (6) | | | Born: 27-May-1997 | | Age: 22 | | Risk: Yellow |

Year	Team	G/GS	Snaps	Att	Comp	C%	Yds	TD	INT/Adj	FUM	ASR	NY/P	Rk	DVOA	Rk	DYAR	Rk	YAR	Runs	Yds	TD	DVOA	DYAR	QBR
2019	NYG		538	320	59.4%	3684	20	17	8		6.1		-10.8%					68	227	2	2.2%		

OK, we're going to pretend that everything goes right for Daniel Jones. Let's try this thought experiment, since people say we're too negative. Let's pretend he gets more accurate. Let's pretend he gets a little faster with his progressions. Let's pretend he develops enough of an arm to occasionally target the deep sidelines. We're already projecting a lot of improvement here. Let's say he becomes a 63 percent passer, gets his yards per attempt up in the range of seven, and still makes a bit too bold of a read from time to time and averages 10 or 12 picks a season. He's not an out-of-structure creator, scrambles a bit but isn't particularly dangerous, and takes a few more sacks than the average quarterback because of his slow release. Do you know who we just invented? It's Ryan Tannehill. The Giants have hemmed and hawwed publicly about who deserves the chance to start at quarterback. It feels unlikely that Jones will earn the job so much as claim it by default, whenever it happens.

Case Keenum

| | | Height: 6-2 | | Weight: 209 | | College: Houston | | | Draft: 2012/FA | | | Born: 17-Feb-1988 | | Age: 31 | | Risk: Yellow |

Year	Team	G/GS	Snaps	Att	Comp	C%	Yds	TD	INT/Adj	FUM	ASR	NY/P	Rk	DVOA	Rk	DYAR	Rk	YAR	Runs	Yds	TD	DVOA	DYAR	QBR
2016	LAR	10/9	596	322	196	60.9%	2201	9	11/10	5	6.3%	6.0	26	-19.5%	31	-183	31	-174	20	51	1	22.2%	25	43.4
2017	MIN	15/14	1017	481	325	67.6%	3547	22	7/10	1	4.0%	7.1	8	28.1%	1	1293	4	1307	40	160	1	58.3%	76	69.7
2018	DEN	16/16	1073	586	365	62.3%	3890	18	15/17	11	6.3%	5.9	29	-12.7%	28	-63	29	-41	26	93	2	31.2%	40	46.9
2019	WAS		502	323	64.3%	3384	21	12	6		5.8		-7.8%					39	97	0	-18.1%		

| 2017: | 57% Short | 25% Mid | 13% Deep | 6% Bomb | aDOT: 8.0 (26) | YAC: 5.6 (11) | ALEX: 0.4 | 2018: | 55% Short | 28% Mid | 10% Deep | 7% Bomb | aDOT: 7.8 (23) | YAC: 4.9 (27) | ALEX: 0.1 |

Keenum threw just 61 passes when his Broncos held the lead in games last year, 384 while trailing. In his breakout 2017 season, he threw 215 passes when the Vikings were leading and 171 while trailing. Across the NFL in 2019, completion rates were 1.7 percentage points higher when a team was leading than trailing. Teams averaged 7.6 yards per pass attempt when leading and 7.3 when trailing. Interception rates rose from 2.0 to 2.5 percent when a team was trailing, sack rates increased slightly, touchdown rates decreased slightly. Quarterbacks throw about 64 percent more passes when trailing than when leading, so Keenum's 2017 season found him in good situations an extremely disproportionate percentage of the time; his 2018 season was at the opposite end of the spectrum. Accounting for the heavy statistical undertow caused by score differentials alone, Keenum's steep decline in 2018 was not surprising at all, and expecting any substantial rebound with Washington, a team unlikely to help any of its quarterbacks build and sustain leads, is foolish. Someday, teams evaluating a quarterback with suspiciously good stats (a 30-year-old career backup suddenly playing at a Pro Bowl level, for instance) will apply the simple litmus test of adjusting for game situations before making any trade/contract decisions. Those teams will avoid a lot of costly mistakes and wasted seasons. Until then, guys like Keenum will be able to turn hot streaks with great teams into future starting opportunities and eight-figure windfalls.

Cody Kessler

| | | Height: 6-1 | | Weight: 220 | | College: USC | | | Draft: 2016/3 (93) | | | Born: 11-May-1993 | | Age: 26 | | Risk: Red |

Year	Team	G/GS	Snaps	Att	Comp	C%	Yds	TD	INT/Adj	FUM	ASR	NY/P	Rk	DVOA	Rk	DYAR	Rk	YAR	Runs	Yds	TD	DVOA	DYAR	QBR
2016	CLE	9/8	349	195	128	65.6%	1380	6	2/3	4	9.7%	5.8	29	-7.6%	22	50	24	80	11	18	0	-37.1%	-9	49.6
2017	CLE	3/0	48	23	11	47.8%	126	0	1/1	0	18.9%	2.7	--	-66.4%	--	-98	--	-73	1	-1	0	--	--	5.1
2018	JAX	5/4	263	131	85	64.9%	709	2	2/2	5	14.5%	3.6	--	-59.7%	--	-458	--	-393	19	123	0	7.5%	20	27.4
2019	PHI		568	371	65.4%	3928	19	11	11		5.9		-4.1%					57	227	1	-8.8%		

| 2017: | 67% Short | 8% Mid | 8% Deep | 17% Bomb | aDOT: 10.7 (--) | YAC: 6.4 (--) | ALEX: -1.1 | 2018: | 51% Short | 37% Mid | 8% Deep | 5% Bomb | aDOT: 6.8 (--) | YAC: 4.1 (--) | ALEX: 0.0 |

Kessler's arm strength, or lack thereof, was what separated him from the real quarterback prospects in the 2015 NFL draft. It's what has kept him on the move despite the mobility and ability to run an NFL offense he has shown in his small sample sizes. Last year for the Jaguars, Kessler attempted 18 deep balls and completed a grand total of four of them. Even those completed deep balls can be seen as a bit of a gift as they came in garbage time against the Titans and were targeting the toasty Malcolm Butler. The Jaguars saw enough and decided he wasn't the heir to Blake Bortles. The Eagles decided to just make this a straight-up backup quarterback swap by signing Kessler to replace Nick Foles. There's no bigger sign that the Eagles are all-in on Carson Wentz than the endorsement of entering the year with Kessler as the main backup.

DeShone Kizer Height: 6-4 Weight: 233 College: Notre Dame Draft: 2017/2 (52) Born: 3-Jan-1996 Age: 23 Risk: Green

Year	Team	G/GS	Snaps	Att	Comp	C%	Yds	TD	INT/Adj	FUM	ASR	NY/P	Rk	DVOA	Rk	DYAR	Rk	YAR	Runs	Yds	TD	DVOA	DYAR	QBR
2017	CLE	15/15	887	476	255	53.6%	2894	11	22/23	9	6.7%	5.4	31	-34.5%	35	-756	35	-889	77	419	5	-3.7%	32	29.4
2018	GB	3/0	62	42	20	47.6%	187	0	2/3	1	7.4%	3.4	--	-102.7%	--	-262	--	-234	5	39	0	134.4%	23	28.2
2019	GB			548	322	58.8%	3678	19	17	12		5.9		-20.2%					82	403	4	12.6%		

2017:	56% Short	22% Mid	14% Deep	8% Bomb	aDOT: 9.5 (9)	YAC: 5.5 (14)	ALEX: 1.2	2018:	44% Short	31% Mid	13% Deep	13% Bomb	aDOT: 10.5 (--)	YAC: 3.2 (--)	ALEX: 4.1

Nurturing young quarterbacks with stable coaching and a proper offensive mind leading the charge is a necessity in the modern NFL. Kizer, a second-round pick just two years ago, did not get those benefits early on. Kizer was initially thrust into the Browns' starting job in 2017, struggling to find consistent success under Hue Jackson's tutelage and with a poor receiving group by his side. He only impressed in flashes, often with deep passes, but his poor pocket awareness, up-and-down accuracy, and overaggressive tendencies were never ironed out. After being moved to Green Bay in exchange for safety Damarious Randall, Kizer struggled in relief duty for Aaron Rodgers in Weeks 1 and 17. The Packers did not make any notable moves at quarterback this offseason, so it appears they believe in Kizer enough to give him another go as the backup, but the hope that the light will ever turn on for him is dwindling.

Drew Lock Height: 6-4 Weight: 230 College: Missouri Draft: 2019/2 (42) Born: 10-Nov-1996 Age: 23 Risk: Yellow

Year	Team	G/GS	Snaps	Att	Comp	C%	Yds	TD	INT/Adj	FUM	ASR	NY/P	Rk	DVOA	Rk	DYAR	Rk	YAR	Runs	Yds	TD	DVOA	DYAR	QBR
2019	DEN			536	329	61.5%	3587	19	17	10		5.5		-18.5%					32	98	1	0.3%		

There's plenty in Lock's film at Missouri for Broncos fans to get excited about. According to Derrik Klassen's charting, Lock was the most accurate of any of this year's draft class when pressured, at 60.8 percent. He was also the third-most accurate when forced outside the pocket, just trailing the Haskins/Murray consensus top two, so he can handle pressure and still perform at a high level. He also had the second-highest accuracy on deep shots in this deep class. Grace under pressure and a strong, accurate arm are two of the most important attributes a passer can have, so Lock's ceiling is quite high, even if he didn't manage to put everything together in college. If there's one thing he needs to work on, it's his poise in the red zone: he completed just 46.3 percent of his passes inside the 20, the worst in the class by a significant margin.

Andrew Luck Height: 6-4 Weight: 234 College: Stanford Draft: 2012/1 (1) Born: 12-Mar-1989 Age: 30 Risk: Green

Year	Team	G/GS	Snaps	Att	Comp	C%	Yds	TD	INT/Adj	FUM	ASR	NY/P	Rk	DVOA	Rk	DYAR	Rk	YAR	Runs	Yds	TD	DVOA	DYAR	QBR
2016	IND	15/15	1013	545	346	63.5%	4240	31	13/13	6	7.6%	6.8	10	7.3%	13	719	11	671	64	341	2	26.2%	93	71.2
2018	IND	16/16	1120	639	430	67.3%	4593	39	15/17	6	4.1%	6.8	12	13.3%	9	1070	7	1152	46	148	0	25.3%	51	71.7
2019	IND			600	400	66.6%	4455	35	12	7		6.8		18.4%					44	177	1	7.6%		

	2018:	52% Short	31% Mid	12% Deep	5% Bomb	aDOT: 7.7 (25)	YAC: 4.6 (30)	ALEX: 0.1

A shoulder injury cost Andrew Luck the 2017 season and now a calf injury has cost him the 2019 offseason. Nobody is worried, though, as Luck announced he could play if it were the regular season, and in between he had perhaps the best season of his career. The rebuilt offensive line and a new scheme under Frank Reich led to the lowest sack rate of his career. He still throws a fine deep ball, as only Drew Brees and Russell Wilson had a higher success rate on bombs than he did, but he ran an offense built more around slants, screens, curls, and outs than the deep cross, fly, and post. Upgrades at receiver beyond T.Y. Hilton, an offseason priority, and a second year under Frank Reich will be the key to improving his efficiency numbers. Of his interceptions, three were caused by receiver drops, a total matched only by Blake Bortles, while he had the only interception SIS charting marked on a throw away all season.

Paxton Lynch Height: 6-7 Weight: 244 College: Memphis Draft: 2016/1 (26) Born: 12-Feb-1994 Age: 25 Risk: Red

Year	Team	G/GS	Snaps	Att	Comp	C%	Yds	TD	INT/Adj	FUM	ASR	NY/P	Rk	DVOA	Rk	DYAR	Rk	YAR	Runs	Yds	TD	DVOA	DYAR	QBR
2016	DEN	3/2	176	83	49	59.0%	497	2	1/2	2	10.2%	5.0	--	-18.8%	--	-46	--	-57	11	25	0	-43.0%	-12	28.8
2017	DEN	2/2	98	45	30	66.7%	295	2	3/4	2	17.9%	4.5	--	-76.3%	--	-224	--	-191	5	30	0	16.5%	5	22.9
2019	SEA			448	277	61.9%	3144	17	12	8		5.6		-18.7%					48	200	2	9.4%		

2017:	53% Short	30% Mid	14% Deep	4% Bomb	aDOT: 8.5 (--)	YAC: 4.0 (--)	ALEX: 2.9

Lynch was drafted in the first round in 2016 but never made an impact in Denver, failing to beat out Trevor Siemian or Brock Osweiler for the starting job there. He was cut just before the start of last season and remained unsigned throughout the year. He now finds himself in a competition with Geno Smith for the backup job with the Seahawks, who were coincidentally the original owners of the pick used to draft Lynch in the first place. If Lynch sees any regular-season action outside of garbage time, something will have gone horribly wrong.

Patrick Mahomes

Height: 6-2   Weight: 225   College: Texas Tech   Draft: 2017/1 (10)   Born: 17-Sep-1995   Age: 24   Risk: Green

Year	Team	G/GS	Snaps	Att	Comp	C%	Yds	TD	INT/Adj	FUM	ASR	NY/P	Rk	DVOA	Rk	DYAR	Rk	YAR	Runs	Yds	TD	DVOA	DYAR	QBR
2017	KC	1/1	63	35	22	62.9%	284	0	1/1	0	5.8%	7.3	--	11.7%	--	54	--	57	7	10	0	9.2%	4	64.8
2018	KC	16/16	1032	580	383	66.0%	5097	50	12/21	9	5.4%	8.1	2	39.9%	1	2031	1	1904	60	272	2	3.0%	39	81.6
2019	KC			576	379	65.8%	4748	38	15	12		7.6		18.0%					59	263	2	10.8%		

2017:   61% Short   24% Mid   8% Deep   8% Bomb   aDOT: 7.7 (--)   YAC: 7.9 (--)   ALEX: -0.6   2018:   47% Short   31% Mid   13% Deep   10% Bomb   aDOT: 9.3 (9)   YAC: 6.8 (2)   ALEX: 4.5

Nine players in history have had over 2,000 DYAR in a season. Three are named Tom Brady, three are named Peyton Manning, two more are Drew Brees and Aaron Rodgers, and now there's Mahomes. The other eight were all in the primes of their careers, at least 28 when having their monster seasons, but Mahomes? Mahomes is just getting started.

Is it too early to put Mahomes in the conversation for greatest quarterback of all time? Of course it is, but a season like his 2018 means we're going to spit out the stats anyway. According to Pro Football Reference, Mahomes' "Adjusted Net Yards Per Attempt Index" (in other words, normalized so 100 is an average season in any given offensive environment) is 134. That is the highest total for any quarterback with at least four career starts, beating out Steve Young's 123. Going down that list and increasing the number of starts needed to qualify is a pretty good way to find the best quarterbacks of all time—you go from Mahomes to Young to Joe Montana to Manning to Brady to Brett Favre. In fact, it's hard to find any stat which doesn't put Mahomes in that kind of company—that's what happens when your one season as a starter is an MVP year. Even the best quarterbacks of all time could only put up a tiny handful of games in this stratosphere, so there's no way Mahomes can keep this up ... right?

Eli Manning

Height: 6-4   Weight: 218   College: Mississippi   Draft: 2004/1 (1)   Born: 3-Jan-1981   Age: 38   Risk: Red

Year	Team	G/GS	Snaps	Att	Comp	C%	Yds	TD	INT/Adj	FUM	ASR	NY/P	Rk	DVOA	Rk	DYAR	Rk	YAR	Runs	Yds	TD	DVOA	DYAR	QBR
2016	NYG	16/16	1061	598	377	63.0%	4027	26	16/26	7	3.8%	6.3	20	-6.5%	20	188	20	192	21	-9	0	-12.5%	0	51.8
2017	NYG	15/15	1018	571	352	61.6%	3468	19	13/17	11	5.6%	5.5	28	-8.2%	23	117	23	-1	12	26	1	-15.1%	-1	43.8
2018	NYG	16/16	1010	576	380	66.0%	4299	21	11/15	7	7.5%	6.3	19	-2.5%	24	337	22	339	15	20	1	-7.4%	4	51.8
2019	NYG			574	376	65.5%	4082	22	13	9		6.2		-5.4%					17	31	0	-10.3%		

2017:   55% Short   32% Mid   7% Deep   6% Bomb   aDOT: 7.4 (32)   YAC: 4.6 (27)   ALEX: 1.9   2018:   55% Short   25% Mid   12% Deep   7% Bomb   aDOT: 7.8 (24)   YAC: 5.7 (9)   ALEX: -0.5

Manning threw 62 curl or comeback routes in 2018 and completed 47 of them for 454 yards. He threw 39 slant routes and completed 28 of them for 339 yards. He completed 40 of 45 screens for 315 yards. In that sense, Pat Shurmur's scheme is doing a lot of heavy lifting for Manning's deficiencies. Manning doesn't have the arm strength to live downfield, nor the timing to live in the middle of the field if it's not a quick-hitter. He was 5-of-15 with two picks on corner routes, and the only pick he threw all season that didn't have much to do with his arm strength was Week 1's pick-six on an angle route. Worse yet, Manning's 7.5 percent sack rate was the highest of his career. New York's move for Kevin Zeitler increases the chances that Manning's 38-year-old body will survive the season, but with Odell Beckham gone, Shurmur is trying to make Manning play like 2017 Case Keenum without Stefon Diggs or Adam Thielen.

Sean Mannion

Height: 6-6   Weight: 229   College: Oregon State   Draft: 2015/3 (89)   Born: 25-Apr-1992   Age: 27   Risk: Green

Year	Team	G/GS	Snaps	Att	Comp	C%	Yds	TD	INT/Adj	FUM	ASR	NY/P	Rk	DVOA	Rk	DYAR	Rk	YAR	Runs	Yds	TD	DVOA	DYAR	QBR
2016	LAR	1/0	16	6	3	50.0%	19	0	1/1	1	0.0%	3.2	--	-108.8%	--	-45	--	-53	1	-1	0	-373.2%	-20	0.4
2017	LAR	5/1	102	37	22	59.5%	185	0	0/0	2	8.3%	4.1	--	-66.6%	--	-141	--	-97	9	-2	0	-33.0%	-6	14.4
2018	LAR	3/0	36	3	2	66.7%	23	0	0/0	0	0.0%	7.7	--	66.0%	--	10	--	14	7	-9	0	40.8%	4	6.4
2019	MIN			500	298	59.6%	3287	17	18	10		5.3		-22.5%					22	44	0	-12.6%		

2017:   70% Short   13% Mid   13% Deep   5% Bomb   aDOT: 7.0 (--)   YAC: 3.3 (--)   ALEX: -3.3   2018:   100% Short   0% Mid   0% Deep   0% Bomb   aDOT: -3.3 (--)   YAC: 13.5 (--)   ALEX: -14.5

As far as "looking the part" goes, Mannion has it all. He is 6-foot-6 and has an arm that can hit any throw on the field. "Looking the part" is where his list of traits of a good quarterback end, though. Mannion is not mobile by any stretch of the imagination and the speed at which he processes the field makes it seem as though he starts each play a half-second behind pace. Granted, that has been enough for Mannion to show out in the preseason at different points. During the 2016 and 2017 preseasons, Mannion threw six touchdowns with just one pick. Still, in four NFL seasons, Mannion has just one start: a meaningless 2017 Week 17 game versus the 49ers where he threw for 169 yards, no touchdowns, and no interceptions on 34 attempts. Mannion is the type of quarterback who will be around five years from now and you will wonder how—or why—considering how little he has ever been asked to play.

Marcus Mariota   Height: 6-4   Weight: 222   College: Oregon   Draft: 2015/1 (2)   Born: 30-Oct-1993   Age: 26   Risk: Red

Year	Team	G/GS	Snaps	Att	Comp	C%	Yds	TD	INT/Adj	FUM	ASR	NY/P	Rk	DVOA	Rk	DYAR	Rk	YAR	Runs	Yds	TD	DVOA	DYAR	QBR
2016	TEN	15/15	963	451	276	61.2%	3426	26	9/11	8	5.4%	7.0	9	11.1%	10	681	13	719	60	349	2	9.5%	52	64.9
2017	TEN	15/15	945	453	281	62.0%	3232	13	15/17	2	5.3%	6.4	17	-3.3%	20	236	19	262	60	312	5	35.6%	114	54.9
2018	TEN	14/13	775	331	228	68.9%	2528	11	8/10	9	11.6%	6.1	24	-8.5%	27	65	27	18	64	357	2	15.1%	86	55.5
2019	TEN			474	315	66.5%	3617	19	12	6		6.6		0.6%					64	357	1	14.6%		

2017:	47% Short	32% Mid	16% Deep	5% Bomb	aDOT: 9.3 (10)	YAC: 4.5 (31)	ALEX: 2.3	2018:	52% Short	30% Mid	12% Deep	7% Bomb	aDOT: 8.1 (21)	YAC: 5.6 (12)	ALEX: 1.6

Four seasons into his NFL career and Marcus Mariota has yet to play 16 games, drawing a round of criticism after missing even Week 17's winner-take-wild-card finale. The culprit that game was a nerve injury on his throwing arm suffered in the season opener that may or may not have affected him for all, much, or some of the season. He remains a riddle, wrapped in a mystery, inside an enigma, a variably average player who fluctuates between superior moments and standing there looking confused until he gets sacked over and over, 11 times against Baltimore alone. For the second consecutive season, he was better under center than from the shotgun, the opposite of his early-career split. He was mediocre in the red zone, where his structured processing and lack of aggressiveness as a thrower may be most prominent. He was no better on third downs than on early downs, but was not too bad in third-and-long (12.3% DVOA). Naturally Derrick Henry's emergence in the second half of the season led to a change in his play—he improved on early downs and declined on third down by about the same amount (-22.3% to 5.6% DVOA on first and second downs, 5.0% to -22.2% DVOA on third downs). Heading into the option year of his rookie contract, unless he is available for every game in 2019 and consistently better, we expect some other team to try to solve the riddle in 2020.

Baker Mayfield   Height: 6-1   Weight: 215   College: Oklahoma   Draft: 2018/1 (1)   Born: 14-Apr-1995   Age: 24   Risk: Green

Year	Team	G/GS	Snaps	Att	Comp	C%	Yds	TD	INT/Adj	FUM	ASR	NY/P	Rk	DVOA	Rk	DYAR	Rk	YAR	Runs	Yds	TD	DVOA	DYAR	QBR
2018	CLE	14/13	906	486	310	63.8%	3725	27	14/14	7	5.5%	7.0	11	8.1%	14	628	12	610	39	131	0	-28.6%	-20	53.9
2019	CLE			566	366	64.5%	4509	33	13	10		7.3		13.8%					46	155	1	-2.6%		

					2018:	44% Short	29% Mid	19% Deep	9% Bomb	aDOT: 9.7 (4)	YAC: 5.5 (14)	ALEX: 1.8

Mayfield was the fourth-highest ranked collegiate quarterback by QBASE—not last year, but ever (only Philip Rivers, Carson Palmer, and Donovan McNabb were higher). In that context, his stellar rookie season wasn't particularly surprising. Baker may seem like an old-school, shoot-from-the-hip kinda player, but he has been an analytical favorite for a while now.

Mayfield's gunner's rep certainly didn't extend to his most notable split, his red zone efficiency. His 42.2% DVOA on 60 snaps inside the 20 was only bettered by Andy Dalton (57.5% on 50 snaps) and Patrick Mahomes (46.1% on an insane 113 snaps). Baker's pinpoint accuracy becomes even more critical when the field shortens, so that is not especially surprising, except for the unusual poise Mayfield displayed, a trait that extended to all areas of the field.

Our projection has Baker in rarefied quarterback air, especially in Fantasyland, so grab him early. If nothing else, he will be fun to have on your team.

AJ McCarron

Height: 6-3   Weight: 220   College: Alabama   Draft: 2014/5 (164)   Born: 13-Sep-1990   Age: 29   Risk: Red

Year	Team	G/GS	Snaps	Att	Comp	C%	Yds	TD	INT/Adj	FUM	ASR	NY/P	Rk	DVOA	Rk	DYAR	Rk	YAR	Runs	Yds	TD	DVOA	DYAR	QBR
2016	CIN	1/0	2	0	0	0.0%	0	0	0/0	0	--	--	--	--	--	--	--	--	0	0	0	--	--	--
2017	CIN	3/0	26	14	7	50.0%	66	0	0/0	0	5.5%	3.8	--	-11.1%	--	0	--	-11	0	0	0	--	--	21.3
2018	OAK	2/0	12	3	1	33.3%	8	0	0/0	1	24.6%	0.3	--	-157.0%	--	-30	--	-26	3	-2	0	-118.4%	-12	0.4
2019	HOU			512	315	61.6%	3636	22	19	7		6.0		-18.0%					48	139	1	-14.9%		

2017:	57% Short	29% Mid	7% Deep	7% Bomb	aDOT: 7.6 (--)	YAC: 8.1 (--)	ALEX: -6.8	2018:	0% Short	100% Mid	0% Deep	0% Bomb	aDOT: 7.0 (--)	YAC: 1.0 (--)	ALEX: 0.0

Adding AJ McCarron to your roster is like picking the nicest GoFundMe color scheme you can find. Like health insurance, there is no compromise in the backup quarterback world. You either have a good one, or you don't. McCarron has no deep ball and little pocket presence, and last year both the Bills and Raiders decided that the two-year, $10-million contract Buffalo gave him in the 2018 offseason was stupid. Pairing Deshaun Watson with this Texans offensive line is foolish; pairing McCarron (who had 12 sacks in 131 dropbacks behind the Whitworth-Zeitler Bengals line) behind the 2019 Texans line is just mean.

Josh McCown

Height: 6-4   Weight: 215   College: Sam Houston State   Draft: 2002/3 (81)   Born: 4-Jul-1979   Age: 40   Risk: N/A

Year	Team	G/GS	Snaps	Att	Comp	C%	Yds	TD	INT/Adj	FUM	ASR	NY/P	Rk	DVOA	Rk	DYAR	Rk	YAR	Runs	Yds	TD	DVOA	DYAR	QBR
2016	CLE	5/3	262	165	90	54.5%	1100	6	6/10	7	10.5%	5.3	--	-34.4%	--	-269	--	-276	7	21	0	-37.8%	-6	35.1
2017	NYJ	13/13	819	397	267	67.3%	2926	18	9/14	11	9.4%	6.2	19	-8.9%	25	62	25	133	37	124	5	24.3%	50	51.9
2018	NYJ	4/3	191	110	60	54.5%	539	1	4/4	0	7.1%	4.3	--	-36.5%	--	-184	--	-223	5	32	0	14.2%	6	35.2

2017:	57% Short	29% Mid	8% Deep	6% Bomb	aDOT: 7.9 (29)	YAC: 4.7 (24)	ALEX: 0.0	2018:	54% Short	28% Mid	8% Deep	10% Bomb	aDOT: 8.0 (--)	YAC: 5.1 (--)	ALEX: 5.3

McCown turned 40 on the Fourth of July and is coming off a year in which he looked like a broken-down journeyman barely capable of even routine passes. He turned a two-month hot streak in 2013 into lucrative gigs with three teams, amassing a 7-31 record as a starter for bad teams with cap space to burn during that stretch. With a weaker quarterback, those teams might have gone 6-32 or something! McCown's a swell dude and everybody's looking forward to having him at the ESPN studios now that he's retired.

Colt McCoy

Height: 6-1   Weight: 216   College: Texas   Draft: 2010/3 (85)   Born: 5-Sep-1986   Age: 33   Risk: Red

Year	Team	G/GS	Snaps	Att	Comp	C%	Yds	TD	INT/Adj	FUM	ASR	NY/P	Rk	DVOA	Rk	DYAR	Rk	YAR	Runs	Yds	TD	DVOA	DYAR	QBR
2017	WAS	1/0	4	0	0	0.0%	0	0	0/0	0	--	--	--	--	--	--	--	--	0	0	0	--	--	--
2018	WAS	3/2	100	54	34	63.0%	372	3	3/4	1	10.9%	5.8	--	-40.8%	--	-119	--	-114	10	63	0	48.3%	30	41.5
2019	WAS			485	305	63.0%	3297	21	16	9		5.8		-17.5%					59	226	1	-9.2%		

								2018:	37% Short	39% Mid	16% Deep	8% Bomb	aDOT: 9.7 (--)	YAC: 4.4 (--)	ALEX: 3.7

McCoy played poorly in a relief appearance and a start before breaking his leg early in the Week 13 loss to the Eagles. McCoy opted for minor surgery as the Skins tried to rush him back before the end of the season; he suffered a setback as a result, which required additional surgery in the early offseason. Jay Gruden irrationally loves McCoy, and the Skins were touting a McCoy-Case Keenum quarterback competition before the injury news and Dwayne Haskins' arrival. But if McCoy is under center, several things have gone very wrong in Washington, and something else will go wrong the moment McCoy absorbs another hit.

Gardner Minshew

Height: 6-1   Weight: 220   College: Washington State   Draft: 2019/6 (178)   Born: 16-May-1996   Age: 23   Risk: Green

Year	Team	G/GS	Snaps	Att	Comp	C%	Yds	TD	INT/Adj	FUM	ASR	NY/P	Rk	DVOA	Rk	DYAR	Rk	YAR	Runs	Yds	TD	DVOA	DYAR	QBR
2019	JAX			509	325	63.9%	3191	13	15	9		5.2		-18.2%					42	131	1	-3.5%		

Headband. Mullet. Mustache. Minshew will have fans sold on his aesthetics in Jacksonville with ease. How good of a quarterback is he? Well, the statistics don't mean much in Mike Leach's Air Raid offense. Minshew was one of the pre-eminent checkdown artists in college football in 2018, rarely threatening the deep field. He's careful with the football—aside from fumbles—and could grow up to be Cody Kessler in an '80s Wrestling package. To get there entirely, he'll have to do a better job under pressure—Derrik Klassen's quarterback charting had him as the second-least accurate quarterback in this class under pressure, and the least accurate outside of the pocket.

Nick Mullens | Height: 6-1 | Weight: 210 | College: Southern Mississippi | Draft: 2017/FA | Born: 21-Mar-1995 | Age: 24 | Risk: Yellow

Year	Team	G/GS	Snaps	Att	Comp	C%	Yds	TD	INT/Adj	FUM	ASR	NY/P	Rk	DVOA	Rk	DYAR	Rk	YAR	Runs	Yds	TD	DVOA	DYAR	QBR
2018	SF	8/8	519	274	176	64.2%	2277	13	10/12	2	6.3%	7.5	6	4.2%	18	286	24	232	18	-16	0	-118.6%	-43	54.9
2019	SF			546	337	61.7%	4259	24	19	7		6.7		-3.6%					32	51	1	-23.2%		

2018: 47% Short 38% Mid 13% Deep 2% Bomb aDOT: 7.4 (31) YAC: 7.0 (1) ALEX: 0.1

Mullens broke many of Brett Favre's passing records at Southern Mississippi before going undrafted in 2017. After a year and a half on San Francisco's practice squad, he got a chance to start on Thursday night against Oakland in Week 9. The 49ers didn't even announce a starter until that day, and had that game been on Sunday, C.J. Beathard's wrist might have recovered and Mullens might have never played last year. Regardless, Mullens shredded the Raiders, going 16-of-22 for 262 yards with three touchdowns and no interceptions, and started every game for San Francisco from that point forward.

You may have read this offseason, perhaps even from an FO alumnus (Hi Cian!), that Mullens deserved to keep his starting job over Jimmy Garoppolo. The best argument you'll find for that in our numbers is his performance with and without pressure. Mullens completely collapsed under pressure—only Alex Smith, Derek Carr, and Josh Rosen were worse—but his DVOA with no pressure was excellent, eighth among qualifying quarterbacks and better than that of Matt Ryan, Tom Brady, or Ben Roethlisberger. This is important, because DVOA without pressure is usually the more accurate predictor of a quarterback's performance in the future. Consider, however, what Mullens' teammates did for him—his average completion gained 7.0 yards after the catch, most in the league. Fifty-seven percent of Mullens' total passing yardage came after the catch, fourth-most among qualifying quarterbacks; two of the players above him (Ryan Tannehill and Blake Bortles) will be backups in 2019. Mullens' arm strength also leaves a lot to be desired. Only 10 percent of his throws were marked as deep outside passes, and only 2 percent were bombs of 26 yards or more, both the fewest of any qualifier. Going forward, defenses will know they can ignore the deep routes, and they will crowd the line of scrimmage and tackle those short completions before receivers have a chance to go for big gains. Mullens impressed with his poise and accuracy and could earn an NFL paycheck for a long time, but there's reason to be skeptical about his ability to last as a starter.

Kyler Murray | Height: 5-10 | Weight: 195 | College: Oklahoma | Draft: 2019/1 (1) | Born: 7-Aug-1997 | Age: 22 | Risk: Yellow

Year	Team	G/GS	Snaps	Att	Comp	C%	Yds	TD	INT/Adj	FUM	ASR	NY/P	Rk	DVOA	Rk	DYAR	Rk	YAR	Runs	Yds	TD	DVOA	DYAR	QBR
2019	ARI			521	330	63.3%	3779	24	16	10		6.3		-7.5%					89	534	4	21.1%		

Numerically, there is little reason to question whether Murray will be a star in the NFL. His numbers last season are hard to comprehend: 69.0 percent completion rate, 11.6 yards per attempt, 42 touchdowns, and seven interceptions to go with 1,001 yards and 12 more touchdowns on the ground. His QBASE projection (see page 441) is modest, mostly because he only started for one year in college, but it's not as if Murray was stuck on the bench behind training camp fodder—he was backing up Baker Mayfield, who went on to win the Heisman Trophy and set the NFL rookie record for touchdown passes. Mayfield and Murray were one of the best pairs of passers any college team ever had, and that unique situation may be fooling QBASE to a degree. The only other worrying statistic is 5 feet, 10 inches, Murray's height at the combine. Only once in the last 70 years has a quarterback that short thrown for 20 touchdowns in a season: Doug Flutie in 1998. That could present some schematic challenges for Kliff Kingsbury, but considering Murray is just 1 inch shorter than Russell Wilson and 2 inches shorter than Drew Brees, it shouldn't be a dealbreaker.

What the numbers can't account for, however, is Murray's unusual path to the NFL. Shortly before the draft, Robert Klemko wrote a piece for *Sports Illustrated* chronicling the unusual history Murray and his father Kevin have had with football, baseball, and the business of pro sports. In the 1980s, the elder Murray made commitments to teams in pro baseball and college football, then walked away from both to enter the NFL draft (sound familiar?). The NFL never gave him much of a chance—and if we're being honest about NFL decision-makers of the time, his skin color was probably a big reason why. He eventually started his own quarterback academy, where his son became his star pupil. The NFL has come a long way since then. Nobody's questioning whether or not the younger Murray has the talent to play football, only if he can be trusted to develop himself into the best player he can be. Some of this is due to the Ouroboros-like nature of 24-7 sports media, which can lead to all sorts of nonsense—Murray went 54-2 as a starter in high school and college, and some have questioned how he'll handle an inevitable losing streak in the NFL, in essence criticizing for Murray for *winning too much*—but there is cause for reasonable skepticism. "For me it was always football," he told Klemko. "But at the same time it wasn't." The Oakland A's have retained his baseball rights in case this whole NFL thing goes south.

Cam Newton

| | | Height: 6-5 | | Weight: 248 | | College: Auburn | | | Draft: 2011/1 (1) | | Born: 11-May-1989 | | Age: 30 | | Risk: Yellow |

Year	Team	G/GS	Snaps	Att	Comp	C%	Yds	TD	INT/Adj	FUM	ASR	NY/P	Rk	DVOA	Rk	DYAR	Rk	YAR	Runs	Yds	TD	DVOA	DYAR	QBR
2016	CAR	15/14	1023	510	270	52.9%	3509	19	14/22	3	6.8%	6.0	25	-13.0%	28	-64	28	-64	90	359	5	-12.5%	-2	53.1
2017	CAR	16/16	1063	492	291	59.1%	3302	22	16/16	9	7.2%	6.0	21	-6.9%	21	141	21	197	139	754	6	6.5%	120	47.7
2018	CAR	14/14	885	471	320	67.9%	3395	24	13/17	6	6.6%	6.4	18	-1.4%	23	321	23	407	101	488	4	2.7%	71	55.9
2019	CAR			530	350	66.1%	3747	25	12	10		6.3		1.4%					108	525	5	8.6%		

| 2017: | 53% Short | 29% Mid | 13% Deep | 6% Bomb | aDOT: 8.9 (14) | YAC: 5.5 (13) | ALEX: 2.5 | 2018: | 49% Short | 35% Mid | 13% Deep | 4% Bomb | aDOT: 7.4 (30) | YAC: 5.4 (15) | ALEX: 1.1 |

As discussed at length in the Panthers essay, Newton's 2018 season essentially breaks down into two distinct sections (see table). In Weeks 1 to 9, Newton's DVOA marked him as a top-ten passer on a par with Andrew Luck. In Weeks 10 to 15, he performed like a bottom-five passer on a par with Blake Bortles. This line of demarcation was particularly exaggerated by his deep passing numbers, but Newton also declined in both short passing and rushing DVOA. He also had fewer rushing attempts and took significantly more sacks—his adjusted sack rate did not increase as much as the raw rate, but the raw rate shows the sheer number of hits he accumulated as his health declined. Newton became less decisive, less accurate, less dynamic, and much, much less effective from Week 10's Thursday night game until the team wisely shut him down for the year in mid-December.

Cam Newton's Second-Half Decline

Weeks	Pass DVOA	Deep Pass	Short Pass	Run DVOA	Runs/Game	Sack Rate	ASR
Weeks 1-9	13.2%	39.5%	27.6%	5.3%	9.1	4.4%	5.9%
Weeks 10-15	-18.7%	-79.5%	14.1%	-3.4%	4.7	7.6%	7.4%

The way Newton's season unfolded leaves us with some major questions for 2019. Newton's DVOA prior to the aggravation of his shoulder injury was not just his highest since his rookie year. It was the first time he even had *positive* DVOA for the first half of a season since 2013. Even absent the debilitating shoulder injury, we would have expected Newton to regress somewhat over the back half of the season. Norv Turner did a remarkable job tailoring his offense to one of the more atypical quarterback talents in the professional game, but the injury deprived us of a clear picture of the evolution of that offense over the full campaign. A healthy Newton would probably have recorded only his second positive passing DVOA since 2013; a hobbled Newton recorded his fourth negative season in five years. For 2019, that means we project Newton somewhere around the middle of the two extremes, but with perhaps the most potential upside of any quarterback ever to have such a mediocre DVOA track record. And of course, all that rushing gives him plenty of fantasy value.

Brock Osweiler

| | | Height: 6-7 | | Weight: 242 | | College: Arizona State | | | Draft: 2012/2 (57) | | Born: 22-Nov-1990 | | Age: 29 | | Risk: N/A |

Year	Team	G/GS	Snaps	Att	Comp	C%	Yds	TD	INT/Adj	FUM	ASR	NY/P	Rk	DVOA	Rk	DYAR	Rk	YAR	Runs	Yds	TD	DVOA	DYAR	QBR
2016	HOU	15/14	977	510	301	59.0%	2957	15	16/21	5	5.4%	5.2	33	-26.8%	33	-558	33	-502	30	131	2	35.5%	54	55.3
2017	DEN	6/4	350	172	96	55.8%	1088	5	5/7	2	5.5%	5.7	--	-16.2%	--	-56	--	-90	14	64	1	-8.5%	2	46.4
2018	MIA	7/5	340	178	113	63.5%	1247	6	4/5	1	8.3%	5.8	--	-17.7%	--	-85	--	-50	8	21	0	-24.0%	-3	37.5

| 2017: | 56% Short | 29% Mid | 9% Deep | 6% Bomb | aDOT: 7.8 (--) | YAC: 5.3 (--) | ALEX: -1.9 | 2018: | 57% Short | 25% Mid | 9% Deep | 9% Bomb | aDOT: 7.9 (--) | YAC: 5.9 (--) | ALEX: 1.4 |

Osweiler threw three touchdowns against the Bears (thanks to several short throw/long run plays) and two touchdowns against the Lions (one of them in garbage time) before turning back into Brock Osweiler, Professional Stumblebum in his final three starts for the Dolphins. Even the "tall guy with big arm" illusion has worn off now that Bill O'Brien, Hue Jackson, and Adam Gase have all kicked Osweiler's tires and moved on, so he's currently a free agent in search of a quarterback guru egomaniac who thinks he can fix him. Maybe he should just stand in front of Raiders headquarters with a sign.

Nathan Peterman

| | | Height: 6-2 | | Weight: 226 | | College: Pittsburgh | | | Draft: 2017/5 (171) | | Born: 4-May-1994 | | Age: 25 | | Risk: Green |

Year	Team	G/GS	Snaps	Att	Comp	C%	Yds	TD	INT/Adj	FUM	ASR	NY/P	Rk	DVOA	Rk	DYAR	Rk	YAR	Runs	Yds	TD	DVOA	DYAR	QBR
2017	BUF	4/2	97	49	24	49.0%	252	2	5/5	2	1.7%	4.9	--	-73.8%	--	-194	--	-195	7	23	0	-84.2%	-18	10.8
2018	BUF	4/2	148	81	44	54.3%	296	1	7/8	0	8.3%	2.9	--	-85.1%	--	-380	--	-500	10	50	1	19.3%	18	9.3
2019	OAK			492	281	57.2%	2980	19	29	7		5.3		-39.5%					61	193	2	-4.8%		

| 2017: | 42% Short | 42% Mid | 13% Deep | 4% Bomb | aDOT: 9.2 (--) | YAC: 2.9 (--) | ALEX: 1.4 | 2018: | 58% Short | 26% Mid | 12% Deep | 4% Bomb | aDOT: 6.6 (--) | YAC: 4.2 (--) | ALEX: -1.2 |

Before the 2017 draft, Jon Gruden called Peterman the most pro-ready quarterback in the class. It should be noted that Gruden never specified what Peterman should go pro in; perhaps he's an excellent shuffleboard player or a Fortnite superstar in the making. As an NFL quarterback, Peterman has been one of the worst to ever play the game, putting up 1970s numbers in a 2010s environment. Peterman has thrown an interception on 9.2 percent of his passes, the worst rate since Tom Flick in the mid '80s. Derek Carr could throw an interception on each of his next 225 passes and still have a better interception rate than Peterman.

Dak Prescott

Height: 6-2 Weight: 226 College: Mississippi State Draft: 2016/4 (135) Born: 29-Jul-1993 Age: 26 Risk: Yellow

Year	Team	G/GS	Snaps	Att	Comp	C%	Yds	TD	INT/Adj	FUM	ASR	NY/P	Rk	DVOA	Rk	DYAR	Rk	YAR	Runs	Yds	TD	DVOA	DYAR	QBR
2016	DAL	16/16	1013	459	311	67.8%	3667	23	4/7	9	5.3%	7.3	4	31.6%	3	1302	4	1220	57	282	6	43.6%	121	81.5
2017	DAL	16/16	1053	490	308	62.9%	3324	22	13/17	4	6.4%	6.3	18	-0.2%	17	375	17	322	57	357	6	46.9%	167	66.7
2018	DAL	16/16	1071	526	356	67.7%	3885	22	8/12	12	9.7%	6.1	26	-8.1%	26	112	25	253	75	305	6	2.0%	45	57.8
2019	DAL			524	352	67.2%	3897	23	12	7		6.5		-0.2%					81	399	4	20.6%		

2017:	50% Short	35% Mid	9% Deep	6% Bomb	aDOT: 8.7 (18)	YAC: 4.4 (33)	ALEX: 0.5	2018:	50% Short	35% Mid	8% Deep	7% Bomb	aDOT: 7.6 (26)	YAC: 5.3 (18)	ALEX: -1.0

Prescott went through a 16-game stretch between Week 8 of the 2017 season and Week 6 of last year in which he threw for less than 200 yards 11 times, completing 62.6 percent of his passes, averaging 190.1 yards per game, throwing 15 touchdowns and 13 interceptions and suffering 44 sacks. That "lost season" coincides roughly with the period from Tyron Smith's injury and Ezekiel Elliott's suspension in 2017 through the arrival of Amari Cooper last year. Most quarterbacks will struggle without their top weapons or pass protectors, of course, but Prescott hovered around replacement level for 16 full games when the offense surrounding him was functioning at less than peak capacity. That should terrify the Cowboys as they prepare to embark upon Prescott's expensive years: the evidence suggests that Prescott must be elevated by his supporting cast to play at a high level, not vice versa. From a fantasy standpoint, Prescott's rushing ability and job security make him a useful QB2 type. Just make sure to plant him on the bench the moment any little thing goes wrong elsewhere in the Cowboys offense.

Philip Rivers

Height: 6-5 Weight: 228 College: North Carolina State Draft: 2004/1 (4) Born: 8-Dec-1981 Age: 38 Risk: Red

Year	Team	G/GS	Snaps	Att	Comp	C%	Yds	TD	INT/Adj	FUM	ASR	NY/P	Rk	DVOA	Rk	DYAR	Rk	YAR	Runs	Yds	TD	DVOA	DYAR	QBR
2016	SD	16/16	1061	578	349	60.4%	4386	33	21/19	9	6.6%	6.8	11	1.4%	18	498	17	435	14	35	0	-9.3%	1	64.5
2017	LAC	16/16	1028	575	360	62.6%	4515	28	10/16	8	4.3%	7.5	2	26.1%	4	1412	2	1505	18	-2	0	-97.2%	-10	57.4
2018	LAC	16/16	964	508	347	68.3%	4308	32	12/16	2	6.1%	7.6	4	27.2%	3	1316	3	1216	18	7	0	-96.5%	-55	70.2
2019	LAC			524	351	67.0%	4356	33	9	4		7.6		27.9%					23	15	0	-21.0%		

2017:	52% Short	29% Mid	11% Deep	8% Bomb	aDOT: 8.9 (13)	YAC: 5.9 (5)	ALEX: 0.9	2018:	53% Short	28% Mid	11% Deep	7% Bomb	aDOT: 8.2 (20)	YAC: 6.1 (6)	ALEX: 1.7

From 2014 to 2016, Rivers appeared to be entering the gradual twilight of his career. He'd average a 7.0% or 8.0% DVOA, he'd rank in the high teens in DVOA and DYAR, his interception total would rise. He looked like he was stepping down from being one of the best in the league to being just an above-average player—still useful, but aging gracefully into his mid-30s. There must be something in the water in Los Angeles, because Rivers has looked as good as he has at any point over the last two seasons. Rivers was especially good on first downs, where his 39.4% DVOA was second behind only Drew Brees.

The question with any quarterback who will be turning 38 during the season is just how much longer can he go. Rivers did see his DVOA drop from 37.2% to 16.1% over the last half of the season. Does that mean he will decline this year? We took the research on first half-second half splits from the Cleveland chapter (page 56) and looked specifically at older quarterbacks who declined in the second half. And just as with improvement by younger quarterbacks, we found no indication that second-half decline by older quarterbacks carries over to the next season.

However, we did find a correlation between age and a quarterback's decline in the second half of the season: a correlation coefficient of -0.20 for quarterbacks over the age of 32. So there may be something to the idea that older quarterbacks decline in the second half more often than younger quarterbacks do. In a perfect world, the Chargers would clinch a playoff berth early and give Rivers some rest down the wire so he'd be fresh for the postseason. But that won't happen in a tough AFC West.

Aaron Rodgers

| Height: 6-2 | Weight: 223 | College: California | Draft: 2005/1 (24) | Born: 2-Dec-1983 | Age: 36 | Risk: Green |

Year	Team	G/GS	Snaps	Att	Comp	C%	Yds	TD	INT/Adj	FUM	ASR	NY/P	Rk	DVOA	Rk	DYAR	Rk	YAR	Runs	Yds	TD	DVOA	DYAR	QBR
2016	GB	16/16	1066	610	401	65.7%	4428	40	7/11	8	5.6%	6.5	18	18.7%	8	1279	6	1299	67	369	4	22.4%	89	76.9
2017	GB	7/7	418	238	154	64.7%	1675	16	6/6	1	8.3%	6.0	22	7.8%	14	334	18	308	24	126	0	48.7%	55	62.6
2018	GB	16/16	1013	597	372	62.3%	4442	25	2/8	6	8.0%	6.3	22	8.1%	12	817	9	694	43	269	2	18.4%	66	60.6
2019	GB			601	385	64.0%	4523	31	11	6		6.4		9.6%					42	220	1	19.0%		

| 2017: | 61% Short | 27% Mid | 6% Deep | 6% Bomb | aDOT: 7.2 (33) | YAC: 5.6 (12) | ALEX: 3.9 | 2018: | 47% Short | 30% Mid | 15% Deep | 8% Bomb | aDOT: 9.1 (10) | YAC: 5.7 (8) | ALEX: 4.5 |

The standard for Rodgers is such that anything below elite is unacceptable. For all the talk of his decline, Rodgers has ranked 14th or better in DVOA in each of the past three seasons. That is good by most standards, but compared to what Rodgers can be at his peak, compounded by the Packers missing the playoffs for two straight years, it has been difficult for Rodgers to fend off the notion that he doesn't have "it" like he used to. The reality is, Rodgers is still one of the best at toeing the line between aggression and caution; the Packers' offense just was not functioning well enough to get the most out of it. Rodgers' +4.0 ALEX on third down trailed only Patrick Mahomes, and the Packers tied for fifth in deep passing frequency, yet Rodgers managed a league-best 1.3 percent adjusted interception rate. It is true that his accuracy suffered a bit in 2018—a three-year-low -0.7 passing plus-minus confirms as much—but he played the entire season on a bum knee that he injured in Week 1. It is fair to expect Rodgers' accuracy to return with a healthy knee and a refreshing look on offense.

Ben Roethlisberger

| Height: 6-5 | Weight: 240 | College: Miami (Ohio) | Draft: 2004/1 (11) | Born: 2-Mar-1982 | Age: 37 | Risk: Yellow |

Year	Team	G/GS	Snaps	Att	Comp	C%	Yds	TD	INT/Adj	FUM	ASR	NY/P	Rk	DVOA	Rk	DYAR	Rk	YAR	Runs	Yds	TD	DVOA	DYAR	QBR
2016	PIT	14/14	921	509	328	64.4%	3819	29	13/25	8	4.0%	7.0	8	12.1%	9	807	8	790	16	14	1	14.8%	7	66.3
2017	PIT	15/15	1038	561	360	64.2%	4251	28	14/18	3	3.6%	7.4	5	21.8%	8	1270	5	1247	28	47	0	-2.1%	6	63.2
2018	PIT	16/16	1086	675	452	67.0%	5129	34	16/20	7	4.4%	7.1	9	14.5%	8	1204	5	1070	31	98	3	37.8%	62	71.8
2019	PIT			612	406	66.3%	4668	31	14	5		6.9		17.1%					28	65	1	-1.3%		

| 2017: | 50% Short | 28% Mid | 14% Deep | 9% Bomb | aDOT: 9.6 (7) | YAC: 5.7 (9) | ALEX: 2.4 | 2018: | 54% Short | 28% Mid | 10% Deep | 8% Bomb | aDOT: 8.0 (22) | YAC: 6.2 (3) | ALEX: 1.4 |

One way of looking at the 2018 Steelers is to realize that for all the craziness surrounding him, Roethlisberger was, at age 36, a steady hand that kept the ship pointed towards the playoffs until the final Sunday of the season. Big Ben ranked highly in all of our advanced metrics, to go along with his cumulative stats, which were buoyed by an exceptional workload. Only three quarterbacks have ever thrown more passes in a single season than Roethlisberger heaved in 2018 (Peyton Manning's 679 in 2010, Drew Bledsoe's 691 in 1994, and Matthew Stafford's insane 727 in 2012). Pittsburgh receivers rewarded Roethlisberger's arm trauma by dropping just 18 of those passes, the second-best drop rate in the NFL after Houston offense which threw it almost 200 fewer times.

In one of the many contradictions around the 2018 Steelers, Roethlisberger got small when the field shrank, posting a -13.2% DVOA inside the red zone. Yet the Steelers managed to finish first in the league in touchdown rate and fourth in scoring average per red zone appearance, so Roethlisberger's relative weakness inside the 20 didn't seem to hurt the team.

Roethlisberger has made plenty of noise about retirement and seemed to lack commitment to the cause in recent years—he has certainly earned the label "drama queen" himself. But it is reasonable to deduce that all the opera in the Steel City has had the effect of hardening his resolve. Pittsburgh extended the quarterback for two more years in April, through his age-39 season, thus nullifying any upcoming contractual hassles and scuttlebutt providing further drama. With Antonio Brown and Le'Veon Bell elsewhere, any doubters as to the real power source in the Steelers' engine room can be unequivocally silenced with another strong year from No. 7. Regardless of how many passes he throws and to whom he aims them, Roethlisberger remains unwise to bet against.

Josh Rosen

| Height: 6-4 | Weight: 226 | College: UCLA | Draft: 2018/1 (10) | Born: 10-Feb-1997 | Age: 22 | Risk: Red |

Year	Team	G/GS	Snaps	Att	Comp	C%	Yds	TD	INT/Adj	FUM	ASR	NY/P	Rk	DVOA	Rk	DYAR	Rk	YAR	Runs	Yds	TD	DVOA	DYAR	QBR
2018	ARI	14/13	781	393	217	55.2%	2278	11	14/17	10	10.0%	4.5	34	-53.7%	34	-1145	34	-1067	23	138	0	25.2%	23	26.1
2019	MIA			516	311	60.4%	3456	17	14	11		5.3		-19.9%					32	186	1	13.8%		

| | | | | | | | | | | | | | | | 2018: | 46% Short | 32% Mid | 14% Deep | 8% Bomb | aDOT: 8.8 (14) | YAC: 4.5 (32) | ALEX: -0.7 |

Rosen started 13 games behind one of the NFL's weakest lines, throwing to the league's thinnest receiving corps in an offense which was shockingly remedial and predictable, even when veteran Sam Bradford was running it. Obviously, this dire offensive environment had an impact on Rosen's statistics. Rosen was sacked 27 times due to blown blocks or unblocked defenders last year. On passes to targets other than Larry Fitzgerald, Christian Kirk, and David Johnson, he was 91-of-184 (49.5 percent) for 872 yards (4.74 yards per attempt), one touchdown, and five interceptions, three of them pick-sixes.

Projecting what Rosen will do when being protected by better linemen than Mason Cole and Colby Gossett and throwing to better receivers than Ricky Seals-Jones and Trent Sherfield is an inexact science, especially since he won't exactly be upgrading to the Greatest Show on Turf in Miami. So Rosen's KUBIAK projection is understandably modest but realistic. If he has a season like the one we project, the Dolphins should feel optimistic about what he can do once he's finally surrounded by a half-decent offense.

Mason Rudolph Height: 6-5 Weight: 235 College: Oklahoma State Draft: 2018/3 (76) Born: 17-Jul-1995 Age: 24 Risk: Yellow

Year	Team	G/GS	Snaps	Att	Comp	C%	Yds	TD	INT/Adj	FUM	ASR	NY/P	Rk	DVOA	Rk	DYAR	Rk	YAR	Runs	Yds	TD	DVOA	DYAR	QBR
2019	PIT			559	333	59.5%	3777	22	16	9		5.6		-9.8%					24	37	1	-3.6%		

When the Steelers picked Rudolph in the third round in 2018, they hoped a bit of Jimmy Garoppolo-like presence and accuracy would emerge. Instead, Rudolph's rookie campaign was unimpressive on the field in preseason (he completed just 55 percent of passes and took seven sacks) and apparently not much better behind the scenes. Ben Roethlisberger isn't going anywhere, and the team seems high on Joshua Dobbs, so this year is vital if the former Oklahoma State product is to emerge as a trade asset, if not a reliable backup or even future starter in Pittsburgh.

Cooper Rush Height: 6-3 Weight: 228 College: Central Michigan Draft: 2017/FA Born: 21-Nov-1993 Age: 26 Risk: Yellow

Year	Team	G/GS	Snaps	Att	Comp	C%	Yds	TD	INT/Adj	FUM	ASR	NY/P	Rk	DVOA	Rk	DYAR	Rk	YAR	Runs	Yds	TD	DVOA	DYAR	QBR
2017	DAL	2/0	15	3	1	33.3%	2	0	0/0	0	0.0%	0.7	--	-147.5%	--	-8	--	-7	2	13	0	60.7%	6	1.0
2018	DAL	1/0	6	0	0	0.0%	0	0	0/0	0	--	--	--	--	--	--	--	--	0	0	0	--	--	--
2019	DAL			534	335	62.7%	3669	20	18	10		5.6		-14.7%					23	35	1	-9.5%		

Rush threw two interceptions each in the final two Cowboys preseason games last year, if that sort of thing matters to you. It doesn't matter to Jason Garrett, who likes his backup quarterbacks as Jason Garrett-like as possible, and Rush even has the proper shade of ginger-colored hair. The Cowboys didn't add any quarterbacks in the offseason, so Rush will once again back up Prescott, with the even more unassuming Mike White third on the depth chart. In summary, Rush is somewhere between Garrett Lite and Kellen Moore Red, Mike White is Rush Extra Lite, and the Cowboys are in big trouble if anything happens to Dak Prescott.

Matt Ryan Height: 6-4 Weight: 228 College: Boston College Draft: 2008/1 (3) Born: 17-May-1985 Age: 34 Risk: Yellow

Year	Team	G/GS	Snaps	Att	Comp	C%	Yds	TD	INT/Adj	FUM	ASR	NY/P	Rk	DVOA	Rk	DYAR	Rk	YAR	Runs	Yds	TD	DVOA	DYAR	QBR
2016	ATL	16/16	1021	534	373	69.9%	4944	38	7/10	4	6.6%	8.2	1	39.1%	1	1885	1	1765	35	117	0	12.7%	32	83.3
2017	ATL	16/16	1026	529	342	64.7%	4095	20	12/9	4	4.8%	7.2	7	19.1%	9	1084	7	1076	32	143	0	43.4%	54	63.7
2018	ATL	16/16	1048	608	422	69.4%	4924	35	7/11	10	6.7%	7.1	7	18.2%	4	1232	4	1352	33	125	3	33.9%	68	68.2
2019	ATL			589	397	67.4%	4699	33	12	5		6.9		17.4%					30	107	0	5.9%		

2017: 51% Short 30% Mid 12% Deep 6% Bomb aDOT: 9.1 (12) YAC: 5.4 (15) ALEX: 1.2   2018: 47% Short 33% Mid 13% Deep 7% Bomb aDOT: 9.0 (12) YAC: 5.1 (22) ALEX: 0.8

We lose sight of it because we're often talking about Drew Brees, Tom Brady, and Aaron Rodgers, but Ryan has been very good for a very long time, finishing in the top 10 in DYAR and DVOA in nine of his 11 seasons. On occasion, he has been one of the four or five best quarterbacks in the NFL. Yet you don't hear much Hall of Fame chatter. He's not a lock by any means, but he's on track, based on Pro Football Reference's Approximate Value statistic. Ryan has a career AV of 166, which is more than some active stars (Brees, Brady, and Rodgers) and all-time greats (Brett Favre, Dan Marino, and Fran Tarkenton) had in their first 11 seasons.

Maybe he's underrated (excuse us, Jalen Ramsey, but you're wrong) because he's boring. A pair of khakis or a can of beige paint would be better interviews. Let's not pretend that a player's charm doesn't influence our perception of him. The more likely reason, of course, is that he hasn't won a Super Bowl. But what if he never does? Can he make it to Canton anyway? He can, but it might take a handful more seasons like last year. KUBIAK's outlook is positive, at least for 2019.

Tom Savage

Height: 6-4   Weight: 228   College: Pittsburgh   Draft: 2014/4 (135)   Born: 26-Apr-1990   Age: 29   Risk: Green

Year	Team	G/GS	Snaps	Att	Comp	C%	Yds	TD	INT/Adj	FUM	ASR	NY/P	Rk	DVOA	Rk	DYAR	Rk	YAR	Runs	Yds	TD	DVOA	DYAR	QBR
2016	HOU	3/2	146	73	46	63.0%	461	0	0/1	1	6.9%	5.5	--	-5.4%	--	31	--	21	6	12	0	32.0%	8	63.1
2017	HOU	8/7	421	223	125	56.1%	1412	5	6/9	8	8.8%	5.4	30	-27.5%	33	-249	31	-252	4	2	0	-54.0%	-3	38.1
2019	DET			525	320	61.0%	3361	20	15	13		5.6		-19.4%					41	54	1	-25.0%		

2017:   46% Short   32% Mid   15% Deep   7% Bomb   aDOT: 9.7 (6)   YAC: 4.1 (35)   ALEX: 2.2

Savage's lead feet and middling arm inhibit his decent processing and accuracy, forever cementing him as a mid- or low-tier backup. He spent last year with three different teams: New Orleans cut him when they traded for Teddy Bridgewater, San Francisco had him on the roster for about six weeks, and he ended the year as Jeff Driskel's backup in Cincinnati. David Fales is his current opponent for the backup job in Detroit.

Matt Schaub

Height: 6-5   Weight: 235   College: Virginia   Draft: 2004/3 (90)   Born: 25-Jun-1981   Age: 38   Risk: Red

Year	Team	G/GS	Snaps	Att	Comp	C%	Yds	TD	INT/Adj	FUM	ASR	NY/P	Rk	DVOA	Rk	DYAR	Rk	YAR	Runs	Yds	TD	DVOA	DYAR	QBR
2016	ATL	4/0	21	3	1	33.3%	16	0	0/0	0	0.0%	5.3	--	-15.0%	--	-1	--	3	2	-2	0	--	--	18.4
2018	ATL	3/0	12	7	5	71.4%	20	0	0/0	1	0.0%	2.9	--	-114.3%	--	-52	--	-54	1	0	0	--	--	65.5
2019	ATL			583	376	64.4%	3965	19	16	9		5.9		-10.6%					45	78	1	-22.6%		

2018:   43% Short   57% Mid   0% Deep   0% Bomb   aDOT: 4.6 (--)   YAC: 1.6 (--)   ALEX: 0.0

Schaub did something in October that he hadn't done in years: he threw several passes in a game. His seven passes in the final minutes of a Falcons blowout loss to the Steelers were the most he had thrown in a game since December 2016. The average cost per throw: about $450,000. After the season, he signed a two-year extension that could pay him up to $3.8 million. Only $750,000 of that, however, is guaranteed. Atlanta holds a team option for the 2020 season.

Trevor Siemian

Height: 6-3   Weight: 220   College: Northwestern   Draft: 2015/7 (250)   Born: 26-Dec-1991   Age: 28   Risk: Yellow

Year	Team	G/GS	Snaps	Att	Comp	C%	Yds	TD	INT/Adj	FUM	ASR	NY/P	Rk	DVOA	Rk	DYAR	Rk	YAR	Runs	Yds	TD	DVOA	DYAR	QBR
2016	DEN	14/14	904	486	289	59.5%	3401	18	10/13	4	7.0%	6.2	21	-7.1%	21	137	22	214	28	57	0	-17.0%	-4	55.8
2017	DEN	11/10	677	349	206	59.0%	2285	12	14/20	5	9.5%	5.6	25	-24.6%	32	-327	33	-242	31	127	1	-11.4%	1	27.8
2019	NYJ			530	313	59.2%	3620	21	19	8		5.8		-25.5%					69	233	2	-14.2%		

2017:   52% Short   31% Mid   12% Deep   5% Bomb   aDOT: 9.2 (11)   YAC: 4.9 (22)   ALEX: 1.7

Disappearing onto the Vikings bench was a great career move for Siemian. When a backup quarterback has a zero-attempt year, NFL coaches and execs think he's shrink-wrapped: he doesn't age or decline in any way, and in fact may become more valuable by sitting on a shelf like some vintage comic. Zero-attempt seasons magically turn guys like Siemian into "established veteran backups" with all sorts of intangible value, keeping them employed into their mid-30s. Siemian's career goal should be to parlay his one four-touchdown game in 2016, plus some other OK performances that year, into Derek Anderson's 13-year career. The next step in that plan: avoid direct eye contact with Adam Gase and hope Sam Darnold doesn't miss a snap.

Alex Smith

Height: 6-4   Weight: 212   College: Utah   Draft: 2005/1 (1)   Born: 7-May-1984   Age: 35   Risk: N/A

Year	Team	G/GS	Snaps	Att	Comp	C%	Yds	TD	INT/Adj	FUM	ASR	NY/P	Rk	DVOA	Rk	DYAR	Rk	YAR	Runs	Yds	TD	DVOA	DYAR	QBR
2016	KC	15/15	917	489	328	67.1%	3502	15	8/11	7	5.5%	6.5	17	9.4%	11	688	12	538	48	134	5	4.8%	26	66.1
2017	KC	15/15	966	505	341	67.5%	4042	26	5/10	2	6.8%	7.1	9	18.3%	10	1026	9	1071	60	355	1	20.3%	85	61.6
2018	WAS	10/10	651	328	205	62.5%	2180	10	5/7	6	6.9%	5.9	31	-13.5%	29	-53	28	95	41	168	1	13.8%	42	49.3

2017:   62% Short   21% Mid   8% Deep   8% Bomb   aDOT: 8.0 (27)   YAC: 5.7 (7)   ALEX: 0.7   2018:   48% Short   32% Mid   14% Deep   7% Bomb   aDOT: 8.6 (15)   YAC: 4.8 (29)   ALEX: 0.3

It feels impolite to mention it, but Smith was playing very poorly before the injury last season. He looked uncomfortable in Jay Gruden's offense, often throwing late or miscommunicating with receivers. His short accuracy was off, and he lapsed into self-parody with his reluctance to challenge defenses with deep passes. Smith only threw for 300-plus yards once, in the blowout loss to the Falcons. He spent the rest of last season stringing together some "game manager" wins in low-scoring victories over the Cowboys, Giants, and Buccaneers before getting hurt. (Smith threw for exactly 178 yards in all three games, in which the Skins scored 20, 20, and 16 points. So at least he was consistent.) Even if Smith hadn't suffered the most gruesome quarterback injury since Joe Theismann, the Skins would probably have been in the offseason quarterback market and on the hook for millions in guarantees. We're glad Smith is getting paid and hope he recovers enough to think about a comeback, or at least be able to participate in neighborhood 5K runs after retirement. But the Skins were foolish to pay so much in money and trade compensation for him, and they can't hide behind "injuries happen" as an excuse for their bad decision.

Geno Smith   Height: 6-3   Weight: 208   College: West Virginia   Draft: 2013/2 (39)   Born: 10-Oct-1990   Age: 29   Risk: Green

Year	Team	G/GS	Snaps	Att	Comp	C%	Yds	TD	INT/Adj	FUM	ASR	NY/P	Rk	DVOA	Rk	DYAR	Rk	YAR	Runs	Yds	TD	DVOA	DYAR	QBR
2016	NYJ	2/1	33	14	8	57.1%	126	1	1/1	1	17.3%	6.2	--	-70.8%	--	-68	--	-83	2	9	0	39.6%	5	30.9
2017	NYG	2/1	66	36	21	58.3%	212	1	0/0	2	8.6%	5.3	--	-41.4%	--	-83	--	-44	4	12	0	6.4%	4	34.5
2018	LAC	5/0	32	4	1	25.0%	8	0	0/0	1	16.8%	-1.0	--	-282.0%	--	-49	--	-55	8	2	0	45.4%	3	0.8
2019	SEA			460	279	60.6%	3285	20	13	8		6.1		-11.2%					54	240	2	9.7%		

2017:   64% Short   28% Mid   8% Deep   0% Bomb   aDOT: 6.5 (--)   YAC: 5.1 (--)   ALEX: -1.0   2018:   50% Short   50% Mid   0% Deep   0% Bomb   aDOT: 2.0 (--)   YAC: 11.0 (--)   ALEX: -11

Smith was most recently relevant for breaking up Eli Manning's 100-game start streak in 2017, a decision which got Ben McAdoo fired. Suffice it to say that Smith will not be replacing Russell Wilson anytime soon, but he fits Seattle's requirements for a backup nicely: he's mobile enough and has a good enough arm to run the Seahawks offense if he needs to, with starting experience to boot. Basically, Tarvaris Jackson 2.0.

Matthew Stafford   Height: 6-2   Weight: 225   College: Georgia   Draft: 2009/1 (1)   Born: 7-Feb-1988   Age: 31   Risk: Yellow

Year	Team	G/GS	Snaps	Att	Comp	C%	Yds	TD	INT/Adj	FUM	ASR	NY/P	Rk	DVOA	Rk	DYAR	Rk	YAR	Runs	Yds	TD	DVOA	DYAR	QBR
2016	DET	16/16	1037	594	388	65.3%	4327	24	10/16	3	6.1%	6.5	16	7.2%	14	761	9	768	37	207	2	29.3%	64	70.5
2017	DET	16/16	1035	565	371	65.7%	4446	29	10/18	11	7.6%	7.0	11	14.9%	11	1004	10	913	29	98	0	0.2%	11	61.7
2018	DET	16/16	1053	555	367	66.1%	3777	21	11/16	6	6.4%	5.9	28	-0.8%	21	396	20	275	25	71	0	1.9%	12	54.0
2019	DET			537	352	65.6%	3890	26	11	6		6.3		7.6%					29	68	1	-3.1%		

2017:   57% Short   26% Mid   9% Deep   8% Bomb   aDOT: 8.7 (19)   YAC: 5.7 (10)   ALEX: 2.1   2018:   59% Short   27% Mid   9% Deep   6% Bomb   aDOT: 7.2 (32)   YAC: 5.5 (13)   ALEX: 1.3

Even in the "toned down" stage of Stafford's career, he has been an extreme boom-or-bust passer. In 2017, Detroit had the widest gap between short passing DVOA and deep passing DVOA despite being just a hair over average on short passing. That gap fell only to fifth-widest in 2018, when Detroit was well below average on short passing but remained top-tier in deep passing. That is not to blame Stafford for making use of Marvin Jones and Kenny Golladay down the field, but the offense's explosive play potential needs to be complemented by reliable play underneath. Stafford's processing in the quick game is not always as sharp as it needs to be. The additions of two tight ends (T.J. Hockenson and Jessie James) and two underneath receivers (Danny Amendola and Jermaine Kearse) should give Stafford better short-passing options that can be open consistently, something he has not had the past two seasons. With a new offensive coordinator and a real chance to impress under second-year head coach Matt Patricia, this has to be the season Stafford ties it all together.

Drew Stanton   Height: 6-3   Weight: 230   College: Michigan State   Draft: 2007/2 (43)   Born: 7-May-1984   Age: 35   Risk: Green

Year	Team	G/GS	Snaps	Att	Comp	C%	Yds	TD	INT/Adj	FUM	ASR	NY/P	Rk	DVOA	Rk	DYAR	Rk	YAR	Runs	Yds	TD	DVOA	DYAR	QBR
2016	ARI	5/1	106	48	19	39.6%	192	2	3/2	0	1.9%	3.8	--	-50.9%	--	-119	--	-84	3	-3	0	--	--	26.9
2017	ARI	5/4	320	159	79	49.7%	894	6	5/5	3	4.3%	5.3	--	-18.3%	--	-75	--	-62	9	7	0	-21.2%	-2	35.9
2019	CLE			554	333	60.1%	3861	25	17	11		6.4		-10.4%					40	40	0	-25.0%		

2017:   36% Short   40% Mid   14% Deep   9% Bomb   aDOT: 11.1 (--)   YAC: 3.8 (--)   ALEX: 1.6

Tyrod Taylor's departure leaves the backup role in the hands of Stanton, who didn't take a snap last year and was last seen posting a -18.3% DVOA in Arizona in 2017. Should he be forced to play any sizable role for the Browns, he will have considerably more talent around him, but Cleveland should still consider the season lost.

Nate Sudfeld

| | | Height: 6-6 | | Weight: 234 | | College: Indiana | | | Draft: 2016/6 (187) | | Born: 7-Oct-1993 | | | Age: 26 | | | Risk: Yellow |

Year	Team	G/GS	Snaps	Att	Comp	C%	Yds	TD	INT/Adj	FUM	ASR	NY/P	Rk	DVOA	Rk	DYAR	Rk	YAR	Runs	Yds	TD	DVOA	DYAR	QBR
2017	PHI	1/0	40	23	19	82.6%	134	0	0/0	0	12.0%	4.2	--	-24.5%	--	-22	--	-17	1	22	0	81.8%	7	31.1
2018	PHI	2/0	11	2	1	50.0%	22	1	0/0	0	0.5%	11.0	--	144.0%	--	20	--	20	2	-2	0	--	--	31.1
2019	PHI		552	339	61.3%	3895		23	16	10		6.1		-6.4%					43	65	1	-15.8%		

| 2017: | 73% Short | 23% Mid | 4% Deep | 0% Bomb | aDOT: 4.3 (--) | YAC: 4.3 (--) | ALEX: -11.0 | 2018: | 50% Short | 50% Mid | 0% Deep | 0% Bomb | aDOT: 4.5 (--) | YAC: 23.0 (--) | ALEX: 0.0 |

Sudfeld was brought into Philadelphia in 2017 after being drafted by Washington the year before. Though Sudfeld is heading into his third season with the team, this will be the first year he is backing up Carson Wentz. He got playing time at the end of the 2017 when the Eagles had locked up a playoff bye, but aside from that, he had been third on the depth chart behind Wentz and Nick Foles. The Eagles placed a second-round tender on Sudfeld this offseason, though, which indicates they either have faith in Sudfeld to develop into a valuable backup, or they desperately wanted to maintain continuity considering Wentz has missed considerable time the past two seasons.

Ryan Tannehill

| | | Height: 6-4 | | Weight: 221 | | College: Texas A&M | | | Draft: 2012/1 (8) | | Born: 27-Jul-1988 | | | Age: 31 | | | Risk: Red |

Year	Team	G/GS	Snaps	Att	Comp	C%	Yds	TD	INT/Adj	FUM	ASR	NY/P	Rk	DVOA	Rk	DYAR	Rk	YAR	Runs	Yds	TD	DVOA	DYAR	QBR
2016	MIA	13/13	758	389	261	67.1%	2995	19	12/16	9	7.2%	6.7	14	-10.8%	25	10	25	92	39	164	1	-7.0%	8	54.6
2018	MIA	11/11	580	274	176	64.2%	1979	17	9/16	5	12.0%	5.5	32	-20.8%	32	-186	31	-251	32	145	0	34.9%	39	35.0
2019	TEN		466	296	63.6%	3412		19	13	9		6.1		-13.0%					41	163	2	7.5%		

| | | | | | | | | | | | | 2018: | 54% Short | 27% Mid | 9% Deep | 10% Bomb | aDOT: 8.6 (16) | YAC: 6.1 (5) | ALEX: 0.9 |

Sometimes, when a player puts up consistently below-average numbers across multiple regimes, a team decides it just means a player is below average and decides they no longer want a below-average player. So it was with Tannehill and Miami. Struggles up front (including particularly an abysmal -86.7% DVOA against a league-leading rate of defensive back blitzes) and a blinkered receiving corps made him even more below average than he had been to date. And now he finds himself in Tennessee, clearly ensconced as a backup, after the Titans gave up a fourth-round pick to get him. He's in a position of opportunity, restructuring his contract for just a one-year deal and now behind a quarterback in the final year of his own deal who has a history of injury problems. Best of all, even a below-average player at backup quarterback is significantly better than what the Titans have had in a number of years. Ryan Tannehill, you're all set to become the most popular man in Nashville, with the possibility some team will make an eight-figure mistake in your favor next offseason. Just don't screw it up.

Tyrod Taylor

| | | Height: 6-1 | | Weight: 216 | | College: Virginia Tech | | | Draft: 2011/6 (180) | | Born: 3-Aug-1989 | | | Age: 30 | | | Risk: Green |

Year	Team	G/GS	Snaps	Att	Comp	C%	Yds	TD	INT/Adj	FUM	ASR	NY/P	Rk	DVOA	Rk	DYAR	Rk	YAR	Runs	Yds	TD	DVOA	DYAR	QBR
2016	BUF	15/15	969	436	269	61.7%	3023	17	6/6	4	9.2%	5.9	27	-2.1%	19	275	19	347	95	580	6	2.1%	65	68.2
2017	BUF	15/14	931	420	263	62.6%	2799	14	4/4	4	10.2%	5.6	26	-7.0%	22	121	22	263	84	427	4	20.8%	110	52.7
2018	CLE	4/3	185	85	42	49.4%	473	2	2/2	3	13.3%	3.9	--	-53.5%	--	-264	--	-258	16	125	1	-6.8%	4	29.1
2019	LAC		463	292	63.0%	3202		16	9	8		6.2		-6.6%					78	333	3	10.3%		

| 2017: | 57% Short | 27% Mid | 8% Deep | 8% Bomb | aDOT: 8.8 (15) | YAC: 4.8 (23) | ALEX: 1.2 | 2018: | 48% Short | 19% Mid | 23% Deep | 11% Bomb | aDOT: 11.1 (--) | YAC: 4.7 (--) | ALEX: 0.5 |

Taylor's trip to Los Angeles reunites him with Anthony Lynn, who was assistant head coach, offensive coordinator, and head coach for Taylor in Buffalo in 2015 and 2016. Those happen to be Taylor's two best seasons, as Lynn was able to get the most out of Taylor's combination of downfield accuracy, dynamic rushing ability, and terrible progression reading. Taylor's still one of the best 40 or so quarterbacks in the league, so even though he's a very different passer than Philip Rivers and would require the offense to change dramatically if he's forced under center, he's still a valuable asset for a team with championship hopes. In all fairness, it should be noted that Taylor was terrible in three starts for Cleveland last season. That puts him in an exclusive club with every other quarterback in Cleveland between Vinny Testaverde and Baker Mayfield.

Mitchell Trubisky

Height: 6-2 Weight: 222 College: North Carolina Draft: 2017/1 (2) Born: 20-Aug-1994 Age: 25 Risk: Yellow

Year	Team	G/GS	Snaps	Att	Comp	C%	Yds	TD	INT/Adj	FUM	ASR	NY/P	Rk	DVOA	Rk	DYAR	Rk	YAR	Runs	Yds	TD	DVOA	DYAR	QBR
2017	CHI	12/12	726	330	196	59.4%	2193	7	7/8	10	8.7%	5.5	27	-16.8%	29	-119	29	-176	41	248	2	9.7%	32	29.2
2018	CHI	14/14	929	434	289	66.6%	3223	24	12/16	6	5.1%	6.7	15	3.6%	19	448	17	540	68	421	3	22.9%	114	72.8
2019	CHI			513	341	66.5%	3777	27	13	12		6.6		1.8%					68	369	3	14.5%		

2017: 57% Short 27% Mid 12% Deep 3% Bomb aDOT: 7.9 (28) YAC: 5.1 (19) ALEX: -2.4 2018: 46% Short 31% Mid 12% Deep 10% Bomb aDOT: 9.3 (8) YAC: 4.9 (28) ALEX: 2.7

Trubisky is, if nothing else, a unique quarterback. Trubisky threw a higher percentage of his passes outside the pocket (19.7 percent) than all but three quarterbacks last season. Likewise, only three quarterbacks scored a higher positive DVOA difference (+42.4%) on throws outside vs. inside the pocket. Though John Fox's offense repressed Trubisky as a rookie, the quarterback still broke the pocket more often than league average and fared better outside the pocket than inside it. The "joke" about Trubisky struggling to throw to his left still rings true, too. The Bears were 31st in both frequency and DVOA on passes to the left in 2017, barely improving to 30th and 29th respectively in 2018. Volatility also remains an issue for the young quarterback. He had 231 DYAR in a fluky Week 4 smashing of the Buccaneers and another 130 against the Lions in Week 10. Conversely, he posted five negative-DYAR performances, and the Bears finished the season with the fifth-most volatile passing offense based on week-to-week DVOA. 2019 is an important season for Trubisky's development with respect to finding a consistent, repeatable process to make his game complete. Roller-coaster production buoyed by his value as a runner is not going to cut it long-term.

Deshaun Watson

Height: 6-2 Weight: 221 College: Clemson Draft: 2017/1 (12) Born: 14-Sep-1995 Age: 24 Risk: Yellow

Year	Team	G/GS	Snaps	Att	Comp	C%	Yds	TD	INT/Adj	FUM	ASR	NY/P	Rk	DVOA	Rk	DYAR	Rk	YAR	Runs	Yds	TD	DVOA	DYAR	QBR
2017	HOU	7/6	464	204	126	61.8%	1699	19	8/8	3	8.5%	7.7	1	23.1%	7	497	14	529	36	269	2	29.3%	70	81.3
2018	HOU	16/16	1093	505	345	68.3%	4165	26	9/14	9	11.6%	6.8	14	9.5%	11	737	10	722	99	551	5	7.8%	95	63.8
2019	HOU			520	338	65.0%	4073	29	13	10		6.7		1.1%					85	481	5	20.2%		

2017: 47% Short 30% Mid 13% Deep 10% Bomb aDOT: 11.5 (1) YAC: 5.3 (16) ALEX: 2.1 2018: 44% Short 38% Mid 12% Deep 6% Bomb aDOT: 8.9 (13) YAC: 5.1 (21) ALEX: -0.3

On 62 dropbacks from Weeks 1 to 9, Watson was sacked just four times on blitzes and averaged 9.3 yards per attempt on his 58 passes. From Week 10 on, Watson was sacked on 12 of his 80 blitz dropbacks and averaged just 7.8 yards per pass, getting shredded by slot blitzes from the Browns, then the Colts, then copycats. It got to the point where Watson had to operate out of empty sets to mitigate the pressure. Now, to be fair to Watson, this would never have happened if the Texans actually had a running game that worked. It's also pretty telling that when we're trying to think of improvement issues for Watson that we're heading to very granular issues like this. He has developed a lot already, improving his footwork and late-play recognition. He's always going to be under pressure, by the way. Feature, not a bug. It's Houston's job to make sure that the linemen they put in front of him don't make him too harried and too run-happy.

Carson Wentz

Height: 6-5 Weight: 237 College: North Dakota State Draft: 2016/1 (2) Born: 30-Dec-1992 Age: 27 Risk: Red

Year	Team	G/GS	Snaps	Att	Comp	C%	Yds	TD	INT/Adj	FUM	ASR	NY/P	Rk	DVOA	Rk	DYAR	Rk	YAR	Runs	Yds	TD	DVOA	DYAR	QBR
2016	PHI	16/16	1127	607	379	62.4%	3782	16	14/19	14	5.4%	5.6	31	-12.0%	27	-36	27	12	46	150	2	-3.6%	16	52.8
2017	PHI	13/13	879	440	265	60.2%	3296	33	7/13	9	6.1%	6.9	12	23.8%	6	1047	8	934	64	299	0	6.7%	52	75.9
2018	PHI	11/11	724	401	279	69.6%	3074	21	7/11	9	7.8%	6.6	16	8.1%	13	545	14	574	34	93	0	-6.8%	7	64.2
2019	PHI			588	397	67.5%	4559	31	11	10		6.9		16.2%					57	187	1	-1.7%		

2017: 47% Short 33% Mid 11% Deep 9% Bomb aDOT: 10.4 (3) YAC: 4.6 (26) ALEX: 3.7 2018: 47% Short 36% Mid 10% Deep 8% Bomb aDOT: 8.2 (19) YAC: 5.0 (24) ALEX: 0.5

Any number of factors can explain Wentz's dip in production last year compared to his near-MVP season in 2017. A diminished receiving corps, turnover regression, and the lack of a healthy offseason all played into Wentz's regression on the stat sheet. More so than anywhere else, the slip in productivity showed up most on third down. Wentz excelled there in 2017, finishing second in conversion rate and first in DVOA. In 2018, without any quality vertical threats in the offense, Wentz fell to 19th and 25th, respectively, and his ALEX on third down fell from +3.7 to +0.5. He was far less aggressive, in part because he was less aggressive in general in 2018, but the offense was not opened up in a way that allowed him to test the sticks as often as he would have liked to. Still, Wentz finished a respectable 14th in DYAR and displayed development as a player that showed up on film, but not necessarily the box score. He showed better patience in the pocket, cleaner mechanics, and a clearer understanding of when to take the short throws versus going for the big play. Health, of course, is the primary question moving forward for the freshly paid quarterback, but Wentz should be able to return to form as the offense around him fills out.

Russell Wilson Height: 5-11   Weight: 204   College: Wisconsin   Draft: 2012/3 (75)   Born: 29-Nov-1988   Age: 31   Risk: Yellow

Year	Team	G/GS	Snaps	Att	Comp	C%	Yds	TD	INT/Adj	FUM	ASR	NY/P	Rk	DVOA	Rk	DYAR	Rk	YAR	Runs	Yds	TD	DVOA	DYAR	QBR
2016	SEA	16/16	1008	546	353	64.7%	4219	21	11/15	7	7.0%	6.7	13	4.0%	15	569	14	599	72	259	1	-12.3%	-1	63.2
2017	SEA	16/16	1063	553	339	61.3%	3983	34	11/15	14	8.1%	6.1	20	2.9%	15	530	13	564	95	586	3	28.9%	154	58.3
2018	SEA	16/16	1069	427	280	65.6%	3448	35	7/11	10	10.4%	6.6	17	11.3%	10	673	11	637	67	376	0	23.3%	83	65.6
2019	SEA			453	295	65.2%	3602	31	8	9		6.8		14.5%					69	369	3	19.9%		

2017:	52% Short	27% Mid	11% Deep	9% Bomb	aDOT: 10.1 (4)	YAC: 4.7 (25)	ALEX: 1.5	2018:	45% Short	31% Mid	13% Deep	11% Bomb	aDOT: 9.7 (5)	YAC: 4.9 (26)	ALEX: 2.8

Wilson was blitzed on 30.7 percent of pass plays in 2018, second in the league behind Joe Flacco. This was a new strategy because Wilson had been below average in blitzes at 22.0 percent in 2017. Seattle's DVOA dropped when Wilson was blitzed, as the team went from 72.3% DVOA and 8.4 net yards per pass against two or three pass-rushers to 49.0% DVOA and 7.4 yards against four pass-rushers, to 16.6% DVOA (6.8 yards) against five or more. It's possible that Seattle's run-heavy tendencies on early downs played into this, as there were fewer pass plays in non-obvious passing situations, so Seattle will have to hope that swapping Mike Iupati for J.R. Sweezy at left guard and another year of continuity for the four other offensive linemen will help them handle blitzes more effectively, giving Wilson a better chance to make plays against extra rushers.

Jameis Winston Height: 6-4   Weight: 230   College: Florida State   Draft: 2015/1 (1)   Born: 6-Jan-1994   Age: 26   Risk: Yellow

Year	Team	G/GS	Snaps	Att	Comp	C%	Yds	TD	INT/Adj	FUM	ASR	NY/P	Rk	DVOA	Rk	DYAR	Rk	YAR	Runs	Yds	TD	DVOA	DYAR	QBR
2016	TB	16/16	1123	567	345	60.8%	4090	28	18/20	10	5.9%	6.4	19	3.6%	16	556	15	539	53	165	1	-23.8%	-19	64.7
2017	TB	13/13	795	442	282	63.8%	3504	19	11/19	15	7.0%	7.1	10	14.3%	12	779	11	684	33	135	1	-21.7%	-14	48.2
2018	TB	11/9	688	378	244	64.6%	2992	19	14/19	7	7.4%	7.0	10	6.9%	15	470	16	489	49	281	1	4.7%	37	68.6
2019	TB			596	379	63.5%	4729	28	17	10		6.8		4.5%					54	254	1	6.3%		

2017:	41% Short	38% Mid	14% Deep	8% Bomb	aDOT: 11.0 (2)	YAC: 4.4 (32)	ALEX: 3.2	2018:	33% Short	43% Mid	17% Deep	7% Bomb	aDOT: 11.1 (1)	YAC: 3.7 (34)	ALEX: 3.2

Winston makes just enough special plays to hold your attention until the next bad one. Take, for instance, his Week 15 performance against the Ravens. On a third-and-20 play late in the second quarter, Winston escaped pressure from linebacker Terrell Suggs, rolled to his left and, on the run, threw a bomb to Mike Evans 50 yards down the field. Then early in the fourth quarter, under no pressure whatsoever, he underthrew Evans, and cornerback Marlon Humphrey came up with the interception.

Winston's ability to extend plays is one of his greatest strengths—and part of the reason he produced the second-best DVOA (-11.6%) on passes when under pressure (Patrick Mahomes had a 7.6% DVOA). It's a nice attribute to have. The thing is, though, performance in such situations isn't stable. Just because Winston played well (relative to other quarterbacks) when under pressure last season doesn't mean that he will do it again this season. A quarterback's performance when *not* under pressure is more telling. That's the scenario 70 percent of the time. If you can't count on a quarterback to execute when things go (mostly) according to plan, how can you count on him to execute when things break down?

Winston can move the chains as well as almost any quarterback, but his performance when not under pressure is a bit of a red flag. It's not horrible; it's just OK. Oddly, when Winston has excelled in pressure situations, he has been ordinary in non-pressure situations. When he has excelled in non-pressure situations, he has been ordinary in pressure situations.

The unsolved mystery that is Winston is now Bruce Arians' to solve. But what if he can't be solved? What if everything Winston has ever done or will do, he's going to do over and over again?

Jameis Winston and Pressure, 2015 to 2018

Season	DVOA w/pressure	Rk	DVOA w/no pressure	Rk
2018	-11.6%	2	47.9%	18
2017	-60.0%	23	74.3%	5
2016	-24.9%	3	45.3%	18
2015	-47.0%	10	44.0%	20

Going Deep

Tyler Bray, CHI: Since entering the league in 2013, Bray has one career pass attempt and one rushing attempt. He failed to complete the pass and fumbled on the run. Aside from that, he is best known for an absurd back tattoo that reads "Bray" where a jersey nameplate would be, with stars layered behind each letter. Trust me, that description does not do it justice.

Matt Cassel, FA: The first time Cassel made an appearance for the Lions in 2018, he threw an interception to Buster Skrine to close out a peculiar 48-17 routing by the Jets in Week 1. The last time Cassel made an appearance, he was sacked by Kentrell Brothers while playing in place of Matt Stafford in the waning minutes of a doomed Week 16 loss. It is safe to say whatever was left of Cassel's veteran value is running dry.

Joshua Dobbs, PIT: Dobbs beat out both Landry Jones and Mason Rudolph for the backup spot in Pittsburgh last offseason, averaging 10.1 yards per attempt in the preseason. When he played in a couple of regular-season blowouts, he struggled (-124.1% DVOA). Assuming Randolph has improved enough for the Steelers to cut Dobbs, teams across the league are no doubt waiting to pounce, a fact that says plenty about the state of backup quarterbacking across the NFL.

Nick Fitzgerald, TB: Not to be cliché, but the NFL is a copycat league. After seeing how the Saints deployed Taysom Hill last season, the Buccaneers wanted a Swiss Army knife of their own, so they signed Fitzgerald, an undrafted free agent out of Mississippi State. They're grooming him to be their third-string quarterback, but to gain the inside track, he'll have to prove himself on special teams. He should be a good fit in the quarterback room; in college, he threw an interception on 3.2 percent of his passes. If he can protect the football, he could be a real home-run threat.

Garrett Gilbert, CLE: Remember the American Alliance of Football, the mayfly of spring football leagues? If you were quick enough to catch any of the action, one familiar name who stood out was Gilbert, who starred for the Orlando Apollos under the tutelage of Steve Spurrier until the AAF choked on its own debt. Two days after the league capsized, Gilbert was signed by Cleveland. His competition for backup is Drew Stanton, who didn't play at all in 2018, so if recency bias is a thing, Gilbert could well win the job.

Kevin Hogan, DEN: Kevinmania ran wild for three quarters in 2016, running for 100 yards in a surprise deployment of the read option and part of Hue Jackson's ever-spinning wheel of quarterbacks. Apart from that, he can be *very* charitably described as a borderline talent with severe accuracy issues. The fact that he beat out Paxton Lynch and replaced Chad Kelly last season says more about Denver's quarterback situation than it does about Hogan.

Tyree Jackson, BUF: Stop us if you've heard this one before. Buffalo grabbed a rookie with a huge arm, but poor accuracy and touch. Jackson was the 2018 MAC Offensive Player of the Year with (the University of) Buffalo, leading the conference with a 13.8-yard aDOT; his lack of fear uncorking the big bomb helped him to a 49-24 TD-INT ratio in four years with the Bulls. ESPN measured him with a 20.5 percent career off-target passing rate, worst of any college quarterback since 2011. Pretty much the dictionary definition of a developmental prospect.

Landry Jones, FA: Jones spent the first five years of his career backing up Ben Roethlisberger in Pittsburgh, a job that requires you to start about one game a year and keep things from collapsing while Big Ben rests up whichever injury acted up this time. Jones was solid in that limited role—some accuracy issues, but his 7.75 career yards per attempt ranks 11th since he came into the league among all quarterbacks with at least 150 career passes. That wasn't enough to beat out Nathan Peterman in Oakland, though, and Jones was released in May.

Kyle Lauletta, NYG: As far as auspicious starts go, it doesn't get much better than 0-of-5 with an interception and an arrest for allegedly hitting a cop with your car. Now behind Daniel Jones in the pecking order for the Giants, Lauletta's preseason work (17-of-35, 194 yards, 1 TD, 2 INT) was lacking as well. He'll be cheap for the time being, but nothing the Giants have seen from Lauletta so far should have them thinking he can be Jones' long-term backup.

Tanner Lee, JAX: A big-armed, 6-foot-4 prospect from a big-time program is getting extra shots to become an NFL quarterback. Collapse and faint, as you will. Lee transferred from Tulane to Nebraska and completed only 57.5 percent of his throws for the Huskers, which was an upgrade on his 53.6 percent rate with Tulane. He's Jacksonville's most experienced backup in-house, battling rookie Gardner Minshew for the job in training camp. There are generally very few quarterbacks on an NFL bench that could compete for an NFL starting job. The Jaguars don't have any of them.

Trace McSorley, BAL: For the 2017 Nittany Lions, McSorley played with Saquon Barkley, DaeSean Hamilton, and Mike Gesicki. He completed 66.5 percent of his passes for 3,570 yards, 28 touchdowns, and 10 picks. For the 2018 Nittany Lions, he played with Miles Sanders. He completed 53.2 percent of his passes for 2,530 yards, with 18 touchdowns and seven picks. Saquon Barkley really is a generational talent! McSorley is seen as a Taysom Hill-type because he ran for 30 touchdowns. Being on the same team as Lamar Jackson should remove the temptation to ever use him in that role.

Jake Rudock, MIA: A noodle-armed Michigan alum drafted by the Lions in the sixth round in 2016, Rudock has lost backup jobs to Dan Orlovsky and Matt Cassel, tossing five passes in between in a brief 2017 appearance. Your basic thirsty effort guy who keeps getting jobs because the last guy gave him a job.

Mark Sanchez, FA: Since 2015, Sanchez has gone 88-of-144 (61.1 percent) for 847 yards (5.88 YPA), four touchdowns, nine interceptions, 19 sacks (a whopping 11.7 percent sack rate) and an 0-3 record as a starter if you are into that sort of thing. That's the sort of production your basic sixth-round rookie can provide, plus the rookie could probably scramble for some yards. Farewell, Sanchize. It's been weird.

Kyle Sloter, MIN: Sloter was a small-school sleeper favorite of the NFL draft community in 2017. He had lost his job at Southern Miss to now-49ers quarterback Nick Mullens, which led Sloter to transfer to Northern Colorado. Sloter initially failed to stick with the Broncos as an undrafted free agent but landed with the Vikings as their third-string and practice squad quarterback. This will be Sloter's first chance at a legitimate backup role as he battles with former Rams backup Sean Mannion.

Easton Stick, LAC: Some thought the Chargers would draft a quarterback early to be the heir apparent behind Philip Rivers. Instead, they stuck with Stick in the fifth round. Stick broke most of Carson Wentz's records at North Dakota State, winning a pair of national titles and finishing with 49 wins with only three losses. He's about as different from Rivers as you can possibly be—an athletic dual-threat quarterback who thrived in an RPO-style system. His arm strength is questionable and it's hard to imagine him running around NFL-quality defenders, but he has enough tools to make him an intriguing prospect.

Jarrett Stidham, NE: A four-star (ESPN, Rivals.com) or five-star (Scout.com, 24/7 Sports) recruit out of high school, Stidham started three games as a true freshman at Baylor, then spent a year at community college before resurfacing at Auburn. Once touted as a possible Day 2 pick, Stidham's play regressed sufficiently in his senior year to drop him to the Patriots in the fourth round (No. 133). He may compete with Brian Hoyer to back up Tom Brady in 2019 but is more likely to spend this year as effectively a professional redshirt.

Alex Tanney, NYG: Better known for his YouTube trick shot videos than his NFL career, Tanney was somehow one Eli Manning injury from playing last year. Now behind Manning and two young quarterbacks, it would not be surprising if he caught on somewhere else by August. Either way, at 31, he's a long shot to do more than ride the bench.

Clayton Thorson, PHI: Though Northwestern did not boast immense talent on offense, it's hard to make a case for Thorson based on a senior season with 5.6 net yards per attempt (including sacks) and almost as many interceptions (15) as touchdowns (17). This Philly fifth-rounder sports the size, arm, and experience of a desirable backup and project, but there is a lot of projecting for the Eagles staff to do.

Davis Webb, NYJ: Since getting selected in the third round of the 2017 draft, Webb was passed over by Geno Smith in the Great Eli Benching Fiasco, lost the backup job to small-program rookie Kyle Lauletta (despite Lauletta's newsworthy reckless driving habits), got punted across northern New Jersey to the Jets, and rode the bench while the desiccated remains of Josh McCown shambled through some ugly starts in relief of Sam Darnold. That's a remarkable set of non-accomplishments. Losing a roster spot to Trevor Siemian in August will come naturally to him.

Mike White, DAL: White threw for 8,540 yards and 63 touchdowns for the Western Kentucky Hilltoppers in 2016 and 2017. He then leapt into the Jason Garrett Cloning Vat, hoping to follow Garrett and Kellen Moore on the path from rarely used backup quarterback to offensive coordinator to head coach to Cowboys company man. But he's stuck behind Cooper Rush in what has become a very crowded queue in recent years.

Running Backs

In the following section we provide the last three years of statistics, as well as a 2019 KUBIAK projection, for every running back who either played a significant role in 2018 or is expected to do so in 2018.

The first line contains biographical data—each player's name, height, weight, college, draft position, birth date, and age. Height and weight are the best data we could find; weight, of course, can fluctuate during the offseason. **Age** is very simple, the number of years between the player's birth year and 2019, but birthdate is provided if you want to figure out exact age.

Draft position gives draft year and round, with the overall pick number with which the player was taken in parentheses. In the sample table, it says that Todd Gurley was chosen in the 2015 NFL draft in the first round with the 10th overall pick. Undrafted free agents are listed as "FA" with the year they came into the league, even if they were only in training camp or on a practice squad.

To the far right of the first line is the player's Risk for fantasy football in 2019. As explained in the quarterback section, the standard is for players to be marked Green. Players with higher than normal risk are marked Yellow, and players with the highest risk are marked Red. Players who are most likely to match or surpass our forecast—primarily second-stringers with low projections—are marked Blue. Risk is not only based on age and injury probability, but how a player's projection compares to his recent performance as well as our confidence (or lack thereof) in his offensive teammates.

Next we give the last three years of player stats. First come games played and games started (**G/GS**). Games played is the official NFL total and may include games in which a player appeared on special teams but did not carry the ball or catch a pass. We also have a total of offensive **Snaps** for each season. The next four columns are familiar: **Runs**, rushing yards (**Yds**), yards per rush (**Yd/R**) and rushing touchdowns (**TD**).

The entry for fumbles (**FUM**) includes all fumbles by this running back, no matter whether they were recovered by the offense or defense. Holding onto the ball is an identifiable skill; fumbling it so that your own offense can recover it is not. (For more on this issue, see the essay "Pregame Show" in the front of the book.) This entry combines fumbles on both carries and receptions. Fumbles on special teams are not included. (That's particularly important for Jalen Richard of Oakland, who fumbled seven times on special teams in 2017.)

The next five columns give our advanced metrics for rushing: **DVOA** (Defense-Adjusted Value Over Average), **DYAR** (Defense-Adjusted Yards Above Replacement), and **YAR** (Yards Above Replacement), along with the player's rank (**Rk**) in both **DVOA** and **DYAR**. These metrics compare every carry by the running back to a league-average baseline based on the game situations in which that running back carried the ball. DVOA and DYAR are also adjusted based on the opposing defense. The methods used to compute these numbers are described in detail in the "Statistical Toolbox" introduction in the front of the book. The important distinctions between them are:

- DVOA is a rate statistic, while DYAR is a cumulative statistic. Thus, a higher DVOA means more value per play, while a higher DYAR means more aggregate value over the entire season.
- Because DYAR is defense-adjusted and YAR is not, a player whose DYAR is higher than his YAR faced a harder-than-average schedule. A player whose DYAR is lower than his YAR faced an easier-than-average schedule.

To qualify for ranking in rushing DVOA and DYAR, a running back must have had 100 carries in that season. Last year, 47 running backs qualified to be ranked in these stats, compared to 47 backs in 2017 and 42 backs in 2016.

Success Rate (**Suc%**), listed along with rank, represents running back consistency as measured by successful running plays divided by total running plays. (The definition for success is explained in the "Statistical Toolbox" introduction in the front of the book.) A player with high DVOA and a low Success Rate mixes long runs with plays on which he was stuffed at or behind the line of scrimmage. A player with low DVOA and a high Success Rate generally gets the yards needed, but rarely gets more. The league-average Success Rate in 2018 was 50 percent. Success Rate is not adjusted for the defenses a player faced.

We also give a total of broken tackles (**BTkl**) according to charting from Sports Info Solutions. This total includes broken tackles on both runs and receptions. Please note that SIS marked broken tackles roughly 8 percent more often in 2017 than in either 2016 or 2018.

The shaded columns to the right of broken tackles give data for each running back as a pass receiver. Receptions (**Rec**) counts passes caught, while Passes (**Pass**) counts total passes

Todd Gurley			Height: 6-1		Weight: 222		College: Georgia				Draft: 2015/1 (10)		Born: 3-Aug-1994		Age: 25		Risk: Red		
Year	Team	G/GS	Snaps	Runs	Yds	TD	Yd/R	FUM	DVOA	Rk	DYAR	Rk	YAR	Suc%	Rk	BTkl	Pass	Rec	Yds	TD	C%	Yd/C	YAC	DVOA	Rk	DYAR	Rk
2016	LAR	16/16	742	278	885	6	3.2	2	-14.4%	37	-66	37	-75	41%	36	56	58	43	327	0	74%	7.6	8.2	-9.9%	39	13	35
2017	LAR	15/15	794	279	1305	13	4.7	5	13.9%	4	268	2	205	53%	5	79	87	64	788	6	74%	12.3	12.3	35.9%	7	236	2
2018	LAR	14/14	825	256	1251	17	4.9	1	23.6%	1	366	1	342	57%	4	42	81	59	580	4	73%	9.8	9.9	6.9%	20	98	12
2019	LAR			238	1118	12	4.7	4	10.5%								70	54	511	2	77%	9.5		16.6%			

thrown to this player, complete or incomplete. The next four columns list receiving yards (**Yds**), receiving touchdowns (**TD**), catch rate (**C%**), yards per catch (**Yd/C**), and average yards after the catch (**YAC**).

Our research has shown that receivers bear some responsibility for incomplete passes, even though only their catches are tracked in official statistics. Catch rate represents receptions divided by all intended passes for this running back. The average NFL running back caught 76 percent of passes in 2018. Unfortunately, we don't have room to post the best and worst running backs in receiving plus-minus, but you'll find the top 10 and bottom 10 running backs in this metric listed in the statistical appendix.

Finally we have receiving DVOA and DYAR, which are entirely separate from rushing DVOA and DYAR. To qualify for ranking in receiving DVOA and DYAR, a running back must have 25 passes thrown to him in that season. There are 53 players ranked for 2018, 62 players ranked for 2017, and 53 players ranked for 2016. Numbers without opponent adjustment (YAR and VOA) can be found on our website, FootballOutsiders.com.

The italicized row of statistics for the 2019 season is our 2019 KUBIAK projection based on a complicated regression analysis that takes into account numerous variables including projected role, performance over the past two years, projected team offense and defense, historical comparables, height, age, experience of the offensive line, and strength of schedule.

It is difficult to accurately project statistics for a 162-game baseball season, but it is exponentially more difficult to accurately project statistics for a 16-game football season. Consider the listed projections not as a prediction of exact numbers, but the mean of a range of possible performances. What's important is less the exact number of yards we project, and more which players are projected to improve or decline. Actual performance will vary from our projection less for veteran starters and more for rookies and third-stringers, for whom we must base our projections on much smaller career statistical samples. Touchdown numbers will vary more than yardage numbers.

Finally, in a section we call "Going Deep," we briefly discuss lower-round rookies, free-agent veterans, and practice-squad players who may play a role during the 2019 season or beyond.

Top 20 RB by Rushing DYAR (Total Value), 2018

Rank	Player	Team	DYAR
1	Todd Gurley	LAR	367
2	Derrick Henry	TEN	280
3	Alvin Kamara	NO	237
4	Marlon Mack	IND	215
5	Melvin Gordon	LAC	208
6	Phillip Lindsay	DEN	201
7	Christian McCaffrey	CAR	167
8	Joe Mixon	CIN	154
9	Ezekiel Elliott	DAL	150
10	Aaron Jones	GB	145
11	Kareem Hunt	KC	131
12	Gus Edwards	BAL	130
13	Chris Carson	SEA	127
14	Kerryon Johnson	DET	124
15	Saquon Barkley	NYG	123
16	James Conner	PIT	100
17	Frank Gore	MIA	87
18	Nick Chubb	CLE	80
19	Mike Davis	SEA	78
20	Mark Ingram	NO	71

Minimum 100 carries.

Top 20 RB by Rushing DVOA (Value per Rush), 2018

Rank	Player	Team	DVOA
1	Todd Gurley	LAR	23.7%
2	Derrick Henry	TEN	23.1%
3	Melvin Gordon	LAC	20.5%
4	Alvin Kamara	NO	18.5%
5	Kerryon Johnson	DET	17.3%
6	Phillip Lindsay	DEN	17.0%
7	Aaron Jones	GB	16.9%
8	Marlon Mack	IND	16.6%
9	Gus Edwards	BAL	14.0%
10	Christian McCaffrey	CAR	9.7%
11	Mike Davis	SEA	8.7%
11	Kareem Hunt	KC	8.7%
13	Joe Mixon	CIN	6.5%
14	Frank Gore	MIA	5.8%
15	Austin Ekeler	LAC	4.7%
16	Kenyan Drake	MIA	4.7%
17	Chris Carson	SEA	3.3%
18	Ezekiel Elliott	DAL	3.0%
19	Saquon Barkley	NYG	2.9%
20	Mark Ingram	NO	2.8%

Minimum 100 carries.

Top 10 RB by Receiving DYAR (Total Value), 2018

Rank	Player	Team	DYAR
1	Kareem Hunt	KC	198
2	Alvin Kamara	NO	197
3	James White	NE	194
4	Tarik Cohen	CHI	184
5	Christian McCaffrey	CAR	183
6	Jalen Richard	OAK	138
7	Austin Ekeler	LAC	131
8	Kenyan Drake	MIA	123
9	James Conner	PIT	112
10	Matt Breida	SF	105

Minimum 25 passes.

Top 10 RB by Receiving DVOA (Value per Pass), 2018

Rank	Player	Team	DVOA
1	Kareem Hunt	KC	79.4%
2	Matt Breida	SF	44.8%
3	Jaylen Samuels	PIT	36.4%
4	Austin Ekeler	LAC	30.3%
5	Adrian Peterson	WAS	22.3%
6	Tarik Cohen	CHI	21.3%
7	Alvin Kamara	NO	19.4%
8	Kyle Juszczyk	SF	18.7%
9	Jalen Richard	OAK	17.4%
10	Tevin Coleman	ATL	17.2%

Minimum 25 passes.

Josh Adams
Height: 6-2   Weight: 217   College: Notre Dame   Draft: 2018/FA   Born: 29-Oct-1996   Age: 23   Risk: Red

Year	Team	G/GS	Snaps	Runs	Yds	TD	Yd/R	FUM	DVOA	Rk	DYAR	Rk	YAR	Suc%	Rk	BTkl	Pass	Rec	Yds	TD	C%	Yd/C	YAC	DVOA	Rk	DYAR	Rk
2018	PHI	14/5	252	120	511	3	4.3	1	-11.0%	34	-12	34	-16	50%	19	16	13	7	58	0	54%	8.3	9.3	-37.9%	--	-19	--
2019	PHI			37	160	1	4.4	1	3.8%								9	7	44	0	78%	6.3		-11.8%			

Adams was never intended to be the Eagles' leading rusher, but the circumstance called for it and he fared better than an undrafted rookie should be expected to. He has a tall, awkward running form, but shows enough balance through contact and speed to make good on the blocks his linemen provide for him. Adams was far more consistent than teammates Corey Clement or Wendell Smallwood. Given the pinch Philadelphia was put in through injuries to their other backs, getting baseline production out of Adams was a win. The downside to Adams is that he is nonexistent in the pass game and can not match Jay Ajayi's explosive potential that ignited the Eagles' run offense down the stretch in 2017. He is a barebones running back who is only useful on two downs and provides minimal upside on those downs. If Adams can develop as a pass-catcher, which he barely did in college, he may work himself into a regular role in 2019, but the offseason additions of Jordan Howard and Miles Sanders will be difficult roadblocks for him to clear.

Jay Ajayi
Height: 6-0   Weight: 221   College: Boise State   Draft: 2015/5 (149)   Born: 15-Jun-1993   Age: 26   Risk: N/A

Year	Team	G/GS	Snaps	Runs	Yds	TD	Yd/R	FUM	DVOA	Rk	DYAR	Rk	YAR	Suc%	Rk	BTkl	Pass	Rec	Yds	TD	C%	Yd/C	YAC	DVOA	Rk	DYAR	Rk
2016	MIA	15/12	582	260	1272	8	4.9	4	9.3%	13	185	7	126	43%	32	59	35	27	151	0	77%	5.6	4.9	-20.7%	47	-14	46
2017	2TM	14/8	509	208	873	1	4.2	3	-5.1%	28	27	27	21	43%	30	59	34	24	158	1	71%	6.6	7.3	-23.6%	55	-18	53
2018	PHI	4/3	120	45	184	3	4.1	1	-17.9%	--	-19	--	5	47%	--	11	6	5	20	0	83%	4.0	6.0	-24.7%	--	-4	--

Ajayi's history of ACL issues is well-documented. He tore his ACL as a freshman at Boise State in 2011, and while he played exceptionally in the Mountain West, many teams were concerned that his knee had long-term issues and would not hold up in the NFL. Prior to 2018, Ajayi's knees had held up fine, though he did fracture a rib and suffer a concussion over that period. Four games into last season, Ajayi's left knee gave in, resulting in a second ACL tear that many teams had feared on draft day four years ago. Despite a fantastic 2017 half-season with the Eagles and a solid start to 2018, Ajayi was not a hot item on the free agent market. It is possible that a second ACL tear, especially troubling for a violent and explosive runner such as Ajayi, renders the former Pro Bowler a shell of his former self. Everyone loves a comeback story and Ajayi would not be the first post-ACL success, but it is hard to blame teams for wanting to steer clear and invest their resources elsewhere before entertaining Ajayi.

Buck Allen   Height: 6-0   Weight: 221   College: USC   Draft: 2015/4 (125)   Born: 27-Aug-1991   Age: 28   Risk: Red

Year	Team	G/GS	Snaps	Runs	Yds	TD	Yd/R	FUM	DVOA	Rk	DYAR	Rk	YAR	Suc%	Rk	BTkl	Pass	Rec	Yds	TD	C%	Yd/C	YAC	DVOA	Rk	DYAR	Rk
2016	BAL	8/0	41	9	34	0	3.8	0	-18.0%	--	-3	--	2	56%	--	3	4	3	15	0	75%	5.0	7.3	-12.1%	--	0	--
2017	BAL	16/0	466	153	591	4	3.9	0	6.2%	13	96	13	67	47%	17	22	60	46	250	2	77%	5.4	4.7	-16.7%	49	-10	51
2018	BAL	14/0	310	41	110	3	2.7	1	-16.3%	--	-16	--	-19	41%	--	9	43	35	196	2	81%	5.6	5.3	-15.4%	42	-4	41
2019	NO			32	145	0	4.5	1	4.0%								30	23	203	2	77%	8.8		16.9%			

A smart player without any standout athletic traits, but with demonstrated basic professional competence at his job, Allen is a solid fit as a roughly replacement-level veteran reserve running back who can do most things adequately when needed. He has not started a game since his rookie year, but has still accumulated over 200 carries and over 100 targets behind an ever-changing cast of starters in Baltimore. Last year, his playing time mostly consisted of mop-up and third-down duty as a cog in the Joe Flacco checkdown machine. The emergence of Lamar Jackson bumped him off the field almost entirely—Allen had only 10 offensive snaps and two touches after Jackson took over as the starting quarterback in Week 11. He latched on with the Saints after the draft, and that "basic competence" skill set should keep him on the fringes of rosters for quite a bit. He just doesn't have the one knockout tool that's going to earn him playing time no matter what.

C.J. Anderson   Height: 5-8   Weight: 224   College: California   Draft: 2013/FA   Born: 2-Feb-1991   Age: 28   Risk: Green

Year	Team	G/GS	Snaps	Runs	Yds	TD	Yd/R	FUM	DVOA	Rk	DYAR	Rk	YAR	Suc%	Rk	BTkl	Pass	Rec	Yds	TD	C%	Yd/C	YAC	DVOA	Rk	DYAR	Rk
2016	DEN	7/7	314	110	437	4	4.0	0	-13.5%	36	-23	35	9	39%	41	17	24	16	128	1	67%	8.0	6.8	-15.4%	--	-2	--
2017	DEN	16/16	617	245	1007	3	4.1	1	-6.9%	34	16	30	74	42%	34	47	40	28	224	1	70%	8.0	7.7	-13.2%	44	1	44
2018	2TM	11/3	152	67	403	2	6.0	0	41.2%	--	141	--	135	67%	--	12	9	5	41	1	56%	8.2	9.0	-34.4%	--	-12	--
2019	DET			105	441	3	4.2	2	0.8%								14	10	72	0	71%	7.2		-10.7%			

There is more to Anderson's story than reviving himself in Los Angeles after being cut midseason by Carolina. In taking over the bulk of the workload from a hobbled Todd Gurley, Anderson changed the complexion of Sean McVay's offense. McVay's scheme is based on wide zone and weak zone; therefore, many of their play-action concepts feed off those looks. However, with Anderson, the Rams ran more duo concepts that did not as effectively blend with the play-action game. They still ran plenty of wide zone, but the system was a little choppier than it had been previously. Anderson's 14 targets in five games (including the playoffs) to Gurley's 88 targets in 17 games also made for a clear difference between the two players and was a tip-off for defenses. In each the two seasons prior, both in Denver, Anderson posted the lowest success rates on first and second down among Broncos running backs with at least 50 carries. He may have some left in the tank, but it has to raise concern that Anderson's only successful stretch in the past three seasons came through one of the league's best offensive minds molding to his strengths—and it still took the offense down a peg in the playoffs.

Cameron Artis-Payne   Height: 5-10   Weight: 212   College: Auburn   Draft: 2015/5 (174)   Born: 23-Jun-1992   Age: 27   Risk: Yellow

Year	Team	G/GS	Snaps	Runs	Yds	TD	Yd/R	FUM	DVOA	Rk	DYAR	Rk	YAR	Suc%	Rk	BTkl	Pass	Rec	Yds	TD	C%	Yd/C	YAC	DVOA	Rk	DYAR	Rk
2016	CAR	3/3	84	36	144	2	4.0	0	-4.5%	--	6	--	21	50%	--	8	1	1	11	0	100%	11.0	15.0	128.6%	--	8	--
2017	CAR	13/0	37	18	95	1	5.3	0	4.1%	--	11	--	10	44%	--	3	1	1	2	0	100%	2.0	6.0	-77.2%	--	-4	--
2018	CAR	9/0	48	19	69	1	3.6	0	31.5%	--	37	--	13	58%	--	1	4	3	15	0	75%	5.0	5.0	-50.3%	--	-8	--
2019	CAR			36	139	0	3.8	1	-7.6%								7	5	31	0	71%	6.3		-20.2%			

Artis-Payne has morphed into a solid special teams player since the Panthers drafted him in the fifth round in 2015, but the backup power runner hasn't started a game on offense since 2016 and his total yards from scrimmage have declined every year. Though a shallow depth chart in theory gives Artis-Payne more opportunities as Christian McCaffrey's direct backup, in practice he was in the same spot last year after C.J. Anderson's release. He still failed to reach 20 carries or 90 total yards, and 56 of his 69 rushing yards came in the meaningless season finale against the Saints. Last year, two wide receivers had more rushing yards for the Panthers. This year, it could easily be two rookie running backs as well.

Kalen Ballage
Height: 6-1 Weight: 228 College: Arizona State Draft: 2018/4 (131) Born: 22-Dec-1995 Age: 24 Risk: Red

Year	Team	G/GS	Snaps	Runs	Yds	TD	Yd/R	FUM	DVOA	Rk	DYAR	Rk	YAR	Suc%	Rk	BTkl	Pass	Rec	Yds	TD	C%	Yd/C	YAC	DVOA	Rk	DYAR	Rk
2018	MIA	12/0	92	36	191	1	5.3	1	1.0%	--	16	--	0	42%	--	2	11	9	56	0	82%	6.2	8.4	-39.6%	--	-17	--
2019	MIA			139	596	3	4.3	4	-5.0%								34	25	201	0	74%	8.0		-7.2%			

Ballage ripped off a 75-yard run against the Vikings in Week 15 and took a bunch of Wildcat snaps in Week 17 against the Bills, mishandling one snap for a fumble. Otherwise, it was an uneventful season for the fourth-round pick. Big-play potential is Ballage's calling card, and the new coaching staff talked Ballage up early in minicamp. He may max out as a change-up back (which was his role in college), but look for him to get more opportunities this year.

Peyton Barber
Height: 5-10 Weight: 228 College: Auburn Draft: 2016/FA Born: 27-Jun-1994 Age: 25 Risk: Yellow

Year	Team	G/GS	Snaps	Runs	Yds	TD	Yd/R	FUM	DVOA	Rk	DYAR	Rk	YAR	Suc%	Rk	BTkl	Pass	Rec	Yds	TD	C%	Yd/C	YAC	DVOA	Rk	DYAR	Rk
2016	TB	15/1	136	55	223	1	4.1	0	-17.2%	--	-19	--	11	47%	--	8	6	5	28	0	83%	5.6	2.8	-10.2%	--	1	--
2017	TB	16/4	254	108	423	3	3.9	2	4.4%	15	63	19	58	57%	3	16	19	16	114	0	84%	7.1	7.1	-11.1%	--	3	--
2018	TB	16/16	616	234	871	5	3.7	1	-12.4%	38	-37	41	-83	44%	36	44	29	20	92	1	69%	4.6	3.2	-35.1%	53	-34	53
2019	TB			174	665	4	3.8	2	-6.4%								26	19	132	1	73%	7.0		-11.3%			

Barber had more carries than all but eight running backs last season: Ezekiel Elliott, Saquon Barkley, David Johnson, Todd Gurley, Adrian Peterson, Jordan Howard, Chris Carson, and Joe Mixon. Of that group, only Johnson was more inefficient than Barber by DVOA. The Buccaneers offensive line was far from blameless, however. Barber often had to earn every inch of his 2-yard runs. Case in point: on one carry against Cleveland, not one, not two, but three Browns hit him in the backfield. He literally dragged the last one—linebacker Jamie Collins—5 yards. He's a tough runner, but given his lack of pass-catching skills, is better suited to a complementary role. Barber should lose some of his carries to Ronald Jones this year, but given how badly Jones struggled as a rookie, it's hard to tell how many.

Saquon Barkley
Height: 6-0 Weight: 233 College: Penn State Draft: 2018/1 (2) Born: 7-Feb-1997 Age: 22 Risk: Green

Year	Team	G/GS	Snaps	Runs	Yds	TD	Yd/R	FUM	DVOA	Rk	DYAR	Rk	YAR	Suc%	Rk	BTkl	Pass	Rec	Yds	TD	C%	Yd/C	YAC	DVOA	Rk	DYAR	Rk
2018	NYG	16/16	853	261	1307	11	5.0	0	3.3%	18	127	14	45	41%	40	94	121	91	721	4	75%	7.9	8.4	-0.7%	28	86	13
2019	NYG			297	1391	12	4.7	3	11.0%								119	87	701	3	73%	8.1		-1.9%			

The list of players with 500 or more receiving yards and 1,250 or more rushing yards in their rookie season: Barkley, Marshall Faulk, Edgerrin James, Billy Sims. That's a Hall of Famer, someone who should be one, and a guy who looked like he'd be one before a catastrophic knee injury. Barkley made an instant impact and the only real problem he has as a player is the circumstantial changes of professional football that have limited just what a running back can add to winning a game. Even down to the little things like not fumbling once all season, Barkley played above the rest of his teammates in reaching the yardage marks he did. It's hard to understand what he could do better, short of taking handoffs and chucking them downfield to open receivers. He truly is a generational back.

Le'Veon Bell
Height: 6-1 Weight: 230 College: Michigan State Draft: 2013/2 (48) Born: 18-Feb-1992 Age: 27 Risk: Yellow

Year	Team	G/GS	Snaps	Runs	Yds	TD	Yd/R	FUM	DVOA	Rk	DYAR	Rk	YAR	Suc%	Rk	BTkl	Pass	Rec	Yds	TD	C%	Yd/C	YAC	DVOA	Rk	DYAR	Rk
2016	PIT	12/12	781	261	1268	7	4.9	4	17.3%	5	277	3	271	56%	3	61	94	75	616	2	80%	8.2	8.9	16.2%	12	165	2
2017	PIT	15/15	945	321	1291	9	4.0	3	7.9%	11	214	5	261	49%	11	79	106	85	655	2	80%	7.7	8.0	2.5%	29	101	11
2019	NYJ			296	1260	11	4.3	3	5.7%								96	71	603	3	74%	8.5		4.7%			

Some of the most legendary running backs in NFL history also engaged in some of the most contentious holdouts:
- John Riggins missed the entire 1980 season while holding out for more money from the Redskins. New coach Joe Gibbs coaxed Riggins out of semi-retirement with the help of a renegotiated contract for 1981 ("I'm bored, I'm broke, I'm back," he famously announced), and Riggins went on to enjoy his signature seasons.
- Eric Dickerson missed the first two games of the 1985 season with a holdout that began in training camp, then rushed for 1,234 yards for the remainder of that season and led the NFL in rushing in 1986. Dickerson's contract demands also led

to his trade to the Colts in 1987 and a prolonged holdout/fiasco/spitting contest in 1990. Dickerson is still holding out for money, this time for participating in Hall of Fame events. The dude's never off brand.

- Emmitt Smith held out for two games in 1993. The Cowboys went 0-2 while giving someone named Derrick Lassic 20 touches per game and hoping no one noticed. Jerry Jones flew to Emmitt's home in a jet filled with money, and Smith returned to lead the NFL in rushing and the Cowboys to the Super Bowl.
- Bo Jackson held out after being drafted by the Buccaneers, who bungled their courtship of the preternaturally talented but obdurate Heisman winner. The Raiders scooped him up, accommodated his baseball passion and didn't antagonize him the way the clueless 1980s Buccaneers braintrust did. Bo knows the rest, and so do you.

One moral of this story is that holdouts don't hurt running backs much; only the late-career Dickerson, pushing 30 and with several 380- to 400-carry seasons on his odometer, showed any ill effects of missing weeks or months of training camp.

Another moral of this story: the free-spirited Riggins was earning just $300,000 when he held out, Dickerson was initially seeking guaranteed disability insurance, and Bo was more motivated by personal freedom than money. Running backs have known for decades that their careers are short and that teams use them as battering rams, then toss them aside. Bell held out for a combination of financial security and respect. He'll get the former from the Jets; whether he gets the latter depends on many forces, only some of which are under his control.

Giovani Bernard Height: 5-8   Weight: 202   College: North Carolina   Draft: 2013/2 (37)   Born: 22-Nov-1991   Age: 28   Risk: Yellow

Year	Team	G/GS	Snaps	Runs	Yds	TD	Yd/R	FUM	DVOA	Rk	DYAR	Rk	YAR	Suc%	Rk	BTkl	Pass	Rec	Yds	TD	C%	Yd/C	YAC	DVOA	Rk	DYAR	Rk
2016	CIN	10/2	394	91	337	2	3.7	1	-2.1%	--	24	--	22	49%	--	17	51	39	336	1	76%	8.6	6.4	22.4%	7	101	10
2017	CIN	16/2	486	105	458	2	4.4	0	3.4%	16	48	24	43	40%	40	22	60	43	389	2	72%	9.0	10.0	-10.3%	41	11	40
2018	CIN	12/4	329	56	211	3	3.8	0	-1.6%	--	16	--	18	41%	--	10	48	35	218	0	73%	6.2	6.5	-11.8%	37	5	37
2019	CIN			56	232	1	4.1	1	-3.3%								55	39	287	2	71%	7.4		-8.6%			

Bernard heads into the last season of his contract coming off his worst season to date, missing time to an MCL injury and ceding snaps to Joe Mixon as Mixon became the integral part of Cincinnati's offense. Bernard will turn 28 in November, and he looks largely extraneous on this depth chart. This will mostly be an audition season for him behind Mixon. If a team values him enough to poach him from the Bengals, he has already shown over the course of his career that he has the talent to lead a committee, if not the body to stand up to 250 touches of punishment. The Bengals drafted two running backs, if you want an idea about how they feel about continuing to pay Bernard.

LeGarrette Blount Height: 6-0   Weight: 247   College: Oregon   Draft: 2010/FA   Born: 5-Dec-1986   Age: 33   Risk: N/A

Year	Team	G/GS	Snaps	Runs	Yds	TD	Yd/R	FUM	DVOA	Rk	DYAR	Rk	YAR	Suc%	Rk	BTkl	Pass	Rec	Yds	TD	C%	Yd/C	YAC	DVOA	Rk	DYAR	Rk
2016	NE	16/8	527	299	1161	18	3.9	2	1.5%	18	131	14	84	44%	28	48	8	7	38	0	88%	5.4	6.1	-31.0%	--	-7	--
2017	PHI	16/11	353	173	766	2	4.4	1	-9.8%	36	-9	37	-5	43%	33	48	8	8	50	1	100%	6.3	5.9	41.4%	--	25	--
2018	DET	16/8	281	154	418	5	2.7	2	-27.9%	46	-125	47	-142	37%	44	24	15	10	67	0	67%	6.7	8.7	-52.5%	--	-38	--

Three things in life are certain: death, taxes, and LaGarrette Blount earning more touches than you thought he was going to. Blount has at least 125 carries in each of the past six seasons, one of just five running backs to do so. Somehow, he always finds his way into a regular role, whether that means being the Patriots' 18-touchdown battering ram or the Lions' backup and emergency plan behind Kerryon Johnson. Blount, in his prime, was a force downhill complemented by stunning shiftiness for someone his size. His age started to show last season, however, and he appeared to have lost some of the oomph that made used to make him effective. Blount's putrid success rate was far worse than Johnson's (53 percent, ranked 12th). As Blount approaches his mid-thirties, the curtains have begun to close on an entertaining and underappreciated career.

Alfred Blue Height: 6-2   Weight: 223   College: Louisiana State   Draft: 2014/6 (181)   Born: 27-Apr-1991   Age: 28   Risk: Yellow

Year	Team	G/GS	Snaps	Runs	Yds	TD	Yd/R	FUM	DVOA	Rk	DYAR	Rk	YAR	Suc%	Rk	BTkl	Pass	Rec	Yds	TD	C%	Yd/C	YAC	DVOA	Rk	DYAR	Rk
2016	HOU	14/2	238	100	420	1	4.2	1	-7.2%	27	6	27	29	45%	24	10	16	12	40	0	75%	3.3	2.3	-59.7%	--	-42	--
2017	HOU	11/0	158	71	262	1	3.7	0	-4.0%	--	14	--	6	42%	--	9	9	7	54	0	78%	7.7	6.0	15.8%	--	15	--
2018	HOU	16/2	461	150	499	2	3.3	0	-23.0%	44	-93	44	-98	41%	39	10	27	20	154	0	74%	7.7	5.4	-20.5%	48	-10	47
2019	JAX			75	325	1	4.3	2	-2.9%								21	15	100	0	71%	6.7		-21.0%			

ALFRED BLUE OWNER'S MANUAL: Alfred Blue will get you the yards you blocked, and perhaps a little more if he happens to bowl over somebody. That second part doesn't happen often, as you might be able to tell from his broken tackle numbers. Do not ask Alfred Blue to catch passes, because you won't like the results. Use as a goal-line battering ram and special-teamer. Do not have high expectations. The Jaguars signed Blue as a true Leonard Fournette backup, which is probably one of the best outcomes for Blue given their stylistic similarities. That is where the comparisons between Blue and Fournette end.

Devontae Booker Height: 5-11 Weight: 219 College: Utah Draft: 2016/4 (136) Born: 27-May-1992 Age: 27 Risk: Red

Year	Team	G/GS	Snaps	Runs	Yds	TD	Yd/R	FUM	DVOA	Rk	DYAR	Rk	YAR	Suc%	Rk	BTkl	Pass	Rec	Yds	TD	C%	Yd/C	YAC	DVOA	Rk	DYAR	Rk
2016	DEN	16/6	497	174	612	4	3.5	4	-21.1%	39	-95	41	-62	45%	27	24	45	31	265	1	69%	8.5	8.3	-31.4%	51	-41	50
2017	DEN	13/0	291	79	299	1	3.8	2	-9.2%	--	-2	--	25	47%	--	18	38	30	275	0	79%	9.2	7.8	7.7%	17	45	25
2018	DEN	16/0	316	34	183	1	5.4	1	9.6%	--	27	--	43	50%	--	21	51	38	275	0	75%	7.2	6.3	-13.5%	39	1	39
2019	DEN			41	175	0	4.2	2	-4.5%								44	35	251	1	80%	7.2		-0.7%			

Booker has seen his carries drop every season in the league, becoming a clear third option behind rookies Phillip Lindsay and Royce Freeman last year. Booker still did lead Denver's running back committee in targets and receptions, but was slightly less efficient than Lindsay. He also blew just as many pass blocks as Lindsay did in a similar number of staps, so his pass-blocking prowess is somewhat overstated as well. A return to the zone-based system Booker excelled in as a rookie might help him bounce back some in 2019, but at the moment, there's nothing Booker does that one of the other two running backs doesn't do better.

Matt Breida Height: 5-11 Weight: 190 College: Georgia Southern Draft: 2017/FA Born: 28-Feb-1995 Age: 24 Risk: Yellow

Year	Team	G/GS	Snaps	Runs	Yds	TD	Yd/R	FUM	DVOA	Rk	DYAR	Rk	YAR	Suc%	Rk	BTkl	Pass	Rec	Yds	TD	C%	Yd/C	YAC	DVOA	Rk	DYAR	Rk
2017	SF	16/0	310	105	465	2	4.4	1	13.0%	5	87	15	79	47%	16	12	37	21	180	1	59%	8.6	7.3	-4.8%	37	16	37
2018	SF	14/13	364	153	814	3	5.3	1	1.3%	23	58	23	97	46%	30	28	31	27	261	2	87%	9.7	8.7	44.8%	2	105	10
2019	SF			99	444	3	4.5	2	4.1%								31	26	205	0	84%	7.9		2.8%			

Breida ran a 4.39 40-yard dash at Georgia Southern's pro day in 2017, and since signing with San Francisco he has been a big play waiting to happen. Of the 45 running backs with at least 200 carries in the last two years, only three have averaged more yards per carry, and only five have averaged more yards per catch. Nineteen of his 306 career runs and receptions have gained 20 yards or more; for comparison's sake, Saquon Barkley has 21 20-plus-yard gains in 352 touches. A normal team would be trying to get Breida more involved in the offense, but the 49ers devoted free agency and draft picks to get other runners and receivers to give the ball to instead. Projecting how the 49ers will use all their running backs this year is like counting all the grains of sand at the beach.

Malcolm Brown Height: 5-11 Weight: 224 College: Texas Draft: 2015/FA Born: 15-May-1993 Age: 26 Risk: Green

Year	Team	G/GS	Snaps	Runs	Yds	TD	Yd/R	FUM	DVOA	Rk	DYAR	Rk	YAR	Suc%	Rk	BTkl	Pass	Rec	Yds	TD	C%	Yd/C	YAC	DVOA	Rk	DYAR	Rk
2016	LAR	16/0	65	18	39	0	2.2	1	-67.0%	--	-44	--	-43	22%	--	4	3	3	46	0	100%	15.3	14.0	166.9%	--	25	--
2017	LAR	11/1	150	63	246	1	3.9	1	-6.9%	--	4	--	-3	33%	--	13	11	9	53	0	82%	5.9	6.6	-24.6%	--	-7	--
2018	LAR	12/0	123	43	212	0	4.9	0	9.7%	--	36	--	37	67%	--	7	7	5	52	1	71%	10.4	7.8	43.5%	--	23	--
2019	LAR			36	163	1	4.5	1	2.4%								13	11	83	1	85%	7.5		10.8%			

Brown did not receive a ton of opportunities in 2018. Just when Todd Gurley's knee issues began to flare up in early December, Brown went down with a season-ending broken clavicle, opening the door for C.J. Anderson to step into the lineup. While a former undrafted free agent normally would not be a high priority to retain in free agency, with long-term questions surrounding Gurley's health, the Rams decided to match the offer sheet Detroit extended to Brown. The Rams' backfield is crowded thanks to the continuing presence of Gurley and the addition of third-round pick Darrell Henderson, but the Rams coaching staff trusted Brown enough to make bringing him back a priority. That should give him a fair shot to have an impact on the ground as a complement to the other two backs in 2019.

Rex Burkhead

Height: 5-10   Weight: 214   College: Nebraska   Draft: 2013/6 (190)   Born: 2-Jul-1990   Age: 29   Risk: Red

Year	Team	G/GS	Snaps	Runs	Yds	TD	Yd/R	FUM	DVOA	Rk	DYAR	Rk	YAR	Suc%	Rk	BTkl	Pass	Rec	Yds	TD	C%	Yd/C	YAC	DVOA	Rk	DYAR	Rk
2016	CIN	16/1	238	74	344	2	4.6	1	42.0%	--	163	--	126	62%	--	24	20	17	145	0	85%	8.5	8.4	7.3%	--	22	--
2017	NE	10/3	196	64	264	5	4.1	1	10.5%	--	56	--	65	53%	--	14	36	30	254	3	83%	8.5	6.1	33.7%	8	102	8
2018	NE	8/4	151	57	186	0	3.3	2	-8.2%	--	1	--	-43	40%	--	14	20	14	131	1	70%	9.4	8.6	-9.1%	--	5	--
2019	NE			44	207	1	4.7	2	6.5%								32	27	243	2	84%	9.0		28.2%			

Injuries blighted Burkhead's second year in New England, just as they did his first. The six-year veteran has never started more than four games in a regular season, and never recorded more than 74 carries or 350 rushing yards. Now entering his age-29 season, Burkhead is approaching the point at which running backs typically acquire more injuries, not fewer. He may have to be carefully managed, as New England did with Danny Amendola, if the Patriots are to get the best out of him.

When healthy, Burkhead's biggest asset for New England is his versatility. A key feature of the game-sealing drive in last year's Super Bowl was Burkhead's ability to be effective as a receiver split wide while also keeping the defense in "base" due to his effectiveness as a rusher. During his most productive season, 2017, he had almost as many yards receiving as rushing, and five of his 13 regular-season touchdowns have come through the air. The problem, other than injuries, is that he is not the best man for the job in either individual phase—he plays second fiddle to Sony Michel on rushing downs, and to James White in the passing game—so his contribution is heavily reliant on getting snaps as a backup and those specific "either-or" packages.

Trenton Cannon

Height: 5-11   Weight: 185   College: Virginia State   Draft: 2018/6 (204)   Born: 23-Dec-1994   Age: 25   Risk: Yellow

Year	Team	G/GS	Snaps	Runs	Yds	TD	Yd/R	FUM	DVOA	Rk	DYAR	Rk	YAR	Suc%	Rk	BTkl	Pass	Rec	Yds	TD	C%	Yd/C	YAC	DVOA	Rk	DYAR	Rk
2018	NYJ	16/0	185	38	113	1	3.0	0	-14.7%	--	-10	--	-31	37%	--	11	25	17	144	0	68%	8.5	6.9	-30.2%	52	-23	51
2019	NYJ			16	68	0	4.3	1	2.8%								18	13	70	0	72%	5.4		-33.1%			

The Jets drafted Cannon after he ran a 4.4-second 40 at his small-program pro day, then talked themselves into thinking they found Tyreek Hill 2.0. They fed Cannon all the screens and jet sweeps the coaching staff could dream up, which wasn't many. Other than a 35-yard catch on a wheel route against the Vikings, Cannon was a big-play threat who didn't produce big plays. Cannon might improve now that he has some experience and the Jets offense is more functional. He may also be a reminder that for every nifty-shifty guy who becomes Tyreek or Darren Sproles, there are at least a dozen other pint-sized college playmakers who don't have what it takes for the NFL.

Chris Carson

Height: 6-0   Weight: 218   College: Oklahoma State   Draft: 2017/7 (249)   Born: 16-Sep-1994   Age: 25   Risk: Red

Year	Team	G/GS	Snaps	Runs	Yds	TD	Yd/R	FUM	DVOA	Rk	DYAR	Rk	YAR	Suc%	Rk	BTkl	Pass	Rec	Yds	TD	C%	Yd/C	YAC	DVOA	Rk	DYAR	Rk
2017	SEA	4/3	152	49	208	0	4.2	0	7.0%	--	33	--	21	43%	--	21	8	7	59	1	88%	8.4	6.6	34.9%	--	26	--
2018	SEA	14/14	454	247	1151	9	4.7	3	3.9%	17	133	12	134	51%	15	61	24	20	163	0	83%	8.2	8.2	21.2%	--	43	--
2019	SEA			229	1026	8	4.5	4	4.3%								25	19	185	1	75%	9.7		13.4%			

Carson's biggest bugaboo entering 2018 was his ability to stay healthy, with injury issues dating back to his time in college. After missing the majority of 2017 due to a fractured leg, the Seahawks had reason to be concerned that the tough runner from Oklahoma State would not always be available. He did end up missing two games in 2018 due to some minor injuries, but when he was on the field, his battering ram style played well with Seattle's desire to recommit to playing bully-ball. Per Sports Info Solutions, Carson led the league in broken tackles on runs with 58, finishing just ahead of Saquon Barkley's 56. If he can stay healthy in 2019, Carson should have every opportunity to repeat his performance on the ground, given that Seattle has no interest in running the ball any less frequently moving forward.

Nick Chubb

Height: 5-11   Weight: 227   College: Georgia   Draft: 2018/2 (35)   Born: 27-Dec-1995   Age: 24   Risk: Green

Year	Team	G/GS	Snaps	Runs	Yds	TD	Yd/R	FUM	DVOA	Rk	DYAR	Rk	YAR	Suc%	Rk	BTkl	Pass	Rec	Yds	TD	C%	Yd/C	YAC	DVOA	Rk	DYAR	Rk
2018	CLE	16/9	395	192	996	8	5.2	0	1.1%	24	80	18	129	50%	19	47	29	20	149	2	69%	7.5	9.1	-4.6%	30	14	32
2019	CLE			261	1184	10	4.5	4	6.6%								36	27	253	1	75%	9.4		9.9%			

For the first six games of his rookie season, Chubb languished behind Carlos Hyde, getting just 16 carries. But in that time he ripped off runs of 63, 41, 19, and 17 yards, demonstrating to everyone not named Hue Jackson that he should have been the starter from Jump Street. In a move the Brad Pitt version of Billy Beane would have appreciated, Cleveland wisely traded Hyde to allow Chubb maximum opportunity, and he rewarded the Browns with 4.67 yards per carry and 80 DYAR over the final ten games. Just as Chubb was feeling good about being the Browns main back, the team signed disgraced Kareem Hunt to share duties once his eight-game suspension is over. That's the NFL for you—*sic transit gloria*, unless you are Tom Brady.

Corey Clement				Height: 5-10		Weight: 220		College: Wisconsin			Draft: 2017/FA			Born: 2-Nov-1994		Age: 25		Risk: Green	
Year	Team	G/GS	Snaps	Runs	Yds	TD	Yd/R	FUM	DVOA	Rk	DYAR	Rk	YAR	Suc%	Rk	BTkl	Pass	Rec	Yds	TD	C%	Yd/C	YAC	DVOA	Rk	DYAR	Rk
2017	PHI	16/0	256	74	321	4	4.3	0	14.5%	--	71	--	71	50%	--	11	15	10	123	2	67%	12.3	12.8	41.7%	--	50	--
2018	PHI	11/0	238	68	259	2	3.8	2	-19.9%	--	-31	--	-28	46%	--	8	25	22	192	0	88%	8.7	12.0	5.8%	21	29	29
2019	PHI			23	97	0	4.3	0	2.0%								13	10	73	0	77%	7.3		-3.6%			

Clement is a reliable pass-catcher and a decent, albeit uninspiring, runner. Heading into 2018, the plan for Clement was to be a sort of "do-it-all" back for the Eagles, with Jay Ajayi being the primary runner and Darren Sproles being the main pass-catcher. Ajayi and Sproles each missed more than half the season with injuries, however, which put the Eagles in a bind. Josh Adams was not a strong enough runner and Wendell Smallwood was not an effective enough pass-catcher to get any value out of a tweener like Clement: defenses just were not worried about Eagles' backs the way they were the previous year, so the run-pass ambiguity of Clement was ineffective. Now, Jordan Howard and Miles Sanders stand above Clement on the depth chart, but neither are as effective in the pass game as he is. As such, Clement's role as a passing-down back could spike this season.

Tarik Cohen				Height: 5-6		Weight: 179		College: North Carolina A&T			Draft: 2017/4 (119)			Born: 26-Jul-1995		Age: 24		Risk: Green	
Year	Team	G/GS	Snaps	Runs	Yds	TD	Yd/R	FUM	DVOA	Rk	DYAR	Rk	YAR	Suc%	Rk	BTkl	Pass	Rec	Yds	TD	C%	Yd/C	YAC	DVOA	Rk	DYAR	Rk
2017	CHI	16/4	360	87	370	2	4.3	2	-6.8%	--	6	--	4	46%	--	33	71	53	353	1	75%	6.7	5.9	-30.6%	58	-64	61
2018	CHI	16/7	495	99	444	3	4.5	3	-12.9%	--	-17	--	0	44%	--	37	91	71	725	5	78%	10.2	7.3	21.3%	6	184	4
2019	CHI			75	347	2	4.7	2	6.9%								82	63	531	2	77%	8.4		9.5%			

If Chicago's offseason moves have told us anything, it is that Matt Nagy does not plan on using Cohen as a bell-cow runner. While the team did trade away Jordan Howard, they signed Mike Davis and drafted David Montgomery to take his place. The two fresh faces provide the same downhill, efficient running style that the Bears do not get out of Cohen. Cohen, instead, is an all-or-nothing runner. Twenty-five of his 99 rushing attempts last season resulted in no gain or a loss, but he ripped off 13 carries of 10-plus yards. For comparison, Howard had 47 runs for no gain or a loss, but just 18 10-plus yard rushes on 250 attempts. Cohen lands on the more extreme end than Howard in both instances. Cohen's value is as a movable pass-catcher. Only five running backs saw more targets than Cohen, and just three earned a higher percentage of their targets from a wide receiver alignment. The goal for Cohen moving forward should not be to take on more carries, but refine what he is already good at: pass-catching and working in space.

Tevin Coleman				Height: 5-11		Weight: 206		College: Indiana			Draft: 2015/3 (73)			Born: 16-Apr-1993		Age: 26		Risk: Yellow	
Year	Team	G/GS	Snaps	Runs	Yds	TD	Yd/R	FUM	DVOA	Rk	DYAR	Rk	YAR	Suc%	Rk	BTkl	Pass	Rec	Yds	TD	C%	Yd/C	YAC	DVOA	Rk	DYAR	Rk
2016	ATL	13/0	353	118	520	8	4.4	1	9.7%	12	86	18	90	45%	25	24	40	31	421	3	78%	13.6	12.1	48.8%	1	136	5
2017	ATL	15/3	425	156	628	5	4.0	1	-6.5%	31	14	32	9	40%	39	31	39	27	299	3	69%	11.1	8.1	41.2%	4	121	6
2018	ATL	16/14	580	167	800	4	4.8	2	-6.4%	30	14	30	8	43%	37	26	44	32	276	5	73%	8.6	8.6	17.2%	10	77	16
2019	SF			141	599	4	4.3	3	1.3%								54	41	425	2	76%	10.4		23.0%			

The last time Coleman played for Kyle Shanahan, he led all NFL running backs in receiving DVOA. Mind you, he has been a pretty good receiver in Shanahan's absence too, and last year he set a career high in rushing yards as well. He now joins Matthew Breida and Kyle Juszczyk, giving San Francisco three running backs who finished in the top 10 in receiving DVOA and top 20 in receiving DYAR in 2018. Coleman can fit in wherever he is needed—over the past three years, he has consistently seen about 70 to 75 percent of his targets out of the backfield, with the rest split fairly evenly between the slot and out wide; his DVOA has consistently been higher on slot/wide throws. Projecting how the 49ers will use all their running backs this year is like sailing to the end of the ocean.

Alex Collins Height: 5-10 Weight: 217 College: Arkansas Draft: 2016/5 (171) Born: 26-Aug-1994 Age: 25 Risk: N/A

Year	Team	G/GS	Snaps	Runs	Yds	TD	Yd/R	FUM	DVOA	Rk	DYAR	Rk	YAR	Suc%	Rk	BTkl	Pass	Rec	Yds	TD	C%	Yd/C	YAC	DVOA	Rk	DYAR	Rk
2016	SEA	11/0	141	31	125	1	4.0	2	-13.0%	--	-6	--	-8	35%	--	7	11	11	84	0	100%	7.6	7.4	35.7%	--	37	--
2017	BAL	15/12	378	212	973	6	4.6	4	15.1%	3	205	6	181	51%	8	64	36	23	187	0	64%	8.1	8.4	-55.6%	62	-92	62
2018	BAL	10/10	311	114	411	7	3.6	3	-9.4%	33	-4	32	-12	47%	26	25	21	15	105	1	71%	7.0	6.5	-6.6%	--	9	--

One of the hardest things about speculating in fantasy football value is that the talent is often weighed against the opportunity. Collins has the talent to be the bruiser part of a good committee. He led the NFL in broken tackles in 2017 and was well on his way to another top-10 campaign in the stat this year. But the Ravens hadn't invested much in him, and three fumbles got him in John Harbaugh's doghouse. There may have been an opportunity for Collins to make this roster at some point before he was arrested in May and charged with possession of marijuana, intent to distribute marijuana, and possession of a handgun. The Ravens waived Collins before details of the arrest even circulated. Any team that wants to pick him up will have to weigh impending NFL discipline for his arrest. If Collins was a former first-round pick, someone probably would have stood up for him. As an end-of-roster, found-money guy? We wouldn't be surprised if he never got another NFL shot.

James Conner Height: 6-1 Weight: 233 College: Pittsburgh Draft: 2017/3 (105) Born: 5-May-1995 Age: 24 Risk: Yellow

Year	Team	G/GS	Snaps	Runs	Yds	TD	Yd/R	FUM	DVOA	Rk	DYAR	Rk	YAR	Suc%	Rk	BTkl	Pass	Rec	Yds	TD	C%	Yd/C	YAC	DVOA	Rk	DYAR	Rk
2017	PIT	14/0	68	32	144	0	4.5	0	10.2%	--	20	--	18	53%	--	4	1	0	0	0	0%	0.0	0.0	-130.7%	--	-7	--
2018	PIT	13/12	718	215	973	12	4.5	4	2.3%	21	99	16	137	49%	24	56	71	55	497	1	77%	9.0	10.0	15.2%	11	112	9
2019	PIT			238	1093	10	4.6	3	6.4%								78	60	519	1	77%	8.6		8.2%			

Conner had a strong 2018, but he wasn't Le'Veon Bell, despite Steelers Nation's ardent desire and insistence that he was every bit as good. More accurately, he presented a productive-enough facsimile without the baggage and team-last attitude, which was fine with most fans of the Black and Gold. Conner is also a cancer survivor and good soldier, so the deck is stacked in his direction.

Pittsburgh had the widest pass-run ratio split in the NFL in 2018, which figured into Conner's effectiveness. With Antonio Brown out of town, that split figures to narrow, which puts the onus on Conner to be as effective with one less weapon to distract defenses. The weapons on display in the passing game surely helped Conner's stalwart third-down splits—on 19 carries he sported an impressive 19.4% DVOA. He was equally good catching passes on the money down, to the tune of a 41.3% DVOA. On the other hand, his effectiveness in the red zone (11.8% DVOA, and only Todd Gurley had more than Conner's nine touchdowns from inside the 5-yard line) wasn't necessarily as aided by the receiving corps.

Dalvin Cook Height: 5-10 Weight: 210 College: Florida State Draft: 2017/2 (41) Born: 10-Aug-1995 Age: 24 Risk: Yellow

Year	Team	G/GS	Snaps	Runs	Yds	TD	Yd/R	FUM	DVOA	Rk	DYAR	Rk	YAR	Suc%	Rk	BTkl	Pass	Rec	Yds	TD	C%	Yd/C	YAC	DVOA	Rk	DYAR	Rk
2017	MIN	4/4	169	74	354	2	4.8	1	7.4%	--	48	--	66	55%	--	23	16	11	90	0	69%	8.2	9.5	-19.0%	--	-5	--
2018	MIN	11/10	490	133	615	2	4.6	2	-13.7%	41	-27	38	-27	41%	41	42	49	40	305	2	82%	7.6	9.3	2.1%	26	45	24
2019	MIN			251	1103	7	4.4	3	3.5%								71	58	464	2	82%	8.0		12.4%			

Something always muddies Cook's evaluation. As a rookie in 2017, he excelled in a surprisingly effective Vikings offense; his blend of speed, vision, and sneaky balance was exactly what Minnesota hoped for when they drafted him. However, that success lasted just four games before he tore his ACL, signaling an early end to a potential Rookie of the Year season. In 2018, Cook managed to play 11 games instead of four, but with the line in disarray and no consistent direction on offense, he was often left drowning behind the line of scrimmage before he had a chance to get anything going. His success rate dropped, and aside from a stellar 136 yards and two touchdowns versus Miami in Week 15, he failed to produce with any meaningful volume. The Miami game was his only 100-plus-yard game, and those two touchdowns were the only scores he found as a runner all season. The good news is that Minnesota's offensive line looks improved and there will be continuity on the offensive coaching staff, along with the addition of Gary Kubiak, who brings a zone-oriented offense geared for Cook. There is not yet enough evidence to say Cook is a great running back, but he has shown flashes. Health permitting, 2019 is as good a chance as any to prove himself.

Isaiah Crowell

Height: 5-11 Weight: 225 College: Alabama State Draft: 2014/FA Born: 8-Jan-1993 Age: 26 Risk: N/A

Year	Team	G/GS	Snaps	Runs	Yds	TD	Yd/R	FUM	DVOA	Rk	DYAR	Rk	YAR	Suc%	Rk	BTkl	Pass	Rec	Yds	TD	C%	Yd/C	YAC	DVOA	Rk	DYAR	Rk
2016	CLE	16/16	568	198	952	7	4.8	2	13.4%	8	169	11	94	39%	40	37	53	40	319	0	75%	8.0	8.4	-2.4%	28	33	28
2017	CLE	16/16	536	206	853	2	4.1	1	-2.9%	26	46	25	57	40%	38	32	43	28	182	0	67%	6.5	6.9	-35.9%	60	-52	59
2018	NYJ	13/6	332	143	685	6	4.8	0	-1.9%	25	37	26	26	36%	46	30	28	21	152	0	75%	7.2	8.2	-6.8%	32	10	34

The Raiders signed Crowell to a one-year deal in March as a hedge against Marshawn Lynch's potential retirement. It was thought he would carve out a significant role in the backfield, but he tore his Achilles in May and will miss the entire 2019 season. It is quite possible that Crowell will never play a snap for the Raiders, either in Oakland or Las Vegas.

Mike Davis

Height: 5-9 Weight: 217 College: South Carolina Draft: 2015/4 (126) Born: 19-Feb-1993 Age: 26 Risk: Green

Year	Team	G/GS	Snaps	Runs	Yds	TD	Yd/R	FUM	DVOA	Rk	DYAR	Rk	YAR	Suc%	Rk	BTkl	Pass	Rec	Yds	TD	C%	Yd/C	YAC	DVOA	Rk	DYAR	Rk
2016	SF	8/1	66	19	50	1	2.6	1	-38.1%	--	-28	--	-25	47%	--	0	5	3	25	0	60%	8.3	5.0	-10.4%	--	1	--
2017	SEA	6/6	176	68	240	0	3.5	0	-23.1%	--	-38	--	-53	29%	--	25	18	15	131	0	83%	8.7	11.2	15.2%	--	26	--
2018	SEA	15/2	393	112	514	4	4.6	0	9.0%	12	80	19	115	52%	14	24	42	34	214	1	81%	6.3	6.9	-0.1%	27	31	28
2019	CHI			84	304	3	3.6	2	-9.2%								16	13	80	0	81%	6.2		-11.9%			

Davis is jumping from one three-headed backfield to another. In Seattle, Davis and Rashaad Penny shared the backup role to Chris Carson. When Carson went down for an early portion of the season, it was Davis who took over. Carson was out most of the time from Week 4 to Week 10, and 75 of Davis' 112 attempts came in that time frame. By season's end, Davis' 52 percent success rate was slightly higher than Carson's 51 percent, and his 58 percent success rate on first-down carries was comfortably ahead of Carson's 52 percent. Of course, there is a "running backs don't matter" joke to be made here somewhere, but Davis' efficiency relative to the starter ahead of him is a testament to his ability. Now in Chicago, Davis will help fill in for Jordan Howard as an efficient downhill runner to complement Tarik Cohen's freer, more reckless running style. Though the Bears also spent a third-round pick on David Montgomery, do not expect Davis to fade into the background this season.

Kenneth Dixon

Height: 5-10 Weight: 215 College: Louisiana Tech Draft: 2016/4 (134) Born: 21-Jan-1994 Age: 25 Risk: Green

Year	Team	G/GS	Snaps	Runs	Yds	TD	Yd/R	FUM	DVOA	Rk	DYAR	Rk	YAR	Suc%	Rk	BTkl	Pass	Rec	Yds	TD	C%	Yd/C	YAC	DVOA	Rk	DYAR	Rk
2016	BAL	12/0	258	88	382	2	4.3	1	5.1%	--	54	--	54	55%	--	34	41	30	162	1	73%	5.4	6.2	-20.6%	46	-14	47
2018	BAL	6/0	152	60	333	2	5.6	2	8.1%	--	38	--	58	55%	--	19	7	6	51	0	86%	8.5	9.0	-0.6%	--	5	--
2019	BAL			26	116	0	4.5	1	3.0%								23	17	117	0	74%	6.9		-12.0%			

It isn't completely uncommon for a good running back stuck in a bad situation to become a good player later in his career. The problem is that most of the players who get limited shots like this change teams before they break out. Priest Holmes toiled behind Errict Rhett and Jamal Lewis. Michael Turner shared a depth chart with LaDainian Tomlinson. Thomas Jones got to play early but split time with Marcel Shipp and Michael Pittman. Dixon has the talent to be a very good NFL back—no back would have survived three seasons on an NFL depth chart with the litany of injuries and suspensions Dixon has endured unless his team thought he had breakout potential. But in Year 4, with Justice Hill nipping at his heels, Dixon would seem much more likely to wind up as a breakout star on a new team than to do it in Baltimore. Dixon should be able to play the passing-down role quite well if given the chance. Will he give himself that chance? He started the season by missing time in OTAs with an undisclosed injury.

Kenyan Drake

Height: 6-1 Weight: 210 College: Alabama Draft: 2016/3 (73) Born: 26-Jan-1994 Age: 25 Risk: Yellow

Year	Team	G/GS	Snaps	Runs	Yds	TD	Yd/R	FUM	DVOA	Rk	DYAR	Rk	YAR	Suc%	Rk	BTkl	Pass	Rec	Yds	TD	C%	Yd/C	YAC	DVOA	Rk	DYAR	Rk
2016	MIA	16/1	109	33	179	2	5.4	0	38.1%	--	60	--	57	42%	--	3	10	9	46	0	90%	5.1	7.1	0.6%	--	8	--
2017	MIA	16/6	477	133	644	3	4.8	2	-11.3%	39	-14	38	30	44%	25	39	48	32	239	1	67%	7.5	6.7	-19.1%	52	-13	52
2018	MIA	16/7	545	120	535	4	4.5	2	4.7%	16	58	22	22	45%	33	41	74	53	477	5	73%	9.0	7.8	14.0%	12	123	8
2019	MIA			156	662	5	4.2	2	0.7%								77	54	499	3	70%	9.2		7.6%			

Drake fell into Adam Gase's 600-unit apartment complex of a doghouse due to poor pass protection. After rushing 91 times for 444 yards and two touchdowns in five games in December of 2017, making it appear that he was poised for a breakout season in 2018, Drake fell behind Frank Gore (fair enough) and, late in the year, Kalen Ballage and Brandon Bolden (what!?). Down the 2018 stretch, he was limited to four to 10 offensive touches per game.

Drake's pass protection is indeed embarrassing. Sports Info Solutions charged him with four sacks due to blown blocks, and Gase's patience evaporated soon after Anthony Barr caused Drake to stumble backwards into Ryan Tannehill during a Vikings sack spree. On the other hand, it takes a coach with a unique vision to keep a prospect with explosive playmaking potential for three years, fail to develop him as a pass protector, yet also fail to either replace him or find ways to work around his deficiency.

Gase's departure was Bastille Day for everyone trapped in his doghouse, and with Gore gone, Drake may get the featured opportunity he deserves. But nothing is guaranteed, and if there's one thing an old-fashioned defensive-minded coach like Brian Flores hates, it's a running back who cannot block.

Chase Edmonds

Chase Edmonds			Height: 5-9		Weight: 205			College: Fordham				Draft: 2018/4 (134)			Born: 13-Apr-1996			Age: 23		Risk: Red	
Year	Team	G/GS	Snaps	Runs	Yds	TD	Yd/R	FUM	DVOA	Rk	DYAR	Rk	YAR	Suc%	Rk	BTkl	Pass	Rec	Yds	TD	C%	Yd/C	YAC	DVOA	Rk	DYAR	Rk
2018	ARI	16/0	198	60	208	2	3.5	1	-18.9%	--	-27	--	-11	45%	--	14	23	20	103	0	87%	5.2	6.1	-27.7%	--	-19	--
2019	ARI			51	196	1	3.9	1	-9.8%								30	20	180	1	67%	9.0		-2.5%			

Edmonds got off to a very slow start, but seemed to figure things out by the end of the year. Through November, he had gained 85 yards on 34 carries; in five games in December, he gained 123 on 26. Kliff Kingsbury praised Edmonds' receiving ability at OTAs and said he would have "a really nice role in the offense." He went on to say David Johnson might get 35 carries or ten catches in a game, so Edmonds' role might be nice, but it's not going to be very big.

Gus Edwards

Gus Edwards			Height: 6-1		Weight: 235			College: Rutgers				Draft: 2018/FA			Born: 13-Apr-1995			Age: 24		Risk: Green	
Year	Team	G/GS	Snaps	Runs	Yds	TD	Yd/R	FUM	DVOA	Rk	DYAR	Rk	YAR	Suc%	Rk	BTkl	Pass	Rec	Yds	TD	C%	Yd/C	YAC	DVOA	Rk	DYAR	Rk
2018	BAL	11/6	286	137	718	2	5.2	0	13.9%	9	130	13	202	63%	1	19	2	2	20	0	100%	10.0	8.5	69.1%	--	10	--
2019	BAL			137	624	3	4.6	3	3.9%								5	4	23	0	80%	5.6		-20.5%			

To the extent that there are problems with Gus Edwards, they are problems that limit him to the head of a committee role. Edwards can't catch passes. His presence on the field heavily locks an offense into a run and is probably a tendency that defenses will key on. But the Gus Bus will run over players and was a find for the Ravens after transferring from Miami to Rutgers to finish his college career. Vision is Edwards' other calling card, something that fits very well with what the Ravens do with Lamar Jackson. He should be a solid depth player and a worthy fantasy pick-up again if anything happens to Mark Ingram.

Austin Ekeler

Austin Ekeler			Height: 5-10		Weight: 195			College: Western State				Draft: 2017/FA			Born: 17-May-1995			Age: 24		Risk: Yellow	
Year	Team	G/GS	Snaps	Runs	Yds	TD	Yd/R	FUM	DVOA	Rk	DYAR	Rk	YAR	Suc%	Rk	BTkl	Pass	Rec	Yds	TD	C%	Yd/C	YAC	DVOA	Rk	DYAR	Rk
2017	LAC	16/0	197	47	260	2	5.5	2	22.7%	--	59	--	61	55%	--	23	35	27	279	3	77%	10.3	9.3	27.1%	12	84	16
2018	LAC	14/3	348	106	554	3	5.2	1	4.9%	15	59	21	73	52%	13	39	53	39	404	3	74%	10.4	10.5	30.3%	4	131	7
2019	LAC			101	522	2	5.2	2	14.0%								46	36	333	1	78%	9.2		14.8%			

It's pretty nice when your backup running back finishes in the top 15 in rushing DVOA and appears near the top of the receiving leaderboards as well. Ekeler was one of seven players last year to have double-digit 15-yard plays as both a rusher and a receiver. The other six were feature players in their respective offenses, all with more than 40 snaps a game. Ekeler averaged just 24.9 snaps and missed a pair of games with a concussion, making his raw totals all the more impressive. It's unlikely that he'd keep his success rate up that high if he had to replace Melvin Gordon as the full-time starter, but Ekeler is a heck of a weapon as a change-of-pace back.

Ezekiel Elliott   Height: 6-0   Weight: 225   College: Ohio State   Draft: 2016/1 (4)   Born: 22-Jul-1995   Age: 24   Risk: Yellow

Year	Team	G/GS	Snaps	Runs	Yds	TD	Yd/R	FUM	DVOA	Rk	DYAR	Rk	YAR	Suc%	Rk	BTkl	Pass	Rec	Yds	TD	C%	Yd/C	YAC	DVOA	Rk	DYAR	Rk
2016	DAL	15/15	716	322	1631	15	5.1	5	15.9%	6	339	1	354	57%	2	69	40	32	363	1	80%	11.3	12.2	26.9%	5	82	11
2017	DAL	10/10	591	242	983	7	4.1	1	11.1%	8	205	7	198	57%	2	42	38	26	269	2	68%	10.3	10.0	-11.2%	43	5	43
2018	DAL	15/15	890	304	1434	6	4.7	6	2.9%	20	149	9	121	50%	18	46	95	77	567	3	81%	7.4	7.5	-3.2%	29	52	20
2019	DAL			310	1414	12	4.6	4	8.1%								91	75	614	2	82%	8.2		12.3%			

Some interesting Elliott splits:
- Elliott rushed 82 times for 315 yards (3.8 yards per carry) in first quarters and 222 times for 1,119 yards (5.04 yards per carry, 74 carries for 374 yards per quarter) in the other three quarters. It's a good thing the Cowboys "established the run" by force-feeding Elliott early; otherwise, opponents might forget that they like to run the ball.
- Elliott caught 16 passes on 16 targets for 92 yards (5.8) and zero (0) first downs on third down-and 10-plus yards last year. Those figures go a long way toward explaining Elliott's negative receiving DVOA despite 77 receptions. Elliott is a dangerous open-field player, of course, but the third-and-long checkdown, rarely effective under any circumstances, is almost guaranteed to fail when opponents know it's a signature move.
- Elliott rushed 35 times for 93 yards (2.7) after his 20th carry in a game. That one speaks for itself, right?

So Elliott was used too predictably in first quarters and inefficiently as a receiver on third-and-long, and he didn't have much left when asked to grind out close wins late in the fourth quarter. It sure sounds like a job for a change-up back, and rookies Tony Pollard and Mike Weber will both get a crack at the role. Elliott led the NFL with 381 offensive touches, but would be more effective on a per-play basis at about 340 or so, assuming they are the right kind of touches.

D'Onta Foreman   Height: 6-0   Weight: 233   College: Texas   Draft: 2017/3 (89)   Born: 24-Apr-1996   Age: 23   Risk: Red

Year	Team	G/GS	Snaps	Runs	Yds	TD	Yd/R	FUM	DVOA	Rk	DYAR	Rk	YAR	Suc%	Rk	BTkl	Pass	Rec	Yds	TD	C%	Yd/C	YAC	DVOA	Rk	DYAR	Rk
2017	HOU	10/1	147	78	327	2	4.2	2	-5.5%	--	10	--	-5	42%	--	14	8	6	83	0	75%	13.8	11.0	39.8%	--	25	--
2018	HOU	1/0	31	7	-1	0	-0.1	1	-177.7%	--	-37	--	-40	0%	--	0	2	2	28	1	100%	14.0	5.0	229.7%	--	28	--
2019	HOU			128	575	4	4.5	4	1.6%								25	19	167	1	76%	8.8		3.5%			

Looking slow and running away from his blockers in a limited sample last year, Foreman essentially had a lost season coming off a torn Achilles in 2017. The number of NFL backs in recent memory who have actually recovered from that surgery is comically low, but the path for playing time is wide open in Houston's dismal backfield. Foreman's career feels like it's at the coin-flip stage. Forced to choose, we'd probably bet on the history of backs who have cratered to this injury (Mikel Leshoure, Arian Foster, Kendall Hunter, et al.) over Foreman's obvious talent.

Leonard Fournette   Height: 6-0   Weight: 228   College: Louisiana State   Draft: 2017/1 (4)   Born: 18-Jan-1995   Age: 24   Risk: Yellow

Year	Team	G/GS	Snaps	Runs	Yds	TD	Yd/R	FUM	DVOA	Rk	DYAR	Rk	YAR	Suc%	Rk	BTkl	Pass	Rec	Yds	TD	C%	Yd/C	YAC	DVOA	Rk	DYAR	Rk
2017	JAX	13/13	564	268	1040	9	3.9	2	2.1%	17	115	11	57	44%	26	55	48	36	302	1	75%	8.4	8.5	7.2%	18	58	21
2018	JAX	8/8	280	133	439	5	3.3	0	-9.3%	32	-4	33	-4	47%	26	17	26	22	185	1	85%	8.4	9.7	9.6%	17	37	26
2019	JAX			249	1085	6	4.4	3	1.3%								62	49	421	1	79%	8.6		12.2%			

Can we suggest a different scheme? In 2018, on runs marked inside zone or outside zone by SIS charters, Leonard Fournette averaged 3.46 yards per attempt on 73 attempts. Only 11 of those attempts were in the red zone. He was up to 3.89 yards on 113 zone attempts in 2017. While Fournette's numbers aren't wildly better on other carries, zone runs do bury a lot of his downhill ability. Fournette's not a back you want laterally shifting and bending—you just want him full-steam through the line of scrimmage.

Fournette has been injured, and he has been buried in small-sample-size theater stats by those who would make fun of drafting a running back No. 4 overall. He also has had some conflicts with management, including being benched for Week 17's meaningless finale last year. While the pick will go down as looking silly no matter what at this point, the Jaguars have a Bugatti that they're treating like an SUV.

Devonta Freeman

Height: 5-8 Weight: 206 College: Florida St. Draft: 2014/4 (103) Born: 15-Mar-1992 Age: 27 Risk: Yellow

Year	Team	G/GS	Snaps	Runs	Yds	TD	Yd/R	FUM	DVOA	Rk	DYAR	Rk	YAR	Suc%	Rk	BTkl	Pass	Rec	Yds	TD	C%	Yd/C	YAC	DVOA	Rk	DYAR	Rk
2016	ATL	16/16	604	227	1079	11	4.8	1	6.4%	14	148	13	179	50%	12	63	65	54	462	2	83%	8.6	7.7	24.9%	6	141	4
2017	ATL	14/14	552	196	865	7	4.4	4	1.5%	18	89	14	105	51%	9	59	47	36	317	1	77%	8.8	6.8	23.6%	13	102	10
2018	ATL	2/2	67	14	68	0	4.9	0	-6.9%	--	1	--	-4	50%	--	2	7	5	23	0	71%	4.6	4.0	-109.8%	--	-30	--
2019	ATL			208	952	7	4.6	2	8.6%								59	46	397	2	78%	8.6		12.0%			

Best-case scenario is that Freeman plays like he did in 2015 and 2016, when he established himself as one of the best dual-threat running backs in the NFL, and the Falcons happily absorb his $9.5-million cap hit in 2020, the fourth-largest among running backs. Worst-case scenario is that he sustains another round of injuries and Ito Smith capably carries the load. In that scenario, Freeman could end up as a candidate for release in the offseason, though Atlanta would have to swallow $6 million in dead money.

Royce Freeman

Height: 5-11 Weight: 229 College: Oregon Draft: 2018/3 (71) Born: 24-Feb-1996 Age: 23 Risk: Yellow

Year	Team	G/GS	Snaps	Runs	Yds	TD	Yd/R	FUM	DVOA	Rk	DYAR	Rk	YAR	Suc%	Rk	BTkl	Pass	Rec	Yds	TD	C%	Yd/C	YAC	DVOA	Rk	DYAR	Rk
2018	DEN	14/8	308	130	521	5	4.0	1	-6.8%	31	10	31	29	46%	29	31	20	14	72	0	70%	5.1	4.2	-32.2%	--	-20	--
2019	DEN			151	685	4	4.5	4	1.6%								27	22	165	1	81%	7.5		4.5%			

We thought a rookie would supplant Devontae Booker in Denver's offense; we just thought it would be Freeman rather than some undrafted free agent. We're still high on Freeman, and he looked great in the offseason program when Philip Lindsay was sidelined. It should also be noted that Freeman was a more effective runner in the first half of the season; he had a -0.5% rushing DVOA before a high ankle sprain cost him some time and left him gimpy the rest of the way. He's a different style of runner than Lindsay, making him a solid change-of-pace option. The question is whether he'll continue to play second fiddle to Lindsay's explosiveness, or if he'll carve out a bigger role for himself going forward.

Wayne Gallman

Height: 6-0 Weight: 215 College: Clemson Draft: 2017/4 (140) Born: 1-Oct-1994 Age: 25 Risk: Green

Year	Team	G/GS	Snaps	Runs	Yds	TD	Yd/R	FUM	DVOA	Rk	DYAR	Rk	YAR	Suc%	Rk	BTkl	Pass	Rec	Yds	TD	C%	Yd/C	YAC	DVOA	Rk	DYAR	Rk
2017	NYG	13/1	325	111	476	0	4.3	3	-5.2%	29	15	31	21	50%	10	31	48	34	193	1	71%	5.7	5.9	-14.6%	48	-2	48
2018	NYG	15/1	155	51	176	1	3.5	2	7.3%	--	30	--	11	39%	--	12	22	14	89	0	64%	6.4	5.8	-63.8%	--	-47	--
2019	NYG			41	176	1	4.3	2	-1.6%								18	13	100	0	72%	7.7		-9.0%			

How many running backs do you know of with 43 broken tackles on less than 250 career touches, and there's no chance they get more work? Gallman even got dragged by the Giants in OTAs and put behind Paul Perkins in media releases. Coming out of Clemson, Gallman was every 2017 draftnik's "underrated" guy because he doesn't have a dramatically great tool. He combines good vision with good power and balance, which is to say he makes playing running back look fairly easy, but not sexy. Five fumbles is an area he needs to do some work on, but other than that, Gallman could be a lead committee back for most teams that don't employ Saquon Barkley.

Melvin Gordon

Height: 6-1 Weight: 215 College: Wisconsin Draft: 2015/1 (15) Born: 13-Apr-1993 Age: 26 Risk: Yellow

Year	Team	G/GS	Snaps	Runs	Yds	TD	Yd/R	FUM	DVOA	Rk	DYAR	Rk	YAR	Suc%	Rk	BTkl	Pass	Rec	Yds	TD	C%	Yd/C	YAC	DVOA	Rk	DYAR	Rk
2016	SD	13/11	659	254	997	10	3.9	2	-8.4%	29	2	29	83	45%	26	52	57	41	419	2	72%	10.2	10.1	21.0%	9	105	9
2017	LAC	16/16	750	284	1105	8	3.9	1	-6.8%	33	21	29	30	40%	41	73	83	58	476	4	70%	8.2	8.5	3.0%	28	76	18
2018	LAC	12/12	524	175	885	10	5.1	1	20.8%	3	210	5	239	53%	9	55	66	50	490	4	76%	9.8	10.7	5.5%	22	72	19
2019	LAC			250	1081	8	4.3	4	4.3%								85	66	622	3	78%	9.4		17.8%			

The Chargers cut Gordon's workload some in 2018, going from 18.6 attempts per game in 2016 and 2017 to 14.6 last season. Gordon responded with his most efficient season to date, finishing with a positive rushing DVOA and averaging more than four yards a carry for the first time in his career. If anything, the season stats underrate how good Gordon actually was; he had a 21.3% DVOA before suffering a knee injury in November, dropping slightly to 17.6% when he came back. Part of Gordon's 2018 success can be attributed to extra rest. In 2017, the Chargers used Gordon on two-thirds of their rushing attempts; that was down under 55 percent even before his injury last season. The emergence of Austin Ekeler as a viable change of pace means that Gordon can occasionally get some drives off; he didn't have 20 carries in a single game for the first time since his rookie season. That's bad for your fantasy team but great for Gordon. If he can keep up last year's yards per carry and attempts per game while playing all 16 games in 2019, he'll top his career high for rushing yards with 50 fewer attempts than he had in 2017. Stay fresh!

Frank Gore

Height: 5-9   Weight: 215   College: Miami   Draft: 2005/3 (65)   Born: 14-May-1983   Age: 36   Risk: Yellow

Year	Team	G/GS	Snaps	Runs	Yds	TD	Yd/R	FUM	DVOA	Rk	DYAR	Rk	YAR	Suc%	Rk	BTkl	Pass	Rec	Yds	TD	C%	Yd/C	YAC	DVOA	Rk	DYAR	Rk
2016	IND	16/16	650	263	1025	4	3.9	2	5.6%	16	159	12	88	49%	19	32	48	38	277	4	81%	7.3	7.6	0.7%	25	40	23
2017	IND	16/16	555	261	961	3	3.7	3	-2.3%	23	66	18	46	44%	23	41	38	29	245	1	76%	8.4	9.5	4.1%	25	35	31
2018	MIA	14/14	330	156	722	0	4.6	1	5.7%	14	86	17	70	50%	19	28	16	12	124	1	75%	10.3	9.6	35.4%	--	49	--
2019	*BUF*			*129*	*581*	*2*	*4.5*	*2*	*5.3%*								*15*	*11*	*104*	*0*	*73%*	*9.4*		*8.6%*			

Forget efficiency for a moment. Gore's only the third running back in the history of DVOA, stretching back to 1986, to even quality for the main running back tables at age 35 or older, joining Emmitt Smith in 2004 and Marcus Allen from 1995 to 1997. The fact that Gore's still standing and playing a significant role for any offense with nearly 15,000 yards under his belt is insane, much less that he's doing it while ranking in the top 20 in both DYAR and DVOA. We must, once again, point out that Father Time is undefeated, and eventually even Gore's exquisite technique will not be enough to keep him in the league. And we'll probably be pointing that out when you're downloading *FOA 2077* into your cyberware implants, and Gore's rushing for 500 yards for the Stuttgart Scorpions.

Derrius Guice

Height: 5-10   Weight: 224   College: Louisiana State   Draft: 2018/2 (59)   Born: 21-Jun-1997   Age: 22   Risk: Yellow

Year	Team	G/GS	Snaps	Runs	Yds	TD	Yd/R	FUM	DVOA	Rk	DYAR	Rk	YAR	Suc%	Rk	BTkl	Pass	Rec	Yds	TD	C%	Yd/C	YAC	DVOA	Rk	DYAR	Rk
2019	*WAS*			*201*	*888*	*5*	*4.4*	*2*	*2.6%*								*33*	*26*	*197*	*0*	*79%*	*7.6*		*-3.9%*			

Per Kareem Copeland's reporting in *The Washington Post*, an infection set in soon after Guice's August ACL surgery, requiring two months of antibiotics and three additional procedures to flush infected tissue out of his knee. The setbacks slowed Guice's recovery significantly; after the draft, Jay Gruden said that Guice "could" be ready for training camp. Washington drafted fellow injury rehab case Bryce Love in the fourth round (Guice responded to the pick with a vague emoji on Instagram), and Adrian Peterson is still around to remind everyone that he's only at his best when getting 20 touches per game from his preferred formations. The best advice we can give fantasy owners is to watch Skins camp very carefully before making any commitments to Guice; even if fully healthy, he could be trapped in a three-back rotation for a weak team.

Todd Gurley

Height: 6-1   Weight: 222   College: Georgia   Draft: 2015/1 (10)   Born: 3-Aug-1994   Age: 25   Risk: Red

Year	Team	G/GS	Snaps	Runs	Yds	TD	Yd/R	FUM	DVOA	Rk	DYAR	Rk	YAR	Suc%	Rk	BTkl	Pass	Rec	Yds	TD	C%	Yd/C	YAC	DVOA	Rk	DYAR	Rk
2016	LAR	16/16	742	278	885	6	3.2	2	-14.4%	37	-66	37	-75	41%	36	56	58	43	327	0	74%	7.6	8.2	-9.9%	39	13	35
2017	LAR	15/15	794	279	1305	13	4.7	5	13.9%	4	268	2	205	53%	5	79	87	64	788	6	74%	12.3	12.3	35.9%	7	236	2
2018	LAR	14/14	825	256	1251	17	4.9	1	23.6%	1	366	1	342	57%	4	42	81	59	580	4	73%	9.8	9.9	6.9%	20	98	12
2019	*LAR*			*238*	*1118*	*12*	*4.7*	*4*	*10.5%*								*70*	*54*	*511*	*2*	*77%*	*9.5*		*16.6%*			

In Sean McVay's first two seasons as the head coach in Los Angeles, Gurley's vision and ability to find the right running lane has played a major role in the Rams' potent outside zone rushing attack. The offensive line has opened some massive holes for him, and Gurley has taken advantage, finishing in the top two in rushing DYAR in both seasons. Gurley does not break many tackles (averaging a broken tackle on 13.3 percent of his touches), which could be an issue for him if the Los Angeles offensive line takes a step back this season after the departure of two of last season's starters, but the holes he has typically had available to him under McVay have been so large that is has not mattered. Gurley's ability in the passing game has also added value to the potent Rams offense, and it will be interesting to see how his role changes as the Rams manage the deteriorating condition of his knees. It might make sense for him to give up some of the tough between-the-tackles carries to preserve his health for the long run. That will certainly be something to monitor in 2019.

Damien Harris   Height: 5-10   Weight: 216   College: Alabama   Draft: 2019/3 (87)   Born: 11-Feb-1997   Age: 22   Risk: Blue

Year	Team	G/GS	Snaps	Runs	Yds	TD	Yd/R	FUM	DVOA	Rk	DYAR	Rk	YAR	Suc%	Rk	BTkl	Pass	Rec	Yds	TD	C%	Yd/C	YAC	DVOA	Rk	DYAR	Rk
2019	NE			42	207	2	4.9	1	17.5%							10	8	62	0	80%	7.7		-1.9%			

A second highy drafted running back in two years was a surprise for a franchise that is usually so in tune with analytics, especially considering that Harris projects more as a direct backup for Sony Michel than a complementary option. A hard-nosed one-cut runner, Harris is noted for his vision and power but not for his agility or speed. Opinions vary on his utility as a receiver and pass-blocker, suggesting he might be able to elevate that aspect of his game. He did have the second-best fumble rate (one fumble every 179.7 touches) of any running back in the Nick Saban era at Alabama. Harris was considered a potential first-round pick ahead of the 2018 draft but opted instead to return to college. He is likely to begin his Patriots career as an early-down and short-yardage backup.

Darrell Henderson   Height: 5-8   Weight: 208   College: Memphis   Draft: 2019/3 (70)   Born: 19-Aug-1997   Age: 22   Risk: Blue

Year	Team	G/GS	Snaps	Runs	Yds	TD	Yd/R	FUM	DVOA	Rk	DYAR	Rk	YAR	Suc%	Rk	BTkl	Pass	Rec	Yds	TD	C%	Yd/C	YAC	DVOA	Rk	DYAR	Rk
2019	LAR			103	480	5	4.7	2	9.5%							16	13	108	1	81%	8.3		3.2%			

Given that Henderson was a third-round pick and is entering a locker room with the highest-paid back in the league in Todd Gurley and a capable backup in Malcolm Brown, you would normally be hesitant to expect much in Year 1. But the Rams traded up to draft Henderson in large part because of the uncertainty surrounding the health of Gurley's knee, and Brown suffered a season-ending injury in 2018 that forced the late-season acquisition of C.J. Anderson. Henderson rushed for over 1,900 yards in his final season at Memphis and had the highest BackCAST projection in this year's running back class. If Gurley's knee results in him being let go down the road, Henderson may become the bell cow at running back in Los Angeles.

Derrick Henry   Height: 6-3   Weight: 247   College: Alabama   Draft: 2016/2 (45)   Born: 4-Jan-1994   Age: 26   Risk: Green

Year	Team	G/GS	Snaps	Runs	Yds	TD	Yd/R	FUM	DVOA	Rk	DYAR	Rk	YAR	Suc%	Rk	BTkl	Pass	Rec	Yds	TD	C%	Yd/C	YAC	DVOA	Rk	DYAR	Rk
2016	TEN	15/1	270	110	490	5	4.5	0	19.6%	4	131	15	139	55%	6	27	15	13	137	0	87%	10.5	9.5	46.9%	--	45	--
2017	TEN	16/2	411	176	744	5	4.2	1	-1.2%	21	56	22	37	48%	15	45	17	11	136	1	65%	12.4	11.8	23.6%	--	31	--
2018	TEN	16/12	401	215	1059	12	4.9	1	23.1%	2	281	2	234	51%	16	55	18	15	99	0	83%	6.6	7.7	-18.0%	--	-4	--
2019	TEN			274	1229	10	4.5	4	5.2%							28	21	192	1	75%	9.2		6.6%			

What is the "real" Derrick Henry? The back who was below average in a committee role the first half of the season, or the player who was by far the most productive rusher in the league the second half of the season? The Titans are banking on the latter and are likely to give Henry every opportunity to keep up his strong play and a leading role in the backfield. New offensive coordinator Arthur Smith kept the same playbook, so expect a heavy diet of outside zone.

Nyheim Hines   Height: 5-8   Weight: 198   College: North Carolina State   Draft: 2018/4 (104)   Born: 12-Nov-1996   Age: 23   Risk: Yellow

Year	Team	G/GS	Snaps	Runs	Yds	TD	Yd/R	FUM	DVOA	Rk	DYAR	Rk	YAR	Suc%	Rk	BTkl	Pass	Rec	Yds	TD	C%	Yd/C	YAC	DVOA	Rk	DYAR	Rk
2018	IND	16/4	499	85	314	2	3.7	1	-11.8%	--	-12	--	-16	46%	--	21	81	63	425	2	78%	6.7	5.5	3.5%	23	79	15
2019	IND			74	298	1	4.0	2	-5.3%							73	60	524	2	82%	8.7		22.7%			

Hines' college performance presaged that he would be at least as much movable chess piece and third-down back as runner, and so it was in 2018, with nearly as many targets as rushing attempts. He was about as effective running from shotgun (his primary role) as he was from under center, and was a favored target on one of the Colts' many screen plays. Second-round pick Parris Campbell has the potential to play a similar sort of movable chess piece role, and Frank Reich confirmed in June that Campbell's presence would probably affect Hines' numbers. Veteran Spencer Ware performs a different sort of threat as a better all-around performer in case the Colts want a less specialized player given Hines' unspectacular rookie performance.

Jordan Howard   Height: 6-0   Weight: 230   College: Indiana   Draft: 2016/5 (150)   Born: 2-Nov-1994   Age: 25   Risk: Red

Year	Team	G/GS	Snaps	Runs	Yds	TD	Yd/R	FUM	DVOA	Rk	DYAR	Rk	YAR	Suc%	Rk	BTkl	Pass	Rec	Yds	TD	C%	Yd/C	YAC	DVOA	Rk	DYAR	Rk
2016	CHI	15/13	654	252	1313	6	5.2	2	12.3%	9	219	5	246	49%	17	51	50	29	298	1	58%	10.3	10.3	-7.5%	36	17	33
2017	CHI	16/16	578	276	1122	9	4.1	1	5.8%	14	160	10	122	42%	35	42	32	23	125	0	72%	5.4	6.7	-53.3%	61	-60	60
2018	CHI	16/15	624	250	935	9	3.7	2	-11.1%	36	-28	40	25	50%	17	26	27	20	145	0	74%	7.3	6.4	-21.9%	50	-13	49
2019	PHI			145	582	4	4.0	1	1.9%								23	17	146	1	74%	8.6		5.6%			

It was common to hear fans and analysts clamoring for Howard to lose snaps in favor of Tarik Cohen, but Howard's touches weren't granted for the sake of it. Howard was the team's designated "on pace" runner. When Chicago was even or ahead of the sticks, he was the back to keep them on schedule and provide the most well-rounded skill set available, even if at the expense of explosive ability. On Howard's 87 second-down carries, the Bears had an average 5.75 yards to go; and 35 percent of his carries required 7 to 10 yards to go. Cohen, for comparison, faced an average 8.15 yards to go and half of his 34 carries required 7 to 10 yards to go. As a result, Howard finished with a higher success rate despite a lower yards per carry. While his overall effectiveness did take a fall last season, a change of scenery in Philadelphia—an excellent offense as is—could be just what Howard needs to find his footing again.

Kareem Hunt   Height: 5-10   Weight: 216   College: Toledo   Draft: 2017/3 (86)   Born: 6-Aug-1995   Age: 24   Risk: Green

Year	Team	G/GS	Snaps	Runs	Yds	TD	Yd/R	FUM	DVOA	Rk	DYAR	Rk	YAR	Suc%	Rk	BTkl	Pass	Rec	Yds	TD	C%	Yd/C	YAC	DVOA	Rk	DYAR	Rk
2017	KC	16/16	670	272	1327	8	4.9	1	11.9%	6	222	4	248	47%	18	89	63	53	455	3	84%	8.6	7.8	15.6%	14	102	9
2018	KC	11/11	503	181	824	7	4.6	0	9.1%	11	134	11	133	55%	7	54	35	26	378	7	74%	14.5	13.0	79.4%	1	198	1
2019	CLE			56	245	2	4.4	2	3.8%								19	16	139	1	84%	8.7		13.6%			

We all know how good Hunt was in Kansas City before getting cut in the wake of a domestic violence incident. John Dorsey, who drafted Hunt for the Chiefs and sat in the front row of the "talent over character" school, didn't hesitate to bring the disgraced running back into his new fiefdom by Lake Erie, happy to eat the eight-game suspension Hunt received for kicking a woman (and, more to the point, having it caught on videotape). Given the Browns already have Nick Chubb and Duke Johnson, the move seemed redundant, even leaving aside the PR implications. But injuries to running backs are a regular part of the NFL leitmotif, and should Hunt become a key cog in a long, long-awaited playoff run in Cleveland, Browns fans won't care much about the optics.

Carlos Hyde   Height: 6-0   Weight: 230   College: Ohio St.   Draft: 2014/2 (57)   Born: 20-Sep-1990   Age: 29   Risk: Green

Year	Team	G/GS	Snaps	Runs	Yds	TD	Yd/R	FUM	DVOA	Rk	DYAR	Rk	YAR	Suc%	Rk	BTkl	Pass	Rec	Yds	TD	C%	Yd/C	YAC	DVOA	Rk	DYAR	Rk
2016	SF	13/13	535	217	988	6	4.6	5	15.3%	7	204	6	98	48%	21	51	34	27	163	3	82%	6.0	5.4	6.2%	19	38	25
2017	SF	16/16	783	240	938	8	3.9	2	-7.4%	35	12	33	14	44%	27	52	89	59	350	0	67%	5.9	5.4	-22.4%	53	-43	58
2018	2TM	14/7	385	172	571	5	3.3	2	-11.0%	35	-18	36	-93	39%	42	28	16	10	33	0	63%	3.3	5.9	-73.3%	--	-51	--
2019	KC			101	447	5	4.4	2	8.9%								29	22	194	1	76%	8.8		10.3%			

In 2016, Hyde was a top-ten rusher on his way to what looked like a very solid career. Since then, however, Hyde's performance has tanked. He averaged just 3.3 yards per carry last season, and has now been deemed expendable by three franchises in just over a year. He's an odd fit in Kansas City, too, with their focus on running backs getting involved in the passing game; Hyde's career-high 59 receptions in Kyle Shanahan's scheme came with a -22.4% receiving DVOA.

Mark Ingram   Height: 5-11   Weight: 215   College: Alabama   Draft: 2011/1 (28)   Born: 21-Dec-1989   Age: 30   Risk: Yellow

Year	Team	G/GS	Snaps	Runs	Yds	TD	Yd/R	FUM	DVOA	Rk	DYAR	Rk	YAR	Suc%	Rk	BTkl	Pass	Rec	Yds	TD	C%	Yd/C	YAC	DVOA	Rk	DYAR	Rk
2016	NO	16/14	530	205	1043	6	5.1	2	11.3%	11	175	10	223	56%	5	46	58	46	319	4	79%	6.9	7.1	10.6%	16	81	12
2017	NO	16/12	571	230	1124	12	4.9	3	11.2%	7	193	8	210	49%	12	56	71	58	416	0	82%	7.2	8.7	-10.7%	42	13	39
2018	NO	12/6	350	138	645	6	4.7	3	2.9%	19	71	20	94	57%	3	24	27	21	170	1	78%	8.1	7.4	-18.8%	46	-7	43
2019	BAL			204	959	6	4.7	3	9.6%								41	31	246	1	76%	7.9		0.7%			

Where Ingram becomes a big upgrade on Gus Edwards is mostly in his ability to catch the ball. From 2015 to 2017, before Alvin Kamara was fully integrated into the Saints offense, Ingram averaged 63 targets a season and proved capable, with positive DVOAs in two of three seasons. Ingram missed time to suspension last year, and was more of a changeup to Kamara when he came back. The Saints and Ravens are very similar offenses as far as how much zone they use, and Ingram should be a sturdy No. 1 back for Baltimore as long as he avoids injury.

Chris Ivory   Height: 6-0   Weight: 222   College: Tiffin   Draft: 2010/FA   Born: 22-Mar-1988   Age: 31   Risk: N/A

Year	Team	G/GS	Snaps	Runs	Yds	TD	Yd/R	FUM	DVOA	Rk	DYAR	Rk	YAR	Suc%	Rk	BTkl	Pass	Rec	Yds	TD	C%	Yd/C	YAC	DVOA	Rk	DYAR	Rk
2016	JAX	11/1	311	117	439	3	3.8	5	-34.3%	42	-125	42	-93	45%	22	22	28	20	186	0	71%	9.3	9.5	-12.0%	42	3	42
2017	JAX	14/3	299	112	382	1	3.4	2	-17.0%	44	-38	42	-50	38%	44	27	28	21	175	1	75%	8.3	9.0	4.4%	24	27	33
2018	BUF	13/1	300	115	385	1	3.3	1	-14.3%	42	-27	37	-45	44%	34	19	21	13	205	0	62%	15.8	15.7	31.3%	--	47	--

Ivory became expendable when the Bills added Frank Gore and was subsequently released. In all honesty, Ivory was expendable long before that, as he has played below replacement level since 2015. We're not sure what the market is for 31-year-old backs who can't catch and average less than 3.4 yards per carry is, but it seems unlikely that Ivory's phone will be ringing off the hook any time soon.

Justin Jackson   Height: 6-0   Weight: 199   College: Northwestern   Draft: 2018/7 (251)   Born: 22-Apr-1995   Age: 24   Risk: Green

Year	Team	G/GS	Snaps	Runs	Yds	TD	Yd/R	FUM	DVOA	Rk	DYAR	Rk	YAR	Suc%	Rk	BTkl	Pass	Rec	Yds	TD	C%	Yd/C	YAC	DVOA	Rk	DYAR	Rk
2018	LAC	13/1	149	50	206	2	4.1	0	-6.0%	--	6	--	39	56%	--	20	19	15	135	0	79%	9.0	10.1	29.9%	--	37	--
2019	LAC			24	97	1	4.1	1	-1.3%								11	9	59	1	82%	6.5		-8.7%			

As an injury fill-in for Melvin Gordon and Austin Ekeler, Jackson had a pretty strong debut for a seventh-round rookie. He burst onto the scene by helping lead a second-half comeback against Pittsburgh in Week 11, with eight carries for 63 yards and a touchdown resulting in a 117.5% rushing DVOA. Take that one game out and his rushing DVOA drops to -25.8%, but Jackson still flashed quickness and slipperiness, especially as a receiver. The Chargers would be happiest if Jackson doesn't see the field much in 2019, but he showed he can provide better-than-replacement-level performance should the injury bug flare up again.

Josh Jacobs   Height: 5-10   Weight: 220   College: Alabama   Draft: 2019/1 (24)   Born: 11-Feb-1998   Age: 21   Risk: Yellow

Year	Team	G/GS	Snaps	Runs	Yds	TD	Yd/R	FUM	DVOA	Rk	DYAR	Rk	YAR	Suc%	Rk	BTkl	Pass	Rec	Yds	TD	C%	Yd/C	YAC	DVOA	Rk	DYAR	Rk
2019	OAK			240	962	6	4.0	4	-6.9%								55	44	342	1	80%	7.8		-1.0%			

When a running back fails to lead his own college team in rushing attempts, it's a red flag. Jacobs ends up with a terrible BackCAST projection in large part because he couldn't out-touch Damien Harris at Alabama. Generally speaking, cream rises to the top, and running backs who become successful NFL players are starting running backs in college. Alvin Kamara is a recent and notable exception, but Kamara was squashed on the bench by a very bad Tennessee coaching staff; you won't find many willing to criticize Nick Saban. When Jacobs was on the field, however, he impressed, smashing through tackles and plowing for yards after contact. He has the size and skills needed to become an every-down starter, and there's every reason to believe he'll outperform his low BackCAST projection.

David Johnson   Height: 6-1   Weight: 224   College: Northern Iowa   Draft: 2015/3 (86)   Born: 16-Dec-1991   Age: 28   Risk: Yellow

Year	Team	G/GS	Snaps	Runs	Yds	TD	Yd/R	FUM	DVOA	Rk	DYAR	Rk	YAR	Suc%	Rk	BTkl	Pass	Rec	Yds	TD	C%	Yd/C	YAC	DVOA	Rk	DYAR	Rk
2016	ARI	16/16	964	293	1239	16	4.2	5	5.1%	17	177	9	139	50%	13	80	121	80	879	4	67%	11.0	8.0	27.7%	4	274	1
2017	ARI	1/1	46	11	23	0	2.1	2	-100.3%	--	-40	--	-34	18%	--	5	9	6	67	0	67%	11.2	7.7	-33.0%	--	-9	--
2018	ARI	16/16	749	258	940	7	3.6	3	-12.6%	40	-42	42	0	38%	43	45	76	50	446	3	66%	8.9	7.7	-17.1%	43	-13	50
2019	ARI			252	1033	6	4.1	3	-2.4%								99	73	690	3	74%	9.5		12.6%			

The Cardinals were widely criticized last year for not using Johnson as a wide receiver more often. All told, 20 percent of his targets last year came when was lined up in the slot or out wide. That's actually quite a bit, among the top 20 for running backs in the league … but it's barely half the rate he had in 2016, when he led all running backs in receiving DYAR. The Cardinals coaches cut way down on his slot/wide usage even though he was much less effective on targets out of the backfield, which is one of the reasons they are not the Cardinals coaches anymore. Arizona's new staff wants nothing more than to spread the field as much as possible, and though Johnson will usually be the only running back on the field, he will frequently motion out into an empty set. It should be a much better fit for Arizona's most versatile weapon.

Duke Johnson
Height: 5-9 Weight: 207 College: Miami Draft: 2015/3 (77) Born: 23-Sep-1993 Age: 26 Risk: Red

Year	Team	G/GS	Snaps	Runs	Yds	TD	Yd/R	FUM	DVOA	Rk	DYAR	Rk	YAR	Suc%	Rk	BTkl	Pass	Rec	Yds	TD	C%	Yd/C	YAC	DVOA	Rk	DYAR	Rk
2016	CLE	16/1	457	73	358	1	4.9	2	11.2%	--	54	--	45	45%	--	35	74	53	514	0	72%	9.7	8.0	19.2%	11	134	6
2017	CLE	16/0	565	82	348	4	4.2	3	15.7%	--	90	--	92	53%	--	51	94	74	693	3	80%	9.4	8.6	6.7%	19	110	7
2018	CLE	16/2	459	40	201	0	5.0	1	7.2%	--	24	--	21	50%	--	20	62	47	429	3	76%	9.1	8.0	12.9%	14	103	11
2019	CLE			35	153	0	4.4	1	0.4%								55	45	407	2	82%	9.1		20.0%			

Sir Duke has been one of the most reliable pass-catching backs over the last three seasons, averaging 58 receptions, with a 76 percent catch rate and just under 13.0% DVOA in that span. But his cumulative numbers dipped last year, and his third-down efficiency (-1.0% DVOA receiving and an awful -33.9% on ten carries) was in the tank. The influx of talent at the skill positions in BrownsTown makes Johnson something of a luxury, and he has reportedly demanded a trade. Some team might be able to acquire a handy weapon on the cheap.

Kerryon Johnson
Height: 5-11 Weight: 213 College: Auburn Draft: 2018/2 (43) Born: 30-Jun-1997 Age: 22 Risk: Yellow

Year	Team	G/GS	Snaps	Runs	Yds	TD	Yd/R	FUM	DVOA	Rk	DYAR	Rk	YAR	Suc%	Rk	BTkl	Pass	Rec	Yds	TD	C%	Yd/C	YAC	DVOA	Rk	DYAR	Rk
2018	DET	10/7	346	118	641	3	5.4	1	17.5%	5	124	15	112	53%	12	35	39	32	213	1	82%	6.7	8.3	-4.8%	31	20	30
2019	DET			225	1076	8	4.8	4	9.3%								57	45	340	1	79%	7.6		-0.6%			

A bevy of things went wrong for Detroit's offense last year, but losing Johnson for the final six games was one of the most significant. Johnson matched pace with or exceeded the production of many of his rookie peers. He led all rookie runners in DVOA, and was second in success rate behind New England's Sony Michel. Johnson was also Detroit's only effective runner out of shotgun. The other three qualifying backs combined for a 37 percent success rate on 78 shotgun carries, yet Johnson managed a 55 percent success rate and nearly 6 yards per carry on 53 shotgun attempts. Coming from Gus Malzahn's downhill spread-gun system at Auburn, Johnson was plenty equipped to handle carries out of shotgun in the NFL. Considering Johnson's injury occurred shortly after Golden Tate was traded and Marvin Jones was lost for the year, losing his athleticism and flexible rushing profile was the nail in the coffin for Detroit's offense.

Aaron Jones
Height: 5-9 Weight: 208 College: Texas-El Paso Draft: 2017/5 (182) Born: 2-Dec-1994 Age: 25 Risk: Red

Year	Team	G/GS	Snaps	Runs	Yds	TD	Yd/R	FUM	DVOA	Rk	DYAR	Rk	YAR	Suc%	Rk	BTkl	Pass	Rec	Yds	TD	C%	Yd/C	YAC	DVOA	Rk	DYAR	Rk
2017	GB	12/4	236	81	448	4	5.5	0	31.3%	--	143	--	134	53%	--	15	18	9	22	0	50%	2.4	3.3	-75.4%	--	-60	--
2018	GB	12/8	376	133	728	8	5.5	1	17.1%	7	146	10	184	55%	6	34	35	26	206	1	74%	7.9	8.5	2.2%	25	33	27
2019	GB			188	917	7	4.9	2	13.9%								50	36	305	1	72%	8.5		0.5%			

Size may be holding Jones back from assuming a full-time role, but when he gets his chances, he does not squander them. Jones is one of the slipperiest runners in the league. He is not the fastest player in a straight line, but few can match his change of direction and explosiveness in tight quarters. Jones makes defenders pay for lazy tackle attempts, generating space by making defenders miss rather than simply blowing past them. Jones racked up 34 10-plus-yard gains on only 214 attempts over the past two seasons, once every 6.29 attempts. Granted, the same creativity and free-flowing rushing style that earns him such gains also makes him prone to taking ugly negative plays, but that is the trade-off a coach accepts with runners of that nature. LeSean McCoy, Saquon Barkley, and Tarik Cohen all suffer from the same boom-or-bust affliction. More impressive, though, is how much Jones grew as a pass-down back from 2017 to 2018. Jones was not trusted as a rookie to handle pass-protection or receiving responsibilities, but took on a larger role in both areas in 2018 and proved himself plenty capable. The under-center offense Matt LaFleur is bringing to Green Bay is not an ideal fit for Jones, but he is explosive enough and has shown quality development that should be rewarded with snaps by the new coaching staff.

Ronald Jones

Height: 6-0   **Weight:** 200   **College:** USC   **Draft:** 2018/2 (38)   **Born:** 2-Aug-1997   **Age:** 22   **Risk: Red**

Year	Team	G/GS	Snaps	Runs	Yds	TD	Yd/R	FUM	DVOA	Rk	DYAR	Rk	YAR	Suc%	Rk	BTkl	Pass	Rec	Yds	TD	C%	Yd/C	YAC	DVOA	Rk	DYAR	Rk
2018	TB	9/0	90	23	44	1	1.9	0	-24.3%	--	-15	--	-24	30%	--	3	9	7	33	0	78%	4.7	6.0	-42.4%	--	-15	--
2019	TB			136	557	4	4.1	3	-4.7%								50	37	279	1	74%	7.5		-11.9%			

When the Buccaneers drafted Jones 38th overall in 2018, they hoped he would bring some explosiveness to their run game. That never happened. He didn't have a single run of at least 10 yards last season. Blame it on the lack of opportunities, but there's more to it. For one, Tampa Bay's run-blocking was inconsistent. Jones was hit behind the line of scrimmage on 11 of his 23 carries. Even when he had room to run, he rarely made anyone miss, breaking only one tackle on a run. The Buccaneers don't think he lacks talent; they think he lacks confidence. So instead of investing in a functional right guard, Tampa Bay has been paying Jones compliments.

Kyle Juszczyk

Height: 6-1   **Weight:** 248   **College:** Harvard   **Draft:** 2013/4 (130)   **Born:** 23-Apr-1991   **Age:** 28   **Risk: Red**

Year	Team	G/GS	Snaps	Runs	Yds	TD	Yd/R	FUM	DVOA	Rk	DYAR	Rk	YAR	Suc%	Rk	BTkl	Pass	Rec	Yds	TD	C%	Yd/C	YAC	DVOA	Rk	DYAR	Rk
2016	BAL	16/7	463	5	22	1	4.4	0	72.5%	--	19	--	19	60%	--	7	49	37	266	0	76%	7.2	5.9	-11.9%	41	6	41
2017	SF	14/10	397	7	31	0	4.4	2	21.3%	--	12	--	7	57%	--	6	42	33	315	1	79%	9.5	6.3	3.7%	27	41	28
2018	SF	16/14	662	8	30	0	3.8	2	-86.7%	--	-29	--	-23	38%	--	6	41	30	324	1	73%	10.8	5.8	18.7%	8	76	18
2019	SF			8	35	0	4.3	0	14.7%								38	28	267	1	74%	9.5		12.1%			

Juszczyk had an excellent receiving DVOA overall last year, but his DVOA on passes out of the backfield was -19.9%. His numbers out wide (or at tight end) were ridiculous: 12 targets, 10 catches, 172 yards. His average depth of target of 5.3 yards was second-highest among running backs last season. It makes you wonder why they bothered throwing to him out of the backfield at all. Now he'll likely lose some of those slot/wide targets to free-agent signee Tevin Coleman. Projecting how the 49ers will use all their running backs this year is like finishing a crossword puzzle when you only have clues for "down."

Alvin Kamara

Height: 5-10   **Weight:** 214   **College:** Tennessee   **Draft:** 2017/3 (67)   **Born:** 25-Jul-1995   **Age:** 24   **Risk: Green**

Year	Team	G/GS	Snaps	Runs	Yds	TD	Yd/R	FUM	DVOA	Rk	DYAR	Rk	YAR	Suc%	Rk	BTkl	Pass	Rec	Yds	TD	C%	Yd/C	YAC	DVOA	Rk	DYAR	Rk
2017	NO	16/3	464	120	728	8	6.1	1	44.5%	1	255	3	255	53%	6	66	100	81	826	5	81%	10.2	8.5	36.4%	6	278	1
2018	NO	15/13	657	194	883	14	4.6	0	18.5%	4	238	3	281	58%	2	43	105	81	709	4	77%	8.8	7.9	19.4%	7	197	2
2019	NO			200	903	10	4.5	4	8.2%								102	82	726	4	80%	8.9		20.8%			

It was always too much to hope that Kamara could replicate his incredible rookie season, but his sophomore year was still very, very good. What he lost in efficiency, he made up in volume: even with Week 17 off, Kamara again surpassed 1,500 total scrimmage yards, increased his carry total by over 50 percent, increased his target total (though not his number of receptions) and recorded 18 touchdowns. He then piled up over 100 scrimmage yards in two straight playoff games, including 96 receiving yards alone against the Rams. During Mark Ingram's absence at the start of the year, Kamara set single-game career highs in carries (19), targets (20), receptions (15), and total yards (190).

With Ingram now in Baltimore, this backfield very much belongs to Kamara. New backup Latavius Murray is a former 1,000-yard rusher, but at 29 he is much less of a threat than Ingram to eat into Kamara's snap count and rushing total in New Orleans. Assuming he plays all 16 games this time around, that should be enough to see Kamara eclipse 200 rushing attempts and 1,600 total yards, further cementing his place as a top-five running back in both fantasy and real-world terms.

Dion Lewis

Height: 5-7   **Weight:** 195   **College:** Pittsburgh   **Draft:** 2011/5 (149)   **Born:** 27-Sep-1990   **Age:** 29   **Risk: Yellow**

Year	Team	G/GS	Snaps	Runs	Yds	TD	Yd/R	FUM	DVOA	Rk	DYAR	Rk	YAR	Suc%	Rk	BTkl	Pass	Rec	Yds	TD	C%	Yd/C	YAC	DVOA	Rk	DYAR	Rk
2016	NE	7/5	163	64	283	0	4.4	1	21.0%	--	74	--	52	59%	--	20	24	17	94	0	71%	5.5	4.9	-31.9%	--	-25	--
2017	NE	16/8	404	180	896	6	5.0	0	27.6%	2	273	1	280	56%	4	60	35	32	214	3	91%	6.7	7.0	32.0%	10	90	12
2018	TEN	16/7	600	155	517	1	3.3	1	-20.1%	43	-69	43	-130	34%	47	53	67	59	400	1	88%	6.8	8.1	-9.8%	35	15	31
2019	TEN			85	357	2	4.2	1	2.2%								57	46	340	1	81%	7.4		3.7%			

Lewis' first season in Tennessee was quite a comedown from what he had experienced in New England. He managed to stay healthy for all 16 games for just the second time, but it did not matter. Pushed into more of a traditional role, he was about as ineffective as Derrick Henry the first half of the season (-8.5% DVOA to Henry's -0.5%) then cratered the second half of the season (-36.3% DVOA) while Henry took off. He still had a role, given Henry's passing-game limitations, but it seems unlikely to be much more than that. He was one of the league's most high-volume screen receivers, as his 25 targets there tied for fourth-most, but only David Johnson in Arizona's dumpster fire had a lower DVOA on such plays.

Phillip Lindsay

| | | Height: 5-8 | | Weight: 190 | | College: Colorado | | | | Draft: 2018/FA | | | Born: 24-Jul-1994 | | | Age: 25 | | Risk: Yellow |

Year	Team	G/GS	Snaps	Runs	Yds	TD	Yd/R	FUM	DVOA	Rk	DYAR	Rk	YAR	Suc%	Rk	BTkl	Pass	Rec	Yds	TD	C%	Yd/C	YAC	DVOA	Rk	DYAR	Rk
2018	DEN	15/8	453	192	1037	9	5.4	0	17.3%	6	203	6	228	49%	22	36	47	35	241	1	74%	6.9	8.5	-10.4%	36	9	36
2019	DEN			181	853	7	4.7	2	10.5%								56	38	305	1	68%	8.0		-13.7%			

The new patron saint of "don't draft running backs," Lindsay didn't even get a Going Deep mention in *FOA 2018* on his way to not only making the Broncos as an undrafted free agent, but making the Pro Bowl. Lindsay's success was based on the vision needed to avoid contact near the line of scrimmage, and then the speed needed to turn that crack of daylight into a huge play. Lindsay had 30 rushes for 10 yards or more on just 192 carries; that rate of big-play success probably isn't sustainable, but it does come from his skill set as opposed to just great blocking or poor defense. Durability concerns likely mean he'll never be a 20-carry-a-game player, but he should be a gem of a 1A for years to come.

Marshawn Lynch

| | | Height: 5-11 | | Weight: 215 | | College: California | | | | Draft: 2007/1 (12) | | | Born: 22-Apr-1986 | | | Age: 33 | | Risk: N/A |

Year	Team	G/GS	Snaps	Runs	Yds	TD	Yd/R	FUM	DVOA	Rk	DYAR	Rk	YAR	Suc%	Rk	BTkl	Pass	Rec	Yds	TD	C%	Yd/C	YAC	DVOA	Rk	DYAR	Rk
2017	OAK	15/15	462	207	891	7	4.3	1	10.1%	9	165	9	131	49%	13	60	31	20	151	0	65%	7.6	8.2	-27.2%	56	-23	54
2018	OAK	6/6	212	90	376	3	4.2	0	-2.3%	--	25	--	51	53%	--	24	20	15	84	0	75%	5.6	6.0	-28.5%	--	-17	--

Lynch retired for the second time in April after a groin/core muscle injury cost him most of 2018. Lynch's two-year stint in Oakland is mostly an odd coda to his career, though it did get him up over the 10,000-yard mark. He had some moments with the Raiders, especially in December of 2017, but when we remember Lynch, we'll remember that 2011 through 2014 stretch where he Beasted all over Seattle, finishing in the top five in DYAR each year and topping out by leading the league in rushing DVOA in 2014. Is that four-year Seattle run enough to punch his ticket to Canton? Peter King thinks so, and he has a vote.

Marlon Mack

| | | Height: 5-11 | | Weight: 213 | | College: South Florida | | | | Draft: 2017/4 (143) | | | Born: 7-Mar-1996 | | | Age: 23 | | Risk: Red |

Year	Team	G/GS	Snaps	Runs	Yds	TD	Yd/R	FUM	DVOA	Rk	DYAR	Rk	YAR	Suc%	Rk	BTkl	Pass	Rec	Yds	TD	C%	Yd/C	YAC	DVOA	Rk	DYAR	Rk
2017	IND	14/0	310	93	358	3	3.8	1	-6.9%	--	6	--	11	41%	--	23	33	21	225	1	64%	10.7	13.5	9.2%	16	38	29
2018	IND	12/10	445	195	908	9	4.7	2	16.8%	8	216	4	177	54%	8	27	26	17	103	1	65%	6.1	7.2	-21.3%	49	-10	48
2019	IND			240	1081	8	4.5	4	5.3%								48	33	248	2	69%	7.5		-16.8%			

Was Mack's hamstring injury that cost him four games early in the season part of the Colts' overall offensive struggles? Perhaps a part of it, but he was fine when he returned in Week 6 and from then on did well as the offense as a whole did well. Even that was a remarkable accomplishment for Mack after an inconsistent rookie year set him up with challengers to his job if he did not perform well in his second season. He was the sort of physical runner he needed to be behind a run game built primarily around inside zone (his most effective high-rep run), outside zone, and power (both with a lower success rate but more yards per play). He was not much of a passing-game player but showed he could be effective enough there if the Colts needed him, even if he was not as versatile a receiver as their other options. Not pursuing a significant free-agent back could be read as a sign of the Colts' comfort with Mack, further buttressed by complimentary words from Chis Ballard and Frank Reich. Injury appears to be the only threat to an even more significant workload in 2019.

Doug Martin Height: 5-9   Weight: 210   College: Boise State   Draft: 2012/1 (31)   Born: 13-Jan-1989   Age: 30   Risk: Yellow

Year	Team	G/GS	Snaps	Runs	Yds	TD	Yd/R	FUM	DVOA	Rk	DYAR	Rk	YAR	Suc%	Rk	BTkl	Pass	Rec	Yds	TD	C%	Yd/C	YAC	DVOA	Rk	DYAR	Rk
2016	TB	8/8	322	144	421	3	2.9	1	-22.0%	40	-82	39	-76	42%	34	33	16	14	134	0	88%	9.6	7.6	24.7%	--	30	--
2017	TB	11/8	289	138	406	3	2.9	1	-22.5%	47	-77	45	-83	35%	46	12	18	9	84	0	50%	9.3	6.7	-30.4%	--	-18	--
2018	OAK	16/9	360	172	723	4	4.2	3	-12.2%	37	-27	39	19	53%	10	19	24	18	116	0	75%	6.4	5.2	-11.7%	--	3	--
2019	OAK			72	273	2	3.8	2	-9.1%								11	9	74	0	82%	8.2		7.5%			

Martin's first year in Oakland was his best year since 2015, which sounds really nice when you phrase it that way. He has been a sub-replacement level player in all but two years of his career, and hasn't been an above-average rusher since his rookie season in 2012. He was just so bad in 2016 and 2017 that anything even close to adequate feels like a revelation. He closed out the year with back-to-back 100-yard rushing days, but those were only worth a total of 9 DYAR, as they came against the worst run defense in the league in Kansas City and a mostly checked-out Denver squad. It's possible he might still have a little more gas in the tank, but any version of the 2019 Raiders that involves Martin getting anything more than a handful of carries is likely not a successful one.

Alexander Mattison Height: 5-11   Weight: 221   College: Boise State   Draft: 2019/3 (102)   Born: 19-Jun-1998   Age: 21   Risk: Green

Year	Team	G/GS	Snaps	Runs	Yds	TD	Yd/R	FUM	DVOA	Rk	DYAR	Rk	YAR	Suc%	Rk	BTkl	Pass	Rec	Yds	TD	C%	Yd/C	YAC	DVOA	Rk	DYAR	Rk
2019	MIN			68	262	3	3.9	3	-3.8%								16	13	105	1	81%	8.1		0.2%			

Nothing encapsulates Mike Zimmer's offensive philosophy better than firing an offensive coordinator whom he believed passed too often, then spending a third-round pick on a milquetoast running back. Mattison is the antithesis of Minnesota's current starter, Dalvin Cook. Mattison is a stout runner who relishes work between the tackles and when forced to take on defenders. He is light on his feet for a runner of his stature, too, though he will not impress the way Saquon Barkley or Alvin Kamara might. Rather than explosiveness, the draw for Mattison is that he is a low-variance runner who will pick up the yards provided to him—exactly what Zimmer wants from the offense. Those yards should be more available in Minnesota than they were last year now that the offensive line is improved. Nobody should expect Mattison to eat into Cook's overall workload, especially on passing downs, but he can serve as a stable presence when Cook needs a rest.

Christian McCaffrey Height: 5-11   Weight: 202   College: Stanford   Draft: 2017/1 (8)   Born: 7-Jun-1996   Age: 23   Risk: Green

Year	Team	G/GS	Snaps	Runs	Yds	TD	Yd/R	FUM	DVOA	Rk	DYAR	Rk	YAR	Suc%	Rk	BTkl	Pass	Rec	Yds	TD	C%	Yd/C	YAC	DVOA	Rk	DYAR	Rk
2017	CAR	16/10	757	117	435	2	3.7	1	-6.2%	30	11	34	14	45%	22	47	113	80	651	5	71%	8.1	7.4	5.7%	21	128	5
2018	CAR	16/16	965	219	1098	7	5.0	4	9.6%	10	167	7	181	55%	5	63	124	107	867	6	86%	8.1	8.0	11.5%	15	183	5
2019	CAR			230	1031	7	4.5	3	6.1%								121	97	813	4	80%	8.4		20.2%			

Now unconstrained by a backfield timeshare, McCaffrey followed up a productive rookie season with a tremendous second year. McCaffrey fully lived up to his LaDainian Tomlinson best-case scenario in Norv Turner's offense, following in Tomlinson's footsteps as only the third player ever to record at least 1,000 rushing yards and 100 catches in the same season. Though the Panthers finished outside the playoff picture, McCaffrey finished third in yards from scrimmage, third in ESPN standard fantasy points, and second in PPR.

McCaffrey was the one starting player to benefit from Carolina's second-half collapse: through Week 9, he had 109 carries for 502 yards (4.6 yards per carry, -4.9% DVOA) and five touchdowns, including four games under 100 yards from scrimmage. In the second half, with Cam Newton visibly impaired, McCaffrey became the offensive workhorse: he surpassed 100 scrimmage yards in every game from Week 10 to Week 16; leapt to 23.2% rushing DVOA (5.45 yards per carry); and ran, caught, or even threw for nine touchdowns in the six games he played alongside Newton (the touchdown pass was to Chris Manhertz in Week 15, Newton's final game). Carolina's league-leading 5.1 yards per carry is likely to regress, as is McCaffrey's personal 5.01 yards per carry—the last team to average more than 5.0 yards per carry in consecutive seasons was the 2011-12 Vikings, while the last *player* to do so (minimum 160 carries per season) was Jamaal Charles in 2010. Even that regression would barely impact his value: between his rushing efficiency and receiving production, McCaffrey has already established himself as one of the league's few elite feature backs ahead of his third professional season.

LeSean McCoy Height: 5-11   Weight: 198   College: Pittsburgh   Draft: 2009/2 (53)   Born: 12-Jul-1988   Age: 31   Risk: Yellow

Year	Team	G/GS	Snaps	Runs	Yds	TD	Yd/R	FUM	DVOA	Rk	DYAR	Rk	YAR	Suc%	Rk	BTkl	Pass	Rec	Yds	TD	C%	Yd/C	YAC	DVOA	Rk	DYAR	Rk
2016	BUF	15/15	645	234	1267	13	5.4	3	28.3%	2	338	2	244	51%	10	65	58	50	356	1	88%	7.1	7.6	21.2%	8	117	7
2017	BUF	16/16	722	287	1138	6	4.0	3	-10.8%	38	-26	41	-7	43%	32	61	78	59	448	2	77%	7.6	6.9	-1.8%	33	48	24
2018	BUF	14/13	490	161	514	3	3.2	0	-26.2%	45	-109	46	-119	37%	45	34	46	34	238	0	74%	7.0	8.5	-24.5%	51	-26	52
2019	*BUF*			*157*	*627*	*3*	*4.0*	*1*	*0.3%*								*37*	*26*	*208*	*1*	*70%*	*8.0*		*-9.3%*			

Brandon Beane says McCoy will still be the Bills' featured back in 2019, and McCoy says he expects to be used in the same role as he was last year. If 2018 had been a one-year blip, then maybe you could hold out some optimism for the 31-year-old back, but signs of decline started in 2017. McCoy doesn't bounce off defenders the way he used to, nor does he have the same burst he once had. With the third-highest cap hit for a running back in football, and just $2.6 million in dead money if he's released, it would not be at all surprising for the Bills to decide to move on from McCoy before the season began.

Elijah McGuire Height: 5-10   Weight: 214   College: Louisiana-Lafayette   Draft: 2017/6 (188)   Born: 1-Jun-1994   Age: 25   Risk: Yellow

Year	Team	G/GS	Snaps	Runs	Yds	TD	Yd/R	FUM	DVOA	Rk	DYAR	Rk	YAR	Suc%	Rk	BTkl	Pass	Rec	Yds	TD	C%	Yd/C	YAC	DVOA	Rk	DYAR	Rk
2017	NYJ	16/2	267	88	315	1	3.6	1	-25.8%	--	-56	--	-38	34%	--	22	26	17	177	1	65%	10.4	8.4	-1.4%	32	18	36
2018	NYJ	8/3	318	92	276	3	3.0	2	-32.1%	--	-90	--	-104	36%	--	25	31	19	193	1	61%	10.2	8.9	8.1%	18	38	25
2019	*NYJ*			*47*	*186*	*1*	*4.0*	*1*	*-5.4%*								*36*	*25*	*175*	*0*	*69%*	*7.0*		*-19.2%*			

McGuire received three starts and lots of touches in December, when the Jets ran out of bodies and ideas in the backfield. He rushed 73 times for 190 yards, 2.7 yards per carry and three touchdowns in five games, which is not good. McGuire only spent two years on the Jets roster because Mike Maccagnan drafted him and Maccagnan was also responsible for finding replacements for him. With Adam Gase eager to put his own stamp on things (picture Harley Quinn with a giant mallet here) and Ty Montgomery in town to back up Le'Veon Bell, McGuire is a very likely training camp cut.

Jerick McKinnon Height: 5-9   Weight: 209   College: Georgia Southern   Draft: 2014/3 (96)   Born: 5-Mar-1992   Age: 27   Risk: Yellow

Year	Team	G/GS	Snaps	Runs	Yds	TD	Yd/R	FUM	DVOA	Rk	DYAR	Rk	YAR	Suc%	Rk	BTkl	Pass	Rec	Yds	TD	C%	Yd/C	YAC	DVOA	Rk	DYAR	Rk
2016	MIN	15/7	510	159	539	2	3.4	0	-11.0%	34	-15	33	-56	42%	35	32	53	43	255	2	81%	5.9	6.3	-10.7%	40	10	36
2017	MIN	16/1	528	150	570	3	3.8	2	-12.7%	40	-24	40	-25	43%	28	43	68	51	421	2	75%	8.3	9.0	-0.4%	31	48	23
2019	*SF*			*117*	*497*	*3*	*4.2*	*2*	*1.1%*								*48*	*36*	*310*	*1*	*75%*	*8.6*		*3.0%*			

McKinnon didn't participate in OTAs, still rehabbing the torn ACL that knocked him out for all of 2018. In an age when many players are filling hybrid roles, McKinnon is pretty strictly a running back—less than ten percent of his targets came from slot/wide positions in his last two years in Minnesota. That means he is competing less with Matt Breida and Tevin Coleman for playing time, and more with Jeff Wilson and Raheem Mostert. Projecting how the 49ers will use all their running backs this year is like solving a Rubik's Cube on acid.

Sony Michel Height: 5-11   Weight: 214   College: Georgia   Draft: 2018/1 (31)   Born: 17-Feb-1995   Age: 24   Risk: Red

Year	Team	G/GS	Snaps	Runs	Yds	TD	Yd/R	FUM	DVOA	Rk	DYAR	Rk	YAR	Suc%	Rk	BTkl	Pass	Rec	Yds	TD	C%	Yd/C	YAC	DVOA	Rk	DYAR	Rk
2018	NE	13/8	320	209	931	6	4.5	1	-2.7%	26	58	24	101	53%	11	23	11	7	50	0	64%	7.1	7.1	-18.4%	--	-3	--
2019	*NE*			*239*	*1056*	*9*	*4.4*	*3*	*8.4%*								*15*	*11*	*91*	*1*	*73%*	*8.2*		*-2.3%*			

For most of the decade following Corey Dillon's departure, the Patriots were the archetypal running-back-by-committee franchise—a season-by-season, week-to-week stable of replaceable backs occasionally featuring big days from the likes of LaMont Jordan, Sammy Morris, Brandon Bolden, and one-week legend Jonas Gray. That has been less the case over recent seasons: after only two backs reached 800 yards for them between 2007 and 2016, the Patriots have had an 800-yard back in each of the past three years. Still, Dillon remains the last Patriots back to have two seasons of 800 rushing yards, and the last player to do so in *consecutive* seasons was Antowain Smith in 2001-02.

Sony Michel was drafted to break that pattern. Michel was the first Patriots rookie to reach 900 rushing yards since Robert Edwards in 1998, and he would surely have reached 1,000 had he not missed two games with a knee sprain suffered in late October. Michel was used almost purely as a between-the-tackles chugger—121 of his 209 runs were marked left guard, middle, or right guard—and he had only eight receptions despite playing a significant role in 16 games (both numbers include the post-season). His six 100-yard rushing days included both AFC playoff victories, and his six postseason touchdowns included the clinching score in Super Bowl LIII. His lack of utility in the passing game limits his fantasy upside, but a healthy Michel is a key component of the team's rebuilt power-rushing attack.

Lamar Miller Height: 5-11 Weight: 212 College: Miami Draft: 2012/4 (97) Born: 25-Apr-1991 Age: 28 Risk: Green

Year	Team	G/GS	Snaps	Runs	Yds	TD	Yd/R	FUM	DVOA	Rk	DYAR	Rk	YAR	Suc%	Rk	BTkl	Pass	Rec	Yds	TD	C%	Yd/C	YAC	DVOA	Rk	DYAR	Rk
2016	HOU	14/14	623	268	1073	5	4.0	2	-10.5%	32	-21	34	29	45%	23	37	39	31	188	1	79%	6.1	6.0	-14.4%	44	-1	44
2017	HOU	16/13	757	238	888	3	3.7	1	-2.8%	25	57	21	42	45%	21	34	45	36	327	3	80%	9.1	8.2	42.7%	2	134	4
2018	HOU	14/14	619	210	973	5	4.6	1	-5.3%	28	28	27	46	44%	35	28	35	25	163	1	71%	6.5	6.8	-19.9%	47	-10	45
2019	HOU			216	888	4	4.1	2	-1.1%								39	31	252	2	79%	8.1		9.5%			

Miller has a demonstrated split of being more effective as a shotgun runner the last two seasons, with a 8.8% DVOA in 120 carries out of the gun in 2017 and a 6.7% DVOA in 96 carries in 2018. Shedding eight pounds this offseason, Miller looks like a better candidate to handle outside zone than inside zone at this point in his career. The Texans are probably hoping that D'Onta Foreman can take most of the pounding while Miller gets into open space. Miller also told the *Houston Chronicle* that he spent more time running routes this offseason, which is something that might be of interest to PPR-league players.

Joe Mixon Height: 6-1 Weight: 228 College: Oklahoma Draft: 2017/2 (48) Born: 24-Jul-1996 Age: 23 Risk: Yellow

Year	Team	G/GS	Snaps	Runs	Yds	TD	Yd/R	FUM	DVOA	Rk	DYAR	Rk	YAR	Suc%	Rk	BTkl	Pass	Rec	Yds	TD	C%	Yd/C	YAC	DVOA	Rk	DYAR	Rk
2017	CIN	14/7	385	178	626	4	3.5	3	1.0%	19	68	17	-1	41%	37	22	35	30	287	0	89%	9.6	10.9	-6.8%	38	13	38
2018	CIN	14/13	596	237	1168	8	4.9	0	6.4%	13	154	8	154	49%	23	46	55	43	296	1	78%	6.9	7.7	-15.3%	41	-5	42
2019	CIN			268	1192	8	4.5	3	5.4%								60	47	378	2	78%	8.0		5.4%			

Massive fantasy football upside is afoot here if everything goes right. Mixon demonstrated his ability as a true three-down back last season, thriving in a broken offense without A.J. Green or Andy Dalton. In theory, if Zac Taylor's offense boosts him with more play-action and better blocking from more two-tight end sets, the easy comparison is that Mixon could have a Todd Gurley-esque season. One big problem with that idea is that the Bengals offensive line is terrible. Another is that it is relying on optimal health from a couple of players who can't seem to stay healthy anymore. However, the ceiling has been raised via the coaching, and you should be prepared to pay for that if you want to target Mixon in fantasy football.

David Montgomery Height: 5-10 Weight: 222 College: Iowa State Draft: 2019/3 (73) Born: 7-Jun-1997 Age: 22 Risk: Red

Year	Team	G/GS	Snaps	Runs	Yds	TD	Yd/R	FUM	DVOA	Rk	DYAR	Rk	YAR	Suc%	Rk	BTkl	Pass	Rec	Yds	TD	C%	Yd/C	YAC	DVOA	Rk	DYAR	Rk
2019	CHI			184	767	7	4.2	4	-1.5%								29	24	209	1	83%	8.7		6.0%			

The Bears must have immense trust in their scouting department to spend a third-round pick on Montgomery. Statistically, Montgomery is a mess. Among notable draft prospects, Montgomery held one of the lowest career rushing success rates at 41.3 percent, placing him between sixth-round picks Trayveon Williams and Travis Homer. He does not counter the poor efficiency with speed or explosiveness: he ran just a 4.63-second 40-yard dash and seldom ripped off long runs. The caveat is Iowa State's offensive line was a disaster, and while he was inefficient overall, Montgomery broke tackles in a way no other back could. His low, compact frame; impeccable balance; and fierce nature make him a nightmare to tackle. Montgomery will bounce and stumble around a few times on most carries before finally being drug to the ground by a swarm of defenders. The hope for Montgomery is that the Bears' nasty interior offensive line can unlock the potential he was never able to reach in a bad college offense.

Ty Montgomery   Height: 6-0   Weight: 221   College: Stanford   Draft: 2015/3 (94)   Born: 22-Jan-1993   Age: 26   Risk: Red

Year	Team	G/GS	Snaps	Runs	Yds	TD	Yd/R	FUM	DVOA	Rk	DYAR	Rk	YAR	Suc%	Rk	BTkl	Pass	Rec	Yds	TD	C%	Yd/C	YAC	DVOA	Rk	DYAR	Rk
2016	GB	15/6	392	77	457	3	5.9	2	17.6%	--	86	--	105	55%	--	25	56	44	348	0	79%	7.9	7.3	-4.2%	32	33	27
2017	GB	8/5	274	71	273	3	3.8	0	2.8%	--	37	--	41	49%	--	12	31	23	173	1	74%	7.5	9.3	-3.7%	35	19	35
2018	2TM	13/0	264	41	188	1	4.6	1	0.9%	--	17	--	25	57%	--	13	40	25	235	0	63%	9.4	8.5	-14.1%	40	-1	40
2019	NYJ			22	94	0	4.4	1	2.3%								17	12	81	0	71%	6.8		-13.7%			

It's hard to tell whether Montgomery's decline the last two years has been the result of the Packers offensive dysfunction or the fact that Montgomery isn't as dynamic or elusive as he looked when catching defenses by surprise back in his rookie year. A 162-yard rushing performance against the Bears in December of 2016 still accounts for over 17 percent of Montgomery's career rushing production, and he hasn't caught 10 passes in a game since he did so in back-to-back games that season. Montgomery may simply be a replacement-level third-down back who has extra name recognition because he played with Aaron Rodgers and had a weird jersey number. He'll get a long look behind Le'Veon Bell, because the Jets are always looking to upgrade their bench to replacement level.

Alfred Morris   Height: 5-10   Weight: 219   College: Florida Atlantic   Draft: 2012/6 (173)   Born: 12-Dec-1988   Age: 31   Risk: N/A

Year	Team	G/GS	Snaps	Runs	Yds	TD	Yd/R	FUM	DVOA	Rk	DYAR	Rk	YAR	Suc%	Rk	BTkl	Pass	Rec	Yds	TD	C%	Yd/C	YAC	DVOA	Rk	DYAR	Rk
2016	DAL	14/0	130	69	243	2	3.5	0	-7.7%	--	3	--	11	52%	--	13	6	3	11	0	50%	3.7	3.7	-53.4%	--	-13	--
2017	DAL	14/5	204	115	547	1	4.8	0	8.4%	10	79	16	99	51%	7	30	9	7	45	0	78%	6.4	6.3	-18.4%	--	-2	--
2018	SF	12/1	250	111	428	2	3.9	2	-30.5%	47	-103	45	-60	41%	38	18	13	8	73	0	62%	9.1	8.4	-6.7%	--	6	--

Did you know that Morris is ninth among active players in career rushing yards? No, really! He likely won't be active for much longer though—he had 4,713 yards in four seasons in Washington but only 1,218 yards in three seasons since, and he was dead last in rushing DVOA last year. If you chart Morris' career yardage by season, you get an almost linear pattern of descent. With Morris unsigned, it appears that descent has reached its final end.

Marcus Murphy   Height: 5-9   Weight: 198   College: Missouri   Draft: 2015/7 (230)   Born: 3-Oct-1991   Age: 28   Risk: Red

Year	Team	G/GS	Snaps	Runs	Yds	TD	Yd/R	FUM	DVOA	Rk	DYAR	Rk	YAR	Suc%	Rk	BTkl	Pass	Rec	Yds	TD	C%	Yd/C	YAC	DVOA	Rk	DYAR	Rk
2016	NO	3/0	1	0	0	0	0.0	--	--	--	--	--	--	--	--	--	1	1	3	0	100%	3.0	1.0	-52.4%	--	-2	--
2017	BUF	1/0	14	7	41	0	5.9	0	11.7%	--	6	--	5	43%	--	0	2	2	7	0	100%	3.5	5.0	-0.7%	--	1	--
2018	BUF	11/1	196	52	250	0	4.8	0	10.6%	--	36	--	31	42%	--	11	19	11	26	0	58%	2.4	3.4	-82.6%	--	-76	--
2019	BUF			16	75	0	4.6	1	6.0%								9	7	53	0	78%	7.5		2.9%			

Murphy has mostly been a practice squad player throughout his four-year career. He has now been forced into action by injuries two years in a row, and shown surprising production for someone who is essentially bottom-of-the-roster fodder—4.9 yards per carry is nothing to sneeze at, even in such a small sample size. With Frank Gore, T.J. Yeldon, and Devin Singletary all joining the team this offseason, Murphy's likely to get forced out by the numbers game, but don't count him out for stealing a spot at the very bottom of the roster yet again. He's not someone who should be starting football games, but you could do worse for a fourth running back.

Latavius Murray   Height: 6-2   Weight: 223   College: UCF   Draft: 2013/6 (181)   Born: 21-Feb-1991   Age: 28   Risk: Yellow

Year	Team	G/GS	Snaps	Runs	Yds	TD	Yd/R	FUM	DVOA	Rk	DYAR	Rk	YAR	Suc%	Rk	BTkl	Pass	Rec	Yds	TD	C%	Yd/C	YAC	DVOA	Rk	DYAR	Rk
2016	OAK	14/12	525	195	788	12	4.0	2	-3.4%	23	46	23	100	49%	16	36	43	33	264	0	77%	8.0	8.5	-9.4%	38	10	37
2017	MIN	16/11	421	216	842	8	3.9	1	-2.3%	24	59	20	58	44%	23	34	17	15	103	0	88%	6.9	8.3	-11.6%	--	2	--
2018	MIN	16/6	461	140	578	6	4.1	0	-4.2%	27	25	29	16	46%	31	18	26	22	141	0	85%	6.4	5.2	-7.5%	33	9	35
2019	NO			158	677	7	4.3	4	2.6%								28	22	189	2	79%	8.6		12.8%			

Playing for the Saints in 2019 should feel to Murray like he has been resurrected in a brand-new body. He arrives in New Orleans after two years playing behind a notoriously bad Vikings line, but prior to that he had two productive seasons behind a Raiders front much closer in quality to the one he should find in New Orleans. Murray had over 2,500 rushing yards from 2015 to 2017, including a 1,000-yard Pro Bowl campaign for the Raiders in 2015, but he spent most of 2018 as the backup to Dalvin Cook and has not recorded a positive DVOA in any season as a major contributor.

In theory the replacement for the departed Mark Ingram, Murray has a skill set that does not quite replace Ingram's like-for-like. His role, usage, and production should be similar though, at least compared to Ingram in 2018. His main job will be spelling Alvin Kamara much as he did Cook in Minnesota, and he should find plenty of short-yardage and red zone work, where the superior Saints line will hopefully see him improve on his thoroughly mediocre Vikings numbers in both areas.

Rashaad Penny   Height: 5-11   Weight: 220   College: San Diego State   Draft: 2018/1 (27)   Born: 2-Feb-1996   Age: 23   Risk: Green

Year	Team	G/GS	Snaps	Runs	Yds	TD	Yd/R	FUM	DVOA	Rk	DYAR	Rk	YAR	Suc%	Rk	BTkl	Pass	Rec	Yds	TD	C%	Yd/C	YAC	DVOA	Rk	DYAR	Rk
2018	SEA	14/0	180	85	419	2	4.9	0	8.9%	--	56	--	53	40%	--	12	12	9	75	0	75%	8.3	8.1	8.3%	--	12	--
2019	SEA			141	629	3	4.5	2	2.4%								24	20	156	0	83%	7.8		5.3%			

It wasn't Penny's fault that Seattle drafted him in the first round instead of trading down further in the 2018 draft to acquire more picks, but that decision will come up in most discussions of the former San Diego State star until he earns a starting job with the team. While Mike Davis, one of the backs on the depth chart ahead of Penny, has since departed for Chicago, Penny still has to contend with entrenched starter Chris Carson for time. Penny had a tendency to dance around in the backfield looking for opportunities to bust a big play as a rookie; while it made for some highlights, it also contributed to him being stopped for no gain or a loss on 21.1 percent of his carries. That may have been part of why he was lower in the pecking order, as Carson was only stopped for no gain or a loss 15.9 percent of the time. If Penny can get moving downfield more effectively in his sophomore season, he will have a better chance to make an impact.

Adrian Peterson   Height: 6-2   Weight: 217   College: Oklahoma   Draft: 2007/1 (7)   Born: 21-Mar-1985   Age: 34   Risk: Red

Year	Team	G/GS	Snaps	Runs	Yds	TD	Yd/R	FUM	DVOA	Rk	DYAR	Rk	YAR	Suc%	Rk	BTkl	Pass	Rec	Yds	TD	C%	Yd/C	YAC	DVOA	Rk	DYAR	Rk
2016	MIN	3/3	84	37	72	0	1.9	1	-49.1%	--	-57	--	-63	38%	--	2	6	3	8	0	50%	2.7	3.7	-109.4%	--	-30	--
2017	2TM	10/7	300	156	529	2	3.4	3	-21.9%	46	-85	46	-79	40%	42	32	19	11	70	0	58%	6.4	5.0	-35.7%	--	-23	--
2018	WAS	16/16	481	251	1042	7	4.2	3	-6.0%	29	26	28	-13	47%	28	56	26	20	208	1	77%	10.4	10.1	22.3%	5	50	21
2019	WAS			92	372	2	4.1	1	-0.4%								13	9	60	0	69%	6.7		-23.6%			

Peterson's 2018 resurgence took most of the analytics community by surprise—it didn't take a math degree to estimate that the future Hall of Famer was cooked when he averaged 3.4 yards per carry for two teams in 2017—but it wasn't nearly as impressive a season as Peterson's yardage total indicates. Peterson averaged just 3.2 yards per rush in the final four games of last season. Set aside his 90-yard touchdown run against the Eagles, and he averaged just 3.2 yards per rush in games 9 to 12 as well. A handful of big plays inflated Peterson's receiving DVOA in a small sample; he wasn't used much as a receiver (just one third-down reception—he gained 52 yards, then fumbled the ball away), and his preference for taking handoffs from an under-center quarterback (185 carries under center last year, just 66 from shotgun) limits what his teams can do when he is in the huddle. Peterson can best help the Skins this season as president of the ACL Recovery Club in the running back room, helping Derrius Guice and Bryce Love turn the corner after significant injuries. If he finds his way back onto the field yet again, Peterson will still provide scattered highlights, plus lots and lots of 3-yard runs between the tackles from an Ace formation.

Bilal Powell   Height: 5-10   Weight: 205   College: Louisville   Draft: 2011/4 (126)   Born: 27-Oct-1988   Age: 31   Risk: Red

Year	Team	G/GS	Snaps	Runs	Yds	TD	Yd/R	FUM	DVOA	Rk	DYAR	Rk	YAR	Suc%	Rk	BTkl	Pass	Rec	Yds	TD	C%	Yd/C	YAC	DVOA	Rk	DYAR	Rk
2016	NYJ	16/4	531	131	722	3	5.5	1	23.1%	3	182	8	197	56%	4	49	75	58	388	2	79%	6.7	7.2	-1.9%	27	49	20
2017	NYJ	15/10	401	178	772	5	4.3	1	-14.8%	42	-43	43	5	35%	45	36	33	23	170	0	70%	7.4	7.0	-30.4%	57	-30	56
2018	NYJ	7/7	208	80	343	0	4.3	2	-19.9%	--	-34	--	-33	44%	--	8	18	11	110	1	61%	10.0	7.6	-14.4%	--	-1	--
2019	NYJ			23	99	0	4.4	0	4.5%								11	8	56	0	73%	7.0		-8.8%			

Powell was medically cleared to return to football in May after undergoing neck surgery last October. He has always been a useful all-purpose committee back, but the market for 31-year-old committee backs coming off neck surgery is understandably slow, and Powell didn't re-sign with the Jets until June. Powell has hung around long enough to reach 10th place on the all-time Jets rushing list, between Adrian Murrell in ninth and Shonn Greene in 11th, which says a lot about Jets history.

Jalen Richard   Height: 5-8   Weight: 207   College: Southern Mississippi   Draft: 2016/FA   Born: 15-Oct-1993   Age: 26   Risk: Green

Year	Team	G/GS	Snaps	Runs	Yds	TD	Yd/R	FUM	DVOA	Rk	DYAR	Rk	YAR	Suc%	Rk	BTkl	Pass	Rec	Yds	TD	C%	Yd/C	YAC	DVOA	Rk	DYAR	Rk
2016	OAK	16/0	237	83	491	1	5.9	0	16.7%	--	76	--	97	49%	--	23	39	29	194	2	74%	6.7	4.9	-8.8%	37	9	39
2017	OAK	16/1	219	56	275	1	4.9	1	-1.4%	--	15	--	15	38%	--	10	36	27	256	1	75%	9.5	9.0	33.3%	9	86	14
2018	OAK	16/1	413	55	259	1	4.7	2	-20.3%	--	-28	--	-7	45%	--	27	81	68	607	0	84%	8.9	7.3	17.4%	9	138	6
2019	OAK			35	152	1	4.3	1	0.2%								70	55	409	2	79%	7.4		2.1%			

Richard carved out a nice little niche for himself last season as the Raiders' primary receiving back. He probably would have had the job by default due to the fact that none of the old guys in the running back meeting room could catch anything at this point, but no, Richard proved himself a legitimate quality safety valve-type player for Derek Carr, finishing third in receiving plus-minus

Theo Riddick   Height: 5-10   Weight: 201   College: Notre Dame   Draft: 2013/6 (199)   Born: 4-May-1991   Age: 28   Risk: Yellow

Year	Team	G/GS	Snaps	Runs	Yds	TD	Yd/R	FUM	DVOA	Rk	DYAR	Rk	YAR	Suc%	Rk	BTkl	Pass	Rec	Yds	TD	C%	Yd/C	YAC	DVOA	Rk	DYAR	Rk
2016	DET	10/8	423	92	357	1	3.9	0	-9.8%	--	-5	--	-1	42%	--	33	67	53	371	5	79%	7.0	7.3	3.9%	21	67	15
2017	DET	16/5	472	84	286	3	3.4	1	-9.5%	--	-3	--	-8	39%	--	31	71	53	444	2	75%	8.4	8.2	-4.6%	36	37	30
2018	DET	14/3	415	40	171	0	4.3	0	-4.7%	--	5	--	13	43%	--	19	74	61	384	0	82%	6.3	6.7	-12.7%	38	4	38
2019	DET			35	150	0	4.3	1	-0.2%								72	54	414	2	75%	7.7		-1.3%			

Riddick is the most extreme case of a running back who is a better pass-catcher than a runner. Player such as James White, Alvin Kamara, and Tarik Cohen are best used as receivers, but they are still capable or better as runners. Riddick, on the other hand, is a well-below-average runner who does not sport the vision, balance, or breakaway speed to threaten under any context. However, few backs in the league are as adept at finding space as a pass-catcher out of the backfield. Riddick has the fifth-most targets among running backs since 2016. Riddick can also play as a legitimate slot receiver, which better serves to hide what Detroit wants to accomplish on a given play considering lining him up in the backfield is not a good look for Detroit if they want to run the ball. As the offense moves away from Jim Bob Cooter's conservative shotgun offense, it would not be surprising to see Riddick phased out of the lineup, especially with the signing of C.J. Anderson this offseason.

Jacquizz Rodgers   Height: 5-6   Weight: 196   College: Oregon State   Draft: 2011/5 (145)   Born: 6-Feb-1990   Age: 29   Risk: N/A

Year	Team	G/GS	Snaps	Runs	Yds	TD	Yd/R	FUM	DVOA	Rk	DYAR	Rk	YAR	Suc%	Rk	BTkl	Pass	Rec	Yds	TD	C%	Yd/C	YAC	DVOA	Rk	DYAR	Rk
2016	TB	10/5	341	129	560	2	4.3	0	0.2%	19	47	22	64	49%	18	22	16	13	98	0	81%	7.5	6.9	9.3%	--	19	--
2017	TB	16/4	168	64	244	1	3.8	0	-7.7%	--	2	--	15	41%	--	15	11	9	74	0	82%	8.2	9.8	30.5%	--	24	--
2018	TB	16/0	368	33	106	1	3.2	1	-7.6%	--	1	--	-7	33%	--	6	45	38	304	0	84%	8.0	6.3	7.1%	19	49	22

Rodgers, 29, is looking to play one more season before he goes to running back heaven. Might he head to Atlanta, where Dirk Koetter is the offensive coordinator? Koetter has been his coach in some capacity in six of his eight seasons. In terms of rushing DVOA, Rodgers hasn't been an above-average back since 2016, so it likely will take a training camp injury before he finds his way back onto an NFL roster.

Jaylen Samuels   Height: 5-11   Weight: 225   College: North Carolina State   Draft: 2018/5 (165)   Born: 20-Jul-1996   Age: 23   Risk: Green

Year	Team	G/GS	Snaps	Runs	Yds	TD	Yd/R	FUM	DVOA	Rk	DYAR	Rk	YAR	Suc%	Rk	BTkl	Pass	Rec	Yds	TD	C%	Yd/C	YAC	DVOA	Rk	DYAR	Rk
2018	PIT	14/3	228	56	256	0	4.6	0	-1.3%	--	17	--	15	52%	--	11	29	26	199	3	90%	7.7	8.3	36.4%	3	79	14
2019	PIT			58	253	1	4.4	2	0.8%								29	25	182	1	86%	7.3		11.8%			

Exhibit 9,148 in the case of *Running Backs Are Fungible vs. the Old-School NFL*, Samuels, an unheralded fifth-round pick a year ago, replaced the injured James Conner (himself filling in admirably for Le'Veon Bell) in the Steelers backfield and reeled off 142 yards against the Patriots. Samuels went on to emulate Bell when it comes to sure-handedness—the former collegiate tight end/H-back caught all but three of his targets, posting a seven-reception performance in the season finale against Cincinnati. Samuels is the kind of versatile talent who helps win division titles even while the rest of the world is still worrying about how much money Bell left on the table by sitting out 2018.

Miles Sanders   Height: 5-11   Weight: 211   College: Penn State   Draft: 2019/2 (53)   Born: 1-May-1997   Age: 22   Risk: Yellow

Year	Team	G/GS	Snaps	Runs	Yds	TD	Yd/R	FUM	DVOA	Rk	DYAR	Rk	YAR	Suc%	Rk	BTkl	Pass	Rec	Yds	TD	C%	Yd/C	YAC	DVOA	Rk	DYAR	Rk
2019	PHI			175	745	5	4.3	4	-0.3%								38	31	221	1	82%	7.1		-5.2%			

In most cases, spending valuable resources on running backs is not advisable, but the Eagles were in a unique position this year. Their running back room had been decimated the previous season and they let their top two running backs walk, yet most of the rest of the roster was stacked. Thus, they had the luxury to burn a second-round pick on a running back. Miles Sanders, the heir to Saquon Barkley at Penn State, feels like Philadelphia's attempt to replace the explosive play ability they dearly missed when Jay Ajayi went down early last season. Sanders ran a 4.49-second 40-yard dash and 6.89-second 3-cone drill at the combine, fitting the electric running style he showed in college. Sanders does not possess impressive power or balance, but the Eagles have one of the best offensive lines in the sport and should be able to grant him many wide-open running lanes that do not necessarily require those two traits. The worry for Sanders early on is that he may need to take on a larger third-down role than he will be ready for considering Jordan Howard is not a threatening pass-catcher. Sanders has the skill set to grow into a quality third-down player, but it may take time for him to grow into the role and Corey Clement could take those snaps early in the year.

Devin Singletary   Height: 5-7   Weight: 203   College: Florida Atlantic   Draft: 2019/3 (74)   Born: 3-Sep-1997   Age: 22   Risk: Blue

Year	Team	G/GS	Snaps	Runs	Yds	TD	Yd/R	FUM	DVOA	Rk	DYAR	Rk	YAR	Suc%	Rk	BTkl	Pass	Rec	Yds	TD	C%	Yd/C	YAC	DVOA	Rk	DYAR	Rk
2019	BUF			40	169	1	4.3	2	-2.8%								7	6	36	0	79%	6.5		-9.7%			

One good thing and one bad thing about the Bills' second-round pick. Per Sports Info Solutions, Singletary had the highest broken tackle rate per 100 touches in college football last season; he's got the balance and sideways zip you might expect from a younger LeSean McCoy. What he doesn't have is speed, running a 4.66 40 at the combine at 203 pounds. That's a speed score of just 86.1; the lowest speed score for a back who went on to be at all productive in the NFL was Ahmad Bradshaw's 87.7. Singletary will have to be faster in pads if he wants to stick at the NFL level.

Wendell Smallwood   Height: 5-10   Weight: 208   College: West Virginia   Draft: 2016/5 (153)   Born: 20-Jan-1994   Age: 25   Risk: Green

Year	Team	G/GS	Snaps	Runs	Yds	TD	Yd/R	FUM	DVOA	Rk	DYAR	Rk	YAR	Suc%	Rk	BTkl	Pass	Rec	Yds	TD	C%	Yd/C	YAC	DVOA	Rk	DYAR	Rk
2016	PHI	13/3	164	77	312	1	4.1	1	-3.4%	--	17	--	9	49%	--	12	13	6	55	0	46%	9.2	8.3	-27.6%	--	-9	--
2017	PHI	8/3	172	47	174	1	3.7	0	-19.5%	--	-20	--	-3	36%	--	11	18	13	103	0	72%	7.9	6.7	14.2%	--	30	--
2018	PHI	16/6	324	87	364	3	4.2	1	3.1%	--	41	--	53	51%	--	18	35	28	230	2	80%	8.2	8.3	11.2%	16	49	23
2019	PHI			25	90	0	3.6	1	-9.1%								15	12	82	0	80%	6.9		-7.8%			

Smallwood was supposed to be pushed down the depth chart by Jay Ajayi and Darren Sproles, but with both missing most of the season, Smallwood again assumed a regular role in the offense. Like most of Philly's backfield last year, Smallwood does not often impress with explosive runs or miraculous broken tackles. However, he did improve in his consistency and baseline level of play last season. He posted career highs in carries and success rate despite the decline and injuries along Philadelphia's offensive line. Smallwood also ended up leading the team's running backs in receptions in place of an injured Sproles. With the additions of Jordan Howard and Miles Sanders, in addition to the competition he already faced with Josh Adams and Corey Clement, Smallwood will presumably become an emergency option.

Ito Smith   Height: 5-9   Weight: 195   College: Southern Mississippi   Draft: 2018/4 (126)   Born: 11-Sep-1995   Age: 24   Risk: Yellow

Year	Team	G/GS	Snaps	Runs	Yds	TD	Yd/R	FUM	DVOA	Rk	DYAR	Rk	YAR	Suc%	Rk	BTkl	Pass	Rec	Yds	TD	C%	Yd/C	YAC	DVOA	Rk	DYAR	Rk
2018	ATL	14/0	311	90	315	4	3.5	1	-13.4%	--	-19	--	-12	48%	--	20	32	27	152	0	84%	5.6	5.9	-17.7%	45	-8	44
2019	ATL			90	350	3	3.9	2	-6.1%								24	20	164	1	83%	8.2		9.8%			

With the departure of Tevin Coleman to the 49ers, Ito "Whoa-oh-oh-oh-oh-oh" Smith slides into the Falcons' RB2 role. Really, though, he's more than that. He's a decent insurance policy in case Devonta Freeman—who sustained knee, foot and groin injuries last season—can't return to 2016 form. As a rookie, Smith wasn't an efficient runner but was a reliable receiver, dropping only one of his 32 targets. Even if Freeman is healthy, Smith figures to still see a good amount of touches. In 2016, when Freeman started every game, Coleman played 34.0 percent of the offensive snaps. In 2017, when Freeman started 14 games, Coleman played 41.4 percent.

Darren Sproles

Height: 5-6 **Weight:** 181 **College:** Kansas State **Draft:** 2005/4 (130) **Born:** 20-Jun-1983 **Age:** 36 **Risk:** N/A

Year	Team	G/GS	Snaps	Runs	Yds	TD	Yd/R	FUM	DVOA	Rk	DYAR	Rk	YAR	Suc%	Rk	BTkl	Pass	Rec	Yds	TD	C%	Yd/C	YAC	DVOA	Rk	DYAR	Rk
2016	PHI	15/5	511	94	438	2	4.7	0	17.6%	--	99	--	83	52%	--	36	71	52	427	2	73%	8.2	7.9	3.0%	24	65	16
2017	PHI	3/0	88	15	61	0	4.1	0	-5.5%	--	2	--	14	40%	--	4	12	7	73	0	58%	10.4	11.9	12.7%	--	16	--
2018	PHI	6/2	146	29	120	1	4.1	0	8.5%	--	19	--	19	41%	--	6	23	15	160	2	65%	10.7	8.5	-3.7%	--	16	--

Injuries are piling up on an aging Darren Sproles. Since breaking his ankle in 2006, Sproles had never missed more than three games in a season before missing 23 in the past two years. A forearm fracture and ACL tear took him out early in 2017, then a lingering hamstring issue that popped up after Week 1 kept him out for three months last season. The Eagles decided to let Sproles walk in wake of the injuries. Considering Sproles is a small, 36-year-old back who never produced in immense volume to begin with, the market for him was unsurprisingly slow. There are too many talented running backs to be going out of one's way for Sproles in his current state.

Chris Thompson

Height: 5-8 **Weight:** 187 **College:** Florida State **Draft:** 2013/5 (154) **Born:** 20-Oct-1990 **Age:** 29 **Risk:** Red

Year	Team	G/GS	Snaps	Runs	Yds	TD	Yd/R	FUM	DVOA	Rk	DYAR	Rk	YAR	Suc%	Rk	BTkl	Pass	Rec	Yds	TD	C%	Yd/C	YAC	DVOA	Rk	DYAR	Rk
2016	WAS	16/0	489	68	356	3	5.2	2	33.9%	--	111	--	99	53%	--	30	62	49	349	2	79%	7.1	5.1	10.6%	17	77	13
2017	WAS	10/1	338	64	294	2	4.6	1	-4.9%	--	9	--	8	42%	--	29	54	39	510	4	72%	13.1	12.2	67.3%	1	223	3
2018	WAS	10/0	308	43	178	0	4.1	1	-30.7%	--	-35	--	-45	30%	--	15	56	41	268	1	75%	6.5	5.3	-17.3%	44	-10	46
2019	WAS			45	209	1	4.6	1	2.4%								79	57	429	1	72%	7.5		-11.9%			

Thompson started last season showing no ill effects from his 2017 broken leg, gaining 128 yards on 11 touches in the season opener and catching 13 passes for 91 yards in the Week 2 loss to the Colts. His production then cooled, and rib and knee injuries sidelined him for much of October and November. When he returned, Mark Sanchez and Josh Johnson were the Washington quarterbacks, leaving Thompson with little to do but catch flare passes and get mobbed by waiting defenders. Thompson is unlikely to ever again average 13.1 yards per catch like he did in 2017, but when healthy he's a serviceable third-down back. He's trapped in a very crowded backfield, however, and could be a roster casualty if both Derrius Guice and Bryce Love prove to be healthy.

Spencer Ware

Height: 5-10 **Weight:** 228 **College:** Louisiana State **Draft:** 2013/6 (194) **Born:** 23-Nov-1991 **Age:** 28 **Risk:** Red

Year	Team	G/GS	Snaps	Runs	Yds	TD	Yd/R	FUM	DVOA	Rk	DYAR	Rk	YAR	Suc%	Rk	BTkl	Pass	Rec	Yds	TD	C%	Yd/C	YAC	DVOA	Rk	DYAR	Rk
2016	KC	14/14	546	214	921	3	4.3	4	-2.7%	22	54	20	72	53%	7	55	42	33	447	2	79%	13.5	11.4	32.7%	2	115	8
2018	KC	13/2	247	51	246	2	4.8	0	9.0%	--	38	--	32	45%	--	19	23	20	224	0	87%	11.2	12.3	56.1%	--	85	--
2019	IND			17	73	0	4.4	1	3.5%								8	6	44	1	75%	7.4		-2.8%			

Kareem Hunt took Ware's job away from him when Ware missed 2017 with an injury. Then when Hunt was hurt, the starting job went to Damien Williams. That means Ware is off to Indianapolis, where he will compete for snaps as the veteran option to a trio of young backs. The Ware who led the Chiefs in carries in 2016 when he finally got an opportunity was an effective bulldozing back who was better than you'd think looking at him in the pass game. Public comments from the Colts and the dollar figure make it look like Marlon Mack should be the lead back, but Ware has a shot to be Mack's backup and displace Nyheim Hines as the third-down back. Or he could just not make the team altogether, as Jordan Wilkins was solid in his own right as Mack's backup last year and Hines is more of a chess piece.

DeAndre Washington Height: 5-8   Weight: 204   College: Texas Tech   Draft: 2016/5 (143)   Born: 22-Feb-1993   Age: 26   Risk: Yellow

Year	Team	G/GS	Snaps	Runs	Yds	TD	Yd/R	FUM	DVOA	Rk	DYAR	Rk	YAR	Suc%	Rk	BTkl	Pass	Rec	Yds	TD	C%	Yd/C	YAC	DVOA	Rk	DYAR	Rk
2016	OAK	14/2	241	87	467	2	5.4	1	7.0%	--	55	--	78	47%	--	14	23	17	115	0	74%	6.8	6.8	-12.9%	--	1	--
2017	OAK	15/0	223	57	153	2	2.7	2	-33.1%	--	-55	--	-34	40%	--	23	45	34	197	1	76%	5.8	4.9	-13.6%	46	1	46
2018	OAK	10/0	70	30	115	0	3.8	1	-19.6%	--	-16	--	-5	55%	--	4	1	1	9	0	100%	9.0	7.0	144.7%	--	8	--
2019	OAK			25	103	0	4.1	1	-3.8%								9	7	47	0	78%	6.8		-8.8%			

One of the worst things you can do when fighting for a roster spot is get hurt. Washington's knee injury in last year's training camp might have cost him a spot on the 53-man roster had preseason sensation Chris Warren not also gotten hurt. As it was, Washington was simply buried on the depth chart, rarely seeing the field even after Marshawn Lynch *also* got hurt. Through three years in the league, Washington has yet to really show anything at the NFL level, and his role keeps getting smaller and smaller. His best path back to relevancy probably involves stealing passing-down reps from Jalen Richard, but it's more likely he's the odd man out in the Oakland backfield.

James White Height: 5-9   Weight: 204   College: Wisconsin   Draft: 2014/4 (130)   Born: 3-Feb-1992   Age: 27   Risk: Yellow

Year	Team	G/GS	Snaps	Runs	Yds	TD	Yd/R	FUM	DVOA	Rk	DYAR	Rk	YAR	Suc%	Rk	BTkl	Pass	Rec	Yds	TD	C%	Yd/C	YAC	DVOA	Rk	DYAR	Rk
2016	NE	16/4	426	39	166	0	4.3	0	7.8%	--	24	--	24	51%	--	16	86	60	551	5	70%	9.2	8.8	20.1%	10	163	3
2017	NE	14/4	384	43	171	0	4.0	0	-9.3%	--	-1	--	8	51%	--	10	72	56	429	3	78%	7.7	6.1	6.4%	20	86	13
2018	NE	16/3	600	94	425	5	4.5	0	1.6%	--	42	--	41	47%	--	14	123	87	751	7	71%	8.6	7.6	13.5%	13	194	3
2019	NE			76	349	1	4.6	1	7.1%								114	83	746	5	73%	9.0		18.0%			

White's 94 rushing attempts in 2018 more than doubled his previous career high, and his 123 pass targets were also significantly more than his previous best. That was not enough for him to qualify for the main rushing leaderboard, but he did finish third in running back receiving DYAR. White is not only the most trusted receiving back on the Patriots, he is one of Tom Brady's most trusted targets, period. No other running back on the roster had even a fifth of his targets, and only Julian Edelman had more targets per game played.

White's usage probably hit its high-water mark in 2018. Edelman's four-game suspension, Josh Gordon's off-field struggles, Rob Gronkowski's injuries, and the lack of other trusted receivers created the conditions for the first 100-target running back of Tom Brady's career—indeed, White is the only back to have even been targeted 80 times in a season by Brady. The extreme production is unlikely to be replicated, but White remains the premier receiving back on the Patriots and one of the most productive pass-catching backs in the league. He should remain one of the more consistent receiving options at any position throughout the 2019 season.

Jordan Wilkins Height: 6-1   Weight: 216   College: Mississippi   Draft: 2018/5 (169)   Born: 18-Jul-1994   Age: 25   Risk: Green

Year	Team	G/GS	Snaps	Runs	Yds	TD	Yd/R	FUM	DVOA	Rk	DYAR	Rk	YAR	Suc%	Rk	BTkl	Pass	Rec	Yds	TD	C%	Yd/C	YAC	DVOA	Rk	DYAR	Rk
2018	IND	16/3	198	60	336	1	5.6	2	15.0%	--	61	--	58	58%	--	9	17	16	85	0	94%	5.3	6.6	-47.8%	--	-34	--
2019	IND			29	123	0	4.2	1	-2.8%								8	7	62	1	88%	8.9		20.8%			

Wilkins had a clear role in 2018: starting running back when Marlon Mack was out, and a non-factor otherwise. He had 44 carries in the Colts' first five games and just 18 in the final 13 (including postseason). He ran the same diet of primarily inside zone, outside zone, and power, and showed he can be reasonably effective. But Indianapolis clearly prefers Mack, and Reich noted as much this offseason, saying Wilkins was battling for a roster spot with former Bills fifth-round pick Jonathan Williams.

Damien Williams Height: 5-11   Weight: 221   College: Oklahoma   Draft: 2014/FA   Born: 3-Apr-1992   Age: 27   Risk: Red

Year	Team	G/GS	Snaps	Runs	Yds	TD	Yd/R	FUM	DVOA	Rk	DYAR	Rk	YAR	Suc%	Rk	BTkl	Pass	Rec	Yds	TD	C%	Yd/C	YAC	DVOA	Rk	DYAR	Rk
2016	MIA	15/0	160	35	115	3	3.3	1	6.3%	--	22	--	9	37%	--	14	31	23	249	3	74%	10.8	9.0	12.5%	14	45	21
2017	MIA	11/4	195	46	181	0	3.9	0	-22.7%	--	-25	--	-28	28%	--	20	28	20	155	1	71%	7.8	7.7	12.2%	15	44	27
2018	KC	16/3	207	50	256	4	5.1	1	26.4%	--	79	--	66	62%	--	9	24	23	160	2	96%	7.0	9.3	33.9%	--	74	--
2019	KC			160	722	7	4.5	1	9.8%								65	50	395	2	77%	7.9		5.5%			

Even with Carlos Hyde coming to Kansas City in free agency, Chiefs offensive coordinator Eric Bieniemy insists that Williams will be the starter, or at least first up among the committee. You don't need us to tell you that Williams doesn't have the raw talent of Kareem Hunt, but he did have a better *rushing* DVOA than Hunt did, albeit in a small sample size. It's perhaps best shown in the red zone: Williams had a 50.8% rushing DVOA inside the 20, with an 80 percent success rate. Hunt managed just 14.9% and 67 percent, respectively. Hunt was much better as a receiver, but Williams' 26.2% DVOA on seven red zone targets isn't terrible either, and he actually had more red zone receptions than Hunt did on fewer targets. It's doubtful that Williams' hot December will last a full season; he would have had the highest DVOA in the league if he had maintained that rate over 100 carries. But, at least in the running game, the Chiefs will probably be alright with Williams carrying the ball.

Jamaal Williams Height: 6-0 Weight: 212 College: BYU Draft: 2017/4 (134) Born: 3-Apr-1995 Age: 24 Risk: Green

Year	Team	G/GS	Snaps	Runs	Yds	TD	Yd/R	FUM	DVOA	Rk	DYAR	Rk	YAR	Suc%	Rk	BTkl	Pass	Rec	Yds	TD	C%	Yd/C	YAC	DVOA	Rk	DYAR	Rk
2017	GB	16/7	443	153	556	4	3.6	0	7.4%	12	108	12	86	48%	14	23	34	25	262	2	74%	10.5	10.2	29.9%	11	84	17
2018	GB	16/8	523	121	464	3	3.8	0	1.7%	22	52	25	26	45%	32	21	41	27	210	0	66%	7.8	8.5	-9.3%	34	11	33
2019	GB			80	351	2	4.4	1	2.9%								37	29	250	1	78%	8.6		11.4%			

In a league littered with thunder-and-lightning duos, Williams is one of the least inspiring "thunders" around. Williams is a tall, thick runner who does his best work reading zone and getting vertical as soon as a hole opens up. He has never fumbled in the NFL, another nod to his reliability. In turn, Williams does not produce many disastrous runs, which endeared him to Green Bay's past coaching staff, but he does not dazzle with any playmaking either. Through 274 carries the past two seasons, Williams has just 17 10-plus-yard runs. He does not have the speed or creativity to get to space very often, let alone make anything of it when he does. Williams' saving grace is that he is a decent pass-catcher, which helps in not identifying him as a clear downhill run indicator when he is in the game as opposed to Aaron Jones. Overall lackluster nature aside, Williams may be better suited for Matt LaFleur's under-center zone run game, and that could keep him firmly in the rotation despite Jones having previously been more productive in every way.

Jeffery Wilson Height: 6-0 Weight: 194 College: North Texas Draft: 2018/FA Born: 16-Nov-1995 Age: 24 Risk: Red

Year	Team	G/GS	Snaps	Runs	Yds	TD	Yd/R	FUM	DVOA	Rk	DYAR	Rk	YAR	Suc%	Rk	BTkl	Pass	Rec	Yds	TD	C%	Yd/C	YAC	DVOA	Rk	DYAR	Rk
2018	SF	6/2	197	66	266	0	4.0	3	-9.4%	--	-2	--	-20	52%	--	9	15	12	98	0	80%	8.2	8.1	4.9%	--	17	--
2019	SF			14	57	0	4.0	1	-1.7%								6	5	30	0	75%	6.6		-13.7%			

Wilson was brought in off the practice squad in Week 12 and went hog-wild a week later against Seattle, rushing for 61 yards and adding 73 more through the air. He had only 172 yards rushing and 17 receiving in four games after that. Given the absurd depth in San Francisco's backfield, there's a decent chance Wilson eventually plays somewhere else this fall. Projecting how the 49ers will use all their running backs this year is like comparing a raven to a writing desk while counting travelers to St. Ives and untying the Gordian Knot.

T.J. Yeldon Height: 6-1 Weight: 226 College: Alabama Draft: 2015/2 (36) Born: 2-Oct-1993 Age: 26 Risk: Green

Year	Team	G/GS	Snaps	Runs	Yds	TD	Yd/R	FUM	DVOA	Rk	DYAR	Rk	YAR	Suc%	Rk	BTkl	Pass	Rec	Yds	TD	C%	Yd/C	YAC	DVOA	Rk	DYAR	Rk
2016	JAX	15/13	576	130	465	1	3.6	2	-24.8%	41	-81	38	-57	38%	42	42	68	50	312	1	74%	6.2	7.1	-27.9%	49	-52	53
2017	JAX	10/0	230	49	253	2	5.2	2	-6.7%	--	4	--	-3	43%	--	13	41	30	224	0	73%	7.5	6.3	-9.9%	40	8	42
2018	JAX	14/5	507	104	414	1	4.0	1	-12.5%	39	-17	35	-22	48%	25	19	79	55	487	4	71%	8.9	8.0	3.0%	24	76	17
2019	BUF			37	159	0	4.3	1	-1.9%								46	34	281	1	74%	8.3		1.9%			

Yeldon ended 2018 as a healthy scratch in Jacksonville and is looking to jumpstart his career in a crowded Buffalo backfield. His best chance of making an impact is as a receiver; LeSean McCoy was terrible catching the ball last year, Frank Gore is no threat as a receiver, and Devin Singletary had just six catches last year at Florida Atlantic. Any significant use as a runner would likely require age to hit McCoy and Gore and inexperience to stall Singletary.

Zach Zenner   Height: 5-11   Weight: 222   College: South Dakota State   Draft: 2015/FA   Born: 13-Sep-1991   Age: 28   Risk: Red

Year	Team	G/GS	Snaps	Runs	Yds	TD	Yd/R	FUM	DVOA	Rk	DYAR	Rk	YAR	Suc%	Rk	BTkl	Pass	Rec	Yds	TD	C%	Yd/C	YAC	DVOA	Rk	DYAR	Rk
2016	DET	14/4	293	88	334	4	3.8	1	-3.1%	--	21	--	9	48%	--	15	23	18	196	0	78%	10.9	11.4	51.4%	--	80	--
2017	DET	8/0	65	14	26	1	1.9	0	-34.5%	--	-17	--	-23	21%	--	2	1	0	0	0	0%	0.0	0.0	-136.6%	--	-4	--
2018	DET	8/1	118	55	265	3	4.8	0	19.3%	--	68	--	77	56%	--	10	10	7	56	0	70%	8.0	9.3	-32.2%	--	-11	--
2019	DET			27	112	0	4.1	1	-2.8%								9	7	48	0	78%	6.9		-1.7%			

Outside of Kerryon Johnson, each of Detroit's running backs succeed in specific ways. For Zach Zenner, the red zone is his sweet spot. Though he barely played in 2017, Zenner was the team's most successful red zone runner in 2016 and 2018. On 11 red zone carries last season, Zenner picked up 53 yards and a 91 percent success rate, meaning he "failed" just one of his 11 attempts. To be fair, Johnson also rocked a 50-plus-percent success rate on a larger sample, but aside from Johnson, nobody in the past few years has been as solid as Zenner in the red zone for Detroit. Unfortunately for Zenner, with Johnson healthy, Riddick still on the roster, and three other running backs being signed or drafted as depth competition, he may struggle to work his way into carries again.

Going Deep

Ameer Abdullah, MIN: Abdullah is an unfortunate example of how fragile and expendable running backs are. As a mid-round rookie in 2015, he posted a top-10 success rate (51 percent) on 143 carries and proved to be a good pass-catcher to boot. A foot injury landed him on the IR for most of the following season, however, and he was never the same player, in part because that particular injury inhibited his quick, jittery running style. He was active on two different teams in 2018 (Detroit, then Minnesota), but only saw four touches the entire season. He may make the Vikings roster as a kick returner.

Bruce Anderson, TB: Of the Buccaneers' undrafted free agents, Anderson, who went to high school 25 miles from Raymond James Stadium in Tampa, has the clearest path to making the team, mainly because he can catch passes. Peyton Barber and Ronald Jones can't. In Anderson's senior season at North Dakota State, he averaged 7.5 yards per carry and caught 12 passes for 199 yards and three touchdowns. Tampa Bay also will try him out as a kick returner.

Rodney Anderson, CIN: Anderson likely would have exploded for Oklahoma last season had he actually been healthy, but a torn ACL in September kept him off the draft radar. Anderson is an excellent receiver and shows versatility in his reads at the line of scrimmage that could lead to him becoming an every-down back. His glaring flaws are a lack of breakaway speed and a total lack of interest as a pass-blocker. Barring an injury, Anderson probably won't see much immediate work for the Bengals, but he does have the talent to be an NFL starter someday.

Ryquell Armstead, JAX: After 13 touchdowns for the Temple Owls on 5.2 yards per tote, Armstead sat out their bowl game to get ready for the NFL draft. He earned an Alex Collins comparison from NFL.com's Lance Zierlein. Like Collins, Armstead is a bigger (220-pound) back who can rumble over tacklers like a bus. He's a good fit for the Jaguars' gap-based scheme and should be a fine change of pace for Leonard Fournette on running downs. Just don't ask him to catch anything.

Kenjon Barner, ATL: Barner—who has bounced from Carolina to Philadelphia to Los Angeles to Philadelphia again to Carolina again to New England to Carolina again—will compete with sixth-round rookie Marcus Green to be the Falcons' primary returner. The big question is whether he can co-exist with punter/kickoff specialist Matt Bosher, who leveled Barner last season and then flexed while standing over him. Barner: "Now I tell my child to take the trash out, and he tells me, 'Shut up before I go get Bosher.'"

Kapri Bibbs, FA: Bibbs is the type of semi-competent, low-bandwidth runner teams like to keep around in case of emergency. In five seasons, Bibbs has yet to top more than 40 touches in a year, hitting a career high last year at 37, most of which were in Washington before he was cut near the end of the season and then signed by Green Bay. Unsigned as of press time, he can provide functional play between the tackles and is plenty serviceable as a pass-catcher.

Brandon Bolden, NE: Bolden returns to New England after a year in Miami, during which his only notable contribution on offense was … er, two touchdowns on two handoffs against the Patriots. Those were his first scores from scrimmage since 2015; though he added a receiving score in a defeat against the Jaguars later in the year, he is likely to revert to his old role as a special teams stalwart with the occasional cameo on offense.

Mike Boone, MIN: An undrafted free agent last year, Boone is the epitome of a project running back. He never cracked more than 120 carries or 30 receptions in a college season, but tore up his pro day workout, running a 4.44-second 40-yard dash and 6.95-second 3-cone drill at 5-foot-10 and 206 pounds. Athletically, he is more than gifted enough to stick around in the NFL, but he has little substance to back it up. Boone saw only 11 carries last season (-4.2% DVOA), none of which came after Week 8 once starter Dalvin Cook returned from injury.

Damarea Crockett, HOU: Crockett ran for 1,062 yards and 11 touchdowns in his freshman season at Missouri, but he was injured in 2017 and got hooked into a timeshare with Larry Rountree III as a junior. Whispers were loud that Crockett didn't care much for new offensive coordinator Derek Dooley and that came through in the effort he put on the field. However, as a UDFA he landed in a perfect spot: the Texans are as RB-needy as any team in the NFL. His weaknesses (dealing with early penetration) wouldn't seem to mesh well with the Texans offensive line, but he's probably the best hope Houston has of someone crashing the party for Lamar Miller and D'Onta Foreman as unquestioned one-two on the depth chart.

Benny Cunningham, JAX: The man who once got to catch passes instead of Todd Gurley because Jeff Fisher is stubborn has remained a capable third-down back. With Tarik Cohen healthy and a little more explosive than Cunningham, Cunningham had little to do in 2018, touching the ball just six times. Now with the Jaguars, he's probably the best third-down back on the roster and has a chance to assume T.J. Yeldon's workload while contributing as a returner.

Trey Edmunds, PIT: Ferrell Edmunds III, known as Trey, is the little-known third brother in the Edmunds pigskin dynasty, along with teammate Terrell and Buffalo linebacker Tremaine. Whereas the whole football world knows about Archie Manning, Gordon Gronkowski and other dads of multiple NFL stars, Ferrell the Second, once a Pro Bowl tight end for the Dolphins, toils away as a high school coach in rural Virginia, with no one asking his advice on sending a trio of sons to the pros. Edmunds spent most of the year on the Pittsburgh practice squad and had no regular-season carries.

Andre Ellington, TB: After missing all of last season, the 2014 fantasy football breakout candidate is back. Reunited with Bruce Arians in Tampa Bay, Ellington will compete for a role on passing downs. For the Cardinals and Texans in 2017, he caught 59 passes for 369 yards and posted a 5.3% DVOA.

Keith Ford, FA: With injuries piling up at the end of the season, the undrafted Ford became relevant in Buffalo for two weeks, carrying the ball 21 times for 79 yards (-15.0% DVOA) and even getting a start. That will likely be the end of his relevancy, as he was released after the Bills spent all offseason starting a running back collection.

Myles Gaskin, MIA: Gaskin was remarkably productive and consistent for four years at the University of Washington. He rushed for between 1,268 and 1,380 yards each year, with 10 to 21 rushing touchdowns, a little receiving value, and a career rate of 5.6 yards per carry. That's a lot of mileage, of course, and Gaskin lacks any one special NFL characteristic. Gaskin is too small to be a between-the-tackles carry-muncher for Kenyan Drake, so it's hard to project a role for him right now besides "the other committee back."

Mike Gillislee, FA: Gillislee's time in the Saints backfield was short-lived and disastrous: his 2.7 yards per carry was bad enough, but he is most remembered for a fumble on opening day that was returned for a touchdown in the one-score defeat against the Buccaneers. He was released the very day Mark Ingram returned from suspension and has not been signed since. Now 29 and still without a team, Gillislee's second year in Buffalo—during which he led all qualifying backs in DVOA and finished fourth in DYAR—will probably stand as the high point of a career that appears already to be nearing its end.

Corey Grant, FA: A player the Jaguars raved about publicly for years, it was a bit surprising that "Tail Lights" Grant didn't get a bigger role last season after averaging 6.6 yards on 62 attempts in 2016-2017. 13 attempts last year led to a -17 DYAR on a -12.5% DVOA, then Grant suffered a Lisfranc injury in Week 5 and hit IR. His combination of explosiveness and open-field evasion probably shouldn't be sitting there in free agency as we go to press, but such is running back life.

Karan Higdon, HOU: Odd player and team combination here: Higdon mainly ran gap plays at Michigan, and the Texans mostly run zone. He also wasn't used much as a receiver at Michigan despite his size and open-field ability, and that's the niche the Texans have for him to slide into. Higdon caught just 16 balls in his entire four-year career at Michigan. It takes a lot of projection for him to see a role with the Texans, but boy is there a wide-open vacuum on the roster trying to suck Higdon into fantasy relevancy.

Brian Hill, ATL: And this is why we invented DVOA. Well, this and Mike Alstott. Hill, who backed up Tevin Coleman in the Falcons' final two games last season, gained 7.9 yards per carry, more than any running back who had 20 carries. Sixty of his 157 yards, however, came on one Week 16 run. In Week 17 against the ghastly Buccaneers run defense, he gained 30 yards on eight carries. His final DVOA: -10.8%. He'll compete with a couple of other Going Deep guys to be the third-string back behind Devonta Freeman and Ito Smith.

Jeremy Hill, FA: After three-plus years as a starter for the Bengals, Hill joined the Patriots last year to fill the role of veteran power back but tore his ACL on opening day and missed the rest of the season. Only 26 years old, Hill may be young enough to get another shot, but he has over 700 carries already to his name and has missed 24 games in his past two seasons. That is not a good record for a back who has also grown less effective in each of his professional seasons to date—from sixth in DYAR in 2014, to 16th in 2015, 25th in 2016, then injured and unranked in 2017 and 2018.

Justice Hill, BAL: The Ravens dealt for Ty Montgomery at last year's trade deadline after remembering that they were pretending Buck Allen was a good receiver and realizing what a mistake that was. They finally fully rectified that by bringing in Hill from Oklahoma State in the fourth round. The speedy scatback isn't breaking any tackles at the line of scrimmage, but he's a mismatch against linebackers and could be settling in for a long career as a premium third-down back à la Theo Riddick. The Ravens have no one in front of him as good as him in his role, so he could get playing time right away.

Dontrell Hilliard, CLE: Hilliard's decent special teams showing put him at the front of the line to take over kick return duties with Jabrill Peppers gone. He may not get many opportunities in Cleveland's crowded backfield unless he channels (unrelated) Dalton Hilliard in summer ball, but the talent is there to contribute if given the chance.

Travis Homer, SEA: A 2019 sixth-round pick from Miami, Homer will be competing for a role as a pass-catching back in his rookie season. Homer had a bit of a fumble problem as a senior, putting the ball on the turf four times over the course of the year, so he may have some work to do to earn the offensive coaching staff's trust and make an impact in Year 1.

Ty Johnson, DET: A calf injury put a damper on Johnson's senior season, but his collegiate career was filled with explosive plays, including 132 yards on 12 carries and 80 yards on two kick returns in Maryland's 2017 upset over Texas. Though not a particularly nuanced or versatile back, as he is neither an efficient runner nor a valuable pass-catcher, Johnson is a 4.40-second 40-yard dash track athlete who can torch a defense if given a sliver of room to run. As Detroit's No. 3 back, he can be a wild-card home run threat out of the backfield and a solid kick returner.

Taiwan Jones, HOU: Now 31 years old, Taiwan Jones caught eyes in the 2011 draft with a 4.32-second 40-yard dash at his Eastern Washington pro day. That's special teams speed even if he doesn't have much else (44 career carries, 25 career targets in eight seasons) to recommend him by. He may wind up with some carries in Houston's backfield because Bill O'Brien did nothing to add to the depth but sign UDFAs.

John Kelly, LAR: Kelly only appeared in four games in his rookie year after being drafted in the sixth round out of Tennessee. He had a decent amount of volume in the games that star running back Todd Gurley missed at the end of the season, but with last year's primary backup Malcolm Brown returning and the Rams drafting Darrell Henderson in the third round, Kelly may struggle to find playing time again.

Bryce Love, WAS: Love was the Heisman runner-up with 2,118 rushing yards and 19 touchdowns for Stanford in 2017. He played through an ankle injury and other undisclosed ailments in 2018, rushing for just 739 yards and looking like a shell of his former self, before suffering an ACL tear in the regular-season finale. Washington is trying to complete a full set of running backs with major injuries, and Love was so explosive in 2017 that he's worth a long look, but he may not be able to do any significant football work until August. Try not to think of all the money he lost working for free last year instead of going pro.

Raheem Mostert, SF: Mostert's first 30 games (spread out over parts of four seasons, with five different teams) resulted in 13 carries for all of 47 yards. Game No. 31 was a Monday nighter in Week 6 in Green Bay last fall, when Mostert rumbled for 87 yards on just 12 carries. He played three more games, running 16 more times for 163 more yards, before a broken forearm ended his Cinderella season. One of San Francisco's top special-teamers, Mostert signed a new three-year deal after the season, but in May underwent a second surgery that added a month to his recovery time. Projecting how the 49ers will use all their running backs this year is like translating the Qur'an into English using a Japanese-to-Russian dictionary.

Detrez Newsome, LAC: Newsome was one of last preseason's standouts, finishing as the ninth-leading rusher and earning a practice squad spot as an undrafted free agent. Pressed into action after Melvin Gordon and Austin Ekeler went down, he then averaged 5.2 yards per touch in some emergency December action. He's the fourth back for a team that usually keeps three on the 53-man roster, but he'll be a solid backup if he can earn a job somewhere.

Qadree Ollison, ATL: One of the larger backs (228 pounds) drafted in April, the fifth-round rookie looks to be headed for the physical, late-game grinder role. In his final season at Pitt, he gained 1,213 rushing yards and averaged 6.3 yards per carry, but he was a bit boom-or-bust, managing only a 44 percent success rate.

Elijhaa Penny, NYG: Between Rashaad and Elijhaa, the Penny family clearly believed in buying the extra vowel. Penny is listed as a fullback and got most of his work as a blocker and special-teamer. The Giants signed him off Arizona's practice squad in Week 3 after ridding themselves of Jonathan Stewart. Penny is a fine, versatile player who offers a lot to a roster. But as the -6 DYAR and -30.1% DVOA on seven carries last year would seem to suggest, he's not a back who should see a lot of time actually running the ball.

Paul Perkins, NYG: Perkins has had about 150 NFL carries and 34 targets, and he has turned them into -18 DYAR rushing and -13 DYAR receiving. He was a favorite of some draftniks as a bowling ball, Devonta Freeman type. Perkins missed the entire 2018 season with a torn pectoral, not that he'd have been playing much behind Saquon Barkley anyway. Some reports surfaced about him challenging Wayne Gallman for the No. 2 job behind Barkley in OTAs. Entering the last year of his rookie deal, Perkins would be lucky to get work, let alone a No. 2 job.

Tony Pollard, DAL: Meet Jaylen Samuels 2.0. Like the Steelers' fifth-round pick last year (who started a few late-season games), Pollard is a running back/receiver/H-back slash player. At Memphis, the Tigers slid him all around the formation, motioning him out of the backfield and often using him as a blocker in bunch-receiver formations. Pollard is smaller than Samuels but more dangerous with the ball in his hands, with both long speed and some tackle-breaking ability. Pollard could be a versatile change-up weapon if deployed creatively, but Jason Garrett will be the one doing the deploying.

C.J. Prosise, SEA: It feels like forever ago that Prosise was a sparkplug at running back as a rookie, particularly in the passing game, but a litany of injuries have prevented him from playing more than six games in a season in his three-year career. In a fairly deep running back room, Prosise will be fighting to make the final roster, but if he can show glimmers of his past receiving prowess (he amassed 62 receiving DYAR on 19 passes in 2016), he may have a shot.

Stevan Ridley, FA: Ridley has dressed for fully one-quarter of the teams in the league in his well-traveled career, most recently with the Steelers. Currently unemployed, Ridley is in his age-30 season, which doesn't bode well for adding another uniform to his collection, unless an injury tidal wave strikes in some NFL city.

Jordan Scarlett, CAR: This year's fifth-round running back projects to have a similar role and skill set to veteran incumbent and 2015 fifth-rounder Cameron Artis-Payne. A pure power back with negligible ability as a receiver, this Florida alum is most likely to earn playing time either on special teams or as an end-of-game pummeler. That usage pattern has not translated into a significant role for Artis-Payne, and there is little reason so far to believe that Scarlett will fare much better.

Rod Smith, NYG: Remove one 45-yard run in 2017 from Smith's career, and he has averaged 3.19 yards per carry in four seasons. Smith was Ezekiel Elliott's little-used backup last year, playing mostly in mop-up situations. The Giants must like Smith's ability to give the featured back high-fives, because they signed him to back up Saquon Barkley.

Benny Snell, PIT: Snell was pretty much the entirety of Kentucky's offense in 2018, so his pedestrian 45 percent success rate has to be taken in context. He scored an impressive 48 touchdowns in Lexington, which speaks to his positive attributes—toughness and power, with the commensurate lack of burst that dropped him to the fourth round. He's pretty much a smaller version of James Conner. If Pittsburgh should make a Super Bowl during Snell's duration on the team, expect a surfeit of features on his great-uncle, Matt, who was the key cog in the Jets' famous upset of the Colts in Super Bowl III.

Roc Thomas, MIN: Similar to teammate Mike Boone, Thomas saw a handful of carries while Dalvin Cook was sidelined, but none following his return. He was signed as an undrafted free agent out of Jacksonville State primarily due to his above-average athletic profile. Aside from being a functional athlete who can do the bare minimum as a runner, Thomas does not possess a ton of value, but may be able to edge out Ameer Abdullah as the No. 4 running back given Abdullah's accumulation of injuries over the years.

Darwin Thompson, KC: When you average 15.3 yards per catch and 6.8 yards per rush, someone's going to take notice. At Utah State, Thompson made a habit of smashing through arm tackles and racked up yards after contact. Not quite as fast on the field as his numbers suggest, he's still an intriguing sixth-round selection. With Kareem Hunt and Spencer Ware out of the picture, there's an opening for Thompson to become a third-down back … and possibly more.

Mark Walton, MIA: Waived by the Bengals after not one, not two, but three arrests in the 2019 offseason. The Dolphins pounced on him, taking the opportunity to add another scatback zone-runner behind Kalen Ballage. Walton contributed -10 DYAR on 14 carries for the Bengals last season and will be in a fight for a roster spot with Kenneth Farrow and Myles Gaskin.

Dwayne Washington, NO: A seventh-round pick of the Lions in 2016, almost 25 percent of Washington's career yards—and 70 percent of his yards last season—came in last season's Week 17 scrimmage between the Saints and Panthers backups. Even as a solid special teams contributor, Washington is more likely to find himself competing with undrafted free agents at the bottom of the depth chart than with Alvin Kamara and Latavius Murray at the top of it.

Mike Weber, DAL: Weber was a regular contributor to the Ohio State offense since 2016, when he rushed for 1,096 yards. He's dependable with the vision and jump-cut ability to find holes at the line of scrimmage, and he's effective enough as a receiver to handle screens and dump-offs. Despite a 4.47-second combine 40, the size-speed-explosiveness package of an NFL starter just isn't there, but Weber has the skill set of a guy who sticks around for years as a third running back.

Charcandrick West, FA: West was released by the Chiefs before the 2018 season started, only to re-sign in December after Kareem Hunt was cut. He peaked in 2015, ranking 15th in DVOA and 20th in DYAR while rushing for 630 yards, but he has been firmly planted as a replacement-level player ever since. If Kansas City finds itself in need of another running back, his familiarity with Andy Reid should come in handy, but at the moment, their depth chart is full.

Kerrith Whyte, CHI: Whyte was the lightning to Devin Singletary's thunder at Florida Atlantic. Singletary got the bulk of the carries, but Whyte served as a capable change-of-pace back with potentially devastating 4.37-second 40-yard dash speed. As much as head coach Matt Nagy continues to put a premium on speed at the skill positions, Whyte could find a role in specific packages or situations. Whyte may even contribute as a returner if Nagy chooses to keep Tarik Cohen off special teams.

Darrel Williams, KC: Williams went undrafted out of LSU, but performed well enough to squeeze onto the Chiefs' 53-man roster. That meant he got same late-season work after the Kareem Hunt release, with 11 of his 13 carries coming in an almost-meaningless Week 17 blowout of Oakland.

Dexter Williams, GB: Landing on a team that has typically done well with athletic late-round and undrafted running backs is perfect for Williams. Williams was buried as a backup for most of his collegiate career, only emerging as a senior, when Notre Dame's offensive line had an uncharacteristically bad season in which they only granted Williams a 45 percent opportunity rate. In turn, Williams was not particularly efficient in his one big season, but he has the tools to develop into a nice pro in a fresh Green Bay environment.

Trayveon Williams, CIN: His college production, including 1,760 rushing yards last season, gave Williams an excellent 57.3% BackCAST rating. However, Williams' lack of power and balance at Texas A&M level do not bode well for a transition to the pros, and his top speed is more of a plus tool than a plus-plus tool for him. Williams' 5-foot-8 frame is well-chiseled and he can pass block, but his development of power is going to be a knockout trait for him—he has to get better at it or he won't have more than a cup of coffee at the NFL level. He'll open the year as the third back behind Joe Mixon and Giovani Bernard.

Wide Receivers

In the following two sections we provide the last three years of statistics, as well as a 2019 KUBIAK projection, for every wide receiver and tight end who either played a significant role in 2018 or is expected to do so in 2019.

The first line contains biographical data—each player's name, height, weight, college, draft position, birth date, and age. Height and weight are the best data we could find; weight, of course, can fluctuate during the off-season. **Age** is very simple, the number of years between the player's birth year and 2019, but birth date is provided if you want to figure out exact age.

Draft position gives draft year and round, with the overall pick number with which the player was taken in parentheses. In the sample table, it says that Antonio Brown was chosen in the 2010 NFL draft with the 195th overall pick in the sixth round. Undrafted free agents are listed as "FA" with the year they came into the league, even if they were only in training camp or on a practice squad.

To the far right of the first line is the player's Risk for fantasy football in 2019. As explained in the quarterback section, the standard is for players to be marked Green. Players with higher than normal risk are marked Yellow, and players with the highest risk are marked Red. Players who are most likely to match or surpass our forecast—primarily second-stringers with low projections—are marked Blue. Risk is not only based on age and injury probability, but how a player's projection compares to his recent performance as well as our confidence (or lack thereof) in his offensive teammates.

Next we give the last three years of player stats. Note that rushing stats are not included for receivers, but that any receiver with at least five carries last year will have his 2018 rushing stats appear in his team's chapter.

Next we give the last three years of player stats. First come games played and games started (**G/GS**). Games played represents the official NFL total and may include games in which a player appeared on special teams but did not play wide receiver or tight end. We also have a total of offensive **Snaps** for each season. Receptions (**Rec**) counts passes caught, while Passes (**Pass**) counts passes thrown to this player, complete or incomplete. Receiving yards (**Yds**) and touchdowns (**TD**) are the official NFL totals for each player.

Catch rate (**C%**) includes all passes listed in the official play-by-play with the given player as the intended receiver, even if those passes were listed as "Thrown Away," "Tipped at Line," or "Quarterback Hit in Motion." The average NFL wide receiver has caught between 58 and 63 percent of passes over the last four seasons; tight ends caught between 64 and 68 percent of passes over the last four seasons.

Plus/minus (**+/-**) is a metric that we introduced in *Football Outsiders Almanac 2010*. It estimates how many passes a receiver caught compared to what an average receiver would have caught, given the location of those passes. Unlike simple catch rate, plus/minus does not consider passes listed as "Thrown Away," "Tipped at Line," or "Quarterback Hit in Motion." Player performance is compared to a historical baseline of how often a pass is caught based on the pass distance, the distance required for a first down, and whether it is on the left, middle, or right side of the field. Note that plus/minus is not scaled to a player's target total.

Drops (**Drop**) list the number of dropped passes according to charting from Sports Info Solutions. Our totals may differ from the drop totals kept by other organizations. Yards per catch (**Yd/C**) is a standard statistic.

We have added a new column this year, listing each player's average depth of target (**aDOT**). This is the average distance beyond the line of scrimmage on all throws to this player, not counting passes listed as "Thrown Away," "Tipped at Line," or "Quarterback Hit in Motion." Long-ball specialists will rank high in this category (Tampa Bay's DeSean Jackson had a 19.4 aDOT, most of any qualifying wide receiver) while players who see a lot of passes on slots and screens will rank low (Tampa Bay's Adam Humphries was lowest at 6.2 aDOT).

Next we list yards after catch (**YAC**), rank (**Rk**) in yards after catch, and **YAC+.** YAC+ is similar to plus/minus; it estimates how much YAC a receiver gained compared to what we would have expected from an average receiver catching passes of similar length in similar down-and-distance situations. This is imperfect—we don't specifically mark what route a player runs, and obviously a go route will have more YAC than a comeback—but it does a fairly good job of telling you if this receiver gets more or less YAC than other receivers with similar usage patterns. We also give a total of broken tackles (**BTkl**) according to Sports Info Solutions charting.

The next five columns include our main advanced metrics for receiving: **DVOA** (Defense-Adjusted Value Over Average), **DYAR** (Defense-Adjusted Yards Above Replacement), and **YAR** (Yards Above Replacement), along with the player's rank in both DVOA and DYAR. These metrics compare every pass intended for a receiver and the results of that pass to a league-average baseline based on the game situations in

Antonio Brown				Height: 5-10			Weight: 186		College: Central Mighican				Draft: 2010/6 (195)			Born: 10-Jul-1988			Age: 31	Risk: Yellow
Year	Team	G/GS	Snaps	Pass	Rec	Yds	TD	C%	+/-	Drop	Yd/C	aDOT	Rk	YAC	Rk	YAC+	BTkl	DVOA	Rk	DYAR	Rk	YAR	Use	Rk	Slot
2016	PIT	15/15	975	154	106	1284	12	69%	+8.1	4	12.1	10.5	59	3.8	56	-1.0	13	11.1%	22	295	7	306	28.3%	6	26%
2017	PIT	14/14	888	163	101	1533	9	62%	+12.0	6	15.2	14.3	17	4.8	27	+0.1	29	20.1%	11	430	1	389	32.3%	2	21%
2018	PIT	15/15	998	168	104	1297	15	62%	-4.2	2	12.5	11.1	46	4.7	34	-0.3	17	1.7%	41	191	19	137	26.4%	10	38%
2019	OAK			161	106	1336	10	66%			12.6							9.6%							

which passes were thrown to that receiver. DVOA and DYAR are also adjusted based on the opposing defense and include Defensive Pass Interference yards on passes intended for that receiver. The methods used to compute these numbers are described in detail in the "Statistical Toolbox" introduction in the front of the book. The important distinctions between them are:

- DVOA is a rate statistic, while DYAR is a cumulative statistic. Thus, a higher DVOA means more value per pass play, while a higher DYAR means more aggregate value over the entire season.
- Because DYAR is defense-adjusted and YAR is not, a player whose DYAR is higher than his YAR faced a harder-than-average schedule. A player whose DYAR is lower than his YAR faced an easier-than-average schedule.

To qualify for ranking in YAC, receiving DVOA, or receiving DYAR, a wide receiver must have had 50 passes thrown to him in that season. We ranked 84 wideouts in 2018, 86 in 2017, and 93 in 2016. Tight ends qualify with 25 targets in a given season; we ranked 49 tight ends in 2018, 51 in 2017, and 46 in 2016.

The final columns measure each player's role in his offense. Usage rate (**Use**) measures each player's share of his team's targets, adjusted for games played. Cincinnati's A.J. Green was targeted on 14.7 percent of his team's targets, but he also missed seven games. Adjusting for those missing games gives Green a usage rate of 26.1 percent, a more accurate assessment of his workload. The final column shows the percentage of each player's targets came when he lined up in the **Slot**

(or at tight end). Cooper Kupp of the Los Angeles Rams saw 100 percent of his targets from the slot, obviously the highest rate in the league; the Seahawks' David Moore had the lowest rate of slot targets at 4 percent. Tight ends have an additional column listing how frequently they were split **Wide**, from a high of 21 percent (Miami's Mike Gesicki) to a low of zero percent (lots of guys).

"Slot" and "Wide" here are defined based on where the players are lined up in relation to the field, not based on where they are lined up in relation to other receivers. For example, if three wide receivers are in a trips bunch that is tight to the formation, all three receivers are marked as "slot" even if no other receiver is further out wide on that same side of the formation.

The italicized row of statistics for the 2019 season is our 2019 KUBIAK projection based on a complicated regression analysis that takes into account numerous variables including projected role, performance over the past two years, projected team offense and defense, projected quarterback statistics, historical comparables, height, age, and strength of schedule.

It is difficult to accurately project statistics for a 162-game baseball season, but it is exponentially more difficult to accurately project statistics for a 16-game football season. Consider the listed projections not as a prediction of exact numbers, but as the mean of a range of possible performances. What's important is less the exact number of yards we project, and more which players are projected to improve or decline. Actual performance will vary from our projection less for veteran starters and more for rookies and third-stringers, for whom we must base our projections on much smaller career statistical samples. Touchdown numbers will vary more than yardage

Top 20 WR by DYAR (Total Value), 2018

Rank	Player	Team	DYAR
1	Tyler Lockett	SEA	464
2	DeAndre Hopkins	HOU	455
3	Michael Thomas	NO	442
4	Mike Evans	TB	412
5	Tyreek Hill	KC	387
6	Julio Jones	ATL	382
7	T.Y. Hilton	IND	359
8	Adam Thielen	MIN	341
9	Keenan Allen	LAC	320
10	Brandin Cooks	LAR	318
11	Robert Woods	LAR	316
12	Tyler Boyd	CIN	305
13	Mike Williams	LAC	262
14	Alshon Jeffery	PHI	251
15	Kenny Golladay	DET	250
16	Davante Adams	GB	246
17	Juju Smith-Schuster	PIT	235
18	Josh Gordon	CLE/NE	193
19	Antonio Brown	PIT	191
20	Amari Cooper	OAK/DAL	187

Minimum 50 passes.

Top 20 WR by DVOA (Value per Pass), 2018

Rank	Player	Team	DVOA
1	Tyler Lockett	SEA	66.3%
2	Mike Williams	LAC	39.2%
3	Mike Evans	TB	25.2%
5	Sammy Watkins	KC	24.1%
4	Tyler Boyd	CIN	24.1%
7	Cooper Kupp	LAR	23.8%
6	Tyreek Hill	KC	23.8%
8	T.Y. Hilton	IND	23.4%
9	Michael Thomas	NO	23.1%
10	DeAndre Hopkins	HOU	22.6%
11	Rashard Higgins	CLE	22.3%
12	Brandin Cooks	LAR	21.5%
13	Alshon Jeffery	PHI	21.1%
14	Josh Gordon	CLE/NE	20.4%
15	Keenan Allen	LAC	18.1%
16	Robert Woods	LAR	17.5%
17	Julio Jones	ATL	15.9%
18	Marvin Jones	DET	15.7%
19	Adam Thielen	MIN	15.2%
20	Chris Hogan	NE	14.3%

Minimum 50 passes.

numbers. Players facing suspension or recovering from injury have those missed games taken into account.

Note that the receiving totals for each team will add up to higher numbers than the projection for that team's starting quarterback, because we have done KUBIAK projections for more receivers than will actually make the final roster.

A few low-round rookies, guys listed at seventh on the depth chart, and players who are listed as wide receivers but really only play special teams are briefly discussed at the end of the chapter in a section we call "Going Deep."

Two notes regarding our advanced metrics: We cannot yet fully separate the performance of a receiver from the performance of his quarterback. Be aware that one will affect the other. In addition, these statistics measure only passes thrown to a receiver, not performance on plays when he is not thrown the ball, such as blocking and drawing double teams.

Davante Adams

Height: 6-1   Weight: 212   College: Fresno St.   Draft: 2014/2 (53)   Born: 12/24/1992   Age: 27   Risk: Green

Year	Team	G/GS	Snaps	Pass	Rec	Yds	TD	C%	+/-	Drop	Yd/C	aDOT	Rk	YAC	Rk	YAC+	BTkl	DVOA	Rk	DYAR	Rk	YAR	Use	Rk	Slot
2016	GB	16/15	915	121	75	997	12	62%	+1.8	9	13.3	11.9	43	5.2	23	+0.6	14	11.3%	21	230	14	216	19.8%	39	28%
2017	GB	14/14	776	117	74	885	10	63%	+4.7	6	12.0	10.1	59	4.5	35	+0.1	23	10.3%	25	215	15	205	23.8%	13	32%
2018	GB	15/15	954	169	111	1386	13	66%	+5.0	5	12.5	11.2	44	4.3	43	-0.5	10	6.1%	30	246	16	264	29.3%	4	32%
2019	GB			159	106	1301	12	67%			12.3							13.8%							

There is no secret that Adams is Aaron Rodgers' preferred pass-catcher. Still, that preference could not have been more pronounced than it was in the red zone last season. Adams was targeted 31 times in the red zone. Twelve other players combined for the rest of the team's 41 targets, and none of them earned more than 10. Furthermore, no player came close to Adams' red zone DVOA, and no player with at least four targets matched his 52 percent catch rate. In Week 2, Rodgers made a check at the line of scrimmage on a called run play, instead signaling for Adams to run a back-shoulder route versus Vikings cornerback Xavier Rhodes. Adams cooked Rhodes on the route and waltzed into the end zone after hauling in a clean pass from Rodgers. The Packers did precious little to boost their skill group this offseason, so Adams is shaping up for another season of carrying a heavy burden.

Nelson Agholor

Height: 6-0   Weight: 198   College: USC   Draft: 2015/1 (20)   Born: 24-May-1993   Age: 26   Risk: Green

Year	Team	G/GS	Snaps	Pass	Rec	Yds	TD	C%	+/-	Drop	Yd/C	aDOT	Rk	YAC	Rk	YAC+	BTkl	DVOA	Rk	DYAR	Rk	YAR	Use	Rk	Slot
2016	PHI	15/14	883	70	36	365	2	53%	-4.9	6	10.1	11.0	52	3.3	73	-1.6	7	-23.3%	86	-60	88	-60	12.7%	81	48%
2017	PHI	16/10	813	95	62	768	8	65%	+2.1	8	12.4	10.6	54	4.9	24	-0.2	12	6.7%	33	141	32	130	16.8%	54	92%
2018	PHI	16/16	985	97	64	736	4	66%	+2.0	4	11.5	10.5	48	5.5	17	-0.2	11	-21.8%	77	-69	78	-33	16.2%	56	78%
2019	PHI			80	51	604	3	64%			11.9							-0.2%							

Agholor has worn a number of hats for the Eagles since being drafted in 2015: slot receiver, designated YAC receiver, deep threat, you name it. Agholor has never been able to figure out the red zone, though, because he does not have the tools to do so. He has speed and yards-after-catch potential, but his route-running can be questionable, and he is not a threat to win contested catch situations. It is difficult for him to be anything more than a screen option in the red zone. As a result, he has posted a negative DVOA in the red zone three seasons a row. Agholor also earned sub-5.0 average depth of target in each of the past two seasons after a horrendous 2016 red zone campaign that asked him to do more. Trading for Golden Tate last season set off an alarm that the Eagles may be done trying to make Agholor anything more than what he is. That said, he is still their best yards-after-catch player and underneath threat, so he should maintain his role for now. 2019 is an important "prove it" year for Agholor.

Keenan Allen

Height: 6-2   Weight: 206   College: California   Draft: 2013/3 (76)   Born: 27-Apr-1992   Age: 27   Risk: Yellow

Year	Team	G/GS	Snaps	Pass	Rec	Yds	TD	C%	+/-	Drop	Yd/C	aDOT	Rk	YAC	Rk	YAC+	BTkl	DVOA	Rk	DYAR	Rk	YAR	Use	Rk	Slot
2016	SD	1/1	27	7	6	63	0	86%	+1.4	0	10.5	7.1	--	3.0	--	-0.5	0	36.8%	--	33	--	29	22.3%	--	38%
2017	LAC	16/15	897	159	102	1393	6	64%	+8.3	8	13.7	9.8	65	4.9	25	+0.7	16	16.5%	14	378	3	378	28.3%	6	54%
2018	LAC	16/14	794	136	97	1196	6	71%	+7.2	4	12.3	8.9	68	4.2	45	-0.3	9	18.1%	15	320	9	296	27.0%	7	64%
2019	LAC			147	98	1290	8	67%			13.2							13.2%							

There may not be a better pure route-runner in all of football than Allen, and few players are able to run themselves into more targets. This offseason, Sports Info Solutions created Targets Above Expectation, which factors in the game situation, pre-snap alignment, route run, and coverage points to figure out how often a receiver would typically be targeted, and then comparing it to actual results. Allen finished second with 7.8 TAE. If there's a receiver out there better at timing his breaks and finding open space, we'd like to see him.

Geronimo Allison   Height: 6-3   Weight: 202   College: Illinois   Draft: 2016/FA   Born: 18-Jan-1994   Age: 25   Risk: Red

Year	Team	G/GS	Snaps	Pass	Rec	Yds	TD	C%	+/-	Drop	Yd/C	aDOT	Rk	YAC	Rk	YAC+	BTkl	DVOA	Rk	DYAR	Rk	YAR	Use	Rk	Slot
2016	GB	10/2	185	22	12	202	2	55%	-0.1	3	16.8	13.7	--	4.2	--	+0.3	1	15.2%	--	47	--	51	5.7%	--	68%
2017	GB	15/2	343	39	23	253	0	59%	-1.6	4	11.0	7.9	--	5.2	--	+0.3	3	-15.0%	--	-8	--	-12	7.7%	--	44%
2018	GB	5/4	241	30	20	303	2	67%	+1.3	2	15.2	12.9	--	5.3	--	+1.0	4	16.8%	--	66	--	46	15.4%	--	23%
2019	GB			77	48	639	4	62%			13.3							5.1%							

Before a hamstring injury derailed Allison's season, he was on pace to be an integral piece of the Green Bay offense—an efficient one, at that. He gained at least 60 yards in each of the first four games of the year (the only four healthy games he played last season) at a clip of 10.0 yards per target. Allison was one of Green Bay's best options to play both inside and outside the slot, a flexibility only Davante Adams shared effectively. Neither Randall Cobb nor any of the rookies who stepped up in Allison's absence were as impressive alternating between each position. Marquez Valdes-Scantling did the most flip-flopping, but his limited route tree did not make the most of the positional flexibility the way Allison could. Indications are now that Valdes-Scantling will man the outside in Matt LaFleur's offense, while Allison assumes more of a slot role in place of a departed Cobb.

Danny Amendola   Height: 5-11   Weight: 186   College: Texas Tech   Draft: 2008/FA   Born: 2-Nov-1985   Age: 34   Risk: Red

Year	Team	G/GS	Snaps	Pass	Rec	Yds	TD	C%	+/-	Drop	Yd/C	aDOT	Rk	YAC	Rk	YAC+	BTkl	DVOA	Rk	DYAR	Rk	YAR	Use	Rk	Slot
2016	NE	12/4	267	29	23	243	4	79%	+4.2	0	10.6	8.8	--	3.2	--	-1.8	0	27.0%	--	85	--	96	7.0%	--	90%
2017	NE	15/8	569	86	61	659	2	71%	+6.9	3	10.8	8.2	76	3.4	62	-0.9	6	8.4%	29	138	34	150	15.4%	61	97%
2018	MIA	15/15	682	79	59	575	1	75%	+5.1	1	9.7	7.4	78	3.9	53	-1.3	2	-6.2%	55	38	55	25	19.1%	36	91%
2019	DET			67	46	449	2	69%			9.8							-3.0%							

If nothing else, bringing in a former Patriots receiver in Amendola to help restructure the offense is a sensible move by Matt Patricia. Especially after the departures of Golden Tate and Eric Ebron, the Lions had few options over the middle of the field to pick up quick yards and punish zone coverages. Amendola is a savant in that regard. In each of the past two seasons, Amendola finished in the top five in percentage of targets from the slot, including a first-place finish with the Patriots in 2017. Though Amendola's volume last season benefitted from other players in Miami's offense missing time, Amendola was quietly heating up through the middle portion of the season before tweaking his knee. In five games between Weeks 6 to 11, he caught 31 passes for 305 yards and a touchdown. A minor knee sprain knocked him out for the better part of two games and slowed down his production for the remainder of the year. The Lions are hoping Amdenola can rediscover the form he was playing at in the middle of last year to fill out their passing attack.

Robby Anderson   Height: 6-3   Weight: 190   College: Temple   Draft: 2016/FA   Born: 9-May-1993   Age: 26   Risk: Green

Year	Team	G/GS	Snaps	Pass	Rec	Yds	TD	C%	+/-	Drop	Yd/C	aDOT	Rk	YAC	Rk	YAC+	BTkl	DVOA	Rk	DYAR	Rk	YAR	Use	Rk	Slot
2016	NYJ	16/8	717	78	42	587	2	54%	+0.6	6	14.0	16.9	3	2.8	84	-1.6	2	-17.9%	81	-31	80	-24	14.1%	71	18%
2017	NYJ	16/15	812	116	63	941	7	56%	-3.4	7	14.9	12.9	34	4.4	38	-0.3	7	-0.1%	47	113	41	99	23.1%	15	33%
2018	NYJ	14/9	682	94	50	752	6	53%	+0.3	1	15.0	16.4	4	3.6	61	-0.6	3	-11.8%	65	6	66	13	21.2%	28	32%
2019	NYJ			104	55	827	6	53%			15.0							-1.2%							

Anderson overcame a midseason ankle sprain and other misadventures to go 27-384-3 in five December games, with a 9-140-1 monster performance against the Packers. Sam Darnold was 3-of-16 with three interceptions on passes to Anderson labeled "deep" in the play by play before both missed time with injuries; they were 7-of-13 on deep passes after Darnold's Week 12 return. Anderson is a legitimate home run threat who never had a legitimate quarterback throwing to him until the new, improved December Darnold appeared. He's a likely candidate for a breakthrough season. After all, even Adam Gase orders a deep shot once in a while.

JJ Arcega-Whiteside

Height: 6-3   Weight: 221   College: Stanford   Draft: 2019/2 (57)   Born: 31-Dec-1996   Age: 23   Risk: Red

Year	Team	G/GS	Snaps	Pass	Rec	Yds	TD	C%	+/-	Drop	Yd/C	aDOT	Rk	YAC	Rk	YAC+	BTkl	DVOA	Rk	DYAR	Rk	YAR	Use	Rk	Slot
2019	PHI			40	24	371	2	60%			15.5							-2.0%							

While the Eagles did need to retool their wide receiver corps this offseason, JJ Arcega-Whiteside is stylistically a bit of a luxury. A former three-star basketball recruit, Arcega-Whiteside is most comfortable working against defenders in tight areas and boxing them away from tough-to-catch passes. His knack for finding inside positioning and always working to the high point before his opponent is mesmerizing. As such, he is a matchup terror in the red zone—just ask Oregon's cornerbacks, who allowed Arcega-Whiteside to catch 14 passes for 302 yards and five touchdowns in three career games against the Ducks. If this skill set sounds familiar to Eagles fans, it is because he is not materially different from Alshon Jeffery. That is not to say the two cannot play in tandem or that Arcega-Whiteside provides nothing different from Jeffery, but it does signal that he will likely be more of a role player early on in his career rather than a regular part of the offense. Tight down-and-distance situations and red zone packages should be where he sees most of his action. That said, Arcega-Whiteside has enough athletic ability and potential to blossom into a solid No. 2 opposite Jeffery, even if that does not occur until 2020 or 2021. After all, Arcega-Whiteside was Stanford's first 1,000-yard receiver since 1999 and first double-digit-touchdown receiver since Ty Montgomery in 2013.

Marcell Ateman

Height: 6-4   Weight: 216   College: Oklahoma State   Draft: 2018/7 (228)   Born: 16-Sep-1994   Age: 25   Risk: Green

Year	Team	G/GS	Snaps	Pass	Rec	Yds	TD	C%	+/-	Drop	Yd/C	aDOT	Rk	YAC	Rk	YAC+	BTkl	DVOA	Rk	DYAR	Rk	YAR	Use	Rk	Slot
2018	OAK	7/6	370	31	15	154	1	48%	-3.9	2	10.3	11.1	--	2.1	--	-3.1	0	-28.5%	--	-38	--	-57	13.2%	--	35%
2019	OAK			15	8	80	0	53%			10.0							-26.6%							

The biggest short-term beneficiary from the Amari Cooper trade was Ateman, who vaulted from the practice squad to a starting role. Things started off so promising with a 50-yard day against Arizona but went downhill rapidly from there, including a 3-for-10 day in Baltimore. Ateman was the only Oakland receiver to underperform his expected catch rate. He entered the offseason penciled in the Raiders' top X receiver, which goes some way to explaining why they brought in four veterans and a rookie, all of whom likely will jump Ateman on the depth chart.

Doug Baldwin

Height: 5-11   Weight: 189   College: Stanford   Draft: 2011/FA   Born: 21-Sep-1988   Age: 31   Risk: N/A

Year	Team	G/GS	Snaps	Pass	Rec	Yds	TD	C%	+/-	Drop	Yd/C	aDOT	Rk	YAC	Rk	YAC+	BTkl	DVOA	Rk	DYAR	Rk	YAR	Use	Rk	Slot
2016	SEA	16/15	896	128	94	1128	7	76%	+12.9	5	12.0	9.0	73	4.9	30	-0.4	12	13.0%	16	263	9	287	23.3%	21	86%
2017	SEA	16/16	855	118	75	991	8	65%	+7.7	3	13.2	13.0	33	3.3	64	-1.5	15	9.6%	28	200	17	218	22.5%	17	80%
2018	SEA	13/13	710	73	50	618	5	68%	+3.2	1	12.4	11.1	45	3.1	73	-1.3	4	6.0%	31	113	37	112	22.8%	22	78%

After a 2018 season marred by a series of injuries, Baldwin hung up the cleats this offseason at the age of 30. Despite playing in some run-heavy offenses over the years, Baldwin finished his career with the second-most receiving yards by an undrafted wide receiver since the merger, behind only Drew Pearson of the Cowboys. While his 2018 season was a far cry from his peak in 2015, when he led the league in receiving touchdowns and receiving DVOA, he was still a key piece of a Seattle passing attack that did not have many weapons beyond him and the deep threat of Tyler Lockett. His departure leaves a major void that the combination of Lockett, David Moore, Jaron Brown, and a gaggle of rookies will have to fill if Seattle is going to match its sixth-place finish in passing DVOA from 2018.

Cole Beasley

Height: 5-8   Weight: 177   College: Southern Methodist   Draft: 2012/FA   Born: 26-Apr-1989   Age: 30   Risk: Yellow

Year	Team	G/GS	Snaps	Pass	Rec	Yds	TD	C%	+/-	Drop	Yd/C	aDOT	Rk	YAC	Rk	YAC+	BTkl	DVOA	Rk	DYAR	Rk	YAR	Use	Rk	Slot
2016	DAL	16/6	604	99	75	833	5	77%	+9.5	4	11.1	6.4	91	5.3	19	+0.7	11	31.0%	5	341	5	342	20.8%	32	86%
2017	DAL	15/4	576	63	36	314	4	57%	-1.3	2	8.7	7.9	79	3.4	60	-0.4	1	-16.9%	74	-22	73	-8	14.0%	69	88%
2018	DAL	16/4	713	87	65	672	3	75%	+5.1	2	10.3	7.5	77	3.3	71	-1.1	5	2.1%	38	100	41	128	16.9%	50	89%
2019	BUF			95	58	633	3	61%			10.9							-8.3%							

Beasley's a slot specialist, consistently ranking in the top 10 in slot/wide ratio. Beasley's 9.6% DVOA in the slot beats Buffalo's leader from last season, Zay Jones and his -8.6% DVOA. He'll be a nice safety blanket for Josh Allen, though there's a bit of a styles clash to worry about. Beasley's average depth of target was just 7.4 yards last season; the closest-targeted Bills receiver last season was Isaiah McKenzie at 8.2. It will be interesting to see if the Bills have Beasley run longer routes, or if they'll try to get Allen to check down a little more often.

Odell Beckham

Height: 5-11 **Weight:** 198 **College:** Louisiana State **Draft:** 2014/1 (12) **Born:** 5-Nov-1992 **Age:** 27 **Risk:** Yellow

Year	Team	G/GS	Snaps	Pass	Rec	Yds	TD	C%	+/-	Drop	Yd/C	aDOT	Rk	YAC	Rk	YAC+	BTkl	DVOA	Rk	DYAR	Rk	YAR	Use	Rk	Slot
2016	NYG	16/16	1002	169	101	1367	10	60%	+0.3	10	13.5	10.9	54	5.2	24	+0.8	32	-1.1%	52	161	29	177	28.8%	4	27%
2017	NYG	4/2	212	41	25	302	3	61%	+0.3	6	12.1	12.9	--	2.6	--	-1.5	4	3.5%	--	57	--	64	28.3%	--	9%
2018	NYG	12/12	716	124	77	1052	6	62%	+1.7	3	13.7	12.2	30	4.1	50	-0.8	18	2.5%	37	151	27	154	29.5%	3	44%
2019	CLE			144	89	1220	9	62%			13.7							8.0%							

AFC North defensive backs had about 48 hours to celebrate Antonio Brown leaving the division before Beckham came bursting through the door. The baffling sequence of events that played out in Dave Gettleman's head is of little interest to Browns fans, who are giddy at the thought of a Baker-to-Odell combo surpassing Roethlisberger-to-Brown, Dalton-to-Green, and Flacco-to-Interchangeable-Tight-End atop the division's passing hierarchy.

Beckham's last two healthy seasons in New York produced top-five usage rates. Less will certainly be more in Cleveland, which has the other pieces on offense to maximize Beckham's talents and minimize the bumfluffery, assuming Odell's ego can handle that. It's never a great sign when a team's fan base isn't all that upset when a star player departs (to be fair, that reaction was split among generational and racial fault lines), but it's hard to see a downside in the move for Cleveland.

Kelvin Benjamin

Height: 6-5 **Weight:** 240 **College:** Florida St. **Draft:** 2014/1 (28) **Born:** 5-Feb-1991 **Age:** 28 **Risk:** N/A

Year	Team	G/GS	Snaps	Pass	Rec	Yds	TD	C%	+/-	Drop	Yd/C	aDOT	Rk	YAC	Rk	YAC+	BTkl	DVOA	Rk	DYAR	Rk	YAR	Use	Rk	Slot
2016	CAR	16/13	801	118	63	941	7	53%	-5.1	8	14.9	12.4	34	3.7	64	+0.1	14	3.0%	46	145	33	128	21.2%	30	37%
2017	2TM	14/14	597	78	48	692	3	62%	+1.5	5	14.4	11.5	46	2.9	71	-0.8	3	8.1%	30	125	36	129	18.5%	41	24%
2018	2TM	15/10	537	67	25	380	1	37%	-11.8	4	15.2	15.6	8	2.6	81	-1.9	1	-26.4%	80	-69	79	-96	15.3%	64	20%

For the second year in a row, Benjamin switched teams midway through the season. Benjamin's off-field attitude in Buffalo was terrible; he refused to work with Josh Allen on routes. That might have been alright if he produced on the field, but Benjamin showed a lack of effort, a lack of speed, and frankly a lack of anything valuable. Benjamin pulled off the double, ranking in the bottom three in both receiving plus-minus and YAC+. He does not offer anything more than veteran depth at this point in his career.

Travis Benjamin

Height: 5-10 **Weight:** 172 **College:** Miami **Draft:** 2012/4 (100) **Born:** 29-Dec-1989 **Age:** 30 **Risk:** Red

Year	Team	G/GS	Snaps	Pass	Rec	Yds	TD	C%	+/-	Drop	Yd/C	aDOT	Rk	YAC	Rk	YAC+	BTkl	DVOA	Rk	DYAR	Rk	YAR	Use	Rk	Slot
2016	SD	14/8	548	75	47	677	4	63%	+3.3	6	14.4	13.3	26	5.2	21	+0.6	4	12.1%	19	144	35	110	15.2%	67	59%
2017	LAC	16/3	566	66	34	567	4	53%	-1.8	6	16.7	16.1	6	6.6	7	+1.1	6	0.5%	43	65	54	76	11.4%	78	54%
2018	LAC	12/3	278	24	12	186	1	50%	-0.5	3	15.5	19.7	--	5.4	--	-1.0	7	-11.7%	--	2	--	-5	6.3%	--	88%
2019	LAC			48	28	434	3	58%			15.5							10.0%							

Benjamin has started 14 games in his three years in Los Angeles; his 161 targets over that time period are the second-most for anyone with fewer than 15 starts over the past three years. He comes in off the bench, gets chucked a few deep bombs (his 15.0 aDOT is the largest for any Chargers receiver with more than five targets over the last three years), and hopefully makes a big play or two. He'll be bumped back up into the third receiver role with Tyrell Williams leaving town, so Los Angeles could stand for him to be a bit more than a speed and deep-ball guy.

Kendrick Bourne

Height: 6-1 **Weight:** 203 **College:** Eastern Washington **Draft:** 2017/FA **Born:** 4-Aug-1995 **Age:** 24 **Risk:** Green

Year	Team	G/GS	Snaps	Pass	Rec	Yds	TD	C%	+/-	Drop	Yd/C	aDOT	Rk	YAC	Rk	YAC+	BTkl	DVOA	Rk	DYAR	Rk	YAR	Use	Rk	Slot
2017	SF	11/0	283	34	16	257	0	47%	-1.0	1	16.1	11.0	--	7.1	--	+2.7	3	-9.7%	--	8	--	-3	8.2%	--	48%
2018	SF	16/8	606	67	42	487	4	63%	+0.5	4	11.6	9.0	67	3.5	65	-0.4	4	-4.5%	51	42	52	45	12.8%	74	52%
2019	SF			28	15	180	2	54%			12.0							-12.2%							

Bourne led all San Francisco wide receivers in targets, receptions, and yards last season, and his reward for that success is a stuffed depth chart that puts his roster spot in serious jeopardy. Though he has lined up in the slot about half the time in his career, he was spending more time out wide in OTAs. That's not necessarily good news. In the slot last season, he had a 3.7% DVOA and a 71 percent catch rate; out wide, those numbers fell to -17.6% and 52 percent. Bourne is taller than San Francisco's other prospects to line up wide, Marquise Goodwin (5-foot-9) and Deebo Samuel (5-foot-11), but he can't hold a candle to their athleticism.

Tyler Boyd

Height: 6-1 Weight: 197 College: Pittsburgh Draft: 2016/2 (55) Born: 15-Nov-1994 Age: 25 Risk: Green

Year	Team	G/GS	Snaps	Pass	Rec	Yds	TD	C%	+/-	Drop	Yd/C	aDOT	Rk	YAC	Rk	YAC+	BTkl	DVOA	Rk	DYAR	Rk	YAR	Use	Rk	Slot
2016	CIN	16/2	739	81	54	603	1	67%	+3.4	2	11.2	9.2	71	3.7	60	-0.9	3	2.4%	47	96	53	85	14.9%	68	85%
2017	CIN	10/1	307	32	22	225	2	69%	+1.2	2	10.2	6.9	--	4.1	--	-0.5	1	19.5%	--	76	--	71	10.3%	--	97%
2018	CIN	14/14	773	108	76	1028	7	70%	+7.4	6	13.5	9.8	55	5.5	17	+0.6	5	24.1%	4	305	12	310	22.9%	21	82%
2019	CIN			126	83	1087	7	66%			13.1							8.3%							

From the void to the Boyd … sorry, that was awful even for us. Boyd came back from a season in Marv Lewis' doghouse to become Cincinnati's most important receiver by honing his skill set in the slot. Boyd was hyper-efficient on underneath routes, catching 29 of 38 dig/drag/out routes for 338 yards, three touchdowns, and 18 other first downs. Then, just when they were baited into the short game, Boyd would strike deep. He was a perfect 8-for-8 on posts, corners, or deep crosses, for 172 yards and a touchdown. Slot production is easier than wide production, but Boyd is in line for a big payday in the final year of his rookie deal. If the Bengals let him get to free agency, he probably won't be coming back.

Miles Boykin

Height: 6-4 Weight: 228 College: Notre Dame Draft: 2019/3 (93) Born: 12-Oct-1996 Age: 23 Risk: Red

Year	Team	G/GS	Snaps	Pass	Rec	Yds	TD	C%	+/-	Drop	Yd/C	aDOT	Rk	YAC	Rk	YAC+	BTkl	DVOA	Rk	DYAR	Rk	YAR	Use	Rk	Slot
2019	BAL			20	11	149	1	55%			13.5							-13.1%							

D.K. Metcalf was regarded as the true physical marvel of the NFL combine because he ran a 4.33-second 40-yard dash and benched 27 reps at 228 pounds. But while Metcalf had enormous struggles in his shuttle measurements, Miles Boykin crushed them. A 6-foot-3, 220-pounder who can do it all, Boykin is the prototype outside receiver the Ravens haven't had since Torrey Smith was healthy. The Ravens traded up in the third round to land Boykin. Most of the talk in Baltimore is cautious because Boykin only had one year of production at Notre Dame, but Boykin's body is an accuracy-improver, and he's more spry than he would appear. Some sort of future on the Kenny Golladay-Vincent Jackson spectrum may be in him, and don't be surprised if he gets playing time sooner rather than later. Baltimore doesn't have many outside receivers who can match Boykin's skill set.

A.J. Brown

Height: 6-1 Weight: 230 College: Mississippi Draft: 2019/2 (51) Born: 30-Jun-1997 Age: 22 Risk: Red

Year	Team	G/GS	Snaps	Pass	Rec	Yds	TD	C%	+/-	Drop	Yd/C	aDOT	Rk	YAC	Rk	YAC+	BTkl	DVOA	Rk	DYAR	Rk	YAR	Use	Rk	Slot
2019	TEN			67	45	601	4	67%			13.4							5.4%							

Like past Jon Robinson wide receiver picks, Brown checked the box on college productivity. Operating primarily out of the slot in Oxford, he was a two-time All-SEC player and second team All-American who set school records for catches, receiving yards, and touchdowns, including a 72 percent catch rate his final season. In Tennessee, the presence of Adam Humphries means he will likely be an outside receiver, most likely the Z to complement Corey Davis. His toughness over the middle and willingness to block make him a good fit for a Tennessee offense likely to be built around the run, even if he is not the sort of vertical threat people outside St. Thomas Sports Park thought the Titans needed.

Antonio Brown

Height: 5-10 Weight: 186 College: Central Mighican Draft: 2010/6 (195) Born: 10-Jul-1988 Age: 31 Risk: Yellow

Year	Team	G/GS	Snaps	Pass	Rec	Yds	TD	C%	+/-	Drop	Yd/C	aDOT	Rk	YAC	Rk	YAC+	BTkl	DVOA	Rk	DYAR	Rk	YAR	Use	Rk	Slot
2016	PIT	15/15	975	154	106	1284	12	69%	+8.1	4	12.1	10.5	59	3.8	56	-1.0	13	11.1%	22	295	7	306	28.3%	6	26%
2017	PIT	14/14	888	163	101	1533	9	62%	+12.0	6	15.2	14.3	17	4.8	27	+0.1	29	20.1%	11	430	1	389	32.3%	2	21%
2018	PIT	15/15	998	168	104	1297	15	62%	-4.2	2	12.5	11.1	46	4.7	34	-0.3	17	1.7%	41	191	19	137	26.4%	10	38%
2019	OAK			161	106	1336	10	66%			12.6							9.6%							

Brown's exit from Pittsburgh was about as acrimonious as any we can remember in recent history, but he finally got his wish, and Oakland gets one of the top receivers in the league. Brown just had his worst season since breaking out as an elite starter in 2013, and he still led the league in receiving touchdowns and likely would have been in the top 10 in receiving yards had he not skipped-slash-been benched in Week 17. Brown made sure to burn all his bridges behind him, slamming both Ben Roethlisberger and Mike Tomlin on social media on his way out. At least now he gets to go to the drama-free situation of, uh, a franchise preparing to move cities while appearing on an HBO series. Get your popcorn ready.

One thing to watch out for as the Raiders and Brown try to get used to one another: no receiver on a Jon Gruden-led offense has ever had more than 153 targets in a season. Brown has been over that number in each of the last six seasons, and at his peak was eating up a third of Pittsburgh's targets. You gotta feed Brown early and often to keep him happy!

John Brown   Height: 5-10   Weight: 179   College: Pittsburg St. (KS)   Draft: 2014/3 (91)   Born: 4-Mar-1990   Age: 29   Risk: Red

Year	Team	G/GS	Snaps	Pass	Rec	Yds	TD	C%	+/-	Drop	Yd/C	aDOT	Rk	YAC	Rk	YAC+	BTkl	DVOA	Rk	DYAR	Rk	YAR	Use	Rk	Slot
2016	ARI	15/6	595	73	39	517	2	53%	-0.6	1	13.3	13.8	19	2.7	88	-1.5	1	-1.9%	57	61	61	69	12.3%	83	39%
2017	ARI	10/5	491	55	21	299	3	38%	-6.4	2	14.2	17.0	3	2.8	73	-0.8	1	-24.4%	83	-51	83	-29	15.3%	62	39%
2018	BAL	16/15	757	97	42	715	5	43%	-11.2	6	17.0	16.9	2	3.8	56	-0.5	1	-12.2%	67	4	67	-7	18.1%	42	51%
2019	BUF			86	44	706	4	51%			16.1							-3.9%							

Bombs away! Brown is a go-route master, a player whose skills really don't start kicking in until he's 15 yards downfield. His receiving DVOA last year wasn't pretty, but he was hurt hard by the switch from the strong-armed, if inaccurate, Joe Flacco to the run-first Lamar Jackson. Brown's DVOA was 3.7% when Flacco was throwing him the ball, but it fell to -42.7% with Jackson under center. Josh Allen has more than a little Flacco in him, so expect to see something closer to the former performance in Buffalo.

Marquise Brown   Height: 5-10   Weight: 170   College: Oklahoma   Draft: 2019/1 (25)   Born: 4-Jun-1997   Age: 22   Risk: Red

Year	Team	G/GS	Snaps	Pass	Rec	Yds	TD	C%	+/-	Drop	Yd/C	aDOT	Rk	YAC	Rk	YAC+	BTkl	DVOA	Rk	DYAR	Rk	YAR	Use	Rk	Slot
2019	BAL			84	48	701	4	57%			14.6							-6.2%							

DeSean Jackson comparisons get thrown around every short, undersized receiver who can blaze it. Hollywood walked the walk at Oklahoma with a huge season, and he wasn't just a slot receiver. The imperative thing for his career will be how good he is at avoiding contact at the line of scrimmage—this wasn't a problem for him in college, but he could do it better, and it would benefit his career. His short-term career in Baltimore is clouded by a Lisfranc injury he suffered in the Big 12 Championship Game. John Harbaugh was optimistic that Brown would be ready for training camp, but the receiver had only done individual drills at OTAs as we go to press. If he's healthy enough, he'll be a starter from Week 1, because there's not much on the depth chart above him.

Hakeem Butler   Height: 6-6   Weight: 225   College: Iowa State   Draft: 2019/4 (103)   Born: 16-May-1996   Age: 23   Risk: Red

Year	Team	G/GS	Snaps	Pass	Rec	Yds	TD	C%	+/-	Drop	Yd/C	aDOT	Rk	YAC	Rk	YAC+	BTkl	DVOA	Rk	DYAR	Rk	YAR	Use	Rk	Slot
2019	ARI			54	34	549	3	63%			16.1							7.6%							

Now writing for *USA Today's* Touchdown Wire, FO alumnus Doug Farrar named Butler one of his top 50 prospects in this year's draft—No. 32, to be precise. He had the highest Playmaker Rating (which does not account for projected draft position) of any wideout in this class (see page 441). So the Cardinals must have been thrilled to find him still available at the start of Day 3. Butler is a raw prospect with worrisome hands, but his height and speed (4.48 40 at the combine) should make him a dangerous deep threat right out of the gate. As Doug noted, Butler led all draftable receivers in 2018 with 19 receptions of 20 air yards or more, gaining 721 yards and scoring four touchdowns on those plays. Butler probably won't catch many passes this year, but the passes he does catch should be game-changers. He averaged nearly 20 yards per reception in college, and that was on an Iowa State team that had four different quarterbacks moving in and out of the lineup. Just imagine what he can do with Kyler Murray.

Antonio Callaway
Height: 5-11 | Weight: 200 | College: Florida | Draft: 2018/4 (105) | Born: 9-Jan-1997 | Age: 22 | Risk: Green

Year	Team	G/GS	Snaps	Pass	Rec	Yds	TD	C%	+/-	Drop	Yd/C	aDOT	Rk	YAC	Rk	YAC+	BTkl	DVOA	Rk	DYAR	Rk	YAR	Use	Rk	Slot
2018	CLE	16/11	766	79	43	586	5	54%	-5.0	4	13.6	14.5	15	5.5	19	+0.2	6	-6.3%	56	40	53	35	14.4%	66	26%
2019	CLE			58	32	477	4	55%			14.9							1.4%							

Callaway's rookie season lived up to his pre-draft billing as a gifted but mercurial player whose character concerns dropped him to the fourth round. Callaway's speed is reflected in his top-15 aDOT, and his shaky hands are reflected in his 54 percent catch rate. He came on in the second half of the season. Odell Beckham's presence should have a salutary effect on the sophomore deep threat, at least on the field. Callaway would be primed to be a breakout player in 2019, but are there enough balls to go around in Cleveland?

Parris Campbell
Height: 6-1 | Weight: 205 | College: Ohio State | Draft: 2019/2 (59) | Born: 16-Jul-1997 | Age: 22 | Risk: Red

Year	Team	G/GS	Snaps	Pass	Rec	Yds	TD	C%	+/-	Drop	Yd/C	aDOT	Rk	YAC	Rk	YAC+	BTkl	DVOA	Rk	DYAR	Rk	YAR	Use	Rk	Slot
2019	IND			79	56	600	4	71%			10.7							-1.5%							

Campbell spent a couple of seasons primarily as a returner before breaking through as the Buckeyes' top receiver in 2018. His outstanding 82 percent catch rate was primarily a product of catching short passes and using his speed to run away from defenders. That could be a good match for what the Colts ask him to do. Playmaker Score is as down on him as you would expect, because receivers who don't have significant production until their senior year tend to underperform in the NFL. Campbell had 705 yards in his college career before 1,063 yards as a senior. There's reason to be concerned here, but starting off in Indianapolis as the third receiver and potential return man seems like the best possible fit.

DeAndre Carter
Height: 5-8 | Weight: 190 | College: Sacramento State | Draft: 2015/FA | Born: 10-Apr-1993 | Age: 26 | Risk: Blue

Year	Team	G/GS	Snaps	Pass	Rec	Yds	TD	C%	+/-	Drop	Yd/C	aDOT	Rk	YAC	Rk	YAC+	BTkl	DVOA	Rk	DYAR	Rk	YAR	Use	Rk	Slot
2018	2TM	14/4	284	25	22	216	0	88%	+3.2	0	9.8	3.1	--	6.8	--	+0.3	1	0.3%	--	24	--	13	5.3%	--	76%
2019	HOU			10	7	70	0	70%			10.0							-11.7%							

Waived by the Eagles midseason, Carter caught on with the Texans as their main punt returner and third receiver while Will Fuller and Keke Coutee struggled with injuries. Carter was mostly used on screens, so don't get too blown away by that high catch rate. If things go right for the Texans this year, Carter probably won't see anywhere near this number of targets again. It was surprising given how agile he looked on punt returns how poor he was at forcing missed tackles in open space. If he is to be more than he was in 2018, that's where he needs to start.

DJ Chark
Height: 6-4 | Weight: 198 | College: Louisiana State | Draft: 2018/2 (61) | Born: 23-Sep-1996 | Age: 23 | Risk: Red

Year	Team	G/GS	Snaps	Pass	Rec	Yds	TD	C%	+/-	Drop	Yd/C	aDOT	Rk	YAC	Rk	YAC+	BTkl	DVOA	Rk	DYAR	Rk	YAR	Use	Rk	Slot
2018	JAX	11/0	291	32	14	174	0	44%	-4.7	2	12.4	10.3	--	3.2	--	-1.5	1	-47.4%	--	-90	--	-95	8.8%	--	34%
2019	JAX			82	45	626	5	55%			13.9							-2.3%							

Chark was exactly the wrong kind of receiver to thrive with the Blake Bortles Jaguars. He's a speed-power receiver who wants to win deep enough to make you respect curls, but Bortles was only able to pick on 5-foot-11 Steven Nelson in Week 5 to make that part of the Jacksonville game plan. Chark could use some extra work on his hands and ball technique as well after having two dropped passes and failing to use his body to effectively corral a couple of other balls. The Jags have a fairly crowded depth chart and, after Chark got lost last year, it's probably best to wait on good news from camp before you believe in him in 2019. To Chark's credit, wideout coach Keenan McCardell praised him in OTAs.

Randall Cobb

Height: 5-11   Weight: 190   College: Kentucky   Draft: 2011/2 (64)   Born: 22-Aug-1990   Age: 29   Risk: Yellow

Year	Team	G/GS	Snaps	Pass	Rec	Yds	TD	C%	+/-	Drop	Yd/C	aDOT	Rk	YAC	Rk	YAC+	BTkl	DVOA	Rk	DYAR	Rk	YAR	Use	Rk	Slot
2016	GB	13/10	681	84	60	610	4	71%	+3.4	1	10.2	6.6	90	6.0	10	+0.6	15	6.6%	35	133	39	131	16.8%	57	81%
2017	GB	15/14	742	93	66	653	4	72%	+4.1	1	9.9	5.8	86	6.2	8	+0.4	9	-6.0%	62	48	61	41	17.7%	47	76%
2018	GB	9/6	466	61	38	383	2	62%	-3.3	4	10.1	8.4	71	6.2	6	+0.1	5	-22.1%	78	-45	76	-50	17.7%	46	90%
2019	DAL			88	56	569	2	64%			10.2							-8.9%							

Cobb opened last season with a 9-142-1 performance in the wild Packers comeback over the Bears, then disappeared due to a bad hamstring, a late-season concussion, and the Mike McCarthy-Aaron Rodgers standoff that reduced his role in recent years to being the flat receiver in the 25 curl-flat patterns the Packers run per game. Cobb turns 29 in August and theoretically has productive years left if used creatively, but leaving McCarthy for Jason Garrett is like falling out of the frying pan and behind the stove to slowly rot until eaten by mice.

Keelan Cole

Height: 6-1   Weight: 194   College: Kentucky Wesleyan   Draft: 2017/FA   Born: 20-Apr-1993   Age: 26   Risk: Green

Year	Team	G/GS	Snaps	Pass	Rec	Yds	TD	C%	+/-	Drop	Yd/C	aDOT	Rk	YAC	Rk	YAC+	BTkl	DVOA	Rk	DYAR	Rk	YAR	Use	Rk	Slot
2017	JAX	16/6	755	83	42	748	3	51%	-1.9	6	17.8	13.3	30	7.0	3	+2.5	6	-7.4%	66	35	65	57	16.0%	55	54%
2018	JAX	16/11	687	70	38	491	1	54%	-4.8	8	12.9	10.2	51	3.6	60	-0.7	1	-21.3%	76	-48	77	-41	13.5%	67	51%
2019	JAX			26	15	165	0	58%			11.0							-12.8%							

Coming out like gangbusters, Cole had a 72.3% DVOA and an 83 percent catch rate over the first two weeks. Over the next 15, he came up with only 338 yards on 59 targets. Six drops in five weeks hurt, and the Jaguars effectively benched him for Donte Moncrief after Cole fumbled in London. Cole does a nice job underneath opening up passing lanes on drag routes, and Blake Bortles accentuated the bleeding for Cole by not being able to take advantage of his speed outside. Still, Cole's going to have to prove he can keep himself on the field by catching balls before he should be trusted again. He also has a long history that suggests he's better as a slot receiver, and he's on a team that has Dede Westbrook.

Corey Coleman

Height: 5-11   Weight: 194   College: Baylor   Draft: 2016/1 (15)   Born: 6-Jul-1994   Age: 25   Risk: Red

Year	Team	G/GS	Snaps	Pass	Rec	Yds	TD	C%	+/-	Drop	Yd/C	aDOT	Rk	YAC	Rk	YAC+	BTkl	DVOA	Rk	DYAR	Rk	YAR	Use	Rk	Slot
2016	CLE	10/10	533	73	33	413	3	45%	-3.6	4	12.5	14.3	14	2.9	81	-1.6	10	-22.9%	85	-57	87	-84	20.9%	31	24%
2017	CLE	9/8	450	58	23	305	2	40%	-6.0	4	13.3	14.7	15	1.1	86	-2.9	2	-21.5%	80	-41	80	-60	18.4%	42	17%
2018	2TM	8/1	132	8	5	71	0	63%	+0.3	1	14.2	14.8	--	1.6	--	-2.0	0	19.6%	--	23	--	28	3.1%	--	0%
2019	NYG			50	29	399	3	58%			13.8							0.6%							

In the span of five months, Coleman went from the Browns to the Bills to the Patriots to the Giants. Broken hands haunted him with the Browns, as he missed time in each of his two seasons in Cleveland and dropped plenty of passes along the way. That said, in both 2016 and 2017, Coleman had one of the highest average depth of target figures in the NFL, top 15 among all qualified receivers. If the Giants are cosplaying the Panthers, Coleman is their Ted Ginn wannabe. 23 DYAR and 19.6% DVOA in a small sample meant that the Giants tendered him at a first-round level, putting him in the conversation for starting duties.

Chris Conley

Height: 6-2   Weight: 213   College: Georgia   Draft: 2015/3 (76)   Born: 25-Oct-1992   Age: 27   Risk: Green

Year	Team	G/GS	Snaps	Pass	Rec	Yds	TD	C%	+/-	Drop	Yd/C	aDOT	Rk	YAC	Rk	YAC+	BTkl	DVOA	Rk	DYAR	Rk	YAR	Use	Rk	Slot
2016	KC	16/11	818	69	44	530	0	64%	+1.6	3	12.0	10.0	63	3.4	69	-0.4	3	1.1%	49	74	56	57	12.8%	79	28%
2017	KC	5/5	293	16	11	175	0	69%	+1.8	0	15.9	14.4	--	4.1	--	-0.1	0	27.2%	--	50	--	49	9.6%	--	13%
2018	KC	16/13	802	52	32	334	5	62%	-3.1	5	10.4	9.0	64	4.4	39	+0.1	4	-1.0%	47	48	50	38	9.5%	83	66%
2019	JAX			66	38	477	3	58%			12.5							-4.9%							

Talented mid-round wideout deals with serious injuries, gets picked up by the Jaguars in the second wave of free agency. Wow, it's like Donte Moncrief got replaced by Donte Moncrief! Conley tore his Achilles in 2017 and rehabbed back to being a bit player in the Chiefs passing game. Some reporters on the ground were saying Conley was the best receiver Jacksonville had in their offseason program. Conley also has some interesting views on Godzilla that he shared with Jacksonville.com: "I grew up watching the Toho Godzilla films with my dad, and so I felt like in the movie I saw a lot of tributes to the older Godzilla films. There were a lot of Easter eggs, and a lot of shots that they shot that were purposely shot to look like they were on a big set, with Godzilla walking around. I thought that was awesome. That brought me back to my childhood. It kind of looked like a live-action person in a suit, even though it was CGI [computer-generated image], so I was a fan of that. I think they've done a good job of kind of honoring the origins of Godzilla." Conley's a self-described nerd, and he definitely should have written this comment for us.

Brandin Cooks

Height: 5-10 Weight: 189 College: Oregon St. Draft: 2014/1 (20) Born: 25-Sep-1993 Age: 26 Risk: Green

Year	Team	G/GS	Snaps	Pass	Rec	Yds	TD	C%	+/-	Drop	Yd/C	aDOT	Rk	YAC	Rk	YAC+	BTkl	DVOA	Rk	DYAR	Rk	YAR	Use	Rk	Slot
2016	NO	16/12	880	118	78	1173	8	67%	+8.7	6	15.0	13.4	24	4.9	31	+0.1	4	11.6%	20	226	16	212	17.8%	48	66%
2017	NE	16/15	1058	114	65	1082	7	57%	+2.1	8	16.6	16.5	4	3.5	57	-1.3	8	14.9%	17	258	13	266	20.0%	34	29%
2018	LAR	16/16	989	117	80	1204	5	68%	+9.1	1	15.1	14.0	19	4.3	41	-1.0	9	21.5%	12	318	10	313	21.7%	26	70%
2019	LAR			118	76	1137	8	64%			15.0							17.0%							

After being traded in back-to-back offseasons, Cooks has found a long-term home in Los Angeles, inking a five-year extension in July last year. He certainly made the Rams' brass look smart in Year 1, serving as a both a potent deep threat and a high-volume target in the Rams' electric aerial attack. Despite playing for three different teams already in the course of his five-year career, Cooks has not finished worse than No. 21 in DYAR or with fewer than 114 targets and 1,082 yards since his rookie season in New Orleans. Given that he only turns 26 in September, Cooks will be a part of the offensive core of the Rams for years to come.

Amari Cooper

Height: 6-1 Weight: 211 College: Alabama Draft: 2015/1 (4) Born: 18-Jun-1994 Age: 25 Risk: Yellow

Year	Team	G/GS	Snaps	Pass	Rec	Yds	TD	C%	+/-	Drop	Yd/C	aDOT	Rk	YAC	Rk	YAC+	BTkl	DVOA	Rk	DYAR	Rk	YAR	Use	Rk	Slot
2016	OAK	16/14	997	132	83	1153	5	63%	+0.8	4	13.9	10.0	64	5.3	18	+0.0	12	8.8%	28	231	13	185	22.9%	24	32%
2017	OAK	14/12	710	95	48	680	7	51%	-7.6	9	14.2	12.2	38	6.0	11	+1.6	6	-9.1%	68	27	67	20	19.8%	36	42%
2018	2TM	15/15	838	107	75	1005	7	70%	+6.4	5	13.4	9.9	53	5.5	15	+1.2	13	8.7%	27	187	20	196	21.9%	25	31%
2019	DAL			138	88	1166	8	64%			13.3							8.1%							

Cooper had some massive games down the stretch for the Cowboys: 18 catches for 292 yards and three touchdowns in two games against the injury-plagued Eagles secondary, an 8-180-2 line against Washington on Thanksgiving, and 13-171-2 in the two playoff games, plus a drawn pass interference call near the goal line to set up a touchdown. Cooper also had some clunkers, continuing a pattern of huge games and vanishing acts which has defined his career. The Cowboys need consistency from Cooper, and while Dak Prescott and Jason Garrett's scheme will have a lot to do with that, Cooper was susceptible to slumps long before his arrival in Dallas. At press time, Cooper hoped to hang Jerrah upside down and shake the money out of his pockets, which was a bad idea because: a) Prescott was still Jerrah's top financial priority, and b) Jerrah is at his least generous when he smells a shakedown. So don't be surprised if Cooper has an All-Pro year, and also don't be surprised if the Cooper situation turns out to be another one of those Cowboys wide receiver cautionary tales (Terry Glenn, Joey Galloway, Terrell Owens, Roy Williams…) in two years.

Keke Coutee

Height: 5-10 Weight: 181 College: Texas Tech Draft: 2018/4 (103) Born: 14-Jan-1997 Age: 22 Risk: Yellow

Year	Team	G/GS	Snaps	Pass	Rec	Yds	TD	C%	+/-	Drop	Yd/C	aDOT	Rk	YAC	Rk	YAC+	BTkl	DVOA	Rk	DYAR	Rk	YAR	Use	Rk	Slot
2018	HOU	6/2	267	41	28	287	1	68%	-2.5	3	10.3	5.1	--	7.5	--	+1.1	2	-10.5%	--	7	--	7	21.9%	--	73%
2019	HOU			95	69	758	5	73%			11.0							10.5%							

Coutee got many targets as an extension of an inconsistent running game, but he also showed the ability to create space whenever he wanted against NFL cornerbacks, and he is an ideal slot receiver who dealt with injuries for essentially all of last season. He had a deep-ball game at Texas Tech that the Texans barely scratched the surface of last year. Coutee and Will Fuller sort of pulled the offense in different directions in 2018. If both are healthy next season, expect the balance to be more towards Fuller than Coutee. Coutee will benefit when he does get the ball with a healthy Fuller though, because safeties won't be able to cheat off Fuller like they would Vyncint Smith or Demaryius Thomas.

Michael Crabtree

Height: 6-2 Weight: 215 College: Texas Tech Draft: 2009/1 (10) Born: 14-Sep-1987 Age: 32 Risk: N/A

Year	Team	G/GS	Snaps	Pass	Rec	Yds	TD	C%	+/-	Drop	Yd/C	aDOT	Rk	YAC	Rk	YAC+	BTkl	DVOA	Rk	DYAR	Rk	YAR	Use	Rk	Slot
2016	OAK	16/16	835	145	89	1003	8	61%	+0.1	11	11.3	11.1	49	2.8	83	-1.4	12	5.3%	40	212	18	171	24.8%	14	49%
2017	OAK	14/14	603	101	58	618	8	57%	-2.7	7	10.7	11.2	49	3.3	65	-0.8	10	-6.5%	64	52	59	54	21.2%	26	33%
2018	BAL	16/16	805	100	54	607	3	54%	-9.7	9	11.2	11.3	41	2.4	83	-1.8	5	-16.6%	74	-33	75	-43	18.9%	37	28%

Not much has generally changed about Crabtree's receiving profile. He has always been drop-prone, and he has never been a dynamic open-field receiver. Last year he completely disappeared when Lamar Jackson took over, perhaps partially because the Ravens didn't use him as a slot receiver and Jackson couldn't target the sidelines quite as well last season. Crabtree is simply less spry than he used to be, something that shows up in broken tackle numbers, but he's always struggled to get YAC with a consistently negative YAC+. Unsigned as we go to press, Crabtree can be a competent complementary receiver for someone, but this was probably his end as a primary target.

Jamison Crowder

Height: 5-8 Weight: 185 College: Duke Draft: 2015/4 (105) Born: 17-Jun-1993 Age: 26 Risk: Red

Year	Team	G/GS	Snaps	Pass	Rec	Yds	TD	C%	+/-	Drop	Yd/C	aDOT	Rk	YAC	Rk	YAC+	BTkl	DVOA	Rk	DYAR	Rk	YAR	Use	Rk	Slot
2016	WAS	16/9	784	99	67	847	7	68%	+2.8	3	12.6	8.1	80	5.6	13	+0.8	11	4.6%	44	129	42	127	16.7%	58	97%
2017	WAS	15/6	674	103	66	789	3	64%	+1.4	8	12.0	7.5	80	5.6	12	+0.6	5	-4.5%	57	64	55	50	20.3%	30	89%
2018	WAS	9/7	428	49	29	388	2	59%	-1.1	2	13.4	10.2	52	7.0	4	+1.6	4	-6.2%	54	23	56	28	18.0%	43	84%
2019	NYJ			104	61	734	4	59%			12.0							-5.5%							

Crowder looked like a rising star in the slot in 2016, but he has just been another guy working the short middle of the field since then. An ankle injury erased the middle of last season for him, hip and hamstring injuries slowed him in 2017, and neither Alex Smith's off-kilter early-season passing or the late-season revolving door at quarterback helped him much. Mike Maccagnan saw a receiver worth $28 million over three years, which may mean that Big Macc stopped midway through 2017, but Crowder is a big upgrade over what the Jets had in the slot last year (Jermaine Kearse and good intentions, basically). Crowder and Quincy Enunwa will run lots of mesh routes and catch lots of 6-yard passes in Adam Gase's system—assuming either of them can stay healthy, that is.

Corey Davis

Height: 6-3 Weight: 209 College: Western Michigan Draft: 2017/1 (5) Born: 11-Jan-1995 Age: 24 Risk: Green

Year	Team	G/GS	Snaps	Pass	Rec	Yds	TD	C%	+/-	Drop	Yd/C	aDOT	Rk	YAC	Rk	YAC+	BTkl	DVOA	Rk	DYAR	Rk	YAR	Use	Rk	Slot
2017	TEN	11/9	516	65	34	375	0	52%	-4.8	2	11.0	11.7	43	3.1	67	-1.4	10	-30.2%	85	-88	85	-97	19.4%	38	28%
2018	TEN	16/16	872	112	65	891	4	58%	-2.7	5	13.7	11.2	43	4.1	49	-0.8	10	-1.2%	48	104	40	90	27.1%	6	62%
2019	TEN			108	62	877	5	57%			14.1							1.0%							

Stephon Gilmore was at the top of our cornerback charting statistics, so Davis's terrific 7-125-1 plus a pass interference penalty in the Titans' blowout win over New England might have been one of the best cornerback-adjusted games of the season. Following up that with 30 yards in a punchless blowout loss to the Colts summarizes simply where Davis is right now. From a scouting perspective, he looks more comfortable when asked to win against individual players in man coverage than he does when asked to win by creating space for himself against zone, though our charting numbers suggest he performed about as well against both. Tennessee loved to target him on slant routes, throwing 15 of their 25 as a team his way, with results suggesting Tennessee should not be throwing slant routes to Davis or really anybody. Even with the additions, his status as a starter is unquestioned, but the next step to justifying the fifth overall pick used to select him is much more consistent performance. Offseason reports were suitably effusive, but bigger numbers in a more crowded room will depend on demonstrating that improvement.

Stefon Diggs

Height: 6-0 Weight: 195 College: Maryland Draft: 2015/5 (146) Born: 29-Nov-1993 Age: 26 Risk: Green

Year	Team	G/GS	Snaps	Pass	Rec	Yds	TD	C%	+/-	Drop	Yd/C	aDOT	Rk	YAC	Rk	YAC+	BTkl	DVOA	Rk	DYAR	Rk	YAR	Use	Rk	Slot
2016	MIN	13/11	693	111	84	903	3	76%	+11.3	5	10.8	8.6	77	3.8	57	-0.8	9	8.2%	29	186	24	218	23.4%	20	69%
2017	MIN	14/14	781	95	64	849	8	67%	+6.8	5	13.3	11.9	41	4.7	30	+0.3	9	24.7%	5	295	9	308	21.4%	25	40%
2018	MIN	15/14	874	149	102	1021	9	68%	+9.7	3	10.0	9.1	61	4.3	42	-0.7	24	-12.0%	66	8	64	20	26.7%	8	42%
2019	MIN			132	87	1015	8	66%			11.7							6.8%							

It seems an exaggeration to say Diggs is underrated, but he is. Diggs has never made an All-Pro or Pro Bowl team. Of course, those are not the best markers for success and recognition, but there are not many players as excellent as Diggs without any accolades to show for it. Diggs is an exceptional route-runner who regularly draws the attention of opposing defenses' best cornerbacks. More so than teammate Adam Thielen, Diggs is the one to dictate coverages and force defenses to respect him on the boundary. More targets over the past couple seasons have been funneled to Thielen in the slot, but it is Diggs' isolation threat that helps ease pressure off the middle of the field for his teammate. Though Diggs was not as productive or efficient in 2018 as he could have been, the repressed passing offense in 2018 compared to 2017 hindered what Diggs could do with a full, vertical route tree. The offense was far more geared to get the ball out immediately over the middle of the field. With a new offensive line and philosophical direction, hopefully Diggs can re-emerge as one of the best receivers in the league.

Josh Doctson
Height: 6-2   Weight: 202   College: TCU   Draft: 2016/1 (22)   Born: 3-Dec-1992   Age: 27   Risk: Green

Year	Team	G/GS	Snaps	Pass	Rec	Yds	TD	C%	+/-	Drop	Yd/C	aDOT	Rk	YAC	Rk	YAC+	BTkl	DVOA	Rk	DYAR	Rk	YAR	Use	Rk	Slot
2016	WAS	2/0	31	6	2	66	0	33%	-0.8	0	33.0	14.4	--	7.5	--	+1.5	0	-9.3%	--	2	--	-3	8.0%	--	0%
2017	WAS	16/14	756	78	35	502	6	45%	-6.7	6	14.3	14.3	18	3.7	48	-0.7	3	-7.1%	65	37	64	22	15.2%	64	30%
2018	WAS	15/12	846	78	44	532	2	56%	+0.2	2	12.1	14.7	12	3.0	75	-1.3	4	-11.5%	64	7	65	21	17.2%	48	32%
2019	WAS			85	48	626	5	56%			13.0							-4.3%							

Doctson on passes listed as "deep" (16-plus yards) in the play-by-play: seven catches for 162 yards (23.1 yards per catch) on 29 targets with four interceptions, one of which came on a Hail Mary. Doctson was a #DraftTwitter favorite back in 2016 by virtue of his ability to run fast in a straight line and catch 50-50 balls against Big 12 defenders. He is very fast and can win jump balls, but no other element of his game developed, despite multiple efforts to force-feed him opportunities in recent years. Washington declined to exercise the fifth-year option on Doctson's rookie contract while penciling him in as a starter for 2019, because that's exactly the type of clear thinking Washington is known for.

Phillip Dorsett
Height: 5-10   Weight: 185   College: Miami   Draft: 2015/1 (29)   Born: 5-Jan-1993   Age: 27   Risk: Yellow

Year	Team	G/GS	Snaps	Pass	Rec	Yds	TD	C%	+/-	Drop	Yd/C	aDOT	Rk	YAC	Rk	YAC+	BTkl	DVOA	Rk	DYAR	Rk	YAR	Use	Rk	Slot
2016	IND	15/7	795	59	33	528	2	56%	-1.7	5	16.0	14.5	10	4.5	39	-0.1	2	10.2%	25	107	50	86	11.3%	88	56%
2017	NE	15/2	377	18	12	194	0	67%	+2.9	1	16.2	18.2	--	5.7	--	+1.0	2	21.6%	--	45	--	40	3.2%	--	56%
2018	NE	16/2	399	42	32	290	3	76%	+3.0	1	9.1	10.5	--	3.1	--	-1.1	3	5.4%	--	56	--	73	7.4%	--	29%
2019	NE			50	32	395	2	64%			12.3							5.6%							

As a first-round pick for the Colts, Dorsett was a bust. As an ancillary target for first the Colts and now the Patriots, Dorsett has been a useful depth piece. Dorsett has been shut out in 15 of his 31 games for the Patriots, and he only started two games last year even during Julian Edelman's absence. But he had at least five targets in every game Edelman missed, finished with positive DVOA for his third straight season, and contributed enough that the Patriots re-signed him to a one-year deal this offseason. If Edelman were to miss time again for any reason, Dorsett may well be the greatest beneficiary, but in a healthy receiving corps his ceiling is likely to stay around two or three targets every other week.

Julian Edelman
Height: 6-0   Weight: 198   College: Kent State   Draft: 2009/7 (232)   Born: 22-May-1986   Age: 33   Risk: Yellow

Year	Team	G/GS	Snaps	Pass	Rec	Yds	TD	C%	+/-	Drop	Yd/C	aDOT	Rk	YAC	Rk	YAC+	BTkl	DVOA	Rk	DYAR	Rk	YAR	Use	Rk	Slot
2016	NE	16/13	875	159	98	1106	3	62%	-4.0	10	11.3	9.1	72	5.0	29	+0.2	12	-9.2%	68	43	65	38	28.9%	3	80%
2018	NE	12/12	747	108	74	850	6	69%	+1.3	8	11.5	7.9	75	4.7	30	+0.1	10	1.7%	42	122	35	124	25.5%	13	82%
2019	NE			134	96	1086	8	72%			11.3							11.2%							

Edelman's 2018 season began with a four-game PED suspension and ended with a Super Bowl MVP and his third championship ring. Now 33 years old, Edelman remains Tom Brady's favorite target and, as Super Bowl LIII demonstrated, arguably the most important non-quarterback cog in the Patriots offensive machine. Edelman's last two seasons have seen his lowest catch rates as a primary starter, but he matched a career high in yards per target in 2018, and his prorated stats would have set a new career high in both yards and touchdowns. His existing chemistry with Brady should ensure that he once again leads the Patriots receivers in targets.

Bruce Ellington Height: 5-9 Weight: 197 College: South Carolina Draft: 2014/4 (106) Born: 22-Aug-1991 Age: 28 Risk: N/A

Year	Team	G/GS	Snaps	Pass	Rec	Yds	TD	C%	+/-	Drop	Yd/C	aDOT	Rk	YAC	Rk	YAC+	BTkl	DVOA	Rk	DYAR	Rk	YAR	Use	Rk	Slot
2017	HOU	11/6	591	57	29	330	2	51%	-4.2	3	11.4	9.2	70	4.7	29	-0.2	5	-24.5%	84	-53	84	-61	15.8%	58	93%
2018	2TM	7/3	273	42	31	224	1	74%	-0.5	3	7.2	4.9	--	3.5	--	-1.9	6	-30.3%	--	-56	--	-54	18.1%	--	86%

Ellington's professional career is one long battle against persistent hamstring injuries: he has been placed on injured reserve with a bad hamstring four separate times by three different teams in the past three seasons—and yes, those numbers are in the correct order. He also joined the Jets on waivers in 2017 but was released after failing his physical, and he signed a one-year deal with the Patriots this past March but was released in May with an injury designation. Even when he has been healthy enough to take the field, Ellington has not been good enough to justify the patience it requires to get him there; he has been at -24.5% DVOA or lower in every season with at least 10 catches. He remains unsigned as of late June.

Quincy Enunwa Height: 6-2 Weight: 225 College: Nebraska Draft: 2014/6 (209) Born: 31-May-1992 Age: 27 Risk: Yellow

Year	Team	G/GS	Snaps	Pass	Rec	Yds	TD	C%	+/-	Drop	Yd/C	aDOT	Rk	YAC	Rk	YAC+	BTkl	DVOA	Rk	DYAR	Rk	YAR	Use	Rk	Slot
2016	NYJ	16/13	873	105	58	857	4	55%	-9.0	7	14.8	9.4	69	6.1	7	+1.1	13	-4.5%	63	69	58	72	19.3%	41	82%
2018	NYJ	11/10	526	68	38	449	1	56%	-6.1	4	11.8	7.7	76	7.5	3	+1.8	9	-32.2%	83	-105	82	-87	19.8%	32	75%
2019	NYJ			78	44	572	4	56%			13.0							-3.9%							

The Jets and their fans have been trying to make Quincy Enunwa a thing since 2015, but Enunwa keeps getting hurt (ankle, hip and hand injuries last season, a neck injury which erased all of 2017) and proving that he's at the mercy of the few ups and many downs of the Jets offense. Enunwa was Sam Darnold's screen-pass binky at the start of last year, targeted for eight screens in the first three games, but missed most of Darnold's Shazam performance in December with an ankle injury. Mike Maccagnan gave Enunwa a four-year, $35-million extension in December that looks like it was structured by a madman, with tons of backloaded money in 2021 and 2022. At first glance, Enunwa looks like a prime candidate for a culture-change cut, but the contract makes him nearly impossible to release; his YAC ability when healthy is truly impressive; and Adam Gase—who sees nothing wrong with throwing eight receiver screens in three games—has reportedly taken a shine to him.

Mike Evans Height: 6-5 Weight: 231 College: Texas A&M Draft: 2014/1 (7) Born: 21-Aug-1993 Age: 26 Risk: Green

Year	Team	G/GS	Snaps	Pass	Rec	Yds	TD	C%	+/-	Drop	Yd/C	aDOT	Rk	YAC	Rk	YAC+	BTkl	DVOA	Rk	DYAR	Rk	YAR	Use	Rk	Slot
2016	TB	16/16	950	173	96	1321	12	55%	+2.3	8	13.8	14.6	9	1.8	94	-1.9	2	10.0%	26	309	6	312	30.2%	1	43%
2017	TB	15/15	884	136	71	1001	5	52%	-2.6	7	14.1	14.2	19	1.7	85	-2.0	4	1.2%	42	149	27	145	24.6%	12	39%
2018	TB	16/16	940	138	86	1524	8	62%	+10.3	6	17.7	15.8	6	3.3	70	-1.0	6	26.3%	3	420	4	417	22.3%	24	29%
2019	TB			141	85	1319	8	60%			15.5							12.3%							

Before last season, the main thing keeping Evans out of the top-five receiver conversation was his lack of efficiency. His numbers were partly the product of Buccaneers quarterbacks force-feeding him targets. In 2018, though, he was better than ever, as he set career bests in not only receiving yards but also catch rate, yards per catch, receiving +/-, DYAR, and DVOA. So why the improvement? Part of the answer is that Jameis Winston targeted him deeper down the field. Also, Winston was more accurate when targeting Evans on passes of at least 21 air yards than when targeting other Tampa Bay receivers, according to John Kinsley's Deep Ball Project. Expect some regression here, but you still can bank on 70 to 80 catches and 1,200 to 1,300 yards.

Larry Fitzgerald Height: 6-3 Weight: 225 College: Pittsburgh Draft: 2004/1 (3) Born: 31-Aug-1983 Age: 36 Risk: Green

Year	Team	G/GS	Snaps	Pass	Rec	Yds	TD	C%	+/-	Drop	Yd/C	aDOT	Rk	YAC	Rk	YAC+	BTkl	DVOA	Rk	DYAR	Rk	YAR	Use	Rk	Slot
2016	ARI	16/16	1052	152	107	1023	6	72%	+7.3	4	9.6	7.1	88	3.4	68	-1.1	16	-6.8%	65	71	57	119	23.7%	19	79%
2017	ARI	16/16	1074	161	109	1156	6	68%	+7.1	5	10.6	8.6	75	3.7	47	-1.1	8	-1.3%	50	147	28	182	27.2%	10	81%
2018	ARI	16/16	872	112	69	734	6	62%	-1.4	2	10.6	9.5	58	3.0	76	-1.7	12	-15.3%	71	-23	72	-4	23.6%	18	89%
2019	ARI			115	69	723	6	60%			10.5							-7.4%							

For two years in a row now, Fitzgerald has pondered retirement after the season, then signed a one-year contract with Arizona, this time for $11 million (or more, with incentives). Though he was the Cardinals' top receiver once again last season, he did so with a career-low 734 yards. Part of that can be blamed on the putrid Arizona offense, but then Fitzgerald has played in putrid Arizona offenses for a good chunk of his career. We have been guilty of writing off Fitzgerald before, when it looked like Michael Floyd was going to steal his spotlight, and he has proved us wrong. Now? His age is a definite cause for concern. Fitzgerald turns 36 just before opening day, and only three wideouts that age or older have ever topped a thousand yards in a season: Joey Galloway, Jimmy Smith, and Jerry Rice, who did it three times. Speaking of Rice, Fitzgerald needs 246 catches to tie his record of 1,549 career receptions. Can he hold off Father Time and put together three or four more years to get that done? It's a longshot, but it bears repeating: we have doubted Fitzgerald before, and he has proved us wrong.

Robert Foster   Height: 6-2   Weight: 194   College: Alabama   Draft: 2018/FA   Born: 7-May-1994   Age: 25   Risk: Red

Year	Team	G/GS	Snaps	Pass	Rec	Yds	TD	C%	+/-	Drop	Yd/C	aDOT	Rk	YAC	Rk	YAC+	BTkl	DVOA	Rk	DYAR	Rk	YAR	Use	Rk	Slot
2018	BUF	13/3	450	44	27	541	3	61%	+3.7	1	20.0	21.4	--	6.2	--	+0.4	1	26.2%	--	135	--	141	11.4%	--	38%
2019	BUF			57	31	523	2	54%			16.9							4.5%							

It's overly simplistic to look at it this way, but the Bills' passing DVOA rose from -65.7% to 7.2% when Foster entered the lineup on a regular basis starting in Week 10. There's obviously a lot more to passing production than one guy, but the undrafted free agent out of Alabama was clearly the best receiver the Bills had last season. Foster's DVOA on deep passes was 49.7%, ranking ninth amidst a group of much more highly acclaimed players. The trouble with Foster, however, is that his game is fairly one-dimensional at the moment, and it's the same dimension John Brown brings to the team from Baltimore. Either one or the other is going to have to start running some shorter routes, or Foster could spend some time on the bench.

Bennie Fowler   Height: 6-1   Weight: 212   College: Michigan State   Draft: 2014/FA   Born: 10-Jun-1991   Age: 28   Risk: Green

Year	Team	G/GS	Snaps	Pass	Rec	Yds	TD	C%	+/-	Drop	Yd/C	aDOT	Rk	YAC	Rk	YAC+	BTkl	DVOA	Rk	DYAR	Rk	YAR	Use	Rk	Slot
2016	DEN	13/0	242	24	11	145	2	46%	-3.0	1	13.2	11.1	--	5.8	--	+2.0	0	-22.2%	--	-16	--	-16	5.2%	--	83%
2017	DEN	16/4	575	56	29	350	3	52%	-5.3	4	12.1	10.2	57	3.7	50	-0.1	3	-9.8%	69	12	70	14	10.0%	82	77%
2018	NYG	10/5	370	27	16	199	1	59%	-1.2	1	12.4	9.9	--	4.8	--	+0.5	6	-18.4%	--	-12	--	-7	7.4%	--	46%
2019	NYG			18	10	115	0	56%			11.5							-14.3%							

When Cody Latimer went down with a hamstring injury in the middle of the season, the Giants called on Fowler. As the third receiver in an offense that didn't cater much playing time to third receivers—seriously, he played 35 snaps in Week 7 and was targeted once—Fowler didn't add much. He is a willing special-teamer, and the Giants re-signed him. And unless one of their lower-round picks or UDFA lottery tickets pays off, the thrilling conclusion of the Latimer/Fowler receiving battle may play out again on our television sets. Probably on Sunday Night Football, since the Giants are always on it.

Will Fuller   Height: 6-0   Weight: 186   College: Notre Dame   Draft: 2016/1 (21)   Born: 16-Apr-1994   Age: 25   Risk: Yellow

Year	Team	G/GS	Snaps	Pass	Rec	Yds	TD	C%	+/-	Drop	Yd/C	aDOT	Rk	YAC	Rk	YAC+	BTkl	DVOA	Rk	DYAR	Rk	YAR	Use	Rk	Slot
2016	HOU	14/13	829	92	47	635	2	51%	-2.4	6	13.5	15.7	4	4.7	35	-0.2	7	-14.8%	77	-15	78	-15	18.0%	45	43%
2017	HOU	10/10	530	50	28	423	7	56%	+1.7	2	15.1	17.4	2	3.5	56	-0.7	0	17.6%	12	126	35	134	15.6%	59	42%
2018	HOU	7/7	375	45	32	503	4	71%	+6.0	0	15.7	16.3	--	5.2	--	+0.6	4	34.6%	--	180	--	190	21.5%	--	40%
2019	HOU			86	51	783	5	59%			15.3							8.1%							

Nationally slept on because of his injuries, DeAndre Hopkins' shadow, and bad quarterbacks in 2017, Fuller is a complete receiver who only has drops as a real weakness. When paired with Deshaun Watson in 2017, Fuller caught 13-of-22 balls for 279 yards and seven touchdowns. He missed some time last year with a lingering hamstring injury, and often that injury kept him from going full-bore, leading to decoy games like Week 5's two-catch, 15-yard effort against the Cowboys. If Fuller could stay healthy for a full season, he would easily be in the Pro Bowl conversation and might be in the All-Pro conversation. The torn ACL that ended Fuller's season will probably set him back a bit heading into training camp, and he is truly one of the biggest open questions of the 2018 season. A healthy Fuller will dominate cornerbacks. A dinged Fuller will have a lot of cascade fallout for the Texans, both in real life and in fantasy football.

Devin Funchess   Height: 6-4   Weight: 232   College: Michigan   Draft: 2015/2 (41)   Born: 21-May-1994   Age: 25   Risk: Yellow

Year	Team	G/GS	Snaps	Pass	Rec	Yds	TD	C%	+/-	Drop	Yd/C	aDOT	Rk	YAC	Rk	YAC+	BTkl	DVOA	Rk	DYAR	Rk	YAR	Use	Rk	Slot
2016	CAR	15/7	494	58	23	371	4	40%	-8.9	5	16.1	14.1	16	4.5	42	+1.0	2	-7.4%	66	26	68	28	11.8%	86	39%
2017	CAR	16/16	853	112	63	840	8	56%	-2.0	4	13.3	13.4	26	4.5	36	+0.2	3	6.8%	32	168	21	157	22.8%	16	38%
2018	CAR	14/12	622	79	44	549	4	56%	-2.0	7	12.5	13.0	22	1.7	84	-1.9	1	-10.5%	62	13	61	30	16.4%	54	39%
2019	IND			72	45	546	5	63%			12.1							1.3%							

Funchess looked like an ascending player a year ago, and now he gets a fresh start in Indianapolis after a recurrence of his drop issues and a back injury helped lead to a down season in 2018. He is primarily an outside receiver, with digs, outs, slants, and comebacks his most common routes. He gives the Colts a different type of receiver than they really had on their roster in 2018, a pure outside complement to T.Y. Hilton. Only on a one-year deal, Funchess benefited financially from a thin receiver group in free agency. There's opportunity here, but he could also be phased out like he was late in the year in Carolina if he is not effective in his role.

Taylor Gabriel   Height: 5-8   Weight: 167   College: Abilene Christian   Draft: 2014/FA   Born: 17-Feb-1991   Age: 28   Risk: Green

Year	Team	G/GS	Snaps	Pass	Rec	Yds	TD	C%	+/-	Drop	Yd/C	aDOT	Rk	YAC	Rk	YAC+	BTkl	DVOA	Rk	DYAR	Rk	YAR	Use	Rk	Slot
2016	ATL	13/3	349	51	35	579	6	71%	+4.4	0	16.5	11.0	51	7.7	1	+1.9	7	33.7%	1	181	25	185	11.8%	85	71%
2017	ATL	16/4	540	51	33	378	1	65%	+0.2	2	11.5	10.3	56	6.6	6	+0.8	7	-8.0%	67	18	68	19	9.9%	84	48%
2018	CHI	16/11	830	93	67	688	2	72%	+5.4	2	10.3	11.9	32	3.2	72	-2.3	6	-10.2%	61	19	59	35	18.6%	38	48%
2019	CHI			88	56	633	3	64%			11.3							-6.1%							

Gabriel needs to be moved back to a slot position. When Gabriel was at his peak under Kyle Shanahan, both in Cleveland and Atlanta, he was primarily a slot player deployed as a field-stretcher. He has blazing 4.45 speed that can uncork the top off a defense, creating space for other pass-catchers underneath. The last time Gabriel posted a positive DVOA from either the slot or out wide was with the Falcons in 2016, when he held a 42.6% rating from the slot as Shanahan's deep threat. In fairness to Matt Nagy, the Bears did use Gabriel as a vertical threat last year, but they did so more often from a wide alignment, not from the slot like Shanahan. With Allen Robinson as an iso threat and Anthony Miller as a fiend for underneath yardage, deploying Gabriel as a slot field-stretcher should be able to work, but it could be the case that Nagy prefers Miller's more versatile route tree out of the slot instead.

Michael Gallup   Height: 6-1   Weight: 205   College: Colorado State   Draft: 2018/3 (81)   Born: 4-Mar-1996   Age: 23   Risk: Yellow

Year	Team	G/GS	Snaps	Pass	Rec	Yds	TD	C%	+/-	Drop	Yd/C	aDOT	Rk	YAC	Rk	YAC+	BTkl	DVOA	Rk	DYAR	Rk	YAR	Use	Rk	Slot
2018	DAL	16/8	739	68	33	507	2	49%	-5.7	1	15.4	14.3	16	5.2	23	-0.1	2	-14.3%	68	-9	68	15	13.4%	69	16%
2019	DAL			78	46	663	6	59%			14.4							5.8%							

Gallup put up some yucky splits in high leverage situations: three catches on eight red zone targets (just one touchdown), 3-of-11 on third-and-10-plus yards (two first downs), 8-of-22 in fourth quarters, 1-of-5 when trailing in the final four minutes. The third-round rookie may have been a little over his head as the team's top outside receiver before Amari Cooper arrived, and Gallup had to play through personal tragedy late in the year when his brother took his own life days before Thanksgiving. Gallup should settle in as the No. 2 receiver across from Amari Cooper, but as the most likely "designated deep threat" in the Cowboys offense, his production will rise and fall based on Dak Prescott's accuracy, the health of the offensive line, and whether Jason Garrett has had any fresh ideas in the previous month.

Pierre Garcon   Height: 6-0   Weight: 210   College: Mount Union   Draft: 2008/6 (205)   Born: 8-Aug-1986   Age: 33   Risk: N/A

Year	Team	G/GS	Snaps	Pass	Rec	Yds	TD	C%	+/-	Drop	Yd/C	aDOT	Rk	YAC	Rk	YAC+	BTkl	DVOA	Rk	DYAR	Rk	YAR	Use	Rk	Slot
2016	WAS	16/16	808	114	79	1041	3	69%	+8.8	2	13.2	10.3	60	4.3	45	-0.1	13	16.3%	14	262	10	256	19.2%	42	27%
2017	SF	8/8	430	67	40	500	0	60%	-2.9	0	12.5	10.0	62	4.7	31	-0.2	3	-3.8%	55	45	63	41	22.5%	18	54%
2018	SF	8/8	379	46	24	286	1	52%	-2.5	3	11.9	9.7	--	4.1	--	-1.0	4	-21.3%	--	-31	--	-37	17.6%	--	63%

Garcon's body may have broken down, as knee, neck, and shoulder injuries ruined his tenure in San Francisco. The 49ers declined his $6-million option for 2019, and he hasn't been heard from since. Assorted online speculation has linked Garcon with any number of teams in need of a veteran receiver—Green Bay, Washington, or Buffalo, just to name three—but it's more likely that he has played his last NFL snap. If so, it's an end to a career that was better than you probably realized; only seven players have caught more passes in the last decade.

Ted Ginn

		Height: 5-11				Weight: 178			College: Ohio State					Draft: 2007/1 (9)			Born: 12-Apr-1985			Age: 34		Risk: Green

Year	Team	G/GS	Snaps	Pass	Rec	Yds	TD	C%	+/-	Drop	Yd/C	aDOT	Rk	YAC	Rk	YAC+	BTkl	DVOA	Rk	DYAR	Rk	YAR	Use	Rk	Slot
2016	CAR	16/8	687	95	54	752	4	57%	-2.9	6	13.9	13.2	29	3.4	70	-1.6	5	-10.8%	72	13	72	15	16.9%	56	37%
2017	NO	15/10	617	70	53	787	4	76%	+10.0	2	14.8	12.6	36	5.4	14	+0.1	9	34.8%	2	259	12	266	14.0%	68	59%
2018	NO	5/3	197	30	17	209	2	57%	-0.4	2	12.3	16.6	--	2.8	--	-1.7	3	-21.6%	--	-21	--	-9	18.3%	--	53%
2019	NO			44	26	368	2	59%			14.2							6.7%							

Ginn's 2017 efficiency was always likely to be a massive outlier given his career averages, and he reverted to a stat line more in keeping with those averages when he made it onto the field in 2018. A knee injury had him in and out of the lineup for much of the regular season, but he returned to play in Week 16 and started both playoff games. At age 34, he was confident enough in his health to issue a standing offer to race anybody for $10,000 or more—though he did not show up for the high-profile "40 Yards of Gold" race-off in June despite his wager being the inspiration for the event. Ginn is the clear favorite to re-emerge from the cluster of competitors for the No. 2 receiver spot in New Orleans, but a host of both personal and circumstantial factors render him unlikely to replicate his 2017 production.

Chris Godwin

		Height: 6-1				Weight: 209			College: Penn State					Draft: 2017/3 (84)			Born: 27-Feb-1996			Age: 23		Risk: Yellow

Year	Team	G/GS	Snaps	Pass	Rec	Yds	TD	C%	+/-	Drop	Yd/C	aDOT	Rk	YAC	Rk	YAC+	BTkl	DVOA	Rk	DYAR	Rk	YAR	Use	Rk	Slot
2017	TB	16/2	449	55	34	525	1	62%	+2.4	2	15.4	13.4	27	5.0	23	+0.8	7	20.5%	10	138	33	130	9.1%	86	44%
2018	TB	16/5	717	95	59	842	7	62%	+1.2	1	14.3	11.9	33	4.2	46	+0.1	10	1.3%	43	105	39	116	15.5%	60	49%
2019	TB			124	75	1020	7	60%			13.6							4.5%							

Once upon a time, we called the inside receiver in a formation the "slot receiver." In a Bruce Arians offense, though, that boring, old label just won't do. We need something that sounds more innovative, more transcendent. Something unique, catchy. Something like … the Larry Fitzgerald role! Sure, it's just another way of saying "dude who catches a lot of footballs," but let's not let thinking get in the way of coach idolatry.

The "Larry Fitzgerald role" label has been slapped on Godwin ever since Arians said in March that he thinks that the Buccaneers receiver can do what Fitzgerald did (and is still doing). "I think Chris Godwin is going to be close to a 100-catch guy, especially because I think he can play in the slot," he said. A hundred catches? How realistic is that? If you assume that Mike Evans catches 80 passes, then not very. One Arians offense has featured two 80-catch players: the 2016 Cardinals (Fitzgerald had 107, and David Johnson had 80). For the round-numbers-obsessed, there is reason to believe that Godwin will pass 1,000 receiving yards, especially with DeSean Jackson out of the picture. Since 2017, Godwin averaged four catches for 73 yards in games in which he played but Jackson didn't.

Kenny Golladay

		Height: 6-4				Weight: 218			College: Northern Illinois					Draft: 2017/3 (96)			Born: 3-Nov-1993			Age: 26		Risk: Yellow

Year	Team	G/GS	Snaps	Pass	Rec	Yds	TD	C%	+/-	Drop	Yd/C	aDOT	Rk	YAC	Rk	YAC+	BTkl	DVOA	Rk	DYAR	Rk	YAR	Use	Rk	Slot
2017	DET	11/5	477	48	28	477	3	58%	+0.7	1	17.0	14.9	--	6.5	--	+1.5	2	21.9%	--	130	--	126	12.4%	--	33%
2018	DET	15/13	904	119	70	1063	5	59%	-0.5	5	15.2	12.9	23	5.0	25	+0.7	10	13.3%	21	250	15	225	23.2%	19	46%
2019	DET			113	70	1031	7	62%			14.7							8.2%							

Golladay enjoyed a fantastic breakout season as a second-year player in 2018, but it's worth re-examining the context with which Golladay was able to produce the way he did. He came on strong down the stretch with Marvin Jones out of the lineup. From Weeks 11 through 16, without Jones, Golladay became the team's leading receiver. Golladay was targeted at an unprecedented rate for him—nearly 10 targets per game over that span. However, Golladay was scraping just below 8 yards per target as the lone quality receiver in the offense, whereas he maintained nearly 10 yards per target before Jones went down. While Golladay could be the focal point of an offense, and his value is not tied directly to Jones, this highlights that Golladay is served best as a secondary or tertiary option who stretches the field, both from the slot and from out wide. He is similar to what Tyrell Williams was for the Chargers: a tall, athletic, vertical and deep-crossing threat who turns into one of the most dangerous ball-carriers in the league once he reels in a pass. Hopefully the new-look Lions offense can allow Golladay to return to a role with slightly less volume, while enabling him to reach peak efficiency.

Marquise Goodwin

Height: 5-9   Weight: 183   College: Texas   Draft: 2013/3 (78)   Born: 19-Nov-1990   Age: 29   Risk: Green

Year	Team	G/GS	Snaps	Pass	Rec	Yds	TD	C%	+/-	Drop	Yd/C	aDOT	Rk	YAC	Rk	YAC+	BTkl	DVOA	Rk	DYAR	Rk	YAR	Use	Rk	Slot
2016	BUF	15/9	638	68	29	431	3	43%	-7.1	3	14.9	15.2	5	2.8	86	-0.9	1	-23.8%	87	-56	86	-50	15.6%	64	26%
2017	SF	16/16	769	105	56	962	2	53%	-0.3	7	17.2	15.3	11	3.4	58	-0.8	7	5.9%	34	155	24	149	17.5%	48	57%
2018	SF	11/8	436	44	23	395	4	52%	-3.2	2	17.2	14.3	--	5.5	--	+0.9	2	1.7%	--	51	--	40	12.2%	--	52%
2019	SF			69	36	576	4	52%			16.0							1.1%							

In June, Goodwin won the inaugural 40 Yards of Gold event, a 16-man tournament of NFL players running 40-yard dashes, defeating Carolina defensive back Donte Jackson in the finals. As such, he was supposed to win a $1-million prize, but as of press time none of the competitors had received their money. Goodwin did, however, receive a "random" drug test from the NFL a few days after the event. What's most impressive is that speed isn't even Goodwin's best athletic trait—he finished 10th in the long jump at the 2012 Olympics in London, and though he failed to make the U.S. team in 2016, he has said he'll compete again for the 2020 games in Tokyo. He is under contract with San Francico through 2021, but presumably the 49ers have OK'd his participation. Goodwin has played in seven of Jimmy Garoppolo's starts in San Francisco, averaging 59.1 yards in those games. That would be almost a 1,000-yard pace over a full season, presuming we ever get a full season where Garoppolo and Goodwin are both healthy.

Josh Gordon

Height: 6-4   Weight: 220   College: Baylor   Draft: 2012/2 (SUP)   Born: 12-Apr-1991   Age: 28   Risk: N/A

Year	Team	G/GS	Snaps	Pass	Rec	Yds	TD	C%	+/-	Drop	Yd/C	aDOT	Rk	YAC	Rk	YAC+	BTkl	DVOA	Rk	DYAR	Rk	YAR	Use	Rk	Slot
2017	CLE	5/5	259	42	18	335	1	43%	-2.5	1	18.6	17.2	--	6.8	--	+2.2	4	-7.8%	--	16	--	13	23.1%	--	38%
2018	2TM	12/12	633	71	41	737	4	58%	-0.4	6	18.0	14.9	11	6.4	5	+2.3	9	20.4%	14	193	18	195	17.7%	45	26%

What Might Have Been, Chapter IV: Gordon's football career, both college and professional, stands as an agonizing cautionary tale against the dangers of drug and alcohol abuse. Gordon has spoken at length about his ongoing battle against the personal demons (most people fixate on his marijuana use, but Gordon has openly stated that weed is far from the worst of his afflictions) that have cost him two full seasons of his professional career and now chunks of four more. Both Gordon and his new employers thought a move to Foxborough and a fresh start would help him gain control over his addictions last season, but he only lasted 11 games with the Patriots before being suspended indefinitely for another violation of the league's substance abuse policy. This is the fourth substance-abuse suspension in Gordon's seven years as a pro, and despite some positive overtures it is not yet clear when or even if he will be cleared again to return to the NFL.

Very much the secondary aspect of the tragedy of Gordon's struggles is just how good he is when he can get on the field. A 2012 supplemental draft pick, Gordon exploded onto the professional scene in his second season with a league-leading 1,646 yards despite questionable quarterbacking and only 14 games played. His advanced stats were also excellent: Gordon's 336 DYAR ranked ninth, and his 14.4% DVOA ranked 17th. He has only added 1,375 yards in the five seasons since, during which he has missed 58 of 80 possible games due to a mixture of team and league punishments, but he still performed as a legitimate No. 1 receiver in 2018 before his latest suspension curtailed his season. If he can ever truly conquer his illness and get back on the field for good, the 28-year-old just about has time to salvage a career that once had oh-so-much potential.

Jakeem Grant

Height: 5-6   Weight: 161   College: Texas Tech   Draft: 2016/6 (186)   Born: 30-Oct-1992   Age: 27   Risk: Red

Year	Team	G/GS	Snaps	Pass	Rec	Yds	TD	C%	+/-	Drop	Yd/C	aDOT	Rk	YAC	Rk	YAC+	BTkl	DVOA	Rk	DYAR	Rk	YAR	Use	Rk	Slot
2016	MIA	16/0	19	1	0	0	0	0%	-0.9	1	0.0	-3.0	--	0.0	--	--	0	-114.2%	--	-9	--	-8	0.2%	--	100%
2017	MIA	16/0	132	23	13	203	2	61%	-0.2	2	15.6	10.5	--	11.4	--	+5.8	9	22.1%	--	60	--	58	4.0%	--	21%
2018	MIA	10/2	282	34	21	268	2	62%	-0.4	2	12.8	8.5	--	6.7	--	+1.3	3	-4.6%	--	21	--	26	12.7%	--	31%
2019	MIA			52	29	321	1	56%			11.1							-18.5%							

Grant was having a high-impact season as a return man that included some solid games on offense (including two touchdowns in the feeding frenzy against the Raiders defense) before suffering an Achilles injury against the Packers. An Achilles injury is a red flag for a 170-pound junebug, because players like Grant can't afford to lose even a millisecond of lateral explosiveness. Grant and Albert Wilson play the same role in an offensive ecosystem, and assuming both are healthy, Wilson should handle most of the screens and slot stuff while Grant concentrates on returns and some five-wide packages. But Wilson is returning from a hip injury, and Grant was a limited OTA participant, so we shouldn't make hasty assumptions until we see who is on the field in training camp.

Ryan Grant   Height: 6-0   Weight: 199   College: Tulane   Draft: 2014/5 (142)   Born: 19-Dec-1990   Age: 29   Risk: Green

Year	Team	G/GS	Snaps	Pass	Rec	Yds	TD	C%	+/-	Drop	Yd/C	aDOT	Rk	YAC	Rk	YAC+	BTkl	DVOA	Rk	DYAR	Rk	YAR	Use	Rk	Slot
2016	WAS	16/1	271	19	9	76	0	47%	-2.9	1	8.4	8.7	--	2.8	--	-1.7	0	-34.9%	--	-35	--	-38	3.2%	--	63%
2017	WAS	16/7	616	65	45	573	4	69%	+4.1	4	12.7	9.7	68	5.2	18	+0.7	7	16.7%	13	146	31	152	12.0%	76	58%
2018	IND	14/10	561	52	35	334	1	67%	+0.3	3	9.5	8.2	72	2.7	80	-1.7	2	-9.8%	59	12	62	14	9.4%	84	26%
2019	OAK			21	12	130	0	57%			10.8							-15.9%							

Grant is coming back to the warm arms of the Gruden family after a 2018 to forget. Two years ago, Grant was one of just five receivers to rank in the top 20 in both YAC+ and receiving plus-minus. That was with Jay's squad in Washington, and it set him up nicely for a free-agent windfall. Things went downhill from there—a failed physical voided a huge payday in Baltimore, and then his stint in Indianapolis ended up disappointing at best. Grant's hoping a healthy season in a more familiar scheme will help vault him back up to 2017's levels, and we'll just quietly forget last season ever occurred.

A.J. Green   Height: 6-4   Weight: 207   College: Georgia   Draft: 2011/1 (4)   Born: 31-Jul-1988   Age: 31   Risk: Yellow

Year	Team	G/GS	Snaps	Pass	Rec	Yds	TD	C%	+/-	Drop	Yd/C	aDOT	Rk	YAC	Rk	YAC+	BTkl	DVOA	Rk	DYAR	Rk	YAR	Use	Rk	Slot
2016	CIN	10/10	554	100	66	964	4	66%	+6.8	3	14.6	12.4	35	3.9	54	-1.1	9	19.1%	9	250	11	232	29.9%	2	24%
2017	CIN	16/16	857	143	75	1078	8	52%	-1.3	6	14.4	13.9	23	4.0	44	+0.2	11	-6.4%	63	73	49	88	29.7%	3	25%
2018	CIN	9/9	457	77	46	694	6	60%	-1.2	4	15.1	12.7	24	3.5	64	-0.4	4	12.4%	23	155	24	145	26.1%	11	47%
2019	CIN			136	79	1160	9	58%			14.7							5.6%							

An increase in slot snaps and a decrease in target percentage brought A.J. Green's productivity way up on a per-snap basis. (Green had a 39.8% DVOA in the slot, but a -12.2% DVOA out wide.) At this point we have sort of hit the age range and injury-proneness equation where Green will be watched like a hawk for any signs of decline. Green is still a terrific receiver, and his mastery of the mental game at an early age was clear and evident. Since he's not quite the level of physical freak that someone like Julio Jones is, it subjectively seems more likely for him to have a leveled decline than one where it all goes at once. Green is in the last year of his four-year, $60-million extension signed in 2015. If allowed to get to free agency, he may be a prime candidate to go ring-chasing and trying to shake the Bengals funk off of him. His health will be a big deal, though, and someone who missed chunks of three of his last four years would not be super-appealing as a free agent.

DaeSean Hamilton   Height: 6-1   Weight: 203   College: Penn State   Draft: 2018/4 (113)   Born: 10-Mar-1995   Age: 24   Risk: Red

Year	Team	G/GS	Snaps	Pass	Rec	Yds	TD	C%	+/-	Drop	Yd/C	aDOT	Rk	YAC	Rk	YAC+	BTkl	DVOA	Rk	DYAR	Rk	YAR	Use	Rk	Slot
2018	DEN	14/5	471	46	30	243	2	65%	-0.9	1	8.1	8.5	--	2.3	--	-2.3	0	-18.1%	--	-20	--	-32	9.4%	--	77%
2019	DEN			79	51	573	3	65%			11.2							-3.1%							

Hamilton ended up closing the season as the Broncos' primary slot receiver when Emmanuel Sanders went down, with all but eight of his targets coming in the last four games of the season. The results were not ideal. Hamilton averaged just 4.8 yards per target in December, dead last among wide receivers with at least 25 targets. His lack of game-breaking speed was a concern pre-draft, but that's still a distressingly bad stat. He says a knee injury slowed him down late last season, though he never appeared on the injury report. If so, perhaps Hamilton can take a significant step forward in 2019; his catching ability and route-running aren't in question, just his ability to do things with the ball in his hands. Hamilton will start the year as either the second or third receiver, depending on Emmanuel Sanders' health.

Mecole Hardman Height: 5-11 Weight: 183 College: Georgia Draft: 2019/2 (56) Born: 12-Mar-1998 Age: 21 Risk: Yellow

Year	Team	G/GS	Snaps	Pass	Rec	Yds	TD	C%	+/-	Drop	Yd/C	aDOT	Rk	YAC	Rk	YAC+	BTkl	DVOA	Rk	DYAR	Rk	YAR	Use	Rk	Slot
2019	KC		55	31	477	3	56%			15.4								-4.9%							

If you want a receiver who can almost make big plays, then Hardman is the man for you. His athleticism is off the charts; a 4.33-second 40-yard dash nearly led the class, and he drew rave reviews for his performance in the individual receiving drills. It just hasn't always shown up on tape. Hardman struggles with contested catches, and he relies more on that athleticism rather than route-running or technique to get open. He has only been playing the position for two years, so there's a lot of potential to grow into a more well-rounded player, but it will take some time.

Maurice Harris Height: 6-3 Weight: 200 College: California Draft: 2016/FA Born: 11-Nov-1992 Age: 27 Risk: Green

Year	Team	G/GS	Snaps	Pass	Rec	Yds	TD	C%	+/-	Drop	Yd/C	aDOT	Rk	YAC	Rk	YAC+	BTkl	DVOA	Rk	DYAR	Rk	YAR	Use	Rk	Slot
2016	WAS	10/0	131	12	8	66	0	67%	+0.6	0	8.3	8.9	--	1.3	--	-3.4	0	-19.7%	--	-7	--	-9	3.2%	--	58%
2017	WAS	6/0	76	6	4	62	1	67%	+0.6	0	15.5	12.2	--	2.0	--	-0.8	0	24.3%	--	18	--	20	3.0%	--	50%
2018	WAS	12/7	462	47	28	304	0	60%	+0.4	3	10.9	10.5	--	3.6	--	-1.8	0	-33.2%	--	-73	--	-66	12.7%	--	60%
2019	NE			28	18	226	2	64%			12.5							8.3%							

Harris appears to be an odd beneficiary of New England's uncharacteristic recent trend toward getting ... bigger? ... at wide receiver. A 2016 undrafted free agent out of Cal, the 6-foot-3 target finally earned a starting gig last year amid the rubble of Washington's offense. Even then, he had more games with zero catches (four) than with 25 yards or more (three), and he would have been within a rounding error of John Ross for the league's worst DVOA given enough targets to qualify for the leaderboard. Harris doesn't have the strong special teams pedigree we usually associate with this sort of Patriots signing, though he has played around 120 snaps in the kicking game over the past three years. It would be something of an upset to see him get significant playing time in New England, unless Bill Belichick likes his special teams utility more than Jay Gruden ever did.

N'Keal Harry Height: 6-2 Weight: 228 College: Arizona State Draft: 2019/1 (32) Born: 17-Dec-1997 Age: 22 Risk: Yellow

Year	Team	G/GS	Snaps	Pass	Rec	Yds	TD	C%	+/-	Drop	Yd/C	aDOT	Rk	YAC	Rk	YAC+	BTkl	DVOA	Rk	DYAR	Rk	YAR	Use	Rk	Slot
2019	NE		75	47	667	4	63%			14.2								2.7%							

The last time the Patriots drafted a wide receiver in the first round, Bill Clinton was the U.S. president and Michael Jordan's Chicago Bulls had just achieved their record-breaking 70th win of the NBA season. Every other team had drafted at least one first-round receiver over the intervening two decades, and the Patriots had drafted a first-round rookie at every other starting position on both offense and defense. While the trade for Brandin Cooks *technically* counts as spending a first-round pick at the position, Cooks was a three-year veteran of a complex NFL offense, who was then traded away after a year of service for a pick higher than the one the Patriots spent on him. The Patriots will certainly hope for a longer period of service from *this* use of the 32nd overall pick.

Harry should, at the very least, step immediately into Chris Hogan's role on offense. A big, broad target with both long speed and short-area quickness, he is comfortable both in the slot and split wide and possesses strong, soft hands and punt-returner agility. The Patriots did not have a strong track record with rookie receivers for most of their two-decade run, but their more recent relative successes—Kenbrell Thompkins and Malcolm Mitchell—have been 6-foot-something receivers who can win with physical attributes while they develop their understanding of the offense. Harry is more talented than any of those players, and he should have both the role and target share to have a strong chance of outproducing all of them.

Rashard Higgins Height: 6-1 Weight: 196 College: Colorado State Draft: 2016/5 (172) Born: 7-Oct-1994 Age: 25 Risk: Green

Year	Team	G/GS	Snaps	Pass	Rec	Yds	TD	C%	+/-	Drop	Yd/C	aDOT	Rk	YAC	Rk	YAC+	BTkl	DVOA	Rk	DYAR	Rk	YAR	Use	Rk	Slot
2016	CLE	16/0	183	12	6	77	0	50%	-0.9	1	12.8	11.7	--	5.2	--	+1.4	1	-26.4%	--	-14	--	-11	2.1%	--	33%
2017	CLE	15/4	664	51	27	312	2	55%	-1.5	2	11.6	9.6	69	5.3	16	+0.7	9	-23.1%	82	-41	81	-50	9.4%	85	92%
2018	CLE	13/1	483	53	39	572	4	74%	+7.6	3	14.7	11.6	38	3.7	57	-1.0	3	22.3%	11	143	28	142	11.6%	76	57%
2019	CLE			31	18	247	2	58%			13.7							0.5%							

With all the noise around the Browns, the player who was by far their most effective receiver in 2018 is almost completely unknown outside Northeast Ohio. Higgins was cut in 2017 and then brought back as a practice squadder, then seized on the opportunity wrought by chaos last year. It helped that the Browns took the speedy Higgins out of the slot and put him on the perimeter, where he thrived once Baker Mayfield took over. Higgy made his bones on first down—his splits drop from a heady 57.9% DVOA on that initial play to 8.1% and -1.9% on succeeding downs, on a virtually equivalent number of targets.

Alas, all that progress and hard work may be for naught now that Odell Beckham is in town. Higgins is nicknamed "Hollywood" and he won points for a creative touchdown celebration, "walking" the red carpet while his teammates/paparazzi jostled to get quality photos. You didn't hear about that, but Odell proposing to a kicking net was jammed down your throat...

Tyreek Hill Height: 5-9 Weight: 185 College: West Alabama Draft: 2016/5 (165) Born: 1-Mar-1994 Age: 25 Risk: Red

Year	Team	G/GS	Snaps	Pass	Rec	Yds	TD	C%	+/-	Drop	Yd/C	aDOT	Rk	YAC	Rk	YAC+	BTkl	DVOA	Rk	DYAR	Rk	YAR	Use	Rk	Slot
2016	KC	16/1	418	83	61	593	6	73%	+3.9	6	9.7	8.0	82	4.5	41	-1.1	26	0.8%	50	87	55	67	15.4%	66	53%
2017	KC	15/13	779	106	75	1183	7	72%	+10.0	3	15.8	11.7	44	6.1	9	+0.4	19	23.6%	7	304	8	303	21.4%	24	42%
2018	KC	16/16	905	137	87	1479	12	64%	+8.3	8	17.0	15.3	10	6.1	8	+0.5	19	23.8%	6	387	5	356	24.0%	17	59%
2019	KC			123	80	1221	11	65%			15.3							21.0%							

Seeing why a team would want to stand by Hill despite all his off-field troubles isn't very difficult. Hill had the second-most DYAR on deep passes with 257; maintaining a 58.2% DVOA on deep balls through 50 targets is a difficult combination of efficiency and volume to match, with only Tyler Lockett's insane season really topping it. Hill is more than just a big-play guy, though. His 40.2% DVOA on third down was fourth-best among players with at least 30 third-down targets; 19 of his 22 third-down catches went for a first down. His speed, his twitch, his agility—we could go on about all the things that make Hill a great player. His long-term future with the team and the league in general depends far more on the ongoing legal and disciplinary situations than it has to do with third-down efficiency. This projection does not assume any kind of league suspension related to his ongoing legal problems.

T.Y. Hilton Height: 5-10 Weight: 183 College: Florida International Draft: 2012/3 (92) Born: 14-Nov-1989 Age: 30 Risk: Yellow

Year	Team	G/GS	Snaps	Pass	Rec	Yds	TD	C%	+/-	Drop	Yd/C	aDOT	Rk	YAC	Rk	YAC+	BTkl	DVOA	Rk	DYAR	Rk	YAR	Use	Rk	Slot
2016	IND	16/16	947	155	91	1448	6	59%	+6.3	10	15.9	13.2	28	3.8	58	-0.4	6	17.3%	12	360	4	333	26.8%	9	76%
2017	IND	16/16	926	109	57	966	4	52%	-0.9	5	16.9	13.4	28	5.3	15	+0.7	3	-3.8%	56	75	48	60	23.2%	14	68%
2018	IND	14/14	763	120	76	1270	6	63%	-0.4	3	16.7	11.8	34	6.0	9	+1.0	8	23.4%	8	359	7	386	22.4%	23	50%
2019	IND			135	82	1279	9	61%			15.6							12.7%							

Did you know: Hilton was targeted 33 times on curl routes in 2018, five more than any other player in the league (former Frank Reich player Zach Ertz was next). For a player who made his reputation as a vertical threat, that's quite a change in usage. On a team bereft of other quality options, he was indispensable and terrific, especially after the Colts' early-season struggles. Luck looked to him in all situations, but particularly on third downs, where his average depth of target was only 9.1 compared to those deep shots that led to his aDOT of 15.0 on first downs. The upgrades around him could make him even more efficient. A full season of health—without the chest and hamstring injuries that cost him two games and the ankle, shoulder, and groin injuries he played through later in the season—might even see his target total rise despite the other options.

Chris Hogan Height: 6-1 Weight: 220 College: Monmouth Draft: 2012/FA Born: 24-Oct-1987 Age: 32 Risk: Green

Year	Team	G/GS	Snaps	Pass	Rec	Yds	TD	C%	+/-	Drop	Yd/C	aDOT	Rk	YAC	Rk	YAC+	BTkl	DVOA	Rk	DYAR	Rk	YAR	Use	Rk	Slot
2016	NE	15/14	830	58	38	680	4	66%	+5.3	4	17.9	14.0	18	6.3	6	+1.4	2	18.0%	11	145	34	158	11.4%	87	56%
2017	NE	9/7	591	59	34	439	5	58%	-1.5	2	12.9	13.3	29	5.0	22	+0.9	2	2.5%	40	71	52	84	17.9%	44	73%
2018	NE	16/7	803	55	35	532	3	64%	+2.2	2	15.2	12.4	28	5.5	16	+1.1	3	14.3%	20	123	34	121	10.3%	80	66%
2019	CAR			27	17	218	2	63%			12.8							6.4%							

The mirror image of new teammate Curtis Samuel, Hogan had a top-10 37.7% DVOA from the slot and a woeful -23.4% DVOA split wide. That was the third-highest difference of any player with at least 10 targets in each role. Hogan had more slot targets than wide targets in every season in New England, but he had positive DVOA from both spots during 2017 and 2016. He will probably step right as Devin Funchess' replacement in his new team's three-wide packages, where his usage and production will depend on whether the coaches prefer the larger Hogan or the more elusive D.J. Moore in the slot role seemingly favored by both.

DeAndre Hopkins   Height: 6-1   Weight: 214   College: Clemson   Draft: 2013/1 (27)   Born: 6-Jun-1992   Age: 27   Risk: Green

Year	Team	G/GS	Snaps	Pass	Rec	Yds	TD	C%	+/-	Drop	Yd/C	aDOT	Rk	YAC	Rk	YAC+	BTkl	DVOA	Rk	DYAR	Rk	YAR	Use	Rk	Slot
2016	HOU	16/16	1086	151	78	954	4	52%	-6.1	4	12.2	11.9	44	3.3	74	-0.6	6	-9.3%	70	43	66	27	27.0%	8	35%
2017	HOU	15/15	1027	174	96	1378	13	55%	-1.7	5	14.4	13.2	31	3.7	49	-0.2	9	13.3%	22	367	4	340	37.0%	1	20%
2018	HOU	16/16	1084	163	115	1572	11	71%	+14.2	1	13.7	11.6	40	3.4	69	-0.9	10	22.6%	10	455	2	433	33.0%	1	33%
2019	HOU			163	104	1450	12	64%			13.9							11.3%							

Hopkins was probably the best wideout in the NFL last year on a pure difficulty basis—he and Michael Thomas were on the same efficiency plane, but Thomas did almost all of his damage in the slot (a much easier position to get open from), while Hopkins' slot targets were few and far between. Hopkins has perhaps the largest catch radius in the NFL, and last year he managed to drop just one pass despite an extremely difficult slate of targets. Regression will come for him in 2019, but most of it will probably be based on the target split of a potentially healthier Keke Coutee and Will Fuller. That could increase Hopkins' efficiency, particularly if Fuller is able to freeze safeties like he can when he runs full speed. Hopkins' battles with Jalen Ramsey are teaching tape for both sides of the position, and his ability to generate space outside is going to be used in coaches' film for years. Oh, he also played the last month of the season with a shoulder injury so severe that he had to go for surgery right after the Colts game. A true warrior, the only thing that Hopkins can do to increase his status now is start winning some playoff games.

Adam Humphries   Height: 5-11   Weight: 195   College: Clemson   Draft: 2015/FA   Born: 24-Jun-1993   Age: 26   Risk: Green

Year	Team	G/GS	Snaps	Pass	Rec	Yds	TD	C%	+/-	Drop	Yd/C	aDOT	Rk	YAC	Rk	YAC+	BTkl	DVOA	Rk	DYAR	Rk	YAR	Use	Rk	Slot
2016	TB	15/4	650	83	55	622	2	66%	-0.1	4	11.3	6.3	92	6.9	2	+1.6	4	-1.9%	56	68	59	77	15.6%	65	74%
2017	TB	16/3	684	83	61	631	1	73%	+4.7	2	10.3	7.1	81	4.6	33	-0.6	8	5.1%	36	112	42	99	13.8%	70	83%
2018	TB	16/10	781	105	76	816	5	72%	+0.6	3	10.7	6.4	84	5.5	20	+0.5	6	6.7%	28	152	26	154	16.7%	52	84%
2019	TEN			71	48	501	2	68%			10.4							-1.0%							

Half of Humphries' body of work was once again a steady diet of curls, out routes, and screens (52 of 105 after 40 of 83 in 2017), but he added dig routes to his repertoire last year (15, one more than curls) and was reasonably effective at all of them. Though Mike Evans looks like a better red zone receiver, Humphries actually had just as many red zone targets in 2018 and was more effective (34.1% DVOA). Reunited with Jon Robinson, who identified him as an undrafted free agent, he fills Tennessee's glaring void at slot receiver and might be able to help out DVOA's 25th-best red zone pass offense. He'll be hard-pressed to match last year's numbers on a Tennessee team likely to spend more time running the ball and less time playing from behind than last year's Buccaneers, but it's the Titans and not your fantasy team that signed him to a four-year, $36-million deal at the start of free agency.

Allen Hurns   Height: 6-3   Weight: 195   College: Miami   Draft: 2014/FA   Born: 12-Nov-1991   Age: 28   Risk: Yellow

Year	Team	G/GS	Snaps	Pass	Rec	Yds	TD	C%	+/-	Drop	Yd/C	aDOT	Rk	YAC	Rk	YAC+	BTkl	DVOA	Rk	DYAR	Rk	YAR	Use	Rk	Slot
2016	JAX	11/11	635	76	35	477	3	46%	-7.8	6	13.6	10.3	61	6.0	9	+1.1	4	-24.0%	88	-71	89	-63	17.9%	46	86%
2017	JAX	10/8	537	56	39	484	2	70%	+5.5	1	12.4	10.1	60	4.5	34	+0.5	7	20.6%	9	149	26	154	17.3%	50	82%
2018	DAL	16/7	452	35	20	295	2	57%	+1.7	1	14.8	12.2	--	3.9	--	-0.1	2	-9.3%	--	9	--	22	6.7%	--	29%
2019	DAL			18	10	116	0	56%			11.6							-12.6%							

Hurns suffered an ankle injury in the playoffs which was so gruesome that everyone forced to write about it simply called it "gruesome." He did not participate in OTAs and is not expected to return to the field until August. There was training camp buzz last year that Hurns would be the Cowboys' go-to receiver, but he was nearly invisible once the season started and got shunted down to the fourth wideout role when Amari Cooper arrived. It's wonderful that the Cowboys exercised Hurns' year-two contract option so he can be (well) paid while rehabbing, but he hasn't been a factor since that fluky 2015 Jaguars season, and he's unlikely to see significant targets this year.

Dontrelle Inman   Height: 6-3   Weight: 205   College: Virginia   Draft: 2011/FA   Born: 31-Jan-1989   Age: 30   Risk: Red

Year	Team	G/GS	Snaps	Pass	Rec	Yds	TD	C%	+/-	Drop	Yd/C	aDOT	Rk	YAC	Rk	YAC+	BTkl	DVOA	Rk	DYAR	Rk	YAR	Use	Rk	Slot
2016	SD	16/16	958	97	58	810	4	60%	+2.2	6	14.0	11.5	47	3.7	62	-0.7	5	5.5%	38	140	37	134	17.8%	47	64%
2017	2TM	12/7	457	44	25	343	1	57%	-0.4	5	13.7	13.0	--	1.2	--	-2.5	0	3.6%	--	54	--	60	11.4%	--	27%
2018	IND	9/4	372	39	28	304	3	72%	+3.3	2	10.9	10.2	--	2.1	--	-1.8	2	9.1%	--	69	--	77	11.3%	--	59%
2019	NE			19	12	138	1	63%			11.5							2.0%							

Inman is a competent though unspectacular outside receiver, so if that is what you need and are missing, he can be effective. So it was in Indianapolis, where he quickly supplanted Ryan Grant on the depth chart and was a useful part for a Colts passing game lacking quality options. Signed by the Patriots in May, he'll be on the roster bubble, and his status and role will depend on how quickly N'Keal Harry adapts to the NFL; whether Demaryius Thomas can recover from injury; and whether he or the speedier Phillip Dorsett provides more value in their role. If it doesn't work out in New England, some other team should be able to find a use for him.

Andy Isabella   Height: 5-9   Weight: 190   College: Massachusetts   Draft: 2019/2 (62)   Born: 18-Nov-1996   Age: 23   Risk: Red

Year	Team	G/GS	Snaps	Pass	Rec	Yds	TD	C%	+/-	Drop	Yd/C	aDOT	Rk	YAC	Rk	YAC+	BTkl	DVOA	Rk	DYAR	Rk	YAR	Use	Rk	Slot
2019	ARI			63	45	586	4	71%			13.0							10.0%							

After the draft, the Cardinals released war room video showing their phone call with the Dolphins that finalized the trade that sent Josh Rosen to Miami in exchange for draft picks, one of which was used to take Isabella. The video is stunning for a few reasons—it was actually Miami that started the negotiations, and Arizona only agreed because they had a chance to grab Isabella. Had Isabella not been on the board, for all we know Rosen might still be with the Cardinals right now. Regardless, the deal was done, and Arizona walked away with the man who led the NCAA with 1,698 receiving yards in 2018, then ran a 4.31 40 at the combine. Playmaker Score (see page 441) found he had a similar resume coming into the NFL as Tyler Lockett, another undersized speed demon with impressive collegiate production.

DeSean Jackson   Height: 5-9   Weight: 169   College: California   Draft: 2008/2 (49)   Born: 1-Dec-1986   Age: 33   Risk: Yellow

Year	Team	G/GS	Snaps	Pass	Rec	Yds	TD	C%	+/-	Drop	Yd/C	aDOT	Rk	YAC	Rk	YAC+	BTkl	DVOA	Rk	DYAR	Rk	YAR	Use	Rk	Slot
2016	WAS	15/15	707	100	56	1005	4	56%	+4.3	6	17.9	17.6	1	5.1	28	+0.3	4	16.4%	13	241	12	233	18.7%	44	58%
2017	TB	14/13	610	90	50	668	3	56%	+2.2	2	13.4	16.4	5	3.8	46	-0.3	1	1.6%	41	105	45	99	17.8%	45	43%
2018	TB	12/10	453	74	41	774	4	55%	+1.3	2	18.9	19.5	1	4.4	38	-0.2	3	12.2%	25	153	25	147	16.4%	53	32%
2019	PHI			95	53	835	6	56%			15.7							5.0%							

Since DeSean Jackson's initial stint in Philly, his value has not been in his own production, but in what he creates for others. Jackson has been unmatched as a deep threat for a decade now and has been instrumental to his teams' passing success. When he was in Washington, for example, then-coordinator Sean McVay often deployed Jackson out of bunch, stack, and tight sets to earn him free releases and enable him to blow the cap off of single-high defenses for open throws underneath. In Tampa Bay, though he never quite found chemistry with quarterback Jameis Winston, Jackson's vertical presense was used more outside as he helped generate space over the middle for the Bucs' big-bodied trio of Mike Evans, Cameron Brate, and O.J. Howard. Every offense Jackson played in over the past four seasons ranked top-10 in passing DVOA. Now back where he started, Jackson provides the Eagles with a deep threat they desperately needed last season.

Alshon Jeffery   Height: 6-3   Weight: 216   College: South Carolina   Draft: 2012/2 (45)   Born: 14-Feb-1990   Age: 29   Risk: Yellow

Year	Team	G/GS	Snaps	Pass	Rec	Yds	TD	C%	+/-	Drop	Yd/C	aDOT	Rk	YAC	Rk	YAC+	BTkl	DVOA	Rk	DYAR	Rk	YAR	Use	Rk	Slot
2016	CHI	12/12	692	94	52	821	2	55%	+2.3	5	15.8	13.4	23	3.7	63	-0.7	6	5.0%	42	132	40	140	22.9%	23	27%
2017	PHI	16/16	927	120	57	789	9	48%	-7.6	4	13.8	14.2	21	3.4	59	-0.4	3	-1.2%	49	108	43	115	21.8%	22	36%
2018	PHI	13/13	771	92	65	843	6	71%	+6.5	4	13.0	11.6	39	4.1	47	-0.5	11	21.1%	13	251	14	270	19.7%	33	39%
2019	PHI			116	74	945	9	64%			12.8							9.6%							

Vertical receivers are often viewed through the lens of speed, but not all of them function that way. Alshon Jeffery seldom beats his opponents in a foot race, but few receivers around the league can match his body control, aggression at the catch point, and soft hands. In fairness, he is not a deep threat in the same way DeSean Jackson or Robby Anderson are, but he is difficult to keep at bay one-on-one beyond 10 yards. He is a poster boy for the "open even when he is not" moniker. For that same reason, Jeffery is a staple for Philadelphia's situational offense. Jeffery posted the team's highest DVOAs on third and fourth down, as well as in the red zone, after also being near the top in both categories in 2017. Carson Wentz, in particular, loved to target Jeffery on third and fourth downs last season, often trusting him most near and beyond the sticks when it mattered most. Jeffery converted 14 of his 25 such targets from Wentz into first downs, good for a team-high 56 percent conversion rate among players with at least 10 targets. That kind of dependability in clutch situations gives the Eagles offense a higher baseline of play than most other offenses enjoy.

Gary Jennings

Height: 6-1			Weight: 214		College: West Virginia				Draft: 2019/4 (120)			Born: 7-Mar-1997			Age: 22	Risk: Green							

Year	Team	G/GS	Snaps	Pass	Rec	Yds	TD	C%	+/-	Drop	Yd/C	aDOT	Rk	YAC	Rk	YAC+	BTkl	DVOA	Rk	DYAR	Rk	YAR	Use	Rk	Slot
2019	SEA			46	26	368	3	57%			14.2							-8.6%							

Jennings was drafted in the fourth round this year out of West Virginia, shortly after news leaked that former Seahawks stalwart Doug Baldwin was likely to retire. While Jennings will not be expected to fully replace Baldwin (and frankly, no rookie should), he will have every opportunity to make an impact as a deep threat, as evidenced by his 17.0 yards per catch in his senior season. Jennings primarily plays in the slot, as Sports Info Solutions recorded him lined up in the slot on 81 percent of plays last season.

Diontae Johnson

Height: 5-11			Weight: 181		College: Toledo				Draft: 2019/3 (66)			Born: 5-Jul-1996			Age: 23	Risk: Red							

Year	Team	G/GS	Snaps	Pass	Rec	Yds	TD	C%	+/-	Drop	Yd/C	aDOT	Rk	YAC	Rk	YAC+	BTkl	DVOA	Rk	DYAR	Rk	YAR	Use	Rk	Slot
2019	PIT			46	30	378	3	65%			12.6							0.5%							

Johnson's collegiate stats at Toledo won't do much for you if you're hoping he's going to replace Antonio Brown anytime soon, especially not his 54 percent catch rate or 45 percent success rate. He didn't test particularly well athletically in the pre-draft process, either. But Brown was hardly a can't-miss prospect himself, and Johnson's ability to cut sharply and knack for finding open spaces are indeed reminiscent of the fellow former MAC product he is tasked to help replace. Besides, those 168 targets that are now in Oakland have to go to someone.

Julio Jones

Height: 6-3			Weight: 220		College: Alabama				Draft: 2011/1 (6)			Born: 3-Feb-1989			Age: 30	Risk: Yellow							

Year	Team	G/GS	Snaps	Pass	Rec	Yds	TD	C%	+/-	Drop	Yd/C	aDOT	Rk	YAC	Rk	YAC+	BTkl	DVOA	Rk	DYAR	Rk	YAR	Use	Rk	Slot
2016	ATL	14/14	705	129	83	1409	6	64%	+7.9	5	17.0	14.5	11	4.7	36	+0.2	9	31.7%	2	458	1	469	28.5%	5	50%
2017	ATL	16/16	766	148	88	1444	3	59%	+3.1	8	16.4	14.2	20	5.5	13	+1.1	17	13.7%	18	313	7	326	28.7%	4	51%
2018	ATL	16/16	818	170	113	1677	8	66%	+10.1	6	14.8	14.5	14	4.0	51	-0.4	13	15.9%	17	382	6	416	28.2%	5	43%
2019	ATL			160	103	1525	10	64%			14.8							16.0%							

Early last season, you might have wondered whether Jones would ever score a touchdown again. Through seven weeks, he ranked third in catches (53) and second in receiving yards (812) but couldn't find the end zone. The explanation is simple: a lack of red zone targets. He saw only three such passes come his way. Over the final 10 weeks, he saw a surge in red zone targets (his 14 were fifth-most), and—voila!—the scoring drought came to an end. Jones exploded for eight touchdowns in the Falcons' final nine games.

The only receiver in NFL history with five straight 1,400-yard seasons, he's a bargain. At $14.3 million per season, his contract ranks 12th among receivers in average annual value, according to Over The Cap. He has two years left on the deal he signed in 2015, but an extension could be in the works. Antonio Brown's reworked contract with the Raiders pays him $16.7 million per season. Jones should eclipse that.

Marvin Jones

Height: 6-2   Weight: 199   College: California   Draft: 2012/5 (166)   Born: 12-Mar-1990   Age: 29   Risk: Red

Year	Team	G/GS	Snaps	Pass	Rec	Yds	TD	C%	+/-	Drop	Yd/C	aDOT	Rk	YAC	Rk	YAC+	BTkl	DVOA	Rk	DYAR	Rk	YAR	Use	Rk	Slot
2016	DET	15/15	879	103	55	930	4	53%	-3.5	9	16.9	14.1	15	4.3	47	+0.0	7	10.9%	23	202	21	200	19.8%	38	9%
2017	DET	16/16	1005	107	61	1101	9	57%	+2.8	1	18.0	16.0	7	3.2	66	-1.2	11	33.8%	3	395	2	385	19.9%	35	21%
2018	DET	9/9	538	62	35	508	5	56%	-0.6	1	14.5	15.5	9	3.1	74	-0.6	3	15.7%	18	142	29	134	20.5%	30	23%
2019	DET			109	65	916	6	60%			14.1							8.3%							

Jones' season was cut short with a knee injury suffered in a Week 10 showdown with the Chicago Bears. To that point, the Lions' passing offense had been serviceable, if uninspiring, but it fell apart in his absence. Putting aside a Week 17 fluke versus a clearly defeated Packers team, just one of the Lions' final five offensive passing DVOA performances was better than Jones' last game in Chicago. Jones' injury coincided with Golden Tate being traded away shortly beforehand, but Jones' presence as the team's primary outside wide receiver was crucial in opening up space over the middle. Jones held the fourth-lowest slot ratio among 84 qualifying receivers after finishing sixth-lowest among 86 qualifying receivers the year before, finishing with team-leading DVOAs from a wide position both seasons. As the Lions' skill group is now refurbished with multiple tight ends and slot receivers who can work the middle of the field and underneath area, a healthy Jones to stretch and threaten the boundary will be a boon to a Detroit offense eager to rebound.

Zay Jones

Height: 6-2   Weight: 201   College: East Carolina   Draft: 2017/2 (37)   Born: 30-Mar-1995   Age: 24   Risk: Green

Year	Team	G/GS	Snaps	Pass	Rec	Yds	TD	C%	+/-	Drop	Yd/C	aDOT	Rk	YAC	Rk	YAC+	BTkl	DVOA	Rk	DYAR	Rk	YAR	Use	Rk	Slot
2017	BUF	15/10	793	74	27	316	2	36%	-11.8	3	11.7	13.1	32	2.3	81	-1.4	1	-35.2%	86	-131	86	-119	16.8%	53	32%
2018	BUF	16/15	941	102	56	652	7	55%	-6.2	4	11.6	12.5	27	2.5	82	-1.9	3	-15.5%	72	-22	71	-11	21.4%	27	57%
2019	BUF			60	33	389	2	55%			11.8							-12.4%							

In his first two NFL seasons, Jones has caught 50 percent of his passes, once you remove tipped balls and plays where the quarterback was hit when he was throwing. That would be fine if Jones was an excellent deep threat, but, well, he's not. Taking into account down, distance, and spot on the field, the average receiver would have caught 60.8 percent of Jones' targets. That's a plus-minus of -18.0, the worst over the last two years by leaps and bounds. It's true that Jones hasn't had the world's most accurate passes thrown to him, and his plus-minus did improve from last in the league as a rookie to seventh worst in 2018. Still, at some point, you have to run out of excuses and start actually hanging on to some passes.

Jermaine Kearse

Height: 6-1   Weight: 209   College: Washington   Draft: 2012/FA   Born: 6-Feb-1990   Age: 29   Risk: Green

Year	Team	G/GS	Snaps	Pass	Rec	Yds	TD	C%	+/-	Drop	Yd/C	aDOT	Rk	YAC	Rk	YAC+	BTkl	DVOA	Rk	DYAR	Rk	YAR	Use	Rk	Slot
2016	SEA	16/15	828	89	41	510	1	46%	-5.3	3	12.4	11.9	40	3.4	71	-1.4	7	-28.7%	91	-114	92	-90	16.0%	62	44%
2017	NYJ	16/14	880	102	65	810	5	64%	+3.8	5	12.5	9.1	71	4.4	40	+0.0	6	5.2%	35	146	30	133	20.7%	28	69%
2018	NYJ	14/9	626	76	37	371	1	49%	-12.6	2	10.0	9.4	59	3.4	68	-0.9	2	-28.8%	82	-95	80	-130	17.2%	49	86%
2019	DET			19	11	107	0	58%			9.7							-19.7%							

Kearse went 16-262-1 during a wild two-game stretch in 2017, fooling the Jets and their fans into thinking that he was more than just a high-effort, low-impact possession target in the slot. Kearse reverted to form with a vengeance last season, but the Jets kept throwing passes to him because they didn't have anyone better. Kearse figures to be a good wide receivers coach someday, but that day is not quite here yet—he signed a one-year deal with Detroit in June, reuniting with Darrell Bevell, his old offensive coordinator in Seattle.

Christian Kirk

Height: 5-10   Weight: 201   College: Texas A&M   Draft: 2018/2 (47)   Born: 18-Nov-1996   Age: 23   Risk: Red

Year	Team	G/GS	Snaps	Pass	Rec	Yds	TD	C%	+/-	Drop	Yd/C	aDOT	Rk	YAC	Rk	YAC+	BTkl	DVOA	Rk	DYAR	Rk	YAR	Use	Rk	Slot
2018	ARI	12/7	542	68	43	590	3	63%	-0.5	3	13.7	9.8	54	5.3	22	-0.1	3	-1.8%	49	57	49	57	19.2%	35	48%
2019	ARI			102	59	778	5	58%			13.2							-2.1%							

Say hello to the only good thing that happened to the Cardinals in 2018. Kirk started hot—in his first six games, he had a catch rate over 80 percent while averaging 12.4 yards per reception—before leveling off, then suffering a broken foot that ended his season. He was much more effective in the slot (22.6% DVOA) than out wide (-25.1%), with 30-some targets in both positions. He was very effective on screens, averaging 9.4 yards on 13 targets; all other Cardinals averaged 4.6 yards on screen plays. But he was also the team's best deep threat, with a catch rate of 69 percent on 14 deep passes; all other Cardinals had a catch rate of 30 percent on deep passes. Some reports said Kirk was Arizona's best receiver in OTAs, and though everyone on this team is going to get some catches, Kirk likely has the highest ceiling in 2019.

Cooper Kupp

Height: 6-2   Weight: 204   College: Eastern Washington   Draft: 2017/3 (69)   Born: 15-Jun-1993   Age: 26   Risk: Yellow

Year	Team	G/GS	Snaps	Pass	Rec	Yds	TD	C%	+/-	Drop	Yd/C	aDOT	Rk	YAC	Rk	YAC+	BTkl	DVOA	Rk	DYAR	Rk	YAR	Use	Rk	Slot
2017	LAR	15/6	740	92	62	869	5	65%	+3.3	7	14.0	9.8	66	6.0	10	+1.7	15	24.8%	4	272	10	266	19.4%	39	94%
2018	LAR	8/8	439	55	40	566	6	73%	+3.9	1	14.2	7.4	79	7.6	2	+2.2	8	23.8%	7	158	23	154	19.9%	31	100%
2019	LAR			111	73	986	8	66%			13.5							13.8%							

The injury that cut short his 2018 season robbed Kupp of a chance to rack up hefty totals, but he was still quite efficient when he was on the field. Kupp was at his best on third and fourth downs, finishing with 63.0% DVOA and 13.3 yards per pass. When Kupp was out of the lineup, it certainly showed in the Rams' overall offensive output, as all five of Los Angeles' games with negative offensive DVOA took place with Kupp injured. He should be fully recovered from his torn ACL by the start of the regular season, which bodes well for the Rams offense moving forward. Kupp is eligible for a contract extension after the 2019 season; barring any lasting influence from his knee injury, he should be a key cog in the Los Angeles offense for years to come.

Jarvis Landry

Height: 5-11   Weight: 205   College: Louisiana State   Draft: 2014/2 (63)   Born: 11/28/1992   Age: 27   Risk: Green

Year	Team	G/GS	Snaps	Pass	Rec	Yds	TD	C%	+/-	Drop	Yd/C	aDOT	Rk	YAC	Rk	YAC+	BTkl	DVOA	Rk	DYAR	Rk	YAR	Use	Rk	Slot
2016	MIA	16/16	892	131	94	1136	4	72%	+6.2	5	12.1	6.6	89	6.6	4	+1.2	30	4.8%	43	174	26	190	27.8%	7	79%
2017	MIA	16/16	932	161	112	987	9	70%	+1.8	7	8.8	6.4	83	4.4	37	-0.7	15	-4.9%	59	98	46	75	27.3%	9	76%
2018	CLE	16/14	957	149	81	976	4	54%	-7.9	6	12.0	11.7	36	3.4	67	-1.6	9	-22.2%	79	-111	83	-121	26.6%	9	75%
2019	CLE			122	76	917	6	62%			12.1							1.4%							

In the wake of the stunning trade that brought his old LSU running mate to Cleveland, there was a lot of chatter about how Landry is on a par just below Odell Beckham as a wideout. Landry's continued rep as a top-flight receiver is Elizabeth Holmes-level fraudulence.

Among receivers with fifty or more targets, only Golden Tate, who cycled across two teams and is now on a third, produced a worse DYAR. Landry was not only miles away from Beckham but also from unheralded teammate Rashard Higgins, 28th overall in DYAR to Beckham's 27th. On third down, supposedly where Landry proves his worth, and where in his last two seasons in Miami he edged into positive DVOA, his 2018 split was brutal, with -21.4% DVOA. Every Brown with four or more red zone targets had a positive DVOA on those plays except Landry, who had 10 more close-in targets and was -34.0% on them. And while his target rate remained high, his catch rate dipped alarmingly. His broken tackles total has also dropped for two straight years. At least the wideout known for catching an 8-yard pass on third-and-10 increased his aDOT, though with Beckham in town Landry is even more likely to work the patch of grass just beyond the line of scrimmage going forward.

Cody Latimer

Height: 6-2   Weight: 215   College: Indiana   Draft: 2014/2 (56)   Born: 10-Oct-1992   Age: 27   Risk: Yellow

Year	Team	G/GS	Snaps	Pass	Rec	Yds	TD	C%	+/-	Drop	Yd/C	aDOT	Rk	YAC	Rk	YAC+	BTkl	DVOA	Rk	DYAR	Rk	YAR	Use	Rk	Slot
2016	DEN	12/1	217	15	8	76	0	53%	-0.6	0	9.5	13.1	--	3.0	--	-1.5	0	-10.9%	--	2	--	0	3.8%	--	31%
2017	DEN	11/1	376	31	19	287	2	61%	+2.4	1	15.1	11.6	--	3.4	--	-0.7	1	21.9%	--	88	--	88	8.1%	--	61%
2018	NYG	6/2	209	16	11	190	1	69%	+2.7	0	17.3	19.9	--	2.1	--	-3.0	0	19.7%	--	40	--	42	7.3%	--	25%
2019	NYG			20	11	141	1	55%			12.8							-9.1%							

There was a ton of noise from Broncos media about how good Latimer was and how he just needed a chance, but Latimer never got a real shake in Denver. Latimer averaged 15.3 targets per year for the Broncos for the duration of his rookie deal, despite being a second-round pick and the depth chart in front of him including guys like Jordan Norwood and Andre Caldwell. He also was out-targeted by Bennie Fowler, which probably made it extra satisfying for Latimer when he won the third receiver job in New York last year—only to get hurt and cede playing time to Fowler over the second half of the season. We hope you appreciate the lengths we've gone to fully flesh out the Bennie Fowler-Cody Latimer war that will rock your Twitter feed in

August. (We'd run with Latimer and give him a real chance, but the Giants will probably target their third receiver about 50 times total this year.)

Marqise Lee Height: 6-0 Weight: 192 College: USC Draft: 2014/2 (39) Born: 11/25/1991 Age: 28 Risk: Yellow

Year	Team	G/GS	Snaps	Pass	Rec	Yds	TD	C%	+/-	Drop	Yd/C	aDOT	Rk	YAC	Rk	YAC+	BTkl	DVOA	Rk	DYAR	Rk	YAR	Use	Rk	Slot
2016	JAX	16/6	817	105	63	851	3	60%	-0.7	5	13.5	12.3	36	5.5	14	+1.0	10	12.2%	18	211	19	192	17.0%	55	40%
2017	JAX	14/14	738	96	56	702	3	58%	+0.8	9	12.5	11.6	45	5.2	20	+0.8	14	3.0%	39	119	38	115	21.5%	23	48%
2019	JAX			93	59	766	3	63%			13.0							4.3%							

A torn ACL ended Lee's season before it began, and Doug Marrone did not expect Lee to be back before the start of training camp. It would be best to take a wait-and-see approach on his health before you go banking on his comeback in fantasy football leagues. Not a thing is owed to Lee after this season as far as guaranteed money on his four-year, $34-million contract, so there is a lot of incentive for him to get back in there. The drag routes he was so successful at in 2017 will probably be more of Dede Westbrook's role in the offense, and while Lee can play outside receiver, we don't have any untainted (read: non-Bortles) data on how he performs there. Lee comes into the year as a known unknown, but he has enough skill to be a solid No. 2 if healthy.

Tyler Lockett Height: 5-10 Weight: 182 College: Kansas State Draft: 2015/3 (69) Born: 28-Sep-1992 Age: 27 Risk: Green

Year	Team	G/GS	Snaps	Pass	Rec	Yds	TD	C%	+/-	Drop	Yd/C	aDOT	Rk	YAC	Rk	YAC+	BTkl	DVOA	Rk	DYAR	Rk	YAR	Use	Rk	Slot
2016	SEA	15/9	558	68	41	597	1	63%	-0.1	2	14.6	10.8	55	5.7	12	-0.2	3	5.5%	39	99	52	105	13.3%	74	44%
2017	SEA	16/8	692	71	45	555	2	63%	+2.5	1	12.3	12.7	35	4.2	42	-1.0	8	-3.4%	54	48	60	68	13.2%	71	68%
2018	SEA	16/14	908	70	57	965	10	81%	+17.7	0	16.9	15.9	5	3.7	58	-1.5	7	66.3%	1	464	1	458	18.5%	39	58%
2019	SEA			96	62	939	10	65%			15.1							21.6%							

Perhaps no receiver on the Seahawks better epitomized the team's passing approach than Lockett in 2018. While he did not see much in the way of volume (only 4.4 targets per game), he was the team's primary deep threat and made those opportunities count in a major way. Lockett's ability to stretch the field deep resulted in him not only leading the league in receiving DVOA and DYAR in 2018, but posting the best receiving DVOA we have ever measured, dating back to 1986.

Best WR Single-Season Receiving DVOA, 1986-2018

Player	Year	Team	DVOA	Pass	Rec	C%	Yards	Yd/Rec	TD	Fum
Tyler Lockett	**2018**	**SEA**	**66.3%**	**70**	**57**	**81%**	**965**	**16.9**	**10**	**1**
Dennis Northcutt	2002	CLE	60.5%	51	40	78%	609	15.2	5	0
John Taylor	1989	SF	56.3%	75	60	80%	1077	18.0	10	1
Jordy Nelson	2011	GB	52.9%	96	68	71%	1263	18.6	15	0
Malcom Floyd	2011	SD	51.9%	70	43	61%	856	19.9	5	0
Tim Dwight	1999	ATL	51.8%	50	32	64%	669	20.9	7	0
John Taylor	1993	SF	51.3%	74	56	76%	940	16.8	5	1
Mike Wallace	2010	PIT	49.5%	89	60	61%	966	16.1	10	1
Ricky Proehl	2001	STL	47.5%	55	40	73%	563	14.1	5	0
Az-Zahir Hakim	1999	STL	46.9%	56	36	64%	677	18.8	8	0
Eric Martin	1987	NO	45.5%	49	30	61%	572	19.1	4	0
Minimum 50 passes.										

Betting on his efficiency numbers to decrease is probably the safest bet in the league this season, but he has a good chance to tally some larger counting stats (outside of touchdowns) now that Doug Baldwin has retired. Lockett is moving into the No. 1 receiver role and will play more out of Baldwin's former position in the slot. His continued connection with Russell Wilson will be critical for Seattle's passing attack to remain successful.

Jordan Matthews

Height: 6-3   Weight: 212   College: Vanderbilt   Draft: 2014/2 (42)   Born: 7/16/1992   Age: 27   Risk: Red

Year	Team	G/GS	Snaps	Pass	Rec	Yds	TD	C%	+/-	Drop	Yd/C	aDOT	Rk	YAC	Rk	YAC+	BTkl	DVOA	Rk	DYAR	Rk	YAR	Use	Rk	Slot
2016	PHI	14/13	844	117	73	804	3	62%	+0.8	10	11.0	10.1	62	3.2	75	-1.8	5	-13.2%	76	-4	76	2	22.1%	27	75%
2017	BUF	10/7	509	36	25	282	1	69%	+1.6	2	11.3	7.3	--	5.0	--	+1.1	3	-0.6%	--	33	--	32	12.1%	--	92%
2018	PHI	14/3	344	28	20	300	2	71%	+2.4	1	15.0	10.6	--	4.2	--	-0.7	4	28.8%	--	84	--	86	5.3%	--	39%
2019	SF			9	5	55	0	56%			11.1							-14.2%							

Had Matthews known that San Francisco was going to draft Deebo Samuel and Jalen Hurd, he likely would have signed elsewhere, with a team where he would have more job security. Alas, he is trapped in Santa Clara after joining a new team for the fourth time in three years. He originally signed with New England in 2018, but was cut in August, then re-signed with Philadelphia in September. His second tenure with the Eagles did not end well—he caught only four passes in his final six games last year, for a measly total of 23 yards. With a long injury history and little upside, Matthews will need a blowaway training camp to stick on a depth chart that's much more crowded now than it was during free agency.

Terry McLaurin

Height: 6-0   Weight: 202   College: Ohio State   Draft: 2019/3 (76)   Born: 15-Apr-1996   Age: 23   Risk: Yellow

Year	Team	G/GS	Snaps	Pass	Rec	Yds	TD	C%	+/-	Drop	Yd/C	aDOT	Rk	YAC	Rk	YAC+	BTkl	DVOA	Rk	DYAR	Rk	YAR	Use	Rk	Slot
2019	WAS			32	19	293	2	59%			15.4							-1.2%							

McLaurin may have had the best pre-draft season in modern draft history. He left Ohio State with just 35 catches in his senior season and a rep as a high-effort special teams guy. He then proved to be uncoverable at the Senior Bowl and sounded like a cross between an offensive coordinator and a junior city councilman in media interviews. He later ran a 4.35-second 40 at the combine, with other fine workout measurables, landing him squarely in the Day 2 draft conversation. The problem with McLaurin is that his game film isn't very good, despite having played with current teammate Dwayne Haskins in a receiver-friendly offense. As impressive as McLaurin is as an athlete and a dude, the Skins may have drafted the next Darrius Heyward-Bey: a guy with speed, brains, and dedication who maxes out as the special teams captain. At least they didn't take him eighth overall.

D.K. Metcalf

Height: 6-4   Weight: 225   College: Mississippi   Draft: 2019/2 (64)   Born: 14-Dec-1997   Age: 22   Risk: Red

Year	Team	G/GS	Snaps	Pass	Rec	Yds	TD	C%	+/-	Drop	Yd/C	aDOT	Rk	YAC	Rk	YAC+	BTkl	DVOA	Rk	DYAR	Rk	YAR	Use	Rk	Slot
2019	SEA			76	44	665	4	58%			15.1							-3.3%							

Metcalf enters the league as an incredibly polarizing receiver prospect after being drafted in the second round from Ole Miss. His supporters see a special athlete (6-foot-3, 228 pounds with a 4.33-second 40-yard dash, 40.5-inch vertical jump, and 27 bench press reps) capable of beating a press corner deep for a touchdown on any given snap. His detractors will point out his poor change-of-direction testing (7.38 seconds in the 3-cone drill and 4.5 seconds in the 20-yard shuttle at the combine), limited route tree, and injury history, as well as the fact that he was not the most productive receiver on his college team, thanks to the presence of fellow second-round pick A.J. Brown. His skill set as a deep threat makes for a good match with Russell Wilson's penchant for chucking it long, and his primary competition for targets will be David Moore, who has exceeded normal expectations for a seventh-round pick but is still far from a sure thing. Time will tell whether Metcalf becomes a star or another Darrius Heyward-Bey, but for 2019, he has a great chance to make an impact playing alongside incumbent No. 1 receiver Tyler Lockett.

Anthony Miller

Height: 5-11   Weight: 201   College: Memphis   Draft: 2018/2 (51)   Born: 9-Oct-1994   Age: 25   Risk: Green

Year	Team	G/GS	Snaps	Pass	Rec	Yds	TD	C%	+/-	Drop	Yd/C	aDOT	Rk	YAC	Rk	YAC+	BTkl	DVOA	Rk	DYAR	Rk	YAR	Use	Rk	Slot
2018	CHI	15/4	576	54	33	423	7	61%	-2.0	4	12.8	11.8	35	5.2	24	+0.4	4	3.9%	36	71	46	87	11.4%	77	82%
2019	CHI			70	44	551	6	63%			12.5							2.5%							

Though other options are on the roster, Matt Nagy appears set on Miller as the team's primary slot receiver. Miller is not a burner down the field, but he plays with the pace and body control of a veteran slot receiver. He knows how to work himself open into space, whether that means adjusting his route stem to the coverage or properly diagnosing where a zone is going to open up. While his overall DVOA out of the slot was slightly negative, Miller was the team's most "clutch" receiver, for lack of better phrasing. On third and fourth down, as well as in the red zone, Miller posted the best DVOA on the team among wide receivers, and trailed only Tarik Cohen in the red zone among all Bears players. Additionally, Miller often has his way with defenders, earning himself a top-20 spot in YAC+ for 2018, one of four rookies to do so. Miller may not provide the same vertical presence out of the slot that Taylor Gabriel could, but the consistency and reliability that he provides is a strong baseline to build on as he develops into one of the league's most complete slot receivers.

Donte Moncrief

Height: 6-2 Weight: 221 College: Mississippi Draft: 2014/3 (90) Born: 6-Aug-1993 Age: 26 Risk: Yellow

Year	Team	G/GS	Snaps	Pass	Rec	Yds	TD	C%	+/-	Drop	Yd/C	aDOT	Rk	YAC	Rk	YAC+	BTkl	DVOA	Rk	DYAR	Rk	YAR	Use	Rk	Slot
2016	IND	9/7	468	56	30	307	7	54%	-2.9	3	10.2	10.6	58	2.6	89	-1.1	4	-1.9%	58	50	63	49	17.4%	53	58%
2017	IND	12/8	614	47	26	391	2	55%	+3.0	4	15.0	14.6	--	3.0	--	-0.7	3	11.4%	--	94	--	88	13.5%	--	19%
2018	JAX	16/14	815	89	48	668	3	54%	-5.3	4	13.9	13.1	21	5.0	26	+0.4	4	-14.8%	69	-14	70	0	16.9%	51	38%
2019	PIT			91	55	740	5	60%			13.5							4.2%							

Moncrief's career has been fairly predictable thus far. In any given year he will catch about half his targets, most of them thrown by a replacement-level quarterback, while turning a couple of passes into long touchdowns and struggling with injuries. Just 25, Moncrief remains a big-play threat, and he managed to stay healthy all of last year while toiling away in Bortlesville. Setting him free in Pittsburgh while letting him streak under Ben Roethlisberger's throws seems like a welcome change, and if good health continues Moncrief would be a strong late-round fantasy play.

Chris Moore

Height: 6-1 Weight: 206 College: Cincinnati Draft: 2016/4 (107) Born: 16-Jun-1993 Age: 26 Risk: Green

Year	Team	G/GS	Snaps	Pass	Rec	Yds	TD	C%	+/-	Drop	Yd/C	aDOT	Rk	YAC	Rk	YAC+	BTkl	DVOA	Rk	DYAR	Rk	YAR	Use	Rk	Slot
2016	BAL	15/0	162	16	7	46	0	44%	-3.8	3	6.6	8.6	--	2.7	--	-2.1	0	-66.1%	--	-68	--	-63	2.5%	--	88%
2017	BAL	13/4	375	38	18	248	3	47%	-1.5	4	13.8	13.2	--	2.3	--	-0.9	3	-14.1%	--	-4	--	-5	8.3%	--	34%
2018	BAL	16/0	467	25	19	196	1	76%	+3.0	0	10.3	11.2	--	3.1	--	-2.5	3	2.5%	--	28	--	23	4.5%	--	48%
2019	BAL			28	16	187	1	57%			11.7							-9.3%							

Moore and punter Sam Koch have hooked up for two deep completions on fake punts in the last two years, and Moore brings obvious speed to the field. Moore grew a bit as a receiver last year, getting some work underneath and catching more than 50 percent of his targets for the first time. Unfortunately for Moore, the Ravens drafted two receivers in the first three rounds, and Jordan Lasley and Jaleel Scott are also lingering on the depth chart. Moore enters the final year of his rookie deal as a long-speed returner and fringe receiver, so even if he doesn't develop further, that combination should draw some interest on the market. Lamar Jackson's development will be important for any breakout predictions, such as the one made by Ravens owner Steve Bisciotti on his team's website.

D.J. Moore

Height: 6-0 Weight: 210 College: Maryland Draft: 2018/1 (24) Born: 14-Apr-1997 Age: 22 Risk: Green

Year	Team	G/GS	Snaps	Pass	Rec	Yds	TD	C%	+/-	Drop	Yd/C	aDOT	Rk	YAC	Rk	YAC+	BTkl	DVOA	Rk	DYAR	Rk	YAR	Use	Rk	Slot
2018	CAR	16/10	732	82	55	788	2	67%	+1.2	1	14.3	8.6	70	7.7	1	+2.2	27	4.1%	35	109	38	126	15.4%	61	35%
2019	CAR			114	71	938	7	62%			13.2							7.7%							

Moore is a yards-after-catch machine in Norv Turner's offense: more than half of his yards came after the catch, and he and Quincy Enunwa were the only receivers to average over 7.0 YAC regardless of whether they lined up in the slot or split wide. Moore's 16.7% DVOA and 87 percent catch rate from the slot suggest that the Panthers should use him there more than they did last year (only 30 of his 83 targets came from the slot), but the difference in his numbers when split wide may be misleading: Moore saw a massive decline in his deep numbers, from 69.4% to -10.9% DVOA, following Week 9—the same period in which Cam Newton's shoulder injury flared up.

The decline in Moore's efficiency when split wide may well say more about Newton's fading arm than Moore's own performance outside the hash marks. We'll have a clearer idea what the coaching staff thinks this September: Moore is probably the most talented of Carolina's current receiving options, particularly in the open field, so the priority should probably be getting him where he can do the most damage before allocating the other players' roles accordingly.

David Moore

| | Height: 6-2 | Weight: 225 | College: East Central (OK) | | Draft: 2017/7 (226) | | Born: 15-Jan-1995 | | Age: 24 | Risk: Green |

Year	Team	G/GS	Snaps	Pass	Rec	Yds	TD	C%	+/-	Drop	Yd/C	aDOT	Rk	YAC	Rk	YAC+	BTkl	DVOA	Rk	DYAR	Rk	YAR	Use	Rk	Slot
2018	SEA	16/7	620	53	26	445	5	49%	-3.5	1	17.1	15.6	7	3.6	62	-1.2	5	-7.4%	57	20	58	21	12.9%	72	4%
2019	SEA			51	30	425	6	59%			14.2							7.8%							

The former seventh-round pick usurped veteran Brandon Marshall as the third receiver in Seattle's run-first offense, serving primarily as a deep threat down the field with a limited route tree. Moore's production faded down the stretch as defenses got more tape on him, but he enters 2019 with a great opportunity to become more than just a fast guy told to run go routes. With Doug Baldwin gone, there is a sizable hole in Seattle's receiving corps, and Moore will have the chance to earn a role as the No. 2 receiver behind Tyler Lockett. He has competition from a host of rookies, including second-round pick D.K. Metcalf, but Moore's past experience playing with Russell Wilson could initially give him a leg up on the young guns.

Jordy Nelson

| | Height: 6-2 | Weight: 217 | College: Kansas State | | Draft: 2008/2 (36) | | Born: 31-May-1985 | | Age: 34 | Risk: N/A |

Year	Team	G/GS	Snaps	Pass	Rec	Yds	TD	C%	+/-	Drop	Yd/C	aDOT	Rk	YAC	Rk	YAC+	BTkl	DVOA	Rk	DYAR	Rk	YAR	Use	Rk	Slot
2016	GB	16/16	1015	152	97	1257	14	64%	+7.6	9	13.0	12.6	32	3.7	61	+0.1	3	19.2%	8	382	3	366	24.6%	16	44%
2017	GB	15/15	806	89	53	482	6	60%	+1.5	3	9.1	11.5	47	2.4	80	-1.5	3	-5.0%	60	58	57	49	17.3%	51	47%
2018	OAK	15/14	845	88	63	739	3	72%	+6.8	1	11.7	9.4	60	3.8	55	-1.0	5	5.7%	32	130	31	114	17.9%	44	44%

For someone supposedly washed up, Nelson had a pretty good final year in Oakland. While obviously no longer the same player who was a touchdown machine in Green Bay, Nelson ended his career with 78 DYAR and a 7.4% DVOA in December, finishing that last month as a top-20 receiver once more. He's lost a step, and it's probably for the best that he's retired now rather than going to camp and fighting for a third receiver slot somewhere, but if an injury occurs somewhere, Nelson wouldn't be the worst guy to call.

DeVante Parker

| | Height: 6-3 | Weight: 209 | College: Louisville | | Draft: 2015/1 (14) | | Born: 20-Jan-1993 | | Age: 26 | Risk: Red |

Year	Team	G/GS	Snaps	Pass	Rec	Yds	TD	C%	+/-	Drop	Yd/C	aDOT	Rk	YAC	Rk	YAC+	BTkl	DVOA	Rk	DYAR	Rk	YAR	Use	Rk	Slot
2016	MIA	15/8	736	88	56	744	4	64%	+4.6	3	13.3	12.5	33	4.2	50	-0.2	6	7.8%	31	141	36	141	20.4%	35	14%
2017	MIA	13/12	678	96	57	670	1	59%	+0.4	3	11.8	12.5	37	3.7	51	-1.0	3	-11.0%	70	12	69	6	20.0%	32	14%
2018	MIA	11/7	411	48	24	309	1	52%	-3.1	1	12.9	13.6	--	3.9	--	-1.1	2	-26.6%	--	-52	--	-59	15.8%	--	15%
2019	MIA			103	58	748	5	56%			12.9							-7.3%							

Welcome to Parker's fifth scholarship year! Parker battled shoulder and quad injuries last year, was a healthy scratch in some games and the fourth receiver in others as the Dolphins appeared to finally lose patience with the former first-round pick. But the new regime signed Parker to a two-year contract, perhaps assuming that Parker's problems were exacerbated by being trapped in Adam Gase's labyrinthine doghouse. Parker still looks like DeAndre Hopkins during minicamps and pregame warmups, so he's worth one more long look to see if he figures things out. Wait … didn't we write that last year?

Zach Pascal

| | Height: 6-2 | Weight: 219 | College: Old Dominion | | Draft: 2017/FA | | Born: 18-Dec-1994 | | Age: 25 | Risk: Red |

Year	Team	G/GS	Snaps	Pass	Rec	Yds	TD	C%	+/-	Drop	Yd/C	aDOT	Rk	YAC	Rk	YAC+	BTkl	DVOA	Rk	DYAR	Rk	YAR	Use	Rk	Slot
2018	IND	16/4	527	46	27	268	2	59%	-2.8	2	9.9	8.9	--	3.0	--	-1.4	2	-20.5%	--	-28	--	-25	7.1%	--	48%
2019	IND			6	4	39	0	67%			9.7							-5.5%							

"Giving over 500 snaps to a UDFA Titans castoff" is a sign of how desperate the Colts were at receiver. Pascal did most of his work in the two regular season games against the Texans, with 11 catches for 124 yards and two touchdowns. He had a 13.3% DVOA against Houston and a -39.2% DVOA against the rest of the league. The offseason additions make him WR4 at best, and Deon Cain looks like the heavy favorite for that role after missing all of last season.

Tim Patrick

Height: 6-5   Weight: 205   College: Utah   Draft: 2017/FA   Born: 23-Nov-1993   Age: 26   Risk: Red

Year	Team	G/GS	Snaps	Pass	Rec	Yds	TD	C%	+/-	Drop	Yd/C	aDOT	Rk	YAC	Rk	YAC+	BTkl	DVOA	Rk	DYAR	Rk	YAR	Use	Rk	Slot
2018	DEN	16/4	393	41	23	315	1	56%	-1.9	2	13.7	10.7	--	4.9	--	+0.1	0	-17.6%	--	-16	--	-20	7.2%	--	44%
2019	DEN			62	35	420	1	56%			12.0							-12.1%							

Patrick got his first NFL opportunity in Denver's December depleted receiving corps and stood out. His -13.9% DVOA that month was basically tied with Courtland Sutton as the top wideout on the team, and he actually led Denver in receiving yards down the stretch. The fact that a double-digit negative DVOA led the Broncos is an indictment of that December attack, but Patrick legitimately impressed considering the circumstances. If Emmanuel Sanders starts the season on PUP as expected, Patrick will likely be the third receiver.

Cordarrelle Patterson

Height: 6-2   Weight: 216   College: Tennessee   Draft: 2013/1 (29)   Born: 17-Mar-1991   Age: 28   Risk: Green

Year	Team	G/GS	Snaps	Pass	Rec	Yds	TD	C%	+/-	Drop	Yd/C	aDOT	Rk	YAC	Rk	YAC+	BTkl	DVOA	Rk	DYAR	Rk	YAR	Use	Rk	Slot
2016	MIN	16/8	531	70	52	453	2	74%	+3.5	2	8.7	4.7	94	6.4	5	+0.4	19	-9.5%	71	17	71	28	12.0%	84	49%
2017	OAK	16/2	431	42	31	309	0	74%	+1.5	1	10.0	5.5	--	6.3	--	+0.6	14	-7.4%	--	17	--	5	7.7%	--	42%
2018	NE	15/5	230	28	21	247	3	75%	+0.7	1	11.8	6.2	--	7.7	--	+0.9	11	0.6%	--	29	--	32	5.3%	--	46%
2019	CHI			13	9	82	1	69%			9.1							-6.3%							

One day there will be a conversation about Patterson being the best kick returner of all time. For now, what is most important for Patterson is how much he can contribute to the Bears aside from returning kicks. Though he has not made good on his first-round status as a typical wide receiver, Patterson has earned a reputation as an effective gadget weapon. When Patterson first left Minnesota for Oakland in 2017, the Raiders experimented with him at running back to get him touches instead of using him primarily as a jet player like the Vikings tended to. The following year, New England took it a step further by embracing him as a running back for certain matchups, in addition to his regular gadget role on end-arounds and screens. Now paired with a spread offensive mind in Matt Nagy, Patterson should get a fair amount of opportunities to show off his electric potential in space. Alongside Tarik Cohen, another hybrid runner/receiver, the Bears can cook up some unique packages to overwhelm defenses.

Breshad Perriman

Height: 6-2   Weight: 212   College: UCF   Draft: 2015/1 (26)   Born: 10-Sep-1993   Age: 26   Risk: Yellow

Year	Team	G/GS	Snaps	Pass	Rec	Yds	TD	C%	+/-	Drop	Yd/C	aDOT	Rk	YAC	Rk	YAC+	BTkl	DVOA	Rk	DYAR	Rk	YAR	Use	Rk	Slot
2016	BAL	16/1	484	66	33	499	3	50%	-5.9	5	15.1	14.3	12	5.2	25	+0.6	2	-8.7%	67	21	70	20	10.3%	90	25%
2017	BAL	11/3	387	35	10	77	0	29%	-7.8	3	7.7	14.4	--	0.5	--	-4.0	0	-71.8%	--	-158	--	-150	9.0%	--	22%
2018	CLE	10/2	218	25	16	340	2	64%	+2.2	0	21.3	18.4	--	4.7	--	-0.4	1	36.6%	--	97	--	86	7.1%	--	28%
2019	TB			71	40	563	4	56%			14.1							0.5%							

Sixteen catches and no drops? After three tumultuous seasons in Baltimore, Perriman lands in Cleveland and suddenly becomes Mr. Reliable? What a turnaround. A year ago, he was barely in this book. Now, Tampa Bay is hoping he can replace DeSean Jackson. The Buccaneers are paying Perriman half of what they would have been paying Jackson, but here's the catch: they're also getting half the player. Perriman's hands and Jameis Winston's arm seem like a less than ideal match.

Dante Pettis

Height: 6-0   Weight: 186   College: Washington   Draft: 2018/2 (44)   Born: 23-Oct-1995   Age: 24   Risk: Red

Year	Team	G/GS	Snaps	Pass	Rec	Yds	TD	C%	+/-	Drop	Yd/C	aDOT	Rk	YAC	Rk	YAC+	BTkl	DVOA	Rk	DYAR	Rk	YAR	Use	Rk	Slot
2018	SF	12/7	452	45	27	467	5	60%	+1.0	1	17.3	11.1	--	7.6	--	+3.0	7	16.8%	--	109	--	114	12.2%	--	63%
2019	SF			93	48	778	6	52%			16.2							1.1%							

In his first eight NFL games, Pettis only caught seven passes for 108 yards and a touchdown. He caught fire late, however—from Weeks 12 to 15, he was among the NFL's top-10 wide receivers with 338 receiving yards and four touchdowns. His best game came in Seattle, where he had starred for the University of Washington; he burned the Seahawks for five catches, 129 yards, and two touchdowns, including a 75-yard gallop that was his longest catch of the year. The 49ers' depth chart is nearly as crowded and convoluted at wide receiver as it is at running back, but Pettis has as good a chance as anyone to be their top wideout this fall.

Trey Quinn   Height: 5-11   Weight: 203   College: Southern Methodist   Draft: 2018/7 (256)   Born: 7-Dec-1995   Age: 24   Risk: Yellow

Year	Team	G/GS	Snaps	Pass	Rec	Yds	TD	C%	+/-	Drop	Yd/C	aDOT	Rk	YAC	Rk	YAC+	BTkl	DVOA	Rk	DYAR	Rk	YAR	Use	Rk	Slot
2018	WAS	3/2	107	10	9	75	1	90%	+2.1	0	8.3	7.3	--	1.9	--	-2.1	0	14.9%	--	22	--	22	10.8%	--	90%
2019	WAS			59	36	380	1	61%			10.6							-13.1%							

Quinn may have been Mr. Irrelevant at the end of the 2018 draft, but he's no longer irrelevant when it comes to Washington's depth chart at wide receiver. Although he's a low-round draft pick who missed most of his rookie year with an ankle injury, Washington has Quinn penciled in to replace Jamison Crowder as the starting slot receiver this season. Quinn has quite a history, setting the national high school receiving yards record at Brabe High School in Louisiana and leading FBS with 114 receptions in 2017. He counters his limited size and speed with strong hands and an understanding of how to get open in zone coverage. He's a carbon copy of the next player listed, so let's hear it for the coincidences of alphabetical order.

Hunter Renfrow   Height: 5-10   Weight: 180   College: Clemson   Draft: 2019/5 (149)   Born: 21-Dec-1995   Age: 24   Risk: Red

Year	Team	G/GS	Snaps	Pass	Rec	Yds	TD	C%	+/-	Drop	Yd/C	aDOT	Rk	YAC	Rk	YAC+	BTkl	DVOA	Rk	DYAR	Rk	YAR	Use	Rk	Slot
2019	OAK			51	35	386	3	69%			11.0							-4.1%							

On tape, Renfrow shows good hands (including a 73 percent catch rate last season) and good instincts. At the combine, he came up small—both literally and figuratively. He's small even for a tiny slot receiver, and he only ran a 4.59 40 with mediocre agility drills. It's a big step up from ACC safeties to NFL slot corners, but Renfrow isn't lacking for competitiveness. You could do worse than being a sure-handed short-yardage guy, and there's a lot to like of Renfrow's tape, as long as you use the zoom feature.

Josh Reynolds   Height: 6-3   Weight: 194   College: Texas A&M   Draft: 2017/4 (117)   Born: 16-Feb-1995   Age: 24   Risk: Green

Year	Team	G/GS	Snaps	Pass	Rec	Yds	TD	C%	+/-	Drop	Yd/C	aDOT	Rk	YAC	Rk	YAC+	BTkl	DVOA	Rk	DYAR	Rk	YAR	Use	Rk	Slot
2017	LAR	16/1	280	24	11	104	1	46%	-3.9	0	9.5	7.4	--	3.1	--	-0.4	1	-31.0%	--	-35	--	-43	4.6%	--	79%
2018	LAR	16/8	611	53	29	402	5	55%	-1.6	2	13.9	11.7	37	4.4	37	+0.4	4	1.9%	40	62	48	52	9.6%	82	79%
2019	LAR			29	16	208	2	55%			13.0							-5.6%							

Reynolds was overshadowed by the starting receiver trio of Cooper Kupp, Brandin Cooks, and Robert Woods for the early part of his second season, but after Kupp went down for the year in Week 10, Reynolds filled his role in the lineup. Forty-one of his 53 targets came after Kupp's injury. He should serve as a valuable depth piece again in his third season.

Paul Richardson   Height: 6-0   Weight: 175   College: Colorado   Draft: 2014/2 (45)   Born: 4/13/1992   Age: 27   Risk: Yellow

Year	Team	G/GS	Snaps	Pass	Rec	Yds	TD	C%	+/-	Drop	Yd/C	aDOT	Rk	YAC	Rk	YAC+	BTkl	DVOA	Rk	DYAR	Rk	YAR	Use	Rk	Slot
2016	SEA	15/0	338	36	21	288	1	58%	+2.9	0	13.7	13.3	--	4.6	--	+0.3	1	7.9%	--	56	--	61	6.8%	--	36%
2017	SEA	16/13	816	80	44	703	6	55%	-2.3	6	16.0	15.4	10	2.8	72	-1.4	5	13.4%	20	161	23	183	15.4%	60	35%
2018	WAS	7/4	368	35	20	262	2	57%	-1.5	0	13.1	13.8	--	2.3	--	-2.0	1	4.1%	--	48	--	54	17.1%	--	56%
2019	WAS			91	47	684	5	52%			14.6							-1.7%							

The Seahawks got results from the 170-pound Richardson in past seasons by letting him run non-stop deep routes up the boundary, resulting in a Russell Wilson bomb or two per game. The Skins spent $40 million on Richardson and possessed zero quarterbacks capable of throwing deep last season, so he was used mostly on screens, hitches, and comebacks. Richardson hurt his shoulder in the season opener and his knee a few weeks later, played through the injuries for a while, caught one deep pass (a 46-yarder) by adjusting to an Alex Smith underthrow against the Panthers, and underwent shoulder surgery after the Falcons loss in November. The injured, undersized, and one-dimensional Richardson is Washington's No. 1 receiver, folks. It takes some effort to create a roster quite this discouraging.

Calvin Ridley

Height: 6-0 | Weight: 189 | College: Alabama | Draft: 2018/1 (26) | Born: 20-Dec-1994 | Age: 25 | Risk: Green

Year	Team	G/GS	Snaps	Pass	Rec	Yds	TD	C%	+/-	Drop	Yd/C	aDOT	Rk	YAC	Rk	YAC+	BTkl	DVOA	Rk	DYAR	Rk	YAR	Use	Rk	Slot
2018	ATL	16/5	644	92	64	821	10	70%	+3.9	9	12.8	10.6	47	5.7	13	+0.7	5	10.2%	26	167	21	175	15.3%	63	49%
2019	ATL			103	66	876	7	64%			13.3							10.4%							

So there's this Hall of Fame-caliber receiver who's mired in a career-long touchdown drought. Then this rookie comes along and makes scoring look easy. Football is crazy. That underscores how much of a game-changer Julio Jones is and how he creates opportunities for teammates. When defenses rolled their coverages toward Jones last season, Ridley took advantage and burst onto the NFL scene by scoring six touchdowns in his first four games. His scoring pace tailed off, but he ultimately hit the 10-touchdown mark, something Jones has done only once and not since 2012. Even if Ridley doesn't score a touchdown on 15.6 percent of catches again, he and Jones will continue to be one of the most fearsome receiver duos in the league.

Seth Roberts

Height: 6-2 | Weight: 195 | College: West Alabama | Draft: 2014/FA | Born: 22-Feb-1991 | Age: 28 | Risk: Blue

Year	Team	G/GS	Snaps	Pass	Rec	Yds	TD	C%	+/-	Drop	Yd/C	aDOT	Rk	YAC	Rk	YAC+	BTkl	DVOA	Rk	DYAR	Rk	YAR	Use	Rk	Slot
2016	OAK	16/6	749	77	38	397	5	49%	-12.3	9	10.4	8.5	78	5.3	20	+0.4	14	-18.6%	83	-37	84	-54	13.0%	76	85%
2017	OAK	15/7	752	65	43	455	1	66%	+1.2	5	10.6	10.0	61	2.5	79	-2.0	2	-5.8%	61	34	66	33	12.5%	74	92%
2018	OAK	15/7	571	64	45	494	2	70%	+3.0	3	11.0	9.1	62	4.7	32	-0.7	4	4.7%	33	86	45	68	13.0%	71	97%
2019	BAL			7	4	42	0	57%			10.5							-15.3%							

A sure-handed slot receiver without much in the way of active jukes, Roberts is probably just a backup for Willie Snead as well as veteran insurance in case some of the Ravens young receivers don't work out or are sent to IR. Roberts caught just five of his 13 deep targets last year, and doesn't do a great job fighting for the ball at the top of his route. He doesn't have a real calling card besides catching the ball underneath—he's almost got a blocking tight end profile, just without the blocking. Still, a little insurance on a depth chart this muddled wasn't a bad idea for Baltimore. Roberts should get used to quick stints with his new teams.

Allen Robinson

Height: 6-2 | Weight: 220 | College: Penn St. | Draft: 2014/2 (61) | Born: 8/24/1993 | Age: 26 | Risk: Yellow

Year	Team	G/GS	Snaps	Pass	Rec	Yds	TD	C%	+/-	Drop	Yd/C	aDOT	Rk	YAC	Rk	YAC+	BTkl	DVOA	Rk	DYAR	Rk	YAR	Use	Rk	Slot
2016	JAX	16/16	1047	151	73	883	6	48%	-10.4	10	12.1	13.5	20	2.8	87	-1.2	5	-12.0%	74	8	73	-16	24.9%	13	33%
2017	JAX	1/1	3	1	1	17	0	100%	+0.6	0	17.0	15.0	--	2.0	--	-2.2	0	123.1%	--	12	--	12	3.0%	--	0%
2018	CHI	13/12	765	94	55	754	4	59%	-2.0	2	13.7	12.0	31	3.9	52	-0.4	9	-4.8%	52	62	47	103	24.3%	15	52%
2019	CHI			116	68	942	7	59%			13.9							0.7%							

Robinson was an upgrade from what the Bears had at wide receiver before him yet not as good as they were hoping he could be. Though his overall catch rate was the best it had been since his rookie season in 2014, Robinson was not the force on critical downs and in the red zone that he should have been. He posted a negative DVOA on third and fourth downs and in the red zone while being the Bears' most targeted player in both areas. He was still the offense's best big-play threat and maintained the highest yards per target on the team, but surely Chicago was looking for the 2015 version of Robinson that led the league in touchdowns (14) and placed eighth in DYAR (318). Another offseason spent with Mitchell Trubisky, a still-developing young passer, may be just what Robinson needs to return to the heights the Bears paid him to reach.

Demarcus Robinson

Height: 6-1 | Weight: 203 | College: Florida | Draft: 2016/4 (126) | Born: 21-Sep-1994 | Age: 25 | Risk: Yellow

Year	Team	G/GS	Snaps	Pass	Rec	Yds	TD	C%	+/-	Drop	Yd/C	aDOT	Rk	YAC	Rk	YAC+	BTkl	DVOA	Rk	DYAR	Rk	YAR	Use	Rk	Slot
2016	KC	16/0	6	--	0	0	0	--	--	--	--	--	--	--	--	--	--	--	--	--	--	--	--	--	--
2017	KC	16/8	586	39	21	212	0	54%	-1.8	3	10.1	11.0	--	2.0	--	-2.0	0	-16.9%	--	-14	--	-12	7.7%	--	51%
2018	KC	16/5	419	33	22	288	4	67%	+0.6	1	13.1	12.1	--	5.3	--	+0.0	4	13.5%	--	68	--	54	5.8%	--	45%
2019	KC			47	30	403	5	64%			13.4							10.8%							

There wasn't much need for Robinson in the Kansas City offense last year, and he ended up starting mostly as an injury replacement when Sammy Watkins was out. Twenty of his 33 targets came in games Watkins didn't play. With Tyreek Hill possibly facing a suspension, rookie Mecole Hardman being a raw prospect, and Watkins a perennial injury risk, Robinson might be tasked with a hefty workload in 2019. It's worth noting that Robinson performed much better with Patrick Mahomes than he did with Alex Smith, but he's really more of a role player without a dominant strength to fall back on. He will, at least, be an upgrade over Chris Conley as the Chiefs' fourth target, but the sooner some of the more talented guys are back, the better for Kansas City's offense.

Chester Rogers

Height: 6-1   Weight: 180   College: Grambling State   Draft: 2016/FA   Born: 12-Jan-1994   Age: 25   Risk: Green

Year	Team	G/GS	Snaps	Pass	Rec	Yds	TD	C%	+/-	Drop	Yd/C	aDOT	Rk	YAC	Rk	YAC+	BTkl	DVOA	Rk	DYAR	Rk	YAR	Use	Rk	Slot
2016	IND	14/2	434	34	19	273	0	56%	-0.6	3	14.4	12.3	--	2.8	--	-0.8	2	5.4%	--	51	--	41	7.1%	--	25%
2017	IND	11/4	445	37	23	284	1	62%	+0.4	2	12.3	9.4	--	4.5	--	-0.5	4	-3.1%	--	28	--	15	11.4%	--	56%
2018	IND	16/10	595	72	53	485	2	74%	+1.3	4	9.2	6.5	81	4.9	28	-1.1	7	-9.7%	58	17	60	24	11.3%	78	93%
2019	IND			26	16	183	1	62%			11.4							-3.2%							

Among receivers, only Antonio Brown and Davante Adams had more targets on screens than Rogers' 19. He was pretty much a pure slot receiver last season, and the selection of Parris Campbell in the second round appeared to make him superfluous. Frank Reich praised his performance in offseason workouts and he could compete with Campbell for return duties, so it is premature to predict he will be cut. But a strong camp by Campbell could push him at least off the active roster and possibly onto the street.

John Ross

Height: 5-11   Weight: 188   College: Washington   Draft: 2017/1 (9)   Born: 27-Nov-1995   Age: 24   Risk: Green

Year	Team	G/GS	Snaps	Pass	Rec	Yds	TD	C%	+/-	Drop	Yd/C	aDOT	Rk	YAC	Rk	YAC+	BTkl	DVOA	Rk	DYAR	Rk	YAR	Use	Rk	Slot
2017	CIN	3/1	17	2	0	0	0	0%	-0.9	0	0.0	23.0	--	0.0	--	+0.0	0	-105.6%	--	-14	--	-13	2.1%	--	50%
2018	CIN	13/10	601	58	21	210	7	36%	-13.3	6	10.0	14.2	18	2.8	78	-1.5	4	-33.3%	84	-96	81	-119	13.5%	68	32%
2019	CIN			57	30	365	2	53%			12.2							-17.6%							

Ross is a true 1990s outside receiver, and by that we mean his route tree is not very advanced. Twenty-nine of his 48 targets fell under "fade," "go," "curl," "post," and "deep cross." Ross was actually wildly unsuccessful on those targets, too, catching just 10 of them for 143 yards. Of course, when you catch just 36 percent of your targets, most plays are rather inefficient! Still, let's not outright dismiss his chances of being productive in a new system, as the talent is certainly there. We'll close with an amazing subtweet of the Marvin Lewis administration from Ross, as told to WCPO9 in Cincinnati: "When I'm having fun, I'm a completely different person than the uptight person I've been the last two years, overthinking and letting things get to me that I shouldn't."

Curtis Samuel

Height: 5-11   Weight: 196   College: Ohio State   Draft: 2017/2 (40)   Born: 11-Aug-1996   Age: 23   Risk: Yellow

Year	Team	G/GS	Snaps	Pass	Rec	Yds	TD	C%	+/-	Drop	Yd/C	aDOT	Rk	YAC	Rk	YAC+	BTkl	DVOA	Rk	DYAR	Rk	YAR	Use	Rk	Slot
2017	CAR	9/4	226	26	15	115	0	58%	-2.1	2	7.7	11.0	--	3.4	--	-2.3	4	-18.3%	--	-12	--	-10	9.9%	--	71%
2018	CAR	13/8	466	65	39	494	5	60%	-2.2	3	12.7	12.3	29	2.8	77	-1.7	14	-5.4%	53	39	54	61	14.9%	65	24%
2019	CAR			91	56	692	4	62%			12.3							0.2%							

Contrary to most of his old scouting reports, Samuel had the second-worst DVOA (-40.1%) from the slot of any receiver last year but was considerably more effective split wide (7.8%)—his was the third-largest DVOA difference in favor of being split wide of any receiver with at least 10 targets in each role. Fortunately, the coaching staff recognized this, splitting Samuel wide on 50 of his 66 targets and bringing in another slot option in Chris Hogan during the offseason. Ideally, this will allow Samuel to increase his effectiveness as a traditional pass-catcher while still allowing him to contribute on the sweeps and end-arounds that generated a couple of bonus rushing scores in 2018.

Deebo Samuel

Height: 6-0   Weight: 214   College: South Carolina   Draft: 2019/2 (36)   Born: 15-Jan-1996   Age: 23   Risk: Yellow

Year	Team	G/GS	Snaps	Pass	Rec	Yds	TD	C%	+/-	Drop	Yd/C	aDOT	Rk	YAC	Rk	YAC+	BTkl	DVOA	Rk	DYAR	Rk	YAR	Use	Rk	Slot
2019	SF			53	33	452	3	62%			13.7							-1.0%							

Samuel gets dinged in our Playmaker Projections (see page 441) for staying in school for his senior season; as a group, wide receivers who hit the NFL as underclassmen have outperformed those who played four years in college. Samuel had good reason for staying in Columbia however: his junior campaign in 2017 was ended by a broken leg after only three games. Mind you, they were three ridiculous games—Samuel had 476 all-purpose yards and scored a half-dozen touchdowns against North Carolina State, Missouri, and Kentucky. The 49ers have a lot of wide receivers on hand, but Samuel will get every chance to win a starting job as the "Z" receiver (a flanker who lines up on the strong side of the formation) in Kyle Shanahan's offense. He's also more than a receiver—he scored four touchdowns on kickoff returns for the Gamecocks and also threw a pair of touchdown passes.

Emmanuel Sanders

Height: 5-11   Weight: 186   College: Southern Methodist   Draft: 2010/3 (82)   Born: 17-Mar-1987   Age: 32   Risk: Red

Year	Team	G/GS	Snaps	Pass	Rec	Yds	TD	C%	+/-	Drop	Yd/C	aDOT	Rk	YAC	Rk	YAC+	BTkl	DVOA	Rk	DYAR	Rk	YAR	Use	Rk	Slot
2016	DEN	16/16	869	137	79	1032	5	58%	+2.4	3	13.1	13.3	27	3.0	79	-0.9	12	-3.3%	61	103	51	82	24.3%	17	41%
2017	DEN	12/11	635	91	47	555	2	51%	-7.1	6	11.8	11.0	50	3.6	54	-0.6	7	-18.2%	75	-40	79	-36	22.0%	21	39%
2018	DEN	12/12	658	99	71	868	4	73%	+6.8	5	12.2	9.7	56	4.3	44	-1.3	10	2.0%	39	113	36	114	23.1%	20	68%
2019	DEN			76	46	529	3	60%			11.6							-5.1%							

A December Achilles' tear is not an ideal situation for any receiver to be facing, much less a 32-year-old veteran. Sanders is still targeting a Week 1 return, and boy, do the Broncos ever need him considering the state of the rest of the receiving corps. The best-case scenario for the Broncos' offense in 2019 likely involves Sanders and Joe Flacco establishing a deep-ball connection. From 2013 to 2016, Sanders consistently had at least 15 percent of his targets listed as bombs at least 26 yards downfield, with plenty of shots in the 16- to 25-yard range as well. That dropped off significantly over the last two seasons, as his quarterbacks had the arm strength of wet rigatoni. Flacco's got a cannon, albeit an inaccurate one, so a healthy Sanders might see his average depth of target bounce back up in 2019.

Mohamed Sanu

Height: 6-2   Weight: 211   College: Rutgers   Draft: 2012/3 (83)   Born: 22-Aug-1989   Age: 30   Risk: Green

Year	Team	G/GS	Snaps	Pass	Rec	Yds	TD	C%	+/-	Drop	Yd/C	aDOT	Rk	YAC	Rk	YAC+	BTkl	DVOA	Rk	DYAR	Rk	YAR	Use	Rk	Slot
2016	ATL	15/15	744	81	59	653	4	73%	+5.7	2	11.1	8.1	81	4.9	32	+0.2	10	6.5%	36	123	44	135	16.2%	61	87%
2017	ATL	15/15	756	96	67	703	5	70%	+4.3	6	10.5	8.0	77	3.7	53	-0.6	8	10.7%	24	179	18	180	20.0%	33	78%
2018	ATL	16/16	830	94	66	838	4	70%	+1.7	2	12.7	8.2	73	6.1	7	+0.8	9	6.4%	29	141	30	154	15.8%	58	84%
2019	ATL			98	63	778	5	64%			12.3							4.7%							

With the emergence of Calvin Ridley and the Falcons' plans to extend Julio Jones, this season could be Sanu's last in Atlanta. His $7.9-million cap hit next season is set to be the seventh highest on the team. He has been dependable in his three seasons as the Falcons' No. 2 receiver, ranking in the top 40 in catches, receiving yards, and touchdown catches. He has even spelled Matt Ryan here and there, throwing a touchdown pass in back-to-back seasons. Both of them were against the Buccaneers, which, when you think about it, is kind of rubbing it in. Take it easy, guys. Tampa Bay has had enough trouble stopping regular quarterbacks.

Tajae Sharpe

Height: 6-2   Weight: 194   College: Massachusetts   Draft: 2016/5 (140)   Born: 23-Dec-1994   Age: 25   Risk: Blue

Year	Team	G/GS	Snaps	Pass	Rec	Yds	TD	C%	+/-	Drop	Yd/C	aDOT	Rk	YAC	Rk	YAC+	BTkl	DVOA	Rk	DYAR	Rk	YAR	Use	Rk	Slot
2016	TEN	16/10	786	83	41	522	2	49%	-5.9	2	12.7	13.2	30	2.1	91	-1.8	3	-9.2%	69	23	69	8	17.5%	49	31%
2018	TEN	16/13	592	47	26	316	2	55%	-2.5	1	12.2	10.9	--	3.2	--	-1.2	1	-4.9%	--	30	--	22	11.1%	--	85%
2019	TEN			7	4	45	0	57%			11.3							-10.8%							

It was not hard to see the writing on the wall for Sharpe after he played just 10 snaps in the final two games. The Titans took the chance to see what else they had at receiver, and then signed Adam Humphries and drafted A.J. Brown in the second round. He had a strong offseason by all accounts and has the versatility across receiver positions to back up the top three. Without special teams value, though, he might be a healthy scratch unless he demonstrates a better most valuable attribute than finding the soft spot in zone coverage, or Brown struggles in his transition to the NFL.

Sterling Shepard

Height: 5-10   Weight: 194   College: Oklahoma   Draft: 2016/2 (40)   Born: 10-Feb-1993   Age: 26   Risk: Green

Year	Team	G/GS	Snaps	Pass	Rec	Yds	TD	C%	+/-	Drop	Yd/C	aDOT	Rk	YAC	Rk	YAC+	BTkl	DVOA	Rk	DYAR	Rk	YAR	Use	Rk	Slot
2016	NYG	16/16	1005	105	65	683	8	62%	-3.3	5	10.5	9.2	70	4.0	53	-0.6	9	-1.8%	55	91	54	101	17.5%	50	89%
2017	NYG	11/10	688	84	59	731	2	70%	+4.5	6	12.4	8.8	72	5.0	21	+0.6	6	4.9%	37	120	37	122	20.1%	31	89%
2018	NYG	16/16	936	107	66	872	4	62%	-2.6	7	13.2	10.2	50	4.7	33	-0.1	9	-0.9%	46	97	42	111	18.5%	40	69%
2019	NYG			108	66	864	6	61%			13.1							1.7%							

Despite playing a lot of slot, Shepard actually has had better success outside the last two seasons in small sample sizes. Shepard doesn't win with his body or by doing the traditional outside receiver stuff—he's not going to separate at the top of his route and turn to catch a curl. Shepard's game is separation right off the snap, and a lot of his successful plays to the outside are on quick routes like drags, digs, and whip routes that quickly enable him to beat his man at the line of scrimmage. One of the grand questions about the direction of the Giants offense is just how much time Shepard and Golden Tate will split in the slot and how that will work out. We'd recommend letting Shepard get his outside.

Trent Sherfield

Height: 6-1   Weight: 205   College: Vanderbilt   Draft: 2018/FA   Born: 26-Feb-1996   Age: 23   Risk: Green

Year	Team	G/GS	Snaps	Pass	Rec	Yds	TD	C%	+/-	Drop	Yd/C	aDOT	Rk	YAC	Rk	YAC+	BTkl	DVOA	Rk	DYAR	Rk	YAR	Use	Rk	Slot
2018	ARI	13/2	343	28	19	210	1	68%	+1.0	0	11.1	11.3	--	2.0	--	-1.9	0	-4.3%	--	18	--	33	7.2%	--	46%
2019	ARI			7	4	44	0	57%			11.1							-13.1%							

Through Week 9, Sherfield was almost exclusively a special-teamer. From Week 10 on, however, he played at least 20 snaps on offense each game, and he had at least one catch in each of Arizona's last six contests. The Cardinals drafted three wide receivers, so if Sherfield wins a roster spot this fall, he will probably be almost exclusively a special-teamer again.

JuJu Smith-Schuster

Height: 6-1   Weight: 215   College: USC   Draft: 2017/2 (62)   Born: 22-Nov-1996   Age: 23   Risk: Green

Year	Team	G/GS	Snaps	Pass	Rec	Yds	TD	C%	+/-	Drop	Yd/C	aDOT	Rk	YAC	Rk	YAC+	BTkl	DVOA	Rk	DYAR	Rk	YAR	Use	Rk	Slot
2017	PIT	14/7	707	79	58	917	7	73%	+8.1	2	15.8	9.9	63	6.7	5	+2.2	8	37.3%	1	317	6	321	15.3%	63	59%
2018	PIT	16/13	960	167	111	1426	7	67%	+3.1	5	12.8	9.0	63	5.8	11	+0.7	12	4.4%	34	235	17	195	24.8%	14	65%
2019	PIT			153	103	1325	9	67%			12.9							13.8%							

The knowing smiles exchanged by Steelers fans as the Antonio Brown saga played out showed that they knew that Smith-Schuster is already a superstar. To wit: only two other receivers—Isaac Bruce in 1995 and Larry Fitzgerald a decade later—have had 100-catch, 1,400-yard seasons in either of their first two seasons. Only Randy Moss has as many 100-yard receiving games (11) before his 23rd birthday as Smith-Schuster. And JuJu already has four touchdowns of 75-plus yards, including two 97-yarders, which doesn't seem real.

Mandatory caution department: JJSS of course was doing all this while opposing defenses were geared to stop Brown, and stepping into the protagonist role isn't always easy for supporting actors. That said, it's rare for a team to lose a player the caliber of Brown and have a player this accomplished standing by in the wings.

Smith-Schuster was demonstrably more efficient on second down than any other, with a 31.4% DVOA while in the red on other plays. Now that he is The Man, that imbalance will need to clear up a bit.

Torrey Smith

Height: 6-1   Weight: 204   College: Maryland   Draft: 2011/2 (58)   Born: 26-Jan-1989   Age: 30   Risk: Green

Year	Team	G/GS	Snaps	Pass	Rec	Yds	TD	C%	+/-	Drop	Yd/C	aDOT	Rk	YAC	Rk	YAC+	BTkl	DVOA	Rk	DYAR	Rk	YAR	Use	Rk	Slot
2016	SF	12/12	643	49	20	267	3	41%	-7.4	5	13.4	13.5	22	3.1	78	-1.2	2	-33.0%	93	-78	90	-69	13.5%	73	36%
2017	PHI	16/14	735	69	36	430	2	54%	-3.9	8	11.9	13.8	24	3.3	63	-1.3	1	-18.2%	76	-29	74	-26	12.7%	73	36%
2018	CAR	11/6	324	31	17	190	2	55%	+0.2	1	11.2	13.4	--	2.8	--	-0.5	3	-10.0%	--	7	--	19	8.4%	--	38%
2019	CAR			11	6	75	0	55%			12.5							-8.4%							

The first sub-200-yard season of his career saw Smith finish eighth on the Panthers in each of targets, yards per game, catch rate, and yards per target. Of the five main Panthers wide receivers, only Jarius Wright had fewer yards per catch than Smith—alarming because Smith built his reputation as a deep threat, but that figure has now declined in each of the past three seasons.

Smith remains fifth of the five major Panthers receivers at this stage in the offseason—even fullback Alex Armah is getting more attention as a possible pass target—so unless something drastic changes ahead of him, it could be another season of two targets per game as he enters his 30s.

Tre'Quan Smith

Height: 6-1 | Weight: 205 | College: Central Florida | Draft: 2018/3 (91) | Born: 7-Jan-1996 | Age: 23 | Risk: Blue

Year	Team	G/GS	Snaps	Pass	Rec	Yds	TD	C%	+/-	Drop	Yd/C	aDOT	Rk	YAC	Rk	YAC+	BTkl	DVOA	Rk	DYAR	Rk	YAR	Use	Rk	Slot
2018	NO	15/7	567	44	28	427	5	64%	+2.8	2	15.3	11.7	--	4.1	--	+0.1	2	22.7%	--	126	--	126	9.0%	--	55%
2019	NO			66	42	593	6	64%			14.1							11.5%							

Smith had the highest Playmaker Rating in the 2018 receiver class, and he had a promising rookie campaign after being forced into a starting role ahead of schedule by the injury to Ted Ginn. A significant majority of his rookie production—268 of his 427 yards—came in just two games against Washington and Philadelphia; Smith had only one other game above 30 receiving yards all year, as Michael Thomas and Alvin Kamara vacuumed up almost all the targets between them. Still, Smith showed enough promise to have Saints fans excited for a breakout in 2019—if he can wrest enough of Drew Brees' attention away from the high-volume stars of the Superdome.

Willie Snead

Height: 5-11 | Weight: 195 | College: Ball State | Draft: 2014/FA | Born: 17-Oct-1992 | Age: 27 | Risk: Yellow

Year	Team	G/GS	Snaps	Pass	Rec	Yds	TD	C%	+/-	Drop	Yd/C	aDOT	Rk	YAC	Rk	YAC+	BTkl	DVOA	Rk	DYAR	Rk	YAR	Use	Rk	Slot
2016	NO	15/4	740	104	72	895	4	69%	+2.5	4	12.4	7.4	87	5.4	17	+0.8	12	12.5%	17	206	20	195	16.6%	59	90%
2017	NO	11/7	259	16	8	92	0	50%	-1.1	1	11.5	7.6	--	4.0	--	-1.2	1	-31.0%	--	-23	--	-22	4.4%	--	81%
2018	BAL	16/10	821	95	62	651	1	65%	+0.1	5	10.5	9.0	66	4.5	36	-0.3	9	-9.8%	60	21	57	20	17.6%	47	91%
2019	BAL			98	59	665	3	60%			11.3							-7.9%							

Snead became a lower-target player with Lamar Jackson, but nobody could have avoided that given how little the Ravens threw. Snead seemed to be one of Jackson's favorite targets and definitely the wideout with whom he had the best rapport. Heading into 2019, Snead's future in Baltimore likely rests on just how much Hollywood Brown can be used outside and retain his efficiency. Snead is a fine slot receiver in the separation-and-catch mold, but he isn't much of a deep threat. Even if the Ravens do move forward with Brown as their slot receiver of the future, Snead has done enough to solidify himself as an Adam Humphries-esque player. Suddenly that kind of player without any red flags makes a lot of money in free agency.

Equanimeous St. Brown

Height: 5-5 | Weight: 214 | College: Notre Dame | Draft: 2018/6 (207) | Born: 30-Sep-1996 | Age: 23 | Risk: Red

Year	Team	G/GS	Snaps	Pass	Rec	Yds	TD	C%	+/-	Drop	Yd/C	aDOT	Rk	YAC	Rk	YAC+	BTkl	DVOA	Rk	DYAR	Rk	YAR	Use	Rk	Slot
2018	GB	12/7	358	36	21	328	0	58%	+0.4	0	15.6	14.5	--	5.7	--	+0.2	4	-7.2%	--	16	--	30	7.9%	--	54%
2019	GB			47	29	365	2	62%			12.6							0.2%							

St. Brown is sort of a lesser version of Marquez Valdes-Scantling. St. Brown, like his teammate, is a tall, long-strider with sub-4.50-second speed. He can be effective stretching the field on post routes, go routes, and the like, but asking him to run routes with any sort of nuance or suddenness is not in his wheelhouse. St. Brown put up a stellar performance in Week 16 versus the Jets in which he caught all five of his targets for 94 yards and landed eighth in DYAR for the week, but the season was effectively over for both teams anyway. He only reached 50-plus receiving yards in two of his other 11 games. As Geronimo Allison comes back from injury and the offense presumably shifts toward more 12 personnel, St. Brown should not be expected to see an uptick in playing time or production.

Kenny Stills

Height: 6-0 | Weight: 194 | College: Oklahoma | Draft: 2013/5 (144) | Born: 22-Apr-1992 | Age: 27 | Risk: Green

Year	Team	G/GS	Snaps	Pass	Rec	Yds	TD	C%	+/-	Drop	Yd/C	aDOT	Rk	YAC	Rk	YAC+	BTkl	DVOA	Rk	DYAR	Rk	YAR	Use	Rk	Slot
2016	MIA	16/16	795	81	42	726	9	52%	-2.7	3	17.3	14.8	8	4.6	38	+0.5	4	6.8%	34	121	45	144	17.4%	52	56%
2017	MIA	16/16	942	105	58	847	6	55%	+1.0	4	14.6	15.2	12	2.7	75	-1.4	4	0.4%	44	107	44	91	18.0%	43	54%
2018	MIA	15/15	745	64	37	553	6	58%	+0.9	3	14.9	16.5	3	3.5	63	-0.6	4	12.6%	22	127	33	105	15.7%	59	54%
2019	MIA			89	46	673	4	52%			14.6							-2.9%							

Stills disappeared during the Brock Osweiler games—seven catches on 13 targets for 57 yards and one touchdown in Osweiler's four starts—then disappeared again when the Dolphins waived the surrender flag in the final three games. The new Dolphins regime decided it was worth almost $10 million in 2019 cap space to see if Stills can regain his 2017 form. Like returning veterans DeVante Parker and Kenyan Drake, he has one year to prove that Osweiler and Adam Gase were the problems and that he can be part of the solution. If not, Stills will either be midseason trade bait or a 2020 cap cut.

Courtland Sutton

Height: 6-3			Weight: 218			College: Southern Methodist				Draft: 2018/2 (40)				Born: 10-Oct-1995				Age: 24			Risk: Red				

Year	Team	G/GS	Snaps	Pass	Rec	Yds	TD	C%	+/-	Drop	Yd/C	aDOT	Rk	YAC	Rk	YAC+	BTkl	DVOA	Rk	DYAR	Rk	YAR	Use	Rk	Slot
2018	DEN	16/9	819	84	42	704	4	50%	-5.9	9	16.8	14.3	17	3.9	54	-0.5	5	1.3%	44	95	44	87	15.4%	62	25%
2019	DEN			101	57	799	6	56%			14.0							-0.5%							

Sutton's rookie year was really three entirely different seasons, which helpfully illustrates how dramatically the specific role a player is asked to play affects their production. For the first half of the season, Sutton was the third receiver behind Emmanuel Sanders and Demaryius Thomas; he put up a 2.5% DVOA as he worked his way into the offense. For the next four games, Sutton was WR2 after Thomas' trade; he took advantage of the increased opportunities and larger role to put up a 15.4% DVOA. He then became the Broncos' top option over the last four weeks when Sanders went down with his Achilles' tear; his DVOA plummeted to -12.1% as he was now matched up against top cornerbacks on the other team. Hopefully, Sanders will be back and Sutton will be able to resume his role as a high-efficiency WR2, as he is not yet quite ready to be the focal point of an offense.

Ryan Switzer

Height: 5-8			Weight: 181			College: North Carolina				Draft: 2017/4 (133)				Born: 4-Nov-1994				Age: 25			Risk: Green			

Year	Team	G/GS	Snaps	Pass	Rec	Yds	TD	C%	+/-	Drop	Yd/C	aDOT	Rk	YAC	Rk	YAC+	BTkl	DVOA	Rk	DYAR	Rk	YAR	Use	Rk	Slot
2017	DAL	16/0	91	7	6	41	0	86%	+1.1	1	6.8	4.7	--	3.0	--	-2.5	2	7.1%	--	11	--	11	1.4%	--	100%
2018	PIT	16/1	302	44	36	253	1	82%	+2.8	1	7.0	3.9	--	3.8	--	-1.6	2	-11.1%	--	5	--	-7	6.6%	--	76%
2019	PIT			26	19	157	0	73%			8.3							-10.7%							

There are few things easier than dehumanizing pro athletes. Hell, we are a publication devoted to reducing their achievements and failures into quantifiable statistics! But taking the time to understand what goes into a player's rise and/or fall is always worthwhile. Take Switzer, an athletic god in his native West Virginia and a standout at North Carolina, who was drafted by goddamn America's Team in the fourth round in 2017. Things couldn't have been rosier. He was even engaged! Then he was traded twice within five months, with the usual amount of compassion—"it's a business, kid, now gimme your playbook."

Switzer told Steelers.com that the deals—along with the stress of moving twice across the country, the new marriage, and the lack of any communication about why he was traded—drove him to the brink of leaving the sport for good. Enter Ben Roethlisberger, who welcomed Switzer with open arms and, more important than Switzer's unremarkable on-field impact, made Switzer feel relevant and cared for once again. As such, he is in the mix for a larger role in the passing game in 2019, rather than getting caught in the pro football backwash that casts off so many players not so fortunate.

Golden Tate

Height: 5-10			Weight: 199			College: Notre Dame				Draft: 2010/2 (60)				Born: 2-Aug-1988				Age: 31			Risk: Green		

Year	Team	G/GS	Snaps	Pass	Rec	Yds	TD	C%	+/-	Drop	Yd/C	aDOT	Rk	YAC	Rk	YAC+	BTkl	DVOA	Rk	DYAR	Rk	YAR	Use	Rk	Slot
2016	DET	16/16	866	135	91	1077	4	67%	+3.0	9	11.8	7.8	84	6.8	3	+0.9	27	-1.8%	54	114	48	111	22.9%	22	43%
2017	DET	16/12	791	120	92	1003	5	77%	+8.6	3	10.9	6.0	85	6.8	4	+1.2	23	9.7%	27	204	16	205	20.9%	27	80%
2018	2TM	15/7	606	114	74	795	4	66%	-3.6	9	10.7	6.7	80	5.7	12	+0.6	29	-27.8%	81	-134	84	-88	20.8%	29	86%
2019	NYG			101	70	753	4	69%			10.8							2.7%							

Freed from Detroit and Philadelphia, Tate will now be asked to do something he hasn't done since 2016: Play outside more. His DVOA splits between slot and outside receiver are interesting. In 2016, he was better on the outside by about 30.0% DVOA. In 2017, he was better in the slot by 33.6% DVOA. In 2018? Better out wide, but in an extremely small sample as you can see from that slot percentage. Tate has been, in the past, a wideout who can win deep balls. For most of the last three years he has been a wideout who wins by breaking tackles and being elusive in space. Tate's average target depth of 6.7 was one of the lowest in the NFL. Screens are probably always going to be a part of his game, but he needs to be able to threaten the intermediate to help the Giants from being too one-dimensional.

Jordan Taylor

Height: 6-5 Weight: 210 College: Rice Draft: 2015/FA Born: 18-Feb-1992 Age: 27 Risk: Red

Year	Team	G/GS	Snaps	Pass	Rec	Yds	TD	C%	+/-	Drop	Yd/C	aDOT	Rk	YAC	Rk	YAC+	BTkl	DVOA	Rk	DYAR	Rk	YAR	Use	Rk	Slot
2016	DEN	16/0	277	25	16	209	2	64%	+1.5	0	13.1	9.8	--	5.3	--	+1.5	2	2.7%	--	32	--	29	4.6%	--	50%
2017	DEN	10/2	258	20	13	142	0	65%	+1.4	0	10.9	11.1	--	3.5	--	-0.9	3	-10.9%	--	3	--	6	5.7%	--	26%
2019	MIN			37	23	285	1	62%			12.4							0.9%							

The Vikings are desperate to replace Laquon Treadwell, so much so that they are rolling the dice on a career backup who missed all of 2018 after offseason hip surgery. Prior to missing all of last year, Taylor earned snaps in Denver as a rotational fourth or fifth wide receiver. He rocks a tall, lean frame that he carries well athletically, showing off the speed to work defenders down the sideline and the acrobatics to make tough catches. If the second trait sounds familiar, it is because a video of Taylor making an Odell Beckham Jr.-like catch during training camp circled around in 2016. He will not be doing that often during regular-season play, but if Taylor can provide the vertical and yards-after-catch presence he flashed in limited action in Denver, he could be some semblance of an upgrade over Treadwell. As a bonus, Taylor has experience returning punts, which is valuable for a Vikings squad now without their punt returner of eight years, Marcus Sherels.

Taywan Taylor

Height: 5-11 Weight: 203 College: Western Kentucky Draft: 2017/3 (72) Born: 2-Mar-1995 Age: 24 Risk: Green

Year	Team	G/GS	Snaps	Pass	Rec	Yds	TD	C%	+/-	Drop	Yd/C	aDOT	Rk	YAC	Rk	YAC+	BTkl	DVOA	Rk	DYAR	Rk	YAR	Use	Rk	Slot
2017	TEN	16/4	246	28	16	231	1	57%	+0.7	0	14.4	13.5	--	3.4	--	-2.7	4	-9.7%	--	6	--	18	6.0%	--	66%
2018	TEN	13/5	444	56	37	466	1	66%	+2.3	5	12.6	13.5	20	4.4	40	-1.4	5	-2.7%	50	43	51	31	16.0%	57	52%
2019	TEN			31	18	248	0	58%			13.8							-1.0%							

Taylor's aDOT is the product of mixed usage, split between short throws designed to create yards after catch like screens and jet sweep passes and deep downfield routes like fly patterns, with a smattering of intermediate routes. He was a favored component of the vertical part of three-level stretch passing plays, though he was not too effective at catching passes there (-26.8% DVOA). Receivers coach Rob Moore said in June the team needed to give Taylor more opportunities, but it's hard to see that happening after adding A.J. Brown and Adam Humphries. Still, he could have a defined role, especially because none of the Titans' other top receivers has his speed.

Trent Taylor

Height: 5-8 Weight: 181 College: Louisiana Tech Draft: 2017/5 (177) Born: 30-Apr-1994 Age: 25 Risk: Blue

Year	Team	G/GS	Snaps	Pass	Rec	Yds	TD	C%	+/-	Drop	Yd/C	aDOT	Rk	YAC	Rk	YAC+	BTkl	DVOA	Rk	DYAR	Rk	YAR	Use	Rk	Slot
2017	SF	15/1	491	60	43	430	2	72%	+1.8	4	10.0	6.9	82	4.3	41	+0.0	7	11.4%	23	114	40	92	10.8%	79	84%
2018	SF	14/0	321	40	26	215	1	65%	-3.0	2	8.3	6.0	--	4.0	--	-0.9	1	-19.4%	--	-21	--	-24	9.2%	--	90%
2019	SF			8	5	47	0	63%			9.5							-13.3%							

Taylor is a short, white, slot receiver, so he always gets compared to Wes Welker. Now he gets to work with Wes Welker, the 49ers' newly hired wide receivers coach. Taylor never fully recovered from back surgery last year, which partly explains his statistical drop-off. He's healthy now, but San Francisco has stacked the depth chart with a lot of new faces at wideout, and his spot on the roster is precarious.

Adam Thielen

Height: 6-2 Weight: 195 College: Minnesota State Draft: 2013/FA Born: 22-Aug-1990 Age: 29 Risk: Green

Year	Team	G/GS	Snaps	Pass	Rec	Yds	TD	C%	+/-	Drop	Yd/C	aDOT	Rk	YAC	Rk	YAC+	BTkl	DVOA	Rk	DYAR	Rk	YAR	Use	Rk	Slot
2016	MIN	16/10	786	92	69	967	5	75%	+12.2	2	14.0	11.2	48	4.3	44	-0.3	9	26.2%	6	270	8	299	15.8%	63	49%
2017	MIN	16/16	1034	142	91	1276	4	64%	+8.1	6	14.0	10.9	52	4.9	26	+0.1	11	10.1%	26	261	11	269	27.5%	7	60%
2018	MIN	16/16	1011	153	113	1373	9	74%	+16.6	2	12.2	9.7	57	3.7	59	-0.7	5	15.2%	19	341	8	335	25.7%	12	70%
2019	MIN			148	96	1196	8	65%			12.5							8.3%							

Nobody in the league has a catch radius quite like Thielen. He does not outmuscle opponents at the catch point like Mike Evans, and he does not flash one-handed catches far away from his body the way Odell Beckham Jr. does. Instead, Thielen has a unique talent to contort his body any way he needs to, be that going low, fighting through traffic, or tip-toeing around the sideline. The ball is somehow always in reach for Thielen, which has helped him earn a top-eight finish in receiving plus-minus three years in a row. The Vikings have regularly put him in position to succeed, too. Thielen saw just 50 percent of his targets from the slot when he first broke out in 2016. That climbed to 60 percent in 2017 and again to 70 percent in 2018. Playing heavily out of the slot works well for Thielen as he is not the route-runner and separator Stefon Diggs is. Being a frequent slot player who gets to expose zones and linebackers more often, there is a fair argument that Thielen's job in Minnesota is "easier" than that of Diggs', but there is no use discrediting a player with Thielen's productivity and dependability.

Demaryius Thomas Height: 6-3   Weight: 224   College: Georgia Tech   Draft: 2010/1 (22)   Born: 25-Dec-1987   Age: 32   Risk: Green

Year	Team	G/GS	Snaps	Pass	Rec	Yds	TD	C%	+/-	Drop	Yd/C	aDOT	Rk	YAC	Rk	YAC+	BTkl	DVOA	Rk	DYAR	Rk	YAR	Use	Rk	Slot
2016	DEN	16/16	890	144	90	1083	5	63%	+1.6	10	12.0	11.1	50	3.6	65	-0.6	11	2.1%	48	172	27	149	26.6%	10	29%
2017	DEN	16/16	886	140	83	949	5	59%	-1.8	10	11.4	10.9	51	3.6	55	-0.7	10	0.2%	46	146	29	151	26.2%	11	34%
2018	2TM	15/15	764	89	59	677	5	66%	+1.4	6	11.5	10.4	49	4.7	31	-0.6	5	0.9%	45	96	43	74	18.2%	41	47%
2019	NE			37	21	246	2	57%			11.7							-1.1%							

The last time he played with an elite quarterback, Thomas was one half of the league's most productive wide receiver duo alongside Emmanuel Sanders. Thomas hasn't reached those heights since, albeit in less than favorable circumstances, and an Achilles injury suffered in late December has his status in doubt for the opening month of next season. Thomas recovered in just eight months from his previous Achilles tear, but that was eight years ago; he remains likely to start 2019 on PUP, aiming to return to the field in mid-October.

When he does return, Thomas should assume a starting role quickly, ideally opposite rookie N'Keal Harry with Julian Edelman in the slot (pending a change in the status of Josh Gordon). Though he will not have the benefit of the offseason work with his new quarterback, he does at least have experience with his new offensive coordinator—Josh McDaniels drafted Thomas and coached him for most of his rookie season in Denver. A healthy Thomas would assuage concerns about New England's receiver depth, and the veteran should enjoy a productive year even it does get off to a belated start.

Michael Thomas Height: 6-3   Weight: 212   College: Ohio State   Draft: 2016/2 (47)   Born: 3-Mar-1993   Age: 26   Risk: Green

Year	Team	G/GS	Snaps	Pass	Rec	Yds	TD	C%	+/-	Drop	Yd/C	aDOT	Rk	YAC	Rk	YAC+	BTkl	DVOA	Rk	DYAR	Rk	YAR	Use	Rk	Slot
2016	NO	15/12	865	121	92	1137	9	76%	+11.4	4	12.4	8.3	79	5.1	26	+1.1	17	31.6%	3	431	2	408	19.6%	40	31%
2017	NO	16/14	851	149	104	1245	5	70%	+14.9	3	12.0	9.8	67	4.1	43	-0.5	14	15.0%	16	330	5	335	28.3%	5	52%
2018	NO	16/16	927	147	125	1405	9	85%	+24.2	3	11.2	8.0	74	4.1	48	-0.0	18	23.1%	9	442	3	473	29.6%	2	59%
2019	NO			145	107	1302	9	74%			12.2							20.5%							

Four wide receivers were drafted in the first round in 2016. Including the postseason, second-round pick Michael Thomas has more catches (352 vs. 289) and yards (4,210 vs. 3,898) than the four of them combined. Thomas posted his third straight year in the top five of DYAR, which is perhaps to be expected given his target share, but also his second top-10 finish in DVOA and the highest catch rate ever for a player with at least 40 targets. Only three players have ever recorded more receiving yards in the first three years of their careers, and all three were first-round picks: Randy Moss, Odell Beckham, and A.J. Green. Unsurprisingly, Thomas led the league in receiving plus-minus, and he had 80 yards or more in eight of his 17 games with Drew Brees at quarterback.

Best WR Single-Season Catch Rate, 1986-2018

Player	Year	Team	Pass	Rec	C%	Yards	Yd/Rec	TD	DVOA
Michael Thomas	**2018**	**NO**	**147**	**125**	**85.0%**	**1405**	**11.2**	**9**	**23.1%**
Ryan Switzer	2018	PIT	44	36	81.8%	253	7.0	1	-11.1%
Austin Collie	2010	IND	71	58	81.7%	649	11.2	8	28.1%
Tyler Lockett	2018	SEA	70	57	81.4%	965	16.9	10	66.3%
Ike Hilliard	2008	TB	59	48	81.4%	424	8.8	4	17.1%
John Taylor	1989	SF	75	60	80.0%	1077	18.0	10	56.3%
Willie Jackson	1996	JAX	42	33	78.6%	486	14.7	3	46.3%
Dennis Northcutt	2002	CLE	51	40	78.4%	609	15.2	5	60.5%
Mike Thomas	2009	JAX	62	48	77.4%	453	9.4	1	8.3%
Wes Welker	2007	NE	145	112	77.2%	1175	10.5	8	20.5%

Minimum 40 passes.

Thomas was the only player in our charting data with a top-five catch rate from both the slot (86 percent, fourth) and outside receiver (83 percent, second) spots. The Saints were creative with their usage, moving Thomas into the slot for 59 percent of his targets, which accounted for 959 of his yards. He had at least 17.5% DVOA, an 80 percent catch rate, and 8.6 yards per target on every down, and the second-highest red zone DVOA of any receiver with at least 20 targets inside the 20. He was effective short (14.5% DVOA, 290 DYAR) and he was effective deep (82.5% DVOA, 152 DYAR)—any way you slice it, Thomas was dominant in 2018. Though his spectacular catch rate is unlikely to be sustained, his third straight season over 1,100 yards gives us every confidence that he will continue to be one of the most productive receivers by just about any measure in 2019.

Laquon Treadwell

Height: 6-2   Weight: 221   College: Mississippi   Draft: 2016/1 (23)   Born: 14-Jun-1995   Age: 24   Risk: Green

Year	Team	G/GS	Snaps	Pass	Rec	Yds	TD	C%	+/-	Drop	Yd/C	aDOT	Rk	YAC	Rk	YAC+	BTkl	DVOA	Rk	DYAR	Rk	YAR	Use	Rk	Slot
2016	MIN	9/1	80	3	1	15	0	33%	+0.2	0	15.0	17.3	--	0.0	--	-4.6	0	-38.8%	--	-8	--	-5	1.2%	--	0%
2017	MIN	16/7	502	35	20	200	0	57%	+0.9	2	10.0	13.2	--	2.9	--	-1.9	0	-18.2%	--	-15	--	-12	6.9%	--	11%
2018	MIN	15/7	543	53	35	302	1	66%	-2.0	6	8.6	6.4	82	3.4	66	-1.4	4	-19.1%	75	-27	74	-24	9.8%	81	33%
2019	MIN			18	12	109	0	67%			9.1							-9.8%							

It's about time to close the book on Treadwell's chances in Minnesota. Treadwell may find success elsewhere down the line, but he has been given every opportunity to be the Vikings' No. 3 with little competition and has yet to prove he is worthy. While 2018 was an improvement in volume, Treadwell posted a negative DVOA on all four downs and was one of the worst YAC receivers in the NFL, which is especially troubling considering tough-fought YAC was a strength of his coming out of Ole Miss. Treadwell's role with the team in 2019 is unclear, but he will likely fall out of favor as the team's third wide receiver and may struggle to even last on the roster through the season. Dramatic, unexpected change needs to be made if Treadwell wants to turn his career around.

Marquez Valdes-Scantling

Height: 6-4   Weight: 206   College: South Florida   Draft: 2018/5 (174)   Born: 10-Oct-1994   Age: 25   Risk: Red

Year	Team	G/GS	Snaps	Pass	Rec	Yds	TD	C%	+/-	Drop	Yd/C	aDOT	Rk	YAC	Rk	YAC+	BTkl	DVOA	Rk	DYAR	Rk	YAR	Use	Rk	Slot
2018	GB	16/10	692	73	38	581	2	52%	-5.6	3	15.3	12.5	26	5.6	14	+0.2	4	-11.3%	63	8	63	30	12.4%	75	56%
2019	GB			102	59	861	5	58%			14.6							3.1%							

Valdes-Scantling was good at one thing last season: getting open down the field. On early downs, the Packers did not always unleash him to do so, but when they needed to move the sticks on third and fourth down, they let him rip. Valdes-Scantling's average target on those downs came 18.4 yards down the field, and he joined Davante Adams and Jimmy Graham as the only Packers to post a positive DVOA on those downs. Considering he is a lanky 6-foot-4 and ran a 4.37-second 40-yard dash coming out of an up-tempo spread offense at South Florida, it is no surprise Valdes-Scantling is at his best when simply trying to out-athlete his opponent. Unfortunately, he proved to be of little use in every other area. He is not an underneath receiver who can win with quick, sharp moves, nor is he a sure-handed receiver who can dominate the catch point. His route tree is limited to vertical routes between the 20s. While that does have value, it hurt the Packers that he was their No. 2 wide receiver last year. Heading into the new year, Valdes-Scantling again seems primed for a heavy role in the offense, but he will need to show development toward being more than an inconsistent one-dimensional player.

James Washington

Height: 5-11   Weight: 213   College: Oklahoma State   Draft: 2018/2 (60)   Born: 2-Apr-1996   Age: 23   Risk: Yellow

Year	Team	G/GS	Snaps	Pass	Rec	Yds	TD	C%	+/-	Drop	Yd/C	aDOT	Rk	YAC	Rk	YAC+	BTkl	DVOA	Rk	DYAR	Rk	YAR	Use	Rk	Slot
2018	PIT	14/6	526	38	16	217	1	42%	-4.7	2	13.6	17.0	--	3.3	--	-1.2	1	-25.1%	--	-37	--	-51	6.3%	--	45%
2019	PIT			74	45	633	5	61%			14.1							8.5%							

When the Steelers selected Washington in the second round last year, the immediate reaction was, "Oh, there they go again!" Pittsburgh's proclivity for turning any drafted wideout into a Pro Bowler can work against those anointed as the Next One, and, unsurprisingly, Washington struggled with route concepts and the professional life in his debut season. That said, Washington had a rookie year that was very comparable to Antonio Brown's initial campaign—both had 16 catches, and Wash had 50 more yards and scored a touchdown, unlike Mr. Big Chest. No one expects Washington to turn into AB, but he is in a good spot with Ben Roethlisberger tossing him balls and, with Brown and Jesse James gone, 206 targets to replace. Washington remains explosive and competitive with the ball in the air, and he would make a good later-round target in your fantasy draft.

Sammy Watkins

Height: 6-1   Weight: 211   College: Clemson   Draft: 2014/1 (4)   Born: 14-Jun-1993   Age: 26   Risk: Green

Year	Team	G/GS	Snaps	Pass	Rec	Yds	TD	C%	+/-	Drop	Yd/C	aDOT	Rk	YAC	Rk	YAC+	BTkl	DVOA	Rk	DYAR	Rk	YAR	Use	Rk	Slot
2016	BUF	8/8	382	52	28	430	2	54%	+0.6	3	15.4	14.1	17	1.9	93	-1.8	2	-1.3%	53	48	64	56	22.8%	25	43%
2017	LAR	15/14	776	70	39	593	8	56%	+3.4	3	15.2	15.5	9	4.7	28	+0.8	2	24.1%	6	216	14	206	15.0%	65	47%
2018	KC	10/9	459	55	40	519	3	73%	+3.8	1	13.0	9.0	65	6.0	10	+1.2	14	24.1%	5	161	22	147	16.3%	55	57%
2019	KC			95	60	836	8	63%			13.9							13.7%							

A funny thing happened to Watkins last season. For the first time in his career, Watkins was not asked to be his team's top deep target. Watkins had the shortest aDOT of the four qualified Chiefs receivers; a new role in which he excelled. Watkins has always been a reliable target on curls and slants, but those two routes alone made up 48 percent of his targets last season, as opposed to 32 percent the year before. In 2017, 52 percent of his targets came more than 10 yards downfield; that fell to 28 percent in Kansas City. With Tyreek Hill possibly suspended to start the season, we may see more deep posts from Watkins in 2019 as the Chiefs look to replace that deep-ball threat.

Dede Westbrook

Height: 6-0   Weight: 178   College: Oklahoma   Draft: 2017/4 (110)   Born: 21-Nov-1993   Age: 26   Risk: Yellow

Year	Team	G/GS	Snaps	Pass	Rec	Yds	TD	C%	+/-	Drop	Yd/C	aDOT	Rk	YAC	Rk	YAC+	BTkl	DVOA	Rk	DYAR	Rk	YAR	Use	Rk	Slot
2017	JAX	7/5	386	51	27	339	1	53%	-2.0	2	12.6	12.0	39	3.7	52	-1.2	3	-21.5%	79	-35	76	-24	22.2%	20	39%
2018	JAX	16/9	805	102	66	717	5	66%	+0.4	8	10.9	8.7	69	5.4	21	+0.4	12	-15.7%	73	-25	73	1	19.4%	34	92%
2019	JAX			115	78	905	6	68%			11.6							-2.0%							

Westbrook fully moved into the slot role, taking almost all of his snaps and receptions from the position. His catch rate spiked, and for the offense he was in, Westbrook wasn't bad. To get to the next echelon, Westbrook will need to cut the drops, and he'll need to improve on the broken tackle numbers. Twelve isn't bad, but Westbrook was one of the most elusive players in the draft, and now he's logging broken tackle numbers that Albert Wilson and Marquise Lee can hit. The next couple of years and how hard he works on these things will be the difference between him becoming the next Golden Tate or the next Jarvis Landry. He's definitely getting the reps with how often Nick Foles targets slot receivers.

Chad Williams

Height: 6-0   Weight: 207   College: Grambling State   Draft: 2017/3 (98)   Born: 19-Oct-1994   Age: 25   Risk: Green

Year	Team	G/GS	Snaps	Pass	Rec	Yds	TD	C%	+/-	Drop	Yd/C	aDOT	Rk	YAC	Rk	YAC+	BTkl	DVOA	Rk	DYAR	Rk	YAR	Use	Rk	Slot
2017	ARI	6/1	100	7	3	31	0	43%	+0.2	0	10.3	17.7	--	2.0	--	-1.9	0	-0.4%	--	7	--	1	3.5%	--	0%
2018	ARI	10/7	430	46	17	171	1	37%	-8.7	3	10.1	13.2	--	0.9	--	-3.0	0	-53.5%	--	-142	--	-139	15.4%	--	13%
2019	ARI			13	7	82	0	54%			11.6							-15.4%							

Though his season wasn't as historically bad as those of teammates Josh Rosen and Ricky Seals-Jones, Williams did have the worst DYAR of any wide receiver in football last year. And he did that on only 46 passes, which means he didn't even qualify for our wide receivers leaderboard. He did not make the top 100 wideouts in catches, but he made the top 50 in targets not caught. It was the worst DYAR ever for a wideout with fewer than 50 targets … so maybe he was as bad as Rosen and Seals-Jones after all. This is why Arizona drafted a bazillion wideouts and why Williams' days in the desert are probably numbered.

Mike Williams

Height: 6-4   Weight: 218   College: Clemson   Draft: 2017/1 (7)   Born: 4-Oct-1994   Age: 25   Risk: Green

Year	Team	G/GS	Snaps	Pass	Rec	Yds	TD	C%	+/-	Drop	Yd/C	aDOT	Rk	YAC	Rk	YAC+	BTkl	DVOA	Rk	DYAR	Rk	YAR	Use	Rk	Slot
2017	LAC	10/1	234	23	11	95	0	48%	-2.8	2	8.6	9.7	--	1.0	--	-3.0	0	-18.0%	--	-10	--	-24	6.8%	--	20%
2018	LAC	16/5	622	66	43	664	10	65%	+4.9	2	15.4	14.7	13	2.7	79	-1.1	8	39.2%	2	262	13	246	13.2%	70	51%
2019	LAC			97	62	918	8	64%			14.8							17.4%							

The loss of Tyrell Williams means there are 65 more targets to go around in the Chargers' receiving corps, and Mike Williams is the guy in line to grab most of 'em. Williams is still a bit boom-or-bust, with a quarter of his games ending with fewer than 20 yards, but his boom was big enough to vault him near the top of our receiving leaderboard. He's not going to have six touchdowns in nine red zone catches again in 2019, and he's going to have to be more than an end zone threat to make the Williams-to-Williams transition as smooth as possible. Seven of Williams' touchdowns came on receptions in the end zone, tied for second-most in the league.

Tyrell Williams

Height: 6-3   Weight: 204   College: Western Oregon   Draft: 2015/FA   Born: 12-Feb-1992   Age: 27   Risk: Red

Year	Team	G/GS	Snaps	Pass	Rec	Yds	TD	C%	+/-	Drop	Yd/C	aDOT	Rk	YAC	Rk	YAC+	BTkl	DVOA	Rk	DYAR	Rk	YAR	Use	Rk	Slot
2016	SD	16/12	891	118	69	1059	7	58%	+0.4	9	15.3	11.9	42	6.0	8	+1.7	8	9.0%	27	201	23	174	20.6%	33	50%
2017	LAC	16/15	852	69	43	728	4	62%	+2.2	4	16.9	14.3	16	7.7	1	+2.6	6	15.4%	15	150	25	142	12.0%	75	56%
2018	LAC	16/10	761	65	41	653	5	63%	+1.2	2	15.9	12.6	25	4.8	29	-0.0	3	12.3%	24	128	32	109	12.8%	73	62%
2019	OAK			82	47	691	4	57%			14.7							0.8%							

Williams led the league in YAC+ in 2016 and 2017, but he dropped out of the top 20 last season. He'll be looking for a bounce-back year in Oakland, but there are some slight concerns. Williams had been the Chargers' big-play receiver ever since he arrived in San Diego. He has 1,159 yards on deep passes (16-plus air yards) in his career, 261 more than any other Charger from that time period. That's all well and good, but Antonio Brown has the most yards on deep passes in football over that time period, and J.J. Nelson's one real skill is an occasional crazy play deep downfield. There's some duplication in Williams' skill set, in other words, especially notable when paired with a quarterback who routinely ranks near the bottom of the league in average depth of target.

Albert Wilson

Height: 5-9   Weight: 186   College: Georgia State   Draft: 2014/FA   Born: 12-Jul-1992   Age: 27   Risk: Yellow

Year	Team	G/GS	Snaps	Pass	Rec	Yds	TD	C%	+/-	Drop	Yd/C	aDOT	Rk	YAC	Rk	YAC+	BTkl	DVOA	Rk	DYAR	Rk	YAR	Use	Rk	Slot
2016	KC	16/5	466	51	31	279	2	61%	-4.4	5	9.0	7.4	86	4.8	34	-0.8	7	-22.1%	84	-37	83	-48	9.5%	92	73%
2017	KC	13/7	538	62	42	554	3	68%	+0.5	7	13.2	6.3	84	7.5	2	+1.5	13	21.4%	8	167	22	157	14.5%	67	71%
2018	MIA	7/3	232	35	26	391	4	74%	+0.8	1	15.0	7.0	--	12.9	--	+6.5	13	10.8%	--	63	--	65	18.1%	--	46%
2019	MIA			80	50	588	2	63%			11.8							-4.2%							

Wilson's 2018 season was the ultimate expression of the last Dolphins regime's malaise/neurosis. Mike Tannenbaum signed the former Chiefs slot weapon to a zany three-year, $24-million contract with loads of guarantees for the first two seasons. Wilson responded with huge games against the Raiders (2-74-1, with big plays on a flea flicker and a shovel pass) and the Bears (6-155-2, with touchdowns on a screen-and-go and a shallow dig where the defense fell asleep). But there's a reason 186-pound jitterbugs are given small roles and short-term contracts: Wilson suffered a hip injury in late October and missed the remainder of the year. Without Wilson, the Dolphins offense turtled up, because Adam Gase just couldn't find a way to generate offense with only Kenny Stills, DeVante Parker, Frank Gore, Kenyan Drake, and so forth.

Wilson was still unavailable for the start of OTAs, but the Dolphins can't cut him without taking a cap hit because of the guarantees in his contract, plus Wilson's ability to turn screens into touchdowns could be a huge boon to Josh Rosen. Wilson's cap number balloons to $10.8 million in 2020 (Tannenbaum's meds either wore off or kicked in), and it's hard to imagine that he will still be on the team when they start to get competitive. But he should be fun to watch this year. If he's healthy.

Robert Woods

Height: 6-0   Weight: 201   College: USC   Draft: 2013/2 (41)   Born: 10-Apr-1992   Age: 27   Risk: Green

Year	Team	G/GS	Snaps	Pass	Rec	Yds	TD	C%	+/-	Drop	Yd/C	aDOT	Rk	YAC	Rk	YAC+	BTkl	DVOA	Rk	DYAR	Rk	YAR	Use	Rk	Slot
2016	BUF	13/10	633	75	51	613	1	67%	+7.2	2	12.0	11.6	45	2.5	90	-1.6	3	7.9%	30	117	46	123	20.1%	37	67%
2017	LAR	12/11	649	85	56	781	5	66%	+4.4	4	13.9	10.6	53	5.2	19	+0.3	6	13.4%	21	172	20	178	22.4%	19	84%
2018	LAR	16/16	1041	130	86	1219	6	66%	+4.1	3	14.2	11.3	42	4.9	27	+0.1	11	17.5%	16	316	11	301	24.3%	16	85%
2019	LAR			131	81	1057	6	62%			13.0							9.0%							

As part of the talented Rams receiving triumvirate, Woods made his hay in the red zone, finishing with 18.7% receiving DVOA inside the 20, best among the Rams' receivers in that area of the field. He also took advantage of Cooper Kupp's absence due to injury and blew his career highs out of the water with 130 targets and 19 carries, finishing 11th in receiving DYAR and second in rushing DYAR among wide receivers. His usage will probably come back to earth a bit with Kupp's return to the lineup, but through Year 2 of the five-year deal he signed in free agency to come home to Los Angeles, Woods has been a smashing success.

Jarius Wright   Height: 5-10   Weight: 182   College: Arkansas   Draft: 2012/4 (118)   Born: 25-Nov-1989   Age: 30   Risk: Red

Year	Team	G/GS	Snaps	Pass	Rec	Yds	TD	C%	+/-	Drop	Yd/C	aDOT	Rk	YAC	Rk	YAC+	BTkl	DVOA	Rk	DYAR	Rk	YAR	Use	Rk	Slot
2016	MIN	8/1	119	14	11	67	1	79%	+0.6	0	6.1	4.0	--	3.8	--	-1.2	1	-1.8%	--	12	--	12	4.7%	--	79%
2017	MIN	16/0	256	25	18	198	2	72%	+2.0	0	11.0	8.2	--	4.9	--	-0.3	1	29.0%	--	84	--	86	4.9%	--	96%
2018	CAR	16/6	528	59	43	447	1	73%	+2.5	2	10.4	6.4	83	4.6	35	-0.4	11	-15.1%	70	-12	69	6	10.9%	79	87%
2019	CAR			49	33	342	1	67%			10.4							-0.7%							

Another Panthers receiver who was more effective from the slot than split wide, Wright's six starts and almost 500 scrimmage yards marked a larger-than-expected contribution for the discount ex-Vikings free agent. Wright's biggest contributions came during the team's second-half fade, during which he had eight straight games of 20 or more yards; when Newton was healthy and the offense was at its best, Wright was held below 10 yards in four of eight contests. That, along with his three fumbles, casts a shadow over his 2019 prospects, and the signing of Chris Hogan from the Patriots will probably reduce Wright's target share even if it doesn't bump him any lower down the pecking order than he was last year.

Going Deep

Tavon Austin, DAL: Austin caught a 64-yard touchdown bomb against the Giants in Week 2 when a defender slipped, and he hauled in a 44-yard pass against the Texans in Week 5 at the end of a Dak Prescott scramble. What little else he did last year consisted mostly of reverses, screens, and shovel passes, with a few critical drops, plus shoulder and groin injuries to erase most of the second half of the season. Austin remains a poor man's Percy Harvin and is getting a little poorer every year. Various members of the Jones clan still think they can make a superstar "web back" (don't ask) out of him, so his roster spot appears secure.

Cameron Batson, TEN: Taywan Taylor's injury created a four-game window of opportunity for this slot man, but that closed with Taylor's return. Signing veteran slot specialist Adam Humphries and drafting A.J. Brown, primarily a slot receiver at Ole Miss, made clear what the Titans' thought of last year's slot options. Special teams is Batson's only route to regular snaps.

Chad Beebe, MIN: It is only natural that Beebe gets compared to Adam Thielen. He is an undrafted, undersized slot receiver paying his dues at the bottom of the depth chart in hopes to climb in the future. The difference, however, is that Thielen dominated the small school circuit in college, while Beebe never cracked 500 receiving yards. Beebe is also not an impressive athlete, clocking a linebacker-esque 4.73-second 40-yard dash at 5-foot-10 and 180 pounds. He may get the inside track on snaps as the No. 4 receiver, especially if the Vikings fully give up on Laquon Treadwell.

Josh Bellamy, NYJ: Bellamy carved out a weird little niche as the Bears' fourth receiver for four solid seasons. Fourth receivers typically either get promoted or get cut and bounce around the league, but Bellamy hung around Chicago from 2015 through 2018, catching 14 to 24 passes per year and earning spot starts due to injuries or just when the Bears opened the game with four receivers. Bellamy is likely to resume that role for the Jets, whose top three receivers all have complicated injury histories.

Braxton Berrios, NE: A 2018 sixth-round pick out of Miami as a short slot receiver and prospective punt returner, Berrios has already been compared to former Patriots short slot receiver and punt returner Danny Amendola because of course he has. Stashed on injured reserve last season, Berrios should get more of a chance to compete this year in a shallow receiving corps.

Jaron Brown, SEA: After signing with Seattle as a free agent in the 2018 offseason, Brown was fairly low on the receiving totem pole in a low-volume passing attack. When he was targeted, he was quite effective, finishing with 58.0% receiving DVOA on 14 receptions (19 targets) with 166 yards and five touchdowns. In drafting D.K. Metcalf, Gary Jennings, and John Ursua, the Seahawks clearly showed they needed more of a threat at receiver to help replace Doug Baldwin this offseason, but the Seattle coaching staff liked how Brown blocked. If nothing else, that should give Brown a chance to keep his spot on the roster.

Noah Brown, DAL: Brown is the perfect fourth wide receiver. He's a big, high-effort core special-teamer who is useful in four-receiver sets and bunch formations because he's fast enough to force the defense to spend a cornerback on him in coverage but a rugged blocker for screens or running plays. And he's a former seventh-round pick, so he works cheap. Look for Brown to catch four or five passes per year for many years to come, maybe climbing up to 15 or 20 in his best years.

Dez Bryant, FA: A torn Achilles on his first day of practice after signing with the Saints in midseason looks to have brought an ignominious end to a hugely productive career. Bryant never saw game action for the Saints, but he left the Cowboys as their all-time leader in receiving touchdowns and fifth all-time in receiving yards. He was a first-team All-Pro in 2014, which was also his best season in DYAR and DVOA (fifth in both). Bryant wants to return and has posted video of himself working out to that effect, but he remains unsigned as of early June. Absent a major injury crisis, the 30-year-old is likely to remain that way.

Martavis Bryant, FA: Bryant faced a full year's suspension last year for violating the league's drug policy, but he received a conditional reprieve at the last moment. Nineteen catches later, the league announced that Bryant had violated that reprieve, and he would be suspended indefinitely. This after missing 20 games in 2015 and 2016 for violating the drug policy. Bryant flashed superstar potential as a rookie, but he hasn't lived up to it since then, and it's quite likely no one will want to put up with the many, many headaches Bryant brings with him.

Deontay Burnett, NYJ: Burnett was a crafty, slippery collegiate route-runner who went 86-1,114-9 in his final season at USC but showed up at his pro day at 177 pounds and ran a 4.70 40 on a not-yet-healed hammy. He bounced from Titans to Jets camp as a UDFA, catching four passes against the Bears in Week 8 for the Jets and five passes for 73 yards in the season finale against the Patriots. Burnett now lists at 186 pounds, and the Jets re-signed him to a one-year deal. He could push Josh Bellamy for the fourth receiver spot.

Brice Butler, MIA: The Cowboys let Butler go when they traded for Amari Cooper last year; falling to the bottom of the 2018 Cowboys receiver depth chart takes some doing. The Dolphins scooped him up during an injury crunch, and Butler caught a 21-yard touchdown pass in the wacky win over the Patriots. Butler is a 29-year-old knockaround journeyman, making him exactly the type of player the Dolphins do not want on the roster.

Deon Cain, IND: The man who succeeded Mike Williams as Clemson's top receiver tore his ACL in training camp and spent his rookie season on injured reserve. General manager Chris Ballard indicated in April that he believed Cain had great upside but cautioned in May that the receiver may not be ready until midseason. If healthy, Cain is more explosive than Devin Funchess, but he's also a sixth-round pick who has done nothing on an NFL field yet.

Dylan Cantrell, LAC: As a sixth-round rookie out of Texas Tech, Cantrell didn't get a snap in 2018, but the Chargers are high enough on him that they promoted him to the main roster in December. Cantrell is a slow, big-bodied receiver, but he had some very intriguing, explosive results at his combine—great scores in the vertical and broad jump. He's not a direct replacement for Tyrell Williams but could be a solid possession option down by the goal line. Dynasty owners await with bated breath for their sleeper pick from last year to pan out.

Austin Carr, NO: Carr has an awesome off-field story as a stem cell donor whose donation saved the life of a cancer patient in 2015. On the field, he has only 97 yards on 14 targets across his first two seasons, and he owes even that production to the churn of the Saints receivers in 2018. He will need to have a very strong summer to remain on the roster as he enters the final year of his rookie contract.

Cody Core, CIN: Core was set ablaze by Bengals fans who were #MadOnline that he dropped a pass on fourth-and-3 with the season at stake against the Ravens. That's more of a reflection of the coaching staff than of Core—he simply isn't the guy you want to replace A.J. Green. Core's a special-teamer. In the final year of his rookie deal, with a new head coach, don't be surprised if Core and his 46 percent catch rate are available at last cuts.

Jawill Davis, GB: Every year a football player suffers an unfortunate yet hilarious injury, and we need to give it the kind of chuckle you feel a little embarrassed about. Davis dislocated his kneecap while dancing. Not after an awesome return. Not after a touchdown. Not celebrating with a teammate. He suffered it dancing in the locker room. Yup. Davis led the Giants with 0.3 points of punt return value last year. Waived in May but claimed by the Packers. Where there's a Jawill, there's a Jaway.

Trevor Davis, GB: Three years into his NFL career, Trevor Davis has been far more productive as a returner than as a receiver. Davis was a speed and yards-after-catch threat coming out of Cal in 2016 but did not have the hands or route-running skill to cut it as a reliable wide receiver. Instead, Davis transitioned those skills to special teams. He finished the 2017 season with a third-best 6.1 points of punt return value, eking out Tyreek Hill's 6.0. Conversely, Davis has just eight career receptions and he scored his lone receiving touchdown as a rookie. Even without much added competition this offseason, Davis will likely remain as strictly a return man.

Alex Erickson, CIN: Based on his punt return profile, you would expect Erickson's game to be based on short-area explosion, but he torches corners in deep coverage more often than you'd think. He caught Bradley Roby napping in Week 11 of 2017, and he beat T.J. Carrie on a go route for 28 yards in Week 16 last year. He's not just a screens-and-slants guy, which is another area of extra value. In total he caught 20 of 29 passes for 167 yards, though he only had -16.4% DVOA. Erickson signed a two-year extension last September for only $4.05 million and is likely to remain a good value proposition for the duration of the deal.

Michael Floyd, BAL: Floyd has caught 24 passes for 220 yards and two touchdowns for his last three teams, dating back to when the Patriots claimed him off waivers from the Cardinals in December 2016. He was also found guilty of DUI (a second offense, which led to his departure from Arizona), received a four-game NFL suspension, and reportedly violated the terms of his house arrest in that span. The Ravens picked up the former deep threat who now averages 9.2 yards per catch because NFL decision-makers honestly believe that 29-year-old athletes with obvious personal problems will magically recreate their 2013-15 production if just motivated properly.

Daurice Fountain, IND: The transition from Northern Iowa to the NFL was a rough one for the fifth-round pick. Staring at opportunity on a thin depth chart, he failed to make the team and spent most of the season on the practice squad, playing just four snaps on offense. He remains an intriguing project, a leaper and high-jump champion who could be a deep-ball specialist or more. There is still opportunity here, just less of it than there was a year ago.

Travis Fulgham, DET: A sixth-round rookie for Detroit, Fulgham walked on and redshirted at Old Dominion during the program's first season in the FBS in 2014. Outside of the red zone, he was not a driving force in the offense until his final season, where he topped 1,000 yards in a campaign that included four 150-plus-yard performances. He is not a burner by any stretch, instead winning through vertical ability and a sneaky ability to fight through contact, which fits Detroit's "type" to a T.

Russell Gage, ATL: Primarily a special teams player last season, the sixth-round draft pick out of LSU saw only 13 offensive snaps in the Falcons' first 12 games. In their final four games, he played 47 snaps and caught six of 10 targets for 63 yards. He'll compete with veteran Justin Hardy and rookie Marcus Green for the team's receiving spots behind Julio Jones, Calvin Ridley, and Mohamed Sanu.

Shelton Gibson, PHI: Now three years removed from college, Gibson is still trying to recreate the downfield success he had in Dana Holgorsen's Air Raid system at West Virginia. He posted two seasons of 20-plus yards per reception in the Big 12, but only has three catches to his name in the NFL, which is made even more disappointing by the fact that the Eagles had a need at deep threat last season that he theoretically could have filled. Unfortunately, he must not have proven capable enough to handle the volume of that role yet, though he still remains an athletic special-teamer.

Terry Godwin, CAR: A seventh-round pick at wide receiver by a team that didn't really need another wide receiver, Godwin will probably have to earn his roster spot the hard way: he played a lot of special teams at Georgia without ever being considered a return specialist, so his path to the active roster is most likely coverage teams. A crisp route-runner with decent deep speed and body control, Godwin's skill set at least appears to match his quarterback's strengths, but there are a lot of strong veterans between him and the offensive lineup.

Marcus Green, ATL: The Falcons have started an annual tradition: drafting multidimensional receivers/special-teamers from Louisiana in the sixth round. Last year it was LSU's Russell Gage with the 194th overall pick; this year it was Louisiana-Monroe's Green with the 203rd overall pick. Green gained 1,048 yards from scrimmage (855 receiving, 193 rushing) for the Warhawks in 2018 and returned kicks and a handful of punts. Atlanta is listing him as a running back rather than a wide receiver, and early on he's likely to see more snaps as a kick returner.

Emanuel Hall, CHI: Consistency is not Emanuel Hall's game. Be that the result of dropping too many passes or missing time via injury, Hall's college career is not a shrine to reliability. However, if you need a home run hitter, Hall is the man to call. A favorite of quarterback Drew Lock at Missouri, Hall was a speed threat on the sideline who, in addition to being the Tigers' best wide receiver, helped create space underneath for crossers and screens. To no surprise, the offense often faltered when he was sidelined by injury. Hall finished his career at Missouri with a stunning 20.8 yards per reception and 12.1 yards per target. He signed with Chicago after going undrafted.

Marvin Hall, CHI: Hall is more kick returner than wide receiver. As a receiver, he is more or less a poor man's version of the Taylor Gabriel, Marquise Goodwin style of speed slot that Kyle Shanahan's offenses tend to feature. Even on kick returns, though, Hall's linear speed is often not enough to make a great impact, rendering the Falcons just 22nd in our kick return ratings last season with Hall fielding a majority of those returns. He signed with Chicago in March.

Justin Hardy, ATL: In his four seasons with the Falcons, Hardy has been decent enough, but he has never risen to the level of a No. 3 receiver. His 22 targets, 14 catches, and 133 receiving yards in 2018 were all career lows, and over the final quarter of the season, rookie Russell Gage played nearly as many offensive snaps.

Kelvin Harmon, WAS: Selected in the sixth round, Harmon is a well-built, hard-nosed boundary receiver who produced back-to-back 1,000-yard seasons playing pitch-and-catch with Ryan Finley at North Carolina State. Harmon has the body control and competitiveness to be effective at plucking contested deep balls, making him a threat to Josh Doctson's role as the perma-project who runs fade routes. Like fellow rookie Terry McLaurin, Harmon has a rep for top-notch intangibles, which could help him stick to the roster.

Dwayne Harris, OAK: Harris led the NFL in yards per punt return last season, mostly thanks to a fluky 99-yard touchdown on Christmas Eve against Denver—one of those plays where the other team touches the ball first, and so there's no risk trying a crazy runback. Take everyone's best return away, and he drops from first to fourth—any stat with a tiny sample size can really be thrown off by one outlier. He also finished in the top 10 in yards per kick return, so he was a fine replacement for Cordarrelle Patterson. Harris even contributed six receptions, but it would be an act of purest optimism to project him to top that number in 2019.

Jalen Hurd, SF: One of the more unusual talents in this year's draft, Hurd first played college football at Tennessee, where he was the tallest, skinniest running back you ever saw. Playing ahead of Alvin Kamara, he ran for more than 2,600 yards in three seasons. He then transferred to Baylor, and in his one season with the Bears, he ran for 209 more yards, but added 69 catches for 946 yards. After the 49ers took him 67th overall, Kyle Shanahan called Hurd the most versatile player he had ever drafted, and both coach and player said Hurd could play wide receiver, running back, or even tight end. The 49ers don't need any more running backs and are quite set at tight end, thank you, so Hurd will be a wideout for now. He'll likely play mostly out of the slot this season, running slats and flants and trying to rack up YAC.

Richie James, SF: A seventh-round rookie out of Middle Tennessee State, James showed a knack for big plays in limited action last year, with a 53-yard catch-and-run against Oakland in Week 9 and a kickoff return for a touchdown against Seattle in Week 15. The 49ers added Jordan Matthews in free agency and drafted a pair of wideouts, so James will likely be limited to special teams in 2019.

Darius Jennings, TEN: Jennings caught 11 of 15 passes for 101 yards and a replacement-level -13.2% DVOA. But where he really excelled was as a kick returner, returning a kickoff opening week in Miami for a score and finishing second in the league behind Andre Roberts with 12.2 points of kick return value. With the additions up the depth chart at wide receiver, special teams remains his route to a roster spot, especially if he can replace Adoree' Jackson on punt returns in addition to his fine kick return work.

Charles Johnson, PHI: Johnson was something of a bottom-of-the-roster fan favorite with the Vikings from 2014 to 2016, when the receiver depth was questionable and Stefon Diggs and Adam Thielen had not fully emerged as the stars they are now. He topped 400 yards for the first and only time in 2014, when he served primarily as an intermediate and deep threat down the sideline. Now, Johnson is one of a handful of players returning to the NFL after a stint in the failed Alliance of American Football; he led the league with both 45 receptions and 687 yards.

KeeSean Johnson, ARI: Arizona's sixth-round pick is no relation to (and is not named for) the other Keyshawn Johnson. This KeeSean was a four-year starter at Fresno State, going over 1,000 yards with eight scores in each of his last two seasons. Johnson ran a 4.6-second 40-yard dash at the combine, so there's no deep speed here. But he has size (6-foot-1, 201 pounds) and quickness (he also returned kickoffs and punts for the Bulldogs) and he could be a dangerous player if Kyler Murray can just give him the damn ball.

Olabisi Johnson, MIN: At a Colorado State program that has quietly developed a knack for producing NFL receivers, Johnson played second fiddle to Preston Williams, a Tennessee transfer. But it was Johnson who got drafted (in the seventh round) while Williams went to the Dolphins as a UDFA. Across the board, Johnson sports a good-not-great profile for a late-round rookie. He has requisite speed, size, and agility to be groomed into a capable receiver with the flexibility to move between slot and flanker, and he was devilishly efficient in college with a 71 percent catch rate and 65 percent success rate as a senior. There is little to indicate a special ceiling, but he could emerge as the Vikings' No. 4 or No. 5 by time the season comes around.

Andy Jones, DET: Not until Golden Tate was traded did Jones see any targets last season. He slowly found opportunities here and there over the last few games before getting a full game's worth of action in a Week 16 "who cares?" sort of contest against the Packers. Jones saw a career-high 12 targets, six receptions, and 50 yards against an injury-riddled, worn-down Packers defense. He had only five catches for 30 yards the rest of the season.

T.J. Jones, FA: Jones carved out a niche for himself in Detroit during the Jim Bob Cooter era, but with a new head coach last year and a new offensive coordinator this year, he is out. Jones was not quite the short-area YAC monster Golden Tate was, nor was he the pterodactyl Marvin Jones and Kenny Golladay were, but he could swap between slot and flanker as a solid chains-mover. Though he never found much volume, Jones was the "duct tape" of sorts for whatever Detroit needed in four-wide receiver sets. Jones was born in Winnipeg so the CFL may be his next stop.

Keith Kirkwood, NO: Another of the large number of undrafted receivers who earned playing time for the Saints in 2018, Kirkwood worked his way onto the field in Week 9 of his rookie year and stayed involved throughout the rest of the season—by the end of the year he had played over 20 percent of the team's offensive snaps, and his 15 total receptions, including playoffs, included at least one catch in eight straight games with Drew Brees at quarterback. Kirkwood is unlikely to break into a regular starting role in 2019, but he should remain involved on both offense and special teams despite fierce competition at the bottom of the roster.

Jake Kumerow, GB: Like a few others in Green Bay last year, Kumerow saw unexpected playing time as result of a shallow receiver group that battled with injuries. Kumerow caught just eight passes, but they were the first and only receptions of his career, and that playing time was the only time he has ever seen snaps on offense since entering the league in 2015. Barring another slew of injuries, it is unlikely he catches more passes in 2019, but he can now say he is more than a career practice squad player.

Brandon LaFell, FA: LaFell became the Raiders' top wide receiver option after the Amari Cooper trade, albeit more or less by default. He put up a 26.9% DVOA on just 16 passes with a catch rate of 75 percent—unsustainable, but his best numbers since 2011. We'll never know if he could keep it up—he ruptured his Achilles in November. At age 33, that's likely career-ending; he says he's going to try to come back, but so far he hasn't received any interest at all.

Jordan Lasley, BAL: As a fifth-round rookie, Lasley made the 53-man roster to start the season but was never activated. At UCLA, Lasley caught passes from Josh Rosen and showed a pattern of immaturity—arrests, team suspensions, mouthing "bitch" at players he caught a touchdown against, that sort of thing—and that helped him slide to the fourth round despite solid play. Like every other receiver on the Baltimore roster, he's now looking up at Hollywood Brown and Miles Boykin, wondering if there's still an opportunity for him here.

Rishard Matthews, NO: A veteran of three straight seasons of 650-plus yards as the No. 2 receiver on the Titans, Matthews asked for and was granted his release last September after seeing his role massively reduced in Matt LaFleur's new-look offense. He eventually caught on with the Jets, where he found an even smaller role, and he had by far the least productive season of his seven-year career (5 catches for 24 yards). The Saints picked him up as a possible depth piece in mid-June.

Ray-Ray McCloud, BUF: At 5-foot-9, 190 pounds, McCloud was deemed too tiny to play in the NFL by draft scouts when the Bills took him in the sixth round last year. That may or may not be true, but it is not a good sign that McCloud was unable to make a dent in the Bills' extraordinarily weak receiver corps in 2018. By the end of the year, he was passed on the depth chart by undrafted free agents and other teams' cast-offs. He could still end up being a gadget player and returner if used properly, but he's going to have to show more than he did last season to even make the roster.

Isaiah McKenzie, BUF: The scrawny McKenzie had just four receptions in a season and a half with Denver before being cut in midseason so an actual receiver could take his place on the depth chart. That's the kind of resume that makes you a starter in receiver-starved Buffalo, where McKenzie ended up with 18 receptions (-23.8% DVOA), two dozen returns and even some emergency running back duty. A significantly more talented Buffalo team is unlikely to need McKenzie to play such a significant role in 2019.

Cameron Meredith, NO: In Cameron Meredith's last healthy season, he recorded 888 yards and four touchdowns for the Bears despite mediocre advanced stats (4.1% DVOA, 45th; 128 DYAR, 43rd). Unfortunately, his last healthy season ended over two years ago—he tore his left ACL in the 2017 preseason, signed with the Saints in free agency the following summer, and has played only six games since mostly due to complications with his knee. If Meredith can regain some measure of health, he could be a valuable depth piece or even starter in a murky talent pool. Alas, judging by recent history, that's a big "if."

Scott Miller, TB: The Bowling Green product was the only offensive player the Bucs drafted in April (sixth round, 208th over-all). Miller, who was not invited to the combine, has breakaway speed and averaged 16.2 yards per catch during a 1,148-yard senior season. Yet the slim receiver (5-foot-11, 174 pounds) has drawn more comparisons to Adam Humphries than DeSean Jackson (5-foot-10, 175 pounds). He'll try to turn some heads with a scrappy, workmanlike effort during training camp.

Dillon Mitchell, MIN: Following the Chip Kelly era, most people would not associate Oregon with a lack of skill player talent, but that was the case in 2018. Mitchell stood well above his peers as his 1,184 receiving yards were nearly triple that of the next-best receiver on the team (Johnny Redd, 433). In turn, Mitchell was not particularly efficient because defenses knew where the ball was going, lending to a rather low 46 percent success rate on receptions. All that usage gave Mitchell an excellent 85.3% Playmaker Rating. The Vikings grabbed him in the seventh round.

Taquan Mizzell, CHI: Mizzell is the insurance policy for Tarik Cohen. Mizzell, like Cohen, is a small, shifty player who is devastating once he gets into space. Though a running back who could play receiver in college and as a rookie, Mizzell is now officially listed as a wide receiver. It is likely he will see time at both positions like he always has, but he may be prioritized as one of Matt Nagy's many gadget receivers.

J'Mon Moore, GB: J'Mon Moore is one of a handful of young Packers receivers the team is hoping can fix their drop issues. As one of Drew Lock's receivers at Missouri, Moore finished his college career with sub-par 54 percent catch rate. Part of his low catch rate can be explained by him being a deep threat, so naturally many of his targets are low-percentage plays, but he also has his fair share of drops on slants, curls, etc. Moore barely saw action as a fourth-round rookie in 2018 despite a thin wide receiver corps and a slew of injuries ahead of him, but with a new opportunity in a different offensive scheme and another offseason to clean up his ball retention, he may be able to earn himself a few more snaps.

Stanley Morgan, CIN: After breaking Nebraska's receiving yardage record twice in his last two seasons, Morgan found him-self undrafted on account of a 6-foot-0, 202-pound body that didn't inspire much confidence. He's got acceleration and speed out of his breaks and displays a lot of route awareness that could lead to early playing time in the right situation. The caveat, of course, is that the last Nebraska receiver that we were this high on for his technical ability was Kenny Bell, whom you probably had forgotten existed until we wrote this comment. Still, with how weak the depth chart is in Cincinnati, Morgan could be a player to watch. No, he is not related to the former Patriots legend.

J.J. Nelson, OAK: The ghost of Al Davis had to smile when the Raiders signed Nelson this offseason. He had the fastest time at the combine back in 2015, running the 40 in just 4.28 seconds. That speed mostly ensured he found a good spot on the bench in Arizona; he had just 81 catches in his four seasons in the desert and couldn't get on the field last year. Speed failing to turn into production sounds like a Davis pick, too, though Nelson is young enough (27) that a second chance might help him turn the corner.

Brandon Powell, DET: Powell was initially a running back at the University of Florida before converting into a short-area and gadget wide receiver. The way Powell moves and approaches yards after the catch, he very much still plays like a running back, which is how many described former Lions receiver Golden Tate's playing style. With Tate now out of the picture, Powell has a chance to assume the role full-time. Though he did not play for most of last season, Powell erupted in a meaningless Week 17 game versus Green Bay, picking up 103 yards on just six receptions, with a lot of that production coming after the catch.

Byron Pringle, KC: The undrafted Pringle was probably going to make the Chiefs roster last year before a hamstring injury in the final preseason game put him on IR. He's an advanced route-runner and coaches praised him during OTAs for strong hands, which was supposed to be his weakness coming out of Kansas State. He's competing with other UDFAs including Gehrig Dieter and Marcus Kemp for a spot at the bottom of the Chiefs' receiver depth chart. But if Tyreek Hill is suspended, he could move up and even become fantasy-relevant.

Terrelle Pryor, JAX: That 77-catch 2016 season sure did fool everyone, didn't it? Pryor was a 27-year-old failed quarterback prospect who appeared poised to play out the string as a fourth wide receiver when he took opponents by surprise with some high-volume games for a 1-15 Browns team with no one else to throw the football to. But Pryor was good copy, so we all made a big deal about what a great receiver he turned into. The Skins fell for it and paid Pryor $8 million to catch 20 passes and sink to the bottom of the depth chart. Both the Jets and Bills—teams that were starting the likes of Jermaine Kearse and Kelvin Benjamin last year—kicked Pryor's tires and decided he wasn't worth it. Pryor is now 30 years old and in Jacksonville, which should be a euphemism for the end of the line for a former big-name prospect.

Damion Ratley, CLE: Ratley ran the fastest 40-yard dash among wideouts at the 2018 combine, but he only averaged 11.1 yards per his 13 catches as a rookie (-14.3% DVOA). There are some tools to work with here, but he hasn't shown the competitiveness needed to consistently make plays, and with a receiver room as deep as it is in Cleveland, he will have trouble seeing the field.

Riley Ridley, CHI: Though unimpressive by measure of volume, Ridley was one of college football's most efficient receivers last season. Based on Bill Connelly's play-by-play breakdown, he posted the third-highest marginal efficiency rating among draft prospects, mostly proving his prowess on curls, slants, comebacks, and any other pattern that could showcase his sudden yet smooth route running. Chicago selected him in the fourth round and his value, especially early on, will depend on how well quarterback Mitchell Trubisky develops as a timing-based passer and how often head coach Matt Nagy works those plays into the offense.

Andre Roberts, BUF: Roberts was forced into offensive action for the Jets late last year due to injuries, catching 10 of 18 targets for 79 yards and a touchdown (-34.3% DVOA). The Bills hope he gets zero plays with Josh Allen and company. Roberts is here because he was an All-Pro returner, leading the NFL in yards per punt return and gross kickoff return yardage, as well as finishing second in yards per kick return, with a pair of touchdowns thrown in for good measure. Some of Allen's passes may *look* like punts, but still.

Aldrick Robinson, CAR: Robinson was one of Kyle Shanahan's original "speed slot" receivers, a role that has now become a staple of the coaching prodigy's offense. Taylor Gabriel, Marquise Goodwin, and others have come after him, but Robinson helped establish the deep threat slot role in Shanahan's offense when the two were together in Washington in 2012 and 2013. He has bounced around plenty since then, including a return to Shanahan in 2017 with the 49ers, but hit a career-high five touchdowns last year as the Vikings' No. 4 receiver, scoring twice during the Vikings-Rams shootout on Thursday Night Football. He signed with Carolina in May.

Eli Rogers, PIT: After tearing his ACL in the 2017 playoff game against Jacksonville, Rogers was a forgotten man last year, coming off the shelf in December and making a minimal impact (10-of-12, 79 yards, -20.8% DVOA). With Antonio Brown gone, however, Rogers' familiarity with the system is an asset, and the twists and turns of the NFL could swing back in his favor.

Rashad Ross, CAR: An undrafted deep threat out of Arizona State in 2013, Ross attained a measure of fame in early spring 2019 as he led the ill-fated Alliance of American Football in receiving touchdowns. He recorded seven touchdowns and 583 yards for the Arizona Hotshots, but the six-year veteran has only nine catches for 192 yards and a single touchdown in the NFL, all for Washington in 2015 and 2016. Otherwise, he has mostly bounced on and off practice squads as an occasional kick returner, which is probably what gives him his best shot to stick in Carolina.

Jaleel Scott, BAL: Scott lost his entire first year to a hamstring injury that landed him as an IR stash. The 2018 fourth-round pick out of New Mexico State had an up-and-down Senior Bowl but flashed the red zone box-out skills to be a threat for Lamar Jackson. With Hollywood Brown and Miles Boykin added in this year's draft, Scott's window to impress the Ravens enough to keep him may simply be as wide as this offseason. In a game of separation, Scott's subpar athleticism means he needs to use every inch of his 6-foot-6 frame to assure a roster spot.

Russell Shepard, NYG: Shepard's agent has an impeccable talent for picking out exactly the right receiver depth charts for him to land on and get some run. Despite being mostly a special-teamer, Shepard has been targeted at least 19 times in each of the last three seasons and has only had one targetless season since 2013. With 47 DYAR on 20.5% DVOA last season, he is second amongst all returning Giants receivers in DYAR and second among all returning Giants receivers in DYAR accumulated by a player with the surname "Shepard." Russell is going to catch 25 balls this year before Daniel Jones realizes he and Sterling are different people.

Darius Slayton, NYG: A 4.39-second 40-yard dash time that never really shows up on the field without a free release got Slayton on the NFL scout radar. It's hard to completely divorce him from Auburn's Jarrett Stidham-led offense, but Slayton had his own issues with tracking and dropping balls that were independent from what Auburn was doing. However, as the only player drafted this year (fifth round) on this Giants depth chart, he's still got athletic upside worth monitoring. It turns out that when you trade Odell Beckham, you open up a target vacuum.

Vyncint Smith, HOU: A size-speed project who doesn't really know where he's going as a receiver half the time, Smith found his way into a meaningful role with the Texans because not only did Will Fuller get hurt, but Keke Coutee also got hurt, and the guy they traded for to fill Fuller's role, Demaryius Thomas, also got hurt. Smith ran a 4.36-second 40-yard dash at his pro day and caught one big touchdown from Deshaun Watson against the Eagles en route to a -3.3% DVOA season with five catches and 91 yards. Smith will likely return to more of a fringe role for now, but Fuller's health issues should keep him in circulation for a possible role.

Auden Tate, CIN: Tate's 4.68-second 40-yard dash time left him on the board until the last few picks of the 2018 draft. His hulking 6-foot-5, 225-pound frame correctly indicates that he's more of a big-bodied Mike Williams (USC)-type than a flyer on the field. The Bengals found 12 targets for him, and he caught just four—good for -48 DYAR and a -65.0% DVOA. If A.J. Green and John Ross happen to stay healthy all season again, you probably won't hear much from Tate in 2019.

Deonte Thompson, NYJ: Thompson signed with the Jets in May but will probably end up in Buffalo in December. He finished both the 2017 and 2018 season with the Bills after starting those seasons with the Bears and Cowboys. He also had a cup of coffee with the Bills between Ravens and Bears stints in 2014. Ending up in Buffalo every winter sounds like some sort of existential punishment. Maybe Thompson was Attila the Hun in a past life and is now paying for it, or something.

John Ursua, SEA: Seattle traded its 2020 sixth-round pick to move back into the 2019 seventh round and grab Ursua, an undersized slot receiver out of Hawaii. With all the uncertainty in the Seattle receiver room thanks to Doug Baldwin's retirement, Ursua will have a real opportunity to make the final roster and potentially even an impact on the field as a rookie. But he's still a seventh-round pick, and with two other rookies with better pedigree in front of him, he may not get many opportunities.

Mike Wallace, FA: Though best remembered for his Pittsburgh days, Wallace had quietly maintained his status as a top-tier deep threat until his broken leg in Week 2 of last year. He ranked top-50 in DYAR in three of his past four qualifying seasons, topping out at 20th in 2014 with the Dolphins.

Kevin White, ARI: The seventh overall pick in the 2015 draft, White's career was doomed by a fragile skeleton, as he has broken bones from the top (shoulder blade) to the bottom (tibia, repeatedly) of his body. He caught only 25 passes in four years in Chicago, the longest a 54-yarder on a Hail Mary when the Bears needed 55 yards to force overtime against New England. The Cards took a no-risk flier on White in March. If it works out, it would be one of the most pleasant surprises of the 2019 NFL season.

Reggie White, NYG: First things first: Reggie White Jr. is the son of a former Chargers and Patriots lineman, not the Hall of Fame pass-rusher. Our former co-worker Matt Waldman of the Rookie Scouting Portfolio passed along a tale of when a veteran scout told him that White was the best receiver to ever come out of Monmouth. Before you brush that away, keep in mind that includes Miles Austin and Chris Hogan. White blew up his pro day with a 4.45-second 40-yard dash and a 6.77-second 3-cone drill. Waldman compares him to Marvin Jones coming out of Cal, another guy who was talented but a little off the radar. White definitely landed on the right depth chart to test that thesis.

Bobo Wilson, TB: For two straight seasons, Wilson, whose given name is Jesus, has spent the first 12 weeks on the practice squad before getting a promotion to the active roster. In his career, he has caught five of six targets for 70 yards and a touchdown. His biggest contribution down the stretch last season was as a kick returner.

Javon Wims, CHI: Wims was a late bloomer in college, and the Bears hope he can repeat that in the NFL. Though he did not play until his junior season and did not take on a major role until he was a senior, he exploded in that final year as a field-stretcher, notching 720 yards and seven touchdowns on only 45 receptions. Wims also flashed that ability versus the Kansas City Chiefs last preseason when he cooked David Amerson on a crosser for a 54-yard gain. In the regular season, he was a bit more limited, with four catches for 32 yards (0.1% DVOA).

Juwann Winfree, DEN: Hopefully, the Broncos have plenty of bubble wrap for Winfree, a sixth-round rookie out of Colorado. He only managed 15 games over the last three seasons thanks to myriad injuries. On the few occasions he did see the field, he impressed: a big, slippery route-runner capable of putting up huge games. If he's healthy—big, huge, Mile High-sized "if" there—he could easily be the Broncos' fifth receiver to start the year, with room to climb on a depth chart that lacks experienced veterans.

Tight Ends

Top 20 TE by DYAR (Total Value), 2018

Rank	Player	Team	DYAR
1	George Kittle	SF	207
2	Travis Kelce	KC	196
3	O.J. Howard	TB	169
4	Mark Andrews	BAL	159
5	Jared Cook	OAK	146
6	Rob Gronkowski	NE	98
7	Jesse James	PIT	96
8	Zach Ertz	PHI	93
9	Kyle Rudolph	MIN	91
10	Benjamin Watson	NO	73
12	Blake Jarwin	DAL	68
11	Eric Ebron	IND	68
13	Vernon Davis	WAS	60
14	Greg Olsen	CAR	57
15	Austin Hooper	ATL	56
16	Tyler Higbee	LAR	54
17	Vance McDonald	PIT	51
19	Evan Engram	NYG	50
18	Chris Herndon	NYJ	50
20	Rhett Ellison	NYG	48

Minimum 25 passes.

Top 20 TE by DVOA (Value per Play), 2018

Rank	Player	Team	DVOA
1	O.J. Howard	TB	44.0%
2	Mark Andrews	BAL	36.2%
3	Jesse James	PIT	27.3%
4	Blake Jarwin	DAL	24.0%
5	Vernon Davis	WAS	19.0%
6	Benjamin Watson	NO	15.2%
7	George Kittle	SF	15.1%
8	Tyler Higbee	LAR	15.0%
9	Greg Olsen	CAR	14.6%
10	Rhett Ellison	NYG	14.4%
11	Jared Cook	OAK	13.8%
12	Rob Gronkowski	NE	13.3%
13	Jordan Thomas	HOU	12.5%
14	Travis Kelce	KC	11.5%
15	Kyle Rudolph	MIN	8.6%
16	Jordan Akins	HOU	8.3%
17	Chris Herndon	NYJ	6.3%
18	Dallas Goedert	PHI	5.1%
19	Evan Engram	NYG	4.8%
20	Vance McDonald	PIT	3.6%

Minimum 25 passes.

Jordan Akins Height: 6-3 Weight: 249 College: Central Florida Draft: 2018/3 (98) Born: 19-Apr-1992 Age: 27 Risk: Green

Year	Team	G/GS	Snaps	Pass	Rec	Yds	TD	C%	+/-	Drop	Yd/C	aDOT	Rk	YAC	Rk	YAC+	BTkl	DVOA	Rk	DYAR	Rk	YAR	Use	Rk	Slot	Wide
2018	HOU	16/6	388	25	17	225	0	68%	-0.2	0	13.2	6.9	30	7.2	5	+1.8	4	8.3%	16	24	24	26	5.0%	47	44%	4%
2019	HOU			25	18	194	2	72%			10.8							5.0%								

While he was healthy and active all season, the Texans never quite seemed to trust Akins as a blocker. To be fair, he wasn't great at it—but he also never got an extended trial over known mediocrity Ryan Griffin. When Akins did play, it was mostly in two-tight end sets. In fact, of his 14 pass targets in one-tight end sets, seven of them were chip/checkdowns. Akins was drafted at an advanced age after a baseball career with the Texas Rangers and looks the part as a big-bodied receiver with enough agility and length to give safeties problems. But the Texans didn't seem to trust it, and they spent a third-round pick on Kahale Warring to challenge Akins' ascension up the depth chart.

Mark Andrews Height: 6-5 Weight: 256 College: Oklahoma Draft: 2018/3 (86) Born: 6-Sep-1996 Age: 23 Risk: Blue

Year	Team	G/GS	Snaps	Pass	Rec	Yds	TD	C%	+/-	Drop	Yd/C	aDOT	Rk	YAC	Rk	YAC+	BTkl	DVOA	Rk	DYAR	Rk	YAR	Use	Rk	Slot	Wide
2018	BAL	16/3	414	50	34	552	3	68%	+4.3	3	16.2	11.4	4	5.7	17	+1.5	1	36.2%	2	159	4	149	9.6%	25	51%	8%
2019	BAL			61	43	578	3	70%			13.4							9.9%								

Andrews showed an interesting split between Joe Flacco and Lamar Jackson. John Brown was the field-stretcher for the Flacco Ravens, so the average depth of target for Andrews' targets through Week 10 was only 9.5. Once Jackson took over, the deep strikes in the offense started running through the middle of the field. Andrews' aDOT jumped to 13.4, and his DVOA increased from 20.2% to 66.1%. Andrews is never going to get on a list of complete tight ends; he's more of a flex guy. But his first season proved that he's quite adept at that, and depending on how Baltimore's receivers shake out this year, he could be in line for a bigger workload than this projection.

Nick Boyle

Height: 6-4 | Weight: 268 | College: Delaware | Draft: 2015/5 (171) | Born: 17-Feb-1993 | Age: 26 | Risk: Green

Year	Team	G/GS	Snaps	Pass	Rec	Yds	TD	C%	+/-	Drop	Yd/C	aDOT	Rk	YAC	Rk	YAC+	BTkl	DVOA	Rk	DYAR	Rk	YAR	Use	Rk	Slot	Wide
2016	BAL	6/0	114	6	6	44	0	100%	+1.4	0	7.3	3.8	--	3.5	--	-1.1	0	-7.7%	--	0	--	2	2.4%	--	83%	0%
2017	BAL	15/11	696	37	28	203	0	76%	+0.5	0	7.3	2.2	51	5.5	15	-0.5	4	-19.3%	45	-32	45	-37	7.0%	42	19%	11%
2018	BAL	16/13	651	37	23	213	0	62%	-1.9	1	9.3	3.5	48	6.1	13	+0.8	2	-26.6%	44	-50	43	-62	6.7%	40	19%	0%
2019	BAL			31	22	201	1	71%			9.1							-4.4%								

One of the first signs that free agency was going to get a little feisty this year was when Boyle pre-emptively signed a three-year, $18-million contract with $10 million in guarantees. Afterwards, it was reported that several teams were angling to make him an offer in the tens of millions. Boyle is an excellent blocking tight end, and that did help Baltimore's offense dominate the edges last year. He's essentially an outlet valve as a passing-game option though, with only one target beyond 15 yards. Boyle's true impact is in adjusted line yards, not DYAR or DVOA.

Cameron Brate

Height: 6-5 | Weight: 235 | College: Harvard | Draft: 2014/FA | Born: 3-Jul-1991 | Age: 28 | Risk: Green

Year	Team	G/GS	Snaps	Pass	Rec	Yds	TD	C%	+/-	Drop	Yd/C	aDOT	Rk	YAC	Rk	YAC+	BTkl	DVOA	Rk	DYAR	Rk	YAR	Use	Rk	Slot	Wide
2016	TB	15/10	709	81	57	660	8	70%	+6.9	4	11.6	9.8	8	2.4	45	-1.4	3	20.4%	8	149	4	146	15.0%	18	65%	7%
2017	TB	16/5	586	77	48	591	6	62%	+2.4	4	12.3	9.5	15	3.0	45	-1.2	3	24.7%	8	154	5	114	12.8%	19	60%	8%
2018	TB	16/2	534	49	30	289	6	61%	-2.9	5	9.6	8.4	15	1.7	49	-1.9	1	-6.8%	31	2	31	-7	7.8%	34	53%	12%
2019	TB			35	24	260	1	69%			10.8							-1.2%								

For the second straight season, Brate saw a decline in targets, catches, receiving yards, and offensive snaps. You might have expected such a drop when the Buccaneers selected O.J. Howard in the first round of the 2017 draft, but it's not clear whether the front office did. In March 2018, Tampa Bay signed Brate to a contract extension that paid him $7 million last season and will pay him $7 million again this season. In a vacuum, that might seem reasonable for one of Jameis Winston's most reliable targets (his 22 red zone touchdowns since 2015 are the most among tight ends). When you're in salary-cap hell, however, that's a bit rich for the No. 2 tight end on your depth chart.

Don't put too much stock in Brate's below-average DVOA last season; he played through a hip injury that eventually required surgery. He should be ready for the start of training camp.

Trey Burton

Height: 6-3 | Weight: 235 | College: Florida | Draft: 2014/FA | Born: 29-Oct-1991 | Age: 28 | Risk: Green

Year	Team	G/GS	Snaps	Pass	Rec	Yds	TD	C%	+/-	Drop	Yd/C	aDOT	Rk	YAC	Rk	YAC+	BTkl	DVOA	Rk	DYAR	Rk	YAR	Use	Rk	Slot	Wide
2016	PHI	15/4	331	60	37	327	1	62%	-2.2	5	8.8	7.8	23	3.6	33	-1.3	3	-27.9%	44	-83	44	-70	10.5%	31	60%	7%
2017	PHI	15/1	300	31	23	248	5	74%	+4.3	1	10.8	9.5	16	1.5	51	-2.0	0	35.0%	3	85	10	86	5.9%	47	68%	6%
2018	CHI	16/16	860	76	54	569	6	71%	+3.1	3	10.5	8.4	16	3.5	42	-1.0	1	-2.7%	27	24	25	36	14.7%	11	58%	5%
2019	CHI			81	53	561	5	65%			10.6							0.0%								

Trey Burton is the skeleton key for Matt Nagy's offense. Listed as a tight end, Burton can play anywhere from in-line, to wing, to slot, to wideout, to fullback. Sixty-six percent of Burton's targets were from a non-tight end position. What makes him so versatile is not so much one specific trait that translates to all positions, but a well-rounded skill set that features quality speed, change of direction, and strength at the catch point. He has a blend of skills that can threaten linebackers, safeties, and cornerbacks in one way or another. Like most young tight ends, it took Burton a while for the gears to start turning. Burton's 54 receptions in his first year with the Bears were nearly as many as the 63 catches he made in four years with the Eagles, most of which were in 2016 and 2017. As a cherry on top, Burton adds value as a trick play threat. Burton famously threw the "Philly Special" touchdown pass to Nick Foles in Super Bowl LII versus the Patriots, made possible in part by his experience as a quarterback in high school.

Charles Clay   Height: 6-3   Weight: 239   College: Tulsa   Draft: 2011/6 (174)   Born: 13-Feb-1989   Age: 30   Risk: Green

Year	Team	G/GS	Snaps	Pass	Rec	Yds	TD	C%	+/-	Drop	Yd/C	aDOT	Rk	YAC	Rk	YAC+	BTkl	DVOA	Rk	DYAR	Rk	YAR	Use	Rk	Slot	Wide
2016	BUF	15/15	871	87	57	552	4	66%	-2.3	7	9.7	8.1	21	3.4	37	-1.2	10	-6.5%	27	4	27	6	20.2%	5	30%	5%
2017	BUF	13/13	577	74	49	558	2	66%	-1.4	5	11.4	7.2	38	5.3	19	+0.2	6	-2.8%	25	22	25	37	19.4%	7	24%	4%
2018	BUF	13/12	504	36	21	184	0	58%	-2.3	3	8.8	7.7	22	4.0	38	-1.2	1	-38.3%	48	-70	47	-65	9.1%	26	46%	0%
2019	ARI			23	15	147	1	65%			9.8							-5.3%								

Why would Arizona pay Clay over $3 million this season when he turned 30 in February and is coming off such a horrible year in Buffalo? This goes beyond Clay's statistical nosedive, which is obvious—his effort was so poor that he was a healthy scratch at some points, dressing in street clothes as the Bills were throwing passes to Jason Croom and Logan Thomas. What if—and this is going to sound heretical, but hear us out—Kliff Kingsbury wants to use Clay as a … as a … *fullback*? Clay began his career as a "FB/TE" in Miami; all seven of his career rushes came in 2013 (each came on either first down or with 1 yard to go; one gained 13 yards, the other six gained a total of 2). At the combine, Kingsbury talked about coaching against Clay's Tulsa teams in college, praising his blocking and running out of the backfield. Having a passable fifth receiver in spread formations who can also give Kingsbury a warm body to use on the occasional short-yardage dive actually makes sense. Either that, or Steve Keim is a bozo.

Jared Cook   Height: 6-6   Weight: 246   College: South Carolina   Draft: 2009/3 (89)   Born: 7-Apr-1987   Age: 32   Risk: Yellow

Year	Team	G/GS	Snaps	Pass	Rec	Yds	TD	C%	+/-	Drop	Yd/C	aDOT	Rk	YAC	Rk	YAC+	BTkl	DVOA	Rk	DYAR	Rk	YAR	Use	Rk	Slot	Wide
2016	GB	10/5	329	51	30	377	1	59%	-1.7	2	12.6	10.5	4	4.9	13	+0.2	3	-11.5%	33	-15	32	-7	13.4%	23	62%	17%
2017	OAK	16/16	796	86	54	688	2	63%	+0.0	5	12.7	9.6	12	3.9	37	-0.6	5	2.1%	19	53	17	76	15.7%	13	59%	14%
2018	OAK	16/14	770	101	68	896	6	67%	+1.8	8	13.2	8.4	17	5.0	24	+0.6	8	13.8%	11	146	5	143	19.3%	5	36%	18%
2019	NO			80	58	695	5	73%			12.0							13.4%								

2019 was far and away Cook's most productive season in his 10-year professional career. His previous best yardage (760) and DYAR (100, ranked 13th) both came in 2011, when he was still on his rookie deal in Tennessee. Since then, he has earned a reputation as a talented but erratic receiver, capable of making spectacular catches—see the famous playoff grab against Dallas during his season in Green Bay—but also capable of dropping easy ones, as his eight drops in 2018 (tied for fifth-most) will attest. His most *efficient* single season remains 2010, but his best multi-year DVOA since departing Tennessee has been the two years he just completed in Oakland.

Cook has basically no competition as the top tight end in New Orleans. The Saints have gone two seasons without a single tight end exceeding 400 yards, but their offense has always been at its best with at least one strong receiving option at that position—whether Jeremy Shockey, Jimmy Graham, Benjamin Watson, or even Coby Fleener, maligned as he was, in 2016. Cook has the most athletic talent of any Saints tight end since Graham, and his fewest drops in a season came the last time he was catching passes from an elite quarterback (Aaron Rodgers, 2016). He can hardly ask for a better situation to continue his late-career resurgence, and he has a great opportunity to take over Graham's former mantle as the second-leading receiver in New Orleans.

Jason Croom   Height: 6-5   Weight: 246   College: Tennessee   Draft: 2017/FA   Born: 28-Feb-1994   Age: 25   Risk: Green

Year	Team	G/GS	Snaps	Pass	Rec	Yds	TD	C%	+/-	Drop	Yd/C	aDOT	Rk	YAC	Rk	YAC+	BTkl	DVOA	Rk	DYAR	Rk	YAR	Use	Rk	Slot	Wide
2018	BUF	15/3	387	35	22	259	1	63%	-1.3	1	11.8	7.8	21	6.2	10	+1.3	3	-19.5%	42	-27	41	-41	7.7%	35	37%	11%
2019	BUF			24	14	171	1	58%			12.2							-4.1%								

Croom was in a dogfight for a roster spot before a hamstring injury sidelined him for most of OTAs. The ex-receiver saw his first game action last season, and while he was better than Charles Clay, that is damning with faint praise. Croom flashed some athleticism at times, but there's a reason the Bills brought in six different tight ends this offseason. Croom's best chance at being relevant in 2019 is if oft-injured Tyler Kroft remains oft-injured.

Vernon Davis

Height: 6-3		Weight: 250		College: Maryland				Draft: 2006/1 (6)			Born: 31-Jan-1984				Age: 35				Risk: Green						

Year	Team	G/GS	Snaps	Pass	Rec	Yds	TD	C%	+/-	Drop	Yd/C	aDOT	Rk	YAC	Rk	YAC+	BTkl	DVOA	Rk	DYAR	Rk	YAR	Use	Rk	Slot	Wide
2016	WAS	16/14	673	59	44	583	2	75%	+4.7	4	13.3	9.0	14	5.4	8	+0.7	11	16.8%	11	96	14	100	9.8%	36	42%	5%
2017	WAS	16/16	803	69	43	648	3	62%	+2.1	4	15.1	10.9	5	7.0	4	+1.8	16	6.7%	16	61	14	37	12.8%	20	29%	7%
2018	WAS	14/8	448	36	25	367	2	69%	+2.7	2	14.7	11.9	2	6.7	6	+1.8	8	19.0%	5	60	13	63	8.3%	32	31%	8%
2019	WAS			48	30	406	3	63%			13.5							6.9%								

Davis arrived in Washington in 2016 at age 32 and appeared to be at the end of the productive phase of his career, but he ended up starting most of the season and catching 44 passes. The Skins signed Davis to a three-year contract, and Davis responded with an even stronger 2017 season. He was still effective on a per-target basis last year, but his playing time declined sharply, in part because Jordan Reed was healthier than usual, in part because … well, he was a 34-year-old tight end. Davis will cost the Skins $6 million in cap space as a No. 2 tight end this year. He'll have to catch a lot of checkdowns from Dwayne Haskins to be worth the money and the roster spot.

Will Dissly

Height: 6-4		Weight: 262		College: Washington				Draft: 2018/4 (120)			Born: 8-Jul-1996				Age: 23				Risk: Yellow						

Year	Team	G/GS	Snaps	Pass	Rec	Yds	TD	C%	+/-	Drop	Yd/C	aDOT	Rk	YAC	Rk	YAC+	BTkl	DVOA	Rk	DYAR	Rk	YAR	Use	Rk	Slot	Wide
2018	SEA	4/4	127	14	8	156	2	57%	-0.3	1	19.5	10.8	--	11.6	--	+7.4	2	30.6%	--	36	--	29	13.7%	--	21%	0%
2019	SEA			52	37	409	5	71%			11.0							7.3%								

Originally drafted for his prowess as a run-blocker, Dissly's effectiveness in Seattle's play-action-heavy passing game was a pleasant surprise early in the 2018 season. Dissly tore his patellar tendon in Week 4, which not only ended his season early but also put his status for the beginning of 2019 in question. Patellar tendon tears can drastically alter a player's career, but former Seahawks tight end Jimmy Graham suffered a similar tear in 2015 and finished second in DYAR the following season. With Dissly, Seattle will have to hope for a similar sort of rebound to his prior performance level.

Jack Doyle

Height: 6-6		Weight: 258		College: Western Kentucky				Draft: 2013/FA			Born: 5-May-1990				Age: 29				Risk: Red						

Year	Team	G/GS	Snaps	Pass	Rec	Yds	TD	C%	+/-	Drop	Yd/C	aDOT	Rk	YAC	Rk	YAC+	BTkl	DVOA	Rk	DYAR	Rk	YAR	Use	Rk	Slot	Wide
2016	IND	16/14	750	75	59	584	5	79%	+6.2	4	9.9	6.3	41	4.2	23	-0.2	7	18.7%	10	131	9	96	13.0%	25	43%	0%
2017	IND	15/15	909	108	80	690	4	74%	+4.0	3	8.6	5.0	50	4.2	33	-0.7	9	-7.5%	29	-2	31	31	24.3%	2	44%	4%
2018	IND	6/6	332	33	26	245	2	79%	+2.3	0	9.4	5.4	43	4.2	36	-0.1	2	-7.4%	33	0	33	15	13.7%	15	48%	6%
2019	IND			83	59	547	5	71%			9.3							3.2%								

Persistent hip problems and eventually a kidney injury ruined Doyle's 2018 season. He was a mainstay on the rare times he was healthy as the Colts' best all-around tight end. He was primarily a short receiver in 2018, with curls, drags, and flats his most common routes. He missed much of the offseason due to injury, but he is expected to be ready for training camp with no issues. Assuming he maintains his health, expect another season of more of the same things seen when he was 100 percent.

Eric Ebron

Height: 6-4		Weight: 250		College: North Carolina				Draft: 2014/1 (10)			Born: 10-Apr-1993				Age: 26				Risk: Green						

Year	Team	G/GS	Snaps	Pass	Rec	Yds	TD	C%	+/-	Drop	Yd/C	aDOT	Rk	YAC	Rk	YAC+	BTkl	DVOA	Rk	DYAR	Rk	YAR	Use	Rk	Slot	Wide
2016	DET	13/13	708	85	61	711	1	72%	+3.1	7	11.7	8.0	22	4.6	14	+0.3	3	20.1%	9	149	5	141	18.1%	12	53%	11%
2017	DET	16/9	552	86	53	574	4	62%	-1.7	6	10.8	7.8	32	4.9	25	+0.3	9	2.0%	20	50	18	24	15.0%	15	47%	10%
2018	IND	16/8	634	110	66	750	13	60%	-4.9	8	11.4	9.6	8	3.8	41	-0.4	6	2.0%	22	68	11	51	17.1%	6	76%	4%
2019	IND			74	46	510	5	62%			11.1							1.5%								

You may have missed it, but there were two different Eric Ebrons on the field in 2018. One was one of the most productive tight ends in the league, and one was one of the least productive. The former appeared in the games primary tight end Jack Doyle played. There, Ebron was a tremendously effective complementary player. He only averaged 3.7 targets per game, but had 100 receiving DYAR, which would have ranked sixth-best among all tight ends. The latter appeared in the games Doyle missed. There, Ebron was an ineffective primary player. He averaged almost nine targets per game and had -73 DYAR (including postseason), which would have ranked third-worst among all tight ends. Including playoff games would also increase his position-leading drop count. The unproductive Ebron was still a good player for your fantasy team, precisely because of that volume and a fluky touchdown total, but the point of the additions at wide receiver was the Colts want to see an offense that does not run through Eric Ebron, because they saw that and it wasn't good.

Tyler Eifert

Height: 6-6   Weight: 251   College: Notre Dame   Draft: 2013/1 (21)   Born: 8-Sep-1990   Age: 29   Risk: Red

Year	Team	G/GS	Snaps	Pass	Rec	Yds	TD	C%	+/-	Drop	Yd/C	aDOT	Rk	YAC	Rk	YAC+	BTkl	DVOA	Rk	DYAR	Rk	YAR	Use	Rk	Slot	Wide
2016	CIN	8/2	428	47	29	394	5	62%	+3.5	1	13.6	8.6	18	5.0	10	+1.0	0	9.6%	15	57	18	79	17.4%	14	50%	6%
2017	CIN	2/1	104	5	4	46	0	80%	+0.8	0	11.5	9.4	--	2.8	--	-4.3	0	11.6%	--	6	--	12	8.0%	--	60%	0%
2018	CIN	4/2	133	19	15	179	1	79%	+3.1	0	11.9	8.2	--	3.6	--	-0.9	1	21.1%	--	36	--	50	15.6%	--	70%	0%
2019	CIN			47	33	374	4	70%			11.3							8.1%								

At some point, you bought a printer. The printer had a ton of bells and whistles. It could scan. It could fax. It could connect wirelessly to things. It worked really well for a few years. Today, that printer gathers dust because every time you turn it on, you face an effort calculus of how to connect it with newer things, dealing with the fact that it's always out of ink and how one of the tracks doesn't quite work because your cat likes to sit on it. In theory it adds a lot of flexibility to your life. In actuality, well, you almost always just sign a PDF and try to send that rather than mess with the printer.

That printer is in better shape than Tyler Eifert's back.

Rhett Ellison

Height: 6-4   Weight: 251   College: USC   Draft: 2012/FA   Born: 3-Oct-1988   Age: 31   Risk: Green

Year	Team	G/GS	Snaps	Pass	Rec	Yds	TD	C%	+/-	Drop	Yd/C	aDOT	Rk	YAC	Rk	YAC+	BTkl	DVOA	Rk	DYAR	Rk	YAR	Use	Rk	Slot	Wide
2016	MIN	15/6	258	14	9	57	0	64%	-0.1	0	6.3	3.8	--	3.8	--	-2.3	0	-51.9%	--	-41	--	-53	2.5%	--	7%	0%
2017	NYG	16/14	538	32	24	235	2	75%	+3.2	1	9.8	5.0	49	5.5	16	+1.1	6	17.7%	11	56	15	57	5.3%	49	3%	3%
2018	NYG	14/12	557	34	25	272	1	74%	+1.7	3	10.9	6.5	36	5.2	21	+0.5	2	14.4%	10	48	20	23	6.7%	41	21%	0%
2019	NYG			35	25	238	1	71%			9.5							-2.2%								

If SIS tracks 14 of your 34 targets as either "chip-flat" or "chip-drag" … you might be a blocking tight end. Ellison is quite handy at that, and the Giants seem to think they're going to run over every NFL defense like it's 1965, so Ellison will probably get plenty of reps to get his technique going. Ellison's on a fairly expensive contract, with a $5.75-million cap hit this year and a $6.25-million cap hit in 2020. It would probably be best for the Giants if they developed a player to take over this role before 2020, but that's nothing against Ellison as a player. He's just not cost-efficient.

Evan Engram

Height: 6-3   Weight: 234   College: Mississippi   Draft: 2017/2 (23)   Born: 2-Sep-1994   Age: 25   Risk: Green

Year	Team	G/GS	Snaps	Pass	Rec	Yds	TD	C%	+/-	Drop	Yd/C	aDOT	Rk	YAC	Rk	YAC+	BTkl	DVOA	Rk	DYAR	Rk	YAR	Use	Rk	Slot	Wide
2017	NYG	15/11	777	115	64	722	6	56%	-7.1	7	11.3	8.5	25	4.7	27	+0.5	7	-8.0%	33	-5	33	-20	20.2%	6	25%	15%
2018	NYG	11/8	475	64	45	577	3	70%	-1.8	2	12.8	5.4	42	8.6	3	+2.8	10	4.8%	19	50	19	32	16.2%	7	54%	2%
2019	NYG			111	71	875	5	64%			12.3							1.7%								

When Engram came out of Ole Miss, he went to the NFL combine and ran a 4.42-second 40-yard dash at 234 pounds. In the year of our Lord 2018, between his now-customary injuries, Engram had a grand total of *seven* deep targets out of 64 total. He had the second lowest aDOT of any receiver with more than 43 targets, at 5.1, ahead of only Ryan Switzer. What exactly is it, you would say, you do here Mr. Shurmur? Engram did finish fourth in broken tackles among tight ends, behind only George Kittle, Vance McDonald, and Travis Kelce. Still, he feels wasted in this offense and with the quarterbacks this team have drafted. Knee and hamstring injuries and concussions plagued Engram in 2018 and had him sitting out early portions of 2019 team activities. He's not built like a Dave Gettleman player because he has very little use in a run-based attack. This might be another situation where some value could be extracted by a smart team that has exactly the sort of shiny trinket Gettleman actually desires.

Zach Ertz

Height: 6-5   Weight: 249   College: Stanford   Draft: 2013/2 (35)   Born: 10-Nov-1990   Age: 29   Risk: Yellow

Year	Team	G/GS	Snaps	Pass	Rec	Yds	TD	C%	+/-	Drop	Yd/C	aDOT	Rk	YAC	Rk	YAC+	BTkl	DVOA	Rk	DYAR	Rk	YAR	Use	Rk	Slot	Wide
2016	PHI	14/12	851	106	78	816	4	74%	+11.4	3	10.5	8.1	20	3.4	39	-1.1	2	3.4%	22	75	17	106	20.0%	6	62%	4%
2017	PHI	14/13	778	110	74	824	8	67%	+4.0	8	11.1	8.0	29	3.4	43	-0.8	4	14.2%	13	154	4	129	22.3%	4	48%	4%
2018	PHI	16/16	1000	155	116	1163	8	74%	+7.7	5	10.0	7.4	27	3.1	46	-1.4	7	1.6%	23	93	8	120	26.2%	3	65%	4%
2019	PHI			133	99	1003	7	74%			10.1							5.5%								

For good reason, Ertz is the preferred option for Philadelphia's quarterbacks in the red zone. Ertz's 26 red zone targets last season were as many as the next two players combined (Alshon Jefffery, 14; Dallas Goedert, 12). He also had exactly 17 red zone targets in each of the two prior seasons, leading the team in 2016 and finishing second in 2017. Ertz is not athletically gifted in the same way Travis Kelce or Rob Gronkowski are, but his sense for how to manipulate space, create leverage, and make plays in traffic make him a nightmare for defenders who can't match his savvy (and most can't). Playing out of the slot better allows Ertz to make use of those traits. He saw 102 targets from the slot, most among tight ends, though his 65 percent target ratio from the slot ranked sixth, a hair behind other notable names such as Kelce and Eric Ebron. If DeSean Jackson can take the top off the defense the way everyone expects him to, the middle of the field will be a buffet for Ertz in 2019.

Gerald Everett

Height: 6-3   Weight: 239   College: South Alabama   Draft: 2017/2 (44)   Born: 25-Jun-1994   Age: 25   Risk: Green

Year	Team	G/GS	Snaps	Pass	Rec	Yds	TD	C%	+/-	Drop	Yd/C	aDOT	Rk	YAC	Rk	YAC+	BTkl	DVOA	Rk	DYAR	Rk	YAR	Use	Rk	Slot	Wide
2017	LAR	16/2	299	32	16	244	2	50%	-3.3	3	15.3	9.5	14	6.8	6	+1.6	1	-17.0%	44	-20	41	-36	6.2%	45	41%	9%
2018	LAR	16/0	380	50	33	320	3	66%	-0.4	0	9.7	6.4	37	4.4	33	+0.0	7	-6.6%	29	2	29	-19	9.1%	27	26%	20%
2019	LAR			53	36	446	3	68%			12.4							6.4%								

Everett's 2019 season will have some significant team-building implications for Los Angeles moving forward, as his performance may dictate whether the Rams feel comfortable letting fellow tight end Tyler Higbee walk at the end of the year. The Rams used their top pick in the 2017 draft on Everett, but Higbee has been the better player of the two in each of Everett's first two seasons. While Everett flashed his potential as an athletic mismatch at times in 2018, particularly on the game-winning touchdown against the Chiefs in Week 11, he'll have to show more than that for the Rams to be confident about their tight end situation moving forward. With Jared Goff's raise on the horizon, Everett could play a key role in keeping other parts of the Los Angeles offense cheap.

Noah Fant

Height: 6-5   Weight: 241   College: Iowa   Draft: 2019/1 (20)   Born: 20-Nov-1997   Age: 22   Risk: Red

Year	Team	G/GS	Snaps	Pass	Rec	Yds	TD	C%	+/-	Drop	Yd/C	aDOT	Rk	YAC	Rk	YAC+	BTkl	DVOA	Rk	DYAR	Rk	YAR	Use	Rk	Slot	Wide
2019	DEN			68	46	505	3	68%			11.0							-2.8%								

There's no doubting Fant's athleticism. That 4.5-second 40 at the combine isn't just shorts and T-shirt speed; that burst shows up on tape. He's a matchup challenge for sure; accelerating off the line to blow past slower defenders, leaping ability to outjump shorter ones, and a terrific catch radius. There are two outstanding questions about Fant which will determine whether he's an every-down player or just a move tight end for passing downs. First, can he play in-line? He was almost exclusively a slot receiver at Iowa, and his blocking leaves much to be desired. Second, can he cut the drops? His tended to lose focus in close coverage, leading to more drops than you'd like to see.

Anthony Firkser

Height: 6-3   Weight: 220   College: Harvard   Draft: 2017/FA   Born: 19-Feb-1995   Age: 24   Risk: Green

Year	Team	G/GS	Snaps	Pass	Rec	Yds	TD	C%	+/-	Drop	Yd/C	aDOT	Rk	YAC	Rk	YAC+	BTkl	DVOA	Rk	DYAR	Rk	YAR	Use	Rk	Slot	Wide
2018	TEN	12/0	181	20	19	225	1	95%	+4.7	0	11.8	6.7	--	5.1	--	+0.8	1	59.3%	--	85	--	85	6.2%	--	55%	5%
2019	TEN			11	8	95	1	73%			11.8							7.3%								

Firkser's receiving DVOA was the best by any tight end with at least 10 targets since Tom Crabtree put up 76.8% DVOA catching passes from Aaron Rodgers in 2012. Firkser would have finished 10th in receiving DYAR had he had enough targets to quality for the ranking tables. A 95 percent catch rate in clearly unsustainable, and the return of Delanie Walker and Jonnu Smith from injury ensures he is no higher than third on the H-back/flex/blocking-optional depth chart and consequently not a roster lock. But anybody who can be successful catching over routes from Blaine Gabbert deserves a look somewhere else if he does not get one in Tennessee.

Antonio Gates | Height: 6-4 | Weight: 260 | College: Kent State | Draft: 2003/FA | Born: 18-Jun-1980 | Age: 39 | Risk: N/A

Year	Team	G/GS	Snaps	Pass	Rec	Yds	TD	C%	+/-	Drop	Yd/C	aDOT	Rk	YAC	Rk	YAC+	BTkl	DVOA	Rk	DYAR	Rk	YAR	Use	Rk	Slot	Wide
2016	SD	14/9	585	93	53	548	7	57%	-5.2	8	10.3	8.7	17	3.5	35	-0.2	4	-6.6%	28	4	28	6	18.9%	9	72%	6%
2017	LAC	16/4	500	52	30	316	3	58%	+0.1	1	10.5	8.9	20	2.2	49	-1.6	1	-3.2%	26	13	26	5	8.8%	35	80%	0%
2018	LAC	16/1	364	45	28	333	2	62%	-0.2	0	11.9	8.2	19	4.5	31	+0.5	5	-7.4%	32	0	32	10	8.9%	30	84%	4%

OK, this time, we think we mean it when we say that Gates is going to retire. He was lured back just before the start of 2018 due to Hunter Henry's ACL tear, and was mostly a non-factor throughout the year. He was acceptable as a third-down safety valve, with a 20.1% DVOA on 22 targets, but apart from that, he was mostly a shadow of the player who was once the best tight end in football. The fact he could provide any value at age 38 is impressive in and of itself and a credit to his skills, but it's time to call it a day and get ready for Canton.

Mike Gesicki | Height: 6-5 | Weight: 247 | College: Penn State | Draft: 2018/2 (42) | Born: 3-Oct-1995 | Age: 24 | Risk: Green

Year	Team	G/GS	Snaps	Pass	Rec	Yds	TD	C%	+/-	Drop	Yd/C	aDOT	Rk	YAC	Rk	YAC+	BTkl	DVOA	Rk	DYAR	Rk	YAR	Use	Rk	Slot	Wide
2018	MIA	16/7	400	32	22	202	0	69%	+1.1	1	9.2	9.2	10	4.4	33	-0.7	3	-37.3%	47	-70	45	-56	7.5%	37	21%	21%
2019	MIA			47	31	345	2	66%			11.1							-2.3%								

Gesicki caught exactly one pass on exactly one target for exactly 5 yards in three separate games last year. This is probably not further evidence of some obsessive Adam Gase mania, but let's leave that door open. Gesicki left college as a vertical-threat tight end, but Gase likes to turn his vertical threats to 90-degree angles, and Gesicki was forced to share the tight end role with Nick O'Leary, who has no discernable skills. Gesicki has breakout potential now that he is not being coached by some comic book supervillain with an overcomplicated master plan. At the very least, he should work his way up to solid foods and two-catch, 20-yard games this season.

Dallas Goedert | Height: 6-5 | Weight: 256 | College: South Dakota State | Draft: 2018/2 (49) | Born: 3-Jan-1995 | Age: 25 | Risk: Green

Year	Team	G/GS	Snaps	Pass	Rec	Yds	TD	C%	+/-	Drop	Yd/C	aDOT	Rk	YAC	Rk	YAC+	BTkl	DVOA	Rk	DYAR	Rk	YAR	Use	Rk	Slot	Wide
2018	PHI	16/8	524	44	33	334	4	75%	+2.4	1	10.1	7.8	20	5.2	22	+0.3	5	5.1%	18	38	21	37	7.5%	36	29%	7%
2019	PHI			57	41	445	3	72%			10.9							1.5%								

No other team has purposefully opted in to a 12 personnel offense to the extent Philadelphia has. Goedert, a rookie out of South Dakota State last season, is the perfect complement to Zach Ertz. Whereas Ertz is more of a hybrid player better suited for the slot, Goedert is an old-school in-line tight end with stunning athleticism. He does not yet win in space the way his athletic profile may suggest, however. Just 29 percent of his targets were from the slot, one of the lowest marks in the league. When he lined up as a standard tight end, his average depth of target was just 5.1 yards. Goedert was more of a short-area player who could outmuscle opponents and burst up the field for a few extra yards once he caught the ball, not someone who was streaking across the field on deeper routes. His athleticism is best served with the ball in his hands. The next step for Goedert will be taking notes from Ertz's route-running and understanding of leverage so that he can bloom into the all-around weapon Philadelphia expects him to be.

Jimmy Graham | Height: 6-6 | Weight: 260 | College: Miami | Draft: 2010/3 (95) | Born: 24-Nov-1986 | Age: 33 | Risk: Green

Year	Team	G/GS	Snaps	Pass	Rec	Yds	TD	C%	+/-	Drop	Yd/C	aDOT	Rk	YAC	Rk	YAC+	BTkl	DVOA	Rk	DYAR	Rk	YAR	Use	Rk	Slot	Wide
2016	SEA	16/15	790	96	65	923	6	69%	+3.7	5	14.2	9.7	9	5.0	12	+0.3	9	25.1%	6	204	2	194	17.4%	13	38%	4%
2017	SEA	16/13	730	96	57	520	10	59%	-3.8	7	9.1	7.9	30	3.7	39	-0.4	6	-6.0%	28	9	27	-4	18.0%	10	43%	27%
2018	GB	16/12	795	89	55	636	2	62%	+0.7	3	11.6	9.4	9	4.7	28	-0.0	5	-6.6%	30	4	28	-18	14.4%	13	57%	8%
2019	GB			77	52	591	6	68%			11.4							4.8%								

Some tight ends are true in-line players, others are better served in a wide receiver role, but most fall somewhere in between. Jimmy Graham is as far toward the wide receiver end of the spectrum as anyone can get. For the past three seasons, Graham has finished with a better DVOA out of the slot than as a traditional tight end, including two straight seasons with negative DVOA from a tight end alignment. The good news is, Green Bay has typically used Graham more often out of the slot than in-line. The bad news is, Matt LaFleur's scheme is centered around what he can do via run-pass conflicts with his tight ends, and Graham provides no such conflict as a slot player who can't block effectively. Monitoring how LaFleur works his scheme around Graham's one-dimensional, though effective, play style will be critical in shaping the success of the Packers' offense.

Virgil Green

Height: 6-5 Weight: 240 College: Nevada Draft: 2011/7 (204) Born: 3-Aug-1988 Age: 31 Risk: Yellow

Year	Team	G/GS	Snaps	Pass	Rec	Yds	TD	C%	+/-	Drop	Yd/C	aDOT	Rk	YAC	Rk	YAC+	BTkl	DVOA	Rk	DYAR	Rk	YAR	Use	Rk	Slot	Wide
2016	DEN	12/11	494	37	22	237	1	59%	-2.0	3	10.8	7.3	28	4.6	16	-0.4	4	-14.8%	37	-19	35	-11	8.7%	39	11%	0%
2017	DEN	16/16	534	22	14	191	1	64%	-0.8	3	13.6	8.0	--	6.6	--	+1.8	1	0.8%	--	12	--	20	3.9%	--	14%	0%
2018	LAC	16/16	674	27	19	210	1	70%	-1.3	4	11.1	5.4	45	5.4	20	+1.2	2	-8.2%	35	-2	35	8	5.3%	45	7%	0%
2019	LAC			20	13	130	2	65%			10.0							-1.6%								

Green has been a prospect who could break out any day now since 2011, and we're all still waiting. Hunter Henry's torn ACL gave Green the best opportunity of his career, but he was out-targeted and out-played by the shambling remains of Antonio Gates. Henry's injury history means there's always a chance the backup tight end could find a place in the spotlight, but with Green's history it would be more likely to see him passed by Sean Culkin or Vince Mayle than it would be for him to finally have a breakout season.

Ryan Griffin

Height: 6-6 Weight: 247 College: Connecticut Draft: 2013/6 (201) Born: 11-Jan-1990 Age: 29 Risk: N/A

Year	Team	G/GS	Snaps	Pass	Rec	Yds	TD	C%	+/-	Drop	Yd/C	aDOT	Rk	YAC	Rk	YAC+	BTkl	DVOA	Rk	DYAR	Rk	YAR	Use	Rk	Slot	Wide
2016	HOU	16/5	507	74	50	442	2	68%	+0.1	6	8.8	6.7	36	3.4	42	-1.1	4	-22.9%	43	-77	43	-62	12.7%	26	31%	3%
2017	HOU	7/6	349	26	13	158	1	50%	-2.5	1	12.2	10.3	9	5.6	13	+1.4	1	-11.0%	37	-6	34	-9	11.1%	26	8%	0%
2018	HOU	14/11	743	43	24	305	0	56%	-5.3	3	12.7	7.6	24	6.3	8	+1.8	2	-13.5%	38	-18	40	-30	10.1%	24	34%	5%

Griffin never seemed to be on the same page as Deshaun Watson last year. Griffin had nine red zone targets in the first six weeks of the season, then didn't get another one all year. In theory, Griffin has the requisite speed and hands to be an underneath target on a good team. That role was often taken by other players with the Texans, and so Griffin was relegated to a "too cute" option trying to threaten downfield where his speed didn't play, or running all the way across a formation to take on a block. Griffin broke his hand in Nashville over draft weekend after the Texans picked Kahale Warring, then was released by the club in May. As we go to press, he's a free agent. Griffin still has the talent to be on an NFL roster, but he needs a more limited role than the one the Texans carved for him in 2018.

Rob Gronkowski

Height: 6-6 Weight: 264 College: Arizona Draft: 2010/2 (42) Born: 14-May-1989 Age: 30 Risk: N/A

Year	Team	G/GS	Snaps	Pass	Rec	Yds	TD	C%	+/-	Drop	Yd/C	aDOT	Rk	YAC	Rk	YAC+	BTkl	DVOA	Rk	DYAR	Rk	YAR	Use	Rk	Slot	Wide
2016	NE	8/6	354	38	25	540	3	66%	+4.5	1	21.6	14.2	1	9.1	1	+5.0	7	44.5%	2	136	7	142	14.1%	21	38%	23%
2017	NE	14/14	905	105	69	1084	8	66%	+7.9	3	15.7	12.2	1	5.0	22	+1.0	12	40.4%	2	339	1	347	21.1%	5	41%	15%
2018	NE	13/11	838	72	47	682	3	65%	+1.8	2	14.5	12.4	1	3.9	40	-0.3	5	13.3%	12	98	6	123	16.1%	8	38%	11%

This offseason has seen a huge amount of column inches devoted to the question of whether "GRONK" will fight the itch to return when the live action resumes, but the analytics case for staying retired is fairly clear: Gronkowski was visibly impaired throughout much of 2018 and had his least productive season with double-digit games played since his rookie year. His DVOA was his lowest of any season with at least eight games played, and though he remains one of the top players at his position as both a blocker and receiver, it would be a shame to see such a special career end with a series of increasingly below-par injury-blighted seasons.

Instead, when we think of Gronk, we still see one of the most talented players of his generation: a four-time All-Pro who has a case to be considered the most complete tight end ever, and at worst the second-best player on a three-time Super Bowl winning roster. When healthy, Gronkowski utterly dominated our numbers. His 2011 season was the best tight end receiving season on record by a country mile. He had six seasons in the top two of DYAR even though he only played more than eight games seven times. He ranked in the top eight of DVOA in seven of his nine seasons despite being opponents' No. 1 coverage priority. He also led all players in touchdown catches from 2010 to 2018 despite losing 29 games to injury, and he is the only tight end in history to average 60 yards per game and 15 yards per catch in his career. Gronkowski will be a deserved Hall of Fame selection, and he is probably the most difficult player to replace thus far in Bill Belichick's time as Patriots head coach.

Demetrius Harris

Height: 6-7 | Weight: 230 | College: Wisconsin-Milwaukee | Draft: 2013/FA | Born: 29-Jul-1991 | Age: 28 | Risk: Yellow

Year	Team	G/GS	Snaps	Pass	Rec	Yds	TD	C%	+/-	Drop	Yd/C	aDOT	Rk	YAC	Rk	YAC+	BTkl	DVOA	Rk	DYAR	Rk	YAR	Use	Rk	Slot	Wide
2016	KC	16/11	459	31	17	123	1	55%	-4.0	6	7.2	6.6	38	2.4	44	-1.8	6	-36.9%	45	-63	39	-69	5.8%	44	39%	13%
2017	KC	16/7	487	35	18	224	1	51%	-4.0	7	12.4	8.1	28	7.2	3	+2.2	3	-23.3%	47	-37	46	-30	6.6%	43	53%	6%
2018	KC	15/3	371	25	12	164	3	48%	-5.0	4	13.7	7.7	23	6.3	8	+1.4	0	-15.6%	39	-14	37	-4	4.7%	48	16%	4%
2019	CLE			29	17	206	3	59%			12.1							1.3%								

Harris was a college basketball player at Wisconsin-Milwaukee (after transferring from someplace called the Mineral Area College), and John Dorsey drafted him for Kansas City based on physical traits. General managers tend to remember guys like that, and Dorsey has brought Harris to his new team in Cleveland to help replace the departed Darren Fells (and perhaps displace incumbent backup Seth DeValve). Harris remains raw but adds athletic depth, and should some targets actually come his way they are likely to be in the red zone—six of his 57 career receptions have gone for touchdowns (including one tossed by Dontari Poe!).

Hunter Henry

Height: 6-5 | Weight: 250 | College: Arkansas | Draft: 2016/2 (35) | Born: 7-Dec-1994 | Age: 25 | Risk: Green

Year	Team	G/GS	Snaps	Pass	Rec	Yds	TD	C%	+/-	Drop	Yd/C	aDOT	Rk	YAC	Rk	YAC+	BTkl	DVOA	Rk	DYAR	Rk	YAR	Use	Rk	Slot	Wide
2016	SD	15/10	573	53	36	478	8	68%	+3.6	2	13.3	9.0	13	5.4	6	+2.2	5	33.4%	3	148	6	140	9.9%	35	43%	8%
2017	LAC	14/13	598	62	45	579	4	73%	+5.8	3	12.9	9.2	19	4.2	32	+0.3	1	32.3%	4	165	3	183	12.4%	23	50%	3%
2019	LAC			86	60	780	7	70%			13.0							17.2%								

Adding a top-five tight end to the second-best passing offense in the league almost seems unfair, but that's what the Chargers get with Henry's return from his torn ACL. Durability has to be a bit of a concern—in addition to the ACL, Henry has missed time with calf and knee injuries, plus a lacerated kidney in 2017. The Chargers will also have to see if Henry's phenomenal numbers stand a likely increase in usage; it's hard not to imagine him with at least 80 targets in a fully healthy season. These are minor quibbles; we were expecting a breakout season in 2018, and with his knee fully recovered, there's no reason not to expect one in 2019.

Christopher Herndon

Height: 6-4 | Weight: 252 | College: Miami | Draft: 2018/4 (107) | Born: 23-Feb-1996 | Age: 23 | Risk: Green

Year	Team	G/GS	Snaps	Pass	Rec	Yds	TD	C%	+/-	Drop	Yd/C	aDOT	Rk	YAC	Rk	YAC+	BTkl	DVOA	Rk	DYAR	Rk	YAR	Use	Rk	Slot	Wide
2018	NYJ	16/12	625	56	39	502	4	70%	+3.4	1	12.9	10.5	6	4.7	29	-0.1	4	6.3%	17	50	18	57	11.1%	22	53%	2%
2019	NYJ			52	34	427	3	65%			12.6							6.6%								

Herndon slipped into the fourth round of the 2018 draft because he was stuck behind David Njoku until his final season, then suffered an MCL injury which kept him out of the Senior Bowl and other pre-draft activities. He quickly earned a starting job for the tight end-starved Jets and demonstrated some traits that could make him a star: body control to adjust to deep routes, the ability to catch away from his body, some rumbling YAC ability. His blocking isn't bad, either. The projection above accounts for a four-game suspension for a DUI car accident, announced just before we went to press.

Jeff Heuerman

Height: 6-5 | Weight: 254 | College: Ohio State | Draft: 2015/3 (92) | Born: 24-Nov-1992 | Age: 27 | Risk: Green

Year	Team	G/GS	Snaps	Pass	Rec	Yds	TD	C%	+/-	Drop	Yd/C	aDOT	Rk	YAC	Rk	YAC+	BTkl	DVOA	Rk	DYAR	Rk	YAR	Use	Rk	Slot	Wide
2016	DEN	12/2	232	17	9	141	0	53%	-0.8	0	15.7	8.8	--	7.6	--	+1.8	2	-5.6%	--	2	--	7	4.0%	--	19%	0%
2017	DEN	14/6	321	18	9	142	2	50%	-3.2	1	15.8	8.6	--	7.0	--	+2.4	2	11.6%	--	20	--	16	3.7%	--	50%	11%
2018	DEN	11/10	555	48	31	281	2	65%	-3.9	3	9.1	5.0	47	4.8	25	-0.4	3	-29.7%	46	-70	46	-44	12.2%	19	21%	10%
2019	DEN			37	26	254	1	70%			9.8							-4.9%								

You may have thought the age of Heuerman being relevant ended the moment the Broncos took Noah Fant in the first round, but hold off just a moment. Tight ends are notoriously slow starters in the NFL, with only five players racking up 50 receptions as a rookie in the 21st century. That likely means Heuerman will continue to play a role for the Broncos in 2019, which may not be ideal. The former third-round pick has struggled with injuries and ineffectiveness in his Denver career. Broncos fans should be hoping Jake Butt or Troy Fumagalli can stay healthy long enough to actually challenge Heuerman for the second tight end spot.

Tyler Higbee   Height: 6-6   Weight: 249   College: Western Kentucky   Draft: 2016/4 (110)   Born: 1-Jan-1993   Age: 27   Risk: Green

Year	Team	G/GS	Snaps	Pass	Rec	Yds	TD	C%	+/-	Drop	Yd/C	aDOT	Rk	YAC	Rk	YAC+	BTkl	DVOA	Rk	DYAR	Rk	YAR	Use	Rk	Slot	Wide
2016	LAR	16/6	405	29	11	85	1	38%	-7.2	4	7.7	6.9	32	2.4	46	-2.5	1	-68.5%	46	-109	46	-111	5.4%	45	14%	7%
2017	LAR	16/16	733	45	25	295	1	56%	-2.6	2	11.8	10.8	6	3.4	42	-0.9	6	-10.4%	36	-9	36	-19	8.7%	36	24%	7%
2018	LAR	16/16	788	34	24	292	2	71%	+1.3	1	12.2	7.0	28	5.7	16	+1.4	4	15.0%	8	54	16	49	6.2%	42	30%	6%
2019	LAR			38	25	269	2	66%			10.8							-0.2%								

In the outstanding Los Angeles passing offense, the Rams did not rely on either of their two tight ends for much in the way of volume, deciding instead to funnel opportunities to their trio of highly touted wide receivers. As a result, Higbee and fellow tight end Gerald Everett have gotten the short end of the stick. Higbee clearly outperformed Everett in receiving DVOA and DYAR, but with the major financial decisions coming up for the Rams elsewhere on the roster, he may not be the highest priority to keep around moving forward. As Higbee enters the final season of his rookie contract, he may be playing to earn a bigger payday somewhere else next season. Still, not bad for a fourth-round pick who is one of the last offensive remnants from the Jeff Fisher era.

T.J. Hockenson   Height: 6-5   Weight: 251   College: Iowa   Draft: 2019/1 (8)   Born: 3-Jul-1997   Age: 22   Risk: Red

Year	Team	G/GS	Snaps	Pass	Rec	Yds	TD	C%	+/-	Drop	Yd/C	aDOT	Rk	YAC	Rk	YAC+	BTkl	DVOA	Rk	DYAR	Rk	YAR	Use	Rk	Slot	Wide
2019	DET			68	45	516	4	66%			11.5							-1.3%								

The true essence of the tight end position is to be a run-pass conflict. Elite tight ends are effective in all facets of the pass game in addition to being useful blockers. A tight end can still be good, even among the best, if he only excels at one or the other, but those who thrive in both areas are a special breed of player. T.J. Hockenson fits the mold of a dual-threat tight end. As a pass-catcher, Hockenson is a bully at the catch point first and foremost, but he has the athleticism to threaten explosive plays and pick up substantial yards after the catch. There is not a route he can not run from the tight end position, and once the ball goes up for grabs, there is not much hope in wrestling it away from him. He caught 75 percent of targets in his final season at Iowa. Hockenson's prowess as a blocker is what makes him so effective, though. In the same vein as Rob Gronkowski, Jack Doyle, and George Kittle, Hockenson can be tied into pulling concepts, thrust into the point of attack on power runs, and used as an effective chip blocker before fanning out into a pattern. The ambiguity Hockenson presents opens many doors for an offensive coordinator to utilize him as a centerpiece for run-pass deception

Austin Hooper   Height: 6-4   Weight: 254   College: Stanford   Draft: 2016/3 (81)   Born: 29-Oct-1994   Age: 25   Risk: Green

Year	Team	G/GS	Snaps	Pass	Rec	Yds	TD	C%	+/-	Drop	Yd/C	aDOT	Rk	YAC	Rk	YAC+	BTkl	DVOA	Rk	DYAR	Rk	YAR	Use	Rk	Slot	Wide
2016	ATL	14/3	405	27	19	271	3	70%	+2.8	2	14.3	10.3	5	3.8	27	-0.4	1	46.8%	1	106	11	95	5.9%	43	25%	4%
2017	ATL	16/8	787	65	49	526	3	75%	+5.8	4	10.7	6.8	40	5.3	17	+0.4	10	9.4%	14	71	13	47	12.4%	21	43%	0%
2018	ATL	16/7	809	88	71	660	4	81%	+8.1	1	9.3	6.8	32	3.3	44	-1.3	9	2.2%	21	56	15	52	14.5%	12	47%	7%
2019	ATL			85	65	631	4	76%			9.7							2.4%								

Since entering the NFL in 2016 as a third-round draft pick, Hooper's production has increased every season, but with that rise has come a drop in efficiency. So he's not Travis Kelce, Zach Ertz, or George Kittle. Only three people in the world are. He's solidly in the next tier of tight ends, though. His 233 DYAR over the past three seasons ranks ninth among tight ends.

O.J. Howard Height: 6-6   Weight: 251   College: Alabama   Draft: 2017/1 (19)   Born: 18-Nov-1994   Age: 25   Risk: Green

Year	Team	G/GS	Snaps	Pass	Rec	Yds	TD	C%	+/-	Drop	Yd/C	aDOT	Rk	YAC	Rk	YAC+	BTkl	DVOA	Rk	DYAR	Rk	YAR	Use	Rk	Slot	Wide
2017	TB	14/14	608	39	26	432	6	67%	+4.0	1	16.6	11.9	2	5.8	12	+1.5	1	32.2%	5	101	7	91	7.4%	39	21%	3%
2018	TB	10/8	436	48	34	565	5	71%	+3.3	2	16.6	11.7	3	6.1	12	+1.8	4	44.0%	1	169	3	160	12.2%	17	57%	6%
2019	TB			75	55	813	5	73%			14.8							20.8%								

Bruce Arians has never really featured tight ends in his offense, unless you count Heath Miller on the Steelers from 2007 to 2011. While with the Cardinals, he said, "We pay Larry (Fitzgerald) and those guys too much money to throw it to the tight ends. They're here to block." Back then, Arians had Rob Housler, John Carlson, and Jermaine Gresham. Now, he has Howard. If Arians can't find a way to feature him, then it's worth questioning whether he was the right hire for this Buccaneers team. With DeSean Jackson and Adam Humphries gone, with the lack of a proven pass-catching running back, and with Jameis Winston's tendency to lean on his tight ends, Howard is in line for a substantial increase in targets. Look for Arians to use him more as a receiver than a true tight end anyway, which shouldn't be much of an adjustment given that Howard lined up in the slot 27 times and out wide three times last season. He should clear 35 catches and 600 yards for the first time in his career—easily.

Hayden Hurst Height: 6-4   Weight: 250   College: South Carolina   Draft: 2018/1 (25)   Born: 24-Aug-1993   Age: 26   Risk: Green

Year	Team	G/GS	Snaps	Pass	Rec	Yds	TD	C%	+/-	Drop	Yd/C	aDOT	Rk	YAC	Rk	YAC+	BTkl	DVOA	Rk	DYAR	Rk	YAR	Use	Rk	Slot	Wide
2018	BAL	12/0	275	23	13	163	1	57%	-2.6	0	12.5	7.5	--	5.7	--	+1.0	2	-17.5%	--	-16	--	-18	5.6%	--	30%	13%
2019	BAL			32	22	228	1	69%			10.4							-3.1%								

With a Jones fracture forcing him to miss the first month of the year, Hurst never really became a consistent part of the offense in his rookie season. The plot twist this year is that Hurst apparently re-dedicated himself in the gym, putting on 20 pounds of muscle despite the fact that, per John Harbaugh (as relayed to Ravens.com), Hurst "hasn't lost one step of speed." Coming out of South Carolina, Hurst showed the speed to be able to threaten the seam, and if his extra pounds help him hold up on blocks, he has a chance to become a complete tight end. That said, it's hard to imagine him getting a real role on this team over Mark Andrews and the newly paid Nick Boyle unless he comes in and blows the coaching staff away this preseason. There's a lot of upside here—something in the vein of Hunter Henry with blocking—but not much guaranteed playing time.

Jesse James Height: 6-7   Weight: 261   College: Penn State   Draft: 2015/5 (160)   Born: 4-Jun-1994   Age: 25   Risk: Green

Year	Team	G/GS	Snaps	Pass	Rec	Yds	TD	C%	+/-	Drop	Yd/C	aDOT	Rk	YAC	Rk	YAC+	BTkl	DVOA	Rk	DYAR	Rk	YAR	Use	Rk	Slot	Wide
2016	PIT	16/13	855	60	39	338	3	65%	-3.9	5	8.7	6.8	33	3.2	43	-0.9	1	-13.7%	34	-26	37	-21	10.0%	34	38%	3%
2017	PIT	16/14	907	63	43	372	3	68%	+0.2	2	8.7	6.1	45	4.5	30	-0.5	4	-12.8%	39	-23	43	2	10.5%	29	22%	2%
2018	PIT	16/7	562	39	30	423	2	77%	+2.4	2	14.1	8.5	14	6.2	11	+1.5	1	27.3%	3	96	7	104	5.8%	43	23%	0%
2019	DET			31	24	259	3	77%			10.8							8.4%								

As far as boring yet ultimately solid tight ends go, you would be hard-pressed to find anyone more fitting than Jesse James. He will not be found screaming down the seam or cutting across the deep middle part of the field, but as an underneath chains-mover, he does his job. James can work leverage, find creases of space between zones, and secure tough catches in traffic, making him a reliable safety blanket for any quarterback looking to find a few cheap yards. Pairing him with T.J. Hockenson also poised the Lions well to play out of 12 personnel with both tight ends attached to the line of scrimmage. Hockenson is a dual-threat tight end with plenty of in-line experience, while James is a solid blocker who regularly sports some of the lowest target shares from a wide receiver position among tight ends. The heavy tight end looks would certainly be a change for Detroit, but James can help them accomplish it if that is what they are aiming for.

Blake Jarwin Height: 6-5   Weight: 246   College: Oklahoma State   Draft: 2017/FA   Born: 16-Jul-1994   Age: 25   Risk: Green

Year	Team	G/GS	Snaps	Pass	Rec	Yds	TD	C%	+/-	Drop	Yd/C	aDOT	Rk	YAC	Rk	YAC+	BTkl	DVOA	Rk	DYAR	Rk	YAR	Use	Rk	Slot	Wide
2018	DAL	16/4	387	36	27	307	3	75%	+2.1	2	11.4	8.3	18	4.1	37	-0.6	5	24.0%	4	68	12	69	6.9%	38	58%	0%
2019	DAL			44	28	320	2	64%			11.4							-1.4%								

A 7-catch, 119-yard, 3-touchdown performance in a nearly meaningless Week 17 game against the Giants (which the Cowboys treated like the Super Bowl for some reason) accounted for 39 percent of Jarwin's yardage, 100 percent of his touchdowns, and a big chunk of his gaudy DVOA figure. Jarwin had some other solid games gobbling up quick outs and finding holes in zones to squat in, and he combines enough athleticism with rumble-after-the-catch ability to be a plausible choice as a starting tight end. Jarwin is expected to platoon with Jason Witten this season, which is a sign that the Cowboys weren't carried away by Jarwin's Week 17 effort, so we shouldn't be either.

Travis Kelce

Height: 6-5   Weight: 255   College: Cincinnati   Draft: 2013/3 (63)   Born: 5-Oct-1989   Age: 30   Risk: Yellow

Year	Team	G/GS	Snaps	Pass	Rec	Yds	TD	C%	+/-	Drop	Yd/C	aDOT	Rk	YAC	Rk	YAC+	BTkl	DVOA	Rk	DYAR	Rk	YAR	Use	Rk	Slot	Wide
2016	KC	16/15	888	117	85	1125	4	73%	+4.8	8	13.2	6.8	34	7.4	4	+2.5	12	26.0%	5	261	1	222	21.7%	4	59%	14%
2017	KC	15/15	875	122	83	1038	8	68%	+7.4	7	12.5	9.6	11	4.9	24	+0.2	18	17.0%	12	197	2	206	24.4%	1	56%	16%
2018	KC	16/16	993	150	103	1336	10	69%	+5.0	6	13.0	9.0	11	5.5	18	+1.1	16	11.5%	14	196	2	206	26.6%	1	66%	8%
2019	KC			135	96	1223	8	71%			12.7							14.2%								

Kelce held the single-season record for receiving yards for a tight end for about three hours before George Kittle broke it at the end of 2018. Easy come, easy go. Definitely more receiver than tight end—74 percent of his pass targets came when he was lined up in the slot or out wide, fourth-most among qualified tight ends—Kelce should be considered the league's best big slot receiver and compared to other players as such. He had a 19.2% DVOA when lined up in the slot; that has him seventh among all receivers with at least 60 slot targets. The people ahead of him are all smaller, shiftier guys such as Tyreek Hill or Brandin Cooks, and then you have the 260-pound Kelce dwarfing the poor nickel corners or safeties asked to keep him in check. Great size, great hands, great YAC ability—Kelce's simply the best at what he does.

George Kittle

Height: 6-4   Weight: 247   College: Iowa   Draft: 2017/5 (146)   Born: 9-Oct-1993   Age: 26   Risk: Yellow

Year	Team	G/GS	Snaps	Pass	Rec	Yds	TD	C%	+/-	Drop	Yd/C	aDOT	Rk	YAC	Rk	YAC+	BTkl	DVOA	Rk	DYAR	Rk	YAR	Use	Rk	Slot	Wide
2017	SF	15/7	591	63	43	515	2	68%	-0.1	7	12.0	7.4	35	6.2	10	+1.6	6	5.6%	17	55	16	59	11.3%	25	44%	2%
2018	SF	16/16	928	136	88	1377	5	65%	-3.9	4	15.6	7.5	25	9.9	1	+4.7	19	15.1%	7	207	1	180	26.5%	2	40%	4%
2019	SF			123	85	1151	7	69%			13.5							13.4%								

The 49ers trailed the Rams 48-24 in the closing minutes of Week 17, but they still called a timeout on defense and made a fourth-down stop to get their offense the ball back. Kittle needed only 9 yards to break Travis Kelce's hours-old record for most yards in a season by a tight end, and he rewarded his teammates' efforts with a 6-yard catch and then a 43-yard touchdown to pass Kelce's mark. It was a trademark Kittle play, as he caught a quick out, slipped two tackles, and scampered to the end zone. Earlier in December, he had scorched the Denver Broncos for 210 yards in the first *half*; even though he was shut out after halftime, he still came within 5 yards of breaking Shannon Sharpe's single-game record for tight ends. Kelce led all players, regardless of position, with 870 total yards after the catch, as well as finishing first in average YAC and YAC+. In April, Matt Barrows of The Athletic reported that more than half of Kittle's yardage had been gained after he suffered "fractured cartilage" in his knee against the Raiders. This is all partly because Kyle Shanahan is a master at scheming tight ends open, and partly because Kittle is a very special player—he led all tight ends with 19 broken tackles. With better health at wide receiver and a roster that is infected with surplus running backs, the 49ers might lean on Kittle less in 2019. His totals may drop as a result, but he'll make up for it in the long run. Kittle should be a star for years to come.

Tyler Kroft

Height: 6-5   Weight: 246   College: Rutgers   Draft: 2015/3 (85)   Born: 15-Oct-1992   Age: 27   Risk: Red

Year	Team	G/GS	Snaps	Pass	Rec	Yds	TD	C%	+/-	Drop	Yd/C	aDOT	Rk	YAC	Rk	YAC+	BTkl	DVOA	Rk	DYAR	Rk	YAR	Use	Rk	Slot	Wide
2016	CIN	14/11	374	12	10	92	0	83%	+1.5	1	9.2	7.7	--	3.1	--	-1.7	0	0.0%	--	5	--	5	2.5%	--	33%	8%
2017	CIN	16/16	829	62	42	404	7	68%	+1.0	4	9.6	6.6	42	4.6	28	+0.5	6	1.3%	21	35	21	45	12.4%	22	45%	5%
2018	CIN	5/2	117	6	4	36	0	67%	+0.6	1	9.0	6.6	--	4.3	--	+0.7	0	-11.7%	--	-2	--	3	3.6%	--	20%	0%
2019	BUF			40	25	281	1	63%			11.2							-6.0%								

Kroft broke his foot on the first day of OTAs, which isn't exactly the best way to ingratiate yourself to your new team. This comes after he missed nearly all of 2018 with a broken foot as well, so that is more than a little concerning. When healthy, Kroft is a nice red zone target; he had a 21.5% DVOA in the red zone in 2017, which ranked 15th among players with at least a dozen targets. Kroft is an above-average second tight end; he'll need to take another step forward if he's going to be a good first-stringer. Just, maybe take that step forward with the non-broken foot, Tyler.

Matt LaCosse   Height: 6-5   Weight: 261   College: Illinois   Draft: 2015/FA   Born: 21-Sep-1992   Age: 27   Risk: Yellow

Year	Team	G/GS	Snaps	Pass	Rec	Yds	TD	C%	+/-	Drop	Yd/C	aDOT	Rk	YAC	Rk	YAC+	BTkl	DVOA	Rk	DYAR	Rk	YAR	Use	Rk	Slot	Wide
2017	2TM	5/1	51	1	0	0	0	0%	-0.3	0	0.0	2.0	--	0.0	--	--	0	-125.2%	--	-9	--	-7	0.5%	--	0%	0%
2018	DEN	15/5	418	37	24	250	1	65%	-2.7	2	10.4	5.9	40	6.0	14	+0.9	1	-7.6%	34	-1	34	-13	6.9%	39	51%	5%
2019	NE			31	21	252	2	68%			12.0							6.0%								

Originally signed as a depth contributor, journeyman Matt LaCosse currently sits atop the Patriots tight end depth chart following the suspension of Benjamin Watson and the release of Austin Seferian-Jenkins. A 2015 undrafted free agent out of Illinois, LaCosse has spent time with the Giants (twice), the Jets (one preseason week only), and the Broncos. The Broncos did not offer him a contract to remain in Denver, enabling the Patriots to sign him as an unrestricted free agent.

LaCosse has only 27 career receptions and a single touchdown to his name, but he brings a solid reputation as a blocker and contributed effectively on special teams in Denver. It would be a surprise to see him remain as the leading tight end after Watson returns, but he has a great opportunity to make an impact in the first four weeks.

Vance McDonald   Height: 6-4   Weight: 267   College: Rice   Draft: 2013/2 (55)   Born: 13-Jun-1990   Age: 29   Risk: Green

Year	Team	G/GS	Snaps	Pass	Rec	Yds	TD	C%	+/-	Drop	Yd/C	aDOT	Rk	YAC	Rk	YAC+	BTkl	DVOA	Rk	DYAR	Rk	YAR	Use	Rk	Slot	Wide
2016	SF	11/11	442	45	24	391	4	53%	-4.6	3	16.3	10.3	6	8.6	2	+4.3	2	6.7%	18	41	19	22	13.3%	24	13%	0%
2017	PIT	10/7	270	24	14	188	1	58%	-1.4	3	13.4	8.7	--	6.3	--	+1.9	3	-2.4%	--	7	--	25	6.4%	--	21%	0%
2018	PIT	15/14	564	72	50	610	4	69%	-0.1	2	12.2	5.2	46	7.7	4	+2.3	16	3.6%	20	51	17	48	11.2%	21	28%	4%
2019	PIT			80	53	668	5	66%			12.6							8.4%								

Big Mac saw as many targets in 2018 as he had the previous two seasons combined, and his catch rate and DVOA went up (his third-down DVOA was a potent 12.5% on 31 targets). It has been a topsy-turvy couple of seasons for McDonald, who signed a rich contract extension in San Francisco, then suffered a debilitating shoulder injury three days later and was subsequently dealt by the new 49ers regime in the offseason. He's clearly *el numero uno receptor cerrado* (that means No. 1 tight end, folks) in Pittsburgh this season, and given the flux on the offensive side of the ball, McDonald could well see another increase in his role.

David Njoku   Height: 6-4   Weight: 246   College: Miami   Draft: 2017/1 (29)   Born: 10-Jul-1996   Age: 23   Risk: Green

Year	Team	G/GS	Snaps	Pass	Rec	Yds	TD	C%	+/-	Drop	Yd/C	aDOT	Rk	YAC	Rk	YAC+	BTkl	DVOA	Rk	DYAR	Rk	YAR	Use	Rk	Slot	Wide
2017	CLE	16/5	501	60	32	386	4	53%	-4.1	4	12.1	10.4	8	4.7	26	-0.3	3	-9.7%	34	-10	37	-2	10.8%	27	23%	16%
2018	CLE	16/14	871	88	56	639	4	64%	-2.9	5	11.4	8.7	13	5.5	19	+0.3	9	-18.1%	41	-63	44	-45	15.8%	9	25%	10%
2019	CLE			78	55	711	6	71%			12.9							15.0%								

The Browns shortened Njoku's routes in his second year, which boosted his catch rate but not his effectiveness. Just 23, the athletic marvel isn't much more polished than when he broke into the league, and he is one of the last remaining Browns with ties to the reviled Sashi Brown. He is also a liability as a blocker—only Kyle Rudolph had more blown blocks at the position in 2018. A whole season with Full Baker and Zero Hue might allow Njoku to blossom into his traits, and with defensive attention drawn by Messrs. Beckham, Chubb, et al., there is no excuse for Njoku in this crucial crossroads season. Our projection system agrees—we like him as a high-quality fantasy pickup.

Josh Oliver   Height: 6-5   Weight: 249   College: San Jose State   Draft: 2019/3 (69)   Born: 21-Mar-1997   Age: 22   Risk: Green

Year	Team	G/GS	Snaps	Pass	Rec	Yds	TD	C%	+/-	Drop	Yd/C	aDOT	Rk	YAC	Rk	YAC+	BTkl	DVOA	Rk	DYAR	Rk	YAR	Use	Rk	Slot	Wide
2019	JAX			32	21	226	2	66%			10.8							-6.8%								

Jacksonville's third-round pick last April, Oliver busted out in 2018 for San Jose State, doubling his freshman-through-junior year receiving yardage for a 1-11 team without much else on offense. Oliver has a promising future as a receiving tight end, but his blocking came under fire from pretty much every scout and draftnik—the desire is there, but he was lacking functional power. The Jaguars don't really have anybody who should out-and-out keep Oliver off the field if he shows promise in training camp and the preseason, but he's probably going to need some development before he plays more than 40 or 50 percent of the snaps. Nick Foles does love his tight ends, though, and Oliver should be looked at carefully whenever he gets a real chance.

Greg Olsen
Height: 6-6 Weight: 254 College: Miami Draft: 2007/1 (31) Born: 11-Mar-1985 Age: 34 Risk: Red

Year	Team	G/GS	Snaps	Pass	Rec	Yds	TD	C%	+/-	Drop	Yd/C	aDOT	Rk	YAC	Rk	YAC+	BTkl	DVOA	Rk	DYAR	Rk	YAR	Use	Rk	Slot	Wide
2016	CAR	16/16	1033	129	80	1073	3	62%	+2.5	3	13.4	11.3	3	4.4	17	+0.2	2	8.3%	17	134	8	123	23.4%	1	72%	4%
2017	CAR	7/7	367	38	17	191	1	45%	-4.0	0	11.2	10.6	7	2.8	47	-1.0	0	-24.5%	49	-44	49	-39	18.2%	9	63%	3%
2018	CAR	9/9	429	38	27	291	4	71%	+2.3	2	10.8	8.8	12	3.1	45	-1.0	0	14.6%	9	57	14	57	12.6%	16	54%	0%
2019	CAR			68	48	494	6	71%			10.3							9.2%								

After being a bastion of health and production throughout his first 10 professional seasons, Olsen has missed 16 games over the past two years with a persistent, recurring foot fracture. Now 34 years old, Olsen posted the lowest DVOA of his career in 2017 before rebounding with one of his highest last year. Offseason reports suggest that the injury is behind him, but that will not be fully confirmed until he returns to live game action.

When healthy, Olsen is Cam Newton's favorite, most consistent target. Olsen recorded at least 800 yards in five straight seasons from 2012 to 2016, and he is normally good for five or six touchdowns a season. The problem is that he now hasn't been fully healthy since October 2017, and those issues do not tend to improve with age. 2018 fourth-round rookie Ian Thomas made a strong case for more playing time during Olsen's absence last season, so even a healthy Olsen may see his snap and target count significantly reduced from their 2016 peak. There are also questions about the health of his quarterback, and the distribution of targets among the deepest and most talented receiving group of that quarterback's career. Olsen should still be the lead tight end in Carolina, but even his best case may be closer to his 2012 or 2013 production (approximately 100 targets, 70 receptions, 800 yards) than that of 2016.

James O'Shaughnessy
Height: 6-4 Weight: 248 College: Illinois State Draft: 2015/5 (173) Born: 14-Jan-1992 Age: 27 Risk: Green

Year	Team	G/GS	Snaps	Pass	Rec	Yds	TD	C%	+/-	Drop	Yd/C	aDOT	Rk	YAC	Rk	YAC+	BTkl	DVOA	Rk	DYAR	Rk	YAR	Use	Rk	Slot	Wide
2016	KC	16/3	111	3	2	-1	0	67%	+0.3	0	-0.5	-0.5	--	0.0	--	-8.1	0	-98.0%	--	-15	--	-16	0.6%	--	0%	33%
2017	JAX	16/1	239	24	14	149	1	58%	-2.4	2	10.6	6.0	--	5.9	--	+1.9	3	-4.1%	--	5	--	4	4.6%	--	42%	4%
2018	JAX	14/9	533	38	24	214	0	63%	-2.2	1	8.9	6.9	31	5.1	23	-0.4	7	-28.9%	45	-49	42	-37	8.2%	33	32%	3%
2019	JAX			19	13	130	0	68%			10.0							-3.9%								

Fun with small sample sizes! O'Shaughnessy had -18 DYAR and a -16.6% DVOA on his short targets, catching 73 percent of them and averaging 5.1 yards after catch. Not only did O'Shaughnessy not catch a single one of his five deep targets, but two of them were picked, as Blake Bortles passes tend to be. Those were good for a -112.7% DVOA anchor on O'Shaughnessy's record. As a blocker/underneath option. O'Shaughnessy is both a) credible and b) replicating the skill set of every tight end on this roster besides Josh Oliver. It's anyone's guess who will get the playing time on this depth chart, but O'Shaughnessy provides a known floor.

Jordan Reed
Height: 6-2 Weight: 236 College: Florida Draft: 2013/3 (85) Born: 3-Jul-1990 Age: 29 Risk: Red

Year	Team	G/GS	Snaps	Pass	Rec	Yds	TD	C%	+/-	Drop	Yd/C	aDOT	Rk	YAC	Rk	YAC+	BTkl	DVOA	Rk	DYAR	Rk	YAR	Use	Rk	Slot	Wide
2016	WAS	12/8	568	89	66	686	6	74%	+6.9	1	10.4	7.5	26	4.0	25	-0.2	12	9.9%	14	102	13	130	19.8%	7	54%	15%
2017	WAS	6/5	233	35	27	211	2	77%	+3.8	0	7.8	6.6	43	2.9	46	-1.6	3	-10.1%	35	-7	35	-18	17.3%	12	60%	17%
2018	WAS	13/8	511	84	54	558	2	64%	-4.7	2	10.3	6.9	29	4.2	35	-0.7	5	-22.2%	43	-80	48	-59	20.9%	4	63%	13%
2019	WAS			89	59	602	5	66%			10.2							-6.6%								

Reed played through reported neck and back injuries last season before missing the last few games of the year with a toe injury. He was just 16-of-29 on third-down targets with only 10 first downs, and his downfield production was almost nonexistent. Reed is no longer the terror he was after the catch five years and 500 injuries ago, so lots and lots of quick outs and bunch-formation screens resulted in lots and lots of six-catch, 55-yard stat lines. Reed can still help a team when about 80 percent healthy, but that's about as healthy as he gets these days.

Kyle Rudolph   Height: 6-6   Weight: 265   College: Notre Dame   Draft: 2011/2 (43)   Born: 9-Nov-1989   Age: 30   Risk: Yellow

Year	Team	G/GS	Snaps	Pass	Rec	Yds	TD	C%	+/-	Drop	Yd/C	aDOT	Rk	YAC	Rk	YAC+	BTkl	DVOA	Rk	DYAR	Rk	YAR	Use	Rk	Slot	Wide
2016	MIN	16/16	969	132	83	840	7	63%	-1.9	7	10.1	6.7	37	4.3	19	-0.2	5	-9.1%	31	-17	34	3	22.5%	2	35%	3%
2017	MIN	16/16	924	81	57	532	8	70%	+5.3	2	9.3	7.6	33	4.0	36	-0.2	6	8.8%	15	88	9	91	15.1%	14	28%	3%
2018	MIN	16/16	925	82	64	634	4	78%	+6.7	1	9.9	6.5	35	3.9	39	-0.7	6	8.6%	15	91	9	59	13.9%	14	46%	7%
2019	MIN			88	61	602	4	69%			9.9							-0.5%								

Overall a quality tight end, Rudolph was uniquely bad as a blocker last season. He surrendered 14 blown blocks in the run game, twice as many as David Njoku's seven in second place. In a year with fewer recorded blown blocks across the league than the previous year, Rudolph single-handedly tried to pull 2018 back toward the mean. Thankfully, Rudolph makes up for his atrocious run blocking by being a reliable pass-catcher. Two years running, he has led the Vikings in DVOA on third and fourth down, and finished among the top seven tight ends in receiving plus-minus. Yards after catch and flashy plays are not part of his skill set, but as far as making the plays you expect a player to, few tight ends compare to Rudolph. The Vikings have Stefon Diggs and Adam Thielen to pick up the slack on Rudolph's lack of explosive plays.

Ricky Seals-Jones   Height: 6-5   Weight: 243   College: Texas A&M   Draft: 2017/FA   Born: 15-Mar-1995   Age: 24   Risk: Green

Year	Team	G/GS	Snaps	Pass	Rec	Yds	TD	C%	+/-	Drop	Yd/C	aDOT	Rk	YAC	Rk	YAC+	BTkl	DVOA	Rk	DYAR	Rk	YAR	Use	Rk	Slot	Wide
2017	ARI	10/1	132	28	12	201	3	43%	-4.8	3	16.8	11.4	3	6.2	9	+2.4	2	-4.6%	27	5	28	13	7.4%	38	21%	11%
2018	ARI	15/5	536	69	34	343	1	49%	-10.7	5	10.1	10.0	7	2.7	47	-2.3	1	-43.7%	49	-158	49	-143	15.4%	10	68%	3%
2019	ARI			28	18	204	2	64%			11.3							0.6%								

Perhaps no veteran on Arizona's roster stands to benefit more from the hiring of Kliff Kingsbury than Seals-Jones. A five-star recruit as a wide receiver out of high school, Seals-Jones was in such high demand that his father has claimed colleges were offering bribes up to $600,000 to sign him. Seals-Jones disappointed at Texas A&M, showing neither speed, nor strength, nor good hands. The Cardinals took a flyer on him in 2017, but he struggled as a tight end for Bruce Arians and even more as a slot player for Steve Wilks. Kingsbury should, in theory, find a way to match Seals-Jones up against smaller defensive backs and let the former basketball player box them out. If Kingsbury can't find a way to get some value out of Seals-Jones, it's doubtful anyone else could either.

Austin Seferian-Jenkins   Height: 6-5   Weight: 262   College: Washington   Draft: 2014/2 (38)   Born: 9/29/1992   Age: 27   Risk: N/A

Year	Team	G/GS	Snaps	Pass	Rec	Yds	TD	C%	+/-	Drop	Yd/C	aDOT	Rk	YAC	Rk	YAC+	BTkl	DVOA	Rk	DYAR	Rk	YAR	Use	Rk	Slot	Wide
2016	2TM	9/2	190	20	13	154	1	65%	-0.5	3	11.8	10.2	--	2.2	--	-1.2	1	15.4%	--	32	--	37	6.7%	--	33%	29%
2017	NYJ	13/10	655	74	50	357	3	68%	+0.9	4	7.1	6.9	39	2.3	48	-2.5	6	-23.4%	48	-83	51	-83	18.7%	8	51%	7%
2018	JAX	5/5	221	19	11	90	1	58%	-1.3	1	8.2	5.8	--	2.7	--	-2.2	0	-25.9%	--	-24	--	-33	11.5%	--	42%	0%

An athletically gifted but erratic player, Seferian-Jenkins was released by the Patriots less than two months after signing a one-year deal as a potential high-profile solution at tight end. New England would have been his fourth team in four seasons. While frequently being the subject of negative off-field publicity, mostly for his struggles with alcohol, he has never had the consistent on-field production that might encourage a team to be more patient with him. He has not been signed by another team at the time of writing.

Irv Smith   Height: 6-2   Weight: 241   College: Alabama   Draft: 2019/2 (50)   Born: 9-Aug-1998   Age: 21   Risk: Red

Year	Team	G/GS	Snaps	Pass	Rec	Yds	TD	C%	+/-	Drop	Yd/C	aDOT	Rk	YAC	Rk	YAC+	BTkl	DVOA	Rk	DYAR	Rk	YAR	Use	Rk	Slot	Wide
2019	MIN			34	25	299	2	74%			11.9							11.5%								

It may not be apparent yet, but Irv Smith Jr. is part of a revolution in the sport. Football is starting to embrace tight ends who can function as H-backs and wing players. The trend is prevalent at the college level—nearly every team plays with a wing or an H-back on a regular basis—but it is not something that has yet become a staple in the NFL. As more such as Smith enter the league, that will change. Smith played as a wing player in many of Alabama's pistol and shotgun looks, often serving as a pulling blocker on run plays and a seam or flat threat in the pass game. He even lined up in the backfield on occasion. As part of Alabama's high-flying pass game, Smith often thrived in space created in part by excellent wide receivers, a luxury he will experience again in Minnesota. As he started just one season in college, Smith will need time to iron out his technique as a blocker and route-runner, but with Kyle Rudolph recently extended, he is comfortably locked into a No. 2 position that will give him the time he needs.

Jonnu Smith

Height: 6-3 Weight: 248 College: Florida International Draft: 2017/3 (100) Born: 22-Aug-1995 Age: 24 Risk: Green

Year	Team	G/GS	Snaps	Pass	Rec	Yds	TD	C%	+/-	Drop	Yd/C	aDOT	Rk	YAC	Rk	YAC+	BTkl	DVOA	Rk	DYAR	Rk	YAR	Use	Rk	Slot	Wide
2017	TEN	16/13	556	30	18	157	2	60%	-1.8	1	8.7	7.2	37	5.3	18	-0.1	4	-30.7%	51	-44	48	-37	6.2%	46	10%	10%
2018	TEN	13/12	610	30	20	258	3	67%	-2.0	3	12.9	5.4	44	9.0	2	+3.7	4	-1.8%	26	11	27	14	8.5%	31	23%	13%
2019	TEN			27	17	167	1	63%			9.8							-8.3%								

The only Titans casualty on Derrick Henry's 99-yard run against the Jaguars in Week 14, Smith was still working his way through MCL rehab in June, but should be ready for the start of the season. Delanie Walker's Week 1 injury created plenty of opportunity for Smith, but he flashed with big plays like a 61-yard catch-and-run score against the Texans and a 29-yard catch-and-run against the Patriots rather than stepping into Walker's role as a sustaining force and main target for the offense. Walker's return and better depth at receiver likely mean less opportunity in the pass game. While his blocking has improved, it is probably not good enough for the Titans to trust him as their primary in-line player, so Smith might find himself in a more limited role in his third season.

Jace Sternberger

Height: 6-4 Weight: 251 College: Texas A&M Draft: 2019/3 (75) Born: 26-Jun-1996 Age: 23 Risk: Yellow

Year	Team	G/GS	Snaps	Pass	Rec	Yds	TD	C%	+/-	Drop	Yd/C	aDOT	Rk	YAC	Rk	YAC+	BTkl	DVOA	Rk	DYAR	Rk	YAR	Use	Rk	Slot	Wide
2019	GB			38	26	272	2	68%			10.4							0.6%								

The track record for rookie tight ends contributing right away is not encouraging, but the Packers may need a miracle from Sternberger. A third-round pick from Texas A&M, Sternberger is a hybrid in-line/H-back player who can do a little bit of everything: block, run routes, pick up yards after the catch. That well-roundedness is a stark change from Green Bay's other two tight ends, Jimmy Graham and Marcedes Lewis. The former is strictly a pass-catcher, mostly from the slot, and the other is only valuable as a blocker. Sternberger proved himself a quality pass-catcher in college as Texas A&M's leading receiver at a clip of 10.7 yards per target, proving he can work the short area just the same as he can be a threat deep over the middle. Likewise, he more than held his own as a blocker in the SEC, both attached to the line of scrimmage and as a wing H-back. That he can be moved all over the formation and provide a number of services makes him unique among Green Bay's tight end corps. Getting meaningful play out of him right away would be huge for Matt LaFleur's tight end-centric offense.

Geoff Swaim

Height: 6-4 Weight: 250 College: Texas Draft: 2015/7 (246) Born: 16-Sep-1993 Age: 26 Risk: Yellow

Year	Team	G/GS	Snaps	Pass	Rec	Yds	TD	C%	+/-	Drop	Yd/C	aDOT	Rk	YAC	Rk	YAC+	BTkl	DVOA	Rk	DYAR	Rk	YAR	Use	Rk	Slot	Wide
2016	DAL	9/6	203	8	6	69	0	75%	+0.7	0	11.5	3.3	--	8.3	--	+2.7	0	-2.3%	--	3	--	4	2.9%	--	0%	0%
2017	DAL	15/2	173	2	2	25	0	100%	+0.7	0	12.5	7.0	--	5.5	--	+0.7	0	69.6%	--	12	--	12	0.4%	--	0%	0%
2018	DAL	9/9	512	32	26	242	1	81%	+2.7	0	9.3	3.3	49	6.3	7	+1.2	2	-11.6%	37	-9	36	-15	10.9%	23	48%	0%
2019	JAX			49	32	293	1	65%			9.2							-10.3%								

Swaim was the main Cowboys tight end who got play in the passing game in the wake of Jason Witten's retirement, and it went so well that the Cowboys begged Witten to unretire. Some creative play-action got Swaim a 43-yard gain against the Texans on Sunday Night Football, and that was pretty much the highlight of his season. A broken wrist suffered in November put him out for the season, and he signed with the Jaguars so that he could be forever linked with Ben Koyack. Well, OK, he signed because Ben Koyack and James O'Shaughnessy are not threatening competition.

Ian Thomas | Height: 6-4 | Weight: 259 | College: Indiana | Draft: 2018/4 (101) | Born: 6-Jun-1996 | Age: 23 | Risk: Green

Year	Team	G/GS	Snaps	Pass	Rec	Yds	TD	C%	+/-	Drop	Yd/C	aDOT	Rk	YAC	Rk	YAC+	BTkl	DVOA	Rk	DYAR	Rk	YAR	Use	Rk	Slot	Wide
2018	CAR	16/6	525	49	36	333	2	73%	+1.5	4	9.3	6.3	38	4.4	32	-0.4	1	0.9%	24	27	23	10	8.9%	29	49%	0%
2019	CAR			36	24	269	1	67%			11.2							-1.0%								

A fourth-round pick out of Indiana, Ian Thomas was expected to spend his first season as the backup to veteran Greg Olsen while the coaches molded his intriguing athleticism into a more refined passing target. Olsen's recurring foot injury forced Thomas into the lineup earlier than planned, and the rookie finished the year with more targets and receiving yards than the veteran despite starting three fewer games. The Panthers expect Olsen back at full health for 2019, but Thomas should have established a role for himself regardless.

What size of role remains to be seen. Almost all of Thomas' 2019 production came in games Olsen either missed entirely (Weeks 2 to 4, then 14 to 17) or left early (Weeks 1 and 13). From Weeks 5 to 11, with Olsen back as the primary tight end, Thomas had just a single target, which he caught for 15 yards. Thomas does need to become more refined and consistent, but that is common for rookie tight ends—even elite players at this position do not usually break out until at least their second season. Olsen has missed 16 games over the past two seasons, so there is a good chance that Thomas will get the opportunity to build on a rookie year that certainly flashed potential.

Jordan Thomas | Height: 6-5 | Weight: 265 | College: Mississippi State | Draft: 2018/6 (211) | Born: 2-Aug-1996 | Age: 23 | Risk: Yellow

Year	Team	G/GS	Snaps	Pass	Rec	Yds	TD	C%	+/-	Drop	Yd/C	aDOT	Rk	YAC	Rk	YAC+	BTkl	DVOA	Rk	DYAR	Rk	YAR	Use	Rk	Slot	Wide
2018	HOU	16/10	470	27	20	215	4	74%	+1.2	1	10.8	6.2	39	4.8	27	+0.9	2	12.5%	13	38	22	44	5.4%	44	22%	0%
2019	HOU			63	41	470	4	65%			11.5							2.6%								

Red zone threat. Nine of Thomas' 27 targets came in the red zone, and he caught seven of them. Thomas has a big frame but was a terrible blocker in 2018—he's actually a converted wideout—but he did at least have the good sense to pick Darren Fells' brain about it during offseason activities. "We talk a lot about blocking, and me and him are getting together over the break," Thomas told reporters at minicamp. "He's come along and helped me a lot, actually." Thomas has to be regarded as the most likely tight end to get playing time in Houston given his seniority on the depth chart and how much more he was used than Jordan Akins last season. He has the physical talent to live up to this projection.

C.J. Uzomah | Height: 6-4 | Weight: 254 | College: Auburn | Draft: 2015/5 (157) | Born: 14-Jan-1993 | Age: 26 | Risk: Green

Year	Team	G/GS	Snaps	Pass	Rec	Yds	TD	C%	+/-	Drop	Yd/C	aDOT	Rk	YAC	Rk	YAC+	BTkl	DVOA	Rk	DYAR	Rk	YAR	Use	Rk	Slot	Wide
2016	CIN	10/8	411	38	25	234	1	66%	-0.8	2	9.4	6.9	30	4.0	24	-0.3	4	-0.2%	23	18	23	-4	11.0%	30	47%	3%
2017	CIN	14/4	213	15	10	92	1	67%	+0.8	1	9.2	5.2	--	5.0	--	+0.7	1	-1.1%	--	7	--	7	3.4%	--	20%	0%
2018	CIN	16/15	840	65	43	439	3	66%	-2.4	4	10.2	7.5	26	4.5	30	+0.0	4	-11.3%	36	-18	39	-9	12.2%	18	47%	2%
2019	CIN			37	26	284	2	70%			10.9							2.6%								

Uzomah's season was a warning against expecting role players to take a step up in higher-volume situations. Through Week 7, Uzomah had been targeted 20 times and had a 33.2% DVOA. From Week 8 on, Uzomah was targeted 46 times and had a -31.4% DVOA. Now, granted, some of that was with Jeff Driskel, and Driskel is not much of an NFL quarterback, but Uzomah even had a -36.2% on throws from Andy Dalton during that stretch. In Week 12 against the Browns, with A.J. Green hurt, the Bengals threw at Uzomah 12 times, completing six for 39 yards. Eight of those targets were curls or outs, as if there was no game plan for Driskel beyond the very basic. Uzomah is a solid move tight end who saw his stats decimated when he was stretched.

Nick Vannett | Height: 6-6 | Weight: 257 | College: Ohio State | Draft: 2016/3 (94) | Born: 6-Mar-1993 | Age: 26 | Risk: Green

Year	Team	G/GS	Snaps	Pass	Rec	Yds	TD	C%	+/-	Drop	Yd/C	aDOT	Rk	YAC	Rk	YAC+	BTkl	DVOA	Rk	DYAR	Rk	YAR	Use	Rk	Slot	Wide
2016	SEA	9/2	84	4	3	32	0	75%	+0.1	1	10.7	6.5	--	4.0	--	-1.2	0	-17.1%	--	-2	--	-2	1.3%	--	0%	0%
2017	SEA	15/4	278	15	12	124	1	80%	+1.5	2	10.3	7.2	--	3.8	--	-0.7	0	31.0%	--	36	--	30	3.0%	--	27%	0%
2018	SEA	15/9	529	43	29	269	3	67%	-0.5	1	9.3	6.5	34	4.8	26	+0.5	1	-6.5%	28	2	30	-6	11.4%	20	32%	5%
2019	SEA			26	17	165	1	65%			9.7							-6.6%								

Vannett is entering a make-or-break season, as the former third-round pick's time in Seattle could come to an abrupt end depending on how this year plays out. After Vannett did not show much through his first two seasons, Seattle drafted Will Dissly in the fourth round in 2018, which does not bode well for Vannett's future role with the Seahawks. The one thing Vannett has going for him at this point is his durability, as both Dissly and veteran Ed Dickson missed large portions of the 2018 season, but his production has not been enough to firmly solidify a starting spot. With Dissly still recovering from a torn patellar tendon, Vannett will need to make the most of his opportunity to keep a role in the 2019 Seattle offense.

Delanie Walker Height: 6-1 Weight: 241 College: Central Missouri Draft: 2006/6 (175) Born: 12-Aug-1984 Age: 35 Risk: Red

Year	Team	G/GS	Snaps	Pass	Rec	Yds	TD	C%	+/-	Drop	Yd/C	aDOT	Rk	YAC	Rk	YAC+	BTkl	DVOA	Rk	DYAR	Rk	YAR	Use	Rk	Slot	Wide
2016	TEN	15/10	707	103	65	800	7	64%	+3.2	6	12.3	9.9	7	4.3	20	-0.4	11	8.4%	16	102	12	102	22.1%	3	67%	6%
2017	TEN	16/11	744	111	74	807	3	67%	+6.7	2	10.9	9.3	17	3.3	44	-1.4	5	-7.6%	32	-3	32	33	22.8%	3	51%	3%
2018	TEN	1/1	39	7	4	52	0	57%	-0.3	0	13.0	6.6	--	5.0	--	+0.7	2	-25.9%	--	-9	--	-2	25.9%	--	57%	14%
2019	TEN			95	64	730	5	67%			11.4							4.6%								

A broken ankle ended Walker's season in Week 1, and the risk color for a 35-year-old receiving tight end coming off that kind of injury is most definitely red. Offseason reports have been suitably optimistic. Though he missed minicamp, he participated in individual drills after estimating in early May he was 85 percent healthy. The decline in his yards after catch numbers will probably continue, notwithstanding last year's small sample size and the arrival of a legitimate slot receiver who gives him competition for middle of the field targets. As long as his recovery proceeds apace, though, he should be in line for a significant role in Tennessee's offense once again.

Darren Waller Height: 6-6 Weight: 238 College: Georgia Tech Draft: 2015/6 (204) Born: 13-Sep-1992 Age: 27 Risk: Green

Year	Team	G/GS	Snaps	Pass	Rec	Yds	TD	C%	+/-	Drop	Yd/C	aDOT	Rk	YAC	Rk	YAC+	BTkl	DVOA	Rk	DYAR	Rk	YAR	Use	Rk	Slot	Wide
2016	BAL	12/3	234	17	10	85	2	59%	-1.2	2	8.5	6.8	--	3.9	--	+0.1	1	-15.1%	--	-10	--	-13	3.4%	--	41%	12%
2018	OAK	4/0	42	6	6	75	0	100%	+1.5	0	12.5	3.2	--	9.3	--	+4.8	1	26.7%	--	15	--	22	4.5%	--	0%	33%
2019	OAK			47	32	350	5	68%			10.9							6.0%								

Waller got a second chance in Oakland after being suspended for 20 games in 2016-17 for substance abuse issues. He caught all six targets thrown at him and flashed some deep-threat potential—the converted wide receiver is far more athletic than you would expect a tight end to be. Jon Gruden calls him one of the league's "best-kept secrets," which is hyperbole, but Waller *did* start OTAs as Oakland's top tight end, and he has as good a chance as any to break out of a crowded and unheralded group there.

Benjamin Watson Height: 6-3 Weight: 255 College: Duke Draft: 2004/1 (32) Born: 18-Dec-1980 Age: 39 Risk: Green

Year	Team	G/GS	Snaps	Pass	Rec	Yds	TD	C%	+/-	Drop	Yd/C	aDOT	Rk	YAC	Rk	YAC+	BTkl	DVOA	Rk	DYAR	Rk	YAR	Use	Rk	Slot	Wide
2017	BAL	16/12	699	79	61	522	4	77%	+4.4	4	8.6	5.4	47	4.1	35	-0.8	4	-7.5%	31	-1	30	20	14.0%	18	34%	0%
2018	NO	16/4	506	46	35	400	2	76%	+5.6	2	11.4	10.5	5	2.5	48	-2.0	0	15.2%	6	73	10	74	9.0%	28	51%	0%
2019	NE			35	25	293	3	70%			11.8							11.2%								

A veteran of New England's 2004 and 2005 title teams, Watson returned to the Patriots this summer almost a decade after first departing for Cleveland. The 38-year-old initially retired at the conclusion of his second stint in New Orleans, but he was persuaded to rejoin his former teammates for one last hurrah.

Watson's flirtation with retirement has already cost him a four-game PED suspension, as the tight end has admitted taking a banned supplement in March when he had no expectation of returning. Last year was his most efficient receiving season since leaving New England in 2009—he is usually found in the lower half of the DVOA table—but that still amounted to only 400 yards even in the high-powered Saints offense. At his peak, the 15-year veteran usually caught 40 to 50 passes for 400 to 600 yards given a 16-game season. On his return to the field after suspension, Watson will probably slot into the lower end of that range as the senior member of a tight-end committee, just one of multiple players who will collectively try to replace the irreplaceable Rob Gronkowski.

Jason Witten   Height: 6-6   Weight: 265   College: Tennessee   Draft: 2003/3 (69)   Born: 6-May-1982   Age: 37   Risk: Green

Year	Team	G/GS	Snaps	Pass	Rec	Yds	TD	C%	+/-	Drop	Yd/C	aDOT	Rk	YAC	Rk	YAC+	BTkl	DVOA	Rk	DYAR	Rk	YAR	Use	Rk	Slot	Wide
2016	DAL	16/16	1018	95	69	673	3	73%	+4.7	3	9.8	6.8	35	3.7	32	-0.6	10	-7.2%	29	0	29	25	19.5%	8	52%	1%
2017	DAL	16/16	1050	87	63	560	5	72%	+6.5	1	8.9	7.4	36	1.7	50	-2.1	1	-0.4%	24	40	20	37	17.8%	11	65%	1%
2019	DAL			53	36	328	3	68%			9.1							-3.8%								

Listening to Witten call Monday Night Football games was like getting trapped in an airport rental car shuttle with a dude mansplaining to his wife on his phone that the couple's financial woes weren't his fault because buying a speedboat is practically an investment. Witten often sounded like he believed that if he stopped talking for a moment, or even slowed down to collect his thoughts, he would cease to exist and the universe itself would blink away to nothingness. Witten was like a telemarketer who was reading the sales pitch off a monitor and didn't want to give you the chance to hang up by pausing for breath, and also the boiler room he was calling from was on fire. You could smell his pits staining midway through the first quarter. It was … unsettling. Witten was in the last stages of a long, slow decline from his Hall of Fame peak when he retired after the 2017 season. Long, slow declines don't reverse themselves after a year off at age 37. But if we all humor him, maybe we won't have to hear him in the booth again for a while.

Going Deep

Mo Alie-Cox, IND: One of the Colts' basketball convert projects, Alie-Cox got his chance when injury issues to the top three tight ends created an opportunity for the former Virginia Commonwealth cager. Alie-Cox had nine catches, including two scores, before injury issues of his own (calf) sent him to injured reserve. Alie-Cox has developed enough as a blocker that the Colts may feel comfortable giving him in-line snaps, but the presence of both Jack Doyle and Eric Ebron means his ceiling is limited barring injury.

Dwayne Allen, MIA: Allen caught just 13 passes for 113 yards in 29 regular-season games as Rob Gronkowski's backup, with no playoff receptions. Brian Flores brought him to Miami for leadership and blocking, but the days of Allen being any sort of offensive weapon are long over.

Dan Arnold, NO: After passing undrafted in 2017 as a receiver out of Division-III Wisconsin-Platteville, Arnold spent his entire rookie season on injured reserve before converting to tight end last summer. He etched himself into trivia lore as the 50th different Saints player to catch a touchdown pass from Drew Brees, but the rest of his debut season was less memorable: -18 DYAR on 19 targets, a red zone fumble against the Cowboys, and a critical end zone drop on the first drive of the NFC Championship Game. Still very much a developmental prospect, Arnold enters the final year of his initial contract in competition with seventh-round pick Alize Mack at the bottom of the tight end depth chart.

Antony Auclair, TB: The Buccaneers have had a lot of holes in their rosters over the years, but one of them hasn't been third-string blocking tight end. The 6-foot-6, 256-pound Auclair, whom Tampa Bay imported from Canada in 2017, saw a surge in playing time down the stretch last season because of injuries, but he remains stuck behind O.J. Howard and Cameron Brate on the depth chart. In his two seasons, he has caught nine passes on 10 targets.

Blake Bell, KC: The Belldozer has made a decent transition from quarterback at Oklahoma to NFL tight end. He has caught just 30 career passes, mostly as a rookie in 2015 when the San Francisco depth chart was a ghost town. His gadgetry potential never came to fruition, so it's his pass blocking and special teams chops that have kept him in the league. He'll be fighting younger, cheaper players for a slot, including converted college quarterback John Lovett—a younger version of Bell, in other words.

Daniel Brown, NYJ: A converted wide receiver out of James Madison, Brown only played 23 offensive snaps in 14 games for the Bears last season and was never targeted on a pass. But the Jets signed him to a one-year contract and he may end up starting the first four games now that Chris Herndon has been suspended. Brown was a seam-stretcher in college and the preseason but has mostly caught short stuff in the regular season. In 2016 and 2017 he had 29 combined catches for 253 yards, a touchdown, and 3.1% DVOA.

Jake Butt, DEN: Butt is recovering from the third ACL tear of his career, injuries which have limited him to just three games in his first two seasons. At least this one was on his left knee, while the first two affected his right. Injuries keep rearing their heads for Butt, who has now slipped behind a first-round rookie (Noah Fant) and last year's starter (Jeff Heuerman). His as-yet unrealized potential may still earn him a seat on the bench, but the arrival of Fant means that Butt's likely to stick to the back of the tight end depth chart.

Derek Carrier, OAK: With Jared Cook having a career year, there wasn't much call for Carrier offensively on the Raiders last season—he was brought in for some occasional run-blocking duties and played on over 75 percent of Oakland's special teams snaps. That special teams versatility is his best chance of making the 53-man roster again in 2019, but the addition of Luke Willson would seem to fill the "veteran blocking tight end" slot at a cheaper price tag than Carrier carries.

Garrett Celek, SF: Celek's role in the passing game was rendered moot by George Kittle's explosion. He saw only eight targets in 15 games, but he still had plenty to offer, playing 277 snaps on offense (and 168 more on special teams). He played most of the year with a broken thumb and ended the year in the concussion protocol, and it remains uncertain whether he will be ready for training camp. He is at risk of losing snaps (and perhaps his entire job) to free-agent signee Levine Toilolo.

Tyler Conklin, MIN: Conklin had a quiet rookie season, but he has an athletic profile that suggests he may be able to develop into a solid backup or situational receiving tight end. He caught just five passes for 77 yards, but 15.4 yards per reception would have ranked among the best in the league if he could sustain that with an increase of volume. Five receptions is not a reliable sample, but he is the type of space-oriented tight end who can work the middle and pick up yards after the catch, and he showed that in those few instances last season.

Seth DeValve, CLE: There are few Browns left from the Sashi Brown era on the Browns roster, and DeValve may go the way of the other Browns sent packing by John Dorsey. DeValve has shown flashes of strong route-running and is in the last year of his rookie deal, so he is still a cost-effective guy to keep around—for the moment. But he is allergic to blocking and with all the other targets around doesn't figure to make much impact. He could find greener pastures elsewhere than Cleveland.

Ed Dickson, SEA: Dickson, a strong run blocker, joined the Seahawks in 2018 as part of their effort to rebuild their running game. He spent the early part of the year on the PUP list and barely participated in the passing game after his return, averaging barely more than one target per game. While he posted strong advanced metrics in his limited role in the Seattle passing game (56 DYAR, 61.4% DVOA), he should not be counted on as an aerial threat at this stage of his career.

Darren Fells, HOU: A blocking tight end-for-hire, Fells can take on edge rushers, has a big shove, and fills a role that nobody could in Houston in 2018. Depending on the development of the other tight ends, he's likely to be the No. 2 on Houston's depth chart. Don't expect much from a fantasy football perspective, but Fells is a solid depth chart addition on a team that has nothing but youngsters outside of him. Fells has also maintained a double-digit positive DVOA when targeted for a pass in each of the last four seasons, including 52 DYAR on a 53.9% DVOA last season.

Zach Gentry, PIT: Jim Harbaugh couldn't resist turning Gentry, once a highly-ranked quarterback prospect out of Albuquerque, into a tight end. He retains the athleticism from his passing days, but to latch on as a pro tight end Pittsburgh's fifth-round pick will need to get much stronger. Scouts also questioned the quality of his hands, though his catch rate at Michigan was 70 percent. The Black and Gold may need him to develop ASAP, with just the oft-injured Vance McDonald and in-line blocker Xavier Grimble in the fold at the position.

Jermaine Gresham, FA: Gresham produced a pair of Pro Bowl campaigns for the Bengals in his younger days, but (like many of us) he has been steadily declining for years and was finally relegated almost exclusively to blocking duties in Arizona last season. Now 31, Gresham was released in March and remains unsigned.

Xavier Grimble, PIT: Pittsburgh is paying a little over $2 million for Grimble, their backup tight end with 22 career catches in five seasons. Athletic ability allows the X-Man to be a strong blocker and get to the second level, but he's no mutant, as proven when one of his rare catches turned into a critical fumble/touchback in the Steelers' painful loss to Denver.

Josh Hill, NO: Despite starting 31 of his 41 games over the past three years and leading all Saints tight ends in offensive snaps in both 2017 and 2018, Hill recorded only 47 total catches and three touchdowns across those three seasons. He has not qualified for the tight end DYAR leaderboard since 2015 (when his -44 DYAR ranked 43rd), and set a career high last year with a mere 185 yards (and 12 DYAR). Hill's spot as the team's notional No. 2 tight end appears secure, but that is not a position he has previously parlayed into production.

Jacob Hollister, SEA: Seattle acquired Hollister from New England for a conditional seventh-round pick in 2020 to add depth at tight end as Will Dissly continues his recovery from a patellar tendon tear. Hollister did not make much of an impact in the passing game in either of his two seasons with the Patriots, which is a bit of a concern for a player whose reputation entering the league was that of a catch-first tight end. There is a decent chance he fails to make the final roster, depending on Dissly's health.

Lance Kendricks, FA: Kendricks enjoyed a quietly solid career with the Rams, but the past two seasons he spent in Green Bay were lackluster. (His receiving DVOA last year was -0.1%, about as close to average as you can get.) Though over the hill, Kendricks was used as a median between pass-catching Jimmy Graham and run-blocking Marcedes Lewis. He was almost exclusively used in-line, which checks out considering Graham was better suited to play from the slot and Kendricks has never been much of a threat out in space. The Packers tried using him as somewhat of a slot player in 2017 but realized their mistake and moved him back to an in-line spot in 2018. Of 49 qualifying tight ends, only one (Virgil Green) saw fewer of his targets from a wide receiver position than Kendricks last year.

Dawson Knox, BUF: A converted quarterback, Knox was a workout wonder at Ole Miss' pro day, and it vaulted him all the way up to the third round. He didn't do much on the field, buried as the sixth target on the Rebels' depth chart, but his 10.5 yards per target, solid hands, and good route-running skills makes him a tempting developmental project. He also may bring with him a voodoo curse, as both Tyler Kroft and Jason Croom injured themselves on the second day of OTAs. More snaps for the developmental guy!

Jordan Leggett, TB: Leggett started a handful of games alongside fellow Jets rookie Chris Herndon last year, catching 14 passes and blocking acceptably. Adam Gase cut him immediately after deactivating Mike Maccagnan's key fob, probably just to flex his new general management muscles. Leggett is a well-built, athletic receiver who caught 15 touchdown passes in his final two Clemson seasons, so there was no logical reason to release him. The Buccaneers snapped Leggett up on waivers within hours. He would be an intriguing breakthrough candidate if the Bucs weren't so loaded at tight end.

Marcedes Lewis, GB: Over the past few seasons, Lewis has transitioned from a low-bandwidth all-around tight end to being almost exclusively a blocker. He performed well in the role as Green Bay's No. 2 last season and did not record even a single blown block in the run game. Conversely, it has been six years since Lewis caught more than 25 passes, and he only caught three last season, so there should be no expectation for receiving production from him.

Alize Mack, NO: A seventh-round draft pick out of Notre Dame, Mack is a receiving tight end most acclaimed for his large frame, leaping ability, and aptitude for contested catches. Though neither an especially elusive route runner nor an overly proficient blocker, Mack has the potential to find work quickly as a red zone and situational target, assuming he can stave off Dan Arnold to make the 53-man roster and work his way onto the field from there.

Foster Moreau, OAK: This fourth-round pick was barely a factor as a receiver at LSU. Instead he earned his team captaincy with his run-blocking. He's a tremendous blocker with power and ideal footwork, especially when asked to run out ahead and clobber a guy in the second level. He tested very well athletically at the combine, especially in the shuttle and jumping drills, so there's a chance he could develop into a receiver at some point, but that's an issue for future development. For 2019, he's just gonna get to clobber some guys on two-tight end sets and special teams.

David Morgan, MIN: Morgan finished second on the Vikings in tight end snaps last season but did so primarily as a blocking tight end. Morgan's only value in the pass game comes as a quick-game outlet. He does not have the athletic tools to stress defenses further, so he is often relegated to blocking and red zone play. With the drafting of Tyler Conklin last year and Irv Smith Jr. this year, Morgan's best hope to hold a prominent role is that he is the best-blocking backup.

Isaac Nauta, DET: Had Georgia's offense not been as littered with wide receiver and pass-catching running back talent as it was, Nauta would have been capable of more volume than he ended up with. He ended his final season with just 430 yards and three touchdowns but did so with an 86 percent catch rate and a 69 percent success rate. To say he was reliable in his limited role would be downplaying his success. Selected by Detroit in the seventh round, Nauta will serve mostly as a Jesse James lite, but he may develop into more down the line.

Nick O'Leary, MIA: O'Leary caught eight passes and was charged with four sacks on blown blocks last season. In other words, he's a tight end who can neither catch nor block. The Dolphins acquired him off waivers at the end of camp last year, gave him seven starts, and signed him to a one-year extension before everyone was fired in December. All of these are real things that happened, and the gibbering madman responsible for it all was rewarded with absolute power over a divisional rival. O'Leary will back up Mike Gesicki this year, or perhaps be released in favor of someone better, because he is not an NFL-caliber player.

Brian Parker, FA: An undrafted free agent back in 2015, Parker got into some game action with the Chiefs as a rookie, then bounced around practice squads for four years. Jake Butt's ACL tear gave him his first extended game action, and even a start late in the year, as he racked up five of his six career receptions in Weeks 14-16. Denver opted not to re-sign him, not even as an exclusive rights free agent.

Niles Paul, FA: The Niles Paul moment happened when Fred Davis was suspended for violating the substance abuse policy in 2014. Paul came in ahead of second-year tight end Jordan Reed and finished third in DVOA and 11th in DYAR among all tight ends. A dislocated MCL in 2015 pushed Paul down the pecking order. Given a chance to hit with the Jaguars on a two-year contract, he could have been James O'Shaughnessy. Instead, after a 65-yard, nine-target game against the Chiefs, Paul sprained his MCL in Week 6 and finished with -9 DYAR on a -18.8% DVOA. He was waived in December. As long as his body can withstand the punishment, Paul, who turns 30 in August, will continue to journey around getting jobs because of how desolate tight end depth charts look.

Logan Paulsen, ATL: Despite playing in 15 games last season for the Falcons and playing the second-most snaps at tight end, Paulsen saw only nine targets (he caught all of them). It was bit odd that Atlanta re-signed Paulsen days after they signed Luke Stocker, a player with a similar skill set (read: blocking), but only $90,000 of Paulsen's $930,000 salary is guaranteed.

Josh Perkins, PHI: Like Zach Ertz and Dallas Goedert, a good portion of Perkins' value is rooted in being able to flex to the slot as a receiver. He can flow in space well and has the athletic ability to threaten after the catch. In Week 2 of last season, Perkins got an extended look as the Eagles were trying to see what they had in many of their young players while backup Nick Foles was in at quarterback, and Perkins ended up with four catches on six targets. Once starting quarterback Carson Wentz returned the following week and the offense turned away from experimentalism, Perkins was back in the shadows. He only saw five more targets the rest of the year.

MyCole Pruitt, TEN: A 2015 fourth-round pick of the Vikings, Pruitt needed injury to Delanie Walker to find a roster spot and injury to Jonnu Smith to find significant playing time. He was better than expected as an in-line player, catching the winning touchdown pass against Washington in Week 16. He will likely compete with Anthony Firkser for a roster spot and a third tight end role, which will probably not be a significant part of Tennessee's offense.

Michael Roberts, FA: Roberts appeared to carve out a niche for himself as a red zone specialist in his second season in 2017. Though only appearing in eight games, Roberts snagged three touchdowns and was the most targeted Lions tight end in the red zone. (Granted, competition was not stiff, but still.) In one week this offseason, Roberts was traded to New England on June 13, failed his physical to cancel the trade, was waived by the Lions on June 14, picked up by Green Bay June 18, and then cut by Green Bay on June 20 for failing his physical there too.

Drew Sample, CIN: The Bengals made Sample a very surprising second-round selection this year. We don't have many flags to extrapolate from, but if Zac Taylor is planning on making the Bengals offense in the vein of Sean McVay's in Los Angeles, Sample was a pick meant to mimic Tyler Higbee. A great blocker at Washington, but with only 46 total receptions in his college career, Sample's athletic testing at the combine—in particular his 4.71-second 40-yard dash time—opened some eyes. We don't have much of a Sample size (pun intended, waiting for your eyeroll to clear) of his receptions, but the projection here is for him to be multi-faceted like Higbee is. Given how limited Sample's receiving was, that might be a bit of a stretch.

Eric Saubert, ATL: With Austin Hooper firmly entrenched as the Falcons' No. 1 tight end and Luke Stocker likely to be the backup, Saubert, a fifth-round draft pick in 2017, will struggle again to see significant offensive snaps. He played 208 total over the past two seasons, and caught 5 of 9 targets last year with 48 yards but -25 DYAR.

Dalton Schultz, DAL: Schultz is a block-first tight end who earned seven starts and 12 receptions as a rookie last year. He'll see action in an offense with a big role for an extra blocker, but there won't be many tight end touches to go around after Blake Jarwin and Jason Witten get fed.

Adam Shaheen, CHI: Shaheen is a remnant of the John Fox era in Chicago that featured more tight ends and under-center formations. Current head coach Matt Nagy, however, runs a spread offense out of the shotgun, which leaves little room for Shaheen to fit in over the more versatile Trey Burton. Shaheen maintained a role last year because the Bears did not have the personnel to run effective three- and four-wide receiver sets, but now that they can, expect Shaheen to fade into the background.

Scott Simonson, NYG: There's a lot of color we can add about Simonson. He was a first-team "All-Northeast-10 Conference" selection for Assumption in 2013. He donated bone marrow to save his sister's life as a fourth-grader. But his NFL career has just been spent journeying around the bottom of various tight end depth charts in anonymity, eventually breaking out to catch a touchdown against the Colts last year in Week 16. He finished with -5 DYAR and a -11.6% DVOA. This is more likely to be Simonson's moment than his foot-in-the-door to real playing time, but we guess we can't Assumption anything.

Kaden Smith, SF: A second-team all-Pac-12 player in 2018, Smith skipped his final two seasons of eligibility at Stanford and was drafted by San Francisco in the sixth round. Smith was respectably productive at school—he topped a thousand yards receiving with seven touchdowns in his two years at Palo Alto, with three straight 100-yard games against Utah, Washington State, and Washington last fall—but between Smith's limited athleticism and George Kittle's presence atop the depth chart, the fantasy potential here is close to zero.

Lee Smith, BUF: Smith's coming home! Smith spent the first four years of his career in Buffalo, mostly in the Doug Marrone era, before spending the last four seasons toiling in Oakland. Smith has never had more than 13 targets in a season, and his 85 percent catch rate is mostly a factor of no one expecting him to have the ball thrown his way. No matter—that's not what he's paid for. Smith is one of the top 10 blocking tight ends in football, with only three blown blocks the last two seasons. He'll be the Bills' second tight end, behind whichever pass catcher wins the top job.

Durham Smythe, MIA: A 2018 fourth-round pick, Smythe was a block-first tight end at Notre Dame, and he caught just six passes (one for 21 yards and five others for 29) in a pair of starts and some scattered snaps last year. He has potential as a blocker if not a receiver, which puts him one up on Nick O'Leary (who has no potential as either) in the race to be Mike Gesicki's backup.

Jeremy Sprinkle, WAS: Sprinkle is an effective blocking tight end who has settled in to a 10- to 20-snap role. All five of his receptions last year came after all heck had broken loose in Washington and Josh Johnson was at quarterback. If he was a threat to move up the depth chart, Sprinkle would have done so by now.

Neal Sterling, KC: Sterling opened last season as the Jets' starting tight end, giving way to youngsters Chris Herndon and Jordan Leggett after a handful of games and landing on injured reserve with a concussion in late October. The Jets re-signed him to back up Herndon this year, then cut him in June. Now in Kansas City.

Luke Stocker, ATL: Because of his familiarity with offensive coordinator Dirk Koetter and tight ends coach Mike Mularkey, the versatile Stocker, who will make $2.9 million this season, has the inside track to usurp Logan Paulsen as the Falcons' primary blocking tight end. He'll catch the occasional pass (15 catches for 165 yards and an 11.4% DVOA last season for the Titans) and will see some work at fullback, too.

Tommy Sweeney, BUF: If this seventh-round pick out of Boston College is going to catch on, it's going to be as an in-line blocker. His hands are solid enough, but he simply does not have the athletic traits needed to be a receiving threat in the NFL; a 4.83-second 40-yard dash isn't going to cut it. With a little polish of his blocking fundamentals, he could be a solid role player for a run-first team; he may need a year or two on the practice squad to get there.

Erik Swoope, OAK: After missing all of 2017, Swoope suffered through another injury-troubled season and finished on injured reserve. He struggled to find a consistent role or spot on the team and lost Eric Ebron backup snaps to Mo Alie-Cox. Oakland's near-barren depth chart creates opportunity for the small sample size superstar (46.7% DVOA on 22 targets in 2016, 47.4% on 10 targets in 2018), but staying healthy and making the roster will be his first challenges.

Logan Thomas, DET: Once deemed a future first-round pick at quarterback early on at Virginia Tech, Thomas finds himself nearly a decade later as a preseason star tight end. Thomas amassed over 100 yards last preseason, mostly over the final two games that help determine final cuts, and that was enough to earn him the No. 3 tight end spot with the Buffalo Bills. Now in Detroit, Thomas faces a tight end room stacked with more depth than in Buffalo, and he will have to show development as a receiver to earn a spot on the 53.

Levine Toilolo, SF: Toilolo was oddly productive in limited action (21-for-24, 263 yards, a touchdown, and 37.3% DVOA) but the Lions knew what they were doing in not prioritizing tight ends in last year's offense. Prior to landing in Detroit, Toilolo was mostly a backup tight end with an emphasis on blocking with the Falcons. In two seasons under Kyle Shanahan in Atlanta, Toilolo caught just 20 passes for 308 yards. Reuniting with his old coach will be nice, but Toilolo was hardly a staple in a less competitive tight end corps in Atlanta, so it will be tough for him to find playing time in a loaded tight end group in San Francisco.

Eric Tomlinson, NYJ: Tomlinson is one of those guys who clung to the Jets roster for several years because Mike Maccagnan thought finding replacement-level talent was an accomplishment. He's a 265-pound extra right tackle type who somehow started 29 games in three seasons and caught 16 passes. The Jets re-signed him in May.

Kahale Warring, HOU: Selected in the middle of the third round, Warring is a size-speed tight end who fits a lot of concepts the Texans do with both his run blocking and his ability to get open in two-tight end sets. The odds of him being a major factor in 2019 are low given how little tight ends are used in Bill O'Brien's offense, but he is an interesting prospect with a basketball history at San Diego State. He could develop into a true No. 1 tight end in time.

Trevon Wesco, NYJ: Wesco caught 26 passes for 366 yards (14.1 yards per catch) and one touchdown in a stacked West Virginia offense. The Jets snagged him in the fourth round. Wesco was a quick-footed, hard-thumping block-first tight end/fullback/H-back who did most of his receiving damage when the opposing defense couldn't account for him, and he projects as the same type of player in the NFL level. Look for Wesco to do the dirty work so Chris Herndon won't have to.

Maxx Williams, ARI: Everything about Williams' career needs to be seen through the eyes of his 2016 knee surgery, one that John Harbaugh said "no other football player has had." In that light, Williams is a feel-good story even if he never lived up to his second-round pick billing. Last year he got some run with the Ravens again and made it to 18 DYAR on an 8.2% DVOA, mostly on short targets (16-of-17, 143 yards, TD). Heading to training camp with the Cardinals, his chances of adding to his -48 career DYAR would appear low.

Luke Willson, OAK: Willson qualified for the tight end leaderboards from 2013 to 2015 in Seattle, and nearly hit the top 10 in DVOA. He fell out of favor there, moved to Detroit to get a full-time opportunity and … nothing. Nineteen targets in 14 games set a new career low, as did his 6.7 yards per reception and -28.6% DVOA. At this point, he's not much more than a blocker and occasional red zone option, but he *is* good at those things. He blew just two blocks last season and could end up as Oakland's second tight end.

Caleb Wilson, ARI: Your Mr. Irrelevant for 2019, Wilson could have a hard time sticking in a crowded tight end room for a coach who hasn't always used a lot of tight ends. A quarterback and receiver coming out of high school, Wilson ended up playing tight end for UCLA, leading the team with 60 catches for 965 yards last year. He's more an oversized slot guy than a true tight end and Wilson's best chance to stick in Arizona is by showing he can be a reliable matchup problem downfield.

2019 Kicker Projections

Listed below are the 2019 KUBIAK projections for kickers. Because of the inconsistency of field goal percentage from year to year, kickers are projected almost entirely based on team forecasts, although a handful of individual factors do come into play:

- More experience leads to a slightly higher field goal percentage in general, with the biggest jump between a kicker's rookie and sophomore seasons.
- Kickers with a better career field goal percentage tend to get more attempts, although they are not necessarily more accurate.
- Field goal percentage on kicks over 40 yards tends to

regress to the mean.

Kickers are listed with their total fantasy points based on two different scoring systems. For **Pts1**, all field goals are worth three points. For **Pts2**, all field goals up to 39 yards are worth three points, field goals of 40-49 yards are worth four points, and field goals over 50 yards are worth five points. Kickers are also listed with a Risk of Green, Yellow, or Red, as explained in the introduction to the section on quarterbacks.

Note that field goal totals below are rounded, but "fantasy points" are based on the actual projections, so the total may not exactly equal (FG * 3 + XP).

Fantasy Kicker Projections, 2018

Kicker	Team	FG	Pct	XP	Pts1	Pts2	Risk
Stephen Gostkowski	NE	30-38	79%	44	135	150	Green
Harrison Butker	KC	27-32	84%	49	131	145	Green
Greg Zuerlein	LAR	27-32	84%	48	129	146	Green
Justin Tucker	BAL	31-35	89%	34	127	146	Green
Adam Vinatieri	IND	28-33	85%	43	127	145	Green
Wil Lutz	NO	27-30	90%	47	127	140	Yellow
Jason Myers	SEA	27-31	87%	46	126	139	Yellow
Mason Crosby	GB	28-35	80%	40	125	139	Green
Brett Maher	DAL	27-34	79%	40	122	136	Yellow
Matt Prater	DET	28-34	82%	38	122	140	Green
Chris Boswell	PIT	27-34	79%	42	122	136	Green
Josh Lambo	JAX	30-34	88%	30	120	137	Yellow
Randy Bullock	CIN	28-33	85%	35	118	131	Yellow
Ka'imi Fairbairn	HOU	25-29	86%	44	118	131	Green
Michael Badgley	LAC	25-28	89%	43	117	130	Yellow
Jake Elliott	PHI	25-31	81%	41	117	130	Green
Eddy Pineiro	CHI	25-32	78%	41	117	130	Red
Aldrick Rosas	NYG	28-32	88%	31	116	130	Yellow
Graham Gano	CAR	25-27	93%	39	113	125	Yellow

Kicker	Team	FG	Pct	XP	Pts1	Pts2	Risk
Steven Hauschka	BUF	26-33	79%	34	113	130	Yellow
Austin Seibert	CLE	23-28	82%	43	111	123	Red
Giorgio Tavecchio	ATL	23-26	88%	41	110	123	Green
Ryan Succop	TEN	26-31	84%	33	110	121	Green
Chandler Catanzaro	NYJ	25-33	76%	34	109	122	Green
Robbie Gould	SF	25-27	93%	34	109	121	Green
Daniel Carlson	OAK	25-30	83%	33	108	121	Yellow
Dustin Hopkins	WAS	27-31	87%	28	108	122	Green
Brandon McManus	DEN	25-32	78%	28	103	116	Yellow
Dan Bailey	MIN	22-29	76%	37	102	114	Yellow
Zane Gonzalez	ARI	21-28	75%	39	102	113	Red
Jason Sanders	MIA	23-27	85%	27	96	108	Yellow
Matt Gay	TB	20-26	77%	35	96	107	Red

Other kickers who may win jobs:							
Kicker	Team	FG	Pct	XP	Pts1	Pts2	Risk
Matthew Wright	PIT	25-31	81%	42	117	130	Red
Elliott Fry	CHI	25-32	78%	41	117	130	Red
Greg Joseph	CLE	23-29	79%	44	114	127	Yellow
Cairo Santos	TB	20-26	77%	35	95	103	Yellow

2019 Fantasy Defense Projections

Listed below are the 2019 KUBIAK projections for fantasy team defense. The projection method is discussed in an essay in *Pro Football Prospectus 2006*, the key conclusions of which were:

- Schedule strength is very important for projecting fantasy defense.
- Categories used for scoring in fantasy defense have no consistency from year-to-year whatsoever, with the exception of sacks and interceptions.

Fumble recoveries and defensive touchdowns are forecast solely based on the projected sacks and interceptions, rather than the team's totals in these categories from a year ago. This is why the 2019 projections may look very different from the fantasy defense values from the 2018 season. Safeties and shutouts are not common enough to have a significant effect on the projections. Team defenses are also projected with Risk factor of Green, Yellow, or Red; this is based on the team's projection compared to performance in recent seasons.

In addition to projection of separate categories, we also give an overall total based on our generic fantasy scoring formula: one point for a sack, two points for a fumble recovery or interception, and six points for a touchdown. Remember that certain teams (for example, the Jaguars) will score better if your league also gives points for limiting opponents' scoring or yardage. Special teams touchdowns are listed separately and are not included in the fantasy scoring total listed.

Fantasy Team Defense Projections, 2019

Team	Fant Pts	Sack	Int	Fum Rec	Def TD	Risk	ST TD	Team	Fant Pts	Sack	Int	Fum Rec	Def TD	Risk	ST TD
NO	108	43.6	15.5	10.1	2.3	Yellow	0.6	BAL	98	40.5	13.4	9.0	2.0	Green	0.6
LAR	108	47.4	14.6	8.6	2.4	Green	0.5	SEA	97	37.5	14.2	9.6	2.0	Green	0.6
DAL	105	43.4	13.4	10.6	2.3	Red	0.5	CLE	97	37.2	14.1	8.8	2.4	Yellow	0.5
PHI	104	41.9	14.6	10.6	2.0	Yellow	0.6	TEN	97	37.4	13.6	7.0	3.0	Yellow	0.6
PIT	104	44.3	14.1	8.8	2.3	Yellow	0.6	JAX	96	38.9	12.5	10.0	2.1	Green	0.4
MIN	103	37.4	13.2	10.3	3.1	Yellow	0.5	CIN	96	34.6	12.4	9.1	3.0	Yellow	0.5
CHI	102	40.5	14.3	8.7	2.7	Green	0.3	SF	95	41.7	10.5	9.4	2.3	Red	0.5
LAC	102	42.0	14.8	9.0	2.1	Yellow	0.5	DEN	95	35.8	12.7	7.7	3.1	Green	0.4
HOU	102	37.9	13.8	8.6	3.2	Yellow	0.5	CAR	93	37.5	12.3	9.1	2.1	Yellow	0.5
BUF	102	39.2	12.2	10.1	3.0	Yellow	0.6	WAS	92	39.0	12.7	8.0	1.9	Green	0.6
DET	100	38.4	12.0	10.5	2.8	Yellow	0.3	NYJ	91	36.5	13.2	8.3	2.0	Yellow	0.6
IND	100	37.3	13.9	10.7	2.2	Red	0.6	NYG	89	38.6	12.1	8.1	1.6	Yellow	0.6
NE	99	40.8	15.9	9.6	1.2	Yellow	0.6	GB	88	35.3	13.3	7.3	1.9	Yellow	0.7
KC	98	37.9	13.5	9.0	2.6	Green	0.5	MIA	82	31.0	11.5	8.2	2.0	Green	0.7
ATL	98	33.9	12.9	9.7	3.2	Yellow	0.6	TB	75	29.8	10.2	6.4	2.0	Green	0.7
ARI	98	37.2	12.4	9.5	2.8	Yellow	0.5	OAK	68	20.3	11.7	6.5	1.8	Green	0.7

Projected Defensive Leaders, 2019

Solo Tackles			Total Tackles			Sacks			Interceptions		
Player	Team	Tkl	Player	Team	Tkl	Player	Team	Sacks	Player	Team	Int
D.Leonard	IND	103	D.Leonard	IND	155	A.Donald	LAR	14.4	D.James	LAC	3.4
L.Vander Esch	DAL	99	B.Martinez	GB	140	J.J.Watt	HOU	13.2	E.Jackson	CHI	3.2
R.Smith	CHI	95	L.Vander Esch	DAL	136	C.Jordan	NO	12.2	J.Poyer	BUF	3.2
B.Wagner	SEA	91	R.Smith	CHI	134	C.Jones	ARI	12.1	E.Apple	NO	3.1
L.David	TB	91	D.Jones	ATL	133	V.Miller	DEN	11.7	K.Byard	TEN	3.1
D.White	TB	89	D.White	TB	129	J.Bosa	LAC	11.6	H.Smith	MIN	3.0
D.Jones	ATL	89	L.Kuechly	CAR	126	M.Garrett	CLE	11.5	S.Gilmore	NE	3.0
B.Martinez	GB	88	B.Wgner	SEA	126	D.Ford	SF	11.5	J.Jenkins	NYG	2.9
K.Alexander	SF	87	K.Alexander	SF	126	K.Mack	CHI	11.1	J.Reid	HOU	2.9
C.Littleton	LAR	87	C.Littleton	LAR	124	F.Clark	KC	11.0	R.Jones	MIA	2.9
D.Davis	NO	85	D.Bush	PIT	123	D.Hunter	MIN	11.0	J.Haden	PIT	2.8
D.Bush	PIT	84	A.Hitchens	KC	121	Y.Ngakoue	JAX	10.8	D.Slay	DET	2.8

College Football Introduction and Statistical Toolbox

In the five-year history of the College Football Playoff (CFP), two programs have dominated all others. The Alabama Crimson Tide have appeared in all five iterations of the playoff to date, claiming two national championships. The Clemson Tigers have appeared in each of the last four playoff fields, claiming two championships themselves. Of the 15 CFP games played to date in national semifinals or national championship matchups, 11 have been won by either Alabama (six) or Clemson (five). The other eight programs that have made at least one CFP appearance have combined to win only four playoff games.

It should come as no surprise that our *Football Outsiders Almanac 2019* college football projections have the Crimson Tide and Tigers leading the way once again. The two programs have combined to produce more top single-game and overall season performances than any other teams over the last five years. They've lost great players to the NFL draft, but still have an enviable wealth of talent returning at key positions. And they have depth to restock their roster holes with recent elite recruiting hauls and proven player development systems. Those elements—recent performance, returning production, and recruiting success—are key ingredients in our projection model, and Alabama and Clemson are quite simply the surest bets in college football.

It is not a sure bet that they'll meet in the postseason for the fifth straight year, however. Alabama projects to be the nation's top team, but they will face what projects to be one too many landmines in the SEC to navigate the season unscathed. The Crimson Tide will face three top-10 opponents in November according to our projections (LSU, at Mississippi State, at Auburn), and they draw their fourth-toughest opponent (projected No. 16 Texas A&M) on the road as well. Alabama is still the most likely team to win the SEC, but they're also likely to take one loss along the way (in fact, probably two) according to our model. The playoff selection committee may favor a team with a strong schedule over one with a weak schedule, but they haven't yet rewarded a two-loss team with a playoff berth.

Clemson, on the other hand, has a relatively clear path to this year's playoff field. The Tigers will be favored every week and boast an individual game win likelihood of at least 80 percent in every conference game according to our projections. Their toughest opponent, Texas A&M, is Alabama's fourth-toughest, and the Tigers get the Aggies in Death Valley instead of College Station. Clemson has a whopping 66.5 percent chance of reaching the playoff this year, higher than any other team we have projected in the preseason to date. That's formidable, but Clemson also played and survived several tight games last season while boasting the nation's highest likelihood to reach the playoff.

If either Clemson or Alabama falls short of the playoff this year, the list of contenders that could take their place is led by a collection of familiar faces. Oklahoma (seeking their fourth playoff appearance), Washington (second), Georgia (second), and Ohio State (third) are each projected with better playoff berth chances than the Crimson Tide, in fact. If a playoff newcomer crashes this year's party, our numbers like Utah, Wisconsin, Mississippi State, Missouri, Miami, and Michigan to be in the mix. Our model has given the eventual playoff teams at least a 10 percent likelihood to reach the playoff at the start of the year in each of the last three seasons. Twelve programs meet that criteria heading into this year.

Of course, only a small fraction of FBS programs measure themselves against College Football Playoff aspirations and appearances, and the top non-playoff contenders will play far more than just a spoiler role. Central Florida and Memphis project to be destined for a fantastic American Athletic Conference championship game at season's end, and Boise State and Fresno State are on a similar collision course in the Mountain West. One of those four teams is most likely to grab a New Year's Six major bowl bid, if Appalachian State doesn't run the table in the Sun Belt and steal that bid away—the Mountaineers rank behind only Clemson as the team most likely to finish the regular season undefeated by our projections.

From the most intriguing non-conference battles to the traditionally fierce rivalry games, the 2019 season promises to deliver once again. And as much as we strive to be accurate with our projections, we're thrilled when college football surprises us along the way. Whether it's Army keeping a power opponent on the ropes deep into the second half by ruthlessly draining the clock with its precision option offense—watch out on September 7, Michigan—or Clemson completing an almost preposterous percentage of third-and-long conversions in a stunning blowout playoff victory, every drive and every play is meaningful. Join us in examining, scrutinizing, and celebrating college football with our rundown of the top 50 teams of 2019.

College Statistics Toolbox

Regular readers of FootballOutsiders.com may be familiar with the FEI and S&P+ stats published throughout the year. Others may be learning about our advanced approach to college football stats analysis for the first time by reading this book. In either case, this College Statistics Toolbox section is highly recommended reading before getting into the conference chapters. The stats that form the building blocks for F/+, FEI, and S&P+ are constantly being updated and refined.

Each team profile begins with a statistical snapshot. The

projected overall and conference records—rounded from the team's projected Mean Wins—are listed alongside the team name in the header. Other stats and rankings provided in the team snapshot and highlighted in the team capsules are explained below.

Drive-by-Drive Data

Fremeau Efficiency Index (FEI): Approximately 20,000 possessions are contested annually in FBS vs. FBS games, an average of 26.6 total game possessions per game. First-half clock-kills and end-of-game garbage drives are filtered out, and the resulting possessions (23.8 per game) are evaluated to determine the success rates of each team's offensive, defensive, and special teams units. Raw possession efficiency rates are adjusted for opponent team unit strength. FEI ratings represent the opponent-adjusted per-possession scoring advantage a team would be expected to have on a neutral field against an average opponent.

Offensive and Defensive FEI: Maximizing success on offensive possessions and minimizing success on opponent possessions begins with an understanding of the value of field position. An average offense facing an average defense may expect to score 2.1 points on average at the conclusion of each drive. If a given drive begins at the offense's own 15-yard line, the average scoring value is only 1.5 points. If it begins at the opponent's 15-yard line, the average scoring value is 4.9 points. Offensive and defensive efficiency is in part a function of the intrinsic value of starting field position.

Drive-ending field position is an important component as well. Touchdowns represent the ultimate goal of an offensive possession, but drives that fall short of the end zone can also add scoring value attributed to the offense. National field goal success rates correlate strongly with proximity of the attempt to the end zone, and an offense that drives deep into opponent territory to set up a chip shot field goal generates more scoring value than one that ends a drive at the edge of or outside field goal range.

The value generated by an offense on a given possession is the difference between the drive-ending value and the value of field position at the start of the drive. Offensive efficiency is the average per-possession value generated or lost by the offense. Defensive efficiency is the average per-possession value generated or lost by the defense. Offensive FEI and Defensive FEI are the opponent-adjusted per-possession values generated or lost by these units, adjusted according to the strength of the opponent defense and offenses faced.

Play-by-Play Data

In January 2014, Bill Connelly introduced a new set of concepts for analysis and debate within the realm of college football stats. At Football Study Hall, a college football stats site within the SB Nation network, he wrote the following: "Over time, I've come to realize that the sport comes down to five basic things, four of which you can mostly control. You make more big plays than your opponent, you stay on schedule, you tilt the field, you finish drives, and you fall on the ball. *Explosiveness, efficiency, field position, finishing drives, and turnovers are the five factors to winning football games.*"

Unlike the Four Factors used by ESPN's Dean Oliver for discussion of basketball, these factors are heavily related to each other. But looking at these factors individually can allow you to quickly home in on a given team's strengths and weaknesses in a way that looking at total yardage or even yards per play cannot.

Success Rates: Efficiency is by far the most predictive and vital of the factors. Without it, you find yourself in unfavorable downs and distances (which can lead to either turnovers or unfavorable downs and distances for your offense or a lack thereof for your defense), and your offense can't stay on the field long enough to generate big plays.

The most effective tool for efficiency measurement is success rate. More than one million plays over the last ten years

1. Alabama Crimson Tide (14-1, 8-0)

2019 Projections		Projection Factors	
F/+	54.3 (1)	2018 F/+	52.8 (1)
FEI	1.33 (1)	2018 FEI	1.52 (1)
S&P+	35.4 (1)	2018 S&P+	36.3 (1)
Total Wins	9.9	5-Year F/+	65.0 (1)
Conf Wins	6.0	5-Year FEI	1.14 (1)
SOS	.037 (9)	5-Year S&P+	33.0 (1)
Conf SOS	.040 (9)	2-Yr/5-Yr Recruiting	3/1
Div Champ	37%	Ret. Offense	67% (56)
Conf Champ	19%	Ret. Defense	59% (80)
CFP Berth	20%	Ret. Total	63% (63)

Projected Win Likelihood by Game

Date	Opponent (Proj Rank)	PWL	Projected Loss Projected Win
Aug 31	vs Duke (58)	96%	
Sep 7	vs New Mexico St. (125)	99%	
Sep 14	at S. Carolina (29)	79%	
Sep 21	vs Southern Miss (78)	99%	
Sep 28	vs Ole Miss (35)	92%	
Oct 12	at Texas A&M (16)	63%	
Oct 19	vs Tennessee (40)	94%	
Oct 26	vs Arkansas (65)	98%	
Nov 9	vs LSU (6)	66%	
Nov 16	at Mississippi St. (7)	51%	
Nov 23	vs W. Carolina (FCS)	100%	
Nov 30	at Auburn (8)	53%	

in college football have been collected and evaluated to determine baselines for success for every situational down in a game. Similar to DVOA, basic success rates are determined by national standards. The distinction for college football is in defining the standards of success. We use the following determination of a "successful" play:

- First down success = 50 percent of necessary yardage
- Second down success = 70 percent of necessary yardage
- Third/Fourth down success = 100 percent of necessary yardage

On a per play basis, these form the standards of efficiency for every offense in college football. Defensive success rates are based on preventing the same standards of achievement.

Equivalent Points and Isolated Points per Play (IsoPPP): All yards are not created equal. A 10-yard gain from a team's own 15-yard line does not have the same value as a 10-yard gain that goes from the opponent's 10-yard line into the end zone. Based on expected scoring rates by field position, we calculate a point value for each play in a drive. Equivalent Points (EqPts) are calculated by subtracting the value of the resulting yard line from the initial yard line of a given play. This assigns credit to the yards that are most associated with scoring points, the end goal in any possession.

With EqPts, the game can be broken down and built back up again in a number of ways. Average EqPts per play (PPP) measures consistency and IsoPPP measures EqPts per play on successful plays only as a way to isolate of explosiveness. For the S&P+ formula, IsoPPP is used, which allows us to ask two specific questions:

1. How frequently successful are you (consistency)?
2. When you're successful, *how* successful are you (magnitude)?

A boom-or-bust running back may have an excellent per carry average and IsoPPP, but his low success rate will lower his S&P. A consistent running back that gains between four and six yards every play, on the other hand, will have a strong success rate but low IsoPPP. The best offenses in the country can maximize both efficiency and explosiveness on a down-by-down basis. Reciprocally, the best defenses can limit both.

S&P+: Along with applying extra weight for plays inside the opponent's 40, plus a selection of other field position and turnover factors, success rate and IsoPPP make up the meat of the S&P+ formula.

As with the FEI stats discussed above, context matters in college football. Adjustments are made to the S&P unadjusted data with a formula that takes into account a team's production, the quality of the opponent, and the quality of the opponent's opponent. To eliminate the noise of less-informative blowout stats, we filtered the play-by-play data to include only those that took place when the game was "close." This excludes plays where the score margin is larger than 28 points in the first quarter, 24 points in the second quarter, 21 points in the third quarter, or 16 points in the fourth quarter.

The combination of the play-by-play and drive data gives us S&P+, a comprehensive measure that represents a team's efficiency and explosiveness as compared to all other teams in college football. S&P+ values are calibrated around adjusted scoring averages. Taking a team's percentile ratings and applying it to a normal distribution of points scored in a given season, can give us an interesting, descriptive look at a team's performance in a given season.

Highlight Yards: Highlight yards represent the yards gained by a runner outside of those credited to the offensive line through adjusted line yards. The ALY formula, much like the same stat in the NFL, gives 100 percent credit to all yards gained between zero and four yards and 50 percent strength to yards between five and 10. If a runner gains 12 yards in a given carry, and we attribute 7.0 of those yards to the line, and the player's highlight yardage on the play is 5.0 yards. Beginning in 2013, we began calculating highlight yardage averages in a slightly different manner: Instead of dividing total highlight yardage by a player's overall number of carries, we divide it only by the number of carries that gain more than four yards; if a line is given all credit for gains smaller than that, then it makes sense to look at highlight averages only for the carries on which a runner got a chance to create a highlight.

Opportunity Rate: Opportunity rate represents the percentage of a runner's carries that gained at least five yards. This gives us a look at a runner's (and his line's) consistency and efficiency to go along with the explosiveness measured by highlight yards.

Havoc Rate: Havoc rate is a quick glance at defensive disruption. It is the sum total of tackles for loss, passes defensed (intercepted or broken up), and forced fumbles divided by total plays. We produce Havoc rate for total defense as well as split into front seven and defensive backfield.

Combination Data

F/+: Introduced in *Football Outsiders Almanac 2009*, the F/+ measure combines FEI and S&P+. There is a clear distinction between the two individual approaches, and merging the two diminishes certain outliers caused by the quirks of each method. The resulting metric is both powerfully predictive and sensibly evaluative.

Projected F/+: Relative to the pros, college football teams are much more consistent in year-to-year performance. Breakout seasons and catastrophic collapses certainly occur, but generally speaking, teams can be expected to play within a reasonable range of their baseline program expectations. The idea of a Football Outsiders program rating began with the introduction of Program FEI in *Pro Football Prospectus 2008* as a way to represent those individual baseline expectations.

As the strength of the F/+ system has been fortified with more seasons of full drive-by-drive and play-by-play data, the Program F/+ measure has emerged. Program F/+ is calculated from five years of FEI and S&P+ data. The result not only represents the status of each team's program power but provides the first step in projecting future success. For each team statistical profile, we provide each team's five-year ratings profile and other projection factors that are included in the formula for the Projected FEI, Projected S&P+, and Projected F/+ ratings.

Recruiting success rates are based on a blend of Rivals. com and 247Sports.com recruiting ratings. The percentile rating for each team's two-year recruiting success and five-year recruiting success reflect the potential impact for both recent star-studded classes and the depth of talent for each team. Our returning experience data represents the percentage of production that returns to the roster this fall rather than a simple count of players labeled as starters. Program F/+ ratings are a function of program ratings and these recruiting and returning production transition factors.

Strength of Schedule: Unlike other rating systems, our Strength of Schedule (SOS) calculation is not a simple average of the Projected F/+ data of each team's opponents. Instead, it represents the likelihood that an elite team (typical top-five team) would win every game on the given schedule. The distinction is valid. For any elite team, playing No. 1 Alabama and No. 130 Connecticut in a two-game stretch is certainly more difficult than playing No. 65 Arkansas and No. 66 Houston. An average rating might judge these schedules to be equal.

The likelihood of an undefeated season is calculated as the product of individual game projected win likelihoods. Generally speaking, an elite team may have a 75 percent chance of defeating a team ranked No. 10, an 85 percent chance of defeating a team ranked No. 20, and a 95 percent chance of defeating a team ranked No. 40. Combined, the elite team has a 61 percent likelihood of defeating all three ($0.75 \times 0.85 \times$

$0.95 = 0.606$).

A lower SOS rating represents a lower likelihood of an elite team running the table, and thus a stronger schedule. For our calculations of FBS versus FCS games, with all due apologies to North Dakota State et al., the likelihood of victory is 100 percent in the formula.

Mean Wins and Win Probabilities: To project records for each team, we use Projected F/+ and win likelihood formulas to estimate the likelihood of victory for a given team in its individual games. The probabilities for winning each game are added together to represent the average number of wins the team is expected to tally over the course of its scheduled games. Potential conference championship games and bowl games are not included.

The projected records listed next to each team name in the conference chapters are rounded from the mean wins data listed in the team capsule. Mean Wins are not intended to represent projected outcomes of specific matchups; rather they are our most accurate forecast for the team's season as a whole. The correlation of mean projected wins to actual wins is 0.69 for all games, 0.61 for conference games.

Win likelihoods are also used to produce the likelihood of each team winning a division or championship. Our College Football Playoff appearance likelihoods are a function of each team's likelihood to go undefeated or finish the season with one loss as well as the strength of the team's conference and overall schedule, factors that the CFP selection committee considers in their process.

The Win Probability tables that appear in each conference chapter are also based on the game-by-game win likelihood data for each team. The likelihood for each record is rounded to the nearest whole percent.

Brian Fremeau and Bill Connelly

1. Alabama Crimson Tide (10-2, 6-2)

2019 Projections			Projection Factors		
F/+	54.3 (1)		2018 F/+	52.8 (1)	
FEI	1.33 (1)		2018 FEI	1.52 (1)	
S&P+	35.4 (1)		2018 S&P+	36.3 (1)	
Total Wins	9.9		5-Year F/+	65.0 (1)	
Conf Wins	6.0		5-Year FEI	1.14 (1)	
SOS	.037 (9)		5-Year S&P+	33.0 (1)	
Conf SOS	.040 (9)		2-Yr/5-Yr Recruiting	3/1	
Div Champ	37%		Ret. Offense	67% (56)	
Conf Champ	19%		Ret. Defense	59% (80)	
CFP Berth	20%		Ret. Total	63% (63)	

Projected Win Likelihood by Game

Date	Opponent (Proj Rank)	PWL	Projected Loss	Projected Win
Aug 31	vs Duke (58)	96%		
Sep 7	vs New Mexico St. (125)	99%		
Sep 14	at S. Carolina (29)	79%		
Sep 21	vs Southern Miss (78)	99%		
Sep 28	vs Ole Miss (35)	92%		
Oct 12	at Texas A&M (16)	63%		
Oct 19	vs Tennessee (40)	94%		
Oct 26	vs Arkansas (65)	98%		
Nov 9	vs LSU (6)	66%		
Nov 16	at Mississippi St. (7)	51%		
Nov 23	vs W. Carolina (FCS)	100%		
Nov 30	at Auburn (8)	53%		

Teams get blown out in bowl games all the time, and that's even true in the College Football Playoff. Oregon demolished Florida State by nearly 40 points in the first ever playoff game. Alabama beat Michigan State 38-0 the next year. Clemson infamously shut out Ohio State 31-0 in 2016. And then Clemson held Notre Dame to a field goal in a 30-3 win in the 2018 semi-finals.

Alabama, however, does not get blown out. Nick Saban's Alabama teams have lost just 15 times since his first year in Tuscaloosa, and most were narrow upsets, such as the infamous kick-six game against Auburn or Clemson's first national championship win over the Tide in 2016 (which was 35-31 thanks to a last-second Deshaun Watson pass).

The 2018 Alabama team, led by Heisman runner-up Tua Tagovailoa, was developing a convincing argument to be The Best Team of All Time. Until their 35-28 win over Georgia in the SEC Championship Game, Alabama had assembled 12 straight contests with an S&P+ postgame win expectancy of 100 percent. They had sat atop the S&P+ rankings every week since Week 2. The Crimson Tide had an S&P+ percentile performance above 90 percent in nine of their 12 regular-season games.

So it was more than a little shocking when Clemson, led by a true freshman quarterback, ran away with the championship game in a 44-16 win. Sure, the S&P+ postgame adjusted scoring margin actually saw something more like a five-point win for the Tigers, but still—the perception was that the Crimson Tide were humbled in a way they hadn't been in years.

But even with that shocking loss, Alabama is still rated as the best F/+ team in college football heading into the 2019 season. Perennially the country's most talented team, Alabama football should have one of its most dangerous editions yet in 2019. That starts with the return of Tagovailoa and his jaw-droppingly talented receiver corps, including Jerry Jeudy, Jaylen Waddle, Henry Ruggs III, and DeVonta Smith. The Tide had the top-rated passing S&P+ attack in 2018, and that's unlikely to change. Alabama's top two running backs left for

the NFL draft, but Najee Harris might be more talented than both, having averaged 6.7 yards per rush with an opportunity rate of 63.3 percent.

The biggest unknown for the offense is probably the impact from coordinator Steve Sarkisian, who rejoined the staff after his time with the Atlanta Falcons. The early expectation is that the Crimson Tide will pull back from the RPOs that Tagovailoa executes so flawlessly in favor of more traditional pro-style passing.

The Crimson Tide defense hardly varies in its year-to-year excellence despite constant departures to the NFL draft. Losing linemen Quinnen Williams and Isaiah Buggs, linebackers Christian Miller and Mack Wilson, and safety Deionte Thompson isn't ideal—nor is losing defensive coordinator Tosh Lupoi—but the Tide regularly go through this much turnover and always seem to come out fine. Linebackers Dylan Moses and Anfernee Jennings, lineman Raekwon Davis, and cornerback Patrick Surtain II should form the core of the 2019 defense, while countless other blue-chippers (like 2019 five-star end Antonio Alfano) will help.

But even as the most talented team in the country and the projected top team in overall F/+, Alabama has just the sixth-best odds to make the playoff according to the F/+ projections. That's due to a brutal schedule, ranked ninth-most difficult. It would be fairly surprising if the Crimson Tide had a loss before Halloween (although don't sleep on 16th-ranked Texas A&M in mid-October, where the Tide have just a 63 percent win probability), but in November they face three opponents ranked in the F/+ top ten: LSU (66 percent), Mississippi State (51 percent), and Auburn (53 percent). They could face another top-ten-ranked team in the SEC Championship Game too.

Despite having just a single real question about this year's team—the impact of continuous coaching staff turnover—the major improvement of the SEC's top half means that the country's best F/+ team doesn't make the playoff in four-fifths of simulated seasons.

2. Clemson Tigers (11-1, 8-0)

2019 Projections

F/+	53.6 (2)
FEI	1.07 (2)
S&P+	29.9 (3)
Total Wins	11.1
Conf Wins	7.6
SOS	.311 (81)
Conf SOS	.587 (80)
Div Champ	90%
Conf Champ	68%
CFP Berth	67%

Projection Factors

2018 F/+	52.7 (2)
2018 FEI	1.22 (2)
2018 S&P+	29.7 (3)
5-Year F/+	54.1 (3)
5-Year FEI	0.91 (2)
5-Year S&P+	25.4 (3)
2-Yr/5-Yr Recruiting	7/6
Ret. Offense	77% (26)
Ret. Defense	52% (100)
Ret. Total	64% (53)

Projected Win Likelihood by Game

Date	Opponent (Proj Rank)	PWL
Aug 29	vs Georgia Tech (69)	98%
Sep 7	vs Texas A&M (16)	76%
Sep 14	at Syracuse (52)	92%
Sep 21	vs Charlotte (118)	99%
Sep 28	at N. Carolina (77)	99%
Oct 12	vs Florida St. (37)	92%
Oct 19	at Louisville (95)	99%
Oct 26	vs Boston College (67)	98%
Nov 2	vs Wofford (FCS)	100%
Nov 9	at NC State (34)	82%
Nov 16	vs Wake Forest (72)	99%
Nov 30	at S. Carolina (29)	78%

The 2018 season was a massive triumph for head coach Dabo Swinney and the Clemson Tigers. They went 15-0 with their fourth consecutive ACC championship, fourth consecutive playoff appearance, and second national championship in that same span. The big gambit by Swinney was to mix in true freshman and five-star recruit Trevor Lawrence at quarterback in the beginning of the year despite returning starter Kelly Bryant. After the first four games, Swinney announced the decision to start Lawrence for the rest of the season, thus allowing Bryant to choose to redshirt the rest of the season so he could transfer and play somewhere else as a senior. Lawrence brought a higher passing acumen to the offense and ended up throwing for over 3,000 yards and 30 touchdowns, including throwing for 300-plus yards and three touchdowns against both Notre Dame and Alabama in the playoff.

Lawrence returns for 2019, as do top receivers Tee Higgins (936 receiving yards and 12 touchdowns) and Justyn Ross (1,000 receiving yards and nine touchdowns), and top running back Travis Etienne (1,658 rushing yards at 8.1 yards per carry and 14 total touchdowns). Many of the bigger pieces to the Clemson title run, though, are now gone. The entire starting defensive line was drafted, along with lockdown cornerback Trayvon Mullen, while left tackle and four-year starter Mitch Hyatt graduated.

Because the Tigers return their quarterback and multiple exceptional skill players, there's a high ceiling for what this offense could become if the floor is well established by the rebuilt offensive line. Clemson's recruiting has improved as they've been winning over the last few years, so there are players like five-stars Jackson Carman (Mullen's replacement at offensive tackle) and Xavier Thomas (a fill-in for their departed defensive ends) who will be called on to step into the vacancies. Assuming those young stars are ready to handle the pressure of carrying on the tradition, things appear on firm ground overall.

The only area on offense without obvious answers is at inside receiver. Former walk-on and longtime third-down target Hunter Renfrow graduated and Amari Rodgers is likely to be out with an ACL injury. At tight end the Tigers are thin after 2018 starter Milan Richard graduated and backup Garrett Williams opted out of his final season to start a career in the military. There's talent inside in the slots, but the Tigers need to fast-track some of it in order to avoid teams splitting their safeties out to cover the outside receivers on third-and-long. The Tigers obliterated both the Fighting Irish and the Crimson Tide on third downs in 2018, going into four-wide spread sets and hitting them for huge plays. Clemson converted 13 of 24 third downs in which they called in a pass for the playoff, with Lawrence going 14-of-23 for 343 yards at 14.9 yards per attempt with three touchdowns and zero interceptions. With an older crew, they could match that lethality in 2019 if they can find a few new receivers capable of punishing defenses that ignore them. Opposing teams won't play the Tigers offense the same in 2019 after what they showed in 2018. Clemson will need some versatility.

The bigger questions are on defense, where eight starters are moving on from S&P+'s No. 3 defense in the country. The Tigers will have a good amount of experience to put on the field; in particular, defensive coordinator Brent Venables has several third- or fourth-year players rising up at linebacker and safety. Sam linebacker Isaiah Simmons was the team's leading tackler, led the backfield in tackles for loss with nine, and at 6-foot-3 and 225 pounds had unreal range and versatility to cover slot receivers one snap and play on the edge the next. Clemson usually deployed him to the wide side of the field in order to cut off offenses from the open space there. He'll be back in 2019 along with strong safety K'Von Wallace and free safeties Tanner Muse and Nolan Turner.

If the Tigers can find more impact players amongst their emerging defensive linemen and inside linebackers, then it's hard to see them as anything but the favorites given the improvements that could occur for an already potent offense. Their schedule (both in the ACC and a non-conference matchup at home with Texas A&M) is "easy" enough that they should have time to work through their various issues without getting eliminated from the playoff.

3. Georgia Bulldogs (10-2, 6-2)

2019 Projections

F/+	53.4 (3)
FEI	0.94 (3)
S&P+	30.7 (2)
Total Wins	10.0
Conf Wins	6.3
SOS	.051 (13)
Conf SOS	.084 (15)
Div Champ	54%
Conf Champ	27%
CFP Berth	28%

Projection Factors

2018 F/+	51.5 (3)
2018 FEI	1.17 (3)
2018 S&P+	32.9 (2)
5-Year F/+	36.8 (7)
5-Year FEI	0.71 (5)
5-Year S&P+	22.7 (5)
2-Yr/5-Yr Recruiting	1/3
Ret. Offense	53% (99)
Ret. Defense	72% (36)
Ret. Total	62% (69)

Projected Win Likelihood by Game

Date	Opponent (Proj Rank)	PWL
Aug 31	at Vanderbilt (61)	95%
Sep 7	vs Murray St. (FCS)	100%
Sep 14	vs Arkansas St. (70)	99%
Sep 21	vs Notre Dame (10)	69%
Oct 5	at Tennessee (40)	85%
Oct 12	vs S. Carolina (29)	89%
Oct 19	vs Kentucky (38)	93%
Nov 2	vs Florida (12)	66%
Nov 9	vs Missouri (15)	76%
Nov 16	at Auburn (8)	51%
Nov 23	vs Texas A&M (16)	76%
Nov 30	at Georgia Tech (69)	98%

Kirby Smart has assembled the most talented top-to-bottom roster outside of Tuscaloosa over the last four years. But Georgia has also been two fourth quarters vs. Alabama away from at least one championship and another playoff appearance. That hump—finally dethroning Smart's mentor—has dominated the offseason discussion about the Bulldogs. Their 35-28 loss in the SEC Championship Game was devastating to the point that their later one-touchdown loss to Texas barely cut through fans' numbness. Were it not for a second-place recruiting class (according to the 247 Sports Composite rankings) that included an incredible five five-star recruits, Georgia fans might even go through the offseason feeling pessimistic for the first time in a few years.

But thanks to the recent influx of elite recruits, Georgia simply has too few roster holes to be considered anything but one of the top three playoff contenders. Jake Fromm returns for his junior season hoping to nudge forward an offense that ranked third in overall S&P+ and fourth in passing S&P+. The Bulldogs offense did just about everything right in 2018—they were top-five in efficiency, top-20 in explosiveness, and top-25 in points per scoring opportunity (although that ill-fated six-play goal-line sequence against Florida will be forever seared into the minds of every Georgia fan).

Their major questions are at offensive coordinator, receiver, and backup running back and quarterback—which are, admittedly, mostly luxury question marks. Smart and company didn't seem to fight too hard to retain Jim Chaney, who left for Knoxville, and James Coley was promoted to the top offensive post. The thought is that little should change conceptually, with significant continuity among most starting personnel.

Second, the biggest actual question mark is probably finding new top receiving targets thanks to the departures of speedy threat Mecole Hardman, top tight end Issac Nauta, reliable Terry Godwin, and top overall target Riley Ridley. Jeremiah Holloman was expected to be the leading receiver after emerging last year, but he was dismissed from the team in late June. Returning wide receiver production is most correlated with next year's offensive S&P+, so the loss of these five key targets is undoubtedly tough. But there are also a number of exciting candidates to fill their shoes. Tight end Charlie Woerner, Miami transfer Lawrence Cager, elite freshmen George Pickens and Dominick Blaylock,

and a number of other upperclassmen suggest a high potential for the passing game, but it may take a little while for Fromm to get completely in sync with his new receivers. And definitely don't think about what happens if Fromm were to go down (although the re-addition of Stetson Bennett IV provides a little insurance).

Third, let's be honest—describing Georgia's backup running back spot as a potential question mark is a kind of a humblebrag about how stacked the rest of this team is. Yes, D'Andre Swift's backfield mate Elijah Holyfield is gone, and he had a 7 percent higher opportunity rate than Swift, but senior Brian Herrien is more than a capable substitute, and he'll have help from shifty James Cook, freshman Kenny McIntosh, and the return of all-world recruit Zamir White, who had consecutive ACL tears delay the start of his college career. More importantly, at least for ensuring steady efficiency levels without Holyfield, is the country's best offensive line. The Georgia offensive line has three five-star recruits who are expected to run with the second team because of the insane talent above them.

The Bulldogs defense might have a few more serious concerns, even if they are still largely first-world problems. Georgia ranked just 53rd in rushing S&P+ last year, eventually allowing LSU and Texas to convert enough third and fourth downs. They only stopped the opposing runner at or behind the line on 18.5 percent of runs (74th). Freshman All-American Jordan Davis is likely to be a big part of the solution, but he will need to play at a consistently high level, and be joined by more impact players beside him (end Malik Herring may be an answer there). Georgia also never got a ton of pressure on opposing offenses in general, and now sack leader D'Andre Walker has graduated. There are again a number of possible candidates to replace and increase his production, including five-stars such as sophomores Brenton Cox and Adam Anderson, freshman Nolan Smith, and JUCO transfer Jermaine Johnson. But while all of these players have all-world talent, none have the experience or production necessary to ease all concerns. Finally, the Bulldogs secondary lost All-American corner Deandre Baker to the NFL. Again, there are plenty of candidates to replace him, including Eric Stokes and Tyson Campbell, who both came on strong late last year, as well as JUCO transfer DJ Daniel, versatile Mark Webb, and freshman Tyrique Stephenson.

Overall, Georgia is in the enviable position of having high-talent answers for seemingly every personnel question heading into 2019. But Georgia also has to contend with a tough schedule that includes Notre Dame's return visit to Athens, dangerous Florida and Missouri teams, and a November slate that includes crossover games against Auburn and Texas A&M.

4. Oklahoma Sooners (11-1, 8-1)

2019 Projections

F/+	51.1 (4)
FEI	0.76 (5)
S&P+	25.0 (5)
Total Wins	10.9
Conf Wins	8.0
SOS	.290 (78)
Conf SOS	.317 (56)
Div Champ	-
Conf Champ	77%
CFP Berth	44%

Projection Factors

2018 F/+	49.5 (4)
2018 FEI	0.79 (5)
2018 S&P+	24.9 (4)
5-Year F/+	45.9 (4)
5-Year FEI	0.73 (4)
5-Year S&P+	23.7 (4)
2-Yr/5-Yr Recruiting	6/11
Ret. Offense	46% (109)
Ret. Defense	81% (13)
Ret. Total	64% (57)

Projected Win Likelihood by Game

Date	Opponent (Proj Rank)	PWL	Projected Loss	Projected Win
Sep 1	vs Houston (66)	98%		
Sep 7	vs S. Dakota (FCS)	100%		
Sep 14	at UCLA (64)	94%		
Sep 28	vs Texas Tech (56)	97%		
Oct 5	at Kansas (111)	99%		
Oct 12	vs Texas (32)	84%		
Oct 19	vs West Virginia (25)	85%		
Oct 26	at Kansas St. (62)	93%		
Nov 9	vs Iowa St. (43)	93%		
Nov 16	at Baylor (44)	86%		
Nov 23	vs TCU (36)	90%		
Nov 30	at Oklahoma St. (27)	74%		

A year after losing Heisman-winning quarterback Baker Mayfield—plus starters at left tackle, center, tight end, and fullback—the Oklahoma Sooners proceeded to field the most explosive offense in the history of the game. Mayfield's replacement Kyler Murray spurned the opportunity to begin what was certain to be a lucrative Major League Baseball career to give college football at least one year's worth of attention, and then became the second collegian ever with both 4,000 passing yards and 1,000 rushing yards, joining former Clemson quarterback Deshaun Watson. The team averaged 48.4 points per game, 11.3 yards per pass, and 6.6 yards per carry, and had almost three runners go for 1,000 rushing yards while two receivers went for over 1,000 receiving yards. That led Murray to go first overall in the NFL draft while four of his offensive linemen and top receiver Marquise Brown were also taken.

The Sooners missed once again on winning the title, however, for the same reason they fell short in 2017: their defense was atrocious. Mike Stoops was fired midseason after Texas beat them 48-45 in the Red River Shootout. Replacement Ruffin McNeil spent the rest of the year trying not to allow their defense to spoil the season with some near-misses against Texas Tech (51-46), Oklahoma State (48-47), and West Virginia (59-56). In the offseason, head coach Lincoln Riley hired new defensive coordinator Alex Grinch, who had coached up an effective unit at Washington State for Mike Leach before spending a year with Ohio State in 2017 when the Buckeyes' defense came apart.

Grinch's plan is to upgrade the Sooners system into a modern, "positionless" unit that features speed and flexibility while emphasizing turnovers. That will probably mean a youth movement in Norman and some growing pains while they search for impact defensive linemen like Grinch had at Washington State. On the bright side, they figure to return six or more starters from last year's unit and will field a much more experienced secondary in 2019. Junior Tre Norwood is back after saving the Sooners in the Big 12 Championship Game by moving from cornerback to safety. Two other starting cornerbacks also return. The fate of the defense may hinge on what they get from defensive end Ron Perkins, nose tackle Neville Gallimore, and defensive end Jalen Redmond, who has been held out to this point with health issues. All have shown flashes; if all three put it all together at the same time, the Sooners defense could surprise.

Riley's offense has a considerably higher floor, even with six starters moving on to the NFL. The Sooners still have 1,000-yard receiver Ceedee Lamb; flex tight end Grant Calcaterra, who dominated in limited opportunities in 2018; and then a deep cast of talented and/or experienced receivers behind them waiting their turn. The running back room is also loaded, with both 1,000-yard rushers (Trey Sermon and Kennedy Brooks) returning. At quarterback the Sooners pounced on the opportunity to start their third consecutive transfer when Alabama's Jalen Hurts determined to play his senior year elsewhere.

The fit here is interesting as Hurts isn't nearly as skilled a passer as Baker Mayfield or Kyler Murray and was ultimately replaced by Tua Tagovailoa at Alabama because of the upgrade that Tua offered in the passing game. In four playoff games before getting benched for Tagovailoa, Hurts completed 43 percent of his passes for 3.7 yards per attempt. He performed better filling in for Tagovailoa against Georgia in the 2018 SEC Championship Game, but did much of his damage scrambling and running, as he had in the past. Riley is developing a well-earned reputation as a quarterback whisperer, but it does seem likely that the Sooners will struggle to maximize their receiving corps to the degree they did in previous seasons.

On the flip side, Oklahoma's run game seems poised to

grow in multiplicity with the infusion of Hurts. At Alabama Hurts ran for 954 yards as a freshman and 855 as a sophomore. He has proven durable getting a workload in the run game and capable in spread-option schemes both pulling the

ball around the edge as well as working between the tackles. If the Sooners can retool the offense around Hurts' not-inconsiderable ability, they should be able to create leeway once more for a rebuilding defense.

5. Ohio State Buckeyes (10-2, 7-2)

2019 Projections

F/+	51.1 (5)
FEI	0.78 (4)
S&P+	24.3 (7)
Total Wins	10.3
Conf Wins	7.4
SOS	.108 (37)
Conf SOS	.121 (23)
Div Champ	49%
Conf Champ	28%
CFP Berth	24%

Projection Factors

2018 F/+	48.4 (5)
2018 FEI	0.67 (7)
2018 S&P+	24.1 (6)
5-Year F/+	57.3 (2)
5-Year FEI	0.90 (3)
5-Year S&P+	26.6 (2)
2-Yr/5-Yr Recruiting	2/2
Ret. Offense	42% (117)
Ret. Defense	85% (9)
Ret. Total	63% (62)

Projected Win Likelihood by Game

Date	Opponent (Proj Rank)	PWL
Aug 31	vs Fl. Atlantic (86)	99%
Sep 7	vs Cincinnati (39)	91%
Sep 14	at Indiana (51)	90%
Sep 21	vs Miami-OH (88)	99%
Sep 28	at Nebraska (49)	88%
Oct 5	vs Michigan St. (23)	83%
Oct 18	at Northwestern (46)	87%
Oct 26	vs Wisconsin (14)	71%
Nov 9	vs Maryland (73)	98%
Nov 16	at Rutgers (108)	99%
Nov 23	vs Penn St. (13)	70%
Nov 30	at Michigan (9)	49%

It's a turbulent but optimistic time for Ohio State. Since the Urban Meyer Buckeyes reached the top of college football in 2014 with postseason wins over Wisconsin, Alabama, and then Oregon to capture the first-ever College Football Playoff title, each subsequent edition of the Buckeyes was basically indistinguishable from the team that came before it. These were the post-Tom Herman offensive coordinator years, with Urban Meyer taking on an increasingly CEO-like role (and the resulting questionable-to-poor coaching hires) and with J.T. Barrett at quarterback.

In that span, from 2015 to 2018, Ohio State narrowly missed out on a repeat trip to the playoff thanks to a fourth-quarter Michigan State field goal in 2015; made the playoff in 2016 but was demolished by Deshaun Watson in the infamous 31-0 game; and then was embarrassed by both Oklahoma and Iowa during the 2017 regular season to fall short of the playoff again. 2018 was a little different. Offensive coordinator Ryan Day took on a greater role and Dwayne Haskins broke just about every passing record that the school had … but the defense fell off a ledge (well, relatively—they still finished 26th in the S&P+). This Big-12-looking team crushed just about everyone on their schedule, including Michigan in a shocking 62-39 win, but the Buckeyes were somehow confounded by Purdue in a 49-20 loss. That margin was enough to keep the Buckeyes out of the playoff for a second straight year, and they had to settle for a lackadaisical Rose Bowl against also-ran Washington. Meyer stepped down due to health reasons in December, Haskins left for the NFL, and defensive coordinator Greg Schiano (along with many other assistant coaches) left the program as well.

Ohio State was one of the steadiest and most predictable programs between 2015 and 2018—an incredibly talented roster with a mostly-constant coaching staff that would always be in a prime position for a playoff spot, even if they hadn't returned to the actual championship game yet. But now

it's really a new era for the Buckeyes as Ryan Day takes over. It's fair to expect a continued focus on the passing game even without Haskins, but the defense should look a bit different under co-coordinators Jeff Hafley and Greg Mattison (whom, along with linebackers coach Al Washington, Day poached from Michigan).

Unlike Schiano's reliance on press-man coverage—which led to diminishing returns in 2018 as the front-line cornerbacks didn't match the play of Ohio State's previous run of first-rounders—the new scheme (re)introduces the hybrid safety/linebacker "Bullet" position and ensures that the Buckeyes will use multiple coverages to better suit their personnel and opponents. The Buckeyes ranked just 62nd in passing S&P+ and 76th in rushing S&P+ in 2018, highlighting the aforementioned problems in the secondary and at linebacker. But with the ascension of some previous top-end recruits—including Chase Young at defensive end, Tyron Vincent and Tommy Togiai in the middle of the line, and Shaun Wade and Jeffrey Okudah in the secondary—Ohio State's defense looks well-positioned to correct their decline.

Ohio State's offense does offer a little uncertainty—with maybe a lower floor, but also a higher ceiling—than Buckeyes fans have gotten used to (the Buckeyes were fourth in overall offensive S&P+ last season). The slightly expanded range of potential outcomes comes from a few factors. First, last season's run game was disappointing, finishing 54th in the S&P+ despite featuring both J.K. Dobbins and Mike Weber. Explosive runs were few and far between (120th in marginal explosiveness), but more importantly, the Buckeyes suddenly started allowing run stuffs (66th in stuff rate, with 18.8 percent stopped at or behind the line). Weber is gone, but Dobbins and a few young four-stars, high-level replacements on the line, and a move toward dedicated runs over RPOs could mean an improvement in the run game. Second, Day will likely be involved with the play calling, but Mike Yurcich comes from Oklahoma State. Third, with Haskins one-and-done, Georgia transfer Justin Fields received instant eligibility and will be the starter at quarterback. His performance in the Ohio State spring game notwithstanding, Fields was the second overall recruit in the country last season and looked strong in (very) limited playtime in Athens as a true freshman. His potential is through the roof, but it's still a major unknown—as is who would come in in relief if he gets injured. Finally, while Haskins was a first-round NFL draft pick for a reason, the Buckeyes also lost three of their top four receivers in Par-

ris Campbell, Johnnie Dixon, and Terry McLaurin. While younger players like Chris Olave have started to emerge and the reliable K.J. Hill elected to stay, replacing those three will be a challenge, even in Day's receiver-friendly offense.

With coaching and personnel changes at linebacker and in the secondary, and a full commitment to Day's vision on offense with Yurcich, the pieces seem to be in place for the Buckeyes to take the half-step forward necessary to return to the College Football Playoff Championship. But there's also the increased risk that comes with so much change—and so much talent up in Ann Arbor.

6. LSU Tigers (9-3, 5-3)

2019 Projections

F/+	49.5 (6)
FEI	0.60 (7)
S&P+	25.8 (4)
Total Wins	9.1
Conf Wins	5.4
SOS	.022 (7)
Conf SOS	.033 (7)
Div Champ	19%
Conf Champ	10%
CFP Berth	9%

Projection Factors

2018 F/+	46.5 (6)
2018 FEI	0.63 (12)
2018 S&P+	24.2 (5)
5-Year F/+	40.2 (5)
5-Year FEI	0.58 (7)
5-Year S&P+	22.3 (6)
2-Yr/5-Yr Recruiting	10/7
Ret. Offense	82% (12)
Ret. Defense	70% (49)
Ret. Total	76% (15)

Projected Win Likelihood by Game

Date	Opponent (Proj Rank)	PWL
Aug 31	vs Ga. Southern (74)	98%
Sep 7	at Texas (32)	77%
Sep 14	vs Nortwestern St. (FCS)	100%
Sep 21	at Vanderbilt (61)	92%
Oct 5	vs Utah St. (30)	86%
Oct 12	vs Florida (12)	68%
Oct 19	at Mississippi St. (7)	43%
Oct 26	vs Auburn (8)	60%
Nov 9	at Alabama (1)	34%
Nov 16	at Ole Miss (35)	79%
Nov 23	vs Arkansas (65)	97%
Nov 30	vs Texas A&M (16)	71%

After finishing 9-4 with another crushing defeat to Alabama in 2017, head coach Ed Orgeron made a few big changes heading into 2018. Matt Canada's jet sweep-heavy offense had failed to make a difference against the Crimson Tide, so Orgeron replaced him with Steve Ensminger, who had coordinated the LSU offense while Orgeron was an interim coach and helped him make the position permanent. Ensminger took LSU back towards becoming an RPO spread offense that kept three receivers on the field and frequently lined up in the shotgun. Then the Tigers welcomed in grad transfer quarterback Joe Burrow, who had lost the battle at Ohio State against Dwayne Haskins, to run the new system.

Their passing (46th in passing S&P+) and success rate (56th) went up somewhat, and they also had a knack for hitting what Bill Connelly called "timely plays"— when they had big plays, they really made them count. Whether that was precise play calling or dumb luck was hard to tell, but Burrow had a solid year with 2,894 yards passing at 7.6 yards per attempt with 16 touchdowns to five interceptions and also 399 rushing yards and seven rushing touchdowns.

In many of LSU's big games in 2018, Burrow came up with key runs in the zone-read game or on the "quarterback stretch" play that turned the NFL's favorite outside zone run into a two-back lead scheme with the running back and tight end blocking while the quarterback carried the ball. Many of their timely plays and conversions occurred as a result of his effective running in short-yardage and red zone situations.

Alabama still punked the Tigers 29-0, but Burrow carried the team to 10 wins and a bowl victory over the Central Florida Knights.

The ensemble returns to make things interesting in 2019. Burrow and his top four receivers are all back, headlined by Justin Jefferson (54 catches for 875 yards and six touchdowns). Up front the Tigers have to replace tight end Foster Moreau, but running back Clyde Edwards-Helaire is back along with four starters on the offensive line. Their biggest question, other than how high Burrow's ceiling will be as a senior, is in pass protection. LSU figures to return sophomore Saahdiq Charles at left tackle. Optimistically in Year 2 of the scheme with improved chemistry in the passing game and know how up front, the Tigers offense could be poised to finally break through in a fashion that LSU fans have been waiting for all decade.

On defense, they have to replace star linebacker, leading tackler, and first-round draft pick Devin White, along with lockdown cornerback Greedy Williams. There's still an awful lot, though, for defensive coordinator Dave Aranda to work with. The defensive front includes former blue-chip recruits Rashard Lawrence and K'Lavon Chaisson. While the secondary is young, it still returns third-year starter Grant Delpit (five sacks and five interceptions in 2018) at strong safety and will feature as many as three former five-star recruits.

Their big challenge will be at inside linebacker, where returning starter Josh Phillips and rising junior Patrick Queen figure to try and replace White's production and sure tackling inside. The Aranda defense utilizes a pass-rushing playmaker in the position White is vacating, and the various power run games in the SEC West generally demand much of a team's linebacker corps. Free safety will also be starting over, probably with former five-star and rising junior Jacoby Stevens. The middle of the Tigers defense is as talented as ever, but whether they'll have the knowhow to lock down the center of the chessboard is another question.

LSU's season will take them to Austin to play Texas in Week 2 before setting them against their normal SEC West slate and a draw from the East that includes a trip to Vanderbilt and Florida at home. Contests with fellow SEC favorites Alabama and Mississippi State are both on the road. It's a pretty brutal schedule, although it normally is for the Tigers. A likely best-case scenario is one in which a one-loss Tigers team still makes the SEC Championship Game or finds some other path to the playoff.

7. Mississippi State Bulldogs (10-2, 6-2)

2019 Projections

F/+	49.0 (7)
FEI	0.69 (6)
S&P+	21.4 (10)
Total Wins	9.5
Conf Wins	5.6
SOS	.046 (10)
Conf SOS	.048 (11)
Div Champ	28%
Conf Champ	14%
CFP Berth	13%

Projection Factors

2018 F/+	44.2 (12)
2018 FEI	0.86 (4)
2018 S&P+	23.2 (8)
5-Year F/+	31.1 (15)
5-Year FEI	0.52 (10)
5-Year S&P+	16.4 (16)
2-Yr/5-Yr Recruiting	23/25
Ret. Offense	59% (81)
Ret. Defense	56% (90)
Ret. Total	57% (92)

Projected Win Likelihood by Game

Date	Opponent (Proj Rank)	PWL
Aug 31	vs UL-Lafayette (100)	99%
Sep 7	vs Southern Miss (78)	99%
Sep 14	vs Kansas St. (62)	97%
Sep 21	vs Kentucky (38)	90%
Sep 28	at Auburn (8)	44%
Oct 12	at Tennessee (40)	82%
Oct 19	vs LSU (6)	57%
Oct 26	at Texas A&M (16)	56%
Nov 2	at Arkansas (65)	93%
Nov 16	vs Alabama (1)	49%
Nov 23	vs Ab. Christian (FCS)	100%
Nov 28	vs Ole Miss (35)	89%

2018 was supposed to be a one-year window for Joe Moorhead's first season in Starkville, since Dan Mullen left the cupboard as stocked as a first-year head coach could ever dream of. Moorhead would only have big names such as quarterback Nick Fitzgerald, running back Aeris Williams, safety Jonathan Abram, and defensive linemen Jeffrey Simmons and Montez Sweat for one year. The latter three would all end up drafted in the first round in 2019. So it's a little disappointing that the Bulldogs only finished 8-5 and dropped all of their matchups against conference heavyweights.

Atypical for Moorhead, the offense was what dragged the Bulldogs down. In their four regular-season losses, Mississippi State would combine for just 16 total points. The offense was necessarily that bad—they ranked 32nd in S&P+ and 28th in FEI—but they definitely were one-dimensional. The rushing offense (sixth in S&P+) was led by Nick Fitzgerald, who finished with nearly 1,300 non-sack rushing yards at a 60.7 percent opportunity rate. The problem was when the Bulldogs faced a team with the defensive talent to slow the run game. The Bulldogs passing game was 93rd in the country in S&P+ and 117th in marginal efficiency as Fitzgerald averaged just 5.2 yards per attempt.

That might change in 2019, as Moorhead's former quarterback at Penn State, Tommy Stevens, joins the Bulldogs. Stevens was underutilized in Happy Valley behind Trace McSorley, but his familiarity with Moorhead's system suggests that the passing offense could take more than a few steps forward in 2019. Most of the Bulldogs' top receivers return, as does top running back Kylin Hill, who will shoulder more of the load. This could be much more representative of the offense that Moorhead actually wants to run.

The defense is almost assuredly going to take a step back given the talent lost, but coordinator Bob Shoop should have a strong linebacker corps with Errol Thompson, Leo Lewis, and Willie Gay Jr. leading the way. Players such as Chauncey Rivers and Kobe Jones will have to step up at defensive end. While the linebacker corps should be a real strength, replacements at safety and on the line will determine the Bulldogs' ceiling for 2019.

8. Auburn Tigers (9-3, 5-3)

2019 Projections

F/+	48.1 (8)
FEI	0.59 (8)
S&P+	22.6 (8)
Total Wins	8.5
Conf Wins	4.8
SOS	.013 (4)
Conf SOS	.017 (3)
Div Champ	10%
Conf Champ	5%
CFP Berth	4%

Projection Factors

2018 F/+	40.7 (15)
2018 FEI	0.55 (15)
2018 S&P+	23.6 (7)
5-Year F/+	39.7 (6)
5-Year FEI	0.63 (6)
5-Year S&P+	20.5 (7)
2-Yr/5-Yr Recruiting	9/8
Ret. Offense	54% (95)
Ret. Defense	67% (59)
Ret. Total	60% (84)

Projected Win Likelihood by Game

Date	Opponent (Proj Rank)	PWL	Projected Loss / Projected Win
Aug 31	vs Oregon (28)	77%	
Sep 7	vs Tulane (97)	99%	
Sep 14	vs Kent St. (120)	99%	
Sep 21	at Texas A&M (16)	54%	
Sep 28	vs Mississippi St. (7)	56%	
Oct 5	at Florida (12)	50%	
Oct 19	at Arkansas (65)	93%	
Oct 26	at LSU (6)	40%	
Nov 2	vs Ole Miss (35)	88%	
Nov 16	vs Georgia (3)	49%	
Nov 23	vs Samford (FCS)	100%	
Nov 30	vs Alabama (1)	47%	

The 2018 season was supposed to be another step forward for the Auburn Tigers after they won the SEC West and played in the conference championship game in 2017. The Tigers returned a strong, veteran lineup on defense as well as quarterback Jarrett Stidham, who had helped key a transition from the normal power-option approach of Gus Malzahn's previous teams to a power/play-action offense. But the offensive line had to start over without line coach Herb Hand (poached by the Texas Longhorns) and four senior starters. The Tigers also struggled to replace running back Kerryon Johnson, who had run for 1,391 tough yards and 18 touchdowns. The 2018 Tigers went 8-5 and struggled to establish any particularly threatening dimensions on offense.

For 2019, everything is going to look pretty different. The offensive line will be able to put four seniors on the field again, highlighted by NFL prospect left tackle Prince Tega Wanogho. At running back, redshirt freshman Jatarvious Whitlow is back after running for 787 yards at 5.2 yards per carry, but on the perimeter the Tigers are starting over. Stidham and the Tigers' top two receivers moved on to the NFL, leaving Malzahn confronted with the need for a youth movement in the passing game in what may be a make-or-break year for his tenure at Auburn.

Seth Williams, who was the team's No. 3 receiver in 2018 as a true freshman, has size at 6-foot-3 and 210 pounds to go get the ball in the air on vertical throws and could be a star in Year 2 as the main target. At quarterback, the battle has come down to redshirt freshman Joey Gatewood (a 6-foot-4, 230-pounder with a big arm and nice mobility) and a true freshman named Bo Nix. The son of Patrick Nix, a star quarterback for Auburn in the mid-'90s, Bo was a transcendent talent in the Alabama high school ranks who won two state championships and was rated a five-star talent by the recruiting services. Nix was an early enrollee for spring practices, and after throwing for nearly 4,000 yards as a high school senior, he's much further along in the passing game than your typical freshman signal-caller. Nix is also quick enough to execute the power-option schemes that still have a presence in the Auburn playbook. Provided that Nix can make good decisions and protect the football, it's a good bet that Malzahn will look to go down swinging and play the talented freshman sooner rather than later to recapture the power/play-action formula that has propelled most of his best teams.

The defense had another very strong season in 2018, finishing sixth in defensive S&P+, except in regards to explosive plays, finishing 78th in IsoPPP. Defensive coordinator Kevin Steele has settled on a nice formula for the Tigers. They play a few base coverages that pressure receivers outside, utilizing the safeties in shallow quarters alignments to jump inside routes and arrive in the run game. Up front, Steele leans on a perpetually loaded defensive line to control the game in the trenches. The Tigers return three starters on their defensive line for 2019, highlighted by tackle Derrick Brown (10.5 tackles for loss and 4.5 sacks) and "Buck" defensive end Nick Coe (7.0 sacks).

Auburn's formula on defense since Steele took over in 2017 has been steady and reliable. If they can re-establish themselves as a power running team with a quarterback who can punish opponents for loading the box, the Tigers have the talent to hang with anyone.

9. Michigan Wolverines (9-3, 7-2)

2019 Projections

F/+	46.9 (9)
FEI	0.55 (11)
S&P+	21.6 (9)
Total Wins	9.4
Conf Wins	6.8
SOS	.055 (15)
Conf SOS	.089 (18)
Div Champ	28%
Conf Champ	16%
CFP Berth	11%

Projection Factors

2018 F/+	45.5 (9)
2018 FEI	0.64 (11)
2018 S&P+	22.0 (10)
5-Year F/+	36.1 (9)
5-Year FEI	0.47 (12)
5-Year S&P+	18.8 (10)
2-Yr/5-Yr Recruiting	19/15
Ret. Offense	76% (30)
Ret. Defense	50% (106)
Ret. Total	63% (68)

Projected Win Likelihood by Game

Date	Opponent (Proj Rank)	PWL
Aug 31	vs Middle Tenn. (92)	99%
Sep 7	vs Army (54)	95%
Sep 21	at Wisconsin (14)	50%
Sep 28	vs Rutgers (108)	99%
Oct 5	vs Iowa (18)	74%
Oct 12	at Illinois (101)	99%
Oct 19	at Penn St. (13)	48%
Oct 26	vs Notre Dame (10)	59%
Nov 2	at Maryland (73)	96%
Nov 16	vs Michigan St. (23)	79%
Nov 23	at Indiana (51)	87%
Nov 30	vs Ohio St. (5)	51%

The Wolverines were firmly in the playoff picture heading into The Game against Ohio State. Having taken just a single loss (by one touchdown, in the opener against Notre Dame), Michigan was favored against the Buckeyes thanks to a top-ten defense and top-25 level offense. Having beaten the in-state rival Spartans a month earlier, the Wolverines had a chance to end the narrative that Jim Harbaugh's team couldn't beat its rivals. But the Buckeyes erased any hope of the Wolverines' first playoff appearance thanks to a dominating offensive performance (the adjusted scoring margin was -33 for the Wolverines, even worse than the actual 62-39 final score). The Wolverines would be similarly demolished by frequent bowl opponent Florida, 41-15. That is a pretty sour end to what looked like a promising season.

But even with those disappointments, Michigan enters 2019 with a big opportunity. Urban Meyer is gone, and no one knows exactly what the Buckeyes will look like. Penn State has also lost a significant amount of talent, so the Big Ten East looks much more open than usual. This is also likely to be Harbaugh's first season at Michigan with a clear starter at quarterback—unbelievably, the Wolverines have started someone different every year of his tenure. Shea Patterson returns with significant receiving talent, including Donovan Peoples-Jones and Nico Collins. Patterson was somewhat underwhelming in 2018 despite the Wolverines ranking ninth overall in passing S&P+; against Ohio State and Florida, Patterson completed fewer than 59 percent of his passes and averaged just 212 passing yards and 6.0 yards per attempt. The Wolverines relied on shorter routes, ranking just 69th in passing marginal explosiveness. And while the passing game was effective overall, the offense struggled significantly on

passing downs, ranking 52nd in passing downs S&P+—basically, if the offense didn't click on early downs, the Wolverines struggled to covert on later ones.

In addition to the benefits from returning starters in the passing game, Michigan fans have reason for optimism with the addition of Alabama co-offensive coordinator Josh Gattis. Gattis promises a long-desired overhaul of the Wolverines offense, instituting a no-huddle "pro-spread" offense, according to the *Detroit Free Press* (Michigan was 123rd in adjusted pace last year). It is possible that Patterson, who averaged 7.7 yards per carry last season, could be increasingly involved in the run game and with throws on the run. Additionally, another year with Ed Warriner and building on the zone-based run scheme with four returning offensive linemen should be good for the run game—that is, if someone emerges as the lead running back. With Karan Higdon gone and Chris Evans out for the season, Michigan will turn to a young back, potentially sophomore Christian Turner or incoming freshman Zach Charbonnet. All things considered, there's enough talent in the unit that even the lack of a clear starter shouldn't be too concerning for the offense.

The defense lost a lot of production, returning just half from last season (106th). Big names such as linebacker Devin Bush, defensive end Chase Winovich, defensive back David Long, and defensive tackle Rashan Gary have all left for the NFL. Defensive coordinator Don Brown will need younger replacements for his stars. Brown has typically relied on an aggressive scheme fueled by havoc (Michigan ranked 23rd in overall havoc rate last year) and press-man coverage. The secondary should be fine thanks to the returning Lavert Hill and incoming five-star freshman Daxton Hill, but there will need to be answers at linebacker and along the line.

10. Notre Dame Fighting Irish (10-2)

2019 Projections

F/+	46.1 (10)
FEI	0.59 (9)
S&P+	19.1 (12)
Total Wins	9.9
Conf Wins	-
SOS	.084 (22)
Conf SOS	-
Div Champ	-
Conf Champ	-
CFP Berth	9%

Projection Factors

2018 F/+	46.2 (7)
2018 FEI	0.67 (8)
2018 S&P+	20.7 (13)
5-Year F/+	35.8 (10)
5-Year FEI	0.51 (11)
5-Year S&P+	18.1 (11)
2-Yr/5-Yr Recruiting	11/10
Ret. Offense	57% (86)
Ret. Defense	55% (95)
Ret. Total	56% (97)

Projected Win Likelihood by Game

Date	Opponent (Proj Rank)	PWL	Projected Loss / Projected Win
Sep 2	at Louisville (95)	99%	
Sep 14	vs New Mexico (115)	99%	
Sep 21	at Georgia (3)	31%	
Sep 28	vs Virginia (45)	91%	
Oct 5	vs Bowling Green (123)	99%	
Oct 12	vs USC (33)	86%	
Oct 26	at Michigan (9)	41%	
Nov 2	vs Virginia Tech (48)	92%	
Nov 9	at Duke (58)	89%	
Nov 16	vs Navy (103)	99%	
Nov 23	vs Boston College (67)	97%	
Nov 30	at Stanford (24)	67%	

The 2018 Notre Dame Fighting Irish had a couple of big factors working in their favor, at least up to the moment where the found themselves facing Clemson in the first round of the playoff. Head coach Brian Kelly made a timely call in 2017 to hire Chip Long from Memphis to help him update the spread offense and mix in some new approaches to power running and RPOs. Then, with the Irish sitting at 3-0 with a big win over Michigan already on the resume, he made a gutsy call to change his quarterback from returning starter and electric athlete Brandon Wimbush to savvy passer Ian Book.

Another big factor was better experience across the offensive line and the entire defense, which maintained the scheme and structure that another 2017 hire (defensive coordinator Mike Elko) had established before leaving for another job (Texas A&M). With Kelly's proactive changes across the program and an experienced team, they were well positioned to take advantage of another favorable factor, the collapse of their competition. On the surface, a schedule including Michigan, Stanford, Virginia Tech, Florida State, and USC looked like a murderer's row, but Syracuse and Michigan were the only opponents the Irish faced who managed to win 10 games in 2018. The 2019 slate figures to be less forgiving. Beyond their home opponents, the Irish travel to Athens to play Georgia, play at Michigan in late October, and finish on the road against Stanford.

One big advantage the Irish will have in 2019 is an offensive line returning four starters from the 2018 playoff unit, including both offensive tackles. Book's No. 2 and no. 3 receivers, Chase Claypool (50 catches, 639 yards) and Chris Finke (49 catches, 571 yards), are back to keep the passing game hum-

ming, and running back Jafar Armstrong (383 rushing yards at 5.3 yards per carry with seven touchdowns) flashed regularly in 2018 and figures to be a star. Returning tight end Cole Kmet is a a solid receiver and at 6-foot-6 and 255 pounds, he can get on the edge.

The defense is a little mixed. On the perimeter, the Irish have tremendous experience and proven talent leading the way. Defensive ends Khalid Khareem, Julian Okwara, and Daelin Hayes had a combined 28 tackles for loss and 14.5 sacks last season and all return. Cornerback Troy Pride Jr. returns, and the Irish also get back corner/nickel Shaun Crawford, who missed last season with a knee injury. The safety tandem of rangy Jalen Elliott (four interceptions in 2018) and hard-hitting Alohi Gilman (94 tackles) also returns. The question marks are in the middle, where Notre Dame lost three exceptional football players in defensive tackle Jerry Tillery (first-round draft pick), linebacker Drue Tranquill (fourth-round draft pick), and linebacker Te'Von Coney (123 tackles, four sacks). The Irish are hoping that returning starter Asmar Bilal can make an effective conversion from rover to middle linebacker to anchor whichever second-year players surround him at the outside linebacker spots. Their ability to play great run defense against teams like Georgia or Michigan will likely hinge on whether they can consistently free up Gilman to drop down and serve as a fourth linebacker.

Notre Dame should be very good again in 2019, but between a tougher schedule and the fact that they have to reload the middle of their defense, a return to the playoff is a tall order.

11. Washington Huskies (10-2, 8-1)

2019 Projections

F/+	44.5 (11)	
FEI	0.56 (10)	
S&P+	17.7 (15)	
Total Wins	10.4	
Conf Wins	7.6	
SOS	.275 (76)	
Conf SOS	.312 (55)	
Div Champ	62%	
Conf Champ	36%	
CFP Berth	29%	

Projection Factors

2018 F/+	46.1 (8)
2018 FEI	0.56 (14)
2018 S&P+	19.9 (14)
5-Year F/+	36.7 (8)
5-Year FEI	0.55 (9)
5-Year S&P+	17.2 (13)
2-Yr/5-Yr Recruiting	14/18
Ret. Offense	67% (55)
Ret. Defense	34% (130)
Ret. Total	50% (118)

Projected Win Likelihood by Game

Date	Opponent (Proj Rank)	PWL	Projected Loss	Projected Win
Aug 31	vs E. Washington (FCS)	100%		
Sep 7	vs California (68)	97%		
Sep 14	vs Hawaii (102)	99%		
Sep 21	at BYU (50)	85%		
Sep 28	vs USC (33)	85%		
Oct 5	at Stanford (24)	65%		
Oct 12	at Arizona (60)	89%		
Oct 19	vs Oregon (28)	80%		
Nov 2	vs Utah (19)	72%		
Nov 8	at Oregon St. (110)	99%		
Nov 23	at Colorado (75)	94%		
Nov 29	vs Washington St. (26)	79%		

Washington lost four games in 2018, but not a single one by more than five points. Unfortunately for the Huskies, but demonstrative of how close they were to bigger things, Washington should have won three of those games based on their S&P+ postgame win expectancies. So it's fair to be a little disappointed, not only because of the final 10-4 record, but also because of the personnel losses—the Huskies are 118th overall in returning production, and dead last in defensive returning production with just 34 percent returning. The losses include longtime quarterback Jake Browning, running back Myles Gaskin, tackle Kaleb McGary, tackling machine Ben Burr-Kirven, and defensive backs Byron Murphy, Taylor Rapp, and Jordan Miller.

It's a new-look Huskies for 2019, so it's good they're led by their most hyped quarterback in years: Georgia transfer Jacob Eason. Eason started at Georgia as a freshman and threw for 2,430 yards with a 55 percent completion rate, but the Bulldogs had just the 91st-ranked passing S&P+ offense and Eason averaged only 5.9 yards per attempt. But the former five-star quarterback is as prototypical as you could hope for, and he returns Browning's top three receiving targets, including Aaron Fuller, Andre Baccellia, and Ty Jones, as well as a number of young tight ends. Given the returning receiving threats and Eason's near-unlimited potential, this could be the most dynamic passing offense of Chris Petersen's Washington tenure. The Huskies also benefit from Salvon Ahmed at running back. Even though Gaskin has been a mainstay of the Washington offense, Ahmed actually bettered him in nearly every statistical category last season, averaging nearly a yard per carry more, and gaining at least 4 yards approximately seven percent more often (55.8 percent). Despite the loss of the quarterback-running back duo, Washington might even be due for an upgrade offensively.

The Huskies defense lost stars at each level, but there's a chance they don't actually fall too far from their elite play from 2018. The Washington defense ranked ninth in defensive FEI last season, shutting down explosive plays and limiting opponents to just 3.7 points per trip inside the 40. They weren't big on creating havoc (just 67th in overall havoc rate), but they played bend-don't-break defense to near-perfection. While Burr-Kiven, Rapp, and Murphy are all gone, there might be some young guys ready to uphold the high standard in Seattle. Sophomore linebackers Ariel Ngata and Joe Tryon were both disruptive in the spring, and Isaiah Gilchrist grabbed two interceptions in the spring game. But beyond the individual players, the most confidence might come from defensive coordinator Jimmy Lake, who has had nothing but elite units at Washington.

12. Florida Gators (8-4, 5-3)

2019 Projections

F/+	43.4 (12)
FEI	0.37 (21)
S&P+	24.6 (6)
Total Wins	8.4
Conf Wins	4.9
SOS	.024 (8)
Conf SOS	.036 (8)
Div Champ	15%
Conf Champ	7%
CFP Berth	6%

Projection Factors

2018 F/+	44.4 (11)
2018 FEI	0.55 (17)
2018 S&P+	23.0 (9)
5-Year F/+	21.2 (24)
5-Year FEI	0.20 (35)
5-Year S&P+	15.9 (18)
2-Yr/5-Yr Recruiting	8/13
Ret. Offense	77% (27)
Ret. Defense	71% (43)
Ret. Total	74% (26)

Projected Win Likelihood by Game

Date	Opponent (Proj Rank)	PWL
Aug 24	vs Miami-FL (22)	67%
Sep 7	vs Tenn-Martin (FCS)	100%
Sep 14	at Kentucky (38)	75%
Sep 21	vs Tennessee (40)	87%
Sep 28	vs Towson (FCS)	100%
Oct 5	vs Auburn (8)	50%
Oct 12	at LSU (6)	32%
Oct 19	at S. Carolina (29)	67%
Nov 2	vs Georgia (3)	34%
Nov 9	vs Vanderbilt (61)	95%
Nov 16	at Missouri (15)	46%
Nov 30	vs Florida St. (37)	85%

The Gators made a sizable jump in Year 1 with Dan Mullen as head coach, climbing from 51st nationally in offensive S&P+ to 15th. They notched big wins over Mississippi State, LSU, and Michigan en route to a 10-win season. Mullen undoubtedly benefited from inheriting a highly experienced offensive line from his predecessor Jim McElwain, but his spread tactics quickly enabled the Gators to get more from their big front and depth at running back.

Lamical Perine and Jordan Scarlett combined to turn 265 carries into 1,602 yards at 6.0 yards per carry with 12 touchdowns. After removing sack yardage, quarterback Feleipe Franks also revealed a mobile side that had not been a part of the offense under McElwain with 95 carries for 452 yards at 4.8 yards per carry with seven touchdowns. The Gators passing game sputtered at times, but Franks threw for 2,457 yards with 24 touchdowns to just six interceptions. Franks returns for 2019 along with Scarlett and four of the top five wide receivers, led by senior Van Jefferson (35 catches for 503 yards and six touchdowns).

But now Mullen has to transition from helping McElwain's offensive recruits realize their potential to rebuilding an offensive line that loses three starters, including both tackles. Departing right tackle Jawaan Taylor ended up being a second-round draft choice, while left tackle Martez Ivey was a four-year starter for the Gators. The prospective first-team line will be comprised mostly of former backups who were rated as three-star recruits, save for Texas transfer and former four-star recruit Jean Delance, who's leading the pack at right tackle. Mullen is no stranger to building strong offensive lines with lower-rated players from his time at Mississippi State, but he'll really need to pull through here to maximize the Gators' returning skill elsewhere.

The passing game should be improved with so much return-ing skill and chemistry between Franks and the receiver corps, but this team leaned on its ability to run the ball in 2018 and will probably need to do so again. The Gators have a wild card with freshman quarterback Emory Jones, who played in just four games in 2018, thus preserving his redshirt. Jones flashed major explosiveness as a runner in Wildcat-style packages designed to help him ease into the offense, although his deployment was often fairly predictable.

Florida's defense also took some tough losses, including three starters who were selected in the NFL draft. On the bright side, defensive end Jabari Zuniga returns after a solid 2018 season (6.5 sacks), multiple defensive backs with starting experience (including both cornerbacks) are back, and steady linebacker David Reese returns in the middle to help direct traffic.

Defensive coordinator Todd Grantham has long been known for generating pressure and teaching pattern-matching coverage, and he'll have another strong cast to execute that vision. What the Gators need is to find a little more up the middle to help stop the run and put teams in obvious passing downs after finishing just 41st in rushing S&P+. Florida has defensive linemen (like 275-pound West Virginia grad transfer Adam Shuler) who are effective in the pass rush on slants and stunts, but they need to find an anchoring nose tackle to give them some power in the box.

The ceiling for the 2019 Gators will be set by how well they can fill out the trenches with new starters on the lines and at linebacker. Beyond their strategic aims to run the ball with spread-option and spread-iso tactics and put opponents in passing downs, Florida needs stout fronts to realize their goal of winning the SEC East division. Currently the road to that title goes through Jacksonville, where they have their annual showdown with big, physical Georgia that hasn't gone Florida's way since Kirby Smart got the Bulldogs going.

13. Penn State Nittany Lions (9-3, 7-2)

2019 Projections

F/+	43.3 (13)
FEI	0.48 (12)
S&P+	18.4 (14)
Total Wins	9.5
Conf Wins	6.6
SOS	.081 (21)
Conf SOS	.085 (17)
Div Champ	18%
Conf Champ	10%
CFP Berth	7%

Projection Factors

2018 F/+	41.8 (14)
2018 FEI	0.50 (20)
2018 S&P+	19.0 (15)
5-Year F/+	32.4 (13)
5-Year FEI	0.46 (13)
5-Year S&P+	16.9 (15)
2-Yr/5-Yr Recruiting	5/12
Ret. Offense	44% (116)
Ret. Defense	68% (55)
Ret. Total	56% (100)

Projected Win Likelihood by Game

Date	Opponent (Proj Rank)	PWL	Projected Loss	Projected Win
Aug 31	vs Idaho (FCS)	100%		
Sep 7	vs Buffalo (89)	99%		
Sep 14	vs Pittsburgh (53)	93%		
Sep 27	at Maryland (73)	94%		
Oct 5	vs Purdue (63)	95%		
Oct 12	at Iowa (18)	54%		
Oct 19	vs Michigan (9)	52%		
Oct 26	at Michigan St. (23)	61%		
Nov 9	at Minnesota (42)	78%		
Nov 16	vs Indiana (51)	93%		
Nov 23	at Ohio St. (5)	30%		
Nov 30	vs Rutgers (108)	99%		

The Nittany Lions took a definite step back on offense in 2018 following Joe Moorhead's move to Mississippi State. After ranking fifth in offensive FEI in 2017, Penn State's offense fell all the way to 44th last season despite featuring numerous senior leaders who have since moved on. Those include quarterback Trace McSorley (and his backup Tommy Stevens, who transferred), running back Miles Sanders, and senior receivers DeAndre Thompkins and Juwan Johnson.

Moorhead's offenses varied between emphasizing efficiency and explosiveness (particularly with Saquon Barkley as the prime boom-or-bust running back), but McSorley certainly seemed to have a gift for the deep ball. Unfortunately, a lack of consistency was partly responsible for the offense's regression to 64th in passing S&P+. McSorley played through injuries throughout the season, and while the passing offense was relatively more explosive (41st in passing marginal explosiveness), it often couldn't connect on more efficient throws (103rd in passing marginal efficiency) and in obvious passing situations (69th on passing downs), with all starting receivers averaging under a 60 percent catch rate.

Sean Clifford now takes over at quarterback. A former four-star recruit, Clifford hasn't seen a ton of action, but he completed five of his seven passes last year for an astounding 195 yards. One of those completions was a 95-yarder, but he nevertheless averaged 25 yards per completion on his other four. The early

indications are that Clifford and Penn State could continue to go deep frequently. Even without Johnson and Thompkins, Penn State returns leading receiver KJ Hamler, who averaged 18.0 yards per catch last season, and young receivers Justin Shorter and Jahan Dotson could be primed for a breakout. Miles Sanders admirably replaced Barkley, offering improved efficiency but lower explosive potential. Now the Nittany Lions will likely feature a running back rotation that starts with Ricky Slade but includes a number of other former blue-chippers, including freshmen Devyn Ford and Noah Cain.

Even with all of its attrition, the offense seems to have highly prized recruits waiting for their breakouts. The defense also features a number of personnel losses, but is still expected to be among the best in the country. Shareef Miller, Kevin Givens, and Robert Windsor are all gone from the line, but Yetur Gross-Matos exploded for 20 tackles for loss last season and could be one of the top defensive ends in the country. He'll need another end to step up without Miller, but Jayson Oweh could be that guy, and Shaka Toney was disruptive as well. But with Micah Parsons looking like a star at linebacker already (he led the team in tackles despite not starting) and incoming freshman linebacker Brandon Smith nearly equaling Parsons' accolades as a recruit, it's possible that the Nittany Lions don't see too much of a drop off from their 11th-place defensive S&P+ ranking last season.

14. Wisconsin Badgers (10-2, 7-2)

2019 Projections

F/+	42.3 (14)
FEI	0.41 (16)
S&P+	20.1 (11)
Total Wins	9.6
Conf Wins	6.6
SOS	.104 (35)
Conf SOS	.107 (20)
Div Champ	50%
Conf Champ	22%
CFP Berth	14%

Projection Factors

2018 F/+	27.1 (33)
2018 FEI	0.24 (37)
2018 S&P+	15.5 (19)
5-Year F/+	34.5 (11)
5-Year FEI	0.57 (8)
5-Year S&P+	18.8 (9)
2-Yr/5-Yr Recruiting	28/32
Ret. Offense	85% (7)
Ret. Defense	60% (78)
Ret. Total	73% (29)

Projected Win Likelihood by Game

Date	Opponent (Proj Rank)	PWL
Aug 30	at South Florida (83)	97%
Sep 7	vs C. Michigan (114)	99%
Sep 21	vs Michigan (9)	50%
Sep 28	vs Northwestern (46)	89%
Oct 5	vs Kent St. (120)	99%
Oct 12	vs Michigan St. (23)	73%
Oct 19	at Illinois (101)	99%
Oct 26	at Ohio St. (5)	29%
Nov 9	vs Iowa (18)	68%
Nov 16	at Nebraska (49)	81%
Nov 23	vs Purdue (63)	95%
Nov 30	at Minnesota (42)	77%

Most prognostications missed Wisconsin's window over the last two years. The Badgers weren't expected to do much in 2017 but rode a veteran defense and star freshman running back Jonathan Taylor over a soft schedule to the Big 10 Championship Game. Then things flipped, with the Badgers picked as high as fourth in 2018 preseason polls only for a retooled and beat-up defense to let Wisconsin down as they went 8-5 against a tougher schedule.

Their 2019 team should be interesting, if nothing else. The offensive line is replacing three starters but has an all-Wisconsin group led by All-Big 10 center Tyler Biadasz, who will likely be flanked by a pair of massive former walk-ons in Josh Seltzner (6-foot-4, 326-pound redshirt sophomore) and Jason Erdmann (6-foot-6, 325-pound redshirt senior). Cole Van Lanen also returns as a starter at left tackle. The Badgers also return their two-headed running back tandem of Jonathan Taylor and Garrett Groshek. Taylor ran for 2,194 yards in 2018 at 7.1 yards per carry with 16 touchdowns and will be running for an NFL contract in 2019. Groshek was brought in on third downs for his pass-catching abilities. Flex tight end Jake Ferguson emerged in 2018 to take the mantle of the departing Troy Fumagalli, who had been drafted, and finished second on the team with 456 receiving yards and four touchdowns. Ferguson is back as a junior alongside leading receivers Danny Davis and A.J. Taylor.

After throwing 26 interceptions over the last two years,

quarterback Alex Hornibrook has grad transferred to Florida State for a fresh start. It seems unlikely that backup Jack Coan pushed him out after a mixed performance in five games. Instead, look for the Badgers to turn to four-star true freshman and early enrollee Graham Mertz. Wisconsin will also likely move to more shotgun looks with Mertz (a spread quarterback in high school) and Coan (at his best in the shotgun zone-read game) competing for the job.

The Badgers defense slipped from fourth in S&P+ in 2017 to 29th in 2018 and had some struggles along the way against some Big 10 West opponents like Northwestern (a 31-17 defeat) and Purdue (a 47-44 victory). They had lots of injuries over the year and struggled to find a pass rush. The six-man rotation at linebacker of 2017 that had generated 24.0 sacks shrunk to a five-man rotation that produced just 14.0 in 2018. In 2019, the defensive line should be healthier and deeper, and the linebacker corps will be bolstered by Alabama transfer Christian Bell and a healthier season from Zach Baun on the outside.

But the schedule is rough, offering home dates against Michigan and Michigan State and a road trip against Ohio State to supplement an improving Big 10 West. Their schedule ends with the road trip against Ohio State, Iowa at home, a road trip to resurgent Nebraska, Purdue at home, and then a road trip to Minnesota. Without experience at quarterback, this doesn't look like a prime year for Wisconsin.

15. Missouri Tigers (9-3, 6-2)

2019 Projections		Projection Factors	
F/+	40.9 (15)	2018 F/+	40.5 (16)
FEI	0.42 (15)	2018 FEI	0.63 (13)
S&P+	17.5 (16)	2018 S&P+	20.8 (12)
Total Wins	9.4	5-Year F/+	13.6 (36)
Conf Wins	5.7	5-Year FEI	0.21 (33)
SOS	.101 (32)	5-Year S&P+	10.7 (30)
Conf SOS	.123 (24)	2-Yr/5-Yr Recruiting	42/39
Div Champ	28%	Ret. Offense	54% (94)
Conf Champ	14%	Ret. Defense	67% (57)
CFP Berth	12%	Ret. Total	61% (81)

Projected Win Likelihood by Game

Date	Opponent (Proj Rank)	PWL	Projected Loss / Projected Win
Aug 31	at Wyoming (93)	99%	
Sep 7	vs West Virginia (25)	75%	
Sep 14	vs SE Missouri St. (FCS)	100%	
Sep 21	vs S. Carolina (29)	77%	
Oct 5	vs Troy (71)	97%	
Oct 12	vs Ole Miss (35)	82%	
Oct 19	at Vanderbilt (61)	86%	
Oct 26	at Kentucky (38)	72%	
Nov 9	at Georgia (3)	24%	
Nov 16	vs Florida (12)	54%	
Nov 23	vs Tennessee (40)	85%	
Nov 29	at Arkansas (65)	88%	

2018 Missouri was an excellent team with an insanely tough schedule. Led by quarterback Drew Lock, the Tigers finished 16th in the F/+ rankings, but their record was just 8-5. Two of those losses came to Georgia and Alabama—completely understandable. Their other three losses were by a combined eight points, to South Carolina, Kentucky, and Oklahoma State. It might seem like a little bit of a missed window of opportunity for Missouri, since Lock has gone to the NFL and the Tigers are now faced with a bowl ban (which is under appeal).

Despite the bowl ban, this could be a very exciting team in 2019. The biggest news is the incoming transfer from Clemson of Kelly Bryant, who decided to leave after Trevor Lawrence grabbed his job. Bryant offers a different skill set than Lock; where Lock was most proficient on downfield throws, Bryant excels at running the zone read and in shorter passes (he averaged just 7.0 yards per attempt as a starter in 2017). Leading receiver Emanuel Hall is gone, but four of the other top receivers do return, including target leader Johnathon Johnson and exciting sophomores Jalen Knox and Kam Scott. If the passing game more closely resembles that of 2017 Clemson, then Tigers fans could expect passing efficiency to stay roughly the same, but for explosiveness to drop significantly. But the decline in passing explosiveness could be counteracted by an improved running game. Even with the departure of Damarea Crockett, the Tigers are likely to have one of the best run games in the SEC. Junior Larry Roundtree III was an efficient, high-volume ballcarrier, and sophomore Tyler Badie showed he deserved carries as a freshman last year, too. The key for this offense will be in finding a few guys who can create explosive plays. Even with Lock and Hall, the Tigers offense was just 86th in overall IsoPPP last season, and it's not completely clear who can be an explosive threat either on the ground or in the passing game.

For years, Missouri's defense was led by an almost disproportionately disruptive defensive line. Led by coach Craig Kuligowski, the line produced stars such as Charles Harris, Shane Ray, Kony Ealy, Michael Sam, Sheldon Richardson, and Aldon Smith. Last year, only tackle Terry Beckner was drafted, and the line's havoc rate fell to 47th. It's not clear if there are early-round draft picks on the current roster, but there are a number of potentially disruptive juniors like Jordan Elliott and Chris Turner, and younger guys like Trajan Jeffcoat. Thankfully most of the secondary and star linebacker Cale Garrett return, so the Missouri defense should be solid again—especially if they can improve their pass rush.

16. Texas A&M Aggies (7-5, 4-4)

2019 Projections		Projection Factors	
F/+	40.8 (16)	2018 F/+	39.9 (17)
FEI	0.38 (18)	2018 FEI	0.50 (21)
S&P+	18.7 (13)	2018 S&P+	21.6 (11)
Total Wins	7.4	5-Year F/+	20.6 (26)
Conf Wins	4.2	5-Year FEI	0.27 (26)
SOS	.007 (1)	5-Year S&P+	15.4 (20)
Conf SOS	.019 (4)	2-Yr/5-Yr Recruiting	12/14
Div Champ	6%	Ret. Offense	62% (71)
Conf Champ	3%	Ret. Defense	49% (108)
CFP Berth	2%	Ret. Total	55% (101)

Projected Win Likelihood by Game

Date	Opponent (Proj Rank)	PWL	Projected Loss / Projected Win
Aug 29	vs Texas St. (109)	99%	
Sep 7	at Clemson (2)	24%	
Sep 14	vs Lamar (FCS)	100%	
Sep 21	vs Auburn (8)	46%	
Sep 28	vs Arkansas (65)	91%	
Oct 12	vs Alabama (1)	37%	
Oct 19	at Ole Miss (35)	69%	
Oct 26	vs Mississippi St. (7)	44%	
Nov 2	vs UTSA (127)	99%	
Nov 16	vs S. Carolina (29)	77%	
Nov 23	at Georgia (3)	24%	
Nov 30	at LSU (6)	29%	

Year 1 for the Jimbo Fisher era at Texas A&M went quite well, with a 9-4 finish, a 74-72 victory in a seven-overtime battle with LSU, and a 52-13 thrashing of North Carolina State in the Gator Bowl. The keys to the season were the discovery of a run game on offense and a leap to 21st place in defensive S&P+ after finishing 52nd in 2017. Fisher added a pair of tight ends to the roster in transfers Jace Sternberger and Trevor Wood. The Aggies played a lot of double-tight end sets with Wood mostly serving as the muscle while Sternberger punished trigger-happy linebackers with 48 catches for 832 yards and 10 touchdowns. With the extra beef on the edges and a brilliant season by center Erik McCoy, Texas A&M paved a way for star running back Trayveon Williams to rush for 1,760 yards at 6.5 yards per carry with 18 touchdowns.

All of those players are gone now, as are the six leading tacklers on defense. The offense will focus around an experienced line, returning quarterback Kellen Mond, and a talented wide receiver corps that was underutilized in 2018 while the ball was given (justifiably) into the hands of Williams and Sternberger. Mond threw for 3,197 yards in 2018 at 7.5 yards per attempt with 24 touchdowns to nine interceptions while adding seven more rushing touchdowns.

The receivers include all the top targets not named Sternberger, highlighted by Quartney Davis (585 yards and seven touchdowns in 2018) with Kendrick Rogers looming as potentially the most potent skill player on the roster. While he finished fifth on the team with 27 catches, Rogers had five touchdowns and flashed the ability to utilize his 6-foot-4, 210-pound size to overpower even LSU's cornerbacks. The obvious move in 2019 would be for A&M to move towards more of a spread concept, where Mond has typically been most comfortable, with some zone-read to help keep the run game going. From that setup they could try to match the formula that helped Fisher win a championship in 2013 when Jameis Winston, surrounded by an NFL-bound tight end and receivers, threw for over 4,000 yards and 40 touchdowns.

On defense, the Aggies lose three starters on the line that combined for 31.5 tackles for loss and 20.0 sacks in 2018, along with their nickel and both inside linebackers. Both cornerbacks return, but pass defense wasn't the strength of the unit, as they were 68th in passing S&P+ and 72nd on passing downs despite getting good pressure from their front four. The secondary is well stocked with big run support players like sophomore Leon O'Neal and Derrick Tucker, but will need to get some stops in the passing game, especially if the offense opens things up and gets the Aggies into some higher-scoring shootouts.

The schedule will be unforgiving with road trips against Clemson, Georgia, and LSU, the latter two of which will close the year, along with their normal matchups against Alabama, Auburn, and then a neutral-site rivalry game with Arkansas in Dallas.

17. Boise State Broncos (11-1, 7-1)

2019 Projections

F/+	37.1 (17)
FEI	0.45 (13)
S&P+	12.6 (24)
Total Wins	11.0
Conf Wins	7.5
SOS	.523 (107)
Conf SOS	.699 (89)
Div Champ	75%
Conf Champ	47%
CFP Berth	3%

Projection Factors

2018 F/+	35.9 (22)
2018 FEI	0.47 (22)
2018 S&P+	12.2 (28)
5-Year F/+	29.6 (16)
5-Year FEI	0.44 (14)
5-Year S&P+	11.2 (27)
2-Yr/5-Yr Recruiting	58/60
Ret. Offense	40% (120)
Ret. Defense	77% (22)
Ret. Total	59% (88)

Projected Win Likelihood by Game

Date	Opponent (Proj Rank)	PWL
Aug 31	vs Florida St. (37)	72%
Sep 6	vs Marshall (80)	97%
Sep 14	vs Portland St. (FCS)	100%
Sep 20	vs Air Force (79)	97%
Oct 5	at UNLV (104)	99%
Oct 12	vs Hawaii (102)	99%
Oct 19	at BYU (50)	78%
Nov 2	at San Jose St. (121)	99%
Nov 9	vs Wyoming (93)	99%
Nov 16	vs New Mexico (115)	99%
Nov 23	at Utah St. (30)	59%
Nov 29	at Colorado St. (106)	99%

The Broncos looked unstoppable for two games last season, demolishing Troy and UConn by a combined 118-27 before losing convincingly to Oklahoma State and then dropping two more games by a combined nine points to finish a slightly disappointing 10-3.

Boise State was incredible on offense but mediocre against the run on defense, too frequently allowing explosive plays (ranking 85th in marginal explosiveness). Though the defense often allowed big plays, they created them just as often with a fierce pass rush (ranking eighth in the country in sack rate), led by Curtis Weaver (9.5 sacks, 15 tackles for loss overall). Weaver returns, but the other top four tackles for loss leaders have moved on. Some of the younger talent will need to provide a second option. But there's otherwise every reason to believe that the Broncos should be similarly solid on defense for 2019.

It could be a different story for the offense, which is in the bottom ten for least returning offensive production. That starts with the loss of quarterback Brett Rypien, who was phenomenally efficient, leading the 26th-ranked passing S&P+ offense (13th in passing marginal efficiency). The offense also loses top running back Alexander Mattison and the top two receiving options, Sean Modster and A.J. Richardson, although CT Thomas and John Hightower should fall in nicely to the top two spots in the rotation. Andrew Van Buren and Robert Mahone should at least equal Mattison's consistency, if not his volume. It would be great if one of the two could produce a few more explosive plays—the Broncos ranked in the 90s in both passing and rushing marginal explosiveness, but each of the top four rushing options averaged less than 4.0 highlight yards per opportunity.

But the Broncos season rests largely on replacing Rypien. Sophomore Chase Cord, senior Jaylon Henderson, and freshman Hank Bachmeier are all fighting for the spot. Bachmeier is the most talented of the three per recruiting rankings and was an early enrollee. Boise State's ceiling will be largely determined by how quickly the new starter can get up to speed.

18. Iowa Hawkeyes (9-3, 6-3)

2019 Projections

F/+	36.1 (18)
FEI	0.42 (14)
S&P+	12.5 (25)
Total Wins	8.9
Conf Wins	6.2
SOS	.098 (30)
Conf SOS	.118 (22)
Div Champ	33%
Conf Champ	14%
CFP Berth	8%

Projection Factors

2018 F/+	38.8 (20)
2018 FEI	0.54 (18)
2018 S&P+	13.3 (23)
5-Year F/+	20.3 (27)
5-Year FEI	0.30 (21)
5-Year S&P+	9.9 (34)
2-Yr/5-Yr Recruiting	43/45
Ret. Offense	72% (39)
Ret. Defense	57% (84)
Ret. Total	65% (49)

Projected Win Likelihood by Game

Date	Opponent (Proj Rank)	PWL	Projected Loss / Projected Win
Aug 31	vs Miami-OH (88)	98%	
Sep 7	vs Rutgers (108)	99%	
Sep 14	at Iowa St. (43)	71%	
Sep 28	vs Middle Tenn. (92)	98%	
Oct 5	at Michigan (9)	26%	
Oct 12	vs Penn St. (13)	46%	
Oct 19	vs Purdue (63)	92%	
Oct 26	at Northwestern (46)	73%	
Nov 9	at Wisconsin (14)	32%	
Nov 16	vs Minnesota (42)	83%	
Nov 23	vs Illinois (101)	99%	
Nov 29	at Nebraska (49)	74%	

The Hawkeyes were strong in 2018, going 9-4 thanks to another top-20 defense by S&P+ and a passing game keyed by junior Nate Stanley throwing to a pair of NFL-bound tight ends in Matt Hockensen and Noah Fant. They narrowly missed the Big 10 title game thanks to three straight losses late in the year—defeats to Penn State, Purdue, and eventual West division champion Northwestern by a combined 12 points.

Replacing those tight ends will be a big theme to 2019, but it's not as straightforward an issue as you'd guess. Fant and Hockensen combined to catch 78 balls for 1,279 yards and 13 touchdowns in 2018, which is solid, but as the team's leading receivers and major talents you'd almost expect them to drop something close to those numbers individually. The Hawkeyes maintained a focus on their normal zone running game in 2018 with running backs Mekhi Sargent and Toren Young turning 295 combined carries into 1,382 yards at 4.7 yards per carry with 14 touchdowns. The offense was fairly plodding in 2018 and not consistent or productive enough on the ground to make for an explosive play-action attack that could create easy throws over the top to the tight ends.

This year, both offensive tackles will be back, and the tight end positions will be manned by sturdy blocker Nate Wiet-

ing and promising Shaun Beyer, who had been waiting his turn and rehabbing a knee injury in prior years. Iowa figures to try and get back to running the ball more effectively with both running backs returning and an older line that's adding a pair of twin brothers to play either guard position in redshirt seniors Levi and Landan Paulsen.

Defensively the Hawkeyes had to fight through some injuries in 2018, and consequently now have much of their defensive backfield set with six out of seven positions currently held by players with starting experience. Defensive backs Geno Stone and Michael Ojemudia had seven interceptions last year, and the linebacker corps settled on a new starting trio over the course of the year that returns for 2019. Up front the Hawkeyes lose Parker Hesse and Anthony Nelson after strong senior seasons, but defensive end A.J. Epenesa had a breakout 2018 with 10.5 sacks and will be back to lead the pass rush.

There's a lot in place for Iowa if they can find new skill talent and a run game to pair with a senior quarterback. The trouble is the schedule; the Hawkeyes have to play fellow Big 10 West contenders Wisconsin, Northwestern, and Nebraska all on the road.

19. Utah Utes (10-2, 7-2)

2019 Projections

F/+	35.3 (19)
FEI	0.31 (25)
S&P+	15.4 (17)
Total Wins	9.7
Conf Wins	7.0
SOS	.243 (70)
Conf SOS	.275 (53)
Div Champ	73%
Conf Champ	31%
CFP Berth	19%

Projection Factors

2018 F/+	39.1 (18)
2018 FEI	0.39 (27)
2018 S&P+	16.8 (17)
5-Year F/+	26.1 (21)
5-Year FEI	0.22 (32)
5-Year S&P+	11.9 (26)
2-Yr/5-Yr Recruiting	39/34
Ret. Offense	90% (3)
Ret. Defense	59% (81)
Ret. Total	75% (21)

Projected Win Likelihood by Game

Date	Opponent (Proj Rank)	PWL
Aug 29	vs BYU (50)	76%
Sep 7	vs No. Illinois (82)	97%
Sep 14	vs Idaho St. (FCS)	100%
Sep 20	at USC (33)	61%
Sep 28	vs Washington St. (26)	67%
Oct 12	at Oregon St. (110)	99%
Oct 19	vs Arizona St. (47)	85%
Oct 26	vs California (68)	93%
Nov 2	at Washington (11)	28%
Nov 16	vs UCLA (64)	92%
Nov 23	at Arizona (60)	81%
Nov 30	vs Colorado (75)	95%

Injuries to quarterback Tyler Huntley and running back Zach Moss—the Utes' two most dynamic offensive skill players—caused them both to miss the last five games of the season and contributed to back-to-back losses to Washington and Northwestern. Now the Utes are hoping to best last season's Pac-12 Championship Game appearance (a 10-3 loss to Washington). They're in a good position to do so—almost every offensive player returns, including Huntley and Moss, as well as receivers Britain Covey and Jaylen Dixon. The defense experiences more important turnover, but should still maintain its high level.

While the offense mostly looks the same in terms of player personnel, Andy Ludwig's return as coordinator does mean a significant shift for the offense. Ludwig was most recently at Vanderbilt, leading the 24th-ranked S&P+ offense, which took advantage of explosive running and solid-enough passing from senior quarterback Kyle Shurmur. It's reasonable to expect a similar focus on the ground game thanks to the combination of Huntley and Moss' legs, but Covey and Dixon also give enough of a passing threat to suggest a higher upside than 2018's 63rd rating in offensive FEI. While the Utes' late-season injury luck likely depressed their offensive ratings, overall improvement will likely require more explosiveness. For all of Huntley and Moss' efficiency, neither was particularly explosive on the ground. But Dixon averaged 18.4 yards per catch as a freshman, suggesting he could be a big part of the answer there.

Unfortunately for Utah's defense, their four primary personnel losses were also their top four leading tacklers, including prolific linebacker Chase Hansen (22 tackles for loss and 27.5 total run stuffs in 2018) and both starting safeties. But it's tough to imagine the Utes dropping off too much defensively—they have played at a top-40 S&P+ level for the past four seasons, climbing to 19th on the strength of those four senior defenders. A drop back to the low 30s or so wouldn't be devastating, as long as it is matched by an expected rise in offensive production.

20. Central Florida Knights (11-1, 7-1)

2019 Projections

F/+	33.9 (20)
FEI	0.38 (19)
S&P+	11.7 (27)
Total Wins	10.6
Conf Wins	7.3
SOS	.517 (104)
Conf SOS	.691 (88)
Div Champ	76%
Conf Champ	43%
CFP Berth	2%

Projection Factors

2018 F/+	45.3 (10)
2018 FEI	0.70 (6)
2018 S&P+	16.5 (18)
5-Year F/+	6.8 (52)
5-Year FEI	0.06 (53)
5-Year S&P+	3.7 (57)
2-Yr/5-Yr Recruiting	66/64
Ret. Offense	54% (96)
Ret. Defense	63% (66)
Ret. Total	58% (90)

Projected Win Likelihood by Game

Date	Opponent (Proj Rank)	PWL
Aug 29	vs Florida A&M (FCS)	100%
Sep 7	at Fl. Atlantic (86)	93%
Sep 14	vs Stanford (24)	64%
Sep 21	at Pittsburgh (53)	77%
Sep 28	vs Connecticut (130)	99%
Oct 4	at Cincinnati (39)	63%
Oct 19	vs E. Carolina (107)	99%
Oct 26	at Temple (55)	78%
Nov 2	vs Houston (66)	92%
Nov 8	at Tulsa (99)	99%
Nov 23	at Tulane (97)	99%
Nov 29	vs South Florida (83)	97%

Scott Frost left the Knights in very good shape when he left for Nebraska, and the Central Florida administration put the team in good hands by hiring Josh Heupel from Missouri. In Year 1 with Heupel as head coach, Central Florida went 12-1 with another AAC championship despite losing star quarterback McKenzie Milton to a nasty leg injury in the regular-season finale before the AAC title game.

Milton will not return in 2019, although there's some hope he'll be able to give things another shot in 2020. They finished the year with true freshman Darriel Mack Jr., who completed 51 percent of his passes at 6.2 yards per attempt while rushing for 337 yards and six touchdowns. At 6-foot-3 and 230 pounds, Mack is a powerful athlete with solid mobility and a strong arm, but he's not fully versed in the Central Florida offense yet and struggled to connect with receivers facing man coverage. They're also adding Notre Dame grad transfer Brandon Wimbush to the mix. Wimbush isn't much more polished as a passer than Mack, but he ran for 14 touchdowns in 2017 and is a more explosive athlete while still boasting a strong arm and a lot of big-game experience.

The design of the Heupel offense is to use wide splits and vertical throws to threaten a defense with quick-strike scores in order to clear out space to run the ball downhill into light boxes and vacated alleys. The Knights will be loaded with runners between Mack, Wimbush, and running back Adrian Killins Jr. (715 rushing yards). Lead receiver Gabriel Davis is also back after catching 53 balls for 815 yards and seven scores. The offensive line will be rebuilt, but they do have Trevor Elbert (Texas A&M transfer) and Parker Boudreaux (Notre Dame transfer) infusing the unit with talent and big Wisconsin tight end transfer Jake Hescock on the edge.

The defensive front that helped the Knights upset Auburn in the Peach Bowl is totally gone now, and the replacements are largely untested. They do have Brendon Hayes returning at defensive end after inflicting 11 tackles for loss in 2018 and Nate Evans at weakside linebacker who had 99 tackles, including 10 tackles for loss. The secondary is the strength of the team now, with three starters back led by Richie Grant, who led the team with 108 tackles while adding six interceptions. The Knights counted on Grant heavily last year to roam in the middle of the field and rob routes in the seams or come up to clean up in the run game. He'll be back to reprise that role.

Central Florida's ceiling will hinge on how things go with all the new blood in the trenches, but the skill talent on either side of the ball is as good as it's been in the last few years.

21. Appalachian State Mountaineers (11-1, 8-0)

2019 Projections

F/+	32.7 (21)
FEI	0.39 (17)
S&P+	10.4 (31)
Total Wins	11.1
Conf Wins	7.7
SOS	.653 (115)
Conf SOS	.898 (104)
Div Champ	90%
Conf Champ	63%
CFP Berth	4%

Projection Factors

2018 F/+	36.9 (21)
2018 FEI	0.52 (19)
2018 S&P+	11.9 (29)
5-Year F/+	14.5 (34)
5-Year FEI	0.27 (25)
5-Year S&P+	4.9 (53)
2-Yr/5-Yr Recruiting	98/104
Ret. Offense	87% (5)
Ret. Defense	61% (77)
Ret. Total	74% (22)

Projected Win Likelihood by Game

Date	Opponent (Proj Rank)	PWL
Aug 31	vs E. Tenn. St. (FCS)	100%
Sep 7	vs Charlotte (118)	99%
Sep 21	at N. Carolina (77)	88%
Sep 28	vs Co. Carolina (119)	99%
Oct 9	at UL-Lafayette (100)	99%
Oct 19	vs UL-Monroe (105)	99%
Oct 26	at S. Alabama (126)	99%
Oct 31	vs Ga. Southern (74)	94%
Nov 9	at S. Carolina (29)	51%
Nov 16	at Ga. State (122)	99%
Nov 23	vs Texas St. (109)	99%
Nov 30	at Troy (71)	86%

F/+ projections don't take coaching changes into account, which is notable because the Mountaineers lost a good one—Scott Satterfield—to Louisville, and because it is former North Carolina State offensive coordinator Eliah Drinkwitz's first season as a head coach. But even with the coaching change, Appalachian State has everything it needs to be the country's premier Group of 5 team in 2019.

Appalachian State has regularly outperformed its talent level, including last season's 11-2 finish, which only included a single touchdown loss to Penn State in the season opener and a surprise loss to Georgia Southern in late October. But Drinkwitz is lucky enough to return the fifth-highest percentage of offensive production in the country, including quarterback Zac Thomas, receivers Corey Sutton and Thomas Hennigan, and junior running backs Darrynton Evans and Marcus Williams Jr.

The return of the core run game is particularly important, since Appalachian State was one of the most run-heavy teams in the country (24th and tenth in standard downs and passing downs run rate, respectively). Despite their reliance on the ground game, they weren't particularly efficient at it, ranking 100th in rushing marginal efficiency and 91st in opportunity rate, but bursting out occasionally for the second-best rushing marginal explosiveness. Darrynton Evans averaged 10.7 highlight yards per opportunity (even if he posted a low 40.2 percent opportunity rate), while quarterback Zac Thomas provided consistency on the ground by gaining 4 or more yards on 59 percent of his carries (and he was third on the team in carries). Virtually none of this ground game infrastructure is lost for 2019.

That's interesting, because Drinkwitz was known for efficient passing games at North Carolina State. Since Thomas is a year older and has an experienced receiving corps, it's possible that the Mountaineers opt for a more balanced attack in 2019.

The defense returns a lower percentage of its 2018 production, but remains mostly intact and should not be a reason for concern. The linebackers were undoubtedly the team's strength, occupying the top four slots on the list of tacklers, as well as ranking 12th in havoc rate. The group loses Anthony Flory, but returns everyone else, which should mean that the

Mountaineers field another top-25 defense. Maybe the only concern is the hire of Ted Roof as defensive coordinator.

Barring issues with coordinators failing to adapt scheme to existing talent, this team has all the makings of another Sun Belt champion—at minimum.

22. Miami Hurricanes (10-2, 7-1)

2019 Projections

F/+	32.5 (22)
FEI	0.28 (28)
S&P+	13.9 (19)
Total Wins	9.8
Conf Wins	6.6
SOS	.332 (85)
Conf SOS	.558 (78)
Div Champ	67%
Conf Champ	17%
CFP Berth	11%

Projection Factors

2018 F/+	27.9 (32)
2018 FEI	0.25 (35)
2018 S&P+	12.7 (27)
5-Year F/+	27.2 (19)
5-Year FEI	0.30 (22)
5-Year S&P+	14.7 (21)
2-Yr/5-Yr Recruiting	17/16
Ret. Offense	63% (67)
Ret. Defense	57% (83)
Ret. Total	60% (86)

Projected Win Likelihood by Game

Date	Opponent (Proj Rank)	PWL
Aug 24	vs Florida (12)	33%
Sep 7	at N. Carolina (77)	88%
Sep 14	vs Beth-Cookman (FCS)	100%
Sep 21	vs C. Michigan (114)	99%
Oct 5	vs Virginia Tech (48)	83%
Oct 11	vs Virginia (45)	81%
Oct 19	vs Georgia Tech (69)	93%
Oct 26	at Pittsburgh (53)	75%
Nov 2	at Florida St. (37)	59%
Nov 9	vs Louisville (95)	99%
Nov 23	at Fl. International (91)	96%
Nov 30	at Duke (58)	78%

The Hurricanes had a whirlwind offseason, first losing defensive coordinator Manny Diaz to the Temple head coaching vacancy, then seeing Mark Richt retire, and finally hiring Diaz back as head coach. Diaz then brought several transfers in through the transfer portal to help overhaul the Miami roster.

The offense added immediate help from former five-star quarterback Tate Martell of Ohio State and grad transfers Tommy Kennedy (a potential left tackle from Butler) and K.J. Osborn (a wide receiver from Buffalo). They also added some fresh edge players in Trevon Hill from Virginia Tech and Jaelan Phillips from UCLA; defensive tackle Chigozie Nnoruka from UCLA; and safety Bubba Bolden from USC. The offensive players will add badly needed skill and experience to a unit that finished 66th in offensive S&P+.

It's still unclear whether Martell will win the starting quarterback job from returning starter N'Kosi Perry, who struggled as a redshirt freshman, throwing for 1,091 yards at just 5.7 yards per attempt with 13 touchdowns to six interceptions. Martell adds more explosiveness in the run game, but while he has always flashed potential, he hasn't done much in the passing game to this point in his career. Either will be handing off regularly to Deejay Dallas, who ran for 617 yards at 5.7 yards per carry with six touchdowns a year ago. The line will

need Kennedy to take hold of the left tackle job to buy time for a young group to develop and hopefully keep massive Navaughn Donaldson (6-foot-6 and 350 pounds) at guard where he has thrived rather than trying him again at tackle where he struggled in 2018.

On defense, the Hurricanes are losing star pass-rusher Joe Jackson (8.5 sacks in 2018), but return all three starting linebackers as well as the starting nickel. Linebackers Shaquille Quarterman and Michael Pinckney had a combined 25 tackles for loss and 8.5 sacks a year ago, while nickel Romeo Finley and young returning cornerback Trajan Bandy had five interceptions. With Jonathan Garvin back at defensive end and incoming talent across the line, the only real challenge is replacing a pair of senior safeties. Rising junior Amari Carter had three passes defended in 2018 as a backup safety and will probably be joined on the back end by Bolden, the USC transfer.

There's a lot of talent across the roster that was either already there or brought in through transfers. The challenge will be for Diaz and new offensive coordinator Dan Enos to develop a culture and system on offense that can plug in talent as easily as the Hurricanes have come to do on defense in recent seasons.

23. Michigan State Spartans (8-4, 5-4)

2019 Projections			Projection Factors	
F/+	31.9 (23)		2018 F/+	29.3 (28)
FEI	0.30 (26)		2018 FEI	0.26 (33)
S&P+	12.6 (23)		2018 S&P+	11.5 (30)
Total Wins	8.2		5-Year F/+	28.8 (17)
Conf Wins	5.5		5-Year FEI	0.33 (20)
SOS	.052 (14)		5-Year S&P+	14.5 (22)
Conf SOS	.057 (13)		2-Yr/5-Yr Recruiting	26/26
Div Champ	5%		Ret. Offense	78% (24)
Conf Champ	3%		Ret. Defense	53% (99)
CFP Berth	2%		Ret. Total	66% (48)

Projected Win Likelihood by Game

Date	Opponent (Proj Rank)	PWL	Projected Loss	Projected Win
Aug 30	vs Tulsa (99)	99%		
Sep 7	vs W. Michigan (81)	96%		
Sep 14	vs Arizona St. (47)	81%		
Sep 21	at Northwestern (46)	68%		
Sep 28	vs Indiana (51)	85%		
Oct 5	at Ohio St. (5)	17%		
Oct 12	at Wisconsin (14)	27%		
Oct 26	vs Penn St. (13)	39%		
Nov 9	vs Illinois (101)	99%		
Nov 16	at Michigan (9)	21%		
Nov 23	at Rutgers (108)	99%		
Nov 30	vs Maryland (73)	94%		

Michigan State's 2018 season demonstrated the cost of only fielding half a team: the Spartans ranked second overall in defensive S&P+ but 112th on offense. As a result, Michigan State suffered losses to Arizona State, Northwestern, Nebraska, and Oregon (in addition to more predictable losses to Ohio State and Michigan) to finish 7-6. Their final record was coincidentally also the final score of their disappointing bowl loss to the Ducks.

Despite the sour finish to a disappointing season, the Spartans could be in a stronger position for 2019, as their top-25 F/+ projection suggests. For one, the poor offense returns 78 percent of its production from last year, which ranks 24th-most in the country. That includes, principally, quarterback Brian Lewerke and running back Connor Heyward, along with two of the top three receivers in Darrell Stewart Jr. and Cody White. There's also hope that sophomore Jalen Nailor could be an explosive threat after averaging 17.3 yards per catch last season as a freshman. To be clear, none of these players' statistics are all that encouraging—Lewerke completed just 54.3 percent of his passes, the two returning receivers caught just 54.0 percent of their targets, and Heyward had only a 42.4 percent opportunity rate—but they were nonetheless the best numbers on the team, and the hope is that another offseason's worth of experience could lead the way for improvement overall.

And in all likelihood, the Spartans defense will remain as tough as ever. The best offense on their schedule last season—Ohio State's—managed just 26 points in just the type of ugly, low-scoring game that the Spartans love to force their opponents into. Michigan State is very successful at creating havoc, ranking fourth in the country, and returns an upperclassman-filled defensive lineup, including tackles for loss leaders Kenny Willekes and Raequan Williams.

The 2019 Spartans are likely a step behind the Wolverines and Nittany Lions and maybe two steps behind the Buckeyes in the Big Ten East. But they are also well-positioned to take advantage of quarterback transitions at the latter two division opponents, and they often get the best of the more talented Wolverines anyway. With some improvement in the passing game—even to a merely average-ranked performance—it's not hard to see the Spartans back as a contender in the Big Ten East.

24. Stanford Cardinal (8-4, 6-3)

2019 Projections			Projection Factors	
F/+	29.9 (24)		2018 F/+	29.8 (27)
FEI	0.33 (24)		2018 FEI	0.24 (36)
S&P+	10.0 (32)		2018 S&P+	13.0 (26)
Total Wins	7.9		5-Year F/+	34.3 (12)
Conf Wins	6.4		5-Year FEI	0.42 (15)
SOS	.115 (39)		5-Year S&P+	17.9 (12)
Conf SOS	.286 (54)		2-Yr/5-Yr Recruiting	21/20
Div Champ	17%		Ret. Offense	45% (112)
Conf Champ	10%		Ret. Defense	63% (70)
CFP Berth	5%		Ret. Total	54% (107)

Projected Win Likelihood by Game

Date	Opponent (Proj Rank)	PWL	Projected Loss	Projected Win
Aug 31	vs Northwestern (46)	79%		
Sep 7	at USC (33)	53%		
Sep 14	at UCF (20)	36%		
Sep 21	vs Oregon (28)	60%		
Sep 28	at Oregon St. (110)	99%		
Oct 5	vs Washington (11)	35%		
Oct 17	vs UCLA (64)	88%		
Oct 26	vs Arizona (60)	87%		
Nov 9	at Colorado (75)	84%		
Nov 16	at Washington St. (26)	43%		
Nov 23	vs California (68)	90%		
Nov 30	vs Notre Dame (10)	33%		

Stanford had a promising team heading into 2018 with the emergence of starting quarterback K.J. Costello and the amazing season of running back Bryce Love in 2017, but things went sideways for the Cardinal and they finished 9-4 and short of repeating as Pac-12 North champions. Love struggled to run behind a retooled and beat-up offensive line, finishing with 739 yards. Costello took over and utilized senior wideouts J.J. Arcega-Whiteside and Trenton Irwin in the passing game along with flex tight end Kaden Smith.

On defense Stanford was just 43rd nationally. Things improved down the stretch when redshirt freshman Gabe Reid won a starting job at outside linebacker and ended up leading the team with 5.5 sacks. The defensive line returns key contributors such as tackle Michael Williams and defensive end Jovan Swann, but the team hasn't fielded a dominant linebacker corps since Blake Martinez graduated after the 12-2 season in 2015. Their secondary will have star cornerback Paulson Adebo, but Stanford is thin in the middle of the defense with a need to find new starters at nickel, both inside linebacker positions, and free safety.

The offense has some pass-protecting skill with returning tackles Walker Little and Devery Hamilton along with center Drew Dalman. The top targets for Costello are mostly gone, but Stanford still has tight end Colby Parkinson back after he had 485 receiving yards and seven touchdowns a year ago as the backup behind Kaden Smith. They've recruited well otherwise and have former blue-chip recruit Osiris St. Brown stepping into a starting role. Rebuilding the rushing attack will be tough after losing guard Nate Herbig and many of the other veterans that cleared a path for Love in 2017.

In 2018, the Cardinal started mixing in more spread looks. They may need to expand that tactic in 2019 in order to make the most of what they have with Costello and Parkinson before they leave for the NFL. The hope otherwise is that the strong recruiting in previous years will yield some stars from the rising ranks.

25. West Virginia Mountaineers (8-4, 6-3)

2019 Projections

F/+	29.5 (25)
FEI	0.38 (20)
S&P+	8.6 (38)
Total Wins	7.9
Conf Wins	5.9
SOS	.085 (23)
Conf SOS	.167 (36)
Div Champ	-
Conf Champ	8%
CFP Berth	2%

Projection Factors

2018 F/+	35.0 (23)
2018 FEI	0.46 (23)
2018 S&P+	13.2 (24)
5-Year F/+	19.6 (28)
5-Year FEI	0.29 (23)
5-Year S&P+	10.3 (32)
2-Yr/5-Yr Recruiting	37/47
Ret. Offense	42% (118)
Ret. Defense	67% (58)
Ret. Total	54% (104)

Projected Win Likelihood by Game

Date	Opponent (Proj Rank)	PWL
Aug 31	vs James Madison (FCS)	100%
Sep 7	at Missouri (15)	25%
Sep 14	vs NC State (34)	68%
Sep 21	at Kansas (111)	99%
Oct 5	vs Texas (32)	66%
Oct 12	vs Iowa St. (43)	76%
Oct 19	at Oklahoma (4)	15%
Oct 31	at Baylor (44)	64%
Nov 9	vs Texas Tech (56)	85%
Nov 16	at Kansas St. (62)	76%
Nov 23	vs Oklahoma St. (27)	59%
Nov 29	at TCU (36)	55%

The Mountaineers went 8-4 and finished in the F/+ top-25, but it felt like a missed opportunity considering the senior talent that has now departed—quarterback Will Grier, receivers David Sills V and Gary Jennings Jr. (and potentially third receiver Marcus Simms, who entered his name in the transfer portal during the spring), and run-stuffing linebacker David Long Jr. Of course, the biggest personnel loss was head coach Dana Holgorsen, who left for the same job at Houston.

Holgorsen's move seems pretty surprising at first—there aren't that many (any?) instances of a head coach willingly moving from a Power 5 job to one in the Group of 5. Of course, Houston is just about as Power 5 as a Group of 5 team can get … and it's also possible that the Mountaineers are due for a drop-off in new head coach Neal Brown's first year.

For one thing, the schedule isn't the easiest. There's the usual Big 12 slate that includes tough games against Texas, Oklahoma, and Oklahoma State, but they also have relatively tough out-of-conference games, including James Madison, Missouri, and North Carolina State.

Second, the Mountaineers' percentage of returning production is among the worst in the Power 5 at 54 percent, 105th overall. As mentioned above, that includes major losses among offensive skill positions and along the offensive line, not to mention defensive losses at linebacker and safety. Two transfers—former Oklahoma quarterback Austin Kendall and Miami's Jack Allison—are fighting to replace Grier. Whoever wins will be heavily reliant on another transfer at receiver—T.J. Simmons, formerly of Alabama and last year's fifth-leading receiver for the Mountaineers. West Virginia will rely on mostly untested depth behind him. At least both Kennedy McKoy and Martell Pettaway return at running back. McKoy had 50 percent more carries and more total rushing yards, but Pettaway was more efficient, gaining 4 or more yards on five percent more of his carries.

Third, the defense had already been in decline from previous years, but there's still no guarantee that the overhaul in players and coaches will amount to a meaningful improvement in Brown's first season.

26. Washington State Cougars (9-3, 6-3)

2019 Projections

F/+	29.3 (26)
FEI	0.36 (22)
S&P+	8.9 (36)
Total Wins	8.6
Conf Wins	5.8
SOS	.150 (49)
Conf SOS	.160 (35)
Div Champ	9%
Conf Champ	5%
CFP Berth	3%

Projection Factors

2018 F/+	34.1 (24)
2018 FEI	0.43 (26)
2018 S&P+	11.3 (31)
5-Year F/+	14.6 (32)
5-Year FEI	0.28 (24)
5-Year S&P+	5.7 (49)
2-Yr/5-Yr Recruiting	64/62
Ret. Offense	58% (84)
Ret. Defense	64% (65)
Ret. Total	61% (77)

Projected Win Likelihood by Game

Date	Opponent (Proj Rank)	PWL
Aug 31	vs N. Mexico St. (125)	99%
Sep 7	vs No. Colorado (FCS)	100%
Sep 13	at Houston (66)	79%
Sep 21	vs UCLA (64)	88%
Sep 28	at Utah (19)	33%
Oct 12	at Arizona St. (47)	66%
Oct 19	vs Colorado (75)	92%
Oct 26	at Oregon (28)	43%
Nov 9	at California (68)	80%
Nov 16	vs Stanford (24)	57%
Nov 23	vs Oregon St. (110)	99%
Nov 29	at Washington (11)	21%

Before the 2018 season, Washington State had a tremendous amount of upheaval and turmoil within the program. Prospective quarterback Tyler Hilinski tragically passed away, much of the coaching staff left, and head coach Mike Leach himself nearly departed for Tennessee before that fell through in dramatic fashion. Consequently, they were not a trendy pick to have a successful season, but there was a lot of talent still around in Pullman when the season started.

A rebuilt offensive line led by NFL first-rounder Andre Dillard had a very strong year, and transfer quarterback Gardner Minshew stepped in and threw for 4,776 yards and 38 touchdowns. The defense slipped after losing coordinator Alex Grinch and star defensive tackle Hercules Mata'afa, but held on to finish 59th and keep the Cougars in games while their offense led the way.

Dillard and Minshew are gone, as is running back James Williams, but there's still quite a bit to work with for Leach and his retooled staff. Gage Gobrud transferred in from a fellow Air Raid program in FCS Eastern Washington to compete for the starting quarterback job with two fifth-year seniors and talented redshirt freshman Cammon Cooper. Under Minshew, the Cougars developed an effective rhythm on offense utilizing checkdown passes to the running backs, and they return freshman Max Borghi after he rushed for 366 yards and eight touchdowns while gaining 374 more yards and four more touchdowns through the air. Beyond the running backs, the top four leading receivers are all back as well. The next quarterback will have big shoes to fill after Minshew's performance, but this wouldn't be the first time that Leach has gotten a program to the point where they could expect to rotate in a different quarterback year after year without losing steam.

On defense, the Cougars have eight starters back and are plugging in West Virginia transfer Lamont McDougle at nose tackle. McDougle had a good freshman year in 2017 before losing his starting spot to some incoming transfers. If McDougle can bring more disruption up front, the Cougars have a lot of speed and experience behind him at linebacker and safety.

27. Oklahoma State Cowboys (9-3, 6-3)

2019 Projections

F/+	29.1 (27)
FEI	0.23 (32)
S&P+	12.8 (22)
Total Wins	8.8
Conf Wins	5.8
SOS	.190 (57)
Conf SOS	.194 (41)
Div Champ	-
Conf Champ	8%
CFP Berth	3%

Projection Factors

2018 F/+	29.3 (28)
2018 FEI	0.20 (40)
2018 S&P+	13.8 (22)
5-Year F/+	22.7 (23)
5-Year FEI	0.25 (29)
5-Year S&P+	13.6 (23)
2-Yr/5-Yr Recruiting	36/36
Ret. Offense	56% (91)
Ret. Defense	68% (56)
Ret. Total	62% (75)

Projected Win Likelihood by Game

Date	Opponent (Proj Rank)	PWL
Aug 30	at Oregon St. (110)	99%
Sep 7	vs McNeese (FCS)	100%
Sep 14	at Tulsa (99)	99%
Sep 21	at Texas (32)	50%
Sep 28	vs Kansas St. (62)	87%
Oct 5	at Texas Tech (56)	73%
Oct 19	vs Baylor (44)	77%
Oct 26	at Iowa St. (43)	62%
Nov 2	vs TCU (36)	69%
Nov 16	vs Kansas (111)	99%
Nov 23	at West Virginia (25)	41%
Nov 30	vs Oklahoma (4)	26%

The Cowboys are the second team in 2018 that finished in the F/+ top 30 but nevertheless lost six games. Oklahoma State did so in peak Big 12 fashion—with a typically elite offense (seventh in S&P+) and mediocre defense (71st in S&P+). Early on it looked like the Cowboys might challenge their in-state rivals for the conference title, especially after demolishing Boise State 44-21 in Week 3. But they followed that win up with an immediate loss to Texas Tech. The Cowboys seemed to play up to their best opponents—beating Texas, West Virginia, and Missouri, and only losing to the Sooners by one point—while also losing to teams like Kansas State, Baylor, and TCU.

Oklahoma State's 2019 season will likely hinge on three questions. First, how will new offensive coordinator Sean Gleeson do replacing Mike Yurich? Second, can Year 2 for Jim Knowles' defense go any better than Year 1? And finally, who will win the quarterback battle to replace Taylor Cornelius?

Yurich led excellent Cowboys offenses from 2013 to 2018 before leaving for the same role at Ohio State, but there is widespread excitement about the hire of Gleeson, former coordinator at Princeton. Gleeson has led some of the most creative offenses in the country—not just the Ivy League—by employing plenty of pre-snap motions, tendency-breaking post-snap options, and the effective use of multiple quarterbacks.

That last point might be good news to the contenders for the starting quarterback spot. The principal two are Spencer Sanders and Hawaii graduate transfer Dru Brown, who will continue to battle it out through fall camp. Brown was prolific at Hawaii, while Sanders seems to offer more potential with his legs and as a long-term starter in Stillwater. Based on the limited data we have through practice observations and the spring game, it looks like either choice should allow the Cowboys to continue to operate at a high level. Either quarterback will benefit from the return of three of the top four receivers, including star Tylan Wallace, as well as running back Chuba Hubbard, who was an extremely efficient backup to Justice Hill.

It's now Knowles' second year as defensive coordinator, and Oklahoma State has a challenge to get back to the standard set by previous defenses. In particular, the Cowboys' run defense (91st in rushing S&P+) and ability to generate havoc—something they used to do well—fell off significantly last year, undermining the defense as a whole. There's some turnover at linebacker and on the defensive line (including tackles for loss leader Jordan Brailford), so Knowles will really be counting on some of the younger guys to step up.

28. Oregon Ducks (8-4, 6-3)

2019 Projections

F/+	28.6 (28)
FEI	0.19 (36)
S&P+	13.8 (20)
Total Wins	8.2
Conf Wins	6.0
SOS	.103 (33)
Conf SOS	.196 (42)
Div Champ	12%
Conf Champ	7%
CFP Berth	3%

Projection Factors

2018 F/+	15.0 (42)
2018 FEI	0.12 (47)
2018 S&P+	7.3 (41)
5-Year F/+	20.9 (25)
5-Year FEI	0.26 (27)
5-Year S&P+	12.6 (25)
2-Yr/5-Yr Recruiting	16/19
Ret. Offense	73% (37)
Ret. Defense	71% (46)
Ret. Total	72% (32)

Projected Win Likelihood by Game

Date	Opponent (Proj Rank)	PWL	Projected Loss / Projected Win
Aug 31	vs Auburn (8)	23%	
Sep 7	vs Nevada (84)	96%	
Sep 14	vs Montana (FCS)	100%	
Sep 21	at Stanford (24)	40%	
Oct 5	vs California (68)	89%	
Oct 11	vs Colorado (75)	92%	
Oct 19	at Washington (11)	20%	
Oct 26	vs Washington St. (26)	57%	
Nov 2	at USC (33)	51%	
Nov 16	vs Arizona (60)	86%	
Nov 23	at Arizona St. (47)	65%	
Nov 30	vs Oregon St. (110)	99%	

The 2018 season looked like the potential breakthrough for Oregon. Quarterback Justin Herbert was getting Heisman and first-round draft buzz and the defense was entering Year 2 with Jim Leavitt with hopes of fielding a solid unit for the first time in several years. Herbert ended up having a solid statistical season, but the Ducks took four losses in Pac-12 play with losses to two of their three main competitors in the North (Washington State and Stanford), while Leavitt was fired. They still finished 9-4, but that includes three wins from an easy non-conference slate and a 7-6 victory over a Michigan State team that looked sort of hopeful on defense but bleak on offense.

However, the Ducks played a lot of younger players in the 2018 season that are now back for 2019. The entire offensive line returns, headlined by left tackle Penei Sewell, who started six games as a true freshman and is the future of Ducks offensive football with his run-blocking talent at 6-foot-6 and 345 pounds. Star receiver Dillon Mitchell graduated, but running back C.J. Verdell is back after rushing for 1,018 yards. The next four receivers also come back. Perhaps most importantly, Herbert is returning in hopes of having a big senior season that can realize his goals for his college career and his standing in the NFL draft.

The defense also played a lot of youth in 2018 and now has multiple starters back. The five main defensive backs in the secondary had 14 interceptions, and the four players responsible for 11 of those picks are back, headlined by safety Jevon Holland (five). Leading tackler Troy Dye will also be back for his fourth consecutive season as a starter at linebacker. He has seen everything the Pac-12 will throw at Oregon and will be able to help new defensive coordinator Andy Avalos (Boise State) get their players lined up.

Oregon has a much tougher non-conference schedule this coming season that includes Auburn and Nevada, plus a road trip against Washington. But that should be navigable with a senior-led team in Year 2 under head coach Mario Cristobal.

29. South Carolina Gamecocks (6-6, 3-5)

2019 Projections

F/+	27.3 (29)
FEI	0.14 (42)
S&P+	14.9 (18)
Total Wins	5.8
Conf Wins	3.2
SOS	.012 (3)
Conf SOS	.030 (6)
Div Champ	1%
Conf Champ	1%
CFP Berth	0%

Projection Factors

2018 F/+	18.3 (38)
2018 FEI	0.25 (34)
2018 S&P+	14.9 (20)
5-Year F/+	3.5 (59)
5-Year FEI	0.02 (60)
5-Year S&P+	7.9 (40)
2-Yr/5-Yr Recruiting	18/21
Ret. Offense	68% (51)
Ret. Defense	64% (64)
Ret. Total	66% (45)

Projected Win Likelihood by Game

Date	Opponent (Proj Rank)	PWL	Projected Loss / Projected Win
Aug 31	vs N. Carolina (77)	88%	
Sep 7	vs Ch. Southern (FCS)	100%	
Sep 14	vs Alabama (1)	21%	
Sep 21	at Missouri (15)	23%	
Sep 28	vs Kentucky (38)	68%	
Oct 12	at Georgia (3)	11%	
Oct 19	vs Florida (12)	33%	
Oct 26	at Tennessee (40)	56%	
Nov 2	vs Vanderbilt (61)	85%	
Nov 9	vs Appalachian St. (21)	49%	
Nov 16	at Texas A&M (16)	23%	
Nov 30	vs Clemson (2)	22%	

S&P+ and FEI differ a good bit in their assessment of Will Muschamp's Gamecocks, same as they did last season. In the 2019 projections, S&P+ rates South Carolina at 18th, while FEI has them all the way down at 42nd. Last season S&P+ rated them at 20th, while FEI had them at 43rd. While the metrics obviously capture different things (FEI is possession-based while S&P+ incorporates both drive and per-play data), they also have different adjustments for conference play, which could form part of their disagreement here. Regardless, that range—18th to 42nd—represents the likely floor and ceiling for the Gamecocks' 2019 team.

South Carolina was a weird team in 2018. They finished as the third-best team (per F/+) to go 7-6 (an unlikely list that also includes Oklahoma State and Michigan State). They basically traded wins and losses for the entire year, which was probably a frustrating watching experience week-to-week for fans.

The Gamecocks had very clearly defined strengths and weaknesses, rather than being just pretty good all around. The pretty good areas included: offensive and defensive passing (22nd and 34th in passing S&P+), creating and preventing explosive plays (29th and 12th in marginal explosiveness), and stopping teams during scoring opportunities (36th in points per scoring opportunity). The pretty bad areas included: the ground game (87th and 85th in rushing S&P+) and efficiency on both sides of the ball, especially on standard downs (65th and 125th in marginal efficiency, and 81st and 88th in standard downs success rate).

Personnel-wise, don't expect the Gamecocks to look all that much different in 2019, for better and worse. Quarterback Jake Bentley, who led that top-25 passing offense, is back, along with two of his top three receivers, as Shi Smith and Bryan Edwards will try to replace top target Deebo Samuel. Both had similar catch rates and average yards per catch, so as long as a third receiver pops up, I wouldn't expect too much of a drop-off even without Samuel's explosive talent. It's a similar story for the running backs, where the top three—even though likely starter A.J. Turner spent time with the cornerbacks during spring practice—should remain the same from last season, and all rotate once again. The offensive line should be set following a strong spring. Besides general improvement running the ball, South Carolina's offense could benefit most from sticking to an identity. Muschamp never seemed fully behind a pass-heavy, hurry-up offense despite his obvious talent at receiver and quarterback.

Defensively it's a little more uncertain. The defensive line looks relatively strong, especially if some of the young tackles step up to their recruiting ratings. But there's some uncertainty behind them as there's basically no depth at corner behind the starting two, and there's still a little uncertainty at linebacker as well.

30. Utah State Aggies (9-3, 6-2)

2019 Projections

F/+	26.9 (30)
FEI	0.35 (23)
S&P+	7.6 (42)
Total Wins	9.2
Conf Wins	6.4
SOS	.220 (65)
Conf SOS	.553 (76)
Div Champ	25%
Conf Champ	16%
CFP Berth	1%

Projection Factors

2018 F/+	38.9 (19)
2018 FEI	0.65 (9)
2018 S&P+	14.2 (21)
5-Year F/+	8.3 (47)
5-Year FEI	0.04 (58)
5-Year S&P+	2.5 (63)
2-Yr/5-Yr Recruiting	105/103
Ret. Offense	46% (110)
Ret. Defense	63% (68)
Ret. Total	54% (103)

Projected Win Likelihood by Game

Date	Opponent (Proj Rank)	PWL
Aug 30	at Wake Forest (72)	81%
Sep 7	vs Stony Brook (FCS)	100%
Sep 21	at San Diego St. (57)	71%
Sep 28	vs Colorado St. (106)	99%
Oct 5	at LSU (6)	14%
Oct 19	vs Nevada (84)	95%
Oct 26	at Air Force (79)	85%
Nov 2	vs BYU (50)	80%
Nov 9	at Fresno St. (41)	56%
Nov 16	vs Wyoming (93)	97%
Nov 23	vs Boise St. (17)	41%
Nov 30	at New Mexico (115)	99%

The Aggies of Utah State had a phenomenal 2018 season, going 11-2 and winning the New Mexico Bowl against North Texas 52-13. Head coach Matt Wells and his staff, including both coordinators, parlayed that success into a promotion and departed to take over at Texas Tech. Utah State immediately replaced them with Gary Andersen, the coach who initially got the ball rolling at the program and had hired such assistants as Matt Wells and Dave Aranda. Andersen was fresh off a disappointing run at Oregon State and readily available, and he filled out his staff quickly with former Boise State quarterback and well-traveled assistant Mike Sanford Jr. as offensive coordinator and former BYU and NFL linebacker Justin Ena as his defensive coordinator.

The 2018 Aggies relied on an up-tempo spread under offensive coordinator David Yost (now at Texas Tech) and scored 47.5 points per game. The offense will change, but quarterback Jordan Love is back after throwing for 3,567 yards at 8.6 yards per attempt with 32 touchdowns to six interceptions and adding seven rushing touchdowns. The Aggies had two running backs split duties, and one of them (senior Gerold Bright) returns, although much of the receiving corps, versatile tight end Dax Raymond, and every offensive lineman save for left tackle Alfred Edwards all graduated.

The main strength of Utah State over the years has been their defense, first established by Andersen himself and carried on by Wells. The defense left for him also lost a lot of senior starters but retains three of the best players. Inside linebacker David Woodward is back after leading the team in tackles (134) and finishing second in tackles for loss (12.5) and sacks (5.0). Disruptive defensive end Tipa Galeai is also back after inflicting 13.5 tackles for loss and 10.0 sacks on the Aggies' opponents in 2018. Finally, cornerback D.J. Williams returns after picking off four passes and breaking up 11.

All the resources and many of the players that helped Andersen initially turn Utah State into an unexpected Mountain West contender are there for him to maintain the tradition.

31. Memphis Tigers (10-2, 7-1)

2019 Projections

F/+	24.6 (31)
FEI	0.14 (41)
S&P+	12.3 (26)
Total Wins	10.4
Conf Wins	6.8
SOS	.654 (116)
Conf SOS	.747 (96)
Div Champ	87%
Conf Champ	37%
CFP Berth	2%

Projection Factors

2018 F/+	12.0 (47)
2018 FEI	0.05 (59)
2018 S&P+	9.2 (36)
5-Year F/+	18.6 (30)
5-Year FEI	0.24 (30)
5-Year S&P+	7.7 (41)
2-Yr/5-Yr Recruiting	75/72
Ret. Offense	79% (23)
Ret. Defense	82% (12)
Ret. Total	80% (7)

Projected Win Likelihood by Game

Date	Opponent (Proj Rank)	PWL
Aug 31	vs Ole Miss (35)	61%
Sep 7	vs Southern (FCS)	100%
Sep 14	at S. Alabama (126)	99%
Sep 26	vs Navy (103)	99%
Oct 5	at UL-Monroe (105)	99%
Oct 12	at Temple (55)	68%
Oct 19	vs Tulane (97)	98%
Oct 26	at Tulsa (99)	97%
Nov 2	vs SMU (94)	97%
Nov 16	at Houston (66)	74%
Nov 23	at South Florida (83)	85%
Nov 29	vs Cincinnati (39)	65%

Memphis looks to be one of the top Group of 5 teams heading into 2019. Playing Central Florida twice and a few close losses last season (including losses to Navy, Central Florida, and Wake Forest by a combined five points) depressed their overall win total, but the Tigers still finished second in the AAC and 47th in F/+.

Now almost everyone returns for 2019, with 79 percent of offensive production and 82 percent of defensive production, which is seventh-most in the FBS. Former four-star quarterback Brady White was granted another year by the NCAA. Second-string running back Patrick Taylor Jr. also returns (and he had over 1,100 yards last season), as does basically every top receiver and Memphis's top havoc-producers on defense.

In fact, 2019's team should be roughly the same as 2018's, minus senior linebacker and top tackler Curtis Akins and running backs Darrell Henderson and Tony Pollard, both of whom were drafted. The loss of Akins shouldn't hurt quite as bad as the departures on offense. The defense wasn't really all that great last year anyway, ranking 87th in overall defensive S&P+ and particularly struggling with explosive plays (95th in marginal explosiveness) and at allowing points during scoring opportunities (averaging 5.04 points allowed every time an opponent crossed the Memphis 40, 108th). They were better against the pass than the run, even with a tackling machine like Akins. But the good news is that basically everyone else

returns, so an upperclassman-laden defense should lead to slightly increased expectations for 2019.

On the other hand, Henderson was a big loss. Henderson averaged 8.9 yards per carry and 12.2 highlight yards per opportunity—and gained at least 4 yards a carry on over half of his carries (50.5 percent). Memphis' heavy rushing attack meant that Henderson would total nearly 2,000 yards on the season. Pollard was also drafted; he had the third-most carries and second-most receiving yards on the team, and he had the highest opportunity rate of the top three backs. So we can't discount their departures, either in the passing game, and for the likely hit to Memphis' rushing marginal explosiveness—which was first in the country.

That said, Taylor is a huge back at 6-foot-3 and over 220 pounds, and averaged 5.4 yards per carry last year. They just need to find a complementary explosive back—but they've got plenty of sophomores and freshmen to choose from. Central Florida is still Central Florida, and Cincinnati is gaining ground, but don't be surprised if Memphis challenges again in an exciting AAC race.

32. Texas Longhorns (7-5, 5-4)

2019 Projections

F/+	24.6 (32)
FEI	0.24 (30)
S&P+	8.9 (35)
Total Wins	7.4
Conf Wins	5.2
SOS	.090 (25)
Conf SOS	.156 (34)
Div Champ	-
Conf Champ	3%
CFP Berth	1%

Projection Factors

2018 F/+	33.5 (25)
2018 FEI	0.37 (28)
2018 S&P+	11.3 (32)
5-Year F/+	13.4 (37)
5-Year FEI	0.10 (47)
5-Year S&P+	9.0 (38)
2-Yr/5-Yr Recruiting	4/9
Ret. Offense	57% (88)
Ret. Defense	40% (122)
Ret. Total	48% (121)

Projected Win Likelihood by Game

Date	Opponent (Proj Rank)	PWL
Aug 31	vs Louisiana Tech (85)	94%
Sep 7	vs LSU (6)	23%
Sep 14	vs Rice (128)	99%
Sep 21	vs Oklahoma St. (27)	50%
Oct 5	at West Virginia (25)	34%
Oct 12	vs Oklahoma (4)	16%
Oct 19	vs Kansas (111)	99%
Oct 26	at TCU (36)	46%
Nov 9	vs Kansas St. (62)	83%
Nov 16	at Iowa St. (43)	55%
Nov 23	at Baylor (44)	57%
Nov 29	vs Texas Tech (56)	81%

The statistical projections don't like Texas as much as the many pundits who were impressed by Texas' 2018 victories over playoff-bound Oklahoma (48-45 in the Red River Shootout) and playoff near-miss Georgia (28-21 in the Sugar Bowl) do. Second-year head coach Tom Herman filled out the 2018 roster by adding a grad transfer left tackle and running back, which helped the Longhorns go from 81st in offensive S&P+ in 2017 to 27th in 2018. The defense had to replace star players at cornerback, free safety, middle linebacker, and nose tackle, slipping from 14th in defensive S&P+ in 2017 to 44th in 2018.

Herman's 2018 and 2019 recruiting classes were both ranked in the top five, but the big question in Texas is whether his reloaded roster has enough quality veterans to support another leap from Big 12 contender to Big 12 champion and playoff team. The best case to be made that it does starts with junior quarterback Sam Ehlinger, who had 3,292 passing yards, 25 passing touchdowns, and 16 rushing touchdowns in 2018. The now-third-year starter has a Tim Tebow-like ap-

proach as a downhill, between-the-tackles runner who made short-yardage scenarios a veritable cinch for the Longhorns. Ehlinger will also be working with his No. 2 and 3 receivers from 2018, seniors Collin Johnson (985 receiving yards, seven touchdowns) and Devin Duvernay (546 receiving yards, four touchdowns). The Longhorns added another grad transfer to the offensive line with two-time All-ACC guard Parker Braun from Georgia Tech; he'll help sophomore running back Keaontay Ingram (708 rushing yards at 5.0 yards per carry) try to become a feature back.

The bigger questions are on defense, where the Longhorns lose eight senior starters. Former blue-chip sophomores are now positioned to lead the defense at rush linebacker, nickel, free safety, joker safety, both cornerback positions, and perhaps even nose tackle. Counting on that many second-year players to be ready to anchor a unit is certainly a tall order. Texas does have seniors at inside linebacker (Jeffrey McCulloch, 33 tackles in 2018), defensive line (Malcolm Roach, 24 tackles), and strong safety (Brandon Jones, 70 tackles) to lead the way. The schedule includes a home date with LSU but only takes the Longhorns outside of the state of Texas on two occasions, to play a rebuilding West Virginia team on the road and to face Iowa State. Certain aspects of these Longhorns appear a year away still, but if a few youngsters break out the schedule is set up to speed them on their return journey to national prominence.

33. USC Trojans (7-5, 5-4)

2019 Projections

F/+	23.3 (33)
FEI	0.16 (40)
S&P+	10.7 (29)
Total Wins	6.7
Conf Wins	5.2
SOS	.087 (24)
Conf SOS	.218 (48)
Div Champ	15%
Conf Champ	7%
CFP Berth	3%

Projection Factors

2018 F/+	9.8 (52)
2018 FEI	-0.08 (78)
2018 S&P+	9.7 (34)
5-Year F/+	31.4 (14)
5-Year FEI	0.39 (16)
5-Year S&P+	17.0 (14)
2-Yr/5-Yr Recruiting	15/4
Ret. Offense	79% (21)
Ret. Defense	43% (117)
Ret. Total	61% (79)

Projected Win Likelihood by Game

Date	Opponent (Proj Rank)	PWL	Projected Loss	Projected Win
Aug 31	vs Fresno St. (41)	66%		
Sep 7	vs Stanford (24)	47%		
Sep 14	at BYU (50)	62%		
Sep 20	vs Utah (19)	39%		
Sep 28	at Washington (11)	15%		
Oct 12	at Notre Dame (10)	14%		
Oct 19	vs Arizona (60)	81%		
Oct 25	at Colorado (75)	78%		
Nov 2	vs Oregon (28)	49%		
Nov 9	at Arizona St. (47)	57%		
Nov 16	at California (68)	74%		
Nov 23	vs UCLA (64)	83%		

2019 hasn't been all that great to the Trojans (and really, 2018 wasn't either). USC finished 5-7, losing five of their last six games, and missed a bowl game. That was despite having the third-highest percentage of blue-chip recruits of any team in the country, with 71 percent of players rated as four or five stars by the 247 Sports Composite. Then, to add insult to injury, Kliff Kingsbury, USC's perfect offensive coordinator hire, left for the Arizona Cardinals head coaching job before coaching a single practice. Of course, missing a bowl, along with the uncertainty surrounding head coach Clay Helton's long-term future, led to USC's worst recruiting class in years—20th, with seven four-stars and 18 three-stars (just a 28 percent blue-chip rate). That included the drama of five-star early enrollee receiver Bru McCoy leaving for Texas, too.

It was a rough couple of months, but there are hints that things are starting to look up. After Kingsbury left, the Trojans reinforced their commitment to the Air Raid by snatching up the next young up-and-coming Air Raider, Graham Harrell. Harrell, the record-setting Texas Tech quarterback, most recently coached quarterbacks and led the offense at North Texas. Harrell is only 34 and doesn't have the sustained record of success that Kingsbury did, but Trojans fans should at least be encouraged that Helton is committing to an offensive identity.

And it's an offensive identity that should fit extremely well with the talent on hand. Harrell will inherit former five-star quarterback JT Daniels, who reclassified to the 2018 recruiting class and started last season, and Jack Sears, who looked good in his start filling in for an injured Daniels last year. Either one has significant upside in Harrell's offense—particularly given his receiving corps. Last year's starting receiver trio of Tyler Vaughns, Amon-Ra St. Brown, and Michael Pittman Jr. all return, which is really a nightmare for Pac-12 opponents given how many passes they are likely to see in a game.

It's a reset year on defense, as only 43 percent of last year's production returns for 2019 (118th). That includes the loss of Cameron Smith and Porter Gustin at linebacker, as well as basically the entire secondary, with four starters departing. USC isn't short on talent though, as a number of young, former top-rated recruits now have a chance to take on starting roles. Defensive linemen Jay Tufele and Marlon Tuipulotu, linebacker Palaie Gaoteote IV, safety Talanoa Hufanga, and corners Olaijah Griffin and Issac Taylor-Stuart were all among the top high school players in the country, and now they should all challenge for starring roles.

Last year's defense struggled to create much pressure (35th in havoc rate) and was weak against the run (68th in rushing defensive S&P+), all too often allowing explosive plays (110th in rushing marginal explosiveness). So there was room for improvement, and maybe some youth in the mix could help. But the strength of last year's defense was in the secondary, which is basically all gone—so nothing is a sure thing.

Given the offensive transition and amount of production needing to be replaced on defense, this likely isn't the year for USC to challenge Washington or Oregon for the conference championship. But then again, with this much talent on the roster, who knows how much progress the team will have made by November?

34. North Carolina State Wolfpack (9-3, 6-2)

2019 Projections

F/+	22.8 (34)
FEI	0.29 (27)
S&P+	6.3 (47)
Total Wins	8.8
Conf Wins	5.5
SOS	.244 (71)
Conf SOS	.344 (57)
Div Champ	6%
Conf Champ	5%
CFP Berth	3%

Projection Factors

2018 F/+	22.4 (37)
2018 FEI	0.33 (30)
2018 S&P+	9.4 (35)
5-Year F/+	18.6 (29)
5-Year FEI	0.25 (28)
5-Year S&P+	9.9 (35)
2-Yr/5-Yr Recruiting	31/42
Ret. Offense	32% (129)
Ret. Defense	74% (31)
Ret. Total	53% (109)

Projected Win Likelihood by Game

Date	Opponent (Proj Rank)	PWL	Projected Loss / Projected Win
Aug 31	vs E. Carolina (107)	99%	
Sep 7	vs W. Carolina (FCS)	100%	
Sep 14	at West Virginia (25)	32%	
Sep 21	vs Ball St. (112)	99%	
Sep 28	at Florida St. (37)	44%	
Oct 10	vs Syracuse (52)	76%	
Oct 19	at Boston College (67)	73%	
Nov 2	at Wake Forest (72)	77%	
Nov 9	vs Clemson (2)	18%	
Nov 16	vs Louisville (95)	97%	
Nov 21	at Georgia Tech (69)	76%	
Nov 30	vs N. Carolina (77)	90%	

The Wolfpack have been defined for the last three years by quarterback Ryan Finley, who threw for 3,928 yards last year as a senior. Finley originally transferred in from Boise State, following offensive coordinator Eli Drinkwitz who was hired from the Broncos. But after 2018, Finley was drafted by the NFL and Drinkwitz left to become head coach at Appalachian State. So the Wolfpack will be starting over with new coordinator and a new quarterback, while head coach Dave Doeren is still in charge at the top.

Doeren opted for continuity, promoting two of his more successful offensive assistants and hiring a new quarterback coach to mold another successful starter from the list of candidates on campus. Most likely the job will go to Finley's backup Matt McKay, a redshirt sophomore from within the state. He'll be working to break in new co-stars since the Wolfpack's 1,000-yard running back Reggie Gallaspy II and two

1,000-yard wide receivers Jakobi Meyers and Kelvin Harmon all graduated. The right side of the offensive line is back and Oregon wide receiver transfer Tabari Hines will join the roster, but it'll be a fairly substantial rebuild.

The defense is another story entirely, bringing back the majority of their impact players and starters from the 54th-ranked defense by S&P+. Star linebacker Germaine Pratt led the team in tackles, tackles for loss, and sacks, but he now moves on. However, both cornerbacks and most of the team's leading tacklers at safety and linebacker will be back. Headlining the unit will be defensive linemen James Smith-Williams and Larrell Murchison, who combined for 17 tackles for loss and 10 sacks a year ago. Doeren has maintained a steady pipeline of big, impact defensive linemen to lead his defenses at North Carolina State, and that building block looks strong and intact for the 2019 season.

35. Ole Miss Rebels (6-6, 3-5)

2019 Projections

F/+	22.7 (35)
FEI	0.21 (34)
S&P+	8.5 (39)
Total Wins	5.9
Conf Wins	2.6
SOS	.012 (2)
Conf SOS	.016 (1)
Div Champ	0%
Conf Champ	0%
CFP Berth	0%

Projection Factors

2018 F/+	0.4 (65)
2018 FEI	0.08 (52)
2018 S&P+	9.8 (33)
5-Year F/+	24.4 (22)
5-Year FEI	0.34 (19)
5-Year S&P+	16.3 (17)
2-Yr/5-Yr Recruiting	27/24
Ret. Offense	30% (130)
Ret. Defense	71% (41)
Ret. Total	51% (116)

Projected Win Likelihood by Game

Date	Opponent (Proj Rank)	PWL	Projected Loss / Projected Win
Aug 31	at Memphis (31)	39%	
Sep 7	vs Arkansas (65)	83%	
Sep 14	vs SE Louisiana (FCS)	100%	
Sep 21	vs California (68)	85%	
Sep 28	at Alabama (1)	8%	
Oct 5	vs Vanderbilt (61)	81%	
Oct 12	at Missouri (15)	18%	
Oct 19	vs Texas A&M (16)	31%	
Nov 2	at Auburn (8)	12%	
Nov 9	vs N. Mexico St. (125)	99%	
Nov 16	vs LSU (6)	21%	
Nov 28	at Mississippi St. (7)	11%	

Few teams have been hurt more by departures over the last two years than Ole Miss. The Rebels had high-profile transfers before last season and their bowl ban, losing stars such as quarterback Shea Patterson to Michigan and Van Jefferson to Florida. It was maybe worse in 2019, with the departure of

quarterback Jordan Ta'amu; three top receivers in A.J. Brown, D.K. Metcalf, and DaMarkus Lodge; tackle Greg Little; and defensive back Zedrick Woods.

Blame it partly on the personnel and coaching losses prior to the 2018 season and partly on uninspired offensive and defensive scheming, but the Rebels finished just 5-7 and 66th in the F/+ rankings last season. That included predictable losses to Alabama and LSU, but also to South Carolina, Vanderbilt, and worst, Mississippi State in the Egg Bowl 35-3. And that was with an offense that ranked sixth overall in offensive S&P+—seventh in marginal efficiency and ninth in marginal explosiveness. Take away the best parts of that offense—Ta'amu, Little, Lodge, Brown, and Metcalf—and what are you left with?

Even with all of the departures, the Rebels have a shocking amount of talent on offense. Quarterback Matt Corral had a strong if brief debut for Ole Miss, and the former top-rated quarterback recruit now has the benefit of playing in Rich Rodriguez's offense. The Rebels also have running back Scottie Phillips, who was explosive with 6.4 highlight yards per opportunity last season, and will likely have five-star freshman back Jerrion Ealy (who was thought to be a high baseball draft pick for a while) too. Elijah Moore and Braylon Sanders should be a nice duo at receiver as well.

So the offense should still have some upside despite the heavy losses. But is there any hope for a defense that was 90th in defensive S&P+ last season? Well, the good news is that 71 percent of last year's production returns in 2019, and there should be plenty of upperclassmen for new defensive coordinator Mike MacIntyre to work with.

MacIntyre is a former Colorado head coach, giving the Rebels two former head coaches as coordinators. Sometimes that works really well, but other times that can be a lot of head coaches in one room. MacIntyre hasn't been a defensive coordinator since 2009 with Duke, but his Colorado defenses were usually solid, given their talent levels. There aren't a ton of obvious stars defensively, but just an improvement to "decent" could do a world of good for the Rebels. That is, of course, if they can survive an insanely talented division slate, with LSU and Texas A&M looking strong, and Alabama continuing to be Alabama.

36. TCU Horned Frogs (8-4, 5-4)

2019 Projections

F/+	22.0 (36)
FEI	0.17 (38)
S&P+	9.2 (38)
Total Wins	7.6
Conf Wins	4.9
SOS	.132 (43)
Conf SOS	.142 (31)
Div Champ	-
Conf Champ	2%
CFP Berth	1%

Projection Factors

2018 F/+	7.8 (56)
2018 FEI	-0.01 (65)
2018 S&P+	6.9 (43)
5-Year F/+	28.2 (18)
5-Year FEI	0.35 (18)
5-Year S&P+	15.8 (19)
2-Yr/5-Yr Recruiting	30/31
Ret. Offense	73% (36)
Ret. Defense	47% (111)
Ret. Total	60% (85)

Projected Win Likelihood by Game

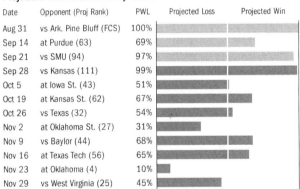

Date	Opponent (Proj Rank)	PWL
Aug 31	vs Ark. Pine Bluff (FCS)	100%
Sep 14	at Purdue (63)	69%
Sep 21	vs SMU (94)	97%
Sep 28	vs Kansas (111)	99%
Oct 5	at Iowa St. (43)	51%
Oct 19	at Kansas St. (62)	67%
Oct 26	vs Texas (32)	54%
Nov 2	at Oklahoma St. (27)	31%
Nov 9	vs Baylor (44)	68%
Nov 16	at Texas Tech (56)	65%
Nov 23	at Oklahoma (4)	10%
Nov 29	vs West Virginia (25)	45%

Gary Patterson's Horned Frogs tend to have up-and-down cycles that hinge on whether they are fielding experienced offensive lines and quarterbacks who can make the most of his perennially effective defenses. The 2018 team wasn't ready to do so after losing several highly experienced offensive linemen and two-year starting quarterback Kenny Hill (who took his own lumps in 2016). They had to shuffle players across the line due to youth and injuries, and sophomore quarterback Shawn Robinson had eight interceptions and three lost fumbles in seven games before a nagging shoulder injury ended his season. They replaced him with Penn transfer Michael Collins, who wasn't the same kind of runner but protected the ball better until he too went down with an injury.

The 2019 team won't have Robinson, who has transferred to Missouri, but they added Kansas State grad transfer quarterback Alex Delton, blue-chip freshman and early enrollee Max Duggan, and Ohio State transfer quarterback Matthew Bald-

win (NCAA waiver pending). The Frogs will likely choose their quarterback based on which player will best protect the ball and take good care of an otherwise great situation. The offensive line is rebuilt now and coming off a strong performance in the Cheez-It Bowl against Cal while leading running backs Sewo Olonilua and Darius Anderson and star receiver Jalen Reagor (1,061 receiving yards and nine scores despite the tumult at quarterback) return.

Patterson's defense sent both defensive ends Ben Banogu and L.J. Collier to the NFL, along with linebacker/defensive end hybrid Ty Summers. But they also return breakout 2017 star Ross Blacklock at defensive tackle after an Achilles injury robbed him of 2018, plus fellow tackle Corey Bethley, a pair of linebackers, both cornerbacks, and a promising safety in Innis Gaines. The best bet is that TCU will once again play their 4-2-5 defense with precision. If one of their four options at quarterback pans out this team is primed to have an up cycle again.

37. Florida State Seminoles (7-5, 5-3)

2019 Projections

F/+	22.0 (37)
FEI	0.12 (45)
S&P+	10.9 (28)
Total Wins	7.2
Conf Wins	4.8
SOS	.072 (17)
Conf SOS	.197 (43)
Div Champ	2%
Conf Champ	2%
CFP Berth	1%

Projection Factors

2018 F/+	-12.8 (88)
2018 FEI	-0.12 (85)
2018 S&P+	1.4 (71)
5-Year F/+	26.3 (20)
5-Year FEI	0.37 (17)
5-Year S&P+	20.0 (8)
2-Yr/5-Yr Recruiting	13/5
Ret. Offense	74% (33)
Ret. Defense	80% (17)
Ret. Total	77% (13)

Projected Win Likelihood by Game

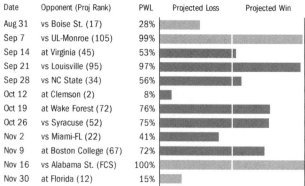

Date	Opponent (Proj Rank)	PWL	Projected Loss	Projected Win
Aug 31	vs Boise St. (17)	28%		
Sep 7	vs UL-Monroe (105)	99%		
Sep 14	at Virginia (45)	53%		
Sep 21	vs Louisville (95)	97%		
Sep 28	vs NC State (34)	56%		
Oct 12	at Clemson (2)	8%		
Oct 19	at Wake Forest (72)	76%		
Oct 26	vs Syracuse (52)	75%		
Nov 2	vs Miami-FL (22)	41%		
Nov 9	at Boston College (67)	72%		
Nov 16	vs Alabama St. (FCS)	100%		
Nov 30	at Florida (12)	15%		

Florida State? What are you doing down here?

After ranking no worse than 19th in F/+ between 2010 and 2016, the Seminoles fell to 35th in Jimbo Fisher's last season in 2017, then all the way down to 88th last year in Willie Taggart's debut season. 88th in F/+ was good for 5-7 as the Seminoles missed a bowl game. Despite continuing to recruit at a high level—last year's team was composed of 67 percent blue-chip recruits, fifth-most in the country, according to SB Nation's Bud Elliot—the later Fisher years had seen a noticeable drop-off in talent at a few key positions.

Nowhere was that more apparent than on the offensive line. The line struggled with injuries before and during the season so much that the starting lineup seemed to change each week. As a result, the line gave up 36 sacks on the year, which was tied for 109th in the country, and they allowed a havoc play on exactly one in five plays, which ranked ninth-worst in the country. Despite elite offensive skill talent everywhere you could look, Florida State was 124th in offensive success rate. With so little offensive production, the defense was often put in tough situations, leading to a decline to 44th both in passing S&P+ and defensive FEI. This was a situation where a slow decline in the team's foundation—its offensive line—eventually manifested in systemic problems.

So on its surface, a projection of 38th in F/+ for 2019 suggests that the Seminoles should improve to roughly their 2017 levels. And in a down ACC, maybe that translates to a big jump in win totals.

But a jump in win totals will require consistency at the line and at quarterback. They should at least have some more bodies in the O-line room this year, with a massive offensive line recruiting class (although you never want to count on freshman offensive linemen to play key roles) and several transfers, including former Northern Illinois lineman Ryan Roberts. And with Deondre Francois dismissed, the offense should belong to James Blackman (Wisconsin transfer Alex Hornibrook will likely back him up). Blackman only saw extensive time against North Carolina State, but he lit up the Wolfpack defense for 424 yards. It's not enough to project too much about his performance in 2019, although he should theoretically have an improved offensive line as well as star receiver Tamorrion Terry to throw to. Add in explosive contributions from junior Cam Akers—an all-world running back recruit who has been held back by the aforementioned offensive line troubles—and you have the makings of a potentially exciting offense. Kendal Briles also joins the staff as a new coordinator, which also increases the Seminoles potential for success in 2019 … although he also brings all of the off-the-field baggage from his time coaching under his father at Baylor.

With this Seminoles team you get the sense that the defense has most of what it needs for success, assuming the offense gets itself together. 37th in defensive S&P+ is obviously much lower than the standard in Tallahassee, but the Seminoles return 80 percent of their defensive production from 2018 (17th-most overall), and the only really irreplaceable name to leave over the offseason might be pass-rusher Brian Burns, with his ten sacks on the season. Even with Burns, the defense only ranked 30th in defensive line havoc rate, so there's still a gap to fill for a young pass-rusher.

When you put all of that together, you get the picture of a team that should take significant steps forward in 2019—stability at quarterback, an improved offensive line, a new offensive scheme that should highlight the depth of skill talent, a more experienced defense, and a weaker ACC—but also one that probably won't be ready to challenge Clemson at the top of the conference.

38. Kentucky Wildcats (7-5, 3-5)

2019 Projections

F/+	20.7 (38)
FEI	0.16 (39)
S&P+	8.8 (37)
Total Wins	6.9
Conf Wins	3.1
SOS	.046 (11)
Conf SOS	.048 (10)
Div Champ	1%
Conf Champ	1%
CFP Berth	0%

Projection Factors

2018 F/+	29.2 (30)
2018 FEI	0.35 (29)
2018 S&P+	13.1 (25)
5-Year F/+	-2.9 (75)
5-Year FEI	-0.04 (72)
5-Year S&P+	3.9 (54)
2-Yr/5-Yr Recruiting	34/33
Ret. Offense	64% (64)
Ret. Defense	39% (127)
Ret. Total	51% (114)

Projected Win Likelihood by Game

Date	Opponent (Proj Rank)	PWL
Aug 31	vs Toledo (76)	87%
Sep 7	vs E. Michigan (98)	98%
Sep 14	vs Florida (12)	25%
Sep 21	at Mississippi St. (7)	10%
Sep 28	at S. Carolina (29)	32%
Oct 12	vs Arkansas (65)	81%
Oct 19	at Georgia (3)	7%
Oct 26	vs Missouri (15)	28%
Nov 9	vs Tennessee (40)	61%
Nov 16	at Vanderbilt (61)	65%
Nov 23	vs Tenn-Martin (FCS)	100%
Nov 30	vs Louisville (95)	97%

The 2018 Kentucky Wildcats were far and away the best team that Mark Stoops has coached since he took over the program in 2013. After back-to-back 7-6 seasons, they finally broke through and went 10-3. There were two big reasons for the timing of their success. One was an offense that finally found an identity as a spread-option running team. Sophomore quarterback Terry Wilson took over and offered fairly modest passing production, with eight touchdowns to 11 interceptions, but he ran the ball 135 times for 547 yards at 4.1 yards per carry (before removing sack yardage) with four touchdowns. That helped clear space for running back Benjamin Snell Jr. to run 289 times for 1,449 yards at 5.0 yards per carry with 16 touchdowns. Receiver Lynn Bowden Jr. was responsible for much of the rest of the offensive output with 67 catches for 745 yards and five touchdowns.

The offensive line that mastered their blocking schemes returns their right side and has a lot in place to help Wilson, Bowden, and new running back A.J. Rose pick up where they left off. What's concerning for this team is the loss of that other factor that helped drive them to 10 wins in 2018: outside linebacker Josh Allen. The seventh overall pick in the 2019 NFL draft had an unreal 17 sacks for Kentucky last season after having seven each of the prior two seasons. When one player is that dominant, there's typically a strong supporting cast behind him that prevented an opponent from using all their resources to take him out of the game. The 2010 Nebraska Cornhuskers had to replace Ndamukong Suh after he led the team in tackles and had 12 sacks, but actually improved because there was so much quality returning across the roster. But the Wildcats are losing six other starters on defense besides Allen, so not only will they certainly lack another generational pass-rushing talent but they may struggle to support whoever replaces him. In an improving SEC East division, Kentucky may take a step back to where they were before the magical 10-win season of 2018.

39. Cincinnati Bearcats (9-3, 6-2)

2019 Projections

F/+	20.3 (39)
FEI	0.20 (35)
S&P+	7.1 (44)
Total Wins	8.6
Conf Wins	5.9
SOS	.207 (61)
Conf SOS	.541 (73)
Div Champ	18%
Conf Champ	10%
CFP Berth	0%

Projection Factors

2018 F/+	30.1 (26)
2018 FEI	0.44 (25)
2018 S&P+	5.4 (50)
5-Year F/+	-4.0 (80)
5-Year FEI	-0.03 (69)
5-Year S&P+	1.5 (68)
2-Yr/5-Yr Recruiting	62/69
Ret. Offense	71% (42)
Ret. Defense	71% (44)
Ret. Total	71% (36)

Projected Win Likelihood by Game

Date	Opponent (Proj Rank)	PWL
Aug 29	vs UCLA (64)	80%
Sep 7	at Ohio St. (5)	9%
Sep 14	vs Miami-OH (88)	94%
Sep 28	at Marshall (80)	79%
Oct 4	vs UCF (20)	37%
Oct 12	at Houston (66)	69%
Oct 19	vs Tulsa (99)	98%
Nov 2	at E. Carolina (107)	99%
Nov 9	vs Connecticut (130)	99%
Nov 16	at South Florida (83)	82%
Nov 23	vs Temple (55)	76%
Nov 29	at Memphis (31)	35%

Luke Fickell's Bearcats were one of the bigger surprises in the Group of 5 last season, going 11-2 in just his second year. The Bearcats were definitely ahead of schedule thanks to Fickell's strong defense, which ranked seventh overall in defensive FEI and 36th in defensive S&P+ (part of the difference in S&P+ and FEI there might be because the Bearcats were excellent in terms of efficiency and overall drive success rate, but allowed some big explosive plays, ranking 77th in

IsoPPP and marginal explosiveness). The good news is that not only is Fickell staying for at least one more season (and with Ryan Day being hired at Ohio State, that door is likely closed for the immediate future), but he returns a significant amount of last season's production, ranking 36th overall. And that production was almost all from young players, suggesting that the Bearcats' success won't be limited to 2018.

Nowhere is that returning production and young talent more apparent than at the offensive skill positions. Freshman quarterback Desmond Ridder had a solid debut as a starter, displacing senior Hayden Moore. While Ridder's overall numbers won't blow your socks off, there are reasons for optimism given his high marginal efficiency and only five interceptions. Unfortunately Ridder won't have receiver Kahlil Lewis any more, but targets were widely spread between five other guys. And that includes running backs junior Michael Warren II and sophomores Tavion Thomas and Charles McClelland, not to mention Ridder's own rushing abilities. However, the offense still has a way to go, especially since they ranked just 99th in standard downs S&P+, leading to too many third-and-longs (46.7 percent). Attrition on the offensive line could be a con-

cern, but transfers and overall excellent recruiting (including Michigan transfer James Hudson) should mitigate some of the concerns.

So we're likely to see an offense improved by significant returnees and more experience at skill positions, but that faces some questions along the line. The defense looks similar in terms of line attrition, but also starts from a higher level of play than the offense. The major losses include leading tackler Malik Clements at linebacker as well as three along the line—especially Cortez Broughton, who led the team in tackles for loss by far. 2018's defense was top-20 in terms of overall havoc creation, so they will need some younger players to step up. But it's hard to bet against a Fickell-coached defense—they are bound to know their fundamentals well and certainly be near the top of the AAC in overall defensive strength.

Overall, Cincinnati's 2019 season likely boils down to how both lines can progress. Given how much Fickell likes to run the ball, can the offense replace its losses on the line and improve its efficiency? And can the defense find some havoc-producers to approach last season's stout run defense that ranked sixth overall in rushing S&P+?

40. Tennessee Volunteers (6-6, 2-6)

2019 Projections

F/+	19.2 (40)
FEI	0.02 (62)
S&P+	12.9 (21)
Total Wins	5.9
Conf Wins	2.3
SOS	.021 (6)
Conf SOS	.023 (5)
Div Champ	0%
Conf Champ	0%
CFP Berth	0%

Projection Factors

2018 F/+	-12.4 (87)
2018 FEI	-0.06 (73)
2018 S&P+	5.5 (48)
5-Year F/+	-4.0 (80)
5-Year FEI	0.10 (48)
5-Year S&P+	10.9 (29)
2-Yr/5-Yr Recruiting	20/17
Ret. Offense	91% (2)
Ret. Defense	76% (25)
Ret. Total	83% (2)

Projected Win Likelihood by Game

Date	Opponent (Proj Rank)	PWL	Projected Loss	Projected Win
Aug 31	vs Ga. State (122)	99%		
Sep 7	vs BYU (50)	71%		
Sep 14	vs Chattanooga (FCS)	100%		
Sep 21	at Florida (12)	13%		
Oct 5	vs Georgia (3)	15%		
Oct 12	vs Mississippi St. (7)	18%		
Oct 19	at Alabama (1)	6%		
Oct 26	vs S. Carolina (29)	44%		
Nov 2	vs UAB (87)	93%		
Nov 9	at Kentucky (38)	39%		
Nov 23	at Missouri (15)	15%		
Nov 30	vs Vanderbilt (61)	77%		

New head coach Jeremy Pruitt, a former Nick Saban defensive assistant, went 5-7 in Year 1 with the Volunteers. His offense ran and threw the ball decently without particularly scaring opponents with either dimension while the defense was pretty weak at most everything save for big-play prevention.

Pruitt was a former defensive backs coach who helped build big time secondaries at Florida State, Georgia, and Alabama before coming to Rocky Top, so their early success in pass defense is likely indicative of a trend. The secondary will have a pair of seniors in Nigel Warrior (safety) and Baylen Buchanan (nickel) leading a trio of sophomores who got a fair amount of action in 2018 such as cornerback Bryce Thompson, who picked off three passes. The defensive front will be rebuilt but

does have experience at inside linebacker with Daniel Bituli and Will Ignont. They will add former five-star recruit Aubrey Solomon on the line after he transferred over from Michigan, where he had flashed major potential as a freshman in 2017.

The offense will have loads of experience from 2018. Quarterback Jarrett Guarantano threw for 1,907 yards and 12 touchdowns. Their top two rushers, top three receivers, and starting tight end are all back. Left tackle Trey Smith had to step down with health issues; the Volunteers may try to replace him with five-star freshman Wanya Morris while also adding Alabama transfer Brandon Kennedy at center. If the new talent on the offensive line can start to push the pile, then the run/pass options of the Volunteers offense may come alive due to a firmer connection between their quarterback and receivers.

41. Fresno State Bulldogs (10-2, 7-1)

2019 Projections

F/+	18.6 (41)
FEI	0.22 (33)
S&P+	5.5 (51)
Total Wins	9.6
Conf Wins	6.6
SOS	.538 (108)
Conf SOS	.744 (94)
Div Champ	66%
Conf Champ	24%
CFP Berth	1%

Projection Factors

2018 F/+	44.0 (13)
2018 FEI	0.64 (10)
2018 S&P+	17.4 (16)
5-Year F/+	-6.4 (85)
5-Year FEI	-0.20 (90)
5-Year S&P+	-4.3 (87)
2-Yr/5-Yr Recruiting	86/84
Ret. Offense	34% (127)
Ret. Defense	41% (120)
Ret. Total	38% (129)

Projected Win Likelihood by Game

Date	Opponent (Proj Rank)	PWL
Aug 31	at USC (33)	34%
Sep 7	vs Minnesota (42)	61%
Sep 21	vs Sacramento St. (FCS)	100%
Sep 28	at N. Mexico St. (125)	99%
Oct 12	at Air Force (79)	78%
Oct 18	vs UNLV (104)	98%
Oct 26	vs Colorado St. (106)	98%
Nov 2	at Hawaii (102)	96%
Nov 9	vs Utah St. (30)	44%
Nov 15	at San Diego St. (57)	61%
Nov 23	vs Nevada (84)	91%
Nov 30	at San Jose St. (121)	99%

Fresno State was one of the most surprising teams of 2018, going 12-2 with only one-score losses to Minnesota and Boise State. Otherwise Fresno State took down UCLA, San Diego State, Boise State in their conference championship rematch game, and Arizona State in their bowl game. The Bulldogs largely won on the strength of an incredible defense that finished 21st in defensive FEI and 12th in S&P+. The only problem? The Bulldogs rank 129th out of 130 FBS teams in terms of returning production.

The losses are pretty devastating, with just 34 percent of offensive production returning and 41 percent on defense. That includes prolific quarterback Marcus McMaryion, who led the 16th-ranked passing S&P+ offense last year, and two of his top receivers (KeeSean Johnson and Jamire Jordan) who combined for 178 targets last season. On defense, the losses include almost the entire starting linebacker corps, including Mountain West defensive player of the year Jeff Allison, and pass breakup leader Anthoula Kelly at defensive back.

The good news is that despite all of the attrition, Jeff Tedford has developed a lot of talent in Fresno. Offensively, likely starting quarterback Jorge Reyna only threw 12 passes last season, but he'll still have a platoon of running backs to help, as well as star tight end Jared Rice. Rice was second on the team in targets and receiving yards in 2018. Defensively, while the linebacker corps is experiencing significant losses, that should be partly offset by a relatively experienced secondary, as well as tackles-for-loss leader Mykal Walker up front.

42. Minnesota Golden Gophers (7-5, 5-4)

2019 Projections

F/+	16.9 (42)
FEI	0.06 (55)
S&P+	9.5 (33)
Total Wins	7.4
Conf Wins	5.1
SOS	.182 (55)
Conf SOS	.223 (51)
Div Champ	10%
Conf Champ	4%
CFP Berth	2%

Projection Factors

2018 F/+	12.9 (45)
2018 FEI	0.07 (53)
2018 S&P+	6.3 (45)
5-Year F/+	7.0 (51)
5-Year FEI	0.05 (55)
5-Year S&P+	6.8 (45)
2-Yr/5-Yr Recruiting	38/46
Ret. Offense	90% (4)
Ret. Defense	66% (61)
Ret. Total	78% (10)

Projected Win Likelihood by Game

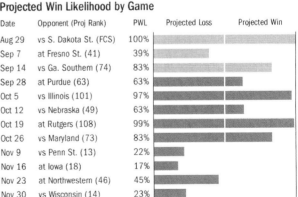

Date	Opponent (Proj Rank)	PWL
Aug 29	vs S. Dakota St. (FCS)	100%
Sep 7	at Fresno St. (41)	39%
Sep 14	vs Ga. Southern (74)	83%
Sep 28	at Purdue (63)	63%
Oct 5	vs Illinois (101)	97%
Oct 12	vs Nebraska (49)	63%
Oct 19	at Rutgers (108)	99%
Oct 26	vs Maryland (73)	83%
Nov 9	vs Penn St. (13)	22%
Nov 16	at Iowa (18)	17%
Nov 23	at Northwestern (46)	45%
Nov 30	vs Wisconsin (14)	23%

Head coach P.J. Fleck with his "row the boat" mantra started to break through the ice up in Minnesota with their 2018 season. Walk-on quarterback Alex Annexstad helped put it together. He was a local Minnesotan who went to IMG Academy in Florida and led them to an undefeated season as a senior and then came back home to Minnesota, bringing with him a pair of four-star offensive linemen: Daniel Faalele and Curtis Dunlap. Annexstad started as a true freshman, as did one of those two tackles. Faalele and Dunlap figure to comprise the right side of the 2019 offensive line, and they are notably massive. Right tackle Faalele is 6-foot-9 and 400 pounds while Dunlap is 6-foot-5 and 350 pounds. From center to left tackle, the Gophers will probably start a trio of 6-foot-5 Minnesotans who got valuable experience in

2018. Fleck also broke in a new pair of running backs last year in Mohamed Ibrahim and Bryce Williams, the former of whom rushed for over 1,000 yards at 5.7 yards per carry with nine touchdowns. The Minnesota offense includes heavy doses of run/pass options; the pass options and play-action shots typically went to Tyler Johnson, who finished with 1,169 receiving yards and 12 touchdowns, but they started a pair of freshmen with him in Rashod Bateman and Chris Autman-Bell who may get more looks in 2019. The formula will be simple: run the ball to the right side behind nearly 800 pounds of force in the freezing cold and see if opponents are even up for it.

On defense, the Gophers managed to finish 39th in S&P+. They had three particularly high-impact performers in inside linebacker Blake Cashman (graduated), defensive end Carter Coughlin (back after getting 9.5 sacks), and safety Jacob Huff (graduated). The Golden Gophers secondary is stocked with experienced players now. Star safety Antoine Winfield is healthy and hoping to lead the unit. Minnesota has the most favorable draw of the Big 10 West contenders, getting Penn State, Maryland, and Rutgers from the East and facing Wisconsin and Nebraska at home.

43. Iowa State Cyclones (7-5, 4-5)

2019 Projections

F/+	16.9 (43)
FEI	0.13 (43)
S&P+	7.2 (43)
Total Wins	6.5
Conf Wins	4.2
SOS	.106 (36)
Conf SOS	.138 (30)
Div Champ	-
Conf Champ	0%
CFP Berth	0%

Projection Factors

2018 F/+	23.8 (36)
2018 FEI	0.31 (31)
2018 S&P+	7.9 (38)
5-Year F/+	4.1 (57)
5-Year FEI	-0.05 (76)
5-Year S&P+	1.6 (67)
2-Yr/5-Yr Recruiting	52/55
Ret. Offense	53% (98)
Ret. Defense	68% (53)
Ret. Total	61% (80)

Projected Win Likelihood by Game

Date	Opponent (Proj Rank)	PWL	Projected Loss / Projected Win
Aug 31	vs Northern Iowa (FCS)	100%	
Sep 14	vs Iowa (18)	29%	
Sep 21	vs UL-Monroe (105)	98%	
Sep 28	at Baylor (44)	44%	
Oct 5	vs TCU (36)	49%	
Oct 12	at West Virginia (25)	24%	
Oct 19	at Texas Tech (56)	58%	
Oct 26	vs Oklahoma St. (27)	38%	
Nov 9	at Oklahoma (4)	7%	
Nov 16	vs Texas (32)	45%	
Nov 23	vs Kansas (111)	99%	
Nov 30	at Kansas St. (62)	60%	

The Cyclones have somehow retained 39-year-old head coach Matt Campbell for a fourth season. After a 3-9 record in Year 1, Campbell has guided the Cyclones to back-to-back 8-5 seasons that have included wins over ranked Oklahoma, TCU, and Memphis in 2017, and then Oklahoma and West Virginia last season. Early media and fans expectations have only gotten higher for 2019, with many expecting Iowa State to finish third in the conference behind Oklahoma and Texas.

The Cyclones deserve raised expectations after their unprecedented run under Campbell. Last season saw freshman Brock Purdy take over at quarterback in Week 3, and despite underwhelming offensive performances against Texas and Drake where he combined to go 25-of-45 for just 283 yards, Purdy led the 21st-ranked passing S&P+ offense. The passing game was equally as efficient as it was explosive, ranking 32nd and 28th in passing marginal efficiency and explosiveness, and Purdy completed 66.4 percent of his passes.

The problem, of course, is that the Cyclones' two best offensive skill players—receiver Hakeem Butler and running back David Montgomery—are both in the NFL now. It was great that Purdy could rely on future NFL talent as a freshman, but how will he and the offense perform without them to lean on? Iowa State's season might hinge to some degree on an answer to that question, but there are some early indications.

First, the run game really wasn't all that efficient last year, ranking just 102nd in rushing S&P+. Montgomery averaged just 4.7 yards per carry. Backup Kene Nwangwu is the likely starter; he brings slightly more explosiveness and a little less efficiency based on his limited performance in 2018 outside of kick returns. But whoever takes over could stand to add a little more efficiency to the run game.

Replacing Butler may be a little more challenging even though there are some interesting options. Senior Deshaunte Jones was the second-most targeted receiver last season, but didn't offer much in big-play ability after averaging just 8.5 yards per catch. Tarique Milton had an impressive freshman season, ranking second in receiving yards despite being just fourth in targets. And Campbell also landed commitments from JUCO transfer Darren Wilson and Arkansas transfer La'Michael Pettway, who brings some explosive-play capability (he had at least one catch of 30-plus yards in four of his last five games as a Razorback). But it's really difficult to overstate how important Butler was to the Cyclones, considering he had more receiving yards than the next four receivers combined.

Campbell's defenses have traditionally been solid, and last year's was no exception at 28th in S&P+. While Iowa State returns 68 percent of its defensive production from a year ago, there are a number of important players returning, including sack leader JaQuan Bailey, a senior-laden defensive line as a whole, and sophomore (and Freshman All-American) linebacker Mike Rose. However, depth at defensive back may be a little light—if there are any questions for a Campbell-coached Iowa State defense, it's likely in the secondary.

44. Baylor Bears (7-5, 4-5)

2019 Projections			Projection Factors		
F/+	15.8 (44)		2018 F/+	-6.3 (80)	
FEI	0.08 (51)		2018 FEI	-0.06 (77)	
S&P+	8.1 (40)		2018 S&P+	2.0 (67)	
Total Wins	7.3		5-Year F/+	10.8 (40)	
Conf Wins	4.3		5-Year FEI	0.22 (31)	
SOS	.193 (59)		5-Year S&P+	11.0 (28)	
Conf SOS	.197 (44)		2-Yr/5-Yr Recruiting	35/35	
Div Champ	-		Ret. Offense	65% (59)	
Conf Champ	1%		Ret. Defense	85% (8)	
CFP Berth	0%		Ret. Total	75% (20)	

Projected Win Likelihood by Game

Date	Opponent (Proj Rank)	PWL	Projected Loss	Projected Win
Aug 31	vs SF Austin (FCS)	100%		
Sep 7	vs UTSA (127)	99%		
Sep 21	at Rice (128)	99%		
Sep 28	vs Iowa St. (43)	56%		
Oct 5	at Kansas St. (62)	59%		
Oct 12	vs Texas Tech (56)	71%		
Oct 19	at Oklahoma St. (27)	23%		
Oct 31	vs West Virginia (25)	36%		
Nov 9	at TCU (36)	32%		
Nov 16	vs Oklahoma (4)	14%		
Nov 23	vs Texas (32)	43%		
Nov 30	at Kansas (111)	99%		

Head coach Matt Rhule has never seemed in any great rush in Waco, recruiting for upside and restocking the roster with raw athleticism with hopes of eventually molding a team with NFL talent. They have also brought in transfers every year and made some significant improvements in Year 2 with a 7-6 finish for 2018. For 2019, they'll be returning talented junior quarterback Charlie Brewer for his third year as their starter while hoping to finally field a strong defense.

The defense was Rhule's calling card at Temple, his previous job, but the Bears have lacked defensive end talent such as Haason Reddick that made the Temple defenses so effective. In 2018 they found at least three good pieces who will be back in 2019 in defensive lineman James Lynch (4.5 sacks), nickel linebacker Blake Lynch, and middle linebacker Clay Johnston (leading tackler). James Lynch played multiple positions across the defensive line but is most effective inside if the Bears can find some impact defensive ends,

while Blake Lynch and Johnston brought an impressive size/speed ratio inside at about 220 pounds apiece. Beyond finding defensive ends, the Bears also need safeties after finishing nearly dead last in IsoPPP in 2019. They committed regular busts and struggled to take clean angles against the run all season.

Baylor is also hoping to finally field a strong offensive line in 2019, but will have to replace the right side. They are hoping that left tackle Connor Galvin, who was thrust into the action last year as a true freshman, is ready to make a leap and be a top performer. Clemson transfer Jake Fruhmorgen may be a piece of the puzzle somewhere along the line, while converted tight end Sam Tecklenburg is now a third-year starter inside for the Bears. If the pieces up front fit, then Brewer has a pair of seniors to help him in wide receiver Denzel Mims (794 yards and nine touchdowns in 2018) and running back Jamycal Hasty (434 rushing yards).

45. Virginia Cavaliers (8-4, 5-3)

2019 Projections			Projection Factors		
F/+	15.7 (45)		2018 F/+	24.1 (35)	
FEI	0.08 (49)		2018 FEI	0.22 (39)	
S&P+	7.9 (41)		2018 S&P+	7.1 (42)	
Total Wins	8.0		5-Year F/+	0.4 (72)	
Conf Wins	4.9		5-Year FEI	-0.05 (74)	
SOS	.232 (67)		5-Year S&P+	1.9 (66)	
Conf SOS	.484 (64)		2-Yr/5-Yr Recruiting	55/56	
Div Champ	13%		Ret. Offense	56% (90)	
Conf Champ	3%		Ret. Defense	72% (38)	
CFP Berth	2%		Ret. Total	64% (55)	

Projected Win Likelihood by Game

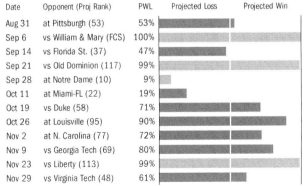

Date	Opponent (Proj Rank)	PWL	Projected Loss	Projected Win
Aug 31	at Pittsburgh (53)	53%		
Sep 6	vs William & Mary (FCS)	100%		
Sep 14	vs Florida St. (37)	47%		
Sep 21	vs Old Dominion (117)	99%		
Sep 28	at Notre Dame (10)	9%		
Oct 11	at Miami-FL (22)	19%		
Oct 19	vs Duke (58)	71%		
Oct 26	at Louisville (95)	90%		
Nov 2	at N. Carolina (77)	72%		
Nov 9	vs Georgia Tech (69)	80%		
Nov 23	vs Liberty (113)	99%		
Nov 29	vs Virginia Tech (48)	61%		

The Cavaliers managed a surprising 8-5 record in 2018, punctuated with a resounding 28-0 win over South Carolina in the Belk Bowl. The ACC was down (outside of Clemson, of course), but Virginia managed to rise above the mediocrity

for one of their best seasons in years—and that's even with losses by four points or less to Indiana, Georgia Tech, and Virginia Tech. The Cavaliers might get another year of ACC instability thanks to a rebuilding Florida State and new hires at Miami, Louisville, North Carolina, and Georgia Tech. So even a performance similar to last season might be enough for a similar or better record.

It's not too often that an offense produces two 1,000-yard rushers (if you include quarterback Bryce Perkins' non-sack yardage) but ranks in the 100s (104th!) in rushing S&P+. But that was the situation for the Cavaliers last year thanks to a dearth of explosive plays and some poor defenses. Still, in the non-opponent-adjusted efficiency metrics, Virginia's ground game shined, ranking 13th in opportunity rate and 12th in stuff rate. Unfortunately the Cavaliers may be overly reliant on the quarterback run in 2019, as they lost Jordan Ellis to graduation. Besides Perkins' high opportunity rate, no other running back besides Ellis (with a 50.7 percent opportunity rate) managed any semblance of efficiency. Backup PK Kier gained 4 yards or more on just nine of his 26 carries last year.

And that's really the major concern for the Hoos in 2019.

They were as reliant as anyone on steady success, ranking 38th in success rate compared to 98th in IsoPPP, but they lose their top two efficient offensive skill players in Ellis and H-back Olamide Zaccheaus. Can Perkins and unproven running backs fill the efficiency void?

At least Perkins will have a defense that returns a significant percentage of its production from last season (72 percent overall, 38th), and his second and third receivers from last year in Hasise Dubois and Joe Reed. Outside of interception machine Juan Thornhill at safety, Bronco Mendenhall's defense should be largely full of experienced upperclassmen who could improve even on last year's 31st ranking in defensive S&P+. The Cavaliers defense could improve on their havoc generation up front—despite ranking 17th overall in havoc rate, they were 126th (!) in defensive line havoc, including no returning linemen with more than two sacks—but the back seven should be electric.

46. Northwestern Wildcats (6-6, 4-5)

2019 Projections			Projection Factors		
F/+	15.0 (46)		2018 F/+	11.9 (48)	
FEI	0.19 (37)		2018 FEI	0.19 (41)	
S&P+	4.2 (57)		2018 S&P+	1.9 (41)	
Total Wins	6.2		5-Year F/+	10.0 (44)	
Conf Wins	4.0		5-Year FEI	0.18 (37)	
SOS	.096 (28)		5-Year S&P+	3.5 (58)	
Conf SOS	.136 (29)		2-Yr/5-Yr Recruiting	44/43	
Div Champ	2%		Ret. Offense	53% (97)	
Conf Champ	1%		Ret. Defense	71% (42)	
CFP Berth	0%		Ret. Total	62% (72)	

Projected Win Likelihood by Game

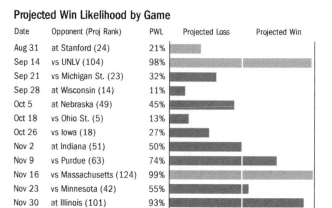

Date	Opponent (Proj Rank)	PWL
Aug 31	at Stanford (24)	21%
Sep 14	vs UNLV (104)	98%
Sep 21	vs Michigan St. (23)	32%
Sep 28	at Wisconsin (14)	11%
Oct 5	at Nebraska (49)	45%
Oct 18	vs Ohio St. (5)	13%
Oct 26	vs Iowa (18)	27%
Nov 2	at Indiana (51)	50%
Nov 9	vs Purdue (63)	74%
Nov 16	vs Massachusetts (124)	99%
Nov 23	vs Minnesota (42)	55%
Nov 30	at Illinois (101)	93%

The Wildcats won the Big 10 West division in 2018, which was their first title under head coach Pat Fitzgerald, although they finished 9-5 and missed being his fourth overall and second consecutive team with 10 wins. Four-year starting quarterback Clayton Thorson is now gone, drafted by the Eagles, and the Wildcats will have to rebuild their team in a tough year.

The expectation is that the job will go to former five-star recruit and Clemson transfer Hunter Johnson, who left after losing the starting job to Kelly Bryant and then seeing Trevor Lawrence on campus. Johnson redshirted in 2018 behind Thorson and is now competing for the top job. He'll have one of Thorson's favorite targets in big senior Bennett Skowronek, a 6-foot-4 receiver who had 562 yards and three scores, as well as running back Isaiah Bowser, who ran for 866 yards as a true freshman. The Wildcats have a

fair amount of their skill talent returning and two very effective starters on the offensive line in center Jared Thomas and tackle Rashawn Slater.

Defense is often where the Wildcats make their living, and they finished 30th in S&P+ in 2018. Most of the key performers are back, headlined by big defensive end Joe Gaziano, who led the team with 7.5 sacks a year ago. Inside linebackers Paddy Fisher and Blake Gallagher are back after leading the team with 127 and 116 tackles respectively. Safeties Travis Whillock and J.R. Pace return to hold down the middle of the defense. Fisher and Whillock were part of a legendary high school defense in Katy, Texas, that excelled at playing "bend don't break" and bringing good fundamentals and tackling to the field and won a championship. That's the name of the game at Northwestern as well, and the Wildcats should play it at a high level once again in 2019.

47. Arizona State Sun Devils (7-5, 5-4)

2019 Projections

F/+	14.2 (47)
FEI	0.11 (46)
S&P+	5.9 (49)
Total Wins	7.2
Conf Wins	5.0
SOS	.239 (69)
Conf SOS	.348 (58)
Div Champ	11%
Conf Champ	5%
CFP Berth	2%

Projection Factors

2018 F/+	14.8 (43)
2018 FEI	0.17 (42)
2018 S&P+	5.0 (52)
5-Year F/+	8.5 (46)
5-Year FEI	0.06 (54)
5-Year S&P+	5.4 (50)
2-Yr/5-Yr Recruiting	32/28
Ret. Offense	52% (103)
Ret. Defense	81% (14)
Ret. Total	66% (44)

Projected Win Likelihood by Game

Date	Opponent (Proj Rank)	PWL
Aug 29	vs Kent St. (120)	99%
Sep 6	vs Sacramento St. (FCS)	100%
Sep 14	at Michigan St. (23)	19%
Sep 21	vs Colorado (75)	81%
Sep 27	at California (68)	63%
Oct 12	vs Washington St. (26)	34%
Oct 19	at Utah (19)	15%
Oct 26	at UCLA (64)	59%
Nov 9	vs USC (33)	43%
Nov 16	at Oregon St. (110)	98%
Nov 23	vs Oregon (28)	35%
Nov 29	vs Arizona (60)	71%

Maybe we all underestimated Herm Edwards at Arizona State. It seemed like a bizarre hire for the Sun Devils, as Edwards hadn't coached in years, but Arizona State nevertheless put together a 7-6 record including a win over the rival Wildcats. Outside of a Week 3 loss to San Diego State, the Sun Devils more or less beat who they were supposed to and lost to better teams (although it is questionable at best whether they "should have" beaten the Aztecs, since the Sun Devils had just a 9 percent postgame win expectancy and were ranked behind the Aztecs in most advanced stats). That was a win for Herm in Year 1—some analysts expected Arizona State to crater in 2018.

But don't expect the Sun Devils to dramatically out-perform expectations in Year 2. They have recruited well enough—ranking 31st using a weighted four-year average—and return 81 percent of their production on defense, but also lose a ton of talent on offense.

The biggest storyline is, as with most schools in a similar position, the quarterback race. With Manny Wilkins' departure, the Sun Devils are deciding between last year's backup Dillon Sterling-Cole, a junior who threw two passes, and two true freshmen, Jayden Daniels and Joey Yellen. Daniels was the sec-ond-rated dual threat quarterback in the country last year (and Edward's highest-rated recruit in his two classes), and the early enrollee was already pushing Sterling-Cole for the starting spot in spring practice. His rushing ability likely gives him a leg up, but he was arguably the most impressive quarterback at the Under Armour All-America game as well. Whomever wins the job unfortunately won't have top receiving target N'Keal Harry to throw to, as Harry was drafted in the first round by the Patriots. However, Brandon Aiyuk and deep threat Frank Darby should provide at least some insurance for the new starter.

Even with the importance of the quarterback race and the talent lost from last season, the Sun Devils were actually much better on the ground than through the air, ranking 19th in rushing S&P+ compared to 50th in passing S&P+. That largely centers on workhorse running back Eno Benjamin, who totaled 1,642 yards on 300 carries last season.

As for the defense, well, it wasn't exactly on par with the offense last year—ranking 86th in defensive S&P+ including 114th in success rate+—but nearly everyone returns from last season. In fact, the Sun Devils rank 14th overall in returning defensive production, so they at least have experience to build upon for 2019.

48. Virginia Tech Hokies (8-4, 5-3)

2019 Projections

F/+	13.6 (48)
FEI	-0.03 (70)
S&P+	10.6 (30)
Total Wins	7.8
Conf Wins	4.8
SOS	.233 (68)
Conf SOS	.482 (63)
Div Champ	13%
Conf Champ	3%
CFP Berth	2%

Projection Factors

2018 F/+	-3.3 (76)
2018 FEI	-0.18 (89)
2018 S&P+	3.9 (55)
5-Year F/+	17.0 (31)
5-Year FEI	0.12 (44)
5-Year S&P+	10.5 (31)
2-Yr/5-Yr Recruiting	24/30
Ret. Offense	60% (77)
Ret. Defense	96% (1)
Ret. Total	78% (11)

Projected Win Likelihood by Game

Date	Opponent (Proj Rank)	PWL
Aug 31	at Boston College (67)	62%
Sep 7	vs Old Dominion (117)	99%
Sep 14	vs Furman (FCS)	100%
Sep 27	vs Duke (58)	69%
Oct 5	at Miami-FL (22)	17%
Oct 12	vs Rhode Island (FCS)	100%
Oct 19	vs N. Carolina (77)	82%
Nov 2	at Notre Dame (10)	8%
Nov 9	vs Wake Forest (72)	80%
Nov 16	at Georgia Tech (69)	65%
Nov 23	vs Pittsburgh (53)	65%
Nov 29	at Virginia (45)	39%

Virginia Tech has had a wild time since Justin Fuente became head coach in 2016, with their win totals dropping every year since he took over. They slipped to 6-7 in 2018, and Fuente's job will likely be at risk if they have another losing season in a struggling ACC. There was a little stability to be had in quarterback Ryan Willis, a transfer from Kansas (of all schools) who threw for 2,716 yards at 7.5 yards per attempt with 24 touchdowns and nine interceptions. Willis also added 354 rushing yards and four touchdowns and was able to execute Fuente's run and pass quarterback option schemes.

The rest of the offense didn't take off, though, and the Hokies lacked a go-to weapon either in the run game or the passing attack. In 2019 they'll hope that Deshawn McClease is ready to shoulder the load at running back, while big receiver Damon Hazelton will get his shot to build on an 802-yard, eight-touchdown season. Fuente has slowly been able to stock the offensive line with more talent than he found waiting for him, but they'll be fairly young in 2019.

Virginia Tech used to rely on excellent defense, but long-time coordinator Bud Foster's normally stout unit collapsed from ninth in S&P+ in 2017 to 77th in 2018. The Hokies lost multiple starters across the unit and struggled to plug all the leaks that sprung up. A big issue was a lack of playmaking from the defensive line, which will be young in 2019 but include a lot of rising talents who were largely defensive ends out of high school who have grown into bigger players, such as tackle Rob Porcher. If the line improves there will be much more experience behind them at linebacker and safety.

49. Nebraska Cornhuskers (7-5, 4-5)

2019 Projections

F/+	13.5 (49)
FEI	0.08 (50)
S&P+	6.6 (45)
Total Wins	6.8
Conf Wins	4.3
SOS	.198 (60)
Conf SOS	.207 (46)
Div Champ	4%
Conf Champ	2%
CFP Berth	1%

Projection Factors

2018 F/+	9.2 (53)
2018 FEI	0.05 (57)
2018 S&P+	5.4 (49)
5-Year F/+	5.6 (54)
5-Year FEI	0.11 (46)
5-Year S&P+	8.5 (39)
2-Yr/5-Yr Recruiting	22/23
Ret. Offense	59% (79)
Ret. Defense	55% (94)
Ret. Total	57% (93)

Projected Win Likelihood by Game

Date	Opponent (Proj Rank)	PWL
Aug 31	vs S. Alabama (126)	99%
Sep 7	at Colorado (75)	67%
Sep 14	vs N. Illinois (82)	85%
Sep 21	at Illinois (101)	92%
Sep 28	vs Ohio St. (5)	12%
Oct 5	vs Northwestern (46)	55%
Oct 12	at Minnesota (42)	37%
Oct 26	vs Indiana (51)	63%
Nov 2	at Purdue (63)	58%
Nov 16	vs Wisconsin (14)	19%
Nov 23	at Maryland (73)	67%
Nov 29	vs Iowa (18)	26%

The general narrative around Scott Frost's Year 2 at Nebraska is that the Cornhuskers are a team on the rise despite finishing 2018 with just a 4-8 record. Part of that is because the Cornhuskers righted the ship after starting 0-6, finishing 4-2 with losses to Ohio State by just five and Iowa by three. Reinforcing that turnaround is the fact that Nebraska finished with 6.7 second-order wins, suggesting that most of the time they would have won three more games than they actually did (in fact, their postgame win expectancies were above 50 percent against Colorado, Troy, and Northwestern).

Frost also has some young talent to build around, including sophomore quarterback Adrian Martinez. Martinez was fourth among FBS freshmen in average passing yards per game last season (237.9), but he and the team were even more effective on the ground—Nebraska ranked seventh overall in rushing S&P+, with Martinez and leading rusher Devine Ozigbo both averaging over a 57 percent opportunity rate and 6.7 yards per carry. Ozigbo is gone, but sophomore Maurice Washington posted similar numbers, albeit with slightly more explosiveness and less efficiency. His status for 2019 is unclear, so Frost brought in JUCO transfer (and former Georgia Tech Yellow Jacket) Dedrick Mills as a power back. Returning receiver JD Spielman will be complemented by freshman early enrollee Wandale Robinson, the top-ranked all-purpose back according to the 247 Sports composite rankings. Quarterback depth is a little thin, however—projected backup Noah Vedral completed just two of nine passes last season.

The Huskers defense returns just 55 percent of its production from last season (94th), with the defensive backs and linebackers hit particularly hard. However, the story from spring practice is that the defense is showing positive signs. This includes former four-star transfer defensive lineman Darrion Daniels (who joins his younger brother Damion), junior defensive back Dicaprio Bootle, and senior linebacker Mohamed Barry.

Although projected at a similar position as they ended last season (in the high 40s) it's likely that their record should better reflect their overall quality. While 7-5 or so might be a disappointing total relative to surging offseason expectations, the reality is that Frost needed (and still needs) to do a good deal of roster work to get the Huskers' talent level up to conference championship contention.

50. BYU Cougars (6-6)

2019 Projections

F/+	10.9 (50)
FEI	0.06 (56)
S&P+	5.7 (50)
Total Wins	6.3
Conf Wins	-
SOS	.191 (58)
Conf SOS	-
Div Champ	-
Conf Champ	-
CFP Berth	0%

Projection Factors

2018 F/+	7.1 (58)
2018 FEI	0.07 (54)
2018 S&P+	6.2 (46)
5-Year F/+	5.0 (55)
5-Year FEI	0.05 (56)
5-Year S&P+	5.1 (52)
2-Yr/5-Yr Recruiting	78/71
Ret. Offense	69% (48)
Ret. Defense	57% (85)
Ret. Total	63% (65)

Projected Win Likelihood by Game

Date	Opponent (Proj Rank)	PWL
Aug 29	vs Utah (19)	24%
Sep 7	at Tennessee (40)	29%
Sep 14	vs USC (33)	38%
Sep 21	vs Washington (11)	15%
Sep 28	at Toledo (76)	65%
Oct 12	at South Florida (83)	72%
Oct 19	vs Boise St. (17)	22%
Nov 2	at Utah St. (30)	20%
Nov 9	vs Liberty (113)	98%
Nov 16	vs Idaho St. (FCS)	100%
Nov 23	at Massachusetts (124)	99%
Nov 30	at San Diego St. (57)	49%

The 7-6 Cougars were very solid on defense in 2018, finishing 33rd in S&P+, and weak on offense, where they were 77th despite returning starters at quarterback and running back. BYU has struggled to find their way on offense in the modern era since the passing attacks that defined their 80s teams has become more commonplace across the game, and they've tried to lean into being a power-option rushing team. They started to find their feet in 2018 after inserting young quarterback Zach Wilson and using him in the read game.

The 2019 Cougars will return Wilson and a fair amount of size and experience on the offensive line, including 2018 standouts Brady Christensen (left tackle) and James Empey (center). Lead rusher Squally Canada is moving on and the Cougars will have to choose the next main back from a committee.

On defense they lost star linebacker Sione Takitaki, who led the team in tackles and tackles for loss, as well as defensive lineman Corbin Kaufusi, who led the team in sacks. There are three other Kaufusi's fighting for a spot on the depth chart and a solid collection of linebackers and safeties with some good playing experience. BYU figures to be stout, but they'll need someone to emerge as a pass-rushing threat for Kalani Sitake to wield in his blitz packages to put it all together. The hidden upside of this team will come from having Wilson in Year 2 as quarterback; his rushing ability helped unlock the offense once he took over last season.

NCAA Win Projections

Projected Win Probabilities For ACC Teams

ACC Atlantic	Overall Wins													Conference Wins								
	12-0	11-1	10-2	9-3	8-4	7-5	6-6	5-7	4-8	3-9	2-10	1-11	0-12	8-0	7-1	6-2	5-3	4-4	3-5	2-6	1-7	0-8
Boston College	-	-	-	1	7	20	30	29	11	2	-	-	-	-	-	2	9	21	32	25	9	2
Clemson	38	43	15	4	-	-	-	-	-	-	-	-	-	66	30	4	-	-	-	-	-	-
Florida State	-	-	4	12	26	28	20	8	2	-	-	-	-	-	7	23	35	24	9	2	-	-
Louisville	-	-	-	-	-	-	-	2	8	28	40	22	-	-	-	-	-	-	2	14	38	46
NC State	1	6	22	33	25	11	2	-	-	-	-	-	-	2	14	31	32	17	4	-	-	-
Syracuse	-	1	3	16	27	26	17	8	2	-	-	-	-	-	1	9	24	34	23	7	2	-
Wake Forest	-	-	-	1	4	16	26	28	18	6	1	-	-	-	-	1	5	15	29	32	16	2

ACC Coastal	12-0	11-1	10-2	9-3	8-4	7-5	6-6	5-7	4-8	3-9	2-10	1-11	0-12	8-0	7-1	6-2	5-3	4-4	3-5	2-6	1-7	0-8
Duke	-	-	-	2	8	19	26	26	14	4	1	-	-	-	2	6	20	30	25	13	4	
Georgia Tech	-	-	-	-	1	5	12	24	29	19	9	1	-	-	-	-	3	12	26	33	22	4
Miami-FL	6	23	35	24	10	2	-	-	-	-	-	-	-	18	37	29	13	2	1	-	-	-
North Carolina	-	-	-	-	-	1	4	11	25	31	21	7	-	-	-	-	1	4	17	32	32	14
Pittsburgh	-	-	1	5	11	21	25	21	11	4	1	-	-	-	3	9	20	31	22	12	3	-
Virginia	-	2	10	23	31	22	9	2	1	-	-	-	-	1	9	22	32	22	10	3	1	-
Virginia Tech	-	2	7	22	27	28	11	3	-	-	-	-	-	1	7	21	32	23	11	4	1	-

Projected Win Probabilities For American Teams

American East	Overall Wins													Conference Wins								
	12-0	11-1	10-2	9-3	8-4	7-5	6-6	5-7	4-8	3-9	2-10	1-11	0-12	8-0	7-1	6-2	5-3	4-4	3-5	2-6	1-7	0-8
Central Florida	20	40	27	11	2	-	-	-	-	-	-	-	-	43	43	13	1	-	-	-	-	-
Cincinnati	-	4	19	33	28	11	4	1	-	-	-	-	-	5	26	38	24	6	1	-	-	-
Connecticut	-	-	-	-	-	-	-	3	12	31	38	16	-	-	-	-	-	-	2	17	45	36
East Carolina	-	-	-	-	-	2	13	27	32	20	6	-	-	-	-	-	1	5	17	33	33	11
South Florida	-	-	-	1	4	15	32	28	15	4	1	-	-	-	-	6	24	38	23	8	1	-
Temple	-	3	14	28	30	17	7	1	-	-	-	-	-	1	7	25	38	24	5	-	-	-

American West	12-0	11-1	10-2	9-3	8-4	7-5	6-6	5-7	4-8	3-9	2-10	1-11	0-12	8-0	7-1	6-2	5-3	4-4	3-5	2-6	1-7	0-8
Houston	-	-	1	8	26	30	25	8	2	-	-	-	-	-	5	27	39	24	5	-	-	-
Memphis	13	35	32	16	4	-	-	-	-	-	-	-	-	25	43	25	6	1	-	-	-	-
Navy	-	-	-	-	-	5	13	22	32	20	7	1	-	-	-	1	7	23	32	27	9	1
SMU	-	-	-	-	2	7	20	28	25	13	4	1	-	-	-	3	15	26	32	19	5	-
Tulane	-	-	-	-	-	4	13	26	32	20	5	-	-	-	-	-	5	19	36	28	11	1
Tulsa	-	-	-	-	-	1	4	13	29	28	19	5	1	-	-	-	1	10	27	35	22	5

Projected Win Probabilities For Big 12 Teams

Big 12	12-0	11-1	10-2	9-3	8-4	7-5	6-6	5-7	4-8	3-9	2-10	1-11	0-12	9-0	8-1	7-2	6-3	5-4	4-5	3-6	2-7	1-8	0-9
						Overall Wins											Conference Wins						
Baylor	-	1	4	14	26	25	22	7	1	-	-	-	-	-	1	5	15	23	29	19	7	1	-
Iowa State	-	1	2	7	16	27	26	15	6	-	-	-	-	-	-	4	12	26	29	20	8	1	-
Kansas	-	-	-	-	-	-	-	-	1	12	57	30	-	-	-	-	-	-	-	-	1	16	83
Kansas State	-	-	-	1	3	11	22	30	23	9	1	-	-	-	-	-	2	7	25	34	23	8	1
Oklahoma	31	41	20	6	2	-	-	-	-	-	-	-	-	34	41	19	5	1	-	-	-	-	-
Oklahoma State	1	7	23	29	24	12	3	1	-	-	-	-	-	1	9	24	29	23	11	3	-	-	-
TCU	-	1	6	19	26	26	15	5	2	-	-	-	-	-	2	8	20	31	25	11	3	-	-
Texas	-	1	5	15	26	27	17	7	2	-	-	-	-	-	3	13	24	31	19	9	1	-	-
Texas Tech	-	-	-	3	6	19	27	26	15	4	-	-	-	-	-	-	4	13	26	30	21	5	1
West Virginia	-	2	10	24	25	21	12	5	1	-	-	-	-	1	8	24	33	21	10	3	-	-	-

Projected Win Probabilities For Big Ten Teams

Big Ten East	12-0	11-1	10-2	9-3	8-4	7-5	6-6	5-7	4-8	3-9	2-10	1-11	0-12	9-0	8-1	7-2	6-3	5-4	4-5	3-6	2-7	1-8	0-9
						Overall Wins											Conference Wins						
Indiana	-	-	1	4	14	30	31	17	3	-	-	-	-	-	-	-	4	13	30	34	16	3	-
Maryland	-	-	-	-	-	3	8	22	29	28	9	1	-	-	-	-	-	2	8	28	37	22	3
Michigan	4	14	31	27	17	5	2	-	-	-	-	-	-	4	22	35	27	10	2	-	-	-	-
Michigan State	-	3	11	28	31	19	6	2	-	-	-	-	-	-	3	14	33	33	15	2	-	-	-
Ohio State	12	31	31	18	7	1	-	-	-	-	-	-	-	14	34	33	15	3	1	-	-	-	-
Penn State	4	16	32	28	15	4	1	-	-	-	-	-	-	3	15	34	31	13	4	-	-	-	-
Rutgers	-	-	-	-	-	-	-	-	4	20	39	30	7	-	-	-	-	-	-	-	4	39	57
Big Ten West	12-0	11-1	10-2	9-3	8-4	7-5	6-6	5-7	4-8	3-9	2-10	1-11	0-12	9-0	8-1	7-2	6-3	5-4	4-5	3-6	2-7	1-8	0-9
Illinois	-	-	-	-	-	-	1	7	30	36	21	5	-	-	-	-	-	-	-	2	17	59	22
Iowa	1	9	21	29	26	11	3	-	-	-	-	-	-	2	11	29	34	18	5	1	-	-	-
Minnesota	-	1	5	13	26	30	18	6	1	-	-	-	-	-	2	11	25	34	21	6	1	-	-
Nebraska	-	-	2	9	22	25	24	12	5	1	-	-	-	-	-	4	15	25	30	20	5	1	-
Northwestern	-	-	1	3	12	25	26	22	9	2	-	-	-	-	-	2	9	21	35	22	10	1	-
Purdue	-	-	-	-	3	11	19	26	22	13	5	1	-	-	-	-	2	13	26	35	19	5	-
Wisconsin	4	19	30	28	14	4	1	-	-	-	-	-	-	4	19	32	30	12	3	-	-	-	-

Projected Win Probabilities For Conference USA Teams

Conf USA East	12-0	11-1	10-2	9-3	8-4	7-5	6-6	5-7	4-8	3-9	2-10	1-11	0-12	8-0	7-1	6-2	5-3	4-4	3-5	2-6	1-7	0-8
						Overall Wins											Conference Wins					
Charlotte	-	-	-	-	-	1	5	17	26	31	17	3	-	-	-	-	1	7	20	34	31	7
Florida Atlantic	-	-	4	20	26	26	16	7	1	-	-	-	-	6	18	29	29	13	4	1	-	-
Florida International	-	-	4	12	27	27	21	7	2	-	-	-	-	-	6	17	33	28	14	2	-	-
Marshall	-	1	7	17	30	26	15	3	1	-	-	-	-	9	28	33	22	7	1	-	-	-
Middle Tennessee	-	-	-	3	9	23	29	22	12	2	-	-	-	1	7	22	31	24	12	3	-	-
Old Dominion	-	-	-	-	-	1	4	17	30	30	15	3	-	-	-	-	1	7	23	37	26	6
Western Kentucky	-	-	-	1	5	14	24	28	19	8	1	-	-	-	1	5	16	28	30	15	4	1
Conf USA West	12-0	11-1	10-2	9-3	8-4	7-5	6-6	5-7	4-8	3-9	2-10	1-11	0-12	8-0	7-1	6-2	5-3	4-4	3-5	2-6	1-7	0-8
Louisiana Tech	-	4	14	27	29	19	6	1	-	-	-	-	-	2	13	32	32	16	4	1	-	-
North Texas	-	1	4	15	24	29	18	8	1	-	-	-	-	2	14	32	28	18	5	1	-	-
Rice	-	-	-	-	-	-	-	-	2	12	31	37	18	-	-	-	-	2	8	28	41	21
Southern Miss	-	-	3	16	26	33	16	5	1	-	-	-	-	8	28	34	21	8	1	-	-	-
UAB	-	3	16	29	31	15	5	1	-	-	-	-	-	3	17	36	28	13	3	-	-	-
UTEP	-	-	-	-	-	-	4	12	28	34	18	4	-	-	-	-	1	4	19	39	28	9
UTSA	-	-	-	-	-	-	2	6	18	35	30	9	-	-	-	-	-	6	21	35	30	8

Projected Win Probabilities For Independent Teams

Independents	12-0	11-1	10-2	9-3	8-4	7-5	6-6	5-7	4-8	3-9	2-10	1-11	0-12
						Overall Wins							
Army*	-	39	42	17	2	-	-	-	-	-	-	-	-
BYU	-	-	2	4	15	23	29	18	8	1	-	-	-
Liberty	-	-	-	-	2	13	24	31	22	7	1	-	-
Massachusetts	-	-	-	-	-	2	10	24	29	23	10	2	-
Notre Dame	5	22	38	26	8	1	-	-	-	-	-	-	-
New Mexico State	-	-	-	-	-	-	2	11	26	32	22	7	-

*Army will play 13 regular season games; for projected overall records, 12-0 means 13-0, 11-1 means 12-1, etc.

Projected Win Probabilities For MAC Teams

MAC East	12-0	11-1	10-2	9-3	8-4	7-5	6-6	5-7	4-8	3-9	2-10	1-11	0-12	8-0	7-1	6-2	5-3	4-4	3-5	2-6	1-7	0-8
						Overall Wins											Conference Wins					
Akron	-	-	-	-	-	1	3	9	23	29	21	12	2	-	-	-	2	10	24	32	26	6
Bowling Green	-	-	-	-	-	-	1	7	20	38	27	7	-	-	-	-	-	4	17	39	30	10
Buffalo	-	1	3	12	25	27	21	8	2	1	-	-	-	2	10	28	32	21	6	1	-	-
Kent State	-	-	-	-	-	-	1	10	27	33	24	5	-	-	-	-	2	9	24	32	26	7
Miami-OH	-	-	-	1	10	25	36	21	6	1	-	-	-	1	8	25	34	22	8	2	-	-
Ohio	9	27	34	21	7	2	-	-	-	-	-	-	-	36	37	21	5	1	-	-	-	-
MAC West	12-0	11-1	10-2	9-3	8-4	7-5	6-6	5-7	4-8	3-9	2-10	1-11	0-12	8-0	7-1	6-2	5-3	4-4	3-5	2-6	1-7	0-8
Ball State	-	-	-	-	-	-	2	6	21	39	25	7	-	-	-	-	1	5	19	35	31	9
Central Michigan	-	-	-	-	-	2	6	21	29	29	12	1	-	-	-	-	3	11	25	33	21	7
Eastern Michigan	-	-	-	3	14	20	30	21	9	2	1	-	-	-	1	7	24	34	21	12	1	-
Northern Illinois	-	-	1	5	18	30	29	14	3	-	-	-	-	2	10	28	34	20	5	1	-	-
Toledo	1	7	22	33	21	11	4	1	-	-	-	-	-	15	36	32	14	3	-	-	-	-
Western Michigan	-	-	3	13	29	31	18	5	1	-	-	-	-	1	10	29	36	18	5	1	-	-

Projected Win Probabilities For MWC Teams

MWC Mountain	12-0	11-1	10-2	9-3	8-4	7-5	6-6	5-7	4-8	3-9	2-10	1-11	0-12	8-0	7-1	6-2	5-3	4-4	3-5	2-6	1-7	0-8
						Overall Wins											Conference Wins					
Air Force	-	-	2	10	24	32	22	8	2	-	-	-	-	-	1	13	39	33	12	2	-	-
Boise State	26	46	22	5	1	-	-	-	-	-	-	-	-	53	43	4	-	-	-	-	-	-
Colorado State	-	-	-	-	-	-	1	8	21	35	27	8	-	-	-	-	-	3	15	37	35	10
New Mexico	-	-	-	-	-	1	4	20	30	29	14	2	-	-	-	-	-	4	15	33	36	12
Utah State	1	12	29	31	18	7	2	-	-	-	-	-	-	14	35	35	14	2	-	-	-	-
Wyoming	-	-	-	1	3	19	29	28	15	4	1	-	-	-	-	1	10	29	39	17	4	-
MWC West	12-0	11-1	10-2	9-3	8-4	7-5	6-6	5-7	4-8	3-9	2-10	1-11	0-12	8-0	7-1	6-2	5-3	4-4	3-5	2-6	1-7	0-8
Fresno State	5	17	32	30	13	3	-	-	-	-	-	-	-	18	45	29	8	-	-	-	-	-
Hawaii*	-	-	-	-	-	-	4	15	26	30	19	5	1	-	-	-	3	11	36	32	16	2
Nevada	-	-	1	5	19	36	27	10	2	-	-	-	-	-	1	9	38	37	13	2	-	-
San Diego State	1	8	27	34	21	8	1	-	-	-	-	-	-	5	27	40	22	5	1	-	-	-
San Jose State	-	-	-	-	-	-	-	3	12	31	38	16	-	-	-	-	-	1	6	25	45	23
UNLV	-	-	-	-	-	-	4	13	28	35	17	3	-	-	-	-	2	9	27	37	21	4

*Hawaii will play 13 regular season games; for projected overall records, 12-0 means 13-0, 11-1 means 12-1, etc.

Projected Win Probabilities For Pac-12 Teams

Pac 12 North	Overall Wins													Conference Wins									
	12-0	11-1	10-2	9-3	8-4	7-5	6-6	5-7	4-8	3-9	2-10	1-11	0-12	9-0	8-1	7-2	6-3	5-4	4-5	3-6	2-7	1-8	0-9
California	-	-	-	-	1	3	14	28	33	17	4	-	-	-	-	-	-	3	13	30	35	18	1
Oregon	-	3	12	25	30	20	8	2	-	-	-	-	-	1	9	27	30	22	9	2	-	-	-
Oregon State	-	-	-	-	-	-	-	-	-	5	34	61	-	-	-	-	-	-	-	-	1	14	85
Stanford	-	2	10	21	30	21	12	3	1	-	-	-	-	3	14	31	28	18	5	1	-	-	-
Washington	15	34	32	14	4	1	-	-	-	-	-	-	-	21	36	29	11	3	-	-	-	-	-
Washington State	-	5	17	27	31	14	5	1	-	-	-	-	-	-	6	22	33	24	12	3	-	-	-
Pac 12 South	**12-0**	**11-1**	**10-2**	**9-3**	**8-4**	**7-5**	**6-6**	**5-7**	**4-8**	**3-9**	**2-10**	**1-11**	**0-12**	**9-0**	**8-1**	**7-2**	**6-3**	**5-4**	**4-5**	**3-6**	**2-7**	**1-8**	**0-9**
Arizona	-	-	-	1	6	18	29	29	14	3	-	-	-	-	-	-	3	10	27	33	21	6	-
Arizona State	-	1	4	12	24	28	21	8	2	-	-	-	-	-	2	10	24	29	24	9	2	-	-
Colorado	-	-	-	-	-	1	5	13	28	28	18	6	1	-	-	-	-	1	3	14	31	34	17
UCLA	-	-	-	-	1	5	13	25	27	19	9	1	-	-	-	1	5	15	30	32	14	3	-
USC	-	-	3	9	19	24	23	15	6	1	-	-	-	-	4	12	25	29	22	7	1	-	-
Utah	5	21	34	25	11	3	1	-	-	-	-	-	-	5	28	34	23	8	2	-	-	-	-

Projected Win Probabilities For SEC Teams

SEC East	Overall Wins													Conference Wins								
	12-0	11-1	10-2	9-3	8-4	7-5	6-6	5-7	4-8	3-9	2-10	1-11	0-12	8-0	7-1	6-2	5-3	4-4	3-5	2-6	1-7	0-8
Florida	1	4	16	28	27	16	6	2	-	-	-	-	-	1	9	21	29	26	12	2	-	-
Georgia	8	26	33	20	10	2	1	-	-	-	-	-	-	14	31	31	18	5	1	-	-	-
Kentucky	-	-	3	6	21	32	25	10	3	-	-	-	-	-	-	2	11	26	28	23	9	1
Missouri	2	14	30	29	16	7	2	-	-	-	-	-	-	5	18	33	28	11	4	1	-	-
South Carolina	-	-	-	2	9	20	28	23	13	4	1	-	-	-	-	3	11	28	31	21	5	1
Tennessee	-	-	-	1	6	19	35	28	9	2	-	-	-	-	-	-	3	12	26	33	22	4
Vanderbilt	-	-	-	-	1	4	14	28	32	17	4	-	-	-	-	-	-	2	8	25	39	26
SEC West	**12-0**	**11-1**	**10-2**	**9-3**	**8-4**	**7-5**	**6-6**	**5-7**	**4-8**	**3-9**	**2-10**	**1-11**	**0-12**	**8-0**	**7-1**	**6-2**	**5-3**	**4-4**	**3-5**	**2-6**	**1-7**	**0-8**
Alabama	7	25	34	23	9	2	-	-	-	-	-	-	-	9	24	34	23	8	2	-	-	-
Arkansas	-	-	-	-	-	3	13	35	40	9	-	-	-	-	-	-	-	-	3	14	41	42
Auburn	1	5	15	26	29	17	6	1	-	-	-	-	-	1	7	17	33	25	13	4	-	-
LSU	2	11	25	30	20	10	2	-	-	-	-	-	-	2	14	29	33	16	5	1	-	-
Mississippi State	4	21	28	29	13	4	1	-	-	-	-	-	-	4	17	39	27	10	3	-	-	-
Ole Miss	-	-	-	1	8	20	32	26	11	2	-	-	-	-	-	1	4	14	33	36	11	1
Texas A&M	-	1	6	15	25	26	18	8	1	-	-	-	-	-	3	11	26	32	20	7	1	-

Projected Win Probabilities For Sun Belt Teams

Sun Belt East	Overall Wins													Conference Wins								
	12-0	11-1	10-2	9-3	8-4	7-5	6-6	5-7	4-8	3-9	2-10	1-11	0-12	8-0	7-1	6-2	5-3	4-4	3-5	2-6	1-7	0-8
Appalachian State	33	47	17	3	-	-	-	-	-	-	-	-	-	74	24	2	-	-	-	-	-	-
Coastal Carolina	-	-	-	-	-	3	9	21	29	25	11	2	-	-	-	-	1	6	18	35	32	8
Georgia Southern	-	-	3	17	37	31	11	1	-	-	-	-	-	-	12	39	37	11	1	-	-	-
Georgia State	-	-	-	-	-	-	-	6	19	36	31	8	-	-	-	-	1	4	19	34	31	11
Troy	-	1	15	33	32	15	3	1	-	-	-	-	-	4	20	39	26	10	1	-	-	-
Sun Belt West	**12-0**	**11-1**	**10-2**	**9-3**	**8-4**	**7-5**	**6-6**	**5-7**	**4-8**	**3-9**	**2-10**	**1-11**	**0-12**	**8-0**	**7-1**	**6-2**	**5-3**	**4-4**	**3-5**	**2-6**	**1-7**	**0-8**
Arkansas State	-	10	31	36	17	5	1	-	-	-	-	-	-	17	39	31	11	2	-	-	-	-
South Alabama	-	-	-	-	-	-	-	2	13	30	37	18	-	-	-	-	-	2	8	27	39	24
Texas State	-	-	-	-	1	4	13	24	29	22	6	1	-	-	-	1	5	22	34	26	10	2
UL-Lafayette	-	-	-	-	-	2	10	26	35	18	7	2	-	-	-	2	11	32	34	16	5	-
UL-Monroe	-	-	-	-	-	-	3	15	29	33	16	4	-	-	-	2	13	31	33	18	3	-

NCAA F/+ Projections

NCAA Teams, No. 1 to No. 130

Rk	Team	Rec	Conf	F/+	MW	CW	SOS	Rk	CSOS	Rk	Div	Conf	CFP
1	Alabama	10-2	6-2	54.3%	9.9	6.0	0.037	9	0.040	9	36.5%	18.6%	19.9%
2	Clemson	11-1	8-0	53.6%	11.1	7.6	0.311	81	0.587	80	90.3%	67.7%	66.5%
3	Georgia	10-2	6-2	53.4%	10.0	6.3	0.051	13	0.084	15	54.4%	26.6%	28.1%
4	Oklahoma	11-1	8-1	51.1%	10.9	8.0	0.290	78	0.317	56	-	77.3%	43.9%
5	Ohio State	10-2	7-2	51.1%	10.3	7.4	0.108	37	0.121	23	49.3%	28.1%	24.2%
6	LSU	9-3	5-3	49.5%	9.1	5.4	0.022	7	0.033	7	19.5%	9.9%	8.8%
7	Mississippi State	10-2	6-2	49.0%	9.5	5.6	0.046	10	0.048	11	27.6%	14.1%	13.4%
8	Auburn	9-3	5-3	48.1%	8.5	4.8	0.013	4	0.017	3	10.3%	5.2%	4.5%
9	Michigan	9-3	7-2	46.9%	9.4	6.8	0.055	15	0.089	18	27.7%	15.8%	10.9%
10	Notre Dame	10-2	-	46.1%	9.9	0.0	0.084	22	-	-	-	-	9.2%
11	Washington	10-2	8-1	44.5%	10.4	7.6	0.275	76	0.312	55	62.3%	35.5%	29.1%
12	Florida	8-4	5-3	43.4%	8.4	4.9	0.024	8	0.036	8	14.6%	7.1%	5.5%
13	Penn State	9-3	7-2	43.3%	9.5	6.6	0.081	21	0.085	17	17.8%	10.1%	7.3%
14	Wisconsin	10-2	7-2	42.3%	9.6	6.6	0.104	35	0.107	20	50.4%	21.7%	14.2%
15	Missouri	9-3	6-2	40.9%	9.4	5.7	0.101	32	0.123	24	28.4%	13.9%	12.0%
16	Texas A&M	7-5	4-4	40.8%	7.4	4.2	0.007	1	0.019	4	6.0%	3.0%	2.1%
17	Boise State	11-1	7-1	37.1%	11.0	7.5	0.523	107	0.699	89	74.9%	47.2%	2.7%
18	Iowa	9-3	6-3	36.1%	8.9	6.2	0.098	30	0.118	22	32.8%	14.1%	8.0%
19	Utah	10-2	7-2	35.3%	9.7	7.0	0.243	70	0.275	53	72.6%	31.2%	19.3%
20	Central Florida	11-1	7-1	33.9%	10.6	7.3	0.517	104	0.691	88	75.9%	43.3%	2.3%
21	Appalachian State	11-1	8-0	32.7%	11.1	7.7	0.653	115	0.898	104	90.3%	63.2%	3.6%
22	Miami-FL	10-2	7-1	32.5%	9.8	6.6	0.332	85	0.558	78	66.9%	16.7%	11.5%
23	Michigan State	8-4	5-4	31.9%	8.2	5.5	0.052	14	0.057	13	5.1%	2.9%	1.6%
24	Stanford	8-4	6-3	29.9%	7.9	6.4	0.115	39	0.286	54	17.1%	9.7%	4.9%
25	West Virginia	8-4	6-3	29.5%	7.9	5.9	0.085	23	0.167	36	-	7.7%	2.3%
26	Washington State	9-3	6-3	29.3%	8.6	5.8	0.150	49	0.160	35	8.7%	5.0%	2.9%
27	Oklahoma State	9-3	6-3	29.1%	8.8	5.8	0.190	57	0.194	41	-	8.2%	3.0%
28	Oregon	8-4	6-3	28.6%	8.2	6.0	0.103	33	0.196	42	11.9%	6.8%	3.5%
29	South Carolina	6-6	3-5	27.3%	5.8	3.2	0.012	3	0.030	6	1.2%	0.6%	0.4%
30	Utah State	9-3	6-2	26.9%	9.2	6.4	0.220	65	0.553	76	24.8%	15.6%	0.7%
31	Memphis	10-2	7-1	24.6%	10.4	6.8	0.654	116	0.747	96	86.7%	37.3%	1.8%
32	Texas	7-5	5-4	24.6%	7.4	5.2	0.090	25	0.156	34	-	3.4%	1.0%
33	USC	7-5	5-4	23.3%	6.7	5.2	0.087	24	0.218	48	15.1%	6.5%	2.9%
34	NC State	9-3	6-2	22.8%	8.8	5.5	0.244	71	0.344	57	6.5%	4.9%	2.8%
35	Ole Miss	6-6	3-5	22.7%	5.9	2.6	0.012	2	0.016	1	0.2%	0.1%	0.1%
36	TCU	8-4	5-4	22.0%	7.6	4.9	0.132	43	0.142	31	-	1.8%	0.6%
37	Florida State	7-5	5-3	22.0%	7.2	4.8	0.072	17	0.197	43	2.5%	1.9%	0.9%
38	Kentucky	7-5	3-5	20.7%	6.9	3.1	0.046	11	0.048	10	1.1%	0.5%	0.3%
39	Cincinnati	9-3	6-2	20.3%	8.6	5.9	0.207	61	0.541	73	18.4%	10.5%	0.4%
40	Tennessee	6-6	2-6	19.2%	5.9	2.3	0.021	6	0.023	5	0.4%	0.2%	0.1%
41	Fresno State	10-2	7-1	18.6%	9.6	6.6	0.538	108	0.744	94	65.8%	24.4%	1.1%
42	Minnesota	7-5	5-4	16.9%	7.4	5.1	0.182	55	0.223	51	9.9%	4.3%	2.0%
43	Iowa State	7-5	4-5	16.9%	6.5	4.2	0.106	36	0.138	30	-	0.3%	0.1%
44	Baylor	7-5	4-5	15.8%	7.3	4.3	0.193	59	0.197	44	-	1.3%	0.4%
45	Virginia	8-4	5-3	15.7%	8.0	4.9	0.232	67	0.484	64	12.8%	3.2%	1.6%
46	Northwestern	6-6	4-5	15.0%	6.2	4.0	0.096	28	0.136	29	2.2%	1.0%	0.4%
47	Arizona State	7-5	5-4	14.2%	7.2	5.0	0.239	69	0.348	58	10.5%	4.5%	2.1%
48	Virginia Tech	8-4	5-3	13.6%	7.8	4.8	0.233	68	0.482	63	12.7%	3.2%	1.5%
49	Nebraska	7-5	4-5	13.5%	6.8	4.3	0.198	60	0.207	46	4.2%	1.8%	0.8%
50	BYU	6-6	-	10.9%	6.3	0.0	0.191	58	-	-	-	-	0.0%

438

Rk	Team	Rec	Conf	F/+	MW	CW	SOS	Rk	CSOS	Rk	Div	Conf	CFP
51	Indiana	6-6	3-6	10.4%	6.4	3.5	0.095	27	0.097	19	0.1%	0.1%	0.0%
52	Syracuse	7-5	4-4	9.9%	7.4	3.9	0.262	74	0.274	52	0.7%	0.5%	0.3%
53	Pittsburgh	6-6	4-4	9.3%	5.9	4.0	0.208	62	0.506	66	4.2%	1.1%	0.5%
54	Army	11-2	-	7.8%	11.2	0.0	0.430	95	-	-	-	-	0.2%
55	Temple	8-4	5-3	7.5%	8.3	5.1	0.520	105	0.544	75	5.4%	3.1%	0.1%
56	Texas Tech	6-6	3-6	7.4%	5.7	3.3	0.118	40	0.129	25	-	0.0%	0.0%
57	San Diego State	9-3	6-2	7.1%	9.0	6.1	0.659	117	0.746	95	31.7%	11.7%	0.5%
58	Duke	6-6	4-4	6.8%	5.7	3.8	0.142	45	0.520	69	2.9%	0.7%	0.3%
59	Ohio	10-2	7-1	6.5%	10.0	7.0	0.816	126	0.923	121	78.9%	45.7%	2.1%
60	Arizona	6-6	3-6	5.8%	5.6	3.2	0.168	51	0.175	37	0.6%	0.3%	0.1%
61	Vanderbilt	4-8	1-7	5.8%	4.4	1.2	0.048	12	0.052	12	0.0%	0.0%	0.0%
62	Kansas State	5-7	3-6	5.7%	5.1	3.1	0.081	20	0.186	39	-	0.1%	0.0%
63	Purdue	5-7	3-6	4.0%	4.8	3.3	0.113	38	0.131	26	0.4%	0.2%	0.1%
64	UCLA	4-8	4-5	4.0%	4.3	3.6	0.097	29	0.220	49	1.2%	0.5%	0.2%
65	Arkansas	5-7	1-7	3.9%	4.6	0.8	0.016	5	0.016	2	0.0%	0.0%	0.0%
66	Houston	7-5	5-3	2.4%	7.0	5.1	0.170	52	0.508	67	11.1%	4.8%	0.2%
67	Boston College	6-6	3-5	1.2%	5.8	2.9	0.103	34	0.216	47	0.1%	0.1%	0.0%
68	California	4-8	2-7	1.2%	4.4	2.5	0.090	26	0.115	21	0.0%	0.0%	0.0%
69	Georgia Tech	4-8	2-6	-0.9%	4.3	2.2	0.073	18	0.155	32	0.3%	0.1%	0.0%
70	Arkansas State	9-3	7-1	-1.8%	9.2	6.5	0.322	84	0.898	105	94.2%	28.3%	1.2%
71	Troy	8-4	6-2	-2.0%	8.4	5.8	0.416	94	0.744	93	7.6%	5.3%	0.2%
72	Wake Forest	5-7	3-5	-2.2%	5.3	2.6	0.174	53	0.204	45	0.0%	0.0%	0.0%
73	Maryland	4-8	2-7	-2.8%	3.9	2.2	0.074	19	0.085	16	0.0%	0.0%	0.0%
74	Georgia Southern	8-4	6-2	-2.9%	7.7	5.5	0.219	64	0.611	82	2.2%	1.5%	0.1%
75	Colorado	3-9	2-7	-3.0%	3.4	1.6	0.124	41	0.134	27	0.0%	0.0%	0.0%
76	Toledo	9-3	6-2	-3.5%	8.8	6.4	0.707	122	0.923	124	61.8%	26.0%	1.1%
77	North Carolina	3-9	2-6	-4.8%	3.3	1.7	0.144	46	0.221	50	0.1%	0.0%	0.0%
78	Southern Miss	7-5	6-2	-6.6%	7.4	6.0	0.138	44	0.923	123	39.3%	19.6%	0.8%
79	Air Force	7-5	5-3	-7.0%	7.0	4.5	0.439	98	0.472	62	0.4%	0.2%	0.0%
80	Marshall	8-4	6-2	-7.0%	7.6	6.0	0.508	102	0.923	119	45.2%	22.6%	1.0%
81	Western Michigan	7-5	5-3	-8.0%	7.4	5.2	0.523	106	0.848	99	16.6%	7.0%	0.3%
82	Northern Illinois	7-5	5-3	-8.4%	6.6	5.2	0.445	99	0.848	98	18.6%	7.8%	0.3%
83	South Florida	6-6	4-4	-9.5%	5.5	3.9	0.317	83	0.495	65	0.4%	0.2%	0.0%
84	Nevada	7-5	4-4	-11.0%	6.7	4.4	0.382	90	0.543	74	2.3%	0.9%	0.0%
85	Louisiana Tech	8-4	5-3	-11.2%	8.3	5.4	0.700	121	0.922	112	18.8%	9.4%	0.4%
86	Florida Atlantic	7-5	6-2	-11.6%	7.4	5.5	0.293	79	0.922	109	29.6%	14.8%	0.6%
87	UAB	8-4	6-2	-13.9%	8.4	5.6	0.746	125	0.922	115	22.5%	11.3%	0.5%
88	Miami-OH	6-6	5-3	-14.4%	6.1	5.0	0.180	54	0.858	100	8.9%	5.2%	0.2%
89	Buffalo	7-5	5-3	-14.6%	7.3	5.2	0.456	101	0.895	103	12.1%	7.0%	0.3%
90	North Texas	7-5	5-3	-16.0%	7.3	5.3	0.849	129	0.922	113	19.3%	9.6%	0.4%
91	Florida International	7-5	5-3	-17.8%	7.2	4.7	0.734	124	0.923	118	10.0%	5.0%	0.2%
92	Middle Tennessee	6-6	5-3	-18.3%	6.0	4.8	0.271	75	0.923	120	12.4%	6.2%	0.3%
93	Wyoming	6-6	3-5	-19.1%	5.6	3.3	0.287	77	0.409	59	0.0%	0.0%	0.0%
94	SMU	5-7	3-5	-21.9%	4.8	3.3	0.510	103	0.671	86	1.3%	0.6%	0.0%
95	Louisville	2-10	1-7	-24.0%	2.2	0.7	0.098	31	0.190	40	0.0%	0.0%	0.0%
96	Western Kentucky	5-7	4-4	-24.1%	5.3	3.5	0.824	127	0.922	111	2.5%	1.3%	0.1%
97	Tulane	4-8	3-5	-25.1%	4.3	2.7	0.217	63	0.530	71	0.4%	0.2%	0.0%
98	Eastern Michigan	6-6	4-4	-27.4%	6.1	3.9	0.725	123	0.912	107	2.9%	1.2%	0.1%
99	Tulsa	3-9	2-6	-28.0%	3.3	2.2	0.308	80	0.537	72	0.1%	0.1%	0.0%
100	UL-Lafayette	5-7	3-5	-28.0%	5.2	3.3	0.341	86	0.723	90	2.1%	0.6%	0.0%
101	Illinois	3-9	1-8	-29.4%	3.1	1.0	0.131	42	0.135	28	0.0%	0.0%	0.0%
102	Hawaii	4-9	2-6	-31.0%	4.4	2.5	0.251	73	0.528	70	0.2%	0.1%	0.0%
103	Navy	4-8	3-5	-32.1%	4.3	3.0	0.313	82	0.689	87	0.4%	0.2%	0.0%
104	UNLV	3-9	2-6	-33.8%	3.4	2.2	0.455	100	0.582	79	0.0%	0.0%	0.0%
105	UL-Monroe	4-8	3-5	-33.9%	4.4	3.4	0.370	89	0.622	84	2.7%	0.8%	0.0%
106	Colorado State	3-9	2-6	-34.9%	3.0	1.7	0.398	91	0.441	60	0.0%	0.0%	0.0%

Rk	Team	Rec	Conf	F/+	MW	CW	SOS	Rk	CSOS	Rk	Div	Conf	CFP
107	East Carolina	4-8	2-6	-38.9%	4.3	1.8	0.436	97	0.557	77	0.0%	0.0%	0.0%
108	Rutgers	2-10	0-9	-39.8%	1.9	0.5	0.058	16	0.060	14	0.0%	0.0%	0.0%
109	Texas State	4-8	3-5	-39.9%	4.3	2.8	0.348	88	0.619	83	0.8%	0.3%	0.0%
110	Oregon State	1-11	0-9	-40.1%	1.5	0.2	0.150	48	0.180	38	0.0%	0.0%	0.0%
111	Kansas	2-10	0-9	-40.2%	1.9	0.2	0.147	47	0.156	33	-	0.0%	0.0%
112	Ball State	3-9	2-6	-42.1%	3.0	1.8	0.649	114	0.895	101	0.0%	0.0%	0.0%
113	Liberty	5-7	-	-43.0%	5.1	0.0	0.679	118	-	-	-	-	0.0%
114	Central Michigan	4-8	2-6	-43.8%	3.9	2.2	0.342	87	0.917	108	0.1%	0.0%	0.0%
115	New Mexico	4-8	2-6	-44.5%	3.6	1.6	0.244	72	0.509	68	0.0%	0.0%	0.0%
116	Akron	3-9	2-6	-44.5%	3.1	2.1	0.859	130	0.901	106	0.1%	0.0%	0.0%
117	Old Dominion	4-8	2-6	-44.6%	3.5	2.0	0.680	119	0.923	122	0.2%	0.1%	0.0%
118	Charlotte	4-8	2-6	-44.8%	3.5	1.9	0.226	66	0.923	117	0.1%	0.1%	0.0%
119	Coastal Carolina	4-8	2-6	-45.0%	4.0	1.8	0.591	112	0.609	81	0.0%	0.0%	0.0%
120	Kent State	3-9	2-6	-45.4%	3.1	2.1	0.183	56	0.848	97	0.0%	0.0%	0.0%
121	San Jose State	3-9	1-7	-46.1%	2.5	1.2	0.545	109	0.644	85	0.0%	0.0%	0.0%
122	Georgia State	3-9	2-6	-46.2%	2.9	1.8	0.576	111	0.732	92	0.0%	0.0%	0.0%
123	Bowling Green	3-9	2-6	-46.6%	2.9	1.8	0.401	92	0.895	102	0.0%	0.0%	0.0%
124	Massachusetts	4-8	-	-47.8%	4.1	0.0	0.691	120	-	-	-	-	0.0%
125	New Mexico State	3-9	-	-48.9%	3.2	0.0	0.166	50	-	-	-	-	0.0%
126	South Alabama	2-10	1-7	-49.0%	2.4	1.3	0.554	110	0.729	91	0.2%	0.1%	0.0%
127	UTSA	3-9	2-6	-49.6%	2.9	1.9	0.434	96	0.922	110	0.0%	0.0%	0.0%
128	Rice	1-11	1-7	-50.9%	1.4	1.4	0.638	113	0.922	114	0.0%	0.0%	0.0%
129	UTEP	3-9	2-6	-51.6%	3.4	1.9	0.827	128	0.922	116	0.1%	0.0%	0.0%
130	Connecticut	2-10	1-7	-53.0%	2.5	0.9	0.409	93	0.467	61	0.0%	0.0%	0.0%

FO Rookie Projections

Over the years, Football Outsiders has developed a number of methods for forecasting the NFL success of highly drafted players at various positions. Here is a rundown of those methods and what they say about players drafted in 2019.

Quarterbacks: QBASE

The QBASE (Quarterback Adjusted Stats and Experience) system analyzes the last 20 years of rookie quarterbacks chosen among the top 100 picks of the NFL draft, and uses regression analysis to determine which factors helped predict their total passing DYAR in Years 3 through 5 of their careers. (We use these years to account for the fact that many highly drafted quarterbacks may not play regularly until their second or even third seasons.)

The primary factor in QBASE is the quarterback's college performance, analyzed with three metrics: completion rate, yards per attempt adjusted based on touchdowns and interceptions, and team passing S&P+ from Football Outsiders' college stats. We then adjust based on strength of schedule and strength of teammates. The latter element gives credit based on the draft-pick value of offensive linemen and receivers drafted in the quarterback's draft year as well as the projected draft position of younger teammates in 2020.

The measurement of past performance is then combined with two other factors: college experience and draft position. The latter factor accounts for what scouts will see but a statistical projection system will not, including personality, leadership, and projection of physical attributes to the next level.

QBASE also looks at the past performance of quarterbacks compared to their projection and using 50,000 simulations, produces a range of potential outcomes for each prospect: Elite quarterback (over 2,500 DYAR in Years 3 through 5), Upper Tier quarterback (1,500 to 2,500 DYAR), Adequate Starter (500 to 1,500 DYAR), or Bust (less than 500 DYAR in Years 3 through 5).

Here are QBASE projections for quarterbacks chosen in the top 100 picks of the 2018 NFL draft:

Player	College	Tm	Rd	Pick	QBASE	Elite	Upper Tier	Adequate	Bust
Kyler Murray	OKLA	ARI	1	1	595	7%	16%	29%	48%
Daniel Jones	DUKE	NYG	1	6	279	4%	12%	27%	57%
Dwayne Haskins	OSU	WAS	1	17	465	5%	14%	29%	52%
Drew Lock	MIZZ	DEN	2	42	99	2%	11%	24%	63%
Will Grier	WV	CAR	3	100	-240	1%	7%	19%	73%

Projections are slightly different from those posted on our website in April because they have been adjusted for each player's actual draft position instead of projected draft position.

Running Backs: BackCAST

BackCAST is Football Outsiders' metric for projecting the likelihood of success for running back prospects in the NFL draft. Historically, a college running back attack is more likely to succeed at the NFL level if he has a good size/speed combination, gained a high average yards per carry, and represented a large percentage of his college team's running attack. Criteria measured include:

- Weight and 40-yard dash time at the NFL combine. BackCAST uses pro day measurements for prospects that did not run at the combine.
- Average yards per rush attempt, with an adjustment for running backs who had fewer career carries than an average drafted running back.
- A measurement of how much each prospect's team used him in the running game during his career relative to an average drafted running back in the same year of eligibility.
- Prospect's receiving yards per game in his college career.

BackCAST considers these factors and projects the degree to which the running back will exceed the NFL production of an "average" drafted running back during his first five years in the NFL. For example, a running back with a 50% BackCAST is projected to gain 50 percent more yards than the "average" drafted running back. BackCAST also lists each running back's "RecIndex," measuring whether the player is likely to be a ground-and-pound two-down back, more of a receiving back, or something in between.

Here are the BackCAST numbers for edge rushers drafted in the first three rounds of the 2019 draft, along with the four later-round picks with the highest BackCAST ratings. Your eyes do not deceive you; most of the top-selected running backs in the 2019 draft were players who did poorly in the BackCAST projections.

Player	College	Tm	Rd	Pick	BackCAST	RecIndex
Josh Jacobs	ALA	OAK	1	24	-39.3%	0.02
Miles Sanders	PSU	PHI	2	53	-25.5%	-0.26
Darrell Henderson	MEM	LAR	3	70	116.1%	0.35
David Montgomery	ISU	CHI	3	73	24.0%	0.06
Devin Singletary	FAU	BUF	3	74	13.6%	0.01
Damien Harris	ALA	NE	3	87	-8.4%	-0.22
Alexander Mattison	BSU	MIN	3	102	-13.0%	-0.02
Trayveon Williams	TAMU	CIN	6	182	57.3%	0.16
Justice Hill	OKST	BAL	4	113	46.5%	-0.03
Bryce Love	STAN	WAS	4	112	39.3%	0.00
Benny Snell	UK	PIT	4	122	35.3%	-0.37

Edge Rushers: SackSEER

SackSEER is a method that projects sacks for edge rushers, including both 3-4 outside linebackers and 4-3 defensive ends, using the following criteria:

- An "explosion index" that measures the prospect's scores in the 40-yard dash, the vertical jump, and the broad jump in pre-draft workouts.
- Sacks per game, adjusted for factors such as early entry in the NFL Draft and position switches during college.
- Passes defensed per game.
- Missed games of NCAA eligibility due to academic problems, injuries, benchings, suspensions, or attendance at junior college.

SackSEER outputs two numbers. The first, SackSEER Rating, solely measures how high the prospect scores compared to players of the past. The second, SackSEER Projection, represents a forecast of sacks for the player's first five years in the NFL. It synthesizes metrics with conventional wisdom by adjusting based on the player's expected draft position (interestingly, not his actual draft position) based on pre-draft analysis at the site NFLDraftScout.com.

Here are the SackSEER numbers for edge rushers drafted in the first three rounds of the 2019 draft, along with three later-round picks and one UDFA who had a high SackSEER Rating.

Name	College	Tm	Rnd	Pick	SackSEER Projection	SackSEER Rating
Nick Bosa	OSU	SF	1	2	22.1	67.4%
Clelin Ferrell	CLEM	OAK	1	4	17.6	49.0%
Josh Allen	UK	JAX	1	7	26.3	87.5%
Rashan Gary	MICH	GB	1	12	22.1	71.8%
Brian Burns	FSU	CAR	1	16	26.6	96.1%
Montez Sweat	MSST	WAS	1	26	25.7	89.7%
L.J. Collier	TCU	SEA	1	29	16.6	40.8%
Ben Banogu	TCU	IND	2	49	12.2	85.6%
Zach Allen	BC	ARI	3	65	19.6	71.8%
Jachai Polite	FLA	NYJ	3	68	15.7	30.3%
Chase Winovich	MICH	NE	3	77	13.5	36.7%
Jaylon Ferguson	LT	BAL	3	85	16.0	65.8%
Oshane Ximines	ODU	NYG	3	95	18.0	80.6%
John Cominsky	CHARLESTON	ATL	4	135	13.7	88.8%
Porter Gustin	USC	NO	UDFA	--	9.7	83.6%
Anthony Nelson	IOWA	TB	4	107	10.5	82.7%
Maxx Crosby	EMU	OAK	4	106	9.4	75.6%

Wide Receivers: Playmaker Score

Playmaker Score projects success for NFL wide receivers using the following criteria:

- The wide receiver's peak season for receiving yards per team attempt and receiving touchdowns per team attempt.
- Differences between this prospect's peak season and most recent season, to adjust for players who declined in their final college year.
- College career yards per reception.
- Rushing attempts per game.
- Vertical jump from pre-draft workouts.
- A binary variable that rewards players who enter the draft as underclassmen.

Like SackSEER, Playmaker Score outputs two numbers. The first, Playmaker Rating, solely measures how high the prospect scores compared to players of the past. The second, Playmaker Projection, represents a forecast of average receiving yards per year in the player's first five seasons, synthesizing metrics with conventional wisdom by adjusting based on the player's expected draft position.

Here are the Playmaker Score numbers for players drafted in the first three rounds of the 2019 draft, along with three later-round picks (and two UDFAs) with a high Playmaker Rating.

Name	College	Team	Rnd	Pick	Playmaker Projection	Playmaker Rating
Marquise Brown	OKLA	BAL	1	25	632	90.8%
N'Keal Harry	ASU	NE	1	32	457	89.6%
Deebo Samuel	SCAR	SF	2	36	347	54.9%
A.J. Brown	MISS	TEN	2	51	500	83.2%
Mecole Hardman	UGA	KC	2	56	303	73.0%
JJ Arcega-Whiteside	STAN	PHI	2	57	549	88.0%
Parris Campbell	OSU	IND	2	59	369	47.0%
Andy Isabella	UMASS	ARI	2	62	405	85.7%
D.K. Metcalf	MISS	SEA	2	64	489	73.0%
Diontae Johnson	TOL	PIT	3	66	346	86.0%
Jalen Hurd	BAY	SF	3	67	282	62.4%
Terry McLaurin	OSU	WAS	3	76	149	21.4%
Miles Boykin	ND	BAL	3	93	170	54.8%
Hakeem Butler	ISU	ARI	4	103	496	93.8%
Dillon Mitchell	ORE	MIN	7	239	239	85.3%
Antoine Wesley	TTU	BAL	UDFA	--	215	82.2%
Greg Dortch	WAKE	NYJ	UDFA	--	260	77.7%
Darius Slayton	AUB	NYG	5	171	260	76.5%

Top 25 Prospects

Every year, Football Outsiders puts together a list of the NFL's best and brightest young players who have barely played. Eighty percent of the draft-day discussion is about first-round picks, and 10 percent is about the players who should have been first-round picks, but instead went in the second round.

This list is about the others.

Everybody knows that Quinnen Williams and Nick Bosa are good. There's a cottage industry around the idea of hyping every draft's No. 1 quarterback as a potential superstar. But players don't stop being promising just because they don't make waves in their rookie seasons. This is a list of players who have a strong chance to make an impact in the NFL despite their lack of draft stock and the fact that they weren't immediate NFL starters.

Previous editions of the list have hyped players such as Geno Atkins, Grady Jarrett, David Johnson, Tyreek Hill, and Jamaal Charles before they blew up. Last year's list included Kenny Golladay, Aaron Jones, Larry Ogunjobi, and Chris Godwin.

Most of these lists are heavily dependent on the depth of incoming draft classes. For instance, this year's list doesn't have many wide receivers, because most of the players either played right away or didn't have the requisite talent. Last year's list was packed with wideouts. This year is heavier on the beef, after a 2018 draft class that was quite strong on the defensive line.

This is the 13th anniversary of the list. We're still relying on the same things we always do: scouting, statistics, measurables, context, ceiling, expected role, and what we hear from other sources. The goal is to bring your attention to players who are still developing in their second and third seasons, even after the draftniks have forgotten them. It's important to note that this list is not strictly about fantasy football (otherwise, there wouldn't be offensive linemen on it) and it's about career potential, not just the 2019 season.

Here's our full criteria:

- Drafted in the third round or later, or signed as an undrafted free agent.
- Entered the NFL between 2016 and 2018.
- Fewer than 500 career offensive or defensive snaps (except running backs, who are allowed just 300 offensive snaps).
- Have not signed a contract extension (players who have bounced around the league looking for the right spot, however, still qualify for the list).
- Age 26 or younger in 2019.

1 EDGE Lorenzo Carter, New York Giants
442 defensive snaps, age 23, 3rd-round pick (2018)

When the Giants snagged Carter in the third round, they were making a bet on tools over production. Carter's 4.50 40-yard dash and explosive results in the vertical and broad jump metrics made him someone who fit the NFL mold of a top edge rusher. His results at Georgia? Not so good. Carter had just 14 sacks despite serious playing time in all four seasons with the Bulldogs. Our SackSEER projection system took the middle ground, projecting him for 18.3 sacks in his first five seasons on the basis of the athleticism.

Carter's early returns have been pretty good: four sacks and 16 hurries. He saw a boost in snap count late in the season as the Giants were playing out the string, after mostly being used behind Kareem Martin and Connor Barwin. He has been drawing hype all offseason from Giants reporters and coaches and seems zeroed in on a breakout season.

Carter has a very safe floor compared to a lot of this list. Even if he's never an edge rushing force, he's got coverage skills and uncommon athleticism that will keep him in the NFL. If his physical profile wins out, you can expect production along the lines of another Georgia product: Bears edge rusher Leonard Floyd.

2 DL Da'Shawn Hand, Detroit Lions
455 defensive snaps, age 23, 4th-round pick (2018)

Hand was the consensus No. 1 recruit in his class coming out of high school in 2014 but didn't live up to expectations at Alabama. He had great technique and strength, but he never became the kind of force you'd expect from his tools. Hand paired that résumé with a subpar combine in which he ran a self-destructive 7.98-second 3-cone drill and fell all the way to the fourth round. The one saving grace was his 34⅜-inch arm length; some NFL teams measure pass-rushers by how much distance they can gain with their arms.

Despite the subpar college career, Hand has become a force for the Lions. He had 14 hurries as a rookie to go along with three sacks and six defeats. He played sterling run defense as well. Sometimes pro-level coaching and training can take an underachieving college player and raise him to the next level. Now Hand gets to line up next to Trey Flowers and Damon Harrison for a full season and enjoy the fruits of their labor.

A PFWA all-rookie team selection, Hand sprained his MCL late in the season, and that's the only reason he's still eligible for the list. Hand is going to grip-and-rip past Lions opponents for a long time.

3 WR Keke Coutee, Houston Texans
267 offensive snaps, age 22, 4th-round pick (2018)

Texas Tech's speedy wideout wasn't deeply appreciated by the "talk to the scouts" crew, who tend to disregard production coming out of lower-profile Air Raid schools. Coutee was also dinged at the NFL combine, where he had subpar showings across the board—aside from his 4.43 40-yard dash time—and where he measured in at 5-foot-9, 181 pounds.

So it said a lot that the Texans still believed he was worth taking in the fourth round. Despite dealing with hamstring troubles all season, Coutee caught 11 balls in his first game in

Week 4. He's got the speed to threaten the deep post from the slot but hasn't been utilized like that yet in Houston. When the Texans tried last year, he was just a step out of sync with Deshaun Watson.

Coutee's seasonal upside depends mainly on Will Fuller's health, but Coutee has the potential to be one of the best slot receivers in the NFL for the next three years. He can win short, he can win deep, and he has the ability when healthy to break tackles in space. All he needs is the opportunity.

4 TE Mark Andrews, Baltimore Ravens
414 offensive snaps, age 22, 3rd-round pick (2018)

Andrews took a lot of flak from NFL teams and the draft community for a complete inability to block in college, but he has been pretty solid as a pass-blocker for the Ravens when he has been called upon. He won't win the line of scrimmage as a run-game player too often, but he has the size to be an obstacle.

What Andrews brings is the ability to be a big part of a passing offense at tight end. He had 958 receiving yards in his junior season and was a core reason Oklahoma's opponents couldn't really handle the offense. If they keyed on the pass offense, Andrews was blocking a small college corner. If they keyed on the run offense, Andrews was a physical mismatch.

When Lamar Jackson took over as the starter, Andrews became the Ravens' primary downfield threat. He finished second among all tight ends in receiving DVOA and had the fourth-highest average depth of target. The 6-foot-5 frame should give him a chance to remain a mismatch for safeties.

5 DT Maurice Hurst, Oakland Raiders
472 defensive snaps, age 24, 5th-round pick (2018)

The easiest players to project onto this list are ones who fall in the draft for reasons over which they have no control. Great player plus bad circumstance usually equals a good opportunity for draft value, which usually increases the odds that a player lands here.

Hurst wrecked shop at Michigan, totaling 32 tackles for loss and 15.5 sacks in three seasons. But alarms went off at the NFL scouting combine because of a heart condition. If your favorite team's medical staff had cleared Hurst, though, it was obvious what kind of player he was. Hurst ended the year with four sacks, six hurries, and three disruptions. After so much of Oakland's draft class firebombed, and the Raiders heavily overdrafted some of their higher picks in 2019, he's probably the brightest ray of light left in the box.

Hurst fits another one of the classic undervalued draft archetypes: the smaller defensive tackle who creates havoc inside yet falls after NFL scouts don't take him seriously because of his size. The patron saint of that category is Aaron Donald, who didn't go in the top 10 despite being the best player in the 2014 draft. We think the Raiders would be very happy if Hurst followed in the more reasonable footsteps of Geno Atkins or Grady Jarrett.

6 RB Jaylen Samuels, Pittsburgh Steelers
228 offensive snaps, age 23, 5th-round pick (2018)

North Carolina State's Swiss Army knife went to Pittsburgh

and immediately showed off his speed and skill in the receiving game. Samuels came out of N.C. State as half-running back, half-tight end. The tweener label was stuck on Samuels. However, the athleticism out of this 225-pound package kind of screams "could be a three-down back" to us.

Samuels posted a 36.4% receiving DVOA out of the backfield in his first season, and while that was inflated by a 90 percent catch rate, Samuels also broke 11 tackles in just 82 touches.

Coming into the year behind James Conner, Samuels will probably be the primary passing-down back. It's possible he never grows beyond that and plays a Danny Woodhead-esque role. But Samuels is also stout enough and has the moves behind the line of scrimmage to play his way into a bigger spot than that. If he does, well, there aren't many running backs that play all three downs in today's NFL. The ceiling might look something like David Johnson, and he gives the Steelers a lot of extra flexibility in theory with his ability to play tight end.

7 EDGE Josh Sweat, Philadelphia Eagles
66 defensive snaps, age 22, 4th-round pick (2018)

Sweat blew up our SackSEER system last offseason, and it's all on athleticism. He ran a 4.53-second 40-yard dash at the NFL combine and had terrific scores in the vertical leap and broad jump as well. Thus, despite classifying him with a lower projection on the basis of his projected draft round, SackSEER still thought he was about as good as any of the pass-rushers who went after the first round (outside of Harold Landry, who should have been drafted in the first). Sweat's 14.5 sacks in three college seasons were not all that impressive, but the tools should make him play above that number.

Sweat's rookie season in Philadelphia was mostly invested in watching the fearsome veterans the Eagles have assembled kick butt and take names. The Howie Roseman Eagles have a long history of young linemen watching early, then getting up to speed quickly once given a chance.

With Michael Bennett and Chris Long departing this offseason, the Eagles roll into the year with Vinny Curry, Derek Barnett, and Sweat all itching for time next to Brandon Graham. It's likely all of them will get a chunk of playing time with how the Eagles run things. Sweat has the most imposing physical profile, and comps well to Vikings star Danielle Hunter in that area. He's going to have to develop like Hunter to get playing time on this line.

8 QB Mason Rudolph, Pittsburgh Steelers
0 offensive snaps, age 24, 3rd-round pick (2018)

Rudolph threw for 13,618 yards and 92 touchdowns at Oklahoma State, giving him plenty of clout with scouts as a potential first-round pick. Instead, he slid to the third round, where the Steelers picked him as a potential future replacement for aging quarterback Ben Roethlisberger. QBASE, our quarterback projection system, gave Rudolph a middling projection. He ate up a lot of cream-puff defenses with the Cowboys in the Big 12, and that, combined with the third-round projection, were the reasons his statistics didn't translate to greatness for QBASE.

Rudolph had a somewhat uneven preseason, throwing a pick-six and completing just 54.5 percent of his passes. However, he did average 7.2 yards per attempt. It's easy to see how and why the Steelers valued him in comparing him to Roethlisberger. Rudolph has great accuracy in the vertical passing game, and he is more than willing to stand in the pocket and take shots to complete those deep balls. If he can develop short-game accuracy and better pocket awareness under pressure, he's got the tools to be an NFL starter. If he stalls out, well, Zach Mettenberger had plenty of fans, too.

Rudolph was getting praise in minicamp for looking more comfortable in the offense in his second year, and he took a lot of first-team reps as Roethlisberger took it easy. This is a big offseason for him, and even the preseason games are going to matter a lot. The early returns look good, and Roethlisberger's interception rate reached a point last season where it's not totally impossible to see the Steelers ready to hand over the reins in the near future.

9 S Ronnie Harrison, Jacksonville Jaguars
328 defensive snaps, age 22, 3rd-round pick (2018)

A massive 80¾-inch wingspan with plus speed makes Harrison a sideline-to-sideline player. He got on the field as a sophomore at Alabama, which is no small feat, and showed versatility and skill. He's most notable for bringing the hammer; he's an impact tackler who can disrupt receivers and runners to create turnovers.

Harrison took over the starting safety role from Barry Church in December after Church was released. Harrison is capable of playing either deep safety or in the box, but projects better in the box as a run-stuffer. The Jaguars have mostly committed to big nickel as a base defense, making Harrison a potential fit like Mark Barron or Patrick Chung in that role. Despite drawing acclaim from most draftniks, Harrison's rookie year man-coverage play was poor, which could limit his ceiling if he doesn't develop that part of his game further.

Minicamp reports about Harrison's speed and body development were quite promising, and defensive coordinator Todd Wash was happy with his work. If Harrison puts it all together, his ceiling is a role along the lines of what Landon Collins did for the Giants on his rookie contract.

10 LB Ja'Whaun Bentley, New England Patriots
138 defensive snaps, age 23, 5th-round pick (2018)

A surprise starter at the beginning of last season as a fifth-round pick, Bentley tore his bicep and went on IR after Week 3, but he had already begun to show promise in that small sample size. He picked off Matthew Stafford and provided three quarterback pressures over the three games. And, of course, Bentley came into the NFL billed as one of the top run-stuff linebackers in the draft and did a solid job at that as well.

Bentley ran a 4.67 40-yard dash at 246 pounds at his Purdue pro day (he wasn't invited to the combine). But it was pretty much unanimous among draft analysts that he wasn't going to be a three-down linebacker at the next level; even the ones

who complimented Bentley's zone coverage believed that he looked stiff in the hips at times.

It's hard to completely cut through the New England offseason rhetoric, but with Jamie Collins back in town the Patriots in theory have enough linebackers to get Bentley off the field in passing situations if that is warranted. Instead, the OTA smoke has been that Bentley may be wearing the helmet communicator and that he was getting snaps over Elandon Roberts with the ones. The intangibles are telling us a story that isn't quite supported by the draft profile, but the intangibles can sometimes speak quite loudly. We buy Bentley as a big part of the Patriots defense this year, even if we are a little skeptical of his ceiling.

11 OL Martinas Rankin, Houston Texans
430 offensive snaps, age 24, 3rd-round pick (2018)

Coming out of Mississippi State, Rankin drew a Justin Britt comp from NFL.com's Lance Zierlein, who believed Rankin would be an instant starter on the interior line. As a college tackle, he struggled with edge speed. But Rankin has the athleticism to be terrific on the interior and his strength will play as more of a plus tool inside.

Rankin was a disaster in his rookie year, but the context of that disaster was that he was confined to playing tackle for most of the first half of the season because of injuries and poor play from other Texans linemen. Of the 15 blown blocks that SIS credited to Rankin, only three of them occurred after Week 5. When Rankin rotated back into things, he was inserted at guard late in the season.

It's worth being skeptical about Rankin's performance in the near term just because the Texans haven't been very good at developing linemen under Bill O'Brien. But when put at guard late in the year, Rankin did just fine. He'll probably be able to do that again in 2019. If he improves at all, the Texans might just have one good offensive lineman.

12 S Tracy Walker, Detroit Lions
267 defensive snaps, age 24, 3rd-round pick (2018)

A small-school background with Louisana-Lafayette left outside observers and draftniks a little less sold on Walker's long-term future than the third-round pick would suggest. Most thought Walker was more of a fit in the later rounds of the draft. A 4.51 40-yard dash at the NFL combine helped get him some extra looks, and an 81½-inch wingspan didn't hurt either. Walker has humongous arms.

The Lions pounced on him, and Walker started to get snaps towards the end of last season. He gave up a 34-yard wheel route to Christian McCaffrey, but he also picked off Cam Newton on a deep cross where he straight up stole the ball from Curtis Samuel. Walker's early play was, overall, quite promising.

Most of Walker's snaps last season were as the deep safety, but he showed enough versatility that the Lions might play him closer to the line of scrimmage in 2019. It's up to how Matt Patricia wants to play things and how much he values that versatility up front. We think he's more valuable up front, but either way, Walker is going to be a strong starter.

13 CB J.C. Jackson, New England Patriots
395 defensive snaps, age 24, undrafted (2018)

Jackson was more than heralded by draftniks and media draft types, and the reason he went undrafted was clearly related to the 5-foot-9 height that made him less than an ideal choice to play on the outside in the NFL. Well, that and the April 2015 armed robbery arrest that lost him his scholarship at Florida. Jackson actually had the speed to play outside, running a 4.46 40-yard dash, but there were enough question marks to keep him out of the draft.

Jackson did not get serious playing time for the Patriots until Week 7, but he snagged three picks and allowed just 5.8 yards per pass. He also played out wide fairly often—he was neither a primary slot nor primary wide guy. Quarterbacks completed only seven of 20 passes targeting Jackson out wide; his most impressive work was probably holding Ben Roethlisberger to 4.8 yards per pass on 10 targets in Week 16.

Jackson was running with the ones in minicamp, though he'll get a push from Jason McCourty. It's hard to imagine him not being a starter given the head start he has on players like Duke Dawson, but let's pump the breaks a little on some of the articles saying could be better than Stephon Gilmore, at least until he leads the NFL in success rate like Gilmore did last year.

14 RB Justin Jackson, Los Angeles Chargers
149 offensive snaps, age 24, 7th-round pick (2018)

Jackson came into a crowded backfield situation behind Melvin Gordon and Austin Ekeler last season and managed to find some snaps with injuries. His college tape revealed a back who could reduce contact and make the nuanced moves that separate the good from the great as far as NFL backs. In his first season, he broke 20 tackles in just 65 touches.

The Chargers mostly used Jackson as a receiver last season; he had a 29.9% DVOA and caught 15 of 19 balls. That's a good result for Jackson mostly because, while he's a good runner, he wasn't exactly making contested catches and looking like a top-tier receiver in college.

The short-term limiter on Jackson is that the Chargers have tied up a ton of money in Melvin Gordon, and Austin Ekeler is also a stellar back in a third-down-focused role. So Jackson's playing time isn't easy to see and his draft status makes it easy for him to get lost in coaching turnover if that comes to pass. But the talent warrants a real opportunity and if he gets it, look out. For what it's worth, Chargers general manager Tom Telesco took Twitter questions this offseason and specifically mentioned Jackson as someone who will have a bigger role this season.

15 WR Deon Cain, Indianapolis Colts
0 offensive snaps, age 23, 6th-round pick (2018)

Here's a promising wideout who didn't get to play at all in 2018 after tearing his ACL in the preseason, and it's a damn shame for him because the players the Colts had set up ahead of him on the depth chart would have been child's play for him to beat out.

Cain ran a 4.43 40-yard dash at 202 pounds, pairing that with an explosive 6.71 3-cone drill time that told the story of his lateral agility. A failed drug test and team discipline helped contribute to his plunge to the sixth round, but Cain managed to hold steady at Clemson in his senior season despite Deshaun Watson leaving. Cain has true outside receiver talent, which is something you don't often see available in the sixth round, with the ability to play to his back shoulder and the speed to make it worthwhile. He's also got great open-field vision.

We leave him this low only because receivers that don't make an impact right away sometimes have trouble taking hold of a depth chart. Parris Campbell's selection likely fills two of the three available starting slots for Colts wideouts for the time being, with T.Y. Hilton also hanging outside. All Cain has to do is beat out Panthers washout Devin Funchess to start getting real targets. Cain stood out last summer, is getting talked up again this summer, and absolutely has the talent to contribute right away. Let's see if he gets the chance this time around.

16 CB Levi Wallace, Buffalo Bills
415 defensive snaps, age 24, undrafted (2018)

An interesting player because of his background, Wallace somehow managed to not draw enough attention to get drafted. Imagine somebody dominant at football. Now imagine that they're dominant on the highest stage of college football. They get invited to all-star games, play well at them, and … nothing. That's what happened to Wallace after leading the SEC in pass breakups and interceptions at Alabama. Scouts criticized his 6-foot-even frame and were not thrilled with his 4.63 40-yard dash at the combine. Wallace, a former walk-on, also didn't start at Alabama until his senior season.

In his first season with the Bills, injuries put Wallace into the lineup and he performed well, breaking up three passes and allowing just 4.6 yards per pass. To be fair to scouts, they did say he'd struggle with stronger, taller NFL wideouts because of his frame. Wallace did not face many of them. His only game against top-notch competition was when Buffalo went to New England in Week 16. The best receiver he played against was Kenny Golladay, and Golladay torched him on a broken play. The rest of the schedule he defended against was full of Keelan Coles, Donte Moncriefs, and that type of receiver.

That doesn't mean that Wallace can't be an effective corner—he showed he could be one, and his background is intriguing. But the lack of top-tier athleticism and the weak schedule could be something pointing at how well he performed being a bit of a fluke. Either way, the instincts should keep Wallace as a capable NFL player.

17 OT Tyrell Crosby, Detroit Lions
128 offensive snaps, age 23, 5th-round pick (2018)

Crosby was a surprise faller in the draft process, as most draftniks assumed he would be a top-50 pick. He played with terrific strength at Oregon and showed above-average athleticism at the combine. Most comments we heard about Crosby this fall tended to be about scouts not liking his body and the way it held its weight. Fast-forward and here's a player who could be a long-term starter at right tackle who was available in the fifth round. The Lions aren't complaining too much.

Crosby barely made it onto the field in his first season because of Rick Wagner and Taylor Decker at tackle. This offseason presented a different opportunity, because the release of T.J. Lang (who subsequently retired) left a gigantic hole at guard. The Lions didn't have settled depth at the position and are looking at Kenny Wiggins and Joe Dahl. That has led to questions about Crosby, and Matt Patricia stopped short of saying that Crosby wouldn't be considered at guard.

It would be an odd fit of talent, and Crosby would have to get more used to working with linemen close to his body rather than just winning with his long arms. But it might be the best way for the Lions to get their optimal starting five on the field this season. If not, Crosby still possesses starting NFL tackle talent, which isn't exactly a common trait. That's why he remains this high on the list.

18 NT Poona Ford, Seattle Seahawks
231 defensive snaps, age 23, undrafted (2018)

Ford went undrafted coming out of Texas because he's downright short for a tackle at just 5-foot-11. However, he did come up with 20.5 tackles for loss at Texas, and he does anchor well enough to play nose tackle in the NFL, given how the standards are changing for defenses. Ford wasn't invited to the combine, but he did notch a sack of Josh Allen in the Senior Bowl.

Ford was outstanding in the preseason for the Seahawks, making the roster as a free agent and eventually kicking veteran free-agent signing Tom Johnson entirely off the team. Ford got some work with the ones as the season went on, notching 17 tackles in his last five games.

With Shamar Stephens departing in free agency, Ford would seem to be a lock for a starting spot. Like DJ Reader a couple of years ago, Ford's upside is limited by his lack of real pass-rush moves. But his floor is so high that he belongs on this list regardless.

19 RB Gus Edwards, Baltimore Ravens
286 offensive snaps, age 24, undrafted (2018)

Edwards will lose his starting job to Mark Ingram, but the first season riding the Gus Bus proved that he's a great fit for the offense that Greg Roman put together. The downside of the Bus is that, no matter how hard he's working on it this offseason, he's not a passing-down back and there's almost zero chance he plays on third-and-longs.

The history of running backs with great rushing DVOA in limited playing time is not exactly as high as you'd like. Lamar Miller became more of a solid back than a great one, and Evan Royster washed out of the league entirely in almost no time. That said, it's worth pointing out that Edwards had a 13.9% DVOA in 2018 that ranked ninth in the NFL, and his Success Rate of 63 percent was the highest for any running back with at least 100 carries since 1993.

This is a unique situation for a number of reasons: Edwards' rookie success, a scheme that probably won't be replicated in the current NFL on a grand scale ever again, and the fact that

Edwards probably won't be a starter. But there's still so much statistical upside and he's such a decisive and smart runner that he belongs on this list.

20 CB Taron Johnson, Buffalo Bills
405 defensive snaps, age 23, 4th-round pick (2018)

Slot cornerback is not a position where the results have a strong year-to-year correlation. Kendall Fuller, for example, was one of the best slots in the business in 2017, but in 2018 after being a big part of the Alex Smith trade, he dropped to 47th among qualifying corners in success rate. But it's worth recognizing how great Johnson was for the Bills last season. Johnson finished with a 67 percent success rate on his 24 targets. He picked off Marcus Mariota and sacked Aaron Rodgers.

Johnson is a pure slot cornerback, checking in at 5-foot-11, 192 pounds at the NFL combine. Coming out of tiny Weber State, where he starred as a true freshman, Johnson plays bigger than his size in the run game. He isn't afraid to get physical and in fact can often get downright grabby in coverage. There's not a lot of upside in Johnson—he already is all that he can be—but good slot cornerbacks are very valuable in the current NFL.

Coming into this year, Johnson appears to be the favorite for slot snaps and Buffalo has only signed old or injury-prone depth at corner, so he should get a chance to demonstrate his talent again.

21 WR DaeSean Hamilton, Denver Broncos
471 offensive snaps, age 24, 4th-round pick (2018)

With Emmanuel Sanders' torn Achilles taking him out of the lineup, Hamilton finally had the slot receiver role all to himself in the final month of 2018. If you split out those games, Hamilton actually had a worse receiving DVOA in that month than he did over his full season, but his December DVOA of -21.1% was not far removed from the team's total of -17.9%. Everyone was struggling.

Hamilton came out of Penn State at 6-foot-1, 203 pounds, with a big slot body and a big slot game. He doesn't always play to that weight in strength, but he's quite nimble and able to find easy separation underneath. He dropped only one pass all season and managed to catch 65 percent of his targets despite most of them being from Case Keenum. He also broke zero tackles in 30 touches.

The reason Hamilton is not higher on this list is that his deep speed is non-existent and he's questionable even in the intermediate range. If Hamilton were a baseball player, he'd be the guy who can't hit much or run the bases but can work walks left and right. Separation is a valuable skill, and perhaps the most valuable one a receiver can have. But if it's all you have, you can't really deliver many knockout blows on your own.

22 OL Joseph Noteboom, Los Angeles Rams
78 offensive snaps, age 24, 3rd-round pick (2018)

After Rodger Saffold left for the Titans in free agency, and after they let John Sullivan walk as a free agent as well, the

Rams are thin up front and are going to have to rely on some draft picks and younger players. Of those, the one with the highest pedigree is Noteboom, who will be transitioning from college tackle to NFL guard.

Noteboom got himself moved up the board in the 2018 draft with his combine measurements. He ran a 4.96 40-yard dash at 309 pounds, and his short shuttle of 4.44 was in the 96th percentile of all offensive linemen who have performed at the combine since 2000.

The reason it didn't get him even higher than the third round is that his tape at TCU was pretty inconsistent. While he has the talent to make most blocks, he doesn't always make them. He also noticeably struggled with power. And with only 78 offensive snaps last year, we don't exactly have a large NFL sample size to rely on in projecting Noteboom's move to guard either. Noteboom is a low-floor prospect, but he's got so much physical talent that he'll probably keep getting chances even if he struggles early.

23 CB Holton Hill, Minnesota Vikings
374 defensive snaps, age 22, undrafted (2018)

Hill was kicked out of Texas for violating team rules, reportedly failing several drug tests while in Austin. On talent alone, though, Hill fits a lot of what the NFL wants out of its cornerbacks. He checked in at 6-foot-1 and 198 pounds at the combine, and he has the length to develop into a terrific press cornerback. He also started for the Longhorns as a true freshman before Tom Herman came to town.

Hill got a chance to jump into the starting lineup in Week 8 with the Vikings suffering from a rash of cornerback injuries. Hill finished his first season with a 63 percent success rate in coverage and allowed the lowest yards per pass of any Viking with more than 20 targets. He did this despite playing a pretty tough quarterback slate: Drew Brees, Aaron Rodgers, Tom Brady, and Russell Wilson were among the quarterbacks that got into his limited reps.

Hill has been suspended for the first four games of the season for "unknowingly" taking a banned substance. He also doesn't exactly have a job waiting for him when he comes back, as the Vikings are deep at cornerback. But his highs are so high that we felt he had to be on the list in spite of those facts.

24 TE Jordan Thomas, Houston Texans
470 offensive snaps, age 23, 5th-round pick (2018)

Of the two Jordan tight end prospects that the Texans have, we'd rate Jordan Akins as the one with the better ceiling even though Thomas is ahead on the depth chart. Akins has the talent to be a true No. 1 stretch tight end, and he demonstrated more skill in the receiving game. Fortunately for Thomas, he A) is 23 years old instead of the 27 that disqualifies Akins

from this list, and B) is ahead of Akins on the depth chart.

Thomas took over as the primary red zone tight end in the middle of the season after Ryan Griffin was found wanting. Thomas fits that role quite well as a 6-foot-5 former wideout at Mississippi State with big hands. A lot of Thomas' big catches actually came on busted plays last season, as tight ends aren't a huge part of the Bill O'Brien offense.

Thomas ran a nice 40 at the combine, but most of his other scores as an athlete were poor. His 20-yard shuttle time of 4.75 seconds was in the first percentile of all tight ends since 2000. However, Thomas also seemed to struggle with college coaching, and the Texans actually brought something out of him last year. He's got the size to be a better blocker than he is. There's an every-down tight end somewhere in here, but Thomas still has some steps to take.

25 DL Nathan Shepherd, New York Jets
343 defensive snaps, age 25, 3rd-round pick (2018)

Shepherd was another guy who saw wide appeal throughout the draftnik community; both those who watched the tape and those who mainly talked to scouts found something to like here. A Canadian entrant from Fort Hays State, Shepherd took well to his one chance at real competition in the Senior Bowl, turning heads before breaking his hand in practice. He has an interesting backstory as well, as a 205-pound high school linebacker who had a late growth spurt.

Unfortunately for Shepherd, the safety of his role took a big hit this offseason when the Jets settled on Quinnen Williams with the No. 3 overall pick. Steve McLendon and Henry Anderson both return as well, leaving the team with five competent interior defenders to go in three spots.

Shepherd had nine hurries and five quarterback hits despite having to win time on a stacked line. A best-case scenario for Shepherd could be following in the footsteps of a similarly sized interior player who was on the list last offseason: Browns defensive tackle Larry Ogunjobi. Of course, to follow in those footsteps, Shepherd has to actually get on the field.

Honorable Mentions

Will Dissly, TE, Seattle Seahawks
D'Onta Foreman, RB, Houston Texans
Trey Hendrickson, DE, New Orleans Saints
Jamarco Jones, OT, Seattle Seahawks
Josey Jewell, LB, Denver Broncos
Harrison Phillips, DT, Buffalo Bills
Will Richardson, OT, Jacksonville Jaguars
Deadrin Senat, DT, Atlanta Falcons
Vince Taylor, DT, Miami Dolphins
Kenny Young, LB, Baltimore Ravens

Rivers McCown

Fantasy Projections

Here are the top 275 players according to the KUBIAK projection system, ranked by projected fantasy value (**FANT**) in 2019. We've used the following generic scoring system:

- 1 point for each 10 yards rushing, 10 yards receiving, or 20 yards passing
- 6 points for each rushing or receiving TD, 4 points for each passing TD
- -2 points for each interception or fumble lost
- Kickers: 1 point for each extra point, 3 points for each field goal
- Team defense: 2 points for a fumble recovery, interception, or safety, 1 point for a sack, and 6 points for a touchdown.

These totals are then adjusted based on each player's listed **Risk** for 2019:

- Green: Standard risk, no change
- Yellow: Higher than normal risk, value dropped by five percent
- Red: Highest risk, value dropped by 10 percent
- Blue: Significantly lower than normal risk, value increased by five percent

Note that fantasy totals may not exactly equal these calculations, because each touchdown projection is not necessarily a round number. (For example, a quarterback listed with 2 rushing touchdowns may actually be projected with 2.4 rushing touchdowns, which will add 14 fantasy points to the player's total rather than 12.) Fantasy value does not include adjustments for week-to-week consistency,

Players are ranked in order based on marginal value of each player, the idea that you draft based on how many more points a player will score compared to the worst starting player at that position, not how many points a player scores overall. We've ranked players in five league configurations:

- Flex Rk: 12 teams, starts 1 QB, 2 RB, 2 WR, 1 FLEX (RB/WR), 1 TE, 1 K, and 1 D.
- 3WR Rk: 12 teams, starts 1 QB, 2 RB, 3 WR, 1 TE, 1 K, and 1 D.
- PPR Rk: 12 teams, starts 1 QB, 2 RB, 2 WR, 1 FLEX (RB/WR), 1 TE, 1 K, and 1 D. Also adds one point per reception to scoring.
- 10-3WR Rk: same as 3WR, but with only 10 teams.
- 10-PPR Rk: same as PPR, but with only 10 teams.

These rankings also reduce the value of kickers and defenses to reflect the general drafting habits of fantasy football players. (We estimated four bench players for each team; for each additional bench spot in your league, move kickers and defenses down 10 to 12 spots.) We urge you to draft using common sense, not a strict reading of these rankings.

An online application featuring these projections is also available at FootballOutsiders.com for a $25 fee. These projections can be customized to the rules of any specific league with the ability to save multiple league set-ups. The online KUBIAK application is updated based on injuries and changing forecasts of playing time during the preseason, and also has a version which includes individual defensive players.

Player	Team	Bye	Pos	Age	PaYd	PaTD	INT	Ru	RuYd	RuTD	Rec	RcYd	RcTD	FL	Fant	Risk	Flex Rk	3WR Rk	PPR Rk	10-3WR Rk	10-PPR Rk
Saquon Barkley	NYG	11	RB	22	0	0	0	297	1391	12	87	701	3	2	293	Green	1	1	1	1	1
Ezekiel Elliott	DAL	8	RB	24	0	0	0	310	1414	12	75	614	2	2	266	Yellow	2	2	3	2	3
Le'Veon Bell	NYJ	4	RB	27	0	0	0	296	1260	11	71	603	3	2	252	Yellow	3	3	5	3	5
Christian McCaffrey	CAR	7	RB	23	0	0	0	230	1031	7	97	813	4	1	247	Green	4	5	2	4	2
Alvin Kamara	NO	9	RB	24	0	0	0	200	903	10	82	726	4	2	238	Green	5	7	4	5	4
Melvin Gordon	LAC	12	RB	26	0	0	0	250	1081	8	66	622	3	2	222	Yellow	6	14	12	11	12
Todd Gurley	LAR	9	RB	25	0	0	0	238	1118	12	54	511	2	2	221	Red	7	15	17	12	19
James Conner	PIT	7	RB	24	0	0	0	238	1093	10	60	519	1	1	215	Yellow	8	17	15	13	17
DeAndre Hopkins	HOU	10	WR	27	0	0	0	0	0	0	104	1450	12	0	214	Green	9	4	6	6	6
David Johnson	ARI	12	RB	28	0	0	0	252	1033	6	73	690	3	2	211	Yellow	10	21	14	15	14
Nick Chubb	CLE	7	RB	24	0	0	0	261	1184	10	27	253	1	2	209	Green	11	22	32	17	32
Julio Jones	ATL	9	WR	30	0	0	0	0	0	0	103	1525	10	0	204	Yellow	12	6	8	7	8
Patrick Mahomes	KC	12	QB	24	4748	38	15	59	263	2	0	0	0	6	387	Green	13	9	25	9	21
Travis Kelce	KC	12	TE	30	0	0	0	0	0	0	96	1223	8	0	162	Yellow	14	11	11	10	9
Joe Mixon	CIN	9	RB	23	0	0	0	268	1192	8	47	378	2	2	201	Yellow	15	27	27	21	27
Davante Adams	GB	11	WR	27	0	0	0	2	12	0	106	1301	12	0	200	Green	16	8	7	8	7
Derrick Henry	TEN	11	RB	25	0	0	0	274	1229	10	21	192	1	2	200	Green	17	28	38	22	44
Dalvin Cook	MIN	12	RB	24	0	0	0	251	1103	7	58	464	2	2	197	Yellow	18	31	24	25	25
JuJu Smith-Schuster	PIT	7	WR	23	0	0	0	3	18	0	103	1325	9	0	189	Green	19	10	10	14	11
Michael Thomas	NO	9	WR	26	0	0	0	2	10	0	107	1302	9	0	187	Green	20	12	9	16	10
George Kittle	SF	4	TE	26	0	0	0	0	0	0	85	1151	7	0	147	Yellow	21	20	21	19	16
Mike Evans	TB	7	WR	26	0	0	0	5	31	0	85	1319	8	0	185	Green	22	13	16	18	18
Leonard Fournette	JAX	10	RB	24	0	0	0	249	1085	6	49	421	1	2	184	Yellow	23	41	36	33	38

Player	Team	Bye	Pos	Age	PaYd	PaTD	INT	Ru	RuYd	RuTD	Rec	RcYd	RcTD	FL	Fant	Risk	Flex Rk	3WR Rk	PPR Rk	10-3WR Rk	10-PPR Rk
Kerryon Johnson	DET	5	RB	22	0	0	0	225	1076	8	45	340	1	2	184	Yellow	24	43	37	34	41
Antonio Brown	OAK	6	WR	31	0	0	0	0	0	0	106	1336	10	0	183	Yellow	25	16	13	20	13
Tyreek Hill	KC	12	WR	25	0	0	0	20	85	0	80	1221	11	0	176	Red	26	18	26	23	26
Devonta Freeman	ATL	9	RB	27	0	0	0	208	952	7	46	397	2	1	176	Yellow	27	51	39	44	45
Zach Ertz	PHI	10	TE	29	0	0	0	0	0	0	99	1003	7	0	135	Yellow	28	29	20	26	15
T.Y. Hilton	IND	6	WR	30	0	0	0	2	10	0	82	1279	9	0	174	Yellow	29	19	23	24	24
Keenan Allen	LAC	12	WR	27	0	0	0	4	18	0	98	1290	8	0	171	Yellow	30	23	19	27	22
Odell Beckham	CLE	7	WR	27	0	0	0	3	16	0	89	1220	9	0	170	Yellow	31	24	22	28	23
Marlon Mack	IND	6	RB	23	0	0	0	240	1081	8	33	248	2	2	170	Red	32	59	57	49	63
Adam Thielen	MIN	12	WR	29	0	0	0	2	10	0	96	1196	8	0	170	Green	33	25	18	29	20
Andrew Luck	IND	6	QB	30	4455	35	12	44	177	1	0	0	0	4	353	Green	34	34	43	31	37
Brandin Cooks	LAR	9	WR	26	0	0	0	6	32	0	76	1137	8	0	166	Green	35	26	29	30	29
Aaron Rodgers	GB	11	QB	36	4523	31	11	42	220	1	0	0	0	3	349	Green	36	37	46	32	40
Hunter Henry	LAC	12	TE	25	0	0	0	0	0	0	60	780	7	0	121	Green	37	39	45	36	39
A.J. Green	CIN	9	WR	31	0	0	0	0	0	0	79	1160	9	0	160	Yellow	38	30	33	35	33
Deshaun Watson	HOU	10	QB	24	4073	29	13	85	481	5	0	0	0	5	344	Yellow	39	44	49	39	42
Josh Jacobs	OAK	6	RB	21	0	0	0	240	962	6	44	342	1	2	158	Yellow	40	69	58	60	64
Amari Cooper	DAL	8	WR	25	0	0	0	3	14	0	88	1166	8	0	158	Yellow	41	32	30	37	30
Baker Mayfield	CLE	7	QB	24	4509	33	13	46	155	1	0	0	0	5	343	Green	42	45	52	40	43
Tyler Lockett	SEA	11	WR	27	0	0	0	12	47	0	62	939	10	0	157	Green	43	33	41	38	46
Evan Engram	NYG	11	TE	25	0	0	0	0	0	0	71	875	5	0	117	Green	44	46	40	42	35
Chris Carson	SEA	11	RB	25	0	0	0	229	1026	8	19	185	1	2	155	Red	45	73	89	65	99
Julian Edelman	NE	10	WR	33	0	0	0	8	53	0	96	1086	8	0	155	Yellow	46	35	28	41	28
Robert Woods	LAR	9	WR	27	0	0	0	14	79	1	81	1057	6	0	154	Green	47	36	34	43	34
Kenyan Drake	MIA	5	RB	25	0	0	0	156	662	5	54	499	3	1	153	Yellow	48	76	53	67	57
Aaron Jones	GB	11	RB	25	0	0	0	188	917	7	36	305	1	1	153	Red	49	77	71	71	82
Phillip Lindsay	DEN	10	RB	25	0	0	0	181	853	7	38	305	1	1	152	Yellow	50	79	68	72	79
O.J. Howard	TB	7	TE	25	0	0	0	0	0	0	55	813	5	0	112	Green	51	50	60	46	49
Sony Michel	NE	10	RB	24	0	0	0	239	1056	9	11	91	1	1	152	Red	52	80	102	73	117
Mark Ingram	BAL	8	RB	30	0	0	0	204	959	6	31	246	1	1	151	Yellow	53	82	76	74	86
Stefon Diggs	MIN	12	WR	26	0	0	0	6	32	0	87	1015	8	0	150	Green	54	38	31	45	31
Matt Ryan	ATL	9	QB	34	4699	33	12	30	107	0	0	0	0	3	335	Yellow	55	53	59	48	50
Damien Williams	KC	12	RB	27	0	0	0	160	722	7	50	395	2	1	149	Red	56	87	66	77	73
Tyler Boyd	CIN	9	WR	25	0	0	0	0	0	0	83	1087	7	0	148	Green	57	40	35	47	36
D.J. Moore	CAR	7	WR	22	0	0	0	10	87	0	71	938	7	0	147	Green	58	42	42	50	47
David Njoku	CLE	7	TE	23	0	0	0	0	0	0	55	711	6	0	107	Green	59	57	65	52	54
Jared Goff	LAR	9	QB	25	4440	31	13	49	154	1	0	0	0	6	332	Green	60	58	62	51	53
Lamar Miller	HOU	10	RB	28	0	0	0	216	888	4	31	252	2	1	145	Green	61	91	82	84	92
Alshon Jeffery	PHI	10	WR	29	0	0	0	0	0	0	74	945	9	0	141	Yellow	62	47	47	53	51
Mike Williams	LAC	12	WR	25	0	0	0	3	19	0	62	918	8	0	141	Green	63	48	55	54	59
Cooper Kupp	LAR	9	WR	26	0	0	0	4	26	0	73	986	8	0	141	Yellow	64	49	48	55	52
Kenny Golladay	DET	5	WR	26	0	0	0	2	11	0	70	1031	7	0	137	Yellow	65	52	54	56	58
Cam Newton	CAR	7	QB	30	3747	25	12	108	525	5	0	0	0	5	323	Yellow	66	62	69	58	60
Jameis Winston	TB	7	QB	25	4729	28	17	54	254	1	0	0	0	5	322	Yellow	67	63	70	61	62
Chris Godwin	TB	7	WR	23	0	0	0	2	12	0	75	1020	7	0	136	Yellow	68	54	50	57	55
James White	NE	10	RB	27	0	0	0	76	349	1	83	746	5	1	136	Yellow	69	110	44	101	48
Vance McDonald	PIT	7	TE	29	0	0	0	0	0	0	53	668	5	0	96	Green	70	66	77	63	68
Sammy Watkins	KC	12	WR	26	0	0	0	4	18	0	60	836	8	0	135	Green	71	55	63	59	69
Jared Cook	NO	9	TE	32	0	0	0	0	0	0	58	695	5	0	95	Yellow	72	67	73	64	66
Calvin Ridley	ATL	9	WR	25	0	0	0	4	22	0	66	876	7	0	134	Green	73	56	56	62	61
Derrius Guice	WAS	10	RB	22	0	0	0	201	888	5	26	197	0	1	133	Yellow	74	118	107	105	130
Jimmy Graham	GB	11	TE	33	0	0	0	0	0	0	52	591	6	0	92	Green	75	71	83	70	75
Ben Roethlisberger	PIT	7	QB	37	4668	31	14	28	65	1	0	0	0	3	317	Yellow	76	72	75	69	70
Jarvis Landry	CLE	7	WR	27	0	0	0	3	18	0	76	917	6	0	131	Green	77	60	51	66	56
Allen Robinson	CHI	6	WR	26	0	0	0	2	11	0	68	942	7	0	130	Yellow	78	61	64	68	71
Delanie Walker	TEN	11	TE	35	0	0	0	0	0	0	64	730	5	0	90	Red	79	74	78	76	72
Russell Wilson	SEA	11	QB	31	3602	31	8	69	369	3	0	0	0	4	315	Yellow	80	75	79	75	74
Tevin Coleman	SF	4	RB	26	0	0	0	141	599	4	41	425	2	1	129	Yellow	81	138	94	121	105
Trey Burton	CHI	6	TE	28	0	0	0	0	0	0	53	561	5	0	87	Green	82	81	88	79	80
Latavius Murray	NO	9	RB	29	0	0	0	158	677	7	22	189	2	2	127	Yellow	83	151	135	131	145
Carson Wentz	PHI	10	QB	27	4559	31	11	57	187	1	0	0	0	5	312	Red	84	84	84	78	76
Drew Brees	NO	9	QB	40	4185	31	9	31	29	2	0	0	0	3	311	Yellow	85	85	86	81	78
David Montgomery	CHI	6	RB	22	0	0	0	184	767	7	24	209	1	2	125	Red	86	161	144	134	148
Austin Hooper	ATL	9	TE	25	0	0	0	0	0	0	65	631	4	0	85	Green	87	86	74	83	67
Sterling Shepard	NYG	11	WR	26	0	0	0	3	16	0	66	864	6	0	124	Green	88	64	67	80	77

Player	Team	Bye	Pos	Age	PaYd	PaTD	INT	Ru	RuYd	RuTD	Rec	RcYd	RcTD	FL	Fant	Risk	Flex Rk	3WR Rk	PPR Rk	10-3WR Rk	10-PPR Rk
Dede Westbrook	JAX	10	WR	26	0	0	0	5	23	0	78	905	6	0	123	Yellow	89	65	61	82	65
Miles Sanders	PHI	10	RB	22	0	0	0	175	745	5	31	221	1	2	123	Yellow	90	163	121	139	137
Kyler Murray	ARI	12	QB	22	3779	24	16	89	534	4	0	0	0	5	307	Yellow	91	88	90	87	81
Corey Davis	TEN	11	WR	24	0	0	0	3	16	0	62	877	5	0	122	Green	92	68	72	85	85
Mark Andrews	BAL	8	TE	23	0	0	0	0	0	0	43	578	3	0	81	Blue	93	92	110	89	97
Robby Anderson	NYJ	4	WR	26	0	0	0	0	0	0	55	827	6	0	120	Green	94	70	85	86	93
Dak Prescott	DAL	8	QB	26	3897	23	12	81	399	4	0	0	0	4	305	Yellow	95	94	92	90	84
Kyle Rudolph	MIN	12	TE	30	0	0	0	0	0	0	61	602	4	0	80	Yellow	96	96	93	91	83
Jordan Reed	WAS	10	TE	29	0	0	0	0	0	0	59	602	5	0	79	Red	97	97	100	92	88
Eric Ebron	IND	6	TE	26	0	0	0	0	0	0	46	510	5	0	79	Green	98	98	112	93	101
Jack Doyle	IND	6	TE	29	0	0	0	0	0	0	59	547	5	0	77	Red	99	100	101	97	91
Stephen Gostkowski	NE	10	K	35	0	0	0	0	0	0	0	0	0	0	135	Green	100	95	97	88	95
Mitchell Trubisky	CHI	6	QB	25	3777	27	13	68	369	3	0	0	0	6	301	Yellow	101	103	96	99	87
Marvin Jones	DET	5	WR	29	0	0	0	0	0	0	65	916	6	0	115	Red	102	78	87	95	96
Tarik Cohen	CHI	6	RB	24	0	0	0	75	347	2	63	531	2	1	115	Green	103	178	80	158	89
DeSean Jackson	PHI	10	WR	33	0	0	0	2	12	0	53	835	6	0	114	Yellow	104	83	98	98	110
Greg Olsen	CAR	7	TE	34	0	0	0	0	0	0	48	494	6	0	74	Red	105	106	128	102	113
Harrison Butker	KC	12	K	24	0	0	0	0	0	0	0	0	0	0	131	Green	106	101	104	94	103
Philip Rivers	LAC	12	QB	38	4356	33	9	23	15	0	0	0	0	2	296	Red	107	113	105	109	94
Greg Zuerlein	LAR	9	K	32	0	0	0	0	0	0	0	0	0	0	129	Green	108	105	106	100	106
Rams D	LAR	9	D	--	0	0	0	0	0	0	0	0	0	0	110	Green	109	107	108	96	104
Jordan Thomas	HOU	10	TE	23	0	0	0	0	0	0	41	470	4	0	69	Yellow	110	117	153	113	134
Mohamed Sanu	ATL	9	WR	30	0	0	0	4	24	0	63	778	5	0	109	Green	111	89	91	110	100
Larry Fitzgerald	ARI	12	WR	36	0	0	0	0	0	0	69	723	6	0	109	Green	112	90	81	111	90
Tom Brady	NE	10	QB	42	4218	29	13	26	38	2	0	0	0	4	294	Yellow	113	120	109	115	98
T.J. Hockenson	DET	5	TE	22	0	0	0	0	0	0	45	516	4	0	69	Red	114	121	151	117	132
Royce Freeman	DEN	10	RB	23	0	0	0	151	685	4	22	165	1	2	108	Yellow	115	191	177	165	177
Marquez Valdes-Scantling	GB	11	WR	25	0	0	0	2	12	0	59	861	5	0	108	Red	116	93	103	112	119
Justin Tucker	BAL	8	K	30	0	0	0	0	0	0	0	0	0	0	127	Green	117	109	113	103	108
Andy Dalton	CIN	9	QB	32	3890	27	13	36	145	1	0	0	0	2	293	Green	118	126	111	120	102
Adam Vinatieri	IND	6	K	47	0	0	0	0	0	0	0	0	0	0	126	Green	119	112	115	104	109
Christopher Herndon	NYJ	4	TE	23	0	0	0	0	0	0	34	427	4	0	66	Green	120	130	166	130	147
Mason Crosby	GB	11	K	35	0	0	0	0	0	0	0	0	0	0	124	Green	121	116	117	108	116
Courtland Sutton	DEN	10	WR	24	0	0	0	2	11	0	57	799	6	0	105	Red	122	99	114	122	131
Peyton Barber	TB	7	RB	25	0	0	0	174	665	4	19	132	1	1	105	Yellow	123	198	186	174	187
Ronald Jones	TB	7	RB	22	0	0	0	136	557	4	37	279	1	2	104	Yellow	124	200	154	176	160
Will Dissly	SEA	11	TE	23	0	0	0	0	0	0	37	409	5	0	64	Yellow	125	142	172	133	149
Saints D	NO	9	D	--	0	0	0	0	0	0	0	0	0	0	104	Yellow	126	123	119	106	112
Dallas Goedert	PHI	10	TE	24	0	0	0	0	0	0	41	445	3	0	64	Green	127	143	161	135	139
Bears D	CHI	6	D	--	0	0	0	0	0	0	0	0	0	0	104	Green	128	124	120	107	114
Noah Fant	DEN	10	TE	22	0	0	0	0	0	0	46	505	3	0	64	Red	129	144	160	137	138
Will Fuller	HOU	10	WR	25	0	0	0	2	10	0	51	783	5	0	103	Yellow	130	102	123	132	140
Chris Boswell	PIT	7	K	28	0	0	0	0	0	0	0	0	0	0	122	Green	131	128	122	114	118
LeSean McCoy	BUF	6	RB	31	0	0	0	157	627	3	26	208	1	0	103	Yellow	132	203	179	185	180
Matt Prater	DET	5	K	35	0	0	0	0	0	0	0	0	0	0	122	Green	133	129	124	116	120
Carlos Hyde	KC	12	RB	29	0	0	0	101	447	5	22	194	1	1	103	Green	134	205	183	187	184
Darren Waller	OAK	6	TE	27	0	0	0	0	0	0	32	350	5	0	62	Green	135	156	182	140	159
Dante Pettis	SF	4	WR	24	0	0	0	2	11	0	48	778	6	0	102	Red	136	104	147	136	154
Gerald Everett	LAR	9	TE	25	0	0	0	0	0	0	36	446	3	0	62	Green	137	157	176	141	155
Wil Lutz	NO	9	K	25	0	0	0	0	0	0	0	0	0	0	120	Yellow	138	133	126	124	124
Christian Kirk	ARI	12	WR	23	0	0	0	4	19	0	59	778	5	0	100	Red	139	108	118	138	136
Jason Myers	SEA	11	K	28	0	0	0	0	0	0	0	0	0	0	119	Yellow	140	139	129	129	129
Steelers D	PIT	7	D	--	0	0	0	0	0	0	0	0	0	0	100	Yellow	141	140	130	118	121
Eagles D	PHI	10	D	--	0	0	0	0	0	0	0	0	0	0	100	Yellow	142	141	131	119	122
Kirk Cousins	MIN	12	QB	31	3947	28	12	42	124	2	0	0	0	3	285	Yellow	143	162	127	143	115
Austin Ekeler	LAC	12	RB	24	0	0	0	101	522	2	36	333	1	1	100	Yellow	144	212	163	197	166
Chiefs D	KC	12	D	--	0	0	0	0	0	0	0	0	0	0	99	Green	145	145	134	123	123
Keke Coutee	HOU	10	WR	22	0	0	0	3	14	0	69	758	5	0	99	Yellow	146	111	99	142	111
Vikings D	MIN	12	D	--	0	0	0	0	0	0	0	0	0	0	99	Yellow	147	147	136	125	125
Ravens D	BAL	8	D	--	0	0	0	0	0	0	0	0	0	0	99	Green	148	148	138	126	126
Ka'imi Fairbairn	HOU	10	K	25	0	0	0	0	0	0	0	0	0	0	118	Green	149	149	139	201	201
Texans D	HOU	10	D	--	0	0	0	0	0	0	0	0	0	0	98	Yellow	150	150	140	127	127
Chargers D	LAC	12	D	--	0	0	0	0	0	0	0	0	0	0	98	Yellow	151	152	141	128	128
Seahawks D	SEA	11	D	--	0	0	0	0	0	0	0	0	0	0	98	Green	152	153	142	191	193
Nyheim Hines	IND	6	RB	23	0	0	0	74	298	1	60	524	2	1	98	Yellow	153	220	116	202	135

Player	Team	Bye	Pos	Age	PaYd	PaTD	INT	Ru	RuYd	RuTD	Rec	RcYd	RcTD	FL	Fant	Risk	Flex Rk	3WR Rk	PPR Rk	10-3WR Rk	10-PPR Rk
Jaguars D	JAX	10	D	--	0	0	0	0	0	0	0	0	0	0	98	Green	154	154	143	194	196
Jake Elliott	PHI	10	K	24	0	0	0	0	0	0	0	0	0	0	117	Green	155	155	145	212	208
Michael Gallup	DAL	8	WR	23	0	0	0	3	18	0	46	663	6	0	97	Yellow	156	114	150	144	157
Tre'Quan Smith	NO	9	WR	23	0	0	0	0	0	0	42	593	6	0	97	Blue	157	115	149	145	156
Vernon Davis	WAS	10	TE	35	0	0	0	0	0	0	30	406	3	0	57	Green	158	165	193	150	167
Darrell Henderson	LAR	9	RB	22	0	0	0	103	480	5	13	108	1	1	97	Blue	159	227	212	204	224
Rashaad Penny	SEA	11	RB	23	0	0	0	141	629	3	20	156	0	1	97	Green	160	230	197	207	204
Golden Tate	NYG	11	WR	31	0	0	0	0	0	0	70	753	4	0	96	Green	161	119	95	146	107
Donte Moncrief	PIT	7	WR	26	0	0	0	0	0	0	55	740	5	0	96	Yellow	162	122	133	147	144
Curtis Samuel	CAR	7	WR	23	0	0	0	6	54	0	56	692	4	0	95	Yellow	163	125	132	148	143
Marqise Lee	JAX	10	WR	28	0	0	0	4	24	0	59	766	3	0	95	Yellow	164	127	125	149	142
Tyler Eifert	CIN	9	TE	29	0	0	0	0	0	0	33	374	4	0	55	Red	165	169	199	156	172
Jerick McKinnon	SF	4	RB	27	0	0	0	117	497	3	36	310	1	1	94	Yellow	166	237	178	217	178
Kenny Stills	MIA	5	WR	27	0	0	0	2	9	0	46	673	4	0	93	Green	167	131	155	151	161
Josh Doctson	WAS	10	WR	27	0	0	0	0	0	0	48	626	5	0	93	Green	168	132	152	152	158
Jamison Crowder	NYJ	4	WR	26	0	0	0	4	21	0	61	734	5	0	93	Red	169	134	137	153	146
DeVante Parker	MIA	5	WR	26	0	0	0	0	0	0	58	748	5	0	93	Red	170	135	146	154	153
Anthony Miller	CHI	6	WR	25	0	0	0	4	20	0	44	551	6	0	92	Green	171	136	162	155	165
Paul Richardson	WAS	10	WR	27	0	0	0	0	0	0	47	684	5	0	92	Yellow	172	137	159	157	164
Jordan Howard	PHI	10	RB	25	0	0	0	145	582	4	17	146	1	0	92	Red	173	246	223	226	233
Lamar Jackson	BAL	8	QB	22	3084	17	10	155	847	6	0	0	0	7	277	Red	174	175	148	160	133
James Washington	PIT	7	WR	23	0	0	0	2	11	0	45	633	5	0	91	Yellow	175	146	164	159	168
D'Onta Foreman	HOU	10	RB	23	0	0	0	128	575	4	19	167	1	2	89	Red	176	254	227	237	237
Marquise Brown	BAL	8	WR	22	0	0	0	6	32	0	48	701	4	0	88	Red	177	158	170	161	171
Sam Darnold	NYJ	4	QB	22	3702	24	16	57	232	2	0	0	0	5	273	Green	178	182	157	164	141
N'Keal Harry	NE	10	WR	22	0	0	0	3	20	0	47	667	4	0	88	Yellow	179	159	165	162	169
John Brown	BUF	6	WR	29	0	0	0	2	10	0	44	706	4	0	88	Red	180	160	181	163	182
Jason Witten	DAL	8	TE	37	0	0	0	0	0	0	36	328	3	0	48	Green	181	184	201	166	174
Mike Gesicki	MIA	5	TE	24	0	0	0	0	0	0	31	345	2	0	47	Green	182	186	214	168	183
Dion Lewis	TEN	11	RB	29	0	0	0	85	357	2	46	340	1	1	86	Yellow	183	261	175	248	176
Blake Jarwin	DAL	8	TE	25	0	0	0	0	0	0	28	320	2	0	47	Green	184	187	228	169	190
Kalen Ballage	MIA	5	RB	24	0	0	0	139	596	3	25	201	0	2	86	Red	185	262	219	249	229
Tyrell Williams	OAK	6	WR	27	0	0	0	2	10	0	47	691	4	0	85	Red	186	164	180	167	181
Marquise Goodwin	SF	4	WR	29	0	0	0	4	25	0	36	576	4	0	84	Green	187	166	192	170	197
Benjamin Watson	NE	10	TE	39	0	0	0	0	0	0	25	293	3	0	44	Green	188	189	240	173	209
DJ Chark	JAX	10	WR	23	0	0	0	2	8	0	45	626	5	0	84	Red	189	167	185	171	186
Jesse James	DET	5	TE	25	0	0	0	0	0	0	24	259	3	0	43	Green	190	192	244	180	213
Taylor Gabriel	CHI	6	WR	28	0	0	0	5	25	0	56	633	3	0	82	Green	191	168	156	172	162
Jimmy Garoppolo	SF	4	QB	28	4314	24	14	46	132	1	0	0	0	3	268	Red	192	193	167	181	150
Josh Allen	BUF	6	QB	23	3317	16	14	111	654	7	0	0	0	6	267	Red	193	194	169	183	151
C.J. Uzomah	CIN	9	TE	26	0	0	0	0	0	0	26	284	2	0	42	Green	194	195	242	186	211
Matthew Stafford	DET	5	QB	31	3890	26	11	29	68	1	0	0	0	3	267	Yellow	195	196	171	184	152
D.K. Metcalf	SEA	11	WR	22	0	0	0	3	18	0	44	665	4	0	81	Red	196	170	188	175	191
Willie Snead	BAL	8	WR	27	0	0	0	3	13	0	59	665	3	0	81	Yellow	197	171	158	177	163
Nelson Agholor	PHI	10	WR	26	0	0	0	2	12	0	51	604	3	0	81	Green	198	172	168	178	170
Tyler Higbee	LAR	9	TE	26	0	0	0	0	0	0	25	269	2	0	41	Green	199	197	246	189	218
Parris Campbell	IND	6	WR	22	0	0	0	7	40	0	56	600	4	0	81	Red	200	173	173	179	173
Devin Funchess	IND	6	WR	25	0	0	0	0	0	0	45	546	5	0	80	Yellow	201	174	187	182	188
Gus Edwards	BAL	8	RB	24	0	0	0	137	624	3	4	23	0	1	80	Green	202	266	265	266	275
David Moore	SEA	11	WR	24	0	0	0	2	10	0	30	425	6	0	79	Green	203	176	218	188	228
Quincy Enunwa	NYJ	4	WR	27	0	0	0	0	0	0	44	572	4	0	79	Yellow	204	177	191	190	195
Irv Smith	MIN	12	TE	21	0	0	0	0	0	0	25	299	2	0	38	Red	205	204	250	198	231
Geronimo Allison	GB	11	WR	25	0	0	0	0	0	0	48	639	4	0	78	Red	206	179	189	192	192
Jamaal Williams	GB	11	RB	24	0	0	0	80	351	2	29	250	1	0	77	Green	207	267	225	267	235
A.J. Brown	TEN	11	WR	22	0	0	0	5	29	0	45	601	4	0	77	Red	208	180	195	193	200
Frank Gore	BUF	6	RB	36	0	0	0	129	581	2	11	104	0	1	77	Yellow	209	268	258	268	272
Jace Sternberger	GB	11	TE	23	0	0	0	0	0	0	26	272	2	0	38	Yellow	210	206	249	200	227
Breshad Perriman	TB	7	WR	26	0	0	0	0	0	0	40	563	4	0	77	Yellow	211	181	202	195	210
Matt Breida	SF	4	RB	24	0	0	0	99	444	3	26	205	0	1	77	Yellow	212	269	237	269	250
Matt LaCosse	NE	10	TE	27	0	0	0	0	0	0	21	252	2	0	36	Yellow	213	211	259	208	245
Ian Thomas	CAR	7	TE	23	0	0	0	0	0	0	24	269	1	0	36	Green	214	213	254	209	238
Cole Beasley	BUF	6	WR	30	0	0	0	0	0	0	58	633	3	0	75	Yellow	215	183	174	199	175
Demetrius Harris	CLE	7	TE	28	0	0	0	0	0	0	17	206	3	0	35	Yellow	216	217	266	213	257
Antonio Callaway	CLE	7	WR	22	0	0	0	3	15	0	32	477	4	0	74	Green	217	185	226	203	236
Geoff Swaim	JAX	10	TE	26	0	0	0	0	0	0	32	293	1	0	35	Yellow	218	218	247	214	221

Player	Team	Bye	Pos	Age	PaYd	PaTD	INT	Ru	RuYd	RuTD	Rec	RcYd	RcTD	FL	Fant	Risk	Flex Rk	3WR Rk	PPR Rk	10-3WR Rk	10-PPR Rk
Andy Isabella	ARI	12	WR	23	0	0	0	0	0	0	45	586	4	0	73	Red	219	188	205	211	215
Adam Shaheen	CHI	6	TE	25	0	0	0	0	0	0	23	218	2	0	33	Green	220	224	260	218	246
Josh Oliver	JAX	10	TE	22	0	0	0	0	0	0	21	226	2	0	33	Green	221	225	263	220	253
Xavier Grimble	PIT	7	TE	27	0	0	0	0	0	0	19	194	2	0	32	Yellow	222	228	269	222	260
Jordan Akins	HOU	10	TE	27	0	0	0	0	0	0	18	194	2	0	32	Green	223	229	270	223	261
Rhett Ellison	NYG	11	TE	31	0	0	0	0	0	0	25	238	1	0	32	Green	224	232	255	225	242
Albert Wilson	MIA	5	WR	27	0	0	0	3	16	0	50	588	2	0	71	Yellow	225	190	194	216	199
Ricky Seals-Jones	ARI	12	TE	24	0	0	0	0	0	0	18	204	2	0	31	Green	226	235	272	229	263
Jeff Heuerman	DEN	10	TE	27	0	0	0	0	0	0	26	254	1	0	30	Green	227	236	257	230	243
Cameron Brate	TB	7	TE	28	0	0	0	0	0	0	24	260	1	0	30	Green	228	239	262	232	252
Jalen Richard	OAK	6	RB	26	0	0	0	35	152	1	55	409	2	1	69	Green	229	270	184	270	185
Ito Smith	ATL	9	RB	24	0	0	0	90	350	3	20	164	1	1	69	Yellow	230	271	256	271	270
Hayden Hurst	BAL	8	TE	26	0	0	0	0	0	0	22	228	1	0	29	Green	231	242	268	236	259
Bills D	BUF	6	D	--	0	0	0	0	0	0	0	0	0	0	98	Yellow	232	209	200	196	198
Nick Boyle	BAL	8	TE	26	0	0	0	0	0	0	22	201	1	0	28	Green	233	243	271	238	262
Tyler Kroft	BUF	6	TE	27	0	0	0	0	0	0	25	281	1	0	28	Red	234	245	267	240	258
Randall Cobb	DAL	8	WR	29	0	0	0	0	0	0	56	569	2	0	67	Yellow	235	199	190	233	194
Brett Maher	DAL	8	K	30	0	0	0	0	0	0	0	0	0	0	116	Yellow	236	214	204	219	214
Luke Stocker	ATL	9	TE	31	0	0	0	0	0	0	18	149	2	0	27	Yellow	237	249	274	242	269
Emmanuel Sanders	DEN	10	WR	32	0	0	0	2	8	0	46	529	3	0	66	Red	238	201	222	235	232
Theo Riddick	DET	5	RB	28	0	0	0	35	150	0	54	414	2	0	66	Yellow	239	272	196	272	202
Luke Willson	OAK	6	TE	29	0	0	0	0	0	0	19	170	2	0	26	Green	240	251	273	245	266
DaeSean Hamilton	DEN	10	WR	24	0	0	0	2	8	0	51	573	3	0	66	Red	241	202	210	239	219
Josh Lambo	JAX	10	K	29	0	0	0	0	0	0	0	0	0	0	115	Yellow	242	219	208	227	220
Chris Thompson	WAS	10	RB	29	0	0	0	45	209	1	57	429	1	1	65	Red	243	273	198	273	206
Broncos D	DEN	10	D	--	0	0	0	0	0	0	0	0	0	0	96	Green	244	221	206	205	203
Lions D	DET	5	D	--	0	0	0	0	0	0	0	0	0	0	96	Yellow	245	222	207	206	205
Hakeem Butler	ARI	12	WR	23	0	0	0	0	0	0	34	549	3	0	64	Red	246	207	248	243	264
Derek Carr	OAK	6	QB	28	4093	25	14	23	43	0	0	0	0	3	250	Red	247	255	203	250	179
Cowboys D	DAL	8	D	--	0	0	0	0	0	0	0	0	0	0	96	Red	248	226	209	210	207
Jonnu Smith	TEN	11	TE	24	0	0	0	0	0	0	17	167	1	0	24	Green	249	256	275	255	271
Demarcus Robinson	KC	12	WR	25	0	0	0	0	0	0	30	403	5	0	64	Yellow	250	208	251	246	265
Chris Conley	JAX	10	WR	27	0	0	0	0	0	0	38	477	3	0	64	Green	251	210	236	247	249
Patriots D	NE	10	D	--	0	0	0	0	0	0	0	0	0	0	95	Yellow	252	234	211	215	212
Mecole Hardman	KC	12	WR	21	0	0	0	3	22	0	31	477	3	0	62	Yellow	253	215	252	252	267
Adam Humphries	TEN	11	WR	26	0	0	0	2	11	0	48	501	2	0	62	Green	254	216	213	254	225
Giovani Bernard	CIN	9	RB	28	0	0	0	56	232	1	39	287	2	1	62	Yellow	255	274	245	274	256
Cardinals D	ARI	12	D	--	0	0	0	0	0	0	0	0	0	0	94	Yellow	256	238	215	221	216
Falcons D	ATL	9	D	--	0	0	0	0	0	0	0	0	0	0	94	Yellow	257	240	216	224	217
Randy Bullock	CIN	9	K	30	0	0	0	0	0	0	0	0	0	0	112	Yellow	258	241	221	244	234
Duke Johnson	CLE	7	RB	26	0	0	0	35	153	0	45	407	2	1	61	Red	259	275	238	275	251
Deebo Samuel	SF	4	WR	23	0	0	0	3	16	0	33	452	3	0	60	Yellow	260	223	253	257	268
Browns D	CLE	7	D	--	0	0	0	0	0	0	0	0	0	0	93	Yellow	261	244	220	228	222
Marcus Mariota	TEN	11	QB	26	3617	19	12	64	357	1	0	0	0	3	245	Red	262	264	217	263	189
Michael Badgley	LAC	12	K	24	0	0	0	0	0	0	0	0	0	0	112	Yellow	263	247	230	253	240
Robert Foster	BUF	6	WR	25	0	0	0	0	0	0	31	523	2	0	59	Red	264	231	261	259	273
Redskins D	WAS	10	D	--	0	0	0	0	0	0	0	0	0	0	93	Green	265	248	224	231	223
Travis Benjamin	LAC	12	WR	30	0	0	0	4	20	0	28	434	3	0	59	Red	266	233	264	261	274
Titans D	TEN	11	D	--	0	0	0	0	0	0	0	0	0	0	93	Yellow	267	250	229	234	226
Giorgio Tavecchio	ATL	9	K	29	0	0	0	0	0	0	0	0	0	0	111	Green	268	252	232	256	241
Bengals D	CIN	9	D	--	0	0	0	0	0	0	0	0	0	0	92	Yellow	269	253	231	241	230
Ryan Succop	TEN	11	K	33	0	0	0	0	0	0	0	0	0	0	110	Green	270	257	233	260	247
Aldrick Rosas	NYG	11	K	25	0	0	0	0	0	0	0	0	0	0	110	Yellow	271	258	234	262	248
Chandler Catanzaro	NYJ	4	K	28	0	0	0	0	0	0	0	0	0	0	109	Green	272	259	239	264	254
Colts D	IND	6	D	--	0	0	0	0	0	0	0	0	0	0	90	Red	273	260	235	251	239
Robbie Gould	SF	4	K	37	0	0	0	0	0	0	0	0	0	0	109	Green	274	263	241	265	255
Panthers D	CAR	7	D	--	0	0	0	0	0	0	0	0	0	0	89	Yellow	275	265	243	258	244

Statistical Appendix

Broken Tackles by Team, Offense

Rk	Team	Plays	Plays w/ BTkl	Pct	Total BTkl
1	TEN	882	127	14.4%	158
2	LAC	897	123	13.7%	151
3	NYG	931	124	13.3%	155
4	KC	957	120	12.5%	148
5	DET	968	120	12.4%	140
6	SEA	937	112	12.0%	131
7	CAR	961	114	11.9%	142
8	DEN	969	105	10.8%	123
9	MIA	813	86	10.6%	106
10	CLE	968	102	10.5%	123
11	NO	965	101	10.5%	123
12	SF	939	92	9.8%	110
13	WAS	912	89	9.8%	106
14	PIT	1017	98	9.6%	124
15	OAK	924	89	9.6%	107
16	LAR	1003	96	9.6%	104
17	PHI	982	93	9.5%	106
18	MIN	952	90	9.5%	113
19	BAL	1081	101	9.3%	127
20	NYJ	921	86	9.3%	106
21	JAX	946	86	9.1%	96
22	CHI	962	87	9.0%	97
23	GB	964	87	9.0%	108
24	ARI	841	75	8.9%	89
25	BUF	958	84	8.8%	97
26	ATL	960	84	8.8%	98
27	TB	1003	87	8.7%	104
28	NE	1029	89	8.6%	97
29	DAL	951	82	8.6%	92
30	IND	1025	84	8.2%	93
31	CIN	892	70	7.8%	81
32	HOU	963	72	7.5%	81

Play total includes Defensive Pass Interference.

Broken Tackles by Team, Defense

Rk	Team	Plays	Plays w/ BTkl	Pct	Total BTkl
1	MIN	932	71	7.6%	81
2	TEN	947	77	8.1%	88
3	NE	964	79	8.2%	87
4	LAR	912	76	8.3%	86
5	NYJ	1004	85	8.5%	94
6	CHI	950	83	8.7%	97
7	DET	885	78	8.8%	87
8	NO	915	81	8.9%	89
9	CAR	899	80	8.9%	92
10	BAL	922	84	9.1%	93
11	SF	963	88	9.1%	110
12	PIT	924	86	9.3%	93
13	JAX	914	87	9.5%	97
14	WAS	931	89	9.6%	100
15	DEN	960	92	9.6%	109
16	NYG	980	95	9.7%	114
17	OAK	938	95	10.1%	112
18	SEA	902	94	10.4%	108
19	LAC	932	98	10.5%	116
20	ATL	979	103	10.5%	124
21	PHI	951	102	10.7%	113
22	IND	944	103	10.9%	111
23	ARI	1002	113	11.3%	127
24	TB	935	106	11.3%	128
25	CIN	1029	117	11.4%	134
26	HOU	969	111	11.5%	133
27	DAL	929	108	11.6%	127
28	GB	955	114	11.9%	131
29	KC	1048	129	12.3%	144
30	CLE	1070	132	12.3%	157
31	MIA	974	125	12.8%	145
32	BUF	914	120	13.1%	129

Play total includes Defensive Pass Interference.

Most Broken Tackles, Defenders

Rk	Player	Team	BTkl	Rk	Player	Team	BTkl	Rk	Player	Team	BTkl
1	C.Riley	NYG	22	7	M.Milano	BUF	18	14	D.King	LAC	16
2	J.Heath	DAL	21	7	A.Ogletree	NYG	18	14	B.Poole	ATL	16
3	J.Schobert	CLE	20	7	J.Smith	DAL	18	19	L.Collins	NYG	15
3	T.Smith	JAX	20	12	A.Bethea	ARI	17	19	J.Joseph	HOU	15
5	H.Reddick	ARI	19	12	J.Whitehead	TB	17	19	R.Ragland	KC	15
5	K.Van Noy	NE	19	14	J.Davis	DET	16	19	S.Williams	CIN	15
7	J.Collins	CLE	18	14	D.James	LAC	16				
7	T.Edmunds	BUF	18	14	D.Kazee	ATL	16				

Top 20 Defenders, Broken Tackle Rate

Rk	Player	Team	BTkl	Tkl	Rate
1	I.Johnson	TB	0	41	0.0%
2	C.Campbell	JAX	2	52	3.7%
3	L.Ryan	TEN	2	46	4.2%
4	P.Desir	IND	3	53	5.4%
5	B.Wagner	SEA	4	70	5.4%
6	J.McCourty	NE	3	51	5.6%
7	D.McCourty	NE	3	47	6.0%
8	N.Lawson	DET	3	43	6.5%
9	L.Vander Esch	DAL	7	99	6.6%
10	C.Hayward	LAC	3	40	7.0%
11	W.Woodyard	TEN	4	51	7.3%
12	L.Kuechly	CAR	7	88	7.4%
13	A.Williamson	NYJ	6	75	7.4%
14	P.Chung	NE	4	49	7.5%
15	Z.Brown	WAS	5	60	7.7%
15	L.David	TB	7	84	7.7%
17	K.Byard	TEN	4	47	7.8%
18	J.Adams	NYJ	7	82	7.9%
19	J.Bynes	ARI	4	45	8.2%
19	R.Melvin	OAK	4	45	8.2%

Broken Tackles divided by Broken Tackles + Solo Tackles.
Special teams not included; min. 40 Solo Tackles

Bottom 20 Defenders, Broken Tackle Rate

Rk	Player	Team	BTkl	Tkl	Rate
1	M.Milano	BUF	18	41	30.5%
2	H.Reddick	ARI	19	46	29.2%
3	A.Ogletree	NYG	18	44	29.0%
4	C.Riley	NYG	22	54	28.9%
5	J.Heath	DAL	21	56	27.3%
6	J.Schobert	CLE	20	55	26.7%
7	R.Ragland	KC	15	42	26.3%
8	B.Poole	ATL	16	47	25.4%
9	J.Whitehead	TB	17	50	25.4%
10	K.Van Noy	NE	19	56	25.3%
11	T.J.Watt	PIT	14	44	24.1%
12	J.Joseph	HOU	15	48	23.8%
13	D.Kazee	ATL	16	53	23.2%
14	J.Haden	PIT	12	42	22.2%
14	J.J.Watt	HOU	12	42	22.2%
16	B.Roby	DEN	12	43	21.8%
17	J.Norman	WAS	11	40	21.6%
18	D.Jackson	CAR	14	51	21.5%
19	A.Walker	IND	14	52	21.2%
20	D.Ward	CLE	11	41	21.2%

Broken Tackles divided by Broken Tackles + Solo Tackles.
Special teams not included; min. 40 Solo Tackles

Most Broken Tackles, Running Backs

Rk	Player	Team	BTkl
1	S.Barkley	NYG	94
2	C.McCaffrey	CAR	63
3	C.Carson	SEA	61
4	J.Conner	PIT	56
4	A.Peterson	WAS	56
6	M.Gordon	LAC	55
6	D.Henry	TEN	55
8	K.Hunt	KC	54
9	D.Lewis	TEN	53
10	N.Chubb	CLE	47
11	E.Elliott	DAL	46
11	J.Mixon	CIN	46
13	D.Johnson	ARI	45
14	P.Barber	TB	44
15	A.Kamara	NO	43
16	D.Cook	MIN	42
16	T.Gurley	LAR	42
18	K.Drake	MIA	41
19	A.Ekeler	LAC	39
20	T.Cohen	CHI	37

Most Broken Tackles, WR/TE

Rk	Player	Team	BTkl
1	G.Tate	PHI	29
2	DJ Moore	CAR	27
3	S.Diggs	MIN	24
4	T.Hill	KC	19
4	G.Kittle	SF	19
6	O.Beckham	NYG	18
6	M.Thomas	NO	18
8	A.Brown	PIT	17
9	T.Kelce	KC	16
9	V.McDonald	PIT	16
11	C.Samuel	CAR	14
11	S.Watkins	KC	14
13	A.Cooper	2TM	13
13	J.Jones	ATL	13
13	A.Wilson	MIA	13
16	L.Fitzgerald	ARI	12
16	J.Smith-Schuster	PIT	12
16	D.Westbrook	JAX	12
19	N.Agholor	PHI	11
19	A.Jeffery	PHI	11
19	C.Patterson	NE	11
19	R.Woods	LAR	11
19	J.Wright	CAR	11

Most Broken Tackles, Quarterbacks

Rk	Player	Team	Behind LOS	Beyond LOS	BTkl	Rk	Player	Team	Behind LOS	Beyond LOS	BTkl
1	L.Jackson	BAL	2	27	29	6	P.Mahomes	KC	16	2	18
2	M.Mariota	TEN	7	21	28	6	C.Newton	CAR	2	16	18
3	J.Allen	BUF	8	16	24	6	D.Prescott	DAL	10	8	18
4	D.Watson	HOU	10	13	23	9	B.Mayfield	CLE	12	5	17
5	J.Winston	TB	7	14	21	10	J.Flacco	BAL	15	0	15

Best Broken Tackle Rate, Offensive Players (min. 80 touches)

Rk	Player	Team	BTkl	Touch	Rate	Rk	Player	Team	BTkl	Touch	Rate
1	A.Ekeler	LAC	39	145	26.9%	11	M.Lynch	OAK	24	105	22.9%
2	S.Barkley	NYG	94	352	26.7%	12	C.Carson	SEA	61	267	22.8%
3	K.Hunt	KC	54	207	26.1%	13	E.McGuire	NYJ	25	111	22.5%
4	D.Lewis	TEN	53	214	24.8%	14	N.Chubb	CLE	47	212	22.2%
5	M.Gordon	LAC	55	225	24.4%	15	O.Beckham	NYG	18	82	22.0%
6	D.Cook	MIN	42	173	24.3%	15	J.Richard	OAK	27	123	22.0%
7	D.Henry	TEN	55	230	23.9%	17	T.Cohen	CHI	37	170	21.8%
8	K.Drake	MIA	41	173	23.7%	18	R.Freeman	DEN	31	144	21.5%
9	K.Johnson	DET	35	150	23.3%	19	S.Diggs	MIN	24	112	21.4%
10	D.Johnson	CLE	20	87	23.0%	20	A.Jones	GB	34	159	21.4%

Top 20 Defenders, Passes Defensed

Rk	Player	Team	PD
1	K.Fuller	CHI	21
2	S.Gilmore	NE	20
3	K.Jackson	HOU	17
3	D.Slay	DET	17
5	J.Bradberry	CAR	15
5	G.Conley	OAK	15
5	M.Humphrey	BAL	15
5	E.Jackson	CHI	15
5	J.Jenkins	NYG	15
5	S.Nelson	KC	15
11	E.Apple	2TM	14
11	M.Claiborne	NYJ	14
11	B.Jones	DAL	14
11	J.Ramsey	JAX	14
15	W.Jackson	CIN	13
15	D.James	LAC	13
15	J.Joseph	HOU	13
15	C.Littleton	LAR	13
15	O.Scandrick	KC	13
20	12 tied with		12

Note: Based on the definition given in the Statistical Toolbox, not NFL totals.

Top 20 Defenders, Defeats

Rk	Player	Team	Dfts
1	L.Kuechly	CAR	38
2	D.Leonard	IND	37
3	A.Donald	LAR	36
4	C.Campbell	JAX	32
5	L.David	TB	30
5	D.Lawrence	DAL	30
7	V.Miller	DEN	29
8	J.J.Watt	HOU	28
9	J.Adams	NYJ	27
9	D.Hunter	MIN	27
9	C.Jones	KC	27
12	C.Jones	ARI	26
12	C.Littleton	LAR	26
14	B.Baker	ARI	24
14	J.Clowney	HOU	24
14	C.Jordan	NO	24
14	M.Milano	BUF	24
14	A.Ogletree	NYG	24
14	J.Sheard	IND	24
14	T.J.Watt	PIT	24

Top 20 Defenders, Run Tackles for Loss

Rk	Player	Team	TFL
1	L.Kuechly	CAR	18
2	C.Campbell	JAX	16
3	J.Collins	CLE	13
3	D.Lawrence	DAL	13
3	D.Leonard	IND	13
3	M.Milano	BUF	13
7	J.Clowney	HOU	12
7	D.Harrison	2TM	12
9	A.Donald	LAR	11
9	J.Sheard	IND	11
9	D.Tomlinson	NYG	11
12	L.David	TB	10
12	J.Hughes	BUF	10
12	K.Short	CAR	10
12	J.J.Watt	HOU	10
16	J.Adams	NYJ	9
16	36-B.Baker	ARI	9
16	J.Casey	TEN	9
16	B.Mayowa	ARI	9
16	A.Muhammad	IND	9
16	A.Walker	IND	9

Includes both tackles and assists.

Top 20 Defenders, Quarterback Hits

Rk	Player	Team	Hits
1	F.Cox	PHI	24
1	Y.Ngakoue	JAX	24
3	A.Donald	LAR	22
4	M.Bennett	PHI	20
5	D.Ford	KC	18
6	C.Dunlap	CIN	17
6	M.Garrett	CLE	17
6	Z.Smith	BAL	17
9	S.Tuitt	PIT	16
9	O.Vernon	NYG	16
11	C.Jones	KC	15
11	G.McCoy	TB	15
11	N.Suh	LAR	15
11	J.J.Watt	HOU	15
11	L.Williams	NYJ	15
16	J.Reed	SEA	14
17	F.Clark	SEA	13
17	J.Hughes	BUF	13
17	M.Judon	BAL	13
17	D.Lawrence	DAL	13
17	S.Richardson	MIN	13
17	P.Smith	WAS	13

Top 20 Defenders, QB Knockdowns (Sacks + Hits)

Rk	Defender	Team	KD
1	A.Donald	LAR	45
2	F.Cox	PHI	38
3	D.Ford	KC	35
3	Y.Ngakoue	JAX	35
5	J.J.Watt	HOU	33
6	M.Garrett	CLE	32
6	C.Jones	KC	32
8	M.Bennett	PHI	31
9	V.Miller	DEN	29
10	F.Clark	SEA	28
10	C.Dunlap	CIN	28
12	Z.Smith	BAL	27
13	D.Lawrence	DAL	26
13	J.Reed	SEA	26
15	B.Chubb	DEN	25
15	O.Vernon	NYG	25
17	S.Tuitt	PIT	24
17	T.J.Watt	PIT	24
19	C.Jones	ARI	23
19	L.Williams	NYJ	23

Full credit for whole and half sacks; includes sacks cancelled by penalty. Does not include strip sacks.

Top 20 Defenders, Hurries

Rk	Defender	Team	Hur
1	A.Donald	LAR	59
2	C.Jordan	NO	49
3	F.Cox	PHI	48.5
3	D.Ford	KC	48.5
5	D.Lawrence	DAL	43.5
6	T.Flowers	NE	42.5
6	M.Ingram	LAC	42.5
8	J.J.Watt	HOU	41.5
9	J.Hughes	BUF	38.5
9	D.Hunter	MIN	38.5
11	R.Kerrigan	WAS	38
11	K.Mack	CHI	38
11	Y.Ngakoue	JAX	38
14	C.Wake	MIA	37
15	C.Heyward	PIT	36
15	T.Suggs	BAL	36
17	C.Campbell	JAX	35.5
17	V.Miller	DEN	35.5
19	C.Jones	KC	35
20	B.Chubb	DEN	34.5
20	J.Clowney	HOU	34.5
20	B.Graham	PHI	34.5

Top 20 Quarterbacks, QB Hits

Rk	Player	Team	Hits
1	P.Mahomes	KC	84
2	D.Watson	HOU	74
3	M.Ryan	ATL	67
4	C.Keenum	DEN	62
5	A.Luck	IND	61
6	K.Cousins	MIN	58
7	D.Prescott	DAL	56
8	N.Mullens	SF	54
9	P.Rivers	LAC	53
10	R.Wilson	SEA	52
11	J.Rosen	ARI	51
11	M.Stafford	DET	51
13	B.Roethlisberger	PIT	50
14	E.Manning	NYG	49
14	A.Rodgers	GB	49
16	J.Allen	BUF	48
16	T.Brady	NE	48
18	C.Wentz	PHI	47
19	R.Tannehill	MIA	46
20	J.Goff	LAR	45

Top 20 Quarterbacks, QB Knockdowns (Sacks + Hits)

Rk	Player	Team	KD
1	D.Watson	HOU	138
2	D.Prescott	DAL	111
2	M.Ryan	ATL	111
4	P.Mahomes	KC	109
5	R.Wilson	SEA	105
6	A.Rodgers	GB	100
7	K.Cousins	MIN	98
8	C.Keenum	DEN	97
9	E.Manning	NYG	95
10	J.Rosen	ARI	93
11	M.Stafford	DET	91
12	D.Carr	OAK	88
12	P.Rivers	LAC	88
14	R.Tannehill	MIA	83
15	A.Luck	IND	80
15	C.Wentz	PHI	80
17	J.Allen	BUF	77
18	B.Roethlisberger	PIT	75
18	J.Goff	LAR	75
20	N.Mullens	SF	71

Includes sacks cancelled by penalties
Does not include strip sacks or "self sacks" with no defender listed.

Top 10 Quarterbacks, Knockdowns per Pass

Rk	Player	Team	KD	Pct
1	R.Tannehill	MIA	83	24.9%
2	N.Mullens	SF	71	22.9%
3	D.Watson	HOU	138	22.8%
4	R.Wilson	SEA	105	20.8%
5	J.Allen	BUF	77	20.3%
6	J.Rosen	ARI	93	20.0%
7	R.Fitzpatrick	TB	54	19.6%
8	D.Prescott	DAL	111	17.9%
9	C.Wentz	PHI	80	17.7%
10	P.Mahomes	KC	109	16.8%

Min. 200 passes; includes passes cancelled by penalty

Bottom 10 Quarterbacks in Knockdowns per Pass

Rk	Player	Team	KD	Pct
1	D.Brees	NO	51	9.5%
2	A.Dalton	CIN	41	10.0%
3	B.Roethlisberger	PIT	75	10.2%
4	B.Mayfield	CLE	56	10.3%
5	J.Flacco	BAL	44	10.5%
6	M.Trubisky	CHI	53	10.7%
7	T.Brady	NE	68	11.0%
8	A.Luck	IND	80	11.5%
9	S.Darnold	NYJ	53	11.5%
10	C.Newton	CAR	61	11.8%

Min. 200 passes; includes passes cancelled by penalty

Top 10 Most Passes Tipped at Line, Quarterbacks

Rk	Player	Team	Total
1	K.Cousins	MIN	18
2	B.Bortles	JAX	14
2	J.Flacco	BAL	14
4	A.Luck	IND	11
4	P.Rivers	LAC	11
6	P.Mahomes	KC	10
6	M.Stafford	DET	10
6	R.Tannehill	MIA	10
9	C.J.Beathard	SF	9
9	N.Mullens	SF	9
9	J.Rosen	ARI	9

Top 10 Tipped at the Line, Defenders

Rk	Player	Team	Total
1	C.Dunlap	CIN	7
2	A.Gotsis	DEN	6
2	E.Ogbah	CLE	6
4	S.Lawson	BUF	5
4	J.Peppers	CAR	5
6	13 tied with		4

2018 Quarterbacks with and without Pass Pressure

Rank	Player	Team	Plays	Pct Pressure	DVOA with Pressure	Yds with Pressure	DVOA w/o Pressure	Yds w/o Pressure	DVOA Dif	Rank
1	N.Foles	PHI	207	23.2%	-48.4%	6.2	24.4%	7.0	-72.8%	5
2	D.Brees	NO	523	23.5%	-51.8%	3.6	67.4%	9.1	-119.2%	22
3	T.Brady	NE	602	23.8%	-66.9%	3.6	63.0%	8.5	-129.9%	27
4	B.Roethlisberger	PIT	718	23.8%	-61.3%	5.7	56.2%	7.7	-117.5%	21
5	J.Goff	LAR	619	25.5%	-67.9%	3.4	69.1%	9.1	-137.0%	30
6	J.Flacco	BAL	404	26.2%	-60.2%	3.6	54.5%	7.3	-114.7%	18
7	A.Luck	IND	686	26.5%	-33.7%	4.5	47.7%	7.8	-81.5%	7
8	B.Mayfield	CLE	529	26.8%	-50.0%	5.1	44.3%	7.9	-94.3%	11
9	A.Dalton	CIN	401	28.2%	-49.9%	4.6	45.3%	7.2	-95.1%	12
10	M.Trubisky	CHI	503	28.2%	-14.1%	5.8	37.9%	7.7	-51.9%	1
11	C.Wentz	PHI	451	28.4%	-64.5%	3.5	57.0%	8.1	-121.5%	23
12	D.Carr	OAK	610	28.7%	-110.5%	2.5	62.6%	7.9	-173.0%	34
13	M.Ryan	ATL	675	28.7%	-50.6%	4.3	64.5%	8.6	-115.1%	20
14	M.Mariota	TEN	414	28.7%	-82.5%	3.1	41.7%	7.8	-124.1%	24
15	M.Stafford	DET	617	29.0%	-56.3%	4.2	29.2%	7.0	-85.5%	10
16	C.Newton	CAR	530	29.1%	-81.6%	2.9	46.6%	7.9	-128.3%	25
17	A.Rodgers	GB	686	29.9%	-59.5%	2.6	70.3%	8.2	-129.8%	26
18	A.Smith	WAS	373	30.8%	-109.8%	2.9	50.7%	7.4	-160.5%	32
19	E.Manning	NYG	635	30.9%	-78.3%	2.9	53.3%	8.1	-131.5%	28
20	R.Fitzpatrick	TB	285	31.2%	-76.0%	5.2	68.1%	10.2	-144.1%	31
21	N.Mullens	SF	293	31.4%	-105.5%	3.5	66.0%	9.3	-171.5%	33
22	B.Bortles	JAX	473	32.3%	-52.4%	4.1	11.2%	6.8	-63.6%	4
23	S.Darnold	NYJ	459	32.5%	-72.0%	3.0	36.4%	7.5	-108.5%	17
24	P.Rivers	LAC	547	32.5%	-21.8%	4.8	76.1%	8.9	-97.9%	13
25	C.Keenum	DEN	638	33.2%	-67.7%	3.1	36.2%	7.4	-103.9%	15
26	J.Winston	TB	446	33.6%	-11.6%	6.2	47.9%	7.7	-59.5%	2
27	R.Tannehill	MIA	318	33.6%	-92.6%	1.9	41.9%	7.6	-134.6%	29
28	P.Mahomes	KC	640	34.2%	7.6%	6.2	92.9%	9.2	-85.3%	9
29	D.Prescott	DAL	615	34.5%	-60.6%	3.2	37.4%	7.7	-98.0%	14
30	K.Cousins	MIN	669	34.5%	-34.3%	4.5	39.2%	7.1	-73.5%	6
31	R.Wilson	SEA	510	36.7%	-33.8%	4.0	73.8%	8.8	-107.6%	16
32	J.Rosen	ARI	456	36.8%	-117.3%	1.8	-2.5%	6.4	-114.8%	19
33	J.Allen	BUF	402	39.3%	-45.4%	5.4	17.2%	6.9	-62.5%	3
34	D.Watson	HOU	626	41.1%	-27.4%	5.3	56.2%	8.1	-83.6%	8

Includes scrambles and Defensive Pass Interference. Does not include aborted snaps.
Minimum: 200 passes.

WR: Highest Slot/Wide Ratio of Targets

Rk	Player	Team	Slot	Wide	Slot%
1	C.Kupp	LAR	54	0	100%
2	S.Roberts	OAK	62	2	97%
3	R.Cobb	GB	56	4	93%
4	C.Rogers	IND	68	5	93%
5	D.Amendola	MIA	72	6	92%
6	D.Westbrook	JAX	93	8	92%
7	W.Snead	BAL	87	8	92%
8	C.Beasley	DAL	78	9	90%
9	L.Fitzgerald	ARI	100	12	89%
10	G.Tate	2TM	96	14	87%
11	J.Wright	CAR	52	8	87%
12	R.Woods	LAR	114	18	86%
13	J.Kearse	NYJ	65	11	86%
14	A.Humphries	TB	88	16	85%
15	T.Boyd	CIN	88	17	84%
16	J.Crowder	WAS	41	8	84%
17	M.Sanu	ATL	81	16	84%
18	J.Edelman	NE	88	18	83%
19	A.Miller	CHI	45	10	82%
20	N.Agholor	PHI	76	18	81%

Min. 50 passes. Slot includes lined up tight.

WR: Highest Wide/Slot Ratio of Targets

Rk	Player	Team	Slot	Wide	Wide%
1	D.Moore	SEA	2	50	96%
2	M.Gallup	DAL	11	59	84%
3	K.Benjamin	2TM	14	56	80%
4	M.Jones	DET	15	50	77%
5	C.Samuel	CAR	16	50	76%
6	C.Sutton	DEN	22	66	75%
7	J.Gordon	2TM	19	55	74%
8	A.Callaway	CLE	21	60	74%
9	R.Grant	IND	14	39	74%
10	M.Crabtree	BAL	29	74	72%
11	M.Evans	TB	40	100	71%
12	A.Cooper	2TM	33	74	69%
13	J.Doctson	WAS	25	54	68%
14	D.Adams	GB	54	116	68%
15	D.Jackson	TB	24	51	68%
16	J.Ross	CIN	19	40	68%
17	R.Anderson	NYJ	30	63	68%
18	D.Hopkins	HOU	54	111	67%
18	L.Treadwell	MIN	18	37	67%
20	D.Moore	CAR	30	53	64%

Min. 50 passes. Slot includes lined up tight.

Top 10 WR Better Lined Up Wide

Rk	Player	Team	Slot	Wide	Slot	Wide	Dif
1	Ty.Williams	LAC	40	25	-15.6%	57.2%	72.7%
2	T.Taylor	TEN	29	27	-19.6%	15.0%	34.6%
3	E.Sanders	DEN	67	29	-4.1%	25.1%	29.2%
4	K.Cole	JAX	36	34	-34.3%	-6.2%	28.1%
5	T.Lockett	SEA	44	32	54.8%	82.4%	27.6%
6	K.Stills	MIA	35	30	1.4%	25.9%	24.5%
7	A.Cooper	2TM	33	74	-6.4%	17.4%	23.8%
8	C.Ridley	ATL	46	48	-1.1%	20.7%	21.8%
9	C.Godwin	TB	47	48	-6.2%	15.1%	21.3%
10	S.Watkins	KC	33	24	15.5%	35.8%	20.3%

Min. 20 targets from each position

Top 10 WR Better Lined Up Slot

Rk	Player	Team	Slot	Wide	Slot	Wide	Dif
1	M.Williams	LAC	34	33	76.4%	0.6%	75.8%
2	A.Robinson	CHI	53	48	27.3%	-39.6%	66.9%
3	A.J.Green	CIN	37	42	39.8%	-12.2%	52.0%
4	C.Kirk	ARI	33	36	22.6%	-25.1%	47.7%
5	T.Hill	KC	81	51	44.8%	-0.5%	45.4%
6	D.Hopkins	HOU	54	111	52.9%	7.9%	44.9%
7	J.Brown	BAL	50	48	4.7%	-26.2%	31.0%
8	K.Allen	LAC	87	50	28.1%	-0.2%	28.3%
9	D.Moncrief	JAX	33	55	3.2%	-24.1%	27.3%
10	S.Diggs	MIN	62	83	4.7%	-19.6%	24.3%

Min. 20 targets from each position

Top 10 TE Highest Rate of Targets from WR Positions (Slot/Wide)

Rk	Player	Team	Tight	Slot	Wide	Back	WR%
1	A.Gates	LAC	5	38	2	0	89%
2	E.Ebron	IND	22	84	4	0	80%
3	J.Reed	WAS	19	53	11	1	76%
4	T.Kelce	KC	40	99	12	0	74%
5	R.Seals-Jones	ARI	19	47	2	1	71%
6	Z.Ertz	PHI	48	102	6	1	69%
7	C.Brate	TB	16	26	6	1	65%
8	J.Graham	GB	31	51	7	1	64%
9	O.J.Howard	TB	17	27	3	0	64%
10	T.Burton	CHI	25	43	4	2	64%

Min. 20 targets from each position

Top 10 TE Lowest Rate of Targets from WR Positions (Slot/Wide)

Rk	Player	Team	Tight	Slot	Wide	Back	WR%
1	V.Green	LAC	24	2	0	1	7%
2	L.Kendricks	GB	17	3	0	5	12%
3	N.Boyle	BAL	24	7	0	6	19%
4	D.Harris	KC	20	4	1	0	20%
5	R.Ellison	NYG	26	7	0	1	21%
6	J.Thomas	HOU	21	6	0	0	22%
7	J.James	PIT	30	9	0	1	23%
8	J.Heuerman	DEN	29	10	5	4	31%
9	V.McDonald	PIT	45	20	3	3	32%
10	J.O'Shaughnessy	JAX	24	12	1	1	34%

Min. 20 targets from each position

Top 10 RB Highest Rate of Targets from WR Positions (Slot/Wide)

Rk	Player	Team	Back	Slot	Wide	Tight	WR%
1	M.Breida	SF	19	5	7	0	39%
2	D.Johnson	CLE	38	18	5	1	37%
3	N.Hines	IND	51	17	13	0	37%
4	T.Cohen	CHI	58	19	12	2	34%
5	T.Gurley	LAR	53	23	3	0	33%
6	J.Samuels	PIT	20	3	6	0	31%
7	A.Blue	HOU	19	3	4	0	27%
8	T.Riddick	DET	48	16	3	7	26%
9	A.Kamara	NO	80	17	10	0	25%
10	T.Coleman	ATL	33	6	5	0	25%

Min. 20 targets from each position

Top 10 Teams, Pct Passes Dropped

Rk	Team	Passes	Drops	Pct
1	HOU	478	12	2.5%
2	PIT	662	18	2.7%
3	CHI	499	14	2.8%
4	LAR	517	15	2.9%
5	DAL	507	16	3.2%
6	SEA	387	14	3.6%
7	MIN	568	21	3.7%
8	TB	607	24	4.0%
9	GB	591	24	4.1%
10	MIA	414	17	4.1%

Adjusted for passes tipped/thrown away.

Bottom 10 Teams, Pct Passes Dropped

Rk	Team	Passes	Drops	Pct
23	TEN	417	22	5.3%
24	ARI	454	25	5.5%
25	CLE	544	30	5.5%
26	NYJ	487	27	5.5%
27	BUF	462	26	5.6%
28	KC	550	34	6.2%
29	DET	544	34	6.3%
30	DEN	546	38	7.0%
31	CIN	511	36	7.0%
32	JAX	497	37	7.4%

Adjusted for passes tipped/thrown away.

Top 20 Players, Passes Dropped

Rk	Player	Team	Total
1	M.Crabtree	BAL	9
1	C.Ridley	ATL	9
1	C.Sutton	DEN	9
1	G.Tate	2TM	9
5	K.Cole	JAX	8
5	J.Cook	OAK	8
5	E.Ebron	IND	8
5	J.Edelman	NE	8
5	T.Hill	KC	8
5	D.Johnson	ARI	8
5	D.Westbrook	JAX	8
5	T.Yeldon	JAX	8
13	S.Barkley	NYG	7
13	D.Funchess	CAR	7
13	M.Gordon	LAC	7
13	S.Shepard	NYG	7
17	11 tied with		6

Top 20 Players, Pct. Passes Dropped

Rk	Player	Team	Drops	Passes	Pct
1	M.Roberts	DET	4	9	30.8%
2	C.Ivory	BUF	5	13	27.8%
3	D.Harris	KC	4	12	25.0%
4	J.Ross	CIN	6	21	22.2%
5	M.Lynch	OAK	4	15	21.1%
6	T.Cannon	NYJ	4	17	19.0%
7	C.Sutton	DEN	9	42	17.6%
8	K.Cole	JAX	8	38	17.4%
8	V.Green	LAC	4	19	17.4%
10	L.Treadwell	MIN	6	35	14.6%
11	C.Brate	TB	5	30	14.3%
11	M.Crabtree	BAL	9	54	14.3%
13	K.Benjamin	2TM	4	25	13.8%
13	D.Johnson	ARI	8	50	13.8%
15	D.Funchess	CAR	7	44	13.7%
16	C.Conley	KC	5	32	13.5%
17	K.Hunt	KC	4	26	13.3%
18	R.Seals-Jones	ARI	5	34	12.8%
19	J.Gordon	2TM	6	41	12.8%
20	J.Brown	BAL	6	42	12.5%
20	P.Lindsay	DEN	5	35	12.5%
20	T.Yeldon	JAX	8	56	12.5%

Min. four drops

Top 20 Yards Lost to Drops by Quarterbacks

Rk	Player	Team	Drops	Yds
1	B.Mayfield	CLE	26	299
2	M.Ryan	ATL	28	285
3	C.Keenum	DEN	38	248
4	T.Brady	NE	26	244
4	S.Darnold	NYJ	21	244
6	A.Rodgers	GB	20	243
7	A.Luck	IND	31	230
8	P.Mahomes	KC	33	225
9	M.Mariota	TEN	15	219
10	B.Bortles	JAX	30	217
11	D.Carr	OAK	27	213
12	C.Wentz	PHI	20	212
13	J.Allen	BUF	19	194
14	J.Flacco	BAL	22	185
15	P.Rivers	LAC	25	184
16	M.Stafford	DET	32	183
17	A.Dalton	CIN	25	161
18	C.Newton	CAR	21	160
19	E.Manning	NYG	28	158
19	A.Smith	WAS	12	158

Based on yardage in the air, no possible YAC included.

Top 20 Intended Receivers on Interceptions

Rk	Player	Team	Total
1	A.Brown	PIT	11
2	M.Evans	TB	8
3	K.Benjamin	BUF	7
3	D.Jackson	TB	7
5	T.Hill	KC	6
6	A.Callaway	CLE	5
6	J.Doctson	WAS	5
6	Z.Ertz	PHI	5
6	D.Funchess	CAR	5
6	Z.Jones	BUF	5
6	J.Ross	CIN	5
6	Ty.Williams	LAC	5
13	R.Anderson	NYJ	4
13	O.Beckham	NYG	4
13	J.Cook	OAK	4
13	M.Goodwin	SF	4
13	O.J.Howard	TB	4
13	C.Kirk	ARI	4
13	J.Reynolds	LAR	4
13	J.Smith-Schuster	PIT	4

Top 10 Plus/Minus for Running Backs

Rk	Player	Team	Pass	+/-
1	C.McCaffrey	CAR	122	+8.2
2	A.Kamara	NO	95	+5.4
3	J.Richard	OAK	79	+3.9
4	T.Cohen	CHI	88	+2.8
5	J.Allen	BAL	40	+2.8
6	D.Lewis	TEN	67	+2.2
7	I.Smith	ATL	30	+2.2
8	M.Breida	SF	31	+2.1
9	J.Samuels	PIT	29	+1.8
10	K.Juszczyk	SF	37	+1.7

Min. 25 passes; plus/minus adjusted for passes tipped/thrown away.

Bottom 10 Plus/Minus for Running Backs

Rk	Player	Team	Pass	+/-
1	D.Johnson	ARI	71	-8.2
2	J.White	NE	117	-5.7
3	S.Barkley	NYG	117	-4.9
4	T.Montgomery	2TM	37	-4.6
5	E.McGuire	NYJ	30	-4.0
6	N.Chubb	CLE	29	-3.6
7	P.Barber	TB	28	-3.3
8	M.Mack	IND	24	-3.3
9	J.Williams	GB	36	-3.0
10	T.Gurley	LAR	75	-2.8

Min. 25 passes; plus/minus adjusted for passes tipped/thrown away.

Top 10 Plus/Minus for Wide Receivers

Rk	Player	Team	Pass	+/-
1	M.Thomas	NO	146	+24.2
2	T.Lockett	SEA	65	+17.7
3	A.Thielen	MIN	147	+16.6
4	D.Hopkins	HOU	159	+14.2
5	M.Evans	TB	131	+10.3
6	J.Jones	ATL	167	+10.1
7	S.Diggs	MIN	134	+9.7
8	B.Cooks	LAR	112	+9.1
9	T.Hill	KC	131	+8.3
10	R.Higgins	CLE	50	+7.6

Min. 50 passes; plus/minus adjusted for passes tipped/thrown away.

Bottom 10 Plus/Minus for Wide Receivers

Rk	Player	Team	Pass	+/-
1	J.Ross	CIN	57	-13.3
2	J.Kearse	NYJ	74	-12.6
3	K.Benjamin	2TM	64	-11.8
4	J.Brown	BAL	93	-11.2
5	M.Crabtree	BAL	99	-9.7
6	J.Landry	CLE	140	-7.9
7	Z.Jones	BUF	99	-6.2
8	Q.Enunwa	NYJ	63	-6.1
9	C.Sutton	DEN	81	-5.9
10	M.Gallup	DAL	65	-5.7

Min. 50 passes; plus/minus adjusted for passes tipped/thrown away.

Top 10 Plus/Minus for Tight Ends

Rk	Player	Team	Pass	+/-
1	A.Hooper	ATL	88	+8.1
2	Z.Ertz	PHI	152	+7.7
3	K.Rudolph	MIN	80	+6.7
4	B.Watson	NO	46	+5.6
5	T.Kelce	KC	144	+5.0
5	M.Andrews	BAL	47	+4.3
7	C.Herndon	NYJ	54	+3.4
8	O.J.Howard	TB	47	+3.3
9	T.Burton	CHI	73	+3.1
10	G.Swaim	DAL	30	+2.7

Min. 25 passes; plus/minus adjusted for passes tipped/thrown away.

Bottom 10 Plus/Minus for Tight Ends

Rk	Player	Team	Pass	+/-
1	R.Seals-Jones	ARI	68	-10.7
2	R.Griffin	HOU	42	-5.3
3	E.Ebron	IND	106	-4.9
4	J.Reed	WAS	81	-4.7
5	G.Kittle	SF	130	-3.9
6	J.Heuerman	DEN	47	-3.9
7	D.Njoku	CLE	86	-2.9
8	C.Brate	TB	48	-2.9
9	M.LaCosse	DEN	36	-2.7
10	C.J.Uzomah	CIN	64	-2.4

Min. 25 passes; plus/minus adjusted for passes tipped/thrown away.

Top 10 Quarterbacks, Yards Gained on Defensive Pass Interference

Rk	Player	Team	Pen	Yds
1	M.Stafford	DET	10	221
2	R.Wilson	SEA	10	205
3	M.Ryan	ATL	9	203
4	D.Brees	NO	13	201
5	M.Trubisky	CHI	10	197
6	A.Luck	IND	10	169
7	T.Brady	NE	8	167
8	E.Manning	NYG	9	164
9	J.Flacco	BAL	8	159
10	B.Roethlisberger	PIT	9	152

Top 10 Receivers, Yards Gained on Defensive Pass Interference

Rk	Player	Team	Pen	Yds
1	T.Lockett	SEA	6	182
2	T.Y.Hilton	IND	6	150
3	B.Cooks	LAR	3	124
4	J.Gordon	2TM	4	116
5	C.Davis	TEN	5	106
6	K.Golladay	DET	5	105
7	M.Jones	DET	4	104
8	M.Thomas	NO	8	102
9	J.Jones	ATL	3	98
10	A.Jeffery	PHI	4	93

Top 10 Defenders, Yards Allowed on Defensive Pass Interference

Rk	Player	Team	Pen	Yds
1	P.Gaines	BUF	3	131
2	D.Jackson	CAR	5	113
3	M.Fitzpatrick	MIA	5	110
4	K.Crawley	NO	4	106
5	S.Nelson	KC	4	101
6	B.Webb	NYG	6	99
7	E.Apple	NO	6	91
8	D.Slay	DET	4	90
9	F.Moreau	WAS	4	81
10	J.Alexander	GB	3	78

Top 20 First Downs/Touchdowns Allowed, Coverage

Rk	Player	Team	Yards	Rk	Player	Team	Yards
1	R.Alford	ATL	43	11	T.Flowers	SEA	34
2	C.Awuzie	DAL	42	12	J.Ramsey	JAX	33
3	E.Apple	2TM	40	12	B.Roby	DEN	33
3	K.Fuller	KC	40	14	R.Melvin	OAK	32
5	A.Jackson	TEN	39	15	D.Trufant	ATL	31
5	S.Nelson	KC	39	16	M.Claiborne	NYJ	30
7	J.Jenkins	NYG	38	16	SL.Griffin	SEA	30
8	J.Bradberry	CAR	36	16	O.Scandrick	KC	30
9	M.Butler	TEN	35	19	K.Fuller	CHI	29
9	M.Lattimore	NO	35	19	B.Skrine	NYJ	29

Includes Defensive Pass Interference.

Top 20 Passing Yards Allowed, Coverage

Rk	Player	Team	Yards	Rk	Player	Team	Yards
1	R.Alford	ATL	826	11	K.Fuller	KC	610
2	B.Roby	DEN	719	12	C.Awuzie	DAL	608
3	E.Apple	2TM	707	13	M.Peters	LAR	561
4	S.Nelson	KC	691	13	J.Ramsey	JAX	561
5	M.Lattimore	NO	684	15	M.Claiborne	NYJ	550
6	J.Jenkins	NYG	659	16	R.Melvin	OAK	544
7	A.Jackson	TEN	650	17	P.Desir	IND	526
8	J.Bradberry	CAR	645	18	M.Adams	CAR	524
9	T.Flowers	SEA	638	19	J.Alexander	GB	518
10	M.Butler	TEN	627	20	SL.Griffin	SEA	516

Includes Defensive Pass Interference.

Fewest Yards After Catch Allowed, Coverage by Cornerbacks

Rk	Player	Team	YAC
1	A.Maddox	PHI	1.4
2	S.Gilmore	NE	1.4
3	R.Darby	PHI	1.5
4	D.Slay	DET	1.8
5	C.Sensabaugh	PIT	1.9
6	T.Waynes	MIN	2.1
7	D.Worley	OAK	2.1
8	A.Bouye	JAX	2.5
9	O.Scandrick	KC	2.6
10	K.Jackson	HOU	2.6
11	J.Haden	PIT	2.6
12	C.Awuzie	DAL	2.6
13	J.Jenkins	NYG	2.7
14	K.Fuller	CHI	2.7
15	D.Trufant	ATL	2.7
16	C.Hayward	LAC	2.8
17	C.Harris	DEN	2.9
18	M.Davis	LAC	2.9
19	SL.Griffin	SEA	2.9
20	T.White	BUF	2.9

Min. 50 passes or 8 games started.

Most Yards After Catch Allowed, Coverage by Cornerbacks

Rk	Player	Team	YAC
1	G.Conley	OAK	9.1
2	G.Haley	NYG	7.0
3	J.Mills	PHI	6.2
4	J.Jackson	GB	5.8
5	B.Roby	DEN	5.7
6	A.Talib	LAR	5.6
7	F.Moreau	WAS	5.5
8	T.Flowers	SEA	5.4
9	P.Williams	NO	5.3
10	X.Howard	MIA	5.3
11	B.Poole	ATL	5.1
12	K.Williams	SF	5.0
13	L.Ryan	TEN	4.9
14	R.Alford	ATL	4.8
15	R.Douglas	PHI	4.8
16	J.McCourty	NE	4.8
17	K.Fuller	KC	4.7
17	B.Skrine	NYJ	4.7
19	W.Jackson	CIN	4.6
20	M.Peters	LAR	4.6

Min. 50 passes or 8 games started.

Fewest Avg Yards on Run Tackle, Defensive Line or Edge Rusher

Rk	Player	Team	Tkl	Avg
1	A.Donald	LAR	38	0.3
2	A.Muhammad	IND	27	0.6
3	J.Clowney	HOU	33	0.8
4	K.Short	CAR	36	0.8
5	J.J.Watt	HOU	42	0.9
6	C.Campbell	JAX	58	1.0
7	C.Jordan	NO	33	1.2
8	D.Philon	LAC	25	1.3
9	T.Coley	CLE	32	1.3
10	A.Billings	CIN	28	1.4
11	J.Mauro	NYG	27	1.4
12	L.Floyd	CHI	31	1.5
13	L.Ogunjobi	CLE	41	1.5
14	M.Ingram	LAC	31	1.6
15	J.Sheard	IND	36	1.6
16	B.Mayowa	ARI	29	1.6
17	A.Woods	DAL	27	1.6
18	B.Graham	PHI	28	1.6
19	D.Harrison	2TM	74	1.6
20	R.Blair	SF	25	1.6

Min. 25 run tackles

Fewest Avg Yards on Run Tackle, LB

Rk	Player	Team	Tkl	Avg
1	M.Milano	BUF	47	2.3
2	L.David	TB	62	2.3
2	A.Walker	IND	62	2.3
4	Z.Brown	WAS	50	2.4
5	A.Klein	NO	51	2.6
6	M.Lee	OAK	47	2.7
7	R.Evans	TEN	42	2.7
8	E.Roberts	NE	44	2.8
9	D.Lee	NYJ	43	2.8
10	J.Bynes	ARI	41	2.9
11	J.Smith	DAL	67	3.1
12	J.Bostic	PIT	40	3.1
13	K.Young	BAL	28	3.1
14	J.Baker	MIA	40	3.3
15	R.McMillan	MIA	78	3.3
16	L.Kuechly	CAR	77	3.3
17	D.Davis	NO	54	3.3
17	A.Ogletree	NYG	54	3.3
19	Z.Cunningham	HOU	63	3.4
20	D.Kennard	DET	35	3.5

Min. 25 run tackles

Fewest Avg Yards on Run Tackle, DB

Rk	Player	Team	Tkl	Avg
1	K.Moore	IND	24	2.3
2	J.Tartt	SF	21	3.5
3	T.J.Carrie	CLE	23	3.5
4	K.Jackson	HOU	40	3.7
5	D.Dennard	CIN	20	4.0
6	K.Coleman	NO	20	4.1
7	A.Phillips	LAC	41	4.1
8	J.Jones	GB	27	4.3
9	B.Baker	ARI	49	4.3
10	W.Parks	DEN	20	4.5
11	D.Swearinger	2TM	22	4.6
12	T.Jefferson	BAL	28	4.9
13	L.Collins	NYG	52	5.0
13	P.Desir	IND	22	5.0
15	T.Mathieu	HOU	27	5.0
16	J.Richards	ATL	22	5.1
17	E.Harris	OAK	20	5.2
17	S.Neasman	ATL	20	5.2
19	V.Bell	NO	40	5.3
20	K.Vaccaro	TEN	29	5.3

Min. 20 run tackles

Top 20 Offensive Tackles, Blown Blocks

Rk	Player	Pos	Team	Sacks	All Pass	All Run	Total
1	M.McGlinchey	RT	SF	4.5	25	7	32
2	J.Davenport	LT	HOU	8.0	28	2	30
3	G.Bolles	LT	DEN	5.5	24	4	28
4	K.Miller	LT	OAK	10.7	20	6	26
4	S.Tevi	RT	LAC	6.8	22	4	26
6	C.Leno	LT	CHI	3.5	23	2	25
6	D.Smith	LT	TB	7.0	16	8	25
8	D.Dawkins	LT	BUF	7.5	19	5	24
9	M.Moses	RT	WAS	5.0	20	3	23
9	R.Reiff	LT	MIN	5.5	19	4	23
9	R.Schraeder	RT	ATL	10.0	21	2	23
9	M.Schwartz	RT	KC	5.0	18	5	23
13	R.Hill	RT	MIN	4.5	18	4	22
13	B.Massie	RT	CHI	2.5	17	5	22
15	C.Clark	LT	CAR	6.0	18	3	21
15	E.Fisher	LT	KC	4.5	16	5	21
15	B.Parker	RT	OAK	10.7	20	1	21
18	L.Collins	RT	DAL	6.0	15	3	20
18	C.Hubbard	RT	CLE	6.5	14	6	20
18	C.Wheeler	RT	NYG	6.3	12	8	20

Top 20 Offensive Tackles in Snaps per Blown Block

Rk	Player	Pos	Team	Sacks	All Pass	All Run	Total	Snaps	Snaps per BB
1	T.Armstead	LT	NO	0.0	0	1	1	602	602.0
2	O.Brown	RT	BAL	1.0	3	0	3	760	253.3
3	R.Stanley	LT	BAL	1.0	4	2	6	1085	180.8
4	J.Matthews	LT	ATL	2.0	6	0	7	1057	151.0
5	R.Wagner	RT	DET	4.0	7	2	9	984	109.3
6	T.Brown	LT	NE	2.0	7	3	10	1089	108.9
7	G.Jackson	RT	OAK	4.0	7	1	8	859	107.4
8	T.Smith	LT	DAL	3.5	7	1	8	849	106.1
9	J.Staley	LT	SF	4.0	9	1	10	1005	100.5
10	M.Feiler	RT	PIT	1.0	6	1	7	676	96.6
11	B.Shell	RT	NYJ	2.0	5	4	9	850	94.4
12	A.Whitworth	LT	LAR	7.5	11	0	11	1037	94.3
13	R.Havenstein	RT	LAR	2.5	6	6	12	1100	91.7
14	D.Dotson	RT	TB	2.5	8	3	11	1005	91.4
15	J.Parnell	RT	JAX	1.0	8	2	10	869	86.9
16	R.Okung	LT	LAC	3.5	9	1	10	866	86.6
17	M.Cannon	RT	NE	2.0	9	1	10	835	83.5
18	R.Ramczyk	RT	NO	1.5	8	4	12	996	83.0
19	A.Villanueva	LT	PIT	4.0	11	2	14	1116	79.7
20	D.Bakhtiari	LT	GB	3.0	11	3	14	1032	73.7

Minimum: 400 snaps

Top 20 Interior Linemen, Blown Blocks

Rk	Player	Pos	Team	Sacks	All Pass	All Run	Total
1	M.Remmers	RG	MIN	4.5	19	8	27
2	D.Feeney	LG	LAC	7.0	23	3	26
3	M.Schofield	RG	LAC	4.8	16	9	25
4	J.Davis	RG	MIA	6.5	15	9	24
4	F.Ragnow	LG	DET	5.0	15	9	24
4	B.Turner	LG	DEN	1.0	14	10	24
7	B.Winters	RG	NYJ	6.0	11	12	23
8	C.McGovern	RG	DEN	1.5	16	4	20
9	A.J.Cann	RG	JAX	5.5	13	6	19
9	C.Erving	LG	KC	2.0	14	5	19
9	M.Person	RG	SF	3.5	13	6	19
12	T.Compton	LG	MIN	7.0	11	7	18
12	T.Larsen	LG	MIA	3.0	11	7	18
12	J.Looney	C	DAL	0.0	11	7	18
12	J.Sweezy	LG	SEA	4.0	12	6	18
16	S.Kelemete	LG	HOU	3.5	14	3	17
16	P.Omameh	LG	2TM	4.0	13	4	17
16	W.Richburg	C	SF	3.5	10	7	17
16	T.Swanson	C	MIA	2.0	9	8	17
16	L.Tomlinson	LG	SF	3.0	9	8	17

Top 20 Interior Linemen in Snaps per Blown Block

Rk	Player	Pos	Team	Sacks	All Pass	All Run	Total	Snaps	Snaps per BB
1	M.Morse	C	KC	0.0	0	1	2	678	339.0
2	J.Thuney	LG	NE	0.5	2	2	4	1119	279.8
3	M.Pouncey	C	PIT	0.0	3	1	4	1102	275.5
4	R.Kelly	C	IND	0.0	1	2	3	778	259.3
5	Q.Nelson	LG	IND	1.0	3	2	5	1137	227.4
6	J.C.Tretter	C	CLE	1.0	2	3	5	1091	218.2
7	B.Fusco	RG	ATL	1.0	1	1	2	436	218.0
8	G.Glasgow	C	DET	0.5	2	3	5	1074	214.8
9	S.Mason	RG	NE	0.5	2	3	5	953	190.6
10	M.Paradis	C	DEN	0.0	1	2	3	569	189.7
11	D.Andrews	C	NE	0.5	3	3	6	1103	183.8
12	W.Schweitzer	LG	ATL	1.5	2	3	5	901	180.2
13	C.Whitehair	C	CHI	0.5	3	3	6	1075	179.2
14	A.Mack	C	ATL	2.0	3	3	6	1057	176.2
15	R.Hudson	C	OAK	0.5	3	3	6	1046	174.3
16	J.Harrison	C	NYJ	0.0	3	0	3	506	168.7
17	M.Yanda	RG	BAL	1.0	7	0	7	1163	166.1
18	M.Skura	C	BAL	1.0	4	4	8	1189	148.6
19	J.Kelce	C	PHI	1.0	6	1	7	1037	148.1
20	R.Bodine	C	BUF	0.5	2	2	4	588	147.0

Minimum: 400 snaps

Top 20 Tight Ends, Blown Blocks

Rk	Player	Team	Sacks	All Pass	All Run	Total
1	K.Rudolph	MIN	0.0	14	1	15
2	D.Njoku	CLE	0.5	7	3	10
3	J.Sprinkle	WAS	1.0	6	2	8
3	L.Thomas	BUF	1.0	5	3	8
5	T.Higbee	LAR	0.5	6	1	7
6	N.Boyle	BAL	1.0	2	4	6
6	G.Celek	SF	0.0	3	3	6
6	Z.Ertz	PHI	0.0	4	2	6
6	D.Fells	CLE	1.0	3	3	6
6	D.Goedert	PHI	1.5	4	2	6
6	R.Griffin	HOU	2.0	2	4	6
6	M.LaCosse	DEN	0.0	5	1	6
6	N.O'Leary	MIA	4.0	2	4	6
6	J.Smith	TEN	1.0	2	3	6
6	J.Thomas	HOU	1.5	3	3	6
6	C.J.Uzomah	CIN	1.0	4	2	6
17	R.Ellison	NYG	1.0	3	2	5
17	L.Toilolo	DET	0.0	4	1	5
19	11 tied with					4

Most Penalties, Offense

Rk	Player	Team	Pen	Yds
1	M.Moses	WAS	16	108
2	D.Dawkins	BUF	15	91
3	J.Davenport	HOU	14	80
4	G.Bolles	DEN	13	85
4	B.Hart	CIN	13	75
6	C.Erving	KC	12	75
6	T.Williams	WAS	12	63
8	L.Collins	DAL	11	64
8	D.Dotson	TB	11	50
8	G.Ifedi	SEA	11	76
8	R.Jensen	TB	11	120
8	B.Parker	OAK	11	65
13	D.Harrison	CLE	10	70
13	A.Redmond	CIN	10	89
13	G.Robinson	CLE	10	65
13	T.Smith	DAL	10	85
17	11 tied with		9	

Includes declined and offsetting, but not special teams or penalties on turnover returns.

Most Penalties, Defense

Rk	Player	Team	Pen	Yds
1	J.Clowney	HOU	13	80
2	R.Alford	ATL	12	82
3	E.Apple	2TM	11	106
3	M.Garrett	CLE	11	37
3	S.Nelson	KC	11	121
3	O.Scandrick	KC	11	63
3	T.White	BUF	11	53
8	M.Fitzpatrick	MIA	10	152
8	M.Ingram	LAC	10	52
8	B.Webb	NYG	10	128
8	A.Witherspoon	SF	10	79
12	T.J.Carrie	CLE	9	79
12	R.Gregory	DAL	9	82
12	B.Hill	NYG	9	55
12	N.Lawson	DET	9	64
12	X.Rhodes	MIN	9	84
17	11 tied with		8	

Includes declined and offsetting, but not special teams or penalties on turnover returns.

Top 10 Kickers, Gross Kickoff Value over Average

Rk	Player	Team	Kick Pts+	Net Pts+	Kicks
1	H.Butker	KC	+3.5	+5.0	108
2	J.Myers	NYJ	+3.4	+4.9	80
3	J.Elliott	PHI	+3.0	+3.1	81
4	J.Tucker	BAL	+2.2	+1.0	88
5	D.Hopkins	WAS	+2.1	+2.8	69
6	G.Joseph	CLE	+2.0	+1.6	67
7	C.Parkey	CHI	+1.9	-1.5	88
8	M.Crosby	GB	+1.2	-4.9	80
9	S.Janikowski	SEA	+1.1	-5.6	72
10	R.Bullock	CIN	+1.0	+2.9	76

Min. 20 kickoffs; squibs and onside not included

Bottom 10 Kickers, Gross Kickoff Value over Average

Rk	Player	Team	Kick Pts+	Net Pts+	Kicks
1	B.McManus	DEN	-4.0	-1.4	69
2	S.Martin	DET	-2.8	+2.8	68
3	P.Dawson	ARI	-2.1	+0.8	31
4	M.Badgley	LAC	-2.1	-0.9	54
5	R.Sanchez	IND	-1.4	-1.5	84
6	C.Santos	2TM	-1.3	-1.4	46
7	M.McCrane	3TM	-1.2	+0.6	20
8	W.Lutz	NO	-1.2	-1.6	99
9	C.Sturgis	LAC	-1.2	+2.4	34
10	D.Bailey	MIN	-1.1	-1.1	62

Min. 20 kickoffs; squibs and onside not included

Top 10 Punters, Gross Punt Value over Average

Rk	Player	Team	Punt Pts+	Net Pts+	Punts
1	A.Lee	ARI	+13.0	+6.5	94
2	T.Way	WAS	+11.4	+6.1	79
3	B.Kern	TEN	+6.4	+2.3	75
4	M.Dickson	SEA	+4.6	-2.2	79
5	T.Morstead	NO	+4.4	+5.3	43
6	C.Johnston	PHI	+4.2	+6.4	61
7	R.Allen	NE	+4.1	+4.5	64
8	S.Martin	DET	+4.0	-3.1	74
9	D.Colquitt	KC	+3.4	+7.0	45
10	R.Dixon	NYG	+3.2	+9.6	71

Min. 20 punts

Bottom 10 Punters, Gross Punt Value over Average

Rk	Player	Team	Punt Pts+	Net Pts+	Punts
1	J.Townsend	OAK	-8.6	-12.0	70
2	D.Jones	LAC	-7.4	-2.7	47
3	C.Bojorquez	BUF	-6.7	-4.3	47
4	M.Haack	MIA	-6.3	-10.5	88
5	B.Colquitt	CLE	-6.1	-10.8	85
6	B.Anger	TB	-5.3	-2.9	58
7	M.Bosher	ATL	-4.7	+1.0	62
8	M.Darr	BUF	-3.8	-1.7	20
9	B.Pinion	SF	-3.0	0.0	69
10	C.Jones	DAL	-3.0	-2.5	60

Min. 20 punts

Top 10 Kick Returners, Value over Average

Rk	Player	Team	Pts+	Returns
1	A.Roberts	NYJ	+14.3	40
2	D.Jennings	TEN	+12.2	22
3	A.Erickson	CIN	+8.6	39
4	Tr.Smith	KC	+7.1	33
5	C.Patterson	NE	+6.8	22
6	J.Grant	MIA	+6.0	18
6	R.James	SF	+5.8	22
8	T.Lockett	SEA	+3.7	19
8	C.Coleman	NYG	+3.0	23
10	M.Murphy	BUF	+2.4	13

Min. eight returns

Bottom 10 Kick Returners, Value over Average

Rk	Player	Team	Pts+	Returns
1	D.Reed	SF	-4.1	11
2	R.Switzer	PIT	-2.8	29
3	C.Samuel	CAR	-2.8	10
4	T.Montgomery	GB	-2.7	10
5	J.Peppers	CLE	-2.5	19
6	R.Penny	SEA	-2.2	8
7	A.Callaway	CLE	-2.2	8
8	P.Cooper	LAR	-2.2	13
9	B.Williams	ARI	-2.2	10
10	D.King	LAC	-2.1	22

Min. eight returns

Top 10 Punt Returners, Value over Average

Rk	Player	Team	Pts+	Returns
1	A.Roberts	NYJ	+10.2	23
2	C.Jones	2TM	+10.1	23
3	J.Grant	MIA	+9.4	14
4	D.Harris	OAK	+9.2	20
5	D.King	LAC	+9.0	23
6	D.Westbrook	JAX	+8.9	19
7	M.Sherels	MIN	+5.7	23
8	T.Hill	KC	+5.7	20
9	T.Cohen	CHI	+4.4	33
10	J.Peppers	CLE	+3.3	25

Min. eight returns

Bottom 10 Punt Returners, Value over Average

Rk	Player	Team	Pts+	Returns
1	D.Pettis	SF	-3.7	9
2	O.Beckham	NYG	-3.6	8
3	A.Humphries	TB	-3.3	21
4	I.McKenzie	2TM	-3.2	16
5	J.Agnew	DET	-3.2	12
6	J.Mickens	JAX	-2.9	11
7	T.Lockett	SEA	-2.7	25
7	R.James	SF	-2.6	12
9	T.Williams	GB	-2.4	12
10	A.Jones	DEN	-2.4	10

Min. eight returns

Top 20 Special Teams Plays

Rk	Player	Team	Plays	Rk	Player	Team	Plays
1	A.Phillips	LAC	17	8	B.Mingo	SEA	12
2	E.Turner	ARI	15	8	J.Olawale	DAL	12
3	J.Bethel	ATL	14	8	S.Perry	MIA	12
3	D.Harris	OAK	14	8	M.Thomas	NYG	12
5	N.Ebner	NE	13	8	C.Ward	KC	12
5	C.Fejedelem	CIN	13	15	K.Grugier-Hill	PHI	11
5	J.Kearse	MIN	13	15	J.Jones	DEN	11
8	J.Coleman	SEA	12	15	A.Moore	HOU	11
8	B.King	NE	12	18	9 tied with		10

Plays = tackles + assists; does not include onside or end-half squib kicks.

Top 10 Offenses, 3-and-out per drive

Rk	Team	Pct
1	LAR	10.9%
2	NO	14.2%
3	TB	14.5%
4	KC	16.0%
5	BAL	17.2%
5	PIT	17.2%
7	LAC	17.4%
8	DET	17.9%
9	CHI	17.9%
9	SF	17.9%

Top 10 Defenses, 3-and-out per drive

Rk	Team	Pct
1	CHI	26.8%
2	JAX	25.7%
3	BUF	25.3%
4	MIN	24.9%
5	ARI	24.6%
6	TB	24.6%
7	BAL	24.3%
8	LAC	23.6%
9	GB	22.7%
10	PIT	22.6%

Bottom 10 Offenses, 3-and-out per drive

Rk	Team	Pct
23	NYG	23.3%
24	CIN	23.8%
25	BUF	24.1%
26	WAS	24.8%
27	JAX	24.9%
28	OAK	25.3%
29	MIA	26.7%
30	SEA	27.8%
31	ARI	29.8%
32	NYJ	30.2%

Bottom 10 Defenses, 3-and-out per drive

Rk	Team	Pct
23	WAS	19.6%
24	NYG	19.5%
25	CLE	18.1%
26	NO	18.0%
27	MIA	18.0%
28	LAR	17.6%
29	ATL	17.6%
30	SEA	16.0%
31	CIN	15.7%
32	KC	13.7%

Top 10 Offenses, Yards per drive

Rk	Team	Yds/Dr
1	KC	41.53
2	NO	39.89
3	LAR	38.99
4	ATL	37.97
5	PIT	37.68
6	TB	36.93
7	NE	35.83
8	CAR	35.83
9	IND	35.07
10	LAC	34.84

Top 10 Defenses, Yards per drive

Rk	Team	Yds/Dr
1	CHI	25.97
2	BUF	26.18
3	BAL	26.34
4	MIN	28.00
5	JAX	28.95
6	HOU	29.21
7	PIT	29.72
8	NE	30.61
9	TEN	30.82
10	ARI	31.02

Bottom 10 Offenses, Yards per drive

Rk	Team	Yds/Dr
23	TEN	30.35
24	CLE	30.31
25	CIN	29.97
26	MIN	29.34
27	WAS	28.20
28	JAX	26.23
29	MIA	25.73
30	BUF	25.12
31	NYJ	23.99
32	ARI	21.18

Bottom 10 Defenses, Yards per drive

Rk	Team	Yds/Dr
23	SEA	34.31
24	CAR	34.32
25	WAS	35.15
26	NYG	35.32
27	MIA	35.85
28	NO	35.93
29	OAK	36.13
30	ATL	37.18
31	CIN	38.14
32	KC	39.57

Top 10 Offenses, avg LOS to start drive

Rk	Team	LOS
1	NO	31.4
2	HOU	30.6
3	LAR	30.5
4	MIN	30.3
5	KC	30.2
6	CHI	29.8
7	NYJ	29.7
8	BUF	29.6
9	IND	29.3
10	CIN	29.1

Top 10 Defenses, avg LOS to start drive

Rk	Team	LOS
1	HOU	25.6
2	KC	25.6
3	NO	26.3
4	WAS	26.5
5	CAR	26.8
6	ATL	27.1
7	SEA	27.2
8	LAR	27.4
9	NYG	27.5
10	IND	27.5

Bottom 10 Offenses, avg LOS to start drive

Rk	Team	LOS
23	DEN	27.4
24	OAK	27.1
25	DET	27.0
26	NYG	26.9
27	JAX	26.7
28	GB	26.4
29	TB	26.3
30	ATL	26.3
31	PIT	26.2
32	SF	25.4

Bottom 10 Defenses, avg LOS to start drive

Rk	Team	LOS
23	TB	29.1
24	NE	29.1
25	JAX	29.1
26	CLE	29.2
27	OAK	29.7
28	GB	29.9
29	DAL	30.1
30	NYJ	30.7
31	SF	31.0
32	BUF	31.4

Top 10 Offenses, Points per drive

Rk	Team	Pts/Dr
1	KC	3.25
2	NO	3.21
3	LAR	2.79
4	IND	2.46
5	LAC	2.43
6	ATL	2.42
7	SEA	2.36
8	NE	2.32
9	PIT	2.32
10	CAR	2.21

Top 10 Defenses, Points per drive

Rk	Team	Pts/Dr
1	CHI	1.43
2	BAL	1.62
3	MIN	1.68
4	HOU	1.71
5	TEN	1.75
6	JAX	1.77
7	NE	1.78
8	LAC	1.83
9	DEN	1.84
10	BUF	1.86

Bottom 10 Offenses, Points per drive

Rk	Team	Pts/Dr
23	CLE	1.83
24	TEN	1.79
25	DEN	1.75
26	WAS	1.66
27	OAK	1.62
28	MIA	1.61
29	NYJ	1.55
30	BUF	1.40
31	JAX	1.24
32	ARI	1.12

Bottom 10 Defenses, Points per drive

Rk	Team	Pts/Dr
23	NYJ	2.19
24	MIA	2.28
25	CAR	2.29
26	SF	2.33
27	NYG	2.36
28	KC	2.41
29	ATL	2.44
30	TB	2.48
31	CIN	2.56
32	OAK	2.61

Top 10 Offenses, Better DVOA with Shotgun

Rk	Team	% Plays Shotgun	DVOA Shot	DVOA Not	Yd/Play Shot	Yd/Play Not	DVOA Dif
1	CHI	80%	4.5%	-30.4%	6.1	4.0	34.9%
2	PIT	79%	22.0%	-12.7%	6.7	4.8	34.6%
3	KC	81%	40.2%	12.3%	7.1	6.3	27.9%
4	ATL	50%	21.8%	-2.2%	6.6	6.1	24.0%
5	IND	74%	14.5%	-7.6%	6.0	6.0	22.1%
6	BAL	80%	6.0%	-15.7%	5.7	4.8	21.7%
7	TB	63%	14.8%	-6.7%	6.8	5.7	21.6%
8	HOU	70%	3.0%	-17.2%	6.1	5.0	20.2%
9	CAR	77%	10.4%	-6.8%	6.4	5.0	17.3%
10	OAK	61%	-0.6%	-15.2%	5.8	5.2	14.5%

Top 10 Offenses, Better DVOA with Play-Action

Rk	Team	% PA	DVOA PA	DVOA No PA	Yd/Play PA	Yd/Play No PA	DVOA Dif
1	NE	31%	76.4%	16.4%	9.8	6.2	59.9%
2	ARI	20%	-3.3%	-54.3%	7.1	4.9	51.0%
3	BUF	24%	12.6%	-33.7%	7.5	5.6	46.3%
4	TEN	29%	33.4%	-12.1%	8.1	6.1	45.6%
5	DAL	25%	29.9%	-7.5%	8.3	6.1	37.4%
6	LAR	36%	56.0%	20.3%	9.4	6.8	35.7%
7	SEA	33%	54.4%	19.6%	9.0	6.5	34.8%
8	MIN	21%	40.3%	6.4%	8.4	6.1	33.8%
9	DEN	25%	23.7%	-4.7%	7.6	5.9	28.4%
10	LAC	22%	63.1%	34.9%	9.3	7.4	28.2%

Bottom 10 Offenses, Better DVOA with Shotgun

Rk	Team	% Plays Shotgun	DVOA Shot	DVOA Not	Yd/Play Shot	Yd/Play Not	DVOA Dif
23	SEA	69%	9.1%	8.3%	5.7	6.3	0.8%
24	GB	73%	11.0%	11.3%	5.8	6.0	-0.3%
25	LAC	57%	20.0%	21.6%	6.3	6.5	-1.6%
26	JAX	69%	-23.1%	-20.0%	5.1	4.3	-3.1%
27	SF	46%	-18.3%	-13.4%	5.5	6.2	-4.9%
28	LAR	39%	18.3%	27.9%	6.4	6.7	-9.5%
29	DEN	56%	-6.8%	9.3%	5.4	5.9	-16.1%
30	BUF	57%	-35.5%	-18.9%	4.9	4.8	-16.5%
31	TEN	53%	-15.3%	4.3%	5.3	5.6	-19.5%
32	ARI	57%	-56.5%	-24.4%	4.1	4.8	-32.1%

Bottom 10 Offenses, Better DVOA with Play-Action

Rk	Team	% PA	DVOA PA	DVOA No PA	Yd/Play PA	Yd/Play No PA	DVOA Dif
23	NYG	24%	8.7%	17.1%	7.7	6.6	-8.4%
24	CAR	29%	6.0%	15.2%	7.3	6.6	-9.2%
25	TB	17%	15.4%	30.0%	8.6	7.7	-14.6%
26	OAK	18%	0.4%	16.1%	6.4	6.7	-15.7%
27	JAX	19%	-31.0%	-13.5%	5.8	5.9	-17.5%
28	PIT	12%	9.0%	30.0%	7.0	7.2	-21.0%
29	GB	20%	5.0%	27.6%	6.4	6.8	-22.6%
30	CIN	25%	-5.2%	19.5%	7.1	5.8	-24.7%
31	MIA	22%	-19.4%	7.4%	7.2	6.3	-26.8%
32	KC	29%	43.4%	74.8%	8.7	8.1	-31.4%

Top 10 Defenses, Better DVOA vs. Shotgun

Rk	Team	% Plays Shotgun	DVOA Shot	DVOA Not	Yd/Play Shot	Yd/Play Not	DVOA Dif
1	MIN	61%	-17.7%	-0.6%	4.8	5.6	-17.1%
2	WAS	65%	-4.3%	11.3%	6.0	5.8	-15.6%
3	SEA	56%	-5.1%	5.5%	5.9	6.3	-10.7%
4	LAC	65%	-6.8%	-1.3%	5.5	5.8	-5.5%
5	DEN	62%	-11.6%	-7.0%	5.9	5.5	-4.6%
6	BUF	59%	-16.5%	-11.9%	5.2	5.0	-4.5%
7	ATL	67%	11.6%	16.1%	6.2	6.1	-4.5%
8	KC	66%	5.3%	9.4%	6.0	6.2	-4.0%
9	CHI	68%	-27.4%	-23.5%	4.9	4.7	-3.9%
10	NE	74%	-0.5%	2.8%	5.8	6.1	-3.3%

Top 10 Defenses, Better DVOA vs. Play-Action

Rk	Team	% PA	DVOA PA	DVOA No PA	Yd/Play PA	Yd/Play No PA	DVOA Dif
1	PIT	15%	-28.6%	18.9%	5.9	6.6	-47.6%
2	CIN	21%	-16.3%	27.0%	7.6	7.4	-43.3%
3	OAK	33%	21.4%	34.1%	7.6	8.1	-12.7%
4	LAC	23%	-6.1%	5.4%	7.5	6.3	-11.5%
5	JAX	27%	-6.8%	1.4%	7.5	5.9	-8.2%
6	HOU	21%	1.5%	9.1%	7.8	6.8	-7.6%
7	TEN	28%	9.8%	11.0%	7.3	6.2	-1.3%
8	DET	27%	23.6%	24.6%	8.1	6.7	-1.0%
9	TB	29%	26.0%	25.5%	8.5	7.3	0.5%
10	IND	28%	11.1%	8.4%	7.8	6.6	2.7%

Bottom 10 Defenses, Better DVOA vs. Shotgun

Rk	Team	% Plays Shotgun	DVOA Shot	DVOA Not	Yd/Play Shot	Yd/Play Not	DVOA Dif
23	IND	62%	1.5%	-10.3%	6.1	4.8	11.8%
24	NO	65%	2.3%	-11.0%	6.2	5.7	13.2%
25	OAK	59%	19.1%	3.1%	7.0	6.0	16.1%
26	NYJ	67%	9.2%	-7.2%	6.2	5.2	16.4%
27	PHI	66%	6.5%	-10.8%	6.0	5.7	17.3%
28	TEN	61%	8.3%	-9.6%	5.6	5.3	17.8%
29	HOU	67%	-0.2%	-18.9%	5.7	5.1	18.6%
30	CLE	70%	5.1%	-17.0%	6.1	4.8	22.1%
31	CAR	63%	15.0%	-8.4%	6.4	5.8	23.4%
32	PIT	69%	7.3%	-16.4%	5.8	4.8	23.7%

Bottom 10 Defenses, Better DVOA vs. Play-Action

Rk	Team	% PA	DVOA PA	DVOA No PA	Yd/Play PA	Yd/Play No PA	DVOA Dif
23	GB	23%	34.9%	12.8%	9.4	6.3	22.1%
24	NO	23%	27.6%	5.2%	8.4	6.9	22.4%
25	BUF	26%	1.4%	-22.1%	6.5	5.6	23.4%
26	NYG	27%	33.0%	9.2%	8.7	6.4	23.8%
27	BAL	19%	10.2%	-15.3%	6.4	5.7	25.5%
28	CLE	20%	21.4%	-7.5%	8.1	6.2	28.9%
29	LAR	23%	25.9%	-4.8%	9.1	6.6	30.7%
30	DAL	22%	33.1%	0.4%	8.1	6.4	32.7%
31	SEA	25%	32.5%	-2.6%	8.5	6.4	35.0%
32	MIN	28%	28.7%	-20.2%	8.6	5.5	48.9%

2018 Defenses with and without Pass Pressure

Rank	Team	Plays	Pct Pressure	DVOA with Pressure	Yds with Pressure	DVOA w/o Pressure	Yds w/o Pressure	DVOA Dif	Rank
1	LAR	609	36.0%	-57.8%	4.2	41.5%	8.4	-99.2%	16
2	PIT	646	34.5%	-70.4%	3.2	52.4%	8.0	-122.8%	29
3	CHI	692	33.4%	-97.5%	2.5	15.2%	7.0	-112.7%	23
4	BUF	553	33.3%	-74.2%	3.3	12.9%	7.0	-87.1%	8
5	JAX	583	33.2%	-72.9%	4.4	35.7%	7.0	-108.7%	22
6	NE	666	33.0%	-41.7%	4.3	34.1%	7.5	-75.8%	5
7	BAL	646	32.8%	-55.0%	4.5	10.9%	6.1	-65.9%	4
8	DAL	612	32.2%	-58.8%	3.7	39.8%	7.8	-98.6%	14
9	MIN	587	32.0%	-82.7%	2.9	35.3%	7.4	-117.9%	28
10	CAR	595	31.6%	-57.1%	4.2	50.4%	8.4	-107.5%	21
11	KC	715	31.5%	-71.0%	3.9	44.0%	8.0	-115.0%	25
12	WAS	616	31.3%	-57.8%	3.6	34.5%	8.3	-92.3%	12
13	NO	666	31.2%	-59.1%	4.3	43.1%	8.6	-102.2%	17
14	GB	601	30.8%	-40.4%	4.0	44.1%	8.0	-84.5%	7
14	LAC	614	30.8%	-57.7%	4.5	29.6%	7.2	-87.3%	10
14	NYG	619	30.8%	-46.1%	4.8	44.1%	8.1	-90.1%	11
17	DEN	612	30.2%	-97.6%	3.3	25.8%	8.1	-123.4%	30
18	SF	612	29.9%	-48.3%	3.7	50.5%	7.9	-98.8%	15
19	PHI	702	29.7%	-51.4%	3.7	35.9%	7.8	-87.3%	9
20	HOU	672	29.0%	-76.3%	3.4	40.9%	7.9	-117.1%	27
21	SEA	613	28.9%	-68.8%	3.1	38.6%	8.3	-107.4%	19
22	ARI	577	28.8%	-91.6%	3.0	40.8%	7.2	-132.3%	32
23	MIA	575	28.5%	-11.9%	5.3	31.2%	8.7	-43.1%	2
24	NYJ	652	28.1%	-47.0%	3.5	37.3%	8.0	-84.3%	6
25	IND	604	28.0%	-28.5%	5.4	24.3%	7.2	-52.8%	3
26	TEN	600	27.6%	-73.1%	3.4	42.8%	7.3	-116.0%	26
27	CLE	695	27.1%	-78.2%	3.9	29.1%	7.3	-107.2%	18
28	CIN	637	26.5%	-61.7%	4.4	45.7%	8.3	-107.4%	20
29	DET	563	26.3%	-57.8%	3.3	55.2%	8.0	-113.0%	24
30	ATL	651	25.7%	-46.2%	3.6	50.2%	8.1	-96.4%	13
31	TB	596	25.0%	-70.2%	3.8	58.7%	8.7	-128.9%	31
32	OAK	519	22.0%	8.5%	6.8	35.5%	8.5	-27.0%	1
	NFL AVERAGE	622	30.0%	-60.5%	3.9	37.8%	7.8	-98.3%	

Includes scrambles and Defensive Pass Interference. Does not include aborted snaps.

Author Bios

Editor-in-Chief and NFL Statistician

Aaron Schatz is the creator of FootballOutsiders.com and the proprietary NFL statistics within *Football Outsiders Almanac*, including DVOA, DYAR, and adjusted line yards. He is responsible each year for both the Football Outsiders NFL team projections and the KUBIAK fantasy football projections. He writes regularly for ESPN+ and *ESPN The Magazine*, and he has done custom research for a number of NFL teams. *The New York Times Magazine* referred to him as "the Bill James of football." Readers should feel free to blame everything in this book on the fact that he went to high school six miles from Gillette Stadium before detouring through Brown University and eventually landing in Auburn, Massachusetts. He promises that someday Bill Belichick will retire, the Patriots will be awful, and he will write very mean and nasty things about them.

Layout and Design

Vincent Verhei has been a writer and editor for Football Outsiders since 2007. In addition to writing for *Football Outsiders Almanac 2019*, he did all layout and design on the book. During the season, he writes the "Quick Reads" column covering the best and worst players of each week according to Football Outsiders metrics. His writings have also appeared in *ESPN The Magazine* and in Maple Street Press publications, and he has done layout on a number of other books for Football Outsiders and Prospectus Entertainment Ventures. His other night job is as a writer and podcast host for pro wrestling/MMA website Figurefouronline.com. He is a graduate of Western Washington University.

College Football Statisticians

Bill Connelly is a college football writer for ESPN. He lives in Missouri with his wife, daughter, and pets. You can find old work of his at SB Nation, at his former SB Nation blog Football Study Hall, and in his books, *Study Hall: College Football, Its Stats and Its Stories* and *The 50 Best* College Football Teams of All Time*.

Brian Fremeau has been analyzing college football drive stats for Football Outsiders since 2006. A lifelong Fighting Irish fan, Brian can be found every home football Saturday in Notre Dame Stadium. He can be found there every day, in fact, due to his campus facility operations responsibilities. He lives in South Bend, Indiana, with his wife and two daughters.

Contributors

Thomas Bassinger was in a bookstore (an actual brick-and-mortar bookstore!) more than a decade ago when he first held a Football Outsiders annual. It was a life-changing moment, like when he discovered the breakaway zigzagging speed of QB Eagles in Tecmo Super Bowl. Now, he's a football outsider on the inside: He writes about the Buccaneers, who repeatedly ignore his advice on kickers (don't draft them) and uniforms (fix them, for the children), for the *Tampa Bay Times*. Among his greatest achievements: breaking the 100-point barrier on Tecmo, beating Jacquizz Rodgers in Connect 4, and appearing in this book. He is a graduate of Penn State University and lives with his family in St. Petersburg, Florida.

Ian Boyd is a history major graduate from the University of Texas, now based in southeast Michigan, who loves studying the trends and stories of college football. You can also find his work at the websites Inside Texas and Football Study Hall.

Tom Gower joined the FO writing staff in 2009. He has degrees from Georgetown University and the University of Chicago, whose football programs have combined for an Orange Bowl appearance and seven Big Ten Titles but are still trying to find success after Pearl Harbor. His work has also appeared at NBCSports.com, NBC Sports World, ESPN.com, and in *ESPN The Magazine*. He roots for the Tennessee Titans.

Derrik Klassen is from the Central Valley of California, though he grew up near Tampa Bay, Florida. Covering the NFL draft gave him his start but studying the NFL itself has taken precedent. He has been published at SB Nation and Bleacher Report, and has worked for Optimum Scouting, doing charting and scouting reports for their NFL Draft Guide.

Bryan Knowles has been covering the NFL since 2010, with his work appearing on ESPN, Bleacher Report and Fansided. A graduate of UC Davis and San Jose State University, he's heard rumors that his teams could eventually win a football game but has yet to see the empirical evidence. He currently co-writes Scramble for the Ball with Andrew Potter.

Rivers McCown has written for ESPN.com, Bleacher Report, *USA Today*, and Deadspin, among other places. He's edited for Football Outsiders, *Rookie Scouting Portfolio*, and *Pre-Snap Reads Quarterback Catalogue*. He lives in Houston, Texas, with his wife, under the control of two cats and two birds. He wants more jobs, and if you don't give them to him, he'll be forced to keep speedrunning video games and helping design randomizer hacks for them.

Chad Peltier was raised in Georgia by Ohio State Buckeyes but graduated from the University of Georgia. This background helped raise the odds that he would have at least one, and sometimes two, playoff-contending college football teams to root for. Based in Atlanta, he also contributes to the SB Nation blog Land Grant Holy Land.

Anglo-Scot (so, Briton) **Andrew Potter** blames Mega Drive classics John Madden Football and Joe Montana Sports Talk Football for his transatlantic love of the gridiron game. He joined Football Outsiders in 2013 to help with the infamous Twitter Audibles experiment, and still compiles Audibles at the Line to this day. He also authors the weekly Injury Aftermath report and co-authors Scramble for the Ball with Bryan Knowles. Though outwardly a fan of the New Orleans Saints, inwardly the Angus resident still yearns for his first gridiron love: NFL Europe's Scottish Claymores.

Mike Tanier has been writing for Football Outsiders publications for 15 years and is now entering his sixth season as an NFL lead columnist for Bleacher Report. He previously wrote for *The New York Times*, Sports on Earth, Fox Sports, and gobs of other magazines and websites. He's the father of two black belts, husband of a Teacher of the Year award winner, and lifelong fan of the Philadelphia Eagles.

Robert Weintraub is the author of the *New York Times* bestseller *No Better Friend: One Man, One Dog, and their Extraordinary Story of Courage and Survival in WWII,* as well as *The Victory Season* and *The House That Ruth Built.* He has also been a regular contributor to Sports on Earth, Slate, Grantland, *Columbia Journalism Review*, and *The New York Times.*

Carl Yedor was born and raised in Seattle, Washington, and his first vivid football memory was "We want the ball, and we're going to score." As an undergrad at Georgetown University, he worked with the varsity football team to implement football research into their strategy and gameplanning, drawing on his coursework in statistics and his high school experience as an undersized offensive guard and inside linebacker. He lives in Arlington, Virginia.

Acknowledgements

We want to thank all the Football Outsiders readers, all the people in the media who have helped to spread the word about our website and books, and all the people in the NFL who have shown interest in our work. This is our 15th annual book as part of the *Pro Football Prospectus* or *Football Outsiders Almanac* series. We couldn't do this if we were just one guy, or without the help and/or support from all these people:

- The entire staff at EdjSports, especially Tamela Triplett and Casey Ramage.
- FootballOutsiders.com Technical Director Dave Bernreuther.
- Cale Clinton, the intern responsible for compiling both The Week in Quotes on our website and The Year in Quotes in this book.
- Mike Harris for help with the season simulation.
- Premium programmer Sean McCall, Excel macro master John Argentiero, and drive stats guru Jim Armstrong.
- Our offensive line guru Ben Muth and injury guru Zach Binney.
- New Football Outsiders senior analyst (and for the purposes of this book, copyeditor extraordinaire) Scott Spratt.
- Nathan Forster, creator of SackSEER and BackCAST, who is also responsible for improvements on Playmaker Score (originally created by Vincent Verhei).
- Jason McKinley, creator of Offensive Line Continuity Score.
- Jeremy Snyder, our incredibly prolific transcriber of old play-by-play gamebooks.
- Roland Beech, formerly of TwoMinuteWarning.com, who came up with the original ideas behind our individual defensive stats.
- Our editors at ESPN.com and *ESPN The Magazine*, in particular Tim Kavanagh.
- Our friends at Sports Info Solutions who have really expanded what we can do with game charting, particularly Dan Foehrenbach and Matt Manocherian.
- Bill Simmons, for constantly promoting us on his podcast, and Peter King, for lots of promotion on The MMQB.
- Michael Katzenoff at the NFL, for responding to our endless questions about specific items in the official play-by-play.
- All the friends we've made on coaching staffs and in front offices across the National Football League, who generally don't want to be mentioned by name. You know who you are.
- Our comrades in the revolution: Doug Drinen (creator of the indispensable Pro Football Reference), Bill Barnwell (our long lost brother), Brian Burke and the guys from ESPN Stats & Information, Ben Baldwin, Neil Paine, Robert Mays, Danny Kelly, Kevin Clark, and K.C. Joyner, plus the kids at Numberfire, the football guys from footballguys.com, and all of the young analysts doing awesome work with NFLscrapR all over Twitter.
- Also, our scouting buddies, including Andy Benoit, Chris Brown, Greg Cosell, Doug Farrar, Russ Lande, and Matt Waldman.
- Joe Alread, Justin Patel, and William Schautz, who handle the special Football Outsiders cards in Madden Ultimate Team, and the other folks at EA Sports who make FO a part of the Madden universe.

As always, thanks to our families and friends for putting up with this nonsense.

Aaron Schatz

Follow Football Outsiders on Twitter

Follow the official account announcing new Football Outsiders articles at **@fboutsiders**. You can follow other FO and *FOA 2019* writers at these Twitter addresses:

Thomas Bassinger: **@tometrics**
Zachary Binney: **@zbinney_NFLinj**
Ian Boyd: **@Ian_A_Boyd**
Bill Connelly: **@ESPN_BillC**
Brian Fremeau: **@bcfremeau**
Tom Gower: **@ThomasGower**
Derrik Klassen: **@QBKlass**
Bryan Knowles: **@BryKno**

Rivers McCown: **@RiversMcCown**
Ben Muth: **@FO_WordofMuth**
Chad Peltier: **@cgpeltier**
Andrew Potter: **@bighairyandy**
Aaron Schatz: **@FO_ASchatz**
Scott Spratt: **@Scott_Spratt**
Mike Tanier: **@MikeTanier**
Vince Verhei: **@FO_VVerhei**
Robert Weintraub: **@robwein**
Carl Yedor: **@CarlYedor61**

Follow Football Outsiders on Facebook
https://www.facebook.com/footballoutsiders

About Sports Info Solutions

The mission of Sports Info Solutions (SIS) is to provide the most accurate, in-depth, timely professional sports data, including cutting-edge research and analysis, striving to educate professional teams and the public about sports analytics. SIS is thrilled to work with nearly every Major League Baseball team and a growing number of National Football League teams in service of that goal.

SIS opened its doors back in 2002 and has been on the leading edge of the advanced statistical study of sports ever since. The early years were dedicated to pioneering the analytical landscape in baseball, where SIS successfully played a large role in the growth of trends such as defensive shifting. More recently, SIS recognized the growing need for football analytics and launched a new operation to mirror its industry-leading baseball data collection operation.

That operation began with a partnership with Football Outsiders in 2015, one that continues to propel the industry forward by linking the most comprehensive, objective data provider with the most reputable source for football analysis.

SIS has built its success thanks to its staff of expert scouts and an army of highly trained video scouts who chart thousands of NFL, FBS, MLB, and MiLB games annually. SIS collects valuable data that cannot be found any place else, and each game is reviewed multiple times to ensure that the data is as accurate as possible. The company records everything from basic box score data to advanced defensive coverages and route information. The company's analysts and programmers dissect the data, producing a variety of predictive studies and analytics that are used by high-profile clients throughout the sports industry.

Sports Info Solutions was founded by John Dewan, who has been a leader in baseball analytics for more than 25 years. From his first partnership with Bill James as the Executive Director of Project Scoresheet to co-founding STATS, Inc. and his 15-year tenure as CEO, companies under John's leadership have continually broken new ground in sports data and analytics.

41 South 2nd Street   Coplay, PA 18037   610.261.2370   FAX 610.261.2307   www.SportsInfoSolutions.com

Made in the
USA
Monee, IL